Elements of Language
Introductory Course
Annotated Teacher's Edition

Lee Odell

Richard Vacca

Renée Hobbs

Judith L. Irvin

Grammar, Usage, and Mechanics
Instructional Framework by

John E. Warriner

HOLT, RINEHART AND WINSTON

A Harcourt Classroom Education Company

Austin · New York · Orlando · Atlanta · San Francisco · Boston · Dallas · Toronto · London

STAFF CREDITS

EDITORIAL

Director
Mescal Evler

Manager of Editorial Operations
Bill Wahlgren

Executive Editor
Kristine E. Marshall

Project Editors
Marcia L. Kelley
Amy Strong

Annotated Teacher's Edition Editors
Eileen Joyce
Susan Lynch

Writing and Editing
Roger Boylan, David Bradford, Susan Britt, Peggy Ferrin, Karen Kolar, Barbara Knaggs, David Knaggs, Kevin Lemoine, Chi Nguyen, Kathryn Rogers, Tressa Sanders, Jennifer Schwan, Mary Shaw

Copyediting
Michael Neibergall, *Copyediting Manager;* Mary Malone, *Senior Copyeditor;* Joel Bourgeois, Gabrielle Field, Suzi A. Hunn, Jane Kominek, Millicent Ondras, Theresa Reding, Désirée Reid, Kathleen Scheiner, Sara Searcy, *Copyeditors*

Project Administration
Marie Price, *Managing Editor;* Lori De La Garza, *Editorial Operations Coordinator;* Tracy Demont, Heather Cheyne, Mark Holland, Marcus Johnson, Jill O'Neal, Joyce Rector, Janet Riley, Kelly Tankersley, *Project Administration;* Gail Coupland, Elizabeth Dickson, Ruth Hooker, Margaret Sanchez, *Word Processing*

Editorial Permissions
Janet Harrington

ART, DESIGN AND PHOTO

Book Design
Senior Design Director
Diane Motz

Teresa Carrera-Paprota, *Designer*
Tim Hovde, *Design Associate*

Cover Design
Joe Melomo, *Design Director*

Graphic Services
Kristen Darby, *Manager*

PRODUCTION
Beth Prevelige, *Prepress Manager*
Simira Davis, *Supervisor*
Joan Lindsay, *Production Coordinator*

MANUFACTURING
Belinda Lopez, *Senior Production Coordinator*
Ben Saffer, *Production Assistant*

Copyright © 2001 by Holt, Rinehart and Winston

All rights reserved. No part of this publication may be reproduced or transmitted in any form or by any means, electronic or mechanical, including photocopy, recording, or any information storage and retrieval system, without permission in writing from the publisher.

Requests for permission to make copies of any part of the work should be mailed to the following address: Permissions Department, Holt, Rinehart and Winston, 1120 South Capital of Texas Highway, Austin, Texas 78746-6487.

Acknowledgments and other credits appear on pages 834–835 and 836–837, which are extensions of the copyright page.

Printed in the United States of America
ISBN 0-03-054793-8
5   048   03 02

PROGRAM AUTHORS

LEE ODELL helped establish the pedagogical framework for the composition strand of *Elements of Language*. In addition, he guided the development of the scope and sequence and the pedagogical design of the Writing Workshops. Dr. Odell is Professor of Composition Theory and Research and, since 1996, Director of the Writing Program at Rensselaer Polytechnic Institute. He began his career teaching English in middle and high schools. More recently he has worked with teachers in grades K–12 to establish a program that involves students from all disciplines in writing across the curriculum and for communities outside their classrooms. Dr. Odell's most recent book (with Charles R. Cooper) is *Evaluating Writing: The Role of Teachers' Knowledge about Text, Learning, and Culture* (1999). He is Past Chair of the Conference on College Composition and Communication and of NCTE's Assembly for Research.

RICHARD VACCA helped establish the conceptual basis for the reading strand of *Elements of Language*. In addition, he guided the development of the pedagogical design and the scope and sequence of skills in the Reading Workshops. Dr. Vacca is Professor of Education at Kent State University. He recently completed a term as the forty-second President of the International Reading Association. Originally a middle school and high school teacher, Dr. Vacca served as the project director of the Cleveland Writing Demonstration Project for several years. He is the co-author of *Content Area Reading; Reading and Learning to Read;* and articles and chapters related to adolescents' literacy development. In 1989, Dr. Vacca received the College Reading Association's A.B. Herr Award for Outstanding Contributions to Reading Education. Currently, he is co-chair of the IRA's Commission on Adolescent Literacy.

RENÉE HOBBS helped develop the theoretical framework for the viewing and representing strand of *Elements of Language*. She guided the development of the scope and sequence; served as the authority on terminology, definitions, and pedagogy; and directed the planning for the video series. Dr. Hobbs is Associate Professor of Communication at Babson College in Wellesley, Massachusetts, and Director of the Media Literacy Project. Active in the field of media education, Dr. Hobbs has served as Director of the Institute on Media Education, Harvard Graduate School of Education; Director of the "Know TV" Project, Discovery Networks and Time Warner Cable; and Board Member, The New York Times Newspaper in Education Program. She works actively in staff development in school districts nationwide. Dr. Hobbs has contributed articles and chapters on media, technology, and education to many publications.

JUDITH L. IRVIN also helped establish the conceptual basis for the reading strand of *Elements of Language*. Dr. Irvin taught middle school for several years before pursuing graduate studies in Reading-Language Arts. She now teaches courses in curriculum, middle school education, and educational leadership at Florida State University. She chaired the Research Committee of the National Middle School Association and was editor of *Research in Middle Level Education Quarterly* for six years. Dr. Irvin writes a column, "What Research Says to the Middle Level Practitioner," for the *Middle School Journal*. Her many publications include *What Research Says to the Middle Level Practitioner* and *Reading and the Middle School Student: Strategies to Enhance Literacy*.

JOHN E. WARRINER was a high school English teacher when he developed the original organizational structure for his classic *English Grammar and Composition* series. The approach pioneered by Mr. Warriner was distinctive, and the editorial staff of Holt, Rinehart and Winston have worked diligently to retain the unique qualities of his pedagogy. For the same reason, HRW continues to credit Mr. Warriner as an author of *Elements of Language* in recognition of his groundbreaking work. John Warriner also co-authored the *English Workshop* series and was editor of *Short Stories: Characters in Conflict.* Throughout his long career, however, teaching remained Mr. Warriner's major interest, and he taught for thirty-two years in junior and senior high schools and in college.

PROGRAM CONSULTANTS

The program consultants reviewed instructional materials to ensure consistency with current research, classroom appropriateness, and alignment with curriculum guidelines.

Ann Bagley
Senior Administrator for Secondary English
Wake County Public Schools
Raleigh, North Carolina

Vicki R. Brown
Professor of Education, Grambling State University
Principal, Grambling Middle School
Grambling, Louisiana

Max Hutto
Supervisor of Middle School Language Arts
Hillsborough County Schools
Tampa, Florida

Beth Johnson
Supervisor of Language Arts
Polk District Schools
Bartow, Florida

Kathleen Jongsma
Associate Professor, Department of Education Chair
Texas Lutheran University
Seguin, Texas

Kaye Price-Hawkins
Language Arts Consultant
Abilene, Texas

Lanny van Allen
Consultant, Texas Center for Reading and Language Arts
The University of Texas at Austin
Austin, Texas

CRITICAL REVIEWERS

The critical reviewers read and evaluated pre-publication materials for this book.

Pupil's Edition

Mary M. Goodson
Pershing Middle School
Houston, Texas

Katherine Grace
Labay Junior High School
Houston, Texas

Dorothy Harrington
Marshall Middle School
Beaumont, Texas

Mary Alice Madden
Lathrop Intermediate School
Santa Ana, California

Mary Ann Norwood
Ligon Middle School
Wake County, North Carolina

LeeAnn W. Packer
Adele C. Young Intermediate School
Brigham City, Utah

Elizabeth G. Pope
Memorial Middle School
Sioux Falls, South Dakota

Judith Shane
Carr Intermediate School
Santa Ana, California

Belinda Small
Davidson Middle School
Crestview, Florida

Michael J. Wallpe
Metropolitan School District
Indianapolis, Indiana

Janice Woo
Union Middle School
San Jose, California

Annotated Teacher's Edition

Jennifer L. Millen
Mabry Middle School
Marietta, Georgia

Mary Ann Norwood
Ligon Middle School
Raleigh, North Carolina

Elizabeth G. Pope
Memorial Middle School
Sioux Falls, South Dakota

Michael J. Wallpe
Metropolitan School District
Indianapolis, Indiana

TEACHER/STUDENT CONTRIBUTORS

The following teachers and students worked with HRW's editorial staff to provide models of student writing for the book.

Teachers

Jane Anderson
Garfield Elementary School
Sand Springs, Oklahoma

Peter J. Caron
Cumberland Middle School
Cumberland, Rhode Island

Dorothy Harrington
Marshall Middle School
Beaumont, Texas

Debra Hester
Richbourg Middle School
Crestview, Florida

Dana Humphrey
North Middle School
O'Fallon, Missouri

Students

Anthony C. Rodrigues
Cumberland Middle School
Cumberland, Rhode Island

Natalie Banta and Amy Tidwell
Olympus Junior High School
Salt Lake City, Utah

Stephanie Thompson
North Middle School
O'Fallon, Missouri

Matthew Hester
Richbourg Middle School
Crestview, Florida

Diana DeGarmo
Garfield Elementary School
Sand Springs, Oklahoma

Genna Offerman
Marshall Middle School
Beaumont, Texas

Tyler Duckworth
Liberty Middle School
Morganton, North Carolina

FIELD TEST PARTICIPANTS

The following teachers participated in the pre-publication field test or review of prototype materials for the *Elements of Language* series.

Nadene Adams
Robert Gray Middle School
Portland, Oregon

Carol Alves
Apopka High School
Apopka, Florida

Susan Atkinson
O. P. Norman Junior High School
Kaufman, Texas

Sheryl L. Babione
Fremont Ross High School
Fremont, Ohio

Jane Baker
Elkins High School
Missouri City, Texas

Martha Barnard
Scarborough High School
Houston, Texas

Jennifer S. Barr
James Bowie High School
Austin, Texas

Leslie Benefield
Reed Middle School
Duncanville, Texas

Gina Birdsall
Irving High School
Irving, Texas

Sara J. Brennan
Murchison Middle School
Austin, Texas

Janelle Brinck
Leander Middle School
Leander, Texas

Geraldine K. Brooks
William B. Travis High School
Austin, Texas

Peter J. Caron
Cumberland Middle School
Cumberland, Rhode Island

Patty Cave
O. P. Norman Junior High School
Kaufman, Texas

Mary Cathyrne Coe
Pocatello High School
Pocatello, Idaho

Geri-Lee DeGennaro
Tarpon Springs High School
Tarpon Springs, Florida

Karen Dendy
Stephen F. Austin Middle School
Irving, Texas

Dianne Franz
Tarpon Springs Middle School
Tarpon Springs, Florida

Continued on page T6

FIELD TEST PARTICIPANTS Continued

Doris F. Frazier
East Millbrook Magnet Middle School
Raleigh, North Carolina

Shayne G. Goodrum
C. E. Jordan High School
Durham, North Carolina

Bonnie L. Hall
St. Ann School
Lansing, Illinois

Doris Ann Hall
Forest Meadow Junior High School
Dallas, Texas

James M. Harris
Mayfield High School
Mayfield Village, Ohio

Lynne Hoover
Fremont Ross High School
Fremont, Ohio

Patricia A. Humphreys
James Bowie High School
Austin, Texas

Jennifer L. Jones
Oliver Wendell Holmes Middle School
Dallas, Texas

Kathryn R. Jones
Murchison Middle School
Austin, Texas

Bonnie Just
Narbonne High School
Harbor City, California

Vincent Kimball
Patterson High School #405
Baltimore, Maryland

Nancy C. Long
MacArthur High School
Houston, Texas

Carol M. Mackey
Ft. Lauderdale Christian School
Ft. Lauderdale, Florida

Jan Jennings McCown
Johnston High School
Austin, Texas

Alice Kelly McCurdy
Rusk Middle School
Dallas, Texas

Elizabeth Morris
Northshore High School
Slidell, Louisiana

Victoria Reis
Western High School
Ft. Lauderdale, Florida

Dean Richardson
Scarborough High School
Houston, Texas

Susan M. Rogers
Freedom High School
Morganton, North Carolina

Sammy Rusk
North Mesquite High School
Mesquite, Texas

Carole B. San Miguel
James Bowie High School
Austin, Texas

Jane Saunders
William B. Travis High School
Austin, Texas

Gina Sawyer
Reed Middle School
Duncanville, Texas

Laura R. Schauermann
MacArthur High School
Houston, Texas

Stephen Shearer
MacArthur High School
Houston, Texas

Elizabeth Curry Smith
Tarpon Springs High School
Tarpon Springs, Florida

Jeannette M. Spain
Stephen F. Austin High School
Sugar Land, Texas

Carrie Speer
Northshore High School
Slidell, Louisiana

Trina Steffes
MacArthur High School
Houston, Texas

Andrea G. Freirich Stewart
Freedom High School
Morganton, North Carolina

Diana O. Torres
Johnston High School
Austin, Texas

Jan Voorhees
Whitesboro High School
Marcy, New York

Ann E. Walsh
Bedichek Middle School
Austin, Texas

Mary Jane Warden
Onahan School
Chicago, Illinois

Beth Westbrook
Covington Middle School
Austin, Texas

Char-Lene Wilkins
Morenci Area High School
Morenci, Michigan

CONTENTS IN BRIEF

PART 1

Communications

Introduction: Thinking About Reading and Writing 2
1. Narration/Description: Sharing Our Stories 16
2. Exposition: Reporting the News 48
3. Exposition: Explaining How 84
4. Exposition: Comparing and Contrasting 118
5. Exposition: Responding to a Novel 152
6. Exposition: Sharing Your Research 186
7. Persuasion: Making a Difference 226

PART 2

Sentences and Paragraphs

8. Writing Effective Sentences 262
9. Learning About Paragraphs 278

PART 3

Grammar, Usage, and Mechanics

Grammar
10. The Sentence 300
11. Parts of Speech Overview: Noun, Pronoun, Adjective 322
12. Parts of Speech Overview: Verb, Adverb, Preposition, Conjunction, Interjection 346
13. The Phrase and the Clause 372
14. Complements 402

Usage
15. Agreement 420
16. Using Verbs Correctly 444
17. Using Pronouns Correctly 474
18. Using Modifiers Correctly 494
19. A Glossary of Usage 518

Mechanics
20. Capital Letters 536
21. Punctuation: End Marks, Commas, Semicolons, Colons 560
22. Punctuation: Underlining (Italics), Quotation Marks, Apostrophes, Hyphens 586
23. Spelling 612
24. Correcting Common Errors 642

PART 4

Quick Reference Handbook

- The Dictionary 680
- Document Design 682
- The History of English 690
- The Library/Media Center 694
- Reading and Vocabulary 704
- Speaking and Listening 719
- Studying and Test Taking 733
- Viewing and Representing 743
- Writing 755
- Grammar at a Glance 768

CONTENTS

Features T28
Communication Assignments T30
Overview of the Program T32
To Our Students T48

PART 1
INTRODUCTION

Communications 1

Thinking About Reading and Writing 2

Reading as a Process 4
   Prereading 5
   While Reading 6
      Model Passage: "Meteorite Hunters," Mary Roach from *Muse* 7
   After Reading 8

Writing as a Process 9
   Prewriting 10
   Writing 11
   Revising 12
   Publishing 13

The Reading-Writing Connection 14

CHOICES: *Viewing and Representing, Careers, Collaborative Writing, Creative Writing* 15

CHAPTER 1
Narration/Description

Sharing Our Stories 16

Chapter Planning Guide T15A
Chapter Overview T15C

Preview 17

READING WORKSHOP: *An Autobiographical Incident* 18
Preparing to Read 18
   READING SKILL ▸ MAKING INFERENCES: FORMING GENERALIZATIONS
   READING FOCUS ▸ CHRONOLOGICAL ORDER
Reading Selection: from *Rosa Parks: My Story*, Rosa Parks
with Jim Haskins 19
Vocabulary Mini-Lesson: *Context Clues* 25
Test-Taking Mini-Lesson: *Making Inferences* 26

WRITING WORKSHOP: *A Life Experience* 27
Prewriting 27
Critical-Thinking Mini-Lesson: *Arranging Ideas*

Writing 32
Framework for an Autobiographical Incident
A Writer's Model: "A Night to Remember" 33
A Student's Model: "In the Net," Anthony C. Rodrigues 35

T8 Contents

Revising 36
First Reading: *Content and Organization*
Second Reading: *Style*
  Focus on Word Choice: *Exact Verbs*

Publishing 39
Proofreading: Grammar Link—*Capitalizing Proper Nouns*
Test-Taking Mini-Lesson: *Writing Description for Tests* 41
Connections to Literature: *Writing a Narrative Poem* 42

FOCUS ON SPEAKING AND LISTENING: *Telling a Story* 45

CHOICES: *Careers, Speech, Drama, Writing, Technology* 47

CHAPTER 2

Reporting the News 48

Exposition

Chapter Planning Guide T47A
Chapter Overview T47C

Preview 49

READING WORKSHOP: *A Newspaper Article* 50
  Preparing to Read 50
      READING SKILL ▶ MAIN IDEA
      READING FOCUS ▶ INVERTED PYRAMID STRUCTURE
  Reading Selection: "Whale Watch: Kids Use Internet to Track Progress of Newly Freed J. J.," Lisa Richardson from *Los Angeles Times; Orange County Edition* 51
  Vocabulary Mini-Lesson: *Multiple-Meaning Words* 56
  Test-Taking Mini-Lesson: *Answering Main Idea Questions* 57

WRITING WORKSHOP: *A Newspaper Article* 58
  Prewriting 58
  Critical-Thinking Mini-Lesson: *Analyzing Cause and Effect*

  Writing 66
  Framework for a News Article
  A Writer's Model: "Principal Approves Longer Passing Period" 67
  A Student's Model: "Mr. Sagers Moves to Cyprus High," Natalie Banta and Amy Tidwell 68

  Revising 69
  First Reading: *Content and Organization*
  Second Reading: *Style*
      Focus on Sentences: *Varying Sentences*

  Publishing 72
  Proofreading: Grammar Link—*Correcting Run-on Sentences*
  Connections to Life: *Writing a Newspaper's Advice Column* 74

FOCUS ON VIEWING AND REPRESENTING
Producing a Newspaper 76

FOCUS ON VIEWING AND REPRESENTING
Producing a TV News Segment 79

CHOICES: *Careers; Crossing the Curriculum: Art, Science; Writing* 83

CHAPTER 3 — Exposition

Explaining How 84

Chapter Planning Guide T83A
Chapter Overview T83C

Preview 85

READING WORKSHOP: *A "How-to" Article* 86
   Preparing to Read 86
      READING SKILL ▶ MAKING PREDICTIONS
      READING FOCUS ▶ FORMING MENTAL IMAGES
   Reading Selection: "Making a Flying Fish," Paula Morrow
      from *Faces* 89
   Vocabulary Mini-Lesson: *Compound Words* 92
   Test-Taking Mini-Lesson: *Making Predictions* 93

WRITING WORKSHOP: *A "How-to" Paper* 94
   Prewriting 94
   Writing Mini-Lesson: *Elaboration—Using Specific Language*

   Writing 98
   Framework for a "How-to" Paper
   A Writer's Model: "A Snowman of Style" 99
   A Student's Model: "Make It Grow," Stephanie Thompson 102

   Revising 103
   First Reading: *Content and Organization*
   Second Reading: *Style*
      Focus on Sentences: *Transitional Words*

   Publishing 106
   Proofreading: Grammar Link—*Using Commas in a Series*
   Test-Taking Mini-Lesson: *Writing Instructions* 108
   Connections to Literature: *Writing a Descriptive Paragraph* ... 109

FOCUS ON VIEWING AND LISTENING
   Viewing and Listening to Learn 112

CHOICES: *Crossing the Curriculum: Science, Speech;
   Careers; Writing* 117

CHAPTER 4

Exposition

Comparing and Contrasting 118

Chapter Planning Guide T117A
Chapter Overview T117C

Preview 119

READING WORKSHOP: *A Comparison-Contrast Essay* 120
   Preparing to Read 120
      READING SKILL ▶ POINTS OF COMPARISON
      READING FOCUS ▶ COMPARISON-CONTRAST STRUCTURE
   Reading Selection: "The Nixon-Kennedy Presidential Debates,"
      Edward Wakin from *How TV Changed America's Mind* 121
   Vocabulary Mini-Lesson: *Prefixes and Suffixes* 126
   Test-Taking Mini-Lesson: *Recognizing Supporting Details* 127

WRITING WORKSHOP: *A Comparison-Contrast Essay* 128
   Prewriting 128
   Critical-Thinking Mini-Lesson: *Evaluating Details*

   Writing 136
   Framework for a Comparison-Contrast Essay
   A Writer's Model: "Puppy Love or Hamster Heaven" 137
   A Student's Model: "A Collection Question," Matthew Hester 138

   Revising 139
   First Reading: *Content and Organization*
   Second Reading: *Style*
      Focus on Sentences: *Combining Sentences*

   Publishing 142
   Proofreading: Grammar Link—*Using Comparatives Correctly*
   Test-Taking Mini-Lesson: *Writing a Classification Essay* 145
   Connections to Life: *Comparing Documentaries* 146

FOCUS ON VIEWING AND REPRESENTING
   Comparing Ideas in Photographs 147

CHOICES: *Careers; Crossing the Curriculum: Art, Music;*
   Creative Writing 151

CHAPTER 5

Exposition

Responding to a Novel 152

Chapter Planning Guide T151A
Chapter Overview T151C

Preview 153

READING WORKSHOP: A Book Review 154
Preparing to Read 154
  READING SKILL ▸ POINT OF VIEW
  READING FOCUS ▸ ELEMENTS OF A NOVEL
Reading Selection: Review of *Catherine, Called Birdy,* Kathleen Odean from *Great Books for Girls* 155
Vocabulary Mini-Lesson: *Wordbusting Strategy (CSSD)* 159
Test-Taking Mini-Lesson: *Answering Questions About Unfamiliar Vocabulary* 160

WRITING WORKSHOP: A Book Review 161
Prewriting 161
Critical-Thinking Mini-Lesson: *Identifying the Elements of a Plot*

Writing 168
Framework for a Book Review
A Writer's Model: "A Review of Natalie Babbitt's *Tuck Everlasting*" 169
A Student's Model: "A Review of *Out of the Storm* by Patricia Willis," Diana DeGarmo 170

Revising 171
First Reading: *Content and Organization*
Second Reading: *Style*
  Focus on Word Choice: *Clichés*

Publishing 174
Proofreading: Grammar Link—*Using Appositives*
Connections to Literature: *Writing a Short Story* 176
Connections to Literature: *Writing an Essay About a Poem's Sound Effects* 178

FOCUS ON VIEWING AND REPRESENTING
Comparing Media: Film, TV, and Literature 181

CHOICES: Careers, Writing, Connecting Cultures, Technology, Creative Writing 185

CHAPTER 6

Exposition

Sharing Your Research 186

Chapter Planning Guide T185A
Chapter Overview T185C

Preview 187

READING WORKSHOP: *An Informative Article* 188
  Preparing to Read 188
    READING SKILL ▶ MAKING INFERENCES: DRAWING CONCLUSIONS
    READING FOCUS ▶ AUTHOR'S PURPOSE
  Reading Selection: "The California Gold Rush," Kathy Wilmore
    from *Junior Scholastic* 189
  Vocabulary Mini-Lesson: *Word Roots* 196
  Test-Taking Mini-Lesson: *Answering Questions About Tables* 197

WRITING WORKSHOP: *A Research Report* 198
  Prewriting 198
  Critical-Thinking Mini-Lesson: *Searching the World Wide Web for
    Information*
  Writing Mini-Lesson: *Paraphrasing*

  Writing 210
  Framework for a Research Report
  A Writer's Model: "The South American Guanaco" 211
  A Student's Model: "Billiards," Genna Offerman 213

  Revising 214
  First Reading: *Content and Organization*
  Second Reading: *Style*
    Focus on Word Choice: *Using Precise Nouns*

  Publishing 217
  Proofreading: Grammar Link—*Capitalizing and Punctuating Titles*
  Test-Taking Mini-Lesson: *Writing an Informative Essay* 219
  Connections to Life: *Creating Visuals to Share Information* 220

FOCUS ON SPEAKING AND LISTENING
  Giving and Evaluating a Research Presentation 222

CHOICES: *Careers, Listening, Crossing the Curriculum: Physical
  Education, Creative Writing* 225

CHAPTER 7

Persuasion

Making a Difference 226

Chapter Planning Guide T225A
Chapter Overview T225C

Preview 227

READING WORKSHOP: *A Persuasive Essay* 228
  Preparing to Read 228
    READING SKILL ▸ FACT AND OPINION
    READING FOCUS ▸ REASONS AND EVIDENCE
  Reading Selection: "The U.S. Has a Garbage Crisis," William Dudley
    from *The Environment: Distinguishing Between Fact and Opinion* 229
  Vocabulary Mini-Lesson: *Dictionary and Thesaurus* 235
  Test-Taking Mini-Lesson: *Answering Questions About Fact and Opinion* 236

WRITING WORKSHOP: *A Persuasive Letter* 237
  Prewriting 237
  Critical-Thinking Mini-Lesson: *Understanding Your Audience*

  Writing 244
  Framework for a Persuasive Letter
  A Writer's Model: "Dear Mr. Matsuo" 245
  A Student's Model: A Letter to the President, Tyler Duckworth 247

  Revising 248
  First Reading: *Content and Organization*
  Second Reading: *Style*
    Focus on Sentences: *Eliminating Stringy Sentences*

  Publishing 251
  Proofreading: Grammar Link—*Punctuating Possessives Correctly*
  Test-Taking Mini-Lesson: *Answering Questions That Ask You
    to Persuade* 253

  Connections to Life: *Writing a Humorous Advertisement* 254

FOCUS ON LISTENING
  Evaluating a Persuasive Speech 256

CHOICES: *Editorial Cartoons, Careers, Crossing the Curriculum: Social
Studies, Speaking* 259

T14 Contents

PART 2 Sentences and Paragraphs 260

CHAPTER 8 Writing Effective Sentences 262

WRITING CLEAR SENTENCES 262
  Sentence Fragments 262
  Run-on Sentences 265
  Stringy Sentences 266

REVIEW A: Revising Sentence Fragments, Run-on Sentences,
and Stringy Sentences 268

COMBINING SENTENCES 269
  Inserting Words 269
  Inserting Groups of Words 271
  Using Connecting Words 272
    Joining Subjects and Verbs 273
    Joining Sentences 274

REVIEW B: Revising a Paragraph by Combining Sentences 276

REVIEW C: Writing Clear Sentences 276

CHAPTER 9 Learning About Paragraphs 278

WHAT IS A PARAGRAPH? 278

WHY USE PARAGRAPHS? 278

WHAT ARE THE PARTS OF A PARAGRAPH? 279
  The Main Idea and Topic Sentence 279
  Supporting Sentences 281
  The Clincher Sentence 282

WHAT MAKES A GOOD PARAGRAPH? 283
  Coherence 283
    Organizing Ideas 283
      Spatial Order 284
      Chronological Order 285
    Words That Connect Ideas 287
  Elaboration 289

Contents T15

WHAT ARE THE TYPES OF PARAGRAPHS? 291
    Narrative Paragraphs 292
    Descriptive Paragraphs 292
    Expository Paragraphs 293
    Persuasive Paragraphs 293

HOW ARE PARAGRAPHS USED IN LONGER PIECES OF WRITING? 294
    Dividing a Longer Piece of Writing into Paragraphs 295

REVIEW A: Writing a Narrative Paragraph 296

REVIEW B: Writing a Descriptive Paragraph 296

REVIEW C: Writing an Expository Paragraph 297

REVIEW D: Writing a Persuasive Paragraph 297

Teaching Strands T297A

PART 3 **Grammar, Usage, and Mechanics** 298

CHAPTER 10

The Sentence
Subject and Predicate, Kinds of Sentences 300

DIAGNOSTIC PREVIEW 300
   A. Identifying Sentences
   B. Identifying Simple Subjects and Simple Predicates
   C. Punctuating and Classifying Sentences by Purpose

SENTENCE OR SENTENCE FRAGMENT? 302

SUBJECT AND PREDICATE 305
   The Subject 305
   The Predicate 307
   Finding the Subject 310
   Compound Subject and Compound Verb 311

KINDS OF SENTENCES 316

CHAPTER REVIEW 319
   A. Identifying Sentences
   B. Identifying the Complete Subject and the Complete Predicate
   C. Identifying Simple Subjects and Simple Predicates
   D. Punctuating and Classifying Sentences by Purpose

Writing Application: *Using Sentence Variety* 321

CHAPTER 11

Parts of Speech Overview
Noun, Pronoun, Adjective 322

DIAGNOSTIC PREVIEW: Identifying Nouns, Pronouns, and Adjectives 322

THE NOUN 323
   Proper Nouns and Common Nouns 324

THE PRONOUN 328
   Personal Pronouns 329
   Reflexive and Intensive Pronouns 330
   Demonstrative Pronouns 332
   Indefinite Pronouns 332
   Interrogative Pronouns 334
   Relative Pronouns 335

THE ADJECTIVE 336
   Proper Adjectives 338
   Demonstrative Adjectives 339

CHAPTER REVIEW 343
   A. Identifying Nouns, Pronouns, and Adjectives
   B. Identifying Common and Proper Nouns
   C. Identifying Pronouns
   D. Identifying Proper and Demonstrative Adjectives
   E. Identifying Nouns, Pronouns, and Adjectives
   Writing Application: *Using Pronouns in a Plot Summary* 345

Parts of Speech Overview
Verb, Adverb, Preposition, Conjunction, Interjection **346**

CHAPTER 12

DIAGNOSTIC PREVIEW: Identifying Verbs, Adverbs, Prepositions, Conjunctions, and Interjections 346

THE VERB 347
   Main Verbs and Helping Verbs 347
   Action Verbs 350
   Linking Verbs 351
   Transitive and Intransitive Verbs 353

THE ADVERB 357
   The Position of Adverbs 358

THE PREPOSITION 360
   The Prepositional Phrase 361
   Preposition or Adverb? 363

THE CONJUNCTION 364

THE INTERJECTION 366

DETERMINING PARTS OF SPEECH 368

CHAPTER REVIEW 369
   A. Identifying Verb Phrases and Helping Verbs
   B. Identifying Action and Linking Verbs
   C. Identifying Transitive and Intransitive Verbs
   D. Identifying Adverbs and the Words They Modify
   E. Identifying Prepositions and Their Objects

F. Identifying Verbs, Adverbs, Prepositions, Conjunctions, and Interjections
G. Determining Parts of Speech

Writing Application: *Using Verbs in a List* 371

CHAPTER 13

The Phrase and the Clause
Prepositional Phrases, Independent and Subordinate Clauses, Sentence Structure **372**

DIAGNOSTIC PREVIEW 372
 A. Identifying Adjective Phrases and Adverb Phrases
 B. Identifying Independent Clauses and Subordinate Clauses
 C. Identifying Types of Sentences

THE PHRASE 374

PREPOSITIONAL PHRASES 375
 Adjective Phrases 377
 Adverb Phrases 381

THE CLAUSE 387
 Independent Clauses 387
 Subordinate Clauses 388

SENTENCE STRUCTURE 394
 Simple Sentences 394
 Compound Sentences 395
 Complex Sentences 397
 Compound-Complex Sentences 398

CHAPTER REVIEW 399
 A. Identifying Adjective and Adverb Phrases
 B. Identifying Independent and Subordinate Clauses
 C. Identifying Clauses
 D. Identifying Types of Sentences

Writing Application: *Using Prepositional Phrases in a Story* 401

Complements
Direct and Indirect Objects, Subject Complements **402**

CHAPTER 14

DIAGNOSTIC PREVIEW: Identifying Complements 402

RECOGNIZING COMPLEMENTS 403

OBJECTS OF VERBS 405
    Direct Objects 405
    Indirect Objects 407

SUBJECT COMPLEMENTS 410
    Predicate Nominatives 410
    Predicate Adjectives 412

CHAPTER REVIEW 417
    A. Identifying Direct and Indirect Objects
    B. Identifying Subject Complements
    C. Identifying Complements
    Writing Application: *Using Complements in a Paragraph* 418

Agreement
Subject and Verb, Pronoun and Antecedent **420**

CHAPTER 15

DIAGNOSTIC PREVIEW 420
    A. Choosing Verbs That Agree in Number with Their Subjects
    B. Choosing Pronouns That Agree with Their Antecedents

NUMBER 422

AGREEMENT OF SUBJECT AND VERB 422

PROBLEMS IN AGREEMENT 425
    Phrases Between Subject and Verb 425
    Indefinite Pronouns 427
    Compound Subjects 429
    Subject After the Verb 432
    The Contractions *Don't* and *Doesn't* 433

AGREEMENT OF PRONOUN AND ANTECEDENT 435

CHAPTER REVIEW 441
    A. Choosing Verbs That Agree in Number with Their Subjects
    B. Changing the Number of Subjects and Verbs
    C. Proofreading for Errors in Pronoun-Antecedent Agreement
    Writing Application: *Using Agreement in Instructions* 443

CHAPTER 16

Using Verbs Correctly
Principal Parts, Regular and Irregular Verbs, Tense **444**

DIAGNOSTIC PREVIEW: Revising Incorrect Verb Forms in Sentences 444

PRINCIPAL PARTS OF VERBS 445
    Regular Verbs 446
    Irregular Verbs 448

TENSE 458
    Progressive Forms 459
    The Verb *Be* 460
    Consistency of Tense 462

SIX CONFUSING VERBS 463
    Sit and *Set* 463
    Rise and *Raise* 464
    Lie and *Lay* 466

CHAPTER REVIEW 471
    A. Using Correct Forms of Irregular Verbs
    B. Writing the Past and Past Participle Forms of Irregular Verbs
    C. Proofreading for Correct Verb Forms
    Writing Application: *Using Verbs in a Description* 473

CHAPTER 17

Using Pronouns Correctly
Subject and Object Forms **474**

DIAGNOSTIC PREVIEW: Revising Incorrect Pronoun Forms
    In Sentences 474

THE FORMS OF PERSONAL PRONOUNS 475
    The Subject Form 477
    The Object Form 481

SPECIAL PRONOUN PROBLEMS 486
    Who and *Whom* 486
    Pronouns with Appositives 488

CHAPTER REVIEW 491
    A. Identifying Correct Pronoun Forms
    B. Identifying Pronouns Used as Predicate Nominatives
    C. Identifying the Correct Forms of Pronouns Used as Subjects, Direct Objects, Indirect Objects, and Objects of Prepositions
    Writing Application: *Using Correct Pronoun Forms in Writing* 493

Using Modifiers Correctly
Comparison and Placement **494**

DIAGNOSTIC PREVIEW: Correcting Errors in the Form, Use, and Placement of Modifiers 494

WHAT IS A MODIFIER? 495
    One-Word Modifiers 495
    Phrases Used as Modifiers 496
    Clauses Used as Modifiers 496

COMPARISON OF ADJECTIVES AND ADVERBS 497
    Regular Comparison 498
    Irregular Comparison 501

SPECIAL PROBLEMS IN USING MODIFIERS 502

DOUBLE NEGATIVES 507

PLACEMENT OF MODIFIERS 509
    Adjectives and Adverbs 510
    Prepositional Phrases 510
    Adjective Clauses 512

CHAPTER REVIEW 515
    A. Identifying the Correct Forms of Modifiers
    B. Correcting Double Negatives
    C. Writing Comparative and Superlative Forms
    D. Correcting Misplaced Phrases and Clauses
    Writing Application: *Using Negative Words in Description* 517

CHAPTER 19

A Glossary of Usage
Common Usage Problems **518**

DIAGNOSTIC PREVIEW: Correcting Errors in Usage 518

ABOUT THE GLOSSARY 519

CHAPTER REVIEW 533
    A. Revising Sentences by Correcting Errors in Usage
    B. Revising Sentences by Correcting Errors in Usage
    Writing Application: *Using Formal English in a Letter* 535

CHAPTER 20

Capital Letters
Rules for Capitalization **536**

DIAGNOSTIC PREVIEW: Correcting Sentences by Capitalizing Words 536

USING CAPITAL LETTERS 537

CHAPTER REVIEW 557
    A. Proofreading Sentences for Correct Capitalization
    B. Correcting Sentences by Using Capital Letters Correctly
    C. Correcting Errors in Capitalization
    Writing Application: *Using Capital Letters in an Essay* 559

CHAPTER 21

Punctuation
End Marks, Commas, Semicolons, Colons **560**

DIAGNOSTIC PREVIEW: Using Periods, Question Marks, Exclamation
    Points, Commas, Semicolons, and Colons Correctly 560

END MARKS 561

COMMAS 566
    Items in a Series 566
    Compound Sentences 568
    Interrupters 570
    Introductory Words, Phrases, and Clauses 572

  Conventional Uses 574
  Unnecessary Commas 575

SEMICOLONS 577

COLONS 579

CHAPTER REVIEW 583
  A. Using Punctuation Correctly
  B. Using Punctuation Correctly

Writing Application: *Using End Marks in a Screenplay* 585

Punctuation
Underlining (Italics), Quotation Marks, Apostrophes, Hyphens **586**

CHAPTER 22

DIAGNOSTIC PREVIEW 586
  A. Proofreading Sentences for the Correct Use of
    Underlining (Italics) and Quotation Marks
  B. Proofreading Sentences for the Correct Use of
    Apostrophes and Hyphens

UNDERLINING (ITALICS) 588

QUOTATION MARKS 590

APOSTROPHES 598
  Possessive Case 598
  Contractions 602
  Plurals 605

HYPHENS 606

CHAPTER REVIEW 609
  A. Using Underlining (Italics), Quotation Marks, Apostrophes,
    and Hyphens
  B. Revising Indirect Quotations to Create Direct Quotations
  C. Punctuating a Dialogue

Writing Application: *Using Apostrophes in a Letter* 611

CHAPTER 23

Spelling
Improving Your Spelling **612**

DIAGNOSTIC PREVIEW 612
    A. Proofreading Sentences for Correct Spelling
    B. Proofreading Sentences to Correct Spelling Errors

GOOD SPELLING HABITS 613

SPELLING RULES 615
    ie and *ei* 615
    Prefixes and Suffixes 616
    Forming the Plurals of Nouns 621

WORDS OFTEN CONFUSED 625

CHAPTER REVIEW 637
    A. Proofreading Sentences for Correct Spelling
    B. Choosing Between Words Often Confused
    C. Proofreading a Paragraph to Correct Spelling Errors
    Writing Application: *Using Correct Spelling in a Personal Letter* 639

SPELLING WORDS 640

CHAPTER 24

Correcting Common Errors
Key Language Skills Review **642**

GRAMMAR AND USAGE 643
    Grammar and Usage Test: Section 1 660
    Grammar and Usage Test: Section 2 662

MECHANICS 664
    Mechanics Test: Section 1 674
    Mechanics Test: Section 2 675

PART 4   Quick Reference Handbook 678

THE DICTIONARY 680
  Types and Contents 680

DOCUMENT DESIGN 682
  Manuscript Style 682
  Desktop Publishing 683
  Graphics 687

THE HISTORY OF ENGLISH 690
  Origins and Uses 690

THE LIBRARY/MEDIA CENTER 694
  Using Print and Electronic Sources 694

READING AND VOCABULARY 704
  Reading 704
  Vocabulary 713

SPEAKING AND LISTENING 719
  Speaking 719
  Listening 727

STUDYING AND TEST TAKING 733
  Studying 733
  Test Taking 737

VIEWING AND REPRESENTING 743
  Understanding Media Terms 743

WRITING 755
  Skills, Structures, and Techniques 755

GRAMMAR AT A GLANCE 768

Diagramming Appendix 790

Index 806

Acknowledgments 834

Photo and Illustration Credits 836

MODELS

READING SELECTIONS

- William Dudley, **"The U.S. Has a Garbage Crisis,"** from *The Environment: Distinguishing Between Fact and Fiction*
- Paula Morrow, **"Making a Flying Fish,"** from *Faces: Happy Holidays*
- Kathleen Odean, review of ***Catherine, Called Birdy,*** from *Great Books for Girls*
- Rosa Parks with Jim Haskins, from ***Rosa Parks: My Story***
- Mary Roach, **"Meteorite Hunters,"** from *Muse*
- Edward Wakin, **"The Nixon-Kennedy Presidential Debates,"** from *How TV Changed America's Mind*
- **"Whale Watch: Kids Use Internet to Track Progress of Newly Freed J. J.,"** from *Los Angeles Times; Orange County Edition*
- Kathy Wilmore, **"The California Gold Rush,"** from *Junior Scholastic*

WRITING MODELS

- Lewis Carroll, **"How Doth the Little Crocodile"**
- Beverly Cleary, ***Ramona Forever***
- David A. Dary, ***The Buffalo Book***
- Isak Dinesen, **"The Ring"**
- Harry Gersh, ***Women Who Made America Great***
- Edwin A. Hoey, **"Foul Shot"**
- **"Introduction to Sharks,"** *Ocean of Know* Web site
- Wolfgang Langewiesche, **"The Spectacle of Niagara"**
- Stephen Mooser, ***Lights! Camera! Scream!***
- Jack Prelutsky, **"Last Night I Dreamed of Chickens"**
- **"Reading for the Blind,"** *Smithsonian*
- **"Side View of Complex,"** *Friends of Volunteers* Web site
- Robert Louis Stevenson, **"Windy Nights"**
- Time-Life Books, ***Forces of Nature***
- **"Volunteering—It's So Easy, a Kid Can Do It,"** *GirlZone* Web site
- Paul Robert Walker, ***Pride of Puerto Rico***
- Mary Whitebird, **"Ta-Na-E-Ka"**

STUDENT MODELS

- Natalie Banta and Amy Tidwell, **"Mr. Sagers Moves to Cyprus High"**
- Diana DeGarmo, **"A Review of *Out of the Storm* by Patricia Willis"**
- Tyler Duckworth, **A Letter to the President**
- Matthew Hester, **"A Collection Question"**
- Genna Offerman, **"Billiards"**
- Anthony C. Rodrigues, **"In the Net"**
- Stephanie Thompson, **"Make It Grow"**

Features

Reading Skills and Focuses

Making Inferences: Forming Generalizations	21
Chronological Order	23
Main Idea	53
Inverted Pyramid Structure	54
Making Predictions	87
Forming Mental Images	91
Points of Comparison	123
Comparison-Contrast Structure	124
Elements of a Novel	156
Point of View	157
Making Inferences: Drawing Conclusions	192
Author's Purpose	194
Fact and Opinion	231
Reasons and Evidence	232

Vocabulary Mini-Lessons

Context Clues	25
Multiple-Meaning Words	56
Compound Words	92
Prefixes and Suffixes	126
Wordbusting Strategy	159
Word Roots	196
Dictionary and Thesaurus	235

Reading Test-Taking Mini-Lessons

Making Inferences	26
Answering Main Idea Questions	57
Making Predictions	93
Recognizing Supporting Details	127
Answering Questions About Unfamiliar Vocabulary	160
Answering Questions About Tables	197
Answering Questions About Fact and Opinion	236

Critical-Thinking/Writing Mini-Lessons

Arranging Ideas	31
Analyzing Cause and Effect	65
Elaboration: Using Specific Language	97
Evaluating Details	135
Identifying the Elements of a Plot	165
Searching the World Wide Web for Information	204
Paraphrasing	206
Understanding Your Audience	240

Focus on Sentences/Word Choice
Exact Verbs	38
Varying Sentences	71
Transitional Words	105
Combining Sentences	141
Clichés	173
Using Precise Nouns	216
Eliminating Stringy Sentences	250

Grammar Links
Capitalizing Proper Nouns	39
Correcting Run-on Sentences	72
Using Commas in a Series	106
Using Comparatives Correctly	142
Using Appositives	174
Capitalizing and Punctuating Titles	217
Punctuating Possessives Correctly	251

Writing Test-Taking Mini-Lessons
Writing Description for Tests	41
Writing Instructions	108
Writing a Classification Essay	145
Writing an Informative Essay	219
Answering Questions That Ask You to Persuade	253

Connections to Literature/Life
Writing a Narrative Poem	42
Writing a Newspaper's Advice Column	74
Writing a Descriptive Paragraph	109
Comparing Documentaries	146
Writing a Short Story	176
Writing an Essay About a Poem's Sound Effects	178
Creating Visuals to Share Information	220
Writing a Humorous Advertisement	254

Designing Your Writing
Illustrating Your Autobiographical Incident	34
Laying Out Your Newspaper	77
Illustrating Steps in a Process	101
Creating a Bar Graph	143
Highlighting a Quotation	166
Creating Headings	209
Using Business Letter Format	246

Viewing and Representing/Speaking and Listening
Telling a Story	45
Producing a Newspaper	76
Producing a TV News Segment	79
Viewing and Listening to Learn	112
Comparing Ideas in Photographs	147
Comparing Media: Film, TV, and Literature	181
Giving and Evaluating a Research Presentation	222
Evaluating a Persuasive Speech	256

Major Communication Assignments

	Introductory Course	First Course	Second Course
Narration/ Description	• Writing About a Life Experience • Writing a Narrative Poem • Telling a Story • Writing a Descriptive Paragraph • Writing a Short Story	• Writing an Eyewitness Account • Writing a Descriptive Essay • Writing a Descriptive Poem • Writing a Short Story • Writing a Personal Narrative	• Writing a Personal Narrative • Writing a Descriptive Essay • Telling a True Story • Writing a Humorous "How-to" Poem
Exposition	• Writing a Newspaper Article • Writing a Newspaper's Advice Column • Producing a Newspaper • Producing TV News • Writing a "How-to" Paper • Writing a Comparison-Contrast Essay • Comparing Documentaries • Writing a Book Review • Writing About a Poem • Writing a Research Report • Giving a Research Presentation	• Writing Instructions • Giving Directions • Writing an Advantages/Disadvantages Essay • Comparing Informative TV or Video Presentations • Making a Documentary Video • Creating Book Jacket Copy • Analyzing a Poem • Analyzing and Designing Book Covers • Writing an Information Report • Giving an Informative Speech	• Writing a Process Explanation • Writing a Cause-and-Effect Essay • Writing a Book Review • Creating a Slide Show Comparing a Book and Its Movie • Writing a Response to a Poem • Holding a Panel Discussion • Writing a Research Report • Giving an Informative Speech Using a Web Site as a Visual • Designing a Web Site
Persuasion	• Writing a Persuasive Letter • Writing an Advertisement	• Writing a Persuasive Essay • Creating a Print Advertisement • Creating Your Own Commercial	• Writing a Persuasive Essay • Writing a Short Story That Persuades • Giving a Persuasive Speech • Creating a Brochure
Research Skills	• Writing a Research Report • Giving a Research Presentation	• Writing a Research Report • Giving an Informative Speech	• Writing a Research Report • Giving an Informative Speech Using a Web Site as a Visual • Designing a Web Site
Creative Writing, Speaking, and Representing	• Writing a Narrative Poem • Telling a Story • Writing a Short Story	• Writing Haiku • Writing a Short Story • Performing a Dramatic Reading	• Writing a Humorous "How-to" Poem • Producing a Scene from a Book • Writing a Fable

	Third Course	**Fourth Course**	**Fifth Course**	**Sixth Course**
	• Writing a Description of a Place • Taking Field Notes • Creating a Video Postcard • Writing a Personal Narrative • Writing a Short Story • Presenting Oral Narratives	• Writing a Personal Reflection • Writing a Free-Verse Poem • Making a Video Reflection • Writing a Short Story • Presenting an Oral Interpretation	• Writing an Autobiographical Narrative • Writing a Narrative for an Application • Creating an Oral History • Writing a Poem that Defines • Writing a Dramatic Scene • Writing a Short Story • Adapting a Scene from a Novel for Film	• Writing a Reflective Essay • Writing a College Application • Creating an Oral History • Creating an Audiovisual Self-Reflection • Writing a Short Story • Planning a Trailer • Writing a Ballad • Writing a Dramatic Scene
	• Writing a Comparison-Contrast Essay • Comparing and Contrasting Media Coverage • Writing a Cause-and-Effect Explanation • Writing a Literary Cause-and-Effect Essay • Presenting an Informative Speech • Writing an Analysis of a Poem • Presenting a Poetry Reading • Writing an I-Search Paper • Making a Video Documentary • Analyzing Network News	• Writing a Comparison-Contrast Essay • Distinguishing the Purposes of Media Forms • Comparing and Contrasting Media Coverage • Writing a Cause-and-Effect Explanation • Participating in Group Discussions • Writing a Problem-Analysis Essay • Giving an Informative Speech • Writing a Literary Analysis • Critiquing a Film • Writing a Research Paper	• Writing an Extended Definition • Comparing and Contrasting Media Coverage • Writing a Progress Report • Writing a Memo • Writing and Delivering an Informative Speech • Writing a Problem-Solution Essay • Writing a Literary Analysis of a Novel • Writing a Historical Research Paper • Exploring Uses of History in Fiction • Creating a Video Documentary	• Writing a Comparison-Contrast Essay • Comparing and Contrasting TV Entertainment Genres • Conducting Interviews • Writing a Causal Analysis • Creating an Informative Speech • Writing a Literary Analysis of a Drama • Writing a Literary Research Paper • Researching a Film • Creating an Investigative Documentary • Examining Characterization in TV Sitcoms • Analyzing TV News • Investigating Problem-Solution in Literature
	• Writing a Persuasive Paper • Making a Persuasive Speech • Writing a Critical Review • Critiquing Persuasion in the Media	• Writing a Position Paper • Writing a Letter of Application • Giving a Persuasive Speech • Creating a Brochure • Creating a Documentary on Print Advertising	• Writing an Editorial • Writing a Sales Letter • Writing and Delivering a Persuasive Speech • Creating a Political Campaign • Writing a Book Review • Preparing and Delivering an Oral Critique • Writing an Ad Evaluation • Creating an Ad Campaign	• Writing a Persuasive Essay • Creating a Parody • Analyzing Media Persuasion • Making a Persuasive Speech • Reviewing a Documentary • Writing a Proposal • Conducting a Panel Discussion • Evaluating a Film Version of a Drama
	• Writing an I-Search Paper • Researching for Fiction Writing • Making a Video Documentary	• Writing a Research Paper • Evaluating Web Sites • Analyzing Research in the Media	• Writing a Historical Research Paper • Exploring Uses of History in Fiction • Evaluating Web Sites	• Writing a Literary Research Paper • Researching a Film • Creating an Investigative Documentary
	• Creating a Video Postcard • Writing a Short Story • Writing a Poem • Presenting a Poetry Reading	• Writing a Free-Verse Poem • Writing a Short Story • Presenting an Oral Interpretation • Making a Video Reflection	• Writing a Dramatic Scene • Writing a Poem that Defines • Writing a Short Story • Adapting a Scene for Film • Preparing and Presenting an Oral Interpretation	• Writing a Short Story • Writing a Ballad • Writing a Dramatic Scene • Creating a Dramatic Reading • Creating a Parody

Elements of Language

Designed for the Information Age

While reading and writing have been traditional topics of instruction for centuries, *what* and *how* students read and write have changed dramatically. Personal computers have become a staple in most homes and classrooms, and the variety of communications coming through television, radio, movies, and the Internet demands that students process information in a number of ways. That's why Holt, Rinehart and Winston has created *Elements of Language.*

Elements of Language is a comprehensive language arts program designed for the Information Age. Through its exciting visual design and use of real-world examples, *Elements of Language* helps students understand that—as global communications guru Marshall McLuhan said—"the medium is the message," whether that medium is a book, a television show, an advertisement, or a Web site.

Structured for Teacher Flexibility

Elements of Language is comprehensive in scope yet structured in a way that gives you the ability to pick and choose the instruction most appropriate for each class. Each book is divided into four main parts—the first three parts developing instructional topics in depth and the fourth part providing a comprehensive reference tool.

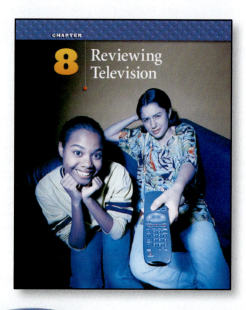

Part 1

Communications

Part 1: Communications is dedicated to an intensive study of a variety of literacies—reading, writing, speaking, listening, viewing, and representing—with an emphasis on writing. Each chapter uses nonfiction texts and real-world documents to explore different modes of communication, such as reviewing a television program, evaluating print ads, or writing a persuasive editorial.

Part 2

Sentences and Paragraphs

Part 2: Sentences and Paragraphs gives students focused instruction in how to revise and improve their sentences through techniques such as combining sentences and varying sentence lengths. After mastering the skills of structuring sentences, students then learn the basics of good paragraphs, including how to achieve unity and coherence and how to use effective transitions between paragraphs in a longer piece of writing.

Part 3

Grammar, Usage, and Mechanics

Part 3: Grammar, Usage, and Mechanics is organized in the classic and effective Warriner's format—rule, followed by example, followed by exercise. Part 3 also contains spelling instruction with spelling rules and an extensive list of words that are often confused.

Part 4

Quick Reference Handbook

Part 4: Quick Reference Handbook gives students an efficient way to access information to help them write, do research, hone speaking and listening skills, learn strategies for studying and taking tests, and develop visual literacy. The Handbook also includes "Grammar at a Glance," a concise overview and reference tool.

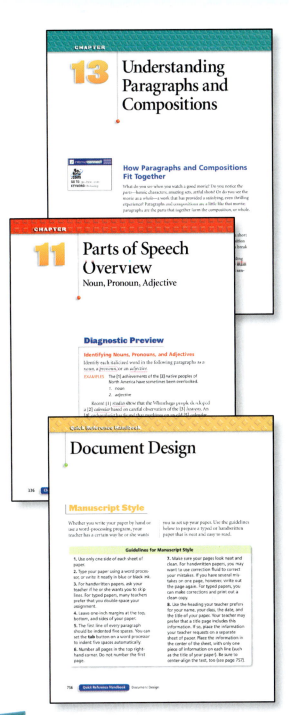

Part 1 Communications
The Reading Workshop

Taking Reading to the Next Level

All readers, even the best, sometimes struggle. **Part 1: Communications** offers strategies and skills developed by the experts to help you address the specific reading needs of your students.

Real-World Focus

Each Communications chapter opens with a **Reading Workshop** that focuses on a reading skill students need to become effective communicators. Each Reading Workshop features nonfiction texts drawn from real-world sources, such as magazines, newspapers, brochures, or Web sites, to model for students the different ways ideas are communicated through writing.

Reading Skills for Life

The **Reading Workshops** teach students strategies for reading and for understanding different kinds of texts.

READING SKILL

Each **Reading Workshop** targets one essential reading skill, demonstrating the strategies active readers use to maximize comprehension.

READING FOCUS

Each **Reading Workshop** focuses on a unique element characteristic of the informational or persuasive text students are studying.

Expert Advice

Dr. Richard Vacca, past president of the International Reading Association and author of *Reading in the Content Areas,* established the conceptual basis for the reading strand in *Elements of Language*. He was pivotal in shaping both the instructional design and the content of the program, and his classroom experience informs the program's practical, real-world strategies for improving communication.

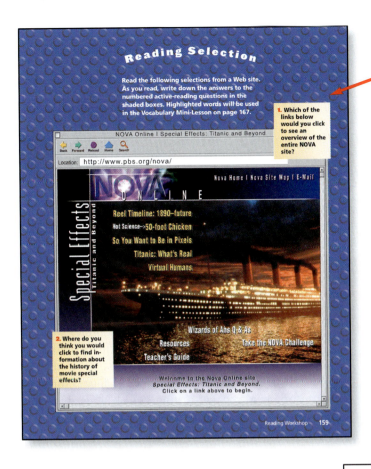

Active-Reading Questions model the thinking and questioning students need to acquire strong reading skills.

Mini-Lessons demonstrate strategies for acquiring an extensive vocabulary and scoring well on standardized tests.

Thinking It Through walks students through the steps needed to analyze a task and identify the critical path to success.

Expert Advice

Judith L. Irvin helped establish the conceptual basis for the middle school reading strand of *Elements of Language*. Dr. Irvin teaches courses in curriculum, middle school education, and educational leadership at Florida State University. She is also chair of the Research Committee of the National Middle School Association and was the editor of *Research in Middle Level Education* for six years.

Part 1 Communications
The Writing Workshop

Writing by Design

A blank page can be one of the most terrifying things any writer faces. *Elements of Language* recognizes that fear and through its **Writing Workshops** guides students step-by-step through the writing process with focused exercises for prewriting, writing, revising, and publishing.

Reading/Writing Connection

The *Pupil's Edition* provides clear connections between reading and writing, easing the transition from reading "writing" to writing "reading." In the Reading Workshop at the start of each chapter, students learn how to read a real-world text and identify the techniques authors use. This instruction prepares students to write a similar piece in the Writing Workshop.

Visual Delivery of Instruction

The step-by-step nature of the instruction is enhanced by its visual presentation. Throughout the Workshop, abundant, colorful graphics convey information and key concepts. A writer's model and a student model—both clearly structured and labeled—provide strong instructional cues for putting pen to paper or fingers to keyboard.

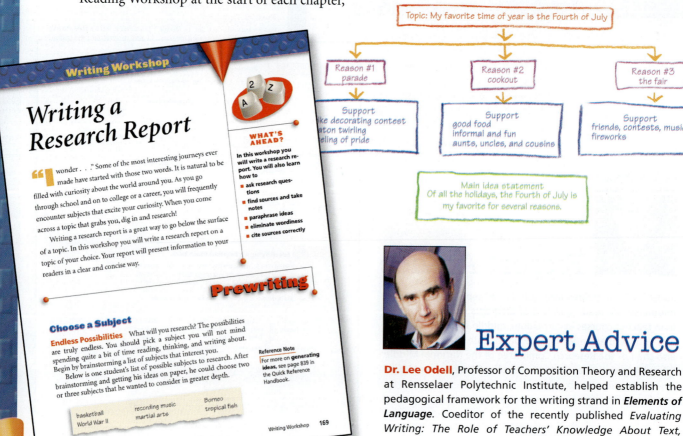

Expert Advice

Dr. Lee Odell, Professor of Composition Theory and Research at Rensselaer Polytechnic Institute, helped establish the pedagogical framework for the writing strand in *Elements of Language*. Coeditor of the recently published *Evaluating Writing: The Role of Teachers' Knowledge About Text, Learning, and Culture* (1999), Dr. Odell guided the development of both the scope and sequence and the instructional design of the Writing Workshops.

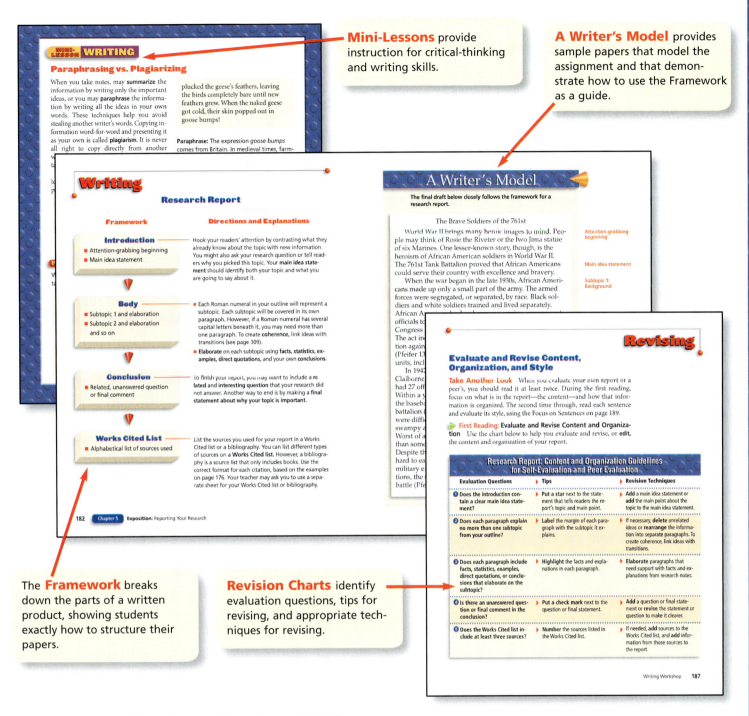

Mini-Lessons provide instruction for critical-thinking and writing skills.

A Writer's Model provides sample papers that model the assignment and that demonstrate how to use the Framework as a guide.

The **Framework** breaks down the parts of a written product, showing students exactly how to structure their papers.

Revision Charts identify evaluation questions, tips for revising, and appropriate techniques for revising.

Features for Developing Style

WORD CHOICE or SENTENCES

Additional instruction and practice help students refine one aspect of their writing style, such as revising wordy sentences or eliminating clichés.

Grammar Link

Instruction and practice show students how to identify and correct common grammatical problems.

Designing Your Writing

This feature teaches students about the visual aspects of writing, helping them choose the most effective design and layout and select the best graphics to convey their message.

T37

Part 1 Communications

Focus on
▶ **Speaking and Listening**
▶ **Viewing and Representing**

Media Literacy and Oral Communication

Today's teenagers are often delighted by the variety and frequency of media. Stimulated from all directions by a multitude of messages, from magazine and television advertising to billboards, movies, and the Internet, students must learn how to understand the power of these messages, how to evaluate them, and how to produce their own messages in a variety of formats. Teaching students to view the media with an analytical eye is a serious responsibility. Students must also learn to receive and interpret verbal messages and to organize ideas and communicate them orally. *Elements of Language* is here to help.

At the end of each Communications chapter, one or more extensive lessons highlight speaking and listening or viewing and representing skills, offering meaningful instruction on ways students can learn to take advantage of the power of the media.

Focus on Viewing and Representing helps students become savvy, critical viewers and creative, responsible media communicators.

Focus on Speaking and Listening encourages students to improve the ways in which they receive and convey oral communications.

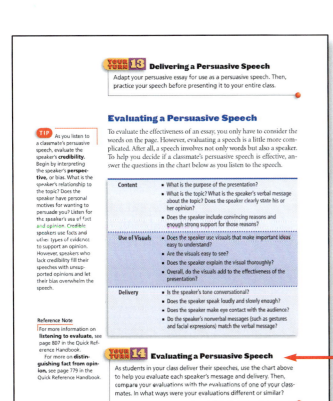

Expert Advice

Renée Hobbs, one of the nation's leading authorities on media education, guided the development of the Viewing and Representing lessons in *Elements of Language*. As the director of the Media Literacy Project at Clark University in Worcester, Massachusetts, Dr. Hobbs works with school districts to develop programs that build the media literacy of students across the nation.

Your Turn puts students' new knowledge to work in real-world situations with hands-on activities.

Features That Connect to Literature and Life

Connections to Life/Connections to Literature features connect chapter concepts to the students' own lives, to the literature they may be reading, and to the communities in which they live.

Foundations for Writing

Part 2 — Sentences and Paragraphs

In **Part 2: Sentences and Paragraphs,** *Elements of Language* focuses on the nuts-and-bolts knowledge students need to become successful writers.

The *Pupil's Edition* presents easy-to-follow instruction on writing complete and effective sentences, combining sentences, and correcting common errors such as fragments, wordiness, and lack of parallel structure.

Students also learn to develop strong paragraphs, focusing on unity and coherence. In grades 10, 11, and 12, students focus on composition structure.

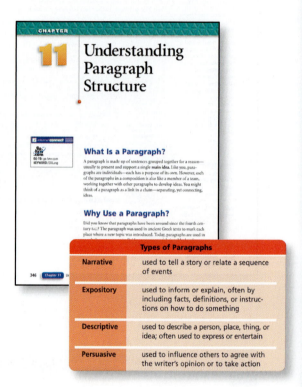

Part 3 — Grammar, Usage, and Mechanics

A confident control of grammar, usage, and mechanics helps to ensure clear and effective communication. In **Part 3: Grammar, Usage, and Mechanics,** *Elements of Language* delivers a comprehensive language skills curriculum that's accessible and effective. Diagnostic Previews give opportunities for diagnosing students' strengths and weaknesses. Reviews A and B provide cumulative assessment, and Chapter Reviews offer additional exercises for ongoing assessments.

Time-Tested Model

Part 3 of *Elements of Language* is based on John Warriner's logical model of instruction—teach students the rule, show examples of the rule in action, and provide immediate practice to reinforce the skill or concept. This time-honored approach has been the authoritative standard for teaching grammar, usage, and mechanics skills for over fifty years.

Warriner's Model for Instruction

"Practice makes perfect," and a multitude of exercises, both written and oral, offer students ample opportunities to practice each rule and learn one concept at a time.

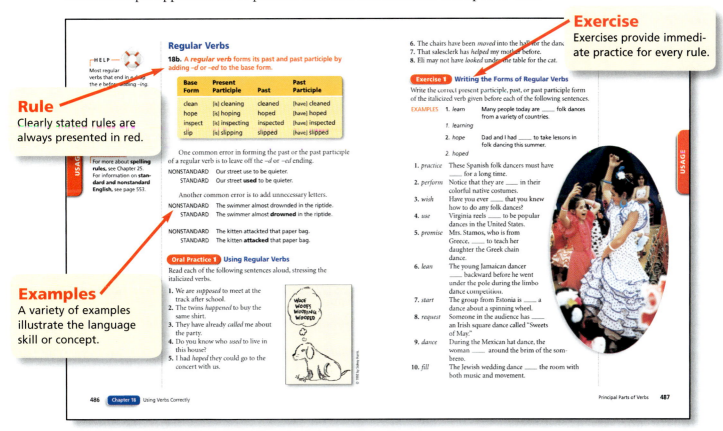

Rule Clearly stated rules are always presented in red.

Examples A variety of examples illustrate the language skill or concept.

Exercise Exercises provide immediate practice for every rule.

Grammar Expert

John E. Warriner, English teacher for thirty years in junior and senior high schools and college, developed the original organizational structure that serves as the basis for the Grammar, Usage, and Mechanics instruction in *Elements of Language*. His well-known and respected pedagogical concept, a clearly stated rule followed by examples and then immediate practice, continues to stand as the ideal model for authoritative grammar, usage, and mechanics instruction.

 **Quick Reference Handbook**

Designed to give students quick and convenient access to key communication concepts, this handbook covers the following topics:

- ▶ The Dictionary
- ▶ Document Design
- ▶ The History of English: Origins and Uses
- ▶ The Library/Media Center
- ▶ Reading and Vocabulary
- ▶ Speaking and Listening
- ▶ Studying and Test Taking
- ▶ Viewing and Representing
- ▶ Writing
- ▶ Grammar at a Glance

Resources to Enrich the Learning Process

Support for Communications Chapters

The wide array of print, visual, and technological resources included with *Elements of Language* gives you the visual and academic support needed to make learning come alive for students.

The **Communications** booklet provides support and practice for the Reading and Writing Workshops with graphic organizers, teaching transparencies, and student worksheets. It includes

- writing prompts
- journal warm-ups
- revising charts
- proofreading practice
- fine art transparencies
- guidelines for peer evaluation and self-evaluation
- additional practice

Designing Your Writing transparencies and worksheets model effective techniques for presenting writing. They teach and demonstrate how the choice of formatting, graphics, and other design elements can affect the intended message.

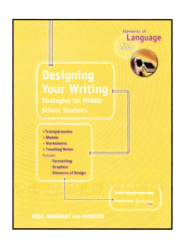

Alternative Readings booklet benefits struggling readers by offering an easier MiniRead, including active-reading questions, for each Reading Workshop. Additional reading strategy options target struggling readers and provide tools they can apply to a range of texts.

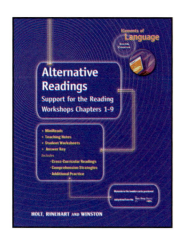

Media Literacy and Communication Skills provides chapter-by-chapter support for speaking, listening, viewing, and representing skills. The package includes videocassettes, *A How-to Handbook,* a set of *Support and Practice* transparencies and worksheets, and *A Teacher's Guide* that pulls these materials together. For more information, see Technology Resources on page T48.

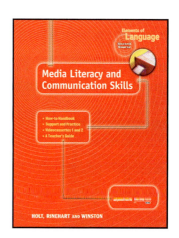

Language Skills

Elements of Language is a comprehensive program of language skills instruction that gives students a solid foundation for effective communication.

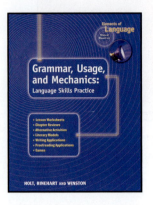

Grammar, Usage, and Mechanics: Language Skills Practice provides additional practice for all grammar, usage, and mechanics rules in Part 3 of the *Pupil's Edition*. Based on Warriner's rule-example-exercise model, this invaluable workbook features exercises, proofreading applications, writing applications, and literary-model activities.

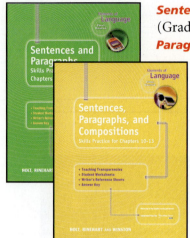

Sentences and Paragraphs (Grades 6–9) and ***Sentences, Paragraphs, and Compositions*** (Grades 10–12) provide up to two pages of additional practice for every exercise in Part 2 of the *Pupil's Edition*.

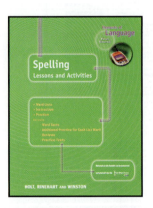

Spelling Lessons and Activities (Grades 6–8) focuses on both sound patterns and word analysis strategies. Analysis and additional practice are included for each word list.

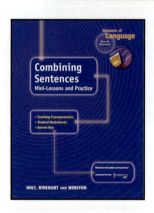

Combining Sentences provides instruction, models, and practice in sentence-combining strategies. This instruction addresses all the basic techniques, such as inserting prepositional or appositive phrases and using compound subjects and verbs.

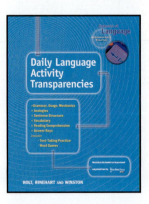

Daily Language Activity Transparencies binder includes
- test-taking practice in analogies, sentence completion, and reading comprehension
- proofreading practice in grammar, usage, and mechanics
- sentence combining
- vocabulary building and word games

Additional Resource

Vocabulary Workshop helps students build their vocabularies and simultaneously prepare for standardized tests. Concepts and skills include analogies, context clues, prefixes, suffixes, roots, synonyms, antonyms, and etymologies.

Vocabulary Workshop Tests assess knowledge of the words and concepts taught in the *Vocabulary Workshop* and provide practice in standardized test formats.

Planning and Assessment

Elements of Language provides several options for planning and assessment, giving you more flexibility for today's diverse classroom.

One-Stop Planner CD-ROM with Test Generator for Macintosh® and Windows®

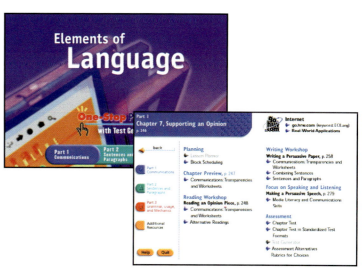

Planning and managing lessons has never been easier than with the *One-Stop Planner CD-ROM*. This convenient, all-in-one planning software program includes all the teaching resources for *Elements of Language*, plus valuable planning and assessment tools. The *One-Stop Planner* provides

- editable lesson plans
- previews of teaching resources
- an easy-to-use test generator

To preview a video segment or transparency, or to print out tests and worksheets for your students, simply select and click.

The **Lesson Planner** focuses on both classroom time and the independent working time needed for the reading, writing, speaking, listening, viewing, and representing lessons in the *Pupil's Edition*.
Teaching Strategies for English-Language Learners provides suggestions for using lessons with students who are not native speakers of English.

Chapter Tests provides short-answer questions in traditional formats for each chapter in the *Pupil's Edition*. The tests include assessment for the Reading and Writing Workshops in Part 1; for the sentences, paragraphs, and compositions instruction in Part 2; and for the grammar, usage, and mechanics skills in Part 3.

Assessment Alternatives includes inventory and evaluation forms for both teachers and students in writing, reading, listening, speaking, viewing, representing, working in groups, and working on projects. Scoring models demonstrate the use of both holistic and analytic rubrics and scales for assessment.

Chapter Tests in Standardized Test Formats offers an additional test for each chapter in the *Pupil's Edition*. Using a range of formats from the most commonly used standardized assessments, these tests include all of the content listed under **Chapter Tests**.

Technology
The Key to Learning in the Information Age

The wide range of dynamic and interactive resources available with *Elements of Language* gives students the opportunity to learn and retain more.

Media Literacy and Communication Skills

Designed to support the speaking, listening, viewing, and representing lessons in *Elements of Language*, this package contains the following materials:

Videocassettes provide video segments that show students and professionals giving speeches and making documentaries. The segments model camera angles and visual effects, and they demonstrate strategies for media analysis.

A How-to Handbook guides students step-by-step through speaking, listening, and media-based activities. The *Handbook* includes sample storyboards, an analysis of camera angles, tips on identifying persuasion in the media, and much more. A glossary of media terms is also included.

Support and Practice contains viewing guides, planning checklists, and transparencies to support each speaking, listening, viewing, and representing lesson in the *Pupil's Edition*. It also includes a summary of each video segment.

A Teacher's Guide includes options for teaching the media literacy and communication skills lessons, including ideas for using the video segments and for guiding students through the projects suggested in the *Pupil's Edition*.

Internet references throughout the *Pupil's Edition* direct students to a new Web site for users of *Elements of Language*. This site links students to activities and projects for each Communications chapter and allows them to put their reading, writing, speaking, and listening skills into action in real-world situations.

The *Elements of Language* Web site is designed to reinforce writing, critical thinking, and media literacy skills. When students see the **go.hrw.com** logo and a keyword in the textbook, they can go to the **go.hrw.com** site, enter the keyword, and link instantly to a dynamic interactive resource.

Language Workshop Interactive Multimedia CD-ROM Software

This award-winning CD-ROM gives your students a complete course of study in grammar, usage, and mechanics.

Each *Language Workshop CD-ROM* includes

- grammar, usage, and mechanics rules in both English and Spanish
- interactive multimedia exercises
- tests and exercises scored by computer
- gradebook updated automatically
- online Diagnostic Pretest that evaluates a student's skill level and recommends a course of study

Writer's Workshop Interactive Multimedia CD-ROM Software

This award-winning interactive CD-ROM program guides students through the eight most common writing assignments, such as writing a personal narrative, preparing an informative report, or composing a persuasive essay.

Features include

- step-by-step guidance through the writing process, from prewriting to publishing
- thesaurus, dictionary, and spell-checker
- bibliography maker for MLA or APA style

All CD-ROMs are available for both Macintosh® and Windows®.

TO OUR STUDENTS

On any given day, you probably watch TV, surf the Internet, read magazines, and listen to CDs. Each day you probably also write papers in school, send e-mails, and talk on the phone. The world of language around you is expanding rapidly. To keep up, you need to become a skilled language user. *Elements of Language* can be an important resource by helping you use language more effectively as you communicate in the twenty-first century.

Elements of Language is divided into four major parts:

- **PART 1 Communications** shows you how to develop the skills you use to **receive** communications through **reading, listening,** and **viewing** and to **send** communications through **writing, speaking,** and **representing.**

- **PART 2 Sentences and Paragraphs** shows you how to develop interesting, clear **sentences** and **paragraphs.**

- **PART 3 Grammar, Usage, and Mechanics** provides instruction and practice with the **building blocks of language**—words, phrases, and clauses—so you can convey meaning clearly and correctly.

- **PART 4 Quick Reference Handbook** is a one-stop **reference guide** to a variety of skills and concepts—in a concise, easily accessible form.

Think of *Elements of Language* as your personal communication resource. As you use this resource, remember that everything is here for a reason. For example, **boldface** type and color draw your attention to important words or ideas; **charts** present information in an easy-to-read form; and **headings** show the organization of ideas.

PART 1 chapters include the following sections:

- **Reading Workshop**—to show you how to develop and improve your reading skills

- **Writing Workshop**—to show you how to use the writing process to develop a piece of your own writing

- **Focus on Speaking and Listening** or **Focus on Viewing and Representing**—to help you master either the skills of speaking and listening or of viewing and representing

You will also encounter the following features in PART 1.

- **Mini-Lessons**—vocabulary and test-taking strategies, as well as writing or critical thinking skills
- **A Writer's Model**—a model of how you might write your own paper
- **A Student's Model**—a paper written by a real student
- **Content and Organization Guidelines for Peer and Self-Evaluation** and **Style Guidelines**—questions, tips, and techniques to help you evaluate and revise *what* you say as well as *how* you say it
- **Designing Your Writing**—pointers on how to present ideas and information visually so your readers can grasp them more easily
- **Connections to Literature** and **Connections to Life**—communication activities related to literature or to the world at large

Here are some of the features you will meet in PART 2 and PART 3.

- **Rules**—the grammar, usage, and mechanics concepts in each Part 3 chapter, numbered in each chapter
- **Exercises**—practice for skills and concepts
- **Tabs**—colored corners on the Part 3 pages that show rule numbers
- **Tips & Tricks**—easy-to-use hints about grammar, usage, and mechanics
- **Style Tips**—information about formal and informal uses of English
- **Help**—pointers to help you understand concepts and complete exercises
- **Computer Tips**—hints for using a computer to help you write better
- **Writing Applications**—activities that link grammar, usage, and mechanics skills and concepts with writing activities

Elements of Language on the Internet

At the *Elements of Language* Internet site, you can dissect the prose of professional writers, crack the codes of the advertising industry, and find out how your communication skills can help you in the real world. You can also submit your work for publication in one of our online galleries. As you move through *Elements of Language*, you will find the best online resources at **go.hrw.com**.

Let this book be your guide to developing your skill as an effective and critical language user—a communicator—in the twenty-first century.

The Authors and Editors

TEACHING TIP

Internet Warning
Activities in the Annotated Teacher's Edition might occasionally suggest that students do research on the Internet. You need to be aware that Internet resources are sometimes public forums and that their content can be unpredictable. The **go.hrw.com** Web site has material designed specifically for *Elements of Language*. The only way students can reach external Internet sites from the *Elements of Language* site is by clicking the Reference section.

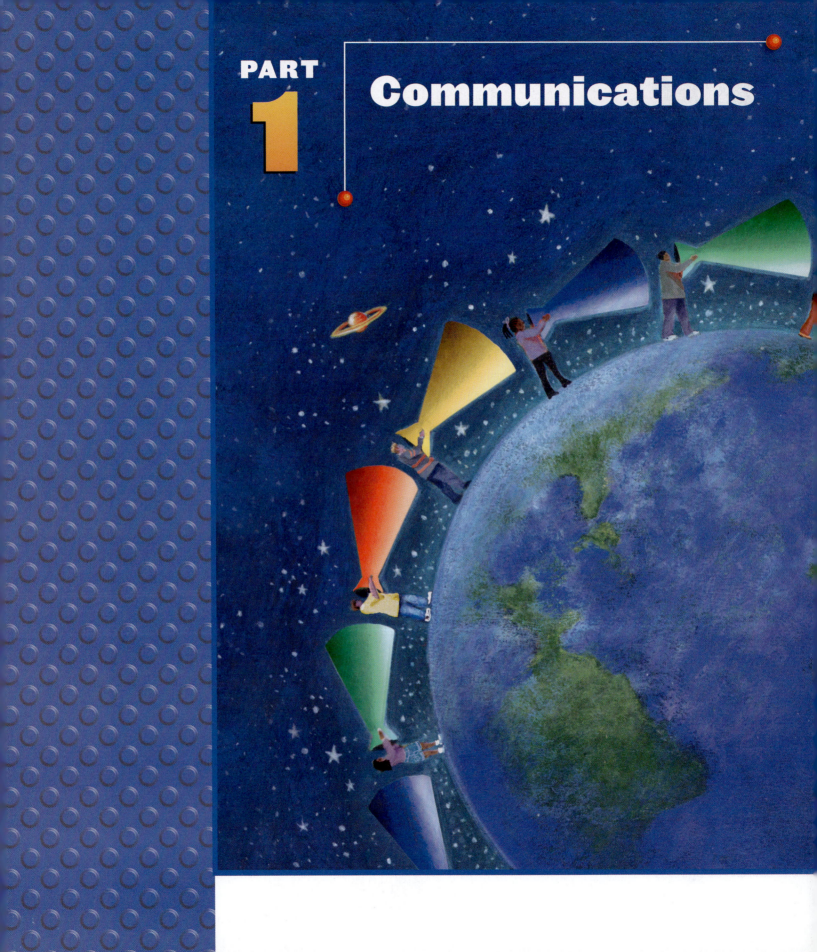

Introduction: Thinking About Reading and Writing

1 Narration/Description: Sharing Our Stories

2 Exposition: Reporting the News

3 Exposition: Explaining How

4 Exposition: Comparing and Contrasting

5 Exposition: Responding to a Novel

6 Exposition: Sharing Your Research

7 Persuasion: Making a Difference

Introduction

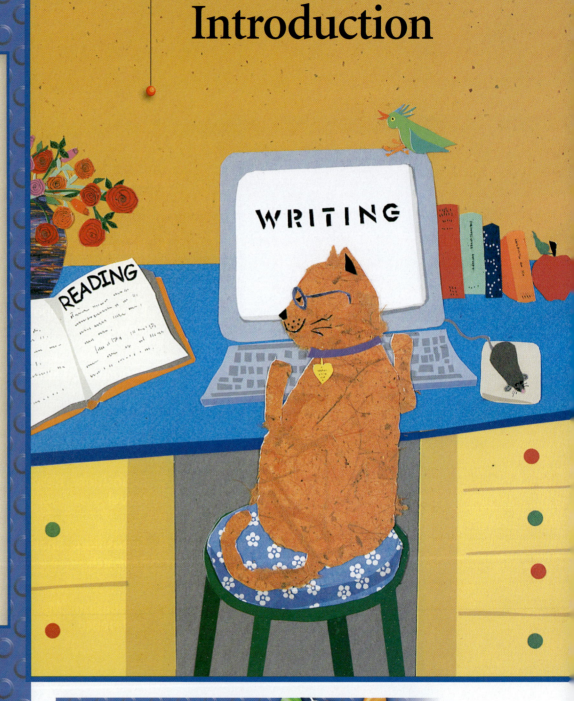

INTRODUCTION

PREVIEWING THE CHAPTER

■ Successful readers and writers use processes and understand the relationships between reading and writing. In this chapter, students will learn about the stages of the reading and writing processes and the interconnections between the two. You may want to use this chapter to introduce the first reading and writing workshops, or you may choose to return to this chapter as necessary throughout the year.

VIEWING THE ILLUSTRATION

■ Point out that the illustration's playful quality may suggest that reading and writing can be fun. Then, explain to students that the artist's use of color and content (the cat appears to read and then type) convey the idea that reading and writing are interactive processes—one helps with the other.

Representing. Invite students to draw their interpretation of how reading and writing work together. Encourage students to use bright colors and to be playful in their art.

CHAPTER RESOURCES

Planning
- *Lesson Planner,* Introductory Ch.
- *ELL Strategies,* Introductory Ch.
- *One-Stop Planner CD-ROM*

Practice
- *Communications,* TPs. 1–9, WS. pp.1–5

Reinforcement
- *Daily Language Activity Transparencies*

Evaluation and Assessment
- *Assessment Package* —*Assessment Alternatives,* Introductory Ch.

Internet
- go.hrw.com (keyword: EOLang 6-0)

Thinking About Reading and Writing

Reading and writing can be a breeze when you race through a gripping mystery novel or dash off an e-mail to a friend. Why, then, can these skills seem difficult when you read a chapter from a science textbook or write a report for social studies?

Practice the Process

Each year, the kinds of things you read and write become more challenging. To master these challenges, you need to keep growing as a reader and as a writer. This growth does not happen all at once. Instead, it is a *process*, or series of steps. Reading and writing are processes, too. To help you grow as a reader and a writer, this chapter will show you some thinking skills and strategies to use

- **before** you read or write,
- **while** you are reading or writing, and
- **after** you read or write.

YOUR TURN 1 — Analyzing the Reading and Writing Processes

- Write down one thing you have read in the past week. It can be anything from a cereal box to a billboard to a Web page. Why did you read it? Did you find it easy or hard to read? What ideas and feelings did it give you?
- Now, write down one thing you have written in the past week—a diary entry, an ad to sell your old bike, or a note to a friend. Where did you get the idea for what you wrote? Why did you write, and who read (or will read) your writing? How did it feel to turn your idea into a piece of writing?

TIP To take a closer look at how you read and write, try using a *learning log*. A **learning log** can simply be a spiral notebook. In this notebook you can make notes about what you have read, explore ideas and connections you have found in a reading selection, and list new words you have learned. You can also make notes that will help you write, including prewriting notes and reflections on pieces you have written.

Meeting INDIVIDUAL NEEDS

LEARNERS HAVING DIFFICULTY
Introduce students to the idea of reading and writing as processes by connecting it to a leisure activity with which students are familiar, such as watching a TV show or a movie. Lead students to see that they usually follow a number of steps when participating in such an activity: hearing or reading about the show or movie, judging their interest level in investing the time to watch the show or movie, and then, afterwards talking to other people about what they viewed. Encourage students to share the steps they used with a specific, recent viewing experience. Then, tell students that the reading and writing processes use similar steps.

YOUR TURN 1

To assess quickly students' responses to the questions, you may ask volunteers to share their answers. Then, you may ask students if they have ever read something that made them want to write a response. Use students' answers to help reinforce the close relationship between the reading and writing processes.

Meeting INDIVIDUAL NEEDS

MULTIPLE INTELLIGENCES

Interpersonal Intelligence. Pair students and have each student take turns reading aloud to his or her partner portions of an article or story with which both are familiar. While one student reads aloud, the other should periodically interrupt the reading to share his or her comments, reactions, or questions. The partners can then discuss the comment, reaction, or question before continuing with the reading. Challenge students to engage each other in a dialogue over the text of what they are reading, and to direct their comments toward a fuller understanding of the story or article. By the end of the story or article, students should have had the opportunity to discuss the text in full. Point out that a good piece of writing provokes discussion. Ask students what they learned by asking questions and sharing their reactions and comments.

WHAT'S AHEAD?

In this section you will learn what effective readers do
- before reading
- during reading
- after reading

Reading as a Process

You are reading an article explaining how to create 3-D images on the computer. What is going on in your mind as your eyes go over the words on the page? Even though neither of you is speaking out loud, you and the writer are having a *dialogue,* or discussion between two people. To understand the writer's message, use the thinking strategies in the following chart *before, while,* and *after* you read.

Strategies Used in the Reading Process

Before You Read: Prereading	• **Preview** the text and **make predictions** about what it contains. • **Build background knowledge** for what you will read by thinking about what you already know about the topic. • Determine your **purpose** for reading by asking questions. • **Focus your mind** on what you are about to do.
While You Read: Reading	• **Adjust your reading rate** based on your purpose for reading, how difficult the text is, and what you already know about the subject. • **Look for patterns of organization** to find the most important ideas. • Revise your **predictions** about the text. • Ask yourself **questions** about the text, and use **fix-it strategies** when you become confused. • **Make connections** between what you are reading and what you already know.
After You Read: Exploring and Extending Your Reading	• Decide whether you achieved your **purpose** for reading. • **Confirm your understanding** of the text's meaning. • **Draw conclusions** and **form generalizations** based on the text. • **Extend** and use the ideas you encountered while reading.

4 Introduction

Prereading

Getting Ready to Read

Athletes and dancers know how important it is to warm up before beginning their activities. Warming up is important for readers, too. Try these warm-up exercises before you read. They will help you improve your reading performance.

- **Preview the text.** Looking over the material before you begin reading helps you know what to expect. Read the title, and quickly read, or **skim,** the chapter titles, the headings and subheadings, and terms in **bold** or *italics*. Look at the pictures and graphics (charts, maps, and so on). Skim a paragraph or two to see if the material seems easy or challenging. Determine the writer's purpose and audience.
- **Make predictions.** A **prediction** is a guess about what lies ahead based on what you already know. What do you think the writer's main idea, or message, will be? How will ideas be organized? As you read, you will find out whether your predictions were right. If any were incorrect, you can adjust them.
- **Build background knowledge.** You spot a newspaper article about young people's allowances. In a flash, you connect the article to your own experience: You would like an increase in your allowance. What you already know about a topic, whether it comes from your own experience or from other things you have read, seen, or heard, is your **prior knowledge.** It is the base you use to build background knowledge about a topic.
- **Determine your purpose for reading.** Knowing *why* you are reading helps you decide how quickly to read and what to focus on. For example, when you read a short story just for fun, you read quickly. If you plan to write a report on the story, you will read more slowly, paying attention to how the writer puts the story elements together. Before you begin reading, make sure you know your purpose.
- **Focus your mind.** From time to time, you will need to read things that do not spark your interest. When that happens, think of the text as a workout. Use it to sharpen your skills for reading things you do enjoy.

TIP These five steps take just a few minutes, but they can make a big difference in how well you read. Make them a habit, and see for yourself.

TEACHING TIP

Getting Ready to Read
Help students understand the prereading strategies by displaying an article on the overhead projector and demonstrating each strategy listed. After you demonstrate each strategy, ask for student comments or questions about the step, and encourage students to think of other ways in which the strategy can be used to promote their own understanding of the article. You can list students' suggestions next to the text on the overhead projector.

Meeting INDIVIDUAL NEEDS

MULTIPLE INTELLIGENCES
Musical Intelligence. Compare the adjustment of one's reading rate to the varying speeds of different kinds of music. Point out that some types of music have a slow pace; similarly, a formal or dense piece of writing will often invite a slower, more thorough reading. Other types of music can have a quick pace, and likewise a piece of writing that is humorous or entertaining may provoke a faster pace of reading. The key is to try to find the natural pace of the piece.

While Reading

Making Sense

As you read, you *interpret,* or make sense of, what the writer is saying. These strategies will help you.

- **Adjust your reading rate.** Pay attention to how quickly you are reading. If you find yourself racing through a text you are reading for information, slow down. If you already know something about the subject of a reading, you may be able to read a bit faster than if the subject is unfamiliar to you.

- **Look for patterns of organization.** Suppose you notice that an article about gorillas has a *cause-and-effect* order. You can then figure out that the **main idea** has something to do with causes and effects, and the **supporting details** will probably tell about causes *or* effects. Other patterns you might see include *comparison-contrast, problem-solution, chronological (time),* and *spatial (location).*

- **Revise your predictions.** As you read, you will begin to see whether your predictions were correct. Say that you predicted that an article would try to persuade you that paper bags are better for the environment than plastic ones. You might find as you read that this prediction was wrong because the article merely explains advantages and disadvantages of each type of bag. Based on this new information, you could predict that the author would tell readers to decide for themselves which type of bag was better.

- **Ask yourself questions.** As you read, make comments, raise questions, and notice what puzzles you. If you find part of the text confusing, try one or more of these **fix-it strategies:** slow down and re-read the confusing part; read it aloud; put the ideas in the text into your own words; or jot down notes about the important points in the text in a notebook or learning log, or on sticky notes.

- **Make connections.** You will remember the ideas in a text if you connect them to what you already know. For example, if you read a story about a child who loves horses, think about the time when you petted a horse at the rodeo. That connection gives your mind a place to store the ideas you read in the story.

In the margin are notes one reader made while reading the passage below.

> Way, way out in the middle of Antarctica, six snowmobiles are driving in a row. The people on the snowmobiles are driving very slowly, moving their heads back and forth, as though searching for a lost mitten. But no one has lost a mitten. The six people are scientists. They're looking for shooting stars—shooting stars that have fallen to Earth.
>
> The scientific name for a shooting star is a meteor. A meteor is a piece of rock that's been hurtling through space for thousands of years; when the rock hits our atmosphere, it burns and breaks into pieces. Most of these pieces are no bigger than a walnut. Once they fall to Earth, they're called meteorites. . . .
>
> The empty white ice fields of Antarctica are a good place to look for rocks that have fallen from space. If you're walking along in the middle of Antarctica and you come upon a rock lying on the ice, you can be pretty sure that rock has fallen from space because the interior of Antarctica has no rocks of its own, just ice and snow. . . .
>
> Most meteorites come from the asteroid belt, a region between Mars and Jupiter that's full of asteroids, big chunks of cosmic rubble left over from the planet-building phase of our solar system. A much smaller number of meteorites. . . come not from the asteroid belt, but from planets. Rocks from Mars have been found on Earth. So have rocks from the Moon. The rocks probably got blasted off the surface of Mars or the Moon and out into space when another body smashed into them. . . .
>
>
>
> Scientists study meteorites because these rocks can tell us things about the places they came from. Rocks from the asteroid belt offer clues to what was going on during the formation of our solar system. Rocks from Mars hold hints about what the planet is made of, its history, and whether anything might ever have lived there.
>
> Mary Roach, "Meteorite Hunters," *Muse*

Margin notes:

- Weird. I wonder what they're doing.
- This sounds informative—it will explain how scientists study shooting stars in Antarctica.
- Hurtling must mean something like flying or moving fast.
- I don't think I'll be doing this anytime soon.
- Wow, those meteorites traveled a long way to get to Earth.
- I wonder how they can tell where a rock came from.
- I want to find out more about what scientists learn from meteorites.

TEACHING TIP

Exploring and Extending
Students may have difficulty exploring and extending their reading. Explain to students that writing is usually an attempt by a writer to engage in a dialogue with a reader. After students have finished reading a piece of writing, they should ask themselves questions such as: Why would someone write a piece like this? Why would someone read it? How does it relate to what I know about the world? How might I use what I read about to help me in the future? Have students use such questions in a class discussion of selections with which everyone is familiar to practice exploring and extending a selection. Write students' comments and suggestions on the chalkboard.

After Reading

Exploring and Extending

The reading process does not stop when you reach "The End." For a while, the writer's ideas echo in your mind. Spend some time exploring and extending those ideas.

- **Decide whether you achieved your purpose for reading.** If you read for information, did you find out what you wanted to know? If you read to be entertained, were you? Could you have read more carefully or chosen a text that fit your purpose better?

- **Confirm your understanding.** Make sure you understood what the author said. You might discuss your ideas about the text with others who have read it. Try to sum up the author's message in your own words. Using a *graphic organizer,* map out the important points in the text to help you remember them.

- **Draw conclusions and form generalizations.** Both conclusions and generalizations require you to connect what is on the page with your own knowledge and experience. Drawing conclusions can help you understand a text better. If you read about a place where people are adjusting cameras and reading from scripts, you might conclude that the place is a movie set because you have seen similar scenes before. Forming generalizations can help you understand the world better. You might generalize from the same text and other experiences that moviemaking is hard work.

- **Extend and use the ideas you encountered while reading.** Try one of these activities.

    1. **Be creative.** You might write a new ending to a story, illustrate a poem, or add music to a set of directions.

    2. **Read on.** If you enjoyed the topic, find out more about it in books and magazines or on the Web. If you liked the writer's style, read more of his or her works.

    3. **Link it with life.** What you read can help you solve a problem or make a decision. For example, after reading about ways to study better, you might try them yourself.

You have seen the reader's important part in the reader-writer dialogue. Now you will look at the part the writer plays.

Reference Note
For more on using graphic organizers as you read, see **text structures,** page 709.

Reference Note
For more on **conclusions,** see page 192. For more on **generalizations,** see page 21.

Writing as a Process

Last night you wrote a story in just half an hour. When your friends read it, though, they had trouble following the plot. Chances are, you did not give yourself enough time. Writing is a process made up of many steps, and each step takes time. The chart below shows the steps of the writing process.

Strategies Used in the Writing Process

Prewriting
- Choose a **form** for your writing and a **topic**.
- Identify your **purpose** and **audience**.
- Draft a sentence that expresses your **main idea**.
- **Gather information** about the topic.
- Begin to **organize** the information.

Writing a Draft
- Draft an **introduction** that gets your reader's attention and states your main idea.
- Provide **background information**.
- Follow a **plan** for putting your ideas in order.
- State your **supporting points** and **elaborate** on them.
- Wrap things up with a **conclusion**.

Revising
- **Evaluate** your draft.
- **Revise** the draft to improve its content, organization, and style.

Publishing
- **Proofread** the draft to find and correct spelling, punctuation, and grammar mistakes.
- **Share** your finished writing with readers.
- **Reflect** on your writing experience.

WHAT'S AHEAD?

In this section you will learn how effective writers
- prewrite
- write
- revise
- publish

TIP Unlike the steps on an escalator, these steps can go both ways. For example, when you evaluate your draft, you may realize that it is short on details. While you are finding more details, you are back in the prewriting stage. When you add those details to your paper, you return to the drafting stage.

Computers have made it easier than ever to revisit these steps. You can now move, insert, or delete sections of text without having to rewrite an entire piece.

Meeting INDIVIDUAL NEEDS

MULTIPLE INTELLIGENCES
Interpersonal Intelligence. Have students identify the process used and the challenges faced by a young adult author. By searching for the author's name on the Web, students may be able to find, and even participate in, an online discussion or interview with the writer. *Be aware that Internet resources are sometimes public forums, and their content can be unpredictable.*

Students may also write to the author in care of the author's publisher. In this case, have students work collaboratively in groups of three or four to write letters. Have one student compose a list of questions to ask the author; have a second student frame the questions with a polite opening and closing; and have a third revise the letter and put it into business letter format. (You can find the publisher's address on the Internet.) Each group member should proofread the letter to identify spelling and grammar errors.

Meeting INDIVIDUAL NEEDS

MODALITY

Visual Learners. Tell students that graphic organizers can help them prepare for a writing assignment. The kinds of graphic organizers they use will depend on their own preferences for arranging information and on the type of writing. A good place to start would be with a simple chart such as the one below. This type of chart can be adapted for many topics and types of writing by adding boxes as necessary.

Introduction:
Thesis Statement:
Supporting Paragraph 1:
Supporting Paragraph 2:
Supporting Paragraph 3:
Conclusion:
Final Comment:

Prewriting

Getting Ready to Write

Before you begin writing, allow yourself plenty of thinking time for each of these prewriting steps.

- **Choose a form.** Sometimes your teacher will assign the form—for example, a report, or a presentation, or a review. When the choice is up to you, you may choose any form, from a journal entry to an editorial to a set of instructions.

Reference Note
For more on **freewriting** and **clustering**, see page 763. For more on **brainstorming**, see page 762.

- **Choose a topic.** To find a topic you will enjoy, try *freewriting, brainstorming,* or *clustering*. Then, narrow your topic. Some topics, such as "the solar system," have too many parts to cover in a short paper. Zero in on just one part, such as "the first moon landing."

- **Identify your purpose and audience.** First, decide why you are writing. Do you want to give information, convince readers to share your opinion, entertain people, or express yourself? Once you know your purpose, think about who will read your writing. What does this audience probably already know about the topic? What will you need to explain?

TIP If you are writing to entertain readers or to express yourself, you probably will not include a main idea statement. Even so, you should figure out the meaning of the specific story you want to tell or what you want readers to understand about you.

- **Draft a sentence that expresses your main idea.** Most informative or persuasive papers, even short ones, have one main idea. Like an umbrella, this main idea covers all of the information in the paper. Having a main idea statement, or thesis statement, before you begin writing can help keep you on track.

- **Gather information about the topic.** For pieces about yourself, you can re-read your diary or talk to your friends and relatives. For other topics, you can read newspapers, books, magazines, and Web sites. You can observe *sensory details* such as sights and sounds, or you can interview people. As you find information, take notes so you will have solid ideas for your writing.

Reference Note
For more on types of **order**, see page 283. For more on **outlines**, see page 765.

- **Begin to organize the information.** Information is easier for readers to understand when it is arranged in a logical order. As you organize your ideas, consider what your readers will need to know first, second, and so on. To help you keep your ideas in order as you write, you may want to make a graphic organizer or an informal outline. Your teacher may also ask you to make a formal outline to guide you in writing some papers.

Making a Start

Now you are ready to begin shaping your ideas into sentences. Do not worry about spelling and grammar at this stage. A draft is like a sketch: No one expects it to be as good as the finished work. You will have plenty of time to improve your writing later.

As you draft your paper, keep your audience in mind. Here are some ways to help your readers follow your ideas.

- **Draft an introduction.** Think of your introduction as a hook set to catch your readers' interest. Bait the hook with an attention-getting question, a surprising quote, an amazing fact, or an unusual image. Then, make sure your readers know what they will find in your paper by including your main idea statement. This sentence should tell readers not only what your topic is, but also the main point you will make about the topic.
- **Provide background information.** Give your readers the background information they will need in order to understand your ideas. You may need to define unfamiliar terms, identify people and places, or provide a bit of history about your topic.
- **Follow a plan or order.** Keep related ideas and details together. Put each separate idea in its own paragraph. You will also need to think about the overall pattern of your paper. In a story, for example, putting events in chronological (time) order helps readers understand which event happened first, next, and so on. You will learn about other patterns later in this book.
- **State your supporting points and elaborate on them.** *Elaborate* means "go into detail." Details help readers understand and accept your main idea. For example, suppose your main idea is "Students at our school should wear uniforms." Show your readers how you arrived at that idea by sharing the facts and examples you have collected.
- **Wrap things up.** Do not just stop writing when you run out of ideas. Leave your readers with a clear sense that you have taken them where your introduction suggested you would. In your conclusion, you might restate your main idea in different words or add a final comment about why that idea is important.

Meeting INDIVIDUAL NEEDS

MULTIPLE INTELLIGENCES
Linguistic Intelligence. Point out to students that every "hook" does not have to be a surprising quote or interesting fact. A good way to get a reader's attention is to use language in a creative way. Grab a reader's attention with a startling image, an unusual word choice, an interesting rhythm of language, or a rhyme. Emphasize to students that *how* one says something is often just as important as *what* is said.

TEACHING TIP

Going Back Over Your Draft
You may want to explain to your students that the term *editing* means different things to different people. While editing can refer to any changes made to a draft, some people use editing to refer only to style and proofreading changes to the exclusion of content and organization changes. Still others consider editing to refer to grammar, spelling, and mechanics changes only.

Meeting INDIVIDUAL NEEDS

MODALITY
Auditory Learners. Tell students that it is important during the revising process to distance themselves from their writing so they can look objectively at it. You might suggest that students read out loud as they re-read their drafts, or tape-record the draft and play it back. This will help students stand back from their own writing and become the reader as they work to revise their papers.

Revising

Going Back Over Your Draft

Editing your draft involves three steps: evaluating, revising, and proofreading. Most writers wait to do the last part of editing, proofreading, until they revise their compositions.

- **Evaluate your draft.** *Evaluating* means "judging"—deciding what works and what does not work. Re-read your draft at least twice. First, look at the big picture. Make sure the content and organization of your paper are as clear as possible for your readers. Then, look at your individual sentences.

- **Revise the draft to improve its content and organization.** Here are five ways to revise the content and organization of your writing:

  1. **Add.** Thoroughly explore your topic by adding sentences or even whole paragraphs of related information or explanations. Add specific words using a thesaurus. Add clue words (*then, later, because*) to help readers follow your thinking.
  2. **Delete.** Take out words or ideas that are not related to your main idea. Cut wordy sentences down to size by getting rid of words or phrases that are repeated and long phrases that do not add to the meaning of your sentences.
  3. **Replace.** Replace any weak support with stronger support.
  4. **Rearrange.** Move words, sentences, and paragraphs around. Try to find the order that will be clearest to your readers.
  5. **Elaborate.** Make your ideas clear to readers by supporting them with facts, examples, sensory details, or quotations.

- **Revise to improve style.** Consider these two points:

  1. **Word Choice** Make sure your words communicate your ideas well. Choose precise words rather than vague ones, and avoid using slang or jargon that your readers might not know.
  2. **Sentences** Make sure that each sentence is easy to understand and holds your readers' attention. Mix short and long sentences, and begin your sentences in a variety of ways. Also, try to use different sentence structures, mixing simple, compound, and complex sentences. Combine short, choppy sentences into longer, smoother ones.

> **TIP** **Peer evaluation,** or having a classmate evaluate your paper, can help you revise your writing. Start by asking your peer evaluator a few questions about your paper. For example, you might ask, "Which is my strongest reason?" Listen to your evaluator's comments, and use the suggestions that will improve your writing.
>
> When you read a classmate's work, consider how clear and interesting the paper is. Make specific comments such as, "Now I see how CDs work," rather than general comments such as, "That was good." Each Writing Workshop in this book includes specific questions for peer review as well as guidelines for peer and self-evaluation.

Publishing

Going Public

You have created a brand-new, one-of-a-kind piece of writing. Now all you have to do is tidy it up and send it out into the world.

- **Proofread the draft.** To your readers, your work *is* you, so polish before you publish. Carefully find and correct every mistake in spelling, capitalization, punctuation, grammar, and usage. Have another person proofread as well. A person less familiar with your writing than you are will be less likely to miss errors.

   Use the following guidelines to edit your final draft. Mark your edits using the proofreading symbols on page 767.

Reference Note
Part 3 of this book, beginning on page 298, will help you find and fix errors in grammar, usage, and mechanics.

Guidelines for Proofreading

1. Is every sentence a complete sentence, not a fragment or run-on? (See pages 262 and 265.)
2. Does every sentence begin with a capital letter and end with the correct punctuation mark? (See pages 537 and 561.)
3. Do singular subjects have singular verbs? Do all plural subjects have plural verbs? (See page 422.)
4. Are verb forms and tenses used correctly? (See pages 445 and 458.)
5. Are the forms of personal pronouns used correctly? (See page 475.)
6. Are all words spelled correctly? (See page 613.)

- **Share your finished writing with others.** Share your writing with the audience you had in mind as you wrote. You might post it on a bulletin board or on the Web, or you might read it into a tape recorder and send the tape to a friend or family member.
- **Reflect on your writing experience.** When you finish a piece, take a few minutes to think about what you learned in writing it. Also, decide whether you want to add that piece of writing to your **portfolio,** a collection of pieces that shows what you have accomplished as a writer. Answer the following questions about a finished piece.

TEACHING TIP

■ **Proofread the Draft**
In addition to explaining the guidelines on this page and the proofreading symbols on p. 767, advise students who proofread their peers' papers to follow these suggestions:
- Carefully read the entire paper.
- Concentrate on finding mistakes; a mistake that you miss could cause a classmate to lose points.
- Offer suggestions for correcting mistakes. If you find a run-on sentence, suggest a solution for fixing it.
- Write neatly and be polite.
- Seek help from your teacher if you are not sure about an error.

TEACHING TIP

■ **Reflect on Your Writing Experience**
Encourage students to make a checklist to evaluate the works in their portfolios. Explain that some items, such as proper spelling, grammar, and punctuation, will be common to all of the works they evaluate, while other items will depend upon the purposes for which the pieces were written. Lead students through a possible evaluation of the passage on meteorites on p. 7.

EVALUATED ELEMENT	GRADE (1–5, 5 IS BEST)	COMMENTS
Interesting Introduction	5	image grabs my attention
Clear Main Idea	4	takes time to understand, but is clear
Well-Organized Reasons	3	could rearrange the paragraphs
Clear Sentences	5	writer uses straightforward language

Meeting INDIVIDUAL NEEDS

LEARNERS HAVING DIFFICULTY

Because students can use a variety of resources and reference materials as they write, revise, and edit, they may need help selecting the appropriate resources. Guide students through the process of selecting appropriate materials by completing the following activity:

You are writing a paper explaining how to make a Spanish omelette. The following resources and references are available: a dictionary, a geographical dictionary, a thesaurus, a World Wide Web page published by a writing teacher about creating interesting introductions, and this book which includes a grammar, usage, and mechanics section. Which reference or resource would you select for each of the situations described below?

- You want to tell the location of Spain.
- You want to hook your audience into reading your paper.
- You want to replace the word *delicious* with a more specific word.
- Your teacher has told you to check your paper for comma errors.

- What was the easiest part of writing this piece? What was the hardest part?
- What do you think is the best thing about this piece?
- What skills did you use well in this piece of writing?

Then, think about your entire portfolio so far. Answer these questions in a learning log or on a page inside your portfolio.

- What writing skills have you improved on since you started your portfolio? What skills still need improvement?
- Which piece in your portfolio do you consider your best? What makes it so good?
- What new types of writing would you like to try? What goals can you set for future pieces of writing?

You have probably noticed that the reading and writing processes are similar. The chart below summarizes those similarities.

The Reading-Writing Connection

	Reading Process	Writing Process
Before	• You think about what you already know about the topic.	• You think about what you already know about the topic. You may do some research to find out more.
	• You determine your purpose for reading.	• You identify your purpose and audience.
	• You scan the text to make predictions about what the text will include.	• You make notes or an outline to plan what the text will include.
During	• As you read, you may take notes on important ideas and details.	• As you write, you follow your prewriting notes or outline.
	• You notice how the writer has organized the text. You look for clue words that help you find the writer's main idea and supporting details.	• You organize your writing and use clue words so that readers can easily follow your main idea and supporting details.
After	• You evaluate how well you met your purpose for reading.	• You evaluate and revise the text to make sure you achieve your purpose for writing.
	• You connect what you have read with the real world and to your own experiences.	• You connect your writing with the real world by publishing your ideas.
	• You reflect on what you have read.	• You reflect on what you have written.

Choices

Choose one of the following activities to complete.

▶ VIEWING AND REPRESENTING

1. Small-Screen Sightings As you watch television over a few days, take notes on when you see people reading and writing. For example, *who* is shown reading or writing? *What, when,* and *where* do they read or write, and *why?* Discuss with others how TV represents readers and writers. In a **paragraph,** explain why you agree or disagree with these representations.

▶ CAREERS

2. In Your Dreams Pick a career that interests you—anything from astronaut to zookeeper. Find out how people in that career use reading and writing. What kinds of things do they read and write? Who writes what they read, and who reads what they write? Present an **oral report** on your findings.

▶ COLLABORATIVE WRITING

3. Learning Through Teaching With a small group, explore the reading and writing processes by writing a **skit** about one or both processes. First, decide who your audience will be (the other members of your own class? a younger class?). Then, split up the tasks: gathering information; writing, revising, and editing drafts; and directing and performing the skit.

▶ CREATIVE WRITING

4. The Choice Is Yours Write about the reading process in one of the following ways.

- Use expressive writing in a **journal entry** about why reading is important.
- Write persuasively—either write an **editorial** sharing your opinion on the importance of reading or write a **review** of something you have read recently in which you note how you used the reading process.
- Use expository writing to create a **report** or **presentation** on the reading process, or write a set of **instructions** for using the process.

PORTFOLIO

▶ CREATIVE WRITING

Remind students that a journal is a type of expressive writing in which they can reveal thoughts, explore feelings, solve problems, and so on. For prewriting, encourage students to brainstorm positive associations with and experiences involving reading. (You might do this as a whole-class activity.)

As they start to write, remind students that they should not worry about coming up with something that they can show the world. Encourage them to explore their feelings and remember specific events.

Although formal revision and proofreading are unnecessary for a journal entry, ask students to read over their entries and add a reflection on what the experience of writing about reading was like. Did they discover anything new about themselves or about reading?

CHAPTER 1

Sharing Our Stories

Use this guide to create an instructional plan that suits the individual needs of your students. Assignments marked by an asterisk (*) may be completed out of class. Times given for pacing lessons are estimated. See pp. 16–17 for chapter-wide resources. Resources listed in this guide are point-of-use resources only.

Curriculum Connections

Connections to Literature pp. 42–44
- Writing a Narrative Poem

Choices p. 47
- Speech
- Drama
- Writing
- Technology

internet connect
GO TO: go.hrw.com
KEYWORD: EOLang 6-1

All resources for this chapter are available for preview on the *One-Stop Planner CD-ROM with Test Generator*. All worksheets and tests may be printed from the CD-ROM.

CHAPTER PLANNING GUIDE

	Chapter Opener pp. 16–17	**Reading Workshop: Reading an Autobiographical Incident** pp. 18–26
DEVELOPMENTAL PROGRAM	30 minutes • Your Turn 1 *p. 17*	100 minutes • Preparing to Read *p. 18* • Reading Selection *pp. 19–20* • First Thoughts in groups *p. 21* • Making Inferences: Forming Generalizations *pp. 21–22* • Your Turn 2 *p. 23* • Chronological Order *pp. 23–24* • Your Turn 3 *p. 24* • Vocabulary Mini-Lesson *p. 25* • Test Taking Mini-Lesson *p. 26*
CORE PROGRAM	20 minutes • Your Turn 1 *p. 17*	75 minutes • Preparing to Read *p. 18* • Reading Selection *pp. 19–20* • First Thoughts *p. 21* • Making Inferences: Forming Generalizations *pp. 21–22* • Your Turn 2 *p. 23* • Chronological Order *pp. 23–24* • Your Turn 3 *p. 24* • Vocabulary Mini-Lesson *p. 25* • Test Taking Mini-Lesson *p. 26*
ADVANCED PROGRAM	15 minutes • Your Turn 1 *p. 17*	60 minutes • Preparing to Read *p. 18* • Reading Selection *pp. 19–20* • First Thoughts *p. 21* • Making Inferences: Forming Generalizations *pp. 21–22* • Your Turn 2 *p. 23* • Chronological Order *pp. 23–24* • Your Turn 3 *p. 24* • Vocabulary Mini-Lesson *p. 25*
RESOURCES — PRINT	• *Communications,* TP. 10, WS. p. 6	• *Alternative Readings,* Ch. 1 • *Communications,* TPs. 11, 12, WS. pp. 7–14
RESOURCES — MEDIA	• *One-Stop Planner CD-ROM*	• *One-Stop Planner CD-ROM*

TP.=Transparency WS.=Worksheet

Writing Workshop: **Writing About a Life Experience** *pp. 27–44*	**Focus on Speaking and Listening:** **Telling a Story** *pp. 45–46*
⏱ **260 minutes** • Choose an Experience; Your Turn 4 *pp. 27–28* • Think About Purpose and Audience; Your Turn 5 *p. 29* • Recall Descriptive Details; Your Turn 6 *p. 30* • Framework; Your Turn 7* *p. 32* • Writer's Model and Student's Model *pp. 33–35* • Evaluate and Revise *pp. 36–37* • Your Turn 8 *p. 38* • Proofreading, Publishing, and Reflecting *pp. 39–40* • Grammar Link *p. 39* • Your Turn 9 *p. 40* • Test Taking Mini-Lesson *p. 41*	⏱ **45 minutes** • Plan Your Story *p. 45* • Practice Your Story* *pp. 45–46* • Share Your Story *p. 46* • Your Turn 11 *p. 46*
⏱ **180 minutes** • Choose an Experience; Your Turn 4 *pp. 27–28* • Think About Purpose and Audience; Your Turn 5 *p. 29* • Recall Descriptive Details; Your Turn 6 *p. 30* • Critical-Thinking Mini-Lesson in groups *p. 31* • Framework; Your Turn 7* *p. 32* • Writer's Model and Student's Model *pp. 33–35* • Evaluate and Revise *pp. 36–37* • Focus on Word Choice *p. 38* • Your Turn 8 *p. 38* • Proofreading, Publishing, and Reflecting *pp. 39–40* • Grammar Link *p. 39* • Your Turn 9 *p. 40* • Test Taking Mini-Lesson *p. 41* • Connections to Literature; Your Turn 10 *pp. 42–44*	⏱ **40 minutes** • Plan Your Story *p. 45* • Practice Your Story* *pp. 45–46* • Share Your Story *p. 46* • Your Turn 11 *p. 46*
⏱ **140 minutes** • Choose an Experience; Your Turn 4 *pp. 27–28* • Think About Purpose and Audience; Your Turn 5 *p. 29* • Recall Descriptive Details; Your Turn 6 *p. 30* • Critical-Thinking Mini-Lesson *p. 31* • Framework; Your Turn 7* *p. 32* • Writer's Model and Student's Model *pp. 33–35* • Evaluate and Revise *pp. 36–37* • Focus on Word Choice *p. 38* • Your Turn 8* *p. 38* • Proofreading, Publishing, and Reflecting; Your Turn 9 *pp. 39–40* • Connections to Literature; Your Turn 10* *pp. 42–44*	⏱ **30 minutes** • Plan Your Story *p. 45* • Practice Your Story* *pp. 45–46* • Share Your Story *p. 46* • Your Turn 11 *p. 46*
• *Communications,* TPs. 13–16, WS. pp. 15–26 • *Designing Your Writing*	• *Media Literacy and Communication Skills* —*Support and Practice*, Ch. 1 —*A How-to Handbook* —*A Teacher's Guide*, Ch. 1
• One-Stop Planner CD-ROM	• *Media Literacy and Communication Skills* —Videocassette 1, Segment A • One-Stop Planner CD-ROM

CHAPTER 1
Sharing Our Stories

CHAPTER OBJECTIVES

- To read an excerpt from an autobiography
- To write an autobiographical incident using narrative and descriptive writing
- To tell a story to classmates

Chapter Overview

Often, people use autobiographical incidents to share their thoughts and feelings about meaningful experiences. In this chapter students will study characteristics of an autobiographical incident and then write one of their own. The Reading Workshop (pp. 18–26) contains an autobiographical selection for students to analyze for its use of time order. The Writing Workshop (pp. 27–44) guides students through the steps of the writing process as they write autobiographical incidents. It also shows them how to add depth to narrative accounts with descriptive language and details. The Focus on Speaking and Listening shows students how to share a story with an audience, using elements of both narration and description. Although the sections of the chapter can be taught separately, they work together to help give students a broad understanding of narrative and descriptive writing and of how this kind of writing can be woven into autobiographical incidents.

Why Study Autobiographical Incidents?

Reading autobiographical incidents can help students learn more about important people, places, and events in the past or in their world today. Autobiographical incidents can teach them about other cultures or time periods or people's triumphs and tragedies. By studying how writers use elements of description and narration to create effective autobiographical incidents, students can also learn how to express their thoughts and feelings more effectively. Learning how writers bring true events to life can also strengthen students' appreciation of descriptive and narrative writing they encounter on their own.

Teaching the Chapter

Option 1: Begin with Literature

You may want to begin teaching about autobiographical incidents by first introducing students to examples of literature that illustrate elements of descriptive and narrative writing. For example, point out how writers use sensory details, action details, and exact verbs in poetry and how they use chronological order in short stories. Then have students read the selection in this chapter (pp. 19–20). Encourage them to notice how the selection uses narration as well as description to make the experience come alive. After reading and analyzing description and narration in literature, students will be prepared to write their own autobiographical incidents in the Writing Workshop (pp. 27–44).

Option 2: Begin with Nonfiction and Writing

Familiarize students with description and narration before turning to literature by starting with the material in this chapter. The autobiographical excerpt (pp. 19–20) in the Reading Workshop can help students understand how writers use narration to tell a story. Then, by writing an autobiographical incident and a narrative poem in the Writing Workshop (pp. 27–44), students may better understand how to arrange information and use descriptive language to create a vivid picture of an event. Afterward, guide students in analyzing descriptive and narrative writing in specific novels, short stories, and poems. See also **Connections to Literature** on pp. 42–44.

Making Connections

■ To the Literature Curriculum

Explain to students that one of the important steps in creating a story is arranging the ideas. For example, readers learn how the Lins adjust to life in the United States through the narration in Lensey Namioka's "The All-American Slurp." Also, reading Mary Whitebird's "Ta-Na-E-Ka" with a focus on the use of time order in narrative writing can help students appreciate the effective arrangement of ideas.

Lesson Idea: Looking at Chronological Order in "Ta-Na-E-Ka" by Mary Whitebird

1. After students have read the story, draw a time line on the chalkboard and have students copy it on their papers. Then have them write five major events that happen to Mary in the time order in which they occur. A sample time line might take the following form:

| Mary borrows $5 from her teacher. | She begins her endurance ritual. | She eats at Ernie's Riverside Restaurant. | She sneaks into Ernie's to sleep. | She returns home after 5 days at Ernie's. |

2. After students complete their time lines, discuss why being able to recognize the order of events might help them understand a story. [Knowing the time order of events makes the story easier to follow.]

3. Introduce students to the nonfiction selection in this chapter (pp. 19–20). Point out that both the selection and "Ta-Na-E-Ka" are written in time order. The instruction on chronological order on pp. 23–24 may help prepare students to write their own stories clearly and logically.

■ To Careers

Explain that autobiographical incidents do not appear only in textbooks—successful people are asked to share stories about their accomplishments in several ways. Suggest that students use newspapers, magazines, and radio or television programs to locate interviews in which professional athletes, business leaders, politicians, or celebrities discuss highlights of their careers. Encourage students to bring in interviews to share with the class.

■ To the Community

In this chapter, students will focus on autobiographical incidents—stories about important experiences that happened to them or to people of historical importance, such as Rosa Parks. Have students work together in small groups to create an oral history about an event that happened in their own community. Direct groups to plan, conduct, and tape-record interviews with a few people, such as prominent citizens or family members, who are willing to share their firsthand experience with a local event, such as celebrating the town's founding or organizing a community garden. Before beginning this activity, you may want to obtain permission from parents or guardians and from the interview subjects whom students will contact.

■ To the Social Studies Curriculum

Clarify for students the pivotal role that Rosa Parks played in the civil rights movement. If possible, show the class the portion of the PBS documentary *Eyes on the Prize* that deals with Parks and the Montgomery bus boycott or show them a segment from a similar video. After viewing the video clip, have the class discuss the significance of what Parks did. You may want to preview the video segment to make sure it is suitable for your students. Alternatively, you might have small groups use the Internet or print sources to research and report information on Rosa Parks. *You need to be aware that Internet resources are sometimes public forums and their content can be unpredictable.*

CHAPTER 1

Sharing Our Stories

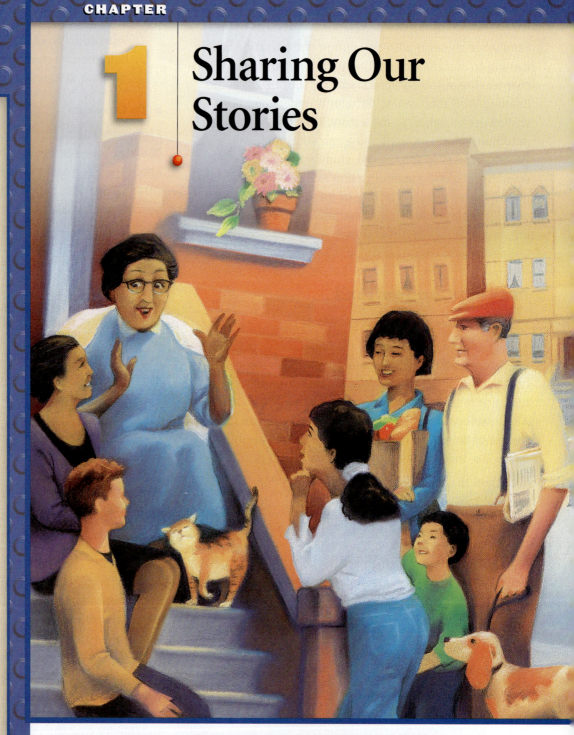

PREVIEWING THE CHAPTER

- The three workshops in Chapter 1 focus on sharing stories through narration and description. Although the workshops can be taught separately, they work together to help students understand how to tell stories effectively. Reading and studying an autobiographical incident can help prepare students to write about their own life experiences. After reading and writing autobiographical incidents, students will be better able to convey stories orally through storytelling. To integrate this chapter with grammar, usage, and mechanics chapters, see pp. T297A–T297B.

INTRODUCING THE CHAPTER

- To introduce the chapter, use the Journal Warmup, Transparency 10, in *Communications*.

VIEWING THE ILLUSTRATION

- Ask students how they know what is happening in the illustration. [A woman is telling a story. Clues include the variety of people that are gathered and the woman's excited expression and gestures.] Then, ask students to comment on the colors and texture of the work. [Colors include blues, yellows, and browns with green and black and the texture is soft. The colors and softness suggest a safe, friendly atmosphere.]

Representing. Ask students to sketch what a gathering in their own communities would look like.

CHAPTER RESOURCES

Planning
- *Lesson Planner, ELL Strategies,* Ch. 1
- Block Scheduling, p. T15A (this book)
- One-Stop Planner CD-ROM

Practice
- *Communications,* Ch. 1
- Writer's Workshop 1 CD-ROM

- Media Literacy and Communication Skills

Extension
- *Designing Your Writing*

Internet
- go.hrw.com (keyword: EOLang 6–1)

PREVIEW

Reading Workshop

Reading an Autobiographical Incident
PAGE 18

Writing Workshop

Writing About a Life Experience
PAGE 27

Focus on Speaking and Listening

Telling a Story
PAGE 45

Motivate

Ask students to think of a funny experience they have had. Encourage each student to relate his or her experience to a classmate. Then, explain to students that in telling this personal experience, they were relating an autobiographical incident. Inform students that they will be reading and writing autobiographical incidents as they explore the material in this chapter.

Do you wonder what it is like to fly over the ocean alone in a small plane? Would you like to know what it is like to live in a different country? You can learn about these experiences by reading *autobiographical incidents*. An **autobiographical incident** is a true story about a specific event in a writer's life. Not only do you learn about the event, but you also learn why the experience is important to the writer. Because writers share, or express, their thoughts and feelings, an autobiographical incident is an example of **expressive writing.**

You also share autobiographical incidents. When you talk with your grandmother about your track meet, for example, you are telling a story about yourself. Writing an autobiographical incident is a great way to express what you think and feel.

GO TO: go.hrw.com
KEYWORD: EOLang 6-1

ELEMENTS OF Literature

Autobiographical Incidents in Literature. For additional examples of autobiography, refer to these works of literature in *Elements of Literature,* Introductory Course: "Brother" from *I Know Why the Caged Bird Sings* by Maya Angelou, pp. 110–112, and the excerpt from *The Land I Lost* by Huynh Quang Nhuong, pp. 281–287.

YOUR TURN 1 — Sharing Experiences

List the topics of three memorable experiences that you would not mind sharing. Then, discuss the following questions with a partner.
- Why are these experiences memorable?
- What did you learn about yourself from these experiences?

YOUR TURN 1

Point out to students that determining whether or not an experience is memorable depends on an individual's feelings and response to the event. Memorable experiences can range from major events, such as winning a statewide musical competition, to minor ones, such as receiving a silly birthday surprise.

Reinforcement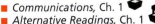
- *Communications,* Ch. 1
- *Alternative Readings,* Ch. 1
- *Daily Language Activity Transparencies*
- *Vocabulary Workshop* and *Tests*
- *Spelling*

Evaluation and Assessment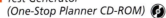
- Test Generator (One-Stop Planner CD-ROM)
- Assessment Package
  — Chapter Tests, Ch. 1
  — Chapter Tests in Standardized Test Formats, Ch. 1
  — Assessment Alternatives, Ch. 1

Reading Workshop

OBJECTIVES
- To read an autobiographical incident in preparation for writing one
- To form generalizations
- To construct a flowchart to chart chronological order
- To use context clues to determine the meanings of unfamiliar words

Quotation for the Day

"Experience is a hard teacher because she gives the test first, the lesson afterward."

(Vernon Law, 1930–   , major-league baseball player, 1950–1951, 1954–1967)

Initiate a discussion on how telling or writing an autobiographical incident helps an individual examine the lessons learned from experience. Encourage students to speculate how time and distance can help put a difficult experience in perspective and enable the writer or speaker to focus on what he or she learned from it.

TEACHING TIP

Preparing to Read
The Reading Selection, an excerpt from *Rosa Parks: My Story,* illustrates the concept of chronological order and also provides an opportunity for students to apply what they learn about making inferences and forming generalizations.

RESOURCES

Reading Workshop
Reinforcement
- *Alternative Readings,* Ch.1

Reading Workshop

Reading an Autobiographical Incident

WHAT'S AHEAD?
In this section you will read an autobiographical incident. You will also learn how to
- form generalizations
- construct a flowchart to understand chronological order

If you want to bring about a change, you have to take action. Many people throughout the history of the United States have dared to do just that. These people stood up for what they believed, and their actions led to positive changes in U.S. society. Rosa Parks is one of those people. On December 1, 1955, in Montgomery, Alabama, Rosa Parks challenged a law that said African Americans must sit in a separate section from whites on public buses. Read about the incident in the excerpt from her autobiography on the next page.

Preparing to Read

READING SKILL

Making Inferences: Forming Generalizations   A **generalization** is a statement that applies to many individuals or experiences, not just a specific person or experience. As you read the following excerpt, think about what you could say about Rosa Parks's experience that would also be true for others who have experienced discrimination.

READING FOCUS

Chronological Order   Rosa Parks tells her story in **chronological order.** She starts with the first event and ends with the last. As you read, pay attention to the order, or **sequence,** of events. How does chronological order help you understand the story?

18   Chapter 1   Narration/Description: Sharing Our Stories

READING PROCESS

PREREADING
Build Background. Ask your students to brainstorm what they know about the civil rights movement. Tell them that knowing some historical facts that relate to the Reading Selection will help them better understand it. Explain that segregation laws, established in many states in the 1800s, required blacks and whites to attend separate schools and to use separate facilities such as restaurants, hospitals, and hotels. African Americans launched the civil rights movement

Reading Selection

Jot down answers to the numbered active-reading questions in the shaded boxes. The underlined words will be discussed in the Vocabulary Mini-Lesson on page 25.

from Rosa Parks: My Story

BY ROSA PARKS
with Jim Haskins

When I got off from work that evening of December 1, I went to Court Square as usual to catch the Cleveland Avenue bus home. I didn't look to see who was driving when I got on, and by the time I recognized him, I had already paid my fare. It was the same driver who had put me off the bus back in 1943, twelve years earlier. He was still tall and heavy, with red, rough-looking skin. And he was still mean-looking. I didn't know if he had been on that route before—they switched the drivers around sometimes. I do know that most of the time if I saw him on a bus, I wouldn't get on it.

1. What is the first event in Rosa Parks's story?

I saw a vacant seat in the middle section of the bus and took it. I didn't even question why there was a vacant seat even though there were quite a few people standing in the back. If I had thought about it at all, I would probably have figured maybe someone saw me get on and did not take the seat but left it vacant for me. There was a man sitting next to the window and two women across the aisle.

2. Do you think the order of the first two paragraphs could be switched? Why?

The next stop was the Empire Theater, and some whites got on. They filled up the white seats,[1] and one man was left standing. The driver looked back and noticed the man standing. Then he looked back at us. He said,

---

1. **white seats:** seats on a public bus that only white people could occupy.

---

in the 1950s to end segregation and demand equality. When Rosa Parks, an African American seamstress, refused to give up her seat to a white person on a Montgomery, Alabama, bus in 1955, she was arrested for disobeying segregation laws. In response, local civil rights leaders, led by Dr. Martin Luther King, Jr., urged African Americans to boycott the city's bus system. In 1956, the Supreme Court declared local and state segregation laws in Montgomery, Alabama, unconstitutional.

Active-Reading Questions

The purpose of the active-reading questions is to help students notice chronological order and to have them make inferences about events in the Reading Selection. Use students' answers as an informal assessment of their understanding of these concepts. Possible answers follow.

ANSWERS

1. Parks boards the Cleveland Avenue bus to go home after work.

2. Students may think that the order could not be switched because events in the second paragraph happen after events in the first paragraph.

Cooperative Learning

Shared Experiences. Divide the class into groups, and have them create "empathy webs." Groups should begin by drawing a circle that contains the sentence "Rosa Parks was asked to give up her seat." Groups should draw connecting circles that contain adjectives describing Parks's feelings. Ask students to share situations (if they feel comfortable doing so) in which they experienced feelings similar to Parks's. Then, have students write those experiences in circles attached to the adjectives shared with Parks. Finally, ask each group to discuss the following:

- How does your experience affect the way you feel about Parks's story?
- Have you learned anything new about society or culture?

Active-Reading Questions
ANSWERS continued

3. Students may say the driver told the black passengers to give up their seats because all the "white seats" were filled and he did not want to let black passengers sit while white passengers stood.

4. The bus driver needed one seat.

5. Students may say that the bus driver was bossy or prejudiced toward African Americans.

6. Students may infer that Parks was tired of giving in to the unfair practice of segregation and could not accept such discrimination any longer without protesting it.

Meeting INDIVIDUAL NEEDS

LEARNERS HAVING DIFFICULTY
You may need to explain to students that the third paragraph on this page begins with a literary technique called a *flashback*. A flashback is an interruption in the present action of a plot to show events that happened at an earlier time.

"Let me have those front seats," because they were the front seats of the black section.[2] Didn't anybody move. We just sat right where we were, the four of us. Then he spoke a second time: "Y'all better make it light on yourselves and let me have those seats."

> **3.** Why did the bus driver tell the black passengers to give up their seats?

The man in the window seat next to me stood up, and I moved to let him pass by me, and then I looked across the aisle and saw that the two women were also standing. I moved over to the window seat. I could not see how standing up was going to "make it light" for me. The more we gave in and complied, the worse they treated us.

> **4.** How many seats did the bus driver need so all the white passengers could sit down?

I thought back to the time when I used to sit up all night and didn't sleep, and my grandfather would have his gun right by the fireplace, or if he had his one-horse wagon going anywhere, he always had his gun in the back of the wagon. People always say that I didn't give up my seat because I was tired, but that isn't true. I was not tired physically, or no more tired than I usually was at the end of a working day. I was not old, although some people have an image of me as being old then. I was forty-two. No, the only tired I was, was tired of giving in.

The driver of the bus saw me still sitting there, and he asked was I going to stand up. I said, "No." He said, "Well, I'm going to have you arrested." Then I said, "You may do that." These were the only words we said to each other. I didn't even know his name, which was James Blake, until we were in court together. He got out of the bus and stayed outside for a few minutes, waiting for the police.

> **5.** Why do you think the bus driver insisted that Rosa Parks move?

As I sat there, I tried not to think about what might happen. I knew that anything was possible. I could be manhandled or beaten. I could be arrested. People have asked me if it occurred to me then that I could be the test case the NAACP[3] had been looking for. I did not think about that at all. In fact if I had let myself think too deeply about what might happen to me, I might have gotten off the bus. But I chose to remain.

> **6.** Why do you think Rosa Parks decided not to give up her seat?

---

2. **black section:** the back of a public bus, where African Americans were allowed to sit.
3. **NAACP:** National Association for the Advancement of Colored People, an organization that fights for the equal treatment of African Americans and other minority groups.

Chapter 1   Narration/Description: Sharing Our Stories

READING PROCESS

READING
Ask Questions. Most people get more out of their reading if they have a specific purpose in mind. One purpose for reading is to find answers to specific questions.

Encourage students to jot down notes and questions about confusing words or passages that they encounter. If students cannot find answers to their questions, help them think through information in the text

Narration/Description: Sharing Our Stories

First Thoughts on Your Reading

1. Based on what you have read, how were Rosa Parks and other African Americans treated during the 1950s?
2. How would you tell Rosa Parks's story in your own words?

Making Inferences: Forming Generalizations

READING SKILL

Read Between the Lines An author will not always give you every detail of a story. Sometimes you will need to make educated guesses about what is happening. Educated guesses are called **inferences**. To make inferences, combine clues that the author provides with what you already know about the subject.

Example: **What you read:** The little boy fell on the floor kicking and screaming while his mother held the football.

+ **What you know:** My mother took my toys away when I was in trouble, and I would get very mad.

Inference: The little boy misbehaved, so his mother took the football away from him.

Reference Note
For more on **inferences**, see page 706 in the Quick Reference Handbook.

One type of inference is a *generalization*. A **generalization** is a statement that applies to many different situations or people even though it is based on specific situations or people.

Example: **What you read:** Emma and Miguel do their math homework. Emma and Miguel make *A*'s in math.

+ **What you know:** I do my homework in science, and I make good grades.

Generalization: Doing your homework usually leads to good grades.

TIP Generalizations use words like *many, usually, some, overall, most,* and *generally.* What clue word does the generalization in the example use?

Notice that the generalization above doesn't apply just to Emma and Miguel or to math homework. It is a general statement that is true for many different people and school subjects.

Read the paragraph on the next page. Then, form a generalization by using personal knowledge as well as information in the paragraph. Use the steps that follow the paragraph if you need help.

Reading Workshop 21

First Thoughts on Your Reading

ANSWERS
Possible responses are given below.

1. Students may infer that Parks and other African Americans were treated unfairly because they were forced by law to sit in a section of a public bus that was separate from the section used by whites.
2. Students should summarize the story showing an understanding of the chronological sequence of events.

Critical Thinking

Synthesis. For additional practice in making inferences, ask students to form a generalization about each of the following sets of statements.

- Grandpa enjoys fly-fishing. Grammy takes line-dancing lessons. My neighbor is retired but works part time at a store. [Many older people lead active lives.]

- Kristin sprained her ankle during a skateboarding exhibition. I bruised my knee when I was in-line skating. My cousin broke his wrist in a skiing accident. [Some sports can be dangerous.]

---

or provide additional information to ensure that they understand what they have read. For example, students may be confused by the interruption in the action at the beginning of paragraph five. Explain that this passage is a flashback—it refers to an event in the past, one that happened when Parks was a child. The flashback provides information that helps to explain Parks's current actions on the bus.

TIP Be careful not to make *faulty generalizations*. If you can find an exception to your generalization, then it is faulty. Faulty generalizations tend to include words like *all, none, never, always,* and *every*.

Faulty Generalization: Doing your homework *always* leads to good grades.

Reference Note
For more on **generalizations**, see page 705 in the Quick Reference Handbook.

In 1848, Elizabeth Cady Stanton and Lucretia Mott organized the first women's rights convention. Through their efforts and the persistence of women after them, women eventually gained the right to own property and to vote. In the 1960s, Cesar Chavez helped migrant workers by forming a union, the United Farm Workers. He began strikes and boycotts that won union members better wages and working conditions. Ed Roberts began the movement for the rights of the disabled when he started a program to help disabled students in the 1960s. Other people joined the cause, and eventually Congress passed the Americans with Disabilities Act in 1990. This act made it illegal to discriminate against people with mental or physical disabilities.

THINKING IT THROUGH — Forming Generalizations

STEP 1 Read the entire passage. Look for similarities and connections between the details in the passage.

Stanton and Mott helped women. Chavez helped migrant workers. Roberts helped disabled people. They all made a difference.

STEP 2 Connect the details in the passage to something you already know.

My parents organized a petition to keep a park from becoming a parking lot. The mayor agreed.

STEP 3 Form a generalization that combines what you read with what you know.

People can often make a difference when they stand up for what they believe.

STEP 4 Check your answer. Make sure your generalization
- is not faulty (look for a faulty generalization clue word)
- is reasonable, based on the information in the passage.

I say *often*, not *always*. My generalization is reasonable because all the details I read were about people who did something and made a difference.

Meeting INDIVIDUAL NEEDS

MODALITY
Visual Learners. Consider using the following graphic to help students visualize the process as they form generalizations.

```
  facts from
   selection
      +
     prior
   knowledge
      =
  generalization
```

YOUR TURN 2 Forming Generalizations

Re-read the reading selection on pages 19–20. Using the steps in the Thinking It Through on page 22, form a generalization about what sometimes happens when people take a stand against something they believe is unfair. Be prepared to support your generalization with information from the reading selection and from your own knowledge.

Chronological Order

It Goes Like This Like a fictional story, an autobiographical incident has a beginning, middle, and end. The writer uses **chronological** (or time) **order** to tell which event happened first, second, third, and so on. If the events were not written in chronological order, you might have a hard time picturing the story in your mind. Read the following autobiographical incident. Which event happened first? second? third?

> While visiting our grandmother, my sister and I decided we would have a picnic lunch. We packed a bag and walked to the field behind my grandmother's house.
>
> We chose a nice, shady spot under a big tree. Tamara had started to spread out the blanket when all of a sudden she began to scream and fling her arms wildly. Before I could ask her what was wrong, I was screaming, too. We both ran to the house.
>
> My grandmother heard the noise and came out to see what was wrong. She found that Tamara and I had been stung several times. We definitely upset a family of yellow jackets when we laid our blanket on top of their nest.

Flowcharts are graphic organizers that can help you see the events of an autobiographical incident in the order in which they occurred. In the flowchart on the next page, notice that only major events of the incident above are listed. Details are left out.

Reading Workshop   23

YOUR TURN 2

Students may say that when people take a stand against what they believe is unfair, they must sometimes face obstacles or hardships. For example, Rosa Parks knew she might be beaten or arrested for refusing to give up her seat on the bus. Students may also offer personal examples of obstacles or hardships.

TEACHING TIP

Chronological Order
To help students understand chronological order, point out that certain words or phrases, such as *now, then, finally, next,* and *before,* are clues to a sequence of events. Have students look for three words or phrases that signal chronological order in the Reading Selection on pp. 19–20. ["When I got off," "twelve years earlier," "then"] Discuss how these words can help readers identify the order of events. For example, you might point out that the word *then* alerts a reader that the action to be described follows action that has just been described.

RESOURCES

Your Turn 2
Practice
- *Communications,* WS. p. 7

Reinforcement
- *Communications,* TP. 11, WS. p. 8

First Event: My sister and I went out to have a picnic lunch. → Second Event: We screamed and ran to the house. → Third Event: We found out we had been stung by yellow jackets.

To tell the difference between a major event and a supporting detail, look for action. For instance, what is more important: that the picnic spot was nice and shady, or that the narrator and her sister screamed and ran to the house? The main event in that paragraph is the action of the narrator and her sister.

YOUR TURN 3 Charting Chronological Order

Copy the following flowchart onto your paper. Then, read the list of events and details taken from *Rosa Parks: My Story* below. Decide which sentences are supporting details and which are major events. Place the major events in the flowchart. When you are done, re-read the reading selection on pages 19–20 to see if you listed the major events in the correct order.

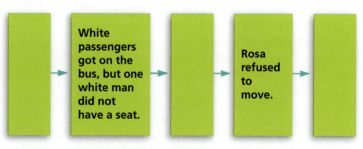

The bus driver told the African American passengers to move.
The bus driver's name was James Blake.
Rosa waited for the police.
Rosa got on the bus after work to go home.
The bus driver was tall, heavy, and had a red face.

ANSWERS

Students should place the following events in order in the flowchart.

- Rosa got on the bus after work to go home.
- The bus driver told the African American passengers to move.
- Rosa waited for the police.

If students have included supporting details in the flowchart, remind them that major events include action.

Wrap It Up

Metacognition. To encourage students to reflect on their own reading processes, have them answer the following question:

1. What insights about autobiographical incidents did you gain from reading this selection?

Then ask students this question:

2. Why do writers use chronological order to tell a story? [to help readers picture events in their minds and to help them understand how the events are related]

READING PROCESS

EXTENDING
Apply What You Read. Tell students that being able to make inferences will make them more effective readers, listeners, and viewers. Have them form generalizations about products they have seen advertised on television. Remind students to follow the steps in **Thinking It Through** on p. 22 as they form their generalizations.

MINI-LESSON VOCABULARY

Context Clues

As you read an autobiographical incident, you may discover that the author uses unfamiliar words to tell about his or her experience. One way to determine the meaning of an unfamiliar word is to use *context clues*. A word's **context** is made up of the words and sentences that surround it. Try using context clues to understand the underlined word in this passage taken from Rosa Parks's autobiography.

> I wasn't frightened at the jail. I was more resigned than anything else. I don't recall being real angry, not enough to have an argument. I was just prepared to accept whatever I had to face. I asked again if I could make a telephone call. I was ignored.
>
> Rosa Parks, *Rosa Parks: My Story*

THINKING IT THROUGH — Using Context Clues

▶ **STEP 1** Look at the context of the unfamiliar word. See if the words and sentences around it provide clues to the word's meaning.

The passage says that Rosa was not frightened or angry. It also says she was "prepared to accept" anything.

▶ **STEP 2** Use the context clues to make a guess at the unfamiliar word's meaning.

Since Rosa was not frightened or angry, and she could accept anything, I think *resigned* means "prepared to accept whatever happens."

▶ **STEP 3** Check your definition by inserting it in the passage in place of the unfamiliar word.

"I wasn't frightened at the jail. I was more prepared to accept whatever happened than anything else." That makes sense.

PRACTICE

Using context clues, figure out the meanings of these words. The words are underlined in *Rosa Parks: My Story*.

1. recognized (page 19)
2. vacant (page 19)
3. complied (page 20)
4. manhandled (page 20)
5. occurred (page 20)

MINI-LESSON VOCABULARY

Context Clues

ANSWERS
Possible responses follow.

1. The passage says that Rosa realizes the bus driver "was the same driver who had put me off the bus back in 1943." I think *recognized* means "identified someone who had been seen before."

2. Rosa sees "a vacant seat in the middle section of the bus" and sits down. *Vacant* might mean "empty." "I saw a[n] empty seat . . . and took it" makes sense.

3. The passage says "we gave in and complied." *Complied* might mean "adapted to another's wishes." "The more we gave in and adapted to others' wishes" makes sense.

4. Rosa fears what will happen after the police arrive. She worries that she might be beaten or manhandled. I think *manhandled* means "treated roughly."

5. In the passage, Rosa does not think she might be a test case for the NAACP. Maybe *occurred* means "came to mind." It works in the sentence to say "People have asked me if it came to mind then that I could be the test case."

RESOURCES

Your Turn 3

Practice
- *Communications,* WS. p. 9

Reinforcement
- *Communications,* TP. 12, WS. p. 10

Vocabulary

Practice
- *Communications,* WS. p. 11

Looking Ahead to Writing

In the Writing Workshop on pp. 27–44, students will be asked to write their own narratives about a life experience. As they work on their drafts, tell students that they might wish to use a chronological order flowchart similar to the one on p. 24 of the Reading Workshop to help them plan the sequence of events.

MINI-LESSON: TEST TAKING

Making Inferences

When you take a reading test, you may be asked to make an inference. Read the passage below and the question following it. How would you answer the question?

> Citizens in Montgomery organized a bus boycott to protest the arrest of Rosa Parks. Leaflets were distributed encouraging African Americans not to ride the bus. Not using public transportation was very difficult for families without cars, so other means of transportation were made available. Black-owned cab companies helped those without cars by charging cheap fares. In addition, car owners and local churches formed car pools.

You can tell from the passage that during the Montgomery bus boycott

A. most African Americans stayed home

B. all African Americans refused to ride the bus

C. many African Americans supported one another

D. all African Americans used taxis to get around

THINKING IT THROUGH — Making Inferences

▶ **STEP 1** Read the passage and the question to see what it is asking you.

"You can tell" tells me I will make an educated guess, or an inference.

▶ **STEP 2** To identify the best response, look at each of the answer choices and ask yourself these questions:
- Is there information in the passage that supports this answer choice?
- Does this statement cover all the information in the passage?
- Is the answer free of faulty generalization words such as *all, none, never, always, every*?

Answer A—The passage does not mention African Americans staying home.

Answer B—Right away I see a faulty generalization clue word—<u>all</u>. I don't know if all African Americans refused to ride the bus.

Answer C—I can find specific information to support this choice.

Answer D—Yes, they did use taxis, but they also carpooled. D also has a faulty generalization word—<u>all</u>.

▶ **STEP 3** After evaluating each answer choice, choose the best one.

I think answer C is the best answer. I can support it with information from the passage.

RESOURCES

Test Taking
Practice
- *Communications*, WS. pp. 12–14

Writing Workshop

Writing About a Life Experience

On the first day of school, you are given your first assignment—*Tell the class one thing you did this summer.* "This is easy," you think. "I'll talk about my rafting trip." You begin by telling when and where you went, and who was with you. Then, you describe the trip, particularly the dangerous parts. As you share your experience, your teacher and classmates learn something about you. You discover something about yourself, too. It is obvious that you like rafting, but your story also reveals that you like action.

You can discover more about yourself through **expressive writing**. In this workshop you will have an opportunity to share your thoughts and feelings about a single experience from your life by writing an **autobiographical incident**. You will use details that tell the reader what happened and how you felt about the incident.

WHAT'S AHEAD?

In this workshop you will write an autobiographical incident. You will also learn how to
- include background information
- create a detail chart
- arrange ideas in chronological order
- choose exact verbs
- capitalize proper nouns

Prewriting

Choose an Experience

Who? Me? What is the one subject you know the best? Why, *you* are, of course. You have probably had many experiences that you can write about. The first step in writing an autobiographical

---

Writing Workshop

OBJECTIVES
- To use the writing process to write and revise an autobiographical incident
- To include background information that will help an audience understand the incident
- To create a chart of action details and sensory details that will help re-create the incident
- To arrange ideas in chronological order
- To replace dull verbs with exact verbs
- To capitalize proper nouns

Quotation for the Day

"My yesterdays walk with me. They keep step, they are gray faces that peer over my shoulder."
(William Golding, 1911–1993, English novelist)

Use this quotation to remind students that they already have all the information necessary to write an autobiographical narrative. To demonstrate the importance of the past to students, ask them to recall a time they learned to do something they now do nearly every day. An example might be riding a bicycle or using multiplication. Ask volunteers to share details from their important lessons.

Meeting INDIVIDUAL NEEDS

STUDENTS WITH SPECIAL NEEDS
Some students may need more individual attention as they try to think of experiences for their autobiographical incidents. Help them uncover topics by asking them direct questions about experiences they are likely to have had or things and people about which they are likely to be enthusiastic. For example, Have you ever gone to (place)? Do you have a pet? Do you remember a special birthday present?

YOUR TURN 4

Sample answers appear below.

I am going to write about losing the spelling bee. This experience is meaningful to me because I learned to accept defeat gracefully.

KEY CONCEPT

incident is choosing one particular experience. If you need help coming up with one, consider these suggestions.

- Think about an experience that defines an emotion. When were you most happy, scared, surprised, sad, or angry?
- Brainstorm with your friends and family members. Ask them to recall a memorable experience that involves you.
- Look at your journals and at letters or pictures you have saved.
- Draw a road map of your life like the one to the left. Start with your birth and list all the important events that have happened to you up to now, such as your first day of kindergarten, the day your little sister was born, and the time your baseball team won the city championship.

You Be the Judge Once you have a list of experiences, you want to choose the one that will make the best autobiographical incident to share with an audience. **The best experience is one that is meaningful, or important, to you.** Ask yourself the questions below to decide which experience is most meaningful.

Question	Example
Do I remember the experience well?	If you cannot remember all the details, you will not be able to provide a complete picture of the experience. For instance, family members may have told you about your first step, but do *you* remember all the details?
Why is this experience important to me?	The reader should know how you felt about this experience or what you learned from it. For example, you might say that forgetting your lines in the school play was your most embarrassing moment.
Am I willing to share this experience with others?	You should feel comfortable letting other people read about your experience. For example, you might not want to share your first crush with the whole class.

YOUR TURN 4 Choosing an Experience

Make a list of your experiences. Then, evaluate each experience by answering the questions in the chart above. Finally, choose an experience and complete the following sentences.

I am going to write about _____.

This experience is meaningful to me because _____.

RESOURCES

Your Turn 4 and 5
Practice
- *Communications,* WS. pp. 15, 16

Think About Purpose and Audience

FYI... You are telling a story to a group of people when someone interrupts to ask, "How old were you?" Before you can speak, your best friend answers, "Third grade, right?" You agree and continue, only to be stopped again with another question. Again, your best friend answers. Why does your best friend understand the story when everyone else does not?

Before you begin writing your autobiographical incident, think about your purpose and audience. **Your purpose is to express your thoughts and feelings by sharing an experience with an audience.** Because you may not know exactly who your audience is, you should write as if your audience knows nothing about you. In order for your audience to understand your incident fully, you will need to provide **background information,** facts that set up the story. The four W's—*What? When? Who? Where?*—will help you think about the information your audience needs.

- **What:** What is the incident? What happened?
- **When:** When did this event happen? How old were you?
- **Who:** Besides you, who was involved?
- **Where:** Where did this event take place? What was this place like?

> *What?* slipped during a dance recital
> *When?* an October night when I was seven years old
> *Who?* me, my parents, my dance teacher, my classmates, and their friends and families
> *Where?* on an auditorium stage that had very bright lights

◄ KEY CONCEPT

TIP Part of your **style**—how you say things—is your **voice**—the *sound* of your writing. Most good writing sounds like speech. You can develop your voice by choosing words that sound like you yet fit your audience and purpose.

Describe the voice in each sentence below:

1. I was so embarrassed! I wanted to crawl under the stage.
2. I doubt that I had ever been as embarrassed as I was at that moment.

YOUR TURN 5 — Thinking About Your Audience

Ask yourself *What? When? Who? Where?* to help you think of background information you should give your audience. Write your answers on a sheet of paper or in a learning log.

LEARNERS HAVING DIFFICULTY
Students may need help selecting a voice appropriate for their audience and purpose. On the chalkboard, write students' descriptions of the voices in the examples from the Tip on this page. Then, ask the class to consider which voice (as described) is more appropriate for the purpose of expressing. [Students may recognize that the voice in the first example is more expressive—the writer told how he or she felt by using concrete, sensory details.] Next, ask each student which voice is more appropriate for a younger audience, and which for an older audience. [Students may agree that the first example might be more interesting to both audiences than the second example]. Finally, ask students whether the voice exhibited in either example would be appropriate for other purposes, such as to inform, to entertain, or to persuade. [The first example would be entertaining; the second example may be suitable for persuasion, where there is less emphasis on expressing feelings; the use of *I* in both examples may make them both unsuitable for most informative writing.]

YOUR TURN 5

Have students create a chart with the headings *What? When? Who?* and *Where?* to help them generate, record, and organize the background information they should provide.

Recall Descriptive Details

You Had to Be There   You ask a friend about the movie he saw the other night. "Oh, it was great! First, the bad guy terrorizes the city. In the end, though, the good guy wins." It doesn't sound so great to you. Why not? Your friend left out the details.

Details will allow your readers to experience an incident just as if they were there. Two types of details that you should include in your essay are *action details* and *sensory details*.

- **Action details** tell what events occurred and what people said.

   After waiting thirty minutes, I finally made it through the ticket line. I raced to the roller coaster only to find another long line.

   "Will I ever get to have fun?" I moaned to my friend.

- **Sensory details** describe what you see, hear, taste, feel, and smell.

   The coaster went click, click, click as it slowly went uphill. Sweat trickled down my neck as we reached the top.

To re-create your memory, picture the incident in your mind. In a chart like the one below, record the details that you "see."

Action Details	Sensory Details
Beginning: lined up backstage, then walked onto stage. My dance teacher said, "Break a leg!"	black leotard and tights, gold sequined belt flowery smell of hair spray announcer's booming voice
Middle: doing a routine with wooden boxes, was supposed to put one foot on the box next to me, missed and slipped—everyone else was on their box except me	heard audience laughing felt hot, face turned red dance teacher had said if we made a mistake to keep smiling
End: curtain dropped, I cried	sobbing, salty tears

Reference Note
For more information and practice on **punctuating dialogue**, see page 594.

KEY CONCEPT

TIP   You can decide if a detail is necessary by asking yourself, "What was most important about my experience?" For instance, if the most important part of your vacation was going whale watching, then your details should be about whales. Leave out the details that do not describe the whales.

 Recalling Details

Create a detail chart like the one above. List action details that happened at the beginning, middle, and end of your incident. Then, list sensory details to go with each action detail.

MINI-LESSON: CRITICAL THINKING

Arranging Ideas

My mom was not happy. Tony and Najla stared at me with open mouths. I hit the ball. It went crashing into the living room window. Tony, Najla, and I were playing baseball in the street. Najla pitched the ball. "I'm in trouble now," I said.

Wait a minute. What just happened? The mother was angry before the ball broke the window? The narrator is in trouble for playing in the street or because the ball crashed into the living room? This story is confusing.

In order to help their readers understand an incident, writers usually tell events in *chronological order*. Using **chronological order** means telling the events of a story in the order that they happened, starting with the first event, going to the second, then the third, and so on. Chronological order helps the reader follow the action of the incident. You can see that a story written chronologically is much easier to understand than one that is not.

Tony, Najla, and I were playing baseball in the street. Najla pitched the ball to me. I hit the ball, and it went crashing into the living room window. Tony and Najla stared at me with open mouths. "I'm in trouble now," I said. My mom was not happy.

PRACTICE

Read the following list of events. Then, rewrite the events in chronological order on your own paper.

- look at the clock, it is 6:50 A.M.
- get dressed, it is 6:55 A.M.
- alarm goes off at 6 A.M.
- grab my books, it is 6:59 A.M.
- get on the bus at 7 A.M.
- take a shower
- jump out of bed
- hit the snooze button
- breathe a sigh of relief, "I barely made it!"

TIP To arrange events in chronological order, you can create a numbered list, draw a **flowchart**, or make a **time line**. Choose one of these methods when you write your answer.

Reference Note
For more on **flowcharts**, see page 23. For more on **time lines**, see page 96.

Cooperative Learning

Time Lines. To give students practice in organizing their ideas in chronological order, have them complete a time line. Divide the class into randomly assigned groups of four or five, and then ask group members to share their memories about the first day of school. Ask the students to create a time line of the events that took place. Refer students to the time line section in the **Quick Reference Handbook** on p. 689 if they need assistance.

MINI-LESSON: CRITICAL THINKING

ANSWERS
A sample numbered list appears below.

1. alarm goes off at 6 A.M.
2. hit the snooze button
3. look at the clock, it is 6:50 A.M.
4. jump out of bed
5. take a shower
6. get dressed, it is 6:55 A.M.
7. grab my books, it is 6:59 A.M.
8. get on the bus at 7 A.M.
9. breathe a sigh of relief, "I barely made it!"

RESOURCES

Critical Thinking
Practice
- *Communications,* WS. p. 18

Quotation for the Day

"The need to write comes from the need to make sense of one's life and discover one's usefulness."

(John Cheever, 1912–1982, American author)

Remind students that they can discover important things about their own lives by writing an autobiographical incident. After students complete their writing assignments, have them write journal entries explaining what they learned about themselves from writing an autobiographical incident.

Meeting INDIVIDUAL NEEDS

LEARNERS HAVING DIFFICULTY

To help students organize their writing, meet with them individually and have them describe to you the autobiographical incident they have chosen. As they talk, take notes about what you perceive to be the beginning, middle, and end of the incident. Have them create simple outlines based on your notes and then check them against the **Framework**.

YOUR TURN 7

If you wish to assign a length to this writing assignment, 500 to 700 words is appropriate.

Timesaver

To quickly assess that students' drafts follow the framework, ask them to use a different colored ink than they used in writing their papers to label the introduction; the beginning, middle, and end of the incident; the conclusion; and one or two examples of background information, action details, and sensory details.

Writing

Autobiographical Incident

Framework	Directions and Explanations

Introduction
- Attention-grabbing opening
- Background information

Start your paper with an **interesting opening.** You might ask a question or give a hint about why this incident is important to you. Or, like the writer of the model to the right, you might set the scene. Provide **background information** by telling your reader what the incident is, who was involved, where the incident took place, and when it happened.

Body
- Beginning of incident (action details and sensory details)
- Middle of incident (action details and sensory details)
- End of incident (action details and sensory details)

- Write the events in **chronological order.**
- Write about the beginning of your incident in the first paragraph of the body, the middle of the incident in the second paragraph, and the end of the incident in the third paragraph.
- Describe each part of the incident using **action details** and **sensory details.**

Conclusion
- Reason this incident is important to you

Explain how this incident affected you. **Why is it important? What does it mean to you?** Leave your reader with a complete picture of what occurred and how you felt.

YOUR TURN 7

Drafting Your Autobiographical Incident

Now it is your turn to write an autobiographical incident. As you write, refer to the framework above and the Writer's Model on the next page.

32 Chapter 1 Narration/Description: Sharing Our Stories

RESOURCES

Writing

Writing Prompts
- *Communications,* TP. 13, WS. p. 19

Extension
- *Designing Your Writing*

Your Turn 7

Practice
- *Communications,* TP. 14, WS. p. 20

A Writer's Model

The final draft below closely follows the framework for an autobiographical incident on the previous page.

A Night to Remember

It was a cool October evening. Excitement and family members filled the auditorium. I was only seven years old, but I was the center of attention. Finally, after weeks of preparation, I would show off all my hard work in a dance recital. Everything would be perfect—so I thought.

I waited backstage all dressed up in my black leotard and tights with a gold sequined belt. My hair was pulled back in a French braid, and a strong flowery smell of hair spray hung around me. In a booming voice, the master of ceremonies announced that my class was next. As I pranced proudly onto the stage and into the hot, bright stage lights, my dance teacher whispered, "Break a leg!"

My dance class was doing a routine with boxes two feet by two feet, made of wood. During part of the routine, the entire class was standing in a line on top of our boxes facing the audience. All I had to do in the next move was put one foot on the box next to mine and keep my other foot on my box. It really was an easy move. I was concentrating so much on maintaining the huge smile I had plastered on my face and keeping my head up that I did not look where I was going. I missed my partner's box altogether and slipped. There I was standing on the stage floor when my classmates were on top of their boxes. I could hear giggles coming from the audience, and I felt the heat rush to my face. I remembered my dance teacher had told my class during rehearsal, "If you make a mistake, keep smiling so the audience will not notice." I did my best to follow her advice as I continued with the routine.

(continued)

Annotations:
- Attention-grabbing opening
- Background information
- Beginning of incident
- Sensory details
- Action details / Middle of incident
- Action details
- Sensory details

Connecting Reading and Writing

To help students in writing their autobiographical incidents, have them refer to the information on chronological order in the Reading Workshop (p. 23). Then, have them read **A Writer's Model** while paying particular attention to its chronological order. As a whole class activity, list the order of major events in the model.

(continued)

End of incident
Sensory details
Action details

Reason this incident is important

> When the curtain dropped, so did my hopes for the evening. I sobbed loudly, tasting the salt from the tears that streamed down my face. I ran backstage, but no one could console me. I just wanted to be left alone.
>
> Recently I realized I *had* been a star that night. I was embarrassed, but I fought the urge to run off the stage. Instead, I finished the routine with a smile on my face. Now when friends and family laugh about the time I slipped during a dance recital, I can laugh too.

Designing Your Writing

Illustrating Your Autobiographical Incident Illustrations, such as drawings or photographs, can enhance your written description and show why an incident is important and meaningful to you. For instance, say you are writing about the time you received your best present—a puppy. You could include a picture of yourself hugging the puppy with a red ribbon around its neck. The picture shows how excited you were when you got your dog. The writer of the Writer's Model included a photo that was taken the exact moment she slipped during the dance recital. The picture definitely illustrates her embarrassment. There are several ways you can include pictures in your paper. You can paste snapshots on a piece of paper, scan pictures on the computer, or even draw your own illustrations.

TECHNOLOGY TIP

Suggest that students use computer graphics software to create pictures or word-processing software to create line drawings, such as diagrams or maps, to accompany their writing. Students may want to paste in clip art to add interest to their word-processor documents, or they may use a CD-ROM drive and software to download photographic images to include in their papers.

34 Chapter 1 **Narration/Description:** Sharing Our Stories

A Student's Model

In the following paper, Anthony C. Rodrigues, a middle school student from Cumberland, Rhode Island, writes about what he learned from a soccer game. Anthony suggests that writers should make "an organizational chart" of action and sensory details to re-create the experience.

In the Net

It was two o'clock on a Sunday afternoon, and I was on my way to my championship soccer game. As I rode up to the field and entered the parking lot, I wondered if this game was going to be like the other years when our team made it to the semifinals but then lost in the championship game. I looked at the field and I remembered seeing the pine trees in the background, but it was difficult to concentrate on their beauty because I was so nervous. *[Background information]*

One by one the players arrived and the coach told us to begin our warm-up drills and to take shots on our goaltender. I wondered if during the game I was going to shoot as well as I had in warm-ups. *[Beginning of incident]*

Finally, it was time. I was in the starting lineup, playing halfback. The whistle blew and the game had officially started. In the first half our team played exceptionally well, but at half time the score was 0–0, and we were all exhausted and cold. In the beginning of the second half we scored a goal. The crowd went up with a roar, and the players were running down the field yelling and screaming. I started to believe that maybe we would win. The second half went on and on. We maintained our 1–0 lead. *[Middle of incident]*

We went on to win the game 1–0. I was so excited that I had won my first championship game in all of my six years playing soccer. I learned that anything is possible if I put my mind and soul into it. *[End of incident / Reason this incident is important]*

Connecting Reading and Writing

Before students write drafts of their autobiographical incidents they may want to review the section **Making Inferences: Forming Generalizations** on pp. 21–22 of the Reading Workshop. Ask students to identify a generalization in **A Student's Model**. ["I learned that anything is possible if I put my mind and soul into it."] Tell students that generalizations often appear in the concluding paragraph of autobiographical writing to sum up what the writer has learned from the experience.

Quotation for the Day

"One of the advantages of the kind of writing I do is that you are your own boss. You shoot your own stock, choose all the scenes, cast all the characters. You're your own everything, really—and the product, then, is yours."

(John Updike, 1932–   , American author)

Use this quotation as a motivation for students to take care in revising and proofreading their writing. Just as the product belongs to the writer, so does the responsibility to make that product as good as it can be. Revising is one process by which this goal is met.

TEACHING TIP

▶ **Elaboration**

Suggest that students make charts like the one below to brainstorm sensory details that they may add to their autobiographical incidents. Explain that such descriptive details help readers experience exactly what is being described.

Sight	Sound	Taste	Touch	Smell

Meeting INDIVIDUAL NEEDS

ENGLISH-LANGUAGE LEARNERS
General Strategies. Students may have difficulty understanding the language in the Self-Evaluation chart on this page. Using a student's draft, go through the evaluation process with students, following the tips given in the chart. Consider rewording the evaluation questions. For example, question 2 could be changed to "Does the introduction answer these questions about the incident: What? Who? Where? When?" Remember to give positive feedback to help learners see what they have done well.

Revising

Evaluate and Revise Content, Organization, and Style

Take Two When you are ready to evaluate your essay or a classmate's, you should read the essay twice. In the first reading, look at the essay's content and organization, using the guidelines below. In the second reading, focus on the sentences, using the Focus on Word Choice on page 38.

▶ **First Reading: Content and Organization** Use the chart below to evaluate and revise your autobiographical incident to make sure it is easy to understand.

Autobiographical Incident: Content and Organization Guidelines for Self-Evaluation and Peer Evaluation

Evaluation Questions	Tips	Revision Techniques
❶ Does the introduction grab the reader's attention?	**Underline** the question or hint that makes the beginning interesting.	If needed, **add** a question or a hint about the incident's importance.
❷ Does the introduction include enough background information to help the reader understand this incident?	**Circle** information about what the incident is, who was involved, where the incident took place, and when it happened.	If necessary, **add** sentences that provide background information for the reader.
❸ Are the action details in chronological order?	**Put a number** by each action detail and check that the numbers match the order in which the action happened.	If necessary, **rearrange** action details so that they are in chronological order.
❹ Do sensory details help the reader experience the incident?	Use a colored marker to **highlight** the sensory details.	**Elaborate** on each action detail as needed by adding sensory details that describe what was seen, heard, tasted, felt, or smelled.
❺ Does the conclusion tell why the incident is important to the writer?	**Put a check mark** next to the passage that explains why the event is important.	If needed, **add** thoughts or feelings that will relate the importance of the incident.

36 Chapter 1 Narration/Description: Sharing Our Stories

RESOURCES

Revising
Practice
- *Communications,* TPs. 15, 16, WS. pp. 21, 22, 23

Narration/Description: Sharing Our Stories

ONE WRITER'S REVISIONS This revision is an early draft of the autobiographical incident on page 33.

> There I was standing on the stage floor when my class- ~~move~~
> mates were on top of their boxes. I missed my partner's
> box altogether and slipped. I could hear giggles coming
> , and I felt the heat rush to my face. ~~elaborate~~
> from the audience. I remembered my dance teacher had
> told my class during rehearsal, "If you make a mistake,
> keep smiling so the audience will not notice."

Responding to the Revision Process

1. Why do you think the writer moved a sentence?
2. Why do you think the writer added information to the paragraph above?

PEER REVIEW

As you look at your peer's autobiographical incident, ask yourself:

- Could the writer add dialogue to elaborate on an event? If so, where?
- What do I think of the writer's experience? Do I know why it is important to the writer?

▶ **Second Reading: Style** You have revised your essay so that it is well organized and complete. Now, you will check that you have written your autobiographical incident using the best possible sentences. One way to improve your sentences is to use *exact verbs*. **Exact verbs** make your writing better because they accurately express a specific action. Look at the following guidelines to see if you need more exact verbs in your essay.

Style Guidelines

Evaluation Question	Tip	Revision Technique
Does the autobiographical incident include verbs that accurately describe specific actions?	Put an **X** through ordinary verbs that are not very descriptive.	**Replace** the dull verbs with more descriptive ones.

Writing Workshop 37

TEACHING TIP

Exact Verbs
To give students practice replacing dull verbs with exact verbs, have them make word wheels. First, ask them to identify a dull verb, such as *sleep* or *move,* and write it in the center of its own wheel. Next, tell them to write alternative exact verbs to replace the dull verb, such as *doze* or *scamper,* on lines, or spokes, extending from the center of the wheel. The wheels can be placed on classroom walls for reference by all students.

Responding to the Revision Process
ANSWER
Students may say that exact verbs—*pranced* and *whispered*—paint a more vivid picture in the reader's mind.

 YOUR TURN 8

To make sure your students follow the revision guidelines on p. 36, have them photocopy or print out a copy of their drafts before they begin to make revisions. Then, after they have revised their drafts, look at the two versions to compare content, organization, and style.

Critical Thinking
Evaluation. Ask students to evaluate the student's use of verbs in **A Student's Model** on p. 35. Which verbs most accurately describe specific actions? [shoot, scored] Which verbs are dull, ordinary, or vague? [looked, went] Ask students for examples of exact verbs that might replace dull verbs. [glanced (looked), jumped (went)]

Focus on Word Choice

Exact Verbs

One of your purposes when you are writing an autobiographical incident is to help your readers see the action. Exact verbs can help you accomplish your goal. Exact verbs make your writing style more vivid and precise. Look at the following examples. Notice how exact verbs paint a more specific picture of an event in your mind—they make the action come alive.

Dull Verbs	Exact Verbs
Jesse *ate* his dinner.	Jesse *gobbled down* his dinner.
Natalie *said,* "I'm leaving!"	Natalie *screamed,* "I'm leaving!"
Brian *went* to the store.	Brian *raced* to the store.

COMPUTER TIP
You can use the thesaurus function in a word-processing program to replace dull verbs with exact verbs. Highlight the verb you want to replace, and the thesaurus will list other verbs with the same or similar meanings. From the list, you can choose the exact verb that accurately describes the action.

ONE WRITER'S REVISIONS

As I ~~walked~~ *pranced* proudly onto the stage and into the hot, bright stage lights, my dance teacher ~~said~~, *whispered* "Break a leg!"

Responding to the Revision Process
How did replacing dull verbs with exact verbs improve the sentence above?

 YOUR TURN 8

Evaluating and Revising Your Autobiographical Incident

- First, evaluate and revise the content and organization of your paper, using the guidelines on page 36.
- Next, use the Focus on Word Choice above to see if you need to replace dull verbs in your paper with exact verbs.
- If a peer evaluated your paper, think carefully about your peer's comments as you revise.

38   Chapter 1   Narration/Description: Sharing Our Stories

RESOURCES

Focus on Word Choice
Practice
- *Communications,* WS. p. 24

Publishing

Proofread Your Narrative

Correctness Counts Errors in your final draft will be distracting to your readers. If you have another person proofread your narrative, you will be less likely to overlook mistakes.

Grammar Link

Capitalizing Proper Nouns

As you write your autobiographical incident, you will use **nouns,** words that name people, places, things, and ideas. There are two kinds of nouns: *common* and *proper.* A **common noun** names any one of a group of persons, places, things, or ideas. A **proper noun** names a particular person, place, thing, or idea, and begins with a capital letter. Here are some examples of common and proper nouns.

Common Nouns	Proper Nouns
city	Boston
religion	Judaism
basketball player	Michael Jordan
teacher	Mr. Williams

Notice that the title *Mr.* is capitalized in the example above. Capitalize a title that comes *immediately* before the person's name.

Example:
Washington, D.C., was named after President George Washington.

Most titles are not capitalized when they are not immediately followed by a name.

Example:
The first president was George Washington.

PRACTICE

Capitalize the proper nouns in the following sentences.

Example:
1. My vacation to visit aunt sue in england was the best.

1. aunt sue → Aunt Sue
   england → England

1. I spent the entire month of july living in london.
2. In one day, we visited the tower of london and buckingham palace.
3. Riding on a boat down the thames river was exciting for my aunt and me.
4. I was hoping to see prince william, but he was in scotland with his father.
5. It took over ten hours for me to travel from london's gatwick airport to george bush intercontinental airport.

For more information and practice on **capitalizing proper nouns,** see page 539.

Writing Workshop 39

Quotation for the Day

"Writers write for themselves and not for their readers."

(Rebecca West, 1892–1983, British writer)

Let this quotation open a discussion among students who agree with West and those who disagree. To stimulate discussion, have students consider the purpose of writing an autobiographical incident—to share their experience with others in order to discover something about themselves.

Grammar Link

Capitalizing Proper Nouns

ANSWERS

1. July, London
2. Tower of London, Buckingham Palace
3. Thames River
4. Prince William, Scotland
5. London's Gatwick Airport, George Bush Intercontinental Airport

TEACHING TIP

Capitalizing Proper Nouns
Some students may have difficulty identifying common and proper nouns. For additional practice, have students identify three common nouns and three proper nouns in a passage in a book they are reading on their own or in the Reading Selection on pp. 19–20. ["driver," "police," "court"; "December," "Court Square," "James Blake"]

RESOURCES

Grammar Link
Practice
- *Communications,* WS. p. 25

TEACHING TIP

Publish Your Essay
Depending on their penmanship, some students may choose to write in cursive style and some may choose manuscript style. In either case, remind students to write legibly as they prepare the final copy of their essay. If their letters are not neat and formed correctly, some words may appear misspelled and the essay's message may be lost. You may want to display legibly written samples in both handwriting styles of published writing that students may use as models.

YOUR TURN 9

As students answer the "Reflect on Your Essay" questions, ask them to write down the steps they found difficult and to consider how they might meet these challenges the next time they have a similar writing assignment.

Wrap It Up

Metacognition. Have students reflect on their writing processes by answering the following question:

1. How do you think writing an autobiographical incident will help you become a more effective writer?

Then, ask students the following question:

2. What four things can you include to help make an autobiographical incident come alive for your readers? [background information, action and sensory details, and exact verbs]

Publish Your Essay

Extra, Extra Read All About It You are finally ready to share your experience with others. After all, that is the purpose of writing an autobiographical incident. How do you go about getting an audience to read your essay?

- One audience could be an older you. Create a scrapbook of your life with the first entry being your autobiographical incident. It will be fun to look back on these memories later in life.
- Make an illustrated book of all the autobiographical incidents from your class. Place the book in your school library for other students to read.
- Create a "Me" poster you could share with your class. Include your autobiographical incident along with pictures and mementos that tell your hobbies, likes and dislikes, and plans for the future.

PORTFOLIO

Reflect on Your Essay

Building Your Portfolio Your essay is finally written and published. Now, take the time to think about *what* you wrote and *how* you wrote. Reflecting on work that you have completed will make you a better writer in the future.

- What did you find difficult when writing about yourself? What did you find easy?
- Think back on all the steps you took before you actually began writing your autobiographical incident. Which of these steps would you use again when writing another paper?

TIP As you proofread your essay, use a dictionary to make sure you have spelled words correctly. Don't guess about the correct spelling.

YOUR TURN 9 Proofreading, Publishing, and Reflecting on Your Essay

- Correct grammar, usage, and mechanics errors. Pay particular attention to the capitalization of proper nouns.
- Publish your essay using one of the suggestions above.
- Answer the Reflect on Your Essay questions above. Write your responses in a learning log, or include them in your portfolio.

MINI-LESSON TEST TAKING

Writing Description for Tests

In an essay test, you may be given a question that asks you to describe a person, place, or thing. Your description should include action details and sensory details. Read the following descriptive writing prompt. How would you answer this type of essay question?

> Think about your friends. Choose one and write a letter to your teacher in which you describe your friend. In your letter, describe in detail what your friend looks like and how your friend acts.

TIP Handwriting is important when answering an essay question. Your teacher or another test grader will not be able to read your answer if your handwriting is not **legible**, or easy to read. To make sure your answer is legible, use your best handwriting. You can print or write in cursive. Choose the style that will be easier for others to read.

THINKING IT THROUGH — Writing a Description

▶ **STEP 1** Read the prompt to see what it is asking you to do. What is your topic? Who is your audience?

The prompt is asking me to write a letter describing a friend. I will describe how my friend Reggie looks and acts. The audience is my teacher.

▶ **STEP 2** List action and sensory details that describe your subject. To picture the details, close your eyes and imagine the subject right in front of you.

Action details: makes good grades, does nice things (shared his sandwich), plays baseball

Sensory details: has curly, short, black hair and brown eyes, is tall (5 feet 3 inches) and thin (about 95 pounds), has a squeaky voice, smells like apples because he always uses apple shampoo

▶ **STEP 3** Decide how you will organize your details. Then, write your description.

First paragraph: I will tell what Reggie looks like.
Second paragraph: I will tell how he acts.

▶ **STEP 4** Read your description, checking for details that allow your reader to see your subject clearly.

I will check to see that I have a really good description of what Reggie looks like and how he acts.

Writing Workshop 41

RESOURCES

Test Taking
Practice
 Communications, WS. p. 26

TEACHING TIP

Writing a Narrative Poem
Before students begin to write a narrative poem, remind them that the autobiographical incidents they have read and written are prose narratives. Then, have students discuss how a prose narrative and a narrative poem are similar and different. [Both have characters and a beginning, middle, and end; narrative poems often are written in stanzas and contain alliteration and figurative language.]

Connections to Literature

Writing a Narrative Poem

Just as there are different types of stories—funny, sad, scary—there are different ways to present them to an audience. One way to present a story is by writing a narrative poem. A **narrative poem** has characters and a beginning, middle, and end. When you wrote your autobiographical incident, you wrote a *prose* narrative. Now you have a chance to be a poet by writing a narrative *poem*.

Start with the Basics It is not difficult to create a poem once you understand how poems are written. Poets say things in unusual ways. They often use very few words, so they have to select their words very carefully. Poets use sounds and figurative language to express their thoughts and feelings and to paint a picture of people, places, things, and actions.

The following list will provide you with the definitions and examples of the most common poetic elements.

Alliteration is the repetition of consonant sounds, especially sounds at the beginning of words.

Sara certainly saw Sam sail to Sardinia.

Bobby built rubber baby buggy bumpers.

Figurative Language is descriptive language that is not meant to be taken literally. Figurative language is used to express an idea by making a comparison that will give readers a clearer picture of the idea. For example, saying a noise is loud is not as clear as comparing the noise to eighty bowlers all making strikes at the same time. Three types of figurative language are *personification*, *simile*, and *metaphor*.

- **Personification** is describing something that is not human, such as an animal or object, as if it were human by giving it human qualities.

  The *joyful* sparrow chirped *hello*.

  Each morning the alarm clock *screams* at me to get out of bed.

- **Simile** compares two different things using the word *like* or *as*.

  Like a statue, I sat motionless.

  The leaves fell as quietly *as* a whisper.

- **Metaphor** compares two different things by saying one is the other.

  He *is* a bottomless pit, eating everything in sight.

  When she first wakes up in the morning, her hair *is* a tangled bird's nest.

Seeing Is Believing Read the narrative poem on the next page. What event is the poet relating? What are his thoughts and feelings? What other examples of alliteration or figurative language can you find?

Foul Shot
by Edwin A. Hoey

With two 60's stuck on the scoreboard
And two seconds hanging on the clock,
The solemn boy in the center of eyes,
Squeezed by silence,
Seeks out the line with his feet,
Soothes his hands along his uniform,
Gently drums the ball against the floor,
Then measures the waiting net,
Raises the ball on his right hand,
Balances it with his left,
Calms it with fingertips,
Breathes,
Crouches,
Waits,
And then through a stretching of stillness,
Nudges it upward.
The ball
Slides up and out,
Lands,
Leans,
Wobbles,
Wavers,
Hesitates,
Exasperates,
Plays it coy
Until every face begs with unsounding screams—
And then
       And then
              And then,
Right before ROAR-UP,
Dives down and through.

Annotations:
- Figurative language: personification—silence is squeezing the boy
- Alliteration—lands and leans
- Alliteration—wobbles and wavers
- Figurative language: personification—the ball is playing it coy

TIP As you read the narrative poem, notice that
- the incident can be the title of the poem
- a narrative poem does not have to be autobiographical
- events are written in chronological order so the reader can understand the incident
- placing one word on a line can emphasize that word or thought
- exact verbs provide an accurate description of the action

Meeting INDIVIDUAL NEEDS

MODALITY

Kinesthetic Learners. To help students emphasize the connection between exact verbs and a specific action, ask students to pantomime the incident about which they want to write. Randomly assign each student to work with a partner. One student will act out the incident while the other takes notes describing the actions. Then, students can trade places and use the notes to help them compose their poems.

Connecting Reading and Writing

Students do not necessarily have to write their narrative poems about autobiographical incidents. Suggest that students having difficulty finding a topic review the Reading Selection on pp. 19–20. To help students develop personally meaningful similes and metaphors, urge them to put themselves in Rosa Parks's shoes, connecting her feelings with their own experiences. For example, a student might compare Parks—when she realizes too late that the bus driver is one she usually avoids—to a butterfly caught in a jar.

TEACHING TIP

The Ball Is in Your Court

For **Your Turn 10**, if students decide to present a dramatic interpretation of their poems, divide the class into randomly selected groups of three or four. Students should present their poems to their groups by following the steps below.

- Stand facing the group while reading the poem aloud or reciting it from memory.
- Make eye contact with your audience as often as possible.
- Vary tone, pitch, and volume of speaking voice to emphasize changes in mood and action.
- Use gestures and facial expressions sparingly for added emphasis.

Hold a class poetry reading to give students an opportunity to share their narrative poems. After each reader finishes, ask the class to identify specific examples of poetic elements—alliteration, personification, similes, metaphors—that they heard in each poem.

Timesaver

To help you evaluate the students' narrative poems, ask students to work in small groups to write two or three lines about each group member's poem after it is read, identifying strengths and weaknesses, and to give these comments to the writer. Students should attach these comments to their poems before turning them in to you for review.

Got the Idea? How did the author of "Foul Shot" fit a story into a poem? As you can see, the author based his poem on a specific incident. The poem describes, in order, the events that happened during a free-throw shot. The poet did not take five pages to describe the incident, nor did he just list the events by saying, "The boy bounced the ball a few times, threw it, and it went into the basket." Instead, he selected his words carefully and used alliteration and figurative language. The poet's words put you there in the gym. You can see the action clearly and feel the crowd's hopes and the boy's nervousness.

The Ball Is in Your Court Now that you have read an example, try writing your own narrative poem by following the steps below.

1. Brainstorm an incident to write about that you don't mind sharing with others. The incident could be the title of your poem.
2. In the first stanza (group of lines), describe where the character is and how he or she feels. You can write about yourself or a **fictional**, or made-up, character.
3. In the second stanza, describe what the character is doing and what he or she is thinking. Remember, each line does not have to be a complete sentence. You can write a phrase or one word on a line.
4. In the last stanza of your poem, tell how the incident ends.

Making It Better Once you have written the basic events that make up your narrative poem, you can revise your poem. You want to make sure you have used the best words to relate your ideas and feelings. Use the following suggestions to add poetic sounds and descriptions to your poem. Remember, a poem does not have to rhyme unless you want it to. There are other poetic elements you can use. Look for places where you can

- make several words that are near each other all begin with the same sound
- give human qualities to a feeling, animal, or object
- compare two unlike things using *like* or *as*
- compare two unlike things by saying one *is* the other

 Writing and Revising a Narrative Poem

Write a narrative poem using the steps above. Then, revise your poem by adding as many of the poetic elements on page 42 as you can. Make a clean copy of your narrative poem and share it with a friend or give a **dramatic presentation** of your poem to your class.

Focus on Speaking and Listening

Telling a Story

The art of storytelling has been around for a very long time. Before people could write, they told stories. Early storytellers would explain things in nature, teach lessons, and retell historical events. The **oral tradition** continued as these stories were passed from one generation to the next.

People still enjoy listening to a good story. In order to make a story entertaining, storytellers plan and practice before sharing a story with an audience. You can use the following guidelines as you prepare to tell a story.

WHAT'S AHEAD?

In this section you will tell a story. You will also learn how to

- keep your audience's attention
- make your story entertaining
- understand your audience's needs

Plan Your Story

To keep your audience's attention, plan to give them what they want—action. Choose an incident that has more "doing" than "describing." Your story will be more interesting if it keeps moving with action details.

You should also plan to tell your story in **chronological order.** You want your audience to be eager to find out what will happen next. Build **suspense** by saving the outcome until the very last moment. Jotting down the events on note cards will help you. Use three note cards, one each for the beginning, middle, and end of your story.

Your audience will also want **background information.** What will the audience need to know to understand your story? Answer this question before you begin practicing.

TIP Use formal language when telling your story. Use informal language, such as slang, only when a character is speaking and you are sure your audience will understand it.

Practice Your Story

Before you tell your story in front of an audience, you will need to practice what you have planned. You will also need to practice making your story entertaining. How do you do that? It's simple.

Focus on Speaking and Listening   45

Focus on Speaking and Listening

OBJECTIVES

- To tell a story to an audience
- To keep an audience's attention by telling a story that contains action, that uses chronological order, and that gives background information
- To use voice, facial expressions, and gestures to make a story entertaining
- To recognize an audience's needs

TEACHING TIP

Plan Your Story

Explain to students that by choosing words that show rather than tell, they are more likely to keep their audience's interest and achieve their purpose: *to entertain*. Depending on the age of their audience, they may need to choose words their audience will understand or explain words that may be unfamiliar to their audience. For example, a student telling a story about snowboarding to kindergartners in Florida would probably have to "show" what snowboarding is.

Students should also be aware of how their language might change based on the occasion. In this case, the occasion is fairly formal—students are speaking to their class. Therefore, using standard English is appropriate. However, students will recognize that in telling the same story to friends in the lunchroom, they would naturally use more informal language.

RESOURCES

Focus on Speaking and Listening
Practice
- *Media Literacy and Communication Skills*

  —*Support and Practice,* Ch. 1
  —*A How-to Handbook*

Teaching Notes
- *Media Literacy and Communication Skills*

  —*A Teacher's Guide,* Ch. 1

Focus on Speaking and Listening   45

Quotation for the Day

"[Writers] tend to have a lot of stories available to them just because they are human beings."

(Robert Penn Warren, 1905–1989, American author and poet)

Remind students that they have already heard, read, or experienced many different stories that are worth telling to an audience—from Rosa Parks's story to their own stories about autobiographical incidents.

TEACHING TIP

Share Your Story
As students share their stories, ask audience members to listen carefully, paying special attention to the purpose of the story and how the storyteller makes it entertaining by using facial expressions, gestures, and his or her voice, including the storyteller's use of regional language to show when a character is speaking. Afterward, have students discuss their ideas about what makes a story well told. Also have students discuss whether they have ever had experiences similar to ones told by the speaker.

YOUR TURN 11

For assessment, make sure students incorporate the elements discussed in **Practice Makes Perfect,** such as varying their voices, using gestures for expression, including background information, and presenting their stories in chronological order.

Wrap It Up

Ask students the following question:

What five things can you do to keep an audience's attention and to make a story entertaining? [tell a story with action, use chronological order, give background information, change the level of your voice to alter mood or to portray characters, and use gestures and facial expressions]

TIP Language, especially sayings or names for things, reflects different regions and cultures. For example, do you say *you, y'all,* or *you guys* when talking to a group? If possible, include in your story the specific words and phrases that a character from a different culture or part of the country might say.

Speak Out Your voice is the most important tool when telling a story, so use it. Practice speaking loudly enough for the people in the back row to hear; talk slowly and clearly enough for your audience to understand you. Also, practice changing the levels of your voice to change the mood. For instance, whispering adds suspense, and yelling suddenly can show surprise. You can even change your voice entirely. Try using different voices so the audience will know when different characters are speaking.

Show and Tell Words alone cannot express a story fully. Facial expressions and gestures are important as well. Don't tell everything; practice showing your actions. If you were telling a story about falling off your mountain bike, you might fall to the floor, grab your knee, and grimace as if in pain. You can include **sensory details** in your story by using gestures, too. For example, covering your ears shows that you heard a loud noise.

Practice Makes Perfect Practice telling your story in front of a friend and let your friend make suggestions on how you can improve your presentation. Make sure that you tell your story to your friend the same way you would tell it to a real audience. Keep the events in order, include background information, and use your voice and gestures.

Share Your Story

As you share your story, maintain eye contact with your audience. By looking at your audience, you can tell what they need. If the faces in your audience look puzzled, give background information or a more detailed explanation. If your audience is distracted or, worse, falling asleep, wake them up by performing an action or speaking in a different voice. The more lively you are, the more your audience will enjoy your story. Have fun. Telling a story should be an enjoyable experience for the audience and for you.

Reference Note
For more on adjusting **volume, rate, pitch** (your voice's highs and lows), and **tone** (or mood), see page 722. For more on **oral interpretation,** see page 725.

YOUR TURN 11 Telling a Story

Follow the guidelines above to share a story and make connections with your classmates. As you tell your story and listen to your classmates' stories, do you notice similar experiences?

RESOURCES

Your Turn 11
Practice and Reinforcement
- Media Literacy and Communication Skills

—Support and Practice Ch. 1, transparencies and worksheets
—Videocassette 1, Segment A

CHAPTER 1 Choices

Choose one of the following activities to complete.

▶ CAREERS

1. When I Grow Up Read an autobiography or biography about a person who has a career that interests you. When you are finished, write a **journal entry** telling one thing that surprised you about the person and the career.

▶ SPEECH

2. Telling Tales All cultures have stories that have been passed on from one generation to the next. These stories, called folk tales, come from the **oral tradition**. Even though folk tales reflect the particular culture that created them, folk tales from different cultures have common features, such as magic and talking animals. Read and compare two folk tales from different cultures, and present your findings to your class in a **speech**.

▶ DRAMA

3. Another Life With a few other classmates, present a **dramatic interpretation** of a play based on the life of a real person. For example, *The Miracle Worker* is about Helen Keller. You can find plays in the drama section of your school or local library.

▶ WRITING

4. Larger Than Life Write a **tall tale**, a story full of exaggerations, by taking a real incident and describing it with larger-than-life details. For instance, you could write about the time you went fishing. The fish you caught weighed two pounds and did not put up much of a fight. In your tall tale, however, the fish weighed twenty pounds, and it took you *and* a friend to drag it into the boat!

▶ TECHNOLOGY

5. You've Got Mail If you have access to e-mail, send an **e-mail message** to a friend describing an event that has just occurred in your life. Make sure you give background information so your friend will understand what happened.

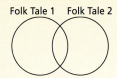
PORTFOLIO

▶ SPEECH

Tell students to look for other common features as they read, such as tricksters, false parents, tests of the hero, and brave youngest daughters and sons. To compare and contrast the two tales, have them make a Venn diagram as shown below. Students can write the common features of the tales in the overlapping area. They can write features unique to each tale in the outside area under each tale's title. Have students share their findings with the class, using their diagrams to help them recall similarities and differences.

Folk Tale 1   Folk Tale 2

▶ DRAMA

In groups of four or five, have students follow these steps to create and present their dramatic interpretations:

1. Choose a play based on the life of a real person.
2. Based on the play, write a skit of up to ten minutes.
3. Storyboard the plot by drawing pictures to outline the action.
4. Assign characters to group members.
5. Gather any props necessary to the characters or the set.
6. Rehearse and perform the piece.

Remind students to speak their lines clearly and loudly and to emphasize their movements so that the audience can see and hear them.

RESOURCES

Sharing Our Stories

Assessment
- *Assessment Package*
  — *Chapter Tests,* Ch. 1
  — *Chapter Tests in Standardized Test Formats,* Ch. 1
  — *Assessment Alternatives,* Ch. 1
- *Test Generator* (One-Stop Planner CD-ROM)

Choices

Rubrics
- *Assessment Package*
  — *Assessment Alternatives,* Ch. 1

CHAPTER 2

Reporting the News

Use this guide to create an instructional plan that suits the individual needs of your students. Assignments marked by an asterisk (*) may be completed out of class. Times given for pacing lessons are estimated. See pp. 48–49 for chapter-wide resources. Resources listed in this guide are point-of-use resources only.

Curriculum Connections

Choices *p. 83*
- Crossing the Curriculum: Art
- Writing
- Crossing the Curriculum: Science

GO TO: go.hrw.com
KEYWORD: EOLang 6-2

All resources for this chapter are available for preview on the *One-Stop Planner CD-ROM with Test Generator.* All worksheets and tests may be printed from the CD-ROM.

	Chapter Opener pp. 48–49	**Reading Workshop: Reading a Newspaper Article** pp. 50–57
DEVELOPMENTAL PROGRAM	⏱ **30 minutes** • Your Turn 1 *p. 49*	⏱ **90 minutes** • Preparing to Read *p. 50* • Reading Selection *pp. 51–52* • First Thoughts in groups *p. 53* • Main Idea *pp. 53–54* • Your Turn 2 *p. 54* • Inverted Pyramid Structure *pp. 54–55* • Your Turn 3 *p. 55* • Test Taking Mini-Lesson *p. 57*
CORE PROGRAM	⏱ **20 minutes** • Your Turn 1 *p. 49*	⏱ **75 minutes** • Preparing to Read *p. 50* • Reading Selection *pp. 51–52* • First Thoughts *p. 53* • Main Idea *pp. 53–54* • Your Turn 2 *p. 54* • Inverted Pyramid Structure *pp. 54–55* • Your Turn 3 *p. 55* • Vocabulary Mini-Lesson *p. 56* • Test Taking Mini-Lesson *p. 57*
ADVANCED PROGRAM	⏱ **15 minutes** • Your Turn 1 *p. 49*	⏱ **45 minutes** • Preparing to Read *p. 50* • Reading Selection *pp. 51–52* • First Thoughts *p. 53* • Main Idea *pp. 53–54* • Your Turn 2 *p. 54* • Inverted Pyramid Structure *pp. 54–55* • Your Turn 3 *p. 55*
RESOURCES — PRINT	• *Communications,* TP. 17, WS. p. 27	• *Alternative Readings,* Ch. 2 • *Communications,* TPs. 18, 19, WS. pp. 28–35
RESOURCES — MEDIA	• One-Stop Planner CD-ROM	• One-Stop Planner CD-ROM

TP.=Transparency WS.=Worksheet

Writing Workshop: Writing a Newspaper Article *pp. 58–75*	**Focus on Viewing and Representing:** Producing a Newspaper *pp. 76–78* / Producing a TV News Segment *pp. 79–82*
⏱ **200 minutes** • Choose and Evaluate an Event; Your Turn 4 *pp. 58–59* • Identify Your Audience; Your Turn 5 *p. 60* • Gather Details; Your Turn 6 *pp. 60–63* • Organize and Evaluate Details; Your Turn 7 *pp. 63–64* • Framework; Your Turn 8* *p. 66* • Writer's Model and Student's Model *pp. 67–68* • Evaluate and Revise *pp. 69–70* • Focus on Sentences in groups *p. 71* • Your Turn 9 *p. 71* • Proofread, Publish, and Reflect *pp. 72–73* • Grammar Link *p. 72* • Your Turn 10 *p. 73*	⏱ **100 minutes** • Make a Plan *pp. 76–77* • Put It Together *pp. 77–78* • Your Turn 12 *p. 78* ⏱ **100 minutes** • Select Your Story *p. 79* • Choose Your Part *pp. 79–80* • Prepare the Script *pp. 80–81* • Practice Your Performance *pp. 81–82* • Record and Evaluate Your News Segment *p. 82* • Your Turn 13 *p. 82*
⏱ **160 minutes** • Choose and Evaluate an Event; Your Turn 4 *pp. 58–59* • Identify Your Audience; Your Turn 5 *p. 60* • Gather Details; Your Turn 6* *pp. 60–63* • Organize and Evaluate Details; Your Turn 7 *pp. 63–64* • Critical-Thinking Mini-Lesson in groups *p. 65* • Framework; Your Turn 8* *p. 66* • Writer's Model and Student's Model *pp. 67–68* • Evaluate and Revise *pp. 69–70* • Focus on Sentences *p. 71* • Your Turn 9 *p. 71* • Grammar Link *p. 72* • Proofread, Publish, and Reflect; Your Turn 10 *pp. 72–73* • Connections to Life; Your Turn 11* *pp. 74–75*	⏱ **75 minutes** • Make a Plan *pp. 76–77* • Put It Together *pp. 77–78* • Your Turn 12 *p. 78* ⏱ **80 minutes** • Select Your Story *p. 79* • Choose Your Part *pp. 79–80* • Prepare the Script *pp. 80–81* • Practice Your Performance *pp. 81–82* • Record and Evaluate Your News Segment *p. 82* • Your Turn 13 *p. 82*
⏱ **100 minutes** • Choose and Evaluate an Event; Your Turn 4 *pp. 58–59* • Identify Your Audience; Your Turn 5 *p. 60* • Gather Details; Your Turn 6* *pp. 60–63* • Organize and Evaluate Details; Your Turn 7 *pp. 63–64* • Critical-Thinking Mini-Lesson *p. 65* • Framework; Your Turn 8* *p. 66* • Writer's Model and Student's Model *pp. 67–68* • Evaluate and Revise *pp. 69–70* • Focus on Sentences *p. 71* • Your Turn 9* *p. 71* • Proofread, Publish, and Reflect; Your Turn 10 *pp. 72–73* • Connections to Life; Your Turn 11* *pp. 74–75*	⏱ **60 minutes** • Make a Plan *pp. 76–77* • Put It Together *pp. 77–78* • Your Turn 12 *p. 78* ⏱ **60 minutes** • Select Your Story *p. 79* • Choose Your Part *pp. 79–80* • Prepare the Script *pp. 80–81* • Practice Your Performance *pp. 81–82* • Record and Evaluate Your News Segment *p. 82* • Your Turn 13 *p. 82*
• *Communications*, TPs. 20–23, WS. pp. 36–47 • *Designing Your Writing*	• *Media Literacy and Communication Skills* —*Support and Practice*, Ch. 2 —*A How-to Handbook* —*A Teacher's Guide*, Ch. 2
• *One-Stop Planner CD-ROM*	• *Media Literacy and Communication Skills* —Videocassette 1, Segment B • *One-Stop Planner CD-ROM*

CHAPTER 2

Reporting the News

CHAPTER OBJECTIVES

- To read a newspaper article to identify the main idea and recognize the structure
- To write a newspaper article
- To plan, design, and publish a newspaper
- To prepare and produce a TV news segment

Chapter Overview

This chapter focuses students' attention on a type of exposition with which they are probably familiar—news reporting—and helps them become more proficient readers and reporters of news. The Reading Workshop (pp. 50–57) provides students with a newspaper article to read and analyze for its main idea and its use of the inverted pyramid structure. In the Writing Workshop (pp. 58–75), students are guided through the steps of the writing process as they research and write their own news articles. In the Focuses on Viewing and Representing students learn how to produce their own newspaper and TV news segment. The sections may be taught separately, but they also work together to give students a strong foundation for reading, writing, and producing news.

Why Study News Reporting?

The news is part of students' lives through newspapers, magazines, radio or television news, and online news. The news helps shape our perceptions of the world around us. Students can become better-informed consumers of the news by reading, analyzing, and writing news articles and by producing newspaper and TV news segments.

Teaching the Chapter

Option 1: Begin with Literature

You might begin teaching about news reporting by introducing students to examples of literature that include elements of news articles. For example, discuss how novels and short stories usually feature people, the *who* of the narrative, and their actions, or *what* they do. Explain that biographies focus on *who* and *what* and also include information on *when* and *where* individuals lived, and often on *how* and *why* they acted in certain ways. Then, as students read the newspaper article in this chapter (pp. 51–52), tell them to look for answers to the *5W-How?* questions. After both reading and analyzing the newspaper article, students can begin writing their own articles.

Option 2: Begin with Nonfiction and Writing

Use the material in this chapter to familiarize students with elements of news writing. The article in the Reading Workshop, along with the activities, can help students understand both the use of the inverted pyramid structure and strategies for identifying main ideas. The Writing Workshop (pp. 58–75) leads students through the steps of writing and revising their own newspaper articles. When returning to literature, students may be more aware whenever literary works include elements of news writing.

Making Connections

■ To the Literature Curriculum

Explain to students that in news articles, the main idea appears at the beginning and is supported by details that follow it. In other forms of exposition, however, the details are arranged so that the main idea may not be obvious until the reader has finished the selection. This arrangement of details appears in both "Storm" from *Woodsong* by Gary Paulsen and "Crow Poets" by Robert Kyle.

Lesson Idea: Identifying Main Idea in "Crow Poets" by Robert Kyle

1. Have students read "Crow Poets." Then, help them identify the key details, which should answer the questions *Who?, What?, When?, Where?,* and *Why?,* and will be found throughout the selection.

2. Draw the following graphic organizer on the chalkboard and jot down the key details that students find. Sample answers from "Crow Poets" have been provided.

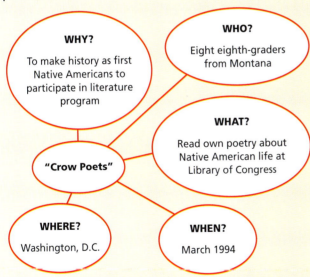

3. Have students work in pairs to use the details to generate a main idea statement. [Eight Native American students from a Montana reservation made history in 1994 when they read their own poetry at the Library of Congress.] Discuss how students decided which details to include in their main idea statements.

4. After discussion, refer students to the article on pp. 51–52 in the Reading Workshop. Point out that details and the main idea are arranged in a pattern known as the inverted pyramid structure. The instruction on main idea and inverted pyramid structure (pp. 53–55) will prepare students for reading and writing news articles on their own.

■ To Careers

After reading and writing newspaper articles, students may better appreciate the complex jobs of reporters and editors. Communicating with working journalists can deepen students' understanding of these careers. If possible, arrange for a newspaper reporter or editor to speak to the class. Students should prepare in advance a list of questions about the education and training needed for the job, challenging and gratifying aspects, and the ingredients of a successful news article. Alternatively, students could send their questions through regular mail or e-mail. See also **Connections to Life** on pp. 74–75.

■ To the Community

A field trip to the editorial or production facilities of a newspaper would introduce students to the work that goes on behind the scenes and help them better appreciate professional newspaper publication, including its use of technology. Alternatively, you might arrange a visit to a local network or cable TV station or a local radio station to enable students to observe the steps involved in putting news stories on the air. Be certain to check with school officials regarding field-trip policies before you plan one.

■ To the Art Curriculum

After designing and laying out their own newspaper, students may be interested in comparing design styles and features of newspapers. Bring in copies of several different newspapers for students to analyze. Students might compare such aspects of design as the masthead and the use of color, type font and size, photographs, and other visual elements. Consider inviting a teacher of art, graphics, or desktop publishing to join the discussion.

CHAPTER 2

PREVIEWING THE CHAPTER

- The four workshops in this chapter explore the content and structure of news reports. While the workshops can be taught separately, when taught together they provide the information and practice to help students develop a thorough understanding of news reporting. After reading and analyzing the components of a newspaper article, then researching and writing their own articles, students will produce a newspaper and a TV news segment. To integrate this chapter with grammar, usage, and mechanics chapters, see pp. T297A–T297B.

INTRODUCING THE CHAPTER

- To introduce the chapter, use the Journal Warm-up, Transparency 17, in *Communications*.

VIEWING THE ILLUSTRATION

- As students view the illustration, point out that the artist arranged the individuals so that a viewer's eyes move in a circle around the illustration. Ask students why each individual faces forward and has an interested and excited expression. [The reporters appear to be looking at the viewer. The artist probably wanted viewers to feel like they are the reporters' focus.]

- **Representing.** Have students illustrate themselves gathering information about a news event. They may show themselves using computers, telephones, or a newspaper. Ask students to pay attention to their facial expressions as they learn of news as well as their choice of color, shape, and line.

CHAPTER 2 Reporting the News

CHAPTER RESOURCES

Planning
- *Lesson Planner*, Ch. 2
- *ELL Strategies*, Ch. 2
- *Block Scheduling*, p. T47A (this book)
- *One-Stop Planner CD-ROM*

Practice
- *Communications*, Ch. 2

- *Media Literacy and Communication Skills*

Extension
- *Designing Your Writing*

Reinforcement
- *Communications*, Ch. 2
- *Alternative Readings*, Ch. 2

PREVIEW

Reading Workshop
Reading a Newspaper Article
PAGE 50

Writing Workshop
Writing a Newspaper Article
PAGE 58

Focus on Viewing and Representing
Producing a Newspaper
PAGE 76

Focus on Viewing and Representing
Producing a TV News Segment
PAGE 79

You and your classmates are riding the bus to school when suddenly the bus stalls. The bus driver tries to start the bus, but is unsuccessful. A trip that normally takes thirty minutes has turned into a two-hour ordeal. This event has made a big impression on you, but you probably will not see it reported on tonight's newscast or in tomorrow's newspaper. What makes some events worth reporting in the news and others not? Newsworthy events are not just recent events. They must also affect many people or simply grab people's attention.

GO TO: go.hrw.com
KEYWORD: EOLang 6-2

YOUR TURN 1 — Looking at the News

Find an example of a news story. You can watch the news on television, listen to the news on the radio, or find a news article in a newspaper or magazine. Then, answer the following questions about the story you found.

- What event is the news story about?
- Who would want to know about this event?
- Why do you think this event made the news?

- Daily Language Activity Transparencies
- *Vocabulary Workshop* and *Tests*
- Spelling

Evaluation and Assessment

- Test Generator (One-Stop Planner CD-ROM)

- Assessment Package
  —Chapter Tests, Ch. 2
  —Chapter Tests in Standardized Test Formats, Ch. 2
  —Assessment Alternatives, Ch. 2

Internet

- go.hrw.com (keyword: EOLang 6–2)

Reading Workshop

OBJECTIVES

- To read a newspaper article in preparation for writing one
- To identify the main idea of a news article
- To recognize the inverted pyramid structure of a news article
- To identify the correct meaning of multiple-meaning words

Quotation for the Day

"There is an art of reading; as well as an art of thinking, and an art of writing."

(Isaac D'Israeli, 1766–1848, English writer)

Write the quotation on the chalkboard. Under it draw three columns labeled *Art of Reading, Art of Thinking,* and *Art of Writing.* Ask students why they think the writer calls each of these activities an art. Jot down students' comments in the appropriate columns. Then, ask students how the three concepts might be interrelated.

TEACHING TIP

Preparing to Read
The material on this page explains the difference between a stated main idea and an implied one. It also introduces the inverted pyramid structure of a news article. These concepts are the instructional focus of the Reading Workshop and will be discussed in more detail on pp. 53–55. The Reading Selection, **"Whale Watch,"** illustrates both of these concepts.

RESOURCES

Reading Workshop Reinforcement
- *Alternative Readings,* Ch. 2

Reading Workshop

WHAT'S AHEAD?
In this section you will read a news article. You will also learn how to
- identify the main idea of a news article
- recognize the pattern of a news article called inverted pyramid structure

Reading a Newspaper Article

Can an orphaned baby whale survive without its parents? Students in California are asking the same question. They have been logging onto the Internet to check the status of the baby whale ever since she was returned to the ocean. What started as a history project focusing on current events has turned into something more. Find out what students have learned from this project by reading the news article on the next page.

Preparing to Read

READING SKILL

Main Idea   The **main idea** is the most important point a writer wants to make. Sometimes the main idea is *stated*. This means it will be written in a sentence or two. Other times the main idea is *implied*, or suggested. In that case, you will have to look for clues to figure out the writer's most important point. As you read the following article, see if you can figure out the main idea.

READING FOCUS

Inverted Pyramid Structure   A news event is made up of many details that answer the *5W-How?* questions.

- *Who* was involved?
- *What* happened?
- *When* did the event take place?
- *Where* did the event occur?
- *Why* did the event happen?
- *How* did the event happen?

News writers organize these details in an **inverted pyramid** (upside-down triangle) **structure** that begins with the most important details and ends with the least important details. Why do you think news articles are organized this way?

Exposition: Reporting the News

READING PROCESS

PREREADING
Set a Purpose for Reading the Selection.
The **Preparing to Read** section explains to students that one of their purposes for reading the newspaper article is to identify the main idea. Tell students that when they read with a purpose, they are more focused in their reading. Setting a purpose for reading also helps readers learn information from their reading and improves their ability to remember what they have read.

Tell students that they also need to

Reading Selection

Read the following news article. In a notebook, write the answers to the numbered active-reading questions in the shaded boxes. The underlined words will be discussed in the Vocabulary Mini-Lesson on page 56.

FROM LOS ANGELES TIMES; ORANGE COUNTY EDITION

Whale Watch: Kids Use Internet to Track Progress of Newly Freed J. J.

BY LISA RICHARDSON

MISSION VIEJO—Marine experts from Sea World are using the latest radio transmission technology to monitor J. J., the newly freed gray whale.

Ten sixth-graders at Barcelona Hills Elementary School in Mission Viejo are doing the same thing, using the Internet.

Since the fifteen-month-old whale was orphaned last year, the group has followed her arrival at Sea World, how she has adapted to her handlers and, most recently, her return to the ocean and ride to freedom Tuesday.

The group has amassed an encyclopedic amount of whale knowledge over the months, and students can spout whale family classifications, whale dietary habits, and whale growth patterns with ease.

The group, students of history teacher Kaye Denison, spent most of Thursday morning on the Internet, checking reports on the whale's progress.

Having followed J. J. for so long, the eleven- and twelve-year-olds have put some thought into why—beyond scientific reasons—saving her life and studying her is important.

They have concluded that even if animals and mammals don't love human beings, it's natural for humans to love them.

At their school, the kids care for frogs, snakes, a chameleon, a skunk, an iguana, fish, and water turtles. They are sure the animals are indifferent toward them, but it doesn't stop them from liking the creatures.

"I heard on the news that you're not lonely and your life is not so stressful with animals in it, and I think it's true," said Sean Kingsmill, twelve.

"I mean, people are lonely," A. J. Young said.

1. What have the sixth-graders been doing for several months?

2. How are the students keeping track of J. J.'s progress?

Active-Reading Questions

The purpose of the active-reading questions is to focus students' attention on the details that support the main idea. Students will also look at how the inverted pyramid structure is used in the article. Use students' answers as an informal assessment of their comprehension. Possible answers are suggested below.

ANSWERS

1. The students have been following the progress of J. J., an orphaned whale that was recently returned to the ocean.

2. Students have been using the Internet to check reports on J. J.'s progress.

TEACHING TIP

Active-Reading Questions
One way of using the active-reading questions is to have each student read silently to the first question and then determine the answer to the question. Then, lead a brief class discussion in which students share and discuss their answers to the first question before you have them go on to the next question.

---

identify their own purposes for reading. Suggest that they skim the selection and jot down their predictions about the important ideas presented in it. The predictions they make will help them figure out what they expect to learn from their reading.

Active-Reading Questions
ANSWERS continued

3. Students may say that the information in this paragraph should appear earlier in the article because the paragraph includes specific information about J. J. This specific information is currently preceded by less important information and quotations from the students about how they feel about animals.

4. The students feel affection for the baby whale.

5. These paragraphs are not necessary for understanding the class's "J. J." project. The paragraphs provide background about other projects students undertook in their ancient history class.

"For example, wouldn't you be lonely if you didn't live at all with anybody, and wouldn't you want a dog or something?"

Learning about the whale has been fun. They know that J. J. weighs more than 17,000 pounds, is 29 feet long, and gains 2 pounds every hour. Killer whales are natural enemies of gray whales, and while adults eat plankton,[1] J. J. existed mostly on a mixture of milk, powdered fish, and warm cream passed through a tube into her stomach.

"It's important to save her because they come from an extinct [endangered] species, and it's good since they're coming back up," said Danielle Howannesian, eleven. "Besides, babies are always cute."

It is largely affection for the baby whale that keeps them interested in her plight.

They sympathized with J. J.'s orphanhood and her efforts to learn survival skills. When she was released, the group felt bad for the whale's disappointed handlers, who said J. J. did not make her typical sound of gratitude before swimming away. But they believe J. J. will miss her handlers after awhile....

For now the group relies on updates posted to the Sea World Web site..., but by next Friday, the satellite tracking system should begin receiving transmissions directly from J. J., and the students will have access to more current information.

But the class doesn't spend all its time on J. J. For another project in Denison's class, the children had to pretend they were Hollywood location scouts and, using computers, map important sites in ancient Egypt. The project was coupled with lessons on chemical warfare in neighboring Iraq and political tension in the region.

"My class is actually an ancient history class, but because we're really involved in current events, we tie in whatever is happening in the world," Denison said.

Members of the "Barcelona Hills J. J. Fan Club"—what one student dubbed the group—say they will follow the whale's progress until they are sure she is safe or has joined a pod of whales.

"We've been with it this long," said Lindsay Murray, twelve. "We have to make sure that she's going to be OK."

---
1. **plankton:** microscopic animals and plants.

3. Do you think the information in the second paragraph above should appear earlier in the article? Why or why not?

4. According to the first paragraph above, why does this project interest students?

5. Is the information in the two paragraphs at the top of this column necessary to understand the class's "J. J." project? Why or why not?

READING PROCESS

READING

Ask Questions. Well-written newspaper articles should clearly answer the *5W-How?* questions. Tell students that by asking themselves these questions as they read the article, they can check their comprehension and more easily identify the main idea. You might suggest that as they read, students jot down answers to the *5W-How?* questions. Asking themselves these questions will also prepare students for answering the questions in **First Thoughts on Your Reading.**

First Thoughts on Your Reading
1. What is this article about?
2. Where are the most important details in the article located?

Main Idea

Behind the Wheel   What do a bicycle wheel and a news article have in common? You may have noticed that the spokes on a bicycle wheel lead directly to the hub, which is the central point of the wheel. News articles also have a central point, or **main idea**. All the details lead the reader to the main idea, which can be stated or implied. A **stated main idea** is one that is written out in a sentence or two.

Example:
Brian Caspar's quick thinking saved his friend's life.

An **implied main idea,** or suggested main idea, is not found in a specific sentence. The reader must look at how the supporting details are related to figure out the implied main idea.

Example:
Brian Caspar found his friend lying unconscious on the floor. After calling 911, Brian began CPR before paramedics arrived. His friend is now in stable condition.

All the details in the example above support the main idea: Brian thought quickly and saved his friend's life.

Read the news article below. Can you identify the main idea? Use the Thinking It Through steps on the next page if you need help.

> To make room for a new playground, Urban Demolition, Inc., used dynamite to demolish the old Paramount Theater on Elm Avenue last Wednesday.
>
> The demolition took approximately nine seconds from start to finish. Dust hovered over Elm Avenue and the surrounding areas for several hours.
>
> Urban Demolition crews estimate that it will take a week for them to clear the rubble.

> **READING SKILL**

> **TIP**   Whether you are reading a newspaper article, a short story, or a research report, you should look for a main idea. Finding the main idea will help you understand the supporting details.

First Thoughts on Your Reading
ANSWERS
Possible answers follow.

1. The article is about ten sixth-graders from Mission Viejo who are using the Internet to follow the progress of an orphaned baby whale named J. J.

2. The most important details can be found in the first three paragraphs.
   - Paragraph 1: Who? [J. J., gray whale] What? [using technology to monitor J. J.]
   - Paragraph 2: Who? [ten sixth-graders] Where? [Mission Viejo] How? [by using the Internet]
   - Paragraph 3: When? [since the whale was orphaned last year] Why? [to learn how J. J. has adapted to her handlers and to her return to the ocean]

Meeting INDIVIDUAL NEEDS

INCLUSION
Drawings can help some students understand what they read. A helper can start by reading the selection aloud to students. Then, the helper and students can use stick figures and simple line drawings to illustrate the main ideas. The helper might work with students to draw ten students inside one circle and J. J. the whale in another. As students read through the story, they can add the important details to the appropriate places in their drawings. Later, students can use the drawings to retell the story or to help remember details.

Cooperative Learning

Main-Idea Pairs. Students can work in pairs to identify the main idea in the article about the demolition on the preceding page. The two students should first collaborate on tentatively identifying the main idea. Then, each student should separately check to see whether all the details in the paragraphs support that idea. If necessary, students should work together to revise their main idea.

YOUR TURN 2

ANSWERS

Students might do this activity as homework. Below are suggested answers.

Step 1. Ten sixth-graders have been using the Internet to follow an orphaned whale's progress because they are concerned about her survival and adjustment to her new home.

Step 2. Most of the details give more information about the students and what they think of the project, about the whale and her progress, and about what kinds of information students can get from the Internet.

RESOURCES

Your Turn 2
Practice
- *Communications*, WS. p. 28

Reinforcement
- *Communications*, TP. 18, WS. p. 29

Your Turn 3
Practice
- *Communications*, WS. p. 30

Reinforcement
- *Communications*, TP. 19, WS. p. 31

THINKING IT THROUGH
Identifying the Main Idea in a News Article

▶ **STEP 1** Identify the main idea by asking, "*Who* (or *what*) did *what* and *why*?"

Urban Demolition, Inc., demolished the Paramount Theater to make room for a playground.

▶ **STEP 2** Check to see that you identified the main idea by asking, "Do all the details support my answer?"

The details tell me how long it took, what happened afterward, and what will happen in the future. They all relate to the demolition.

YOUR TURN 2 — Identifying the Main Idea

Re-read the news article on pages 51–52. Then, use the Thinking It Through steps above to identify the article's main idea.

READING FOCUS

Inverted Pyramid Structure

Why Save the Best for Last? After dinner, you can have dessert. After you clean your room, you can see your friends. Have you ever asked yourself, "Why do I have to *wait* for all the good stuff?" You don't have to wait when you read a news article.

News articles are arranged in an **inverted pyramid structure.** An inverted pyramid is an upside-down triangle. The wide part of the triangle holds the *lead*. The **lead,** which can be more than one paragraph long, is the beginning of a news article. It summarizes the most important information about an event by answering the *5W-How?* questions: *Who? What? When? Where? Why?* and *How?* Readers who are in a hurry can understand the event by reading just the lead.

The rest of the news article provides readers with more information about the event. The details are presented in order from most important to least important. Why? If an article is longer than the amount of space the news editor has set aside for it, some of the information will need to be cut. Cutting is easy when the least important details are at the end of the article. The news

Lead
(5W-How?
questions)
Details
Details
Details

READING PROCESS

EXTENDING
Apply What You Read. First, review with students the predictions they made in the **Preparing to Read** section of the Reading Workshop. Most students probably had to adjust their predictions. Remind students that predictions are a tool for reading, not an indication of how well they read, and that most readers need to adjust their ideas as they read.

Then, explain to students that they can set purposes when reading other articles by editor can start at the end and cut details until the article fits its assigned space. An inverted pyramid structure saves time for both the reader and the news editor.

Cut to Fit Edie, a newspaper editor, has room for a four-paragraph article, but the following article has five paragraphs. Notice how Edie rearranged the details so that the important ones are at the beginning, then cut the unimportant details so the article now has only four paragraphs.

> Malcolm Scott, CEO of Happy Faces Corporation, announced plans today to build a new amusement park west of downtown.
>
> ~~"I can't wait for the park to open," said eleven-year old Hector Garza. "I will be the first one in line."~~
>
> "We want to give people, especially kids, a fun and exciting place to visit," said Scott.
>
> The park will be a good source of entertainment, say city officials. It will also create jobs and bring additional money to the community from tourists.
>
> Construction for the new amusement park will begin in September and should be completed by the end of April. The grand opening is scheduled for the beginning of May.

Answers to who, what, and where

Answers to why

Answers to how and when

TIP The paragraphs in a newspaper article are usually very short, sometimes only one or two sentences. Shorter paragraphs with fewer details make reading a news article easier and more efficient.

TIP How does an editor decide which details are less important than others? You already know that the *most* important details answer the *5W-How?* questions about the topic. Among the details that follow the lead, those judged more important than others might be ones that

- are more recent
- concern more readers
- are more attention-grabbing

YOUR TURN 3 — Editing a News Article

Make a copy of the news article on pages 51–52. In a group, reread it with news editors' eyes.

- After reading, discuss whether the answers to the *5W-How?* questions are in the lead. If they are not, rearrange the paragraphs so that the answers are at the beginning.
- Then, cut the least important details in the article so it will fit in a space for a fifteen-paragraph article. You will need to cut four paragraphs. Use the second Tip in the margin above to decide which details are less important.

Wrap It Up

Metacognition. Ask students to reflect on their reading processes by answering the following question:

1. How does what you have learned about reading the news help you identify the main idea in an article?

Then, ask students this question:

2. How does the structure of a news article differ from that used in other informative writing? [uses an inverted pyramid structure instead of building toward the main idea]

YOUR TURN 3
ANSWERS

The lead, which consists of the first three paragraphs, answers the *5W-How?* questions.

Students may suggest cutting any of the following paragraphs:

Paragraph 8: Details about other animals that the students take care of do not support the main idea.

Paragraphs 9 and 10: Quotations about how animals help with loneliness and stress do not directly relate to the J. J. story.

Paragraphs 16 and 17: Information about other class projects is not important to the story about tracking J. J.'s progress.

---

applying what they have learned about prereading. Have students select news articles and then work in pairs to examine articles to locate important details. Ask students to use these details to identify the main idea of the story. Point out that the inverted pyramid format enables readers to skim quickly introductory paragraphs of an article to see if they are interested in reading more.

MINI-LESSON VOCABULARY

Multiple-Meaning Words

ANSWERS
Possible answers follow.

1. I know that a marine is a kind of soldier, but in the sentence, *marine* is an adjective that tells what kind of experts the people are. I think *marine* may have something to do with the ocean because the article is about a whale, an ocean animal. "Ocean experts from Sea World . . ." makes sense.

2. The paragraph describes how much knowledge the students have about whales, and that they "can spout" this information "with ease." I usually think of water running from a spout, so maybe in this case *spout* means "talk freely."

3. I know that *concluded* means "completed or brought to an end." In this sentence, *concluded* follows the statement that students "have put some thought into" a question. Maybe *concluded* means "reached a decision after thinking about something." "They have reached a decision after thinking that . . ." makes sense.

4. The article says that students pretended "they were Hollywood location scouts." I know that a scout is a person sent to get information and that scouts come to high schools to look for the best sports players. Maybe location scouts are people who look for the best movie location.

5. I know that a pod is a part of some fruits or vegetables, but the sentence says that students will follow the (orphaned) whale until it joins a pod. Maybe the word *pod* means "a group." ". . . Until they are sure she is safe or has joined a group of whales" makes sense.

MINI-LESSON VOCABULARY

Multiple-Meaning Words

When you read the newspaper, do you ever get confused by a word you have known for years? When that happens, you have probably stumbled upon a **multiple-meaning word,** a word with more than one meaning.

- A multiple-meaning word can have two or more very different definitions.

Examples:
Marcus *filed* the papers. (to put in place)

The band members *filed* onto the field. (to move in a line)

- A multiple-meaning word can be used as more than one part of speech.

Examples:
If you know the answer, raise your *hand*. (part of the body—noun)

Can you *hand* me the hammer, please? (to give by hand—verb)

THINKING IT THROUGH — Understanding Multiple-Meaning Words

The following steps can help you find the correct meaning of a multiple-meaning word. The example below is from the reading selection.

Example:
"Members of the 'Barcelona Hills J. J. Fan Club'—what one student <u>dubbed</u> the group . . ."

▶ **STEP 1** Look at how the word is used in the passage. What do the words and sentences around it tell you?

▶ **STEP 2** Check your definition in the original sentence. Ask yourself, "Does this definition make sense?"

I think <u>dubbed</u> means "you record over the original," but that definition doesn't make sense here.

The sentence says that one student <u>dubbed</u> the class the "Barcelona Hills J. J. Fan Club." It sounds like <u>dubbed</u> means "to name."

"Members of the Barcelona Hills J. J. Fan Club—what one student <u>named</u> the group . . ." That makes sense to me.

PRACTICE

Use the steps above to define the following multiple-meaning words. The words are underlined for you in the reading selection.

1. marine (page 51)
2. spout (page 51)
3. concluded (page 51)
4. scouts (page 52)
5. pod (page 52)

56   Chapter 2   **Exposition:** Reporting the News

RESOURCES

Vocabulary Practice
- *Communications,* WS. p. 32

Test Taking Practice
- *Communications,* WS. pp. 33–35

MINI-LESSON TEST TAKING

Answering Main Idea Questions

Just as a lead will tell you the most important points of a news article, a main idea will tell you the central point of a reading passage. When you take a reading test, you may be asked to identify the main idea of a reading selection. Read the following passage and question. How would you answer the question?

> Gray whales exhibit a number of interesting behaviors. They often show their flukes, or tails, when they dive. A diving whale is said to be *sounding*. Gray whales can also leap out of the water and fall back, creating a big splash. This type of behavior is called *breaching*. *Spyhopping* occurs when a whale peeks its head vertically out of the water, possibly to see above the surface. You can see the behaviors of gray whales off the west coast of the United States from late fall until early spring.

What is the main idea of this passage?

A. Whale watching is a fun activity.
B. Whales can leap out of the water.
C. Spyhopping allows whales to see above the surface.
D. Gray whales display many interesting behaviors.

THINKING IT THROUGH — Identifying the Main Idea

STEP 1 Decide what the question asks.
I need to find the main idea.

STEP 2 Look at what all the details have in common. The details should point to the main idea. **Hint:** Pay attention to the first and last sentences. Sometimes you may find a sentence that states the main idea.
All of the details describe the behaviors of gray whales. The first sentence tells me that gray whales have different behaviors, and the last sentence tells me where and when I can see them.

STEP 3 State the main idea in your own words. Then, look for an answer that closely matches your own. Rule out answers that are obviously wrong.
Gray whales exhibit three different behaviors. Answer choice D says something like that.

STEP 4 Check to make sure that the details in the paragraph or passage support your answer.
The different behaviors of gray whales are sounding, breaching, and spyhopping. Those details support my answer.

Looking Ahead to Writing

In the Writing Workshop on pp. 58–75, students will be asked to write their own news articles. As students work on their articles, remind them to check that their leads answer the *5W-How?* questions. As they prepare their drafts, students may wish to refer to the inverted pyramid structure on pp. 54–55 for help in structuring their articles.

Writing Workshop

OBJECTIVES

- To write a newspaper article
- To choose a newsworthy event
- To identify the audience
- To organize and evaluate details using the inverted pyramid structure
- To analyze cause and effect
- To vary sentence structure and correct run-on sentences

Quotation for the Day

"The First Duty of a newspaper is to be Accurate. If it be Accurate, it follows that it is Fair."

(Herbert Bayard Swope, 1882–1958, American reporter, in a letter to the *New York Herald Tribune*)

Write the quotation on the chalkboard and ask students to explain the difference between the words *fair* and *accurate*. [*Fair* means that both sides of an issue are presented; *accurate* means that the ideas or facts presented are true.] Then, discuss with students why a newspaper report should be both fair and accurate.

TEACHING TIP

Choose and Evaluate an Event
Instead of choosing a current event about which to write an article, students might consider choosing a historical event. They can write about the event as if it had just taken place. Suggest that students brainstorm topic ideas by listing events they have read about in their history textbooks. They might also skim the table of contents and index of their history textbooks for ideas.

Writing Workshop

WHAT'S AHEAD?

In this workshop you will write a newspaper article. You will also learn how to

- choose a newsworthy event
- organize and evaluate details
- analyze cause and effect
- vary sentence structure
- correct run-on sentences

Writing a Newspaper Article

The headlines read "Mayor Honors Sixth-Grade Student," "Wind Rips Roof off Middle School," and "Girl Saves Brother from Shark Attack." Interesting events occur every day everywhere—even where you live. Would you like to be the one to tell the story? You can, by writing a news article.

News articles are a form of **expository**, or **informative**, writing. They provide readers with information about events that have happened recently. In this Writing Workshop you will write a newspaper article. Your article will explain an interesting event of your choice.

Prewriting

Choose and Evaluate an Event

Look and Listen Interesting events will not just fall into your lap. To find one, you may need to do a little digging. You won't be digging with a shovel, though. Instead, you will use your eyes and ears. Here are some suggestions you can use to find an event that has already happened.

- Talk to presidents and sponsors of clubs at your school about events that have happened recently.
- Ask members of local organizations, such as the PTA or city council, about recent decisions they have made.
- Make a list of recent events you have observed firsthand.

Is It Worth It? Would you spend all your time gathering, organizing, writing, revising, and publishing information about an event if no one is going to find your article interesting? Of course not. **Make your time and the readers' time worthwhile by writing about an event that is newsworthy.** An event is newsworthy if it has at least one of the following characteristics.

KEY CONCEPT

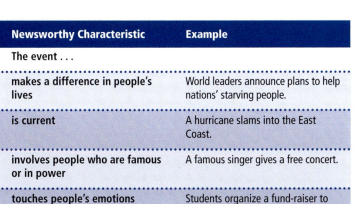

Newsworthy Characteristic	Example
The event . . .	
makes a difference in people's lives	World leaders announce plans to help nations' starving people.
is current	A hurricane slams into the East Coast.
involves people who are famous or in power	A famous singer gives a free concert.
touches people's emotions	Students organize a fund-raiser to help an animal shelter buy supplies.

TIP Events can have more than one newsworthy characteristic. For instance, a school newspaper's story about the volleyball team's win in the state tournament is current *and* touches people's emotions. Reporters look for events with more than one newsworthy characteristic so more people will read their articles.

An article's newsworthiness also depends on the purpose of the newspaper. For example, school or community newspapers generally focus on local events. However, city and national newspapers focus on a range of events, from local to worldwide.

YOUR TURN 4 Choosing and Evaluating an Event

- Make a list of events that have happened recently in your school or community.
- Then, evaluate each event on your list by looking for newsworthy characteristics. (Assume you are writing for a community or school newspaper.)
- Choose the event with the greatest number of newsworthy characteristics as the subject of your news article.

Critical Thinking

Evaluation. Students can use local newspapers to practice evaluating whether or not events described in news articles are newsworthy. Provide the class with a collection of recent newspapers. Have students circle a variety of headlines and read the articles. Then, using the chart on this page as a reference, students can list newsworthy characteristics of events discussed in the articles. Finally, discuss as a class why some events proved more or less newsworthy.

Before students choose an event, have them take some time to determine whether investigating this event would lead them into a situation where they would invade someone's privacy or cause embarrassment. For the purpose of this assignment, students should avoid covering an event that could have these unpleasant consequences.

RESOURCES
Your Turn 4
Practice
- *Communications*, WS. p. 36

Meeting INDIVIDUAL NEEDS

MULTIPLE INTELLIGENCES
Interpersonal Intelligence. To give students a chance to receive helpful feedback on their choices of event and audience, divide the class into pairs. Have each student in turn present his or her event and thoughts about an appropriate audience. Partners can ask questions or make suggestions.

For example, if students do not think the topic will interest enough people, they might ask, "How can you interest more people in the topic?" Or, if students think a topic is interesting but too broad, they might help narrow it by saying, "I really like that idea, but most people will probably want to know more about _____." Encourage students to write down any changes, additions, or suggestions they find helpful.

YOUR TURN 5
Students may wish to survey family members, neighbors, and school friends to determine the level of others' interest in the events they chose for their news articles. Surveying can help students identify the most appropriate audience for their articles.

Identify Your Audience

Who Wants to Know? The school board meeting is over. Your teacher wants to know if the school board approved a pay raise for teachers, but you want to know what the board decided about school uniforms.

Different events interest different people. The people who will be interested in the event you have chosen are your **audience**. To figure out the audience for your news article, ask yourself, "Who will be interested in this event, and why?"

Here is how a student identified his news article's audience.

> Event: I am writing about the principal approving a longer passing period between classes at my school.
>
> Audience: I think teachers and students will be interested because this event happened at school, and the longer passing period will affect them.

YOUR TURN 5 Identifying Your Audience

In your notebook, complete the sentences below to identify the audience for your news article.

Event: I am writing about ____.

Audience: I think ____ will be interested because ____.

Gather Details

Just the Facts Your friend tells you he saw a famous sports star. You want to know all about it. "Who? When? Where? Tell me!" you beg.

Just as you want all the facts of your friend's encounter with a sports star, **your audience will want all the facts of the newsworthy event.** Answers to the *5W-How?* questions will provide your readers with the facts, or details, of the event. The following chart shows specific questions you should try to answer as you gather the details for your news article.

KEY CONCEPT

RESOURCES

Your Turn 5
Practice
- *Communications*, WS. p. 37

Who?	Who was involved in the event? (Names are important, but also try to get other details about the people involved, such as titles, ages, or professions.)
What?	What was the event?
When?	When did the event occur? (Get the time and date of the event.)
Where?	Where did the event take place? (Find out the address or location.)
Why?	Why did the event happen?
How?	How did the event happen? (List the smaller events that made up the event.)

The *5W-How?* questions will give your audience the basic information about the event, but some readers will want to know even more. To help your audience fully understand the event, find the answers to these questions as well.

- What are the effects of the event?
- How do people feel about the event?

TIP A news article's **voice** is *objective,* or factual. When you write a news article, use words that simply state the facts. For instance, instead of writing about a "cute cocker spaniel," stick to the facts and write about a "one-year-old cocker spaniel." The dog's age is a fact because it can be proven. "Cute," on the other hand, is a matter of opinion.

Get to the Source You know what information you need, but how do you go about getting the answers to your questions? **Gather details for your news article by interviewing people who witnessed the event or played a part in it.** Even if *you* observed the event firsthand, you should still talk to other people.

As you interview, take notes about what people say, but also record a few direct quotations. In other words, write down what people say word-for-word instead of summarizing. Readers find direct quotations interesting because they have more force than a summary. You can see the power of a direct quotation in the example on the next page.

KEY CONCEPT

TIP In an interview, avoid asking questions with *yes* or *no* answers. Instead, ask questions that will give you more information, such as, "What do you think about the longer passing period?"

MULTIPLE INTELLIGENCES
Bodily-Kinesthetic Intelligence.
Role-playing is a good way to have students practice conducting their own interviews. Students can re-enact a recent event, with two reporters live on the scene. Ask students to act out the scene in front of the class, having student reporters interview and ask questions. Afterward, discuss with the class whether their questions successfully elicited helpful facts and details from those interviewed. Ask students which quotes would be good to use in a news article and what they learned about interviewing by role-playing.

TEACHING TIP

Get to the Source
Discuss proper interviewing practices with students. Explain that there are two types of interviews: the informal "person-on-the-street" type at the scene of an event, and a more formal interview at a person's home or place of business. If students intend to interview people, they should call ahead, introduce themselves, explain the nature of the interview, and request a short appointment. Remind students to prepare their questions and carry a notebook and pen or pencil and a tape recorder, if one is available. At the end of the interview, a polite thank-you is in order. Make sure you check with school officials regarding parental permission for such interviews.

Cooperative Learning

Working Collaboratively. If you wish to provide students the opportunity to work collaboratively as they prewrite, write, and revise a news report, form groups of four of different abilities. Explain that *collaboration* means that students work together to create a final product. Together, students will compose, revise, edit, and publish a news article. So that everyone in the group is occupied at all times, each student should act as a facilitator for a specific task. Have students choose one of the following roles:

- Reader: reads the list of events, the quotations, and the details that the group gathers
- Compiler: leads group in organizing the details of the chosen event in an inverted pyramid structure
- Scribe: helps group write the lead and the body of details composed by members
- Proofreader: monitors the correction of grammar, usage, and punctuation errors

TIP Your job as a reporter is to present a balanced picture of news events. That means you should present a range of different opinions. You will not include your *own* opinions about the event. To give his audience a balanced picture of the event, the student reporting on the extended passing period got direct quotations from people on both sides of the issue.

Summary: Neil Armstrong was the first man to walk on the moon. Armstrong felt his first step was an exciting moment not only for him but for the rest of the world as well.

Direct Quotation: Neil Armstrong was the first man to walk on the moon. As he made his first step he said, "That's one small step for [a] man, one giant leap for mankind."

The following example shows the notes one student took as he interviewed people. Notice that he includes details that answer the *5W-How?* questions, information about the effects of the event, and people's reactions to it. The student also recorded direct quotations that support some of the details.

Who? Principal Reyes

What? He approved a longer passing period between classes.

When? He announced it at today's pep rally.

Where? Main Street Middle School

Why? Principal Reyes agreed that students needed more time to go to their lockers and the restroom between classes.

How? Morgan Sykes passed a petition around last Wed. and Thurs. It was given to Principal Reyes on Fri.—134 people signed it.

What are the effects of the event? Starts Oct. 7. Classes—5 minutes shorter except 7th period. Passing period—5 minutes longer. School is still over at 3:00 P.M.

How do people feel about the event?
Negative reaction: Toby Washington, 7th grade: "I like my classes. I don't want them to be five minutes shorter. Those five minutes give me a chance to start my homework."

Positive reaction: Paul Brook, 6th-grade history teacher: "I'm so happy that instruction will not be interrupted by students leaving class to go to the restroom or their lockers."

Positive reaction: Joanna Tran, 6th grade: "The extra time will help me clear my head after one class and gear up for the next."

YOUR TURN 6 — Gathering Details

Gather details and direct quotations for your news article by interviewing people involved in and affected by the event. Remember that you are looking for answers to the *5W-How?* questions, information about the effects of the event, and people's reactions to the event.

Organize and Evaluate Details

Go Ahead, Spoil Them! Your readers not only want information about an event, they want to read the most important information first. Give your readers what they want by organizing the details you have gathered in an inverted pyramid structure. **In an inverted pyramid structure, the most important details appear at the beginning of a news article, and the least important details appear at the end.** The inverted pyramid structure of a news article looks like this:

Reference Note
For more on **inverted pyramid structure,** see page 54.

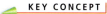 KEY CONCEPT

> Lead (answers the *5W-How?* questions)
> Most important details
> Less important details
> Least important details

To arrange your details in an inverted pyramid structure, start by identifying the details that will go in the *lead*. The **lead** is the beginning of an article, and it provides the answers to the *5W-How?* questions. If your audience reads only the lead, they will still have an idea of what happened.

Once you know which details go in the lead, evaluate the remaining details, and arrange them in descending, or decreasing, order of importance. How do you organize details from most important to least important? Look at your details about the effects of the event and people's reactions to it. Think about your audience and ask yourself the questions on the following page.

YOUR TURN 6

You might review the punctuation of direct quotations so that students are adequately prepared to write down a quotation correctly during an interview. Explain how important it is to use accurate quotations in a news article. For more information on the use of commas and quotation marks with direct quotations, see pp. 590–595.

Critical Thinking

Metacognition. Ask students to select one or two of their best quotations and write them on a piece of paper. Have students answer these questions about each quotation.

1. Why do you think this is a good quotation? What will it add to your article?

2. Are you satisfied with the questions you asked? Why or why not?

3. After conducting interviews for quotations, what would you do differently next time? Please explain.

Have students share their answers and observations in small groups or with the class.

RESOURCES

Your Turn 6
Practice
- *Communications,* WS. p. 38

Meeting INDIVIDUAL NEEDS

LEARNERS HAVING DIFFICULTY
To help students organize their details in order of importance, suggest that after they identify the details that make up the lead, they break down the organizing task further. Have them take the remaining details and divide them into several groups related to the main idea. For example, they could have details about people involved in a fund-raising event, details describing the event, and quotations about the effects of the event. By putting details into smaller topic groups, students may find it easier to determine which are the most or least important details and where the details belong in the pyramid structure.

YOUR TURN 7

Students may find it helpful to draw a large inverted triangle on their papers, filling in the triangle as they complete **Your Turn 7**. To assess their work, have students write each *5W-How?* question over the part of the lead that answers it.

- **Which details would give my audience a better understanding of the event?** The answer to this question will point to the most important details, the ones that will follow the lead.
- **What additional information is likely to interest my *whole* audience?** You have identified information for the lead and other important details of the event. Look over your remaining notes. What *other* information is likely to interest *all* your readers? This information, though less important than the lead, is important enough for the middle of the article.
- **What information might interest *just a few members* of my audience?** Your audience may contain a group with a special interest in certain details. The "least important" details may still be of interest to this group. These types of details go at the end of the article.

This is how the student writing about the passing period change arranged the details for his news article.

Reference Note
For more on **evaluating details**, see the second Tip on page 55.

> Lead: answers to the 5W-How? questions
>
> Most important details:
> —information about when the passing period starts and the effect on class time, passing period time, and school hours
>
> Less important details:
> —information about how students feel about the longer passing period
> —positive quotation from Joanna Tran and negative quotation from Toby Washington
>
> Least important details:
> —information about teachers appreciating the extra time as much as the students do and positive quotation from Paul Brook

YOUR TURN 7 — Organizing and Evaluating Details

Organize your details in an inverted pyramid structure. First, place the answers to the *5W-How?* questions in the lead. Then, arrange the remaining details from most important to least important by asking yourself the questions that appear at the top of this page.

RESOURCES

Your Turn 7
Practice
- *Communications,* WS. p. 39

Critical Thinking
Practice
- *Communications,* WS. p. 40

MINI-LESSON CRITICAL THINKING

Analyzing Cause and Effect

Have you ever set a series of dominoes upright in a row? When the first domino in line tips over, it causes the next one to fall, which causes the next one to fall, and so on. Analyzing a cause-and-effect chain is like watching a chain of dominoes, because it involves looking at how one thing leads to another.

Below is an example of a cause-and-effect chain. Can you see how each cause leads to an effect, which then causes another effect, and so on?

Your news article will explain the causes and the effects of an event. As you write, make sure that the relationships between the causes and effects are clear. If you leave out a portion of the cause-and-effect chain, your audience may not fully understand the event. For example, suppose your little brothers are happily playing together in the living room. You leave to get a snack. When you come back, one brother is crying, and the other brother is yelling. What happened? You missed what caused your brothers to fight. Causes and effects need to be connected clearly in order for them to make sense.

PRACTICE

Create five cause-and-effect chains. The following causes will be the first step in each chain. Use your imagination and experience to complete the chains. Each chain should have at least three steps.

1. A river overflows due to heavy rain.
2. A tornado is seen near town.
3. Sixth-grade students take snacks to a local nursing home.
4. Ms. Martinez, a science teacher, wins the Teacher of the Year award.
5. Greg Goldstein sings off-key during the choir's concert.

MINI-LESSON CRITICAL THINKING

Analyzing Cause and Effect

ANSWERS

Possible answers are shown below. Answers do not include the causes listed in the pupil's text.

1. Houses along the riverbanks are flooded. People climb to their roofs and await rescue.
2. Someone calls the fire department. The fire department sounds an emergency alert siren. People run for shelter.
3. Residents ask students to stay and play board games. Students and residents are happier.
4. A story about the award appears in the local newspaper. Many people read the article. Several parents write to Ms. Martinez to congratulate her.
5. He stops and coughs very heavily. The choir director hears the cough. She gives Greg a critical look.

Taking a Second Look

Analyzing Cause and Effect. Have students redo the **Practice** exercise. This time, instead of having each item be the cause, or the first step in the chain, reverse the process and have each item be the last effect in the chain. Students should work backward to find a cause. For example, the first item might read: Severe weather strikes our town. We receive several inches of rain within a few hours. A river overflows due to heavy rain.

Quotation for the Day

"I am convinced more and more day by day that fine writing is next to fine doing, the top thing in the world."

(John Keats, 1795–1821, English poet)

Write the quotation on the chalkboard. Have students offer ideas about what Keats meant by "fine doing." [searching for beauty or doing good deeds] Then, have students answer the following questions in their journals. Do you think that writing is of such great importance? Why or why not?

TEACHING TIP

Directions and Explanations

To better manage the body of their news articles, students might benefit from a review of paragraphing. Explain that the first sentence after the attention-grabbing opener of the lead paragraph answers the *Who did what?* question and is like a topic sentence that states the main idea. Remind students to indent the opening sentence. Then, indicate that some of the *5W-How?* details make up the supporting sentences in the first paragraph. Emphasize that in news reports, paragraphs are sometimes quite short. However, with the exception of direct quotations, paragraphs should be longer than one sentence. Remind students to use appropriate transition words and phrases whenever possible to connect the ideas in the paragraphs.

If you wish to assign a length to the students' news articles, 500 to 700 words is appropriate.

Writing

News Article

Framework **Directions and Explanations**

Lead
- Attention-grabbing opening
- Answers to the *5W-How?* questions

Capture your audience's attention by beginning your article with an unusual or interesting detail.

Detail	Several animals escaped from Pete's Pets on Friday.
Unusual Detail	Charlie the chimpanzee led several of his animal friends on a daring escape from Pete's Pets on Friday.

Then, write a sentence that answers, at least, "*Who* did *what?*" Finally, give the remaining answers to the *5W-How?* questions.

Keep in mind your lead may be one to three short paragraphs, depending on the amount of information you gathered.

Body
- Most important details
- Less important details
- Least important details

- Organize the remaining **details** in an inverted pyramid structure. Refer to your responses to Your Turn 7 for the order of these details. Be sure the remaining details include information about the effects of the event and people's reactions to it.
- Group the details in short paragraphs.
- Place **direct quotations** after the details they support.

 **Writing Your News Article**

Now it is your turn to write a news article. As you write,
- keep your audience in mind
- order your details so that the most important ones come first and the least important ones come last
- refer to the framework above and to the Writer's Model on the next page

66 Chapter 2 Exposition: Reporting the News

RESOURCES

Writing
Writing Prompts
- *Communications,* TP. 20, WS. p. 41

Your Turn 8
Practice
- *Communications,* TP. 21, WS. p. 42

A Writer's Model

The final draft below closely follows the framework for a news article on the previous page.

Principal Approves Longer Passing Period

A major change has taken place at Main Street Middle School: The period between each class is now five minutes longer. Principal Alan Reyes approved the longer passing period. His decision was announced at today's pep rally in Loftus Gymnasium.

Eighth-grader Morgan Sykes started the petition that led to the longer passing period. She passed the petition to other students last Wednesday and Thursday. When Principal Reyes received it last Friday, 134 students had signed it.

Principal Reyes agreed that students need extra time between classes. With a longer passing period, students will not have to leave class to go to their lockers or the restroom.

The longer passing period will go into effect on Monday, October 7. From now on, each class except seventh period will be five minutes shorter, and the passing periods will be five minutes longer. School will still be over at 3:00 P.M.

Most students are happy about the change, and they are already making plans for the extended passing time. Sixth-grader Joanna Tran said, "The extra time will help me clear my head after one class and gear up for the next."

At least one student disapproved of the new passing period. "I like my classes. I don't want them to be five minutes shorter," said seventh-grader Toby Washington. "Those five minutes give me a chance to start my homework."

Most teachers will enjoy the extra time as much as the students will. "I'm so happy that instruction will not be interrupted by students leaving class to go to the restroom or their lockers," said sixth-grade history teacher Paul Brook.

Side labels:
- Attention-grabbing opening
- Answer to *where*
- Answers to *what* and *who*
- Answer to *when*
- Answer to *how*
- Answer to *why*
- Most important details
- Less important details
- Quotation
- Quotation
- Least important details
- Quotation

Connecting Reading and Writing

Have students refer to the section and graphic on the inverted pyramid structure on pp. 54–55 in the Reading Workshop. Ask a student to draw an enlarged copy of the graphic on the chalkboard. After students have read **A Writer's Model,** discuss as a class how the model follows the inverted pyramid structure. As part of the discussion, ask volunteers to write in the proper place on the graphic the lead and details from the article. Students should use the model's side labels to guide them.

TEACHING TIP

A Writer's Model
Students may need some help with using quotations in their own writing. Have them refer to **A Writer's Model** to see how direct quotations are handled. Explain that when a second person is quoted after a detail, that direct quotation belongs in a separate paragraph to indicate a new person is speaking about the same detail.

Connecting Reading and Writing

Before students read **A Student's Model,** ask them to review the chart on newsworthy characteristics of an event on p. 59. Then, after students have read the model, have them jot down those characteristics that apply and decide how newsworthy the event is.

A Student's Model

When you write a news article, you want to choose a newsworthy topic. Natalie Banta and Amy Tidwell, reporters for Olympus Junior High's online newspaper the *Olympian,* write about an important school event—the principal leaving.

Mr. Sagers Moves to Cyprus High

Attention-grabbing opening

Answers to *who, what, why,* and *how*

Maybe you have heard the rumor about Principal Sagers leaving Olympus Junior High School. Well, it is true. Mr. Sagers was promoted to be the principal of Cyprus High.

Answer to *when*

Most important details

The new principal of Olympus Junior High (OJH) will be Linda Mariotti. She has been the assistant principal at Bonneville and at Granite High, a coordinator at the Jones Center, and a language specialist. We will meet her next September.

When we asked Principal Sagers what he would miss the most about OJH, he answered that he would miss the attitude of the community. "Everyone seems to have high expectations of learning," he said.

Less important details

Some of Principal Sagers's greatest accomplishments have been in the area of technology. He said, "We've achieved a lot [in the area of technology] in the last two years. We've also tried to create a positive climate and beautify the school." If Principal Sagers were not leaving, he would continue increasing literacy. "The goal was to identify all students not reading on their grade level. We're using technology as a vehicle to enhance instruction," he said.

Least important details

It is hard to go to a new school for everyone, but Principal Sagers said, "The first year at a new high school [for a principal] is extremely difficult. It's always hard to start over as a new leader."

Revising

Evaluate and Revise Content, Organization, and Style

Check and Check Again As you look over a peer's article or your own, you should do at least two readings. First, focus on the article's content and organization. The guidelines below will help you edit your article. Then, in your second reading, go back and look for ways to make sentences stronger by using the Focus on Sentences on page 71.

▶ **First Reading: Content and Organization** Use the chart below to look for ways to improve the content and organization of your news article. Respond to questions in the left-hand column. If you need help answering the questions, use the tips in the middle column. If necessary, make the changes suggested in the right-hand column.

TIP Try using a **reference source** when you revise the content and organization of your article and edit it for style. Reference sources such as the dictionary, a thesaurus, and Part 3 of this book can help you improve your article.

News Article: Content and Organization Guidelines for Self-Evaluation and Peer Evaluation

Evaluation Questions	Tips	Revision Techniques
❶ Does the lead answer the 5W-How? questions?	**Circle** the answers to the questions *who, what, when, where, why,* and *how*.	If needed, **add** answers to the 5W-How? questions at the beginning of the news article.
❷ Are details in the body given in order from most important to least important?	**Put a star** next to the details that help the reader better understand the event. **Put a check** next to the details that are not as important and could be cut.	If necessary, **rearrange** the details so those with a star next to them directly follow the lead and those with a check are at the end of the article.
❸ Does the body include details that explain the effects of the event and people's reactions to it?	**Underline** the details that explain the effects. **Put a box** around the details that show people's reactions.	**Add** details that explain the effects and people's reactions if these details are missing.
❹ Does the article include quotations that support the details of the article?	**Highlight** each quotation. **Draw an arrow** to the detail each quotation supports.	If needed, **elaborate** the details by adding quotations.

Writing Workshop 69

RESOURCES

Revising
Practice
- *Communications,* TPs. 22, 23, WS. pp. 43, 44, 45

Quotation for the Day

"I am an obsessive rewriter, doing one draft and then another and another, usually five."

(Gore Vidal, 1925– , American writer)

Write the quotation on the chalkboard. Ask students what value they see in revising their work. Lead them to understand that revision is a necessary step in creating work that is as good as it can be.

Timesaver

To reduce the amount of time you might spend helping students with revisions, consider asking the more skilled writers to act as peer writing consultants. Students who do not understand something can ask one of these writers for help. Any problems students cannot resolve should be highlighted and brought to you.

TEACHING TIP

▶ **Elaboration**
Discuss with students that elaboration does not necessarily mean adding a lot of words or explanation. Students can also elaborate by using simple comparisons.

Example: The motorist rescued the iguana from under a parked car.

Problem: Needs elaboration to answer the questions "What is the iguana doing?" and "Why does it need rescuing?"

Revised example: The motorist rescued the iguana, which crouched under a parked car like the last fighter at the Alamo. Twitching its broken tail like an angry lion, the iguana did not surrender easily. It seemed unaware of the danger of nearby traffic.

Writing Workshop 69

Responding to the Revision Process
ANSWERS

1. Changing the order of the paragraphs allows the more important details in the lead to come first. The paragraph that begins with "The longer passing period" should come second, because it assumes that the writer has already explained what the longer passing period is.

2. This sentence was added to tell *why* extra time is needed.

LEARNERS HAVING DIFFICULTY
Many students need assistance with how to select and use reference materials and resources when revising and editing final drafts. Provide some strategies such as the following.

For help with spelling:

- Select a dictionary. Sound out the word and divide it into syllables. Then, find a guide word at the top of a page close to the spelling you have arrived at, locate your word on the page, and check the word for accuracy.

- Look in this textbook. You can find spelling rules and a list of commonly misspelled words on pp. 615–641.

- Use the spellchecker software on your computer.

For help with grammar, usage, and punctuation:

- Look in the index of a grammar handbook. You will find listed after each concept pages in the grammar handbook that explain the concept and give examples.

PEER REVIEW
As you look at a peer's news article, ask yourself these questions:

- What makes this article newsworthy?
- How do people feel about this event? Is more than one viewpoint presented?

ONE WRITER'S REVISIONS This revision is an early draft of the news article on page 67.

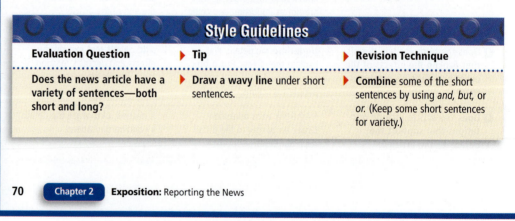

Responding to the Revision Process

1. Why do you think the writer changed the order of the two paragraphs?
2. How did adding a sentence improve the writing?

▶ **Second Reading: Style** Now that you have revised the content and organization of your news article, you can **edit** the individual sentences. You can improve your sentence style by using a variety of sentences—short sentences and long sentences. An article with too many short, choppy sentences or too many long, complex sentences will be difficult to read. To give your article a variety of sentence lengths, use the following guidelines.

Style Guidelines

Evaluation Question	▶ Tip	▶ Revision Technique
Does the news article have a variety of sentences—both short and long?	▶ Draw a wavy line under short sentences.	▶ Combine some of the short sentences by using *and*, *but*, or *or*. (Keep some short sentences for variety.)

Chapter 2   Exposition: Reporting the News

Exposition: Reporting the News

Varying Sentences

A news article presents the facts simply and quickly. That does not mean, however, that all its sentences will be short. A series of short sentences can bore the audience. To vary your sentences, use *and*, *but*, or *or* to combine two short sentences.

All Short Sentences: An ice storm surprised downtown workers last night. Road crews responded. They were not prepared for the severity of the storm. The storm continued until 10:00 P.M. Roads remained icy. Workers found they had two options. They could risk driving. They could stay in their offices.

A Variety of Sentences: An ice storm surprised downtown workers last night. Road crews responded**,** **but** they were not prepared for the severity of the storm. The storm continued until 10:00 P.M.**,** **and** roads remained icy. Workers found they had two options. They could risk driving**, or** they could stay in their offices.

Focus on Sentences

TIP A comma generally comes before the *and, but,* or *or* that connects two short sentences.

ONE WRITER'S REVISIONS

School will still be over at 3:00 P.M.

Most students are happy about the change**, and** ~~They~~ are already making plans for the extended passing time.

Responding to the Revision Process
How did combining the sentences improve the writing?

 **Evaluating and Revising Your News Article**

Evaluate and revise the content and organization of your news article, using the guidelines on page 69. Then, use the Focus on Sentences above. If your class did peer evaluations, consider your peer's comments as you revise.

Writing Workshop 71

RESOURCES
Focus on Sentences
Practice
- *Communications*, WS. p. 46

Publishing

Proofread Your News Article

Upon Close Inspection . . . Mistakes in a news article will distract readers from the facts. Have another person proofread your article to find mistakes you might have missed.

Grammar Link

Correcting Run-on Sentences

Sometimes when you write, your pencil cannot keep up with your thoughts. When this happens, you may write *run-on sentences*. A **run-on sentence** is really two or more sentences that are written as one.

Mick loves old movies he also loves to read.

One way to correct a run-on sentence is to divide the sentence into separate sentences.

Mick loves old movies. He also loves to read.

You can also turn a run-on sentence into a compound sentence by adding a comma and *and*, *but*, or *or*.

Mick loves old movies**,** **but** he also loves to read.

Example:

1. I like the longer passing period my friend does not.

1. I like the longer passing period. My friend does not.

    I like the longer passing period, but my friend does not.

PRACTICE

Correct the run-on sentences to the right. First, divide the run-on sentence into separate sentences. Then, rewrite the run-on sentence as a compound sentence by adding a comma and *and*, *but*, or *or*. If a sentence is correctly punctuated and is not a run-on, write *C* on your paper.

1. The passing period will be five minutes longer school will still be over at 3:00.
2. Morgan Sykes talked at the pep rally she received a standing ovation.
3. The students signed the petition asking for a longer passing period the principal agreed with them.
4. Students can use the extra time to go to their lockers they might use the time to go to the restroom.
5. Students will not miss important information by leaving class to go to their lockers or the restroom.

For more information and practice on correcting **run-on sentences,** see page 265.

Grammar Link

Correcting Run-on Sentences

ANSWERS

1. The passing period will be five minutes longer. School will still be over at 3:00.

    The passing period will be five minutes longer, but school will still be over at 3:00.

2. Morgan Sykes talked at the pep rally. She received a standing ovation.

    Morgan Sykes talked at the pep rally, and she received a standing ovation.

3. The students signed the petition asking for a longer passing period. The principal agreed with them.

    The students signed the petition asking for a longer passing period, and the principal agreed with them.

4. Students can use the extra time to go to their lockers. They might use the time to go to the restroom.

    Students can use the extra time to go to their lockers, or they might use the time to go to the restroom.

5. C

Quotation for the Day

"Clarity is the cornerstone of effective communication—and effective communication is the foundation of good writing."

(David Petersen, 1946– , American writer and editor)

Write the quotation on the chalkboard and discuss the meaning of *clarity*. [state of being clear and free of confusion] Explain that errors in grammar, usage, or mechanics can distort or obscure meaning and inhibit effective communication. Tell students that clarity is especially important in a published news report. A news reader needs a clear picture of an event.

RESOURCES

Grammar Link
Practice
- *Communications,* WS. p. 47

Publish Your News Article

Spread the News Before you publish your article, you will need to write a *headline*. A **headline** is an attention-grabbing title for a news article. A good headline will summarize the event in a short sentence that contains an action verb. Action verbs are important because they tell the reader specifically what happened. Look at the examples below.

Examples:
Sixth-Graders **Adopt** Terence the Tarantula
Teachers **Ban** Homework Next Week

After writing a headline for your article, publish it using one of the following ideas.

- With your classmates, publish your articles together in a newspaper and distribute it to your class.
- Record your article on videotape and show it to your class as part of a news segment. See pages 79–82 for more information.
- Submit your article to your school or community newspaper.

Reflect on Your News Article

Building Your Portfolio Now, take time to reflect on what you have done. Answer these questions.

- How is a lead for a news article like other introductions for other types of writing? How is it different?
- Would you use interviewing to gather information for other types of writing? Why or why not?

YOUR TURN 10 — Proofreading, Publishing, and Reflecting on Your News Article

- Correct spelling and punctuation mistakes. Make sure your article does not contain run-on sentences.
- Write a headline for your article and publish your article using one of the suggestions above.
- Answer the questions from Reflect on Your News Article above. Record your responses in a learning log, or include them in your portfolio.

COMPUTER TIP

Make your news article look like a real one by typing it in **columns,** or vertical rows. Measure the width of a real newspaper column and set the margins of your document to the same width. Then, select the justify option to make straight edges at both the left and right margins.

Before you print your article, use the print preview feature to see what it will look like. You can usually find the print preview feature in the toolbar.

PORTFOLIO

Wrap It Up

Metacognition. Ask students to reflect on the process of preparing a news article by answering the following question in their journals.

1. What did you learn about the process of collecting information about an event?

Then, ask the students this question:

2. Why are news articles written in an inverted pyramid structure? [so that the least important details come last and can be cut from the article if space is tight]

TEACHING TIP

Publish Your News Article
Depending on their penmanship, some students may choose to write in cursive style and some may choose manuscript style. In either case, remind students to write legibly as they prepare the final copy of their news article. If their letters are not neat and formed correctly, some words may appear misspelled and information may be lost.

YOUR TURN 10

Explain to students that proofreading for a single purpose each time they read nets more results than trying to catch all errors at once. Have students re-read their drafts several times—each time editing for a specific purpose, such as to check for consistency of verb tense, subject-verb agreement, and correct punctuation.

TEACHING TIP

Writing a Newspaper's Advice Column

Before students read the **Connections to Life** feature, introduce the topic by providing a variety of advice columns from the local newspaper. Choose columns that have appropriate subject matter, such as sibling rivalry, peer pressure, and parental authority. Ask students which columns they liked and why. Point out that the advice columns' format is problem-solution. In other words, the letters pose a problem and the columnist's answer offers a solution. For this feature, allow students the option of writing a traditional essay that uses the problem-solution structure.

Students who choose the traditional essay may find it helpful to use the graphic organizer below.

QUESTION	YOUR RESPONSE
What is the problem?	
What are the effects?	
What are the causes?	
What are the possible solutions?	
Which solution works best?	
Why is it the best solution?	
What do you recommend?	

Connections to Life

Writing a Newspaper's Advice Column

You have a problem, and you are unsure how to solve it. Of course, you could turn to a friend or relative for help. Would you consider writing to the newspaper? Newspapers feature a special kind of **problem-solution writing** called an advice column. Newspaper advice columns provide information on how to solve all sorts of problems, from personal and financial to car and home repair. They are designed to be entertaining as well as informative.

What Is Your Problem? Advice columns consist of two parts—the readers' problems and the columnist's answers. Newspapers publish these letters and responses to offer help not only to the person writing the letter but also to other readers who may have a similar problem. Maybe you can identify with this reader's problem below:

> Dear Pat the Problem Solver,
> My little brother always gets me in trouble by starting arguments. Then, when my mom comes to see what we are arguing about, he blames me for starting it. I try to explain my side of the story, but it's my word against his. What can I do to keep from being accused of a crime I have not committed?
>
> *Falsely Accused*

Help Is on the Way What is the solution? An advice columnist does more than just provide the reader with an answer. In a response, you can usually find these items.

- **a restatement of the problem** The first thing an advice columnist does is restate the reader's problem. By restating the problem, the columnist lets the reader know that he or she understands what is wrong.

- **a solution** The next part of the response is the advice. Columnists give readers advice that they can actually use. The advice columnist will offer a solution that the reader can carry out to make the situation better.

- **an example** The final part of the response is an example that shows that the recommended solution really works. The advice columnist may give a personal example or one from someone else who tried the same solution. Readers are more likely to try the advice if they read that the solution has already worked in another situation.

Read the response Pat the Problem Solver wrote to Falsely Accused on the next page. The elements listed above are labeled for you.

Chapter 2 Exposition: Reporting the News

Dear Falsely Accused,
    Brothers and sisters often start arguments and then try to pass the blame to someone else. There are two ways you can handle this type of situation. One way is to avoid arguing. When your brother wants to start a fight, walk away and ignore him. However, if you simply cannot hold your tongue, the second way is to discuss (not argue about) the issue in front of your parents. This will keep your little brother (and you) in line. When my little sister wanted to argue, I would ignore her or tell her we should ask our parents what they thought. Suddenly, she would drop the issue. My sister no longer had the fun of seeing me mad or in trouble. Good luck!

Pat

Restatement of the problem

Solution

Example

YOUR TURN 11 — Writing a Newspaper's Advice Column

Pretend you are an advice columnist. Choose one of the following letters. Then, use the guidelines on page 74 to write a response. To publish your response, consider producing a newspaper in which you include an advice column or presenting your response in an oral presentation.

    My father is coach of the soccer team. He made someone else goalie even though he knew that I wanted the position and that I am a good goalie. He said he didn't choose me because he didn't want to show favoritism. Can you help?

A Fan of Fairness

    I just moved to a small school where everyone else has known each other since kindergarten. It has been really hard to make friends, and my shyness doesn't help. Do you have any suggestions?

New Kid in Town

Cooperative Learning

Problem-Solution Relationships. To help students better understand problem-solution relationships, you may want to provide an opportunity for students to compose orally both a problem and a solution. Have students work in randomly selected groups of four to brainstorm a problem and a solution. Two students should collaborate on stating a problem and asking for advice. The other two students should collaborate on a response that includes a restatement, a solution, and an example. Then, have students reverse roles and brainstorm another problem and solution. Finally, have the groups present their work to the class.

YOUR TURN 11

Have students work in pairs to decide how to restate each problem. The solutions should be reasonably easy to carry out, and logical examples should show how the solution has already worked.

Critical Thinking

Analyzing Problems and Solutions. Explain that problem-solution patterns can be found in various types of writing—from newspaper editorials to fiction. Choose a story, such as "Belling the Cat," and have students identify the problem, the solution, the reason supporting the solution, and the probable audience. Help students evaluate the solution by asking them to comment on the probable or actual result of the solution. Finally, have students identify an editorial containing a problem-solution pattern, identifying the same elements mentioned above and presenting their findings to the class.

Focus on Viewing and Representing

OBJECTIVES

- To organize news articles into sections of a newspaper
- To write editorials, giving a stated opinion, supporting reasons, and a call to action
- To design the layout of a newspaper
- To produce a newspaper

Quotation for the Day

❝ 'What is the use of a book,' thought Alice, 'without pictures or conversations?' ❞

(Lewis Carroll, 1832–1898, English writer and mathematician)

After writing the quotation on the chalkboard, ask students if they agree or disagree with Alice's statement. Then, explain that news articles do not have much space for descriptive writing or dialogue. As a class, discuss how quotations, photos, and cartoons enrich a newspaper.

Cooperative Learning

Working Collaboratively. If you want students to write editorials collaboratively, you might form groups of four students comprised of two pairs. Have groups brainstorm problems they have observed in their school or community. What needs improvement, and why? Help groups form opinion statements.

Once an opinion statement is drafted, the first student pair can find support to back up the opinion.

Have the second pair of students draft the editorial and the first pair evaluate and revise it. The second pair can then proofread for mistakes.

Focus on Viewing and Representing

Producing a Newspaper

WHAT'S AHEAD?

In this section you will produce a newspaper. You will also learn how to

- organize news articles into sections
- write editorials
- design the layout of a newspaper

You and your classmates have written a variety of news articles that would interest others, so why not publish them in your own newspaper? Working with a small group, you can follow the guidelines below to produce a newspaper.

Make a Plan

Use What You Have   To fill the pages of your newspaper, you can use the articles you and your group members wrote in the Writing Workshop. First, gather the articles together. Then, put the ones about school events in one stack and ones about community events in another stack.

Hand Out Assignments   Your newspaper should include school articles and community articles. If you need more of one type of article, brainstorm a list of story ideas and choose a "reporter" to investigate and write an article.

In addition to school and community news, you will also need two *editorials* and an *editorial cartoon*. **Editorials** are articles that try to persuade readers to think or act a certain way. For instance, you may want to persuade others that your community needs to create bike lanes on busy streets. In the editorial, you would clearly state your opinion and support it with evidence—facts and examples. At the end of the editorial, you would ask your readers to take some action, such as signing a petition or changing a habit. You can also express your opinion in an **editorial cartoon.** Drawing a cyclist riding on top of cars because no room is available on the street would show that bike lanes are needed.

TIP   The outline of an editorial looks like this:

Opinion statement
    First reason
        Fact or example
    Second reason
        Fact or example
    Third reason
        Fact or example
Call to action

Reference Note

For more on **persuasive writing,** see page 237. For more on **editorial cartoons,** see page 752 in the Quick Reference Handbook.

Chapter 2   Exposition: Reporting the News

RESOURCES

Focus on Viewing and Representing
Practice

- *Media Literacy and Communication Skills*
  —*Support and Practice,* Ch. 2
  —*A How-to Handbook*

Teaching Notes

- *Media Literacy and Communication Skills*
  —*A Teacher's Guide,* Ch. 2

Extension

- *Designing Your Writing*

Exposition: Reporting the News

The Name Game   Before you put your paper together, you should decide on an original name for your newspaper. The name should be related to your school or community and appeal to readers. For example, if your school's mascot is an alligator, you could call your newspaper the *Gator Gazette*.

Put It Together

To put your newspaper together, use the instructions in Designing Your Writing below.

Designing Your Writing

Newspaper Layout   If your newspaper is clearly organized and appeals to the eye, people will be eager to read it. Your newspaper will consist of four pages. Each page will represent a section.

Page 1—The front page will have a **flag,** the title of the newspaper and the date of publication, across the top. It will also include the most newsworthy school article and the most newsworthy community article.

Page 2—School news section

Page 3—Community news section

Page 4—Editorial section

Follow these steps to design the layout of your newspaper.

- First, draw what each newspaper page will look like on an $8\frac{1}{2}'' \times 11''$ piece of paper. Use ××× to represent headlines, ≡ to indicate articles written in columns, and ⊠ to stand for pictures or graphics. As you design the layout, keep in mind the following guidelines.

  1. Articles in a newspaper should fill a square or rectangular block. Blocks help readers know where an article begins and ends. Look at the examples to the right.
  2. Generally, headlines should not be placed side by side. Headlines attract readers to the article because they are written or typed in a larger size than the articles. If two headlines are next to one another, readers will have difficulty separating them. Look at the difference in the examples to the right.
  3. Each page should have one image. Your group can paste or scan actual photographs onto the pages. If you do not have photographs, you can draw pictures. Make sure that the picture or photograph is related to the topic of the article.

TIP   You can add more pages to your newspaper by including other sections, such as sports, movie reviews, and classified ads.

Poorly Designed

Well Designed

Meeting INDIVIDUAL NEEDS

ENGLISH-LANGUAGE LEARNERS

General Strategies. Assigning group editorials may be more productive if English-language learners are well integrated into groups with English-proficient speakers. To limit confusion for English-language learners, you may want to suggest that only one person in each group do the actual writing, while all members engage in brainstorming and generating ideas.

MULTIPLE INTELLIGENCES

Spatial Intelligence. Students may benefit from the challenge of laying out a newspaper and estimating how much space is needed for articles. Have each student take a page and work collaboratively to find solutions to layout problems. Bring newspapers to class so that students can see examples of layouts.

TECHNOLOGY TIP

Many software programs have newsletter and newspaper templates that may be used for formatting. If available, have students use the feature. It will save them time, instantly show effects of changes they make, and provide them with useful computer experience that is applicable to many "real-world" settings.

Focus on Viewing and Representing   **77**

Critical Thinking

Evaluation. Have pairs of students evaluate the content and design of the completed newspaper. Lead students to devise evaluation questions such as these:

- Is there a variety of news stories about the school and community?
- Does each story answer the *5W-How?* questions?
- Do editorials clearly express opinions that are supported by facts or examples?
- Are the layouts well designed according to the guidelines in **Designing Your Writing?**

When students have finished their evaluations, have them compare them to those done by other teams.

YOUR TURN 12

Discuss classroom rules for collaborative work. Explain that each student is expected to help complete the group's assigned task, is responsible for his or her own behavior, and will take turns, use time wisely, share information and materials willingly, and help another if requested. Share with students your decisions about how you will grade their work.

Wrap It Up

Metacognition. Ask students to reflect on their experience of producing a newspaper by having them answer the following questions:

1. How do you think you performed in your group?
2. Would you have preferred a different task? Why or why not?

Then, ask students this question:

3. How do you support an opinion statement in an editorial? [reasons supported with facts and examples]

Here is an example of one group's drawing of their newspaper's layout.

Front page   **School news**   **Community news**   **Editorials**

- After you have decided on the placement of the articles, you can begin to make the pages of the newspaper. Tape two $8\frac{1}{2}" \times 11"$ pieces of paper together like a book. Fold the taped paper in half to make four pages. Set your newspaper pages aside.

Reference Note
For more on laying out articles in **columns,** see the Computer Tip on page 73.

- On separate pieces of paper, write or type the articles in columns that are two or three inches wide. On an $8\frac{1}{2}" \times 11"$ piece of paper, you can fit three 2-inch columns or two 3-inch columns. You also need to write or type the flag and headlines, and draw or print the images.
- Finally, glue the flag, the articles, the headlines, and the pictures onto the pages of the newspaper.

TIP If a news article is too long to fit within the block you have assigned to it, you can cut the article from the bottom. The least important details are at the end because you arranged them in an inverted pyramid structure.

YOUR TURN 12   Producing a Newspaper

In a group, use the following steps to produce a newspaper.

- First, decide whether the articles you wrote in the Writing Workshop are school news or community news.
- Next, assign some reporters to write editorials and others to draw editorial cartoons. If you need more school or community articles, assign reporters to write them, too.
- Then, use the guidelines in Designing Your Writing on pages 77–78 to design the layout of your newspaper.
- Finally, when your newspaper is complete, place it in your school's library so other students can read it.

Chapter 2   Exposition: Reporting the News

RESOURCES

Your Turn 12
Practice and Reinforcement

- *Media Literacy and Communication Skills —Support and Practice,* Ch. 2, transparencies and worksheets

Focus on Viewing and Representing

Producing a TV News Segment

Watching a news segment on TV can affect you differently than simply reading a newspaper article or listening to a news story on the radio. The visual images that you see on TV can make you feel as if you are witnessing an event firsthand. In this section you and a few classmates will work together to produce a short news segment (around three minutes) that will help others experience the excitement of a news event.

WHAT'S AHEAD?

In this section you will produce a television news segment. You will also learn how to

- recognize the different roles of a television production team
- convert a news article into a script
- perform, record, and evaluate your news segment

Reference Note

For more on **newsworthy characteristics**, see page 59.

Select Your Story

Look over the articles you and your group members wrote for the Writing Workshop. Which one is most newsworthy? Which news article has the greatest potential for interesting visuals? Identify the news article that is both newsworthy and has visual interest, and use it as the story for your news segment.

Choose Your Part

In your group, decide who will play each of the following roles.

- **Producer** The producer coordinates the production and is a link between the camera person and the anchor and reporter. The producer signals the camera person to start and stop taping and points to the anchor or reporter to begin talking. He or she also keeps the cue cards ready for the anchor and reporter to use if they need help with their lines.
- **Camera Person** The camera person is responsible for operating the video camera and taping the news segment.

Focus on Viewing and Representing

OBJECTIVES

- To produce a television news segment
- To recognize the different roles of a TV production team
- To convert a news article into a script
- To perform, record, and evaluate a news segment

Quotation for the Day

"Being specific sometimes involves no more than choosing the right word or phrase."
(Ronald Munson, 1939– , American author and teacher)

Write the quotation on the chalkboard or on an overhead transparency. Ask several students to express it in their own words. Students can also freewrite their answers to this question: How does this idea apply to a TV news segment? [Time constraints force TV newscasters to be very precise.]

TEACHING TIP

Choose Your Part
If you do not have video equipment readily available, consider some of these options for producing a news segment. Contact your local high school staff to see if they have equipment. If you have a community cable channel, contact the station for assistance. Finally, camera stores may lend a rental camera as a community service.

RESOURCES

Focus on Viewing and Representing Practice
- Media Literacy and Communication Skills
  —Support and Practice, Ch. 2
  —A How-to Handbook

Teaching Notes
- Media Literacy and Communication Skills
  —A Teacher's Guide, Ch. 2

Cooperative Learning

Choosing a Part. Groups often have trouble deciding who will participate in a specific role. One way to avoid this problem is to have all students in the class who want to be producers stand in one area of the classroom, camera persons in another, and so on. Then, form groups of four students with a mixture of ability levels and with each role represented.

Critical Thinking

Analysis and Evaluation. Provide students with the opportunity to compare a news article to a news segment on the same subject or event in a class discussion.

Students can compare the presentation of ideas and the points of view by considering these questions: Are events told or shown in the same way and in the same order? Are events included in one story and left out of the other? What attitudes are conveyed in each story?

Students may also evaluate the purposes and effects by asking these questions: What is the purpose of each story? Can news articles and news segments be entertaining, persuasive, and expressive as well as informative? What is the overall effect of each story?

- **Anchor** The anchor introduces the news story and the reporter. The anchor almost always sits behind a desk in the studio. Your group can create a studio by setting up a table or desk and chair in front of a solid-color background.
- **Reporter** The reporter presents the details of the event, usually from the scene where the event occurred. If your group cannot get to the scene, the reporter can sit in the studio. Sometimes the reporter sits beside the anchor. Other times the reporter is located in a different part of the studio. The reporter may also interview people who witnessed or were involved in the event.

Prepare the Script

A script tells what will be *said* and *shown* in the news segment. It consists of two parts, audio and video. The audio part includes the music and words that people will hear in your news segment. The video part shows what people will see as they watch your news segment. Look at the example below.

Video: What Is Seen	Audio: What Is Heard
Shot of the studio with anchor behind desk (Begin taping when music starts.)	Begin music
Move in to a close-up shot of anchor	Fade music
Close-up shot of anchor (Put camera on pause.)	Anchor: Good evening. I'm Fatima Rahman. Tonight we bring you a story about the decision of Main Street Middle School's Principal Reyes to extend the passing period. We go now to our reporter on the scene, Kyle Lucas. Kyle . . .
Close-up shot of reporter outside principal's office (Begin taping when reporter speaks.)	Reporter: Thank you, Fatima. I'm here at Main Street Middle School where today Principal Reyes announced . . .

Your group is now ready to write its own script. To turn the news article you have chosen into a script for the news segment, fold a piece of paper in half to create two columns. Label one column *Video* and the other *Audio*. Then, follow the steps below.

Writing a Script

Step 1	**Write the anchor's dialogue.** In your article's lead, find the answer to the question "Who did what?" The answer will be what the anchor says to introduce the news story. The anchor will also introduce the reporter.
Step 2	**Write the reporter's dialogue.** The reporter will tell the remaining information in the lead and the body of the news article. The reporter will also interview the real people involved in the event or classmates playing the parts. This way, the quotes that are in the article will also be in the news segment.
Step 3	**Write the camera shots.** Next to the dialogue, write the directions for the camera person. The camera person will need to know what images to shoot and when to start and stop taping.
Step 4	**Make cue cards.** Transfer the dialogue to large pieces of poster board. Write in big letters so the anchor and reporter can use the cards for reference.
Step 5	**Decide on hand signals.** The producer will give hand signals to tell the rest of the group when to start and stop. That way, the producer's voice will not be heard on the videotape.

TIP Your group may choose to complete the steps in this chart together, or you may assign specific tasks to different group members.

Practice Your Performance

Practice does make perfect, so you should have several practice sessions before filming your news segment. Time your practices so your group can be sure the segment will not run more than the time your teacher allows.

All for One and One for All Each group member should practice his or her role.

- The **producer** should be familiar with the script so that he or she knows when to use hand signals. He or she should also keep the cue cards ready and in order during taping so the anchor and reporter can use them.

TIP Check with your teacher to see if your school has video equipment. If not, you can perform your news segment live.

TECHNOLOGY TIP

Most computer software programs can generate pages in a table format with columns and gridlines. Students may format their script in columns as shown in the model on p. 80 to help them make changes. To distinguish between the parts for the anchor and reporter, students can use a different type style or font.

Wrap It Up

Metacognition. Ask students to answer the following questions:

1. In the section called Record and Evaluate Your News Segment, you asked three questions. What criteria, or standards, for language and presentation were addressed by each question? [The first question addressed the need for clear, complete details; the second question addressed the need for clear, steady camera shots; and the third question addressed the need for good diction and eye contact.]

2. What other criteria for language and presentation should be met in an effective multimedia presentation? [Answers will vary. Examples include attention-grabbing phrasing and effective pacing.] Apply these additional criteria to your product, draw conclusions about language and presentation (supported by reasons and evidence), and use these conclusions to form a judgment about your overall message.

3. What did the medium itself contribute to the overall message? Think about what would be gained or lost if the message were presented in the print medium.

YOUR TURN 13

Students' news segments should include the following elements:

- a written script that focuses on an interesting event

- well-rehearsed and confident deliveries by the anchor and the reporter (both should look directly into the camera and deliver lines without stumbling)

- smooth camera work by the camera person (little or no blurring or shaking)

TIP Anchors and reporters should dress appropriately. Anchors usually dress professionally, and reporters dress for the scene. For instance, a reporter on location at city hall may wear a suit, but a reporter at a football game may wear jeans.

TIP Good news segments flow smoothly from beginning to end. If you notice long shots of the anchor or reporter without audio, you should retape those parts to improve the flow of your segment.

- The **camera person** should practice using the video recorder. He or she should know how to start, stop, pause, and focus the camera. The camera person should also practice moving in for close-ups and pulling back for long shots.

- The **anchor** and **reporter** should be familiar with their lines so that they depend on cue cards as little as possible. Unless they are interviewing someone, they should practice looking directly into the camera when speaking. The anchor and reporter should speak slowly, clearly, and loudly enough for the microphone to pick up their voices.

All Together, Now Once your group has practiced a few times and feels confident, do one practice run with the camera. As you watch the video, look for errors your group can avoid the next time you tape. For instance, if the camera person notes problems with shaking or blurring, he or she can try to avoid those same mistakes by holding the camera more steady and focusing more carefully. The anchor and reporter can listen for misreadings or quiet voices. The producer can make sure the transitions between shots are smooth.

Record and Evaluate Your News Segment

Now that you have practiced, make a final tape. Follow the instructions in your script to create your news segment.

When taping is complete, evaluate your news segment. How does it look? With your group, watch the video and ask yourselves the following questions about language, medium, and presentation.

- **Language:** Are the details of the event told clearly and completely?
- **Medium:** Do the sounds and images used enhance the written story?
- **Presentation:** Do the anchor and reporter speak clearly and look directly into the camera? Are camera shots steady and focused?

YOUR TURN 13 Producing a TV News Segment

Follow the guidelines beginning on page 79 to produce a TV news segment. When you finish, share it with your classmates.

RESOURCES

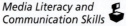

Your Turn 13
Practice and Reinforcement

- *Media Literacy and Communication Skills*
  —*Support and Practice,* Ch. 2, transparencies and worksheets
  —Videocassette 1, Segment B

CHAPTER

 Choices

Choose one of the following activities to complete.

▶ CAREERS

1. Behind the News There are many careers in the field of journalism, such as newspaper reporter, TV reporter, newspaper editor, TV anchor, and TV producer. Research one of these careers to find out the education and training required and the average salary a person in that position would make. You may call your local TV station or newspaper, contact a university, or use the Internet to find information. Use what you learn to write a **report**.

▶ CROSSING THE CURRICULUM: ART

2. Express Yourself Editorial cartoons use pictures and symbols to express opinions about different events. You can create an **editorial cartoon** about a current situation in your school or community. The cartoon should show the event and your opinion about it. Limit the words in your cartoon to the title and, if necessary, brief dialogue between characters.

▶ WRITING

3. What's the Story? Turn your newspaper article into a **short story**. Your story should include everything that your article does—the details of the newsworthy event and the people involved. However, your purpose will be to entertain rather than to inform. Use plenty of descriptive language and action verbs to make the reader feel as if he or she actually witnessed the event.

▶ CROSSING THE CURRICULUM: SCIENCE

4. Tell Me Why Write a brief **article** that answers a frequently asked *why* question about science. Begin the article with a question, such as "Why do people get the hiccups?" or "Why do leaves change colors and fall in autumn?" Then, do enough research to answer the question. Ask your science teacher to help you find the most up-to-date material. Submit your article to a class or school newspaper.

PORTFOLIO

▶ CAREERS

Consider having students write reports of 500–700 words. Students should plan their reports by first outlining the introduction, body, and conclusion. For each part, students can write questions they hope to answer with their research. Discuss appropriate resources. [library, school guidance counselor, government employment information publications, Web sites, and people in the community] *If students use the Internet, they should know that Internet resources are sometimes public forums and their content may be unreliable.*

▶ WRITING

Explain to students that writers often start with real events and transform them into fictional stories. To get students thinking about how to change a news story into a short story, select **A Writer's Model** to use as an example. With the students, start to compose orally a short story about Morgan Sykes and her efforts. Write the following tips on the chalkboard for students to refer to as they write: Use your imagination to create a major character, create a problem or conflict for that character, choose a point of view, visualize the scenes, use sensory language in descriptions, and add additional details, characters, and dialogue.

▶ CROSSING THE CURRICULUM: SCIENCE

To guide students in selecting a *why* question, brainstorm ideas with the students or have them give you several questions on a piece of paper. Help students narrow their topics to something they can cover in 500–700 words.

RESOURCES

Reporting the News
Assessment
- *Assessment Package*
  —*Chapter Tests*, Ch. 2
  —*Chapter Tests in Standardized Test Formats*, Ch. 2
  —*Assessment Alternatives*, Ch. 2
- *Test Generator*
  (One-Stop Planner CD-ROM)

Choices
Rubrics
- *Assessment Package*
  —*Assessment Alternatives*, Ch. 2

CHAPTER PLANNING GUIDE

CHAPTER 3

Explaining How

Use this guide to create an instructional plan that suits the individual needs of your students. Assignments marked by an asterisk (*) may be completed out of class. Times given for pacing lessons are estimated. See pp. 84–85 for chapter-wide resources. Resources listed in this guide are point-of-use resources only.

Curriculum Connections

Connections to Literature *pp. 109–111*
- Writing a Descriptive Paragraph

Choices *p. 117*
- Crossing the Curriculum: Science
- Crossing the Curriculum: Speech
- Writing

GO TO: go.hrw.com
KEYWORD: EOLang 6-3

 All resources for this chapter are available for preview on the *One-Stop Planner CD-ROM with Test Generator*. All worksheets and tests may be printed from the CD-ROM.

		Chapter Opener *pp. 84–85*	**Reading Workshop:** **Reading a "How-to" Article** *pp. 86–93*
DEVELOPMENTAL PROGRAM		⏱ **20 minutes** • Your Turn 1 *p. 85*	⏱ **90 minutes** • Preparing to Read *p. 86* • Making Predictions *pp. 87–88* • Reading Selection *pp. 89–90* • First Thoughts in groups *p. 91* • Forming Mental Images *p. 91* • Your Turn 2 *p. 91* • Test Taking Mini-Lesson *p. 93*
CORE PROGRAM		⏱ **15 minutes** • Your Turn 1 *p. 85*	⏱ **75 minutes** • Preparing to Read *p. 86* • Making Predictions *pp. 87–88* • Reading Selection *pp. 89–90* • First Thoughts *p. 91* • Forming Mental Images *p. 91* • Your Turn 2 *p. 91* • Vocabulary Mini-Lesson *p. 92* • Test Taking Mini-Lesson *p. 93*
ADVANCED PROGRAM		⏱ **15 minutes** • Your Turn 1 *p. 85*	⏱ **60 minutes** • Preparing to Read *p. 86* • Making Predictions *pp. 87–88* • Reading Selection *pp. 89–90* • First Thoughts *p. 91* • Forming Mental Images *p. 91* • Your Turn 2 *p. 91* • Vocabulary Mini-Lesson *p. 92*
RESOURCES	**PRINT**	• *Communications,* TP. 24, WS. p. 48	• *Alternative Readings,* Ch. 3 • *Communications,* TP. 25 WS. pp. 49–54
	MEDIA	• *One-Stop Planner* *CD-ROM*	• *One-Stop Planner CD-ROM*

TP.=Transparency   WS.=Worksheet

Writing Workshop: Writing a "How-to" Paper *pp. 94–111*	**Focus on Viewing and Listening: Viewing and Listening to Learn** *pp. 112–116*
240 minutes • Choose a Topic *pp. 94–95* • Purpose and Audience; Your Turn 3 *pp. 95–96* • Plan Your Paper; Your Turn 4 *p. 96* • Writing Mini-Lesson *p. 97* • Framework; Your Turn 5* *p. 98* • Writer's Model and Student's Model *pp. 99–102* • Evaluate and Revise *pp. 103–104* • Focus on Sentences in groups *p. 105* • Your Turn 6 *p. 105* • Proofread, Publish, and Reflect on Your Paper *pp. 106–107* • Grammar Link *p. 106* • Your Turn 7 *p. 107* • Test Taking Mini-Lesson *p. 108*	**60 minutes** • Charts and Graphics *pp. 112–113* • Your Turn 9 *p. 113* • Computer Software *p. 114* • Your Turn 10 *p. 115* • TV and Video *pp. 115–116* • Your Turn 11* *p. 116*
160 minutes • Choose a Topic *pp. 94–95* • Purpose and Audience; Your Turn 3 *pp. 95–96* • Plan Your Paper; Your Turn 4 *p. 96* • Writing Mini-Lesson *p. 97* • Framework; Your Turn 5* *p. 98* • Writer's Model and Student's Model *pp. 99–102* • Evaluate and Revise *pp. 103–104* • Focus on Sentences *p. 105* • Your Turn 6* *p. 105* • Proofread, Publish, and Reflect on Your Paper *pp. 106–107* • Grammar Link *p. 106* • Your Turn 7 *p. 107* • Test Taking Mini-Lesson *p. 108* • Connections to Literature; Your Turn 8* *pp. 109–111*	**45 minutes** • Charts and Graphics *pp. 112–113* • Your Turn 9 *p. 113* • Computer Software *p. 114* • Your Turn 10 *p. 115* • TV and Video *pp. 115–116* • Your Turn 11* *p. 116*
100 minutes • Choose a Topic *pp. 94–95* • Purpose and Audience; Your Turn 3 *pp. 95–96* • Plan Your Paper; Your Turn 4 *p. 96* • Framework; Your Turn 5* *p. 98* • Writer's Model *pp. 99–100* • Designing Your Writing *p. 101* • Evaluate and Revise *pp. 103–104* • Your Turn 6* *p. 105* • Proofread, Publish, and Reflect on Your Paper *pp. 106–107* • Grammar Link *p. 106* • Your Turn 7 *p. 107* • Connections to Literature; Your Turn 8* *pp. 109–111*	**45 minutes** • Charts and Graphics *pp. 112–113* • Your Turn 9 *p. 113* • Computer Software *p. 114* • Your Turn 10 *p. 115* • TV and Video *pp. 115–116* • Your Turn 11* *p. 116*
• *Communications,* TPs. 26–30, WS. pp. 55–66 • *Designing Your Writing*	• *Media Literacy and Communication Skills* —*Support and Practice,* Ch. 3 —*A How-to Handbook* —*A Teacher's Guide,* Ch. 3
• *One-Stop Planner CD-ROM*	• *Media Literacy and Communication Skills* —Videocassette 1, Segment C • *One-Stop Planner CD-ROM*

CHAPTER PLANNING GUIDE

CHAPTER 3

Explaining How

CHAPTER OBJECTIVES

- To read a "how-to" article and learn how to make predictions and form mental pictures from specific language
- To write a "how-to" paper
- To learn how to do or make something from graphics, computer software, TV, and videos

Chapter Overview

Clear explanations of processes help people understand how things operate in the world. In this chapter, students will examine "how-to" explanations and share what they know by writing their own. The Reading Workshop (pp. 86–93) provides a "how-to" article for students to analyze for its use of specific language. The Writing Workshop (pp. 94–111) guides students through the steps of the writing process as they write their own "how-to" papers. The Focus on Viewing and Listening shows students how to follow instructions presented in a variety of formats. While the sections of the chapter can be taught independently, they also work together to help give students an in-depth look at how exposition and visual devices are used to explain a process.

Why Study "How-to" Explanations?

Understanding how to follow and describe processes can help students better navigate their worlds as they daily follow processes at school and at home. Studying "how-to" explanations can help students follow instructions that they read or view independently, and also help them learn how to give instructions that enable others to follow a process.

Teaching the Chapter

Option 1: Begin with Literature

If literature is the main focus of your curriculum, you might introduce this chapter after studying fiction and biographical selections in which authors use exposition to explain processes. Emphasize that authors use time order and specific language—numbers, descriptive words, exact verbs, comparisons, and transitions—to clarify the steps in processes. Then, have students read the article in this chapter and point out the way the author uses chronological order and specific language. Once they have read and analyzed process writing in fiction and nonfiction, students will be ready to write their own "how-to" papers.

Option 2: Begin with Nonfiction and Writing

You can begin with the materials in this chapter to familiarize students with expository writing that explains a process. The article in the Reading Workshop (pp. 89–90) can help students understand the way authors use exposition to explain how to do or make something. Then, by writing a "how-to" paper in the Writing Workshop (pp. 94–111), students will be better able to follow or to give instructions. When they return to literature, students may be better prepared to identify and analyze explanations of processes in literature. See also **Connections to Literature** on pp. 109–111.

Making Connections

▪ To the Literature Curriculum

Explain to students that writers use specific language to help readers "see" the processes that they are explaining. For example, the descriptive words in an excerpt from *Volcano* by Patricia Lauber can help clarify ideas or help students visualize something.

Lesson Idea: Specific Language in the Excerpt from *Volcano* by Patricia Lauber

1. Explain these kinds of specific language: *numbers, descriptive words, exact verbs, comparisons,* and *transitions*. Help students identify examples of each.

2. After students read the excerpt from *Volcano,* have them locate in it examples of specific language. Tell students to list in a chart like the one below examples of each type of specific language that they find.

Specific Language
Numbers "8:32 A.M." "212 degrees Fahrenheit"
Descriptive Words "bowl-shaped crater" "fan-shaped area of destruction"
Exact Verbs "flattened" "uprooted"
Comparisons ". . . Mount St. Helens was like a giant pressure cooker." "Ash fell like snow that would not melt."
Transitions "meanwhile" "then"

3. Next, ask students to think about how these examples of specific language help them visualize as they read. Have them discuss why they think writers might use specific language to explain a process. [It helps readers follow the steps.]

4. After discussion, introduce students to the article in this chapter (pp. 89–90) and ask them to identify several examples of specific language. Point out that both the article and the excerpt are works of nonfiction in which the use of specific language can help readers form mental images of a process.

▪ To Careers

Tell students that knowing how to follow instructions and how to give clear directions are essential skills in the workplace. Invite speakers who work in a variety of fields, such as construction, food service, medicine, or law enforcement, to speak to your class about processes they use every day and about the instructions they give others.

▪ To the Community

In this chapter, students will focus on following and giving instructions. Have partners create a set of directions that explains how to get from one place to another in their community. Tell them to organize the directions in spatial order and to use specific language to describe landmarks, geographical directions, and distance. Ask partners to draw a map to accompany their directions.

▪ To the Health Curriculum

Have students working in small groups choose an emergency, such as a burn, a nosebleed, or a type of injury associated with your geographic area, such as frostbite or snakebite. Then, have each group find the first-aid process for the emergency they selected. Students might search in health textbooks, Red Cross manuals, or scout handbooks. Allow time for groups to explain the steps in the first-aid process to the class.

CHAPTER 3

CHAPTER 3 Explaining How

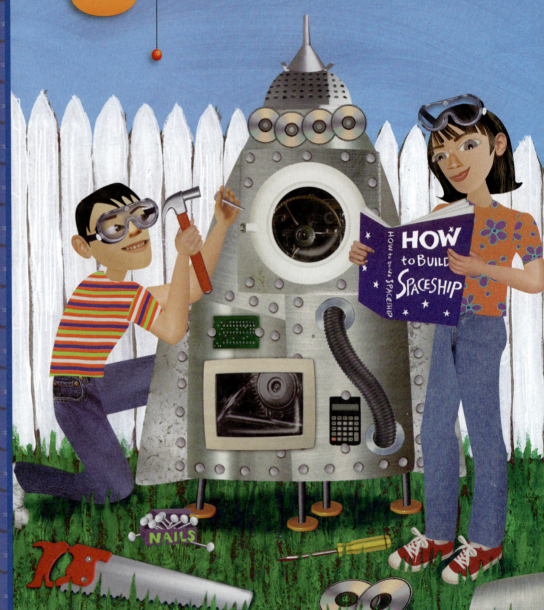

PREVIEWING THE CHAPTER

- The three workshops in this chapter focus on explaining how to complete a process. The workshops can be taught separately, but they also work together to help students read, write, view, and listen to instructions more effectively. Reading and analyzing a "how-to" article can help prepare students to write their own "how-to" papers. After reading and writing "how-to" explanations, students may be better able to follow directions as they are viewing and listening. For help in integrating this chapter with grammar, usage, and mechanics chapters, see pp. T297A–T297B.

INTRODUCING THE CHAPTER

To introduce the chapter, use the Journal Warm-up, Transparency 24, in *Communications*.

VIEWING THE ILLUSTRATION

- Help students notice the contrast of realistic details, such as the compact discs, calculator, and book, with the fantasy detail (the spaceship) in the illustration. Also, note the contrast of dark colors (red, blue, green, and black) with white, silver, and pink. Finally, explain that the illustration reflects the focus of the chapter, a "how-to" process—building a spaceship.

Representing. Have students sketch a design of a machine or other invention constructed of ordinary items. Students might explain how it works to the class.

CHAPTER RESOURCES

Planning
- *Lesson Planner, ELL Strategies*, Ch. 3
- Block Scheduling, p. T83A (this book)
- *One-Stop Planner* CD-ROM

Practice
- *Communications*, Ch. 3
- *Writer's Workshop 1* CD-ROM

- Media Literacy and Communication Skills

Extension
- *Designing Your Writing*

Reinforcement
- *Communications*, Ch. 3

PREVIEW

Reading Workshop

Reading a "How-to" Article
PAGE 86

Writing Workshop

Writing a "How-to" Paper
PAGE 94

Focus on Viewing and Listening

Viewing and Listening to Learn
PAGE 112

Here is a riddle for you: How are you and a computer alike? Computers follow a set of instructions to perform a function, and so do you. Think about it. In math class, for instance, your teacher tells you how to turn an improper fraction into a mixed number. This evening, you may heat up a frozen dinner by following the instructions on the box. The instructions you listen to, view, and read are all designed to teach you to complete a process.

Once you know how a process is done, you can share that information by giving instructions. Whether you share instructions orally, in writing, or through a demonstration, your goal is still the same: to teach others what you know.

GO TO. go.hrw.com
KEYWORD: EOLang 6-3

YOUR TURN 1 — Examining a Process

Find an example of instructions for how to do or how to make something. Share your example with a partner and discuss the following questions.

- Do the instructions tell you how to do something or how to make something? What process do they explain?
- Do you think you could follow the instructions? Why or why not?

Reading Workshop

OBJECTIVES

- To read a "how-to" article in preparation for writing a "how-to" paper
- To make predictions
- To form mental images from specific language
- To discover the meanings of compound words

Quotation for the Day

"So before writing, learn to think."

(Nicolas Boileau-Despréaux, 1636–1711, French critic and poet)

Write the quotation on the chalkboard and ask students to consider how the quotation applies to a writer who explains a process in a "how-to" article. Guide students to understand how first thinking through a process and visualizing each of the steps might help a writer compose a clear and complete "how-to" explanation.

TEACHING TIP

Preparing to Read
The material on this page introduces two concepts, forming mental images and making predictions. These concepts will be the instructional focus of the Reading Workshop. Instruction on making predictions appears on pp. 87–88. Forming mental images will be taught in greater depth on p. 91. The Reading Selection, **"Making a Flying Fish,"** will provide students with an opportunity to apply what they learn about both concepts.

Reading Workshop

Reading a "How-to" Article

WHAT'S AHEAD?

In this section, you will read a "how-to" article. You will also learn how to

- make predictions
- form mental images from specific language

Holidays are a special time for families and friends to gather together and celebrate. Holidays are also a great time to do fun activities. Maybe you have made a card for Valentine's Day, planned a picnic for the Fourth of July, or planted a tree for Earth Day. You will read about one of these activities on the following pages. You will also read about a holiday activity that children take part in halfway around the world. Every May fifth, Japanese children make windsocks called *koinobori* (koi•nō´bô•ri) to hang outside their homes to celebrate Children's Day. The instructions for making *koinobori* appear in "Making a Flying Fish" on page 89.

Preparing to Read

READING SKILL

Making Predictions   A **prediction** is a guess you make about what will happen next. As you read instructions, you may predict what you will do with the supplies that are listed, what the outcome of a step will be, or what the final product will look like. Predictions give you a purpose for reading. You can find out whether your prediction is right by reading further and finding out what happens.

READING FOCUS

Forming Mental Images   Writers of "how-to" articles use **specific language** to name and describe the parts and the activities involved in a process. As you read the "how-to" article on page 89, look for words and phrases that create a picture in your mind of the steps for making a windsock.

86   Chapter 3   **Exposition:** Explaining How

RESOURCES

Reading Workshop Reinforcement
- *Alternative Readings*, Ch. 3

Making Predictions

READING SKILL

I Wonder What Will Happen As you enter your math class, you see that you have a substitute teacher. You go to your seat, get out your review, and begin studying for the test you are about to take. After the bell rings, the substitute announces that the test has been canceled for today. Your friend will have the same substitute teacher later that day, so you go to tell her that her test will be canceled, too. How do you think she will react to the news that the test has been canceled? What if you find out your friend spent four hours studying last night? Now, what do you think her reaction will be? Has your prediction changed?

In life, you are constantly making predictions and adjusting them. For instance, your mind may follow this pattern:

1. what you know	There is no math test today.
2. your prediction	My friend will be happy.
3. new information	My friend studied for four hours.
4. adjusted prediction	My friend will not be happy.

Your mind also makes predictions when you read. The flowchart below shows what your mind is doing as you make a prediction.

Your mind . . .

takes what you already know about the subject → adds information from your reading → forms a prediction that makes sense

As you read on, your mind . . .

checks to see that your prediction is right **or** corrects your prediction using new information

---

Meeting INDIVIDUAL NEEDS

LEARNERS HAVING DIFFICULTY
Students who are having difficulty making predictions may find that filling in the flowchart on this page will help them organize their thoughts. Have students copy the flowchart onto a piece of paper, labeling the ovals *What I already know; New information from reading; My prediction for the next step.* Suggest that they jot down on a piece of paper new information in the first paragraph of what they are reading before filling in the chart. Guide them to use what they wrote in the first two ovals to make a logical prediction before reading further.

Try making a prediction now. The following paragraph is from a set of "how-to" instructions for an Earth Day activity. Read the list of materials and steps. Think about what you already know about the subject. Then, make a prediction about what you think the next step will be. If you need help, use the steps in the Thinking It Through below the instructions.

> To plant a tree, you should gather the following materials: tree, shovel, mulch, and a watering can. First, dig a hole twice as deep as the tree's container. The hole should also be twice as wide as the container. Second, remove the container and place the tree in the hole. Then, using the same soil you removed, fill the hole. When the hole is completely filled, apply a two-inch layer of mulch around the base of the tree.

THINKING IT THROUGH: Making Predictions

▶ **STEP 1** Read a part of the passage. Ask yourself, "What is the passage explaining or telling?"

The passage is telling me how to plant a tree.

▶ **STEP 2** Consider the information you have just read. Ask yourself these questions:
- "Does the information remind me of anything?"
- "What do I already know about this information?"

The information reminds me of the time when I helped my mom plant a tree in our backyard. I already know about the materials because we used the same materials.

▶ **STEP 3** Use what you already know, plus clues from the passage, to make a guess about what will happen next.

I have already been told to plant the tree, but I haven't been told to use the watering can yet. I think the next step will tell me to water the tree.

Chapter 3   Exposition: Explaining How

READING PROCESS

PREREADING
Build Background. Tell students that knowing some background information that relates to the Reading Selection can help them better understand the new information they pick up as they read. Explain that they will be reading about how to make the flying carp streamers that are part of the annual celebration of Children's Day in Japan. The carp design, which appeared in

Exposition: Explaining How

Read the following article. In a notebook, write down the answers to the numbered active-reading questions in the shaded boxes. If necessary, use the Thinking It Through steps on page 88 for the questions that ask you to make a prediction. The underlined words will be used in the Vocabulary Mini-Lesson on page 92.

Making a Flying Fish

by Paula Morrow
from FACES

Japanese boys and girls have their own special day each year on May 5. It is called Children's Day and is a national holiday. This is a time for families to celebrate having children by telling stories, feasting, going on picnics, or visiting grandparents. . . .

A special feature of Children's Day is the *koinobori* (koi•nō´bô•ri) that families display in their yards—one for each child in the family. A tall pole is placed in the garden. . . . Fish made of cloth or strong paper are attached to the pole. Each fish has a hoop in its mouth to catch the wind. The largest fish is for the oldest child, and the smallest is for the youngest.

These fish represent a kind of carp known as a strong fighter. These carp battle their way upstream against strong currents. When the *koinobori* dance in the wind, they remind the children of carp leaping up a waterfall. This is

1. Based on this paragraph, predict what materials might be discussed later in the selection.

the seventeenth century, can be traced to a Chinese legend in which a carp that could successfully swim up a waterfall turns into a dragon. Because a dragon is considered a god in Japan, a carp came to be thought of as a symbol of success. By flying carp streamers in the sky, Japanese parents wish their children success in the future.

Active-Reading Questions
The purpose of the active-reading questions is to encourage students to make predictions about what will happen next in the article and to form mental images to help them picture the steps in a process. Use students' answers as an informal assessment of their understanding of both concepts. You may want to have students write their answers to the active-reading questions in a learning log. Possible answers follow.

ANSWERS

1. Students may predict that the following materials will be discussed later in the selection: "a tall pole," "cloth or strong paper," "a hoop."

Active-Reading Questions
ANSWERS continued

2. Students may predict that they could use the needle and thread to sew the material.

3. Students may predict that the fabric "sleeve" will be used for the body of the fish.

4. Students may say that they know the fringe will be 5 inches long because the author instructs them to "make cuts 5 inches deep."

5. Students may say that the word "Finally" signals the last step in the process.

Meeting INDIVIDUAL NEEDS

MULTIPLE INTELLIGENCES

Linguistic Intelligence. To help students understand the difference between vague and specific words, you might generate an example on the chalkboard like the following.

Vague Verbs	Specific Verbs
spoke	shouted
walked	strolled
threw	hurled

Vague Adjectives	Specific Adjectives
good	delicious
sad	crushed
ugly	hideous

Vague Nouns	Specific Nouns
vegetable	cabbage
color	violet
planet	Venus

RESOURCES

Your Turn 2
Practice
- *Communications,* WS. p. 49

Reinforcement
- *Communications,* TP. 25, WS. p. 50

---

supposed to inspire children to be equally brave and strong.

You can make your own *koinobori* and fly it from a pole or hang it from your window on May 5. In that way, you can share Children's Day with the boys and girls of Japan.

You need an 18- by 30-inch piece of lightweight cloth (cotton, rayon, or nylon), felt-tip markers, a needle and thread, scissors, a narrow plastic headband, and string.

> **2. Make a prediction about what you might do with the needle and thread based on this paragraph.**

First, choose a piece of cloth with a bright, colorful pattern or decorate it yourself with felt-tip markers. Fold the fabric in half lengthwise, with the bright side on the inside. Sew a seam ½ inch from the long (30-inch) edge, making a sleeve.

> **3. What do you predict the "sleeve" will be used for?**

On one end of the sleeve, make a 1-inch-wide hem by turning the right side of the fabric over the wrong side. Then, sew the hem, leaving three 1-inch-wide openings about 5 inches apart.

Make cuts 5 inches deep and 1 inch apart all around the unhemmed end of the sleeve to form a fringe. This is the fish's tail.

> **4. How do you know how long the fringe will be?**

Next, turn the sleeve right side out. With . . . a felt-tip marker, add eyes near the hemmed (head) end (away from the fringed tail).

Thread the narrow plastic headband into the hem through one of the openings. Continue threading it until the open part of the headband is hidden.

Then, tie a 12-inch-long piece of string to the headband at each of the three openings. Tie the loose ends of the strings together.

Finally, hang your windsock from the strings on a tree limb, a clothes pole, or the eaves of your house. On windy days, it will dance like a carp swimming upstream against a waterfall!

> **5. What word lets you know this is the last step?**

one-inch opening · Sleeve · one-inch hem · right side of fabric · wrong side of fabric

90 Chapter 3 **Exposition:** Explaining How

READING PROCESS

READING
Make Personal Connections. Tell students that they can deepen their understanding about what they read by relating their own personal experiences to the information in a selection. As students read "Making a Flying Fish," have them relate the Japanese tradition of making *koinobori* to celebrate Children's Day to holiday processes familiar to them, such as making holiday decorations or preparing a special Thanksgiving dish.

First Thoughts on Your Reading

1. Could you picture the steps for making a *koinobori*? Why or why not?
2. Were your predictions about the materials, the needle and thread, and the "sleeve" correct? If not, identify the information in the selection that helped you adjust your predictions.

Forming Mental Images

It's All in Your Head Pictures in your first books probably helped you understand the words. Even though the books you read today may lack pictures, you can create your own **mental images**—pictures in your mind—using the words on a page.

Most writers of "how-to" instructions know that they should use specific language to describe a process. As a reader, you can use these specific words and phrases to come up with a mental image.

The chart below gives examples of different kinds of specific language. As you read, think about how these examples help a reader *visualize*, or create a mental picture of, a process.

 READING FOCUS

TIP Drawing the instructions you read will help you understand a process better. Drawing can make it easier to picture a process. What do you picture when you read, "Turn the poster over and shake gently to remove any excess glitter"? Is it something like this?

Specific Language	Examples
Numbers	12 x 15 inches, 3 pieces, 450 degrees
Descriptive Words	small circle, large piece of fabric, hollow pipe
Exact Verbs	fold, turn, hang, sprinkle, twist
Comparisons	sew cloth like a sleeve, fold like a hot dog bun
Transitions	after, first, next, finally; above, below, behind, into

YOUR TURN 2 Forming a Mental Image

Find examples of specific language in the selection on pages 89–90. Choose one example and draw a picture of what you see in your mind. Share your drawing with a classmate who drew the same example and discuss the similarities and differences.

Reading Workshop **91**

First Thoughts on Your Reading
ANSWERS
Possible responses are given below.

1. Some students may say that the author's detailed, step-by-step instructions made picturing the steps easy. Others may have needed diagrams or pictures to visualize the steps.
2. Some students will say they made correct predictions. If students needed to correct their predictions, ask them to describe what clues the author provided after they made a prediction.

Wrap It Up

Metacognition. Ask students to reflect on their reading processes by answering the following questions.

1. Which step in this "how-to" article did you find most difficult to understand? Why?

Then, ask the following question.

2. How do readers form predictions? [They take what they already know about a subject and add information from the reading.]

YOUR TURN 2
ANSWERS
Here are examples of specific language from the Reading Selection.

"18- by 30-inch piece,"
"bright, colorful pattern,"
"fold," "sew,"
"dance like a carp swimming upstream,"
"first," "next," "finally"

READING PROCESS

EXTENDING
Connect to the World. Tell students that connecting what they have read to something in the world outside the classroom can make their reading more meaningful. After they have read the selection on pp. 89–90, have students use the resources of the school or public library to research a process that is followed during a celebration in another culture. Have students share their findings with the class.

Reading Workshop **91**

MINI-LESSON: VOCABULARY

Compound Words

ANSWERS
Possible responses follow.
1. *Felt-tip* breaks down to *felt* and *tip*. *Felt* is a fabric of wool. *Tip* means "point or end." A felt-tip marker must have a point made of fabric. "You need . . . *fabric-pointed* markers" makes sense.
2. *Headband* breaks down to *head* and *band*. The *head* is the part of the body above the neck. A *band* is a ring of material that encircles. A headband must be a ring of material that encircles the head. "Thread the narrow plastic *ring of material that encircles the head* into the hem" makes sense.
3. The two parts of *windsock* are *wind* and *sock*. A windsock could be an object that looks like a sock and tells something about the wind. "Finally, hang your *object that looks like a sock and tells something about the wind* from the strings on a tree limb" makes sense.
4. *Upstream* breaks down to *up* (the direction) and *stream* ("a current of water"). Upstream must mean going up or against the flow of water. "It will dance like a carp swimming *against the flow of water*" makes sense.
5. *Waterfall* breaks down to *water* and *fall*. *Water* is the liquid of rivers and streams. *Fall* means "to drop." A waterfall must mean liquid that drops down. "It will dance like a carp swimming upstream against *liquid that drops down*" makes sense.

Taking a Second Look

Compound Words. Emphasize context instead of word parts. Tell students that a word's context is formed by the words that surround it. Explain that context often provides clues to an unfamiliar word's meaning. Then, have students use context clues to determine the meanings of the words in **Practice**.

MINI-LESSON: VOCABULARY

Compound Words

As you read a "how-to" article, you may find words that are unfamiliar to you. Some of these unfamiliar words may be *compound words*. **Compound words** are formed by putting together two or more words to make a new word. A compound word might be written as one word, as separate words, or as a hyphenated word.

Examples: roadrunner
free fall
ice-skating
hand-me-down

THINKING IT THROUGH
Discovering the Meanings of Compound Words

Here is one example of a compound word from "Making a Flying Fish":

You need an 18- by 30-inch piece of lightweight cloth.

▶ **STEP 1** Break the compound word down into its parts.

Lightweight breaks down to light and weight.

▶ **STEP 2** Define each of the parts.

The word light means "not very heavy." Weight means "how much something weighs."

▶ **STEP 3** Use the definitions of the parts to come up with a full definition.

Lightweight must mean "not weighing very much."

▶ **STEP 4** Check that your definition makes sense by inserting the definition for the compound word into the sentence.

"You need an 18- by 30-inch piece of not weighing very much cloth." The definition makes sense to me.

PRACTICE

Define the meanings of the following compound words by using the steps in the Thinking It Through above. The words are underlined in "Making a Flying Fish."

1. felt-tip (page 90)
2. headband (page 90)
3. windsock (page 90)
4. upstream (page 90)
5. waterfall (page 90)

92   Chapter 3   Exposition: Explaining How

RESOURCES

Vocabulary
Practice
■ *Communications*, WS. p. 51

Test Taking
Practice
■ *Communications*, WS. pp. 52–54

MINI-LESSON: TEST TAKING

Making Predictions

Some reading tests may ask you to make predictions. Read the following passage and question. How would you answer the question?

> Several Mexican holidays are celebrated in the United States. One is Cinco de Mayo. Cinco de Mayo is a national holiday in Mexico. On May 5, 1862, a small group of Mexican patriots defeated an invasion by the French army in Puebla, Mexico. Today, Cinco de Mayo is recognized as a celebration of not only that victory but also of Mexican culture.

Based on the information in this paragraph, what might the next paragraph be about?

A. how the French invaded Mexico
B. other Mexican victories
C. how Cinco de Mayo is celebrated
D. French holidays

THINKING IT THROUGH — Making Predictions

▶ **STEP 1** Read the passage and the question. Try to answer the question in your own words.

▶ **STEP 2** Look for an answer choice that closely matches your own.

▶ **STEP 3** If no answer choice matches your prediction exactly, look at each answer choice and ask,
- "Does the choice make sense?"
- "Is this choice supported by information in the passage?" If you cannot support the choice, then it is not the correct one.

If you answer "yes" to both questions, you may have found the right answer.

I think the next paragraph will talk more about other Mexican holidays.

The answer choices don't really say the same thing as my prediction, so I will go to the next step.

A—The author has already told me how the French invaded Mexico.

B—The author does not mention other Mexican victories.

C—The passage says that Cinco de Mayo is celebrated to honor Mexican culture. The author could discuss how it is celebrated.

D—The passage is talking about a Mexican holiday, not French holidays.

I think the correct answer is C.

Looking Ahead to Writing

In the Writing Workshop on pp. 94–111, students will be asked to write their own "how-to" papers using specific language to explain how to make something. As they work on their drafts, suggest that they refer to the examples of different kinds of specific language in the chart on p. 91 of the Reading Workshop.

TEACHING TIP

Making Predictions
Model the think-aloud process for your students by following the steps in **Thinking It Through** to arrive at the correct answer to the sample question.

Writing Workshop

OBJECTIVES

- To use the writing process to write a "how-to" paper
- To create a time line
- To elaborate ideas with specific language
- To use transitional words
- To use commas in a series

Quotation for the Day

"We are wiser than we know."

(Ralph Waldo Emerson, 1803–1882, American author)

Write the quotation on the chalkboard and use it to initiate a discussion about skills students have but may not recognize. Point out to students that every day they do things that require several steps to complete, yet the process has become automatic. Tell students that they will be choosing a process that they have knowledge about and breaking it down into steps for the purpose of instructing others.

Cooperative Learning

Products List. To help your students generate ideas for "how-to" products, divide the class into randomly assigned small groups. Give each group a large piece of paper and a few colored markers. Ask each group member to contribute at least three products to a list of possible writing topics, using the list of questions on this page as a springboard. Then, have groups display their lists at the front of the room for all class members to refer to when choosing a topic.

Writing Workshop

WHAT'S AHEAD?

In this workshop you will write a "how-to" paper. You will also learn how to

- create a time line
- elaborate ideas with specific language
- use transitional words
- use commas in a series

Writing a "How-to" Paper

"Mmm, mmm. No one makes a smoothie as well as you do!" Everyone knows how to make something, whether it is a simple product such as a delicious fruit smoothie or a more complicated one such as a two-level treehouse. Whether the process is easy or difficult, making things takes knowledge and talent. What special skills do you have?

In this workshop you will have an opportunity to share your knowledge with others by writing a "how-to" paper. You will use specific details and **transitional words,** words that connect one idea to another, to give exact instructions for making a product.

Prewriting

Choose a Topic

I Know, I Know Follow the rule successful writers live by: *Write about what you know.* Brainstorm a list of products that you have successfully made before. Consider the following questions.

- Look around your house. What have you built or made?
- What school projects have you made in the past?
- What is your favorite recipe to make?

How Do I Decide? Once you have listed several products, you will need to evaluate them to choose the best one to write about. The chart on the next page shows how one student decided on one of three topics by asking questions about each topic.

Topic	Have I made this product before, and do I know the process well?	Does this process have a manageable number of steps (between three and five)?
Paper swan	yes	no—it has over five steps
Snowman decoration ✓	yes	yes—it has about five steps
Soapbox car	not really—I helped my big brother make it	no—this probably takes more than five steps

After evaluating each of his topics, the student whose chart appears above chose the topic that had the most *yes* answers. His "how-to" paper will tell others how to make a snowman decoration.

Think About Purpose and Audience

Show Some Consideration Your friend teaches you a great magic trick. You amaze your little brother with the trick, and he begs you to teach it to him. After you explain it twice, your brother is still confused. Obviously, you need to explain the trick to him in a different way.

Your purpose for writing instructions is to teach someone how to make something. That person could be a teacher, a friend, or even a young child. Before you begin to write, you should consider what information your audience will need. To do that, use the steps in the Thinking It Through below.

KEY CONCEPT

Considering Your Audience

STEP 1 Identify your audience.

My audience will be fourth-graders.

STEP 2 What words should you define so your audience can understand the process?

The snowman decoration has a muffler. Fourth-graders may not know that a muffler is a scarf.

STEP 3 Ask yourself, "What steps caused me trouble?" How can you make those steps clearer?

I had a problem keeping the sequin eyes in place. I used straight pins to hold them until the glue dried.

TIP Not only do you have a speaking voice, you also have a writing voice. Your writing **voice** shows the attitude you have about a topic. Since you are writing instructions, use a clear, straightforward voice. To do that, leave out information that may distract the reader from the steps you are trying to explain. Get right to the point and focus on the instructions.

YOUR TURN 3

To help you assess students' choices of topic and audience, have students write the following information on a sheet of paper: their "how-to" topic and the audience for their paper; at least two unfamiliar words related to the process and their definitions; and at least one step in the process that could confuse readers and its clear explanation.

Meeting INDIVIDUAL NEEDS

MULTIPLE INTELLIGENCES
Logical-Mathematical Intelligence. Some students may prefer to first write out each step on a separate note card before ordering their steps on a time line. Students can then experiment with the order of the cards until they appear to be in a logical and reasonable sequence. It may be helpful for students to work with a classmate and read the steps out loud. Once students are satisfied with the order, ask them to write the steps of the process on their time lines.

YOUR TURN 4

For assessment, check that students' time lines list three to five steps in the order in which they must be performed, omitting any distracting steps. Also, make sure their lists of materials are complete, accurate, and clear.

YOUR TURN 3 — Choosing a Topic and Thinking About Your Audience

Brainstorm a list of products that you have made. Then, make a chart like the one on page 95 and evaluate each product as a possible topic for your "how-to" paper. Choose the product that has the most "yes" answers in the chart.

Once you have a topic, choose an audience. Then, think about the information your audience will need by completing the steps in the Thinking It Through on page 95.

Plan Your Instructions

As Easy as 1, 2, 3 Imagine the frustration of trying to build a model car if the instructions described painting the model before the car was even put together. **Putting steps in the correct order makes the process easier to understand.** Most "how-to" papers are written in **chronological order,** or time order.

One way to think of the steps in chronological order is to imagine yourself making the product. As you perform each step, write it on a time line, recording the **progression,** or order, of the process. Then, look over your steps and add anything you left out.

KEY CONCEPT

TIP Look over your time line for steps that may distract the reader. Ask yourself, "Does my audience already know how to do this step?" If the answer is "yes," then you do not need that step.

For example, if you were writing instructions for making a peanut-butter-and-jelly sandwich, it would not be necessary to tell readers to open the jar of jelly. They would already know to do that.

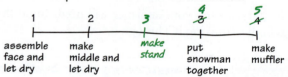

Steps to make a snowman decoration:

1	2	3	4 (̶3̶)	5 (̶4̶)
assemble face and let dry	make middle and let dry	make stand	put snowman together	make muffler

Next, brainstorm the materials you need to make the product. Think carefully about everything you need. If you forget to list a material, your reader will not be able to make the product.

YOUR TURN 4 — Planning Your Instructions

Write the steps for making your product in chronological order on a time line. Then, list the needed materials.

RESOURCES

Your Turn 3 and 4
Practice
- *Communications,* WS. pp. 55, 57

Reinforcement
- *Communications,* TP. 26, WS. p. 56

Writing
Practice
- *Communications,* WS. p. 58

MINI-LESSON WRITING

Elaboration: Using Specific Language

Suppose a friend gave you the following recipe for making Zesty Bagels. Could you follow the directions?

Zesty Bagels

Step 1: Gather materials—pan, bagels, sauce, olives, mushrooms, cheese.

Step 2: Place bagels on pan and pour sauce.

Step 3: Put on toppings.

Step 4: Bake.

As you read the steps, you probably asked yourself many questions. *How many bagels do I need? What are the measurements for the toppings? How long do I bake the bagels and at what temperature?* The recipe leaves you guessing because your friend's directions are not specific.

To help a reader understand a process, you should write your instructions using **specific language.** For example you can give *numbers* to tell how much or how many, such as "six plain bagels." You can also describe supplies using *descriptive words*, such as "finely chopped mushrooms." *Exact verbs* (V) and *transitions* (T) will help tell a reader exactly what to do and where to put supplies.

V
Sprinkle black olives, mushrooms, and
　　　　　　　　　T
cheese evenly **over** the sauce.

Notice how specific language eliminates all guesswork in the recipe below.

Zesty Bagels

Step 1: Gather these materials: a cookie sheet, 6 plain bagels cut in half, 18-ounce jar of spaghetti sauce, ¼ cup chopped black olives, 6 finely chopped mushrooms, and 1 cup grated Parmesan cheese.

Step 2: Place bagel halves on cookie sheet. Evenly spread 1 tablespoon of spaghetti sauce over the face of each bagel.

Step 3: Sprinkle black olives, mushrooms, and cheese evenly over the sauce.

Step 4: Bake in oven at 350 degrees for 15–20 minutes. When done, remove from oven and cool.

PRACTICE

Read the following steps. Then, rewrite the instructions, adding specific language. For more information on specific language, see the chart on page 91.

Directions for Preparing a Can of Soup

Step 1: Gather supplies.

Step 2: Heat soup.

Step 3: Serve.

MINI-LESSON WRITING

Elaboration: Using Specific Language

ANSWERS

Possible responses for preparing a can of condensed soup on a burner follow.

Step 1: Gather the following supplies: an electric or hand-held can opener, 1 10-1/2 ounce can of condensed soup, 1 can of water, 1 medium-sized cooking pot, and 1 long-handled spoon.

Step 2: Combine the soup and water in the pot. Then, simmer on low heat for about 7 minutes, stirring occasionally.

Step 3: When done, remove the pot from the burner and ladle the soup into a bowl. Serve piping hot.

Quotation for the Day

"Writing is manual labor of the mind: a job, like laying pipe."

(John Gregory Dunne, 1932–   , American writer)

Write the quotation on the board and ask students how writing a "how-to" paper is like the job of laying pipe. [It is a step-by-step process, a project done in a specific order] Students may extend the analogy further by expressing that the water will flow through the pipe only if it is placed correctly, and their written instructions will be clear only if the steps are in logical order.

Meeting INDIVIDUAL NEEDS

ENGLISH-LANGUAGE LEARNERS
General Strategies. Some students might be uncertain about how to catch an audience's attention in English. You may want to offer examples of attention-grabbing introductions from students' writing and explain how these introductions catch a reader's attention. These examples may also be useful:

Have you ever wanted to make your own greeting cards?

If you love to work with your hands and don't mind getting messy, then this is a project for you.

I never thought I could . . . until I did this project.

YOUR TURN 5

If you wish to assign a length to students' writing assignments, 500 to 700 words is appropriate. To help you assess the "how-to" papers, you may wish to have students label each part according to the framework on this page.

Writing

"How-to" Paper

Framework | Directions and Explanations

Introduction
- Attention-grabbing opening
- Identification of product
- Reason(s) for making the product

Grab your reader's attention quickly with an interesting introduction. For example, you could **ask questions** to get your reader involved in your paper. Also, **clearly state reasons** why your reader will want to learn to make the product you will explain.

Body
- List of materials
- Step 1 (with specific language)
- Step 2 (with specific language)
- Step 3 (with specific language) and so on

In the first body paragraph, **list the materials your reader needs** to make the product. One way to list the materials is to put them in the order in which your readers will use them. Another way is to group similar types of materials together. Then, write the steps in the correct **chronological order**. As you write, you should

- place each step in a **separate paragraph**
- elaborate on each step with **specific language**. Specific language includes numbers, exact verbs, comparisons, transitions, and descriptive words. (See mini-lesson on page 97.) Transitions are especially useful because they create **coherence**. That is, they show how all the ideas connect.

Conclusion
- Restatement of reason(s) and/or
- Suggestions for using or displaying the product

Restate the reasons for making the product. You can also suggest **ways to use or display** the product.

YOUR TURN 5 Drafting Your "How-to" Paper

Now it is your turn to draft a "how-to" paper. As you write, refer to the framework above and the Writer's Model on the next page.

98   Chapter 3   **Exposition:** Explaining How

RESOURCES

Writing
Writing Prompts
- *Communications,* TP. 27, WS. p. 59

Extension
- *Designing Your Writing*

Your Turn 5
Practice
- *Communications,* TP. 28, WS. p. 60

A Writer's Model

The final draft below closely follows the framework for a "how-to" paper on the previous page.

A Snowman of Style

Are you at home with nothing to do? Are you eager to do something fun? If so, you can make a snowman. It is easy and fun, and you can make one without snow.

Picture a plump snowman with bright shiny eyes, a muffler, and a black hat. You can make the same winter wonder with these materials, which you can find at many hobby and craft stores:

- a 5-inch, a 4-inch, and a 3-inch foam ball
- two 12-inch black pipe cleaners
- one 1-inch orange pipe cleaner
- a 2-inch piece of black yarn
- three medium-size buttons
- two medium-size sequins
- a 1- × 15-inch piece of bright cloth
- an 8½- × 11-inch piece of black paper
- a 2-inch black pompom
- two straight pins
- scissors
- white glue

The first step is making the snowman's face and hat. The orange pipe cleaner will be the nose. Push the pipe cleaner into the center of the smallest foam ball until it sticks out about ½ inch. Next, make the mouth using the black yarn. Happy snowmen wear smiles. Confused snowmen have mouths like a series of mountain peaks. Choose an emotion for your snowman, and glue the black yarn down to match the feeling you are trying to create. To make the eyes, glue down the two sequins. Use the straight pins to pin the eyes in place while they dry.

(continued)

Annotations:
- Attention-grabber
- Identification of product
- Reasons for making the product
- List of materials
- Step one

Connecting Reading and Writing

To help students write their own "how-to" papers, have them refer to the information on forming mental images in the Reading Workshop on p. 91. Then, have them read **A Writer's Model** while paying attention to the writer's use of specific language. As a whole-class activity, call on volunteers to identify examples of numbers, exact verbs, comparisons, transitions, and descriptive words that they find in the model. ["12-inch"; "cut"; "mouths like a series of mountain peaks"; "next"; "circle of black paper"]

TECHNOLOGY TIP

If students are using a computer to draft their papers, remind them to save their drafts frequently by using the save as feature and renaming the document each time they revise a draft (for example, *Draft 1, Draft 2*, etc.). This will make it easier for students to find passages in a past draft that were deleted in the current draft, or to recover wording and organization from old drafts.

Critical Thinking

Evaluation. To "test" the content and organization of **A Writer's Model**, spread the materials for the project on a table in the classroom. Separate the class into randomly selected groups of six students. Then, have groups take turns using the materials to follow the directions in the model. While one group is working with the materials, the other groups could make lists of questions they have about the steps, write ideas for how to improve the model, and brainstorm suggestions for how to modify the snowman (as described in the last paragraph of the model). After each group has tested the model, ask students to discuss the importance of clear writing in a "how-to" explanation and how they could apply what they have learned to their own writing.

(continued)

Snowmen often wear hats. You can make one by cutting a 3-inch circle of black paper. Pin the circle to the top of the snowman's head. Glue the black pompom to the center of the paper, and set the head aside to dry.

Step two   Next, you will make the snowman's middle using the 4-inch foam ball. Cut one of the black pipe cleaners in half to make the arms. Shape each pipe cleaner like a tree branch or jagged line. Then, push each arm in place on the sides of the ball. The three black buttons will make the snowman's shirt. Glue them down the front of the ball. Set the middle aside to dry.

Step three   While you are waiting for the face and middle to dry, you can make a stand to keep your snowman from falling over. Cut a 1- × 5-inch piece of black paper. Form it into a ring by gluing the ends together.

Step four   When everything is dry, you are ready to put the snowman's body together. Take your last black pipe cleaner and cut four 2-inch pieces. Push two of the pipe cleaners in the top of the 4-inch foam ball 1 inch apart. Push the other two pipe cleaners in the bottom of the 4-inch ball 1 inch apart. Make sure you use two pipe cleaners because they will keep the snowman from wobbling. Then, push the snowman's head on top of the pipe cleaners to attach it to the 4-inch ball. Push the 5-inch ball on the bottom pipe cleaners to finish making the snowman's body.

Step five   The final step is making a muffler for your snowman. A muffler is a long fringed scarf that wraps around the neck. The strip of cloth will make the muffler. Create fringe by making cuts into each end of the fabric. Once that is done, tie the muffler around the snowman's neck.

Suggestions   You can make a variety of snow people by changing the style of the hat and clothing. Make a snow woman or snow child. Give your snow person a job. Doctors wear stethoscopes around their necks, and movie stars wear sunglasses. **Restatement of reasons** No matter what type of snowman you choose to create, making one is easy and fun.

Designing Your Writing

Illustrating Steps in a Process When you are writing a "how-to" paper, consider using pictures to help readers understand what you are writing about. You can show readers how to complete individual steps by drawing pictures of the materials and using arrows or lines to show the action that will take place. You can also provide an illustration of the final product so that readers will know what their product should look like. To illustrate your "how-to" paper, you can print or scan images using a computer, cut out pictures from magazines, or even draw graphics by hand. Below is an illustration drawn by the writer of the Writer's Model to help readers understand one step in his "how-to" paper.

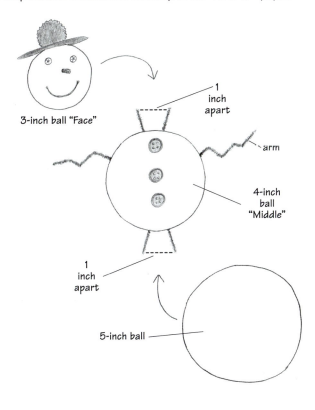

TEACHING TIP

Designing Your Writing
Before students begin to create pictures to illustrate their "how-to" papers, have them look in "how-to" manuals and craft books to find examples of effective illustrations. A school librarian may be able to set aside some books for your class. If students are writing their papers about products they have made in the past, they may want to take pictures of them and, if possible, label the pictures to show different stages of the processes they are describing. Point out that every step in a process does not need to be illustrated; students should illustrate only one or two of the most difficult steps.

TECHNOLOGY TIP

If students have access to a computer with photo or graphics-editing software, they can alter their scanned images by enlarging, shrinking, stretching, copying, cutting, and coloring. They also can add patterns or freehand drawings. You might ask students who use this software to show the class samples of their images at different stages of the editing process and explain how the pictures were manipulated.

Writing Workshop

Connecting Reading and Writing

After students have read **A Student's Model**, invite them to jot down responses to the following questions:

- What is the most difficult or challenging step in the "how-to" paper?
- Why is the step difficult to imagine or to do?
- How would an illustration make the instructions clearer?

Next, ask students to suggest at least two places in **A Student's Model** where they would need to see an illustration. [Students may suggest illustrations that show how to cut the ivy leaves at an angle and how to hook the ivy on the trellis.] Suggest that students use the questions above when they revise their own "how-to" papers to evaluate the need for illustrations.

A Student's Model

It is important to have detailed knowledge and enthusiasm about the product you are explaining in your "how-to" paper. Stephanie Thompson wrote the following paper as a middle school student in St. Peters, Missouri. In it, she shares her knowledge and enthusiasm as she provides the instructions for growing ivy.

Make It Grow

Attention-grabbing opener

Have you ever tried growing ivy from a clipping? It is not as hard to do as it might seem. To get started, the following supplies are needed: an existing ivy plant, a fence or trellis for the ivy to climb, a pan about two inches deep, water, and sunlight.

List of supplies

Step one

First, cut about seven or eight leaves from the ivy plant. Make sure that you cut above where the leaf joins the stem, and cut at the same angle as the leaf grows. Then, fill the pan with water and place each leaf in the water. Let the leaves soak until they form roots that are about three to four inches long.

Step two

Step three

When the roots reach the desired length, it is time to find the best location for the ivy to grow. Although ivy is a hardy plant, it does need some care when it is grown from a clipping. Look for a place where there is plenty of sunlight, good drainage, and where no animals can damage it. Make sure that there is a fence or trellis in the location for the ivy to climb.

Step four

Next, hook the ivy leaves on to the fence or trellis so that the roots are almost touching the ground. As they receive sunlight and moisture from the dew, the roots will grow into the ground and the leaves will continue to sprout upward. In no time the ivy will be covering the fence or trellis, and you can start all over again!

Revising

Evaluate and Revise Content, Organization, and Style

Two Is Better Than One When revising your paper or a peer's, you should read the rough draft twice. First, look at the content and organization, using the guidelines below. The second time you read, concentrate on the sentences, using the Focus on Sentences on page 105.

▶ **First Reading: Content and Organization** Use the chart below on your first reading. It will help you evaluate a "how-to" paper and revise its content and organization.

"How-to" Paper: Content and Organization Guidelines for Self-Evaluation and Peer Evaluation

Evaluation Questions	Tips	Revision Techniques
❶ Does the introduction give a reason for making the product?	▶ **Put brackets** around the reason.	▶ If needed, **add** a reason for making the product.
❷ Does the body list all the materials needed to make the product?	▶ **Circle** all the supplies needed to make the product.	▶ **Add** any supplies that have been left out.
❸ Are the steps of the process in the correct chronological order? Is each step in a separate paragraph?	▶ **Write a number** next to each step in the margin of the paper.	▶ If needed, **rearrange** the steps so they are in the correct order and so that each step is in its own paragraph, as needed.
❹ Is each step described with specific language?	▶ **Underline** numbers, descriptions, comparisons, verbs, and transitions.	▶ If necessary, **elaborate** on the steps by adding specific details.
❺ Does the conclusion restate the reason for making the product and/or give suggestions on how to use the product?	▶ **Put a star** beside the sentence that restates the reason. **Draw a wavy line** under the suggestions for using the product.	▶ If needed, **add** a restatement of the reason for making the product. **Add** some suggestions for how to use the product.

Quotation for the Day

"If [the audience is] satisfied with your poor performance, you will not easily make it better."

(Ralph Waldo Emerson, 1803–1882, American author)

Write the quotation on the chalkboard and ask students how the audience in the quotation relates to the role of peer editor in the classroom. [If the peer editor does not identify unclear writing, the author may not revise it. An awareness of weaknesses in writing will help the author to identify and correct errors in the future.]

TEACHING TIP

▶ **Elaboration**
To help students elaborate in the body of their papers by adding specific details, ask them to close their eyes and visualize the steps in the process. Then, ask students to add to their instructions sensory words and details that help them better picture in their minds each of the steps in the process.

Writing Workshop 103

RESOURCES

Revising
Practice
- *Communications,* TPs. 29, 30, WS. pp. 61, 62, 63

Responding to the Revision Process

ANSWERS

1. The sentence adds specific language comparing the shape of the pipe cleaner to a tree branch or a jagged line to help readers visualize what to do.

2. The writer broke the paragraph into two so that each main step of the process would have its own paragraph, making it easier for readers to follow the directions.

ONE WRITER'S REVISIONS Here is an early draft of the "how-to" paper on pages 99–100.

> Next, you will make the snowman's middle using the 4-inch foam ball. Cut one of the black pipe cleaners in half *[elaborate: Shape each pipe cleaner like a tree branch or jagged line.]* to make the arms. Then, push each arm in place on the sides of the ball. The three black buttons will make the snowman's shirt. Glue them down the front of the ball. Set the middle aside to dry. *[rearrange: ¶]* While you are waiting for the face and middle to dry, you can make a stand to keep your snowman from falling over. Cut a 1- × 5-inch piece of black paper. Form it into a ring by gluing the ends together.

PEER REVIEW

When looking over a peer's paper, ask yourself these questions:

- Would I be able to make this product? Why or why not?

Responding to the Revision Process

1. How does adding a sentence improve this part of the instructions?
2. How does breaking the one paragraph into two paragraphs make the instructions clearer?

▶ **Second Reading: Style** You have improved the content and organization of your paper. Now you will concentrate on the style of your sentences. One way to improve your style is to use transitional words, such as *first, next,* and *finally*. Transitional words connect one idea to another. The following guidelines will help you.

Style Guidelines

Evaluation Question	Tip	Revision Technique
Do transitional words connect one step to another, creating coherence?	▶ **Highlight** each transitional word.	▶ **Add** transitional words to paragraphs that need them.

104 Chapter 3 **Exposition:** Explaining How

Transitional Words

A reader should be able to follow your ideas as easily as a driver follows road signs. Adding **transitional words** between your thoughts will steer the reader in the right direction. Notice how the underlined transitional words make this paragraph easy to read and understand.

Focus on Sentences

> To make a tie-dyed shirt, <u>first</u> you will need to wrap rubber bands around several parts of a T-shirt. <u>Next</u>, fill a tub or sink with dye. <u>Then</u>, dunk the shirt into the dye. Rinse the shirt with water and hang to dry. <u>Finally</u>, take off the rubber bands when the shirt is completely dry.

TIP Listed below are common transitional words for chronological order, the order used to explain a process.

after	next
before	often
finally	then
first	when

ONE WRITER'S REVISIONS

> The orange pipe cleaner will be the nose. Push the pipe cleaner into the center of the smallest foam ball until it sticks out about ½ inch. ^*Next,* ~~You will~~ make the mouth using the black yarn.

Responding to the Revision Process

How did adding a transitional word make this part of the instructions clearer?

YOUR TURN 6 — Evaluating and Revising Your "How-to" Paper

First, improve content and organization using the guidelines on page 103. Then, use the Focus on Sentences above to add transitional words to your paper. If a peer evaluated your paper, consider his or her suggestions as you revise.

RESOURCES

Focus on Sentences
Practice
- *Communications,* WS. p. 64

Quotation for the Day

"It is not who does the most tricks, but the total package."

(Brian Orser, 1962– , Canadian Olympic ice skater)

Write the quotation on the chalkboard and ask students to discuss what they think it means. Lead them to understand that informative writers are obligated to give their readers all the information they can—especially when trying to teach them to do or make something—and that the proofreading and publishing stage of the writing process is when the final touches are put on a piece of writing.

Grammar Link

Using Commas in a Series

ANSWERS

1. Glue the eyes, hold them with a pin, and allow them to dry.
2. My snowman has green eyes, a red scarf, and blue buttons.
3. Miguel gave his snow teen a headset, a T-shirt, and a book bag.
4. A snow baby has a bib, cap, or bow.
5. C

Publishing

Proofread Your Paper

Clear the Path Reading a paper full of errors is like running an obstacle course: Progress is often slow. If you *and* a peer proofread your paper, you are more likely to catch distracting mistakes.

Grammar Link

Using Commas in a Series

When you write a "how-to" paper, you may list materials or give directions in a series. A series consists of three or more items written one after the other.

Use commas to separate three or more items in a series.

Incorrect   Get out a pen, and paper.
Correct   Get out a pen, a ruler, and paper.

To make the meaning of a sentence clear, use a comma before the *and* or *or* in a series.

Unclear   Lori's favorite sandwiches are turkey, ham and cheese. [Does Lori have two or three favorite sandwiches?]
Clear   Lori's favorite sandwiches are turkey, ham, and cheese.

Do not use commas if *all* of the items are joined by *and* or *or*.

Incorrect   You can throw, or roll, or bounce the ball.
Correct   You can throw or roll or bounce the ball.

PRACTICE

Some of the sentences below need commas. Refer to the rules to the left to decide when to use commas. If a sentence needs commas, rewrite the sentence, adding commas where they are needed. If a sentence is correct, write C.

Example:
1. Your snow woman could have long hair a lace collar and earrings.
1. *Your snow woman could have long hair, a lace collar, and earrings.*

1. Glue the eyes hold them with a pin and allow them to dry.
2. My snowman has green eyes a red scarf and blue buttons.
3. Miguel gave his snow teen a headset a T-shirt and a book bag.
4. A snow baby has a bib cap or bow.
5. You can place your snowman on a shelf or a table or a countertop.

For more information and practice on **commas,** see page 566.

RESOURCES

Grammar Link
Practice
- *Communications,* WS. p. 65

Exposition: Explaining How

Publish Your Paper

Tell Them How It Is Done   Since you are the expert, you can share your instructions with others. How do you get your paper to your audience? Use the following suggestions to get people to read your "how-to" paper.

- If you wrote your "how-to" paper for a younger audience, make copies of your instructions and give them to an elementary teacher. If your audience is your classmates, ask your teacher if you can demonstrate how to make your product in class.
- Gather all the "how-to" papers in your class and organize them into categories such as recipes, crafts, and decorations. Compile a "how-to" book and place it in your school's library.

Reflect on Your Paper

Building Your Portfolio   Now that you are finished writing and publishing, take a moment and reflect on your "how-to" paper. Remember your purpose for writing, and think about how your paper will achieve that purpose. Reflecting on a paper you have already completed will help make your next one better.

- Which step in your paper is the easiest to follow? What makes this step clear and easy to understand?
- You created a time line to list your steps in order. In what other types of writing would a time line be useful?
- Take time to examine all the papers in your portfolio. What is one goal you would like to work toward to improve your writing?

PORTFOLIO

YOUR TURN 7 — Proofreading, Publishing, and Reflecting on Your Paper

- Correct any grammar, usage, and mechanics errors. Pay attention to spelling and punctuation, particularly the use of commas in a series.
- Publish your paper so others can use your instructions.
- Answer the questions from Reflect on Your Paper above. Record your responses in a learning log, or include them in your portfolio.

COMPUTER TIP

If you have access to a word processor, use its **spellchecker** feature when you edit your paper to catch and correct misspelled words. However, a spellchecker cannot check homonyms such as *its* (showing possession) and *it's* (it is).

TEACHING TIP

Publish Your Paper
Some students may choose to write their "how-to" explanations in cursive style and some may choose manuscript style. In either case, remind students to write legibly as they prepare the final copy of their papers, for if their papers are not neat and clear, the reader may have difficulty following the steps of the "how-to" paper. You may want to display legibly-written samples in both handwriting styles of published writing that students may use as models.

Critical Thinking

Evaluation. Help students evaluate their portfolios and set goals to improve their writing. Ask them to look over past edits, the teacher's comments, and peer revisions and then make a T-chart of their strengths and weaknesses. Next, direct them to write down their goals as writers and how they plan to accomplish the goals. Give them suggestions such as peer editing; using a computer, a dictionary, or a thesaurus; or peer tutoring.

Wrap It Up

Metacognition. Ask students, "What part of writing a 'how-to' paper was most difficult for you? Why?"

YOUR TURN 7 — ANSWER

Possible answers for the reflection question on time lines include historical accounts, short stories, biographies, and autobiographies.

TEACHING TIP

Writing Instructions
Give students the following mnemonic device to help them remember different ways to elaborate on steps when responding to a test prompt that asks them to write instructions.

Naughty **d**ogs **e**at **c**at **t**reats.

Numbers
Descriptive words
Exact verbs
Comparisons (simile, metaphor)
Transitions

Explain to students that adding some or all of these elements will make their instructions clearer and easier to follow.

MINI-LESSON: TEST TAKING

Writing Instructions

Sometimes an essay test may ask you to write instructions, such as how to do or how to make something. Read the prompt to the right. How would you respond to this prompt on a test?

A new student in your school needs to find the cafeteria. Write the directions for walking from your classroom to the cafeteria.

THINKING IT THROUGH — Writing Instructions for Tests

▶ **STEP 1** Read the prompt. Find out
- what it is asking you to explain
- who your audience is

The prompt is asking me to explain how to get from my classroom to the cafeteria. A new student will be reading my instructions.

▶ **STEP 2** List the materials, if any, you would need to complete the process. Provide definitions of key terms, if necessary.

The new student will not need any materials to learn the way to the cafeteria. There are no terms to define.

▶ **STEP 3** Create a time line to list the steps of the process in order.

Step 1	Step 2	Step 3	Step 4
Turn right out of the classroom door.	Go to the end of the hall and turn right again.	Take the first left.	Go through the double doors, and the cafeteria will be on your left.

▶ **STEP 4** Write your instructions in paragraphs. Remember to use specific language.

I will give specific locations and use directions, such as right and left.

▶ **STEP 5** Review your instructions, checking to make sure that
- you listed any materials needed
- your steps are in order
- you have not left out any steps
- you have included specific language

I don't need materials, and my steps are in order. I can add a specific detail to step 3, though. The first left will come after a water fountain. I also need to explain where the student will find the double doors in Step 4.

108 Chapter 3 Exposition: Explaining How

RESOURCES

Test Taking
Practice
- *Communications*, WS. p. 66

---

108 Exposition: Explaining How

Connections to Life

Writing a Descriptive Paragraph

You are reading instructions for building a basketball backboard. Does having a picture of the backboard in your mind make understanding the instructions easier? It certainly does. You know what the final product looks like, so you already have an idea of what you need to do to make it.

Here's an opportunity for you to help the readers of your "how-to" paper. You will write a **descriptive paragraph** about the product they will make. The written description will help your audience create a mental picture, making the instructions easier to follow.

Do You See What I See? To describe something another person has not seen, you can use descriptive words and phrases to paint a picture in that person's mind. What kinds of descriptive words and phrases help someone picture an object? The following chart provides some examples for you.

Descriptive Words and Phrases	Definitions	Examples
Sensory Details	Details that express what you experience through your five senses—What you hear, see, taste, touch, and smell	sight—blue, tall, leaning hearing—pops, hisses, whispers taste—sweet, salty, sour touch—hot, soft, rough smell—smoky, fresh, spicy
Location Words	Words that describe where something is located	across from next to on the top to the right near to the left
Figurative Language	**Simile**—Language that compares two unlike things using *like* or *as*	The wire is rigid and curled *like* corkscrew pasta. The eyes are *as* shiny *as* emeralds.
	Metaphor—Language that compares two unlike things saying one *is* the other	The string *is* a lifeline keeping the two parts together.

TEACHING TIP

Writing a Descriptive Paragraph
Before students begin to read the **Connections to Literature** section, ask a volunteer to describe orally an object (a musical instrument, a woodworking tool, or an exotic animal) for the class. The student should describe the object as completely as possible and then call on classmates to guess what the object is. Point out to students that the descriptive words and phrases the student used in his or her description helped listeners to picture the object. Then, refer students to the chart of descriptive words and phrases on this page.

Meeting INDIVIDUAL NEEDS

MODALITY
Visual Learners. Students may need help deciding which spatial order to use in their descriptive paragraphs. Suggest that carefully studying a visual representation of their product will help them determine the best spatial order to use. To help them visualize their product, students can draw a rough sketch, create a labeled diagram, or take a snapshot. After studying the image and deciding on the best spatial order, students can gather accurate sensory details and location words to help them write their paragraphs.

First Things First To write a descriptive paragraph, you first need to decide what *spatial order* you are going to use to organize your description. **Spatial order** organizes the details according to their location. You might describe a product from right to left, from top to bottom, or from far away to close up. Choosing an order first will help you be organized as you observe and list all the important details about your product.

For instance, if you choose to describe your product from the left to the right, you will look at the left side of the product and list the details. Then, you will observe the middle of the product, and then the right side, writing down details as you go. You should describe what the product looks like, but you should also consider other sensory details. Does your product make a sound? How does it taste or smell? What does it feel like? Make sure you use location words to tell where the sensory details are located.

To help organize your details in the spatial order that you chose, list them in a chart as you observe your product. The chart below shows a top-to-bottom order for describing a foam snowman.

Spatial Order	Sensory Details and Location Words
Top	small foam ball, black hat on top, fluffy pompom in the center, green sequin eyes, orange nose, black yarn mouth that smiles
Middle	medium foam ball; soft, blue muffler around his neck; three black buttons down the front; black arms stick out
Bottom	large foam ball, black stand made out of paper

Ready, Set, Write Once you have your information in a chart, you are ready to write a descriptive paragraph. All you have to do is follow the order that you chose and write complete sentences using the details that you listed.

When you are finished with your first draft, **elaborate** on your description by adding figurative language. To add figurative language, look at the details to see what comparisons you can make. In the chart above, for instance, the snowman has a mouth that smiles. To whom can a smiling snowman be compared? The snowman smiles like a child with a new toy. The snowman also has green eyes

---

110 Chapter 3 Exposition: Explaining How

made of sequins. Can you compare his eyes to anything?

Now Picture This The following is an example of a descriptive paragraph that could be included with the Writer's Model on pages 99–100. You can see how the writer uses sensory details, figurative language, location words, and spatial order to describe the snowman decoration. Do you see how adding description will help readers make the snowman?

> My snowman is not a typical snowman made of snow. He does not have to be kept outdoors, and he will not melt. Instead, my snowman is a decoration made of three foam balls, 3 inches, 4 inches, and 5 inches in diameter. He can be placed anywhere and enjoyed anytime. The smallest foam ball is my snowman's head. On top of the head sits a black hat with a fluffy, black pompom in the center. The snowman's eyes are green, sparkling sequins, and his nose is bright orange. The black yarn of his mouth is made to smile like a child with a new toy. The middle foam ball makes his body. He is dressed with a soft, blue muffler around his neck and three shiny black buttons down his front. His arms are also black, and they stick out from his body like branches of a tree. The largest foam ball is on the bottom, and it sits in a circular stand made of black paper. The stand is an anchor keeping the snowman in place.

description begins at the top

sensory details and figurative language

description moves to the middle

sensory details and figurative language

description ends at the bottom

figurative language

 Writing and Revising a Descriptive Paragraph

Write a descriptive paragraph using the suggestions above. Remember to

- use spatial order to organize your paragraph
- describe the product with sensory details and location words
- revise your paragraph by adding figurative language

When you have finished writing and revising, make a final draft and include it with your "how-to" instructions.

TEACHING TIP

Now Picture This

To help students prepare to write their own descriptive paragraphs, have them read the descriptive paragraph on this page and identify one or two specific examples of the following types of descriptive words and phrases.

- sensory details [Touch and sight: "fluffy, black pompom"]
- similes ["The black yarn of his mouth is made to smile like a child with a new toy."]
- metaphors ["The stand is an anchor keeping the snowman in place."]
- location words ["in the center"]

Timesaver

To help you quickly assess students' paragraphs, ask them to identify in the margin of their papers the spatial order they used when writing their paragraphs. Also, ask them to circle and label one or two sensory details, location words, and similes or metaphors that they used to describe their products.

YOUR TURN 8

To evaluate the accuracy of students' descriptive paragraphs, check that the details match those used in the "how-to" instructions.

Writing Workshop

Focus on Viewing and Listening

OBJECTIVES

- To listen to and watch instructions given in different forms
- To understand instructional charts and graphics
- To summarize "how-to" instruction in computer software
- To take notes while watching directions on TV or in a video

Quotation for the Day

"*The joy of life is variety.*"

(Samuel Johnson, 1709–1784, English lexicographer, critic, and writer)

Write the quotation on the chalkboard and ask students to tell different ways they have seen instructions presented. You might prompt them by mentioning instructional videos and diagrams in books. [wall charts, illustrations in books, computer software, or television shows] Tell students they will explore some of these instructional methods in this lesson and will hone their viewing and listening skills.

TEACHING TIP

Charts and Graphics
If possible, photocopy and post some examples of charts and graphics on a classroom bulletin board for the entire class to refer to while completing this workshop.

Focus on Viewing and Listening

WHAT'S AHEAD?

In this section you will learn how to listen to and watch instructions in different forms. You will also learn how to

- understand instructional charts and graphics
- summarize "how-to" instruction in computer software
- take notes while watching directions on TV or video

Viewing and Listening to Learn

You and your friend are neck and neck as you swim to the side of the pool. You both turn at the same time, but you come out ahead. Why? You know how to do a flip turn. You hold on to the lead and declare a victory as you touch the other side.

"Where did you learn to do that?" your friend asks.

You confess, "I learned how from TV."

Instructions come in many forms. Not only can you read a how-to paper, you can also learn how to do or make something from **charts and graphics, computer software,** and **"how-to" videos** or **TV shows.** To follow instructions in these forms, you will need to work on your viewing and listening skills.

Charts and Graphics

Charts and graphics provide you with the same information as a "how-to" paper. Both tell the materials, the instructions, and the order in which you should do the instructions. However, charts and graphics do not rely only on words. They *show* the steps in a process by using pictures, symbols, and labels.

One type of chart is a flowchart. Look at the flowchart on the next page. The steps are easy to follow because arrows direct you from one step to another. Labels, such as Step 1, Step 2, and Step 3,

112   Chapter 3   **Exposition:** Explaining How

RESOURCES

Focus on Viewing and Listening
Practice

- *Media Literacy and Communication Skills,*
  —*Support and Practice,* Ch. 3
  —*A How-to Handbook*

Teaching Notes

- *Media Literacy and Communication Skills,*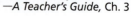
  —*A Teacher's Guide,* Ch. 3

Exposition: Explaining How

also help you see the order of the steps, and the instructions are brief and to the point.

How to Make a Friend

Step 1: Introduce yourself to someone new by smiling, giving your name, and asking the new person his or her name. → **Step 2:** Begin a conversation. You might offer help or make a friendly joke. → **Step 3:** Plan to talk or meet again. You could ask for the new person's phone number or an e-mail address, or name a date and time for your next meeting.

Now, look at the graphic below. This type of graphic is called a diagram. The diagram shows how to fold a blanket like a sleeping bag. As on the flowchart, the steps are labeled, but pictures and symbols give the instructions. These features make it easy to understand what the diagram is demonstrating.

Step 1   Step 2   Step 3   Step 4

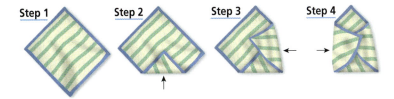

Understanding Charts and Graphics

Answer the following questions about the flowchart and diagram above.

- What material do you need to make the sleeping bag? How is the material presented?
- How are the instructions presented in the flowchart and the graphic? Do words, pictures, or symbols tell you what to do?
- What order is used in the flowchart and the graph (chronological? spatial?)? How is that order shown in each?

Critical Thinking

Evaluation. To help students evaluate varying types of media, arrange students in randomly assigned small groups. Each group will choose a topic (such as computers, aviation, or plants) to look up on a CD-ROM encyclopedia or in a variety of other media (print, video, graphic, etc.). Each student within the group will be responsible for evaluating how one medium conveys information. Have students think about the purpose and effect of each medium. Students should report to their group why the media they researched would be good for some purposes but not for others. [For example, a video showing how a flower blossoms would be good for illustrating that process. However, a flowchart is more effective when explaining a more "invisible" process like photosynthesis.]

Computer Software

Most software, including word-processing programs, computer games, and encyclopedias, comes with built-in "how-to" instructions, usually called a help menu. Help menus are set up differently from one program to another, but you can usually get to one by using the help button in the toolbar or on the keyboard. The help menu will list the features of the program. Click on the feature you are interested in, and a help box will appear, giving you specific directions. Here is an example of a help box.

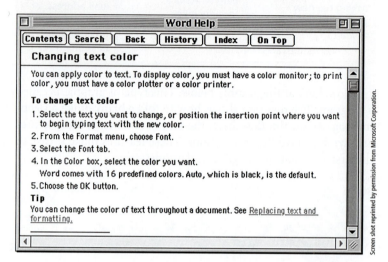

You may find that you go to the same item in a help menu again and again. How can you remember the steps in a process so that you don't have to keep returning to the menu? Summarizing the instructions in a flowchart can help you remember them. To do that, read each step and write down only the important words and details. Use arrows to show the sequence of steps. A flowchart for the instructions in the help box above might look like this:

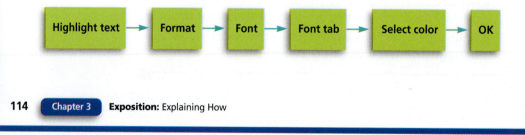

Chapter 3 **Exposition:** Explaining How

Summarizing Instruction

Create a flowchart that summarizes the steps in the following help box.

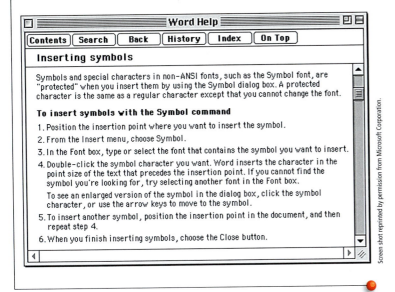

TV and Video

There are "how-to" programs and videos about a variety of topics, but popular ones include cooking, exercise, and home repair. "How-to" programs and videos are very helpful—not only do you *hear* the directions, you also *see* the steps.

When you watch "how-to" instructions on TV or on video, you are doing two things at once. First, you are *listening to* and *viewing* the information. At the same time, you are *trying to understand* how to do the steps in the process. If you are watching a TV program, you cannot ask questions. If you are watching a video, you might hit "pause" or "rewind," but having control over the VCR is not always possible. However, you can get a better understanding of the steps of a process if you take notes. The

YOUR TURN 10

ANSWER

Students' flowcharts may show the following sequence of steps.

- Position cursor (step 1)
- Select Symbol from menu (step 2)
- Select font (step 3)
- Double-click symbol (step 4)
- Reposition cursor and double-click symbol (step 5)
- Close (step 6)

Wrap It Up

Metacognition. Ask students to reflect on their own viewing and listening by answering the following question.

1. What do you think is easiest—following "how-to" instructions in charts, in graphics, or on videos and TV programs? Why do you find this method the easiest?

Then, ask students these questions.

2. How do charts and graphics show the steps in a process? [They use labels, pictures, and symbols.]

3. How can you best understand the steps in "how-to" instructions on TV or on a video? [You can take notes.]

TEACHING TIP

Taking Notes to Learn
You may want to do this activity in class. You will also want to preview the video and inform parents of the material you will be presenting in the video. Start the activity by modeling the note-taking guidelines for students. Then, ask them to do a guided practice, using the pause button to assess your students' note-taking skills.

YOUR TURN 11

To assess students' notes, check the following.

- Are the outlined steps numbered and in a logical, sequential order?
- Are there notes on each step? Do the notes mention important facts and ideas?

To evaluate students' sentences, check whether the information in them summarizes the major points contained in the notes.

---

following chart gives useful suggestions for taking quick and complete notes while viewing "how-to" instructions.

TIP The guidelines below can apply to viewing *any* informative video. Always watch for important facts, on-screen graphics, and ideas emphasized through repetition or dramatic phrasing. In addition, always take a minute after viewing to record important points and to think about the video producer's purpose.

Note-Taking Guidelines

Guidelines	Tip
Prepare to listen.	Think about your purpose for listening, and prepare to focus on the message by eliminating distractions.
Listen to each step.	Clue words such as the transitions *first, second, then,* and *finally* will let you know when a step begins and ends.
Create an outline of the steps.	Organize your notes by numbering steps as they are presented.
Take notes on each step.	Do not try to write every word. Instead, make a note of each major idea and its support. Listen for words and phrases that are repeated. Watch for on-screen graphics.
Listen for a conclusion.	Major points may be repeated.
Check your notes.	Make any necessary additions or corrections. Summarize the information while it is still fresh in your mind. If possible, discuss the message with others who viewed it. Compare your different perceptions of the message, and add to your notes any points you may have missed.

YOUR TURN 11 Taking Notes to Learn

- Watch a "how-to" program on TV or find a "how-to" video at a video rental store or at your local library.
- Use the note-taking guidelines above to take notes.
- After viewing the video, take five minutes to complete the following sentence starters:

  The producers created this video to ____.

  The most important facts or ideas were ____.

RESOURCES

Your Turn 11
Practice and Reinforcement
- Media Literacy and Communication Skills,

—*Support and Practice,* Ch. 3, transparencies and worksheets
—Videocassette 1, Segment C

CHAPTER 3 Choices

Select one of the following activities to complete.

▶ CROSSING THE CURRICULUM: SCIENCE

1. How Did That Happen? Use your science book to find information on how something occurs, such as how fish breathe underwater or how taste buds work. Create a **flowchart** or **graphic** that shows the steps of the process. You can use drawings, magazine cutouts, or computer art to illustrate the steps.

▶ CROSSING THE CURRICULUM: SPEECH

2. You Be the Teacher Choose a product and learn how to make it by listening to someone or by watching a "how-to" program. Then, demonstrate how to make it for your class. Select something entertaining, unique, or appealing to others your age.

Give clear, precise **directions** as you show classmates how to make the product. Use visuals to help your audience understand the process.

▶ CAREERS

3. Do You Have What It Takes? Choose a career that interests you. Find out what sort of training, education, and skills you would need to pursue that career by looking in books in the library, using informational Web sites, or interviewing people who are in that career field. Write a **letter** to a friend explaining how to enter the profession you choose.

▶ WRITING

4. Games People Play Invent a game. Your game could be a board game, an athletic game, a card game, or any other type of game. Write the **instructions** for playing your game. First, state the goal of the game. Is the goal to advance to the center of the board, put a ball through a basket, or get rid of all of your cards? Next, write all the steps required for playing the game. Finally, provide the instructions and materials needed to play the game for a group of your classmates.

PORTFOLIO

▶ CROSSING THE CURRICULUM: SPEECH

Ask students to follow these steps for demonstrating how to make a product using a visual display:

1. Choose a product that you know how to make, that can be explained in three to five steps, and that will interest your classmates.
2. Write directions, using specific language and chronological order.
3. Decide which steps would benefit most from visual aids, such as charts, posters, graphics, and illustrations.
4. Create the visual aids you will use.
5. Demonstrate each step, reciting your written directions to the class. Be sure to speak clearly and slowly and to make eye contact with members of the audience.
6. Use visuals when appropriate to help your classmates understand each step.

▶ CAREERS

Ask students to research careers in print or on-line trade or professional journals and occupational handbooks. Students may also conduct telephone, e-mail, or in-person interviews. However, you may want to obtain permission from parents or guardians and from the parties students contact before beginning work on this assignment. Ask students to write a friendly letter to share their findings, using an informal tone and including a greeting, body, and closing. Suggest that students send their letters either conventionally or electronically.

RESOURCES

Explaining How
Assessment
- *Assessment Package*
  —Chapter Tests, Ch. 3
  —Chapter Tests in Standardized Test Formats, Ch. 3
  —Assessment Alternatives, Ch. 3
- *Test Generator* (One-Stop Planner CD-ROM)

Choices
Rubrics
- *Assessment Package*
  —Assessment Alternatives, Ch. 3

CHAPTER PLANNING GUIDE

CHAPTER 4

Comparing and Contrasting

Use this guide to create an instructional plan that suits the individual needs of your students. Assignments marked by an asterisk (*) may be completed out of class. Times given for pacing lessons are estimated. See pp. 118–119 for chapter-wide resources. Resources listed in this guide are point-of-use resources only.

Curriculum Connections

Choices *p. 151*
- Crossing the Curriculum: Art
- Creative Writing
- Crossing the Curriculum: Music

GO TO: go.hrw.com
KEYWORD: EOLang 6-4

All resources for this chapter are available for preview on the *One-Stop Planner CD-ROM with Test Generator*. All worksheets and tests may be printed from the CD-ROM.

		Chapter Opener pp. 118–119	**Reading Workshop: Reading a Comparison-Contrast Essay** pp. 120–127
DEVELOPMENTAL PROGRAM		⏲ **25 minutes** • Your Turn 1 *p. 119*	⏲ **100 minutes** • Preparing to Read *p. 120* • Reading Selection *pp. 121–122* • First Thoughts in groups *p. 123* • Points of Comparison *p. 123* • Your Turn 2 *p. 124* • Comparison-Contrast Structure *pp. 124–125* • Your Turn 3 *p. 125* • Test Taking Mini-Lesson *p. 127*
CORE PROGRAM		⏲ **20 minutes** • Your Turn 1 *p. 119*	⏲ **90 minutes** • Preparing to Read *p. 120* • Reading Selection *pp. 121–122* • First Thoughts *p. 123* • Points of Comparison *p. 123* • Your Turn 2 *p. 124* • Comparison-Contrast Structure *pp. 124–125* • Your Turn 3 *p. 125* • Vocabulary Mini-Lesson *p. 126* • Test Taking Mini-Lesson *p. 127*
ADVANCED PROGRAM		⏲ **15 minutes** • Your Turn 1 *p. 119*	⏲ **60 minutes** • Preparing to Read *p. 120* • Reading Selection *pp. 121–122* • First Thoughts *p. 123* • Points of Comparison *p. 123* • Your Turn 2 *p. 124* • Comparison-Contrast Structure *pp. 124–125* • Your Turn 3 *p. 125* • Vocabulary Mini-Lesson *p. 126*
RESOURCES	**PRINT**	• *Communications,* TP. 31, WS. p. 67	• *Alternative Readings,* Ch. 4 • *Communications,* TPs. 32, 33, WS. pp. 68–75
	MEDIA	• *One-Stop Planner CD-ROM*	• *One-Stop Planner CD-ROM*

TP.=Transparency WS.=Worksheet

T117A

Writing Workshop: Writing a Comparison-Contrast Essay pp. 128–146	**Focus on Viewing and Representing: Comparing Ideas in Photographs** pp. 147–150
🕐 **175 minutes** • Choose Two Subjects; Your Turn 4 *pp. 128–130* • Purpose and Audience; Your Turn 5 *pp. 130–131* • Points of Comparison; Your Turn 6 *pp. 131–132* • Support and Organize; Your Turn 7 *pp. 132–133* • Develop a Main Idea Statement; Your Turn 8 *p. 133* • Arranging Details; Your Turn 9 *p. 134* • Framework; Your Turn 10; Models* *pp. 136–138* • Evaluate and Revise *pp. 139–140* • Focus on Sentences in groups; Your Turn 11 *p. 141* • Proofread, Publish, and Reflect on Your Essay *pp. 142–144* • Grammar Link *p. 142* • Your Turn 12 *p. 144* • Test Taking Mini-Lesson *p. 145*	🕐 **40 minutes** • Photographs vs. Reality *p. 147* • Photographs Provide Information *pp. 148–150* • Your Turn 14 *p. 150*
🕐 **140 minutes** • Choose Two Subjects; Your Turn 4 *pp. 128–130* • Purpose and Audience; Your Turn 5 *pp. 130–131* • Points of Comparison; Your Turn 6 *pp. 131–132* • Support and Organize; Your Turn 7 *pp. 132–133* • Develop a Main Idea Statement; Your Turn 8 *p. 133* • Arranging Details; Your Turn 9 *p. 134* • Framework; Your Turn 10; Models* *pp. 136–138* • Evaluate and Revise *pp. 139–140* • Focus on Sentences; Your Turn 11* *p. 141* • Proofread, Publish, and Reflect on Your Essay *pp. 142–144* • Grammar Link *p. 142* • Your Turn 12 *p. 144* • Test Taking Mini-Lesson *p. 145* • Connections to Life; Your Turn 13* *p. 146*	🕐 **30 minutes** • Photographs vs. Reality *p. 147* • Photographs Provide Information *pp. 148–150* • Your Turn 14 *p. 150*
🕐 **120 minutes** • Choose Two Subjects; Your Turn 4 *pp. 128–130* • Purpose and Audience; Your Turn 5 *pp. 130–131* • Points of Comparison; Your Turn 6 *pp. 131–132* • Support and Organize; Your Turn 7 *pp. 132–133* • Develop a Main Idea Statement; Your Turn 8 *p. 133* • Arranging Details; Your Turn 9 *p. 134* • Critical-Thinking Mini-Lesson *p. 135* • Framework; Your Turn 10; Models* *pp. 136–138* • Evaluate and Revise *pp. 139–140* • Focus on Sentences; Your Turn 11* *p. 141* • Proofread, Publish, and Reflect on Your Essay *pp. 142–144* • Your Turn 12 *p. 144* • Connections to Life; Your Turn 13* *p. 146*	🕐 **20 minutes** • Photographs vs. Reality *p. 147* • Photographs Provide Information *pp. 148–150* • Your Turn 14 *p. 150*

• *Communications,* TPs. 34–37, WS. pp. 76–90
• *Designing Your Writing*
	• *Media Literacy and Communication Skills*
	  —*Support and Practice,* Ch. 4
	  —*A How-to Handbook*
	  —*A Teacher's Guide,* Ch. 4

• One-Stop Planner CD-ROM	• One-Stop Planner CD-ROM

CHAPTER 4
Comparing and Contrasting

CHAPTER OBJECTIVES

- To read a comparison-contrast essay, identifying points of comparison and comparison-contrast structure
- To write a comparison-contrast essay
- To compare information in photographs

Chapter Overview

Most good decision-making processes involve comparing and contrasting. This chapter is designed to help students make effective comparisons when they read and write and when they examine photographs. The Reading Workshop (pp. 120–127) provides a comparison-contrast article for students to read and analyze. The Writing Workshop (pp. 128–146) guides students through the steps of the writing process as they write a comparison-contrast essay. Focus on Viewing and Representing teaches students to compare information and ideas in photographs. The three parts of the chapter may be taught separately; however, teaching them together can help students develop a thorough knowledge of how to use the techniques of comparing and contrasting and how to apply them in different contexts.

Why Study Comparing and Contrasting?

Comparing and contrasting concepts, decisions, and activities can help students assess ideas and make informed choices. Being able to identify points of comparison can help students develop analytical skills and identify the key elements of a situation. Applying to other situations this process of classifying items may help students relate new information to old or familiar situations.

Teaching the Chapter

Option 1: Begin with Literature

If literature is the focus in your classroom, you might introduce the chapter after studying drama, fiction, or poetry in which writers use comparing and contrasting. Discuss how comparison-contrast structures can highlight similarities and differences of character, theme, or plot development. Then, have students read the article in this chapter (pp. 121–122) and discuss with them its organizational structure. After reading and analyzing comparison-contrast structure, students will be ready to begin writing comparison-contrast essays in the Writing Workshop on pp. 128–146.

Option 2: Begin with Nonfiction and Writing

Use the material in this chapter to introduce the concept and explain the process of comparing and contrasting. The article in the Reading Workshop (pp. 120–127) and its activities illustrate both the meaning of points of comparison and the two basic types of comparison-contrast structure. The Writing Workshop (pp. 128–146) leads students through the steps of writing and revising comparison-contrast essays. When returning to literature, students may be better prepared to appreciate comparison-contrast structures in literature.

Making Connections

■ To the Literature Curriculum

Authors use comparing and contrasting in literature to emphasize similarities and differences in characters and settings and to explore theme-related ideas. For example, in the story "The Fun They Had" by Isaac Asimov, a girl finds an old book, then compares her world with the past portrayed in it.

Lesson Idea: Comparing and Contrasting in "The Nightingale" by Hans Christian Andersen

1. After students read the story, work with them to list similarities and differences between the birds. Then, have them categorize these qualities [appearance, personality]. Explain that the categories will form points of comparison.

2. Explain that similarities and differences can be shown on a graphic known as a Venn diagram. On the chalkboard draw two large overlapping circles. Point out that outside sections represent the differences between the birds and that the overlapping section includes details that the birds have in common. Before students fill in the details, you might write in the boldface words that appear in the sample diagram shown below.

3. Discuss with students how comparing and contrasting the two birds helped them focus on themes of the story. You might ask: What qualities does the live bird have that the artificial bird lacks? [compassion, wisdom, variety of action] What point do you think Andersen is making? [Plain things can be more precious than lavish, artificial things.] Did the story's structure make you want to keep reading? Why or why not? [The structure, which highlights the competition between the birds, helps hold reader interest.]

4. After discussion, introduce students to the article on pp. 121–122 in this chapter. Explain that the article uses a comparison-contrast structure similar to Andersen's.

■ To Careers

Tell students that knowing how to compare and contrast ideas, techniques, and potential actions are essential skills in the workplace. Have the class list careers in which they are interested. Then invite parents, guardians, or other local citizens who work in those fields to speak to the class about how using comparison and contrast can help them to make good decisions in their jobs. Tell students to take notes about two careers that interest them. Then, have them work in groups to discuss how comparing and contrasting can help people make decisions at work. See also **Connections to Life** on p. 146.

■ To the Community

Help students understand how their learning can extend beyond school by pointing out that many school activities have counterparts in the community. For example, if your school has a student government, ask a member to talk with the class about what his or her job entails. Then, invite a city council member to talk about that role. Have students list similarities and differences between the two positions.

■ To the Art Curriculum

The Focus on Viewing and Representing concentrates on analyzing photographs by comparing and contrasting them to real objects and to each other. Point out to students that paintings and sculptures are also works of art that can be compared to real objects and to each other. Invite an art teacher to talk to the class about the similarities and differences between two styles of painting. The teacher might use prints or slides in the presentation.

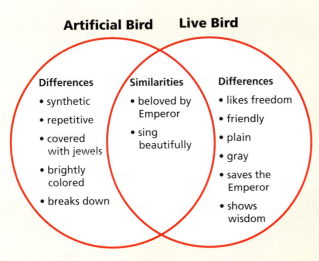

CHAPTER 4

PREVIEWING THE CHAPTER

- The three workshops in this chapter focus on comparing and contrasting. Each workshop may be taught separately, but taught together they can help students develop a thorough understanding of comparing and contrasting. Reading a comparison-contrast essay prepares students for writing an essay that compares and contrasts two subjects. Students may then be prepared to use this process while viewing photographs. For help in integrating this chapter with grammar, usage, and mechanics chapters, see pp. T297A–T297B.

INTRODUCING THE CHAPTER

- To introduce the chapter, use the Journal Warm-up, Transparency 31, in *Communications*.

VIEWING THE ILLUSTRATION

- This illustration shows a diver's view of both land and sea. Point out that the view is divided by the deep blue horizontal line of the water's surface. Create a Venn diagram with students that identifies points of comparison and contrast above and below water. Tell students the artist's use of perspective helps represent the elements of comparison.

Representing. Have students sketch an illustration that contains two different points of view. Ask them to share with the class the significance of the subjects, colors, lines, and shapes in their illustrations.

CHAPTER 4 Comparing and Contrasting

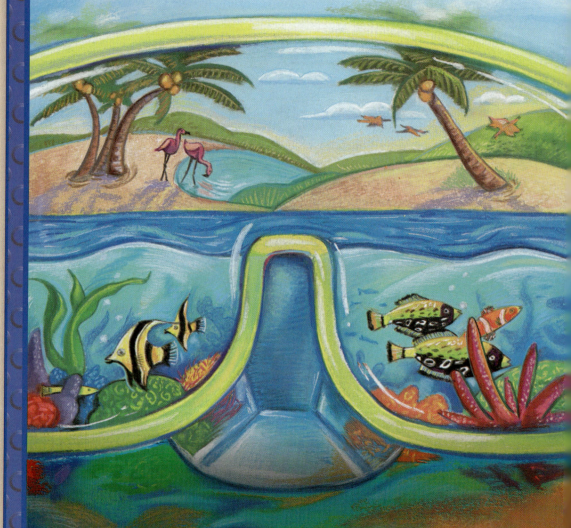

CHAPTER RESOURCES

Planning
- *Lesson Planner, ELL Strategies*, Ch. 4
- Block Scheduling, p. T117A (this book)
- One-Stop Planner CD-ROM

Practice
- *Communications*, Ch. 4

- Media Literacy and Communication Skills

Extension
- *Designing Your Writing*

Reinforcement
- *Communications*, Ch. 4
- *Alternative Readings*, Ch. 4

PREVIEW

Reading Workshop

Reading a Comparison-Contrast Essay
PAGE 120

Writing Workshop

Writing a Comparison-Contrast Essay
PAGE 128

Focus on Viewing and Representing

Comparing Ideas in Photographs
PAGE 147

Motivate

Activate thinking about comparing and contrasting by having students work in pairs to compare their favorite sports. Ask them to think about characteristics to compare, such as skills, strategies, and methods of scoring. After partners complete their comparisons, have volunteers share the results with the class. Discuss with students how comparing items helps them make decisions and judgments.

ELEMENTS OF Literature

Comparing and Contrasting in Literature. In *Elements of Literature*, Introductory Course, the poem "The Toaster" by William Jay Smith, p. 186, compares a machine to a dragon, and the poem "Steam Shovel" by Charles Malam, p. 190, compares a machine to a dinosaur.

Baked potato or salad? Art or band? You make choices every day. Sometimes those choices are easy, such as deciding on a baked potato for lunch. Other choices require more thought, such as choosing an elective in school. How do you make these important decisions? One way is to **compare** and **contrast** the two choices: You can look at how the two things are alike and how they are different. Once you understand the similarities and differences, you are ready to make a decision.

Comparing and contrasting is useful in other ways, too. Comparison-and-contrast structure may be used to define something unfamiliar by comparing it to something well known. For instance, did you know that the English sport rugby is like American football? Comparing and contrasting two subjects is a great way to share useful or interesting information with others.

internet connect
GO TO: go.hrw.com
KEYWORD: EOLang 6-4

YOUR TURN 1

ANSWERS
Possible answers follow.
- In fifth grade, students have one classroom teacher; in sixth grade, they have several teachers.
- In both fifth and sixth grades, there is a lot of homework.

Check that each group names at least one similarity and one difference between the two grades.

YOUR TURN 1 — Practicing Comparing and Contrasting

Answer the following questions, and then discuss them with a few classmates. Share your group's findings with the class.
- How are fifth grade and sixth grade different?
- How are fifth grade and sixth grade alike?

- *Daily Language Activity Transparencies*
- *Vocabulary Workshop* and *Tests*
- *Spelling*

Evaluation and Assessment
- *Test Generator* (One-Stop Planner CD-ROM)

- *Assessment Package*
  —*Chapter Tests*, Ch. 4
  —*Chapter Tests in Standardized Test Formats*, Ch. 4
  —*Assessment Alternatives*, Ch. 4

Internet
- go.hrw.com (keyword: EOLang 6–4)

Reading Workshop

OBJECTIVES

- To read a comparison-contrast essay in preparation for writing an essay
- To identify points of comparison
- To examine two comparison-contrast structures
- To identify the meanings of unfamiliar words using prefixes and suffixes

Quotation for the Day

"Nothing is good or bad but by comparison."

(Thomas Fuller, M.D., 1654–1734, English physician, writer, and compiler)

Ask students to consider how they use comparing and contrasting when they make decisions about which after-school activity to undertake or which binder to purchase for school, for example. Help students see that, when making decisions, comparing and contrasting becomes a matter of evaluation, of figuring out which activity or object is better and why.

TEACHING TIP

Preparing to Read
The material on p. 120 introduces concepts that will be discussed in more depth on pp. 123–125. Points of comparison and comparison-contrast structures are the focuses of instruction in the Reading Workshop. The Reading Selection, **"The Nixon-Kennedy Presidential Debates,"** illustrates both of these concepts.

RESOURCES

Reading Workshop Reinforcement
- *Alternative Readings,* Ch. 4

Reading Workshop

Reading a Comparison-Contrast Essay

WHAT'S AHEAD?
In this section you will read a comparison-contrast essay. You will also learn how to
- identify points of comparison
- examine two comparison-contrast structures

The two men faced each other down, ready for the big fight. One was the clear favorite; the other was a rookie. Who would win? The event had all the drama of a boxing match, but this was a debate. The following comparison-contrast essay shows how television made the presidential debate between John F. Kennedy and Richard M. Nixon different from previous ones. The debate was not just a war of words. Other elements made one candidate more successful than the other. Read on to see if you can identify those winning elements.

Preparing to Read

READING SKILL

Points of Comparison Not every similarity and difference between two subjects is important, so an author must choose the most important areas to compare and contrast. These areas are called the author's **points of comparison**.

READING FOCUS

Comparison-Contrast Structure The **structure**, or organization, of a comparison-contrast essay can help a reader see the similarities and differences more clearly. A writer may give all the information about one subject and then all the information about the other subject, or the writer may shift back and forth between the subjects. As you read Edward Wakin's essay on the next page, try to follow the organization he uses.

Chapter 4 Exposition: Comparing and Contrasting

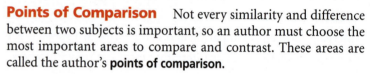

PREREADING
Set a Purpose. Explain to students that they will get more out of their reading when they read with a purpose in mind. Tell students that the teacher-set purposes for the Reading Selection on pp. 121–122 are to look for points of comparison and to follow the comparison-contrast structure of the essay.

Point out that students also need to identify their own purposes for reading. Suggest that they might begin by skimming the

Exposition: Comparing and Contrasting

Reading Selection

Read the following essay. In a notebook, jot down answers to the numbered active-reading questions in the shaded boxes. The underlined words will be discussed in the Vocabulary Mini-Lesson on page 126.

from HOW TV CHANGED AMERICA'S MIND

The  Presidential Debates

BY EDWARD WAKIN

A trim, tanned presidential candidate dressed smartly in dark suit, dark tie, and blue shirt stood at the podium on the left in the Chicago studio of WBBM–TV. He looked <u>vigorous</u>, confident, and businesslike.

His opponent at the other podium wore a light suit, pale tie, and a shirt with a collar that was too big for him. He looked tired, nervous, and in need of a shave.

1. In the first two paragraphs, are the two candidates shown as being similar or different? How?

Both faced the <u>pitiless</u> eye of TV cameras carrying the first televised presidential debate. For one hour of prime time on all three networks, 75 million Americans watched on the evening of September 26, 1960.

2. Whose appearance does the writer describe first, Nixon's or Kennedy's? Whose experience does he describe first?

The candidate on the left side, Democrat John F. Kennedy, looked nothing like the underdog he was supposed to be. An <u>unproved</u> junior senator from Massachusetts, he faced the highly experienced Republican candidate, Richard M. Nixon.

Kennedy needed national exposure. Nixon was seasoned and already nationally known. Twice elected vice president, Nixon had prepared himself for eight years to take over from President Dwight D. Eisenhower.

TV critic Robert Lewis Shayon described the televised debate as if it were a boxing match: "The atmosphere was clearly that of a prizefight: the referee (producer) instructing the champ and the challenger (the candidates), the seconds (advisors) milling around, and the 'come out fighting' handshake."

Reading Workshop **121**

Meeting INDIVIDUAL NEEDS

LEARNERS HAVING DIFFICULTY
If students are not clear which candidate's appearance is described first, they will have difficulty answering active-reading question 2. Help them by pointing out that paragraph 4 indicates that Kennedy is on the left side. Then, refer them back to paragraph 1. Ask them where the candidate being described is standing. [on the left] For students having difficulty understanding the text, you might also clarify that a podium is a stand for speakers or readers.

Active-Reading Questions
The purpose of the active-reading questions is to encourage students to think about points of comparison and comparison-contrast structure while reading the essay. Use students' answers to assess informally their comprehension of comparing and contrasting.

ANSWERS

1. In the opening paragraphs the author emphasizes differences between Nixon and Kennedy by describing how they dressed and how they looked.

2. The writer describes Kennedy's appearance and experience first.

Reading Selection and making predictions about its subject matter. From their predictions, students can determine what they expect to learn from the selection—their purpose for reading.

Reading Workshop **121**

Active-Reading Questions
ANSWERS continued

3. Nixon addresses his opponent—Kennedy—while Kennedy addresses the national television audience.

4. Nixon and Kennedy come across to the audience differently. Nixon appears "uncomfortable" and nervous, while Kennedy seems "assured" and "energetic."

5. When listening to Kennedy speak, Nixon wipes "perspiration from his brow." Kennedy looks "attentive, alert, and self-assured" while listening to Nixon speak.

6. Kennedy and Nixon are similar in that neither of them says anything particularly "memorable" or newsworthy during the debate.

The rules of the match called for an eight-minute opening statement by Kennedy followed by eight minutes from Nixon. Then a panel of four reporters would ask questions.

Kennedy won.

He won on style and image—two key ingredients for success on TV. Nixon challenged and rebutted[1] what Kennedy said as if he were out to win debating points. He addressed Kennedy rather than the TV viewers.

On the other hand, as the celebrated chronicler[2] of presidential campaigns Theodore H. White noted, Kennedy "was addressing himself to the audience that was the nation."

> **3.** Whom does each of the candidates address during the debate?

Kennedy came across as assured, energetic, dynamic. The camera was his friend.

Nixon came across as uncomfortable and ill at ease.

Nixon lost not on what he said, but on how he appeared. TV viewers saw Nixon as a gray man against the studio's gray backdrop. They saw Nixon forcing nervous smiles and perspiring under the studio lights. He "looked terrible," historian David Culbert stated.

> **4.** Are Kennedy and Nixon alike or different in the way they come across to the audience?

At one point, the camera showed Nixon wiping perspiration from his brow and upper lip as he listened to Kennedy. When the camera was on Kennedy listening, he looked attentive, alert, and self-assured.

> **5.** When listening, what does each candidate do?

Neither candidate said anything that was memorable or headline making. The importance of style and image became obvious when audience reactions to the televised and radio versions were compared. Those who heard the debate on radio thought Nixon had won!

> **6.** What similarity do Kennedy and Nixon share?

But what counted was the televised debate. Half the country had watched it. White had a clear verdict: "In 1960 television had won the nation away from sound to images, and that was that."

---

1. **rebutted:** provided opposing arguments in a debate.
2. **chronicler:** person who records historical events.

READING PROCESS

READING
Ask Questions. Inform students that asking the *5W-How?* questions (*who, what, where, when, why,* and *how*) of the text when they get stuck in their reading will help them determine meaning. For example, students might ask, "What were the rules of the debate?" or "Why was the Nixon-Kennedy debate important?" Students should jot down answers to their questions as they read.

Exposition: Comparing and Contrasting

First Thoughts on Your Reading
1. Name one thing about Kennedy and Nixon that the author compares.
2. Was the article's organization easy to follow? Why or why not?

Points of Comparison

The Same, Only Different? Your two closest friends are probably both alike and different. To help someone understand these two friends, however, you wouldn't discuss every similarity and difference. Is it really important to know that one friend has a blue bike helmet while the other has a white bike helmet? You would focus on more important areas, such as personality and hobbies. These main areas would be your **points of comparison.**

A writer does not always announce points of comparison directly. A reader can usually figure out what they are, though, by looking at the details the writer provides.

Look back at the first two paragraphs of "The Nixon-Kennedy Presidential Debates" on page 121. Can you identify the first point of comparison? If you have trouble, look at the chart below.

> READING SKILL

THINKING IT THROUGH
Identifying Points of Comparison

▶ **STEP 1** Does the first paragraph talk about one subject or both? Write down the topic of the paragraph.

The first paragraph is about what Kennedy wore and how he looked confident.

▶ **STEP 2** Read the next paragraph and write down what it is about.

This paragraph is about what Nixon wore and how he looked tired and nervous.

▶ **STEP 3** Identify the author's first point of comparison. Repeat the process until you have identified all points of comparison.

The author talks about the candidates' overall appearance. This is the first point of comparison.

> **TIP** Sometimes you can identify the point of comparison by reading one paragraph. If an author provides information about both subjects in one paragraph, you can skip Step 2.

First Thoughts on Your Reading

ANSWERS
Possible answers are suggested below.

1. The author compares Nixon and Kennedy in terms of physical appearance.

2. The article's organization was easy to understand because the author clearly explains how the two candidates are alike and different in various ways—from how they look and act to their political backgrounds and how they come across to the TV audience.

YOUR TURN 2

ANSWERS

Possible answers include:
- the candidates' overall appearance
- the candidates' levels of political experience
- whom the candidates seem to be addressing during the debate
- what each candidate does while the other is speaking
- what the candidates say during the debate

Critical Thinking

Metacognition. Before students complete **Your Turn 2,** have them re-read the essay. Ask students to place a sticky note next to each place in the text where they get confused or have a question. Suggest that they adjust their reading speeds, slowing down or stopping to re-read passages that they find confusing. After students finish re-reading the essay, discuss how strategies like varying reading speeds, re-reading, and asking questions can improve their understanding.

TEACHING TIP

Comparison-Contrast Structure
Although both organizational methods are good ways to structure comparison-contrast essays, each method seems to suit slightly different situations. The block method may work best when the audience is familiar with one of the two subjects under discussion. In this case, the more familiar subject can be dealt with first, and the relevant points of comparison or contrast can be mentioned without a great deal of explanation. When both subjects are relatively unfamiliar to the audience, the point-by-point method (which doesn't require readers to remember new information for longer periods of time, as the block method does) may be easier for readers to follow.

TIP Paragraphs providing background information may interrupt the author's points of comparison. You should keep reading to find details that describe one subject or both.

READING FOCUS

YOUR TURN 2 Identifying Points of Comparison

Use the steps in the Thinking It Through on page 123 to identify and list the points of comparison in the reading selection that begins on page 121. You will use your list of points of comparison in the Your Turn on the next page. **Hint:** You should find at least four points of comparison.

Comparison-Contrast Structure

A Question of Style Everything has a style. Sports cars have a specific look. You dress in a certain way. Even a comparison-contrast piece has a particular appearance. Not all comparison-contrast writings look just alike, though, because they can be organized in different ways. Two common patterns of organization for comparison-contrast writing are the *block style* and the *point-by-point style*. You can identify the structure of a comparison-contrast piece by looking at the points of comparison.

Block Style A comparison-contrast piece organized in the **block style** discusses all the points of comparison for the first subject and then all the points of comparison for the second subject. Suppose you are reading a comparison-contrast article about going to the movies versus renting a video. The points of comparison are *cost* and *choice of movies*. Here is how a writer using the block style would organize the article.

Subject 1: going to the movies	cost
	choice of movies
Subject 2: renting a video	cost
	choice of movies

In block style, the writer would first discuss going to the movies. The writer would tell about the ticket prices and the choices of movies available. Then, the writer would discuss renting a video. You would read about how much a video costs and what choices you have when renting a video.

RESOURCES

Your Turn 2
Practice
- *Communications,* WS. p. 68

Reinforcement
- *Communications,* TP. 32, WS. p. 69

Your Turn 3
Practice
- *Communications,* WS. p. 70

Reinforcement
- *Communications,* TP. 33, WS. p. 71

Point-by-Point Style A comparison-contrast piece organized in the **point-by-point style** goes back and forth between two subjects. It explains how the two subjects are alike and different for *one* point of comparison. Then, it explains how they are alike and different for the *next* point of comparison, and so on. The example below shows how the movies-versus-video comparison would be organized in point-by-point style.

Point of Comparison 1: cost	going to the movies
	renting a video
Point of Comparison 2: choice of movies	going to the movies
	renting a video

In point-by-point style, the writer would discuss cost first. You would read about how much going to the movies costs in comparison to renting a video. Then, you would read about the choice of movies you have when you go to the movies, followed by a discussion of the choice of movies available at a video store.

TIP Did you notice how the point-by-point style always discussed movies first and videos second? This **predictable order** makes it easy for a reader to understand and follow the points of comparison.

? Look back at the block style organization on the previous page. What is predictable about the order in the block style?

YOUR TURN 3 Identifying Comparison-Contrast Structure

Use your list of points of comparison from Your Turn 2 to identify the organization of the reading selection. Overall, does the article tend to use the block style or the point-by-point style? Support your answer with examples from the essay. **Hint**: Do all the details about Kennedy come before the details about Nixon (block style), or do the details switch back and forth between Kennedy and Nixon (point-by-point style)?

Reading Workshop   **125**

Wrap It Up

Metacognition. Ask students to reflect on their reading processes. Give them a few minutes to jot down answers to the following question.

1. Which part of the Reading Selection gave you the most difficulty? Why?

Then, ask students the following question.

2. What are two basic styles of comparison-contrast structure? [the block style and the point-by-point comparison]

YOUR TURN 3

ANSWER

Using their lists from **Your Turn 2**, students should say that the article uses the point-by-point style. Possible examples from the essay follow.

The writer first discusses Kennedy's appearance, then Nixon's. Next, the writer describes Kennedy as an "unproved junior senator" and Nixon as "seasoned and already nationally known." When the writer describes how the candidates came across on camera, he first describes Kennedy, then Nixon.

READING PROCESS

EXTENDING
Apply What You Read. Discuss with students how their individual purposes for reading helped them better understand the selection. Then, explain to students that they can apply what they have learned about comparing and contrasting to life outside of the classroom. Have students read about two careers that interest them and identify the points of comparison they would use to analyze the similarities and differences between the two careers.

Reading Workshop   **125**

MINI-LESSON VOCABULARY

Prefixes and Suffixes

ANSWERS
Possible answers are given below.

1. The root *vigor* means "strength or vitality." With the suffix –*ous*, *vigorous* means "characterized by strength." "He looked *characterized by strength*" makes sense.

2. The root *pity* means "sorrow for another's suffering." With the suffix –*less*, *pitiless* means "without sorrow." "Both faced the *without sorrow . . . cameras*" sort of makes sense. I guess the cameras didn't have emotions.

3. The root *prove* means "to test or establish as true." With the prefix *un*– and the suffix –*ed*, *unproved* means "not tested or established as true." A *"not established as true* junior senator" makes sense.

4. The root *dyna*– means "power." With the suffix –*ic*, *dynamic* means "the nature of power." "Kennedy came across as . . . *the nature of power*" means he appeared powerful.

5. The root *act* means "a thing done." With the prefix *re*– and the suffix –*ion*, *reactions* must mean "the act of doing a thing again." "When audience *acts of doing a thing again . . .* were compared" doesn't make sense. I think "audience *responses*" makes better sense.

Taking a Second Look

Prefixes and Suffixes. Have students use context clues rather than affixes to determine the meanings of the words in **Practice**. Point out to students that context clues often appear in the words that surround the unfamiliar word.

MINI-LESSON VOCABULARY

Prefixes and Suffixes

A comparison-contrast piece may contain unfamiliar words. Knowing the meanings of common *prefixes* and *suffixes* may help you figure out these words' meanings. A **prefix** is a word part added *before* the root. A **suffix** is a word part added *after* a root. The **root** is the main part of the word. The charts below provide you with the definitions of common prefixes and suffixes.

Prefix	Definition	Example
un–	not	uneven
re–	again	rerun
pre–	before	preview
semi–	half	semifinals

Suffix	Definition	Example
–ous	characterized by	victorious
–ion	act or condition of	inspection
–ic	nature of	angelic
–less	without	careless

THINKING IT THROUGH Using Prefixes and Suffixes

Here is an example based on the word *uncomfortable* from page 122.

▶ **STEP 1** Separate any prefixes or suffixes from the word's root. Define the root.

Un– is a prefix and –able is a suffix. Comfort is the root. It means "free from worry."

▶ **STEP 2** Add the prefix or suffix to the root, and define the word. If you have another prefix or suffix, add it and define the word.

I'll add –able. Comfortable means "able to be free from worry." I'll add un–. Uncomfortable means "not able to be free from worry."

▶ **STEP 3** Check your definition by placing it in the original sentence.

"Nixon came across as not able to be free from worry and ill at ease." That works.

PRACTICE

Using the steps above, figure out the meanings for the following words underlined in "The Nixon-Kennedy Presidential Debates."

1. vigorous (page 121)
2. pitiless (page 121)
3. unproved (page 121)
4. dynamic (page 122)
5. reactions (page 122)

126 Chapter 4 Exposition: Comparing and Contrasting

RESOURCES

Vocabulary Practice
- Communications, WS. p. 72

Test Taking Practice
- Communications, WS. pp. 73–75

Exposition: Comparing and Contrasting

MINI-LESSON: TEST TAKING

Recognizing Supporting Details

Maybe you have had this experience: Your friend tells you, "I met this person the other day who reminds me so much of you." Your first question would probably be "How are we alike?" You want **supporting details** that show how this other person is like you. A reading test may ask you to identify supporting details that show how two subjects are alike or different. Suppose the following passage and the question below it were in a reading test. How would you answer the question?

> Sonja and Maria sometimes seem like the same person. First, they look alike, since each has shiny black hair and big brown eyes. They also have the same interest in collecting stamps from all over the world. They have similar families, too. Sonja has four brothers and Maria has three brothers. Although they complain about their brothers sometimes, each is proud to be the only sister.

What is similar about Sonja and Maria's appearance?

A. They like to wear the same clothes.
B. They both have dark hair and brown eyes.
C. They both have beautiful curly hair.
D. They both are the only sister.

THINKING IT THROUGH: Recognizing Supporting Details

▶ **STEP 1** Identify what detail the question is asking about.

This question asks about the girls' appearance.

▶ **STEP 2** Scan the passage to find the section where this detail is discussed.

The passage doesn't use the word "appearance," but it talks about what the girls look like.

▶ **STEP 3** Find the place in the passage that gives you the answer.

The sentence about their "shiny black hair and big brown eyes" holds the answer.

▶ **STEP 4** Look for the choice that best matches your answer. It may not be stated in the same words, but it should mean the same thing.

Choice D talks about their families. That leaves choices A, B, and C. Clothes are not mentioned, so choice A is not right, and choice C does not match the information in the passage. Choice B is the correct answer.

Looking Ahead to Writing

In the Writing Workshop on pp. 128–146, students will be writing their own comparison-contrast essays. Remind them of the importance of choosing significant points of comparison. Suggest that they review the **Points of Comparison** section on pp. 131–132 when they are preparing to write.

Writing Workshop

OBJECTIVES

- To use the writing process to write a comparison-contrast essay
- To choose and narrow two subjects
- To find points of comparison
- To evaluate supporting details
- To improve choppy sentences
- To use comparatives correctly

Quotation for the Day

"Good order is the foundation of all things."

(Edmund Burke, 1729–1797, British statesman, orator, and writer)

Write this quotation on the chalkboard and explain that one way in which order is particularly important to a comparison-contrast essay is that the two subjects to be compared and contrasted must be examined and their similar and dissimilar qualities identified before writing begins. Identifying qualities to compare and contrast ensures that the comparison-contrast structure will work for a topic.

Meeting INDIVIDUAL NEEDS

ENGLISH-LANGUAGE LEARNERS
General Strategies. Have English-language learners work with English-proficient students to brainstorm subjects. Encourage pairs to begin by discussing similar and dissimilar elements in cultures they have experienced. Students can use the discussion to choose subjects for their writing or to simply practice comparing and contrasting.

Writing Workshop

WHAT'S AHEAD?

In this workshop you will write a comparison-contrast essay. You will also learn how to

- choose and narrow two subjects
- find points of comparison
- evaluate supporting details
- improve choppy sentences
- use comparatives correctly

Writing a Comparison-Contrast Essay

You and your best friend wear the same brand of tennis shoes, save your allowances, and spend too much time on the phone. You seem exactly alike, but are you really? You keep your room neat and organized, while your friend's room is always messy. You love Mexican food, but your friend prefers Thai food. You and your friend share many similarities, but you also have differences. Whenever you recognize that two things are both alike and different, you are comparing and contrasting.

You can understand many things by comparing and contrasting two subjects. In letters, reports, journal entries, and tests, you will find many occasions to write about how two subjects are alike and different. This workshop will prepare you.

Prewriting

Choose and Narrow Two Subjects

Apples and Oranges? Maybe you have heard this statement: "That's like comparing apples and oranges!" This expression means that you should only compare things that are alike,

128   Chapter 4   **Exposition:** Comparing and Contrasting

such as a red apple with a green one. If you think about it, though, comparing apples and oranges makes sense. They are similar enough to be compared, yet different enough to contrast with each other. **When you choose two subjects for your comparison-contrast essay, make sure they have basic similarities as well as differences.**

You should also choose two subjects you know well. For example, you probably know apples and oranges well enough to give specific details about their similarities and differences. What other subjects do you know well? **Brainstorm** about these categories:

- two TV shows
- two people, such as relatives, friends, or movie or sport stars
- two holidays
- two sports
- two musical groups

Set Your Limits The two subjects you choose should be narrow enough for you to write about in an essay. For instance, you could compare apples and oranges in a short essay, but to compare fruits and vegetables, you would need to write a book. Use the steps in the following Thinking It Through to figure out if you need to narrow your subjects.

◀ KEY CONCEPT

TIP One way to choose two subjects for a comparison-contrast essay is to pick a category first. Then, select two subjects within that category. For example, apples and oranges are part of the same category—fruit. Apples and motorcycles are from two different categories—food and transportation—so comparing them would be difficult.

TECHNOLOGY TIP

Suggest that students who have access to a computer and an encyclopedia on CD-ROM use the encyclopedia's search function to find subject ideas. To begin their search, they may want to use broad categories and then focus in on more specific subcategories.

THINKING IT THROUGH — Narrowing Your Subjects

STEP 1 Write down a possible subject you know well.

big pets and small pets

STEP 2 Ask yourself, "Can I break down my subjects into smaller or more specific groups?"

These subjects seem too big. Maybe I should focus on pets I have actually had, like dogs, cats, fish, hamsters, and hermit crabs.

STEP 3 Choose two specific groups that could be discussed in an essay. These are your narrowed subjects.

Since I have a dog and a hamster as pets, I can talk about those in a short essay. They will be my two subjects.

Choosing and Narrowing Subjects

Make a list of possible subjects to compare and contrast. Consider the following questions to help you choose two subjects you can write about in your essay.

- Are the subjects alike enough to make a comparison?
- Do I know enough about the subjects to provide details?
- Are the subjects narrow enough to discuss in an essay? (Use the Thinking It Through steps on page 129.)

Consider Purpose and Audience

A Reason for Everything   Comparing apples and oranges might make sense, except for just one thing: Who cares about them? Most people already know how apples and oranges are alike and different. In other words, there is no strong **purpose** or **audience** for the essay. To determine a specific purpose and audience, first ask yourself the reason for comparing and contrasting the two subjects. Then, ask yourself who would be able to use the information.

Subjects: dogs and hamsters

Purpose: What is the reason for comparing and contrasting dogs and hamsters?
✓ to help people choose a family pet
 to help students from other countries understand two American pets

Audience: Who would be able to use this information?
✓ students and families who want a pet
 students from other countries who do not have dogs or hamsters as pets

---

The student whose chart is shown above chose to help other students and families decide on a family pet. Because her essay will help readers choose a pet, the student will need to provide more information about caring for these pets. Once you have identified your purpose and audience, you can decide what background information or definitions to include in your essay.

RESOURCES

Your Turn 4
Practice
- *Communications,* WS. p. 76

Your Turn 5
Practice
- *Communications,* WS. p. 77

YOUR TURN 5 — Considering Purpose and Audience

Determine your specific purpose and audience for the subjects you have chosen. Create a chart like the one on page 130. Then, think about the background information and definitions your audience will need. Use the following questions to guide you.

- What is the reason for comparing and contrasting the two subjects you have chosen?
- Who would be able to use this information?
- What background information will I need to provide?
- What words will I need to define?

TIP The **voice** of your essay should match your purpose. For example, with a serious purpose such as helping families choose a dog, you would choose words that give specific, direct information: You might refer to a "Lab-Poodle mix" instead of "a mutt." If you want to show the humor in caring for dogs, you might use words that express a lighter tone, such as *pooch, pup,* or *canine comrade.*

 KEY CONCEPT

Think of Points of Comparison

Generally Speaking How are your two subjects alike? How are they different? As you answer these questions, **begin to notice the larger areas in which you find both similarities and differences.** These areas will be the points of comparison that will help you organize your essay.

THINKING IT THROUGH — Choosing Points of Comparison

Here is how to choose the points of comparison for your comparison-contrast essay.

▶ **STEP 1** Think about the subjects of your comparison-contrast essay. What points do they share?

When I think of dogs and hamsters, I think about how they look and act, what they need to survive, how they relate to people, and how long they live.

▶ **STEP 2** Choose two or three of these points of comparison for your essay. Select the ones that you know well so you can provide specific details.

Because I take care of both pets, I can give lots of details about what they need. I also know how they relate to people.

 YOUR TURN 5

To assess the responses, ask students to exchange their charts with a neighbor to check that each question has been answered completely. Students may want to refer to these charts as they write their essays.

TEACHING TIP

Think of Points of Comparison

Discuss further with students how points of comparison are found. Explain that a point of comparison is an idea about two subjects that allows them to be sensibly compared and contrasted with each other. If there are no points of comparison or if the points of comparison don't make sense, comparing and contrasting won't be effective. You might ask volunteers to suggest one pair of subjects that has no clear point of comparison (for example, roller coasters and marathon running) and one pair that has a clear point of comparison (for example, a flute and a saxophone).

YOUR TURN 6

Ask each student to tell a partner his or her two points of comparison. Students should evaluate whether their partners' points are shared by both topics and are supportable.

TEACHING TIP

Gather Support and Organize Information

You may want to guide students when they are selecting and using reference materials and resources by using the following suggestions.

- Warn them not to copy directly from reference materials.
- Discuss reliable and authoritative resources they can use.
- Remind them that they can also use their reference materials and resources while revising and editing their essays.
- Point out that using reference materials such as the dictionary and the thesaurus can also improve their writing.
- *You need to be aware that Internet resources are sometimes public forums and their content can be unpredictable.*

TIP Since you are writing to inform, you want to be sure your details are accurate. If you are unsure about a detail, use **reference materials** and other **resources**. Look up and verify your information in books, in magazines, or on the Internet. You can also verify information by asking teachers or friends who are experts on the subjects you have chosen.

YOUR TURN 6 Choosing Your Points of Comparison

Decide on the points of comparison you will use by following the steps in the Thinking It Through on page 131.

Gather Support and Organize Information

A Leg to Stand On Strong bones support your body just as details support a good essay. How do you get details that will provide the support your ideas need? Start by listing as many details as possible for each point of comparison. Just be sure each detail relates directly to your point of comparison. If it does not, it will weaken, not support, your point.

Getting Organized A Venn diagram can help you organize your details. To make a Venn diagram, draw two overlapping circles like the ones in the student's example below. In the example, the points of comparison are listed to the left of the circles. Each circle represents one of the subjects. The overlapping section includes the details that the subjects have in common. The sections that do not overlap include the details that make each subject different.

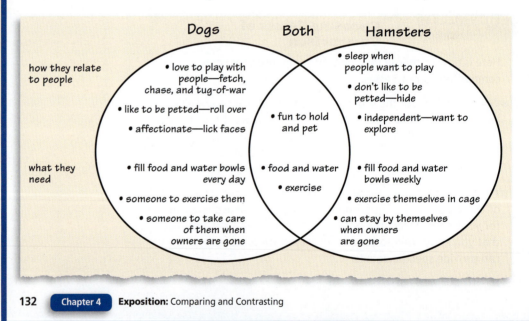

132 Chapter 4 Exposition: Comparing and Contrasting

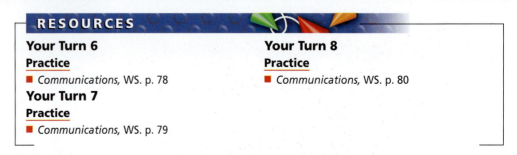

RESOURCES

Your Turn 6
Practice
- *Communications,* WS. p. 78

Your Turn 7
Practice
- *Communications,* WS. p. 79

Your Turn 8
Practice
- *Communications,* WS. p. 80

Exposition: Comparing and Contrasting

Gathering and Organizing Support

Brainstorm a list of details for your two points of comparison. Organize your details in a graphic organizer like the Venn diagram on page 132.

Reference Note
For more on **evaluating details,** see page 135.

Develop a Main Idea Statement

My Point Is . . .   Have you ever had a conversation with someone who gives you an endless list of details? The entire time that person is talking, you are thinking, "What is the point of all this?" In an essay, you can get to the point by writing a **main idea statement,** or **thesis.** This statement is similar to a topic sentence for a paragraph except that it summarizes the main idea of the entire essay. The main idea statement for your comparison-contrast essay will tell readers the subjects you are comparing and contrasting, the purpose of your essay, and your points of comparison. You can write a main idea statement in one or two sentences. See how one student wrote a main idea statement in the example below.

> **Subjects:** dogs and hamsters
>
> **Purpose:** helping students and families decide on a family pet
>
> **Points of comparison:** how dogs and hamsters relate to people and what dogs and hamsters need
>
> **Main idea statement:** Dogs and hamsters both make good family pets, but they are different in the way they relate to people and in their needs.

 Writing a Main Idea Statement

Think about the subjects, purpose, and points of comparison for your comparison-contrast essay. Then, write a main idea statement to communicate these ideas.

Writing Workshop   **133**

Meeting INDIVIDUAL NEEDS

MODALITY
Visual Learners. Suggest that students use graphic organizers to arrange their details. Some students may want to use a simple chart, while others may want to use outlines or conceptual maps to organize details around their main ideas. Encourage students to use the graphic organizer that will best help them organize their details. Refer them to Arranging Ideas on p. 764 in the Quick Reference Handbook.

Ask students to work in pairs to check each other's work. If the points of comparison are arranged in the same order for each subject, the peer evaluator may place a check at the top of the page.

Arranging Details

What Goes Where?   You will organize your essay using the block style, which presents all the information about one subject and then all the information about the other subject. Here is how the student using the block style would arrange the points of comparison for dogs and hamsters.

> Subject 1: Dogs
>   how they relate to people
>   what they need
> Subject 2: Hamsters
>   how they relate to people
>   what they need

As you can see, the block style presents the points of comparison in the same order for both subjects. For each subject, how the pet relates to people is discussed first, and what the pet needs is discussed second. Follow the same structure in your essay.

TIP   For short comparison-contrast essays, the block style is a good way to group similar ideas together. The arrangement of ideas based on similarities is called **logical order.** However, there are other ways to achieve logical order. The chart on page 125 shows the point-by-point style. Still another type of structure is the **modified block style.** In this style, all the *similarities* for the points of comparison are discussed. Then all the *differences* for the points of comparison are discussed. The modified block style looks like this:

Similarities of rugby and football:	rules
	equipment
Differences between rugby and football:	rules
	equipment

YOUR TURN 9 Arranging Details

Arrange the points of comparison for your comparison-contrast essay as in the student example above. Check to see that the points of comparison are in the same order for each subject.

134   Chapter 4   **Exposition:** Comparing and Contrasting

RESOURCES

Your Turn 9
Practice
- *Communications,* WS. p. 81

Critical Thinking
Practice
- *Communications,* WS. p. 82

MINI-LESSON: CRITICAL THINKING

Evaluating Details

When you write a comparison-contrast essay, it is important that your details provide **logical support** for the points of comparison. A feature of logical support is *relevance*. **Relevant details** are related to the point they support. Examine the Venn diagram to the right. Can you identify any details that do not support the point of comparison "appearance"? The details that do not support the point of comparison "appearance" would be either listed with a different point of comparison or removed from the essay.

PRACTICE

Look at the example below and evaluate the details for each point of comparison. Decide whether any detail does not belong with the point of comparison where it is listed.

TEACHING TIP

Evaluating Details

Point out to students that as they arrange and evaluate details, they may find they need to modify or change their points of comparison. For example, if they find that they have many details under one category, they may want to subdivide that category into two separate points of comparison.

MINI-LESSON: CRITICAL THINKING

Evaluating Details

ANSWERS

Details that do not belong under the points of comparison:

- I have a Scottish Terrier named Piper.
- My friend has a German Shepherd named Lady.
- wiry hair
- wiry hair with softer undercoat

Quotation for the Day

"I even have loved spending an entire day seeking the buried treasure of one right word."

(Ralph Schoenstein, 1933– , American author)

Write the quotation on the chalkboard and discuss why selecting precise words is important in writing. [Students may say that precise words help make a writer's ideas clear to a reader.] Why would using precise words be especially important when comparing and contrasting things? [Each thing needs to be carefully described so that the similarities and differences between the things become obvious.]

Meeting INDIVIDUAL NEEDS

MULTIPLE INTELLIGENCES

Logical-Mathematical Intelligence. Compare the framework to an addition equation. Point out that a conclusion should make clear that the main idea stated in the introduction and supported in the body is true. Similarly, a sum in math is the result of the first addend plus the second. To reach a conclusion, then, every point in an essay must in some way help to prove, or strengthen, the main idea statement.

If you wish to assign a length to the students' writing assignment, 500 to 700 words is appropriate. Check to make sure students are following the framework on this page.

Writing

Comparison-Contrast Essay

Framework	Directions and Explanations

Introduction
- Attention-grabbing opener
- Main idea statement

Pull your reader in right away with an **interesting beginning.** You could begin with a mysterious statement which you go on to explain, as the writer of the model to the right did. You could also begin with a funny story or a question. Then, include your **main idea statement** so that the reader understands exactly what you are comparing and contrasting.

Body
- Subject #1
  Point of comparison #1
  (with logical support)
  Point of comparison #2
  (with logical support)
- Subject #2
  Point of comparison #1
  (with logical support)
  Point of comparison #2
  (with logical support)

Here you will point out how the two subjects are alike and different for at least two points of comparison.
- Present your first subject by discussing both **points of comparison** in the first body paragraph.
- When you present your second subject in the next paragraph, discuss the **points of comparison** in the same order.

To help you discuss the similarities and differences, use **transitional words.** Transitional words that show similarities are *also, like, in addition,* and *another.* Transitional words that point out the differences are *on the other hand, but, however,* and *unlike.*

Conclusion
- Summary of body paragraphs

Briefly **sum up** the result of the comparison. **Relate** your summary to the main idea you included in the first paragraph.

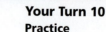 **Drafting Your Essay**

Write a comparison-contrast essay. As you write, refer to the framework above and the Writer's Model on the next page.

136 Chapter 4 **Exposition:** Comparing and Contrasting

RESOURCES

Writing

Writing Prompts
- *Communications,* TP. 34, WS. p. 83

Your Turn 10

Practice
- *Communications,* TP. 35, WS. p. 84

136 Exposition: Comparing and Contrasting

A Writer's Model

The final draft below closely follows the framework for a comparison-contrast essay on the previous page.

Puppy Love or Hamster Heaven?

Your friends have one, maybe even two or three. The neighbors have one. Does it seem that everyone has one but you? No, it is not the latest video game, but something much more fun—a family pet. Dogs and hamsters both make good family pets, but they are different in the way they relate to people and in their needs.

Dogs and hamsters are both fun to hold and pet, but they relate to people in different ways. For instance, dogs enjoy human contact. They love to play fetch, chase, and tug-of-war with their owners. Dogs like to be petted, and most dogs will roll over to have their bellies rubbed. Dogs are also affectionate and love licking their owners' faces. However, dogs need lots of care, too. They need fresh food and water every day, and they need regular exercise. They also need someone to take care of them when their owners go out of town.

Hamsters are very different from dogs. Having contact with people is not important to them. They like to sleep when people want to play. Unlike dogs, hamsters do not like being petted. Many will hide when their owners want to pick them up. Hamsters are also very independent. They like to spend their time exploring. Hamsters may be low on affection, but they need less daily care than dogs do. They need food and water just as dogs do, but an owner usually fills up the food and water dishes only once a week. Hamsters need exercise too, but they get their exercise by running on wheels in their cages. If their owners go out of town, hamsters can be left alone.

Dogs and hamsters both make good pets. Dogs provide plenty of affection, but they are also high maintenance. Hamsters are definitely low maintenance, but they are also less cuddly. The choice is yours.

Attention-grabbing opener

Main idea statement

Subject 1: First point of comparison
Supporting details

Second point of comparison
Supporting details

Subject 2: First point of comparison
Supporting details

Second point of comparison
Supporting details

Summary of body paragraphs

Connecting Reading and Writing

Before students begin reading **A Writer's Model,** have them review the comparison-contrast structure section of the Reading Workshop on pp. 124–125. Ask students to list the points of comparison between puppies and hamsters as they read the essay, making a note of the order in which they are presented. This may help students recognize the block style used in the essay.

Connecting Reading and Writing

Students may benefit from reading **A Student's Model** with an awareness of points of comparison. Before students read the model, refer them to the points of comparison section of the Reading Workshop on pp. 123–124. Students should notice that the model uses two points of comparison and that both points are supported by relevant details.

A Student's Model

When you write a comparison-contrast essay, make sure you have a purpose for writing. Matthew Hester, a middle school student from Laurel Hill, Florida, wants to help his audience make a decision. He compares two types of collections that may interest beginner collectors.

A Collection Question

Attention-grabbing opener

Collecting is very popular today. Collectors have their own magazines, television shows, and Internet sites. If you are thinking about starting a collection, I suggest considering trading cards or airplane models.

Main idea statement

They are both good investments and fun, but they differ in storage and use.

Subject 1: First point of comparison

Collecting trading cards is an enjoyable hobby. They are easy to store and transport in bags, boxes, or notebooks.

Second point of comparison

Trading cards with friends is a super way to spend an afternoon. Cards also provide adventure and challenge as you seek that one card essential to completing your set.

Subject 2: First point of comparison

Model collecting differs from card collecting in several ways. Model airplanes require more storage space than cards do and are more difficult to transport due to their larger size.

Second point of comparison

However, models do allow for more realistic play. The zooming and swooshing of miniature airplanes give the feeling of being in the center of the action.

Summary of body paragraphs

Trading cards and model airplanes both make good collections due to their current and possible future value. This makes them a wise investment for your allowance dollars. Trading cards are excellent choices if you have limited storage space and enjoy a challenge. Model airplanes are better if your storage space is unlimited and you enjoy live-action play. If you have trouble deciding, join me in collecting both. Either way, start your collection today!

Chapter 4 **Exposition:** Comparing and Contrasting

Revising

Evaluate and Revise Content, Organization, and Style

Double Vision Look twice when you evaluate a peer's paper or your own. On the first reading, concentrate on content and organization, using the guidelines below. The second time you read the essay, pay attention to the sentences, using the Focus on Sentences on page 141.

▶ **First Reading: Content and Organization** Use this chart to evaluate and revise your essay so the ideas are clear.

Comparison-Contrast Essay: Content and Organization Guidelines for Self-Evaluation and Peer Evaluation

Evaluation Questions	Tips	Revision Techniques
❶ Does the introduction state the main idea?	▶ **Underline** the main idea statement.	▶ **Add** a main idea statement if one is missing.
❷ Does the first body paragraph discuss the first subject with at least two points of comparison?	▶ **Put a star** next to each point of comparison.	▶ If there is no clear point of comparison, **add** one or **revise** an existing one.
❸ Does the second body paragraph discuss the second subject using the same points of comparison in the same order?	▶ **Draw a wavy line** under each point of comparison.	▶ If the same points of comparison are not used, **add** one or **revise** an existing one. **Rearrange** the points of comparison if they are not in the same order.
❹ Do relevant details logically support each point of comparison for both subjects?	▶ **Put a check mark** next to the supporting details for each point of comparison. **Underline** any details that do not support the point of comparison.	▶ If needed, **elaborate** on a point of comparison by adding details. **Delete** details that do not directly support the point of comparison.
❺ Does the conclusion summarize the body paragraphs and refer to the main idea?	▶ With a colored marker, **highlight** the summary.	▶ If needed, **add** a brief summary that is related to the main idea.

Writing Workshop **139**

Quotation for the Day

❝This is one of the most important things a teacher can share with students: that a piece of writing can be manipulated and molded like clay.❞

(Meredith Sue Willis, 1946–   , American author and teacher)

Share this quotation with the class and ask students to discuss how clay and writing are similar. Point out that a piece of writing, like clay, is "reshaped" many times before it reaches its final form. The students' drafts of their comparison-contrast essays are just one step in the shaping process.

TEACHING TIP

▶ **Elaboration**
So that students can discover areas in need of elaboration in their work, have them read their papers and ask themselves questions such as the following: "Why is this so?" "How do I know this?" "What do I mean by this?" and "Can I give an example or an anecdote that shows this?" Asking these questions will help students see areas that need further explanation, support, or development.

RESOURCES

Revising
Practice
- *Communications,* TPs. 36, 37, WS. pp. 85, 86, 87

Responding to the Revision Process

ANSWERS

1. The writer deleted the sentence because the detail was not relevant to the point of comparison.

2. The writer added the sentence because the sentence elaborates the idea that having contact with people is not important to hamsters.

Cooperative Learning

Peer Review. Consider pairing students who have chosen very different topics. Students should take turns evaluating each other's points of comparison. Students may indicate in the margins if the points are clear to them or, if necessary, mark areas that need more details.

MODALITY

Auditory Learners. To help students identify choppy sentences, you may want to have them read their essays aloud into tape recorders and then listen to their recordings while underlining places on their papers that need revision.

PEER REVIEW

As you evaluate a peer's paper, ask yourself the following questions:

- What points of comparison does the writer discuss?
- Who will be able to use this information?

ONE WRITER'S REVISIONS This revision is an early draft of the essay on page 137.

> Hamsters are very different from dogs. Having contact with people is not important to them. They like to sleep when people want to play. ~~I have to go to bed by 10:30.~~ Unlike dogs, hamsters do not like being petted. *Many will hide when their owners want to pick them up.* Hamsters are also very independent. They like to spend their time exploring.

delete

elaborate

Responding to the Revision Process

1. Why do you think the writer deleted a sentence in the paragraph above?
2. Why do you think the writer added a sentence to the paragraph?

▶ **Second Reading: Style** During your first reading, you looked at what you said in your essay and how you organized your ideas. Now, focus on how your essay *sounds*. Good writing has an easy rhythm that is not choppy. To achieve an easy rhythm, writers use a variety of sentences in their essays. They avoid long series of short sentences by combining two short sentences into one sentence. Use the following guidelines to evaluate the rhythm of your writing.

Style Guidelines

Evaluation Question	Tip	Revision Technique
Are sentences combined so that they are not choppy?	▶ **Underline** any short sentence that repeats several words or a phrase from the sentence before or after it.	▶ **Combine** sentences by cutting repeated words and inserting necessary words or phrases.

140 Chapter 4 Exposition: Comparing and Contrasting

Focus on Sentences

Combining Sentences

Good writers use some short sentences. Too many short sentences are a problem. Many short sentences in a row bore readers. The ideas in the previous three sentences are important for writers to know, but you might have found it difficult to pay attention to them. Their choppy sound and their repeated words and phrases probably bothered you. Combining short, choppy sentences can be as easy as moving a word or phrase from one sentence to another.

Choppy Sentences	~~The car was~~ black. The car was hot. [move a word]
Combined Sentence	The black car was hot.
Choppy Sentences	Jamal played disc golf. ~~He played~~ in the afternoon. [move a phrase]
Combined Sentence	Jamal played disc golf in the afternoon.

ONE WRITER'S REVISIONS

They love to play fetch and tug-of-war with their owners. ~~Dogs also like to play~~ chase.

Responding to the Revision Process

How does combining the two sentences improve the writing?

Evaluating and Revising Your Comparison-Contrast Essay

First, evaluate and revise the content and organization of your essay, using the guidelines on page 139. Then, use the Focus on Sentences above to see if you need to combine any choppy sentences. Finally, if a peer evaluated your paper, think carefully about his or her comments as you revise.

COMPUTER TIP

If you have access to a computer, speed up the revision process by using the cut-and-paste feature. You can rearrange the details in your comparison-contrast essay by cutting words and sentences and then pasting them in a new location. Cutting and pasting saves you the trouble of typing the information twice.

Writing Workshop   141

Quotation for the Day

"He who does not expect a million readers should not write a line."

(J. W. Goethe, 1794–1832, German poet, dramatist, and thinker)

Read the quotation to the class and ask students to freewrite about ways they could publish their essays so they could reach a large number of readers. Have students share their ideas later in the lesson when they discuss methods of publishing.

Meeting INDIVIDUAL NEEDS

INCLUSION

You may to wish to have students work through the practice items with a helper. For each sentence, the helper can tap out on a desktop the number of syllables in a word to help students determine the correct comparative form. If students are unsure about whether to use *more* or *–er* to form the comparative of a two-syllable modifier, they can also look up the modifier in a dictionary.

Grammar Link

Using Comparatives Correctly

ANSWERS

1. more lovable
2. smaller
3. more playful
4. more frequently
5. easier

Publishing

Proofread Your Essay

Reference Note
For more on **proofreading**, see page 13.

Look Out Two sets of eyes are better than one when trying to find mistakes. After you proofread your essay, see if you can catch more mistakes by enlisting the help of another proofreader.

Grammar Link

Using Comparatives Correctly

In a comparison-contrast essay, you have to make comparisons. When you make comparisons between two subjects, you use the **comparative** form of adjectives and adverbs. To write comparatives correctly, follow the guidelines.

The comparative form of one-syllable modifiers is usually made by adding *–er*.

Modifier	Comparative Form
fast	faster

Some two-syllable modifiers form the comparative by using *more*.

Modifier	Comparative Form
nervous	more nervous

Modifiers with three or more syllables use *more* to form the comparative.

Modifier	Comparative Form
successful	more successful

Be sure not to use *–er* together with *more*. That combination is never correct.

Incorrect Mandy always arrives more earlier than Liza.

Correct Mandy always arrives *earlier* than Liza.

PRACTICE

Complete each of the following sentences with the correct form of the given modifier.

Example:
1. quickly — Sam finished his test ____ than Liam.
1. more quickly

1. **lovable** — I think dogs are ____ than hamsters are.
2. **small** — Hamsters are ____ than dogs.
3. **playful** — Hamsters are ____ at night than during the day.
4. **frequently** — Dogs have to be fed ____ than hamsters.
5. **easy** — Do you think hamsters are ____ to take care of than dogs?

For more information and practice on **comparatives**, see page 497.

142 Chapter 4 **Exposition:** Comparing and Contrasting

RESOURCES

Publishing
Extension
- Designing Your Writing

Grammar Link
Practice
- *Communications*, WS. p. 89

Publish Your Essay

Experience to the Rescue Your experience with the two subjects you wrote about in your comparison-contrast essay can provide information that people need and want. What is the best way to reach the audience who will benefit from your experience?

- Does the topic of your comparison-contrast essay relate to a school subject? Did you compare two sports? two artists? two countries? Make copies of your essay and share them with teachers. They might use your essay in their classes.

- Display your essays and those of your classmates on a wall in your school. Invite teachers, parents, and other students to view the "Authors' Wall."

Designing Your Writing

Creating a Bar Graph A quick and visual way to show your readers the similarities and differences between two subjects is to provide a bar graph. Each point of comparison can be a separate graph. Some word-processing programs allow you to create graphs, or you can draw one by hand. Either way, make sure you use colors and provide a **legend,** or explanation of what each color represents. Colors will help your reader identify each subject in your graph. Below, see how the writer of the Writer's Model used a bar graph that includes a legend to compare the needs of hamsters and dogs.

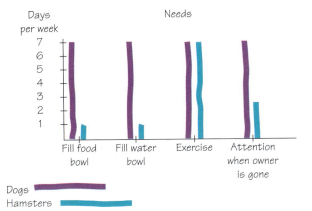

TEACHING TIP

Publish Your Essay
If students are writing essays by hand, they may choose to write in cursive or manuscript style. Point out to students that they need to write legibly as they prepare their essays for publishing since words with letters that are not formed correctly may appear misspelled. You may want to display examples of clearly written samples, in both cursive and manuscript styles, for students to use as models.

TIP By looking at the bar graph to the left, readers can tell which pet needs more daily care.
? Do you know which pet has more needs?

Writing Workshop   143

Wrap It Up

Metacognition. Ask students to reflect on their writing processes by answering the following questions.

1. Which part of the processes was most challenging for you? Why?

2. What could you do to make this part of the process easier for you?

Then, ask students the following question.

3. Why is it important to use a structure such as block style, point-by-point style, or modified block style when writing a comparison-contrast essay? [These structures present the comparative information in a meaningful way for the reader, help the writer organize material, and provide a logical way to highlight points of comparison.]

TEACHING TIP

Proofreading, Publishing, and Reflecting on Your Essay
Tie the proofreading step to grammar instruction by having students look specifically for the problem addressed in the **Grammar Link** as they proofread their papers.

YOUR TURN 12

You might have students create a sheet in their portfolios on which they list both proofreading errors they found in their papers and their corrections. Have students date their entries.

You can lead students in a reflective discussion by asking volunteers to share with the class their responses to the questions.

Reflect on Your Essay

Building Your Portfolio Take time to reflect both on the process of comparing and contrasting two subjects and on the process of writing your essay. Thinking about how you wrote this assignment will help you when you write your next paper.

- Do you think the two subjects you wrote about are more similar or more different? Why?
- Before you wrote your essay, you arranged your ideas in a certain order. Did you find that helpful? Why or why not?
- Think about the reason why you compared the two subjects you chose. How does your essay achieve that purpose?

YOUR TURN 12 Proofreading, Publishing, and Reflecting on Your Essay

- Correct grammar, usage, and mechanics errors.
- Publish your essay by following one of the suggestions on the previous page.
- Answer the questions from Reflect on Your Essay above. Record your responses in a learning log, or include them in your portfolio.

HAGAR THE HORRIBLE reprinted with special permission of King Features Syndicate, Inc.

MINI-LESSON: TEST TAKING

Writing a Classification Essay

A common question on essay tests is one that asks you to classify the similarities and differences between two subjects or the good and bad points about one subject. You must quickly determine how to generate ideas. A T-chart can help. Suppose the prompt to the right appeared on a writing test. How would you approach it?

Think about your language arts class and your science class. They are alike in some ways and different in other ways. Write a composition in which you explain how your language arts and science classes are alike and how they are different.

THINKING IT THROUGH — Writing a Classification Essay

▶ **STEP 1** Identify what the prompt is asking you to do.

It asks me to explain how my language arts and science classes are alike and different.

▶ **STEP 2** Think of at least two points of comparison. Then, create a T-chart and fill it in with supporting details.

	Similarities	Differences
What I learn	information about people and events	L. A. – grammar, writing Sci. – plants, animals
What I do	homework write papers read	L. A. – act out plays, write essays Sci. – labs, draw diagrams

▶ **STEP 3** Plan how you will develop your essay.

I'll use block style. I'll talk all about language arts in the first body paragraph and science in the second body paragraph.

▶ **STEP 4** Write your essay. Make sure to elaborate on the supporting details from your T-chart with facts, examples, and explanations.

RESOURCES

Test Taking
Practice
- *Communications,* WS. p. 90

TEACHING TIP

Comparing Documentaries
When assigning **Your Turn 13**, give students specific suggestions about where they can find two documentaries on the same subject. In addition to viewing documentaries on broadcast networks, students may choose to check out videos from the library or local stores. Tell them that libraries and stores usually carry lists of video titles that students can consult.

You may need to provide an alternative assignment for students who do not have access to television or videos at home. Consider asking these students to use both newspapers and magazines to locate two articles that cover the same event. Then, have the students adapt the questions on p. 146 to compare the two versions.

Critical Thinking
Evaluation. Ask students to work together in randomly selected small groups to develop a checklist for evaluating documentaries. Students should be sure to analyze and judge the following: information, attention-grabbing features, soundtrack, camera work, and role of narrator. Have students develop general statements that describe what each element should look like in an effective documentary and then evaluate a specific documentary.

YOUR TURN 13
To help you assess their essays, ask students to underline the sentence that identifies the purpose for each documentary.

Connections to Life

Comparing Documentaries

Is truth stranger than fiction? Many filmmakers and writers would answer with a booming "Yes!" Filmmakers who want to show that truth is interesting will make a *documentary*. A **documentary** is a nonfiction film that creatively portrays an actual event, person, place, thing, or issue.

Filmmakers have the same reasons for producing documentaries as writers have for writing essays, articles, stories, or poems. Their purposes are *to inform, to entertain, to persuade,* and *to express themselves.* Like many writers, filmmakers may also have the purpose of *making money.* Every documentary will have at least one of these purposes. In fact, a documentary, like a written work, may have several purposes.

Two of a Kind? For this assignment, you will compare the purposes of two documentaries on the same topic. To do that, ask yourself the questions to the right.

- Does the filmmaker provide facts and explanations about a topic? If so, the purpose may be **to inform.**
- Does the filmmaker focus on a famous person, a funny event, or an attention-grabbing topic? Does the documentary contain flashy graphics, an appealing soundtrack, and eye-catching camerawork? If so, the purpose may be **to entertain.**
- Does the filmmaker appeal to viewers' emotions and try to get the viewers to think a certain way? If so, the purpose may be **to persuade.**
- Does the filmmaker explore a topic using a first-person narrator who reveals his or her inner thoughts about the topic? If so, the purpose may be **to express.**
- Does the filmmaker focus on a popular topic? If so, the purpose may be **to make money.** The larger the audience a documentary attracts, the more ads the network can sell.

YOUR TURN 13 Comparing Documentaries

View two documentaries on the same topic. As you watch, take notes on how information is presented in each, using the questions above as a guide. Then, write a paragraph or two comparing the two documentaries. Discuss how the documentaries' purposes are similar, and how they are different.

146 Chapter 4 **Exposition:** Comparing and Contrasting

Focus on Viewing and Representing

Comparing Ideas in Photographs

When you look at a photograph of yourself, what do you see? You see yourself, right? The picture shows the color of your eyes and hair, the shape of your nose and mouth, and the style of clothing you wear. Actually, while the person in the picture certainly seems to look like you, it is not the *real* you.

Photographs vs. Reality

Many people believe that photographs truly represent reality, but they do not. In truth, photographs, like all illustrations, only resemble an actual person, place, thing, or event. What you see in a photograph is not the same as what you see in real life because photographs have the following unique characteristics.

- **Photographs are two-dimensional and flat.** If you took a picture of the palm of your hand, could you turn the picture over and see the top of your hand? No. The photograph shows only one side. In real life, you can view all sides.

- **Photographs are easily reproduced and distributed.** It is easy to make copies of your birthday party pictures and send them to relatives and friends. Although it might be fun, it would be impossible to reproduce the real party over and over again.

- **Photographs contain a single point of view.** When you look at a head-on photograph of a baseball player hitting a baseball, you are looking at the action from the photographer's point of view. You do not see what the hitter sees. Photographers use the element of point of view to show how an image looks from a specific position.

WHAT'S AHEAD?

In this section you will compare ideas in photographs. You will also learn how to

- explain the difference between a photograph of an object and the real object
- analyze how photographs provide information

Meeting INDIVIDUAL NEEDS

INCLUSION
Students who have a visual impairment may need assistance with this workshop. You might want to pair students with a helper to point out and describe details as they complete the exercises in this section.

Critical Thinking
Evaluation. Camera angle (point of view), context (which can be altered by cropping), and captions are three elements of photography discussed in this feature. You may want to have students compare other elements of illustration in general, such as style and media. Have students identify different styles of photographs (such as symbolic or realistic) and then find two examples of photos of similar subjects in different styles.

Alternatively, have students compare representations of the same subject in two different media, such as a photograph vs. a drawing. In both cases, have students discuss what the illustrator gains and what he or she loses when he or she chooses to use a certain style or medium.

TIP Photography is not the only media form that provides information.
? Can you think of any others? **Hint:** The paragraph to the right can give you a few answers.

Photographs Provide Information

Even though looking at a photograph is not the same as actually seeing the real thing, photographs are helpful because they provide information in an easily accessible way. For example, if you want to know what a Tasmanian devil looks like, you could visit the nearest zoo, fly to Tasmania, or look at a photograph. The easiest choice, of course, would be to look at a photograph.

Photographs are also a powerful partner to the written and spoken word. In a newspaper, for instance, you might read about an erupting volcano. Not until you look at the picture that accompanies the article would you fully understand the massive destruction the volcano caused. Because photographs are so powerful and easy to reproduce, they are a popular form of media. Look in any magazine, newspaper, or textbook and you will find many photographs. You should be aware, however, that the information photographs provide can be changed by adjusting the *camera angle*, by *cropping* the photograph, and by using *captions*.

Up, Down, Sideways
A photographer can change the appearance of a person, place, thing, or event by changing the **camera angle.** Look at the examples below. In the picture on the left, the photographer stood on a ladder and shot the picture looking down. Do you see how the boy looks small and rather fragile? Now, look at the picture on the right taken of the same boy from a low angle. From this point of view, the boy looks big and powerful, even a little intimidating.

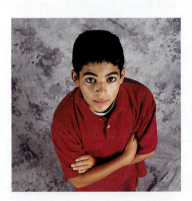 

What's Missing? Photographs can be **cropped,** or cut, so background details do not distract the viewer from the main subject. However, cropping can change the meaning of a picture, as you can see below. In the picture on the left you see a spaceship hovering in the sky. In the picture on the right, though, you see what was cut from the first picture. Aliens are not landing; a girl is holding the spaceship by a string.

More Than Words Some photographs have **captions,** which are like titles. A caption provides viewers with a summary of what is shown in a picture. Captions can be neutral, giving only facts, or they can show a positive or negative attitude toward the subject. Look at the pictures and captions below and on the next page. You can see that the images are the same, but the captions show two very different attitudes toward grizzly bears.

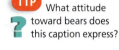 **TIP** What attitude toward bears does this caption express?

Enjoying the spring weather, a mother bear and her young relax by the riverside.

Focus on Viewing and Representing **149**

Critical Thinking

Analysis/Evaluation. Have students compare a moving image from an electronic medium (like TV) with a still photograph. Select similar subjects; for example, a TV commercial for a product which can also be found prominently featured (in photographic medium) in a print ad. Have students notice every similarity and difference that they can about the treatment of the product in the still and moving versions, but also guide students to compare specific points, such as point of view of the camera in both media, captions or other text, cropping (in the photo) vs. types of shots (close-ups, long shots) in the moving image, and the idea or message about the product conveyed in both media. (You may want to post a picture of the print ad next to the TV monitor, then replay the ad several times.) Summarize students' responses in a Venn diagram.

Next, ask students to discuss the purposes and effects of advertising the same product in two different media: Why would an advertiser be willing to invest in both types of advertising? What different purposes and effects might the advertiser be trying to achieve? Ask students to support their ideas with evidence from the Venn diagram.

Wrap It Up

Metacognition. Ask students the following question.

1. What did you learn from this activity about how you view the information in photographs?

Then, ask students this question.

2. List some ways in which the information in photographs can be changed. [cropping, changing camera angles, using captions]

ANSWERS
Possible answers follow.

- First caption: "A young girl was found earlier today, looking lost and tired."

- Second caption: "Children are enjoying the current summer weather by cooling off outside."

- The two photographs convey very different scenes. In the first photo, the cropping of the background makes it seem as if the girl is alone and perhaps abandoned. The second photo shows more of the scene. After looking at it, I realized that the girl was not alone and that she had probably been playing.

Timesaver

To quickly assess students' responses to the questions in **Your Turn 14,** consider having them work in randomly assigned small groups to check their answers. Ask them to discuss why they responded to each photograph as they did. Then, have group representatives present the findings of their discussions.

TIP The purpose of any illustration is to illustrate an idea. Illustrators make choices about what style and medium will best suit their purpose. For example, the photograph to the right uses a realistic style, complementing the informative caption. The choice of photography as a medium also contributes to the informative purpose. Could a **?** different medium (such as a cartoon) or a different style (one using symbols to represent bears, for example) be as effective in complementing the caption text? Explain.

Here is the same picture with a different caption. Notice how the caption changes what you "see" in the photo.

Rangers warn park visitors not to approach mother grizzly bears. They will fiercely protect their cubs.

Your Turn 14 — Comparing Ideas in Photographs

- Look at the photograph on the left below, while covering up the photo next to it. How do you feel about the subject? Write a caption for the photograph that summarizes what you see and expresses your feelings.

- Next, look at the photograph on the right. How do you feel about the subject now? Write a caption for the photograph that summarizes what you see and expresses your feelings.

- Finally, write a paragraph in which you compare the two photographs. Explain how the differences in the way each photo is presented may have affected the captions you wrote.

150 Chapter 4 **Exposition:** Comparing and Contrasting

RESOURCES

Your Turn 14
Practice and Reinforcement

- *Media Literacy and Communication Skills* —*Support and Practice,* Ch. 4, transparencies and worksheets

CHAPTER 4 Choices

Choose one of the following activities to complete.

▶ CAREERS

1. Tool Time Comparing and contrasting two subjects is a favorite tool of journalists, consumer advocates, scientists, sports commentators, and campaign managers for politicians. Find examples of how comparing and contrasting is used in these fields or in other fields. Then, write a **report** that describes examples of how people in their fields make comparisons.

▶ CROSSING THE CURRICULUM: ART

2. An Eye for Detail Sharpen your powers of observation by creating two **illustrations** in which several details have been changed from one to the other. For instance, if you drew two illustrations of a pizza with many toppings, the second would be slightly different from the first because you added, removed, or changed the toppings. Once your two illustrations are drawn, ask a partner to circle the items that are different.

▶ CREATIVE WRITING

3. It's Like This Compose a **humorous poem** about a person, place, thing, or idea using similes. A simile is a comparison of two unlike things using *like* or *as*. For example, you could write a simile poem about happiness that begins, "Happiness is like a day without homework." In the rest of the poem, you would explain in a funny way the ways in which these two things are alike.

▶ CROSSING THE CURRICULUM: MUSIC

4. The Beat Goes On Does your favorite musician or band follow the same formula from one CD to the next? Find specific examples that show how the musician or band has changed or stayed the same over time. You might focus on lyrics, style, vocals, or other areas. Give a **multimedia presentation,** using audio or audiovisual clips to demonstrate your points.

▶ CREATIVE WRITING
Inform students that their humorous poems are more likely to entertain readers if, as writers, they keep in mind the elements of poetry. Remind them that poetry has rhythm; may include rhyme; and contains imagery, or language that appeals to the senses.

Give students the following suggestions for creating humorous comparisons.
- compare emotions to something
- compare a person to an animal
- use "funny" noun phrases when comparing two things, such as comparing baby owls to cotton balls

▶ CROSSING THE CURRICULUM: MUSIC
Have students work in pairs to create their multimedia **reports** and presentations. Students might use these guidelines in preparing their presentations:
- Choose a band or musician whose style has changed over time.
- Find examples of the band's or musician's style from different CDs, tapes, or videos.
- Make a T-chart, list, or Venn diagram to show how the band's or musician's style has changed. [different rhythms, different clothes or hairstyles, new themes in the lyrics]
- Decide which songs or video clips you will play to illustrate your points.
- Assemble all the materials and equipment you will need to make your presentation.
- Test the equipment to make sure it is working.
- Decide who will do which tasks during the presentation and then practice giving the presentation.

Choices 151

RESOURCES

Comparing and Contrasting
Assessment
- *Assessment Package*
  —Chapter Tests, Ch. 4
  —Chapter Tests in Standardized Test Formats, Ch. 4
  —Assessment Alternatives, Ch. 4

- *Test Generator*
  (One-Stop Planner CD-ROM)

Choices
Rubrics
- *Assessment Package*
  —Assessment Alternatives, Ch. 4

Choices 151

CHAPTER PLANNING GUIDE

CHAPTER 5

Responding to a Novel

Use this guide to create an instructional plan that suits the individual needs of your students. Assignments marked by an asterisk (*) may be completed out of class. Times given for pacing lessons are estimated. See pp. 152–153 for chapter-wide resources. Resources listed in this guide are point-of-use resources only.

Curriculum Connections

Connections to Literature
pp. 176–180
- Writing a Short Story
- Writing an Essay About a Poem

Choices *p. 185*
- Writing
- Connecting Cultures
- Technology
- Creative Writing

---

internet connect

 GO TO: go.hrw.com
KEYWORD: EOLang 6-5

 All resources for this chapter are available for preview on the *One-Stop Planner CD-ROM with Test Generator*. All worksheets and tests may be printed from the CD-ROM.

T151A

	Chapter Opener *pp. 152–153*	**Reading Workshop: Reading a Book Review** *pp. 154–160*
DEVELOPMENTAL PROGRAM	⏱ **30 minutes** • Your Turn 1 *p. 153*	⏱ **90 minutes** • Preparing to Read *p. 154* • Reading Selection *p. 155* • First Thoughts in groups *p. 156* • Elements of a Novel *p. 156* • Your Turn 2 *p. 156* • Point of View *pp. 157–158* • Your Turn 3 *p. 158* • Test Taking Mini-Lesson *p. 160*
CORE PROGRAM	⏱ **25 minutes** • Your Turn 1 *p. 153*	⏱ **90 minutes** • Preparing to Read *p. 154* • Reading Selection *p. 155* • First Thoughts *p. 156* • Elements of a Novel *p. 156* • Your Turn 2 *p. 156* • Point of View *pp. 157–158* • Your Turn 3 *p. 158* • Vocabulary Mini-Lesson *p. 159* • Test Taking Mini-Lesson *p. 160*
ADVANCED PROGRAM	⏱ **20 minutes** • Your Turn 1 *p. 153*	⏱ **60 minutes** • Preparing to Read *p. 154* • Reading Selection *p. 155* • First Thoughts *p. 156* • Elements of a Novel *p. 156* • Your Turn 2 *p. 156* • Point of View *pp. 157–158* • Your Turn 3 *p. 158* • Vocabulary Mini-Lesson *p. 159*
RESOURCES — PRINT	• *Communications,* TP. 38, WS. p. 91	• *Alternative Readings,* Ch. 5 • *Communications,* TPs. 39, 40, WS. pp. 92–99
RESOURCES — MEDIA	• *One-Stop Planner CD-ROM*	• *One-Stop Planner CD-ROM*

TP.=Transparency   WS.=Worksheet

Writing Workshop: Writing a Book Review *pp. 161–180*	Focus on Viewing and Representing: Comparing Media: Film, TV, and Literature *pp. 181–184*
⏱ **210 minutes** • Select and Read a Novel; Your Turn 4* *pp. 161–163* • Purpose and Audience; Your Turn 5 *pp. 163–164* • Gather and Organize Details; Your Turn 6 *pp. 164, 166* • Preparing Your Evaluation; Your Turn 7 *p. 167* • Framework; Your Turn 8* *p. 168* • Writer's Model and Student's Model *pp. 169–170* • Evaluate and Revise; Your Turn 9 *pp. 171–173* • Proofreading, Publishing, and Reflecting *pp. 174–175* • Grammar Link *p. 174* • Your Turn 10 *p. 175*	⏱ **75 minutes** • Read the Book and Watch the Show *pp. 181–183* • Compare the Book and Movie or TV Show *pp. 183–184* • Your Turn 13* *p. 184*
⏱ **180 minutes** • Select and Read a Novel; Your Turn 4* *pp. 161–163* • Purpose and Audience; Your Turn 5 *pp. 163–164* • Critical-Thinking Mini-Lesson in groups *p. 165* • Gather and Organize Details; Your Turn 6 *pp. 164, 166* • Preparing Your Evaluation; Your Turn 7 *p. 167* • Framework; Your Turn 8* *p. 168* • Writer's Model and Student's Model *pp. 169–170* • Evaluate and Revise *pp. 171–172* • Focus on Clichés *p. 173* • Your Turn 9 *p. 173* • Proofreading, Publishing, and Reflecting *pp. 174–175* • Grammar Link *p. 174* • Your Turn 10 *p. 175* • Connections to Literature: Analyzing a Poem; Your Turn 12* *pp. 178–180*	⏱ **60 minutes** • Read the Book and Watch the Show *pp. 181–183* • Compare the Book and Movie or TV Show *pp. 183–184* • Your Turn 13* *p. 184*
⏱ **140 minutes** • Select and Read a Novel; Your Turn 4* *pp. 161–163* • Purpose and Audience; Your Turn 5 *pp. 163–164* • Critical-Thinking Mini-Lesson *p. 165* • Gather and Organize Details; Your Turn 6* *pp. 164, 166* • Preparing Your Evaluation; Your Turn 7 *p. 167* • Framework; Your Turn 8* *p. 168* • Writer's Model and Student's Model *pp. 169–170* • Evaluate and Revise *pp. 171–172* • Focus on Clichés *p. 173* • Your Turn 9* *p. 173* • Proofreading, Publishing, and Reflecting *pp. 174–175* • Your Turn 10 *p. 175* • Connections to Literature: Writing a Short Story; Your Turn 11* *pp. 176–177*	⏱ **45 minutes** • Read the Book and Watch the Show *pp. 181–183* • Compare the Book and Movie or TV Show *pp. 183–184* • Your Turn 13* *p. 184*

• *Communications,* TPs. 41–44, WS. pp. 100–111
• *Designing Your Writing*
	• *Media Literacy and Communication Skills*
	  —*Support and Practice*, Ch. 5
	  —*A How-to Handbook*
	  —*A Teacher's Guide*, Ch. 5

• One-Stop Planner CD-ROM	• *Media Literacy and Communication Skills* —Videocassette 2, Segment D • One-Stop Planner CD-ROM

CHAPTER 5
Responding to a Novel

CHAPTER OBJECTIVES

- To read a book review to identify the elements of a novel and a writer's point of view
- To write a book review including a summary and an evaluation
- To compare a book and a film in the same genre

Chapter Overview

In their daily lives, students frequently encounter written and oral evaluations. In this chapter, students will examine one kind of evaluation—a book review—and then share their responses to a novel by writing a book review. The Reading Workshop (pp. 154–160) contains a book review for students to read, giving them an opportunity to identify the elements of a novel that the reviewer focuses on and to identify her point of view. The Writing Workshop (pp. 161–180) guides students through the steps of the writing process as they write their own book reviews. The Focus on Viewing and Representing explains how to compare a book and a film in the same genre. The three parts of this chapter can be taught independently, but they also work together to help students develop a basic understanding of how to evaluate books and other media.

Why Study Book Reviews?

Students read or hear evaluations daily—in publications, in conversations with friends, or on TV and radio programs. For example, they might read an article that rates a new product or watch a game in which an announcer evaluates an athlete's performance. By studying book reviews students can learn both how to evaluate carefully what they read and how to write responses to literature.

Teaching the Chapter

Option 1: Begin with Literature

You might introduce this chapter after studying short stories and novels. Explain that reviewers analyze such elements as character, plot, and setting when evaluating a work of fiction. Have students read the book review in this chapter (p. 155), noting which elements of a novel the review analyzes and how the reviewer's choice of words helps to reveal her point of view. Once students have analyzed the review, they can begin work on their own book reviews in the Writing Workshop (pp. 161–180).

Option 2: Begin with Nonfiction and Writing

You might begin with the nonfiction reading and information in this chapter. The book review in the Reading Workshop (p. 155) provides students with a basic introduction to the way a reviewer analyzes and evaluates a book. Then, by writing a book review in the Writing Workshop (pp. 161–180), students may be better prepared to evaluate books and other media that they read or view independently. When they return to literature, students may be better able to identify elements of a novel or a short story and also better understand how to use a reviewer's analysis to judge if they want to read a work of literature. See also **Connections to Literature** on pp. 176–180.

Making Connections

■ To the Literature Curriculum

Explain to students that reviewers focus on one or more of these elements—character, plot, and setting—when they evaluate a story or a novel. Reading Gary Paulsen's "Storm" with a focus on its main character, a dog named Storm, can help students evaluate this excerpt from *Woodsong*.

Lesson Idea: Elements of a Novel in "Storm," from *Woodsong* by Gary Paulsen

1. Introduce students to these elements of a novel: plot, character, and setting. Have them start a word map for the character Storm by writing his name in the center circle. Tell students to fill out the map as they read the excerpt or after they have finished it. A sample word map follows.

2. Next, encourage students to think about how they responded to Storm as they read. You might ask if they found Storm appealing. Have students discuss why they think a reviewer might focus on the plot, characters, and setting of a novel in evaluating the whole work. [By analyzing its important parts, a reviewer can evaluate the book's strengths and weaknesses.]

3. After this discussion, introduce students to the book review in this chapter (p. 155). Point out that in her review, the writer focuses on Catherine, the main character of *Catherine, Called Birdy*.

■ To Careers

Tell students that many careers depend on a person's ability to think critically and to evaluate works of literature or other media. Encourage students to locate reviews in newspapers, in magazines, or on radio or television. The reviews may evaluate restaurants, books, musical recordings or performances, plays, television programs, or movies. If possible, invite a local book or movie reviewer to speak with the class about the criteria he or she uses in evaluating works for review. Alternatively, have students bring in reviews to share with the class.

■ To the Community

Introduce students to readily available community resources that may be useful for locating books on their community that interest them. Ask volunteers to suggest places in their community that might carry such material [local library, bookstore, historical society]. You might plan a field trip to one of these locations, after arranging to have a librarian, archivist, or bookstore clerk available to speak to the class about the organization and content of the materials they oversee. Prior to the trip, have students choose an author or subject to research. While on site, suggest that students jot down notes about items they locate. You may want to obtain permission from parents or guardians before beginning work on this assignment.

■ To the Health Curriculum

To practice evaluating information, have students work in small groups to assess whether or not people in their grade eat healthful lunches. Have each group create a six-column chart with the following headings: *Grains*; *Vegetables*; *Fruit*; *Dairy*; *Protein* (meat, poultry, fish, beans, eggs, nuts); and *Fats/Oils/Sweets*. Explain that, starting from the left, these headings indicate foods that should be eaten in the greatest to the least quantity each day. Next, have each group poll a different set of students in their grade on what they ate for lunch the day before, checking off the correct columns as students answer. Then, make a chart on the chalkboard on which groups work together to show the totals for each column. Encourage students to use the results to write statements evaluating whether or not their fellow students eat healthful lunches.

CHAPTER 5

PREVIEWING THE CHAPTER

- The three workshops in this chapter focus on making evaluations. While the workshops can be taught separately, they also work together to help students learn to read, write, and view critically. Reading and analyzing a book review can help prepare students to write their own book reviews. After both reading a review and writing one, students will be asked to compare a book and a film in the same genre. To integrate this chapter with grammar, usage, and mechanics chapters, see pp. T297A–T297B.

INTRODUCING THE CHAPTER

- To introduce the chapter, use the Journal Warm-up, Transparency 38, in *Communications*.

VIEWING THE ILLUSTRATION

- Have students focus on how the artist's use of color and texture in the illustration helps the novel come to life for the reader. [Shadows and lines help create realistic textures on the woman's dress, the ripples of water on the page, the dragon's scales, and the armor. The colors white and yellow light up the book, making the boy's face glow.] Finally, point out how the shadowy world of the reader creates a stage effect, as if the book's characters were actors in a play.

Representing. Have students use shadow, light, and color to illustrate the coming to life of their favorite book.

CHAPTER 5 Responding to a Novel

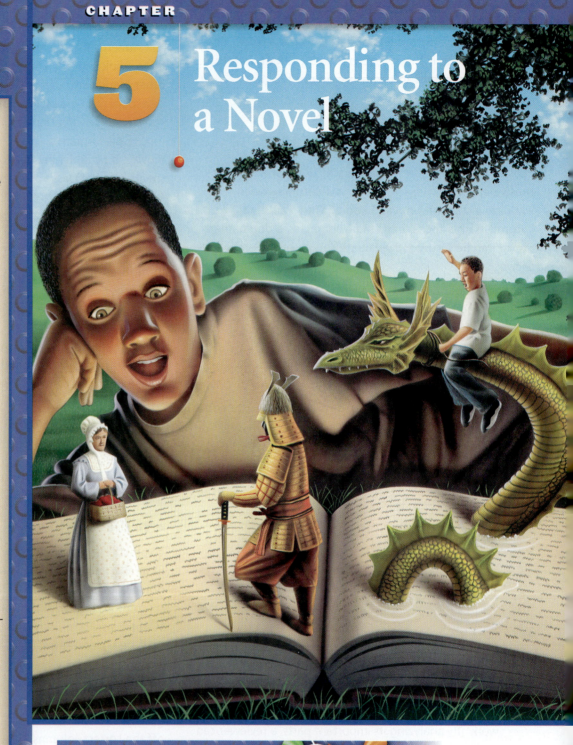

CHAPTER RESOURCES

Planning
- *Lesson Planner, ELL Strategies,* Ch. 5
- *Block Scheduling,* p. T151A (this book)
- *One-Stop Planner CD-ROM*

Practice
- *Communications,* Ch. 5
- *Media Literacy and Communication Skills*

Extension
- *Designing Your Writing*

Reinforcement
- *Communications,* Ch. 5
- *Alternative Readings,* Ch. 5
- *Daily Language Activity Transparencies*
- *Vocabulary Workshop* and *Tests*
- *Spelling*

PREVIEW

Reading Workshop

Reading a Book Review
PAGE 154

Writing Workshop

Writing a Book Review
PAGE 161

Focus on Viewing and Representing

Comparing Media: Film, TV, and Literature
PAGE 181

You stand staring at the rows of bookshelves in your school library. You need to choose a book to read, but how can you? With so many books to choose from, it sometimes seems impossible to settle on just one.

One way to choose a book is to read a book review. A **book review** tells what a book is about and the reviewer's opinion of the book. You can find book reviews in many newspapers and magazines. Some sites on the World Wide Web are devoted entirely to book reviews.

Book reviewers help readers sort through the many choices they have when deciding what to read. Reviewers base their ideas about books on careful reading and on knowledge of what makes a book good. You can be a book reviewer, too. You can use your skills as a reader to judge a book. Then, by sharing your ideas, you will help others decide if a book might be good to read.

internet connect
GO TO: go.hrw.com
KEYWORD: EOLang 6-5

YOUR TURN 1 — Reviewing a Book

With a partner, think of a book that you liked and give two reasons why you liked it. Then, think of a book you disliked and give two reasons why you disliked it. Discuss your reasons.

Motivate

Ask students what they remember most about a favorite novel. Discuss whether the novels they remember most strongly are the ones they liked the best. Help students understand the elements on which reviewers of a novel base their evaluations.

ELEMENTS OF Literature

Evaluating Literature. In *Elements of Literature,* Introductory Course, see "Dentistry" from Mark Twain's novel *The Adventures of Tom Sawyer,* pp. 150–153, for a selection in which the elements of character and plot are important, and "Eleven" by Sandra Cisneros, pp. 328–330, for a story that highlights character.

YOUR TURN 1

Encourage students to think of a work of fiction that they have read. To help them express their opinions about the books, have them complete these sentences:

- I liked _____ because _____ and _____.
- I disliked _____ because _____ and _____.

Preview 153

Evaluation and Assessment
- Test Generator (One-Stop Planner CD-ROM)
- Assessment Package
  —*Chapter Tests,* Ch. 5
  —*Chapter Tests in Standardized Test Formats,* Ch. 5
  —*Assessment Alternatives,* Ch. 5

Internet
- go.hrw.com (keyword: EOLang 6–5)

Reading Workshop

OBJECTIVES

- To read a book review in preparation for writing a book review
- To identify the elements of a novel
- To identify a writer's point of view
- To use a "wordbusting" strategy to figure out the meanings of unfamiliar words

Quotation for the Day

"All good books are alike in that they are truer than if they really happened and after you are finished reading one you will find that all that happened to you and afterwards it belongs to you...."

(Ernest Hemingway, 1899–1961, American writer)

Write the quotation on the chalkboard, and ask students to write journal entries about a book or a story they have read that made them feel as if they were part of the world portrayed. Tell students that a reviewer's job is to evaluate how well an author pulls the reader into a story.

TEACHING TIP

Preparing to Read
The material on this page introduces two concepts—the elements of a novel and point of view. These concepts are the focuses of instruction in the Reading Workshop and will be explored in greater depth on pp. 156–158. The Reading Selection provides students with an opportunity to apply what they learn about each of these concepts.

RESOURCES

Reading Workshop Reinforcement
- *Alternative Readings*, Ch. 5

Reading Workshop

Reading a Book Review

WHAT'S AHEAD?
In this workshop you will read a book review. You will also learn how to
- identify the elements of a novel
- identify a writer's point of view

"Hilarious," "humorous," and "sarcastic" are words a reviewer uses in the review of the book *Catherine, Called Birdy*. Does this description make you interested in knowing more about the book? Read the following book review to see more of the reviewer's ideas about the book. Will it be a "thumbs up" or "thumbs down" review?

Preparing to Read

 READING FOCUS

Elements of a Novel A novel does not just happen. A writer must put certain parts, or **elements,** into a book. Plot, character, setting, and a problem—a novel must have these elements, just as a baseball team needs a pitcher, a catcher, infielders, and outfielders. Reviewers focus on the elements of a novel when they read novels and when they write reviews about them. Notice which elements are mentioned in the review of *Catherine, Called Birdy* by Karen Cushman.

READING SKILL

Point of View We all have an attitude sometimes. Book reviewers specialize in having an attitude, and they will let you know what it is. The attitude of the reviewer (or of any writer) toward his or her topic is sometimes called the **point of view.** A book review will often end with a statement telling you whether the reviewer recommends reading the book. Long before you reach the end of a review, though, you will know how the reviewer feels. The reviewer's point of view will come across in the words he or she uses to talk about the book. What is the point of view of the reviewer of *Catherine, Called Birdy*?

154 Chapter 5 Exposition: Responding to a Novel

PREREADING
Set a Purpose. Explain to students that they can be more focused on what they read if they set specific purposes before they read. Point out that the teacher-set purposes for reading the review on p. 155 are to identify the elements of a novel and the reviewer's point of view.

Tell students that they also need to find their own purposes for reading in order to get more out of what they read. In reading a review, for example, they might first skim

Reading Selection

Read the following book review. In a notebook or on a separate sheet of paper, jot down answers to the numbered active-reading questions in the shaded boxes. The underlined words will be discussed in the Vocabulary Mini-Lesson on page 159.

from Great Books for Girls

Catherine, Called Birdy

BY KAREN CUSHMAN. 1994. CLARION. AGES 12–14.

Reviewed by Kathleen Odean

Catherine, daughter of a small-time nobleman in medieval England, is hilarious. In a diary format she records her daily life, the outrages she suffers as a girl, and her often humorous assessment of things. She longs to be outside frolicking instead of inside sewing, and she chafes at her lessons in ladylike behavior. Birdy is the sort of girl who organizes a spitting contest and starts a mud fight. She makes a list of all the things girls cannot do, such as go on a crusade,[1] be a horse trainer, laugh out loud, and "marry whom they will." She battles with her father, who wants to marry her off to the highest bidder, no matter how repulsive. Many of her best sarcastic remarks are reserved for him, and she irritates him whenever possible. She has a lively sense of humor and a palpable love of life. Few fictional characters are so vivid and funny—do not miss this one.

> **1.** Who or what is the focus of the reviewer's comments?

> **2.** What does the reviewer think about the book?

> **3.** Does this review make you want to read the book? Why or why not?

1. **crusade:** In the eleventh, twelfth, and thirteenth centuries, Christian nations repeatedly sent armies to the Holy Land, the region that is now made up of parts of Israel, Jordan, and Egypt. These armies repeatedly tried but failed to win back the Holy Land from the Muslims. These missions were called crusades.

Active-Reading Questions

The purpose of the active-reading questions is to have students identify both the elements of a novel and a writer's point of view. Use students' answers as an informal assessment of their understanding of these concepts. Possible answers follow.

ANSWERS

1. The reviewer focuses on the novel's main character, Catherine.

2. The reviewer likes this novel. She uses words such as "hilarious" and "humorous" to describe the main character and urges readers not to miss reading the book.

3. Some students may want to read the book because of the reviewer's positive evaluation. Others may or may not want to read the book, depending on their interest in historical fiction or in this character.

---

it and jot down guesses about its content. These guesses can help them figure out what they expect to learn from reading the review.

First Thoughts on Your Reading

ANSWERS

Possible responses are given below.

1. Students may say that Catherine is "funny," "sarcastic," "lively," rebellious, and full of life.
2. The reviewer's main point is that people should read the novel because Catherine is such an engaging character.

Critical Thinking

Analysis. For additional practice in identifying elements of a novel or story, have students make a chart like the one on this page. Then, ask them to select a story from their literature book and complete the chart by categorizing the elements of a story into plot, main character, and setting. Have volunteers explain which events they included.

ANSWERS

Possible answers follow.

- The reviewer describes how Catherine keeps a diary, "organizes a spitting contest," "starts a mud fight," lists "the things girls cannot do," and "battles with her father" about getting married.

- Catherine, the daughter of a nobleman, is the main character. She is energetic, forceful, and spirited.

- in medieval England

First Thoughts on Your Reading

1. According to the review, what is the main character of *Catherine, Called Birdy* like?
2. What is the reviewer's main point?

READING FOCUS

Elements of a Novel

A Recipe for Greatness When you cook, you must have certain ingredients for a dish to turn out well. A spaghetti dinner, for example, needs pasta and a good sauce.

Good stories and novels have several ingredients, or **elements**. A book reviewer will tell you about the elements of a particular novel. The reviewer will also let you know if he or she thinks the novelist got the recipe right. The chart below defines some elements of stories and novels and provides examples from a fairy tale you may know.

Elements of Stories and Novels	Examples from "Snow-White"
The **plot** is a series of related events that make up a story. The events revolve around a central problem, or **conflict**, which must be resolved before the story ends.	A jealous queen wants to kill her beautiful stepdaughter, Snow-White. Snow-White hides in the forest. She lives in a cottage with seven dwarfs. The queen tricks Snow-White into eating a poisoned apple that makes her appear dead. Snow-White is rescued by a prince.
The **main character** is the central person in the story.	Snow-White is the main character.
The **setting** is the time and place of a story.	The story is set a long time ago in a forest.

Identifying Elements of a Novel in a Book Review

Re-read the review of *Catherine, Called Birdy* on page 155. Find the elements of the novel by answering the following questions.

- **Plot:** What does the reviewer tell you about what happens?
- **Character:** Who is the main character? What is she like?
- **Setting:** Where and when do the events take place?

156 Chapter 5 Exposition: Responding to a Novel

RESOURCES

Your Turn 2

Practice
- *Communications*, WS. p. 92

Reinforcement
- *Communications*, TP. 39, WS. p 93

156 Exposition: Responding to a Novel

Point of View

Grade "A" Quality   A book reviewer's job is to evaluate, or judge the quality of, a novel. A reviewer's **point of view** often comes through in the way he or she discusses the elements of the novel. Positive or negative words reveal the reviewer's attitude toward the book.

Read the following review of the fairy tale "Snow-White." Look for the reviewer's point of view by noting which elements the reviewer mentions and whether he or she uses positive or negative words. If you need help, the Thinking It Through that follows the review will guide you.

> READING SKILL

> **TIP**   Reviewers use **positive words** (such as *powerful, exciting, fascinating,* and *funny*) to praise or compliment a novel. They use **negative words** (such as *weak, boring, unrealistic,* and *silly*) to criticize a novel.

> The character of Snow-White is unbelievably good and beautiful, but she is also much too trusting. Her beauty keeps the hunter and wild animals from harming her and provides her a charming home in the forest. However, her beauty does not hide her helplessness. She knows that the queen is trying to kill her, yet she continues to talk to strange women who come to the dwarfs' house. Three times she accepts deadly gifts from the disguised evil queen. Three times she survives. Anyone else would probably not be so lucky. Her character leaves the reader wondering how she manages to live happily ever after.

THINKING IT THROUGH — Identifying Point of View

▶ **STEP 1**   You can make a chart like the one on the next page to analyze a book review. In the middle column, note positive or negative words and phrases the reviewer uses to discuss each element. You may write *none* if the reviewer does not discuss a certain element.

▶ **STEP 2**   Based on the negative or positive words that the reviewer uses, decide what his or her point of view is. Write the point of view in the right-hand column of the chart. If the element is not discussed, you may leave the space blank.

TEACHING TIP

Point of View
To give students additional practice in understanding point of view, you may want to have them rewrite the review of "Snow-White" on this page. Tell them to substitute positive words and phrases for the negative ones that the reviewer uses to describe Snow-White. Then, have students compare the two versions of the review. Encourage them to note how positive or negative words and phrases help reveal point of view.

READING PROCESS

READING
Make Predictions. Tell students that they can enhance their understanding of a selection by pausing as they read to make predictions about what they read. Before students read the last sentence of the review, have them think about the information that they already have and predict the reviewer's evaluation of the novel. Will the reviewer recommend the book or not? Have students read the last sentence to check the accuracy of their predictions.

Wrap It Up

Metacognition. Encourage students to reflect on their reading processes by answering the following question:

1. Which did you find more difficult to identify—the elements of the novel or the reviewer's point of view? Why?

Then, ask students the following question:

2. How can you identify a reviewer's point of view? [through both the elements the reviewer mentions and the positive or negative words]

Meeting INDIVIDUAL NEEDS

ENGLISH-LANGUAGE LEARNERS

General Strategies. Some students may find **Your Turn 3** challenging because their grasp of the vocabulary used in the review might be limited. Consider pairing these students with English-proficient students who can help them identify and interpret positive and negative terms.

Partners might read the review and make lists on a separate sheet of paper, using one color for positive words about the main character and another for negative ones. Then, the partners could look up in a dictionary the words they have identified and discuss their meanings in the context of the review.

YOUR TURN 3

ANSWERS

A sample response follows.

Plot: none

Main Character: Positive terms the reviewer uses to describe Catherine are "hilarious," "lively sense of humor," "vivid," and "funny."

Setting: none

The reviewer's point of view is that the novel is worth reading because its main character is so appealing.

Element	Positive or Negative Words and Phrases	Reviewer's Point of View
Plot	none describing plot	
Main Character	positive: good, beautiful, lucky negative: unbelievably, much too trusting, helplessness	Snow-White is beautiful, but that does not make her a great character.
Setting	positive: charming negative: none	There is not enough information to tell.

▶ **STEP 3** Put it all together. Look at the positive and negative words and phrases and decide what the reviewer thinks.

> The reviewer does not think "Snow-White" is a good story because the main character is too helpless and unbelievably lucky.

YOUR TURN 3 Identifying a Reviewer's Point of View

Re-read the review of *Catherine, Called Birdy* on page 155. Then, use the Thinking It Through steps to identify the reviewer's point of view. Be prepared to explain *why* you think the reviewer takes the point of view you have identified.

158   Chapter 5   **Exposition:** Responding to a Novel

READING PROCESS

EXTENDING

Read Other Works. Discuss with students how the purposes for reading established earlier helped them get more meaning out of the review.

Explain that they might further their understanding of book reviews by reading other reviews of *Catherine, Called Birdy*. Have students use library reference books to locate these reviews, read them, and identify the reviewers' points of view.

MINI-LESSON VOCABULARY

Wordbusting Strategy (CSSD)

A reviewer may use very specific words to communicate exactly what he or she thinks of a book. Often, the word *good* is just not good enough.

When you come across an unfamiliar word in a book review, you can use a four-part strategy called **Wordbusting**. The letters **CSSD** can help you remember the steps of the strategy. Use only as many steps as it takes to understand the word.

- **Context** Use clues from the words and sentences around the word.
- **Structure** Look for familiar roots, prefixes, or suffixes.
- **Sound** Say the word aloud. It may sound like a word you know.
- **Dictionary** Look up the word.

THINKING IT THROUGH — Using the Wordbusting Strategy

Here is an example of Wordbusting, using the word *outrages* from the review of *Catherine, Called Birdy*.

▶ **Context:** "In a diary format she records her daily life, the *outrages* she suffers as a girl, and her often humorous assessment of things."

In the sentence, *outrages* are something she suffers. *Suffers* tells me that *outrages* are bad.

▶ **Structure:** out + rage + s

Rage means "anger," so the word must have something to do with getting mad.

▶ **Sound:** ou̇t′ rāj′ iz

It sounds like *out* and *rage*. I think an *outrage* must be something that makes you mad.

▶ **Dictionary:** *Outrages* are acts that hurt someone or disregard a person's feelings.

My definition is pretty close.

PRACTICE

Use the Wordbusting strategy to figure out the meanings of the words to the right. The words are underlined in the review of *Catherine, Called Birdy* on page 155, so you can see the context of each word. After each definition, list the steps of CSSD that you used for that word.

1. assessment
2. frolicking
3. chafes
4. repulsive
5. palpable

Reading Workshop 159

RESOURCES

Your Turn 3
Practice
- *Communications*, WS. p. 94

Reinforcement
- *Communications*, TP. 40, WS. p. 95

Vocabulary
Practice
- *Communications*, WS. p. 96

MINI-LESSON VOCABULARY

Wordbusting Strategy (CSSD)

ANSWERS
Possible responses follow.

1. I used context—Catherine's "assessment of things"—and structure (the word is made of *assess*, which means "to judge") to determine that an *assessment* is a judgment.

2. I used context to determine that *frolicking* is an enjoyable activity that Catherine prefers over sewing. The word means "having fun."

3. The context for *chafes* indicates that Catherine dislikes lessons in being ladylike but enjoys mud fights. I did not find clues in the word's structure or sound, so I checked in a dictionary. *Chafes* means "feels irritated or annoyed."

4. The context for the word *repulsive* indicates that it is negative. The structure consists of *repulse*, which means "repel." The dictionary defines *repulsive* as "disgusting."

5. I had to use the dictionary to find the definition of *palpable*. I did not find enough clues from the word's context or in its structure or sound. *Palpable* means "obvious or plain."

Taking a Second Look

Wordbusting Strategy. Using the meanings of the words in **Practice**, have students work in groups of three to create word maps for each word. As an example, write the word *repulsive* inside a circle, surrounded by circles containing a synonym (*hateful*), an antonym (*likable*), and related words (*unpleasant, awful*).

Reading Workshop 159

Looking Ahead to Writing

In the Writing Workshop (pp. 161–180) students will be asked to write a book review for a young adult novel. As they work on their drafts, tell students that they can use a chart like the one on p. 158 of the Reading Workshop to help them record positive or negative words and phrases that reflect their reactions to different elements of the novel that they read.

MINI-LESSON TEST TAKING

Answering Questions About Unfamiliar Vocabulary

Reading tests may ask you to identify the meanings of new words. The words may be technical or specialized terms that you normally do not use. To figure out their meanings, you must find clues in the reading passage. Look at the reading passage below and the test question that follows it. Then, use the Thinking It Through steps to figure out the answer.

In the Middle Ages, books and other documents had to be copied by hand. Professional writers, called scribes, copied documents onto a kind of paper made from sheepskin. Often, many scribes sat together in a scriptorium, writing with ink and quill pens made from feathers. Scribes left wide margins on pages so that artists could draw colorful illustrations. When the handmade pages were complete, they were sewn together into a book.

You can tell from the passage that a scriptorium is

A. a person who copies documents
B. a pen made from feathers
C. a room where scribes work
D. a book made from sheepskin

THINKING IT THROUGH — Answering Questions About Unfamiliar Vocabulary

▶ **STEP 1** Read the whole passage and get a sense of what it is about.

The passage is about how scribes copied documents in the Middle Ages.

▶ **STEP 2** Look at the context of the word. Pay attention to words near the new term that may provide a clue to the word's meaning.

The passage tells me that scribes sat in a scriptorium. I can tell from the words "sat" and "in" that a scriptorium is a building or room.

▶ **STEP 3** Check your answer against the items in the test question.

A is wrong. The people who copied are scribes.

B does not match my answer.

C matches my answer. This is correct.

D is wrong. The scribes would not sit in a book.

RESOURCES

Test Taking

Practice

- *Communications*, WS. pp. 97–99

Writing Workshop

Writing a Book Review

You have just taken a journey. Maybe you went back in time or visited a foreign land. Perhaps you fought dragons, danced with royalty, and conquered evil. How did you do these wonderful things? You read a book, of course.

You think that all your friends should visit the world in the book you have just read. You can show your friends this world by writing a **book review.** In this workshop you will write a book review about a young adult novel. You will summarize the book and tell whether you think it is worth reading.

WHAT'S AHEAD?

In this workshop you will write a book review. You will also learn how to

- preview and summarize a novel
- identify the elements of a plot
- replace clichés with your own words
- use appositives

Prewriting

Select a Novel

Plucky Heroines in the City   For this review, you will read a young adult novel. Think of the types of characters or settings you like to read about in novels. Then, look for a book with the type of character or setting that interests you most. To find a book, you might

- browse in bookstores—in person or online
- ask friends for recommendations
- go to the HRW Web site
- ask a librarian or media specialist for suggestions
- read some book reviews
- look for a new book by one of your favorite authors

Writing Workshop

OBJECTIVES

- To use the writing process to write a book review
- To preview and summarize a novel
- To identify the elements of a plot
- To replace clichés with more original wording
- To use appositives

Quotation for the Day

"Sure you use things—you even use yourself and try not to tell yourself about it. You use whatever you can get your hands on, but you're not really using a person; you use something attached to a person—some suggestion, some episode, some quirk or trait of character."

(Robert Penn Warren, 1905–1989, American author and poet)

Share the quotation with students and discuss how a reviewer who judges books might use things in much the same way a writer does. For example, a reviewer might focus on a particular event or character trait. Help students recognize that each reader is likely to focus on a different aspect of a book and will have a unique response to it. The job of a reviewer is to tell how a book makes him or her feel personally.

TEACHING TIP

Select a Novel
To help students select a novel they would like to read and review, divide the class into small groups. Ask each group to brainstorm a list of "top 10" young adult novels. Then, have groups share their lists with the rest of the class by reading them aloud.

Be sure to monitor students' use of the Internet as a source of novel reviews, as the content of certain Internet sites and forums may not be appropriate.

Meeting INDIVIDUAL NEEDS

STUDENTS WITH SPECIAL NEEDS

Some students may benefit from "viewing" a few minutes of a novel to help them preview and select a novel for their assignment. Try showing the opening scenes of a videotaped version of a novel to give students an impression of the story. You will probably want to preview the video and inform parents of the material you will be presenting in the video. Another alternative would be to have students listen to the first chapter of an appropriate book on tape.

LEARNERS HAVING DIFFICULTY

You may wish to work closely with some students to help them take notes while reading. One method is to read a chapter of a novel aloud with a small group of students. Then, have students make a chart like the one shown on p. 164 and decide together what notes to make. Students can discuss their personal reactions and opinions. Have them identify an important quotation and think of questions they may have about the chapter.

TIP You can use a library's **card** or **online catalog** to find a book. These catalogs list books by their titles, by their authors' names, and by their subjects. For more on **libraries** and **catalogs** see page 695 and page 698 in the Quick Reference Handbook.

Preview of Coming Attractions Once you have found several possible choices for your book review, **preview** each one to make your final decision. One student previewed *Tuck Everlasting* by Natalie Babbitt by following the steps in the Thinking it Through below.

THINKING IT THROUGH — Previewing a Novel

▶ **STEP 1 Look at the cover.** Is there something that makes you interested in the book?

The front cover has a mysterious pair of eyes on it. The back cover has a quotation that makes me curious about the book.

▶ **STEP 2 Read the book jacket summary.** What does the summary tell you?

The story is about a young girl who is kidnapped by a family who drank from a spring that lets them live forever.

▶ **STEP 3 Skim some pages.** Do you like the way the characters are shown? Do you see any interesting action taking place?

There are lots of examples of dialogue, and I like to hear the characters talking. Somebody escapes from jail.

▶ **STEP 4 Consider what you have found.** Does the book look interesting? Do you want to know more about the characters?

Yes, I want to know more about these characters. I think that this is a good choice for me.

Read Your Novel

KEY CONCEPT

TIP As you read, keep in mind the deadline for your review. Set aside time to read each day and set goals for how many pages you will read.

Please Note . . . As you read the book you have chosen, remember that you will be writing about it later. Keep nearby a sheet of paper divided into three columns. Label the columns *plot*, *setting*, and *main character*. Fill in the columns by answering the questions at the top of the next page as you read. Include page numbers next to important notes. The page numbers will help you if you need to go back and re-read some sections of the novel.

Plot	Setting	Main Character
■ What are the key events of each chapter? ■ What problem does the main character face? ■ How is the problem solved?	■ Where does the story take place? ■ When does the story take place? ■ How much time passes in the story?	■ Name: ■ Age: ■ What does the character look like? ■ What does the character like to do or play or eat?

YOUR TURN 4 — Selecting and Reading a Novel

Brainstorm a list of the types of novels you like to read. Follow the Thinking It Through steps on page 162 to preview a few novels and choose one that you think you will enjoy. Then, read your book and take notes in a three-column chart based on your answers to the questions above. Save your notes for later.

TIP Keep notes on your reaction to the book. Record your **opinions**, any **quotations** that you like, and **questions** you have about the book. As you read, jot down notes about anything that jumps out at you.

Think About Purpose and Audience

The Big Picture You have read your book and are ready to tell people what you think. Before you begin, think about

■ the **purpose** of your book review
■ the people who will be reading it (your **audience**)

Your purpose for writing a book review will be closely linked to your audience and to *their* purpose for reading the review. Here are some questions and possible responses to help you think about your audience and their purpose.

Who is the audience for my book review?	Why might these people read my book review?	What types of information might interest my audience?
classmates community librarian	to decide whether to read a book to decide whether to get a book for the library	What is the book about? What type of book is it? (mystery, fantasy, western, general fiction, and so on)
parents	to decide if a book is right for younger readers	How easy (or difficult) is it to read?
gift shoppers	to decide whether to buy a book as a gift	How much does it cost?

RESOURCES

Your Turn 4
Practice
■ *Communications*, WS. p. 100

The audience for the review of *Tuck Everlasting* will be the student's classmates. Their purpose for reading will be to decide whether to read the book themselves. This audience will probably want to know what the book is about, but not how it ends. They might also be interested in knowing how easy or difficult the book is to read.

YOUR TURN 5 — Thinking About Purpose and Audience

Use the chart at the bottom of page 163 to help you consider your audience and their purpose for reading your review.

Gather and Organize Details

You Get the Idea If you want people to read the book you have chosen, you need to say more about it than "It's good." You need to give them a *summary* of the book. A **summary** of a piece of writing includes only the key ideas of the piece. When you summarize a novel, you will briefly retell the important events. The notes that you took while you read your novel and the instructions on page 166 will help you write your summary.

There Is More to the Story If a story were plot alone, it would not be much fun to read. Readers will be more interested in plot events if they know something about the people and places involved. When you write a summary, include a description of the characters and the setting. The chart below contains examples from *Tuck Everlasting*.

Character	Who is the main character? What is he or she like?	The main character is Winnie. She is a spoiled only child who is bored and tired of being told what to do.
Setting	Where and when does the story take place?	The novel is set in 1880 in the village of Treegap.
Plot	What problem does the main character face? How does he or she deal with the problem?	Winnie has to decide if she should keep the Tucks' secret—the fountain the Tucks drink from that gives them eternal life. She decides to help them. Helping them makes her brave.

164   Chapter 5   Exposition: Responding to a Novel

YOUR TURN 5

To evaluate students' charts, ask them to exchange their work with a partner and to check that each question has been answered completely. Students may ask each other questions to clarify any points on the chart they do not understand.

Meeting INDIVIDUAL NEEDS

MODALITY
Auditory Learners. Some students may want to use tape recorders to record information about character, setting, and plot to use in writing summaries of their novels. Students can record important information while they are reading a novel, creating oral notes. Before writing their summaries, suggest that they listen for relevant details and stop the tape while they write these details on a chart similar to the one shown on this page.

RESOURCES

Your Turn 5
Practice
- Communications, WS. p. 101

Critical Thinking
Practice
- Communications, WS. p. 102

MINI-LESSON: CRITICAL THINKING

Identifying the Elements of a Plot

Once upon a Time Most fairy tales begin with "Once upon a time . . ." and end with ". . . happily ever after." The plot in between is usually easy to follow. Novels, on the other hand, usually have a more complicated plot. However, they, too, follow a plot pattern.

- Most stories begin with a **basic situation** in which you learn about the characters and the setting.
- The main character usually runs into a **conflict**, or problem, early in the story.
- This problem sets in motion a series of events, or **complications**, that make up the action of the story.
- All of these events build to a high point, the **climax**. The climax is the most exciting moment in the plot.
- Following the climax is the **resolution**, or outcome. In this part of the story, we see how everything works out for the main character.

A **plot line** helps you figure out all the important steps of a plot. Below is an example of a plot line for *Tuck Everlasting*.

Basic Situation: Winnie considers running away.

Conflict: Winnie discovers that the Tucks drank from a spring that lets them live forever. They kidnap her.

Complications: The Tucks explain to Winnie why no one should know about the spring. An evil stranger discovers the secret. Mrs. Tuck accidentally kills the stranger.

Climax: Winnie and the Tucks help Mrs. Tuck escape from jail.

Resolution: The Tucks continue to live forever. Winnie has a full life and never drinks from the spring.

PRACTICE

Create a plot line for the novel that you read.
(**Hint:** As you decide which events are the most important, think about what sticks out in your mind. What are the events that any reader would need to know for the story to make sense?)

Cooperative Learning

Plot Line. To help students understand the elements of a plot, divide the class into groups of five and let the groups develop a plot line for a familiar story the members all know or have read. Assign one of the following tasks to each member of the group:

- identify the basic situation
- identify the conflict
- identify the complications that make up the story's action
- identify the climax
- identify the resolution

Then, members of the group may work together to draw and complete a plot line for the story. Have groups each choose a spokesperson to share their work with the class.

MINI-LESSON: CRITICAL THINKING

ANSWER
Check that students' plot lines include all of the important events for their individual stories and that they are correctly labeled.

Order! Order! You may want to begin your summary with details about character and setting. Then you can start summarizing the plot. Follow **chronological order,** telling what happens in the beginning and middle of the novel but do not tell how the novel ends, unless your audience is a group (such as librarians) who would prefer to know. **When you write your summary, use transitions like** *first, next,* **and** *last* **to link the details of the plot together.**

KEY CONCEPT

YOUR TURN 6 Gathering and Organizing Details

Record details from your reading notes about plot, main character, and setting in a chart like the one on page 164. Put a number next to each detail in your chart to show the order in which you will present the details when you write your summary.

Designing Your Writing

Highlighting a Quotation Book reviews sometimes highlight a quotation from the book. The stand-alone quotation sparks the reader's curiosity. To include a quotation, follow these guidelines.

- Select a quotation by thinking about what the main character says or does at an important moment in the book.
- Set the quotation apart from the rest of your book review by placing it directly below your title and indenting it on both sides. List the title and author of the book beneath the quotation, indented on the left side. Here is an example.

> A Review of Natalie Babbitt's Tuck Everlasting
>
> She would try very hard not to think of it, but sometimes, as now, it would be forced upon her. She raged against it, helpless and insulted, and blurted at last, "I don't want to die."
>
> Tuck Everlasting, by Natalie Babbitt
>
> If you could live forever just by drinking water, would you do it? The Tuck family unknowingly does just that in Natalie Babbitt's fantasy novel Tuck Everlasting. . . .

YOUR TURN 6

When students are ready to write their summaries, you may want to ask them to make fresh copies of their charts, using the correct chronological order. You will be able to evaluate neatly written charts more easily, and students will be able to see more clearly how details will be arranged in chronological order.

TEACHING TIP

Gathering and Organizing Details
Before students begin to record notes from their reading and arrange the details in a chart, you may want to remind them to write this work legibly. Students should choose whichever style of writing allows them to write most clearly, cursive or manuscript. Since the reading and recording process will take several days, students may have to repeat their work if they are unable to read their own writing.

TECHNOLOGY TIP

If students are using word-processing software to write their book reviews, suggest that they make the quotation from the novel stand out by using italics or by setting it inside a tinted box.

RESOURCES

Your Turn 6
Practice
- *Communications,* WS. p. 103

Extension
- *Designing Your Writing*

Your Turn 7
Practice
- *Communications,* WS. p. 104

Preparing Your Evaluation

Four Stars   After you have prepared notes for your book's summary, you should think about your *evaluation*. The evaluation is the last part of a book review. In an **evaluation,** you

- tell readers why you like or dislike the book
- include a recommendation to read or not to read the book

It is important to know whether or not you would recommend the book. After all, you want your **point of view,** or attitude, about the book to come across throughout your review. Also, remember who your audience is when you make your recommendation. For example, you might think a book is too easy to read, but if your audience is younger readers, the reading level might be just right for them.

Here are two example evaluations based on *Tuck Everlasting.*

> The question of whether Winnie would drink from the spring remained open through the whole book. I could tell she might go either way, so the suspense was great. I enjoyed watching Winnie discover a world beyond her sheltered life. I would recommend <u>Tuck Everlasting</u> to readers who wonder what it might be like to live forever and who like suspense and fantasy.

> Winnie's conflict over whether she would tell the Tucks' secret ended early in the book. From then on, I knew exactly how the book would end, and I found too many parts of the story unbelievable. I thought Winnie was weak and boring. She liked rules and order too much, and she hated getting dirty. I would not recommend the book except to big fans of fantasy.

TIP Your **voice** shows your **point of view,** or attitude, about the book. Use positive words for characters and events that you like. Use negative words to describe characters you do not like and parts of the plot that do not work. For more on **point of view,** see page 157.

TIP Many people know what types of books they like to read. If you tell your audience whether the book is a mystery, a western, a historical novel, a fantasy, or another type of book, it helps them decide whether to read it. Not all books fit into the above categories, so you may simply describe your book as "a novel for young adults."

YOUR TURN 7 — Preparing Your Evaluation

Write an evaluation of the young adult novel you read for your book review. State clearly why you like or dislike the book and whether you think others should read the book or not.

Writing

Book Review

Framework	Directions and Explanations
Introduction ■ Attention grabber ■ Statement of author and title	Get your readers' attention by **introducing the topic of the book** in an interesting way. You may use a quotation, dialogue, a question, a metaphor or simile, or a slice of action to get your readers' attention. Be sure to identify the **author and title.** You might also tell readers what **type of book** it is: mystery, fantasy, historical fiction, and so on.

Body
■ Summary
   Details about setting
   Details about main character
   Details about plot
	A **plot summary** should follow **chronological,** or time, **order.** Start with the beginning events, followed by the middle events, but do not reveal the novel's ending unless you think your audience would prefer to know it.
	   Use **transition** words to give your paper *coherence.* In a **coherent** composition, one idea flows logically to the next. For more on **transitions,** see page 287.

Conclusion
■ Evaluation
   Reason
   Recommendation
	Write your **evaluation.** Give readers at least one **reason** why you like or dislike the book. Finally, make a **recommendation** to your readers: Should they read the book or not?

YOUR TURN 8 Drafting Your Book Review

Now it is your turn to draft a book review. As you write,

- keep your audience in mind
- refer to the framework above and the Writer's Model on the next page

168   Chapter 5   **Exposition:** Responding to a Novel

RESOURCES

Writing
Writing Prompts
■ *Communications,* TP. 41, WS. p. 105

Your Turn 8
Practice
■ *Communications,* TP. 42, WS. p. 106

Quotation for the Day

"To note an artist's limitations is but to define his talent."

(Willa Cather, 1873–1947, American writer)

Write the quotation on the chalkboard. Point out to students that they should notice a novel's weak points as well as its strong points when they read. They can keep these strengths and weaknesses in mind when they write a book review. Explain that analyzing a piece of literature for both its most and least successful qualities will allow them to make a more balanced assessment.

YOUR TURN 8

If you wish to assign word length, suggest that their book reviews be between 500 and 700 words long. To check that students' reviews adhere to the framework on this page, have them use colored markers to label the introduction, body, and conclusion. Use students' labeled drafts to assess how well they understand the concept of a book review.

A Writer's Model

The final draft below closely follows the framework for a book review.

A Review of
Natalie Babbitt's *Tuck Everlasting*

If you could live forever just by drinking water, would you do it? The Tuck family unknowingly does just that in Natalie Babbitt's fantasy novel *Tuck Everlasting*. Living forever is complicated, though, especially when other people discover the secret.

Winnie, a **lonely**, **sheltered**, and **spoiled** only child, lives in a house at the edge of a village called Treegap. One hot August day in 1880, she discovers the Tuck family and the magic spring that lets them live forever. The Tucks are kindhearted, but they do not want anyone to know their secret. To keep Winnie from telling what she has seen, the Tucks kidnap her and take her to their home. There, Mr. Tuck explains why no one else should know about the spring. He feels that living forever is a lonely and empty experience. No one has ever talked to Winnie about such important things before. Winnie begins to see the world a bit differently and becomes friends with the Tucks. The next day, however, an evil stranger threatens to tell the secret. Mrs. Tuck gets upset and accidentally kills the man when he tries to take Winnie away. The Treegap constable takes Mrs. Tuck to jail. Next, Winnie **bravely** helps rescue Mrs. Tuck from jail. Winnie **courageously** struggles with some tough decisions. For starters, she must decide whether to keep the Tucks' secret. She also faces the opportunity to drink from the spring and live forever with the Tucks.

Tuck Everlasting is excellent. It is full of suspense as Winnie makes choices, takes risks, and learns about life. Although it is a fantasy book, it contains some truths about life. I recommend it to anyone who has ever dreamed about living forever or has had to make a tough choice.

TIP The highlighted words show the writer's point of view about the book's main character.

Attention grabber

Statement of author and title

Summary: Details about main character

Details about setting

Details about plot

Evaluation and reason

Recommendation

Writing Workshop 169

Connecting Reading and Writing

To help students write their own book reviews, have them review the information on elements of a novel in the Reading Workshop on p. 156. Then, ask them to read **A Writer's Model** while paying close attention to structure and organization. As a whole class activity, list the elements of the novel analyzed in the review. [main character—Winnie; setting—Treegap, 1880s; plot—Winnie discovers how the Tucks can live forever and must decide whether to keep their secret]

Connecting Reading and Writing

Before students write their drafts, ask them to review the section on point of view in the Reading Workshop on pp. 157–158. For additional practice, students may want to jot down words that indicate how the reviewer feels about the character Mandy in *Out of the Storm*. ["resented," "detested," "pitied herself"]

A Student's Model

When you write a book review, you want your point of view about the book to be obvious. Diana DeGarmo, a sixth-grade student from Sand Springs, Oklahoma, makes her feelings known by clearly describing the main character and her situation in the following book review.

A Review of
Out of the Storm by Patricia Willis

Attention grabber — When single mother Vera lost her job in Garnet Creek, the family had to move to a new town.

Statement of author and title — Patricia Willis, author of *Out of the Storm*, wrote this story from the viewpoint of Mandy, Vera's twelve-year-old daughter.

Summary — Mom and nine-year-old Ira adjusted to the new setting quickly, but Mandy resented everything about their new location. She held on to a dream that she and her deceased father had, and that dream prevented her from accepting her new life. She resented living with grumpy Aunt Bess and detested having to tend the sheep.

Mandy lived with her unhappiness and pitied herself until several incidents happened that made her realize that she was not the only kid who did not have a perfect life. She also found that others had dreams and perhaps by forgetting herself and helping someone else, she might find real happiness.

Evaluation — I think if a reader is looking for a book that tells of a family's struggle to live, *Out of the Storm* by Patricia Willis would be a good choice. I really liked this book because it showed characters learning to tough out bad situations. I also like the book's motto, "Sometimes it takes something Bad to make you see the Good."

Revising

Evaluate and Revise Content, Organization, and Style

A Second Look Once you have written a first draft, you need to think about how to improve it. Do this by taking a break from your review and then reading the draft twice. In the first reading, focus on your ideas. Do they make sense? Are they in the right order? The guidelines below will help you decide. In the second reading, look at your words and sentences. The Focus on Word Choice on page 173 will help you.

▶ **First Reading: Content and Organization** Use the following chart to evaluate and revise your book review.

COMPUTER TIP

If you are writing your review using a computer, you can use several word-processing features to help you revise. As you use the Self-Evaluation chart below, use the underlining feature for Tips 1, 3, and 5. For Tip 2, highlight or color the text on your screen.

Book Review: Content and Organization Guidelines for Self-Evaluation and Peer Evaluation

Evaluation Questions	Tips	Revision Techniques
❶ Does the introduction grab the reader's attention and give the book's author and title?	**Put a check mark** next to any interesting statements. **Underline** the title and author of the book.	**Add** a quotation, question, or interesting statement to the introduction. **Add** the book's title and author if necessary.
❷ Does the summary include information about the book's setting and main character?	**Highlight** the book's setting. **Draw a wavy line** under information about the main character.	**Elaborate** with details about the book's setting and main character.
❸ Does the summary retell the book's major plot events? Does it give details that would interest readers?	**Put a star** next to each major plot event. **Underline** any information that would appeal to the review's audience.	**Delete** unimportant plot events and information. **Add** any important plot events missing from the summary.
❹ Does the summary show how the major events are connected?	**Draw a box around** each word that shows how the events are related.	**Add** transition words or **rearrange** events to make their order clearer.
❺ Does the conclusion include a clear evaluation with at least one reason? Does it include a recommendation?	**Underline** the evaluation. **Draw two lines** under the reason or reasons given for it. **Circle** the recommendation.	**Add** reasons to the evaluation, if necessary. **Add** a recommendation, if necessary.

Writing Workshop   **171**

Quotation for the Day

"I found that, having started writing books, I was always having to write one more to kind of make up for the deficiencies of the one I'd just completed."

(John Dos Passos, 1896–1970, American author)

Use this quotation to show students that most writers recognize the need to improve their work. Motivate students to improve their book reviews by encouraging them to remember that even the work of professional authors needs to be evaluated and revised.

TECHNOLOGY TIP

Suggest to students who are using computers that before they print out a draft, they adjust the line spacing and margins to make room for handwritten corrections on the printout. Tell them to use double-spacing and a wide right margin. When they are ready to print a final draft, they can reset the spacing and margins.

TEACHING TIP

▶ **Elaboration**

To help students improve their summaries, ask them to elaborate with sensory words and details about the setting and main character of the books they read. First, suggest that students refer to the charts they made while reading the novel and taking notes about it. Then, ask them to look for vivid adverbs, adjectives, and sensory details to use in describing the setting and the main character. Suggest that they add the most relevant details to their reviews.

RESOURCES

Revising

Practice
- *Communications,* TPs. 43, 44, WS. pp. 107, 108, 109

Evaluating Student Writing

The ancillary *Assessment Alternatives* contains a variety of assessment forms, including Inventories and Evaluation Forms and rubrics: Six-Point Scales, Four-Point Scales, and Six Trait Scales.

Responding to the Revision Process
ANSWERS

1. The writer added adjectives to the first sentence in order to elaborate on information about the book's main character, Winnie.

2. The writer deleted a sentence about an unimportant plot event because it did not help the audience understand the book.

3. The writer added the last sentence to retell one of the book's major plot events.

Critical Thinking

Evaluation. Ask pairs of students to work together to evaluate their drafts. First, ask them to exchange papers and read each other's book reviews. Then, direct them to use the peer evaluation guidelines on p. 171 and the style guidelines on this page to assess the review and to determine what information, if any, their partner might add, delete, or change to improve the review's content, organization, or style. Students may write their comments in the margins of their partner's paper or on a separate sheet.

ONE WRITER'S REVISIONS This revision is an early draft of the book review on page 169.

elaborate

Winnie *, a lonely, sheltered, and spoiled only child,* lives in a house at the edge of a village called Treegap. One hot August day in 1880, she discovers the Tuck family and the magic spring that lets them live for-

delete

ever. ~~She had been following a frog into the forest.~~ The Tucks are kindhearted, but they do not want anyone to

add

know their secret. *To keep Winnie from telling what she has seen, the Tucks kidnap her and take her to their home.*

PEER REVIEW

If you are evaluating a peer's book review, ask yourself these questions:
- Do I understand what the book is about?
- Do I know what the writer thinks of the book?
- Does the book review make me want to read the book? Why or why not?

Responding to the Revision Process

1. Why do you think the writer elaborated by adding words to the first sentence?
2. Why do you think the writer deleted a sentence from the paragraph above?
3. Why do you think the writer added the last sentence?

▶ **Second Reading: Style** Now that you have looked at the big picture, it is time to focus on your sentences. There are many ways to edit sentences. One way is to eliminate *clichés*. **Clichés** are expressions that have been used so often they have lost their original meaning. When you hear or read a cliché, you probably do not even bother to picture the image in your mind. As a writer, the last thing you want is to have your readers ignore your ideas. The following guidelines will help you make your writing clear and original.

Style Guidelines

Evaluation Question	Tip	Revision Technique
Does the review contain any overused phrases?	Circle every word or phrase that you think is a cliché.	Replace each cliché with your original words.

Chapter 5 Exposition: Responding to a Novel

Clichés

When you are writing about a book you have read, you may want to use certain familiar expressions. However, clichés will weaken the punch of your writing. Here are some examples of clichés. See if you can think of others.

It is **raining cats and dogs.**   She is **as busy as a bee.**

Replacing clichés with more original wording will make your meaning clearer and your writing more interesting.

The rain is pummeling the ground.

She zips around from 7:00 A.M. until 7:00 P.M. each day.

Focus on Word Choice

ONE WRITER'S REVISIONS

There, Mr. Tuck explains why no one else should know about the spring. He feels that living forever is ~~no bowl of cherries~~ a lonely and empty experience.

Responding to the Revision Process

How did replacing the cliché "bowl of cherries" with another phrase improve the sentence above?

Evaluating and Revising Your Book Review

- First, evaluate and revise the content and organization of your review by using the guidelines on page 171.
- Next, replace any clichés in your writing. Use the guidelines on page 172 and the Focus on Word Choice above to help you.
- If a peer read your paper, think carefully about his or her comments before you revise.

RESOURCES
Focus on Word Choice
Practice
- *Communications*, WS. p. 110

Cooperative Learning

Book Discussion Group. Encourage students who have read and reviewed the same book to act as critics by engaging in an in-class book discussion group. First, explain that effective critics not only share their own opinions but also listen with open minds to the opinions of their peers. The objective of a book discussion is for students to gain a fuller understanding of a book by investigating new points of view; the objective is not for any individual to prove the correctness of a review. When you begin the discussion, have critics give their reviews one at a time. To ensure that students listen to their peers, you might make group members responsible for summarizing their peers' reviews. After each review, allow students a few minutes to discuss the review.

Responding to the Revision Process
ANSWER
Students may say that replacing the cliché "no bowl of cherries" with the more original wording "a lonely and empty experience" helps make the meaning of the sentence clearer and creates a more vivid picture in readers' minds.

YOUR TURN 9

To help you evaluate students' papers, ask for copies of their drafts before they start revising. Check these drafts against their revised book reviews to make sure they have followed the evaluation guidelines on pp. 171–172. If students have difficulty improving content and organization or replacing clichés, cite specific examples from their paragraphs to help them understand the changes they must make.

Quotation for the Day

"Proofreading is like the quality-control stage at the end of an assembly line."

(John R. Trimble 1940–   , American writer and teacher)

Write the quotation on the chalkboard. Explain to students that just as a factory worker must check that the products made on an assembly line meet certain standards, writers must find and correct errors to make sure their writing is as polished as possible. After discussing the quotation, encourage students to compare proofreading with another process by brainstorming their own similes.

Grammar Link

Using Appositives

ANSWERS

1. The novel, <u>a fantasy for young adults,</u> is set a long time ago in a small village.
2. The main character, <u>Winnie Foster,</u> learns many things in the book.
3. Angus Tuck, <u>head of the Tuck family,</u> talks to Winnie about the loneliness of living forever.
4. Mae Tuck, <u>a character in the book,</u> accidentally kills a man.
5. The Tuck's son <u>Jesse</u> wants Winnie to drink from the spring.

Publishing

Proofread Your Book Review

Getting It Right   Now you need to proofread, or **edit,** your book review. If you have too many errors in your book review, your readers may not take your recommendation seriously. To make sure you catch every error, also have a classmate proofread your review.

Grammar Link

Using Appositives

An **appositive** is a noun or pronoun that identifies or describes another noun or pronoun. An **appositive phrase** includes an appositive and its modifiers. Appositives and appositive phrases often answer the question *Who?* or *What?*

Appositive: My Spanish teacher, **Ms. Alvarez,** was born in Cuba. [*Ms. Alvarez* identifies *who* the Spanish teacher is.]

Appositive Phrase: I am interested in geology, **the study of the earth and rocks.** [*The study of the earth and rocks* explains *what* geology is.]

Appositives that are not essential to the sentence are set off with **commas.**

Our new gym teacher, **Mr. Samson,** trained as a gymnast. [The name *Mr. Samson* is extra information. Commas must be used to set it off.]

Commas are not needed if the appositive is essential to the meaning of the sentence.

My brother **Abdul** wants to be a gymnast. [The speaker has more than one brother.]

PRACTICE

Copy the sentences below on your own paper. Underline the appositive in each sentence, and insert commas where needed.

Example:

1. Last week I read *Tuck Everlasting* a novel about living forever.

1. Last week I read *Tuck Everlasting*, <u>a novel about living forever</u>.

1. The novel a fantasy for young adults is set a long time ago in a small village.
2. The main character Winnie Foster learns many things in the book.
3. Angus Tuck head of the Tuck family talks to Winnie about the loneliness of living forever.
4. Mae Tuck a character in the book accidentally kills a man.
5. The Tucks' son Jesse wants Winnie to drink from the spring. (They have two sons.)

For more information and practice on **punctuating appositives,** see page 570.

174   Chapter 5   Exposition: Responding to a Novel

RESOURCES

Grammar Link

Practice

- *Communications,* WS. p. 111

Publish Your Book Review

Read All About It   Finally, your book review is finished. Your goal was to write a review that would inform others about a book. How will you get your audience to read your review? Here are some suggestions.

- Find a Web site or online bookstore that asks for reader reviews of young adult literature, and send in your review.
- Create a reading suggestion bulletin board in your classroom. Post a copy of your book review there. If you have access to a school Web site, help create a Web page for all the book reviews written by your classmates.
- Deliver your book review as an **oral response** to the novel. Summarize the book for your listeners, and then explain your evaluation. Be sure to provide clear reasons why you like or dislike the book.

Reflect on Your Book Review

Building Your Portfolio   Take time to think about your book review now that it is finished. What did you learn from it? Good writers are always learning from their writing. You can, too, by answering the following questions.

- What did you find easy or difficult about writing a summary?
- When else could you use summary writing?
- Which evaluation guideline (page 171) was most helpful in evaluating and revising your book review? Why?

 **Proofreading, Publishing, and Reflecting on Your Book Review**

- Correct any punctuation, spelling, or grammar errors in your book review. Look closely at any appositives you used.
- Publish your book review so that others can read it.
- Answer the questions from Reflect on Your Book Review above. Record your responses in a learning log, or include them in your portfolio.

Writing Workshop   **175**

Connections to Literature

Writing a Short Story

Like a novel, a short story has characters, a setting, and a conflict. Because short stories are usually only a few pages long, they deal with just a few characters, a single setting, and a simple plot. As a result, short stories often seem more focused than novels. The challenge in writing a short story is getting the focus just right. Here is an opportunity to write your own short story.

Read All About It Read the beginning of the story "Ta-Na-E-Ka." Notice how the writer introduces the main character, setting, and conflict.

> As my birthday drew closer, I had awful nightmares about it. I was reaching the age at which all Kaw Indians had to participate in Ta-Na-E-Ka. Well, not all Kaws. Many of the younger families on the reservation were beginning to give up the old customs. But my grandfather, Amos Deer Leg, was devoted to tradition. He still wore handmade beaded moccasins instead of shoes and kept his iron-gray hair in tight braids. He could speak English, but he spoke it only with white men. With his family he used a Sioux dialect. . . .
>
> *Eleven* was a magic word among the Kaws. It was the time of Ta-Na-E-Ka, the "flowering of adulthood." It was the age, my grandfather informed us hundreds of times, "when a boy could prove himself to be a warrior and a girl took the first steps to womanhood."
>
> "I don't want to be a warrior," my cousin Roger Deer Leg confided to me. "I'm going to become an accountant."
>
> "None of the other tribes make girls go through the endurance ritual," I complained to my mother.
>
> Mary Whitebird, "Ta-Na-E-Ka"

Plot a Course Every project needs a plan. Here is a plan to help you write your story.

1. **Brainstorm characters, settings, and conflicts.** Make a chart like the one below to generate ideas. For each column, think of all the possibilities you can imagine. One example is given.

Main Character	Setting	Conflict
Hector, an 11-year-old detective	a shopping mall	A storm knocks out all the electricity.

TEACHING TIP

Plot a Course
To spark ideas for characters, settings, and plots, ask students to think about experiences they have had that might make a good story. Students may use the following methods to turn real-life people, places, and events into fiction:

- alter factual information
- use their imaginations to invent details
- add description and dialogue

---

176   Chapter 5   Exposition: Responding to a Novel

2. **Choose a main character, a setting, and a conflict.** To create a story beginning, select one idea from each column in your chart. You can mix and match, choosing the character, setting, and conflict that give you the most interesting ideas.

3. **Generate details about character and setting.** To come up with details, answer the following questions.

Main Character	■ What does he or she like to do? ■ How old is the character? ■ What does he or she look like?
Setting	■ Where does the story take place? ■ When does the story take place? ■ What **sensory details** will help the reader imagine the setting?

4. **Map out the plot of your story.** Think of details for your plot, using the questions that follow. You may want to use a plot line like the one shown on page 165.

Questions:
- What events happen because of the conflict?
- How can you create **suspense,** keeping the reader wondering what will happen next?
- What happens first, second, or later?
- What event will be the climax?
- How will the conflict be settled?

Getting Started Once you map out your plot, start writing. If you need help getting started, look again at the first paragraphs of "Ta-Na-E-Ka." You may find it easier to begin in the middle of your story, and then write the beginning and the ending. Finally, remember that a good story has suspense, dialogue, description, and sensory details, and that its resolution ties up loose ends.

YOUR TURN 11 — Writing a Short Story

Write a draft of a short story by following the steps you have just read. Exchange your draft with a partner. Read your partner's draft and look for the story elements of character, setting, and plot. Are any missing? Share your ideas with your partner. Then, revise your story as necessary.

After you have written the story, consider preparing a **dramatic interpretation** of it to present to your class. (For information on **dramatic interpretation,** see page 725 in the Quick Reference Handbook.)

Meeting INDIVIDUAL NEEDS

MODALITY

Visual Learners. Students may want to draw sketches of the main character, the setting, or the conflict to help them generate and visualize details. Students might focus on one scene or character or do several sketches. Some students may want to think of the story as a comic strip and depict one major event per panel.

YOUR TURN 11

To help students review each other's stories, write the following checklist on the chalkboard: 1. main character, 2. setting, 3. plot. As students work with partners to review each other's stories, they can use the checklist and write the appropriate number above the sentence or phrase. After all three elements are correctly labeled, students should put a check mark at the top of the page.

TEACHING TIP

Writing an Essay About a Poem's Sound Effects

To help students prepare to write their essays, read a suitable poem aloud to the class. As you read, ask students to listen for the sound effects (rhyme, rhythm, and repetition) that the poet uses and to identify examples that they think help create a certain mood or feeling.

Connections to Literature

Writing an Essay About a Poem's Sound Effects

Poets play with words to give their readers new ways of looking at the world. In just a few words, a poem can express a wealth of meanings. Many poems rely partly on the sounds of words to convey meaning. You can recognize and appreciate a poem's **sound effects** when you understand some of the special techniques poets use. In this section, you will choose a poem and write an essay analyzing its sound effects.

Sound Effect Check Poets often choose and arrange words to create sound effects. They may try to imitate a specific sound (such as the wind's howling or a bee's buzzing) or to create a mood (such as excitement or joy). Sound effects may provide a clue to a poem's meaning. Three kinds of sound effects are rhyme, rhythm, and repetition.

Rhyme is the repetition of vowel sounds and all sounds following them.

   shelf and *elf*   *comb* and *gnome*

Rhyme is used to emphasize ideas, organize the poem, and entertain the reader.

Rhythm is a musical quality created by the repetition of stressed (´) and unstressed (˘) syllables in a line or by the repetition of certain sounds.

You may notice the rhythm of words when you talk. Poets sometimes emphasize the rhythm and pattern of words to imitate actions described in the poem.

> Hŏw dóth thĕ líttlĕ crócŏdíle
> Ĭmpróve hĭs shíniĭng táil,
> Ănd póur thĕ wátĕrs ŏf thĕ Níle
> Ŏn évĕry góldĕn scále!
>
> Lewis Carroll,
> "How Doth the Little Crocodile"

Repetition is the effect of repeating a word, phrase, or line throughout a poem. Repetition creates rhythm, helps organize a poem, and emphasizes feelings or ideas. Notice the repetition in the following poem.

> Last night I dreamed of chickens,
> there were chickens everywhere,
> they were standing on my stomach,
> they were nesting in my hair,
> they were pecking at my pillow,
> they were hopping on my head,
> they were ruffling up their feathers
> as they raced about my bed.
>
> Jack Prelutsky,
> "Last Night I Dreamed of Chickens"

Jump In Read the poem on the next page. What sound effects can you find? (Hint: Read the poem aloud, and listen.)

> Whenever the moon and stars are set,
>   Whenever the wind is high,
> All night long in the dark and wet,
>   A man goes riding by.
> Late in the night when the fires are out,   5
> Why does he gallop and gallop about?
>
> Whenever the trees are crying aloud,
>   And ships are tossed at sea,
> By, on the highway, low and loud,
>   By at the gallop goes he.   10
> By at the gallop he goes, and then
> By he comes back at the gallop again.
>
> Robert Louis Stevenson, "Windy Nights"

First Impressions
In order to analyze a poem's sound effects, you need to hear them. Read the poem aloud, and jot down your impressions or feelings about it. The following questions can help you identify your response to any poem. Sample responses to "Windy Nights" are provided.

- What did you think about when you read the poem? *I thought about a windy night and the kinds of sounds that the wind makes.*
- Do you like the poem? Why or why not? *Yes, I like the way it repeats words.*

A Closer Look
Now it is time to read the poem again. This time, listen more closely to its sound effects. Think about the following questions as you re-read the poem. Find examples in the poem to answer the questions. (Note the line numbers where you find your examples. You will need to use those examples for support in your essay.)

- Does the poem use rhyme?
- Does the poem have rhythm?
- Does the poem use repetition?
- What do the sound effects add to the poem? Would the poem be as effective without the sound effects?

What's the Plan?
By now, you have a lot of information about the poem. You know what you think about it and the sound effects it uses. The next step is to organize your ideas before you draft your essay. Use the notes that you have taken on the poem, and put your ideas in a graphic organizer like the one below.

Introduction
- Mention the poem's title and author.
- Explain what the poem is about.

↓

Body
- Explain how sound effects are used in the poem.
- Provide one quotation or example from the poem for each type of sound effect.

↓

Conclusion
- State whether you like the poem.
- Explain why you do or do not like it.

For Example Below is an analysis of the sound effects in "Windy Nights." Notice that the writer mentions the three kinds of sound effects in the poem and provides examples with their line numbers.

> "Windy Nights" by Robert Louis Stevenson is a poem about the noises of a windy night. The poet talks about a man riding a horse, but he is really talking about the wind. The sound effects in the poem help me hear and feel a windy night.
>
> The poem uses rhyme, rhythm, and repetition. The rhyming words are in a regular pattern. For example, the words at the ends of every other line rhyme ("set" and "wet" in lines 1 and 3). Then, there are two rhymes in the last two lines of each stanza ("out" and "about" in lines 5 and 6). This reminds me of the way the wind keeps coming back over and over. The rhythm of the poem also reminds me of the wind. Words like "whenever" (lines 1, 2, and 7) and "gallop" (lines 6, 10, 11, and 12) have the rhythm of a galloping horse. The repetition of these words makes the idea of the wind seem even stronger. The repetition of the word "by" in the last four lines makes me think of a night when the wind will not stop.
>
> I like the poem "Windy Nights." At first, I did not know why the poet talks about a man riding. Then, the repetition of the word "gallop" made me realize that the rider is the wind. I like the way the sound of the poem makes the meaning come alive.

YOUR TURN 12 — Writing About a Poem's Sound Effects

- Find a poem you like that contains sound effects. (Ask your teacher or librarian to help you find poems.)
- Jot down your response to the poem. How do the sound effects help express the poem's meaning?
- Use the questions and the graphic organizer on page 179 to prepare a short essay that analyzes the sound effects in the poem.
- Revise your essay and check your final copy for spelling, punctuation, and grammar errors.

Timesaver

Ask students to label the three parts of their analyses (introduction, body, conclusion) when they finish writing. You can use the labels to scan their essays for correct organization and content before they begin revising. To make sure students understand the concept of sound effects, ask them to circle or highlight one or two examples in their essays.

YOUR TURN 12

Give students an opportunity to present their essays. They can read them aloud to the class or create a bulletin board display in which they post both their essays and the poems they selected to analyze.

Comparing Media: Film, TV, and Literature

WHAT'S AHEAD?

In this section you will compare a book and a film or TV show of the same type. You will also learn how to

- identify the elements of a novel and techniques used in a film
- make generalizations about a genre

"I will wait until the movie comes out." So many books are made into films that you might be tempted to stop reading and only see movies. What would you lose if you did that? Books, movies, and television all tell stories, but they tell them in different ways.

Read the Book and Watch the Show

Use Your Critical Eye For this workshop you will work with a partner to compare the main characters in books and movies or TV shows of the same type or *genre*. **Genre** (zhän′rə) is a French word meaning "type" or "class." Works of the same genre share certain characteristics. For example, the main character in detective novels, films, and TV shows is often a private investigator who has one faithful friend but who tends to make other people angry. The investigator also shows great determination, especially if he or she gets injured while trying to solve the mystery.

Other genres include fantasy/science fiction, westerns, animal stories, war/spy stories, sports stories, and historical fiction. Can you think of an example for each of these genres?

Be Choosy With your partner, select a genre. From that genre, each of you should select a book that you have read before. Then, you should each watch a different film or TV show from the same genre. The following chart will give you some ideas.

Possible Book and Movie/ TV Combinations by Genre

To make sure that students understand the concept of classifying by genre, ask volunteers to provide examples of two or three characteristics that are shared by other popular types of books, TV shows, and films, such as westerns or science fiction. Write the examples on the chalkboard.

LEARNERS HAVING DIFFICULTY

You may want students to make a direct comparison between a book and its movie version. After students have read the book, select a key scene; then, discuss characterization and the point of view of the narrator in that scene. Explain that in this context, point of view refers to the viewpoint from which the story is told.

Next, view (on videotape) the same scene in the film version of the book. Have students compare the presentation of characters and point of view in each medium. Explain that in film, point of view can be *omniscient* (the viewer knows what all characters know), or *limited* (the viewer only knows what the main character knows). The filmmaker can establish point of view by letting the camera roam among all the characters or by following just one character. (See pp. 182–183 for information on how filmmakers show characterization.) In the students' opinions, were the director's decisions about how to show character and point of view effective? Conclude the discussion by evaluating the total impact of each version, focusing on how effectively the scene's major idea or theme was presented in the book and in the film.

Possible Book and Movie/TV Combinations by Genre

Genre	Books	Movies/TV Shows
Science Fiction Stories	*Fantastic Voyage* by Isaac Asimov *The Time Machine* by H. G. Wells	*The Day the Earth Stood Still* *Star Trek*
Animal Stories	*Call of the Wild* by Jack London *The Yearling* by Marjorie Kinnan Rawlings	*Wild America* *Fly Away Home*
War Stories	*Number the Stars* by Lois Lowry *Zlata's Diary* by Zlata Filipovic	*The Diary of Anne Frank* *Empire of the Sun*
Sports Stories	*Hoops* by Walter Dean Myers *The Contender* by Robert Lipsyte	*Brian's Song* *Wild Hearts Can't Be Broken*
Mysteries	*I Am the Cheese* by Robert Cormier *The A.I. Gang: Operation Sherlock* by Bruce Coville	*Fairy Tale: A True Story* *From the Mixed-Up Files of Mrs. Basil E. Frankweiler*
Westerns	*Jimmy Spoon and the Pony Express* by Kristiana Gregory *The Long Chance* by Max Brand	*Shane* *Gunsmoke*

TIP Rent the video or check it out from the library. If you do not see a combination that you like in the chart above, talk to a librarian or your teacher to get suggestions.

Reading at the Movies Books, TV, and films have their own **media languages**—special ways of making meaning. The boldface terms below give you some of the language *you* will need to talk about the effects of these media.

How to Be a Character To create a believable character, a writer uses *characterization*. **Characterization** is the process of showing a character's personality. The writer can directly tell you what a character is like by using **description**. Writers can also indirectly show you what a character is like. When a writer uses **narration** (telling the events of a story) to tell us what a character is doing, for example, we get ideas about that character's personality. Another way that writers give us indirect information about character is through **dialogue**.

Like novelists, filmmakers and TV writers use narration and dialogue. Films and TV, though, have some additional techniques for showing character.

Chapter 5 **Exposition:** Responding to a Novel

- **Facial expression and body movement:** Close-ups of actors' faces help reveal characters' feelings. A character may show confidence or fear by the way she walks. A nervous character might constantly wiggle a foot or play with a pen while he is talking.
- **Sound:** Music can be used to say something about characters. For example, the appearance of a threatening character may be accompanied by scary music. A filmmaker may also use different types of music to reflect a character's changing moods.

Tools of the Trade The Venn diagram below reviews some of the tools available to writers, TV show producers, and filmmakers. As you read the book and watch the TV show or movie you have chosen, think about how these tools are used to create character as well as other elements, such as setting and conflict.

writer — both — TV/filmmaker

description | narration dialogue | close-ups movement sound

Compare the Book and Movie or TV Show

What's the Difference? After you have read your book and watched your movie or TV show, you will compare the main characters in your two examples. The following charts compare the main characters in two fairy tales: a print version of "Sleeping Beauty" and a TV movie version of *Cinderella*. Make similar charts for the book and film or TV show you chose.

Story: "Sleeping Beauty" by Charles Perrault

Main Character and Description	Techniques Used to Create Element
The princess: She is lovely, sweet tempered, and clever. She sings and dances. She doesn't do much in the story, but everyone loves her.	Description: The princess is described to us. Narration: The narrator explains what happens to the princess, who does not take any action. Dialogue: There are only a few lines of dialogue, and they don't tell us much.

Focus on Viewing and Representing

Meeting INDIVIDUAL NEEDS

ADVANCED LEARNERS
After students have read the book and watched the TV show or movie, ask them to think about what effect or influence the genre they analyzed has on an audience. For example, in what way might the fairy tales on pp. 183–184 influence young readers?

Students should indicate not only specific differences between a printed story and a TV show or a movie [imagination from verbal description versus visual impact] but also how these differences may affect a young audience. Students may wish to present their analyses to the class.

TEACHING TIP

What's the Difference?
To help students begin to compare a book and a movie or TV show, suggest that they start by thinking about the purpose of film versus the purpose of print. Both media can entertain. What do students think makes an artist choose to entertain through one medium over the other? Then, have students identify one quality in each medium that is done well and describe its effect. A character in a book, for example, might have a compelling way of speaking. In this example, the writer's use of dialogue (speech) has created a memorable character. The best part of a movie or a TV show might be the way the camera always homes in on small details and on the facial expressions of the characters. Such a technique might give viewers a sense of being able to see and know things that the characters cannot, and so make the viewer feel more involved in the movie or TV show.

Wrap It Up

Metacognition. Ask students to reflect on their own viewing and representing by answering the following question:

1. What did you find most challenging about comparing different media?

Then, ask students the following questions:

2. What does the word *genre* mean? ["type" or "class"]

3. What are three methods of characterization that a writer uses to tell you about what a character in a book is like? [description, narration, dialogue]

4. What are four techniques a filmmaker or a TV director can use to reveal character? [narration, dialogue, camera use, sound]

YOUR TURN 13

Check that students compare in their charts the purpose of the book and the movie or TV show, the effects each had on them as readers and viewers, and the tools used by the author and filmmaker or TV director. Also, make sure their generalizations are well supported with specific examples.

Movie: *Cinderella*

Main Character and Description	Techniques Used to Create Element
Cinderella: She is pretty, sweet, and kind, but her costumes are plain and tattered. She wants to be treated with respect.	Narration: The fairy godmother narrates what is happening. Facial expressions: Close-ups of Cinderella show her sadness when her family treats her badly and her joy when she dances with the prince. Sound: Cinderella sings happy songs when she is happy. She also sings songs that tell us about her dreams. Dialogue: The things she says tell us how she feels.

Reference Note
For more on **generalizations**, see page 705 in the Quick Reference Handbook.

Once you have completed your chart, get together with your partner to make a generalization about the main character in the genre you chose. Here is how you and your partner might make a generalization about the main character in a particular genre.

What you learned (about main character in that genre)
+ What you already know
―――――――――――――――――――
Generalization

Working with a partner, the student whose charts are shown above made the following generalization about the main character in a fairy tale.

TIP A **generalization** is a statement, based on specific examples, about the general characteristics of something. Be careful not to overgeneralize: Your generalization should be based on at least two books and at least two movies or TV shows.

> The main character in a fairy tale is often a girl who is sweet and beautiful and loves to sing.

This generalization can be supported by information in the chart, plus what the student's partner discovered, plus what both students know from hearing other fairy tales.

YOUR TURN 13 Comparing Media and Making Generalizations

Choose a book and a movie or TV show from the same genre. Follow the steps on pages 181–184 to make a chart comparing the main characters in the book and the movie or TV show. Then, working with a partner, make a generalization about the main characters in that genre. Support your generalization with evidence from your partner's and your own charts.

RESOURCES

Your Turn 13
Practice and Reinforcement
- Media Literacy and Communication Skills

—*Support and Practice*, Ch. 5, transparencies and worksheets
—Videocassette 2, Segment D

CHAPTER 5 Choices

Choose one of the following activities to complete.

▶ CAREERS
1. Everybody's a Critic
Report on a movie or book for a television review show. Have a partner review the same book or movie with you. Each of you will decide whether you like it. Then present the book or movie **reviews** to the rest of the class. Discuss why you and your partner do or do not agree.

▶ WRITING
2. That's What I Think
Share your thoughts about a novel by writing **e-mails** or **letters** to a pen pal. Discuss the main character, setting, and plot, as well as your reactions. Discuss your pen pal's book, too. Write at least two letters or e-mails each.

▶ CONNECTING CULTURES
3. It's a Small World The German "Aschenputtel," the Chinese "Yeh-Shen," and the English "Cinderella" are different versions of the same story. Read them, or read several versions of another story. Create **charts** comparing the stories' characters, settings, and plot events.

▶ TECHNOLOGY
4. Virtual Critic
Collaborate with a group to create a **database** of reports on educational computer games. As a group, decide which elements you want to evaluate or rank (sound effects, difficulty level, graphics, the goal of the game, and so on). Then, create **forms** for evaluating the games. Each member should then choose a game, play it, and complete the form. Once you have all the information, the group will create a database **record** about each of those games.

▶ CREATIVE WRITING
5. All Together Now
Collaborate in writing a **short story** with a group of classmates. Each person in the group should write a paragraph. Discuss and revise the paragraphs as a group. Read your final version to the class, and discuss your experience of working as a group.

PORTFOLIO

▶ WRITING
Ask students to follow these steps for writing e-mail or conventional letters:
1. Think of who might be interested in the novel you are reading.
2. Write your thoughts about the novel, including your responses to the main character, setting, and plot. Mention what you like and dislike about the novel and ask your reader for his or her reactions, too.
3. Use the following form for a friendly letter: the date; a greeting; the body, in which you discuss the novel; and a friendly closing.
4. Finish your letter, then check it for errors in grammar, spelling, and punctuation. If you write your letter by hand, make sure that your handwriting is neat and legible.

▶ TECHNOLOGY
The following are guidelines to help students work collaboratively on forms for evaluating computer games and to create a database record about each game.
1. Ask each group to compose a form in which they list four or five elements to evaluate. Then, they should organize the form in logical order and create a ranking system. Possibilities include ranking the elements in a game on a scale of *1* to *5* or from *poor* to *excellent.*
2. Ask each group member to use the form to evaluate a new game. Members may want to evaluate and revise their form after using it.
3. After students have completed the forms, ask groups to use a computer database program to enter and organize their findings into database records. Students may demonstrate the database for the class.

RESOURCES
Responding to a Novel
Assessment
- *Assessment Package*
  —*Chapter Tests,* Ch. 5
  —*Chapter Tests in Standardized Test Formats,* Ch. 5
  —*Assessment Alternatives,* Ch. 5
- *Test Generator (One-Stop Planner CD-ROM)*

Choices
Rubrics
- *Assessment Package*
  —*Assessment Alternatives,* Ch. 5

Choices **185**

CHAPTER 6

Sharing Your Research

Use this guide to create an instructional plan that suits the individual needs of your students. Assignments marked by an asterisk (*) may be completed out of class. Times given for pacing lessons are estimated. See pp. 186–187 for chapter-wide resources. Resources listed in this guide are point-of-use resources only.

Curriculum Connections

Choices *p. 225*
- Listening
- Crossing the Curriculum: Physical Education
- Creative Writing

GO TO: go.hrw.com
KEYWORD: EOLang 6-6

All resources for this chapter are available for preview on the *One-Stop Planner CD-ROM with Test Generator.* All worksheets and tests may be printed from the CD-ROM.

CHAPTER PLANNING GUIDE

	Chapter Opener pp. 186–187	**Reading Workshop: Reading an Informative Article** pp. 188–197
DEVELOPMENTAL PROGRAM	**30 minutes** • Your Turn 1 *p. 187*	**100 minutes** • Preparing to Read *p. 188* • Reading Selection *pp. 189–191* • First Thoughts in groups *p. 192* • Making Inferences: Drawing Conclusions *pp. 192–193* • Your Turn 2 *p. 193* • Author's Purpose *pp. 194–195* • Your Turn 3 *p. 195* • Test Taking Mini-Lesson *p. 197*
CORE PROGRAM	**20 minutes** • Your Turn 1 *p. 187*	**90 minutes** • Preparing to Read *p. 188* • Reading Selection *pp. 189–190* • First Thoughts *p. 192* • Making Inferences: Drawing Conclusions *pp. 192–193* • Your Turn 2 *p. 193* • Author's Purpose *pp. 194–195* • Your Turn 3 *p. 195* • Vocabulary Mini-Lesson *p. 196* • Test Taking Mini-Lesson *p. 197*
ADVANCED PROGRAM	**15 minutes** • Your Turn 1 *p. 187*	**75 minutes** • Preparing to Read *p. 188* • Reading Selection *pp. 189–190* • First Thoughts *p. 192* • Making Inferences: Drawing Conclusions *pp. 192–193* • Your Turn 2 *p. 193* • Author's Purpose *pp. 194–195* • Your Turn 3 *p. 195* • Vocabulary Mini-Lesson *p. 196*
RESOURCES — PRINT	• *Communications,* TP. 45, WS. p. 112	• *Alternative Readings,* Ch. 6 • *Communications,* TPs. 46, 47, WS. pp. 113–120
RESOURCES — MEDIA	• *One-Stop Planner* CD-ROM	• *One-Stop Planner* CD-ROM

TP.=Transparency   WS.=Worksheet

Writing Workshop: **Writing a Research Report** pp. 198–221	**Focus on Speaking and Listening:** **Giving and Evaluating a Research Presentation** pp. 222–224
⏲ **275 minutes** • Choose a Subject; Your Turn 4 pp. 198–199 • Purpose, Audience, and Voice; Your Turn 5 p. 200 • Ask Questions; Your Turn 6 p. 201 • Find and List Sources; Your Turn 7 pp. 202–203, 205 • Take Notes; Writing Mini-Lesson; Your Turn 8 pp. 205–207 • Organize and Outline; Your Turn 9 pp. 207–208 • Write a Main Idea Statement; Your Turn 10 p. 209 • Framework; Models; Your Turn 11* pp. 210–213 • Evaluate and Revise; Your Turn 12 pp. 214–216 • Proofread, Publish, and Reflect pp. 217–218 • Grammar Link; Your Turn 13 pp. 217–218 • Test Taking Mini-Lesson p. 219	⏲ **100 minutes** • Giving a Research Presentation pp. 222–223 • Your Turn 15 p. 223 • Evaluating, Get the Message, Special Delivery, Put It All Together pp. 223–224 • Your Turn 16 p. 224
⏲ **180 minutes** • Choose a Subject; Your Turn 4 pp. 198–199 • Purpose, Audience, and Voice; Your Turn 5 p. 200 • Ask Questions; Your Turn 6 p. 201 • Sources; Mini-Lesson in groups; Your Turn 7* pp. 202–205 • Take Notes; Writing Mini-Lesson; Your Turn 8 pp. 205–207 • Organize and Outline; Your Turn 9 pp. 207–208 • Write a Main Idea Statement; Your Turn 10 p. 209 • Framework; Models; Your Turn 11* pp. 210–213 • Evaluate and Revise pp. 214–215 • Focus on Word Choice; Your Turn 12 p. 216 • Proofread, Publish, and Reflect pp. 217–218 • Grammar Link; Your Turn 13 pp. 217–218 • Test Taking Mini-Lesson p. 219 • Connections to Life; Your Turn 14* pp. 220–221	⏲ **75 minutes** • Giving a Research Presentation pp. 222–223 • Your Turn 15 p. 223 • Evaluating, Get the Message, Special Delivery, Put It All Together pp. 223–224 • Your Turn 16 p. 224
⏲ **120 minutes** • Choose a Subject; Your Turn 4 pp. 198–199 • Purpose, Audience, and Voice; Your Turn 5 p. 200 • Ask Questions; Your Turn 6 p. 201 • Sources; Mini-Lesson; Your Turn 7* pp. 202–205 • Take Notes; Writing Mini-Lesson; Your Turn 8* pp. 205–207 • Organize and Outline; Your Turn 9* pp. 207–208 • Write a Main Idea Statement; Your Turn 10 p. 209 • Framework; Models; Your Turn 11* pp. 210–213 • Evaluate and Revise pp. 214–215 • Focus on Word Choice; Your Turn 12* p. 216 • Proofread, Publish, and Reflect pp. 217–218 • Grammar Link; Your Turn 13 pp. 217–218 • Connections to Life; Your Turn 14 pp. 220–221	⏲ **60 minutes** • Giving a Research Presentation pp. 222–223 • Your Turn 15 p. 223 • Evaluating, Get the Message, Special Delivery, Put It All Together pp. 223–224 • Your Turn 16 p. 224

• *Communications,*
  TPs. 48–51,
  WS. pp. 121–137
• *Designing Your Writing*
	• *Media Literacy and Communication Skills*
	  —*Support and Practice,* Ch. 6
	  —*A How-to Handbook*
	  —*A Teacher's Guide,* Ch. 6

• One-Stop Planner CD-ROM	• *Media Literacy and Communication Skills* —Videocassette 2, Segment E • One-Stop Planner CD-ROM

CHAPTER 6
Sharing Your Research

CHAPTER OBJECTIVES

- To read an informative article, gather data, draw conclusions, and determine an author's purpose
- To write a research report
- To present and evaluate an oral report

Chapter Overview

Much of the reading we do in our daily lives comes from informational texts, such as newspaper reports, magazine articles, product information, and Internet articles. This chapter is designed to help students write an informative research paper and present their information orally. The Reading Workshop (pp. 188–197) presents an informative article for students to read to locate information, draw conclusions, and determine the author's purpose. The Writing Workshop (pp. 198–221) gives students an opportunity to follow a step-by-step process for researching and writing a report. The Focus on Speaking and Listening redirects students' research into a peer-evaluated oral presentation. Although the sections of the chapter may be taught independently, teaching them together will prepare students for developing interesting research reports.

Why Study Ways to Share Your Research?

Guiding students to realize that everyone at times looks for information and shares it with others can help them understand that research is not an isolated academic task. Presenting this research in writing or as a speech could influence the decisions of others. By learning to be effective researchers and presenters, students also develop critical thinking and organizational skills essential for daily life.

Teaching the Chapter

Option 1: Begin with Literature

If literature is the basis of instruction in your classroom, you could introduce the chapter after having students read a piece of informative literature, such as a biography or a nonfiction essay. Help students use the literature to draw conclusions and determine an author's purpose. Then, have them read **"The California Gold Rush"** (pp. 189–191) and complete its accompanying instruction. Once students have read and analyzed an informative report, they will be ready to write their own research reports.

Option 2: Begin with Nonfiction and Writing

Familiarize students with informative writing by beginning with the material in this chapter. The Reading Workshop (pp. 188–197) presents research strategies, including drawing conclusions and determining an author's purpose, that students can use as they read various sources. The Writing Workshop (pp. 198–221) leads students through the steps of writing and revising research reports. As they develop their skills with nonfiction, students can apply these skills to other informative literature selections.

Making Connections

■ To the Literature Curriculum

Explain that literary works present information for readers to think about and question. Students can read research about rattlesnakes in the science essay "Snakes, The Facts and the Folklore" by Hilda Simon. In "Scanning the Heavens" by George Beshore, they can read about the conclusions that astronomers in China formed centuries before their Western counterparts did. Students can draw their own conclusions when reading "The Mysterious Mr. Lincoln" by Russell Freedman. These works as well as other pieces of literature may become the basis for further study or research that students can share with others.

Lesson Idea: Drawing Conclusions Based on "The Mysterious Mr. Lincoln" by Russell Freedman

1. After students read "The Mysterious Mr. Lincoln," have them refer to the paragraphs on pp. 130–131 about Frederick Douglass. Then, have students write the topic and details about it in a graphic organizer based on the **Thinking It Through** strategy on p. 193 of the Reading Workshop. A sample chart is shown below.

Frederick Douglass	
What I Read	Topic: Frederick Douglass Details: He was a "fiery abolitionist writer and editor" who was born a slave but later escaped to become free.
+ What I Know	
Conclusion	

2. Discuss relevant facts students already know about Frederick Douglass, abolitionists, or the Civil War. Have them add these facts to the organizer. [For example: An abolitionist wants to outlaw slavery. Editors write their opinions to persuade people to their points of view.]

3. Work with students to draw conclusions using the facts they have at hand. Point out that they are combining facts they read with facts they already know to draw a logical conclusion. [For example: During the war, Frederick Douglass probably wrote articles about getting rid of slavery, and the articles aroused people's emotions.] Discuss other conclusions students can draw from the article.

4. Next, introduce the informative article "The California Gold Rush" (pp. 189–191). Use the instruction on drawing conclusions on pp. 188, 192–193 to prepare students for drawing logical conclusions when they research and write research reports.

■ To Careers

To show students how research is part of daily life, discuss careers with which students are familiar, such as programmer, doctor, and store owner, and the ways in which these people conduct research and report on it. Invite family members or others from the community to class to discuss research in their workplaces, especially the processes and sources they use and the ways in which they present their research.

■ To the Community

One way to connect research to students' community is to suggest that students research and report the history of their community. They could research such questions as: Who were the first people to live in this community, and why did they choose this place to live? How has this community changed over the years? Have groups divide up the research and writing tasks. Ask family and community members to help by providing information and by serving as guest speakers.

■ To the Social Studies Curriculum

"The California Gold Rush" explores some of the reasons why people move from place to place. Discuss the article and have students brainstorm other reasons why people move. Encourage them to research and report on either a historical migration, such as the westward expansion, or a current population shift, such as migration to Sunbelt states. If possible, coordinate the research with the social studies teacher, who may be able to provide resources for students' research.

CHAPTER

6

PREVIEWING THE CHAPTER

- The three workshops in this chapter focus on the process of conducting and sharing research. Each workshop may be taught separately but, taught together, they help students learn how to research, write, present, and evaluate a report. Reading the informative article **"The California Gold Rush"** (pp. 189–191) prepares students for writing their own informative reports. For help in integrating this chapter with grammar, usage, and mechanics chapters, see pp. T297A–T297B.

INTRODUCING THE CHAPTER

- To introduce the chapter, use the Journal Warm-up, Transparency 45, in *Communications*.

VIEWING THE ILLUSTRATION

- This illustration depicts a boy surrounded by plants and animals from Africa, the subject of his report. Have students look closely at the composition of the scene, particularly its balance. [The three seated students are balanced by the standing student, the monkey, and the giraffe.] Help students see that the idea of the art is to show how a report containing visual details can make writing come to life.

Representing. If your students could bring the subject of a report on hurricanes to life, how would they depict it? Allow students to sketch their ideas on paper.

CHAPTER

6 Sharing Your Research

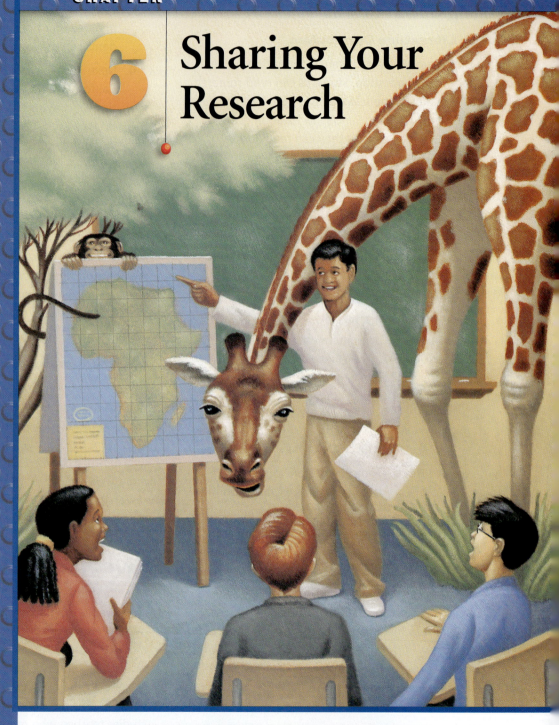

CHAPTER RESOURCES

Planning
- *Lesson Planner, ELL Strategies*, Ch. 6
- Block Scheduling, p. T185A (this book)
- One-Stop Planner CD-ROM

Practice
- *Communications*, Ch. 6
- *Media Literacy and Communication Skills*

- *Writer's Workshop 1 CD-ROM*

Extension
- *Designing Your Writing*

Reinforcement
- *Communications*, Ch. 6
- *Alternative Readings*, Ch. 6
- *Daily Language Activity Transparencies*

PREVIEW

Reading Workshop

Reading an Informative Article
PAGE 188

Writing Workshop

Writing a Research Report
PAGE 198

Focus on Speaking and Listening

Giving and Evaluating a Research Presentation
PAGE 222

You just heard the greatest CD of all time. You want to know everything about the group—Where are they from? How do they get ideas for songs? What other recordings have they made? Finding answers to these questions requires research.

From sixth-graders to research scientists, people need to find and share information with others. One way for people to share this information is by writing a research report. Research reports are based on reliable sources—experts, informative books or articles, videotapes, or Internet sources. A research report writer pulls together information from different sources and presents it along with his or her own thoughts on a subject.

GO TO: go.hrw.com
KEYWORD: EOLang 6-6

YOUR TURN 1 — Seeking Information

With a few classmates, make a list of some subjects you have researched in the past, such as a hobby or sport, something in nature, or an interesting person. Then, discuss these questions:

- What sources did your group use to find information?
- Which sources were easy to use? Why? Which sources were difficult to use? Why?

Motivate

Discuss ways in which we all do research, formally or informally. For example, ask students how they would find out which store has the best prices on bicycles. Explain that researching and presenting a topic will help students learn interesting information.

ELEMENTS OF Literature

Research Reports in Literature. For examples of informative writing in *Elements of Literature*, Introductory Course, refer students to "A Glory over Everything," from *Harriet Tubman: Conductor on the Underground Railroad* by Ann Petry, pp. 138–145.

YOUR TURN 1

After each student shares his or her ideas and insights about the sources he or she used, have another group member summarize what that student said about a particular source. Assess with these questions:

- **Listening:** Do students interpret each speaker's message? Do students' responses indicate that they understand the major ideas and supporting evidence? Do they ask questions to clarify any statements that are unclear?
- **Speaking:** Do students support their ideas with evidence, elaboration, and examples? Do they clarify their ideas when other group members ask questions about them?

- *Vocabulary Workshop* and *Tests*
- *Spelling*

Evaluation and Assessment
- *Assessment Package*
  —*Chapter Tests,* Ch. 6
  —*Chapter Tests in Standardized Test Formats,* Ch. 6
  —*Assessment Alternatives,* Ch. 6

- *Test Generator* (One-Stop Planner CD-ROM)

Internet
- go.hrw.com (keyword: EOLang 6–6)

Reading Workshop

OBJECTIVES

- To read an informative article in preparation for writing a research report
- To draw conclusions
- To recognize an author's purpose for writing
- To use word roots to identify the meanings of unfamiliar words

TEACHING TIP

Preparing to Read
The material on this page introduces the concepts of drawing conclusions and determining an author's purpose. These concepts are the focuses of instruction in the Reading Workshop and will be discussed in greater depth on pp. 192–195. The Reading Selection **"The California Gold Rush"** on pp. 189–191 illustrates both concepts.

Quotation for the Day

"What one knows is, in youth, of little moment; they know enough who know how to learn."
(Henry Adams, 1838–1918, American historian)

Write the quotation on the chalkboard or on an overhead transparency, and explain that in this context the word *moment* means "importance." Then, ask students how the quotation applies to reading informative articles. [Students may suggest that reading informative articles is one way in which a person learns. Understanding how to read an informative article, therefore, helps a person acquire knowledge.]

RESOURCES

Reading Workshop Reinforcement
- *Alternative Readings,* Ch. 6

Reading Workshop

Reading an Informative Article

WHAT'S AHEAD?
In this section you will read an informative article. You will also learn how to
- draw conclusions
- recognize an author's purpose for writing

What is a gold rush? Who were the original Forty-Niners? Why is California known as "the Golden State"? You will find the answers to these questions and more as you read "The California Gold Rush," the informative article on the next page.

Preparing to Read

READING SKILL

Making Inferences: Drawing Conclusions An **inference** is an idea a reader forms, based in part on what he or she has read, seen, or experienced. One type of inference is a *conclusion*. Readers draw **conclusions** by putting together the pieces of information a writer presents and adding their own knowledge to that information. For example, details such as an eye patch, a wooden leg, and a parrot perched on a person's shoulder are clues that can lead readers to conclude that the person being described is a pirate. As you read the following article, try to draw conclusions about the gold rush in California.

READING FOCUS

Author's Purpose An **author's purpose** is the reason the author writes a piece. In the following article, Kathy Wilmore answers questions like these about the California gold rush: *Who was involved? What did they do? Why? How did it start? How did it turn out?* The fact that the article answers such questions gives you a clue about why the author wrote it.

188   Chapter 6   Exposition: Sharing Your Research

READING PROCESS

PREREADING
Setting a Purpose. Explain to students that having a purpose in mind as they read is especially helpful when researching because it allows them to sift out information that is not relevant to the question they are trying to answer. Point out that **Preparing to Read** sets drawing conclusions and determining an author's purpose as two purposes for reading **"The California Gold Rush."**

Explain that in their independent reading, students will set their own purposes. Suggest

Reading Selection

Read the following selection. In a notebook, jot down answers to the numbered active-reading questions in the shaded boxes. Underlined words will be used in the Vocabulary Mini-Lesson on page 196.

from Junior Scholastic

THE CALIFORNIA GOLD RUSH

BY KATHY WILMORE

1 For seventeen years—ever since leaving his New Jersey home at age eighteen—James Wilson Marshall kept moving farther and farther west in search of a better life. In 1845, he went to California, which was part of Mexico then, and things finally seemed to turn around for him. A businessman named John A. Sutter gave him a job building a sawmill in a remote wilderness area in northern California. Build it, Sutter told him, and you can run the place for me. Sutter was looking to make a tidy profit; Marshall was just hoping to make a living. But on January 24, 1848, Marshall was momentarily distracted from his work. A glint of light caught his eye—and sleepy California was never the same again.

1. Why do you think the author tells you so much about James Marshall?

"To See the Elephant"

In January 1848, California had a population of only 15,000 people. By the time December 1849 came around, the population was up to 100,000 and climbing. Why such a boom? Blame it on that glint that caught James Marshall's eye.

One cold and rainy day soon after, Marshall arrived at Sutter's house with "some important and interesting news." Sutter studied the stuff that Marshall had brought and

Reading Workshop 189

Active-Reading Questions
ANSWERS continued

2. The glint was gold.

3. The first miners arrived in 1849, or '49.

4. Students may say that the author includes these quotations because they add interest and authenticity to the report. These eyewitness accounts allow the reader to see what happened during the gold rush through the eyes of someone who experienced the events firsthand.

---

2. What was the glint that caught Marshall's eye?

realized it was gold. He was not happy.

4 "I told [my employees] that I would consider it as a great favor if they would keep this discovery secret only for six weeks, so I could finish [building] my large flour mill at Brighton.... [I]nstead of feeling happy and contented, I was very unhappy, and could not see that it would benefit me much, and I was perfectly right in thinking so."[1]

5 Sutter's employees promised not to tell, but word leaked out. . . .

6 By 1849, the gold rush was on. People poured into California from all points of the compass. They arrived by ship or overland trails, crossing North America by wagon train, riding horses or mules, and even on foot.

7 These hopeful thousands, the first large wave of whom arrived in 1849, were known as Forty-Niners. Many had sold everything they owned to pay their way to California.

3. Why were the first miners called Forty-Niners?

8 Ask a Forty-Niner why, and he or she was likely to reply, "I am going to see the elephant"—that is, to find something wonderful and rare.

---

[1]. From "The Discovery of Gold in California" by Gen. John A. Sutter, *Hutchings California Magazine* (November 1857).

"A Dog's Life"

9 Dreaming of gold was easy, but finding it was anything but. Miners faced hours of strenuous work. Some were able to reach out and pick up a gold-filled nugget, but that was rare.

10 Most miners spent hours slamming pickaxes into rocky soil, or scooping up panfuls of riverbed mud and rinsing it to find tiny grains of gold. They lived in rough, makeshift camps far from "civilization," with little shelter from cold mountain winds and rain. As William Swain described camp life in a letter sent home in 1850:

11 "George, I tell you this mining among the mountains is a dog's life. . . . [T]his climate in the mines requires a constitution like iron. Often for weeks during the rainy season it is damp, cold, and sunless, and the labor of getting gold is of the most laborious kind. Exposure causes sickness to a great extent for, in most of the mines, tents are all the habitation [home] miners have."[2]

4. Why do you think the author includes quotes such as this one in the article?

Making a Go of It

12 Thousands of Forty-Niners made the trek to California with the idea

---

[2]. From a letter from California by William Swain, January 6 & 16, 1850.

---

190 | Chapter 6 | **Exposition:** Sharing Your Research

READING PROCESS

READING

Make Personal Connections. Explain to students that when they find a connection between what they read and events or situations in their own lives, they will understand what they read on a deeper, more personal level. Ask students to write about one or two ways in which the Reading Selection on pp. 189–191 connects to their lives. To prompt them, ask questions such as these: Have you ever discovered something exciting? Has your family ever moved from one of striking it rich, then returning home to spend their wealth. But for every Forty-Niner whose labor paid off handsomely, countless others had to find other ways of making a living.

13   Among those were thousands of Chinese. Word of "Gold Mountain"—the Chinese name for California—lit new hope among poverty-stricken peasants in China. In 1849, only 54 Chinese lived in California; by 1852, the number had risen to 14,000.

14   Chinese miners faced the resentment of many white Forty-Niners who saw them as unfair competition. . . . Looking for less risky ways of earning a living, many Chinese turned to service work: cooking meals, toting heavy loads, and washing clothes. Miners happily plunked down money for such services.

15   The Chinese were not the only Forty-Niners to make a go of things at something other than mining. One of the biggest success stories was that of a Bavarian <u>immigrant</u> named Levi Strauss. Strauss, a tailor, hoped to make his fortune by making and selling tents. But he found that another item he made was more popular: the heavy-duty work pants that became known as those "wonderful pants of Levi's." His blue jeans business prospered, and Strauss became one of the wealthiest men in California.

From Fortune to Misfortune

What of Sutter and Marshall, the men who started it all?

Sutter's workers all quit and poured their efforts into finding gold. When the first Forty-Niners arrived, they overran Sutter's land, wrecked his mills and farmlands, and even killed his cattle for food. . . .

> **5. Do you think Sutter was right to be unhappy when Marshall first discovered gold? Why or why not?**

Marshall's hope of earning a living by running the mill was destroyed when the workers quit and it was wrecked by treasure seekers. He became a drifter, then a poor farmer.

The Golden State

For California, however, the gold rush brought long-lasting benefits. California had become U.S. territory as a result of the treaty ending the Mexican War. That was signed on February 2, 1848—just eight days after Marshall spied that first glint of gold. California became the thirty-first state on September 9, 1850. In that short time, it grew from a place of scattered <u>settlements</u> to one of bustling seaports and boomtowns. Whether or not they ever had the thrill of "seeing the elephant," thousands of restless Forty-Niners found a place to call home. ■

Active-Reading Questions
ANSWERS continued

5. Sutter was probably right to be unhappy about the gold discovery since his workers quit to prospect for gold. In addition, Sutter's land and mills were ruined by miners, who overran his property and killed his livestock.

---

place to another in search of new opportunities? Have you ever done exhausting physical work? How did you feel in these situations? Remind students to write only about experiences they feel comfortable sharing with you and their classmates.

First Thoughts on Your Reading

ANSWERS

Possible answers follow.

1. The author wrote the article to provide information on the events that led to the start of the gold rush, insight into the people who participated in the gold rush, and details about the lives of the Forty-Niners.

2. The people who were successful had to be both hard-working and lucky. In addition, they had to be able to endure physical hardship and to recognize opportunities for success—through mining, services to miners, or businesses that supplied miners.

TEACHING TIP

Making Inferences: Drawing Conclusions

Remind students that drawing conclusions is part of everyday life. Ask students what they would conclude if they saw a very long line of people waiting to get in to see a movie. Discuss with students that the conclusion they drew—that the movie was very popular—came from the evidence they saw (the line of people) combined with their previous personal experience (there is a long line at the movies only when a movie is very popular). Have students share other conclusions they have drawn from everyday activities.

First Thoughts on Your Reading

1. Why do you think the author wrote this article?
2. What qualities helped people succeed during the gold rush?

READING SKILL

Making Inferences: Drawing Conclusions

Add It Up Suppose you are watching a mystery on TV in which a character sneaks into a room, then races from the room carrying a small box. Another character enters the room and screams, "My jewelry has been stolen!" What happened? In order to understand the story, you will need to draw a *conclusion*.

A **conclusion** is a judgment a reader makes about a text based on details the author provides and on what the reader already knows about the subject. Here is an example.

> **What you read:** The Maximizer, the most powerful superhero, has captured the evil Dr. Z. Suddenly, Dr. Z throws a glowing liquid at the Maximizer, who collapses.
>
> + **What you know:** In other comic books, the superhero usually has one big weakness, which his or her enemy discovers at some point.
>
> **Conclusion:** Dr. Z has discovered the Maximizer's weakness. The glowing liquid makes the Maximizer helpless.

Read the following paragraph and try to draw a conclusion based on the details in it. If you have trouble reaching a conclusion, use the Thinking It Through steps on the next page.

> In 1901, the first cars were being mass-produced in the United States. They were popular and sold well. In that same year, a huge oil field was discovered at Spindletop, near Beaumont, Texas. Within three months, the population of Beaumont had grown from nine thousand to fifty thousand.

READING PROCESS

EXTENDING

Apply What You Read. Tell students that when they draw conclusions as they read, they are being active participants in the reading experience. Active involvement in their reading will help students become better readers. Suggest that students choose a magazine article, newspaper article, or short story that they have recently read. Ask them to follow the steps in **Thinking It Through** on p. 193 as they draw conclusions from their reading.

THINKING IT THROUGH

Drawing Conclusions

▶ **STEP 1** Identify the topic of the passage and look for the details about it.

Topic: cars and oil

Details: Cars were mass-produced, and a huge oil field was discovered in the same year. The town where oil was discovered grew.

▶ **STEP 2** Think about what you already know about the topic. How can you connect the details to your own knowledge or experiences?

I know cars use oil and gasoline. I also know people rush to places where big discoveries are made—the way the Forty-Niners rushed to California—because they hope to get rich.

▶ **STEP 3** Connect your knowledge or experiences you recalled from Step 2 with the details you identified in Step 1 to draw a conclusion about the subject.

Conclusion: People knew cars would need oil, so many people rushed to the place where it was discovered, hoping to get rich.

YOUR TURN 2 Drawing Conclusions

Use the Thinking It Through steps above to draw conclusions about the following parts of "The California Gold Rush." Read each passage listed and draw a conclusion by answering the question that follows each item on the list. Be prepared to support your conclusions with details from the reading selection.

- Paragraphs 3 and 4: Why did Sutter react as he did to the discovery of gold?
- Paragraph 15: What did the gold rush have to do with one businessman's making a fortune from the sale of work pants?
- The section titled "From Fortune to Misfortune": Was the gold rush lucky for Sutter? Why?

Reading Workshop **193**

Meeting INDIVIDUAL NEEDS

LEARNERS HAVING DIFFICULTY
To help students who have difficulty understanding the **Thinking It Through,** ask questions such as the following:

- What important things happened in 1901? How are cars and oil related?
- What happened to the population of California during the gold rush? What reason did people have for moving all the way to California?
- What was happening in Beaumont, Texas, in 1901? Why would it make sense for people to move there? What might they be hoping for?

Sample responses follow.

- Sutter was unhappy about the discovery of gold. He predicted that his workers would quit in order to mine for gold.
- Levi Strauss made tents and work pants for the miners. The durable work pants became so popular that Strauss made a fortune from his blue jeans.
- The gold rush wasn't lucky for Sutter. His land was overrun with miners, who destroyed his mills, his farmlands, and his cattle.

Your Turn 2
Practice
- *Communications,* WS. p. 113

Reinforcement
- *Communications,* TP. 46, WS. p. 114

TEACHING TIP

Author's Purpose
In the classroom, display a poem, play, comic book, journal, editorial, novel, encyclopedia, magazine ad, and page of television listings. Guide students as they sort the pieces into groups that have similar purposes. [To inform: television listings, encyclopedia; To express: poem, journal; To entertain: play, comic book, novel; To persuade: editorial, magazine ad] Discuss with students how they made their choices and how discovering an author's purpose can help them figure out their own purposes for reading.

READING FOCUS

Author's Purpose

What's the Point? When you read a comic book, you usually are reading to be entertained. The creator of that comic book most likely wrote it for exactly that purpose. Sometimes, though, writers use the comic-book form in order to express themselves—to tell about something meaningful that happened to them or to share their own feelings about something they think is important. Whether they write comic books or research reports, writers write for a **purpose,** or reason. Being aware of an author's purpose can help you set your own purpose for reading.

The following chart explains the four main purposes for writing. In the right-hand column, it gives clues that you can look for in a piece of writing to figure out an author's purpose.

Purpose	Explanation	Clues
to inform	Informative writing teaches something. It answers *Who? What? Where? When? Why?* and *How?* questions. It can explain the way bats navigate, how a firefighter made a daring rescue, or how to play a game.	• dates • names of real people and places • facts, maps, and charts • helpful headings • quotations from real people
to express a belief or feeling	Expressive writing shares a writer's beliefs or feelings about something. Poems and personal essays are examples of expressive writing.	• words about feelings • use of *I* • value words like *best, worst, great*
to be creative or entertain	Creative writing tells a story, uses drama or humor, or plays with language. Examples include novels, short stories, poems, and plays.	• a story with a beginning, middle, and end • dialogue • rhyme • humor • suspense
to influence or persuade	Persuasive writing tries to convince the reader to share the writer's opinion or to take some action. Examples include editorials, persuasive essays, reviews, and advertisements.	• opinions supported by reasons, facts, or examples • words like *should, must, have to* • value words like *best, worst, great*

Can you figure out the author's purpose in the following passage? You can if you look for clues from the chart on page 194.

> Although history tells about the taming of the American West, an important part of that story is often left out. History books should emphasize the contributions of Chinese immigrants. Chinese workers provided much of the labor for early railroads and took jobs that others considered too dangerous. They suffered from low pay, unfair laws, and frequent attacks by other groups. These people who helped to build the modern West should be honored.

Here is how one student identified clues in this paragraph to figure out the author's purpose.

Clues	What They Tell Me About Purpose
The paragraph includes facts about Chinese workers in the West.	The purpose could be to inform. These facts also seem to back up an opinion, though, so I think the purpose is probably to persuade.
The word should is used twice.	The purpose is definitely to persuade.

YOUR TURN 3 — Identifying the Author's Purpose

- Re-read "The California Gold Rush" on pages 189–191. Alone or with a partner, look for clues from the chart on page 194.
- List the clues you find and identify the purposes they point to, as in the above example.
- Finally, look over your list of the clues and purposes you have found in the article, and choose the purpose that you have listed most often.

Reading Workshop 195

Wrap It Up

Metacognition. Ask students to reflect on their own reading processes by answering the following question:

1. What did you learn from this article that you didn't already know?

Then, ask students this question:

2. On what two things should readers base conclusions? [clues the author provides and information the reader already knows]

YOUR TURN 3

Charts may vary, but students should conclude that the author's purpose is to inform. A sample chart is shown below.

CLUES	WHAT THEY TELL ABOUT PURPOSE
James Marshall discovered gold in California while working for Sutter.	Facts about real people and places suggest that the purpose is to inform.
Marshall found gold on January 24, 1848.	Dates suggest that the purpose is to inform.
The quotations express feelings.	If the writing were expressive, the feelings would be the writer's own, not those of others.

RESOURCES

Your Turn 3
Practice
- *Communications,* WS. p. 115

Reinforcement
- *Communications,* TP. 47, WS. p. 116

MINI-LESSON VOCABULARY

Word Roots

An informative article on a subject you know little about may contain unfamiliar words. You can often figure out the meaning of a word if you recognize its *root*. A **root** is the main part of a word. For example, the words *personality* and *impersonal* have the same root—*person*. Word roots like *person* can stand alone, but some roots cannot. The chart to the right gives examples of such roots. These roots need word parts called *prefixes* and *suffixes* to become words. A **prefix** is a word part that may be added to the beginning of a root to change the root's meaning. A **suffix** may be added to the end of a root. (For more on **prefixes** and **suffixes**, see page 126.)

Word Root	Meaning	Examples
–civi–	relating to townspeople	uncivilized
–migr–	to move	migrate
–popul–	people	unpopular

THINKING IT THROUGH — Using Word Roots

Here is an example based on a word from the reading selection.

▶ **STEP 1** Peel off the prefixes and suffixes to identify the unfamiliar word's root.

The word is <u>population</u>. I can peel off the suffix -ation. That leaves <u>popul</u>-.

▶ **STEP 2** Use what you know about the root and the word's context to come up with a definition for the unfamiliar word.

I know <u>popul</u>- means "people." The words around <u>population</u> tell me how many people lived in California. <u>Population</u> must mean "the number of people."

▶ **STEP 3** Replace your definition in the original sentence to see if it makes sense.

"In January 1848, California had <u>a number of only 15,000 people</u>." That makes sense to me.

PRACTICE

Use the steps above to define the following words. They are underlined for you in the reading selection. For help with meanings of prefixes and suffixes, see pages 715–716.

1. momentarily (page 189)
2. civilization (page 190)
3. laborious (page 190)
4. immigrant (page 191)
5. settlements (page 191)

196 Chapter 6 Exposition: Sharing Your Research

MINI-LESSON VOCABULARY

Word Roots

ANSWERS

1. Peel off the suffix *–arily*. That leaves *moment*, which means "a short amount of time." Substitute the meaning "for a short amount of time" to make sense in the sentence: ". . . Marshall was *for a short amount of time* distracted from his work."
2. Remove the suffix *–ization*. That leaves *civil*, which means "about the citizens." Substitute the meaning "an organized group of citizens" to make sense in the sentence: "They lived in rough, makeshift camps far from *an organized group of citizens* . . ."
3. Peel off the suffix *–ious*. That leaves *labor*, which means "exhausting work." Substitute the meaning "exhausting kind of work" to make sense in the sentence: ". . . getting gold is of the most *exhausting kind of work*."
4. Peel off the prefix *im–*. That leaves *migrant*, which means "someone who moves from place to place." Substitute the meaning "a person who moves into a new place" to make sense in the sentence: "One of the biggest success stories was that of a Bavarian *person named Levi Strauss who moved into a new place*."
5. Remove the suffix *–ments*. That leaves *settle*, which means "to establish a place to live." Substitute the meaning "places to live" to make sense in the sentence: ". . . it grew from a place of scattered *places to live* to one of bustling seaports . . ."

Taking a Second Look

Word Roots. As an alternative strategy, have students use context clues to infer the meanings of the **Practice** words. The definition of *population*, for example, can be inferred from the phrase "of only 15,000 people."

RESOURCES

Vocabulary
Practice
■ *Communications,* WS. p. 117

Test Taking
Practice
■ *Communications,* WS. pp. 118–120

Exposition: Sharing Your Research

MINI-LESSON TEST TAKING

Answering Questions About Tables

Informative texts, including passages found on reading tests, often list factual information in table form. A table, which may have one or many columns, organizes facts into categories to help a reader quickly find information. The categories are usually listed as column headings. To read a table, read the column headings, and then look at the information in each column. When looking at information in the form of dates, notice the amount of time between dates.

The table to the right contains information about important discoveries in history. Study the information, and answer the question below the table.

Century	Discovery
16th	the fact that Earth circles the sun the existence of bacteria
17th	the power of gravity
19th	how to generate electrical current the existence of electrons
20th	bacteria-killing antibiotics the structure of DNA

According to the information in the chart, for how many centuries did people know about bacteria without knowing how to kill bacteria?

A. 20 **B.** 4 **C.** 2 **D.** 16

THINKING IT THROUGH — Answering Questions About Tables

▶ **STEP 1** Read the question, and identify the information you need to find in the chart.

I need to find when bacteria were discovered and when something that kills bacteria was discovered.

▶ **STEP 2** Identify the information in the chart that you can use to answer the question.

The chart says bacteria were discovered in the 16th century and antibiotics were discovered in the 20th century.

▶ **STEP 3** Decide what you need to do with the information to come up with an answer.

I need to figure out how long it was between these discoveries. If I count—16, 17, 18, 19, 20—I get five centuries.

▶ **STEP 4** If none of the choices matches your answer, cross out any choices you know are wrong. Then, review the question and chart to choose between the remaining answers.

Five centuries is not a choice. A and D are the centuries when the discoveries were made. Because 20 − 16 = 4, only four centuries passed between the discoveries. My choice is B.

Looking Ahead to Writing

In the Writing Workshop for this chapter (pp. 198–221), students are asked to choose a topic and write a research paper. Students will realize, as they pull together their notes from various sources, that they will need to understand each author's purpose and be able to draw conclusions about the information they have gathered. Have students refer again to the **Thinking It Through** steps on p. 193 and the chart on p. 194 as they plan, research, and write their papers. Also, have students refer to the Reading Selection as an example of how to incorporate gathered information into a cohesive research report.

Writing Workshop

OBJECTIVES

- To use the writing process to write a research report
- To ask questions to guide research
- To find and list reliable sources
- To take organized notes
- To use precise nouns
- To capitalize and punctuate titles correctly

Quotation for the Day

"We wholly conquer only what we assimilate."
(André Gide, 1869–1951, French writer)

Write the quotation on the chalkboard, and explain to students that *assimilate* means "to absorb into the mind." Then, ask students to discuss how this statement relates to prewriting. [Prewriting involves gathering facts and putting together data from various sources for their reports.] Lead students to understand that it is only when writers have assimilated the data they have collected that they are in control of their information and ready to write their reports.

Writing Workshop

WHAT'S AHEAD?

In this workshop you will write a research report. You will also learn how to

- ask questions to guide your research
- find and list reliable sources
- take organized notes
- use precise nouns
- capitalize and punctuate titles correctly

Writing a Research Report

Have you heard about a snake that grows to be thirty feet long? Did you know that some gladiators in ancient Rome were women? When you find out an unusual fact, the first thing you want to do is tell someone else about it. Writers of research reports feel exactly the same way. They dig into subjects they are curious about, and then, through writing, they share what they have learned. In this workshop you will have the opportunity to exercise your curiosity about a topic that interests you and tell others about what you discover.

Prewriting

Choose and Narrow a Subject

What Grabs You? How did the Grand Canyon get there? Why do chipmunks hibernate? Asking questions like these can help you choose an interesting subject for your research report. Here are more strategies to help you brainstorm subjects.

- Take a survey of your classmates' hobbies *(in-line skating, coin collecting, building model boats . . .)*
- Make an "I wonder" log *(I wonder why cats purr . . . , how helicopters fly . . . , who discovered electricity . . .)*
- Browse a television guide or magazine or newspaper for interesting subjects *(people in the news, medical marvels, strange animals, space technology . . .)*

198   Chapter 6   **Exposition:** Sharing Your Research

---

198   Exposition: Sharing Your Research

Pin It Down   Once you have listed several possible subjects, you can choose the most interesting one. **You will need to focus on a part of the subject small enough to cover in one report.** For example, suppose that volcanoes fascinate you. Can you imagine the amount of research it would take to cover everything there is to know about volcanoes? To make it easier on yourself, you need to narrow that subject down to a focused topic. Your focused topic might be an active volcano in Hawaii. Here are more examples of narrowing a broad subject to a focused topic:

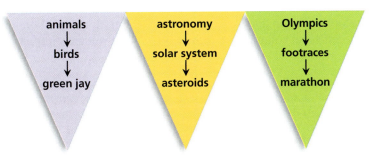

Here is how one writer narrowed a subject to a focused topic.

animals
↓
unusual animals
↓
guanaco

I like animals, but "animals" is too much to write about in a research report. I need to narrow this subject.

I want to write about an animal that most people have never heard of.

In an article about a wild animal ranch, I read about guanacos. I had never heard of a guanaco, and I doubt many other people have either.

TIP   Once you have your focused topic, make a plan to be sure you have enough time to complete your report. Divide the total time you are given among these activities:

- finding information (1/8 of total time)
- taking notes (1/4)
- organizing your notes (1/8)
- writing the first draft (1/4)
- revising (1/8)
- proofreading and publishing your report (1/8)

 **Choosing and Narrowing a Subject**

Brainstorm some subjects that interest you, and choose one you want to research. Then, use an upside-down triangle to find a focused topic. Record your thoughts as you narrow your topic.

Think About Purpose, Audience, and Voice

The *Why* of It   Your **purpose** is your reason for writing. You have two purposes for writing a research report: to discover information for yourself, and to share what you learn with others.

The *Who* of It   The **audience** for your report will be people who share your interest in the topic but do not already know a great deal about it. In most cases, that audience will include your classmates and teacher. You need to think about your audience before you begin doing your research. Ask yourself the questions in the left-hand column of the chart below. One student's responses appear in the right-hand column.

1. What does my audience already know about my topic?	They probably know nothing more about the guanaco than I do.
2. What does my audience need to know?	what it is, where it lives, what it looks like, what it does
3. What kind of information would my audience find interesting?	any unusual or surprising facts that I discover

The *How* of It   The sound of your writing is your **voice**. When your purpose is to inform, you should select a voice that sounds knowledgeable and interesting. Express your ideas in a clear, direct way, without using slang or clichés.

Confusing and slangy	I bet you never heard of a humpless camel-like thing.
Clear and interesting	Visitors to the Andes Mountains may spot a creature resembling a tiny camel without a hump.

YOUR TURN 5 — Thinking About Purpose, Audience, and Voice

Your purpose is to discover information and share it with others. Answer the questions in the chart above to consider how you might communicate what you learn with your readers.

Meeting INDIVIDUAL NEEDS

STUDENTS WITH SPECIAL NEEDS
To help students understand the concepts of audience, purpose, and voice, have small groups role-play teaching a simple topic to two different audiences. For example, students might act out teaching first-graders in a fun way how to make a paper airplane, in contrast to teaching sixth-graders about the same topic. After the role-playing, help students discuss the differences in voice in the scenarios as the audience changed.

YOUR TURN 5
To help you assess how realistic students are about their audience's interest in and knowledge of their topics, have them discuss with a small group of peers their answers to the three questions in the chart on this page. Students should take notes on peers' responses and, if necessary, revise their own answers.

RESOURCES

Your Turn 5
Practice
■ *Communications*, WS. p. 122

Your Turn 6
Practice
■ *Communications*, WS. p. 123

Ask Questions

The K-W-L Method   When you think about your topic, you are probably full of questions such as: *What does it look like? Where does it come from? What does it do?* Research begins with questions like these. Of course, there are some things you already know about your topic.

You can use a K-W-L chart to list what you already **K**now about a topic, what you **W**ant to know about it, and what you **L**earned about it through research. Look at how one student organized his ideas about the topic of guanacos. As he finds answers to his questions, he will list them in the right-hand column.

What I Know	What I Want to Know	What I Learned
A guanaco is part of the camel family. It lives in South America.	What does a guanaco look like? What do guanacos do? Do humans and guanacos get along?	

TIP   You might discover new questions once you begin doing research. Add them to your chart only if they really fit your topic. As one student researched his topic, he came up with and evaluated these questions:

Where do other members of the camel family live?	Other camels are not part of my topic. I won't add this question.
Why are there fewer guanacos now than there used to be?	This fits my topic. I'll add it to my K-W-L chart.

YOUR TURN 6   Asking Questions

Create a K-W-L chart like the one above on your own paper. In the left column, list everything that you already know about your topic. In the middle column, list the questions you have about your topic. Leave the right column of your chart blank. You will fill it out as you do your research.

TIP   Another way to organize what you already know about a topic and what you would like to know is to create a cluster diagram. For more on **clustering,** see page 763 in the Quick Reference Handbook.

Writing Workshop   **201**

Meeting INDIVIDUAL NEEDS

ENGLISH-LANGUAGE LEARNERS
General Strategies. To help students improve their question-asking skills, review question words (*who, what, when, where, why, how*) and model using the words in questions related to a single topic. Then, have students work in small groups to brainstorm questions for their own topics.

Cooperative Learning
Group Review. Ask students to form small groups according to the similarity of their topics. Each group's task will be to check its members' K-W-L chart questions to determine if they have thought through all the possible questions related to their topic. Have group members write their comments on a separate sheet of paper or on sticky notes.

YOUR TURN 6

The questions students ask should be reasonable questions specifically related to their topics and should be easily answered with research. Check that students' questions are logical enough to form the backbone of a report.

TEACHING TIP

Find Sources

You may wish to assist students in selecting and using reference materials that they may need later when they are revising and editing their final drafts.

For help with spelling:

- Sound out the word, dividing it into syllables. Write what each part sounds like. Select a dictionary and find a guide word at the top of a page close to the spelling you have. Then, locate the word you need on the page and check your spelling for accuracy.
- Look in your textbook to find spelling rules and a list of commonly misspelled words on pp. 612–641.
- Use the spellchecking program on a computer.

For help with grammar, usage, and mechanics:

- Look in the index of a grammar handbook. For instance, if you need help punctuating a compound sentence, first look up *Compound sentence*. Under this head, you will find the subhead *comma with* and the pages that teach that concept.

Critical Thinking

Evaluation. Ask students to think about a research paper on the future of computers. Discuss with them which of these sources would be appropriate for the paper and why.

- an encyclopedia with a copyright date of 1978 [no; not current data]
- a recent Internet article by a computer science professor [yes; probably a reliable expert]
- a recent science fiction novel [no; fiction, not fact]
- a conversation with an uncle who sells computer software [no; probably not an expert on future computers]

TIP Some sources are better than others for research. Look for nonfiction sources created by people or organizations likely to know a great deal about the topic. In other words, look for **authoritative** sources. For example, you would get better information on African snakes from a *National Geographic* article than from a movie about the adventures of a fictional explorer.

KEY CONCEPT

Reference Note

For more on using the **media center,** see page 694 in the Quick Reference Handbook.

KEY CONCEPT

Find Sources

Who Has the Answers? You now have a focused topic and a list of questions about it. What do you do next? Research! The best place to start your research is in the library, but that is just the beginning. You will look in several places to find answers to your questions. Some of the resources you can use include

- books
- encyclopedias
- magazine and newspaper articles
- interviews and guest speakers
- the Internet and CD-ROMs
- television programs and videos

Keep in mind that information does not always have to come from print sources. You can also find answers to your questions by watching a documentary; listening to an informative program on the radio; or reading charts, maps, and other graphics.

You will not find all of the information you need in a single source. You should plan to use at least three different kinds of sources. For example, you could find information on your topic in a book, in a magazine article, and on the Internet (a resource for information on all topics). Using a variety of sources will help you find complete answers to your research questions. If you have trouble finding sources **relevant,** or related, to your topic, go to the media center or ask your school's media specialist for help.

Make a List of Sources

Who Said That? When everyone talks at once, it is hard to remember who said what. You may have the same problem when you do research. When you find information about your topic in several different places, you may not remember where you found a particular fact. You will need to keep track of where you find the answers to your questions. **Make a numbered list of all of the sources you find that might be helpful in your research.** In your list, include information about each source. The chart on the next page tells you what information you need for each type of source you might use. The listings in the chart follow the style of the Modern Language Association (MLA).

202   Chapter 6   **Exposition:** Sharing Your Research

Information on Sources

Books: Author. Title. City where book was published: Name of Publisher, copyright year.

Ricciuti, Edward R. What on Earth Is a Guanaco? Woodbridge, CT: Blackbirch Press, 1994.

Magazine and Newspaper Articles: Author (if known). "Title of Article." Name of Magazine or Newspaper Date article was published: page numbers.

Lambeth, Ellen. "Here Comes Paco Guanaco: In the Hilly Grasslands of South America, a Camel Is Born." Ranger Rick Nov. 1996: 4-8.

Encyclopedia Articles: Author (if known). "Title of Article." Encyclopedia Name. Edition number (if known) and year published.

Goodwin, George G. "Guanaco." Collier's Encyclopedia. 1997.

Television or Radio Programs: "Title of Episode." Title of Program. Name of host (if known). Network. Station Call Letters, City. Date of broadcast.

"In the Land of the Llamas." NOVA. PBS. WNPB, Morgantown. 4 Dec. 1990.

Movie or Video Recordings: Title. Name of Director or Producer (if known). Format (videocassette or videodisc). Name of Distributor, year.

The Living Edens: Patagonia. Videocassette. PBS Home Video, 1997.

Internet Sources: Author. "Title." Name of Web site. Date of electronic publication. Name of Sponsoring Institution. Date you accessed information <Internet address>.

Note: Some sites may not list all of the above information. Include what the site does list and skip the items it does not list.

"Gwen the Guanaco." Victory Ranch. 26 Jan. 1999 <http://www.victoryranch.com/gwen.htm>.

Other Electronic Sources: Author (if known). "Title." Title of Database or CD-ROM. Medium (CD-ROM or Database). Copyright date.

Sentman, Everett. "Guanaco." Grolier 1998 Multimedia Encyclopedia. CD-ROM. 1997.

TIP Why should you keep track of your sources?

- You may need to find a source again if you come up with another interesting question later in your research.
- Your readers may want to go to your sources to learn more about your topic.
- Your teacher may expect you to include a list of sources to show the research you did.

TEACHING TIP

Information on Sources
Explain to students that one way to document information is through parenthetical citations. In parentheses directly following the information cited in the research report, the student will list the author's last name (or title if no name is listed) and the page number where the information was found. The works that appear in parenthetical citations must also appear in the Works Cited list, or list of sources. See MLA's style guide for more on parenthetical citations.

Meeting INDIVIDUAL NEEDS

MODALITY
Visual Learners. As they find sources, students may want to list their sources according to type of resource. For example, they could list in one column all the books; in another all the Internet sources; in another the magazine articles, etc. With such organization, students can glance quickly to see whether or not they have a balance of sources. Remind students, however, that they will need to alphabetize the source lists they attach to their reports.

TECHNOLOGY TIP

Before students begin their research on the Internet, discuss with them sensible safety guidelines. For example, remind them that just as they wouldn't talk to or give personal information to strangers on the street, they should not divulge personal information to people on the Internet.

Meeting INDIVIDUAL NEEDS

INCLUSION

Consider providing assistance to those students who need help with the steps of an Internet search. Have students work with helpers who can assist them in locating category menus, discuss the ones most likely to have the necessary research facts, and generally guide the students through menu choices.

MINI-LESSON CRITICAL THINKING

Searching the World Wide Web for Information

As students search the World Wide Web for information, you need to be aware that Internet resources are sometimes public forums and their content can be unpredictable.

Have students draw a flowchart to diagram the steps of each search. Have them refer to the diagrams as they explain which search was more successful.

MINI-LESSON CRITICAL THINKING

Searching the World Wide Web for Information

The World Wide Web contains enormous amounts of information. One way you can find what you need is to use a *search engine*. A **search engine** is a Web site that allows you to hunt for information. By typing a **keyword**—a word related to your topic—into the search engine, you will get a list of possible sites.

Another way to find information from a search engine is to use a *directory*. A **directory** lists categories of information. Each category is divided into smaller and smaller subcategories that you can follow until you find a site that relates to your topic.

Below is a path a student took through categories and subcategories in a directory. The main menu, where he began his search, is on the left. The highlighted choice shows the category the student chose. His choice leads to the next list of subcategories and finally to a list of sites with information about guanacos and other mammals.

TIP Remember, not all Web sites are equal. For your research report, choose sources such as universities, government sites, and major newspapers and broadcast networks. When you get a list of sites, look first at those that have URLs (addresses) ending in *.org* (nonprofit organizations), *.edu* (educational institutions), and *.gov* (U.S. government agencies). (For more on **evaluating Web sites,** see page 703.)

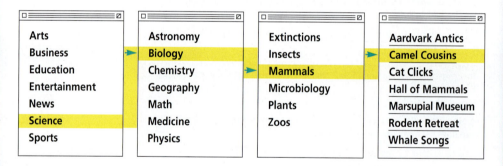

PRACTICE

Search the Internet two different ways for Web sites on the topic of your research report. In your first search, type a keyword into a search engine. In your second search, go through the categories and subcategories in a directory. Which search proved to be more successful? Compare your results with those of your classmates.

Chapter 6 Exposition: Sharing Your Research

RESOURCES

Critical Thinking
Practice
- *Communications,* WS. p. 124

Your Turn 7
Practice
- *Communications,* WS. p. 125

YOUR TURN 7 **Finding and Listing Sources**

Find at least five sources you might use for researching your focused topic. Follow the instructions on page 203 to list important information about these sources. Give each source a number to help you identify sources when you take notes later. For now, do not worry about the order of items in your list. You will alphabetize your source list later (by author's last name or by title, if no author is given).

COMPUTER TIP

Write down the address of any Web site you come across that looks helpful, even if you are not using it right away. You will be able to find the site again quickly by calling up the exact address.

Take Notes

Getting the Facts Once you have identified sources, begin looking for answers to your research questions. Remember, you are looking for answers to the questions in your K-W-L chart. **Your questions will guide your research process.** Record each answer you find, along with information about where you found it. The guidelines below will help you take notes.

- Use a separate note card or a sheet of paper for each new note.
- At the top of each note card, write the question that the notes on the card answer.
- Write the number of the source at the top of each note, so you will always be able to tell exactly where you found the information.
- **Summarize** information explained in a long passage. Even with shorter passages, **paraphrase,** or write the ideas in your own words. If you copy exact words from a source, put them in quotation marks.
- If the information is from a printed book or article, put the page number at the end of your note.

KEY CONCEPT

TIP While you research, keep your K-W-L chart handy. In the "What I Learned" column, write in the authors or titles of the sources where you found your answers. This will help you focus on using a variety of sources. It will also help you see quickly which of your questions still need answers.

Reference Note

For more on **paraphrasing** and **summarizing,** see pages 706 and 709 in the Quick Reference Handbook.

```
Source number ─────────────────────── ③
Question  ─ What is a guanaco?

Notes in your own ┌ - member of the camel family
          words  └ - small and South American


Page number ─────────────────── page 127
```

Writing Workshop   **205**

TEACHING TIP

Paraphrasing

Explain to students that plagiarism is the use of someone else's ideas as your own. Therefore, even paraphrasing a source can constitute plagiarism if the writer does not acknowledge the source of those ideas in a Works Cited list.

Be aware of the common signs of plagiarism in student writing:

- sophisticated vocabulary that is not quoted or cited
- a number of sentences or a paragraph written in a different style from the rest of the writing
- information, opinions, and ideas not usually known by the average student and not attributed to any source

MINI-LESSON — WRITING

Paraphrasing

ANSWERS

Here are possible answers.

1. Plagiarism: specific words and phrases are the same.
2. Paraphrase: the ideas are the same but the words are different.

MINI-LESSON WRITING

Paraphrasing

Paraphrasing means putting information from a source into your own words. Copying an author's words and presenting them as your own is **plagiarizing.** Plagiarizing is the same as stealing another writer's work. If you want to use a writer's exact words, put them in quotation marks and identify the source.

The passages below show the difference between paraphrasing and plagiarizing. The paraphrase on the left tells the ideas of the source passage in different words. The plagiarized passage on the right copies long strings of words which are printed in boldface.

> **Source Passage:** Guanacos, South American members of the camel family, lack the familiar humps of Asian and African camels. Slim and long-legged, guanacos move quickly and gracefully over the rugged terrain of their native Andes Mountains.
>
> **Paraphrase:** Although it is part of the camel family, the South American guanaco does not have a hump like its cousins in Asia and Africa do. It is slim, has long legs, and can run fast in its habitat, the Andes Mountains.
>
> **Plagiarism:** As **members of the camel family,** guanacos **lack the familiar humps of Asian and African camels.** They are able to **move quickly and gracefully over rugged terrain.** They live in the Andes Mountains.

PRACTICE

Read each source passage below, then the passage to its right. Tell whether the passage paraphrases or plagiarizes the source. Explain your answer in a sentence or two.

Source Passage

1. Manifest Destiny was the belief in the nineteenth century that the United States would eventually stretch across the entire continent, from the Atlantic Ocean to the Pacific Ocean.

2. The first settlers from the United States reached northeastern Texas in 1815, encouraged by the Mexican government, which controlled the territory at that time.

Paraphrase or Plagiarism?

1. People believed in the nineteenth century that the United States would eventually reach from the Atlantic Ocean to the Pacific Ocean. This belief was called Manifest Destiny.

2. The government of Mexico encouraged people from the United States to move to its territory of Texas. The first settlers moved to the northeast part of the state in 1815.

206 Chapter 6 Exposition: Sharing Your Research

RESOURCES

Writing

Practice
- *Communications,* WS. p. 126

Your Turn 8

Practice
- *Communications,* WS. p. 127

YOUR TURN 8 — **Researching Your Topic and Taking Notes**

Using the sources you found earlier, locate answers for your research questions. Take notes from each source, being careful to put the information in your own words. Note the source of each piece of information you find by putting its source number on your note card.

TIP To make the most of your time, skim long passages looking for key words, ones that relate to your topic. Then, read only the sections that contain the key words.

Organize Your Information

Getting It Together   A pile of notes will be about as useful to your readers as a box full of bicycle parts. Both need to be put together in a logical way to be of any use. Once you have gathered information from your sources, you will need to organize those ideas into categories. The questions you wrote on the top of your note cards will help you. Group together note cards that answer the same question. Each group of cards will become a paragraph in your report. If you find some note cards that do not seem to belong to any group, set them aside for now.

Outline Your Report

Planning It Out   An **outline** is a plan for your report. It shows how you are grouping the information you have gathered and the order in which you will present the information in your report. One type of outline you can make is an *informal outline*. An **informal outline** lists a report's major **subtopics,** or categories of information related to your topic. It also lists the specific facts that make up each subtopic.

To identify the subtopics for your informal outline, first change the questions from your K-W-L chart into headings. A **heading** is a phrase that covers all the items listed below it. For example, the question "Where do guanacos live?" could be turned into the heading "Where guanacos live." As you turn your questions into headings, write each heading on a piece of paper, leaving several lines after it blank. Then, under each heading, write facts from your note cards or jot down a few words that will remind you what to include when you write your report.

Reference Note

For more on **outlines,** both informal and formal, see page 765 in the Quick Reference Handbook.

Writing Workshop   **207**

YOUR TURN 8

Check that students' notes help answer the research questions and are written in the students' own words. Write any questions or suggestions you have for students on their note cards and draw a box around them so that students can easily separate queries from notes.

TEACHING TIP

Organize Your Information
Remind students that as they group their notes, one way to organize ideas is to use a graphic organizer, such as a conceptual map. Using the conceptual map below to model the process, start by writing on the chalkboard the topic *guanacos*. Then, use the questions from the K-W-L chart on p. 201 to create ovals connected to the topic box. Explain to students that they can use the questions they wrote on the top of their note cards to help them create their conceptual maps. Refer students who need more help organizing ideas to pp. 764–766 in the Quick Reference Handbook.

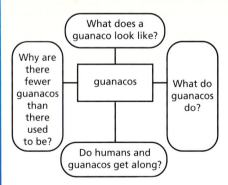

Meeting INDIVIDUAL NEEDS

MULTIPLE INTELLIGENCES
Bodily-Kinesthetic Learners. Some students may prefer to reorder their note cards on the floor or on a large table to create their informal outline. Suggest that students use a different-colored index card for each research question. First, have them arrange these cards in a logical order. Then, they can spread out the rest of their note cards and put them in a logical order under the appropriately-colored heading card. From this ordered file of all their research, students can write their informal outline.

Timesaver

To help you quickly assess that students' questions are reflected in headings and that their outlines are in logical order, ask them to turn in their K-W-L charts with their outlines. Keep in mind that students' questions may have changed since they made their K-W-L charts.

YOUR TURN 9

You may want to check students' headings before having them write their notes below the headings. Students should have developed appropriate headings that are in a logical order for the report. Once students write their notes below each heading, have them talk through their outlines with partners. Encourage partners to query parts they don't understand as well as parts that need more or less detail.

TIP Review your outline to make sure you have at least two pieces of information under each body heading. If you don't, you may need to do a bit more research. You can also check any note cards you set aside to see if they fit under one of the headings. If not, you will not use those cards for this report.

Reference Note
For help in making **graphic organizers** like conceptual maps and time lines, see pages 765 and 766 in the Quick Reference Handbook.

The partial informal outline below shows the information the student writing about guanacos will use in his research report.

```
Body:      Where guanacos live
               Andes Mountains of South America
               how guanacos handle their habitat
               protected reserves
           What guanacos look like
               similarities to camels—legs, hoofs, neck, lips
               differences—ears, no hump, height, fur color
           What guanacos do
               spit cud accurately
               run fast and early in life
               swim across streams and between islands
           How guanacos get along with people
               carrying loads
               wool used for coats and robes
               hunted for meat
```

TIP Instead of an informal outline, you might create a **conceptual map** to organize your information. At the top of a conceptual map is a circle containing the topic. Extending out from the topic circle are circles containing subtopics. Circles containing facts and other information connect to the subtopics that they explain. Another useful tool for organizing information from various sources is a **time line.** You can use a time line to show the time order of events in history.

YOUR TURN 9 — Organizing Your Notes and Creating an Informal Outline

Group your notes based on the questions they answer. Then, create an informal outline by following these steps:

- Turn questions into headings.
- List your headings on a sheet of paper, leaving several blank lines after each.
- Write notes under each heading telling which information you will include from your note cards. You do not need to use complete sentences.

208   Chapter 6   Exposition: Sharing Your Research

RESOURCES

Your Turn 9
Practice
- *Communications,* WS. p. 128

Extension
- *Designing Your Writing*

Your Turn 10
Practice
- *Communications,* WS. p. 129

Designing Your Writing

Creating Headings To help readers see how your ideas are organized, include a descriptive heading before each section of your report. If you are writing on a computer, put your headings in boldface print or underline them using word-processing features. If you are typing or hand-writing your report, print the headings in capital letters or underline them.

Write a Main Idea Statement

Tell It Like It Is To make sure your readers remember the major points you make about your topic, include a *main idea statement* in your introduction. A **main idea statement,** or **thesis,** tells readers the topic of a piece of writing and the main points the writer will make about the topic. Here is how you can develop a main idea statement for your report.

THINKING IT THROUGH
Writing a Main Idea Statement

STEP 1 Identify the major points in your outline.
> strange looking, unusual talents, useful to humans, threatened by hunting

STEP 2 Combine the major points in a single sentence.
> Guanacos are strange-looking animals with unusual talents, and they are useful to humans but threatened by hunting.

STEP 3 If your step 2 sentence is long, condense the ideas into a more compact main idea statement.
> Guanacos are unusual animals that are useful to humans but threatened by hunting.

YOUR TURN 10 Writing a Main Idea Statement

Use the Thinking It Through steps above to develop a clear and compact main idea statement for your research report.

TEACHING TIP

Write a Main Idea Statement
Once they begin writing their research reports, students may find that they either have too much or too little information in their outlines and must change their thesis statements. For example, a student writing about the causes of pollution might change a broad thesis statement like the following: "Pollution from nearby factories and increased traffic have caused pollution problems" to "Pollution from nearby factories has caused the pollution of Fisher Pond."

YOUR TURN 10

To assess main idea statements, check that the main idea statement includes two or three of the major headings of the outline in the order shown there. If a main idea statement is not stated succinctly, you may have to meet with students individually to help them edit their statements.

Quotation for the Day

"Nothing goes by luck in composition. It allows of no tricks. The best you can write will be the best you are."

(Henry David Thoreau, 1817–1862, American writer)

Write the quotation on the chalkboard, and ask students to write journal entries about how writing well relates to being their best. [Students might discuss how good writing demands a certain honesty, the same way being the best at anything demands real ability rather than tricks or gimmicks.]

Meeting INDIVIDUAL NEEDS

MODALITY
Auditory Learners. As students begin to draft paragraphs for the body of their research reports, suggest that each softly read aloud one heading and the notes related to it and then set the notes aside. The student should then write a paragraph on that subtopic, incorporating the information read aloud. Once their paragraphs are completed, students can return to their notes to determine if they left out any information or if they need to elaborate further or reorder information.

YOUR TURN 11

Check to be sure that students are following the framework on this page. If you wish to assign a length to the students' essays, suggest that drafts be 500 to 700 words long.

Writing

Research Report

Framework   **Directions and Explanations**

Introduction
- Attention-getting beginning
- Main idea statement

One way to grab your readers' attention is to begin with a colorful description of something related to your topic. Your **main idea statement** should clearly identify your topic and the major points in your report.

Body
- Heading 1 facts
- Heading 2 facts
and so on

The headings in your informal outline represent subtopics. **Each subtopic will be covered in its own paragraph. Support** each subtopic with facts and explanations from your research, and **elaborate** on your support by explaining each fact or example.

Conclusion
- Restatement of main idea

In addition to restating your main idea, your conclusion may be a good place to share information that did not fit in the body of your report. The Writer's Model, for example, tells what is being done to solve the problem discussed in the report.

List of Sources
- Alphabetized by author

A list of sources is also called a **Works Cited list** or **bibliography.** List only the sources you actually used for your report. See the chart on page 203 for how to list different kinds of sources.

YOUR TURN 11 Drafting Your Report

Write the first draft of your report. Use the framework above and the following Writer's Model to guide you.

210   Chapter 6   **Exposition:** Sharing Your Research

RESOURCES

Writing
Writing Prompts
- *Communications,* TP. 48, WS. p. 130

Your Turn 11
Practice
- *Communications,* TP. 49, WS. p. 131

A Writer's Model

The final draft below closely follows the framework for a research report on the previous page.

The South American Guanaco

Visitors to the Andes Mountains may spot a creature resembling a tiny camel without a hump. This animal is the guanaco, a South American member of the camel family. Guanacos are unusual animals that are useful to humans but threatened by hunting.

For thousands of years guanacos have grazed on tough grasses in the high plains and hills of the Andes Mountains. They can be found from southern Peru to the tip of South America. Their blood can handle the thin mountain air. Steep, rocky paths are no problem for guanacos because they are nimble like mountain goats and have thick, padded soles that protect their feet. Their only wild enemy is the mountain lion, but people have hunted the guanaco so much that the species is in danger. Some herds live in protected reserves in Argentina and Chile.

Like other camels, the guanaco has long legs, two-toed hoofs, a long neck, and floppy lips. It can survive without water for long periods of time, just like a desert camel. The guanaco looks different from the humped camel. It has pointed ears and a slender body, and it stands less than four feet high. In some ways it looks more like a deer or an antelope than a camel. It is reddish brown with a dark gray head and a pale belly.

The guanaco has some strange talents. Like other kinds of camels, the guanaco helps its stomach digest grass by chewing it up again after it has been in the stomach for a while. This rechewed grass, or cud, comes in handy when another animal bothers the guanaco. It can accurately hit whatever is annoying it with smelly green spit, with no warning at all. The guanaco

(continued)

Attention grabber

Main idea statement

Heading 1:
Where guanacos live

Heading 2:
What guanacos look like

Heading 3:
What guanacos do

Connecting Reading and Writing

Remind students that readers will be drawing conclusions from the paragraphs in their research reports. Have students review the material on drawing conclusions in the Reading Workshop on pp. 192–193. Then, have students read **A Writer's Model** on this page, drawing conclusions and noting the evidence that leads to the conclusions. Finally, ask them to review their own drafts, looking for details and evidence that might help readers draw conclusions from the information in their reports.

MULTIPLE INTELLIGENCES
Spatial Intelligence. Suggest that students use color-codes as they review their drafts. They may use one color to highlight the thesis statement and conclusion, another for the main ideas in the paragraphs, and a third color to highlight words that provide supporting details. By focusing on the colors, students can check the flow of their drafts.

TEACHING TIP

Remind your students of the proper format for a research paper. In this book, **A Writer's Model** and **A Student's Model** have not been double-spaced, due to space considerations. Most writing guides, however, recommend double-spacing for both the body and the list of sources in a research paper.

(continued)

can also run fast and swim well. Almost as soon as they are born, guanacos can race to safety if their mothers spot danger. Adult guanacos can run as fast as thirty-five miles an hour. Guanacos swim almost as well as they run. They easily cross cold, fast-running mountain streams. Believe it or not, they even swim in the ocean. They have been seen swimming from island to island off the coast of Chile in the Pacific Ocean.

Heading 4: How guanacos get along with people

Guanacos are helpful to people and are in trouble because of them. People use guanacos to carry loads on the prairies and in the mountains of South America. Their wool is also used for making coats. Newborn guanacos are often killed so that their silky wool can be made into beautiful robes called *capas*. The number of guanacos has also been reduced by hunters, who kill them for their meat.

Restatement of main idea

To help the guanaco survive the threat of people hunting it for meat and hides, this unusual little camel will need to be protected. Some South American countries are already taking steps that may help guanacos to be plentiful again.

List of Sources

Burton, John A. The Collins Guide to the Rare
    Mammals of the World. Lexington: The Stephen
    Greene Press, 1987.
Goodwin, George G. "Guanaco." Collier's
    Encyclopedia. 1997.
"Guanaco." Wildlife Gallery. Fota Wildlife Park.
    26 Jan. 1999 <http://www.zenith.ie/fota/
    wildlife/guanaco.html>.
Lambeth, Ellen. "Here Comes Paco Guanaco: In the
    Hilly Grasslands of South America, a Camel Is
    Born." Ranger Rick Nov. 1996: 4–8.

TIP A research report and its *List of Sources* are normally double-spaced. Because of limited space on these pages, A Writer's Model and A Student's Model are single-spaced. The *Elements of Language* Internet site provides a model of a research report in the double-spaced format. To see this interactive model, go to **go.hrw.com** and enter the keyword **EOLang 6-6**.

TEACHING TIP

Remind students that the *List of Sources* is alphabetized by the author's last name or by the source title if no author is given. As they prepare their source lists, students should use as models the entries on this page and those in the chart on page 203.

A Student's Model

Genna Offerman, a sixth-grader from Marshall Middle School in Beaumont, Texas, wrote about a game many people enjoy—billiards. Below is an excerpt of her research report.

Billiards

. . . Billiard games are played on a rectangular table. This table has rubber cushions around its inside upper edge and is covered with a felt cloth. A billiard table has six holes, called pockets, where the balls go. Many billiard games require fifteen numbered balls. Balls one through eight are all solid colors, and balls nine through fifteen are white with a colored stripe. Also, for some billiard games, a white cue ball is used. A player uses a cue stick, which is made of wood, to hit the white cue ball into a numbered ball. The goal is to get the numbered ball into a pocket.

Subtopic 1: Equipment needed to play billiards

The game of billiards has been around since the 1400s. It was developed in Europe from the game croquet, which is played on the lawn with mallets and balls. When croquet was moved indoors, people began playing it on a table that was made green to resemble grass. By the 1600s, the game of billiards had become so popular that Shakespeare mentioned it in the play *Antony and Cleopatra*.

Subtopic 2: History of billiards

No one knows when billiards came to the United States, but from an early date the game was popular. American woodworkers were producing billiard tables by the 1700s, and George Washington was said to have won a game in 1748. In 1850, Michael Phelan wrote the first American book on the game. . . .

Subtopic 3: History of billiards in the United States

List of Sources

Billiards: The Official Rules and Records Book. Iowa City: Billiard Congress of America, 1966.

"Billiards." 1997 Grolier Multimedia Encyclopedia. CD-ROM. 1997.

Connecting Reading and Writing

Have students review the concept of determining an author's purpose in the Reading Workshop on pp. 194–195. Then, ask students to read **A Student's Model** and to record clues that indicate the author's purpose. Finally, have them go back and check their own drafts to make sure that their purpose is clear and will be evident to the reader.

Quotation for the Day

"Blot out, correct, insert, refine,
Enlarge, diminish, interline;
Be mindful, When invention fails,
To scratch your head,
and bite your nails."

(Jonathan Swift, 1667–1745,
Irish satirist)

Ask students to brainstorm in small groups lists of actions connected with revision. Then, share the quotation with the class and discuss how many of the actions the students listed are mentioned in the quotation. Students may have used different words, such as *elaborate* instead of *enlarge* or *insert* instead of *interline,* but the meanings will be similar. Emphasize that writers throughout history have performed these actions to improve their work.

TEACHING TIP

▶ **Elaboration**
To help students elaborate with examples in their research reports, have them exchange papers with a peer. Ask the peer editors to look for and highlight sentences in which the addition of an example such as a fact, statistic, direct quotation, or expert opinion would further clarify the point the writer is making. Then, have students look through their notes to find additional information that they could use as examples. If students add an example from a source that is not listed in their Works Cited list or bibliography, remind them to add the source to their source list.

Revising

Evaluate and Revise Content, Organization, and Style

Double Duty To make the information in your research report as clear as possible for your readers, you will need to read it at least twice. First, evaluate the content and organization, using the guidelines below. Then, check your writing style using the guidelines on page 215.

▶ **First Reading: Content and Organization** Use the following chart to evaluate the content and organization of your report. The tips in the middle column will help you decide how to answer the questions in the left column. If you answer *no* to any question, use the Revision Technique to improve that part of your writing.

Research Report: Content and Organization Guidelines for Self-Evaluation and Peer Evaluation

Evaluation Questions	Tips	Revision Techniques
❶ Does the introduction contain a main idea statement that identifies the topic and major points of the report?	▶ **Highlight** the main idea statement.	▶ **Add** a main idea statement or **revise** the main idea statement to give complete information about the topic, if needed.
❷ Does each paragraph in the body explain only one part of the topic?	▶ **Label** each body paragraph with the type of information it provides about the topic.	▶ **Rearrange** ideas so each paragraph covers only one part of the topic, or **delete** ideas that do not belong.
❸ Does each paragraph contain facts that give clear information about the topic?	▶ **Put a check mark** above each fact that explains the topic.	▶ **Add** facts to any paragraph with fewer than two check marks.
❹ Does the conclusion restate the report's main idea?	▶ **Circle** the sentence that puts the main idea statement in different words.	▶ If needed, **add** a sentence that states the main idea in another way.
❺ Does the report include information from at least three sources?	▶ **Number** the items on the list of sources.	▶ **Elaborate** on the ideas in your report by using information from another source as needed.

214   Chapter 6   Exposition: Sharing Your Research

RESOURCES

Revising
Practice
■ *Communications,* TPs. 50, 51, WS. pp. 132, 133, 134

ONE WRITER'S REVISIONS These are revisions of an early draft of the research report on pages 211–212.

> The guanaco can also run fast and swim well. Almost as soon as they are born, guanacos can race to safety if their mothers spot danger. Adult guanacos can run as fast as thirty-five miles an hour. ~~This is another way that they are like antelopes and deer.~~ Guanacos swim almost as well as they run. They easily cross cold, fast-running mountain streams. Believe it or not, they even swim in the ocean. ^*They have been seen swimming from island to island off the coast of Chile in the Pacific Ocean.*

delete

elaborate

Responding to the Revision Process

1. How did deleting a sentence improve the passage above?
2. Why was it important for the writer to add the final sentence?

PEER REVIEW

When you are reviewing another student's report, ask yourself these questions:

- Does this report explain information clearly enough for me to tell someone else about this topic?
- What part of this report caught my interest the most? Why?

▶ **Second Reading: Style** When sharing information with others, you should communicate your ideas as clearly as possible. One way to do this is to use *precise nouns* in your writing. **Precise nouns** name a person, place, thing, or idea in a specific way. Look for places in your writing where you can be more precise by changing a vague noun to one that is more specific.

Style Guidelines

Evaluation Question	▶ Tip	▶ Revision Technique
Does the report use specific words to name people, places, things, and ideas?	▶ Put a star above each specific noun.	▶ If possible, replace vague nouns with more precise ones. (You may find more specific words in your notes.)

Writing Workshop

Meeting INDIVIDUAL NEEDS

ADVANCED LEARNERS
Suggest that students develop a fun way to practice using precise nouns. They can also share some of the facts discovered during research and the writing process. For example, students could create a crossword puzzle, a question-and-answer game show, or riddles. Students could share their games with other students as a warm-up or follow-up to their presentations.

Timesaver

Have students highlight changes in their revised drafts. This will help you identify student revisions, and it will help students identify improvements they made in their writing.

Responding to the Revision Process
ANSWER
Adding the precise nouns *guanacos, grasses,* and *Andes* creates a clearer picture.

YOUR TURN 12

Suggest that students read their revised reports out loud to a partner so that they can check for awkwardness, choppy sentences, and other organization and style issues. Have them record the partner's suggestions for improvements on their drafts.

Focus on Word Choice

Using Precise Nouns

When you read the word *flower*, what image comes to mind? You might picture a daisy, while another reader might think of a buttercup or a daffodil. *Flower* is a vague noun because it lets the reader choose what to picture. When you write, give your readers the right picture by using *precise nouns* such as *honeysuckle* or *violet*. **Precise nouns** name people, places, things, or ideas in a specific way. Look at the sentences below. Which one tells you exactly what the writer had in mind?

Vague The author Luis Valdez created a *program* for *people*.
Precise The author Luis Valdez created a *theater company* for *farm workers*.

Replace vague nouns in your writing with more precise ones that will get your picture across. Precise nouns will help your readers learn about your topic.

 TIP If you have trouble coming up with a precise noun, look up the vague noun in a **thesaurus.** Among the synonyms for the vague noun, you will often find more specific ones that you might use to revise your writing.

> **ONE WRITER'S REVISIONS**
>
> For thousands of years, ~~the animals~~ *guanacos* have grazed on tough plants in the high plains and hills of the *Andes* mountains.
> (*grasses* replacing *plants*)

Responding to the Revision Process
How do you think the changes the writer made improve the sentence above?

YOUR TURN 12 — Evaluating and Revising Content, Organization, and Style

Review the first draft of your report. Then, improve your report by using the Content and Organization Guidelines on page 214, the Focus on Word Choice above, and peer comments.

RESOURCES

Focus on Word Choice
Practice
- *Communications,* WS. p. 135

Publishing

Proofread Your Report

Polish It You want your readers to focus on learning about your topic, not on finding errors. Look over your report carefully and correct any mistakes. Use the following Grammar Link to make sure your sources are written correctly.

TIP You can use other **resources** to help you proofread your report, such as a dictionary or a spellchecker.

Grammar Link

Capitalizing and Punctuating Titles

Sources of information for research reports are listed in a certain way. You may see the title of a source listed inside quotation marks, written in italics, or underlined. Some words are capitalized, and others are not. Here are three rules about how to write titles.

Titles of major works should be underlined or typed in *italics*. Major works include books, encyclopedias, magazines, newspapers, databases, Web sites, movies, and television series. Underline these titles when you type or hand-write your report. If you are using a computer, you can use the *italics* function.

Put titles of short works inside quotation marks. These include chapters of books; articles from encyclopedias, magazines, and newspapers; individual pages from Web sites; and titles of single episodes in a TV series.

Capitalize the important words in a title. The only words you will not capitalize in a title are articles (*a, an, the*), conjunctions (*and, but, or*), and prepositions with fewer than five letters (*to, for, with, in,* and so on). However, capitalize the first and last words of a title, no matter what they are.

PRACTICE

Rewrite the following titles. Capitalize each correctly and place it inside quotation marks or underline it.

Example:
1. Newspaper article: students stop disaster on playground
1. "Students Stop Disaster on Playground"

1. Magazine article: with a song in his heart
2. Book: the giant guide to the internet
3. Movie: the iron giant
4. Whole Web site: the science of lightning
5. Episode in a TV program: the perfect pearl

For more information and practice on **punctuating titles,** see pages 588 and 595.

Writing Workshop **217**

RESOURCES

Grammar Link
Practice
- *Communications,* WS. p. 136

Quotation for the Day

"He who hesitates is sometimes saved."

(James Thurber, 1894–1961, American humorist, cartoonist, and author)

Have students discuss how stopping and looking for spelling, grammar, and mechanics errors during the publishing stage can "save" their reports. [Students may say that since these errors confuse and distract readers, they are worth correcting.]

TEACHING TIP

Capitalizing and Punctuating Titles
Review with students the **Information on Sources** chart on p. 203, pointing out the capitalization and punctuation for each bibliographic format. Then, ask volunteers to write some entries on the chalkboard. Work as a class to correct any errors. For more information about format style, refer students to the *MLA Handbook for Writers of Research Papers.*

Grammar Link

Capitalizing and Punctuating Titles

ANSWERS

Underlined titles can also appear in italics.

1. "With a Song in His Heart"
2. The Giant Guide to the Internet
3. The Iron Giant
4. The Science of Lightning
5. "The Perfect Pearl"

Writing Workshop **217**

TEACHING TIP

Publish Your Report
Some students may choose to write in cursive while others may choose manuscript style. In either case, remind them that their handwriting must be legible in their final drafts. Display published models of legible cursive and manuscript handwriting to help students understand the importance of legibility.

Wrap It Up

Metacognition. After students have published their research reports, have them reflect on the process by responding to this question:

1. Which are your strongest and weakest research skills?

Then, ask this question:

2. How are you supposed to document your research? [Keep and submit a list of all sources used in the research of a topic.]

YOUR TURN 13

Have students work in pairs to check each other's source lists for capitalization, punctuation, and alphabetical order. Suggest that they review the source list in **A Writer's Model** on p. 212 before they start. Ask partners to comment on sticky notes if they find any problems.

Publish Your Report

Share the Wealth   Now you can share what you have learned with an audience. Here are some ideas:

- With other students who wrote on similar topics, create and illustrate a book of research reports. This book might be kept in the classroom for independent reading or placed in the library for all students to enjoy.
- Make a display that includes your report and helpful illustrations. Place it in a hallway display case or the library, or share it with other classes.
- Try adapting your report into a children's book. Retell the most interesting facts and details in language children can understand. Work with a partner to illustrate your book.

PORTFOLIO

Reflect on Your Report

Building Your Portfolio   Take some time to think about how you researched your topic and wrote your report. Did you achieve your purpose? What would you do differently next time? Consider these questions:

- Where in your report do you think you did the best job of clearly answering a research question? Why do you think this was the best part?
- What kinds of information sources were useful? Would you use these types of sources for a future report?

YOUR TURN 13

Proofreading, Publishing, and Reflecting on Your Report

- Correct any errors in spelling, punctuation, and sentence structure. Be particularly careful about writing titles of sources correctly.
- Publish your report for an audience of interested readers. You might use one of the suggestions above.
- Answer the Reflect on Your Report questions above. Record your responses in a learning log, or include them in your portfolio.

218   Chapter 6   **Exposition:** Sharing Your Research

MINI-LESSON: TEST TAKING

Writing an Informative Essay

In a research report you explain what you have learned about a topic. Some writing tests, though, will ask you to explain something about *yourself*. You may be asked to explain something that is important or enjoyable to you. Because these essays clarify, or make clear, your relationship to a topic, they are sometimes called **clarification essays**.

You can organize your ideas for a clarification essay just as you organized the information in your research report by using an informal outline. You will also elaborate on your ideas by using explanations. Read the following prompt, and think about how you would respond.

> Everyone has a place that is important to him or her. It may be a place with special memories or a place that makes a person feel comfortable. Choose a place that is important to you, and write an essay about it. Explain three things that make this place special or tell three reasons why the place is special to you.

THINKING IT THROUGH: Responding to an Informative Prompt

STEP 1 Read the prompt to see what you must do. Identify the topic, audience, and format.

> I'm going to write an essay that tells three reasons why a place is special to me. A specific audience was not named so I'll write to my teacher.

STEP 2 Choose a topic for your answer.

> My grandfather's workshop is special to me.

STEP 3 Brainstorm ideas about your connection to the topic.

> Things that make his workshop special:
> 1. good smells—oil, wood, sawdust
> 2. the furniture Grandpa makes
> 3. the jewelry box I made for Mom

STEP 4 Write your essay. In each body paragraph, elaborate on your connection to the topic.

> 1. smells—linseed oil & turpentine, fresh-cut pine, nose-tickling sawdust
> 2. furniture—high chair in progress, repairing Grandma's rocker, refinishing dresser
> 3. jewelry box—carved top, smooth finish

RESOURCES

Test Taking
Practice
 Communications, WS. p. 137

TEACHING TIP

Showing Them
Remind students that visuals can complement or extend meaning. Visuals that complement meaning serve to further explain or illustrate ideas in written or spoken text. A visual that extends meaning, however, would be a springboard for the text that surrounds it. For example, an interesting satellite photo of Mars might inspire a report on new discoveries about Mars.

Cooperative Learning
Visual Consultant Groups. Have students work in randomly assigned groups of four. Students should highlight places in their research reports where they think a visual might work. Have them consult with the group to see if members agree. Members can then brainstorm ideas about the most effective visuals to use. Have students draw quick sketches of their visuals and share them with the group before spending time creating the final versions.

Connections to Life

Creating Visuals to Share Information

Showing Them Think back to the time when you were first learning to read. Remember how the books had pictures? You used the pictures to figure out what was being said. **Visuals** help readers and listeners of all ages understand the topic better. In this section you will learn how you can boost your audience's understanding by creating or finding a visual to include in your report.

The most obvious kind of visual is a **photograph** or **drawing**. The writer of the research report on guanacos, for example, found this photograph in a book. He photocopied it and included it in his report.

Make a Choice Before you create a visual, you must first decide two things: what information you are going to show and how you are going to show it. To decide what information to show, read your report and find anything your audience may need help understanding. Then, decide how you can put that information in a visual. The chart on the next page gives you some examples.

Get the Picture Once you have made your decision about what kind of visual will be most helpful for your audience, you will need to create or find it. You might use one of the following ideas.

- Draw it freehand.
- Trace it, using tracing paper or a projector.
- Photocopy it if you have access to a copier.
- Cut it out of a magazine or newspaper if you have permission.
- Create it in a computer program.
- Download it from an Internet source if you have permission to do so.

When you create your own graphic, use color carefully. In general, use no more than three colors in a graph, chart, or time line. Color attracts attention, but too many colors distract the reader and make information hard to find. A map, however, may need more than three colors to contrast all adjoining states and countries.

TIP If you will use your visual in a **multimedia presentation,** have a friend hold your visual at the front of the room while you look at it from the back of the room. Make sure the visual is easy to read and understand even from across the room. Do some lines need to be bolder? Do some words need to be bigger? Would color help?

Type of Information and Examples	Best Visual to Use and Example
a series of events or a schedule Examples: • series of events in a historical period • schedule for a bus route	time line Jan. 24, 1848 — Gold discovered at Sutter's Mill Feb. 2, 1848 — California becomes a U.S. territory 1849 — Miners rush to California Sept. 9, 1850 — California becomes 31st U.S. state
statistics: facts that involve numbers Examples: • the percentage of people who ride bicycles • number of votes received by each student council candidate	chart such as a pie chart 20% never 45% occasionally 35% frequently
an area's physical features, political divisions, or other geography-related topics Examples: • The mountains, valleys, lakes, and rivers of Utah • The location of one of Canada's provinces—Prince Edward Island	map 

YOUR TURN 14 — Using Visuals

Use these steps to create a visual for your research report.
- Decide what information to show and the best visual to use.
- Create or find your visual, making sure it is large and clear.
- List the source if you have copied, cut out, or downloaded the visual. For a reminder about how to list sources, see page 203.

TEACHING TIP

Time Line
Explain to students that time lines can run horizontally as well as vertically. Vertical time lines read from the top down; horizontal time lines read from left to right. To ensure that students can interpret (and therefore create their own) time lines, ask them these questions about the time line in the chart on this page:

- Which event happened first?
- What happened in 1849?
- When did California become a state?

Meeting INDIVIDUAL NEEDS

INCLUSION
Have students work with a helper to determine what kind of visual would be most effective. After brainstorming ideas, the helper could sketch out one or two visuals and work with the student to choose and refine one.

YOUR TURN 14

For assessment, you may wish to take the following steps.

- Check that students' visuals are used at appropriate points in their reports and provide effective support.
- Make sure that students' visuals are legible.
- Check to see that students listed sources for their visuals, if necessary.

Focus on Speaking and Listening

OBJECTIVES

- To give and evaluate a research presentation
- To turn a research report into notes for a speech
- To practice formal speaking skills
- To identify important parts of a presentation
- To evaluate a speech

Quotation for the Day

"Let us dare to read, think, speak and write."

(John Adams, 1735–1826, second president of the United States)

Read the quotation out loud and inform students that after reading, thinking, and writing, researchers often share their findings in an oral presentation. Tell students that they will present their own research reports to the class just as researchers present their findings to colleagues.

TEACHING TIP

Giving a Research Presentation

Remind students that just as they can go back to the prewriting stage at any point during the writing process—to gather more support, for example—they can do the same in the speaking process. Also, tell students to note the sources of their examples and other evidence on their speech note cards—the audience will find a speech more believable if they know the speaker has used reliable sources.

WHAT'S AHEAD?

In this section you will give and evaluate a research presentation. You will also learn how to

- turn your research report into notes for a speech
- practice formal speaking skills
- identify important parts of a presentation
- evaluate a speech

TIP Have a partner help you practice by answering these questions about your presentation.

- Are there any points in the speech that are not clear?
- Does the visual (if one is used) help me better understand the information?

Giving and Evaluating a Research Presentation

Researchers sometimes present their findings in a formal presentation or speech. A research presentation tells an audience the important points a researcher has discovered. Here is your chance to share your research findings through oral presentations and to discover what your classmates learned.

Giving a Research Presentation

Even the most interesting report can sound dull if a speaker reads it word for word. A good speaker looks at the audience while presenting information. To make this possible, speakers use note cards to remind themselves of the points they want to make. They also practice their speeches until they are comfortable with what they are saying. To turn your research report into a research presentation, follow these guidelines.

- Look back at the informal outline you created for your research report. Each heading in your outline can be a separate note card.
- On each note card, neatly write words or phrases from your notes, outline, or report that will help you remember the points you want to share with your audience. Write major ideas only (including key evidence and examples), but plan to elaborate or clarify your ideas as you speak.

222 Chapter 6 **Exposition:** Sharing Your Research

- Number the note cards in the order that you will present them.
- Practice your speech out loud. Because the occasion for giving your speech is fairly formal, use standard English and avoid using slang or clichés. Consider your volume and rate, speaking loudly and slowly. Everyone in your audience—including people at the back of the room—should be able to understand you.
- If you use a visual, practice holding it up or pointing to it.
- Practice making eye contact by having a friend listen to you or by looking at yourself in a mirror.

YOUR TURN 15 — Giving an Oral Research Presentation

Follow the guidelines on page 222 and above to present the information in your research report to your class.

TIP You can add a note to your cards to remind you when to use your visual during your speech.

Reference Note
For more on **formal speaking,** see page 719 in the Quick Reference Handbook.

Evaluating a Research Presentation

Why are some speeches more interesting than others? Speakers grab the audience's interest with *what* they say and *how* they say it. The *what* is the **content,** or the ideas a speaker presents. The *how* is the speaker's delivery. **Delivery** includes how the speaker talks, uses gestures, and makes eye contact with the audience. When you evaluate a presentation, you will look at the content of the speech and the speaker's delivery.

Get the Message To evaluate the content of a research presentation, you will need to consider how clear and organized the speaker's information is. Here is how one student evaluated the content of a classmate's speech.

TIP Monitor your understanding as you listen to the speech. If you are confused about something the speaker said, wait until he or she is finished to raise your hand and ask a question for clarification.

Content	Comments
Can you understand the main ideas in the speaker's verbal message?	He says guanacos are unusual animals that are in trouble.
Can you identify support for the speaker's main ideas?	He describes what guanacos look like and what they do. He also talks about how they are being hunted.
Does the speaker seem to understand the topic well?	He really knows about guanacos. I wish he would explain how they swim. Overall content: great

Focus on Speaking and Listening **223**

RESOURCES

Focus on Speaking and Listening
Practice
- Media Literacy and Communication Skills
  —*Support and Practice,* Ch. 6
  —*A How-to Handbook*

Teaching Notes
- Media Literacy and Communication Skills
  —*A Teacher's Guide,* Ch. 6

YOUR TURN 15

Check that students were able to speak on their topics clearly and with little hesitation. Make sure that any conclusions they drew were clear and that their visuals were effective in presenting complicated facts or data or in giving helpful examples. Note whether students were able to speak without reading their notes and whether they made eye contact with the audience.

Critical Thinking

Evaluation. Consider having students work in randomly assigned groups of four or five to develop their own criteria for evaluating the research report presentations. Suggest that students first brainstorm characteristics of interesting as well as ineffective speakers. Have students list those characteristics in a two-column chart with the heads *Effective Speakers* and *Ineffective Speakers.* Then, have group members use their charts to brainstorm evaluation criteria to use regarding the speeches they will hear. Suggest that they organize their criteria under the heads *Content* and *Delivery* and share them with the class.

Wrap It Up

Metacognition. Ask students to think about their own presentations and the presentations of other students. Have them respond to this question:

1. If you were going to give this presentation again next week, what would you change? If you wouldn't change anything, explain why not.

Then, ask students this question:

2. What steps should you take to prepare for giving an oral research report? [Re-read the report, create numbered note cards from the outline, and practice the speech.]

YOUR TURN 16

Have students turn in their charts and their evaluations. Check that students' evaluations take into account aspects of good content and good delivery.

Special Delivery A speaker who mumbles or says "um" frequently draws attention to his or her delivery. When you listen to a speech, you may only notice a speaker's delivery if there are problems such as these. When a speaker's delivery is good, you can focus on the content of the speech. To identify good delivery, answer these questions as you listen.

Delivery	Comments
• Does the speaker talk loudly and clearly enough?	• He was easy to understand except when he turned to point at the map.
• Does the speaker look at the audience?	• He is mostly looking at his notes.
• Do the speaker's nonverbal signals (gestures or voice) emphasize important ideas in the verbal message?	• He emphasizes things with his voice, but not with gestures.
• If visuals are used, are they helpful?	• The map and picture both help me understand the topic better. Overall delivery: good

TIP Many speakers use technology to incorporate visuals into their presentations. They might use a VCR, a monitor, an overhead projector, or presentation software to present and enhance their ideas. To evaluate whether a presenter has used technology effectively, think about whether the technology helps the presenter achieve his or her purpose—to inform. Does the technology contribute to the presentation, or does it distract from the presenter's ideas?

Put It All Together As you listen to a speech, use charts like the one on page 223 and the one above to make notes about content and delivery. Considering both the content and the delivery of a presentation takes concentration, so try to limit your distractions. You may want to sit closer to the speaker and put away everything except your evaluation charts and a pen or pencil.

Reference Note
For more on **eliminating barriers to effective listening,** see page 727 in the Quick Reference Handbook.

YOUR TURN 16 **Evaluating an Oral Presentation**

Evaluate a research presentation by one or more of your classmates. Create charts like those on page 223 and this page to evaluate both the content and delivery of the speech.

224 Chapter 6 Exposition: Sharing Your Research

RESOURCES

Your Turn 16
Practice and Reinforcement
- Media Literacy and Communication Skills
  —*Support and Practice,* Ch. 6 transparencies and worksheets
  —Videocassette 2, Segment E

CHAPTER Choices

Choose one of the following activities to complete.

▶ CAREERS

1. Expert Guidance When you see someone doing an exciting job on television, you might wonder how you might someday get that job. Choose a career that interests you. Then, ask classmates or adults you know to refer you to someone with that job. Interview this person, and ask what education and training are needed to get into that career. Present your findings by creating a **career guide** with other students who choose this activity.

▶ LISTENING

2. My Kind of Tune Do you enjoy hip-hop, country, or some other kind of music? Research the important elements of a particular style of music, and choose a recording of that style of music. Then, write a **review** that evaluates how well the recording uses the elements of its musical style. Give a **multimedia presentation** in which you share your review and play the recording.

▶ CROSSING THE CURRICULUM: PHYSICAL EDUCATION

3. Hall of Fame Make a **trading card** for a famous athlete of the past. Include a picture of the athlete, important dates, records, and other interesting facts you uncover in your research. You might consider choosing one of these athletes: Jim Thorpe, Jackie Joyner-Kersee, Sonja Henie, or Satchel Paige.

▶ CREATIVE WRITING

4. A Fresh Angle Try one of the following ideas to share information about your research topic: Write an entertaining **letter** about your topic to someone you think might be interested in it, or write a **short story** that uses the information you learned researching your topic. You could also write a **poem** about your topic, describing or explaining it in a creative way. Share your writing with others by mailing it, reading it aloud, or posting it on a bulletin board.

 PORTFOLIO

▶ CAREERS
Before they interview people about their jobs, have students who have chosen this activity work together to prepare three to five questions to ask. If students plan to interview members of the community, you may want to obtain prior permission from parents or guardians and from the parties students will contact. Once members of the group have collected information on the careers of their choice, have them meet to decide how they will format and produce the career guide.

▶ LISTENING
Tell students that to review a piece of music is to judge how well the music measures up to important features, or criteria, that have been established. Explain that they will determine their criteria by deciding which musical features (such as rhythm, tempo, vocals, and instrumentation) are important to the style of music they have chosen.

▶ CREATIVE WRITING
Show and discuss examples of letters, stories, and poems that both entertain and provide information. Talk about

- who would be interested in getting a letter about students' topics
- what might be the setting, characters, and plot of a short story related to their research topics
- the emotions students have about their topics that they can express in a poem

Then, have students choose a form of writing for their topics.

RESOURCES

Sharing Your Research
Assessment
- *Assessment Package*
  —*Chapter Tests,* Ch. 6
  —*Chapter Tests in Standardized Test Formats,* Ch. 6
  —*Assessment Alternatives,* Ch. 6

- *Test Generator (One-Stop Planner CD-ROM)*

Choices
Rubrics
- *Assessment Package*
  —*Assessment Alternatives,* Ch. 6

CHAPTER 7

Making a Difference

Use this guide to create an instructional plan that suits the individual needs of your students. Assignments marked by an asterisk (*) may be completed out of class. Times given for pacing lessons are estimated. See pp. 226–227 for chapter-wide resources. Resources listed in this guide are point-of-use resources only.

Curriculum Connections

Choices *p. 259*
- Editorial Cartoons
- Crossing the Curriculum: Social Studies
- Speaking

GO TO: go.hrw.com
KEYWORD: EOLang 6-7

All resources for this chapter are available for preview on the *One-Stop Planner CD-ROM with Test Generator*. All worksheets and tests may be printed from the CD-ROM.

	Chapter Opener pp. 226–227	**Reading Workshop: Reading a Persuasive Essay** pp. 228–236
DEVELOPMENTAL PROGRAM	⏱ **30 minutes** • Your Turn 1 *p. 227*	⏱ **100 minutes** • Preparing to Read *p. 228* • Reading Selection *pp. 229–230* • First Thoughts in groups *p. 231* • Fact and Opinion *pp. 231–232* • Your Turn 2 *p. 232* • Reasons and Evidence *pp. 232–234* • Your Turn 3 *p. 234* • Test Taking Mini-Lesson *p. 236*
CORE PROGRAM	⏱ **20 minutes** • Your Turn 1 *p. 227*	⏱ **75 minutes** • Preparing to Read *p. 228* • Reading Selection *pp. 229–230* • First Thoughts *p. 231* • Fact and Opinion *pp. 231–232* • Your Turn 2 *p. 232* • Reasons and Evidence *pp. 232–234* • Your Turn 3 *p. 234* • Vocabulary Mini-Lesson *p. 235* • Test Taking Mini-Lesson *p. 236*
ADVANCED PROGRAM	⏱ **15 minutes** • Your Turn 1 *p. 227*	⏱ **60 minutes** • Preparing to Read *p. 228* • Reading Selection *pp. 229–230* • First Thoughts *p. 231* • Fact and Opinion *pp. 231–232* • Your Turn 2 *p. 232* • Reasons and Evidence *pp. 232–234* • Your Turn 3 *p. 234* • Vocabulary Mini-Lesson *p. 235*
RESOURCES — PRINT	• *Communications*, TP. 52, WS. p. 138	• *Alternative Readings*, Ch. 7 • *Communications*, TPs. 53, 54, WS. pp. 139–146
RESOURCES — MEDIA	• One-Stop Planner CD-ROM	• One-Stop Planner CD-ROM

TP.=Transparency   WS.=Worksheet

Writing Workshop: Writing a Persuasive Letter *pp. 237–255*	Focus on Listening: Evaluating a Persuasive Speech *pp. 256–258*
⏱ 240 minutes • Choose an Issue; Opinion Statement; Your Turn 4 *pp. 237–238* • Consider Audience and Purpose; Your Turn 5 *p. 239* • Develop Reasons and Evidence; Your Turn 6 *pp. 241–242* • Choose a Call to Action; Your Turn 7 *pp. 242–243* • Framework; Models; Your Turn 8* *pp. 244–247* • Evaluate and Revise *pp. 248–249* • Focus on Sentences in groups *p. 250* • Your Turn 9 *p. 250* • Proofread, Publish, and Reflect *pp. 251–252* • Grammar Link; Your Turn 10 *pp. 251–252* • Test Taking Mini-Lesson *p. 253*	**⏱ 40 minutes** • Listen with a Purpose *pp. 256–257* • Develop Criteria *pp. 257–258* • Your Turn 12* *p. 258*
⏱ 180 minutes • Choose an Issue: Opinion Statement; Your Turn 4 *pp. 237–238* • Consider Audience and Purpose; Your Turn 5 *p. 239* • Critical-Thinking Mini-Lesson in groups *p. 240* • Develop Reasons and Evidence; Your Turn 6 *pp. 241–242* • Choose a Call to Action; Your Turn 7 *pp. 242–243* • Framework; Models; Your Turn 8* *pp. 244–247* • Evaluate and Revise *pp. 248–249* • Focus on Sentences *p. 250* • Your Turn 9 *p. 250* • Proofread, Publish, and Reflect *pp. 251–252* • Grammar Link; Your Turn 10 *pp. 251–252* • Test Taking Mini-Lesson *p. 253* • Connections to Life; Your Turn 11* *pp. 254–255*	**⏱ 30 minutes** • Listen with a Purpose *pp. 256–257* • Develop Criteria *pp. 257–258* • Your Turn 12* *p. 258*
⏱ 120 minutes • Choose an Issue; Opinion Statement; Your Turn 4 *pp. 237–238* • Consider Audience and Purpose; Your Turn 5 *p. 239* • Critical-Thinking Mini-Lesson *p. 240* • Develop Reasons and Evidence; Your Turn 6 *pp. 241–242* • Choose a Call to Action; Your Turn 7 *pp. 242–243* • Framework; Models; Your Turn 8* *pp. 244–247* • Evaluate and Revise *pp. 248–249* • Focus on Sentences *p. 250* • Your Turn 9* *p. 250* • Proofread, Publish, and Reflect *pp. 251–252* • Grammar Link; Your Turn 10* *pp. 251–252* • Connections to Life; Your Turn 11* *pp. 254–255*	**⏱ 20 minutes** • Listen with a Purpose *pp. 256–257* • Develop Criteria *pp. 257–258* • Your Turn 12* *p. 258*

• *Communications,*
  TPs. 55–58
  WS. pp. 147–159
• *Designing Your Writing*
	• *Media Literacy and Communication Skills*
	  —*Support and Practice,* Ch. 7
	  —*A How-to Handbook*
	  —*A Teacher's Guide,* Ch. 7

• *One-Stop Planner CD-ROM*	• *Media Literacy and Communication Skills* —Videocassette 2, Segment F • *One-Stop Planner CD-ROM*

CHAPTER PLANNING GUIDE

CHAPTER 7

Making a Difference

CHAPTER OBJECTIVES

- To read a persuasive essay to identify fact and opinion and to recognize how writers use reasons and evidence to persuade readers
- To write a persuasive letter
- To evaluate a persuasive speech

Chapter Overview

This chapter is designed to help students recognize persuasion as readers and listeners and master the art of persuasion as writers and speakers. The Reading Workshop (pp. 228–236) contains a persuasive essay offering solutions to the garbage crisis in the United States. The Writing Workshop (pp. 237–255) guides students through the steps of the writing process as they write a persuasive letter. In the Focus on Listening, students learn how to evaluate the content and delivery of a persuasive speech. The workshops in this chapter may be taught independently, but teaching them together can provide students with a more complete understanding of the uses and power of persuasion.

Why Study Persuasion?

Students experience persuasion through messages from the media and from their peers—messages that tell them what to do, think, and feel. Knowing how to recognize persuasive techniques can help students make intelligent decisions when they are assailed with powerful messages. Understanding persuasion can also enable them to use logical arguments in their own writing and speaking.

Teaching the Chapter

Option 1: Begin with Literature

If literature is the focus in your classroom, your students may be familiar with persuasion as it is used by characters in literature. Encourage them to think about whether these characters influence others through the power of emotions or whether they use reason. After discussion, have students read the persuasive essay in the Reading Workshop on pp. 229–230. Ask them to compare persuasion in literature and in the essay. [The essay is more direct and rational.] Students' observations, along with the information in the Reading Workshop, can help them prepare for writing their own persuasive letters.

Option 2: Begin with Nonfiction and Writing

Introduce students to the elements of persuasion discussed in this chapter. The persuasive essay in the Reading Workshop (pp. 228–236) is developed through the use of facts, opinions, reasons, and evidence. The accompanying information can help students as they write persuasive letters. Their increased understanding of the elements of persuasion can prepare students to examine the tools of persuasion when they return to literature.

Making Connections

■ To the Literature Curriculum

Writers of fiction, poems, and plays use many techniques to influence readers. Yoshiko Uchida's story "The Bracelet" uses descriptive language and emotional appeal to convince readers how unfairly Japanese Americans were treated. In "The Sneetches" by Dr. Seuss, humor and rhyme persuade readers to question how the world works.

Lesson Idea: Persuasion in "The Sneetches" by Dr. Seuss (Theodor Geisel)

1. Have partners alternate reading aloud the stanzas of "The Sneetches." Encourage students to listen closely for the plot, rhyme, and humor.

2. Then, have students read the poem silently, taking notes on the reasons for the Sneetches' actions. Students might work in pairs to complete a chart like the one below. A sample response follows. After completing the chart, point out how Seuss reveals, through humor, the absurdity of the Sneetches' actions.

What the Sneetches Do	Reasons for Their Actions
Star-Belly Sneetches will not play with or be friends with Plain-Belly Sneetches.	They think that the stars on their stomachs make them better.
Plain-Belly Sneetches act sad and lonely.	They have been made to feel inferior to Star-Belly Sneetches due to their lack of stars.
Plain-Belly Sneetches pay McBean for stars.	Plain-Belly Sneetches want to be special like Star-Belly Sneetches.
Star-Belly Sneetches pay Mr. McBean to remove their stars.	Star-Belly Sneetches want to look different to make themselves special.
The Sneetches spend all their money adding and removing stars, forgetting who originally had stars and who did not.	The Sneetches all want to look like special Sneetches.
The Sneetches forget about the stars and learn to live together as equals.	Sneetches realize that with or without stars on their bellies, they are all the same and all special.

3. Discuss with students whether they think the reasons for the Sneetches' actions are logical or emotional. [They are based on an emotional response.]

4. Next, ask students to describe Dr. Seuss's message and his techniques for conveying it. [We should recognize and treat everyone as equal; with humor, emotional appeal.] Are his techniques effective? [Yes.] Why or why not? [Made-up words, humor, rhyme make the message clear, enjoyable, memorable.]

5. After discussion, direct students to the persuasive essay in the Reading Workshop (pp. 229–230). Point out that the writer persuades readers using reasons and evidence. The material on fact, opinion, reasons, and evidence will help students with their persuasive letters.

■ To Careers

Use this chapter to help students think about career choices that use persuasion, such as law enforcement, politics, and sales. Suggest that students create a list of questions about these and other careers to distribute to community members who hold these jobs. Possible questions include: *Why did you choose your career? What is the best part of your job? Do you enjoy persuading people how to think or act?* After collecting the responses, students might report on how the questionnaire affected their ideas about careers. Consider obtaining permission from parents or guardians and from the parties students contact before beginning work on this assignment. See also **Connections to Life** pp. 254–255.

■ To the Community

Techniques of persuasion can be used to convince people to take actions that benefit the community. Persuasive messages might be broadcast as public-service announcements on local radio and television stations promoting such local efforts as cleaning up conservation land or volunteering in nursing homes. Have students work in groups to create public-service announcements to broadcast on the school's intercom system or on the local cable access channel.

■ To the Science Curriculum

Students may not be aware that people often use scientific data to support arguments or to persuade others. Invite students to use science to convince others about the benefits of recycling. Have them work in groups to select a topic for research in books, in magazines, and on the Internet. Possibilities include the process of recycling water or glass or the uses for recycled scrap tires, newspapers, and plastics. Have groups use the information they gather to create posters persuading others to recycle. Students may wish to display these posters in the school. *You need to be aware that Internet resources are sometimes public forums and their content can be unpredictable.*

CHAPTER 7

PREVIEWING THE CHAPTER

- The three workshops in this chapter explore the elements and forms of persuasion. The workshops may be taught separately, but teaching them together can increase students' understanding of persuasive techniques used in reading, writing, and speaking. The Reading Workshop focuses on how to read a persuasive essay. The Writing Workshop guides students through the steps of writing a persuasive letter. The Focus on Listening explains how students may evaluate a persuasive speech. To integrate this chapter with grammar, usage, and mechanics chapters, see pp. T297A–T297B.

INTRODUCING THE CHAPTER

- To introduce the chapter, use the Journal Warm-up, Transparency 52, in *Communications*.

VIEWING THE ILLUSTRATION

- Challenge students to explain why this artwork fits the chapter called "Making a Difference." [The girl is making a difference or improving the world by picking up trash.] Point out how the girl and the trash are outlined in black. What is the effect of the outlining? [It makes the girl and the trash stand out from the background environment, emphasizing the ugliness of the trash and the positive action of the girl.]

Representing. Have students draw or find illustrations of a person making a difference in the world. Ask students to comment on how the person fits in or is different from the environment.

CHAPTER 7 Making a Difference

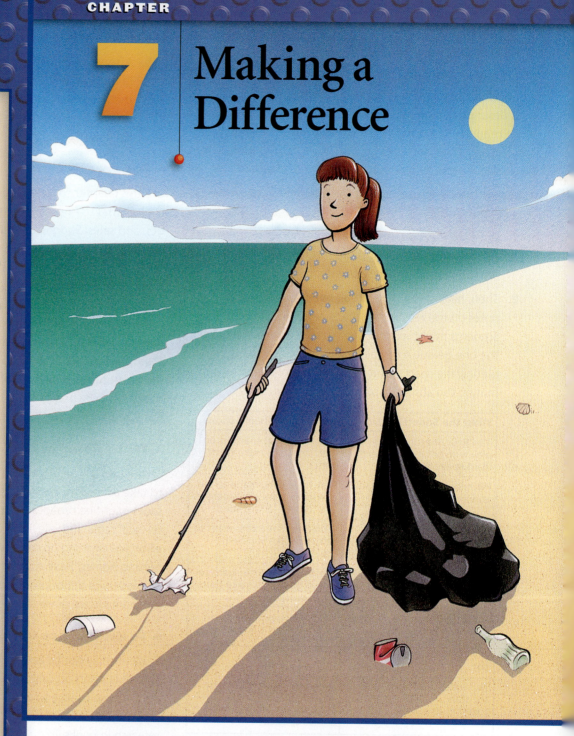

CHAPTER RESOURCES

Planning
- *Lesson Planner,* Ch. 7
- *ELL Strategies,* Ch. 7
- Block Scheduling, p. T225A (this book)
- *One-Stop Planner CD-ROM*

Practice
- *Communications,* Ch. 7

- *Media Literacy and Communication Skills*

Extension
- *Designing Your Writing*

Reinforcement
- *Communications,* Ch. 7
- *Alternative Readings,* Ch. 7

226

PREVIEW

Reading Workshop

Reading a Persuasive Essay
PAGE 228

Writing Workshop

Writing a Persuasive Letter
PAGE 237

Focus on Listening

Evaluating a Persuasive Speech
PAGE 256

"Pleasepleasepleasepleaseplease?!" This may be how young children attempt to get their way, but by now you probably know that whining and repetition are not effective when you are older. You are more likely to get what you want through the art of **persuasion**—convincing others by giving reasons that make sense. Whether you are trying to persuade others or others are trying to persuade you, good reasons make all the difference.

Persuasion comes in many forms. A spoken request from a friend is usually casual and unplanned. The kind of persuasion you read or write is more carefully structured. It includes an opinion and specific reasons to support the opinion. The kind of persuasion you view, including TV ads and billboards, adds pictures and even jingles that appeal to your emotions as well as to your mind.

GO TO: go.hrw.com
KEYWORD: EOLang 6-7

YOUR TURN 1 — Discovering Persuasion

In a small group, discuss the following questions.
- What makes a spoken request convincing? a TV ad? a billboard?
- Is one of these types of persuasion usually more persuasive than the others? Which one? Why?

Motivate

Ask students if they have ever convinced someone to take them somewhere or help them do something. Have students work in pairs to reenact such a scene and to identify what they did or said that convinced the other person.

ELEMENTS OF Literature

Persuasion in Literature. In *Elements of Literature*, Introductory Course, see "Ta-Na-E-Ka" by Mary Whitebird, pp. 16–23, and "A Glory over Everything" by Ann Petry, pp. 138–145, for examples of characters who use persuasion effectively.

YOUR TURN 1

As students share their ideas and insights about persuasive messages, have one group member speak and another summarize that student's comments. Assess students' discussion using the following guidelines:
- Speaking: Do students support their ideas with evidence, elaboration, and examples? Do they clarify any ideas that group members question?
- Listening: Do students' responses indicate that they understand important ideas and evidence? Do they share their own interpretations of each speaker's overall message? Do they ask questions to clarify unclear ideas?

- *Daily Language Activity Transparencies*
- *Vocabulary Workshop* and *Tests*
- *Spelling*

Evaluation and Assessment
- *Assessment Package*
  —*Chapter Tests,* Ch. 7
  —*Chapter Tests in Standardized Test Formats,* Ch. 7
  —*Assessment Alternatives,* Ch. 7
- *Test Generator* (One-Stop Planner CD-ROM)

Internet
- go.hrw.com (keyword: EOLang 6–7)

Reading Workshop

OBJECTIVES

- To read a persuasive essay in preparation for writing a persuasive letter
- To identify facts and opinions
- To recognize the reasons and evidence writers use to persuade readers
- To use a dictionary and a thesaurus to identify the meanings of unfamiliar words

Quotation for the Day

"The chief danger in life is that you may take too many precautions."

(Alfred Adler, 1870–1937, Austrian psychiatrist)

Write the quotation on the chalkboard, and have students reflect on it by freewriting. Ask volunteers to share their thoughts. Point out that Adler is suggesting that people are often too afraid to take a stand and share ideas. Briefly discuss with students how taking a stand is a brave and exciting act.

TEACHING TIP

Preparing to Read
The instruction on this page is an introduction to concepts that will be discussed in depth on pp. 231–234. Distinguishing fact from opinion and identifying reasons and evidence are the key concepts in the Reading Workshop.

RESOURCES

Reading Workshop Reinforcement
- *Alternative Readings*, Ch. 7

Reading Workshop

Reading a Persuasive Essay

WHAT'S AHEAD?

In this section you will read a persuasive essay. You will also learn how to

- identify facts and opinions
- recognize the reasons and evidence writers use to persuade readers

You finish your lunch, and then you throw away the wrapper and bag. You pry a new computer game out of layers of plastic and cardboard, tossing the packaging away before you play the game. You even drag your broken desk chair out to the curb to be picked up on trash day. Think about the amount of stuff you throw away every day, and multiply that amount by 300 million, the estimated population of the United States. That is a lot of garbage! The author of the following essay will try to persuade you to change your ways. Will you be convinced?

Preparing to Read

READING SKILL

Fact and Opinion Strong *opinions* often inspire people to write persuasive essays. To be effective, though, a writer must support opinions with **facts,** or statements that can be proved true. As you read the following essay, watch out for statements of **opinion,** which cannot be proved.

READING FOCUS

Reasons and Evidence In the courtroom dramas you see in movies and on TV, do jurors accept a lawyer's argument without question? Of course not. Even TV lawyers provide *reasons* and *evidence* to convince juries of their cases. Writers have the same duty to their readers. They must support their opinions with enough reasons and evidence to persuade their readers. See if William Dudley, the writer of the following essay, has done a convincing job.

228 Chapter 7 Persuasion: Making a Difference

READING PROCESS

PREREADING
Activate Prior Knowledge. Tell students that activating background knowledge can make them aware of how much they already know about a subject and help them realize that this knowledge may be used for comprehending new information. Before they turn to the Reading Selection on pp. 229–230, ask students to jot down answers to the following questions:

- How much garbage do you usually throw out in a day? What kinds of things do you

Reading Selection

Read the following essay. In a notebook, jot down answers to the numbered active-reading questions in the shaded boxes. Underlined words will be used in the Vocabulary Mini-Lesson on page 235.

from The Environment:
Distinguishing Between Fact and Opinion

The U.S. Has a GARBAGE CRISIS

BY WILLIAM DUDLEY

1   America is a "throwaway" society. Each year Americans throw away 16 billion disposable diapers, 1.6 billion pens, and 220 million tires. For the sake of convenience, we tend to throw these and other used goods away rather than repair or recycle them. The average American household generates 350 bags, or 4,550 gallons, of garbage per year. This comes out to a total of 160 million tons of garbage a year. We have to change our throwaway lifestyle before we are buried in it.

> **1. What opinion does the writer express in this paragraph?**

2   We are running out of places to put all the garbage we produce. About 80 percent of it is now buried in landfills. There are 6,000 landfills currently operating, but many of them are becoming full. The Environmental Protection Agency estimates that one-half of the remaining landfills will run out of space and close within the next five to ten years.

> **2. What reason does the writer give in this paragraph?**

3   Can we simply build new landfills to replace the old ones? The answer is no. For one thing, we are running out of space. We cannot afford to use up land that is needed for farms, parks, and homes.

4   In addition, many landfills contain toxic chemicals that can leak into and pollute underground water supplies. In New York City, over seventy-five wells had to be closed because of such toxic waste poisoning.

> **3. Which statements in paragraph 4 can be proved? How?**

5   One suggested alternative to landfills is to burn the trash. In some states, large incinerators are used to burn garbage, and the heat that is generated is used to produce electricity. But this solution

---

Active-Reading Questions

The purpose of the active-reading questions is to encourage students to think about how to distinguish between fact and opinion and to recognize reasons and evidence in the Reading Selection. Use students' answers as an informal assessment of their grasp of these concepts. Possible answers follow.

ANSWERS

1. The writer's opinion is that Americans need to change their lifestyles so they do not throw away so much garbage.

2. He says that many landfills are almost full, and others will be full within the next five to ten years—there is less space to put garbage.

3. Both statements in paragraph 4 could be proved by checking with the appropriate authorities.

Connecting Reading and Writing

Explain to students that the Reading Selection is a good model for their own writing. Point out how the writer begins the essay with an attention-grabbing opening sentence and includes a clear main idea statement at the end of the first paragraph. The first sentence in each paragraph is well supported by other sentences in the paragraph. Students can make use of the same structure in their own writing.

---

throw out most often?
- What is recycling?
- Do you think recycling is a good idea? Why or why not?

As they read the Reading Selection, have students note how information in the essay adds to their knowledge or affects their opinions.

Active-Reading Questions

ANSWERS continued

4. Evidence that illustrates the problems with burning trash includes the facts that burning trash releases poisonous chemicals into the air and that burned garbage produces "leftover ash," which can be poisonous, and "still has to be buried somewhere."

5. The example serves as a reason that proves the writer's point: Many people do not think that "the amount of garbage we produce" causes problems.

> **4.** What evidence supports the writer's reason that there are problems with burning trash?

has drawbacks. Burning trash pollutes the air with dioxin and mercury, which are highly poisonous. Furthermore, burning does not completely solve the landfill problem. Leftover ash produced by burning is often highly toxic, and it still has to be buried somewhere.

6   The only real solution to the garbage crisis is for Americans to reduce the amount of trash they throw away. There are two methods of doing this. One is recycling—reusing garbage. Bottles can be washed and reused. Aluminum cans can be melted down and remade. Currently in the U.S., only 11 percent of solid waste is used again as something else. . . .

7   We must also reduce the amount of garbage we produce in the first place. We should use less plastic, which is hard to recycle and does not <u>decompose</u> in landfills. Much garbage is useless packaging. Consumers should buy foods and goods that use less packaging. We also should buy reusable products rather than things that are used once and thrown away. . . .

8   A woman in California was asked about garbage. She replied, "Why do we need to change anything? I put my garbage out on the sidewalk and they take it away." Attitudes like hers must be changed. We have to face the inevitable question posed by Ed Repa, manager of the solid waste <u>disposal</u> program at the National Solid Waste Management Association: "How do you throw something away when there is no 'away'?"

> **5.** How does this example help the writer make his point?

230 Chapter 7 **Persuasion:** Making a Difference

READING PROCESS

READING

Self-Check. Tell students that skilled readers realize when they are not making sense of what they read. Good readers can change their reading speeds by slowing down or stopping to re-read when they are confused. Explain that reading a passage aloud, asking questions, and rephrasing sentences are other strategies that readers use to check their understanding.

As students read the Reading Selection, ask them to place a sticky note next to each place

First Thoughts on Your Reading
1. What is the author trying to convince the reader to do?
2. Which parts of the essay were convincing to you? Why?

Fact and Opinion

Is That a Fact? Maybe you have seen a TV show in which a detective asks witnesses for "just the facts." *Facts,* not opinions, will help the detective solve the case. Facts also help writers persuade readers because **facts** are statements that can be proved true. Facts may include numbers, dates, or measurements.

Opinions, on the other hand, are impossible to prove. An **opinion** is a person's judgment. Phrases such as "I believe," "I feel," or "I think" indicate an opinion. Telling readers what *should* be done is another sure clue that an opinion is being expressed. Judgment words such as *best, worst, greatest,* and *prettiest* may be clues that a statement is an opinion. The following pairs of statements show the difference between facts and opinions.

Fact	The city council passed the proposal **five to one.**
Opinion	**I think** the city council made a **smart** decision.
Fact	Our school buses were made in **1995.**
Opinion	The school board **should** buy newer buses.
Fact	Jefferson was the **third** president.
Opinion	Jefferson was the country's **best** president.

Try identifying facts and opinions in the paragraph below. If you have trouble, follow the steps on the next page.

> The city should encourage people to ride bicycles for short trips. Bicycles do not pollute. Taking several short car trips can create more pollution than a longer drive. If people tried bicycling for these short trips, they would enjoy it. Cyclists travel at slower speeds, which allows them to take in nature's sights and sounds. I think an ad campaign could convince people to stop depending on cars for all of their transportation.

First Thoughts on Your Reading
ANSWERS
Sample answers appear below.
1. The author wants to convince readers to reduce the amount of trash they produce every day.
2. Students might identify the following parts as convincing: the statistics about how much trash Americans throw away (paragraph 1), the dwindling number of landfills available (paragraph 2), the number of New York City wells closed by toxic leakage (paragraph 4), and the dangers of incinerating trash (paragraph 5). Students might find these parts convincing because they use specific information to portray the seriousness of the garbage problem.

TEACHING TIP

Is That a Fact?
Caution students that just because a statement is not true, it is not automatically an opinion. For example, although the statement "The moon is made of green cheese" can easily be proved false, it is not an opinion. It is an untrue statement.

in the selection where they need to slow down, re-read portions of the text, ask questions, or rephrase sentences. After they finish reading the essay, discuss with students which strategies they found most useful to improve their understanding of the selection.

YOUR TURN 2

Three sentences with facts follow.
1. "The average American household generates 350 bags, or 4,550 gallons, of garbage per year." (paragraph 1)
   The fact is supported by statistics.
2. "In addition, many landfills contain toxic chemicals that can leak into and pollute underground water supplies." (paragraph 4)
   The fact can be proved true.
3. "Burning trash pollutes the air with dioxin and mercury, which are highly poisonous." (paragraph 5)
   The fact can be proved true.

Three sentences that contain opinions follow.
1. "We have to change our throwaway lifestyle before we are buried in it." (paragraph 1)
   In judging what people "have to" do, the sentence includes an opinion.
2. "Consumers should buy foods and goods that use less packaging." (paragraph 7)
   The use of the word *should* indicates that the sentence includes an opinion.
3. "Attitudes like hers must be changed." (paragraph 8)
   The use of the word *must* indicates that the sentence includes an opinion.

TEACHING TIP

Reasons and Evidence
For homework, have students find and analyze an editorial or other public document that takes a position on an issue. Ask students to use the instruction in the Reading Workshop to complete the following:
- Identify and record the facts, opinions, reasons, and evidence in the article.
- Evaluate the author's ability to communicate the position clearly and logically.

TIP Quiz a classmate by writing five sentences on your paper from the essay. Then, have your partner identify each sentence as either a fact or an opinion. Your partner should also explain his or her answers.

READING FOCUS

THINKING IT THROUGH — Identifying Fact and Opinion

▶ **STEP 1** Read the paragraph. Look for clues, such as *should*, *good*, *bad*, or *I believe*, that signal an opinion.

Sentences with opinion clues: "The city <u>should</u> encourage people to ride bicycles for short trips." "If people tried bicycling for these short trips, they would <u>enjoy</u> it." "<u>I think</u> an ad campaign could convince people to stop depending on cars for all of their transportation."

▶ **STEP 2** Read the paragraph again to identify facts. Look for numbers, measurements, or things that can be proved.

Sentences with fact clues: "Bicycles <u>do not pollute</u>." "Taking several short car trips can create <u>more pollution</u> than a longer drive." "Cyclists travel at <u>slower speeds</u>. . . ."

YOUR TURN 2 — Identifying Fact and Opinion

Re-read the essay on pages 229–230, and look for fact and opinion clues. Identify three sentences that contain facts and three sentences that contain opinions, and explain how you can tell.

Reasons and Evidence

Building a Case Have you ever tried to build a human pyramid? The base of the pyramid needs to have more people, and stronger people, than the top does. Look at the following diagram of a persuasive essay. Notice how it looks like a pyramid.

232 Chapter 7 Persuasion: Making a Difference

RESOURCES

Your Turn 2
Practice
■ *Communications*, WS. p. 139
Reinforcement
■ *Communications*, TP. 53, WS. p. 140

The opinion in a persuasive essay is like the person at the top of a human pyramid. The *reasons* are like the people in the middle row who support the person on top. The *evidence* in a persuasive essay is like the group of people who form the base of a human pyramid. Persuasive writing must have support to be strong, just as a human pyramid needs strong supporters.

Reasons   A **reason** explains *why* the writer holds a particular opinion. In a persuasive essay the writer will usually write one or two paragraphs explaining each reason. For example, in the paragraph on page 231, the writer who wanted the city to encourage bike riding gave the reason that it would help reduce air pollution.

Evidence   Just saying that bicycling reduces air pollution is not convincing. The city council or mayor would need evidence before believing the reason. **Evidence** is the support for a reason, the specific *facts* and *examples* that illustrate the reason. You already know that a **fact** is a statement that can be proved true. An **example** is an event or illustration that shows one specific instance of a reason. Here is evidence a writer used to support a reason in an essay about creating more community bike trails. Would this reason be as convincing without the evidence?

> **Reason:** Many people enjoy bike riding.
>
> **Fact:** 80% of the students at my school own bicycles.
>
> **Example:** When I ride my bike in my neighborhood, I always see lots of other people riding bikes, too.

> **TIP**   Using reasons and evidence to support an opinion is called making a *logical appeal*. A **logical appeal** persuades because it makes sense. There are two other ways persuasive writers appeal to readers. While logical appeals try to persuade your head, **emotional appeals** try to persuade your heart. Humane Society ads showing adorable puppies and kittens up for adoption are examples of emotional appeals. Finally, **ethical appeals** try to persuade you by making the presenter seem trustworthy. One example of an ethical appeal would be a public service announcement featuring a respected celebrity speaking sincerely about a serious issue.

See if you can spot the reasons and evidence in the paragraph on the next page. The graphic organizer below it will help you check your answers.

> **TIP**   In paragraph 3 on page 229, the writer addresses a *counterargument*. A **counterargument** is a reader's **objection** to the writer's opinion. A writer can address a counterargument by presenting a reason that explains why the objection is either incorrect or unimportant.

Meeting INDIVIDUAL NEEDS

LEARNERS HAVING DIFFICULTY
To help students understand the concept of counterargument, you might ask them the following questions:

- What is something that you would like to ask a family member or friend to do?
- Why might the person say "no"?
- What could you do or say to change the "no" to "yes"?

Explain to students that their attempts to change "no" to "yes" represent a counterargument.

READING PROCESS   *Continued on p. 234*

EXPLORING
Evaluate Fact and Opinion. Tell students that being able to evaluate a writer's opinion will help them better understand persuasive writing. Have students evaluate the validity of the author's opinion in the Reading Selection by using what they have learned about fact and opinion on pp. 231–232. They might

Wrap It Up

Metacognition. Have students reflect on their reading processes by answering the following question:

1. How does knowing the difference between fact and opinion help you as a reader?

Then, ask students the following question:

2. What three things are essential for building a persuasive argument? [opinion, reasons, evidence]

ANSWERS
A sample response follows.

Opinion Statement: Americans need to stop throwing away so much garbage.

Reason 1:
We do not have enough places to put all the garbage.

Evidence:
- Of the 6,000 remaining landfills, many will "run out of space" within the next five to ten years.
- We have little space in which to build new landfills.
- Some landfills have been closed because they leak chemicals into underground water supplies.

Reason 2:
An alternative solution—burning trash—does not solve the trash problem.

Evidence:
- "Burning trash pollutes the air. . . ."
- The "leftover ash" is often toxic and still must "be buried somewhere."

People should donate supplies to the Helping Hands Community Assistance Program now. The supplies of clothing, shoes, and blankets are very low. There are only four coats, six blankets, and one pair of shoes now available. The director says that they need enough clothing for twenty adults and ten children. Also, winter is coming soon. Winter always brings a higher demand for warm clothing. Last winter some families left empty-handed because supplies were gone.

TIP The sentence that identifies the issue and the writer's opinion on the issue is called the **opinion statement**.

The writer of the paragraph above used reasons and evidence to be as persuasive as possible. Here is a graphic organizer showing how she built her case. Notice how the graphic organizer is shaped like a pyramid. The reasons and evidence hold up the opinion.

YOUR TURN 3 — Identifying Reasons and Evidence

Re-read "The U.S. Has a Garbage Crisis" on pages 229–230. Then, create a graphic organizer like the one above. Fill in your boxes with the writer's opinion, his reasons for that opinion, and the evidence that supports each of his reasons. (Hint: You will find this information in paragraphs 1–5 of the reading selection.)

Chapter 7 Persuasion: Making a Difference

READING PROCESS

wish to use the following questions to guide their evaluation:
- Does the writer's opinion seem fair?
- Is it supported by facts?
- Are the facts taken from reliable sources?

Allow time for students to share their evaluations and discuss any differences in their conclusions.

Persuasion: Making a Difference

MINI-LESSON VOCABULARY

Dictionary and Thesaurus

Persuasive writing asks you to take a side on an issue. To make an intelligent decision, you need to be sure you understand all of the words you read. You can use reference books to find an unfamiliar word's meaning. Here are two examples.

- **Dictionary** In a dictionary you will find the word's definition, its pronunciation, its part of speech, examples of how it is used, and its history.

- **Thesaurus** In a thesaurus you will find other words that are *synonyms* of the unfamiliar word. **Synonyms** are words that have almost the same meaning, such as *happy* and *glad*.

Dictionaries can sometimes be confusing when they list several definitions for one word. To find the right definition of a word, use the following steps.

THINKING IT THROUGH — Choosing the Right Definition

Here is an example based on the word *convenience* from the reading selection on page 229.

STEP 1 Look up the word in a dictionary. Read the entire definition.

<u>Convenience</u> means: 1. personal comfort 2. a favorable condition

STEP 2 Use each of the meanings in the context of the reading selection. Decide which meaning makes the most sense in the sentence.

"For the sake of <u>personal comfort</u> we tend to throw things away." That sounds good.

"For the sake of <u>a favorable condition</u> we tend to throw things away." That sounds strange. I think the first definition is correct in this context.

PRACTICE

Look up the words to the right in a dictionary. Use the steps above if the word has more than one definition. Write the correct definition of the word. Then, look the word up in a thesaurus and find a synonym that is familiar to you. Write that word next to the definition.

1. generates (page 229)
2. toxic (page 229)
3. incinerators (page 229)
4. decompose (page 230)
5. disposal (page 230)

Reading Workshop **235**

MINI-LESSON VOCABULARY

Dictionary and Thesaurus

ANSWERS
Possible answers follow.

1. *Generates* means "produces" and "brings into being." The first meaning works in context: "The average American household produces 350 bags . . . of garbage per year."
   Correct definition: "produces"
   Synonym: creates

2. *Toxic* means "affected by a deadly or poisonous substance" and "poisonous." The second meaning works in context: ". . . Many landfills contain poisonous chemicals."
   Correct definition: "poisonous"
   Synonym: harmful

3. *Incinerators* means "furnaces for burning trash." There is only one definition.
   Synonym: trash burners

4. *Decompose* means "to break up into parts" and "to decay or rot." The second meaning works in context: "We should use less plastic, which . . . does not decay in landfills."
   Correct definition: "to decay or rot"
   Synonym: break down

5. *Disposal* means "a machine to grind up garbage," "a way of settling an issue or problem," and "the act of throwing something away." The third meaning works best in context: ". . . question posed by Ed Repa, manager of the solid waste throwing away program . . ."
   Correct definition: "the act of throwing something away"
   Synonym: elimination

RESOURCES

Your Turn 3
Practice
- *Communications,* WS. p. 141

Reinforcement
- *Communications,* TP. 54, WS. p. 142

Vocabulary
Practice
- *Communications,* WS. p. 143

Reading Workshop **235**

Looking Ahead to Writing

In the Writing Workshop for this chapter (pp. 237–255), students will write a persuasive letter. As they work on the drafts of their letters, students will need to develop an opinion statement, reasons, and evidence. They may wish to refer to the diagram on p. 232 of the Reading Workshop for guidance.

MINI-LESSON TEST TAKING

Answering Questions About Fact and Opinion

When you take a reading test, you may be asked to identify statements of fact or opinion. Suppose the following paragraph and question were in a reading test. How would you approach them?

> New equipment should be purchased for Esperanza Park. The existing playground equipment is old and dangerous. Three children have received serious cuts from the jagged metal edges of the swing set. The equipment is seventeen years old and cannot be repaired. The city should make Esperanza Park a fun, safe place to play for children and families in the city.

Which of the following is an OPINION expressed in this passage?

A. Children have gotten hurt on the playground.

B. The playground equipment should be repaired.

C. The playground equipment contains jagged metal edges.

D. Esperanza Park should be made safer for children.

THINKING IT THROUGH Identifying Fact and Opinion

▶ **STEP 1** Determine what the question is asking you to do.

The question asks me to find an opinion in the passage. An opinion is a statement that makes a judgment and can't be proved.

▶ **STEP 2** Eliminate choices that do not answer the question. If the question asks for a fact, eliminate opinions. If it asks for an opinion, eliminate facts.

Choice A says "children have gotten hurt." This is a fact because you could ask parents whether their children have been hurt. C says the equipment has "jagged metal edges." This could be proved by looking at the equipment.

▶ **STEP 3** Look at the remaining choices to make sure that each is the kind of statement the question asks for. Then, choose the answer that is stated in the passage. (If the question asks you to identify an opinion, look for opinion clue words.)

The remaining choices are B and D. Choice B is an opinion because it uses the word should, but the passage says the equipment "cannot be repaired." Choice D also uses the word should, so it is an opinion, too. The last sentence of the passage says this in different words. I'll choose D.

RESOURCES

Test Taking
Practice
- *Communications*, WS. pp. 144-146

Writing Workshop

Writing a Persuasive Letter

When you were younger, did you write letters to ask someone for a special toy? Maybe you wanted a certain doll or a new bicycle, so you described the toy and explained why you wanted it. Were you later thrilled to discover that your wish had been granted?

Now that you are older, you may know that letters can achieve results more important than toys. Here is your opportunity to use the power of persuasive writing to make a difference in the world around you. This workshop will teach you how to write a persuasive letter that will help make a positive change in your school, neighborhood, or town. The thrill of making a difference can be even more satisfying than receiving a new toy!

WHAT'S AHEAD?

In this workshop you will write a persuasive letter. You will also learn how to

- develop reasons and evidence
- predict and answer objections
- choose and focus a call to action
- revise stringy sentences
- use possessives correctly

Writing Workshop

OBJECTIVES

- To use the writing process to write a persuasive letter
- To develop reasons and evidence
- To predict and answer objections
- To choose and focus a call to action
- To revise stringy sentences
- To use possessives correctly

Quotation for the Day

"The vital, successful people I have met all had one common characteristic. They had a plan."
(Marilyn Van Derbur, former Miss America)

Use the quotation above to illustrate the importance of the prewriting stage of the writing process. Remind students that having a plan will make their writing processes more organized and their finished products more focused.

Prewriting

Choose an Issue

Dare to Care   Given a choice between soup or sandwiches for lunch, you might answer, "I don't care." For you, the kind of food is not an issue. In persuasive writing, though, *issues* are important. An **issue** is a topic with at least two sides about which people disagree. **In a persuasive letter the writer tries to make the reader agree with his or her opinion on an issue.** Persuasive letters also may ask readers to take action on an issue.

 KEY CONCEPT

Meeting INDIVIDUAL NEEDS

STUDENTS WITH SPECIAL NEEDS
You may need to give some students additional guidance in selecting issues. Sometimes students tend to choose issues that are too broad or too narrow. To help students avoid this problem, ask them to identify topics related to their issues. If they can list three or four topics, then their subjects are probably specific enough and can be covered adequately in a short persuasive letter. If students can list more than four or fewer than three topics, then their issues are probably too broad or too narrow.

Have students exchange statements with a partner. The partners can check to make sure that each has a clear issue and opinion on the issue. You can circulate among the pairs and work individually with students who need assistance clarifying either their issue or their opinion.

TIP Make sure you choose an issue that gets people fired up, not just a topic. For example, "school hours" is a topic that can be explained, while "making the school day longer" is an issue about which many people disagree.

KEY CONCEPT

TIP An opinion statement may also be called a **thesis statement**.

Take Your Pick The issue you choose should be one that is important to you. If you do not feel strongly about an issue, how can you convince your readers to care about it? Ask yourself what issues most affect your world. Completing the following sentence starters will help you identify issues that matter to you.

My school would be a better place if ____.

I become upset when I see ____.

Little by Little You should also choose an issue that is small enough for one person or group to have an effect. For example, one student chose the issue of littering. Although she also felt strongly about the issue of homelessness, she felt that by taking on a smaller issue, she would be better able to make a difference. She also knew that an anti-littering campaign for her soccer league would be an issue she could tackle in a letter.

Write Your Opinion Statement

Take a Stand If you have chosen an issue that is important to you, you probably already know what your opinion on it is. You simply need to put that opinion into words. **An opinion statement should clearly state what the issue is and where the writer stands on it.** Here is how the writer who chose the issue of recycling came up with her opinion statement.

> **issue:** litter at soccer games
> **+ how I feel about it:** soccer fields should be kept free of litter
> **opinion statement:** We need to start an anti-littering campaign to keep the soccer fields clean.

YOUR TURN 4 Choosing an Issue and Writing an Opinion Statement

Brainstorm issues that might make your community or the world a better place. Choose an issue that is both important to you and small enough to tackle in a letter. Write down your opinion about the issue. Then, put the issue and your opinion together into a single clear sentence—your opinion statement.

238 Chapter 7 Persuasion: Making a Difference

RESOURCES

Your Turn 4
Practice
- Communications, WS. p. 147

Your Turn 5
Practice
- Communications, WS. p. 148

Consider Audience and Purpose

Dear Sir or Madam . . .   You would not ask the President of the United States to shorten the school day. Yes, the President can do many things, but your request is likely to get lost in the shuffle of national issues. Because your **purpose** is to persuade your reader, it is important to write to someone who cares about the issue and can do something about it. **Contacting the right audience to consider your request is an important part of your letter's effectiveness.** Identify local people who have the power to do what you want. Your audience may be one person or a group of people. Notice how one student used the following questions to help identify her specific audience.

KEY CONCEPT

What part of your community does the issue involve?	Starting an anti-littering campaign at the soccer fields would involve my soccer league.
What is the specific name of the person or group you need to contact?	My league handbook says the president of the Eastside Soccer League is Jake Matsuo.
What do you know about this person or these people? (How old are they? What interests or concerns them? Why might they disagree with you, or object to your opinion?)	I know he's an adult, and he is interested in soccer. I think he is interested in keeping things running smoothly and in keeping fees low for players. He might object to my opinion if he thinks an anti-littering campaign would be time-consuming or expensive.

TIP   In writing, **voice** reflects your tone and attitude. To persuade readers, you need to use a believable voice. In other words, you should sound as if you know what you are talking about and you take the issue seriously. You should also appeal to your audience by making it clear that you understand and care about their interests.

YOUR TURN 5   Considering Audience and Purpose

Your purpose is to persuade someone who has the power to grant your request. Use the questions above to figure out who that person or group of people is and think about what you know about them.

Cooperative Learning

Analysis Groups. Students may benefit from working collaboratively to identify audience and purpose for their letters. Divide the class into randomly selected groups of three or four. Then, have students present their issues and work with the group to identify the person or organization that could help resolve each issue. Students should write down the reasons the group gives about why the person or organization would be helpful. You may wish to have a representative from each group share one issue and the group's analysis with the class.

Meeting INDIVIDUAL NEEDS

LEARNERS HAVING DIFFICULTY
Students may have difficulty understanding the concept of selecting a voice appropriate to a particular audience. Remind students that when they speak, they use different voices for different audiences. To illustrate this in a humorous way, ask a student to act out the following examples of persuasion:

- convincing a baby not to eat sand
- persuading a friend to share a sandwich
- persuading a teacher to grant a homework extension

Students should understand that just as a speaker can select different voices to suit different audiences, so can a writer.

YOUR TURN 5

To help you quickly assess the students' comprehension of the concept of audience and purpose, ask them to write one sentence that identifies their audience and states how they think their audience feels about the issue.

MINI-LESSON CRITICAL THINKING

Understanding Your Audience

ANSWERS
Here are possible answers.

1. **Possible objection:** The principal is worried that the students involved with the after-school tutoring sessions will miss their transportation home. **Possible reason:** To ensure that students will not miss their transportation, tutors will be responsible for keeping sessions on schedule.

2. **Possible objection:** Parents might object to their children working with a tutor parents do not know. **Possible reason:** To address parents' concerns, the school could provide an opportunity for parents to meet the tutors.

3. **Possible objection:** The older students might object to the extra time required to tutor. **Possible reason:** To provide additional motivation, tutors will receive extra credit for volunteering their time.

MINI-LESSON CRITICAL THINKING

Understanding Your Audience

Imagine sweltering under the hot summer sun at the beach when a vendor selling mugs of steaming hot chocolate comes along. Are you tempted to buy? Of course not. The vendor has forgotten the basic rule of persuasion: Appeal to your audience's interests. Once you know your audience's interests, you can predict their main **objection,** or reason why they might disagree with you. Objections often revolve around how much time or effort a proposed change would take, or how much the change would cost. By appealing to your audience's interests, you can make objections such as these seem less important.

TIP An objection is also called a **counterargument.**

THINKING IT THROUGH — Addressing Objections

You want to persuade the city council to support a Latino cultural festival. Here's how to address their objection.

▶ **STEP 1** Identify the main reason your audience might disagree with you.

The city council might say that having a Latino cultural festival would be expensive.

▶ **STEP 2** Consider what is important to this audience.

- saving money
- bringing people together

▶ **STEP 3** Based on your audience's interests, identify a reason for your opinion that makes the audience's objection seem less important.

The festival can be a fun activity for the community, and it can be inexpensive. To save money, volunteers can organize the festival, and vendors can pay a fee to sell food and crafts.

PRACTICE

Suppose that you want to organize a tutoring program at your school. Older students would tutor younger students for one hour after school. Using the Thinking It Through steps above, identify a possible objection each of the audiences to the right might have. Then, list reasons that would address each audience's objection. Explain each reason.

1. the school principal
2. parents
3. students who would serve as tutors

RESOURCES

Critical Thinking
Practice
- *Communications,* WS. p. 149

Develop Reasons and Evidence

Answering the Big Question Understanding your audience's interests will help you to answer their main question—"Why should I care?" **Your audience will want to know the reasons why they should accept your opinion.** You can begin developing solid reasons by asking why your opinion makes sense.

Your opinion needs more support than reasons alone, though. Evidence must support each reason for the reasons to be believable. **Facts,** which can be proved true, and **examples,** which illustrate a point, can provide support for reasons. See how the following reason is supported by a fact and an example.

Reason: Volunteers help people.

Fact: Since 1961, Peace Corps volunteers have helped people in 134 countries around the world.

Example: My older sister volunteers by helping two fourth-graders with their math homework.

In the chart below, a student lists several reasons to begin an anti-littering campaign. In the middle column, the student gives facts and examples to support each of her reasons. In the right-hand column, she decides whether each reason and its supporting evidence will appeal to her audience.

> **TIP** The facts and examples should also provide **logical support** for your reasons. If they are not **relevant,** or clearly connected to the reason, your audience may become confused.

Reasons	Supporting Evidence	Appealing to Audience?
An anti-littering campaign will make people aware of the trash problem.	My parents had to pick up trash left by others. That made them be more careful not to litter.	Yes. Most people want to enjoy the games and not worry about litter.
An anti-littering program will earn money.	By recycling, we can earn 32 cents for each pound of cans. This money can help pay for clinics to train new coaches.	Yes. If we pay for clinics with recycling money, the league won't have to raise fees to cover these things.
Participating in an anti-littering program helps players earn badges in Scouts.	I can earn 2 badges. Several players I know participate in Scouts.	No. This will help a few of us, but not the president of the soccer league.

Meeting INDIVIDUAL NEEDS

MULTIPLE INTELLIGENCES
Interpersonal Intelligence. Arrange students in randomly assigned groups of five or six. Have group members work collaboratively to evaluate each other's supporting evidence. Students may use the following questions to determine the appeal of each other's supporting evidence for a particular audience:

- Does the evidence suggest that the audience's life will be improved?
- Does the evidence suggest that the audience will save money or time?
- Does the evidence suggest that the audience will feel better?

Group members should provide feedback and discuss any points that are unclear.

Cooperative Learning

Organization Groups. Students might benefit from working collaboratively to create a graphic organizer to organize their reasons and evidence. Suggest that students look back at the graphic organizer on p. 234 and ahead at the framework on p. 244. Allow students to decide on the form the organizer should take, but remind them that it should help them as they move from prewriting to drafting.

Meeting INDIVIDUAL NEEDS

ADVANCED LEARNERS
Some students may want to contact outside sources in person for information about their topics. For example, if students are writing to the city council to address a particular issue, they might visit a city council meeting to see how decisions are made. Or if they are trying to convince the school administration to have a food drive, students might visit a local food bank to discover what the food needs are and how food is distributed. You may want to obtain permission from parents or guardians and from the parties students intend to contact before beginning work on this assignment.

YOUR TURN 6

Check that each student has listed at least two reasons and that each reason is supported by evidence and an explanation of why the evidence is convincing. You may need to work with students who have difficulty deciding whether their reasons will appeal to their audiences.

Reference Note
For more on **facts** and **examples**, see page 233.

From the chart on the previous page, you can tell that this student realized that the last reason might not appeal to her audience. The president of a soccer league is probably more interested in soccer than in scouting. The student thought about possible objections the president might have to the project. Then, she came up with a reason that would take his objection into account. See her revision in the chart below.

New Reason	Supporting Evidence	Appealing to Audience?
This project will not take very much time or effort.	Teams will make posters and rotate collecting the recycling containers. Parents and players do all the work.	Yes. He won't have to find people to do the work. This reason will also show that picking up trash and recycling is not too much trouble, which I think might be his objection.

TIP It is not enough just to give evidence. You also need to explain why your evidence is convincing. In the chart on page 241, the student explained in the Supporting Evidence column the meaning of each piece of evidence. ("This money can help pay for clinics to train new coaches.") This kind of explanation is called **elaboration**.

KEY CONCEPT

YOUR TURN 6 Developing Reasons and Evidence

- Create a chart like the one on page 241, listing reasons and evidence to support your opinion. (Use the library to find facts to support your reasons.) Use the right-hand column to decide whether each reason will appeal to your audience.
- Replace any reasons that will not appeal to most of your audience. You should have at least two good reasons, each supported by facts or examples.

Choose and Focus a Call to Action

911 Means Action! When you dial 911, the operator knows instantly that you are asking for help. In a way, your persuasive letter is also a 911 call because it includes a *call to action*. **A call to action tells readers how they can respond to your ideas.** To get your readers to take action, your call to action must be both *reasonable* and *specific*.

RESOURCES

Your Turn 6
Practice
- *Communications*, WS. p. 150

Your Turn 7
Practice
- *Communications*, WS. p. 151

A **reasonable** request is financially possible and within the audience's power. There is no point in asking a local audience to spend billions of dollars to end all wars or to house all homeless people. Instead, your call to action should focus on smaller actions. Suggesting that your audience sign a petition or volunteer a few hours of time is not too much to ask.

A **specific** request is clear and tells exactly what you want readers to do about an issue. How can a reader tell whether "Please do more for our children" is a call for more sidewalks or for a new playground? The specific call to action, "Start a tutoring program for elementary students," would be more effective.

THINKING IT THROUGH

Writing a Call to Action

Here is how to write a reasonable and specific call to action.

▶ **STEP 1** Decide exactly what action you want to take place.

I want to see trash picked up and recycled at our soccer games.

▶ **STEP 2** State the call to action in concrete terms so there is no confusion about what you are asking.

Maybe my call to action is too vague. I can ask the league to get recycling containers and put them at the soccer fields.

▶ **STEP 3** Address your call to action directly to the audience.

"Please buy and place recycling bins for aluminum cans at the soccer fields. Then, ask teams to participate in the anti-littering campaign."

YOUR TURN 7

Choosing and Focusing a Call to Action

Decide what you want to ask your readers to do about the issue you have chosen. Then, use the steps above to write a **call to action** that is reasonable, clear, and specific. Be direct, but remember a call to action is a request. Therefore, be polite, too.

Critical Thinking

Analysis. Ask students to bring in examples of advertisements that have calls to action. Display the ads, and arrange the students in randomly assigned groups of five or six. Each group should choose and analyze one ad. Direct groups to identify the call to action and then decide whether it is reasonable and specific. If the call is not specific, you might ask the group to suggest ways to reword or revise it to make it specific. The group may write a call to action for the ad and share both the ad and the writing with the class.

YOUR TURN 7

Offer students the following checklist to evaluate their own or a peer's call to action.

- Is the call reasonable or does it ask too much?
- Does the call explain exactly what to do?
- Will the call motivate the audience?

Writing Workshop **243**

Quotation for the Day

"Nothing is ended with honour which does not conclude better than it began."
(Samuel Johnson, 1709–1784, English writer)

Write the quotation on the chalkboard, and use it as the basis for a discussion about endings of persuasive letters. Explain that attention-grabbing introductions, supporting middle paragraphs, and well-written endings all work together to build a convincing case.

Cooperative Learning

Letter-Writing Groups. Suggest that students work in small groups to collaborate on a letter. Students should prepare a message that reflects the group members' shared opinions and should use "we" instead of "I" in the body of the letter. Students should plan and write the letter as a group, and each member should read it for sense and for grammatical or mechanical errors before signing it. Explain that a letter signed by more than one individual often has more influence on its reader.

TEACHING TIP

Drafting Your Persuasive Letter

Some students may want to know the best order in which to place their reasons. Suggest that students place the strongest reason last, the second-strongest reason first, and the other reasons in the middle.

YOUR TURN 8

If you wish to assign a length to the students' letters, 500 to 700 words is appropriate.

Persuasive Letter

Framework	Directions and Explanations

Introduction
- Attention-grabbing opening
- Opinion statement

Grab your readers' interest right away with an **interesting beginning.** For example, you could begin your letter with an anecdote (a brief story), or a question. Next, include a clear **opinion statement** that tells your audience exactly what you think about the issue you have chosen.

Body
- Reason #1
  Evidence supporting reason #1
- Reason #2
  Evidence supporting reason #2
  and so on

- Support your opinion with at least two good reasons. Write a **paragraph for each reason.** You can arrange your body paragraphs in **order of importance,** starting with the most important reason, or in **climactic order,** ending with the most important reason.
- Support each of your reasons with at least one specific **fact** or **example** each.
- **Elaborate** support by explaining the meaning of each fact or example or by summing up your point.

Conclusion
- Summary of reasons
- Call to action

Remind your audience why this issue is important by **summarizing** your reasons in a single sentence. Next, tell your audience what they should do about the issue with a reasonable and specific **call to action.**

YOUR TURN 8 Drafting Your Persuasive Letter

Now, it is your chance to write a first draft of a persuasive letter. As you write, refer to the framework above and the Writer's Model on the next page.

244   Chapter 7   **Persuasion:** Making a Difference

RESOURCES

Writing
Writing Prompts
- *Communications,* TP. 55, WS. p. 152

Extension
- *Designing Your Writing*

Your Turn 8
Practice
- *Communications,* TP. 56, WS. p. 153

A Writer's Model

The final draft below closely follows the framework for a persuasive letter on the previous page.

Dear Mr. Matsuo:

    My soccer team won its game last Saturday. I was happy and excited until I started walking toward the parking lot. I passed cups and candy wrappers left in the stands and six trash cans overflowing with aluminum cans. Seeing all the trash that people did not throw away and the cans that could be recycled bothered me. With your help, we can improve the Eastside Soccer League. We need to start an anti-littering campaign to keep the soccer fields clean.

    An anti-littering campaign would help people become aware of the trash problem. Since I talked to my family about the problem, they have noticed how bad the trash is, too. After last Saturday's game, they made sure they picked up their trash so that they were not contributing to the problem. Letting people know there is a problem is the first step to solving it.

    If we make recycling part of the plan, the anti-littering campaign can earn money. By recycling aluminum cans, the Eastside Soccer League can earn 32 cents per pound. Since there are twelve trash cans at the soccer fields that each can hold about two pounds of cans, and there are fifteen games in the season, we could earn as much as $115.20. This money could be used to pay for clinics to train new coaches. That way, more people could get involved in the league because training would be available.

    Finally, this project will take little time and effort. This can be a project for the parents and the players. Each team will make posters encouraging people to be responsible for their trash. Also, the two teams playing the last game on a field will pick up trash left in the stands and empty the two recycling containers on their field. Once all twelve

(continued)

Margin annotations:
- Attention-grabbing opening
- Opinion statement
- Reason #1: Help people become aware
- Evidence (example)
- Elaboration
- Reason #2: Earn money
- Evidence (facts)
- Elaboration
- Reason #3: Easy to do
- Evidence (examples)

Connecting Reading and Writing

Before students read **A Writer's Model**, ask them to review the information on reasons and evidence on pp. 241–242 in the Reading Workshop. Have students use the Thinking It Through steps in **Critical-Thinking Mini-Lesson** on p. 240 to evaluate and discuss the letter. You may want to point out the margin annotations next to **A Writer's Model** that highlight the supporting evidence for each reason.

TECHNOLOGY TIP

Business Letter Format
Many word-processing programs have features that format documents as business letters. They also may have tools for addressing envelopes. If computers are available, encourage students to practice formatting business letters and envelopes. If computers are not available, have students refer to p. 758 for information on addressing envelopes correctly.

Reference Note
For more on **business letters,** see page 758 in the Quick Reference Handbook.

TIP If you have access to a computer, show your reader that you are serious about your issue by typing your letter. If you do not have access to a computer, write your letter using your best cursive or printing.

Elaboration

Summary of reasons

Call to action

(continued)

> containers are emptied, one parent can drive the cans to the recycling center. This work will take just a few minutes of time. Since the teams already rotate playing times, no one team will be stuck with this chore every week.
>
> An anti-littering campaign will help people become aware of the trash problem and earn money for the league without becoming a time-consuming or expensive project. Please buy and place recycling bins for aluminum cans at the soccer fields. Then, ask teams to participate in the anti-littering campaign.
>
> Sincerely,
>
> *La Vonne Barton*
> LaVonne Barton

Designing Your Writing

Business Letter Format To add to your persuasive letter's impact, use a business letter format like the one below.

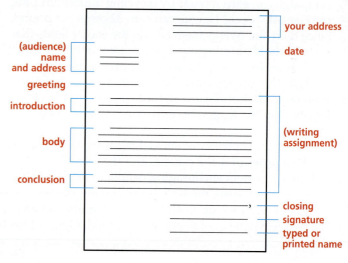

- your address
- date
- (audience) name and address
- greeting
- introduction
- body (writing assignment)
- conclusion
- closing
- signature
- typed or printed name

Persuasion: Making a Difference

A Student's Model

Concern for the global, rather than local, environment prompted sixth-grader Tyler Duckworth to write a letter to the President of the United States.

My name is Tyler Duckworth, and I am a sixth-grade student at Liberty Middle School in Morganton, North Carolina. I think the first thing you should do, Mr. President, is take specific action to protect our environment. As an avid reader of books about science, I am concerned about the natural wonders of our nation and of the world being preserved both for my generation and for future generations.

First of all, the pollution of our earth seems to be on the increase; factories, cars, and people continue to pollute. Statistics show that acid rain is on the increase, and the hole in the ozone layer is widening at an alarming rate. I feel action must be taken now, before it is too late. . . .

Also, the land in the rain forests is essential to our survival. Each year, more and more land in the rain forests is destroyed. If man continues to destroy the rain forests, the species present in them and the plant life present in them can never be replaced. The action taken must be firm and bound by law.

I believe that you, Mr. President, care about our country. You have stated in many speeches that I have listened to and in many articles that I have read that you care about our environment. It is essential that you, as our leader, do what is necessary to preserve the earth for future generations.

In my dad's office, he has a quote that reads, "We do not inherit the earth from our ancestors; we borrow it from our children." That, too, is my belief as a twelve-year-old citizen of the greatest country in the world. Mr. President, I ask you to please act now to save our country and our world.

Annotations:
- Opinion statement
- Reason #1: Increasing pollution
- Evidence (facts)
- Reason #2: Losing rain forests
- Evidence (facts)
- Reason #3: President's record
- Evidence (facts)
- Call to action

Connecting Reading and Writing

Before students write drafts of their persuasive letters, you may want to have them review the section on fact and opinion on pp. 231–232 of the Reading Workshop. Then, ask students to identify an opinion in **A Student's Model**. [I feel action must be taken now, before it is too late.]

Quotation for the Day

"There should be no distinction between what we write down and what we really know."

(Allen Ginsberg, 1926–1997, American poet)

Read the quotation aloud, and ask students to brainstorm how the writing process helps them to clarify and organize their thoughts. Point out that the revising stage allows writers to fine-tune their writing and to clearly express what they know.

TEACHING TIP

▶ **Elaboration**
Remind students that they should elaborate by explaining why their evidence is convincing. If students' evidence needs elaboration, you might suggest that they read their facts or examples to a partner and then state their explanations aloud while their partner takes notes. Students can then use these notes to help them compose their explanations.

Revising

Evaluate and Revise Content, Organization, and Style

COMPUTER TIP
Use a computer to help you revise the content of your paper. You can find many reference materials on CD-ROM, and you can use the Internet as a resource. For example, if you need additional support for a reason, you can look up facts on reliable Web sites or on a CD-ROM version of an encyclopedia.

Twice Is Nice Double the persuasive power of your letter by giving it at least two readings. In the first reading, focus on the content and organization of your first draft. The guidelines below can help. In the second reading, look at the individual sentences using the Focus on Sentences on page 250.

▶ **First Reading: Content and Organization** When you edit your letter, you evaluate what you have written and revise it to make it better. Use the following guidelines to make your letter more persuasive. First, answer the questions in the left-hand column. If you need help answering the questions, use the tips in the middle column. Then, use the revision techniques in the right-hand column to make necessary changes.

Persuasive Letter: Content and Organization Guidelines for Self-Evaluation and Peer Evaluation

▶ Evaluation Questions	▶ Tips	▶ Revision Techniques
❶ Does the introduction have a clear opinion statement?	▶ **Underline** the opinion statement.	▶ **Add** an opinion statement, or **revise** a sentence to state your opinion clearly.
❷ Does the letter give at least two reasons to support the opinion?	▶ **Put stars** next to the reasons that support the opinion.	▶ If necessary, **add** reasons that support the opinion.
❸ Does at least one piece of evidence support each of the reasons?	▶ **Circle** evidence that supports each reason. **Draw a line** to the reason each piece of evidence supports.	▶ If necessary, **add** facts or examples to support each reason. **Rearrange** evidence so it is close to the reason it supports.
❹ Does the letter explain each fact and example?	▶ **Put a check mark** next to each explanation.	▶ **Elaborate** by adding explanations for each fact and example.
❺ Does the conclusion include a specific and reasonable call to action?	▶ **Draw a wavy line** under the call to action.	▶ **Add** a call to action, or **revise** the call to action to make it more specific and reasonable.

248   Chapter 7   Persuasion: Making a Difference

RESOURCES

Revising
Practice
- *Communications*, TPs. 57, 58, WS. pp. 154, 155, 156

ONE WRITER'S REVISIONS This revision is an early draft of the letter on page 245.

> With your help, we can improve the Eastside Soccer League. <ins>We need to start</ins> An anti-littering campaign <ins>to keep the soccer fields clean</ins> ~~would help~~. **revise**
>
> An anti-littering campaign would help people become aware of the trash problem. Since I talked to my family about the problem, they have noticed how bad the trash is, too. After last Saturday's game, they made sure they picked up their trash so that they were not contributing to the problem. <ins>Letting people know there is a problem is the first step to solving it.</ins> **elaborate**

Responding to the Revision Process

1. Why did the writer revise the sentence at the end of the first paragraph?
2. Why did the writer add a sentence to the end of the second paragraph?

▶ **Second Reading: Style** You have taken a look at the big picture of your letter. In your second reading, you will look at the pieces of that picture by focusing on the sentences. One way to improve your writing is to make stringy sentences more compact. The following guidelines and the Focus on Sentences on the next page will help you evaluate your sentences.

PEER REVIEW
As you read a peer's persuasive letter, ask yourself these questions:
- Who is the target audience for this letter? Does the writer appeal to their interests?
- What is the strongest piece of support? What makes it stand out?

Style Guidelines

Evaluation Question	Tip	Revision Technique
Does the writer avoid long sentences made up of strings of ideas connected by *and*, *but*, or *so*?	**Highlight** long sentences that use *and*, *but*, or *so* to join two or more complete thoughts—ideas that can stand alone.	**Break** a long sentence with two or more complete thoughts into two shorter sentences.

Writing Workshop 249

Responding to the Revision Process
ANSWERS

1. The sentence was not a clear opinion statement. The revised sentence is more specific.
2. The added sentence elaborates on a reason to support the opinion statement.

Meeting INDIVIDUAL NEEDS

LEARNERS HAVING DIFFICULTY
Some students may have trouble identifying stringy sentences. One way to illustrate the effects of stringy sentences is to read examples aloud to the class. Exaggerate breathlessness and overemphasize each conjunction while reading.

TEACHING TIP

Eliminating Stringy Sentences
Tell students that they should select a style appropriate to their purpose. Because stringy sentences can sound like spoken language, they may be appropriate if the purpose is to express or entertain. For the purpose of persuading, advise students to avoid stringy sentences. Instead, encourage them to choose other stylistic elements, such as the use of analogy (concrete comparisons to explain and emphasize important points) or the use of vocabulary (active verbs and vivid adjectives to create a dynamic sounding, persuasive style).

Responding to the Revision Process
ANSWER
Each sentence now contains one complete thought. Also, in this case, three sentences are easier to read and understand.

YOUR TURN 9
To assess students' use of the content and organization guidelines on p. 248, ask students to list on the backs of their drafts the evaluation questions they used during the revision process, along with the specific actions they took as a result of their evaluations.

Focus on Sentences

Reference Note
For more on **parts of speech**, see Chapter 12.

TIP If part of the sentence does not express a complete thought, that part will not be able to stand alone in its own sentence.

Eliminating Stringy Sentences

When your purpose is to persuade, your style should also be persuasive. Avoid using stringy sentences. Reading long, stringy sentences is like listening to a person who goes on and on. They bore readers, and a bored reader is an unconvinced reader. To eliminate stringy sentences, follow these steps.

- First, find the conjunctions *and*, *but*, or *so* in a very long sentence. Put a slash mark before each conjunction.
- Then, see if each part has a subject and a verb. If each part of the sentence has both a subject and a verb and expresses a complete thought, then it can stand alone.
- Revise a stringy sentence by breaking it into two or more separate sentences. Each complete thought may have its own sentence.

ONE WRITER'S REVISIONS

> My soccer team won its game last Saturday ~~so~~ I was happy and excited until I started walking toward the parking lot ~~and~~ I passed cups and candy wrappers left in the stands and six trash cans overflowing with aluminum cans.

Responding to the Revision Process
How did breaking the sentence above into three sentences improve it?

YOUR TURN 9

Evaluating and Revising Your Persuasive Letter
Use the guidelines on page 248 and page 249 to evaluate and revise the content, organization, and style of your letter. If a peer read your letter, consider his or her comments as you revise.

RESOURCES

Focus on Sentences
Practice
- *Communications*, WS. p. 157

Publishing

Proofread Your Letter

Edit for Oomph Careless mistakes decrease the persuasive power of your letter. Proofread your letter for mistakes in grammar, spelling, and punctuation.

Grammar Link

Punctuating Possessives Correctly

The **possessive** form of a noun or pronoun shows ownership. Using possessives helps writers make their points more concisely. Read the example below.

the playground equipment at our school
our school's playground equipment

Here are four rules to remember about possessives.

To form the possessive case of a singular noun, add an apostrophe and an *s*.

girl's sweatshirt   car's bumper

To form the possessive case of a plural noun ending in *s*, add only the apostrophe.

books' pages   stores' signs

Do not use an apostrophe to make a noun plural. If you are not sure when to use an apostrophe, ask yourself, "Does the noun possess what follows?" If you answer *yes*, you need an apostrophe.

Do not use an apostrophe with possessive personal pronouns. These pronouns include *its, yours, theirs, his, hers,* and *ours.*

The dog missed **its** owner.

PRACTICE

Write the following sentences on your own paper, adding apostrophes where they are needed. If a sentence is correct, write *C* next to the sentence on your paper.

Example:
1. In visitors eyes, our towns trash is its biggest problem.
1. *In visitors' eyes, our town's trash is its biggest problem.*

1. Recycling helps meet the citys goals as outlined in its long-range plan.
2. Other towns have recycling programs.
3. Theirs are successful. Ours still needs the councils approval.
4. The countys landfill is quickly filling up from the four towns trash.
5. Voters signatures filled page after page of one groups petition.

For more information and practice on **possessives**, see page 598.

Writing Workshop **251**

RESOURCES
Grammar Link
Practice
- *Communications,* WS. p. 158

Quotation for the Day
"A good book is the best of friends, the same today and forever."
(Martin Tupper, 1810–1889, English writer)

Read the quotation aloud to students. Discuss with students how their own writing is a permanent record of what they are thinking at a given time.

Meeting INDIVIDUAL NEEDS

ENGLISH-LANGUAGE LEARNERS
General Strategies. Latin-based languages, such as Spanish, phrase possessives this way: "the book of the student." Explain that the sentences below mean the same thing but that the first and second sentences sound awkward in English.

That is the sandwich of Jason.

That sandwich belongs to Jason.

That is Jason's sandwich.

Grammar Link

Punctuating Possessives Correctly

ANSWERS

1. Recycling helps meet the city's goals as outlined in its long-range plan.
2. Other towns have recycling programs. C
3. Theirs are successful. Ours still needs the council's approval.
4. The county's landfill is quickly filling up from the four towns' trash.
5. Voters' signatures filled page after page of one group's petition.

Writing Workshop **251**

Publish Your Letter

Post It! Publishing a persuasive letter is simple. It requires an envelope, a correct address, and a stamp. Just mail it to the person or the individual people in your target audience. Here are two other ways to reach your readers.

- Even if you will not be mailing your letter, but handing it to someone you know well, use a business envelope to show that you mean business.
- If you have access to e-mail, you can send the letter electronically. Make sure you carefully type the message to avoid introducing mistakes. Be sure to confirm your readers' addresses before sending your letter.

Reflect on Your Letter

Building Your Portfolio The best way to judge your letter's effectiveness is to see what response you get. You may have to wait a while. Factors you may not know about may lead to a "No," a vague response such as "We will consider your request," or no response at all. However, you can judge your letter in the context of your entire portfolio by answering the following questions.

- What are my strengths as a writer? What did I do well in this piece and in other pieces in my portfolio? Which piece was my best or favorite? Why?
- What writing skills do I need to work on? If I had the chance, what would I do differently in this piece or in other pieces in my portfolio? Why?
- What are my goals as a writer now? What kinds of writing does my portfolio seem to be missing? What would I like to try next?

YOUR TURN 10 — Proofreading, Publishing, and Reflecting on Your Persuasive Letter

- Correct mistakes in punctuation, spelling, capitalization, and grammar. Pay particular attention to possessives.
- Publish your letter to your target audience.
- Answer the Reflect on Your Letter questions above. Record your responses in a learning log, or include them in your portfolio.

252 Chapter 7 **Persuasion:** Making a Difference

MINI-LESSON: TEST TAKING

Answering Questions That Ask You to Persuade

Some writing tests ask you to choose and support an opinion on an issue. Your response may be a persuasive letter or essay. If the following prompt were on a test, how would you approach it?

> The city council has a limited budget for a new park. It is trying to decide between spending money for large shade trees or for an in-line skating path. Decide how you think the money should be spent. Then, write a letter convincing the city council to vote in favor of your decision. Give three reasons for your opinion.

THINKING IT THROUGH — Writing a Persuasive Essay

▶ **STEP 1** Identify the task the prompt is asking you to do.

The prompt asks me to decide how the council should spend the money. I have to write a letter stating my opinion and give three reasons to support it.

▶ **STEP 2** Decide on your opinion.

I like in-line skating, but I think trees are more important.

▶ **STEP 3** Develop three reasons to support your opinion.

1. More people will enjoy trees.
2. Trees give shade, which makes the park more comfortable.
3. Trees take time to grow, so we need to plant them now. A skating path can be added any time.

▶ **STEP 4** Develop evidence (facts and examples) to support your reasons.

1. All people appreciate trees. I only know people my age who skate.
2. Summer temperatures are in the 90s. Shade will keep the playground and picnic tables cool even in hot weather.
3. We planted a tree when I was six, and it is still not as tall as our house.

▶ **STEP 5** Write your essay. Include your opinion in the introduction, make each reason a paragraph—with support—and give a call to action in your conclusion.

▶ **STEP 6** Edit (evaluate, revise, proofread) your essay.

Writing Workshop **253**

RESOURCES

Test Taking
Practice
- *Communications,* WS. p. 159

TEACHING TIP

Writing a Humorous Advertisement
To give students a better understanding of how humorous advertisements work, have them bring in print ads or even videotapes of television ads that they find funny. You may want to preview the ads before sharing them with the class. Work together as a whole class to analyze what makes the ads funny and to identify their use of the techniques that are discussed on pp. 254–255.

Connections to Life

Writing a Humorous Advertisement

Is all persuasive writing serious? Not at all. Many people, in fact, find humor more persuasive than logic. Advertisers often rely on humor to persuade their audiences to buy their products. Humorous advertisements usually include these elements: a specific **product** being sold; a **reason** for buying the product, and funny **sounds** or **visuals**. Here is an example of a humorous print ad. Can you identify the elements?

Must be the **Grow Strong Vitamins** you gave her...

Grow Strong Vitamins give your children the boost they need to grow strong bones and healthy bodies. Who knows what your child could do with **Grow Strong Vitamins**? Try them and see!

A Little Imagination To come up with an idea for a humorous ad, begin by identifying a product you would like to advertise. Next, think of a brand name for your product. Brainstorm a list of reasons why people should buy your product. Then, choose a humorous way to get one of those reasons across to an audience. Consider these techniques.

- **Exaggeration** Exaggerate one of the claims of your product. This is the technique the ad on page 254 uses, exaggerating how strong and healthy children who use Grow Strong Vitamins become.

- **Irony** To create humor, say or show the opposite of what readers expect. You might show a family riding in a car. The dad says, "How much longer?" Then, the mom says, "Are we there yet?" The slogan would read, "Kids aren't the only ones who look forward to the fun at Giggles Amusement Park."

- **Silliness** Use silly sounds, voices, words, or visuals, or create a silly character to pitch your product. Talking animals, aliens, and cartoon characters are all used to sell products. For example, a cartoon version of a computer virus might complain about an antivirus software that keeps killing him off.

Sell It Once you have a good idea of what will be in your ad, you can produce it. Create one of these types of ads.

- **Radio Ad** You can turn your idea into a radio ad if the humor is in the words and sounds you include. To do this, you will need to write a script, create sound effects, and record the ad.

- **Print Ad** If the words and pictures are the funny parts of your idea, you can create a print ad like the one on page 254. You may create your ad by cutting and arranging pictures and words, or you might try creating it on a computer with copyright-free pictures.

- **Television Ad** If both sounds and visuals are important in your ad, turn your idea into a television commercial. You should write a script for the ad and find a good location to shoot, as well as any costumes or props that are important for your idea. Cast classmates to act in your ad if you wish, and videotape it using your school's video equipment.

(For information about **speaking,** see page 719. For information about **graphics,** see page 687. For information about **video production,** see page 79.)

YOUR TURN 11 Writing a Humorous Advertisement

Using the guidelines above, develop an idea for a humorous advertisement. Then, produce the ad as a radio ad, print ad, or television ad, and share it with your class.

TEACHING TIP

Sell It
Take a moment to explain to students what "copyright-free" means. Copyright-free means that no person or organization owns the rights to a particular text or illustration. Images that are copyright-free are often filed and maintained by a particular organization, such as a government agency or the Library of Congress, but these organizations are not paid for the use of the image or word.

YOUR TURN 11

Have students evaluate their own ads based on the following criteria.

Language
- Does the script or text of the ad contain elements of humor, such as exaggeration, irony, or silliness?

Medium
- Does the medium (print, radio, or video) suit the ideas in the ad?

Presentation
- Once the text of the ad and the medium were selected, how well was the plan carried out? For a print ad, did the images and the text work well together? For a radio ad, did the pitch and tone of the voice match the verbal message? For a TV ad, did the audio and video elements work well together?

Overall Message:
- How could the overall effect of the ad be improved?

You can use students' evaluations to aid you in your assessment.

Focus on Listening

OBJECTIVES

- To evaluate a persuasive speech
- To identify a purpose for listening
- To develop criteria for evaluating persuasive messages
- To analyze a speaker's delivery and persuasive techniques

Quotation for the Day

"I dearly love to persuade people. There can hardly be a greater pleasure (of a selfish kind) than to feel you have brought another person around to your way of thinking."

(James Hinton, 1822–1875, English philosopher)

Read the quotation aloud. After a brief class discussion, ask students to freewrite a journal entry about the power of persuasion.

TEACHING TIP

Listen with a Purpose

Tell students that when listening to a persuasive speech, it is important to recognize the difference between facts and opinions, because the speaker probably will not announce when a statement is merely an opinion. Explain to students that the speaker's purpose may be to influence—not necessarily to provide the clearest possible presentation of facts. To help students distinguish between fact and opinion, review pp. 231–232 of the Reading Workshop. Then, remind students to listen carefully to distinguish between fact and opinion when they hear a persuasive speech.

WHAT'S AHEAD?

In this section you will evaluate a persuasive speech. You will also learn how to

- identify your purpose for listening
- develop criteria for evaluating persuasive messages
- analyze a speaker's delivery and persuasive techniques

Reference Note

For more on **evaluating a speech,** see page 730 in the Quick Reference Handbook.

Evaluating a Persuasive Speech

If you think you lack experience in evaluating persuasive speeches, think again. If you read magazines, watch TV commercials, or notice billboards, you are highly qualified. Any time you laugh at a clever advertisement or roll your eyes at a weak one, you are evaluating persuasion.

Listen with a Purpose

All persuasive messages, including advertisements, are created for the purpose of convincing people to do something or to believe something. When you listen to an ad or a persuasive speech, you may want to get information. However, your *main* purpose for listening will probably be to see whether you agree with the speaker's opinion. To do that, you must evaluate the speaker's message. Here are the elements to evaluate in a persuasive speech.

- **Content** is driven by the speaker's purpose. Since the speaker's purpose is to persuade, you can expect the content to include opinions, reasons, and evidence.
- **Delivery** refers to how the speaker delivers the message.
- **Believability** refers to whether or not you can believe the speaker.

Not all persuasive messages try to convince through solid evidence. Many persuasive speakers (and advertisers) also draw from a grab bag of *persuasive techniques.* **Persuasive techniques** rely on

256   Chapter 7   **Persuasion:** Making a Difference

RESOURCES

Focus on Listening Practice
- *Media Literacy and Communication Skills*
  —*Support and Practice,* Ch. 7
  —*A How-to Handbook*

Teaching Notes
- *Media Literacy and Communication Skills*
  —*A Teacher's Guide,* Ch. 7

emotional impact to "sell" an idea or product. Here are four of the most common persuasive techniques.

- **Bandwagon** A speaker may use this method to make you feel that everyone else is doing something, so you should do it, too. The statement "Everyone agrees that recycling is important" is an example of the bandwagon approach.
- **Testimonial** A speaker may try to persuade you with an example from his or her own experience, or a **testimonial**. For example, the speaker might say, "Volunteering at our local animal shelter has been a great experience for me."
- **"Plain Folks"** This method is used to make people feel that the speaker understands them. A speaker may try to show that he or she shares the concerns of the audience members. "Like you, I'm concerned about the cost of school supplies. Getting the supplies we need can be difficult when prices keep going up."
- **Emotional Appeals** This technique uses the audience's own emotions to get them on the speaker's side. An emotional appeal might tap into listeners' concern for others by telling sad stories about young refugees. Other appeals might spur the audience's school spirit or their anger about animal cruelty.

TIP Persuasive techniques are sometimes called **propaganda** techniques. They are used not only to sell products, but also to convince others to share an opinion. Listeners should be careful not to be convinced by propaganda alone. They should demand that a persuasive speaker also give solid support for his or her opinions.

Develop Criteria

Use the elements of a persuasive speech to develop *criteria* for evaluation. **Criteria** are standards you use to judge something. To develop criteria for a persuasive speech, first identify and interpret (or understand) these separate items of each element.

- **Content** Consider the **verbal elements:** major ideas and supporting reasons and evidence, facts and opinions, persuasive techniques.
- **Delivery** Consider the **nonverbal elements:** posture, gestures, eye contact, voice, facial expressions.
- **Believability** Consider the speaker's **perspective,** or attitude. For example, believable speakers are considerate of their audiences. They think about what their audiences will find persuasive. In contrast, speakers who try to force their opinions on their audiences without considering their audiences' views will be less believable.

Ask yourself what each item above would be like in a successful speech. The Thinking It Through steps on the next page can help.

TEACHING TIP

Develop Criteria
Remind students that they can use the criteria they generate here to evaluate their own oral presentations, either in rehearsal or after they make their presentations to the class.

Cooperative Learning

Criteria Groups. Have students work in randomly selected groups of three or four to devise a list of criteria for evaluating a persuasive speech based on each item listed for content, delivery, and believability. Each member of the group should contribute at least one question to the group list. The group should work together to finalize a sheet of evaluation questions, which may be used by group members to evaluate a persuasive speech.

TEACHING TIP

Evaluate a Speech
Have the entire class evaluate the same persuasive speech on video. Look in your school or local library or video rental store for some of the following titles:

- *The Speeches Collection* from Mpi Home Video includes speeches by Dr. Martin Luther King, Jr., and Robert F. Kennedy, among others.
- *Greatest Speeches of All-Time* from The Nostalgia Company includes persuasive speeches from world leaders of the twentieth century.

You will probably want to preview the video and inform parents and guardians of the material you will be presenting.

Wrap It Up

Metacognition. Help students reflect on evaluating persuasive speeches by asking this question:

1. How has evaluating persuasive speeches affected the way you will listen to speeches in the future?

Then, ask students the following question:

2. What are four persuasive techniques that rely on emotional impact? [bandwagon, emotional appeal, "plain folks," and testimonial]

YOUR TURN 12

Ask students to exchange their evaluations with a partner. They should compare not only their overall impressions of the speech but also the specific criteria they used. Have each partner record the similarities and differences between their impressions in a notebook.

THINKING IT THROUGH — Developing Criteria

▶ **STEP 1** Choose one item of a persuasive speech to evaluate, and ask yourself, "What should this be like in a persuasive speech?"

What should <u>eye contact</u> be like in a persuasive speech?

▶ **STEP 2** Brainstorm an answer to your question.

A speaker should try to look at various audience members, not just one or two people. This will make the speaker seem more honest and believable.

▶ **STEP 3** Turn your answer into a statement that says what a speaker should do when giving a persuasive speech. Then, develop criteria for the rest of the items listed on page 257.

A speaker should make eye contact with the audience often.

Reference Note
For more on **telling fact from opinion,** see page 231.

Evaluate a Speech

Once you have a list of criteria, you are ready to evaluate a persuasive speech. You may want to make a chart with your criteria in one column and space for notes in another. As you listen, remember your purpose. Do you agree with the speaker's opinion? To convince, speakers should support opinions with facts. Be sure you distinguish between facts and the speaker's opinions.

TIP As you listen to any speech, monitor your understanding, or make sure that everything the speaker is saying makes sense to you. Is anything confusing? If the situation allows, ask clarification questions to have any confusing points explained more clearly. After the speech, you might also look up in a dictionary or thesaurus any unfamiliar word the speaker uses.

YOUR TURN 12 — Evaluating a Persuasive Speech

- Follow the steps in the Thinking It Through above to develop criteria for evaluating a speech. Make sure your criteria cover content, delivery, and believability items.

- Listen to a persuasive speech and make notes about how the speaker does or does not meet each of your criteria. Does the speaker convince through evidence or "sell" through emotion? Afterward, rewrite any illegible notes, and add explanations for any short or confusing notes.

- Write a brief evaluation of the speech using the information in your notes. If other students evaluate the same speech, compare your impressions in a small group. Was the speaker effective? Why or why not?

258 Chapter 7 Persuasion: Making a Difference

RESOURCES

Your Turn 12
Practice and Reinforcement

- *Media Literacy and Communication Skills*
  —*Support and Practice,* Ch. 7, transparencies and worksheets
  —*Videocassette 2, Segment F*

CHAPTER 7 Choices

Choose one of the following activities to complete.

▶ EDITORIAL CARTOONS

1. The Politics of Art An editorial cartoon is a humorous drawing that tries to persuade readers to believe something. Editorial cartoons are usually located on the opinion page of the newspaper. Find an editorial cartoon and analyze it. Answer questions such as these: What is the artist trying to convince readers to believe? How does the drawing help the cartoonist make his or her persuasive point? Were you persuaded by the cartoon? Why or why not? Create a **bulletin board display** that includes the cartoon and a one-paragraph analysis.

▶ CAREERS

2. Persuasion in Practice Lawyers, advertisers, and newspaper columnists use persuasion every day. Research one of these careers. How do people in these professions get others to think a certain way? Do they use logical, emotional, or ethical appeals? (See tip on page 233.) Summarize what you learn about the career in a short **essay**.

▶ CROSSING THE CURRICULUM: SOCIAL STUDIES

3. On the Go What place would you propose to visit as a class field trip? In a small group, create a petition with specific educational reasons for your selection. Your petition should begin with a short **letter** explaining where you want to go and why. The letter should be followed by a **form** with spaces for students to sign their names and list their grade level.

▶ SPEAKING

4. Talk Them into It Make a **persuasive speech** to your class, either on the issue you chose for your letter or on another issue that is important to you. Make sure your opinion and call to action are clear. Support your opinion with reasons and evidence, and organize them in a way that will make sense to your listeners.

◀ PORTFOLIO

Choices **259**

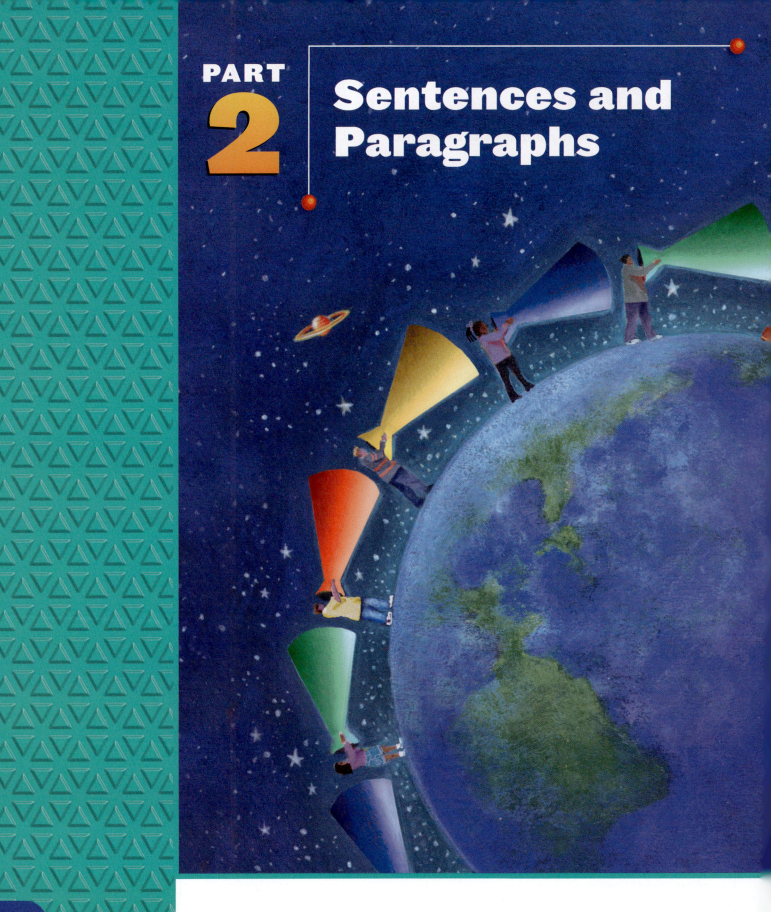

PART 2
Sentences and Paragraphs

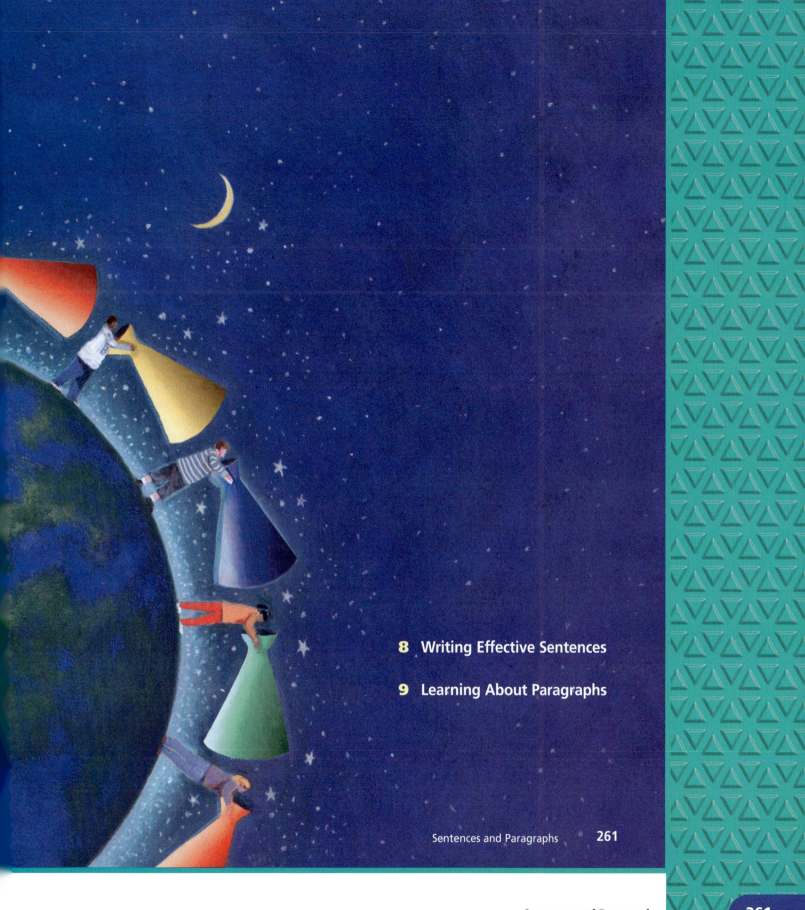

8 Writing Effective Sentences

9 Learning About Paragraphs

CHAPTER 8

PREVIEWING THE CHAPTER

- Complete sentences are the foundation of effective writing. In this chapter, students will learn how to identify and revise sentence fragments as well as run-on sentences and stringy sentences. Students will also learn strategies for combining sentences. You may use this chapter to teach the concept of complete and effective sentences and also as a reference that students might use throughout the year.

CHAPTER 8

Writing Effective Sentences

Writing Clear Sentences

Your goal in writing should always be to communicate clearly with your reader. A clear sentence gives your reader just enough information. It does not leave out any important pieces, and it does not run together or string together too many ideas at once. Clear sentences make it easier for your reader to understand what you are saying. You can learn how to spot three enemies of clear writing: *sentence fragments*, *run-on sentences*, and *stringy sentences*.

Sentence Fragments

What kind of sentence could you write about this picture? You might write something like this:

> The high jumper flips backwards over the bar.
>
> *or*
>
> Look at how high the bar is!
>
> *or*
>
> How does she know where to jump?

These groups of words say different things, but they have something in common. Each is a *complete sentence*. A **complete sentence** is a group of words that expresses a complete thought.

262 Chapter 8 Writing Effective Sentences

CHAPTER RESOURCES

Planning
- One-Stop Planner CD-ROM

Practice and Extension
- *Sentences and Paragraphs,* for Ch. 8
- *Combining Sentences,* Teaching Notes

Evaluation and Assessment
- Assessment Package
  —*Chapter Tests,* Ch. 8
  —*Chapter Tests in Standardized Test Formats,* Ch. 8
- Test Generator (One-Stop Planner CD-ROM)

A part of each thought is expressed by the verb: *flips, look, is, does know, jump.* Another part is expressed by the subject: *high jumper, you, she.* [The *you* is understood in the second sentence even though it is not expressed: (You) Look at how high the bar is!]

A **sentence fragment** is a part of a sentence that is punctuated as if it were a complete sentence. A fragment is confusing because it does not express a complete thought. The following word groups are the example sentences—with some important words left out. Notice how unclear the word groups are when written as fragments.

> Flips backwards over the bar. [The subject is missing. *Who* or *what* flips?]
>
> At how high the bar is. [The verb and the understood subject are missing. *What about* how high the bar is?]
>
> Where to jump. [This word group has a subject and a verb, but it does not express a complete thought. *What about* where to jump?]

Use this simple three-part test to help you decide whether a word group is a sentence fragment or a complete sentence.

1. Does the group of words have a *subject*?
2. Does the word group have a *verb*?
3. Does the word group express a *complete thought*?

You know the word group is a complete sentence if you answer "yes" to all three questions above. If you answer "no" to a question, the word group is a sentence fragment.

Exercise 1 Recognizing Fragments

Decide which of the following word groups are sentence fragments and which are complete sentences. Write *S* for a complete sentence; write *F* for a fragment.

1. We visited the pet shop in the mall.   1. S
2. A bright-eyed hamster chewing on pieces of carrot.   2. F
3. Named him Mustard.   3. F
4. Has pouches inside each fat cheek.   4. F
5. The pouches are for carrying food.   5. S

TIPS & TRICKS

Sometimes a fragment is really a part of a nearby sentence. You can correct the fragment by attaching it to the sentence that comes before or after it.

FRAGMENT
Mark is practicing his hook shot. **Because he wants to try out for the basketball team.**

SENTENCE
Mark is practicing his hook shot because he wants to try out for the basketball team.

When you attach a fragment to a sentence, be sure to check your new sentence for correct punctuation.

Writing Clear Sentences   263

Writing Clear Sentences

OBJECTIVES

- To identify and revise sentence fragments
- To identify and revise run-on sentences
- To identify and revise stringy sentences

Quotation for the Day

"You've got to know when to turn around."
(John Roskelley, 1950– , mountain climber)

Discuss with students how this quotation relates to writing sentences. [*The time for a writer to "turn around" is when he or she needs to revise.*] Explain that writers often write quickly to get an idea down on paper. As a result, the idea may come out as a sentence fragment or as a run-on or stringy sentence.

Meeting INDIVIDUAL NEEDS

MULTIPLE INTELLIGENCES
Bodily-Kinesthetic Intelligence. Students may benefit from copying the three numbered questions on this page onto index cards and then referring to the cards as they complete **Exercises 1** and **2.** Students may choose to circle or underline subjects and verbs within each word group.

Internet

- go.hrw.com (keyword: EOLang)

RESOURCES
Writing Clear Sentences Practice
- *Sentences and Paragraphs,* WS. pp. 1, 2, 3, 4, 5, 6, 7, 8, 9, 10

Cooperative Learning

Fragment Revision. To help students see that there are many ways to revise sentence fragments, you may want to let randomly selected pairs of students work on **Exercise 2**. Have each pair produce two revised versions of each fragment, with each student responsible for one of the versions.

Exercise 2 Revising Fragments

ANSWERS

Here are sample revisions.
1. I was watching TV alone.
2. I was watching a movie about aliens invading from space.
3. S
4. I had to light a candle because the batteries in the flashlight were dead.
5. I heard a strange noise in the backyard.
6. After our dog started to bark, I wondered what was outside.
7. I crept slowly to the door and looked out.
8. I saw two small, glowing eyes in the dark.
9. I laughed when I saw it was just the cat from next door.
10. S

Relating to Literature

Poets may use fragments in their writing. They are using "poetic license"—breaking the rules of formal writing to achieve an effect. Encourage students to look through books of poetry for examples of sentence fragments. Have students share their examples with the class. Ask students what effect the poets might have been trying to achieve by using sentence fragments. [*to create rhythm or rhyme; to evoke a mood by focusing on sensory words and phrases; to emphasize key ideas through repetition*]

6. Newspaper in lots of little shreds.   **6.** F
7. Making his cage quite comfortable.   **7.** F
8. He is plump and has white and tan fur.   **8.** S
9. A diet of mostly fruit, vegetables, and grain.   **9.** F
10. If you decide to raise hamsters.   **10.** F

COMPUTER TIP

If you are using a computer, you can use a word-processing program to help eliminate sentence fragments. Using the cut and paste commands, you can easily try attaching a fragment to both the sentence before it and the sentence after it. Doing so will allow you to see which sentence makes more sense. Check your writing for correctness and completeness after making changes.

Exercise 2 Revising Fragments

Some of the following word groups are sentence fragments. First, identify the fragments. Then, revise each fragment by (1) adding a subject, (2) adding a verb, or (3) attaching the fragment to a complete sentence. You may also need to change the punctuation and capitalization in your revised sentence. If a word group below is already a complete sentence, write *S* on your paper.

EXAMPLE   1. It a stormy Wednesday night.
   1. *It was a stormy Wednesday night.*

1. Was watching TV alone.
2. A movie about aliens invading from space.
3. Suddenly, the lights went out on the whole block.
4. Because the batteries in the flashlight were dead.
5. A strange noise in the backyard.
6. After our dog started to bark.
7. Crept slowly to the door and looked out.
8. Two small, glowing eyes in the dark.
9. When I saw it was just the cat from next door.
10. Maybe I should stop watching scary movies.

CALVIN & HOBBES © 1989 Watterson. Reprinted with permission of Universal Press Syndicate. All rights reserved.

Learning for Life

Using Fragments. Explain to students that sentence fragments appear often in newspapers, advertisements, and TV commercials; on street signs and the Internet; at bus stops; and in subway stations and airports. Ask students to give examples of sentence fragments in these places. [*a street sign that says "Parking 9:00 A.M. to 5:00 P.M. only"; an advertisement that says "Because you care"; a subway sign that says "Tokens here"*] Have

Run-on Sentences

A **run-on sentence** is actually two or more sentences run together without proper punctuation as if they were one sentence. It is often hard to tell where one idea in a run-on ends and the next one begins.

Like sentence fragments, run-on sentences usually appear in your writing because you are in a hurry to get your thoughts down on paper. This mistake happens when you leave out the correct end punctuation (period, question mark, or exclamation point) or when you use a comma to separate the sentences.

There is more than one way to revise a run-on sentence. You can break the run-on into two complete sentences, or you can link the two ideas with a comma and a coordinating conjunction such as *and*, *but*, or *or*.

RUN-ON   In 1962 John Glenn became the first American to orbit Earth, he made his second space flight on the space shuttle *Discovery* in 1998, when he was 77 years old.

CORRECT   In 1962 John Glenn became the first American to orbit Earth**.** **H**e made his second space flight on the space shuttle *Discovery* in 1998, when he was 77 years old.
[The sentence has been broken into two complete sentences.]

or

In 1962 John Glenn became the first American to orbit Earth**,** **and** he made his second space flight on the space shuttle *Discovery* in 1998, when he was 77 years old.
[Two complete ideas have been linked by a comma plus *and*.]

NOTE A comma alone is not enough to link two complete ideas in a sentence. If you use just a comma between two complete ideas, you create a run-on sentence.

RUN-ON   Sally Ride was the first American woman in space, she was a member of a shuttle crew.

CORRECT   Sally Ride was the first American woman in space**.** **S**he was a member of a shuttle crew.

Reference Note
For more information about and practice using **commas with coordinating conjunctions,** see page 568.

TEACHING TIP

Run-on Sentences
Students may overuse one method of revising run-ons, such as dividing them into separate sentences. To help students avoid overusing one strategy, remind them that good writing contains a variety of sentence structures. Some run-ons will be better divided into separate sentences (when the ideas are not closely related), while others will be better joined in one sentence by a comma and a coordinating conjunction or by a semicolon (when the ideas are closely related).

---

students discuss why fragments are used in these cases. [*Fragments are used when there is limited space and when people in a hurry need just basic information.*] Emphasize that while sentence fragments are acceptable in these contexts, they are not acceptable in formal writing because they may confuse a reader.

Timesaver

Save time in assessing **Exercise 3** by having students underline each revision they make. The underlining will help you spot the changes.

Critical Thinking

Metacognition. After students have completed **Exercise 3,** read aloud each item and ask students how they determined whether or not the sentence was a run-on. Some strategies that students might have used are underlining or circling subjects and verbs, using a mental checklist, or crossing out words. Ask a student to take notes on the strategies mentioned by the class and read the complete list aloud when you complete the review.

TECHNOLOGY TIP

Suggest that students look for stringy sentences in their own writing by using the word-count function in a word-processing program. To calculate the average words-per-sentence ratio, students should use the function to count the total number of sentences and the total number of words. By dividing the number of words by the number of sentences, students should find the average word-per-sentence count. Papers with sentences averaging more than twelve words should be checked. They may contain stringy sentences.

Exercise 3 **Identifying and Revising Run-on Sentences**

Decide which of the following groups of words are run-ons. Revise each run-on by (1) making it into two separate sentences, or (2) using a comma and a coordinating conjunction. You may have to change the punctuation and capitalization, too. If the group of words is already correct, write *C*.

Here are possible revisions.

1. and
2. C
3. ⊙
4. ⊙
5. C
6. , but
7. , but
8. C
9. C
10. ⊙

1. People constantly search for faster ways to communicate, the Internet is one tool that helps people share information quickly.
2. The earliest form of the Internet was designed over thirty years ago, and it was created to be used by the military.
3. The Internet has changed a great deal since then now it can be used by almost anyone who uses a computer.
4. The first e-mail program was invented in 1972, e-mail is a way to send messages from one computer to another.
5. Twenty years later, scientists in Switzerland created the World Wide Web, and *Internet* quickly became a household word.
6. The scientists planned to use the Web to share research with scientists in other parts of the world the new invention soon interested businesses and government organizations.
7. The programs that make the Internet and the World Wide Web work are very complicated they are not hard to use.
8. Many schools and libraries have computers that are connected to the Internet and the World Wide Web.
9. The World Wide Web began with four newsgroups in 1991, but it soon included millions of sites.
10. Many sites on the World Wide Web focus on school subjects, news, and hobbies, these sites can be useful sources of information.

Stringy Sentences

For variety, you will sometimes want to join sentences and sentence parts with *and*. If you string many ideas together with *and*, though, you create a **stringy sentence.** Stringy sentences ramble on and on. They do not give the reader a chance to pause between ideas.

STRINGY   The ostrich is the largest living bird, and it stands nearly eight feet tall, and it weighs over three hundred pounds when it is fully grown, and this speedy bird can run up to forty miles an hour!

BETTER   The ostrich is the largest living bird. It stands nearly eight feet tall, and it weighs over three hundred pounds when it is fully grown. This speedy bird can run up to forty miles an hour!

In the revised version, only two ideas are linked by *and*. These ideas can be combined into one sentence because they are closely related. Notice that a comma is used before the word *and*. The comma is also necessary to show a slight pause between the two complete ideas.

Exercise 4 Identifying and Revising Stringy Sentences

Some of the following sentences are stringy. Revise each stringy sentence by breaking it into two or more sentences. If an item is already correct, write C.   Possible revisions follow.

1. Thomas and José were playing softball at school, ~~and~~ Thomas hit the ball very hard, and then he saw it roll under the steps of the library.
2. Thomas peered under the dark steps to recover his ball, ~~and~~ when he reached for it, he saw a giant raccoon, ~~and~~ Thomas wasn't sure what to do next!
3. José told Thomas that raccoons are fierce fighters, and then José warned him not to anger the raccoon, ~~and~~ by this time, other softball players had gathered to offer advice.
4. Thomas finally rolled the ball out from under the steps with a baseball bat. The raccoon stayed completely still, and it hissed and looked fiercely at the group. Then Thomas saw why the raccoon was behaving so strangely.   **4. C**
5. Five baby raccoons were hiding behind the mother, ~~and~~ they were too small to protect themselves, ~~and~~ the mother raccoon was trying to frighten the softball players away!

Writing Clear Sentences   **267**

Meeting INDIVIDUAL NEEDS

INCLUSION
Previewing vocabulary for students should make the exercises and examples throughout this chapter less difficult. Give students a list of difficult words in each lesson and have the students locate the words in the text. Here are some words from the chapter that students may find difficult: *fragment, backward, aliens, crew, orbit, bacteria, float, missionaries, amateurs, myth, ritual.* Then, ask students to work with a helper to look up the meanings of the words in a dictionary. They can jot down the appropriate definitions on the list. Students can use their lists as they work through the chapter.

ENGLISH-LANGUAGE LEARNERS
General Strategies. Many students can eliminate stringy sentences in a focused exercise, yet once they begin to write compositions, the stringy sentences reappear in their writing. Give students the following strategy for finding stringy sentences in their own work: Starting at the beginning of a piece of writing, students should highlight the text until they come to the end of a sentence, whether there is punctuation at that point or not. Then, they should highlight the next sentence in a different color. After all the sentences are highlighted, students can examine the text to see how individual sentences are connected, looking especially for three or more sentences connected by "and."

Review A: Revising Sentence Fragments, Run-on Sentences, and Stringy Sentences

Decide which of the following word groups are fragments, run-ons, or stringy sentences. Then, revise each of these word groups to make it clear and complete. Remember to add correct capitalization and punctuation. If a word group is already clear and complete, write *C* for *correct*.

1. Not all animals see the world in the same way humans see the world.
2. See only light and dark shapes.
3. Squids and octopuses have very advanced eyes they see almost as well as humans.
4. The jeweled squid lives deep underwater in the Indian Ocean, it has white, blue, and red lights around its eyes to help it see in the dark water.
5. Several other sea creatures have their own "headlights," and these lights are sometimes produced by helpful bacteria, and the fish store the bacteria in special skin pouches.
6. Some owls can catch mice in total darkness by hearing alone others can find a mouse by the light of one candle placed nearly a quarter of a mile away from the mouse.
7. Grazing animals must have a wide field of vision so that they will know when an enemy is coming.
8. Rabbits and deer eyes on the sides of their heads.
9. Mammals that hunt other animals for food must be able to judge distance well, therefore their eyes are usually located toward the front of their faces.
10. Most apes do not hunt other animals for food, but their eyes are in much the same position as human eyes, and apes also see the same range of colors humans see.

Review A: Revising Sentence Fragments, Run-on Sentences, and Stringy Sentences

ANSWERS
Here are some sample revisions.

1. C
2. Fragment; Some animals see only light and dark shapes.
3. Run-on; Squids and octopuses have very advanced eyes. They see almost as well as humans.
4. Run-on; The jeweled squid lives deep underwater in the Indian Ocean. It has white, blue, and red lights around its eyes to help it see in the dark water.
5. Stringy; Several other sea creatures have their own "headlights." These lights are sometimes produced by helpful bacteria. The fish store the bacteria in special skin pouches.
6. Run-on; Some owls can catch mice in total darkness by hearing alone. Others can find a mouse by the light of one candle placed nearly a quarter of a mile away from the mouse.
7. C
8. Fragment; Rabbits and deer have eyes on the sides of their heads.
9. Run-on; Mammals that hunt other animals for food must be able to judge distance well. Therefore, their eyes are usually located toward the front of their faces.
10. Stringy; Most apes do not hunt other animals for food. Their eyes are in much the same position as human eyes. Apes also see the same range of colors humans see.

Combining Sentences

Good writers usually use some short sentences, but they don't use them all the time. An entire paragraph of short sentences makes writing sound choppy. For example, notice how dull and choppy the following paragraph sounds.

```
Quicksand is really just sand. The
sand is wet. The sand is loose. You can
sink in quicksand. It will not actually
suck you down. You might get caught in
quicksand. You can lie on your back. You
can float. Then you can roll or wriggle.
Your movements must be slow. You can get
to solid ground this way.
```

Now, see how the writer has revised the paragraph by combining some of the short sentences. Notice how sentence combining has helped to eliminate some repeated words and ideas. The result is a smoother paragraph that has much more variety.

```
Quicksand is really just wet, loose
sand. You can sink in quicksand, but it
will not actually suck you down. If you
are caught in quicksand, you can lie on
your back and float. Then you can slowly
roll or wriggle to solid ground.
```

You can combine sentences in several different ways. Sometimes you can insert a word or a group of words from one sentence into another sentence. Other times you can combine two related sentences by using a connecting word.

Inserting Words

One way to combine two sentences is to pull a key word from one sentence and insert it into the other sentence. Sometimes you can just add the key word to the first sentence and drop the rest of the second sentence. Other times you will need to change the form of the key word before you can insert it.

TIPS & TRICKS

To get ideas for a variety of ways to organize your ideas into sentences, look at sentences written by professional authors. Try imitating the style of a favorite author by using similar sentence structures in your own sentences or paragraphs.

Combining Sentences

OBJECTIVES

- To combine sentences by inserting words and groups of words
- To combine sentences by joining subjects and verbs
- To combine complete sentences

Quotation for the Day

"Writing is exploration. You write to find out what you're writing."

(E. L. Doctorow, 1931– , American writer and editor)

After you write the quotation on the chalkboard, ask students to respond to Doctorow's idea. In what ways do writers find out what they are writing about when they combine sentences? [*Ideas often become clearer and descriptions more vivid.*]

RESOURCES

Combining Sentences

Practice
- *Sentences and Paragraphs,* WS. pp. 11–22

Extension
- *Combining Sentences,* WS. pp. 1–20

Meeting INDIVIDUAL NEEDS

MULTIPLE INTELLIGENCES

Musical Intelligence. To help students grasp the importance of sentence combining to strong writing, ask them what a rock concert would be like if the guitarists played everything in one chord and at the same tempo or beat. What would they think of the performance? Then, point out that if a writer repeats the same patterns and words in short, choppy sentences, the writing can be as dull as a one-note song. Remind students that combining sentences eliminates repetition and improves the flow and rhythm in writing.

ENGLISH-LANGUAGE LEARNERS

Spanish. Adding key words that are adjectives may be confusing to some Spanish speakers. In Spanish, descriptive adjectives usually follow the nouns they modify. In addition, when an adjective appears before the noun, it often has a different meaning. Working through **Exercise 5** orally can help focus attention on the placement of adjectives in relation to the nouns they modify. You might point out that the words *retreating* and *moving* in sentences 4 and 5 are verb forms called participles and are used as adjectives.

TIPS & TRICKS

When you change the forms of key words, you often add endings such as *–ed*, *–ing*, *–ful*, and *–ly* to make adjectives and adverbs.

EXAMPLES
skill → skilled
crash → crashing
use → useful
quiet → quietly

	Using the Same Form
Original	Dr. Martin Luther King, Jr., was a civil rights leader. He was an American.
Combined	Dr. Martin Luther King, Jr., was an **American** civil rights leader.

	Changing the Form
Original	He was famous for his brilliant speeches. His fame was international.
Combined	He was **internationally** famous for his brilliant speeches.

Exercise 5 Combining Sentences by Inserting Words

Each of the following items contains two sentences. Combine the two sentences by taking the italicized key word from the second sentence and inserting it into the first sentence. The directions in parentheses will tell you how to change the form of the key word if you need to do so.

EXAMPLE
1. Chief Joseph was a Nez Perce Indian chief who fought for his people. He was a *brave* fighter. (Add *–ly*.)

1. Chief Joseph was a Nez Perce Indian chief who fought bravely for his people.

1. The name Joseph was given to his father by missionaries. The missionaries were *Christian*.   **1. Christian**
2. His name, Hin-mah-too-yah-lat-ket, means "thunder rolling down the mountains." That is his *Nez Perce* name.   **2. Nez Perce**
3. Chief Joseph fought the United States Army to defend his people's homeland. The fighting was *fierce*. (Add *–ly*.)   **3. fiercely**
4. When he realized he could not win, he led the Nez Perce band more than one thousand miles. The band was in *retreat*. (Add *–ing*.)   **4. retreating**
5. Chief Joseph's surrender speech is famous. The speech is *moving*.   **5. moving**

Inserting Groups of Words

Often, you can combine two related sentences by taking an entire group of words from one sentence and adding it to the other sentence. When the group of words is inserted, it adds detail to the information in the first sentence.

ORIGINAL The first known baseball game was played in 1846. It was played in Hoboken, New Jersey.

COMBINED The first known baseball game was played in 1846 **in Hoboken, New Jersey.**

ORIGINAL The game ended with a score of 23–1. It was played by the New York Baseball Club and the Knickerbockers.

COMBINED **Played by the New York Baseball Club and the Knickerbockers,** the game ended with a score of 23–1.

ORIGINAL The players were all amateurs. They were in the first organized baseball league.

COMBINED The players **in the first organized baseball league** were all amateurs.

Sometimes you will need to put commas around the group of words you are inserting. Ask yourself whether the group of words renames or identifies a noun or pronoun in the sentence. If it does, it is an *appositive phrase* and generally needs a comma or commas to set off the word group from the rest of the sentence.

ORIGINAL The All-American Girls Professional Baseball League had ten teams at its 1948 peak. The league was the subject of a 1992 movie.

COMBINED The All-American Girls Professional Baseball League, **the subject of a 1992 movie,** had ten teams at its 1948 peak.

ORIGINAL Baseball is a sport that is popular with people of all ages. It is played in countries around the world.

COMBINED Baseball**, a sport that is popular with people of all ages,** is played in countries around the world.

TIPS & TRICKS

If you move a phrase from one sentence to the *beginning* of the other sentence, you may need to add a comma after the introductory phrase.

Reference Note

For more information about and practice using **commas with appositive phrases,** see page 570.

After you combine two sentences, be sure to read your new sentence carefully. Then, ask yourself the following questions:

- Is my new sentence clear?
- Does it make sense?
- Does it sound better than the two shorter sentences?

If you answer "no" to any of the above questions, try to combine the sentences in a different way. Then, ask yourself the questions again.

Exercise 6 — Combining Sentences by Inserting Word Groups

Combine each pair of sentences by taking the underlined word group from the second sentence and inserting it into the first sentence. Be sure to add commas if they are needed.

EXAMPLE
1. Jorge read *Storm Chaser: Into the Eye of a Hurricane* for his science report. Jorge is <u>a boy in my class</u>.

1. Jorge, *a boy in my class,* read *Storm Chaser: Into the Eye of a Hurricane* for his science report.

1. *Storm Chaser* is an exciting book. It is <u>by Keith Elliot Greenberg</u>.
2. The book is a true story about a pilot named Brian Taggart, who flies a P-3 airplane. He flies the airplane <u>directly into dangerous storms</u>.
3. Taggart works for the National Oceanic and Atmospheric Administration. He is <u>trained in the study of weather</u>.
4. Scientists aboard his P-3 collect information about hurricanes. The scientists collect this information <u>using computers and other machines</u>.
5. Pilots like Brian help weather forecasters predict where and when a storm will hit land. These pilots are <u>called "hurricane hunters."</u>

Reference Note
For more information about and practice using **conjunctions,** see page 364.

Using Connecting Words

Another way you can combine sentences is by using connecting words called **conjunctions.** Conjunctions allow you to join closely related sentences and sentence parts.

Crossing the Curriculum

Science. Consider using the following activity to give students another opportunity to practice sentence combining. Ask students to collect information on water conservation from their science textbooks or from science magazines. Then, have them work in randomly selected groups of three or four to prepare a list of suggestions for conserving water at home. Encourage students to include both sentences and fragments in their lists. Each group should then pass its list to another group, who will write a paragraph that combines the sentences in the list using the techniques learned in class.

Exercise 6

ALTERNATIVE LESSON
Ask students to rewrite **Exercise 6** as a paragraph that includes complete and varied sentences. Remind students to check for commas after introductory elements, in compound sentences, and with nonessential clauses.

1. by Keith Elliot Greenberg
2. directly into dangerous storms
3. Trained in the study of weather,
4. Using computers and other machines,
5. Called "hurricane hunters,"

Joining Subjects and Verbs

Sometimes two sentences are so closely related that they have the same subjects or verbs. If two sentences have the same subject, you can combine them by making a *compound verb.* If the sentences have the same verb, you can combine them by making a *compound subject.*

The conjunction you use is important. It tells your reader how the two subjects or verbs are related to one another.

- Use *and* to join similar ideas.

ORIGINAL   The Sun Dance is an American Indian tradition. The Spirit Dance is an American Indian tradition.

COMBINED   **The Sun Dance and the Spirit Dance** are American Indian traditions. [compound subject]

- Use *but* to join contrasting ideas.

ORIGINAL   Mike will cook the main course. Mike will buy the dessert.

COMBINED   Mike will **cook** the main course **but buy** the dessert. [compound verb]

- Use *or* to show a choice between ideas.

ORIGINAL   Sara Tallchief may be elected president of the student council. Frances O'Connor may be elected president of the student council.

COMBINED   **Sara Tallchief or Frances O'Connor** may be elected president of the student council. [compound subject]

TIPS & TRICKS

When you use the conjunction *and* to link two subjects, your new compound subject will be plural. Remember to make the verb plural, too. A verb must agree with the subject in number.

EXAMPLE
Carlos and Hannah play on the same team. [The plural subject *Carlos and Hannah* takes the plural verb *play.*]

TEACHING TIP

Joining Subjects and Verbs
Students may need a reminder that a compound subject joined by *and* usually takes a plural verb. You may wish to review the two exceptions to this rule as well. (Two subjects that refer to one thing, such as *peanut butter and jelly,* or two subjects preceded by *each* or *every,* such as *each door and window,* require a singular verb.) You may also point out that in a sentence like the first combined example on this page, the predicate nominative *traditions* is plural to agree in number with the compound subject *sun dance and spirit dance.*

Exercise 7 Combining Sentences by Joining Subjects and Verbs

Use *and, but,* or *or* to combine each of the following pairs of sentences. If the sentences have the same verb, make one sentence with a compound subject. If the sentences have the same subject, make one sentence with a compound verb. The hints in parentheses will help you.

EXAMPLE   1. The climbing perch is a fish that can walk. The mudskipper is a fish that can walk. (Join with *and.*)

1. *The climbing perch and the mudskipper are fish that can walk.*

Combining Sentences   273

MINI-LESSON   Continued on p. 274

Identifying Subjects and Verbs. Review with students the definitions of *subject* and *verb.* Then, ask students to identify the <u>subjects</u> and **verbs** in the following sentences.

1. <u>Clowns</u> **are** just people in funny makeup.
2. <u>Each</u> **creates** his or her special face.
3. Using white greasepaint, <u>clowns</u> **paint** over their faces.
4. Then <u>they</u> **draw** a lot of red around the mouth.

Combining Sentences   273

Exercise 7 Combining Sentences by Joining Subjects and Verbs

ANSWERS

1. Climbing fish and mudskippers have side fins that work much like feet.
2. Mudskippers walk on mud flats and even climb trees.
3. Walking catfish are native to the East Indies but have been seen in Florida.
4. You might find walking catfish or climbing perch in warm, muddy water.
5. Mudskippers can hop more than a yard at a time and can catch insects as the insects fly.

---

1. Climbing fish have side fins that work much like feet. Mudskippers have side fins that work much like feet. (Join with *and*.)
2. Mudskippers walk on mud flats. Mudskippers even climb trees. (Join with *and*.)
3. Walking catfish are native to the East Indies. They have been seen in Florida. (Join with *but*.)
4. You might find walking catfish in warm, muddy water. You might find climbing perch in warm, muddy water. (Join with *or*.)
5. Mudskippers can hop more than a yard at a time. Mudskippers can catch insects as the insects fly. (Join with *and*.)

Joining Sentences

Sometimes you may want to combine two related sentences that express equally important ideas. You can connect the two sentences by using a comma and *and*, *but*, or *or*. The result is a **compound sentence**.

| ORIGINAL | A group of frogs is called an *army*. A group of turtles is called a *bale*. |
| COMBINED | A group of frogs is called an *army*, **and** a group of turtles is called a *bale*. |

Other times you may want to combine two sentences that are related in a special way. One sentence helps explain the other sentence by telling *who*, *what*, *where*, *when*, *why*, or *how*.

274 Chapter 8 Writing Effective Sentences

MINI-LESSON

5. Because of the mouth's importance, <u>clowns</u> **pay** special attention to it.
6. The <u>mouth</u> **reveals** a clown's personality.
7. Many <u>clowns</u> often **wear** a rubber nose.
8. <u>They</u> **may** also **wear** wigs on their heads.
9. A <u>wig</u> **can make** them appear bald or **can give** them a mop of curly blue hair.
10. Baggy <u>pants</u> and floppy <u>shoes</u> **complete** the costume.

Review the answers as a class.

274 Writing Effective Sentences

A good way to combine these sentences is to add a connecting word that shows the special relationship. In this kind of sentence combining, you create a *complex sentence.*

ORIGINAL The drawbridge was pulled up. The enemy knights could not get into the castle.

COMBINED **When** the drawbridge was pulled up, the enemy knights could not get into the castle.

ORIGINAL Their leader had not counted on the princess. The princess knew how to operate the drawbridge.

COMBINED Their leader had not counted on the princess, **who** knew how to operate the drawbridge.

Some connecting words that you can use to create complex sentences are given below. The word that you choose will depend on what you want your sentence to say.

Reference Note
For more about **complex sentences,** see page 397.

after	before	so that	when	who
although	how	that	whether	whom
as	if	until	which	whose
because	since	what	while	why

Exercise 8 Combining Complete Sentences

Following are five pairs of short, choppy sentences that need improving. Make each pair into one sentence by using the connecting word given in parentheses. Be sure to change the capitalization and the punctuation where necessary.

EXAMPLE 1. Planets move quickly. Stars move slowly. (but)
1. *Planets move quickly, but stars move slowly.*

1. I would like to learn more about stars. They are interesting and beautiful. (because)
2. Planets do not give off light of their own. Stars do. (but)
3. Some stars are fainter than our sun. Some are many times brighter. (and)
4. Our sun will change. The change will be slow. (but)
5. We must continue to study the stars and planets. We will understand how we fit into our vast universe. (so that)

Review B — Revising a Paragraph by Combining Sentences

ANSWERS

Here is a sample revision.

Some of the world's oldest cities have been found in Sumer, the land between the Tigris and the Euphrates rivers. These early cities began as farm villages. Eventually, Sumerian merchants began to trade with their neighbors in the mountains. The Sumerians sold the mountain people grains, and the mountain people sold them lumber, stone, and copper. Over five thousand years ago, Sumerians invented a system of writing to keep track of their trading. We know much about how ancient Sumerians lived because they left us many written records.

Review B — Revising a Paragraph by Combining Sentences

The following paragraph sounds choppy because it has too many short sentences. Use the methods you have learned in this section to combine some of the sentences. After you have revised the paragraph, read the choppy version and the new version aloud. You will notice how much better the paragraph sounds after you have revised it.

EXAMPLE   Ancient cities provide information. The information is about how people lived.
Ancient cities provide information about how people lived.

```
    Some of the world's oldest cities
have been found in Sumer. Sumer is the
land between the Tigris and the
Euphrates rivers. These early cities
began as villages. The villages were
made of farms. Eventually, Sumerian mer-
chants began to trade with their neigh-
bors in the mountains. The Sumerians
sold the mountain people grains. The
mountain people sold the Sumerians lum-
ber, stone, and copper. Over five thou-
sand years ago, Sumerians invented a
system of writing. They invented their
writing system to keep track of their
trading. We know much about how ancient
Sumerians lived. They left us many writ-
ten records.
```

Review C — Writing Clear Sentences

The following paragraph is hard to read because it contains some sentence fragments and run-on sentences as well as choppy and stringy sentences. Identify **two** fragments, **one** run-on, and **two** stringy sentences. Then, revise those sentences using the methods you have learned. Also, combine sentences in at least **two** other places.

Sumo wrestling is an unusual sport, not only because of the unique and impressive appearance of the athletes. On average weigh 330 pounds and dress in traditional loincloths. Sumo is based in myth. It is also based in ritual. There is a myth that the Japanese people gained control of Japan when a god won a sumo match with another leader. From a rival group. The earliest sumo matches, dating back over 1500 years, were rituals performed to ensure a good harvest, and sumo later became a way to entertain royalty, and Japan then entered a time of military rule, and sumo wrestlers were used in fighting. When peace returned, sumo became entertainment again, it came to be known as the national sport of Japan. The ritual elements of early sumo remain today. At tournaments, each day opens with a colorful and exciting ritual performed by the wrestlers. The ritual is called *dohyo-iri*. *Dohyo-iri* means "entering the ring." In this ceremony the wrestlers enter the ring, and then the highest ranked wrestler comes into the ring, and he claps and stomps on the ground in a very formal way, and when he is finished other highly ranked wrestlers repeat the clapping and stomping. The ceremony symbolically drives evil spirits away. The world got to see this ceremony when it was part of the 1998 Winter Olympics opening ceremony in Nagano, Japan.

HELP

To make sure you catch all of the errors listed in the instructions, try one of the following methods. (After you correct the errors, remember to choose two other places to combine sentences.)

- Use a sticky note to label each type of sentence error you find; then, see which sentence errors listed in the instructions you have not yet found.
- Make a copy of this paragraph and highlight each type of error in a different color.

Review C **Writing Clear Sentences**

ANSWERS

Sentences 2 and 6 are sentence fragments. Sentence 8 is a run-on sentence. Sentences 7 and 13 are stringy sentences.

Here is a sample revision.

Sumo wrestling is an unusual sport because of the unique and impressive appearance of the athletes, who on average weigh 330 pounds and dress in traditional loincloths. Sumo is based in myth and ritual. There is a myth that the Japanese people gained control of Japan when a god won a sumo match with a leader from a rival group. The earliest sumo matches, dating back over 1500 years, were rituals performed to ensure a good harvest. Sumo later became a way to entertain royalty. Japan then entered a time of military rule, and sumo wrestlers were used in fighting. When peace returned, sumo became entertainment again and came to be known as the national sport of Japan. The ritual elements of early sumo remain today. At tournaments, each day opens with a colorful and exciting ritual performed by the wrestlers. The ritual is called *dohyo-iri*, which means "entering the ring." In this ceremony the wrestlers enter the ring, and then the highest ranked wrestler formally claps and stomps on the ground. When he is finished, the other highly ranked wrestlers repeat the clapping and stomping. The ceremony, which the world got to see at the 1998 Winter Olympics opening ceremony in Nagano, Japan, symbolically drives evil spirits away.

RESOURCES

Writing Effective Sentences

Assessment

- *Assessment Package*
  —*Chapter Tests,* Ch. 8
  —*Chapter Tests in Standardized Test Formats,* Ch. 8
- *Test Generator (One-Stop Planner CD-ROM)*

CHAPTER 9

PREVIEWING THE CHAPTER

■ This chapter discusses the reasons for using paragraphs and the parts of a paragraph, including main idea, topic sentence, supporting sentences, and a clincher sentence. Students will study how to organize their ideas in paragraphs by using spatial and chronological orders. Students will also study how to show ideas are related by using transition words and elaboration. At the end of the chapter, students will have an opportunity to identify and write four kinds of paragraphs—narrative, descriptive, expository, and persuasive. You can use this chapter to teach the components of paragraph structure and as a reference tool that students may refer to as they write during the year.

CHAPTER 9

Learning About Paragraphs

GO TO: go.hrw.com
KEYWORD: EOLang

What Is a Paragraph?

A *paragraph* is a group of related sentences. Often a paragraph is part of a longer piece of writing. For example, in a paper about a visit to a wildlife park, one paragraph might focus on the apes and monkeys. Other paragraphs in the paper could each focus on another type of animal. In this way, the paragraphs would give readers a clear idea of what they might experience at the wildlife park.

Why Use Paragraphs?

Has a friend ever sent you a letter made up of one enormous paragraph? Did you find it hard to follow his or her ideas? Breaking a long piece of writing into paragraphs is more than just a way to give your reader's eyes a rest. Breaking writing into paragraphs is like providing a map for your reader. Paragraphs guide your reader through a piece of writing by showing where one idea (or setting, or speaker) ends and the next begins. Paragraphs also make it easier for your reader to understand the main point of a piece of writing.

278 Chapter 9 Learning About Paragraphs

CHAPTER RESOURCES

Planning
■ One-Stop Planner CD-ROM

Practice and Extension
■ *Sentences and Paragraphs,* for Ch. 9

Internet
■ go.hrw.com (keyword: EOLang)

Evaluation and Assessment
■ Assessment Package
 —Chapter Tests, Ch. 9
 —Chapter Tests in Standardized Test Formats, Ch. 9

■ Test Generator (One-Stop Planner CD-ROM)

What Are the Parts of a Paragraph?

Paragraphs are not all alike, but many of them have the same parts. Most paragraphs have a *main idea, a topic sentence,* and *supporting sentences*. In some paragraphs a *clincher sentence* ends the paragraph and ties the details together.

The Main Idea and Topic Sentence

All of the sentences in a paragraph usually point to a single main idea. This **main idea** is the main point, or central message, of the paragraph. Sometimes an author states the main idea in a **topic sentence.** When a paragraph has a topic sentence, it is often the first or second sentence of the paragraph. Sometimes, though, the topic sentence comes in the middle or at the end of the paragraph. In the following paragraph, the topic sentence comes at the end. Notice that all of the other sentences in this paragraph support, or point to, the main idea stated in the topic sentence.

> He thought he had failed in his life's work. Others agreed with him. He died poor and bitterly disliked. To us today, this rejection seems strange. He had helped to free five South American countries from Spanish rule. He had won major victories on the battlefield. He was anything but a failure. Over time, people began to accept the truth. Monuments were built to honor him. People started to celebrate his birthday. Today, Simón Bolívar is regarded as one of Latin America's greatest heroes.

 **Identifying Main Ideas and Topic Sentences**

How good are you at identifying main ideas and topic sentences? Each of the following paragraphs has one main idea. Read each paragraph, and try to identify its main idea. If the

Some paragraphs, such as those in narrative writing, will have a main idea without including a topic sentence. When reading a paragraph without a topic sentence, the reader must find the main idea by paying attention to the supporting details. A main idea that is not directly stated in a topic sentence is called an **implied main idea.** In your own writing, especially writing you do for school or on tests, you should generally tell readers the main idea of every paragraph with a topic sentence.

What Are the Parts of a Paragraph?   279

Meeting INDIVIDUAL NEEDS

MODALITY
Visual Learners. Draw the graphic organizer below on the chalkboard.

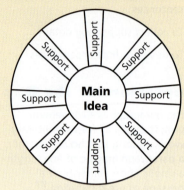

Use the drawing to explain that a paragraph can be compared to a wheel. The main idea or topic sentence is the hub, and the supporting sentences are the spokes. To highlight the comparison, provide students with a paragraph to cut up into sentences. Ask a student to tape the topic sentence onto the wheel's hub. Have other students tape the remaining sentences onto the wheel's spokes.

Exercise 1

ALTERNATIVE LESSON
After students have completed the section on supporting sentences on p. 281, have them return to **Exercise 1** and identify the supporting sentences in the paragraphs. Then, ask students to identify the types of support the sentences provide—facts, statistics, sensory details, or examples.

---

paragraph has a <u>topic sentence</u>, tell what it is. If there is no topic sentence, state the <u>main idea</u> in your own words.

1. <u>Unlike domestic cattle today, the wild buffalo on the plains were very hardy animals.</u> They lived and thrived when other animals, especially cattle, might have died. When winter blizzards hit the plains and prairies, the buffalo did not drift with the storm like cattle. Instead, they faced into the storm, either standing still waiting for the storm to pass or slowly heading into it. In this way the storm passed faster for the buffalo than it did for cattle, who would drift with the storm and frequently die from the elements.

   David A. Dary, *The Buffalo Book*

2. m.i.—As a boy, future baseball star Roberto Clemente had poor playing conditions and primitive equipment.

2. It was a warm tropical evening in Puerto Rico. Roberto Clemente was playing with a group of boys on a muddy field in Barrio San Antón. It was nothing at all like the great stadium in San Juan. There were bumps and puddles, and the outfield was full of trees. The bat in Roberto's hand was a thick stick cut from the branch of a guava tree. The bases were old coffee sacks. The ball was a tightly-knotted bunch of rags.

   Paul Robert Walker, *Pride of Puerto Rico*

3. <u>Comets, asteroids, and meteors are the speed demons of the solar system.</u> The average comet moves at 129,603 miles per hour; an asteroid's average speed is 39,603 miles per hour. Using radar, astronomers have clocked one meteor whizzing along at 164,250 miles per hour.

   Time-Life Books, *Forces of Nature*

280   Chapter 9   Learning About Paragraphs

Learning for Life

Writing Paragraphs. Tell students that the ability to write well-constructed paragraphs is a skill that they will probably use in the workplace. For example, students may need to write effective paragraphs for job applications, in memos to co-workers and supervisors, and in cover letters. For practice, ask students to think of a job that they would

Supporting Sentences

Supporting sentences have details that support, explain, or prove the main idea. Supporting sentences may be *facts*, *examples*, or other kinds of details such as *sensory details*.

- **Facts** are statements that can be tested and proved true. They can be checked in reference books or through firsthand observations. They often include **statistics,** or information based on numbers.
- **Examples** are specific instances of an idea. T-shirts and sunglasses are examples of things you wear.
- **Sensory details** are details that you see, hear, taste, touch, or smell. They make descriptions come alive for the reader.

In the following paragraph, notice that the writer uses a sensory detail and three facts. The supporting sentences explain the main idea that is stated in the first sentence.

Your bones resist breaks in two ways.	Topic sentence
Not only are they as strong as steel, but they also have the ability to stretch like a rubber	Example Sensory detail
band. Bone is made of hard mineral crystals.	Fact
These crystals give bone enough strength to withstand thousands of pounds of weight	Fact
without breaking. Also in bone is a stretchy material, called fiber, which prevents bone from easily snapping when bent.	Fact

Exercise 2 Collecting Supporting Details

Perhaps you collect details about the life of your favorite movie actor or TV star. In the same way, you can gather details about your main idea for a paragraph. Choose one of the main ideas on the following page. Then, make a list of three or four details that support it. Try to use at least one fact, one example, and one sensory detail.

Exercise 2 Collecting Supporting Details

ANSWERS

Possible answers follow.

1. Skateboarding requires skill.
   Details:
   - No handlebars or pedals are involved.
   - Your feet and weight control your turns.
   - Bumpy surfaces can make you lose your balance.
2. My room is always messy.
   Details:
   - My closet is full of sports equipment that spills into the room.
   - I keep my clean and dirty clothes in two piles on the floor.
   - Old magazines and papers clutter my desk.
3. I cannot stand storms.
   Details:
   - The boom of thunder scares me.
   - I am afraid of lightning.
   - I live near a river and worry about floods.

TEACHING TIP

The Clincher Sentence

Advise students not to use weak and redundant clinchers such as "Those are the reasons I like spring." Remind them that their clincher sentences should emphasize or effectively restate the main idea.

EXAMPLE
1. Main Idea: Stamp collecting is a useful hobby.
1. Details: (1) Stamps can be educational.
(2) One stamp series shows drawings of twenty different insects.
(3) The drawings are brightly colored.

1. Skateboarding (or another sport) requires skill.
2. My room is always messy (or neat).
3. I cannot stand snakes (or spiders, worms, or storms).

The Clincher Sentence

Once you have written a topic sentence and supporting sentences that reinforce your main idea, you may want to give your paragraph a strong finish. One way to do this is to make the concluding (last) sentence of your paragraph a *clincher sentence*. A **clincher sentence** ties together the information in your supporting sentences and reminds your reader of the importance of your main idea. Notice how the last sentence of the following paragraph ties the whole paragraph together.

> The shark's survival, which goes back 400 million years, is threatened by only one serious predator—humans. Commercial and sport fishers take more than one million sharks a year from the Gulf of Mexico alone. Each year fewer than seventy-five shark attacks on people are reported, most of which are not deadly. Clearly, we are much more dangerous to sharks than they are to us.
>
> "Introduction to Sharks," *Ocean of Know* Web site

Not every paragraph needs a clincher sentence. However, clincher sentences are often a good way to make your main idea stick in the reader's mind.

Exercise 3 Developing a Clincher Sentence

Write a clincher sentence for each of the following short paragraphs. Remember that a clincher sentence wraps up the information in a paragraph without just repeating it.

1. Guide dogs for the blind are more than just pets. They go almost everywhere with their owners. Unlike most pets, guide dogs wear special harnesses that help them direct their owners safely through unfamiliar places. Because they are trained to ignore strangers unless the strangers are in their owners' way, guide dogs should not be petted while they are working.

2. Every year, lightning kills many people. This happens because many people do not know what to do when a thunderstorm strikes. Some try to take shelter under tall trees that attract lightning strikes. Others think that if they only hear thunder and see no lightning there is no danger of being struck.

TIPS & TRICKS
To write a clincher sentence that is different from the topic sentence, refer to the paragraph's supporting sentences. You might begin a clincher sentence with a phrase like "For these reasons. . . ." Be careful of standard phrases like this one, though. A standard phrase will not work in every case. It also becomes repetitive when overused.

What Makes a Good Paragraph?
Coherence

A good paragraph needs more than a clear main idea and supporting details, facts, or examples. It also needs to have *coherence*. *Coherence* occurs when the details in a paragraph are arranged and connected in a way that makes sense to the reader. You can create coherence by following two steps. First, arrange your ideas in an order that helps your reader understand them. Then, connect your ideas with transitional words and phrases (like *first* and *then* in this paragraph), which will be discussed starting on page 287.

Organizing Ideas

To help get your ideas across clearly, arrange the information in your paragraphs in a sensible way. Here are two useful ways to order information.

- *Spatial order* presents details according to their location.
- *Chronological order* presents details in the order in which they happen.

Quotation for the Day

"I think the whole glory of writing lies in the fact that it forces us out of ourselves and into the lives of others."

(Sherwood Anderson, 1876–1941, American writer)

After reading the quotation, ask students the following questions: How does writing make us aware of others? Why is it important that writing be clear and organized?

In discussion, guide students to realize that a writer writes for specific audiences. By presenting ideas in a clear, organized fashion, the writer helps ensure that the audience will grasp his or her ideas.

Relating to Literature

Screenplays usually include stage directions that use spatial order to describe a scene's setting. Have students consult the opening stage directions for a screenplay, such as Sir Arthur Conan Doyle's "The Adventure of the Speckled Band," on pp. 409–423 of *Elements of Literature,* Introductory Course. Have them notice the order in which details are listed and discuss how spatial order makes a setting easier to picture.

Spatial Order   If you were describing the inside of a house, you probably would not include a description of the couch in a paragraph about the bathroom. You would not describe the kitchen sink in a paragraph about the bedroom, either. If you did, your reader would be confused about what can be found where.

Spatial order organizes details according to their location. When you describe something—a room or a sports arena, for example—you often use spatial order to give details as your eyes move from left to right or right to left. You might also arrange details from far away to close up or from close up to far away. Notice how the writer of the following paragraph uses spatial order to describe the view of Niagara Falls from above.

> . . . At altitude you see it all at once. You see Lake Ontario on one side, Lake Erie on the other, and linking them the thirty-four-mile Niagara River. Then, coming down lower, you see the falls themselves—where the river, along a front almost a mile wide, plunges over a 167-foot cliff and flows off through a deep, narrow gorge seven miles long. . . .
>
> Wolfgang Langewiesche, "The Spectacle of Niagara"

284   Chapter 9   Learning About Paragraphs

Exercise 4 **Using Spatial Order to Develop Paragraphs**

How would you describe a pond or creek, a city street, or the contents of a fish tank? Work in a group with one or two other students. Choose one of the subjects below, and list the details that describe it. Then, arrange the details in spatial order.

1. a grocery store
2. a bicycle
3. a park or building near your school
4. a painting or photograph you have seen
5. a local park or playing field

HELP

When writing a descriptive paragraph, brainstorm and arrange ideas at the same time by creating a map or sketch. For example, if you are describing a bicycle, sketch it. Then label the sketch with details that describe each of the bicycle's parts. Use the labels as notes for your descriptive paragraph.

Chronological Order

What happens after Dorothy is blown by a tornado to the land of Oz? How do you build a model ship in a bottle? What causes a solar eclipse? When you answer these questions, you explain how the event or action happens over time. To explain how something happens, you use chronological, or time, order.

Chronological order helps you tell a story (what happens to Dorothy in the land of Oz) or explain a process (how to build a model ship in a bottle).

- **Using chronological order to tell a story** Some stories are true, and some are made-up. The following paragraph is from a book of fiction.

> Strangely, when Ramona's heart was heavy, so were her feet. She trudged to the school bus, plodded through the halls at school, and clumped home from the bus after school. The house felt lonely when she let herself in, so she turned on the television set for company. She sat on the couch and stared at one of the senseless soap operas Mrs. Kemp watched. They were all about rich people—none of them looking like Howie's Uncle Hobart—who accused other people of doing something terrible; Ramona didn't understand exactly what, but it all was boring, boring, boring.
>
> Beverly Cleary, *Ramona Forever*

What Makes a Good Paragraph? **285**

MULTIPLE INTELLIGENCES
Logical-Mathematical Intelligence. To help students understand other ways to organize ideas and details to support a main idea, have them list ways to organize a group of students [*by age, alphabetical order, interests*] and foods [*by food group or color*]. Post the list where students can view it as they complete the chapter.

NOTE Paragraphs that tell a story do not always have a main idea. However, as you see in the paragraph on the previous page, the events in the paragraph do follow one another. This makes the paragraph easy to understand.

- **Using chronological order to explain a process** When your friend explains how to make a certain meal, he or she is explaining a process. The instructions for that process will be in step-by-step (chronological) order.

Notice how the writer of the following paragraph uses chronological order. He explains, step by step, how to get ready to make a simple movie using clear film and markers.

> After you have assembled your materials you will need a place to work. A desk or drawing table that is well lighted is best. Tape down a sheet of white construction paper on top of the desk. Next, unwind some of the film from the reel and tape it down to the construction paper with clear tape.
>
> Stephen Mooser, *Lights! Camera! Scream!*

NOTE There are two other ways to organize ideas in paragraphs. One way is in *order of importance*. When you use **order of importance,** you arrange details from most important to least important or from least important to most important. For instance, if you were writing a paragraph about your summer vacation, you could begin with the least exciting detail and save the most exciting detail for the end of the paragraph. The other way to organize ideas is in *logical order*. When you use **logical order,** you arrange ideas into groups. For example, if you were writing about frogs, you could discuss their diet at the beginning of the paragraph and their life cycle at the end.

Exercise 5 **Using Chronological Order to Develop Paragraphs**

Telling a story can be fun. Explaining a process can be easy. In this exercise you will develop these skills.

1. Write a group story. Work as a whole class or in smaller groups. Begin with one of the following "starters" or with one of your own. Then, take turns adding a sentence to the story. Be sure the events of the story are in chronological order.
   a. Late one night, a Texas rancher named Ellison looked out across his pastures. He was amazed to see big, strange lights bouncing playfully across the land.
   b. Monika was exploring a cave last weekend when she discovered a small pile of very old bones. At first the bones were a mystery.
2. Choose one of the following processes. Then, list three or more steps needed to complete the process. List the steps in chronological order.
   a. how to introduce yourself to someone
   b. how to make a paper airplane
   c. how to prepare a healthful lunch

Words That Connect Ideas

Carefully arranged ideas help make a paragraph coherent. Sometimes it is easy to tell how ideas are related. In a story, for example, one event usually follows another. This order helps you understand what happens in the story.

Sometimes, though, the reader needs help to see how ideas are arranged. Special words help show how ideas are related. These words are called *transitional words and phrases.* They are connectors that tie one idea to another, one sentence to another, or one paragraph to another. The following chart lists some common transitional words and phrases.

Transitional Words and Phrases

Showing Similarities	also	another
	in addition	too
	and	like
Showing Differences	although	however
	but	instead
Showing Causes and Effects	as a result	since
	because	so

(continued)

COMPUTER TIP

If the computers at your school are arranged in a network, you may be able to use them to do collaborative writing. Some types of computer networks allow writers sitting at different computers to work together on the same piece, to read each other's work, and to make suggestions and comments that all group members can see.

Exercise 5 Using Chronological Order to Develop Paragraphs

ANSWERS
Sample responses follow.

1b. ... First, Monika decided to take pictures of her discovery. Then, she marked a trail back to the entrance of the cave so that she could find it again. The next day, she returned to the cave with an assistant and some tools. They used brushes to clean the bones and special tools to measure them. They appeared to be prehistoric animal bones. Finally, they packed up the bones and took them to a museum for further analysis.

2a. First, get the attention of the person you want to meet. Usually, you can do this by smiling at him or her. Next, look the person in the eye, extend your right hand for a handshake, and say, "Hello, I'm _____." You might also want to add some information about yourself. Finally, be sure to say how pleased you are to have met the person.

Relating to Grammar

Students may benefit from knowing that the transitional words and phrases that appear in the chart on pp. 287–288 are also parts of speech. Remind students that parts of speech can change, depending on how a word is used in a sentence. The word *above,* for example, can be used as an adjective, an adverb, or a preposition. You may categorize the words in the chart according to their parts of speech for more practice.

TEACHING TIP

Transitional Words and Phrases

Transitional words and phrases are one way for students to create **unity** in paragraphs; however, as students write their compositions, you may want to provide these additional strategies:

- Before drafting, organize ideas using a cluster diagram and cross out ideas that are not related to the main idea.

- Use precise words consistently. (This strategy will also increase coherence in writing.) In a paragraph about types of terriers, the writer should include specific words such as *cairn terrier* more often than vague words such as *dog*.

Cooperative Learning

Transitions. Select a paragraph from a magazine or newspaper to provide students with additional practice in using transitional words. Have students form groups of three. Then, ask group members to cut small strips of paper and write one transition word from the chart on pp. 287–288 on each strip. Then, give each group a copy of the paragraph with its transitions left out and ask group members to insert the strips of paper in the proper places. When groups have finished, ask them to discuss with the class why they placed the transitional words where they did.

(continued)

Transitional Words and Phrases		
Showing Time	after before finally first	next second then when
Showing Place	above around across behind	here nearby there under
Showing Importance	first last	mainly most important

The following paragraph is about Babe Didrikson Zaharias, a great athlete. In 1932, she was the entire winning track "team" for an insurance company in Dallas, Texas. Notice how the underlined transitional words connect the ideas.

> Even as the teams entered the stadium, the loudspeakers were calling them for the parade onto the field. <u>When</u> the Illinois Women's Athletic Club was called, twenty-two athletes marched forward. A <u>second</u> club fielded fifteen girls, <u>another</u> twelve. All in all there were more than 200 female athletes on the field. <u>Then</u> they called the team of the Employers' Casualty Insurance Company of Dallas, Texas.... One lonely girl marched bravely down the field. The crowd roared.
>
> Harry Gersh, *Women Who Made America Great*

NOTE If you have trouble connecting ideas with transitional words, your paragraph may lack *unity*. A paragraph has **unity** when all of its sentences work together to support the main idea. For example, a paragraph about your pet turtle might describe the markings on its shell, but not what your pet cat looks like. The information about your cat is not related to your main idea.

Exercise 6 Identifying Transitions

The transition words in the following paragraphs show how one idea is related to another. Identify the transitions in each of the paragraphs. Use the chart on pages 287–288 to help you.

> 1. Building an igloo calls for skill and experience. First, the builder locates a site in firmly packed snow. Next, while standing in the outlined igloo, the builder cuts the snow into blocks of different sizes. Large blocks are used for the bottom layer, and thinner blocks are used for the walls. After the blocks are cut, the builder trims the top edge of each block to help the walls slope inward. Finally, the blocks are stacked to create a dome.

> 2. A polar bear's fur looks white at a glance, but a closer look reveals a different color. Each hair is a transparent tube. When the hairs are clear, the bear appears to be white. However, tiny green plants called algae can grow inside the hairs. As a result, the bear looks green.

Elaboration

A good paragraph *elaborates* (explains or illustrates) the supporting facts and details so that the reader has a clear picture of the main idea. To elaborate, illustrate your main idea by using more than one detail, fact, or example.

The following paragraph has a main idea and supporting details, but the writer has not elaborated on the idea.

```
The Great Pyramid at Giza, Egypt, is
one of the Seven Wonders of the Ancient
World. The pyramid is one of the most
famous structures in the world. Built
about 4,500 years ago as the tomb of
King Khufu, the Great Pyramid is also
one of the largest monuments to a
single person.
```

Reference Note
For more on **supporting details,** see page 281.

Critical Thinking

Metacognition. Below are two questions students may ask themselves as they evaluate the need for elaboration in a piece of writing.

- Do the details or supporting sentences in this paragraph tell me everything I need to know about the main idea?
- What information about the main idea is missing that I would like to know?

When revising their own writing, students should try to answer these questions. If students are evaluating a peer's paper, they should write notes based on each question on a separate sheet and attach it to the peer's paper.

What Makes a Good Paragraph? **289**

 Continued on p. 290

Elaborating with Prepositional Phrases. Writers often use prepositional phrases to elaborate on supporting facts and details. Refer students to pp. 361–362 for a quick overview of prepositional phrases. Then, ask students to identify the prepositional phrases in the following paragraph. Prepositional phrases are underlined.

Icebergs come <u>in different shapes and sizes</u>. An iceberg may be domed, <u>with a rounded top</u> <u>like that</u> <u>of an old mountain</u>. It

Now, read the revised paragraph. Notice how the writer has elaborated on the main idea and details by including more information.

> The Great Pyramid at Giza, Egypt, is one of the Seven Wonders of the Ancient World. The pyramid is one of the most famous structures in the world. **New fact:** In fact, it is visited by more than a million tourists each year. **New detail:** Many millions more recognize its familiar shape from postcards and photographs. Built about 4,500 years ago as the tomb of King Khufu, the Great Pyramid is also one of the largest monuments to a single person. **New fact:** At 450 feet, it is almost one and one-half times as tall as the Statue of Liberty and nearly three times taller than the Arc de Triomphe in Paris.

Exercise 7 Elaborating Details

The paragraph on the next page does not have enough elaboration. Add details, facts, or examples to improve the paragraph.

Timesaver

Have students work in small groups to complete **Exercise 7.** This will save you time in assessment if you select one paper from each group and use it to evaluate every member of the group on an equal basis.

MINI-LESSON

may be blocky, a great squared slab <u>of floating ice</u>. It may also be tabular, almost <u>like a tombstone</u> <u>on its side</u> adrift <u>at sea</u>. Some icebergs are small, but many are huge. <u>In 1956,</u> a naval icebreaker <u>in the Antarctic</u> measured a tabular iceberg <u>at about 12,500 square miles</u>. That's two-and-a-half times the size <u>of the state</u> <u>of Connecticut</u>.

Most of us do not think about the importance of electricity until the power goes out. Many everyday activities require electricity. After sundown, our reliance on electric power increases. Can you imagine how different life must have been before we had electricity and appliances?

What Are the Types of Paragraphs?

There are four different types of paragraphs.

Types of Paragraphs	
Narrative	used to tell a story or recount an event
Descriptive	used to describe a person, animal, scene, or object
Expository	used to provide information, including facts, instructions, and definitions
Persuasive	used to share opinions and convince others to agree with those opinions and sometimes take action

Which type of paragraph you write depends on your *purpose for writing*. If you want to **entertain** your readers or **express** yourself, you may write narrative or descriptive paragraphs. If you want to **inform** your readers about something or **explain** something, you may write expository or narrative paragraphs. If your purpose is to **influence** or **persuade** your readers to agree with your opinion about an issue, you will probably write persuasive paragraphs.

Different types of paragraphs can be written about the same subject. Notice that each of the following paragraphs is about volunteer activities, but each represents a different type of paragraph.

TIPS & TRICKS

When elaborating, look closely at each supporting sentence. Ask yourself whether you can add any information to explain or illustrate what you say in each sentence.

RESOURCES

What Are the Types of Paragraphs?
Practice
- *Sentences and Paragraphs,* WS. p. 30

TEACHING TIP

Narrative Paragraphs
Remind students that chronological order means that the events are told in the order that they occur. Reinforce this idea by asking students to create a short time line based on the paragraph about Joseph J. Gebhardt.

Reference Note
For more on **chronological order,** see page 285.

Narrative Paragraphs

Narrative paragraphs tell a story or describe an event or sequence of events. In narrative paragraphs, details are usually arranged in chronological order. Short stories are examples of narrative writing. However, narrative writing is also found in newspaper articles and in history books—anywhere that a writer wants to recount events from beginning to end.

> Joseph J. Gebhardt started reading for the blind around 1967. For years he had been playing guitar with a local band . . . and had bought a reel-to-reel recorder with the idea of immortalizing them. One night he heard an ad seeking readers for the blind and decided he'd had enough of being drowned out by . . . trombones. For a while he read *Science* magazine, but later he concentrated on *Smithsonian,* which he's been reading ever since.
>
> "Reading for the Blind," *Smithsonian*

Descriptive Paragraphs

Reference Note
For more on **spatial order,** see page 284.

Descriptive paragraphs create a mental picture of a person, animal, scene, or object by describing the details. The following paragraph uses spatial order to describe the plan for a monument to be built in honor of volunteers.

> Atop the monument will be a bald eagle with its thirty-foot wings outstretched, as if ready to take flight. At the base of the monument will be a nine-foot-tall, black granite monolith dedicated to all volunteers who have died during a volunteer activity. . . . Extending outward from the monument will be The Walls of Tribute. These walls, along with other Walls of Tribute located throughout the complex, will contain the names of volunteers who have given one thousand hours or five years of volunteer service.
>
> "Side View of Complex," *Friends of Volunteers* Web site

Expository Paragraphs

Expository paragraphs are used to explain subjects or ideas. Expository paragraphs can list facts or explain a process. Some expository paragraphs, like the one below, follow a **cause-and-effect** pattern. This paragraph explains the effects (or results) of a massive, volunteer cleanup.

Cause	In 1997, approximately 175,000 volunteers picked up at least three million pounds of garbage along the coasts of the United States.
Effect	As a result, both people and sea animals can enjoy cleaner and safer environments. Glass
Effect	bottles, lumber, and syringes are less of a threat to barefooted beachgoers. Fewer
Effect	seabirds, fish, and crabs will die entangled in plastic can holders, fishing nets, and fishing line. People put trash in the oceans, but by volunteering their time to help clean up after themselves, people are also the solution to the problem.

TEACHING TIP

Expository Paragraphs

Ask students to identify the transitional phrase in the expository paragraph that connects the cause to the effects. [*"As a result" connects the cause—volunteers picked up garbage along the coast—with the effects—ways the environment is cleaner and safer for both people and sea animals.*]

Persuasive Paragraphs

Persuasive paragraphs express an opinion about an issue. An **issue** is a topic about which people might disagree. A writer uses supporting details, or reasons, in a persuasive paragraph to convince readers to agree with his or her opinion. Sometimes, the writer of a persuasive paragraph encourages readers to take action on a particular issue.

> . . . Your community is really one of your best friends. It's only natural that you give something back as a way to say thanks. That could include raising money for a local charity, volunteering to clean
> *(continued)*

TEACHING TIP

Persuasive Paragraphs

Explain that the main idea of the model persuasive paragraph is an implied one. Help students identify the main idea by asking them the following questions.

- What do the supporting sentences focus on? [*volunteer activities*]

- What does the writer of the paragraph want you to do or think? [*People should volunteer in their communities.*]

- What is the implied main idea? [*People should give back to their communities by volunteering.*]

Exercise 8 **Identifying Types of Paragraphs**

If students have trouble finding paragraphs to identify, you may want to provide them with paragraphs from their literature, social studies, or science textbooks. Alternatively, you may want to have students work in groups of four and have each group member be responsible for finding one type of paragraph. *If your students use the Web for this exercise, be aware that Internet resources are sometimes public forums and their content can be unpredictable.*

How Are Paragraphs Used in Longer Pieces of Writing?

OBJECTIVE

- To divide a piece of writing into paragraphs

Quotation for the Day

"The house praises the carpenter."

(Ralph Waldo Emerson, 1803–1882, American poet, essayist, and philosopher)

Discuss with students how well-constructed paragraphs are a reflection of a writer's abilities. Ask students to freewrite about why it makes sense to build their writing skills.

TEACHING TIP

How Are Paragraphs Used in Longer Pieces of Writing?
When discussing introductory and concluding paragraphs, offer students the image of a sandwich. Suggest that the introductory and concluding paragraphs are like the bread, and the paragraphs in between, which supply supporting details, are like the filling.

(continued)
up your neighborhood, visiting nursing home residents on a regular basis, or collecting food for a local shelter. The possibilities are endless and whatever you do, your community will be grateful.

"Volunteering—It's So Easy, a Kid Can Do It," *GirlZone* Web site

Exercise 8 **Identifying Types of Paragraphs**

In a group with two or three students, look for examples of each of the four types of paragraphs: narrative, descriptive, expository, and persuasive. To find your paragraphs, look in magazines, newspapers, or books, or on Web sites. As a group, answer the following questions for each paragraph.

1. Which type of paragraph would you say this is? Why?
2. What was the writer's purpose for writing each paragraph—to entertain, express, inform, or influence? Was the writer successful in achieving his or her purpose? Why or why not?

Reference Note
For more on identifying **author's purpose,** see page 194.

Reference Note
For more on writing **introductory** and **concluding paragraphs,** see pages 755 and 756 in the Quick Reference Handbook.

How Are Paragraphs Used in Longer Pieces of Writing?

Paragraphs can exist by themselves, or they can be grouped together as a longer piece of writing. To make a longer piece of writing complete from beginning to end, there are two types of paragraphs you should add to the **body,** or main part, of a piece. These are *introductory paragraphs* and *concluding paragraphs.*

An **introductory paragraph** is like an introduction between two people. It gives your ideas a chance to say "hello" to the reader. An introductory paragraph is a way to get the reader interested in—and ready for—your ideas.

At the opposite end of a longer piece of writing is the **concluding paragraph.** It says "goodbye" to the reader, leaving him or her with a clear idea of what your piece was about.

RESOURCES

How Are Paragraphs Used in Longer Pieces of Writing?
Practice
- *Sentences and Paragraphs,* WS. p. 31

Dividing a Longer Piece of Writing into Paragraphs

When you write a paper or article, you should divide it into paragraphs. There are two main reasons you should do this:

- to give your reader's eyes a rest,
- to give your reader a chance to pause, and
- to show a change.

Writing nonstop without paragraph breaks is much like talking nonstop without taking a breath. If you talk without changing your tone of voice or without pausing now and then, people listening to you will have a hard time following what you are saying. Changes and breaks are as important to good writing as they are to clear speech.

To help make your reader aware of each idea in your composition, start a new paragraph when one of the following occurs:

- you need to express a new or different main idea
- you explain a different part of your subject or another step in the process
- you provide a different reason to support your opinion
- the time or location changes
- a different person or character speaks

Exercise 9 Dividing a Piece into Paragraphs

The following selection needs to be divided into separate paragraphs. Decide where to begin new paragraphs by watching for any of the changes noted above.

```
    Some jobs are dangerous, and some
jobs are a little scary. For a biospe-
leologist (bī′o•spē′lē•äl′ə•jist)—a
scientist who studies life underground—
a day on the job can be both. The bugs and
salamanders a biospeleologist collects may
not be dangerous, but getting to them is.
```
(continued)

Meeting INDIVIDUAL NEEDS

LEARNERS HAVING DIFFICULTY
Suggest that students follow the steps below when dividing a piece of writing into paragraphs. Encourage them to write down their answers until they become familiar with the process.

1. After every sentence, stop and ask, "What is this sentence about?"

2. Then ask, "Does the topic of this sentence tie into the topic of the sentence or sentences that came before it?"

3. If the answer to question 2 is *yes*, then the sentence belongs in the same paragraph.

4. If the answer to question 2 is *no*, then the sentence belongs in a new paragraph.

Exercise 9 Dividing a Piece into Paragraphs

ANSWERS
A paragraph break should occur after the second sentence and after the sixth sentence.

TECHNOLOGY TIP

Students can test where to place the paragraph breaks by typing the piece into a word-processing program. Then, they can experiment with different breaks without having to retype each version.

> **Review A** Writing a Narrative Paragraph
>
> **ANSWER**
> Here is a sample response.
>
> Once upon a time, there was a boy named Himderella. He lived in a lonely castle with his wicked baby brothers, who constantly made fun of him. Then, one day, Himderella was invited to a ball given by the Princess Meow Meow, who ruled all the kingdom. Princess Meow Meow was a star triathlete, so Himderella knew he would have to work hard to impress her. Every day, he trained in his spare time by running, swimming, and cycling. When the day of the ball arrived, Himderella snuck out the back door and confidently rode up to Princess Meow Meow's on his sporty mountain bike.
>
> **Review B** Writing a Descriptive Paragraph
>
> **ANSWER**
> Here is a sample response.
>
> My favorite food is leftover spaghetti. I love it because the flavors of tomato, garlic, and basil have blended into a tangy red sauce. I also like the way the spaghetti clumps together into one big noodle on my fork and makes a squishy sound when it drops on my plate. Some things are just better after you leave them alone for a while.

(continued)

```
Sometimes, these scientists lower them-
selves thousands of feet into rocky
caverns that have never seen the light of
day. Other times, they crawl through cold
underground streams that are only inches
from the rock top above them. Either way,
these scientists are searching for blind
scorpions; small, jumping bugs called
springtails; and other creatures that live
in total darkness. This job is not for
people afraid of the dark or of bugs. It
is a job, though, for people with a sense
of adventure and an interest in finding
out just how the world under our feet
really works.
```

Review A Writing a Narrative Paragraph

Narration can be used to tell true stories or made-up stories. Write a narrative paragraph in which you use chronological (time) order to organize the details. Before writing your paragraph, review the order of your details to make sure the order makes sense. Here are some ideas to get you started.

- Tell how you learned to do a new activity such as riding a bike, swimming, or using a computer.
- Retell a children's story you remember.

Review B Writing a Descriptive Paragraph

Write a descriptive paragraph. Remember to use details to give the reader a sense of how your subject looks, smells, feels, sounds, and tastes. Use spatial order to arrange your details. Here are some ideas for a topic.

- Describe a person or place that is important to you.
- Describe your favorite food.

Review C **Writing an Expository Paragraph**

You will probably use expository writing more often than narrative, descriptive, or persuasive writing. You will use it to answer test questions or to give instructions. Write an expository paragraph to explain what you know about a subject. Remember to support your main idea by using details, facts, and examples. Here are a few ideas for subjects.

- Explain how to do something simple, such as making a sandwich.
- Explain why you enjoy your favorite hobby or activity.

Review D **Writing a Persuasive Paragraph**

Simply asking for something does not always get you what you want. To be persuasive, sometimes you have to *write* about what you want. Write a persuasive paragraph. Remember to give your reader reasons to believe your ideas. Here are some ideas for topics.

- Share your opinion about a school or community issue. For example, you might propose a recycling center for paper and cans at your school, or you might suggest that your community build a new public pool.
- Ask a local business to contribute to a fund-raiser for your school club.

Review C **Writing an Expository Paragraph**

ANSWER
Here is a sample response.

Let me tell you how to make a great sandwich. First, get some really grainy bread and slice a couple of pieces from it. Next, open a jar of your favorite condiment—I recommend honey mustard—and spread it on one side of each piece of bread. Good! Now your bread is ready for the filling, so put whatever you want on only one slice. Many people enjoy eating sandwiches made of ham and cheese, tuna fish, or vegetables, such as eggplant. Once you have placed the filling on one slice of bread, take the other slice and press it firmly on top of the filling. Now you are ready for the final touch: take a knife, slice the sandwich in half, and gobble it up.

Review D **Writing a Persuasive Paragraph**

ANSWER
Here is a sample answer.

I believe that our neighborhood would benefit greatly from the addition of a new public pool. In our state, the summers are long and hot. Often, temperatures hover in the ninety- to one-hundred-degree range. However, many residents of our community do not have air conditioning in their homes. A pool would give people the opportunity to cool off during the hottest part of the summer. In addition, a pool would provide a safe place for children to play and for adults to get exercise. Supporting the construction of a neighborhood pool means supporting the health and happiness of our community.

RESOURCES

Learning About Paragraphs
Assessment
- *Assessment Package*
  —*Chapter Tests,* Ch. 9
  —*Chapter Tests in Standardized Test Formats,* Ch. 9
- *Test Generator (One-Stop Planner CD-ROM)*

Teaching Strands

This teaching-strand chart shows you some connections between grammar instruction and the writing assignments in Part 1 of this book.

The *Elements of Language* grammar handbook is designed to be a flexible teaching tool that accommodates many teaching philosophies and styles. For example, some teachers will prefer to use the handbook as a reference source, having students refer to it only as the need for explicit grammar instruction arises. Others will use the handbook as a teaching text, having their classes work through the instruction, examples, and exercises in a more methodical fashion. Your personal teaching style and the needs of your students will determine the best way for you to teach this material.

 GO TO: go.hrw.com
KEYWORD: EOLang

 All resources for this chapter are available for preview on the *One-Stop Planner CD-ROM with Test Generator.* All worksheets and tests may be printed from the CD-ROM.

Writing Assignments	Rationale
AUTOBIOGRAPHICAL INCIDENT (Chapter 1)	Autobiographical writing calls for using first-person pronouns correctly, which requires understanding case, pronoun-antecedent agreement, and subject-verb agreement. Using quotations and contractions in dialogue to show informal speech patterns is common. Consistent verb tense and clue words advance the story coherently.
NEWSPAPER ARTICLE (Chapter 2)	Newspaper articles report specific factual details without editorializing. Fitting text in a contained space necessitates concise writing and use of precise verbs and nouns. Varying both sentence structure and sentence length adds interest. Quotations must be capitalized and punctuated accurately.
"HOW-TO" PAPER (Chapter 3)	"How-to" instructions create images through precise adjectives and adverbs, while words or phrases indicating location complete the mental picture. Transitional words can indicate the order of steps. Commas separate a series of steps or parts of a list; a colon may precede the list.
COMPARISON-CONTRAST ESSAY (Chapter 4)	Comparison-contrast essays need comparative forms of modifiers used with precise nouns to provide specific details. Transitional words or phrases signal the order of comparison. To avoid too many short, choppy sentences, writers should use sentence-combining techniques.
BOOK REVIEW (Chapter 5)	To describe a plot and offer an opinion when writing a book review, writers rely on carefully chosen positive and negative words, fresh descriptions, and words signaling order of events. Correct pronoun case must be used to show the author's point of view. Appositives are an easy way to provide additional information.
RESEARCH REPORT (Chapter 6)	Because research reports require a sophisticated writing style, students need to use correctly spelled, formal language to incorporate information and quotations from many sources. Writing a report demands attention to sentence structure, capitalization, and punctuation. Phrases and clauses create sentence variety, but sentence fragments should be avoided.
PERSUASIVE LETTER (Chapter 7)	Strong, clear action verbs and their objects help a writer to emphasize points and to build a case in a persuasive essay. Challenging questions and exclamations help clarify the writer's stance. Careful capitalization, clearly punctuated sentences, and correctly used words help avoid confusion.

Links to Grammar	Links to Usage	Links to Mechanics
▶ personal and possessive pronouns (Ch. 11)	▶ pronoun-antecedent agreement (Ch. 15); pronoun case (Ch. 17)	▶ capitalizing the pronoun *I* (Ch. 20)
▶ verbs, adverbs (Ch. 12)	▶ agreement (Ch. 15); tense (Ch. 16)	▶ punctuating contractions (Ch. 22)
▶ sentences classified by purpose (Ch. 10)		▶ punctuating quotations (Ch. 22)
▶ common and proper nouns (Ch. 11); action verbs, conjunctions (Ch. 12)	▶ subject-verb agreement with compound subjects or verbs (Ch. 15); principal parts of verbs (Ch. 16)	▶ capitalizing nouns (Ch. 20); commas, conjunctions, semicolons with compounds (Ch. 21)
▶ sentence structure (Ch. 13)	▶ using *don't* and *doesn't* (Ch. 15); using *who* and *whom* (Ch. 17)	▶ capitalizing and punctuating direct quotations (Ch. 22)
▶ adjectives (Ch. 11); adverbs and prepositions (Ch. 12)	▶ comparison of modifiers (Ch. 18); *between, among; good, well; than, then* (Ch. 19)	▶ using commas to separate two or more adjectives (Ch. 21); using colons with a list (Ch. 21)
▶ adjective and adverb phrases (Ch. 13)	▶ using modifiers (Ch. 18)	▶ commas with interrupters (Ch. 21)
▶ adjectives, nouns (Ch. 11); adverbs, conjunctions (Ch. 12)	▶ comparison of adjectives and adverbs, double comparisons (Ch. 18)	▶ spelling suffixes and prefixes (Ch. 23)
▶ sentences (Ch. 10); complements (Ch. 14)	▶ pronoun case (Ch. 17)	▶ semicolons, end punctuation (Ch. 21)
▶ adjectives (Ch. 11); adverbs (Ch. 12)	▶ comparison of modifiers, double negatives (Ch. 18)	
▶ pronouns (Ch. 11); complements (Ch. 14)	▶ pronoun-antecedent agreement (Ch. 15); pronoun case (Ch. 17)	▶ apostrophes with contractions and possessives (Ch. 22)
▶ clauses and phrases (Ch. 13)		▶ commas with interrupters (Ch. 21)
▶ independent and subordinate clauses, sentence structure (Ch. 13)	▶ formal, standard usage (Ch. 19)	▶ punctuating compound and complex sentences (Ch. 21); spelling (Ch. 23)
▶ sentences, fragments, subjects, predicates (Ch. 10); adverb and adjective phrases (Ch. 13)	▶ subject-verb agreement with intervening phrases, with indefinite pronouns, with compound subjects, and with subjects after verbs (Ch. 15)	▶ capitalization of titles (Ch. 20); punctuation of direct quotations (Ch. 21 & Ch. 22); capitalizing and punctuating sources (Ch. 20–22)
▶ transitive and intransitive verbs (Ch. 12); direct and indirect objects, subject complements (Ch. 14)	▶ principal parts of verbs (Ch. 16)	▶ apostrophes with contractions (Ch. 22); words often confused (Ch. 23); capitalizing the first word in a sentence (Ch. 20)
▶ kinds of sentences (Ch. 10)	▶ pronouns, including *whom*, as objects, nominative case pronouns (Ch. 17)	▶ end marks (Ch. 21)

PART 3: Grammar, Usage, and Mechanics

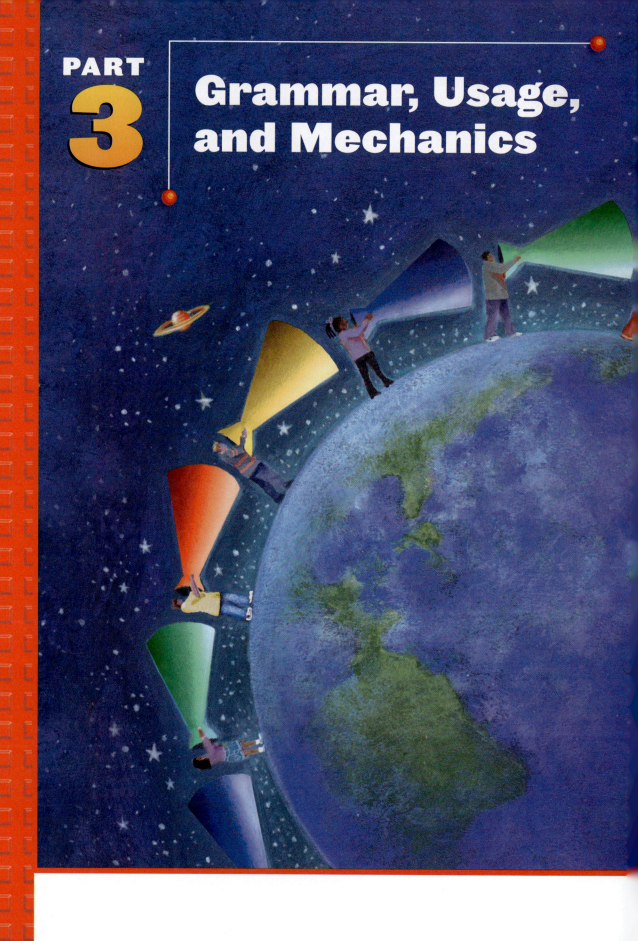

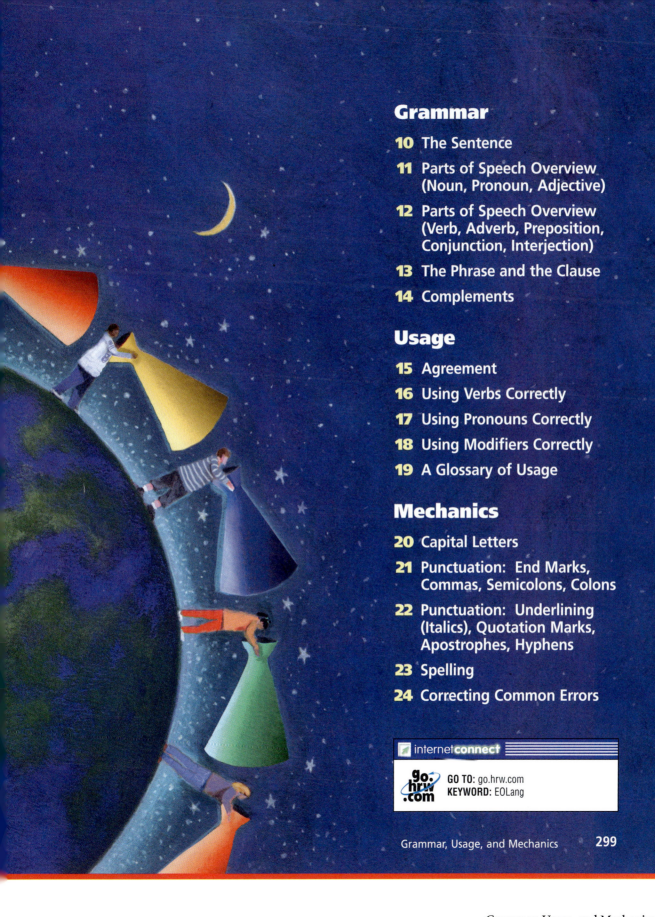

Grammar

10 The Sentence
11 Parts of Speech Overview (Noun, Pronoun, Adjective)
12 Parts of Speech Overview (Verb, Adverb, Preposition, Conjunction, Interjection)
13 The Phrase and the Clause
14 Complements

Usage

15 Agreement
16 Using Verbs Correctly
17 Using Pronouns Correctly
18 Using Modifiers Correctly
19 A Glossary of Usage

Mechanics

20 Capital Letters
21 Punctuation: End Marks, Commas, Semicolons, Colons
22 Punctuation: Underlining (Italics), Quotation Marks, Apostrophes, Hyphens
23 Spelling
24 Correcting Common Errors

internet connect

GO TO: go.hrw.com
KEYWORD: EOLang

CHAPTER 10

PREVIEWING THE CHAPTER

- This chapter begins by explaining the difference between a complete sentence and a sentence fragment. Then, subjects and predicates and compound subjects and compound verbs are discussed. The chapter ends with a brief explanation of the four kinds of sentences: declarative, imperative, interrogative, and exclamatory.

- The chapter closes with a **Chapter Review** including a **Writing Application** feature that asks students to create a comic strip using at least one of each of the following sentence types: declarative, imperative, interrogative, and exclamatory.

- For help in integrating this chapter with writing chapters, see the **Teaching Strands** chart on pages T297A–T297B.

USING THE DIAGNOSTIC PREVIEW

- The **Diagnostic Preview** can be used to determine your students' understanding of the difference between sentences and sentence fragments, of simple subjects and simple predicates, and of punctuating and classifying sentences by purpose. Because the preview is divided into three separate parts, you may want to use one part at a time to determine the areas in which students are having problems.

CHAPTER 10

The Sentence
Subject and Predicate, Kinds of Sentences

Diagnostic Preview

A. Identifying Sentences

If a word group is a sentence, add a capital letter at the beginning and punctuate the sentence with an appropriate end mark. If a word group is not a sentence, write *sentence fragment*.

EXAMPLES 1. followed the trail on the map
   1. sentence fragment

   2. the López twins come from Nuevo Laredo, Mexico
   2. The López twins come from Nuevo Laredo, Mexico.

1. we read the postcards from our Asian pen pals.
2. our school has a homework hot line.
3. definitely mailed the invitations yesterday   *3. frag.*
4. Will you practice guitar before dinner?
5. going to the Washington Monument   *5. frag.*

B. Identifying Simple Subjects and Simple Predicates

Identify the simple subject and the simple predicate in each of the following sentences.

300   Chapter 10   The Sentence

CHAPTER RESOURCES

Planning
- *One-Stop Planner CD-ROM*

Practice and Extension
- *Grammar, Usage, and Mechanics,* p. 1
- *Language Workshop CD-ROM*

Internet
- go.hrw.com (keyword: EOLang)

Evaluation and Assessment
- *Assessment Package*
  —*Chapter Tests,* Ch. 10
  —*Chapter Tests in Standardized Test Formats,* Ch. 10
- *Test Generator (One-Stop Planner CD-ROM)*

EXAMPLES 1. Last year my family traveled to Mecca, Saudi Arabia.
   1. *family*—simple subject; *traveled*—simple predicate

   2. The crowded corner market is having a sale.
   2. *market*—simple subject; *is having*—simple predicate

> **HELP**
> A subject or a predicate in Part B may be compound.

6. My grandmother plays mah-jongg with my friends and me every Saturday.
7. The farmers have plowed the fields and will plant potatoes.
8. At night you can rent roller skates for half price at the rink near my house.
9. On the sand lay a beautiful seashell.
10. On Saturday, Amy, Theo, and I walked through Chinatown and took pictures.
11. Many students in our class have volunteered for the charity softball game.
12. Where did you put Isabella's fuzzy, green wool sweater?
13. *Island of the Blue Dolphins* by Scott O'Dell is one of my favorite books.
14. Beyond the large rocks at the far end of the beach is a small cave.
15. During the last week of vacation, my brother, sister and I hiked through the rain forest.

C. Punctuating and Classifying Sentences by Purpose

For each of the following sentences, add the appropriate end mark. Then, classify each sentence as *declarative*, *interrogative*, *imperative*, or *exclamatory*.

EXAMPLES 1. Have you read this poem by José Garcia Villa
   1. *Have you read this poem by José Garcia Villa?—interrogative*

   2. We sampled a Cuban dish at the international fair.
   2. *We sampled a Cuban dish at the international fair.—declarative*

16. Please answer the phone. **16.** imp.
17. What a good time we had! **17.** exc.
18. Has anyone seen the cat? **18.** int.
19. They sat on a bench and played checkers. **19.** dec.
20. Whose book is this? **20.** int.

Diagnostic Preview

GRAMMAR

Sentence or Sentence Fragment?

Rule 10a *(pp. 302–304)*

OBJECTIVES

- To identify sentences and sentence fragments and write revisions, using capital letters and end marks as needed
- To identify and revise sentence fragments

TEACHING TIP

Motivation. Introduce the subject of sentences and sentence fragments by comparing the sentence to a car. A car needs both a body and an engine to work; in a similar way, a sentence needs both a subject and a verb to be complete. Ask volunteers for a list of subjects and verbs, and write students' suggestions on the chalkboard. Have students combine the subjects and verbs to practice forming sentences.

TECHNOLOGY TIP

Students using computers may have access to a grammar-checking program. Ask students to investigate whether or not their programs check for sentence fragments. Have students share their findings with the class.

---

21. Hang that jacket in the hall closet**.** **21. imp.**
22. How we laughed**!** **22. exc.**
23. Water is composed of oxygen and hydrogen**.** **23. dec.**
24. Call this number in case of an emergency**.** **24. imp.**
25. Did you say to turn left here**?** **25. int.**

Sentence or Sentence Fragment?

10a. A *sentence* is a word group that contains a subject and a verb and that expresses a complete thought.

A sentence begins with a capital letter and ends with a period, a question mark, or an exclamation point.

EXAMPLES **O**ctavio Paz won a Nobel Prize in literature**.** [The subject is *Octavio Paz,* and the verb is *won.*]

Stop**.** [The understood subject is *you,* and the verb is *Stop.*]

Do you collect coins**?** [The subject is *you,* and the verb is *Do collect.*]

I actually rode on an elephant**!** [The subject is *I,* and the verb is *rode.*]

A *sentence fragment* is a word group that looks like a sentence but either does not contain both a subject and a verb or does not express a complete thought.

SENTENCE FRAGMENT	Visited an old Spanish mission in San Diego. [The subject is missing. Who visited the mission?]
SENTENCE	My family visited an old Spanish mission in San Diego.
SENTENCE FRAGMENT	Alonzo's sisters and brothers. [The verb is missing. What did Alonzo's sisters and brothers do?]
SENTENCE	Alonzo's sisters and brothers planned a surprise party for his birthday.

Reference Note

For information on the **understood subject,** see page 316.

 **TIPS & TRICKS**

To tell whether a group of words is a sentence or a sentence fragment, ask yourself these three questions:

1. What is the subject?
2. What is the verb?
3. What is the complete thought the word group expresses?

If you cannot answer any one of these questions, the word group may not be a sentence.

RESOURCES

Sentence or Sentence Fragment?
Practice
- *Grammar, Usage, and Mechanics,* pp. 2–4
- *Language Workshop CD-ROM,* Lesson 31

SENTENCE FRAGMENT	As I walked to school yesterday. [This thought is not complete. What happened as I walked to school yesterday?]
SENTENCE	As I walked to school yesterday, I saw Mr. Saunders walking his dog.

NOTE A word group that has a subject and a verb and that expresses a complete thought is called an **independent clause.** An independent clause can stand alone as a sentence. A word group that has a subject and a verb but does not express a complete thought (such as *As I walked to school yesterday*) is called a **subordinate clause.**

Exercise 1 Identifying Sentences

Identify each of the following word groups as a *sentence* or a *sentence fragment*. If a word group is a sentence, rewrite the sentence, using a capital letter at the beginning and adding an end mark.

EXAMPLE 1. my aunt and uncle raise shar-peis
   1. sentence—My aunt and uncle raise shar-peis.

1. my aunt, my uncle, and my cousins at their house in the country last weekend   1. frag.
2. after dinner, Aunt Marie told me about the history of the shar-pei breed.   2. sent.
3. bred these dogs in China   3. frag.
4. just look at all that loose, wrinkled skin.   4. sent.
5. protected them from injury during a fight   5. frag.
6. gentle and a lot of fun with children   6. frag.
7. playing catch with Queenie   7. frag.
8. the little balls of fur were Queenie's new puppies.   8. sent.
9. have you ever seen such a sight as these puppies?   9. sent.
10. what a good time we had!   10. sent.

Reference Note
For more about **independent and subordinate clauses,** see page 387.

STYLE TIP

In speech, people often use sentence fragments. Such fragments usually are not confusing because the context and the speaker's tone of voice and expressions help to complete the meaning.

Professional writers, too, may use sentence fragments to create specific effects in their writing. However, in your writing at school, you should use complete sentences.

Reference Note
For more information on **revising sentence fragments,** see page 264.

Meeting INDIVIDUAL NEEDS

LEARNERS HAVING DIFFICULTY
General Strategies. Some students may show little interest in differentiating between sentences and sentence fragments because students may feel that a message can be easily communicated without using a complete sentence. Remind students that writing is an important form of communication and that to be competent writers, they must use complete sentences.

MULTIPLE INTELLIGENCES
Interpersonal Intelligence. Arrange students in pairs to practice forming sentences. Each student will write a different verb on each card in a set of five index cards and five different subjects on another set of cards. Each partner will take turns selecting subject and verb cards at random and writing a sentence using the cards. Partners will continue forming sentences until each card has been used.

TEACHING TIP

Exercise 1 You may wish to have the class work through **Exercise 1** once as guided practice. Then, you could have each student write his or her own sentences as independent practice.

MINI-LESSON

Understood *You* as Subject. Write the following words on the chalkboard, and ask students to identify them as complete sentences or sentence fragments.
1. Run! [*sentence*]
2. The broken stairs. [*fragment*]
3. Be quiet. [*sentence*]
4. For her. [*fragment*]

Remind students that a sentence can consist of a verb and the understood subject *you* (as in items 1 and 3).

Exercise 2 Identifying and Revising Sentences and Sentence Fragments

POSSIBLE ANSWERS

1. Having been introduced to the guest of honor, we took our places at the table.
2. sentence
3. Dragonflies were dancing in the air around the garden.
4. sentence
5. sentence
6. This sculpture is one of the only examples of Aztec art in this area.
7. His pocket contained three pennies, a quarter, a bus token, and four acorns.
8. sentence
9. Along with an electric guitar, a mandolin, and kettledrums, the group played an instrument popular in Africa, the kalimba.
10. sentence

Review A Writing Complete Sentences

POSSIBLE ANSWERS

1. Grandmother sent us a postcard from the Philippines.
2. It was cold at the skating rink.
3. My brother helped me with my science project.
4. I dream of being a surfer on a huge wave.
5. How hungry you would be at lunchtime if you didn't eat breakfast!
6. It is too late for a game of checkers.
7. Is that the American Falls or the Horseshoe Falls?
8. Our family welcomed the Cuban family next door.
9. What time is your mom picking us up?
10. The governor of my state is running for president.

COMPUTER TIP

If sentence fragments are a problem in your writing, a computer may be able to help you. Some style-checking programs can find fragments for you. Such programs are useful, but they are not perfect. It is best to check each sentence yourself. Make sure each sentence has a subject and a verb and expresses a complete thought.

Exercise 2 Identifying and Revising Sentences and Sentence Fragments

Some of the following word groups are sentences, and others are sentence fragments. If a word group is a sentence, write *sentence*. If a word group is not a sentence, add words to make the word group a sentence.

EXAMPLE   1. A common custom worldwide.
          1. *Weddings are a common custom worldwide.*

1. Having been introduced to the guest of honor.
2. Hold your horses there, young fellow.
3. Dancing in the air around the garden.
4. It will be on your right.
5. Just how does a fire extinguisher work?
6. One of the only examples of this type of Aztec art in this area.
7. Three pennies, a quarter, a bus token, and four acorns.
8. He called Sunday night.
9. An instrument popular in Africa, the kalimba.
10. How we laughed at that movie!

Review A Writing Complete Sentences

Some of the following word groups are sentences. If a word group is a sentence, rewrite it, adding a capital letter and end punctuation. If a word group is not a sentence, rewrite it, adding a subject or a verb, a capital letter, and end punctuation to make it a sentence.

EXAMPLE   1. wrote a play
          1. *Our language arts class wrote a play.*

1. sent us a postcard from the Philippines
2. it was cold at the skating rink
3. helped me with my science project
4. a surfer on a huge wave
5. was hungry at lunchtime
6. it is too late for a game of checkers
7. is that the American Falls or the Horseshoe Falls
8. the Cuban family next door
9. what time is your mom picking us up
10. the governor of my state

Subject and Predicate

Sentences consist of two basic parts: *subjects* and *predicates*.

The Subject

10b. The *subject* tells *whom* or *what* the sentence is about.

EXAMPLES **Lois Lenski** wrote *Strawberry Girl*.

The tooth with a point is called a canine.

To find the subject, ask yourself *who* or *what* is doing something or *about whom* or *what* something is being said.

EXAMPLES **My best friend** sits next to me in science class. [*Who* sits? My best friend sits.]

Science class is very interesting this year. [*What* is interesting? Science class is.]

The Position of the Subject

The subject may come at the beginning, in the middle, or even at the end of a sentence.

EXAMPLES After school, **Theresa** went to band practice.

Under our house was **a tiny kitten**.

Exercise 3 Identifying Subjects

Identify the subject in each of these sentences.

EXAMPLE 1. The final score was tied.
1. The final score

1. Many games use rackets or paddles.
2. Tennis can be an exhausting sport.
3. Badminton rackets don't weigh very much.
4. Table-tennis paddles are covered with rubber.
5. Racquetball uses special rackets.
6. In Florida, citrus trees grow an important crop.
7. After three to five years, fruit grows on the new trees.
8. Does Florida grow all of the citrus fruit in the nation?
9. California also grows oranges and other citrus fruit.
10. From Texas comes the Star Ruby grapefruit.

Subject and Predicate

Rules 10b–e (pp. 305–310)

OBJECTIVES

- To identify complete subjects and simple subjects in sentences
- To identify predicates in sentences
- To complete sentences by providing predicates
- To identify complete predicates and verbs in sentences

ENGLISH-LANGUAGE LEARNERS
General Strategies. One potentially problematic rule for students is the rule that complete sentences must have stated subjects (except, of course, for imperative sentences). Especially in conversation, students sometimes imply subjects but don't directly state them. Students may need extra coaching to help them see that neglecting to state the subjects of their sentences can be confusing to their audience. Tell students that a sentence should not leave an audience wondering who or what is being discussed.

RESOURCES

Subject and Predicate
Practice
- *Grammar, Usage, and Mechanics,* pp. 5, 6, 7, 8, 9
- *Language Workshop CD-ROM,* Lessons 24, 25

Meeting INDIVIDUAL NEEDS

MULTIPLE INTELLIGENCES
Linguistic Intelligence. Tell students to imagine they are writing the script for a movie. Ask each student to write one sentence about the topic of his or her film. Students' sentences should name the main character of the film and tell what the main character does. After students have written their sentences, point out that their main character is the subject of their sentence and the predicate is what the character does.

If you leave the simple subject out of a sentence, the sentence will not make sense.

EXAMPLES
The Korean . . . is closed today.

A brightly colored . . . sat on the windowsill.

Complete Subject and Simple Subject

The **complete subject** consists of all the words needed to tell *whom* or *what* the sentence is about. The **simple subject** is part of the complete subject.

10c. The **simple subject** is the main word or word group that tells *whom* or *what* the sentence is about.

EXAMPLES   **The Korean market** is closed today.
     complete subject   The Korean market
     simple subject   market

A brightly colored blue jay sat on the windowsill.
     complete subject   A brightly colored blue jay
     simple subject   blue jay

Sometimes the same word or words make up both the simple subject and the complete subject.

EXAMPLES   In the canyon, **we** saw hawks. [*We* is both the complete subject and the simple subject.]

Little Rascal is the story of a boy and his pet raccoon. [The title *Little Rascal* is both the complete subject and the simple subject.]

NOTE   In this book, the term *subject* generally refers to the simple subject unless otherwise indicated.

Exercise 4   Identifying Complete Subjects and Simple Subjects

Identify the **complete subject** of each of the following sentences. Then, underline the **simple subject**.

EXAMPLE   1. From the chimney came a thick cloud of smoke.
          1. a thick <u>cloud</u> of smoke

1. Several <u>tents</u> were set up in the park.
2. Have <u>you</u> heard the new CD by Gloria Estefan?
3. <u>News</u> travels fast in our town.
4. Above the fort, the <u>flag</u> was still flying.
5. Beyond those distant mountains lies an ancient American Indian <u>village</u>.

6. Those newspaper reporters have been interviewing the mayor all morning.
7. On the shelf was a beautiful blue bowl.
8. According to folklore, Pecos Bill made the Grand Canyon.
9. The blue candles burned all night long.
10. In the drawer were some chopsticks.

The Predicate

10d. The *predicate* of a sentence tells something about the subject.

EXAMPLES Lois Lenski **wrote *Strawberry Girl*.**

The tooth with a point **is called a canine.**

Exercise 5   Identifying Predicates

Identify the predicate in each of the following sentences.

EXAMPLE 1. Many people would like to have a robot.
1. would like to have a robot

1. Robots are machines with "brains."
2. The robot's brain is a computer.
3. Not all robots look like humans.
4. Some robots look like toy cars.
5. One robot explored some of the surface of Mars.
6. Many companies use robots.
7. Cars of the future may be guided by robots.
8. Some household jobs can be done by robots.
9. A robot could clean your room.
10. You might like to have a robot to help with your daily chores.

The Position of the Predicate

The predicate usually comes after the subject. Sometimes, however, part or all of the predicate comes before the subject.

EXAMPLES **Quickly** we **learned the layout of the small Hopi village.**

At the entrance to the science fair were maps of the exhibits.

Exercise 6 Identifying Predicates

Write each of the following sentences. Then, underline the predicate.

EXAMPLE   1. At noon we went to a Mexican restaurant.
1. At noon we <u>went to a Mexican restaurant</u>.

1. Our family <u>likes different kinds of food</u>.
2. Last night Dad <u>prepared spaghetti and a salad for supper</u>.
3. Sometimes Mom <u>makes chow mein</u>.
4. With chow mein she <u>serves egg rolls</u>.
5. At the Greek bakery we <u>buy fresh pita bread</u>.
6. Tomorrow Erica <u>will make German potato salad</u>.
7. Lately, tacos <u>have become my favorite food</u>.
8. Carefully, I <u>spoon grated lettuce and cheese into a tortilla</u>.
9. After that <u>come the other ingredients</u>.
10. In the United States, people <u>enjoy a wide variety of foods</u>.

Exercise 7 Writing Predicates

Make a sentence out of each of the following words or word groups by adding a predicate to fill the blank or blanks.

EXAMPLE   1. _____ everyone _____
1. *With a shout of joy, everyone took a paddle and began to row.*

or

As the waves crashed against the raft, everyone grabbed for the sides.

1. Foamy white water _____.
2. The hot summer air _____.
3. A strong current _____.
4. _____ the eyes of every person on board _____.
5. The lightweight paddles _____.
6. _____ dangerous rocks and swirls _____.
7. Quick action by everyone _____.
8. A sleek, blue rubber raft _____.
9. The man in the white helmet and blue life jacket _____.
10. _____ the people in this photograph _____.

— HELP —

Although the example in Exercise 7 shows two possible answers, you need to give only one answer for each item.

Exercise 7 Writing Predicates

POSSIBLE ANSWERS

1. Foamy white water roars through the canyon.
2. The hot summer air chapped my skin.
3. A strong current pulled the raft.
4. When the raft went over a rock, the eyes of every person on board widened in amazement.
5. The lightweight paddles floated down the river.
6. Around the bend dangerous rocks and swirls threatened the raft.
7. Quick action by everyone prevented a disaster.
8. A sleek, blue rubber raft almost overturned.
9. The man in the white helmet and blue life jacket saved the little girl's life.
10. Despite all the problems, the people in this photograph arrived safely on shore.

Complete Predicate and Simple Predicate

The *complete predicate* consists of a verb and all the words that describe the verb and complete its meaning.

10e. The *simple predicate,* or *verb,* is the main word or word group in the complete predicate.

EXAMPLES The nurse **lifted the patient carefully.**

complete predicate   lifted the patient carefully
simple predicate (verb)   lifted

I **saw a picture of a Siberian tiger.**

complete predicate   saw a picture of a Siberian tiger
simple predicate (verb)   saw

HELP
In this book, the simple predicate is generally called the *verb*.

Exercise 8 Identifying Complete Predicates and Verbs

Identify the complete predicate of each of the following sentences. Then, underline the verb.

EXAMPLE 1. For several reasons, space travel fascinates me.
1. For several reasons *fascinates me*

1. My class traveled by train to Houston, Texas.
2. In Houston my classmates and I visited the Lyndon B. Johnson Space Center.
3. The center displays moon rocks.
4. At the center, astronauts train for their flights.
5. In one room we saw several unusual computers.
6. On the way home, we stopped at the Astrodome for a tour.
7. The stadium covers nine-and-a-half acres of land.
8. Several teams play there.
9. Every year the Astrodome attracts thousands of tourists.
10. Actually, I had more fun at the space center.

The simple predicate may be a single verb or a **verb phrase** (a verb with one or more helping verbs).

EXAMPLES Yoshi **went** to Japan last summer. [single verb]

The park **is located** near a lake. [verb phrase]

We **should have planned** a picnic. [verb phrase]

Reference Note
For information on **helping verbs,** see page 347.

Critical Thinking

Analysis. Challenge students to write five sentences each that contain as many words in the complete subject as in the complete predicate. Students should start with a sentence that contains four words in each part, then a sentence with five words in each part, adding one word with each new sentence until they finish the fifth sentence with eight words in both the complete subject and complete predicate. Give students the following example of a final sentence:

> My uncle Chris, an aspiring and talented magician, once pulled ten white rabbits from his hat.

Write volunteers' sentences on the chalkboard.

Timesaver

To save grading time, you may want to go over the odd-numbered sentences in **Exercise 8** orally. For students who need additional practice, assign the even-numbered sentences as written work.

> **NOTE** The words *not* and *never* and the contraction *–n't* are not verbs. They are never part of a verb or verb phrase.
>
> **EXAMPLE** Kendra **should**n't **have added** another hot pepper to the sauce.

Exercise 9 Identifying Complete Predicates and Verbs

Identify the complete predicate in each of the following sentences. Then, underline the verb.

EXAMPLE 1. The Liberty Bell was made in England.
 1. was made in England

1. I am writing a report on the Liberty Bell.
2. The Pennsylvania Assembly ordered the Liberty Bell.
3. Thomas Lester had made the bell in London.
4. In 1752, the bell was cracked by its own clapper.
5. American patriots hid the bell from the British army.
6. The bell was not brought back to Philadelphia until 1778.
7. The Liberty Bell cracked again in 1835.
8. This bell has been rung on many historic occasions.
9. The bell is exhibited in the Liberty Bell Pavilion.
10. We will be seeing it on our field trip to Philadelphia.

Finding the Subject

Sometimes it may be difficult to find the subject of a sentence. In such cases, find the verb first. Then, ask yourself *Who?* or *What?* before the verb.

EXAMPLES Next semester you may take art or music. [The verb is *may take*. *Who* may take? *You* may take. *You* is the subject of the sentence.]

Can your sister drive us to the park? [The verb is *Can drive*. *Who* can drive? *Sister* can drive. *Sister* is the subject of the sentence.]

Please read the first chapter. [The verb is *read*. *Who* should read? *You* should read. *You* is the understood subject of the sentence.]

Reference Note
For more information on **understood subjects,** see page 316.

Exercise 9
ALTERNATIVE LESSON
Have students review parts of speech by finding the following items in sentences 1, 3, 5, and 8:

1. a pronoun [*I*]
3. a preposition [*in*]
5. three nouns [*patriots, bell, army*]
8. three adjectives [*This, many, historic*]

Cooperative Learning
Students may be better able to understand verb phrases if they start by building sentences around them. Arrange students in groups of three. Have one member of each group write action verbs on index cards labeled *AV*. Have another member write helping verbs on other index cards, labeled *HV*. The third member should write linking verbs on cards labeled *LV*. Have each group then practice combining one AV or LV card with one or two HV cards to compose four sentences that contain verb phrases made from the verbs on the index cards. Students may need to review linking verbs and helping verbs on pages 347 and 351. Ask each group to read its sentences aloud.

Compound Subject and Compound Verb

Compound Subject

10f. A *compound subject* consists of two or more subjects that are joined by a conjunction and that have the same verb.

The parts of a compound subject are most often connected by *and* or *or*.

EXAMPLES **Minneapolis** and **St. Paul** are called the "Twin Cities." [The two parts of the compound subject have the same verb, *are called*.]

Will **Mrs. Jones** or **Ms. Lopez** chaperone our field trip? [The two parts of the compound subject have the same verb, *Will chaperone*.]

Flutes, clarinets, and **oboes** are all woodwind instruments. [The three parts of the compound subject have the same verb, *are*.]

Reference Note
Notice that **commas** are **used to separate three or more parts of a compound subject.** For more about this use of commas, see page 566.

Exercise 10 Identifying Compound Subjects

Identify the compound subjects in each of the following sentences.

EXAMPLE   1. October and June are my favorite months.
   1. *October, June*

1. Wild ducks and geese migrate south each year.
2. Stars and planets form a galaxy.
3. Someday dolphins and people may be able to communicate with each other.
4. Baseball and soccer are the two most popular sports at my sister's school.
5. Eggs and flour are two ingredients in pancakes.
6. Every year bugs and rabbits raid our vegetable garden.
7. Pizza or ravioli will be served.
8. At a party, balloons or horns make the best noisemakers.
9. Dachshunds, Chihuahuas, Lhasa apsos, and Pekingese ran around in the yard.
10. In the Tower of London are famous jewels and crowns.

RESOURCES

Compound Subjects and Compound Verbs
Practice
- *Grammar, Usage, and Mechanics,* pp. 10, 11, 12, 13, 14
- *Language Workshop CD-ROM,* Lessons 24, 25

Meeting INDIVIDUAL NEEDS

INCLUSION

Ask students to use a tape recorder to dictate short descriptive paragraphs about their favorite books or TV programs. Have them use as many compound subjects and compound verbs as possible.

LEARNERS HAVING DIFFICULTY

Some students may benefit from working the exercises with advanced students. Assign an exercise to groups of two or three students. Encourage them to talk about the sentences and to analyze the problems they have with the sentences. You may want to walk about the room to verify that the information is being explained adequately.

Exercise 12 Writing Compound Subjects and Compound Verbs

POSSIBLE ANSWERS

1. Jake and Max are beginning a stamp collection.

Compound Verb

10g. A **compound verb** consists of two or more verbs that are joined by a conjunction and that have the same subject.

A connecting word such as *and* or *but* is used to join the parts of a compound verb.

EXAMPLES   Ben **overslept** but **caught** his bus anyway.

Conchita **hums**, **sings**, or **listens** to the radio all day.

My father **bought** a Chinese wok and **cooked** vegetables in it.

HELP—
Remember to include helping verbs when you are identifying verbs in Exercise 11.

Exercise 11 Identifying Compound Verbs

Identify the compound verbs in the following sentences.

EXAMPLE   1. I have proofread my paper and made a final copy.
 1. have proofread, made

1. Mai and her parents left Vietnam and arrived in California in 1994.
2. Julie received good grades and made the honor roll.
3. Every week, our band practices together and writes songs.
4. Before supper I usually set the table or peel the vegetables.
5. Floyd asked for a watch but received a bike instead.
6. We gathered firewood and headed back to camp.
7. Last week everyone gave a speech or recited a poem.
8. The referee will call a rain delay or postpone the game.
9. I remembered the bread but forgot the milk.
10. The Greek restaurant has closed but will reopen soon.

Exercise 12 Writing Compound Subjects and Compound Verbs

Make sentences by adding compound subjects or compound verbs to fill in the blanks in the following word groups.

EXAMPLES   1. ____ are coming to the party.
 1. *Fran and Terry are coming to the party.*

 2. At the mall, we ____.
 2. *At the mall, we ate lunch and went to a movie.*

1. ____ are beginning a stamp collection.

MINI-LESSON

Finding Compound Subjects and Compound Verbs. Write the following sentences on the chalkboard:

1. Marco and Anna played their guitars.
2. Anna played her guitar and sang for us.
3. Marco and Anna played their guitars and sang for us.

Ask the class to identify the verb in the first sentence [*played*] and to find the subject by asking who played [*Marco, Anna*].

2. _____ were my favorite teachers last year.
3. The creature from outer space _____.
4. At the end of the play, the cast _____.
5. Last week _____ were interviewed on a talk show.
6. In the garage are _____.
7. During the storm, we _____.
8. At the front door were _____.
9. After school, my friends _____.
10. He _____ before the birthday party.

Review B — Identifying Subjects and Verbs

Identify the subjects and verbs in each of the following sentences.

EXAMPLE 1. In the history of African American music are many unforgettable names.
 1. names—subject; are—verb

1. You may recognize the man in the picture on this page.
2. Most people immediately think of his deep, raspy voice.
3. Ray Charles is called the father of soul music.
4. He lost his sight at the age of seven and became an orphan at fifteen.
5. However, misfortune and trouble did not stop Ray Charles.
6. His musical genius turned his troubles into songs.
7. Today, the songs of Ray Charles are heard all over the world.
8. Do his songs contain different musical styles?
9. Gospel, jazz, blues, and even pop are all part of his sound.
10. His special style and powerful performances have drawn fans to Ray Charles for nearly fifty years.

A sentence may have both a compound subject and a compound verb.

EXAMPLES
    S   **S** **V**   **V**
Zina and **I bought** corn and **fed** the ducks.

      S   **S** **V**   **V**
Carrots and **celery are** crunchy and **satisfy** your appetite.

HELP
Some of the subjects and verbs in Review B are compound.

NOTE Sometimes a sentence will contain more than one subject and verb, but neither the subject nor verb will be compound.

EXAMPLES

S V   S V
I like apples, but my **sister prefers** oranges.
[compound sentence]

S V
In San Antonio, **we toured** the Alamo, while our
S V
friends visited the Riverwalk.
[complex sentence]

S V   S V
David wipes the table, and **Cindy dries** the dishes
S V
that **Dad has washed**.
[compound-complex sentence]

Reference Note
For more information about **compound, complex,** and **compound-complex sentences,** see page 395.

STYLE TIP

In your own writing, you can combine ideas by creating compound subjects and verbs. Combining sentences in this way will help make your writing smoother and easier to read. Compare the examples below.

CHOPPY
Susan went hiking in the mountains. Mark went hiking, too. Aunt Connie went with them.

REVISED
Susan, Mark, and Aunt Connie went hiking in the mountains.

Reference Note
For more information on **combining sentences,** see page 269.

Exercise 13 Identifying Compound Subjects and Compound Verbs

Identify the compound subject and the compound verb in each of the following sentences.

EXAMPLE 1. Tina and Julia washed the dog and dried it.
        1. *Tina, Julia—subject; washed, dried—verb*

1. Alice and Reiko sang and played the piano.
2. Either Dwayne or I will find the coach and ask his advice.
3. Patrick and she read the same biography of Dr. Martin Luther King, Jr., and reported on it.
4. Roses and lilacs look pretty and smell good.
5. The dentist or her assistant cleans and polishes my teeth.
6. In many traditional Japanese homes, doors or partitions are framed in wood, left open in the middle, and then covered with rice paper.
7. Larry and she washed the dishes but did not dry them.
8. The lamb and its mother had leapt the fence but were still inside the yard.
9. Fish, rays, turtles, and dolphins live in the Gulf of Mexico and often swim near the shore.
10. Did Uncle Ted or his children call or visit you on their way through town?

Learning for Life

Creating an Advertisement. Point out to students that one well-written sentence can have a stronger effect than a series of weaker sentences. Advertisers often use one powerful sentence to get their audience's attention.

Ask students to collect examples of effective advertisements that use a single, powerful sentence. You may want students to focus on advertising that supports a specific cause or relays an important message. Students can post examples of effective

Review C — Identifying Subjects and Predicates

Identify the complete subject and the complete predicate in each of the following sentences. Then, underline the simple subject and the verb.

HELP
Some of the subjects and verbs in Review C are compound.

EXAMPLE
1. Reports and legends of huge apelike creatures fascinate many people.
   1. subject—*Reports* and *legends* of huge apelike creatures; predicate—*fascinate* many people

1. These creatures are known as *Yeti* in the Himalayas and as *Rakshas* in Katmandu.
2. American Indians of the Northwest call them *Mammoth*.
3. *Sasquatch* and *Bigfoot* are other common names for these mysterious creatures.
4. Since 1818, they have been seen and described by people in the United States and Canada.
5. According to most accounts, Bigfoot adults are very strong and large and smell very bad.
6. Their huge footprints have been measured and cast in plaster by eager searchers.
7. However, these reports and bits of evidence generally do not convince scientists.
8. Not one live Bigfoot has ever been captured by either scientists or the general public.
9. As a result, the Bigfoot is simply a fantasy to most people.
10. Still, in pockets of deep wilderness across the country might live whole families of these shy creatures.

Review D — Writing Sentences

Tell whether each of the following sentence parts can be used as a *subject* or a *predicate*. Then, use each sentence part in a sentence. Begin each sentence with a capital letter, and end it with the correct mark of punctuation. Use a variety of subjects and verbs in your sentences.

EXAMPLE
1. will drive us home
   1. predicate—Will your mother drive us home?

1. my favorite book
2. watched a good mystery

Review C — Identifying Subjects and Predicates

ANSWERS

1. subj.—These <u>creatures</u>; pred.—<u>are known</u> as *Yeti* in the Himalayas and as *Rakshas* in Katmandu
2. subj.—American <u>Indians</u> of the Northwest; pred.—<u>call</u> them *Mammoth*
3. subj.—<u>Sasquatch</u> and <u>Bigfoot</u>; pred.—<u>are</u> other common names for these mysterious creatures
4. subj.—<u>they</u>; pred.—Since 1818, <u>have been seen</u> and <u>described</u> by people in the United States and Canada
5. subj.—Bigfoot <u>adults</u>; pred.—According to most accounts, <u>are</u> very strong and large and <u>smell</u> very bad
6. subj.—Their huge <u>footprints</u>; pred.—<u>have been measured</u> and <u>cast</u> in plaster by eager searchers
7. subj.—these <u>reports</u> and <u>bits</u> of evidence; pred.—However, generally <u>do</u> not <u>convince</u> scientists
8. subj.—Not one live <u>Bigfoot</u>; pred.—<u>has</u> ever <u>been captured</u> by either scientists or the general public
9. subj.—the <u>Bigfoot</u>; pred.—As a result, <u>is</u> simply a fantasy to most people
10. subj.—whole <u>families</u> of these shy creatures; pred.—Still, in pockets of deep wilderness across the country <u>might live</u>

Review D — Writing Sentences

POSSIBLE ANSWERS

1. subject: My favorite book is *Black Beauty*.
2. predicate: During the storm, the family watched a good mystery.

---

advertisements on the class bulletin board.
Have students design their own ads that feature a single sentence as a slogan or attention-grabber.
Students can create ads for a student election or a school event such as a play or bazaar.
After students have written their sentences, have them meet with partners to evaluate their ads' effectiveness. Partners should also proofread each other's work.

Review D   **Writing Sentences**

POSSIBLE ANSWERS continued

3. subject: The flying saucer is the subject of my little brother's drawing.
4. subject: The oldest house in town is being made into a museum.
5. predicate: My neighbor prepares delicious Korean food.
6. predicate: The tiger growled and bared its teeth.
7. subject: The shiny red car and the bicycle are pictured on page 49.
8. predicate: Juan caught a huge fish.
9. predicate: No one can borrow your skates.
10. subject: The best tacos and enchiladas in town are served at Washington Middle School.

Kinds of Sentences

Rules 10h–k *(pp. 316–318)*

OBJECTIVE

- To classify sentences as declarative, imperative, interrogative, or exclamatory and to provide the correct punctuation

---

3. the flying saucer
4. the oldest house in town
5. prepares delicious Korean food
6. growled and bared its teeth
7. the shiny red car and the bicycle
8. caught a huge fish
9. can borrow your skates
10. the best tacos and enchiladas in town

Kinds of Sentences

Sentences may be classified according to purpose.

10h. A *declarative sentence* makes a statement and ends with a period.

EXAMPLES   Our media center has several computers.

Patrick Henry lived in Virginia.

10i. An *imperative sentence* gives a command or makes a request. Most imperative sentences end with a period. A strong command ends with an exclamation point.

EXAMPLES   Please pass the potatoes. [request]

Sit down. [command]

Stop shouting! [strong command]

The subject of a command or a request is always *you*, even if the word *you* never appears in the sentence. In such cases, *you* is called the **understood subject**.

EXAMPLES   [**You**] Please pass the potatoes.

[**You**] Stop shouting!

10j. An *interrogative sentence* asks a question and ends with a question mark.

EXAMPLES   Did the Apollo 13 spacecraft reach the moon?

How old are you?

Reference Note

For information on **how sentences can be classified according to structure,** see page 394.

RESOURCES

Kinds of Sentences

Practice

- *Grammar, Usage, and Mechanics,* pp. 15–16
- *Language Workshop CD-ROM,* Lesson 30

10k. An *exclamatory sentence* shows excitement or expresses strong feeling and ends with an exclamation point.

EXAMPLES What a difficult assignment that was!

I got her autograph!

Exercise 14 Classifying Sentences by Purpose

Write each of the following sentences, and add an appropriate end mark. Identify the sentence as *declarative*, *interrogative*, *imperative*, or *exclamatory*.

EXAMPLE 1. What a funny show that was
1. *What a funny show that was!—exclamatory*

1. Please help me find my umbrella. **1. imp.**
2. How happy I am! **2. exc.**
3. Have you and your sister been to the new video store on Congress Avenue? **3. int.**
4. Go east for three blocks, and look for a yellow mailbox next to a red door. **4. imp.**
5. My father and I are cleaning the attic together later this afternoon. **5. dec.**
6. What a delicious salad this is! **6. exc.**
7. During our last summer vacation, we toured the garment district in New York City. **7. dec.**
8. Do you like barbecued chicken? **8. int.**
9. My surprise visit last month pleased both my grandmother and Aunt Gabriela. **9. dec.**
10. When is your next piano lesson? **10. int.**

Review E Classifying Sentences by Purpose

For each of the sentences on the following page, add an appropriate end mark. Then, identify each sentence as *declarative*, *imperative*, *interrogative*, or *exclamatory*.

EXAMPLE 1. Have you ever seen the Grand Canyon
1. *Have you ever seen the Grand Canyon?—interrogative*

STYLE TIP

Be careful not to overuse exclamation points in your writing. Save them for sentences that really do show strong emotion. When used too much, exclamation points lose their effect.

OVERUSED

For her birthday, Katy's parents threw her a bowling party! About twenty friends and family members attended, and we all had a great time! I had two strikes in one game!

IMPROVED

For her birthday, Katy's parents threw her a bowling party. About twenty friends and family members attended, and we all had a great time. I had two strikes in one game!

TEACHING TIP

Activity. Write the three different end marks on the chalkboard, and ask students to write a sentence using each end mark. While students are writing, list the four categories *declarative*, *imperative*, *interrogative*, and *exclamatory* on the chalkboard. Then, as volunteers read their sentences aloud, write student examples under each category heading. Ask students to describe the categories in their own words, judging from the example sentences.

Meeting INDIVIDUAL NEEDS

ENGLISH-LANGUAGE LEARNERS

General Strategies. Students might be able to create different kinds of sentences more easily if you give them a simple declarative sentence and ask them to form the other three types of sentences starting from this base.

EXAMPLE

The game was exciting.

Was the game exciting?

Please tell me whether the game was exciting.

Wow! The game was exciting!

Meeting INDIVIDUAL NEEDS

LEARNERS HAVING DIFFICULTY
To give extra practice in using the four sentence types, cut out magazine pictures that are colorful, vivid, and suitable for writing prompts. Give one to each student, along with instructions to write a short descriptive paragraph based on what is in the picture. Tell each student to use one interrogative, one imperative, one exclamatory, and at least two declarative sentences in the paragraph.

STYLE TIP

In any kind of writing, correct end punctuation is important. However, it is especially important in written conversations. The punctuation helps a reader know how a speaker says something. A sentence can mean very different things when its end punctuation is changed. Try reading the following sentences aloud to hear the difference.

DECLARATIVE
  He's my hero.
INTERROGATIVE
  He's my hero?
EXCLAMATORY
  He's my hero!

1. We enjoyed our vacation in the Southwest.   1. dec.
2. Dad took these photographs when our family visited the Grand Canyon.   2. dec.
3. Our guide spoke both Spanish and English.   3. dec.
4. How pretty the sunset is!   4. exc.
5. Don't stand so close to the edge. [or !]   5. imp.
6. Did you buy any turquoise-and-silver jewelry?   6. int.
7. It was quite chilly at night.   7. dec.
8. What a great movie we saw about the canyon!   8. exc.
9. Did you take the short hike or the long one?   9. int.
10. Look at us riding on mules in this canyon.   10. imp.

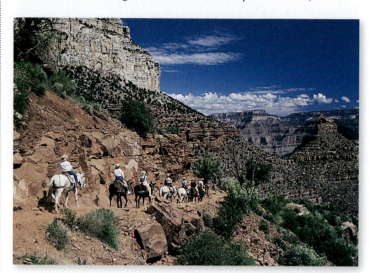

318   Chapter 10   The Sentence

CHAPTER 10

Chapter Review

A. Identifying Sentences

For each of the following word groups that is a sentence, add a capital letter at the beginning and punctuate the sentence with an appropriate end mark. If a group is not a sentence, write *sentence fragment*.

1. burned brightly throughout the night **1. frag.**
2. he studies computer programming after school**.**
3. the band sounds so wonderful tonight**!**
4. whenever the mountains are covered with fog **4. frag.**
5. over the past two thousand years **5. frag.**
6. be seated**.**
7. behind us barked the dogs**.**
8. just as I neared the castle's drawbridge **8. frag.**
9. should we sand the wood now**?**
10. the artist carving the totem pole **10. frag.**

B. Identifying the Complete Subject and the Complete Predicate

Write each of the following sentences. Then, underline the complete subject once and the complete predicate twice.

11. *Black Beauty* is a story about a horse.
12. Sometimes bats fly into our chimney.
13. A wonderful smell of baking bread came from the kitchen and filled the house.
14. The chief will speak to you now.
15. Milk and cheese can help you develop strong bones.
16. Two eagles and a hawk live near our house.
17. Adele peeled and ate the orange.
18. Several knights guarded the castle and drove off the dragon.
19. Under the lettuce was my tomato.
20. Will Ahmad and Nadim set the table before lunch?

Using the Chapter Review

To assess student progress, you may want to compare the types of items missed on the **Diagnostic Preview** with those missed on the **Chapter Review**. If students have not made significant progress, you may want to refer them to **Chapter 24: Correcting Common Errors, Exercises 1** and **2**, for additional practice.

C. Identifying Simple Subjects and Simple Predicates

HELP
Sentences in Part C may contain compound subjects and compound verbs.

For each of the following sentences, write the simple subject and the simple predicate.

21. The winner is Mr. Otis Kwan!
22. Suddenly, the clock stopped.
23. Many cactuses have grown in the garden.
24. Have you ever eaten yakitori?
25. Yancy and Rollo will meet us at the shopping mall.
26. When did they reach the summit of Mount Fairweather?
27. Yellow, orange, and red have always been my favorite colors.
28. Prince and Princess jumped the fence and barked at my brother's friend.
29. The sports banquet will be held on April 4.
30. We bought milk and bread but forgot the eggs.

D. Punctuating and Classifying Sentences by Purpose

Write each sentence, adding an appropriate end mark. Then, classify each sentence as *declarative, imperative, interrogative,* or *exclamatory.*

31. Listen to them! [or .]   31. imp.
32. What music they make!   32. exc.
33. My name is Lucy.   33. dec.
34. Tell me more about your trip to Romania.   34. imp.
35. How long has Marlon played the zither?   35. int.
36. I will ask her to come over for dinner.   36. dec.
37. Who is the star of the film?   37. int.
38. Stop it now!   38. imp.
39. I'm so happy to see you!   39. exc.
40. Which pair of shoes did you decide to buy?   40. int.

RESOURCES

The Sentence

Review
- *Grammar, Usage, and Mechanics,* pp. 17, 18, 19, 20

Assessment
- Assessment Package
  — *Chapter Tests,* Ch. 10
  — *Chapter Tests in Standardized Test Formats,* Ch. 10
- *Test Generator* (One-Stop Planner CD-ROM)

Writing Application
Using Sentence Variety

Sentences Classified by Purpose As a special project, your social studies class is creating a comic book. Each class member will contribute a comic strip about a particular historical event or historical person. In your comic strip, include at least one of each of the four kinds of sentences—declarative, imperative, interrogative, and exclamatory.

Prewriting First, jot down some ideas for the characters and story line of your comic strip. You may want to look through your social studies book for ideas. Then, plan the frames of your comic strip. Think about how you could include the four types of sentences in your characters' dialogue. For example, what request or command could a character make?

Writing Use your prewriting notes to help you make a draft of your comic strip. Use word balloons to add the dialogue to the pictures. As you write, you may decide to add details. Keep in mind that you will be able to add details in the pictures that go with the words.

Revising Ask a friend to read your cartoon. Are your characters' conversations clear? Can your friend follow the story line? If not, you may need to add, revise, or rearrange sentences.

Publishing Check your comic strip for errors in grammar, spelling, and punctuation. Make sure that you have used all four kinds of sentences and that you have used periods, question marks, and exclamation points correctly for each kind of sentence. You and your classmates may want to photocopy all the comic strips and gather them in a folder for each member of the class.

Chapter Review **321**

Writing Application
(p. 321)

OBJECTIVE
- To create a comic strip using at least one of each of the following sentence types: declarative, imperative, interrogative, and exclamatory

Writing Application
Tip. Visual students may prefer to draw their cartoon panels before they attempt to create a verbal story line.

Scoring Rubric. While you will want to pay particular attention to students' use of complete sentences and of types of sentences, you will want to evaluate the students' overall writing performance. You may want to give a split score to indicate development and clarity of the composition as well as grammar skills.

Critical Thinking
Synthesis. One way students can use each of the four kinds of sentences is to present them in dialogue. Point out to students that interrogative and declarative sentences can be used to ask and answer questions on their topics. Exclamatory sentences can be used to express their enthusiasm for the subject. Imperative sentences can be used to tell the reader to take some action.

RESOURCES
Writing Application
Extension
-  *Grammar, Usage, and Mechanics,* p. 23
-  *Language Workshop CD-ROM,* Lessons 24–25, 30–31

Chapter Review **321**

CHAPTER Parts of Speech Overview
Noun, Pronoun, Adjective

PREVIEWING THE CHAPTER

- This chapter should help students use nouns, pronouns, and adjectives effectively in their writing. The first part of the chapter defines the noun and explains the difference between proper nouns and common nouns. Next, the chapter focuses on pronouns and their antecedents and discusses the different types of pronouns. Then the chapter explains adjectives, including proper and demonstrative adjectives.

- The chapter closes with a **Chapter Review** including a **Writing Application** feature that asks students to write a plot summary and a description of the characters for a short science fiction movie spoof. Students should make sure the pronouns refer clearly to their antecedents.

- This chapter may serve as a resource for students who are having problems using these parts of speech correctly in their writing.

- For help in integrating this chapter with writing chapters, see the **Teaching Strands** chart on pp. T297A–T297B.

USING THE DIAGNOSTIC PREVIEW

- You can use the **Diagnostic Preview** to determine students' knowledge of nouns, pronouns, and adjectives, but even students who can identify these parts of speech may not use them effectively in their writing. Evaluating writing samples should reveal weaknesses.

Diagnostic Preview

Identifying Nouns, Pronouns, and Adjectives

Identify each of the italicized words in the following sentences as a *noun*, a *pronoun*, or an *adjective*.

EXAMPLE 1. Her older *brother* has an *important* test today.
   1. brother—noun; important—adjective

1. The *Romans* built a huge system of roads, *some* of which are still used.
2. Last summer we visited *Alaska,* which is our *largest* state.
3. *Which* of the projects does *that* illustrate?
4. The *Hawaiian* dancers wore *colorful* costumes.
5. *The* bubbling volcano, *inactive* for years, is now a popular tourist attraction.
6. The campers enjoyed *themselves* as they watched the sun set behind the *mountains.*
7. "*That* notebook is *mine,*" Angela said.
8. *They* made a touchdown just before the final *whistle.*
9. *Colombo* is the capital *city* of Sri Lanka.
10. The pen with the *blue* ink is *hers.*

CHAPTER RESOURCES

Planning
- One-Stop Planner CD-ROM

Practice and Extension
- *Grammar, Usage, and Mechanics,* p. 24
- Language Workshop CD-ROM

Internet
- go.hrw.com (keyword: EOLang)

Evaluation and Assessment
- *Assessment Package*
  —Chapter Tests, Ch. 11
  —Chapter Tests in Standardized Test Formats, Ch. 11
- Test Generator (One-Stop Planner CD-ROM)

The Noun

11a. A *noun* is a word or word group that is used to name a person, place, thing, or idea.

Persons	parents, Scott, teacher, Ms. Theresa Vargas, sister, linebackers, baby sitter
Places	White House, states, Nairobi, school
Things	rocket, desks, ocean, hamster, computer, Newbery Medal, Golden Gate Bridge
Ideas	danger, freedom, kindness, fears, dream

Notice that some nouns are made up of more than one word. A *compound noun* is a single noun made up of two or more words used together. The compound noun may be written as one word, as a hyphenated word, or as two or more words.

One Word	daydream, Iceland
Hyphenated Word	self-esteem, sister-in-law
Two Words	Rita Rodriguez, family room

Exercise 1 Identifying Nouns

Identify the nouns in the following sentences.

EXAMPLE 1. Clara Barton was the founder of the American Red Cross.
 1. Clara Barton, founder, American Red Cross

1. Clara Barton was born in Massachusetts.
2. She was educated in a rural school and grew up with a love of books.
3. She began her career as a teacher.
4. During the Civil War, however, she distributed medicine and other supplies.
5. Later she helped find soldiers who were missing in action.

11a

The Noun
Rule 11a *(pp. 323–328)*

OBJECTIVES

- To identify nouns in sentences
- To classify nouns in sentences as common or proper
- To revise sentences by substituting proper nouns for common nouns
- To answer questions with complete sentences and to identify each proper noun used in the sentences

INCLUSION
You may wish to use the chapter exercises in a variety of tutoring situations, such as cross-age tutoring, peer tutoring, and community volunteer tutoring. Because student expectations and success are directly related, tutors should establish specific time lines and goals for student performance. Clear, prompt feedback along with measurable, valid criteria for evaluation will help build trust and mutual respect and will boost students' self-esteem.

The Noun
Practice
- *Grammar, Usage, and Mechanics,* pp. 25, 26–27
- *Language Workshop CD-ROM,* Lesson 1

TEACHING TIP

Activity. Have students identify common and proper nouns in articles from publications for students. Then, ask volunteers to read sentences from the articles, and have the class identify the common and proper nouns. Have each volunteer underline the nouns as they are identified, once for a common noun and twice for a proper noun. Display students' articles and lists in the classroom.

Meeting INDIVIDUAL NEEDS

ENGLISH-LANGUAGE LEARNERS
General Strategies. In Spanish, some proper nouns differ from those in English. When discussing an absent person, a Spanish speaker will insert a definite article before a title. For example, "Dr. Hernandez is retired" translates as *El doctor Hernandez está jubilado*. Also, titles such as *doctor* (Dr.), *señor* (Mr.), *señora* (Mrs.), and *general* (General) are not capitalized preceding a name. Therefore, Spanish speakers may say "I saw the general Powell" instead of "I saw General Powell." You may want to emphasize that the article is omitted in English and that the title is capitalized.

---

6. She organized the American Red Cross and was its president for many years.
7. She raised money for the Red Cross and worked with victims of floods and other disasters.
8. Her kindness touched the lives of countless men, women and children.
9. Her life has been an inspiration to many people who have followed in her footsteps.
10. What a remarkable career and legacy she left the people of the world!

Proper Nouns and Common Nouns

A ***proper noun*** names a particular person, place, thing, or idea and begins with a capital letter. A ***common noun*** names any one of a group of persons, places, things, or ideas. It is usually not capitalized.

Reference Note
For information about **capitalizing proper nouns,** see page 539.

Common Nouns	Proper Nouns
woman	Aunt Josie
teacher	Jaime Escalante
city	Los Angeles
country	Germany
continent	Asia
monument	Lincoln Memorial
team	Karr Cougars
book	*Barrio Boy*
holiday	Chinese New Year
religion	Judaism
language	Swahili

Exercise 2 Identifying Common and Proper Nouns

Identify the nouns in the following sentences, and label them *common* or *proper*.

EXAMPLE 1. The people of Japan celebrate many holidays.
  1. people—common; Japan—proper; holidays—common

1. The picture below is of the Snow Festival in Sapporo.
2. Many groups work together to build these giant sculptures of snow.
3. Do you recognize any of the statues or buildings?
4. Is that the Statue of Liberty made out of snow?

5. In the historic city of Kyoto each June, you can see a parade of spears.
6. A popular fair in Tokyo offers pickled radishes.
7. Many villages are colorfully decorated for the Feast of the Lanterns.
8. Toshiro said that his town enjoys the Star Festival every summer.
9. Several flowers, among them the iris and the lily, have their own special days.
10. The birthday of Buddha is observed in April.

Exercise 3 Substituting Proper Nouns for Common Nouns

In the sentences on the next page, substitute a proper noun for each italicized common noun. You may need to change or leave out some other words in each sentence. You may also make up proper names to use. Answers will vary.

Looking at Language

Word Origins. Like most English words, nouns often change meaning over time. Share the following nouns and their changes in meaning with students.

lunch—In the 1500s, a *lunch* was a large chunk of something, such as bread or meat.

caboose—*Caboose* first entered the English language in the late 1700s. Back then, the word had nothing to do with trains. It meant "the kitchen of a ship."

bead—The word *bead* once meant "prayer."

EXAMPLE 1. The *principal* awarded the *student* the prize for the best creative essay.
1. Ms. Chen awarded Paula Perez the prize for the best creative essay.

1. The *student* is from a *city*.   **1. Marc/San Francisco**
2. Usually, my *uncle* looks through the *newspaper* after we finish dinner.   **2. Uncle Dean/The Washington Post**
3. The *child* watched a *movie*.   **3. Ali/The Wizard of Oz**
4. A *teacher* asked a *student* to talk about growing up in Mexico.   **4. Ms. Miller/Imelda**
5. My *cousin* read that *book*.   **5. Sarah/Island of the Blue Dolphins**
6. Surrounded by newspaper reporters, the *mayor* stood outside the *building*.   **6. Mayor Bose/City Hall**
7. Does the *girl* go to this *school*?   **7. Rosie/Central High**
8. That *singer* wrote the *song*.   **8. Loretta Lynn/"Coal Miner's Daughter"**
9. My *neighbor* bought her husband a new *car* for his birthday last Saturday.   **9. Mrs. Berkowitz/Volvo**
10. When he was a college student, the *coach* played for that *team*.   **10. Coach Johnson/the Pirates**
11. The *painting* is in a *museum*.   **11. La Calunnia/the Uffizi Gallery**
12. The *officer* directed us to the *bridge*.   **12. Officer Potts/Congress Avenue Bridge**
13. My relatives, who are originally from a *town*, now live in a *city*.   **13. Eureka/San Diego**
14. The librarian asked my *classmate* to return the *book* as soon as possible.   **14. Jorge/The Wind in the Willows**
15. That *newspaper* is published daily; this *magazine* is published weekly.   **15. The New York Times/the Nation**
16. Ted read a *poem* for the *teacher*.   **16. "The Raven"/Mrs. Long**
17. That *state* borders the *ocean*.   **17. Massachusetts/Atlantic Ocean**
18. The owner of that store visited a *country* during a *month*.   **18. Italy/May**
19. A *man* flew to a *city* one day.   **19. Mr. Kim/Paris**
20. Last week the *president* talked about the history of our *nation*.   **20. President Clinton/the United States**

Exercise 4 Using Proper Nouns

Developers are planning to build a new shopping mall in your neighborhood. They are trying to find out what kinds of stores and other attractions the community would like at the mall. The developers have prepared the following survey.

Answer each question with a complete sentence. Underline each proper noun that you use.

EXAMPLE   1. When would you be most likely to go to the mall?
   1. I would be most likely to visit the mall on <u>Saturdays</u>, especially in <u>August</u> and <u>November</u>.

New Mall Questionnaire
1. What stores would you most like to see at the mall?
2. What would you be most likely to buy at the mall?
3. What types of movies would you prefer to see at the mall theater?
4. What restaurants would you like to have in the mall's food court?
5. Would you go to the mall arcade? If so, what games would you play?
6. What brands of clothes do you prefer?
7. Would you purchase books or magazines at the mall? If so, what books or magazines interest you?
8. To what clubs, organizations, or associations do you belong?
9. What special or seasonal events would attract you to the mall?
10. At what nearby malls do you sometimes shop?

ANSWERS
Exercise 4
Responses will vary, but each response should be a complete sentence and all proper nouns should be underlined.

Review A Identifying and Classifying Nouns

Identify the nouns in the following sentences, and label them *common* or *proper*.

EXAMPLE   1. In 1989, President George Bush gave General Colin Powell a big job.
   1. 1989—common; President George Bush—proper; General Colin Powell—proper; job—common

Cooperative Learning

To give students practice in naming proper nouns, have students complete a team race on a social studies topic that they are studying. Divide the class into groups of four. Give each group a social studies category, and have the groups write as many proper nouns as they can in five minutes. All group members are responsible for generating answers. (Some possible categories include states and their capitals, continents, oceans, rivers, countries, presidents, and battles.) Have one student in each group record the group's ideas, one student make sure the answers are proper nouns, and two students act as prompters. One prompter can mention letters in the alphabet not yet used as initial letters in the group's ideas. The other prompter can mention areas in the category overlooked by the group (for example, state capitals of Western states).

Viewing the Illustration

Ideas for Writing. Discuss with students the feelings that soldiers might have during a military conflict and how soldiers might feel about meeting a general. Ask each student to pretend that he or she is one of the soldiers pictured in the photo and to write a diary entry that a soldier might have written that day.

The Pronoun

Rule 11b *(pp. 328–335)*

OBJECTIVES

- To rewrite sentences, replacing nouns with pronouns
- To identify pronouns in sentences
- To identify pronouns as personal, reflexive, or intensive
- To identify pronouns as indefinite or demonstrative
- To identify pronouns as relative or interrogative

1. He appointed Powell leader of the Joint Chiefs of Staff.
2. Powell became one of the top military officers in the United States.
3. In the photo here, he is shown talking with soldiers during the Persian Gulf War.
4. Do you think the troops were excited to meet the general?
5. Powell grew up in the Bronx, a neighborhood in New York City.
6. His parents came to the United States from Jamaica.
7. Powell graduated from the City College of New York.
8. There he joined the Reserve Officers' Training Corps.
9. Did you know that Powell was awarded the Purple Heart during the Vietnam War?
10. In his speeches, he often encourages students to graduate from high school.

The Pronoun

11b. A ***pronoun*** **is a word that is used in place of one or more nouns or pronouns.**

In each of the following examples, an arrow is drawn from a pronoun to the noun or nouns it stands for in the sentence.

EXAMPLES   When Cindy Davis came to the bus stop, **she** was wearing a cast.

The trees and bushes are dry; **they** should be watered.

This stable is large. **It** has stalls for thirty horses.

The word or word group that a pronoun stands for is called its ***antecedent.***

EXAMPLES   My **aunt** sold her car. [*Aunt* is the antecedent of *her.*]

Anthony, call your mother. [*Anthony* is the antecedent of *your.*]

Reference Note

For information about choosing **pronouns that agree with their antecedents,** see page 435.

RESOURCES

The Pronoun

Practice

- *Grammar, Usage, and Mechanics,* pp. 28, 29, 30, 31, 32
- *Language Workshop CD-ROM,* Lesson 2

Sometimes the antecedent is not stated because the reader can understand the meaning of the sentence without it.

EXAMPLES Call **your** mother. [The antecedent of *your* is clearly the person to whom the sentence is directed.]

They beat **us** fair and square. [The antecedent of *They* is clearly the team that the speaker played against. The antecedent of *us* is clearly the team of which the speaker is a member.]

Exercise 5 Substituting Pronouns for Nouns

In each of the following sentences, replace the repeated nouns with pronouns.

EXAMPLE 1. Viviana set up Viviana's game on the table.
1. Viviana set up her game on the table.

1. The passengers on the departing ocean liner waved to the passengers' friends on shore.   1. their
2. The test was so long that I almost didn't finish the test.   2. it
3. Rachel's neighbors asked Rachel to baby-sit.   3. her
4. Carlos said that Carlos had already cleaned Carlos's room.   4. he/his
5. The directions were long, but the directions were clear.   5. they
6. Mom was born in Nigeria, and Mom speaks French, English, Spanish, and Italian.   6. she
7. Ask those police officers if the police officers know the way to Alhambra Avenue.   7. they
8. The twins saved the twins' money; now, that new bicycle built for two is the twins'.   8. their/theirs
9. Did Warren's aunt fix some tacos for Warren?   9. him
10. Our whole family spent the weekend at home, but our whole family had the best time ever.   10. we

Personal Pronouns

A ***personal pronoun*** refers to the one speaking (***first person***), the one spoken to (***second person***), or the one spoken about (***third person***). Personal pronouns have both singular and plural forms.

EXAMPLE **I** am sure **he** told **you** about **their** plans.

The Pronoun 329

Meeting INDIVIDUAL NEEDS

MODALITIES

Kinesthetic Learners. Have students work at the chalkboard as you dictate sentences containing pronouns. Ask students to circle the pronouns and to draw arrows to the pronouns' antecedents. Students can also point to themselves, other students, and objects around the classroom to act out different types of pronouns. These activities may aid students' understanding of the relationships between pronouns and their antecedents.

Relating to Writing

Point out to students that they can use pronouns to improve their writing. Using personal pronouns allows students to avoid repeating common or proper nouns that are the topics of their writing, and possessive pronouns help to clarify ownership in a passage. Discuss pronoun usage with students, and have students list their own reasons for using different types of pronouns in their writing. Students can use their ideas to revise writing assignments.

HELP

Do not confuse the possessive pronoun *its* with the contraction *it's*. The pronoun *its* means "belonging to it." The contraction *it's* means "it is" or "it has." The apostrophe shows that letters have been left out.

Some other possessive pronouns that are often confused with contractions are *their*, meaning "belonging to them," (confused with *they're*, meaning "they are") and *your*, meaning "belonging to you" (confused with *you're*, meaning "you are").

Reference Note

For more information about **words that are often confused**, see page 625.

Personal Pronouns		
	Singular	Plural
First person	I, me, my, mine	we, us, our, ours
Second person	you, your, yours	you, your, yours
Third person	he, him, his, she, her, hers, it, its	they, them, their, theirs

The **possessive pronouns**—*my, mine, our, ours, your, yours, her, hers, his, its, their,* and *theirs*—are personal pronouns that are used to show ownership or possession.

EXAMPLES Nina stored **her** suitcase under **her** bed.

Is that paper **yours** or **mine**?

NOTE Some teachers prefer to call some possessive forms of pronouns (such as *my, your,* and *our*) adjectives. Follow your teacher's instructions regarding possessive forms.

Reflexive and Intensive Pronouns

A *reflexive pronoun* refers to the subject and is necessary to the basic meaning of the sentence. An *intensive pronoun* emphasizes its antecedent and is unnecessary to the basic meaning of the sentence.

Reflexive and Intensive Pronouns	
First person	myself, ourselves
Second person	yourself, yourselves
Third person	himself, herself, itself, themselves

REFLEXIVE   We enjoyed **ourselves** at the party.

She bought **herself** a new set of Spanish lesson tapes.

INTENSIVE   David **himself** bought a sandwich.

The award will be presented by the principal **herself**.

Exercise 6 Identifying Pronouns

Identify all of the pronouns in each of the following sentences.

EXAMPLE 1. I lent her my camera.
1. I, her, my

1. The dentist asked me several questions before examining my teeth.
2. Dad asked the mechanics working on his car to call him about his bill.
3. Our cousins have decided they will visit Peru.
4. She asked herself where she could have put her book.
5. He washed the mats thoroughly and put them out in the sun to dry.
6. Here is a postcard from Egypt for you and me.
7. We helped ourselves to tacos and refried beans.
8. You gave us your support when we needed it.
9. He had to do his social studies homework before playing soccer with us.
10. I found the weak battery and replaced it myself.

Exercise 7 Identifying Types of Pronouns

In each of the following sentences, identify the italicized pronoun as *personal*, *reflexive*, or *intensive*.

EXAMPLE 1. Eric gave *her* a flower.
1. personal

1. Darren *himself* did not know where the gifts were hidden.
2. Did Teri offer *them* directions to the community center?
3. Elena is a very good actress, and *she* always learns her lines very quickly.
4. Kara treated *herself* to a short nap after a long day.
5. Although *it* fell from the top branches of the elm tree, the chipmunk was not injured.
6. Have *you* told Dennis about the new sports complex?
7. Tracy and Ed carried the aquarium to the car *themselves*.
8. Brian and Erin just arrived home, so *they* have not started their homework assignment yet.
9. Rosalia congratulated *herself* on meeting her goal.
10. The dog made *itself* dizzy by chasing its own tail.

TIPS & TRICKS

If you are not sure whether a pronoun is reflexive or intensive, use this test: Read the sentence aloud, omitting the pronoun. If the meaning of the sentence stays the same, the pronoun is intensive. If the meaning changes, the pronoun is reflexive.

EXAMPLES
Jeremy repaired the tire **himself**. [Without *himself,* the meaning stays the same. The pronoun is intensive.]

The children enjoyed **themselves** at the park. [Without *themselves,* the sentence doesn't make sense. The pronoun is reflexive.]

TEACHING TIP

Exercise 6 After students read the **Note** on p. 330, you may have told them whether you want possessive pronouns to be labeled as pronouns or as adjectives. Your decision will determine whether *my* in sentence 1, *his* in sentence 2, *Our* in sentence 3, *her* in sentence 4, *your* in sentence 8, and *his* in sentence 9 should be identified as pronouns.

Cooperative Learning

Divide the class into groups of five, and ask each group to write a paragraph on a topic such as a field trip, project, or sporting event. One student begins by writing a sentence containing a personal pronoun and underlining the pronoun. The students take turns adding related sentences, each of which contains an underlined example of another type of pronoun: reflexive, possessive, demonstrative, or indefinite. Each group should write three five-sentence paragraphs so that each student writes three sentences using the same type of pronoun. Ask a volunteer from each group to read one of the sentences aloud.

Demonstrative Pronouns

A *demonstrative pronoun* points out a specific person, place, thing, or idea.

Demonstrative Pronouns			
this	that	these	those

EXAMPLES What is **that**?

This is the uniform once worn by Satchel Paige.

These are the shoes he used to wear.

Are **those** really his autographs?

Reference Note
For information on **adjectives,** see page 336.

NOTE *This*, *that*, *these*, and *those* can also be used as adjectives. When these words are used to modify a noun or pronoun, they are called **demonstrative adjectives.**

PRONOUN **This** is a delicious papaya. [*This* refers to *papaya.*]
ADJECTIVE **This** papaya is delicious. [*This* modifies *papaya.*]

PRONOUN **That** is the stamp my cousin sent from Sweden. [*That* refers to *stamp.*]
ADJECTIVE **That** stamp was the first in my collection. [*That* modifies *stamp.*]

Indefinite Pronouns

Reference Note
For more information on **indefinite pronouns,** see page 427.

An *indefinite pronoun* refers to a person, a place, a thing, or an idea that may or may not be specifically named.

Common Indefinite Pronouns			
all	each	more	one
any	either	much	other
anybody	everybody	neither	several
anyone	everyone	nobody	some
anything	few	none	somebody
both	many	no one	something

332 Chapter 11 Parts of Speech Overview

EXAMPLES   **Everyone** in the class was invited to the party.

None of the boys knew **much** about camping.

NOTE Most words that can be used as indefinite pronouns can also be used as adjectives.

PRONOUN   **Some** are bored by this movie.
ADJECTIVE   **Some** people are bored by this movie.

Exercise 8   Identifying Pronouns

Identify the italicized pronoun in each of the following sentences as *indefinite* or *demonstrative*.

EXAMPLE   1. *Someone* has been sitting in my chair.
            1. indefinite

1. Are you asking *anyone* to the dance this weekend?
2. *This* is my jacket; that one must be yours.
3. *Something* is different about your hair.
4. *That* was the funniest thing I have ever seen a kitten do!
5. *This* is good, but Chrissy's report is better.
6. The armadillo paused at the puddle and drank *some* of the water.
7. Are *those* the socks you are wearing with those shoes?
8. We have to choose between *these* and the ones we looked at yesterday.
9. Linda did more sit-ups than *several* who tried before her.
10. *Nobody* knows the answer to that.

Review B   Identifying Pronouns

Identify the pronoun or pronouns in each of the following sentences.

EXAMPLE   1. Everyone in my class likes going on field trips.
            1. *Everyone; my*

1. Last week, we really enjoyed ourselves at the National Museum of African Art.
2. It has been part of the Smithsonian Institution in Washington, D.C., since 1979.

Crossing the Curriculum

Math. Point out to students the connection between numbers and indefinite pronouns: both name quantities. Most indefinite pronouns name a vague quantity, but some, such as *one* and *none*, are very precise. Discuss this connection with students. Students can even arrange the pronouns according to quantity, from *none* to *all*, along a number line such as the following one:

0	1	2	3	4	5...
none, no one	each, one	both, either, neither	few	some	many

TEACHING TIP

Review B If you have instructed students to classify possessive pronouns as adjectives, the following pronouns should not be included in the answers: *its* in sentence 3, *our* in sentences 4 and 7, *her* in sentence 8, and *my* in sentence 9.

Critical Thinking
Metacognition. Point out to students that there are probably too many pronouns to memorize all of them by type. Ask students what their strategies are for remembering the different types of pronouns. Have students rate the effectiveness of and describe their strategies. Students having trouble with pronouns should develop new strategies. Have students meet in groups to share and compare their ideas.

3. In 1987, the museum's collection was moved to its present underground facility.
4. Our teacher, Ms. Martinez, told us about the museum before we went there.
5. She said the entrance is made of pink granite.
6. I was surprised by the six domes on top.
7. Everyone had at least one question to ask our museum guide.
8. We enjoyed hearing her lively explanations of the artwork.
9. This is a photograph of one of my favorite objects at the museum.
10. Do you like it?

Mask, Bassa Peoples, Liberia. Wood, pigment, bone or ivory, iron (9½" X 5¾" X 4½"). National Museum of African Art, Eliot Elisofon Archives, Smithsonian Institution, #88-5-1. Photo Credit: Franko Khoury.

Interrogative Pronouns

An *interrogative pronoun* introduces a question.

Interrogative Pronouns				
what	which	who	whom	whose

EXAMPLES **What** is the first event in the contest?

Who is going to represent our team?

To **whom** is the e-mail addressed?

Which of the books are you reading?

Whose is the car in the driveway?

Relative Pronouns

A *relative pronoun* introduces a subordinate clause.

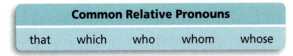

Common Relative Pronouns

that   which   who   whom   whose

Reference Note
For information on **subordinate clauses,** see page 388.

EXAMPLES Harry S. Truman, **who** became president when Franklin D. Roosevelt died, surprised many people with his victory over Thomas Dewey in 1948.

Robins are among the birds **that** migrate south for the winter.

Exercise 9 Identifying Relative and Interrogative Pronouns

Identify the italicized pronouns in each of the following sentences as *relative* or *interrogative*.

EXAMPLE 1. *Which* of those snow sculptures do you think will win the prize?

1. interrogative

1. The only student *that* could complete the obstacle course was Sophia.
2. *What* was the name of the volcano that erupted in Washington?
3. *What* was causing that sound outside your room at night?
4. "*Who* left all of those markers on the floor yesterday?" asked Ms. Jackson.
5. Lilacs, *which* are known throughout the world for their fragrant flowers, grow best in northern climates.
6. The new teacher, *whom* we have not yet met, will start Monday.
7. *Which* of you remembers the name of the author of "The Celebrated Jumping Frog of Calaveras County"?
8. *Whose* turn is it to take out the trash?
9. The light bulb, *which* had been flickering for a few days, finally burned out.
10. To *whom* did you lend your textbook?

The Pronoun 335

The Adjective

Rule 11c (pp. 336–342)

OBJECTIVES

- To identify adjectives and the words they modify in sentences
- To complete a story by adding appropriate adjectives
- To identify adjectives, including proper adjectives, in sentences
- To change proper nouns into proper adjectives and to use the adjectives in sentences
- To distinguish between demonstrative pronouns and demonstrative adjectives

TEACHING TIP

Activity. Ask students to supply words that describe the similarities and differences between an orange and a baseball. Students might begin by saying that both objects are round. You might want to draw a Venn diagram on the chalkboard and ask students to suggest words that describe both items and words that apply to only one item or the other. Tell students that the words listed in the diagram are all adjectives.

Exercises You may wish to have students complete **Exercise 10** as guided practice and **Exercise 11** as independent practice.

STYLE TIP

Some adjectives are more specific and vivid than others. You can make your writing more interesting by replacing dull adjectives with more vivid ones.

ORIGINAL
Mr. Sato is a **nice** man. [The adjective *nice* is dull and doesn't really say much about Mr. Sato.]

REVISED
Mr. Sato is a **generous** man. [The adjective *generous* is more specific about Mr. Sato.]

Reference Note
For information on using *a* and *an*, see page 520.

11c The Adjective

11c. An *adjective* is a word that is used to modify a noun or a pronoun.

To **modify** a word means to describe the word or to make its meaning more definite. An adjective modifies a noun or pronoun by telling *what kind*, *which one*, *how many*, or *how much*.

What Kind?	Which One or Ones?	How Many or How Much?
gentle dog	**sixth** grade	**two** tickets
Irish town	**these** books	**full** pitcher
scary movie	**other** people	**most** players
purple shoes	**any** CD	**no** work

Adjectives usually come before the words they modify. Sometimes, however, an adjective comes after the word it modifies.

EXAMPLES The dog is **gentle**. [The predicate adjective *gentle* modifies *dog*.]

The sea, **blue** and **sparkling**, stretched out before us invitingly. [The adjectives *blue* and *sparkling* modify the noun *sea*.]

NOTE The adjectives *a*, *an*, and *the* are called **articles**.

Exercise 10 Identifying Adjectives

Identify each *adjective* in the following sentences. Do not include *a*, *an*, or *the*.

EXAMPLE 1. The sky was clear, and the night was cold.
1. clear, cold

1. A silvery moon rode down the western sky.
2. It shed a pale light on the quiet countryside.
3. Long meadows spread out between two hills.
4. The smell of the wild grass was strong.
5. The only sound we heard was the sharp crackle of the fire.

336 Chapter 11 Parts of Speech Overview

RESOURCES

The Adjective

Practice

- *Grammar, Usage, and Mechanics,* pp. 33, 34, 35, 36–37
- *Language Workshop CD-ROM,* Lesson 3

6. Suddenly, several stars came out.
7. I watched until the entire sky glowed with bright stars.
8. I was lonely and happy at the same time.
9. I finally became sleepy and longed for my warm bed.
10. Soon I went indoors and fell into a deep sleep.

Exercise 11 Identifying Adjectives and the Words They Modify

Identify the adjectives and the words they modify in the following sentences. Do not include *a, an,* or *the.*

EXAMPLE 1. It costs five dollars to go to that movie.
 1. *five—dollars; that—movie*

1. I have a free ticket for the last game.
2. We ate spicy crawfish, and they were delicious.
3. The new neighbor is helpful and nice.
4. The bear, angry and hungry, surprised the campers.
5. Many students compete in the regional events.
6. Will country musicians play at the county fair?
7. Despite the long delay, we remained cheerful.
8. A shiny coin stared up at me from the the icy sidewalk.
9. Take one booklet and pass the rest to the next row.
10. A few colorful birds perched in the tall, green trees on the bank of the river.

Exercise 12 Writing Adjectives for a Story

The following story is about a cave exploration. Copy the sentences, adding an appropriate adjective for each blank. Underline the adjectives you add.
Adjectives will vary.

EXAMPLE 1. Exploring caves is ____ on ____ days.
 1. *Exploring caves is fun on hot days.*

1. Have you ever been in a ____ cave like the one shown at right?   1. real
2. Would you say it looks ____ and ____?   2. dark/scary 3. huge
3. My father and I explored this ____ cave once.
4. It was ____ but ____, too.   4. frightening/fun
5. We found some ____ rock formations.   5. strange
6. We also heard ____ sounds.   6. weird

COMPUTER TIP

Some software includes a thesaurus feature. You can use the computer thesaurus to find synonyms to replace dull or overused adjectives in your writing. Always check the meaning of an unfamiliar adjective in a dictionary, though, to make sure it is just the right word.

TEACHING TIP

Exercise 10 Students might identify *my* in sentence 9 as an adjective, depending upon your instructions regarding the **Note** on p. 330.

Meeting INDIVIDUAL NEEDS

ENGLISH-LANGUAGE LEARNERS
Spanish. In Spanish most adjectives are placed after the nouns they modify. The words *the beautiful woman*, for example, are expressed as *la mujer bella*. When the adjective modifies a plural noun in Spanish, the adjective changes form to agree with the noun. For example, *the beautiful women* is expressed as *las mujeres bellas*. Reinforce the correct positioning of adjectives in English, and remind students that in English the forms of almost all adjectives remain the same even when they modify plural nouns.

Critical Thinking

Evaluation. As students complete writing assignments, ask them to consider their choice of adjectives by asking "Is there a fresher or more precise adjective I can use?" Students can incorporate an evaluation of their adjectives into their revision steps.

MINI-LESSON   Continued on p. 338

Punctuating Adjectives in a Series.
Often two or more adjectives are used before a noun to make its meaning more specific. Remind students of the rules regarding comma usage with series of adjectives.

1. Use commas to separate two or more adjectives before a noun.

   Try this healthful, tasty snack.

2. Do not place a comma between an adjective and the noun directly following it.

Relating to Vocabulary

Give students practice in choosing adjectives that can make their writing more interesting. Write the following sentences on the chalkboard. Have students replace the underlined adjectives with more vivid adjectives without changing the meanings of the sentences.

1. The <u>cold</u> wind made us shiver.
2. Our neighbor has a <u>cute</u> kitten.
3. We all think he is a <u>nice</u> person.
4. It's a <u>pretty</u> night.
5. She is a <u>good</u> soccer player.

7. My father took some ____ photographs. **7. interesting**
8. We looked up and saw ____ bats flying above our heads. **8. black**
9. After exploring for about ____ hours, we were ready to see the sky again. **9. three**
10. Spelunking, as cave exploring is called, can be a very ____ experience, if you have a ____ guide. **10. fascinating/good**

Proper Adjectives

A **proper adjective** is formed from a proper noun and begins with a capital letter.

Proper Nouns	Proper Adjectives
Japan	**Japanese** islands
Easter	**Easter** Sunday
Queen Victoria	**Victorian** drama
Sioux	**Sioux** customs

Reference Note
For information on **capitalizing proper adjectives,** see page 548.

HELP
Some proper nouns, such as *Easter* and *Sioux,* do not change spelling when they are used as proper adjectives.

Exercise 13 Identifying Adjectives

Identify all of the adjectives in the following sentences. Then, underline each proper adjective. Do not include the articles *a, an,* or *the.*

EXAMPLE 1. The Navajo weaver made a blanket on a wooden loom.
1. *Navajo,* wooden

1. Music can express sad or happy feelings.
2. The quartet sang several Irish songs.
3. The gold watch with the fancy chain was made by a famous Swiss watchmaker.
4. She is a Balinese dancer.
5. On vacation, Mom enjoys long, quiet breakfasts.
6. Many Australian people are of British origin.
7. The Egyptian mummies are on display on the first floor.
8. We are proud of Joshua.
9. The movie is based on a popular Russian novel.
10. In Canadian football, a team has twelve players on the field at one time.

338 Chapter 11 Parts of Speech Overview

MINI-LESSON

Jameel's gift to me was a colorful, hand-woven basket. (no comma before *basket*)

Write the following sentences on the chalkboard, and ask volunteers to add the necessary commas.

1. The ripe[,] juicy apples are ready to eat.
2. Would you enjoy a cool[,] refreshing swim in the lake?
3. Winston is a cute[,] affectionate[,] playful dog.

Exercise 14 Writing Proper Adjectives

Change the following proper nouns into proper adjectives. Then, use each proper adjective in a sentence.

EXAMPLE   1. France
          1. French—We bought French bread at the bakery.

1. England
2. Inca
3. Hinduism
4. Celt
5. Alaska
6. Thanksgiving
7. Shakespeare
8. Korea
9. Navajo
10. Boston

HELP

You may want to use a dictionary to help you spell the adjectives in Exercise 14.

Demonstrative Adjectives

This, that, these, and *those* can be used both as adjectives and as pronouns. When they modify nouns or pronouns, they are called **demonstrative adjectives.** When they are used alone, they are called **demonstrative pronouns.**

ADJECTIVE   What are **these** skates doing in the living room?
PRONOUN   What are **these** doing in the living room?

ADJECTIVE   I prefer **that** brand of frozen yogurt.
PRONOUN   I prefer **that.**

Reference Note

For more information on **demonstrative pronouns,** see page 332.

Exercise 15 Identifying Demonstrative Pronouns and Demonstrative Adjectives

In each of the following sentences, identify the italicized word as a *demonstrative pronoun* or a *demonstrative adjective.*

EXAMPLE   1. Who gave you *those* beautiful flowers?
          1. demonstrative adjective

1. *That* is the strangest hot-air balloon I have ever seen!
2. Will *those* squirrels find enough to eat during the winter?
3. My dog, Manda, has been chewing on *this* piece of rawhide for three weeks.
4. *These* are the only shoes I can find that will fit you.
5. According to the guidebook, *those* are the largest trees in North America.

The Adjective   339

Relating to Literature

Have students read and discuss a story such as "What Do Fish Have to Do with Anything?" by Avi, in which descriptive adjectives are used to create a mood or describe a character. Ask students what mood is created or how a character is described in the story and which adjectives help convey the mood or description.

TEACHING TIP

Reviews You may wish to use **Review D** as guided practice. Then, have students complete **Review E** as independent practice.

---

6. Is *that* your final offer?
7. The geese always return to *these* same lakes.
8. What do you plan to do with *that* lump of clay?
9. I'm afraid she's gone too far *this* time.
10. Can *this* be the same person I knew back in third grade?

Review C — Identifying Adjectives

Identify the adjectives in the following sentences. Do not include *a*, *an*, or *the*.

EXAMPLE 1. I enjoy visiting the large railroad museum in our city.
   1. large, railroad

1. Museums can be interesting.
2. Large cities have different kinds of museums.
3. Some museums display sculpture and paintings.
4. These museums may focus on one special kind of art.
5. For example, they might specialize in Chinese art or Mexican art.
6. Other museums feature birds, sea creatures, dinosaurs, and other animals.
7. A curator holds an important job in a museum.
8. A curator needs to know many facts about a particular display.
9. Some valuable objects must be displayed in a stable environment.
10. Some people prefer displays of modern art, while others enjoy exhibits of folk art.

Review D — Identifying Nouns, Pronouns, and Adjectives

Identify all of the nouns, pronouns, and adjectives in each of the following sentences. Do not include *a*, *an*, or *the*.

EXAMPLE 1. I think models make a great hobby.
   1. I—pronoun; models—noun; great—adjective; hobby—noun

1. Do you have a favorite hobby?
2. Models are enjoyable and educational.

340   Chapter 11   Parts of Speech Overview

Learning for Life

Continued on pp. 341–343

Writing a Letter to the Editor. A responsible citizen will have opinions on current issues and should be able to express those opinions clearly and convincingly. Have students write a letter to the editor of their school or classroom newspaper on a topic of their choice. Point out that the careful use of nouns, pronouns, and adjectives will make their opinions clearer and their arguments more effective.

  Bring copies of student newspapers to class, and have students select several good

3. They require little space.
4. I keep mine on a bookshelf my dad and I built ourselves.
5. Models are packaged in kits.
6. My favorite models are historic ships and antique planes.
7. On my last birthday, my parents gave me two model kits of biplanes.
8. They came with directions in several languages.
9. Many of the tiny parts are designed for an exact fit.
10. Do you think the bright decals add a realistic look?

Review E Identifying Nouns, Pronouns, and Adjectives

Identify all of the nouns, pronouns, and adjectives in each of the following sentences. Do not include *a*, *an*, or *the*.

EXAMPLE 1. Pueblos are practical housing for people in hot, dry regions.
 1. Pueblos—noun; practical—adjective; housing—noun; people—noun; hot—adjective; dry—adjective; regions—noun

1. The brown building in the photograph contains several individual homes.
2. *Pueblo* is a Spanish word for a structure like this and for a town.
3. This building is located at the Taos Pueblo in New Mexico.

Viewing the Illustration
You may wish to have students research and report on the types of housing and other patterns of living used by American Indians in different parts of North America before European settlement of the continent. You might use this activity in conjunction with the Library/Media Center section in the **Quick Reference Handbook.** The project could be a cooperative activity in which group members work on specific parts of the project and each presents some aspect of the report to the class. Reports should connect the geographic location and climate to the types of housing, food, clothing, and customs of the different Native American groups.

examples of letters to the editor to display on the class bulletin board. Students can use these as inspiration and as models for their own letters.

Arrange students in small groups to brainstorm for possible topics. Each group member should decide on his or her own topic and position and should write a list of at least three points to support the argument. Students can then work individually on their letters. Refer students to **Chapter 7: Making a Difference,** p.226 for guidelines

GRAMMAR

Review F Writing Sentences Using Nouns, Pronouns, and Adjectives

POSSIBLE ANSWERS

1. Did you know that <u>Chicago</u> is very windy?
2. Iris asked me to name <u>my</u> favorite color.
3. I bought <u>eight</u> apples at the fruit stand.
4. John gave <u>himself</u> a bruise on his shin when he bumped into the open dishwasher door.
5. Uncle Otis and Aunt Dottie enjoyed the <u>Hawaiian</u> luau.
6. Where did you put <u>the</u> vases for the flowers?
7. I believe <u>they</u> said she would be here in twenty minutes.
8. <u>This</u> sweater fits better than the other one.
9. <u>Everybody</u> thought the assignment was easy.
10. There can never be too much <u>kindness</u> in the world.

---

4. Can [you] tell how pueblos are made?
5. [They] are built of <u>adobe</u>.
6. People make <u>adobe</u> by mixing <u>mud</u> with <u>grass</u> or <u>straw</u>.
7. [They] shape the <u>mixture</u> into <u>bricks</u> and let [them] bake in the sun.
8. <u>Buildings</u> made with <u>this</u> material stay <u>cool</u> during the summer months.
9. [Anyone] on a <u>visit</u> to the <u>Southwest</u> can find <u>other</u> pueblos like <u>this</u> [one].
10. <u>Old</u> <u>pueblos</u> built by the <u>Hopi</u> and the <u>Zuni</u> fascinate [me].

Review F Writing Sentences Using Nouns, Pronouns, and Adjectives

Write ten original sentences using the parts of speech given below. In each sentence, underline the word that is the listed part of speech.

EXAMPLE 1. an adjective that comes after the word it describes
           1. *Our guide was very <u>helpful</u>.*

1. a proper noun
2. a possessive pronoun
3. an adjective that tells *how many*
4. a reflexive pronoun
5. a proper adjective
6. an article
7. a third-person pronoun
8. a demonstrative adjective
9. an indefinite pronoun
10. a noun that names an idea

342   Chapter 11   Parts of Speech Overview

Learning for Life

on persuasive writing.

Caution students to keep their letters under two hundred words in length. Remind them to use pronouns and nouns to refer clearly to their topics and their arguments. Also, point out that precise adjectives can make their writing clear and vivid.

After students have finished writing, pair them to evaluate each other's work. Peer evaluators should be able to name the topic and position of the letter and identify the supporting reasons and conclusion. Partners

Chapter Review

A. Identifying Nouns, Pronouns, and Adjectives

Identify each italicized word or word group in the following sentences as a *noun*, a *pronoun*, or an *adjective*.

1. My *best* friend plays *soccer*.
2. *We* went to *Boston* last summer.
3. Help *yourself* to some *Chinese* food.
4. What a *beautiful* garden *Mrs. Murakami* has!
5. *These* directions were *accurate*.
6. *That* is a fast *merry-go-round*.
7. Juana invited *us* to *her* fiesta.
8. A *sharp* knife is *necessary* for making a wood carving.
9. Almost *everyone* in the band takes private music *lessons*.
10. *This* story is my *favorite* one.

B. Identifying Common and Proper Nouns

Identify the nouns in the following sentences, and label each *common* or *proper*.

11. The religion our family practices is Islam.
12. Was Spanish the first language your mother spoke?
13. The musicians in the band play guitars, keyboards, and drums.
14. My favorite movie is Willy Wonka and the Chocolate Factory.
15. Many American tourists visit London in the summer.

C. Identifying Pronouns

Identify all of the pronouns in each of the following sentences.

16. My cat ate all of its food this morning.
17. Each of the girls said someone had already told her about the band concert.
18. I brought a casserole to the potluck dinner and put it in the oven.

19. The doctor herself removed his bandages.
20. Did anyone notice the person who delivered the package?
21. "I think this winter is going to be long and cold," he said to himself.
22. Didn't you ask him not to do that?
23. That book is not the one that I wanted to read.
24. We asked ourselves if he really intended to come to our party.
25. Which of the sweaters is yours?

D. Identifying Proper and Demonstrative Adjectives

Identify the adjectives in the following sentences. Do not include the articles *a*, *an*, or *the*. Then, label each [proper adjective] and each (demonstrative adjective).

26. The [Easter] holiday lasted for one short week.
27. The apple, glossy and red, rolled out of the bag and across the smooth table.
28. The rain was steady throughout (that) gloomy afternoon.
29. Would you like (these) [French] pastries, or would you rather have those?
30. The [Siamese] cat is playful, but (that) old tabby is aloof.

E. Identifying Nouns, Pronouns, and Adjectives

Identify each *noun*, [pronoun], and *adjective* in the following sentences. Do not include the articles *a*, *an*, and *the*.

31. [Someone] told [me] about the movie.
32. [We] are moving to Belgium, a European country.
33. J. S. Bach, a German composer, wrote many pieces for the harpsichord.
34. "Is [this] the tape [you] wanted?" asked Mr. Imagi.
35. Ted talked [himself] into the purchase of a new computer.
36. [Some] of the old songs are lovely.
37. These colors are brighter than [those].

RESOURCES

Parts of Speech Overview

Review
- *Grammar, Usage, and Mechanics*, pp. 38, 39, 40

Assessment
- Assessment Package
  —*Chapter Tests*, Ch. 11
  —*Chapter Tests in Standardized Test Formats*, Ch. 11
- *Test Generator* (One-Stop Planner CD-ROM)

38. Professor Auerbach herself will present the award to us.
39. The Swedish car in the driveway is ours.
40. Does anybody know when the city of San Antonio was founded?

Writing Application
Using Pronouns in a Plot Summary

Pronouns and Antecedents You are in a filmmaking class at the community center and need ideas for a project. The theme of the project is science fiction movie spoofs. Write a plot summary for a short movie. Explain the plot of the movie, and describe the characters. Be sure that the pronouns you use refer clearly to their antecedents.

Prewriting In a spoof, a writer imitates and makes fun of another work. Imagine several science fiction movie spoofs—for example, *There's an Alien in My Soup* or *Nerds from Neptune*. Choose the idea that you like the best. Then, brainstorm some ideas for a simple plot. Jot down brief descriptions of the setting and the characters in the movie.

Writing Use your notes to help you write your first draft. Summarize what happens in the movie from beginning to end. Describe each character as you introduce him or her. Keep the props and costumes simple—you are working on a low budget.

Revising Ask a friend to read your movie idea. Is the plot interesting? Is it funny? Can your friend tell which character is performing each action? If not, you may need to revise some details. Check to make sure each pronoun refers clearly to its antecedent.

Publishing Read your summary one more time to catch other errors in spelling, grammar, and punctuation. You may want to develop one scene from your plot summary. With the help of several classmates, dramatize this scene in front of the class. Use simple masks and props to create the effect of science fiction.

Reference Note
For more about **developing plots**, see Chapter 5.

Chapter Review **345**

RESOURCES

Writing Application
Extension
- *Grammar, Usage, and Mechanics,* p. 43
- *Language Workshop CD-ROM,* Lessons 1, 2, 3

CHAPTER 12

PREVIEWING THE CHAPTER

- This chapter should help students recognize and understand the functions of verbs, adverbs, prepositions, conjunctions, and interjections.

- The material in this chapter can be referred to when teaching any of the composition chapters and will be of special help to students when they study **Chapter 10: The Sentence.**

- The chapter closes with a **Chapter Review** including a **Writing Application** feature that asks students to write ten sentences using the verb *be* at least twice as a helping verb and at least three times as a linking verb.

- For help in integrating this chapter with writing chapters, see the **Teaching Strands** chart on pages T297A–T297B.

USING THE DIAGNOSTIC PREVIEW

- You could use the **Diagnostic Preview** to gauge students' familiarity with verbs, adverbs, prepositions, conjunctions, and interjections. You may want to assign only the exercises students are likely to find troublesome.

CHAPTER 12 Parts of Speech Overview
Verb, Adverb, Preposition, Conjunction, Interjection

Diagnostic Preview

Identifying Verbs, Adverbs, Prepositions, Conjunctions, and Interjections

Identify each of the italicized words or word groups in the following sentences as a *verb*, an *adverb*, a *preposition*, a *conjunction*, or an *interjection*.

EXAMPLE 1. A tornado *is* a terrible *and* violent storm.
 1. is—verb; and—conjunction
 1. v./prep.

1. The tornado *struck* our neighborhood *without* warning.
2. We do *not* have a basement in our house. 2. adv.
3. I grabbed my dog Muffin *and* ran *into* the bathroom, the safest room in the house. 3. conj./prep.
4. Muffin and I were *tightly* wedged *between* the sink and the bathtub. 4. adv./prep.
5. *Either* the house was shaking *or* I was, and the air *became* very cold. 5. conj./v.
6. *Suddenly,* a siren went *off.* 6. adv./adv.

346 Chapter 12 Parts of Speech Overview

CHAPTER RESOURCES

Planning
- One-Stop Planner CD-ROM

Practice and Extension
- *Grammar, Usage, and Mechanics,* p. 44
- Language Workshop CD-ROM

Internet
- go.hrw.com (keyword: EOLang)

Evaluation and Assessment
- Assessment Package
 —Chapter Tests, Ch. 12
 —Chapter Tests in Standardized Test Formats, Ch. 12
- Test Generator (One-Stop Planner CD-ROM)

7. A tornado *had been sighted* right *in* the area.   **7. v./prep.**
8. Then everything suddenly *grew* calm—it seemed almost *too* calm.   **8. v./adv.**
9. I *was* ready for the worst, *but* the tornado did not touch my house *or* any other home in the area.   **9. v./conj./conj.**
10. *Well,* I was frightened, *but* I was not hurt.   **10. int./conj.**

The Verb

12a. A *verb* is a word that expresses action or a state of being.

EXAMPLES   We **went** to Boston last April.

Is a firefly a kind of beetle?

Every complete sentence has a verb. The verb says something about the subject.

In this book, verbs are classified in three ways — (1) as *main* or *helping* verbs, (2) as *action* or *linking* verbs, and (3) as *transitive* or *intransitive* verbs.

Main Verbs and Helping Verbs

In many sentences, a single word is all that is needed to express the action or the state of being.

EXAMPLES   The dog **barked** all night.

Brett **throws** the ball a long way.

Mr. Rivera **is** the new English teacher.

In other sentences, the verb consists of a main verb and one or more helping verbs.

A **helping verb** (also called an *auxiliary* verb) helps the **main verb** to express action or a state of being.

EXAMPLES   **can** speak

will learn

should have been fed

Reference Note
For more information about **verbs**, see page 444.

TIPS & TRICKS

Remember, a verb cannot be a helping verb unless there is another verb for it to help. If a verb such as *was* or *had* is the only verb in a sentence, it is not a helping verb.

EXAMPLES
I **had** called my grandmother already. [*Had* is helping the main verb, *called*.]

They **had** a good time at the nature center. [*Had* is the only verb; there is no other verb for it to help.]

The Verb   **347**

RESOURCES

The Verb
Practice
- *Grammar, Usage, and Mechanics,* pp. 45, 46, 47, 48, 49, 50, 51
- *Language Workshop CD-ROM,* Lesson 4

Meeting INDIVIDUAL NEEDS

MODALITIES

Visual Learners. If you are teaching more than one part of speech at one time, a permanent classroom display or poster will probably help students remember the names of the parts of speech. Include the names of the parts of speech being covered, lists of examples from the textbook, and model sentences.

HELP

The word *not* and its contraction, *–n't*, are adverbs telling *to what extent*; neither is part of a verb phrase.

Together, the main verb and its helping verb or verbs are called a *verb phrase*.

EXAMPLES Many students **can speak** Spanish.

I **will be learning** all the state capitals tonight.

The dog **should have been fed** by now.

Commonly Used Helping Verbs					
am	being	do	have	must	were
are	can	does	is	shall	will
be	could	had	may	should	would
been	did	has	might	was	

NOTE Some words can be used as both helping verbs and main verbs.

HELPING VERB   I **do** wash the dishes.
MAIN VERB   I will **do** the dishes.

Sometimes a verb phrase is interrupted by another part of speech.

EXAMPLES Suzanne **should** not **call** so late at night. [The verb phrase *should call* is interrupted by the adverb *not*.]

The scientists **did**n't **think** the asteroid would hit the earth. [The verb phrase *did think* is interrupted by *–n't*, the contraction for *not*.]

Did you **watch** Shania Twain's new video? [The verb phrase *Did watch* is interrupted by the subject *you*.]

Exercise 1   Identifying Verb Phrases and Helping Verbs

Identify the verb phrase in each of the following sentences. Then, underline the helping verb or verbs.

EXAMPLE   1. We are going to Arizona this summer.
    1. <u>are</u> going

1. The Petrified Forest <u>has</u> long attracted many tourists.

2. Its spectacular beauty has captured their imaginations.
3. Visitors can see the Painted Desert at the same time.
4. The colors of the desert do not remain the same for long.
5. Specimens of petrified wood are exhibited at the tourist information center.
6. Have you ever seen a piece of petrified wood?
7. A guide will gladly explain the process of petrification.
8. Visitors can purchase the fossilized wood as a souvenir.
9. Tours of the Petrified Forest are not recommended for amateur hikers.
10. Hikes must be arranged with park rangers.

Exercise 2 — Using Verb Phrases in Original Sentences

Use each of the following word groups as the subject of a sentence with a verb phrase. Make some of your sentences questions. Underline each helping verb and the main verb in each sentence.

EXAMPLE   1. your neighbor's dog
          1. Can your neighbor's dog do tricks?

1. my bicycle
2. the astronauts
3. a tiny kitten
4. the hard assignment
5. a famous singer
6. some strange footprints
7. my grandmother
8. the subway
9. a funny costume
10. the refreshments
11. the Los Angeles Dodgers
12. his favorite movie
13. the bird watchers' club
14. the new computer chip
15. Queen Elizabeth
16. her school picture
17. today's newspaper
18. a slice of bread
19. the pencil sharpener
20. my calendar

Review A — Identifying Verbs

Identify the verbs in each of the following sentences. Be sure to include helping verbs.

EXAMPLE   1. Fairy tales are sometimes called folk tales.
          1. are called

1. Long ago, many people could not read.

 Link to Literature

2. Instead, they would memorize stories.
3. Then they would tell the stories to their family members and friends.
4. In this way, the people, or folk, passed the tales on from generation to generation.
5. Finally, some people wrote the collected stories.
6. Two German brothers, Jakob and Wilhelm Grimm, published a famous collection of German folk tales.
7. The brothers had heard many of the tales from their older relatives.
8. Their collection of stories became extremely popular all over the world.
9. "Sleeping Beauty," "Cinderella," and "Rumpelstiltskin" were all preserved by the brothers Grimm.
10. In your library, you can probably find these tales and many others, too.

Action Verbs

An *action verb* expresses either physical or mental activity.

PHYSICAL ACTIVITY   I **have used** a computer in math class.
                         Please **cook** dinner, Jerome.

MENTAL ACTIVITY   Fran **understands** the science assignment better than anyone else does.
                         The magician **is thinking** of a number.

Exercise 3 Identifying Action Verbs

Identify the action verb in each of the following sentences.

EXAMPLE   1. The Maricopa people live in Arizona.
           1. live

1. The Maricopa make unusual pottery.
2. For this pottery they use two kinds of clay.
3. One kind of clay forms the bowl or platter itself.
4. The other kind of clay colors the pottery.
5. First, the potters mold the clay by hand.
6. Then, they shape it into beautiful bowls and vases.
7. With the second type of clay, the potters create designs.

Exercise 3
ALTERNATIVE LESSON
Have students review nouns and pronouns by finding the following items in the first three sentences.

1. one proper noun and one common noun [*Maricopa, pottery*]
2. three nouns and one pronoun [*pottery, kinds, clay; they*]
3. one pronoun [*itself*]

Viewing the Illustration
Exploring the Subject. The Maricopa were originally one of several American Indian groups of the Yuman people. They were primarily an agricultural people who planted along riverbanks. Today, they are accomplished artisans whose pottery is made to be functional.

8. They often <u>etch</u> designs on the pottery with a toothpick.
9. Each family of potters <u>has</u> its own special designs.
10. These designs <u>preserve</u> Maricopa traditions from generation to generation.

Linking Verbs

A *linking verb* connects, or links, the subject to a word or word group that identifies or describes the subject.

EXAMPLES Sandra Cisneros **is** a writer. [The verb *is* connects *writer* with the subject *Sandra Cisneros*.]

The firefighters **had appeared** victorious. [The verb phrase *had appeared* connects *victorious* with the subject *firefighters*.]

The new superintendent **was** she. [The verb *was* connects *she* with the subject *superintendent*.]

Some Linking Verbs Formed from the Verb *Be*		
am	has been	may be
is	have been	might be
are	had been	can be
was	will be	should be
were	shall be	would have been

Other Linking Verbs			
appear	grow	seem	stay
become	look	smell	taste
feel	remain	sound	turn

Some verbs may be either action verbs or linking verbs, depending on how they are used.

ACTION   They **sounded** the bell for a fire drill.
LINKING Mom **sounded** happy about her new job. [The verb *sounded* links *happy* with the subject *Mom*.]

STYLE TIP

In the sentence *The new superintendent was she,* the pronoun *she* after the linking verb may sound strange. Many people would use *her* in informal speech. However, in formal, standard English, *she* is the correct form in this sentence.

Reference Note

For more about **pronouns following linking verbs,** see page 411. For information on **formal and informal language,** see page 519.

The Verb 351

Relating to Writing

For students who understand the difference between action and linking verbs, assign independent writing for further practice. Have each student write one paragraph describing someone's personality. Students can consider happiness, sense of humor, friendliness, talents, and other traits. Have each student use and underline at least three different linking verbs and three different action verbs.

TECHNOLOGY TIP

For help in completing the **Relating to Writing** assignment above, students could use online dictionaries linked to the HRW Web site (go.hrw.com) to check the spellings of their verbs.

TIPS & TRICKS

If you are not sure if a verb is being used as a linking verb or an action verb, try substituting *is* or *are* for the verb. If the sentence still makes sense, the verb is probably a linking verb. If the sentence does not make sense, the verb is probably an action verb.

EXAMPLES
James **looks** taller. [*James is taller* makes sense; here, *looks* is a linking verb.]

James **looks** out the window. [*James is out the window* does not make sense; here, *looks* is an action verb.]

HELP

Remember to include helping verbs in your answers to Exercise 5.

ACTION   The judge **will look** at my science project.
LINKING   Ann **will look** funny in her gorilla costume. [The verb phrase *will look* links *funny* with the subject *Ann*.]

Exercise 4 Identifying Linking Verbs

Identify the linking verbs or verb phrases in the following sentences.

EXAMPLE   1. Peanut soup made from fresh roasted peanuts tastes good.

1. tastes

1. Peanuts remain an important crop around the world.
2. The peanut, which is high in protein, is native to South America.
3. Peanuts grow ripe underground.
4. The seeds are the edible part of the plant.
5. The peanut has become an important ingredient in more than three hundred common products, such as wood stains, shampoo, printer's ink, and soap.
6. Of course, roasting peanuts smell wonderful.
7. Peanut butter was the invention of a St. Louis doctor in 1890.
8. Before then, thanks to George Washington Carver, the peanut had become one of the major crops of the South.
9. Carver, a scientist who experimented with peanuts and other plants, had been a slave.
10. It may seem strange, but Carver once prepared an entire dinner out of peanuts.

Exercise 5 Identifying Action Verbs and Linking Verbs

Identify the verb in each of the following sentences as an *action verb* or a *linking verb*.

EXAMPLES   1. One of the most successful business leaders in the United States is John Johnson.

1. *is*—linking verb

2. Johnson publishes many popular magazines.

2. *publishes*—action verb

1. The photograph at right shows John Johnson as a success.
2. Johnson's life has not always been easy.
3. The small Arkansas town of his childhood had no high school.
4. Therefore, Johnson's mother moved to Chicago.
5. In Chicago, Johnson attended high school with classmates Redd Foxx and Nat "King" Cole.
6. During the Great Depression of the 1930s, Johnson's family grew very poor.
7. However, Johnson studied hard.
8. He became an honor student, the class president, and the editor of the high school newspaper.
9. Johnson started his first magazine with a loan.
10. Now he is the owner of a group of companies worth $200 million per year.

Transitive and Intransitive Verbs

A *transitive verb* is a verb that expresses an action directed toward a person, place, thing, or idea. With transitive verbs, the action passes from the doer—the subject—to the receiver of the action. Words that receive the action of a transitive verb are called *objects*.

EXAMPLES Tamisha **entertained** the child. [The object *child* receives the action of the verb *entertained*.]

Felipe **visited** San Juan. [The object *San Juan* receives the action of the verb *visited*.]

An *intransitive verb* tells something about the subject or expresses action without the action passing to a receiver, or object.

EXAMPLES The children **smiled**.

The horses **galloped** across the prairie.

I **am** here.

Reference Note
For more about **objects in sentences,** see page 405.

Viewing the Illustration
Exploring the Subject. Born in 1918 in Arkansas City, Arkansas, John Johnson attended high school and college in Chicago, Illinois. After working for an in-house publication for an insurance company, he went on to found several magazines, including *Ebony* and *Jet*.

Meeting INDIVIDUAL NEEDS

LEARNERS HAVING DIFFICULTY
You may want to omit for the moment the concepts of transitive and intransitive verbs. Students may grasp these concepts more easily in connection with **Chapter 14: Complements.**

ENGLISH-LANGUAGE LEARNERS
General Strategies. Because many languages use different sentence structures, students may need to be reminded that the basic order of English sentences is subject-verb-object. Languages such as Japanese and Korean follow a subject-object-verb pattern, and Arabic follows a verb-subject-object pattern. You may want to monitor students' work to ensure that they use the English subject-verb-object pattern.

The Verb 353

MINI-LESSON
Continued on p. 354

Transitive and Intransitive Verbs. Students often have difficulty differentiating between transitive and intransitive verbs. Emphasize to students the meaning of the prefix *trans–* by brainstorming for related words, such as *transit* and *transcontinental*. Point out that *trans–* indicates action *through* or *across*. A transitive verb, then, expresses an action from the subject to the object *through* the verb, whereas an intransitive verb does not take a direct object.

The Verb 353

Cooperative Learning

Have students work in groups of three to write sentences with transitive verbs. One student can provide the subject, one can provide a transitive verb, and the third can supply the object of the verb. Each group member can then write the sentence and check to make sure it is correct. After every sentence, have the group members change roles so that after six sentences each student has thought of two subjects, two transitive verbs, and two objects. Challenge each group to keep their sentences on a single topic. Ask for volunteers to share their group's sentences with the class.

Meeting INDIVIDUAL NEEDS

MULTIPLE INTELLIGENCES
Bodily-Kinesthetic Intelligence.
Have pairs of students write a paragraph describing a real or imaginary event. Students can act out the verbs in their paragraphs, such as by miming a batter hitting a baseball and a spectator cheering. Tell students to use transitive and intransitive verbs in their paragraphs, to underline each verb, and to identify it as transitive or intransitive.

NOTE Not everything that follows a verb is an object. Many words or word groups that come after the verb give more information without receiving the action of the verb.

EXAMPLES Tameka writes **poetry.** [The object *poetry* receives the action of the transitive verb *writes.*]

Tameka writes **daily.** [The word *daily* tells when she performs the action of the intransitive verb *writes,* but *daily* does not receive the action and is not an object.]

Tameka writes **in the morning.** [The word group *in the morning* tells when she performs the action of the verb *writes,* but *in the morning* does not receive the action and is not an object.]

Some action verbs may be either transitive or intransitive, depending on how they are used in a sentence.

EXAMPLES My cousin Julio **plays** baseball on a Caribbean League team. [transitive]

My cousin Julio **plays** every week. [intransitive]

Kanani **studies** Chinese each day after school. [transitive]

Kanani **studies** hard. [intransitive]

NOTE Linking verbs are intransitive.

EXAMPLES This soup **tastes** too salty. [The linking verb *tastes* does not express any action for an object to receive. When used as a linking verb, *tastes* is intransitive.]

Does the box **seem** heavier than it should be? [The linking verb *Does seem* does not express any action for an object to receive. *Does seem* is intransitive.]

Exercise 6 Identifying Transitive and Intransitive Verbs

For each of the following sentences, identify the italicized verb as *transitive* or *intransitive*.

354 Chapter 12 Parts of Speech Overview

MINI-LESSON

Students can practice using the following graphic with different subjects, verbs, and objects to explore the differences between transitive and intransitive verbs.

SUBJECT → TRANSITIVE VERB → OBJECT

Students can discuss their examples in small groups.

EXAMPLE 1. Computers *affect* our lives every day.
   1. transitive

1. Computers *make* calculations incredibly quickly.
2. They *perform* many tasks that people often find boring and difficult.
3. Many businesses *benefit* from these machines.
4. Home computers *work* in similar ways.
5. They *do* word processing, a very useful operation for writers.
6. They also *run* programs for thousands of challenging games.
7. Handy pocket computers *fit* easily into a purse, bag, or backpack.
8. My mother *bought* a tiny computer not much larger than a credit card.
9. The information in its memory *appears* on the screen at the touch of a button.
10. Addresses, phone numbers, notes, and other information on the screen *help* my mother with her work.

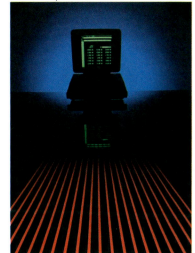

Exercise 7 Using Transitive and Intransitive Verbs

Write an appropriate verb for each of the following sentences. Then, identify the verb as *transitive* or *intransitive*.

EXAMPLE 1. He ____ my older brother's best friend.
   1. is—intransitive
      or
      knows—transitive

1. Aunt Teresa ____ us about some of the traditions of the Cherokee.
2. Our experiment with plants and photosynthesis ____.
3. Billy and I ____ green beans and carrots.
4. By noon, the hot sun ____ the ice.
5. Everything ____ fine to me.
6. In the twilight, a shrimp boat ____ into the bay.
7. ____ these hurdles, Jason.
8. ____ Bogotá the capital of Colombia?
9. Wow! What a crazy tie that ____!
10. Several African nations ____ elections this year.

HELP

Although the example in Exercise 7 gives two possible answers, you need to write only one answer for each item.

Answers may vary.
1. told—t
2. ended—i
3. picked—t
4. melted—t
5. seems—i
6. cruised—i
7. Jump—t
8. Is—i
9. is—i
10. held—t

The Verb 355

Relating to Speaking

Have students work in groups of five to review the types of verbs they have studied (action, linking, helping, transitive, and intransitive). Each group member should choose a different type of verb to review, and should then take a turn presenting a lesson to the group on that verb type. The lesson should include a definition of the verb type, a list of verbs of that type, and three example sentences using that type of verb. Group members are responsible for answering other students' questions on their type of verb.

Relating to Writing

Point out to students that using a variety of verb types helps make a piece of writing more interesting and engaging. Encourage students to include in their revision step in the writing cycle a quick check of the verb types in their draft. Students can use the quick check to vary their verbs.

Review B Identifying Verbs

Identify the verb in each of the following sentences. Be sure to include helping verbs. Then, tell whether the verb is used as an *action* or *linking verb*. Then, tell whether it is *transitive* or *intransitive*.

EXAMPLE 1. Can you form the letters of the sign language alphabet?
  1. Can form—action, transitive

1. The alphabet chart at left is helpful.   1. link./int.
2. Perhaps you and a friend could practice together.   2. act./int.
3. At first, it may be a challenge.   3. link./int.
4. Many people communicate with these letters as well as thousands of other signs.   4. act./int.
5. Many people use forms of sign language.   5. act./tran.
6. For example, referees, coaches, and football players sometimes give signals in sign language.   6. act./tran.
7. Some stroke victims must learn sign language during their recovery period.   7. act./tran.
8. Scientists have taught very simple signs to gorillas and chimpanzees.   8. act./tran.
9. These animals have been talking to people and to each other in sign language.   9. act./int.
10. In the picture below, the gorilla on the left and the woman are having a conversation in sign language.   10. act./tran.

The Adverb

12b. An *adverb* is a word that modifies a verb, an adjective, or another adverb.

Just as an adjective makes the meaning of a noun or a pronoun more definite, an adverb makes the meaning of a verb, an adjective, or another adverb more definite.

EXAMPLES Reporters **quickly** gather the news. [The adverb *quickly* modifies the verb *gather*.]

The route is **too** long. [The adverb *too* modifies the adjective *long*.]

Our newspaper carrier delivers the paper **very early.** [The adverb *very* modifies another adverb, *early*. The adverb *early* modifies the verb *delivers*.]

Adverbs answer the following questions:

Where?	How often?	To what extent?
When?	*or*	*or*
How?	How long?	How much?

EXAMPLES Please put the package **there.** [*There* modifies the verb *put* and tells *where*.]

I will call you **later.** [*Later* modifies the verb phrase *will call* and tells *when*.]

Softly, I shut my door. [*Softly* modifies the verb *shut* and tells *how*.]

Alannah **always** reads science fiction novels. [*Always* modifies the verb *reads* and tells *how often*.]

Would you please **briefly** explain what you mean? [*Briefly* modifies the verb phrase *Would explain* and tells *how long*.]

An owl hooted **very** late last night. [The adverb *very* modifies the adverb *late* and tells *to what extent*.]

The lemonade was **too** sour. [*Too* modifies the adjective *sour* and tells *how much*.]

HELP

Often, adverbs can be recognized by the suffix *–ly*. Remember, however, that not all adverbs end in *–ly* and not all words that end in *–ly* are adverbs.

ADVERBS
swam   **quickly**
left   **later**

ADJECTIVES
only   friend
early   flight

The Adverb 357

RESOURCES

The Adverb

Practice
- *Grammar, Usage, and Mechanics,* pp. 52, 53, 54
- *Language Workshop CD-ROM,* Lesson 5

Cooperative Learning
Have students work in groups of five to make lists of common adverbs. Each group member can take one of the categories in the **Words Often Used as Adverbs** chart. After each group member has written a number of adverbs for his or her category, have the group discuss which adverbs can be placed in more than one category. Have the groups present their lists to the class.

Have students review their adverbs to see that many are formed by adding –ly to an adjective (*bad—badly*), but also tell students that not all adverbs end in –ly (*well, too,* and *very,* for example) and that not all words ending in –ly are adverbs (*lovely, silly*).

STYLE TIP

In your own writing, try not to overuse the adverb *very*. Replace it with a less common adverb, or revise the sentence so that other words carry more of the descriptive meaning.

EXAMPLE
The runt of the litter is still very small.

REVISED
The runt of the litter is still **quite** small.
or
The runt of the litter **weighs just one pound and is only six inches long.**

HELP
The word *not* and its contraction, *–n't,* are adverbs.

Words Often Used as Adverbs	
Where?	here, there, away, up, outside
When?	now, then, later, soon, ago
How?	clearly, easily, quietly, slowly
How often? or How long?	never, always, often, seldom frequently, usually, forever
To what extent? or How much?	very, hardly, almost, so, really most, nearly, quite, less, only

The Position of Adverbs

Adverbs may come before, after, or between the words they modify.

EXAMPLES **Quietly,** she will tiptoe from the stage. [*Quietly* comes before *will tiptoe,* the verb phrase it modifies.]
She will **quietly** tiptoe from the stage. [*Quietly* comes between *will* and *tiptoe,* the verb phrase it modifies.]
She will tiptoe **quietly** from the stage. [*Quietly* comes after *will tiptoe,* the verb phrase it modifies.]

Exercise 8 Identifying Adverbs

Identify the adverb in each of the following sentences. Then, give the word or words each adverb modifies.

EXAMPLE 1. Williamsburg is a very interesting place.
 1. very—interesting

1. Visitors to Williamsburg can truly imagine what life must have been like in the 1700s.
2. As you can see in the photo on the opposite page, Williamsburg was carefully built to resemble a small town of the past.
3. On one street a wigmaker slowly makes old-fashioned powdered wigs.
4. Nearby, a silversmith designs beautiful candlesticks, platters, and jewelry.

5. Down the block the bookbinder <u>skillfully</u> crafts book covers out of leather.
6. His neighbor, the blacksmith, <u>is certainly</u> important because he makes shoes for horses.
7. In colonial times people <u>could seldom afford</u> new shoes for themselves.
8. <u>Nowadays</u>, many curious tourists <u>visit</u> the bootmaker's shop.
9. Another <u>very popular</u> craftsman makes lovely musical instruments.
10. Williamsburg <u>definitely</u> gives tourists the feeling that they have visited the past.

Exercise 9 Identifying Adverbs and the Words They Modify

Each of the following sentences contains at least one adverb. Identify each adverb. Then, give the word each adverb modifies. Be prepared to tell whether the word modified is a verb, an adjective, or an adverb.

EXAMPLE 1. If you look closely at a world map, you can quite easily find Brazil.

1. closely—look; quite—easily; easily—can find

1. The nation of Brazil actually covers almost half of the continent of South America.
2. A large portion of the Amazon rain forest grows there.
3. Many people have become more active in the preservation of the rain forest.
4. The loss of the rain forest may seriously affect the planet's climate.
5. Very early in the sixteenth century, Brazil was colonized by the Portuguese.
6. The country later became an independent republic.
7. Brazilians often say *Bom día,* which means "good day" in Portuguese.
8. In Brazil, sports fans can almost always find a soccer game in progress.
9. Brasília, the capital of Brazil, is an extremely modern city.
10. My aunt travels frequently, but she hasn't been to Brasília.

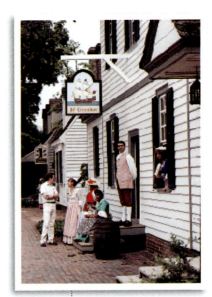

HELP
In the example sentence in Exercise 9, *look* is a verb, *easily* is an adverb, and *can find* is a verb.

Exercise 9 Identifying Adverbs and the Words They Modify

ANSWERS
1. actually—covers (verb); almost—half (adjective)
2. there—grows (verb)
3. more—active (adjective)
4. seriously—may affect (verb)
5. Very—early (adverb); early—was colonized (verb)
6. later—became (verb)
7. often—say (verb)
8. almost—always (adverb); always—can find (verb)
9. extremely—modern (adjective)
10. frequently—travels (verb); n't—has been (verb)

The Adverb

Meeting INDIVIDUAL NEEDS

ADVANCED LEARNERS
To give students further practice using adverbs, have them use adverbs in descriptive paragraphs. Here are possible topics:

1. getting a new pet
2. cooking
3. taking care of a child
4. visiting an animal park

Each student should use at least five adverbs to help make the paragraph clear and interesting. Have students underline the adverbs.

The Preposition

Rule 12c (pp. 360–364)

OBJECTIVES

- To identify prepositions and their objects
- To use appropriate prepositions in sentences
- To distinguish between adverbs and prepositions

TIPS & TRICKS

Many prepositions can be remembered as "anywhere a cat can go."

EXAMPLES
up the tree
behind the sofa
under the bed
through the door

Exercise 10 Writing Appropriate Adverbs

Write the following sentences. Then, fill in each blank with an appropriate adverb. Use a different adverb in each sentence.

EXAMPLE 1. ____ I learned some Spanish words.
1. Quickly, I learned some Spanish words.

Adverbs will vary.

1. I ____ watch TV after school. **1. never**
2. You will ____ bait a hook yourself. **2. soon**
3. My little sister crept down the stairs ____. **3. quietly**
4. Do you think that you can ____ find the answer to the math problem? **4. easily**
5. She is ____ eager for lunch. **5. very**
6. In the evening, the African drums beat ____. **6. loudly**
7. People in the highest balcony could ____ hear the speakers onstage. **7. not**
8. Does thunder ____ follow lightning? **8. always**
9. Would you dim the light ____ for me? **9. slightly**
10. The sky over Honolulu was ____ clear that I could see for miles. **10. so**

The Preposition

12c. A *preposition* is a word that shows the relationship between a noun or a pronoun and another word in the sentence.

EXAMPLES   Your math book is **underneath** your coat, Allen. [The preposition *underneath* shows the relationship of *coat* to *book*.]

The one **behind** us honked his horn. [The preposition *behind* shows the relationship of *us* to *one*.]

Notice how changing the preposition in the following sentences changes the relationship between *hit* and *net*.

I hit the ball **over** the net.
I hit the ball **into** the net.
I hit the ball **under** the net.
I hit the ball **against** the net.
I hit the ball **across** the net.

360   Chapter 12   Parts of Speech Overview

RESOURCES

The Preposition
Practice

- *Grammar, Usage, and Mechanics,* pp. 55, 56, 57
- *Language Workshop CD-ROM,* Lesson 6

Commonly Used Prepositions

aboard	between	past
about	beyond	since
above	by	through
across	down	throughout
after	during	till
against	except	to
along	for	toward
among	from	under
around	in	underneath
at	into	until
before	like	up
behind	of	upon
below	off	with
beneath	on	within
beside	over	without

Some prepositions are made up of more than one word. These are called **compound prepositions.**

Some Compound Prepositions

according to	in addition to	next to
aside from	in place of	on account of
because of	in spite of	out of

The Prepositional Phrase

A preposition always has at least one noun or pronoun as an object. This noun or pronoun is called the **object of the preposition.** The preposition, its object, and any modifiers of the object make up a **prepositional phrase.** Generally, the object of the preposition follows the preposition.

EXAMPLES The pile **of dry leaves** had grown much larger. [The preposition *of* relates its object, *leaves*, to *pile*. The adjective *dry* modifies *leaves*.]

Reference Note

For more information about **prepositional phrases,** see Chapter 13.

Meeting INDIVIDUAL NEEDS

ENGLISH-LANGUAGE LEARNERS
Spanish. In Spanish, the single preposition *a* can be translated as *in, on, at,* and as many other English prepositions. Therefore, you may want to give students extra practice in using prepositions of place. The following rules and examples may prove helpful.

1. Use *in* for cities, states, and countries. [*We live* in *Denver,* in *Colorado,* and in *the United States.*]

2. Use *on* for streets. [*We live* on *Harris Street.*]

3. Use *at* for addresses that include the number. [*We live* at *112 Harris Street.*]

Have students use the correct prepositions in sentences of their own.

The Preposition 361

Learning for Life

Writing and Performing a Skit. Discuss with students the comedy skits they have seen on TV. Point out that skits can also play a more serious role in education, in training films for the military or for businesses, and in helping people adjust to a

Continued on pp. 362–363

new environment, such as a new school.
Brainstorm with students for topics on which a new student at your school might need instruction or advice. Arrange students in groups of four to select a topic and to prepare a skit to perform for the

Meeting INDIVIDUAL NEEDS

LEARNERS HAVING DIFFICULTY
Allow students to use the **Commonly Used Prepositions** list on p. 361 when they are completing **Exercises 11–13.** Make sure students understand that for a word to be a preposition, it must have an object.

MODALITIES
Auditory Learners. Students can practice using prepositional phrases in sentences by working as a group to create variations on given sentences. One student will give a sentence with a prepositional phrase, such as "The dog walked by the bushes." Other students will create new sentences by changing the preposition or prepositional phrase. Once they have created several sentences, another student should give a new sentence with a preposition, and the other students can continue the activity.

TIPS & TRICKS

When you are looking for the object of a preposition, be careful. Sometimes the object comes before, not after, the preposition.

EXAMPLES
This is the movie that I told you about on Tuesday. [*That* is the object of the preposition *about*.]

STYLE TIP

Ending a sentence with a preposition is becoming more accepted in casual speech and informal writing. However, in formal writing it is generally best to avoid doing so.

He poured sauce **over the pizza**. [The preposition *over* relates its object, *pizza*, to *poured*. The article *the* modifies *pizza*.]

A preposition may have more than one object.

EXAMPLES This flea collar is **for cats** and **dogs**. [The preposition *for* has the two objects *cats* and *dogs*.]

My big sister had to decide **between the University of Wisconsin** and **Carroll College**. [The preposition *between* has the two objects *the University of Wisconsin* and *Carroll College*.]

Exercise 11 Identifying Prepositions and Their Objects

Identify the prepositional phrase in each of the following sentences. Underline the preposition, and circle its object.

EXAMPLE 1. Otters are related to weasels and minks.
1. to (weasels) and (minks)

1. Yesterday afternoon, we planted a sapling behind the (garage).
2. I bought a pattern for a (sari).
3. They live near the (airport).
4. For his (birthday), my brother wants a guitar.
5. The pictures won't be developed until (Friday) or (Monday).
6. I received a letter from my (aunt) and (uncle).
7. The largest of all (falcons) is the arctic falcon.
8. What are the answers to the third and fourth (questions)?
9. There are many uses for (peanuts).
10. I think that you might need a graphing calculator for that (problem).

Exercise 12 Using Prepositions

Using the treasure map on the next page, give an appropriate preposition for each of the following sentences. Be sure to use a variety of prepositions. Prepositions may vary.

EXAMPLE 1. Can you find the *X* _____ this map?
1. on

1. Our rowboat rests _____ Mournful Beach. **1.** on
2. Follow the path _____ the treasure. **2.** to

Learning for Life

rest of the class.
Students' skits should last between three and five minutes and should focus on solving a problem related to a common situation at their school. One group member can play the new student; the other group members can offer help and advice.
After each group has written a rough draft of its skit, group members should work together to fine-tune the script, focusing on making the skit both informative and entertaining. Special attention

3. Notice that Skull Rock lies ___ the cliff.   **3.** on
4. A sandy path leads ___ the stone ruins.   **4.** from
5. Did you jump ___ the fallen tree along the cliff?   **5.** over
6. Don't slip ___ the path up Lookout Hill!   **6.** on
7. Walk ___ the river.   **7.** across
8. Go ___ the waterfall!   **8.** under
9. You need not walk ___ the woods.   **9.** through
10. The treasure is ___ the open field and the gnarled oak tree.
    10. near

Preposition or Adverb?

Some words may be used as both prepositions and adverbs. Remember that a preposition always has at least one noun or pronoun as an object. An adverb never does. If you can't tell whether a word is used as an adverb or a preposition, look for an object.

PREPOSITION   Clouds gathered **above** us. [*Us* is the object of the preposition *above*.]

ADVERB   Clouds gathered **above**. [no object]

TEACHING TIP

Extension. To emphasize map-reading skills, you may want to use the exercise below as an oral activity or to write the questions on the chalkboard for students to answer in writing.

1. When you reach the stone ruins, which direction should you turn? [*west* or *left*]

2. Which part of the journey will probably take longer, from the fallen tree to the waterfall or from the waterfall to the gnarled oak? [*from the fallen tree to the waterfall*]

ADVANCED LEARNERS

Provide students with copies of simple directions found with a recipe, a board game, a detergent, or another product. Have students write *prep.* over the prepositions, *obj.* over the objects of verbs, and *o.p.* over objects of prepositions. Then, discuss how the use of prepositional phrases can make directions more understandable.

MODALITIES

Visual Learners. Have students find pictures that show action scenes. Have each student describe the scene by writing five sentences containing prepositions. Then, have two students exchange pictures and sentences. Students should circle prepositions in their partners' sentences and then discuss what prepositions were used and why.

should be paid to the use of the parts of speech discussed in this chapter.

After allowing some rehearsal time, have each group perform its skit for the class.

Groups could also perform their skits as part of an orientation for incoming students at the beginning of the next academic year.

PREPOSITION Meet me **outside** the gym tomorrow morning.
[*Gym* is the object of the preposition *outside*.]

ADVERB Meet me **outside** tomorrow morning. [no object]

Exercise 13 Identifying Adverbs and Prepositions

Identify the italicized word in each of the following sentences as either an *adverb* or a *preposition*.

EXAMPLE 1. *Above* us, wispy clouds filled the sky.
1. preposition

1. Before it rains, bring your bike *in*. **1. adv.**
2. Had you ever seen an authentic Chinese New Year Parade *before*? **2. adv.**
3. Bright red and green lights sparkled *down* the street. **3. prep.**
4. Smoke from the campfire quickly disappeared *in* the heavy fog. **4. prep.**
5. Andy turned the log *over* and found fat, squirming worms. **5. adv.**
6. A submarine surfaced *next to* an aircraft carrier. **6. prep.**
7. Will we read a poem by Nikki Giovanni *next*? **7. adv.**
8. Turn that stereo *down* right now! **8. adv.**
9. Millicent, did you remember to send a thank-you note *to* Mr. Bernstein? **9. prep.**
10. What kind *of* dog is that? **10. prep.**

The Conjunction

12d. A *conjunction* is a word that joins words or groups of words.

A **coordinating conjunction** joins words or word groups that are used in the same way.

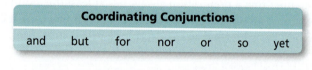

Coordinating Conjunctions						
and	but	for	nor	or	so	yet

CONJUNCTIONS JOINING WORDS
beans **and** rice movies **or** television
sad **but** true Egypt, Italy, **and** Spain

TIPS & TRICKS

You can remember the coordinating conjunctions as FANBOYS:

For
And
Nor
But
Or
Yet
So

The Conjunction

Rule 12d *(pp. 364–366)*

OBJECTIVE
- To identify conjunctions in sentences

TEACHING TIP

Activity. Point out to students that a *junction* is the place at which two roads join. Explain that a *conjunction* is a word that joins words, phrases, or clauses. Have students use the conjunction *and* to join the sentences *I walked to the store*, and *I bought groceries*. [*I walked to the store*, **and** *I bought groceries*.]

RESOURCES

The Conjunction
Practice
- *Grammar, Usage, and Mechanics,* pp. 58–59
- *Language Workshop CD-ROM,* Lesson 7

CONJUNCTIONS JOINING PHRASES	go for a walk **or** read a book after breakfast **but** before lunch cooking dinner **and** fixing breakfast
CONJUNCTIONS JOINING CLAUSES	I wanted to call, **but** it was late. The deer ran, **for** they smelled smoke. We knocked on the door, **and** they answered.

NOTE The word *for* can be used either as a conjunction or as a preposition.

CONJUNCTION	The zebra turned toward the watering hole, **for** it was getting thirsty. [*For* joins the two sentences.]
PREPOSITION	The zebra lay down in the shade **for** a nap. [*For* shows the relationship between the object *nap* and the verb *lay*.]

Reference Note
For information on using **commas to join words, phrases, or clauses,** see page 566.

Reference Note
For more information on using **prepositions,** see page 360.

Correlative conjunctions are pairs of conjunctions that join words or word groups that are used in the same way.

Correlative Conjunctions

both . . . . and	not only . . . but also
either . . . . or	whether . . . or
neither . . . . nor	

EXAMPLES **Both** Michael Jordan **and** David Robinson planned to play in the charity softball game. [two nouns]

Chris turned **neither** to the west **nor** to the east. [two prepositional phrases]

Not only did Babe Didrikson Zaharias set world records in track and field, **but** she **also** won more than fifty golf tournaments. [two independent clauses]

Exercise 14 Identifying Conjunctions

Identify the conjunction in each of the following sentences.

EXAMPLE 1. Lena or I will pitch at batting practice.
   1. *or*

The Conjunction **365**

GRAMMAR

The Interjection
Rule 12e *(pp. 366–367)*

OBJECTIVE

- To complete sentences by providing interjections

Meeting INDIVIDUAL NEEDS

ENGLISH-LANGUAGE LEARNERS
General Strategies. Explain to students that interjections are used to make language more colorful, to get the listener's attention, and to express strong emotions. Most languages include interjections. You could ask students who speak other languages to share interjections from those languages with the class. You may want to have students first submit to you in writing the meaning of their interjections, so you can determine the suitability for class discussion of each interjection.

---

12 e

STYLE TIP

The conjunction *so* is often overused. Whenever you can, reword a sentence to avoid using *so*.

EXAMPLE
The scarves were on sale, so Hector bought two.

REVISED
Because the scarves were on sale, Hector bought two.

1. Julio and Roger joined the soccer team.
2. Whether it rains or not, we will be there.
3. Many Chinese plays include dancing and acrobatics.
4. The squirrels are burying nuts, for the long, cold winter will be here soon.
5. Did Nancy finish her final book report, or is she still working on it?
6. Not only strong but also graceful, the eagle is a beautiful bird.
7. He is not here, nor has he called.
8. The Boys Choir of Harlem will be singing tonight, so we bought tickets.
9. I already addressed the envelope but have not taken it to the post office yet.
10. I have enough money for either popcorn or juice.

The Interjection

12e. An ***interjection*** **is a word that expresses emotion.**

An interjection has no grammatical relation to the rest of the sentence.

Often, an interjection is followed by an exclamation point.

EXAMPLES   **Aha!** I knew you were hiding there.

            Oops! I punched in the wrong numbers.

            Is that a wasp? **Ouch!**

Sometimes an interjection is set off by a comma or a pair of commas.

EXAMPLES   **Well,** what do you think?

            The fish weighed, **oh,** about three pounds.

            It's time to go, **alas.**

Common Interjections			
aha	hey	ouch	whew
alas	hooray	ow	wow
aw	oh	ugh	yikes
goodness	oops	well	yippee

Chapter 12 Parts of Speech Overview

RESOURCES

The Interjection
Practice
- *Grammar, Usage, and Mechanics*, p. 60
- *Language Workshop CD-ROM*, Lesson 8

Exercise 15 **Writing Interjections**

Have you ever heard the expression "an accident waiting to happen"? How many accidents are waiting to happen in the picture below? Write appropriate interjections to complete the following sentences that the people in the picture might say.

EXAMPLE
1. ____, Vince, have you seen my other roller skate anywhere?

1. Oh, Vince, have you seen my other roller skate anywhere?   Interjections will vary.

HELP

In Exercise 15, use a variety of interjections from the list on the previous page.

1. ____! I almost sat on the cat.   **1.** Oops
2. ____! Watch out for that book!   **2.** Hey
3. ____! Something on the stove is burning.   **3.** Uh-oh
4. ____, Lila! Be careful with that milk!   **4.** Oh dear
5. ____, we will have to get a new cord for our lamp.   **5.** Oh no
6. Something smells bad, ____.   **6.** ugh
7. Down the stairs comes Dad with, ____, the biggest present I've ever seen!   **7.** oh my
8. At last the party is over, ____.   **8.** whew
9. ____! Look out for the roller skate.   **9.** Yikes
10. The party was, ____, interesting to say the least.   **10.** well

Determining Parts of Speech

12f. The way a word is used in a sentence determines what part of speech it is.

Remember that you cannot tell what part of speech a word is until you know how it is used in a particular sentence. The same word may be used as different parts of speech.

VERB	Do you **like** guacamole?
PREPOSITION	That looks **like** guacamole.
ADVERB	The cat climbed **up**.
PREPOSITION	The cat climbed **up** the tree.
NOUN	We threw pennies into the wishing **well**.
ADJECTIVE	Janice isn't feeling **well**.
ADVERB	Did you do **well** on the test?
INTERJECTION	**Well**, what did he say?

HELP—
You may want to review Chapter 11 before completing Review C.

Review C Identifying Parts of Speech

Identify the italicized word or words in each of the following sentences as a noun, a pronoun, an adjective, a verb, an adverb, a preposition, a conjunction, or an interjection.

EXAMPLE   1. Some scientists *study* bones.
            1. study—verb

1. The fans lined up *outside* the stadium.   1. prep.
2. *She* always drives to work.   2. pro.
3. Those *plants* grow best in sandy soil.   3. n.
4. *Either* Rhea *or* Susan bought paper cups for the party.   4. conj.
5. Their parents *own* a card store.   5. v.
6. N. Scott Momaday has written several books, *but* I have read only one of them.   6. conj.
7. *Oops*! I dropped my backpack.   7. int.
8. We play *outdoors* every day until dinner time.   8. adv.
9. This videotape looks *new*.   9. adj.
10. You don't sound *too* happy.   10. adv.

368   Chapter 12   Parts of Speech Overview

RESOURCES

Determining Parts of Speech
Practice
- *Grammar, Usage, and Mechanics*, p. 61
- *Language Workshop CD-ROM*, Lesson 9

GRAMMAR

Determining Parts of Speech
Rule 12f (p. 368)

OBJECTIVE
- To identify the parts of speech of words

TEACHING TIP

Activity. In reviewing parts of speech, emphasize that many words can be used as more than one part of speech. You may want to have students look in a dictionary to find words that can be used as many parts of speech.

List the following words on the chalkboard, and have students create example sentences showing these words used as different parts of speech.

1. light [noun, verb, adverb, adjective]
2. fake [noun, verb, adjective]
3. turn [noun, verb]
4. well [noun, adverb, adjective, verb, interjection]

Meeting INDIVIDUAL NEEDS

MODALITIES
Kinesthetic. Arrange students in groups, and have each group use colored construction paper to make eight sets of five cards—one set each for nouns, pronouns, adjectives, verbs, adverbs, prepositions, conjunctions, and interjections. Each set of cards should show examples of that part of speech and should be a different color. Ask the groups to take a minimum of three cards from each set and to create three complete sentences by stringing the parts of speech together appropriately. Students can use extra words, as necessary, but they must make use of all the parts of speech that they select.

Chapter 12 Chapter Review

A. Identifying Verb Phrases and Helping Verbs

Identify the verb phrase in each of the following sentences. Then, underline each helping verb.

1. Tolbert could not see his brother in the fog.
2. Does Nguyen know the words to the song?
3. Dana might come to the party after all.
4. You should have brought your friend home for our special Chinese dinner last night.
5. Will you join the dance?

B. Identifying Action and Linking Verbs

Identify the verb in each of the following sentences as an *action verb* or a *linking verb*.

6. Ivan will be a superb guitar player someday. 6. link.
7. Our dog Tadger brought an old bone home yesterday. 7. act.
8. The whole-wheat bread smelled delicious. 8. link.
9. Jacqui smelled the exhaust of the huge truck in the next lane of the freeway. 9. act.
10. Will you look for me in the parade tomorrow? 10. act.

C. Identifying Transitive and Intransitive Verbs

For each of the following sentences, identify the italicized verb as *transitive* or *intransitive*.

11. Francisco *opened* the door to the cellar. 11. tran.
12. Even the judge *seemed* uncertain about the answer. 12. int.
13. The piano player *performs* twice each night. 13. int.
14. We *performed* the play three times that weekend. 14. tran.
15. We *dine* every night at seven. 15. int.

Using the Chapter Review

To assess student progress, you may want to compare the types of items missed on the **Diagnostic Preview** with those missed on the **Chapter Review.** You may want to work on specific goals with individual students who are still having difficulty mastering essential information.

D. Identifying Adverbs and the Words They Modify

Identify the adverb or adverbs in each of the following sentences. Then, give the word each adverb modifies.

16. Mr. Chavez never watches television, but he listens to the radio often.
17. Carefully open the dryer, and check to see whether the clothes are too wet.
18. Did you awake very early?   18. early–Did awake/very–early
19. Our old cat creeps gingerly from room to room.
20. Recently, I received an extremely interesting letter from my pen pal in Italy.

E. Identifying Prepositions and Their Objects

Identify the prepositional phrase in each of the following sentences. Underline the preposition once and its object twice.

21. Tanya's pet hamster likes sleeping [behind the computer].
22. Has your house ever lost power [during a thunderstorm]?
23. Some animals hunt only [between dusk and dawn].
24. Bring me the largest head [of lettuce], please.
25. [According to my father], my uncle was a carpenter.

F. Identifying Verbs, Adverbs, Prepositions, Conjunctions, and Interjections

Identify each italicized word or word group in the following sentences as a *verb*, an *adverb*, a *preposition*, a *conjunction*, or an *interjection*.

26. I always have fun *at* a water park.   26. prep.
27. You *can slide* as fast as a sled down the huge water slide.   27. v.
28. *Wow*! What a truly exciting ride that is!   28. int.
29. Some parks *rent* inner tubes *inexpensively*.   29. v./adv.
30. You *may become* tired, *but* you won't be bored.   30. v./conj.

RESOURCES

Parts of Speech Overview
Review
- *Grammar, Usage, and Mechanics*, pp. 62, 63, 64

Assessment
- Assessment Package
  —Chapter Tests, Ch. 12
  —Chapter Tests in Standardized Test Formats, Ch. 12
- Test Generator (One-Stop Planner CD-ROM)

G. Determining Parts of Speech

Identify the italicized word in each of the following sentences as a *verb*, an *adjective*, an *adverb*, a *preposition*, or an *interjection*.

31. *Well*, I suppose you know what you are doing. **31.** int.
32. Ms. Jefferson will not be back in school until she is *well*. **32.** adj.
33. When I sat down on the couch, my sister moved *over*. **33.** adv.
34. The bowls are in the cupboard *over* the sink. **34.** prep.
35. Did you *test* the batteries before you installed them? **35.** v.

Writing Application
Using Verbs in a List

Helping Verbs and Linking Verbs   You and your classmates have decided to list some goals for the coming year. The theme for your lists is "How I Can Make the World a Better Place." Write a list of ten or more goals or resolutions for yourself. Make each of your resolutions a complete sentence. In your list, use the verb form *be* at least two times as a helping verb and three times as a linking verb.

Prewriting   First, think of some realistic goals you can set for yourself. List as many goals as you can.

Writing   From your list, choose the resolutions that seem the most important and the most manageable. Write each of them as a complete sentence.

Revising   Read through your list. Are your resolutions clear and specific? Will you really be able to keep them? If not, revise or replace some of the resolutions.

Publishing   Be sure that you've used a form of the verb *be* as a helping verb twice and as a linking verb three times. Make sure that all of your sentences are complete. Identify each helping verb and linking verb. Do a final check for errors in grammar, spelling, and punctuation. You and your classmates may want to have everyone in the class submit one or two of their favorite resolutions and compile a list of resolutions for the entire class. Post the list on the bulletin board.

Reference Note
For information on **complete sentences,** see page 262.

RESOURCES
Writing Application
Extension
- *Grammar, Usage, and Mechanics,* p. 67
- *Language Workshop CD-ROM,* Lessons 4–9

CHAPTER 13

The Phrase and the Clause

Prepositional Phrases, Independent and Subordinate Clauses, Sentence Structure

PREVIEWING THE CHAPTER

- After briefly introducing the phrase, this chapter explains prepositional phrases and discusses how they are used as adjective phrases and adverb phrases. The chapter then defines the clause and explains independent and subordinate clauses. The section on subordinate clauses includes treatment of adjective and adverb clauses. Finally, the chapter discusses sentence structure, focusing on simple and compound sentences but also including a look at complex and compound-complex sentences.

- The chapter closes with a **Chapter Review** including a **Writing Application** feature that asks students to write a narrative using adverb and adjective phrases.

- For help in integrating this chapter with writing chapters, see the **Teaching Strands** chart on pages T297A–T297B.

USING THE DIAGNOSTIC PREVIEW

- Use the **Diagnostic Preview** to evaluate students' understanding of prepositional phrases, independent and subordinate clauses, and sentence structure. You may want to assess **Parts A, B,** and **C** separately to help you determine which areas might require more emphasis. Going over the answers orally in class may serve as a helpful review for some students, particularly auditory learners.

Diagnostic Preview

A. Identifying Adjective Phrases and Adverb Phrases

Identify the prepositional phrase in each of the following sentences, and tell whether the phrase is used as an *adjective phrase* or an *adverb phrase*. Then, give the word or words that the phrase modifies.

EXAMPLE 1. This newspaper article on weather patterns is interesting.

 1. on weather patterns; adjective phrase—article

1. adv.   1. The hikers are ready for a break.
2. adv.   2. Yesterday we rode our bikes through the park.
3. adj.   3. That store has something for everyone.
4. adv.   4. The Reverend Jesse Jackson spoke at the convention.
5. adj.   5. Most children like books with colorful pictures.
6. adj.   6. Students from both South America and North America attended the meet.

372   Chapter 13   The Phrase and the Clause

CHAPTER RESOURCES

Planning
- One-Stop Planner CD-ROM

Practice and Extension
- Grammar, Usage, and Mechanics, p. 68
- Language Workshop CD-ROM

Internet
- go.hrw.com (keyword: EOLang)

Evaluation and Assessment
- Assessment Package
  —Chapter Tests, Ch. 13
  —Chapter Tests in Standardized Test Formats, Ch. 13
- Test Generator (One-Stop Planner CD-ROM)

7. I wear heavy wool socks under my hiking boots. 7. adv.
8. Joel and Tina are participating in the Special Olympics. 8. adv.
9. The door to the secret room is locked. 9. adj.
10. According to the map, Tony's farm is just ahead. 10. adv.

B. Identifying Independent Clauses and Subordinate Clauses

For each of the following items, identify the italicized word group as either an *independent clause* or a *subordinate clause*.

EXAMPLE   1. Marco got the tables ready *while Nestor set up the chairs.*
          1. subordinate clause

11. *When school is out,* these halls seem quite lonely. 11. sub.
12. As far as I can tell, the red piece goes right here, and *the green piece goes under there.* 12. ind.
13. *If you exercise regularly,* your endurance will increase. 13. sub.
14. Just before the train sped across the road, *the bell rang,* and the gate went down. 14. ind.
15. Geronimo, who was a leader of the Apache, *died in the early part of the twentieth century.* 15. ind.

C. Identifying Types of Sentences

Identify each of the following sentences as *simple, compound, complex,* or *compound-complex.*

EXAMPLE   1. Mom is late, but she will be here soon.
          1. compound

16. Jaleel learned several African folk tales and recited them. 16. s.
17. Raccoons and opossums steal our garbage as the dogs bark at them from inside the house. 17. cx.
18. The school bus stopped suddenly, but no one was hurt. 18. cd.
19. The dance committee has chosen a Hawaiian theme, so the volunteers will decorate the gym with flowers and greenery while Todd finds the right music. 19. cd.-cx.
20. Luis Gonzalez stepped up to the plate, and the crowd roared enthusiastically. 20. cd.

Diagnostic Preview

The Phrase

Rule 13a (p. 374)

OBJECTIVE
- To identify groups of words as phrases or sentences

Reference Note
For more about **clauses**, see page 387.

The Phrase

13a. A *phrase* is a group of related words that is used as a single part of speech and that does not contain both a verb and its subject.

EXAMPLES   could have been looking [no subject]

in the backyard [no subject or verb]

NOTE If a word group has both a subject and a verb, it is called a *clause*.

EXAMPLES   The coyote howled. [*Coyote* is the subject of the verb *howled*.]

when the Peytons left [*Peytons* is the subject of the verb *left*.]

Phrases cannot stand alone as sentences. They must be used with other words to make a complete sentence.

PHRASE   **in the box**
SENTENCE   We put the tapes **in the box.**

Exercise 1 Identifying Phrases and Sentences

Identify each of the following word groups as *a phrase* or *not a phrase*.

EXAMPLE   1. some people enjoy skiing
          1. not a phrase

1. not a phrase	1. ski lifts are used for Alpine skiing
2. phrase	2. down the snowy hills
3. not a phrase	3. slalom skiers race through gates
4. phrase	4. during the race
5. phrase	5. before the other skiers
6. not a phrase	6. skiers love the Colorado slopes
7. phrase	7. with tiny snowflakes on my face
8. phrase	8. for a hot cup of soup
9. not a phrase	9. we sat beside the cozy fire
10. not a phrase	10. maybe I can go again next year

374   Chapter 13   The Phrase and the Clause

RESOURCES

The Phrase
Practice
- *Grammar, Usage, and Mechanics*, p. 69
- Language Workshop CD-ROM, Lesson 22

Prepositional Phrases

13b. A *prepositional phrase* includes a preposition, the object of the preposition, and any modifiers of that object.

Prepositions show the relationship of a noun or pronoun to another word in the sentence. The noun or pronoun that follows a preposition is called the *object of the preposition.* A preposition, its object, and any modifiers of the object are all part of the prepositional phrase.

EXAMPLES　The man **from Singapore** was giving a speech. [The preposition *from* shows the relationship between the object *Singapore* and the noun *man.*]

The tree **in front of the window** blocks our view. [The compound preposition *in front of* shows the relationship between the object *window* and the noun *tree. The* modifies *window.*]

Please hand me the book **on the long, green table.** [The preposition *on* shows the relationship between the object *table* and the noun *book. The* adjectives *the, long,* and *green* modify *table.*]

A preposition may have more than one object.

EXAMPLES　Aaron showed his arrowhead collection to **Tranh** and **her.** [The preposition *to* has two objects.]

The dinner of **baked chicken, salad,** and **two vegetables** also came with dessert. [The preposition *of* has three objects.]

Exercise 2　Identifying Prepositional Phrases and Their Objects

For each of the following sentences, identify the prepositional phrase and circle the object or objects of the preposition.

EXAMPLE　1. Dinosaurs and other giant reptiles roamed across the earth sixty-five million years ago.
1. across the (earth)

1. Although some of the (dinosaurs) were enormous, others were quite small.

Reference Note
For more about **objects of prepositions,** see page 361.

Prepositional Phrases
Rules 13b–d *(pp. 375–387)*

OBJECTIVES

- To identify prepositional phrases and their objects in sentences
- To complete sentences by using prepositional phrases
- To identify adjective phrases and the words they modify
- To complete sentences by using adjective phrases
- To identify adverb phrases and the words they modify
- To write sentences using adverb phrases

TEACHING TIP

Motivation. Ask students to suggest humorous answers to the question "Where would be a bad place to have a picnic?" Start students off by writing on the chalkboard *in traffic* and *on a yak.* Write students' suggestions on the chalkboard, and then point out that the groups of words are all prepositional phrases that tell *where* the action happens. If added to the sentence *Do not have a picnic . . . ,* each of the phrases would modify the verb phrase *Do have.*

RESOURCES
Prepositional Phrases
Practice
- *Grammar, Usage, and Mechanics,* pp. 70–71, 72, 73, 74–75
- *Language Workshop CD-ROM,* Lessons 22, 23

Meeting INDIVIDUAL NEEDS

ENGLISH-LANGUAGE LEARNERS
General Strategies. In some languages, prepositions come after their objects. For example, *in the house* would be "the house in." Other languages do not always use prepositions, so that *I went to the train station* would be "I go arrive train station." If your English-language learners use similar constructions in English, ask them how the phrases are spoken in their native languages. Then, explain how prepositions are used in English by pointing out the differences in usage.

MULTIPLE INTELLIGENCES
Bodily-Kinesthetic Intelligence. Pair students, and give each pair an object such as a paperweight. Partners can take turns writing prepositional phrases and demonstrating them by using the object. For example, they might position the object "under the desk" or "on my head." Challenge each pair to act out and list at least ten such phrases.

Musical Intelligence. Many songs make use of prepositional phrases. You can give students the example of the old Thanksgiving song "Over the River and Through the Woods." Have students compose their own songs, using prepositional phrases to describe a journey. Students can set their songs to well-known melodies or to original tunes and can perform their compositions for the class.

---

2. The drawing on this page includes a triceratops, thirty feet long, and a saltopus, not quite three feet long.
3. Many dinosaurs fed on plants and vegetables.
4. Dinosaurs with sharp teeth ate flesh.
5. Can you imagine seeing this flying reptile, the pterodactyl, above you?
6. It once lived in Europe and Africa.
7. Until a few years ago, scientists believed that all dinosaurs were coldblooded.
8. According to recent studies, however, some dinosaurs may have been warmblooded.
9. Many scientists say that birds and crocodiles may be related to dinosaurs.
10. Some people in science even claim that birds are living dinosaurs.

Exercise 3 Identifying Prepositional Phrases and Their Objects

Identify the prepositional phrase in each of the following sentences. Underline each preposition, and circle its object or objects.

EXAMPLE 1. The package was for my brother and me.
1. *for* my brother and me

1. The Sahara is a huge desert that lies south of the Mediterranean.

2. We waited until lunchtime.
3. The house across the street has green shutters.
4. Do not make repairs on the brakes yourself.
5. Maura said that the word *lasso* comes from a Spanish word that means "snare."
6. May I sit between you and him?
7. The woman in the blue uniform is my aunt.
8. The *Cherokee Phoenix* was the first newspaper printed in an American Indian language.
9. He is saving money for a stereo and a guitar.
10. The messenger slipped the note under the door.

Exercise 4 Writing Appropriate Prepositional Phrases

Write the following sentences, filling in each blank with an appropriate prepositional phrase. Answers will vary.

EXAMPLE 1. We saw Jason ____.
    1. We saw Jason at the mall.

1. My favorite comedian will appear ____.
2. That bus always arrives ____.
3. The fans ____ cheered every score.
4. The children tumbled ____.
5. The light ____ is broken.
6. Our car waited ____.
7. ____ sat a bald eagle.
8. A rich vein of gold ran ____.
9. ____ dashed a frightened squirrel.
10. His grandmother told us a story ____.

1. at the party
2. after five o'clock
3. at the game
4. in the yard
5. over the door
6. at the curb
7. On the branch
8. through the mountain
9. Across the street
10. about Mexico

Adjective Phrases

13c. A prepositional phrase that modifies a noun or pronoun is called an *adjective phrase*.

In other words, an adjective phrase is a prepositional phrase that is used as an adjective.

ADJECTIVE **Icy** chunks fell from the skyscraper.
ADJECTIVE PHRASE Chunks **of ice** fell from the skyscraper.

Reference Note
For more information about **adjectives,** see page 336.

Critical Thinking

Metacognition. After students have completed the exercises, have them think of the strategies they use to identify prepositional phrases. Do they first find the preposition and then the object? How do they determine which other words are part of the prepositional phrase? Do they make sure that what they think is a prepositional phrase does not contain a subject and verb?

Meeting INDIVIDUAL NEEDS

ENGLISH-LANGUAGE LEARNERS
General Strategies. To help students see how adjective phrases can help make descriptions precise, bring several pictures of the same type of object to class. For example, you could use several magazine advertisements of cars. Ask students to use adjective phrases to identify and distinguish among the objects.

Timesaver

Because **Exercises 5** and **6** are similar, you may want to use **Exercise 5** as an oral review. You could then assign only the even-numbered sentences of **Exercise 6** to assess students' progress. For those who still need additional practice, assign the odd-numbered sentences as written work.

STYLE TIP

You can use adjective phrases to add details to your writing or to combine ideas into one sentence.

ORIGINAL
His favorite pastime is reading books.

REVISED
His favorite pastime is reading books **about space exploration.**

ORIGINAL
The squirrel was in the top of the tree. The squirrel chattered at me.

REVISED
The squirrel **in the top of the tree** chattered at me.

Adjective phrases answer the same questions that single-word adjectives answer.

> What kind? Which one?
> How many? How much?

EXAMPLES Mr. Arnaud ordered a dinner **of boiled crawfish.** [The adjective phrase modifies the noun *dinner*. The phrase answers the question *What kind?*]

The one **with the big pockets** costs a little more. [The adjective phrase modifies the pronoun *one*. The phrase answers the question *Which one?*]

There was enough room **for only three people.** [The adjective phrase modifies the noun *room*. The phrase answers the question *How much?*]

Notice in these examples that an adjective phrase generally follows the word it modifies.

Exercise 5 Identifying Adjective Phrases

Identify the adjective phrase in each of the following sentences. Then, give the word that the phrase modifies.

EXAMPLE 1. Diego Rivera was a famous painter from Mexico.
1. from Mexico—painter

1. People throughout the world enjoy Rivera's art.
2. One photograph on the next page shows an indoor mural that he painted.
3. Rivera often painted the walls of buildings.
4. His murals are beautiful examples of popular twentieth-century art.
5. Rivera's artworks often include symbols of Mexican culture.
6. His work with other Mexican artists was also very important.
7. Rivera was a major influence on the mural artist Juan O'Gorman.

378 Chapter 13 The Phrase and the Clause

8. O'Gorman's mural on the left beautifies a university library.
9. O'Gorman does not paint his murals; instead, he uses tiny pieces of colored tile.
10. The complicated pattern upon the library walls fascinates everyone who sees it.

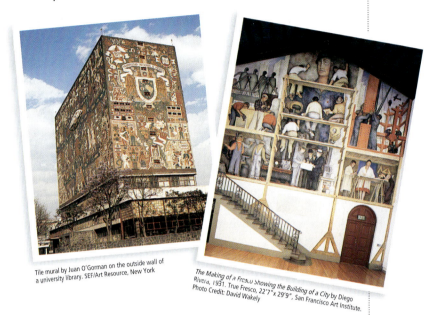

Tile mural by Juan O'Gorman on the outside wall of a university library. SEF/Art Resource, New York

The Making of a Fresco Showing the Building of a City by Diego Rivera, 1931. True Fresco, 22'7" x 29'9", San Francisco Art Institute. Photo Credit: David Wakely

More than one adjective phrase may modify the same noun or pronoun.

EXAMPLE   That painting **of sunflowers** **by van Gogh** is famous. [The two adjective phrases, *of sunflowers* and *by van Gogh,* both answer the question *Which painting?*]

An adjective phrase may also modify the object of another adjective phrase.

EXAMPLE   A number **of the paintings** **by that artist** are landscapes. [The adjective phrase *of the paintings* answers the question *What kind of number?* The adjective phrase *by that artist* answers the question *Which paintings?*]

Viewing the Art
Diego Rivera was born in Mexico on December 8, 1886. He began to study art at the age of ten and eventually studied in Spain and France. Rivera was one of the leaders of the revolutionary movement in Mexican public wall painting that began in the 1920s. His murals conveyed a message of national identity to the public.

Meeting INDIVIDUAL NEEDS

ADVANCED LEARNERS
Challenge students to write sentences that contain a second adjective phrase that modifies the object of the first adjective phrase in the sentence. Students can also work in small groups to create sentences containing strings of adjective phrases, each of which modifies the object of the preceding phrase. Have students share their sentences with the class.

Crossing the Curriculum

Science. Point out to students that **Exercise 6** shows how adjective phrases can be used in scientific description. Tell students that adjective phrases are an important part of classification, especially in distinguishing one species or substance from another. Ask each student to write a brief paragraph or two on a scientific topic of his or her choice. (Students who have difficulty choosing a topic may want to discuss possibilities with their science teachers.) Have students describe the topic using at least six adjective phrases, and have them underline the phrases.

MULTIPLE INTELLIGENCES

Spatial Intelligence. You may wish to provide each student with a sample design or picture, and then pairs of students can practice using adjective phrases in conjunction with drawing. Each student can use adjective phrases to describe the design or picture to a partner. The partner then uses the student's description to draw the design or picture without having seen it. Partners can compare the finished drawings with the originals and brainstorm for adjective phrases that would have helped make the drawing more accurate.

HELP—
Some sentences in Exercise 6 contain more than one adjective phrase.

Exercise 6 Identifying Adjective Phrases

Identify each adjective phrase in the following sentences. Then, give the noun or pronoun the phrase modifies.

EXAMPLE 1. This book about birds of North America has won many awards for photography.

1. about birds—book; of North America—birds; for photography—awards

[*Of flight* and *in the survival* both modify *importance*.]

1. It explains the importance of flight in the survival of the bird population.
2. The key to successful flight is the structure of the feather.
3. As you can see, the shaft and the vane are the two main parts of a feather.
4. The area inside the quill of a feather is hollow.
5. Barbs on the shaft form a feather's vane.
6. The curves in the vane and the notches of the feather permit easy, quick movement.
7. The wings of airplanes resemble birds' wings.
8. Feathers on the wings and tails of birds often are quite showy.
9. Fast-flying birds like swifts usually have pointed wings.
10. Have you ever seen any of the birds that have these kinds of feathers?

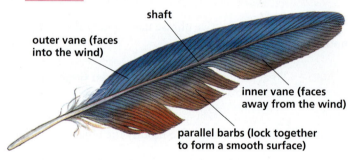

Exercise 7 Writing Adjective Phrases

Fill in the blank in each of the following sentences with an appropriate adjective phrase. Answers will vary.

EXAMPLE 1. That storm _____ might be dangerous.
1. That storm *from the east* might be dangerous.

380 Chapter 13 The Phrase and the Clause

1. The shelf ____ is too high to reach.
2. I certainly hope that my gorilla costume wins a prize ____.
3. The girl ____ is one of my best friends.
4. The argument ____ really wasn't very important.
5. My favorite birthday present was the one ____.
6. Give your ticket to the man ____.
7. Did you see a bear on your trip ____?
8. Put the groceries ____ away, please.
9. My sister is the girl ____.
10. As I looked around the house, I noticed that an African design decorated the wall ____.

1. in the kitchen
2. for originality
3. in that picture
4. over tickets
5. from Aunt Rita
6. at the gate
7. to Montana
8. on the counter
9. with blond hair
10. of the living room

Reference Note
For more about **adverbs**, see page 357.

Adverb Phrases

13d. A prepositional phrase that is used to modify a verb, an adjective, or an adverb is called an **adverb phrase.**

In other words, an adverb phrase is a prepositional phrase that is used as an adverb.

ADVERB   We walk **there** every Saturday.
ADVERB PHRASE   We walk **along the lake** every Saturday.

Adverb phrases answer the same questions that single-word adverbs answer.

> When?   Where?   Why?
> How?   How often?   How long?

EXAMPLES   The statue stands **next to a large oak tree.** [The adverb phrase modifies the verb *stands* and answers the question *Where?*]

Ready **by dawn,** the travelers set out early to reach the capital. [The adverb phrase modifies the adjective *Ready* and answers the question *When?*]

Are these jeans long enough **for you**? [The adverb phrase modifies the adverb *enough* and answers the question *How?*]

Prepositional Phrases   **381**

Meeting INDIVIDUAL NEEDS

LEARNERS HAVING DIFFICULTY
Write the sentence *We rode our bicycles* on the chalkboard. Ask students to suggest adverb phrases to complete the sentence, and write these phrases on the board as well. Remind students that their adverb phrases should modify the verb *rode*. Then, review students' phrases and lead the class to see that the phrases answer the same questions as single-word adverbs: *When? Where? Why? How? How often? How long?*

ENGLISH-LANGUAGE LEARNERS
General Strategies. Some students may have problems deciding which preposition to use when writing adverb phrases about transportation. If students are confused about the uses of *in* and *on,* tell them that as a general rule, *on* is used for vehicles that carry only one person: "get *on* a motorcycle or bicycle." For vehicles that carry several people, *in* is used: "get *in* the car or canoe." For vehicles that carry about twenty or more people, *on* is again used: "get *on* the plane or train."

Exercise 8

ALTERNATIVE LESSON
Have students identify the verb in sentences 1, 2, 7, and 9. Then, have them classify each verb as an action verb or a linking verb. [1. *hung*—action verb; 2. *is*—linking verb; 7. *jogs*—action verb; 9. *were*—linking verb]

Relating to Literature
If Lloyd Alexander's short story "The Stone" is in students' literature book, ask students to read and discuss it. Then, ask them to identify as many adverb phrases as possible in the first four paragraphs. You may want to read those paragraphs aloud, omitting the adverb phrases to demonstrate how different the story would be without them.

HELP
Be sure to ask yourself what question the phrase answers. Often, a phrase that comes right after a noun looks as though it is modifying that noun, but it is actually answering the question *When?*, *Where?*, or *How long?* about the verb. In the last example to the right, *over the bridge* does not tell us *which* bikes, but *where* we rode them.

HELP
Remember, an adverb phrase modifies a verb, an adjective, or an adverb.

NOTE Adverb phrases may appear anywhere in a sentence. They may come before or after the words they modify. Also, other words may come between an adverb phrase and the word or words it modifies.

EXAMPLES **After swimming lessons,** Aunt Helen drove us home.

Dad has been afraid **of snakes** since he was a boy.

We rode our bikes **over the bridge.**

Exercise 8 Identifying Adverb Phrases

Identify the adverb phrase used in each of the following sentences. Then, write the word or words the phrase modifies.

EXAMPLE 1. My hamster disappeared for three days.
1. *for three days*—*disappeared*

1. That mirror hung in the front hall.
2. The cat is afraid of thunderstorms.
3. The normally graceful acrobat plunged into the net but did not hurt herself.
4. Jimmy Smits will speak at our school.
5. Mom discovered several field mice in the cellar.
6. With great courage, Rosa Parks disobeyed the bus driver.
7. She jogs around the reservoir every morning.
8. For a beginner, he plays well.
9. Soon, my shoes were full of sand.
10. We have planted several new varieties of day lilies along the fence.

As with adjective phrases, more than one adverb phrase can modify the same word.

EXAMPLE Cesar Chavez worked **with the United Farm Workers for many years.** [Both adverb phrases, *with the United Farm Workers* and *for many years,* modify the verb *worked.*]

382 Chapter 13 The Phrase and the Clause

An adverb phrase may be followed by an adjective phrase that modifies the object of the preposition in the adverb phrase.

EXAMPLE   Yesterday we went **to an exhibit of rare coins.** [The adverb phrase *to an exhibit* modifies the verb *went.* The adjective phrase *of rare coins* modifies *exhibit,* the object of the preposition in the adverb phrase.]

Exercise 9   Identifying Adverb Phrases

Identify the adverb phrase used in each of the following sentences. After each phrase, give the word or words the phrase modifies.

EXAMPLES   1. On Passover evening, we prepare a Seder, which is a Jewish holiday meal and ceremony.
   1. On Passover evening—prepare
   2. Passover celebrates a time long ago when Jewish slaves freed themselves from their masters.
   2. from their masters—freed

1. On Passover, many of our relatives visit our home.
2. We always invite them for the Seder.
3. Our whole family helps with the preparations.
4. Soon, everything is ready for this special meal.
5. In this photograph you can see how beautiful our holiday table is.
6. Holding all the special Passover foods, the Seder plate is displayed in the center of the table.
7. On the plate is a roasted egg representing new life.
8. Horseradish, which represents slavery's bitterness, is placed near the egg.
9. The other carefully arranged foods are also used during the Passover feast.
10. Throughout the entire meal, everyone enjoys a variety of delicious foods.

Looking at Language

Colloquialisms. Discuss with students the impact that colloquialisms have on the English language. Colloquialisms, the colorful expressions used in everyday conversation, usually have understood meanings that are different from the literal meanings of the words used. Colloquialisms give our speaking and writing a casual, conversational tone. Share with students the following colloquial expressions, each of which contains a prepositional phrase.

Would you **get off my back**?

Is Dad **in the doghouse** again?

Success is **just around the corner.**

Our experiment **went down the tubes.**

He's **gone off the deep end.**

See if students can come up with other colloquialisms that contain prepositions.

GRAMMAR

Prepositional Phrases   383

Learning for Life

Continued on pp. 384–385

Writing a Travel Brochure. Bring to class a number of travel brochures, and discuss with students the descriptions and directions found in the texts. You may want to have students circle the prepositional phrases they find.

If possible, have someone from the area visitors' bureau speak to the class about local attractions. Ask the class to suggest their own favorite sites as well, and list the

GRAMMAR

Exercise 10 Writing Sentences with Adverb Phrases

POSSIBLE ANSWERS
Sentences will vary. Here are some possibilities:

1. Down the hall walked Mr. Ramond.
2. The mascot stood by them.
3. I saw them in the mall.
4. The ball rolled under the car.
5. She stepped onto the diving board.
6. We held the banners high over our heads.
7. This basket was made by a Navajo woman.
8. Through the sky the rocket rose.
9. I will arrive at five o'clock sharp.
10. Those sculptures were imported from Egypt.

Relating to Writing

Ask students to examine pieces of their own writing for the use of prepositional phrases. Ask if they can see places where they could add prepositional phrases to make their meanings clearer or to make their writing more detailed and interesting. Have students make revisions and then exchange papers to share constructive feedback.

Exercise 10 Writing Sentences with Adverb Phrases

Write ten sentences using the following word groups as adverb phrases. Underline each phrase. Then, draw an arrow from the phrase to the word or words it modifies.

EXAMPLE
1. for the airport
1. My grandparents left for the airport.

1. down the hall
2. by them
3. in the mall
4. under the car
5. onto the diving board
6. over our heads
7. by a Navajo woman
8. through the sky
9. at five o'clock sharp
10. from Egypt

Review A Identifying Adjective and Adverb Phrases

Each of the following sentences contains a prepositional phrase. Identify each phrase, and label it *adjective phrase* or *adverb phrase*.

EXAMPLES
1. Wilma Rudolph won three gold medals in the 1960 Olympic games.
1. in the 1960 Olympic games—adverb phrase

2. Rudolph overcame many obstacles in her life.
2. in her life—adjective phrase

1. Wilma Rudolph did not have the childhood you might expect of a future Olympic athlete.
2. She and her twenty-one sisters and brothers were raised in a needy family.
3. Rudolph suffered from polio and scarlet fever when she was four years old.
4. Illnesses like these were often deadly.
5. For many years afterward, Rudolph used a leg brace when she walked.
6. Still, she never lost sight of her dreams.
7. She battled the odds against her.
8. With her family's help, she exercised hard every day.
9. All of her hard work made her strong.
10. Years later, she gained fame as a world-class athlete.

384   Chapter 13   The Phrase and the Clause

Learning for Life

various places on the chalkboard. Tell students to imagine they are directing a visitor to one of the sites listed. Ask "How would you use prepositional phrases to describe the place and direct someone to it?"

Have students work in groups to create travel brochures for a site (or two or three related sites) listed on the chalkboard. As students write the text for their brochures, encourage them to use adjective and

384   The Phrase and the Clause

Review B **Identifying Adjective and Adverb Phrases**

Each of the following sentences contains at least one prepositional phrase. Identify each prepositional phrase, and label each one *adjective phrase* or *adverb phrase*.

EXAMPLES
1. In China, farmers are considered the backbone of the country.
   1. *In China*—adverb phrase; *of the country*—adjective phrase

2. With over one billion people to feed, China asks much from its farmers.
   2. *With over one billion people to feed*—adjective phrase; *from its farmers*—adverb phrase

1. Many of the Chinese people are farmers.
2. They generally work their farms by hand.
3. Chinese farmers usually use hand tools instead of large machines.
4. Farmland throughout China is carefully prepared, planted, and weeded.
5. Farmers also harvest their crops with great care.
6. In the hills, the Chinese make flat terraces.
7. As you can see, water from high terraces can flow to lower terraces.
8. Farmers build ridges around the terraces so that the terraces can be flooded during the growing season.
9. In flat areas, water is pumped out of the ground.
10. Another Chinese method of irrigation is shown in the lower picture.

Prepositional Phrases **385**

Review C — Using Prepositional Phrases in Sentences

POSSIBLE ANSWERS

1. Among the papers in the recycling bin, Dani <u>found</u> what she needed.
2. I <u>can see</u> over the fence, but my brother cannot.
3. Where is the <u>package</u> for your sister?
4. The automobile <u>moved</u> toward him.
5. What do you <u>know</u> about the schedule?
6. Tom <u>did</u> not <u>finish</u> his paper before class.
7. Few flowers <u>will grow</u> along the wall.
8. No sound <u>came</u> through the door.
9. The dog <u>hid</u> under the table.
10. In the evening we <u>will attend</u> the concert.
11. We <u>walked</u> our bicycles across the narrow bridge.
12. Did the escaped canary <u>fly</u> near you and Anna Maria?
13. Five passengers <u>were</u> aboard the sailboat when we saw it.
14. Lori <u>went</u> to the Grand Canyon.
15. Marcus and the kitten <u>slept</u> beneath the handmade quilt.
16. According to the scientist our proposal <u>needed</u> work.
17. What <u>is</u> beyond the farthest planet?
18. His face was <u>pale</u> next to the blue helmet.
19. A flock of birds <u>perched</u> upon the highest tree branch.
20. The <u>present</u> from my brother and me is on that table.

HELP

Although two possible answers are shown in the example, you need to write only one sentence for each item in Review C.

Review C — Using Prepositional Phrases in Sentences

Use each of the following prepositional phrases in a sentence. Then, underline the word or word group that the prepositional phrase modifies.

EXAMPLE 1. across the street
1. They <u>live</u> across the street.
   or
   The <u>store</u> across the street is open.

1. among the papers
2. over the fence
3. for your sister
4. toward him
5. about the schedule
6. before class
7. along the wall
8. through the door
9. under the table
10. in the evening
11. across the narrow bridge
12. near you and Anna Maria
13. aboard the sailboat
14. to the Grand Canyon
15. beneath the handmade quilt
16. according to the scientist
17. beyond the farthest planet
18. next to the blue helmet
19. upon the highest tree branch
20. from my brother and me

Review D — Writing Sentences with Adjective Phrases and Adverb Phrases

Use each of the following phrases in two separate sentences. In the first sentence, use the phrase as an adjective. In the second sentence, use the phrase as an adverb.

EXAMPLE 1. in Indiana
1. The people in Indiana are called "Hoosiers."
   We once lived in Indiana.

1. from California
2. in my class
3. along the path
4. under the bridge
5. behind you
6. throughout the summer
7. at the beginning
8. around the corner
9. during dinner
10. on the patio

The Clause

13e. A *clause* is a word group that contains a verb and its subject and that is used as a sentence or as part of a sentence.

Every clause contains a subject and a verb. However, not all clauses express complete thoughts. Clauses that express complete thoughts are called **independent clauses.** Clauses that do not express complete thoughts are called **subordinate clauses.**

Independent Clauses

13f. An *independent* (or *main*) *clause* expresses a complete thought and can stand by itself as a sentence.

EXAMPLES

S V
Gertie practices soccer every day.

S V
She has improved a great deal.

S V
Her team won yesterday's game.

When an independent clause stands alone, it is called a sentence. Usually, the term *independent clause* is used only when such a clause is joined with another clause.

SENTENCE **He worked on the jigsaw puzzle.**

INDEPENDENT CLAUSE After Kevin had fed the cats, **he worked on the jigsaw puzzle.**

The Clause 387

RESOURCES

The Clause
Practice
- *Grammar, Usage, and Mechanics,* pp. 76, 77, 78, 79, 80, 81–82

Review D Writing Sentences with Adjective Phrases and Adverb Phrases

POSSIBLE ANSWERS

1. My friend from California is trying out for the Olympics.
   The package came from California.
2. The winner in my class was Tim.
   In my class I met Alice, who became my best friend.
3. The trees along the path are oaks.
   Along the path the baby stumbled.
4. The water under the bridge looks peaceful.
   Under the bridge the boat sailed.
5. The wall behind you has a serious crack.
   Look behind you!
6. The parties throughout the summer are planned for out-of-doors.
   Throughout the summer and into the fall, the flowers bloomed.
7. The chapters at the beginning of the book are the most memorable.
   Did you know at the beginning of the project that you would learn so much?
8. The house around the corner is painted blue.
   Walk to the end of the block and go around the corner to find the shop.
9. Richard's silence during dinner was unusual.
   The phone rang during dinner.
10. Rain interrupted lunch on the patio.
    I saw the missing kitten on the patio.

The Clause

Rules 13e–i *(pp. 387–394)*

OBJECTIVES

- To identify clauses as independent or subordinate
- To identify adjective clauses in sentences
- To write sentences using adjective clauses
- To identify adverb clauses in sentences
- To write sentences using adverb clauses

The Clause 387

Meeting INDIVIDUAL NEEDS

MODALITIES

Auditory Learners. One way to help students recognize the difference between independent and subordinate clauses is to read clauses aloud in a manner that exaggerates the incomplete nature of the subordinate clause. Here are some examples that you can read to the class:

1. Though the meal was delicious . . .
2. After you mow the lawn . . .
3. While Ray was riding his bike . . .

Ask students to react to what you read. Point out that all three clauses leave the listener wanting information that an independent clause would provide but that a subordinate clause does not.

HELP

A subordinate clause that is capitalized and punctuated as if it were a sentence is a **sentence fragment.** Avoid using sentence fragments in your writing.

Reference Note

For more on **correcting sentence fragments,** see page 262.

Subordinate Clauses

13g. A *subordinate* (or *dependent*) *clause* does not express a complete thought and cannot stand by itself as a complete sentence.

EXAMPLES
      S V
if you finish on time

         S V
which we found on the sidewalk

Subordinate means "lesser in rank or importance." A subordinate clause must be joined with at least one independent clause to make a sentence and express a complete thought.

SUBORDINATE CLAUSES	that Dad cooked for us
	if you set realistic goals
	before the sun sets

SENTENCES	We all enjoyed the dinner **that Dad cooked for us.**
	If you set realistic goals, you are more likely to succeed.
	Before the sun sets, I need to mow the lawn.

Notice the words that begin the subordinate clauses: *that, if,* and *before.* The chart below lists some other words that can signal the beginning of a subordinate clause.

Words Often Used to Begin Subordinate Clauses			
after	because	that	wherever
although	before	though	whether
as	how	unless	which
as if	if	until	while
as long as	since	when	who
as much as	so that	whenever	whom
as though	than	where	whose

388   Chapter 13   The Phrase and the Clause

Exercise 11 — Identifying Independent and Subordinate Clauses

For each of the following items, identify the italicized word group as either an *independent clause* or a *subordinate clause*.

EXAMPLES
1. I'll do the experiment *if you will record the results.*
    1. subordinate clause
2. Ignacio, *who is an artist,* painted the banner.
    2. independent clause

1. *While Dad was sleeping,* we decorated the house for his birthday party.
2. Just as Terri came in the door, *the phone rang.*
3. Somalis, *who traditionally raise and export livestock,* are nomadic.
4. Before you accept the invitation, *ask your mother.*
5. Do you know *when the train should arrive?*
6. *Although he was better at social studies,* he loved art.
7. Two uniformed soldiers guarded the entrance *where an iron gate stood.*
8. When the snows melt, *these streams will fill and rush down to the valley.*
9. That art paper *that you are using* really soaks up ink.
10. *Toni Morrison,* whose parents were once sharecroppers, *won the Pulitzer Prize.*

1. sub.
2. ind.
3. sub.
4. ind.
5. sub.
6. sub.
7. sub.
8. ind.
9. sub.
10. ind.

Reference Note
For information about **nouns,** see page 323.
For information about **pronouns,** see page 328.

Adjective Clauses

13h. An *adjective clause* is a subordinate clause that modifies a noun or pronoun.

Like an adjective or an adjective phrase, an adjective clause may modify a noun or a pronoun. Unlike an adjective phrase, an adjective clause contains both a subject and verb.

ADJECTIVE	a **white** cat
ADJECTIVE PHRASE	a cat **with white fur** [With white fur does not have a subject and verb.]
ADJECTIVE CLAUSE	a cat **that has white fur** [That has white fur has a subject, *that,* and a verb, *has.*]

Critical Thinking
Metacognition. After students complete **Exercise 11,** ask them to write brief answers to the following questions:

1. How did the way you read the items in **Exercise 11** help you decide whether the items were independent or subordinate clauses?
2. How did you use the examples on pages 387 and 388 to help you identify subordinate clauses?

Meeting INDIVIDUAL NEEDS

MODALITIES
Visual/Kinesthetic Learners. Write the following sentences on the chalkboard, using a differently colored chalk for the adjective clauses. For each sentence, ask a volunteer to draw an arrow from the adjective clause to the word it modifies.

1. The dancer, **who looked familiar,** was my mother's friend. [*dancer*]
2. Let's go to the store **that is having the best sale.** [*store*]
3. We went to the lake on Friday, **which was my birthday.** [*Friday*]
4. The boy **who fell down the stairs** was not hurt. [*boy*]

Meeting INDIVIDUAL NEEDS

ENGLISH-LANGUAGE LEARNERS

Spanish. Because the Spanish relative pronoun *que* can mean *that*, *which*, or *who*, Spanish speakers may tend to use *that* even in cases where *who* or *which* would sound more natural in English. You may want to show them some sentences containing *that*, *which*, and *who* in adjective clauses, allowing them to investigate in which situations each is used.

Spanish. In Spanish it is considered awkward to end a clause with a verb. For example, in an English sentence such as *I like the book that Maria is reading*, the Spanish speaker may invert the subject and the verb in the adjective clause. You may want to give students a list of sentences containing adjective clauses that end in verbs, and emphasize the subject-verb order. Also, suggest that students practice reading the sentences aloud.

An adjective clause usually follows the noun or pronoun it modifies and tells *Which one?* or *What kind?*

EXAMPLES   The runner **who came in second** was Tina. [The adjective clause modifies the noun *runner* and answers the question *Which one?*]

I would like a dog **that I could take for long walks.** [The adjective clause modifies the noun *dog* and answers the question *What kind?*]

Exercise 12 Identifying Adjective Clauses

Identify each adjective clause in the following sentences.

EXAMPLE   1. Her coat was lined with fleece that kept her warm.
1. *that kept her warm*

1. Jordan, whose aunt once rode on the space shuttle, is visiting her this summer.
2. Grandfather gave me that arrowhead, which has been in our family for generations.
3. The doctor looked at the notes that the nurse had written.
4. What was the name of the man who helped us?
5. Panama hats, which are prized far and wide, are woven of jipijapa leaves.
6. We could not have done it without Harry, whose skill saved the day.
7. Have you heard of Sister Juana Ines de la Cruz, the Mexican nun who championed women's rights in 1691?
8. Argentina's pampas, where fine herds of cattle graze, offer ranchers rich and vast grasslands.
9. Since ancient times, Asian ginger has been prized for the tang that it gives many dishes.
10. Ric, whom Doris calls "The Prince," is always a good sport.

Exercise 13 Using Adjective Clauses in Sentences

Write ten sentences using the following word groups as adjective clauses.

EXAMPLE   1. where I grew up
1. *This is the street where I grew up.*

1. which had been imported from Japan
2. who is always on time
3. that live in this ecosystem
4. where the roses grow
5. whose short stories appear in your text
6. whom you talked about yesterday
7. that was having a sale
8. which may or may not be true
9. for whom our school is named
10. whose hard work made this event possible

Adverb Clauses

13i. An *adverb clause* is a subordinate clause that modifies a verb, an adjective, or an adverb.

Like an adverb or an adverb phrase, an adverb clause may modify a verb, an adjective, or another adverb. Unlike an adverb phrase, an adverb clause contains a subject and verb.

ADVERB	**Shyly,** the toddler hid behind her mother.
ADVERB PHRASE	**With a shy smile,** the toddler hid behind her mother. [*With a shy smile* does not have a subject and verb.]
ADVERB CLAUSE	**Since the toddler was shy,** she hid behind her mother. [*Since the toddler was shy* has a subject, *toddler,* and a verb, *was*.]

An adverb clause answers the following questions: *How? When? Where? Why? To what extent? How much? How long?* or *Under what conditions?*

EXAMPLES **After he had moved the books,** Marvin dusted the shelves. [The adverb clause tells *when* Marvin dusted the shelves.]

Then he put the books back **where they belonged.** [The adverb clause tells *where* he put the books.]

He cleaned his room **because it was very messy.** [The adverb clause tells *why* he cleaned his room.]

— HELP —

Introductory adverb clauses are usually set off by commas.

EXAMPLES
After we built the campfire, we roasted hot dogs.

Although the song is good, it is not one of their best.

Reference Note

For more information on **using commas to set off introductory elements,** see page 572.

Exercise 13 Using Adjective Clauses in Sentences

POSSIBLE ANSWERS

1. The TV, which had been imported from Japan, was twenty years old when we replaced it.
2. George, who is always on time, is wearing his cap and gown.
3. In science class we will study endangered organisms that live in this ecosystem.
4. That is the garden where the roses grow.
5. Avi, whose short stories appear in your text, is a popular writer.
6. The new baby, whom you talked about yesterday, is sweet.
7. The store that was having a sale was very crowded.
8. The story I heard, which may or may not be true, is spreading throughout the school.
9. In social studies class we are studying George Washington, for whom our school is named.
10. Mrs. Asher, whose hard work made this event possible, is wearing the pink dress.

The Clause **391**

GRAMMAR

Exercise 14

ALTERNATIVE LESSON
For a quick review of parts of speech, ask students to find the following items in the designated sentences:

1. an adjective [*Tiny*]
2. a pronoun [*you*]
4. a verb phrase [*must be fed*]

TEACHING TIP

Exercise 15 You may wish to have students complete the first ten items as guided practice and the last ten items as independent practice.

Exercise 15 Writing Sentences with Adverb Clauses

POSSIBLE ANSWERS

1. When I save enough money, I will buy a new CD.
2. Dad will be home soon if things go according to the schedule.
3. Since we have lived here, we have painted the house twice.
4. After the assembly was over, the homecoming parade began.
5. Before school starts, we will choose new shoes.
6. Although we couldn't speak Japanese, our guests could speak English.
7. Melanie is older than she is but younger than Marc.
8. Because they were going to the rink, their ice skates were strung over their shoulders.
9. Until the sun set, we could still read the map.
10. While the lions are drinking from the river, the people on the photo safari take pictures.

STYLE TIP

In most cases, deciding where to place an adverb clause is a matter of style, not correctness.

As he leapt across the gorge, Rex glanced back at his alien pursuers.

Rex glanced back at his alien pursuers as he leapt across the gorge.

Which sentence might you use in a science fiction story? The sentence to choose would be the one that looks and sounds better in the context—the rest of the paragraph to which the sentence belongs.

Exercise 14 Identifying Adverb Clauses

Identify each adverb clause in the following sentences.

EXAMPLE 1. Call when you can.
1. when you can

1. Tiny wildflowers sprang up wherever they could.
2. Unless you want to sink, do not pull that large plug at the bottom of the boat.
3. Wind blew softly across the sand dunes while the caravan made its way home.
4. As soon as the cows come in, they must be fed.
5. To our surprise, when we entered the woods, a dozen armadillos were foraging right in front of us.
6. Although the piano had not been used for some time, it was still in tune.
7. Unless the shipment arrives today, the order will not be ready on time.
8. Because the airplane had been painted yellow, it was easily seen from the ground.
9. I'm not going if you're not going.
10. I had never heard anyone sing as he did.

Exercise 15 Writing Sentences with Adverb Clauses

Write twenty sentences using the following word groups as adverb clauses.

EXAMPLE 1. as soon as he can
1. He will be here as soon as he can.

1. when I save enough money
2. if things go according to the schedule
3. since we have lived here
4. after the assembly was over
5. before school starts
6. although we couldn't speak Japanese
7. than she is
8. because they were going to the rink
9. until the sun set
10. while the lions are drinking from the river

Chapter 13 The Phrase and the Clause

11. as long as the band plays
12. whenever the train arrives at the station
13. unless the dog is on a leash
14. wherever you see grasshoppers
15. although the trail was steep
16. when Alexa won the marathon
17. so that we could use the computer
18. while the storm was raging
19. than you are
20. as though they had run ten miles

Review E   Identifying Clauses

For each of the following sentences, identify the italicized clause as an *independent clause* or a *subordinate clause*. Then, identify each subordinate clause as an *adjective clause* or an *adverb clause*.

EXAMPLE   1. Those Japanese sandals *that you are wearing* are zoris.

1. subordinate clause—adjective clause

1. *Camels stamped and bellowed in annoyance* when packs were put on them.
2. Aloe plants, *which originated in Africa,* are now widely available in the United States.
3. As far as scientists can tell, *there is no connection between these two events.*
4. *If you adjust the blinds,* you won't have that glare on your monitor.
5. *The castanets,* which were quite old, *had been Melanie's grandmother's.*
6. *You were always singing* when you were little.
7. Three Indian elephants patiently towed the logs *that had just been cut.*
8. Stay with us *as long as you want.*
9. *Southeast Asia depends heavily on the seasonal rain* that the monsoons bring.
10. The Forbidden City, *where China's emperors lived,* is enclosed by walls.

1. ind.
2. sub.—adj.
3. ind.
4. sub.—adv.
5. ind.
6. ind.
7. sub.—adj.
8. sub.—adv.
9. ind.
10. sub.—adj.

Exercise 15   Writing Sentences with Adverb Clauses

ANSWERS continued

11. I want to stay as long as the band plays.
12. Whenever the train arrives at the station, someone will meet you.
13. Unless the dog is on a leash, it is not welcome on the trail.
14. Wherever you see grasshoppers, there are probably many others hidden in the grass.
15. The climbers were not winded although the trail was steep.
16. When Alexa won the marathon, we all celebrated with her.
17. We signed a list so that we could use the computer in turn.
18. While the storm was raging, the family was cozy by the fire.
19. Hank is taller than you are.
20. The horses looked as though they had run ten miles.

Review F — Writing Sentences with Clauses and Prepositional Phrases

POSSIBLE ANSWERS

1. I like the still life of the boots with a cowboy hat.
2. The salesperson who told us about computers works at Computer Magic.
3. Under the surface of the clear lake, we could see the lost mask.
4. Since the club meets in the afternoon, we will not be able to go shopping.
5. Would you like a new outfit for yourself, Bobbie?
6. If you walk through the puddles, your shoes will get wet.
7. Over the treetops, the clouds looked like cotton balls.
8. Before we ate dinner, the light had faded.
9. The sweet peas that grow along the fence smell like perfume.
10. The puppy raced toward us wagging his tail.

Sentence Structure

Rules 13j–m (pp. 394–398)

OBJECTIVES

- To identify sentences as simple or compound
- To classify sentences according to structure

HELP—Although two possible answers are shown in the example, you need to write only one sentence for each item in Review F.

Reference Note
For information about **independent clauses** and **subordinate clauses,** see page 387.

Review F — Writing Sentences with Clauses and Prepositional Phrases

Use each of the following phrases and clauses in a sentence. Then, underline the word that the phrase or clause modifies.

EXAMPLE 1. under the flat rock
1. Under the flat rock lived many odd insects.
or
The insects under the flat rock wriggled.

1. with a cowboy hat
2. who told us about computers
3. under the surface
4. since the club meets in the afternoon
5. for yourself
6. through the puddles
7. over the treetops
8. before we ate dinner
9. that grow along the fence
10. toward us

Sentence Structure

Simple Sentences

13j. A **simple sentence** has one independent clause and no subordinate clauses.

A simple sentence may have a compound subject, a compound verb, or both. Although a compound subject has two or more parts, it is still considered a single subject. In the same way, a compound verb or verb phrase is considered one verb.

EXAMPLES
S V
My **mother belongs** to the Friends of the Library.
[single subject and single verb]

S S V
Argentina and **Chile are** in South America.
[compound subject]

394   Chapter 13   The Phrase and the Clause

RESOURCES

Sentence Structure
Practice
- *Grammar, Usage, and Mechanics,* pp. 83, 84, 85, 86
- *Language Workshop CD-ROM,* Lesson 29

```
         S        V                  V
```
Jeannette read *Stuart Little* and **reported** on it. [compound verb]

```
       S           S        V
```
The **acrobats** and **jugglers did** amazing tricks and
```
       V
```
were rewarded with a standing ovation. [compound subject and compound verb]

Compound Sentences

13k. A *compound sentence* consists of two or more independent clauses, usually joined by a comma and a connecting word.

In a compound sentence, a coordinating conjunction (*and, but, for, nor, or, so,* or *yet*) generally connects the independent clauses. A comma usually comes before the conjunction in a compound sentence.

EXAMPLES I forgot my lunch, **but** Dad ran to the bus with it.

She likes sweets, **yet** she seldom buys them.

Notice in the second example above that, usually, a sentence is compound if the subject is repeated.

Sometimes the independent clauses in a compound sentence are joined by a semicolon.

EXAMPLES The blue one is mine; it has my initials on it.

The spider is not an insect; it is an arachnid.

Reference Note
For more information about **using commas with conjunctions,** see page 568. For more about using **semicolons,** see page 577.

Sometimes you can combine two simple sentences to make one compound sentence. Just connect the two simple sentences by using a comma and *and, but, for, nor, or, so,* or *yet*.

ORIGINAL
The rain has stopped. The sky is still dreary and gray.

COMBINED
The rain has stopped, **but** the sky is still dreary and gray.

Combining sentences this way can help make your writing smoother and more interesting.

Exercise 16 Identifying Simple Sentences and Compound Sentences

Identify each of the following sentences as *simple* or *compound*.

EXAMPLE 1. That story by Lensey Namioka is good, and you should read it.

1. compound

1. My dad and I like tacos, and we're making them for dinner.   1. cd.
2. Some trees and shrubs live thousands of years.   2. s.
3. It rained, but we marched in the parade anyway.   3. cd.
4. Mr. Edwards will lead the singing, for Ms. Cruz is ill.   4. cd.

Meeting INDIVIDUAL NEEDS

ENGLISH-LANGUAGE LEARNERS
General Strategies. Investigate with students the conjunctions that can be used in compound sentences. Write the following paragraph on the chalkboard, and list the conjunctions to one side. Have students fill in each of the blanks with the appropriate conjunction. Discuss with students their choices and the differences between the words.

Mario had an important soccer game early Saturday morning, ____ [*so*] he decided to go to bed early. He felt confident about the game, ____ [*yet* or *but*] he went to bed feeling anxious. The next morning Mario woke up late, ____ [*for*] he had forgotten to set the alarm. Mario had no time to take a shower, ____ [*but* or *yet*] he did manage to eat breakfast. Neither of his parents could give him a ride, ____ [*but* or *yet*] Mario didn't panic. He could get a ride with a teammate, ____ [*or*] he could walk to the game. His team was counting on him.

 Continued on pp. 396–397

Creating Compound Sentences.
Students may have no difficulty identifying compound sentences but may have trouble forming them. Remind students that if they want to combine two simple sentences to make a compound sentence, the two simple sentences must have related ideas. Discuss with students the differences between the following compound sentences:

TECHNOLOGY TIP

Have students conduct a search on the World Wide Web for sites that deal with famous bridges in the United States. Ask students to create a bookmark for each site and to group the bookmarks together in a folder. Later, allow other students in your classes to use these folders. *Preview any Internet activity that you suggest to students. Because these sites are public forums, their content can be unpredictable.*

5. s.   5. My aunts, uncles, and cousins from Costa Rica visited us last summer.
6. cd.   6. I had worked hard all morning, and I still had not finished the job by lunchtime.
7. s.   7. Abe peeled and chopped all of the onions and dumped them into a huge pot.
8. cd.   8. All ravens are crows, but not all crows are ravens.
9. s.   9. Chippewa and Ojibwa are two names for the same American Indian people.
10. cd. 10. I liked this movie best; it was the most exciting one.

Review G Identifying Simple Sentences and Compound Sentences

Identify each of the following sentences as *simple* or *compound*.

EXAMPLE 1. Have you or Sandy ever seen the movie *The Bridge on the River Kwai*?
         1. simple

1. My stepbrother is only eight years old, and he is fascinated by bridges.   1. cd.
2. We buy postcards with pictures of bridges, for he likes to collect them.   2. cd.
3. He has several cards of stone bridges.   3. s.

396   Chapter 13   The Phrase and the Clause

MINI-LESSON

Jeb is on the soccer team, and his brother Michael plays baseball.
Jeb is on the soccer team, and he has a brother.

Students should recognize that in the first sentence both independent clauses are about sports; the ideas are related. The two independent clauses in the second sentence have no such unifying idea and should be

4. Stone bridges are strong but are costly to build. **4.** s.
5. Many bridges are quite beautiful. **5.** s.
6. The Central American rope bridge shown here is one kind of suspension bridge. **6.** s.
7. The modern bridge on the previous page is another kind of suspension bridge. **7.** s.
8. Suspension bridges may look dangerous, yet most are safe. **8.** cd.
9. Bridges must be inspected regularly. **9.** s.
10. My stepbrother collects postcards of bridges, and I collect postcards of towers. **10.** cd.

Complex Sentences

13l. A *complex sentence* contains one independent clause and at least one subordinate clause.

Subordinate clauses usually begin with a word such as *who, whose, which, that, after, as, if, since,* and *when.* A subordinate clause can appear at the beginning, in the middle, or at the end of a complex sentence.

EXAMPLES   Before Chen planted his garden, he made a sketch of the layout.

independent clause	S V he made a sketch of the layout
subordinate clause	S V Before Chen planted his garden

When bees collect pollen, they fertilize the plants that they visit.

independent clause	S V they fertilize the plants
subordinate clause	S V When bees collect pollen
subordinate clause	S V that they visit

left as two separate sentences.

Write the following pairs of sentences on the chalkboard, and ask students to tell whether they could be combined to make compound sentences.

1. The house is almost finished.
   The family will move in next month. [*yes*]

2. Penguins are my favorite animals.
   Karen's family went to the wildlife park. [*no*]

Compound-Complex Sentences

13m. A sentence with two or more independent clauses and at least one subordinate clause is a *compound-complex sentence.*

EXAMPLE   I picked up the branches that had fallen during the storm, and Rosa mowed the grass.

independent clause	S V I picked up the branches
independent clause	S V Rosa mowed the grass
subordinate clause	S V that had fallen during the storm

Exercise 17 Classifying Sentences by Structure

Identify each of the following sentences as *simple, compound, complex,* or *compound-complex.*

EXAMPLE   1. It was raining, but the sun was shining when we looked out the window.
   1. compound-complex

1. Cuba's capital is Havana, and this beautiful city has been the center of Cuban culture since 1552.
2. The heavy branches of an oak tree hung over our table and shaded us from the sun.
3. When you are looking at a work by Monet, stand back at least fifteen or twenty feet.
4. As it happens, you're right and I'm wrong.
5. Seashells filled Liz's suitcase and spilled onto the floor.
6. According to our records, your next appointment isn't until next month, but we do thank you for your call.
7. The Internet and other forms of electronic communication are shaping the world's future.
8. Because opinions are still divided, further discussion will be necessary.
9. The clock's minute hand is moving, but the second hand has stopped.
10. Between Asia and Africa lies a land bridge that is known as the Sinai Peninsula.

Answers:
1. cd.
2. s.
3. cx.
4. cd.-cx.
5. s.
6. cd.
7. s.
8. cx.
9. cd.
10. cx.

TEACHING TIP

Activity. Draw on the chalkboard a chart with a column for each type of sentence structure. Ask for a volunteer to write a simple sentence in the first column. Then, show students how clauses can be added to the simple sentence to create the other three structures. Add a second independent clause to make a compound sentence, and write the sentence in the second column. Fill in the other columns in a similar fashion. Then, have another student write a new simple sentence, and repeat the process, asking for volunteers to suggest clauses to add to build the other sentence structures.

Crossing the Curriculum

Mathematics. Hand out copies of an article or paragraph that demonstrates well-developed writing style. You might use a magazine article or part of a selection from your literature textbook.

Have students analyze the sentence structure in the piece by labeling each sentence *simple, compound, complex,* or *compound-complex.* Then, have them count the number of sentences of each type to come up with four separate totals. Finally, ask students to create a simple bar graph to show how many sentences of each type of structure the piece contains.

CHAPTER 13

Chapter Review

A. Identifying Adjective and Adverb Phrases

Identify the prepositional phrase in each of the following sentences, and tell whether the phrase is used as an *adjective phrase* or an *adverb phrase*. Then, give the word or words that the phrase modifies.

1. The crowd waved banners during the game.
2. That book about the Underground Railroad is interesting.
3. Have you seen the pictures of the Wongs' new house?
4. The water in my glass was cold.
5. Uncle Eduardo carefully knocked the snow off his boots.
6. You should travel to Utah if you have never seen a beautiful desert.
7. Do you have the new CD by the Three Tenors?
8. The swings in the park are a bit rusty.
9. A clown handed balloons to the children.
10. The mail carrier left a package on the front porch.

B. Identifying Independent and Subordinate Clauses

For each of the following items, identify the italicized word group as either an *independent clause* or a *subordinate clause*.

11. sub.   11. Yamile and her family enjoyed their vacation in Indonesia, *which is a country made up of thousands of islands.*
12. sub.   12. *Whenever he pressed the button,* another buzzer sounded.
13. ind.   13. After Luis worked out on the weight machines and swam ten laps in the pool, *he took a shower.*
14. sub.   14. Bring an extra sweatshirt with you *if you have one.*
15. ind.   15. *Martin enjoys speaking Japanese* when he visits the Nakamuras.
16. ind.   16. Before you leave for school, *do you always remember to brush your teeth?*
17. sub.   17. Is Rena the one *who went to New Zealand?*
18. ind.   18. *Did our grandmother ever tell you* how she came to this country from Latvia?

Chapter Review **399**

Using the Chapter Review

To assess student progress, you may want to compare the types of items missed on the **Diagnostic Preview** with those missed on the **Chapter Review.** You may want to work on specific goals with individual students who are still having difficulty mastering essential information.

19. sub.   19. *Unless you don't like getting wet and working outside all day,* we could use your help at the Spanish club car wash on Saturday.

20. ind.   20. Mr. Boylan, whom we met several times at school events, *is the author of a novel.*

C. Identifying Clauses

For each of the following sentences, identify each italicized clause as an *adjective clause* or an *adverb clause*.

21. adv.   21. *When you have a chance,* send me an e-mail.
22. adj.   22. Anyone *who knows Vita* can tell you how smart she is.
23. adv.   23. *When the Castillo family arrived at the ski lodge that evening,* they went right to bed.
24. adj.   24. The theater company, *which had come to town only that afternoon,* put on a spectacular show.
25. adj.   25. Sherlock Holmes, *whose creator was Sir Arthur Conan Doyle,* is probably the most famous fictional detective in literature.

D. Identifying Types of Sentences

Identify each of the following sentences as *simple, compound, complex,* or *compound-complex.*

26. s.   26. Sir Ernest Shackleton was an Antarctic explorer.
27. cd.-cx. 27. He wanted to be the first man to reach the South Pole, and in 1908, he led a party that came within ninety-seven miles of the pole.
28. s.   28. In 1914, he led the British Imperial Trans-Antarctic Expedition to Antarctica.
29. cx.   29. Shackleton intended to cross Antarctica, which no one else had ever crossed before.
30. cx.   30. Before the expedition could land, Shackleton's ship, the *Endurance,* was trapped in the ice of the Weddell Sea for ten months.
31. cd.   31. Finally, the ice crushed the ship, and Shackleton and his men were stranded on the ice for five more months.
32. cd.-cx. 32. The men escaped the ice in small boats, and they landed on Elephant Island, where they lived in a makeshift camp.

RESOURCES

The Phrase and the Clause

Review
- *Grammar, Usage, and Mechanics,* pp. 87, 88, 89

Assessment
- *Assessment Package*
  —Chapter Tests, Ch. 13
  —Chapter Tests in Standardized Test Formats, Ch. 13
- *Test Generator (One-Stop Planner CD-ROM)*

33. Shackleton and five other men sailed to South Georgia Island, where they sought help from Norwegian whalers.
34. Shackleton's first attempts to return to Elephant Island did not succeed, but he finally rescued his crew on August 30, 1916.
35. Shackleton's expedition failed to cross Antarctica, but he brought all of his men home safely.

Writing Application
Using Prepositional Phrases in a Story

Using Prepositional Phrases to Add Detail The Friends of Animals Society is having a contest for the best true-life pet story. The winner of the contest will have his or her story published in the local newspaper. Write a brief story to enter in the contest. In your story, tell about an unusual pet that you have heard about or known. Use at least five adjective phrases and five adverb phrases in your story.

Prewriting First, you will need to choose a pet about which to write. Then, jot down details about how the animal looks and how it acts. In your notes, focus on a specific time when the animal did something funny or amazing.

Writing Begin your draft with an attention-grabbing paragraph. Introduce and describe your main character. Be sure that you have included any human characters that play a part in the story. Also, describe the story's setting—for example, your kitchen, your neighbor's backyard, or the woods.

Revising Ask a friend to read your draft. Depending on what your friend tells you, you may need to add, cut, or rearrange details. Make sure you have used at least five adjective phrases and five adverb phrases.

Publishing Check your story carefully for errors in grammar, spelling, and punctuation. You and your classmates may want to collect your stories into a booklet. Along with your stories, you might include pictures or drawings of the pets you have written about.

Chapter Review   401

RESOURCES

Writing Application
Extension
- *Grammar, Usage, and Mechanics,* p. 92
- *Language Workshop CD-ROM,* Lessons 22, 23, 29

CHAPTER 14

Complements
Direct and Indirect Objects, Subject Complements

PREVIEWING THE CHAPTER

- The first part of this chapter asks students to look at incomplete sentences and to evaluate when a complement is needed. The second section deals with direct and indirect objects. The last section of the chapter defines subject complements and explains the two types, predicate nominatives and predicate adjectives.

- You may want to refer to this chapter throughout the year, especially as students work on revising and proofreading the compositions assigned in **Chapters 1–7**.

- The chapter closes with a **Chapter Review** including a **Writing Application** feature that asks students to write a paragraph using at least three direct objects and two indirect objects.

- For help in integrating this chapter with writing chapters, see the **Teaching Strands** chart on pages T297A–T297B.

USING THE DIAGNOSTIC PREVIEW

- You could use the **Diagnostic Preview** to gauge students' understanding of sentence completeness, especially as it relates to the classification of objects and subject complements. The preview might be used as a tool to determine which students have problems identifying and using complements correctly.

Diagnostic Preview

Identifying Complements

Identify each complement in the following sentences as a *direct object*, an *indirect object*, a *predicate nominative*, or a *predicate adjective*.

EXAMPLE 1. Many forests are cold and snowy.
   1. *cold*—predicate adjective; *snowy*—predicate adjective

HELP—
Some sentences in the Diagnostic Preview have more than one complement.

1. i.o./d.o.
2. p.a.
3. p.n./p.n.
4. d.o./d.o.
5. i.o./i.o./d.o.
6. p.a./p.a.
7. d.o.
8. d.o./d.o.
9. p.a.
10. i.o./d.o./d.o.
11. p.a.

1. We made our parents a family tree for their anniversary.
2. The sun disappeared, and the wind suddenly grew cold.
3. The home of the former president is now a library and museum.
4. The newspaper published an article and an editorial about ex-Mayor Sharon Pratt Dixon.
5. My uncle gave my sister and brother ice skates.
6. After the long hike, all of the Scouts felt sore and sleepy.
7. Leaders of the Ojibwa people held a meeting last summer.
8. I wrote my name and address in my book.
9. Your dog certainly appears healthy to me.
10. They always send us grapefruit and oranges from Florida.
11. Most stars in our galaxy are invisible to the human eye.

CHAPTER RESOURCES

Planning
- One-Stop Planner CD-ROM

Practice and Extension
- Grammar, Usage, and Mechanics, p. 93
- Language Workshop CD-ROM

Internet
- go.hrw.com (keyword: EOLang)

Evaluation and Assessment
- Assessment Package
  —Chapter Tests, Ch. 14
  —Chapter Tests in Standardized Test Formats, Ch. 14
- Test Generator (One-Stop Planner CD-ROM)

12. Did the workers capture an <u>alligator</u> in the sewer system?
13. Our trip on the Staten Island ferry became an <u>adventure</u>.
14. The air show featured <u>balloons</u> and <u>parachutes</u>.
15. The maples are becoming <u>gold</u> and <u>red</u> early this year.
16. My parents bought <u>themselves</u> several Celia Cruz <u>CDs</u>.
17. Aunt Kathleen gave <u>Ricardo</u> and <u>me</u> <u>tickets</u> for the show.
18. The two most popular sports at my school are <u>football</u> and <u>volleyball</u>.
19. The water in the pool looked <u>clean</u> and <u>fresh</u>.
20. My mother's homemade Sabbath bread tastes <u>delicious</u>.

12. d.o.
13. p.n.
14. d.o./d.o.
15. p.a./p.a.
16. i.o./d.o.
17. i.o./i.o./d.o.
18. p.n./p.n.
19. p.a./p.a.
20. p.a.

Recognizing Complements

14a. A *complement* is a word or word group that completes the meaning of a verb.

Every sentence has a subject and a verb. Sometimes the subject and the verb can express a complete thought all by themselves.

EXAMPLES
    S   V
Adriana swam.

         S   V
The puppy was sleeping.

Often, however, a verb needs a complement to complete its meaning.

           S   V
INCOMPLETE My aunt found [*what?*]

           S   V   C
COMPLETE My aunt found a **wallet.** [The noun *wallet* completes the meaning of the verb *found*.]

           S   V
INCOMPLETE Sarah bought [*what?*]

           S   V   C   C
COMPLETE Sarah bought **herself** a new **jacket.** [The pronoun *herself* and the noun *jacket* complete the meaning of the verb *bought*.]

| TIPS & TRICKS |
You can remember the difference in spelling between *complement* (the grammar term) and *compliment* (an expression of affection or respect) by remembering that a compl**e**ment compl**e**tes a sentence.

Recognizing Complements
Rule 14a (pp. 403–405)

OBJECTIVE
- To complete sentences by adding complements

TEACHING TIP

Motivation. Write three columns of words on the chalkboard: subjects, verbs, and complements. The words can be based on a topic of your choice, such as school sports or favorite music. You can enlist students' help in coming up with the list of words. Then, have students create as many sentences as they can by combining words from the three columns. (They can add words such as articles and adjectives, if necessary.) The sentences can be silly or humorous in meaning, as long as they make sense syntactically and the words are used as subjects, verbs, and complements, as indicated by the columns on the board.

RESOURCES
Recognizing Complements
Practice
- *Grammar, Usage, and Mechanics,* p. 94
- *Language Workshop CD-ROM,* Lesson 26

GRAMMAR

TIPS & TRICKS

To find the complement in a sentence, try this trick. Cross out all the prepositional phrases first. Then, look for the subject, verb, and any complements that are in the rest of the sentence.

EXAMPLE
James threw the ball ~~over the defender~~ and ~~into the receiver's arms~~. [The subject is *James*. The verb is *threw*. *Defender* and *arms* cannot be complements because they are both in prepositional phrases. The complement is *ball*.]

Reference Note
For more about **adverbs**, see page 357. For more about **prepositions** and **prepositional phrases**, see pages 360 and 361.

INCOMPLETE	The longcase clock was [*what?*] (S V)
COMPLETE	The longcase clock was an **antique**. (S V C) [The noun *antique* completes the meaning of the verb *was*.]
INCOMPLETE	The elephant seemed [*what?*] (S V)
COMPLETE	The elephant seemed **tired**. (S V C) [The adjective *tired* completes the meaning of the verb *seemed*.]

An adverb is never a complement.

ADVERB	The koala chews slowly. [The adverb *slowly* modifies the verb by telling *how* the koala chews.]
COMPLEMENT	The koala chews eucalyptus **leaves**. [The noun *leaves* completes the meaning of the verb *chews* by telling *what* the koala chews.]

A complement is never a part of a prepositional phrase.

OBJECT OF PREPOSITION	Hannah is riding to her friend's house. [The noun *house* is the object of the preposition *to*.]
COMPLEMENT	Hannah is riding her **bicycle**. [The noun *bicycle* completes the meaning of the verb phrase *is riding* by telling *what* Hannah is riding.]

Exercise 1 Writing Complements

Write an appropriate complement to complete each of the following sentences.   Answers will vary.

EXAMPLE   1. The class seemed ____ to go on the field trip.
           1. *happy*

1. postcard
2. her
3. programmer
4. fine
5. firefighter
6. cloudy/dark
7. me

1. Yesterday, Uncle Joe sent me a ____ in the mail.
2. Did you lend ____ your calculator?
3. After college, she became a ____ in Chicago.
4. This puppy looks ____ to me, Doctor.
5. Is your brother still a ____ in Montana?
6. The sky was ____ and ____ that winter night.
7. Give ____ a hand, please.

Meeting INDIVIDUAL NEEDS

INCLUSION
Have a helper work with students in a quiet area where they can read the example sentences aloud. Reading aloud might help students hear incomplete sentences and recognize the need for complements. Then, have the helper work with the students to complete **Exercise 1**.

8. Was that ___ in the dinosaur costume?
9. My little brother ran into the house and showed us a ___.
10. Next on the program for the recital, the middle school chorus will sing ___.

Objects of Verbs

Direct objects and *indirect objects* complete the meaning of transitive verbs.

Direct Objects

The direct object is one type of complement. It completes the meaning of a transitive verb.

14b. A *direct object* is a noun, pronoun, or word group that tells *who* or *what* receives the action of the verb.

A direct object answers the question *Whom?* or *What?* after a transitive verb.

EXAMPLES My brother bought a **model**. [My brother bought *what*? Bought a *model*. The noun *model* receives the action of the verb *bought*.]

Jan called **somebody** for the assignment. [Jan called *whom*? Called *somebody*. The pronoun *somebody* receives the action of the verb *called*.]

Corey studied **Mother Teresa** in his history class. [Corey studied *whom*? Studied *Mother Teresa*. The compound noun *Mother Teresa* receives the action of the verb *studied*.]

A direct object may be a compound of two or more objects.

EXAMPLES Did the car have spoked **wheels** and a **spoiler**? [The compound direct object of the verb *Did have* is *wheels* and *spoiler*.]

She needed **glue**, **paint**, and **decals** for her model. [The compound direct object of the verb *needed* is *glue, paint,* and *decals*.]

Reference Note
For more information about **transitive verbs**, see page 353.

Objects of Verbs **405**

Meeting Individual Needs

ENGLISH-LANGUAGE LEARNERS
General Strategies. To reinforce the idea that a direct object can answer the question *Whom?* as well as *What?*, write the following sentences on the chalkboard and ask students to identify the direct objects and to tell which question they answer.

1. I can't find David anywhere. [*David—Whom?*]
2. Melanie hugged her grandmother. [*grandmother—Whom?*]
3. Don't tickle her! [*her—Whom?*]
4. My dog greeted me and wagged its tail. [*me—Whom?; tail—What?*]

Reference Note
For more about **linking verbs,** see page 351.

Link to Literature

A direct object can never follow a linking verb because a linking verb does not express action.

LINKING VERB   Julia Morgan **was** an architect. [The verb *was* does not express action; therefore, *architect* is not a direct object.]

Exercise 2   Identifying Direct Objects

Identify each direct object in the following sentences. Remember that a direct object may be compound.

EXAMPLE
1. Do you enjoy books and movies about horses?
1. books, movies

1. If so, then you probably know some stories by Marguerite Henry.
2. Her books about horses have thrilled readers for more than forty years.
3. Henry has written many popular books, such as *Misty of Chincoteague* and *King of the Wind.*
4. Her book *King of the Wind* won the Newbery Medal in 1949.

Wesley Dennis, illustration from *King of the Wind* by Marguerite Henry. Illustration © 1947; copyright renewed 1976 by Morgan and Charles Reid Dennis.

406   Chapter 14   Complements

MINI-LESSON

Action Verbs and Linking Verbs. Remind students that linking verbs do not take objects because they do not express action. Review the differences between action verbs and linking verbs. Unless students feel confident in recognizing these types of verbs, they may become frustrated when trying to identify direct and indirect objects.

5. The book tells the adventures of the boy Agba and his beautiful Arabian horse.
6. Agba fed milk and honey to the newborn colt.
7. Sometimes the playful colt bit Agba's fingers.
8. The head of the stables often mistreated Agba and the young colt.
9. Later, the boy and the horse left their home and traveled to England.
10. Read *King of the Wind*, and learn more about the adventures of Agba and his horse.

Wesley Dennis, illustration from *King of the Wind* by Marguerite Henry. Illustration © 1947; copyright renewed 1976 by Morgan and Charles Reid Dennis.

Indirect Objects

The indirect object is another type of complement. Like the direct object, the indirect object helps complete the meaning of a transitive verb. If a sentence has an indirect object, it must also have a direct object.

14c. An *indirect object* is a noun, pronoun, or word group that usually comes between the verb and the direct object. An indirect object tells *to whom* or *to what* or *for whom* or *for what* the action of the verb is done.

EXAMPLES I gave that **problem** some thought. [The noun *problem* is the indirect object of the verb *gave* and answers the question "*To what* did I give some thought?"]

Dad bought **himself** some peanuts. [The pronoun *himself* is the indirect object of the verb *bought* and answers the question "*For whom* did Dad buy peanuts?"]

Luke sent **David Robinson** a fan letter. [The compound noun *David Robinson* is the indirect object of the verb *sent* and answers the question "*To whom* did Luke send a fan letter?"]

TIPS & TRICKS

Here is a trick you can use to see whether a word is an indirect object. Move the word from before the direct object to after it, and add either *to* or *for*. If the sentence still makes sense, you know the word is an indirect object in the original sentence.

EXAMPLE
Carol sold Steve her old television.

Carol sold her old television **to** Steve. [The sentence means the same thing either way.]

Objects of Verbs   407

RESOURCES

Indirect Objects
Practice
- *Grammar, Usage, and Mechanics,* pp. 96, 97–98
- *Language Workshop CD-ROM,* Lesson 27

Meeting INDIVIDUAL NEEDS

MULTIPLE INTELLIGENCES
Visual-Spatial Intelligence.
Provide students with a list of sentences containing direct and indirect objects. Ask them to choose one sentence each and to draw a picture that depicts the action described in the sentence and shows the direct and indirect objects.

Exercise 3

ALTERNATIVE LESSON
Ask students to find the prepositional phrases in sentences 1, 6, 7, and 8, and to identify each as an adjective phrase or an adverb phrase.

[1. *In Ecuador*—adverb phrase; *of his relatives*—adjective phrase; 6. *about Ecuadoran heroes*—adjective phrase; 7. *into the Andes Mountains*—adverb phrase; 8. *from the train*—adverb phrase]

Reference Note
For more information about **prepositional phrases** and **objects of prepositions,** see page 375.

HELP
Some sentences in Exercise 3 do not have indirect objects.

If the word *to* or *for* is used, the noun, pronoun, or word group following it is part of a prepositional phrase and cannot be an indirect object.

OBJECTS OF PREPOSITIONS	The ship's captain gave orders to the **crew.**
	Vinnie made some lasagna for **us.**
INDIRECT OBJECTS	The ship's captain gave the **crew** orders.
	Vinnie made **us** some lasagna.

Like a direct object, an indirect object can be compound.

EXAMPLES She gave **Ed** and **me** the list of summer activities. [*Ed* and *me* are indirect objects of the verb *gave.* They answer the question "*To whom* did she give the list?"]

Did the peacock show **you** and your **sister** its tail feathers? [*You* and *sister* are indirect objects of the verb *Did show.* They answer the question "*To whom* did the peacock show its tail feathers?"]

Exercise 3 Identifying Direct and Indirect Objects

Identify the direct objects and indirect objects in the following sentences. Remember not to confuse objects of prepositions with direct objects and indirect objects.

EXAMPLE 1. Gabriel sent me a postcard from Ecuador.
1. me—indirect object; postcard—direct object

1. In Ecuador, Gabriel visited many of his relatives.
2. His aunt Luz and uncle Rodrigo showed him the railroad in San Lorenzo.
3. They also visited the port in Esmeraldas.
4. Ecuador exports bananas and coffee.
5. Gabriel's cousin showed him some other sights.
6. She told Gabriel stories about Ecuadoran heroes.
7. Gabriel and his relatives rode a train high into the Andes Mountains.
8. They took photos from the train.
9. Gabriel enjoyed his visit to Ecuador.
10. He brought us some unusual souvenirs.

Exercise 4 **Writing Direct and Indirect Objects**

Write an appropriate direct or indirect object to complete each of the following sentences. Answers may vary.

EXAMPLE 1. This weekend we are painting the ____.
1. kitchen

1. The President made a ____ on television last night.
2. Did your dad teach ____ those magic tricks?
3. Wow! The governor wrote ____ a letter!
4. Then Marianne asked ____ the question in all our minds.
5. A mechanic replaced the truck's ____.
6. Save ____ a place at your table.
7. Are you still studying ____?
8. Okay, I'll owe ____ two hours' use of my skateboard.
9. Have you taken ____ for a walk?
10. Sam made ____ a table in shop class.

1. speech
2. you
3. me
4. Mr. Liu
5. alternator
6. Lenny
7. French
8. Brenda
9. Rex
10. his mom

Review A **Identifying Direct and Indirect Objects**

Identify the direct objects and indirect objects in the following sentences.

EXAMPLE 1. Have you ever given board games much thought?
1. board games—indirect object; thought—direct object

1. For centuries, people have enjoyed games of strategy.
2. Interest in strategy games has given us chess and checkers.
3. My brother showed me a book about different kinds of board games.
4. Board games reflect many different interests and appeal to all kinds of people.
5. Some games teach players lessons useful in careers and sports.
6. Of course, word games can give people hours of fun.
7. During the more difficult word games, Mrs. Hampton sometimes helps Chen and me.
8. Do you like trivia games?
9. Sharon's uncle bought Ronnie and her one of the new quiz games.
10. A popular television show inspired the game.

HELP
Some sentences in Review A do not have indirect objects.

Meeting INDIVIDUAL NEEDS

ENGLISH-LANGUAGE LEARNERS
Spanish. Before students begin Review A, you may want to remind Spanish speakers that in Spanish, the direct object pronoun generally precedes the verb. You might want to ask a student to write on the chalkboard a short sentence in Spanish containing a direct object. Ask the student to label the parts and rewrite the sentence in English. Label the parts of the English sentence, emphasizing the difference in the position of the direct object. Allow students to use the model while working on Reviews C, D, and E.

Objects of Verbs

Subject Complements

Rules 14d–f (pp. 410–416)

OBJECTIVES

- To identify predicate nominatives in sentences
- To identify predicate adjectives in sentences

TEACHING TIP

Activity. Write the following sentences on the chalkboard, and ask students what the sentences have in common.

> Corinna is enthusiastic.
> The president of the club is Victor.
> My dog is tired.

Lead students to see that the sentences each include the linking verb *is* and a word in the predicate that identifies or describes the subject of the sentence. Discuss with students which words in the predicates are adjectives (*enthusiastic, tired*) and which is a noun (*Victor*). Point out that these words are all subject complements because they identify or describe the subject.

TIPS & TRICKS

To find the subject complement in a question, rearrange the sentence to make a statement.

EXAMPLE
Is Crystal the pitcher for the softball team?
Crystal is the **pitcher** for the softball team.

Reference Note
For more about **linking verbs**, see page 351.

TIPS & TRICKS

Remember that some linking verbs (such as *appear, feel, grow, smell,* and *taste*) can also be used as action verbs.

LINKING VERB
The yogurt **smells** sour.

ACTION VERB
I **smell** fresh bagels.

In sentences with verbs like these, first decide whether the verb is used as a linking verb or an action verb. Then, determine what kind of complement, if any, the sentence contains.

Subject Complements

14d. A ***subject complement*** is a word or word group that is in the predicate and that identifies or describes the subject.

A linking verb connects a subject complement to the subject.

EXAMPLES Mrs. Suarez is a helpful **neighbor.** [The subject complement *neighbor* identifies the subject *Mrs. Suarez*. The linking verb *is* connects *Mrs. Suarez* and *neighbor.*]

The airport appears very **busy.** [The subject complement *busy* describes the subject *airport*. The linking verb *appears* connects *airport* and *busy.*]

What smells so **good**? [The subject complement *good* describes the subject *What*. The linking verb *smells* connects *What* and *good.*]

He was the **one** in the middle of the line, in fact. [The subject complement *one* identifies the subject *He*. The linking verb *was* connects *He* and *one.*]

The author of that story is **Anne McCaffrey.** [The subject complement *Anne McCaffrey* identifies the subject *author*. The linking verb *is* connects *author* and *Anne McCaffrey.*]

Subject complements always complete the meaning of linking verbs, not action verbs.

Common Linking Verbs					
appear	become	grow	remain	smell	stay
be	feel	look	seem	sound	taste

The two kinds of subject complements are the *predicate nominative* and the *predicate adjective*.

Predicate Nominatives

14e. A ***predicate nominative*** is a word or word group that is in the predicate and that identifies the subject or refers to it.

RESOURCES

Subject Complements
Practice

- *Grammar, Usage, and Mechanics,* pp. 99, 100, 101, 102–103
- *Language Workshop CD-ROM,* Lesson 28

A predicate nominative may be a noun, a pronoun, or a word group that functions as a noun. A predicate nominative is connected to the subject by a linking verb.

EXAMPLES   Seaweed is **algae**, as I remember. [The noun *algae* is a predicate nominative following the linking verb *is*. *Algae* identifies the subject *Seaweed*.]

Was the first runner-up really **he**? [The pronoun *he* is a predicate nominative completing the meaning of the linking verb *Was*. *He* identifies the subject *runner-up*.]

NOTE Expressions such as *It's I* and *That was she* may sound awkward even though they are correct. In informal situations, many people use *It's me* and *That was her*. Such expressions may one day become acceptable in formal situations as well. For now, however, it is best to follow the rules of standard, formal English in all formal speaking and writing.

Reference Note
For more about **formal and informal English,** see page 519.

Be careful not to mistake a direct object for a predicate nominative. A predicate nominative always completes the meaning of a linking verb.

DIRECT OBJECT   My brother admired the **acrobat**. [*Acrobat* is the direct object of the action verb *admired*.]

PREDICATE NOMINATIVE   My brother became an **acrobat**. [*Acrobat* is the predicate nominative completing the meaning of the linking verb *became*.]

A predicate nominative may be compound.

EXAMPLES   Maya Angelou is a great **poet** and **storyteller**. [*Poet* and *storyteller* are predicate nominatives. They identify the subject *Maya Angelou* and complete the meaning of the linking verb *is*.]

Is the shark a **fish** or a **mammal**? [*Fish* and *mammal* are predicate nominatives. They refer to the subject *shark* and complete the meaning of the linking verb *Is*.]

Yesterday was my **birthday, Labor Day,** and the first **day** of the week! [*Birthday, Labor Day,* and *day* are predicate nominatives. They identify the subject *Yesterday* and complete the meaning of the linking verb *was*.]

Meeting INDIVIDUAL NEEDS

ENGLISH-LANGUAGE LEARNERS
General Strategies. You may want to write the following sentences on the chalkboard to remind students that a few of the linking verbs in the box on p. 410 (for example, *smell*, *sound*, *taste*, *look*, and *feel*) can also be used as action verbs:

1. She smelled fresh bread in the kitchen.
2. They sounded the gong at dinner time.
3. Taste this sauce!
4. I looked at the picture.
5. I could feel a cool breeze.

LEARNERS HAVING DIFFICULTY
Before students begin doing exercises on subject complements, you might want to give them some practice with linking verbs. Bring newspaper or magazine articles to class, and assign each student a page or two in which to find linking verbs.

TEACHING TIP

Exercise 5 You may wish to have students complete the first ten items as guided practice and the last ten items as independent practice.

Meeting INDIVIDUAL NEEDS

ENGLISH-LANGUAGE LEARNERS
Spanish. Because English has one verb *be* while Spanish has both *estar* and *ser*, Spanish-speaking students may have difficulty reading sentences using forms of *be*, such as those in **Exercises 5** and **6**. Before students can find subject complements in the exercises, you may need to focus on forms of *be* with them.

Looking at Language

Metaphors. Most metaphors use the *subject + linking verb + predicate nominative* pattern to make a comparison. Explain to students that a metaphor is a figure of speech that describes one thing by comparing it to another, unrelated thing. Share with students the following metaphors, pointing out the subject + linking verb + predicate nominative pattern:

> Your smile is a beam of sunlight.
> The ocean was an angry monster.
> Fear is a gray veil.

Challenge students to come up with their own metaphors to share with the class.

HELP
Some sentences in Exercise 5 have a compound predicate nominative.

STYLE TIP
Be careful not to overuse the linking verb *be* in your writing. Read your writing. Do you get the feeling that nothing is happening, that nobody is doing anything? If so, you may have used too many *be* verbs. When possible, replace a dull *be* verb with a verb that expresses action.

BE VERB
My father **is** a cabinet maker.

ACTION VERB
My father **makes** cabinets.

Exercise 5 Identifying Predicate Nominatives

Identify the predicate nominative in each of the following sentences.

EXAMPLES
1. Mount Rushmore is a national memorial.
1. memorial
2. Is that bird a finch or a sparrow?
2. finch, sparrow

1. San Juan is the capital of Puerto Rico.
2. Her mother will remain president of the P.T.A.
3. Athens, Greece, has long been a center of art and drama.
4. The platypus and the spiny anteater are mammals.
5. The object of Juan Ponce de León's quest was the Fountain of Youth.
6. The peace pipe, or calumet, is a symbol of honor and power among American Indians.
7. Quebec is the largest province in Canada.
8. In 1959, Hawaii became our fiftieth state.
9. That bird must be an eagle.
10. The fourth planet from the sun is Mars.
11. Didn't she eventually become a senator?
12. He remained an umpire for over thirty years.
13. You are not the only one in the room.
14. Hiawatha was a real person.
15. Aren't you the oldest daughter in your family?
16. Could the problem with the engine be an empty gas tank?
17. Lucy Craft Laney was the founder of the Haines Normal and Industrial Institute.
18. For more information about Sadaharu Oh, Japan's great baseball star, a good source is "Move Over for Oh-San" in *Sports Illustrated*.
19. Was the author Chaim Potok or Amy Tan?
20. Be an example for others.

Predicate Adjectives

14f. A ***predicate adjective*** is an adjective that is in the predicate and that describes the subject.

A predicate adjective is connected to the subject by a linking verb.

EXAMPLES   By 9:30 P.M., I was very **tired.** [The adjective *tired* describes the subject *I*.]

I believe that Jacob is **Nigerian.** [The adjective *Nigerian* describes the subject *Jacob*.]

Like a predicate nominative, a predicate adjective may be compound.

EXAMPLES   The blanket felt **soft** and **fuzzy.** [Both *soft* and *fuzzy* describe the subject *blanket*.]

The cave looked **cold, damp,** and **uncomfortable.** [*Cold, damp,* and *uncomfortable* all describe the subject *cave*.]

Exercise 6   Identifying Predicate Adjectives

Identify the predicate adjective in each of the following sentences.

EXAMPLES   1. The porpoise seemed friendly.
   1. friendly
   2. Does that alligator look hungry?
   2. hungry

1. Everyone felt ready for the test.
2. Those fresh strawberries smell delicious.
3. The front tire looks flat to me.
4. Everyone appeared interested in the debate.
5. That scratch may become worse.
6. She is talented in music.
7. During the movie, I became restless and bored.
8. Van looks upset about his grades.
9. Queen Liliuokalani was quite popular with the Hawaiian people.
10. The computer program does not seem difficult to Dana.
11. After a two-hour nap, the baby was still sleepy.
12. These ants are quick and industrious.
13. Even in winter, pine trees stay green.
14. Remain calm in an emergency, and do not panic.
15. This machine has always been inexpensive but efficient.

COMPUTER TIP

If you do overuse *be* verbs in your writing, a computer can help you fix the problem. Use the computer's search function to find each occurrence of *am, are, is, was, were, be, been,* and *being* in a piece of your writing. For each case, decide whether you need to use the *be* verb. If possible, replace it with an action verb, or revise the sentence some other way to add variety.

HELP

Some sentences in Exercise 6 have a compound predicate adjective.

Subject Complements   413

Cooperative Learning

To help students learn the difference between predicate nominatives and predicate adjectives, divide the class into groups of two and ask each pair to make a list of words that would complete the sentence *The room is. . . .* One student can write adjectives, the other articles and nouns. Partners can check each other's lists and suggest further items for each category. Ask each student to share one of his or her subject complements, and have the class identify the word as a predicate adjective or a predicate nominative.

Crossing the Curriculum

Science. Point out to students that predicate adjectives are useful in scientific descriptions. Have students write a few sentences in which they use a series of predicate adjectives to describe a scientific topic, such as the characteristics of a species or the symptoms of a disease. Students can share their sentences in small groups.

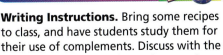

Continued on pp. 414–415

Writing Instructions. Bring some recipes to class, and have students study them for their use of complements. Discuss with the class the importance of complements in clearly written instructions.

Then, ask students to think about how they would give instructions on how to prepare their favorite food or how to play a favorite sport or game, and have them write a set of instructions. Students could meet in small groups to choose a process that can be performed in four or five steps.

GRAMMAR

Timesaver

Let students check each other's answers to **Review B**. Divide students into groups of four, and ask them to exchange papers within their groups. Have students follow these guidelines to check answers:

1. Does each word given as a subject complement identify or describe the subject of the sentence?
2. Is each complement labeled *predicate nominative* a noun or pronoun?
3. Is each complement labeled *predicate adjective* an adjective?

Each student's paper should be reviewed by all three other group members, and each reviewer should sign the paper.

Meeting INDIVIDUAL NEEDS

MODALITIES
Visual Learners. Have students use graphic organizers such as the following to show how word order can help them identify complements in a declarative sentence.

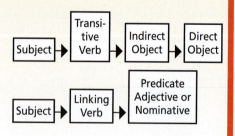

---

16. A giraffe's legs are very skinny.
17. The hikers were hot and thirsty after the long trek.
18. Isn't that statue African?
19. Don't be jealous of Tiger, the new kitten.
20. Is that myth Greek or Roman?

Review B Identifying Subject Complements

Identify each subject complement in the following sentences, and label it a *predicate nominative* or a *predicate adjective*.

EXAMPLE 1. The character Jahdu is a magical trickster.
1. trickster—predicate nominative

1. A trickster is a character who plays tricks on others.
2. Tricksters have been popular in many folk tales throughout the world.
3. Jahdu, however, is the creation of Virginia Hamilton.
4. Her collections of folk tales, such as *The Dark Way* and *In the Beginning,* are very enjoyable.
5. Jahdu may be her most unusual hero.
6. He certainly seems clever and playful.
7. Even Jahdu's home, a forest on the Mountain of Paths, sounds mysterious.
8. Jahdu can stay invisible by using special dust.
9. He can become any object, from a boy to a taxicab.
10. Why are tricksters like Jahdu always such entertaining characters?

HELP
A sentence in Review B may have a compound subject complement.

Link to Literature

HELP
Some sentences in Review C have more than one complement or a compound complement.

Review C Identifying Complements

Identify each complement in the following sentences, and label it a *direct object*, an *indirect object*, a *predicate nominative*, or a *predicate adjective*.

EXAMPLE 1. One pet of President Theodore Roosevelt's family was Algonquin, a pony.
1. Algonquin—predicate nominative

1. Some presidents' pets have become famous. **1. p.a.**
2. Someone may have shown you the book by President George Bush's pet, Millie. **2. i.o./d.o.**
3. Millie, a spaniel, became an author. **3. p.n.**

414   Chapter 14   Complements

Learning for Life

Remind students to write the steps in chronological order and to imagine the reader of their instructions performing the steps.

After students have finished writing, have them meet with a partner for peer evaluation. Students should make sure the instructions are clear and should pay particular attention to whether complements have been used effectively. Partners may find it beneficial to mime the actions of each other's directions.

4. With the help of Mrs. Bush, Millie told a great deal about her days at the White House.   **4.** d.o.
5. President Richard Nixon's best-known pet was Checkers, a cocker spaniel.   **5.** p.n.
6. President Bill Clinton had both a cat named Socks and a dog named Buddy.   **6.** d.o./d.o.
7. President William Howard Taft kept a pet cow.   **7.** d.o.
8. Some presidential pets looked quite strange at the White House.   **8.** p.a.
9. A pet mockingbird was a favorite companion of Thomas Jefferson.   **9.** p.n.
10. Calvin Coolidge's raccoon, Rebecca, appeared comfortable at the White House.   **10.** p.a.

Review D Identifying Complements

Identify each complement in the following sentences as a *direct object*, an *indirect object*, a *predicate nominative*, or a *predicate adjective*.

EXAMPLE   1. Have you ever seen a sari or a bindi?
    1. sari; bindi—direct object

HELP
Some sentences in Review D have more than one complement or a compound complement.

1. Many women from India wear these items.   **1.** d.o.
2. A sari is a traditional Indian garment of cotton or silk.   **2.** p.n.
3. Women wrap the sari's long, brightly printed cloth around their bodies.   **3.** d.o.
4. As you can see, the softly draped sari is both graceful and charming.   **4.** p.a./p.a.
5. Some women buy themselves cloth woven with golden threads for an elegant look.   **5.** i.o./d.o.
6. As you might imagine, sari wearers can become quite chilled in the winter.   **6.** p.a.
7. In cold climates, Indian women wear their beautiful, lightweight garments under sturdy winter coats.
8. Another traditional ornament for many Indian women is the colored dot in the middle of their foreheads.   **7.** d.o.   **8.** p.n.
9. The word for the dot is *bindi*.   **9.** p.n.
10. The bindi gives the wearer a look of beauty and refinement.   **10.** i.o./d.o.

Meeting INDIVIDUAL NEEDS

MULTIPLE INTELLIGENCES
Intrapersonal Intelligence. As an alternative to **Review E**, you might want to tell students to imagine they are writing letters to new pen pals they have never met in person. Have students reflect on how they would describe themselves in their letters. Encourage students to focus on their personality traits, likes and dislikes, goals, hobbies, and so on. Then, have each student write eight sentences he or she could use in the letter: two with direct objects, two with indirect objects and direct objects, two with predicate nominatives, and two with predicate adjectives. Ask students to underline the complements and to label each one by type.

Review E **Writing Sentences with Complements**

Write a sentence using each of the following kinds of complements. Underline the complement or complements in each sentence. Use a variety of subjects and verbs in your sentences.

EXAMPLES
1. a compound predicate nominative
1. My aunt is a swimmer and a jogger.
2. a direct object
2. Lindsey tossed Sabra the softball.
3. a pronoun used as a predicate nominative
3. The winner of the science fair is she.

1. a predicate adjective
2. an indirect object
3. a direct object
4. a predicate nominative
5. a compound predicate adjective
6. a compound predicate nominative
7. a compound direct object
8. a compound indirect object
9. a pronoun used as an indirect object
10. a pronoun used as a direct object

Answers will vary. Possible responses are given.
1. My pen is blue.
2. Give Melanie a hand with that box.
3. Did you lend Ray that book?
4. Her father is a dentist.
5. Flannel feels soft and warm.
6. The finalists are Leila, Ryan, and she.
7. Mrs. Cuomo made lasagna and manicotti.
8. We should take Todd and Sheila a housewarming present.
9. Please paint us a picture, Mr. Sato.
10. Bake it at 350° for one hour.

CHAPTER 14

Chapter Review

A. Identifying Direct and Indirect Objects

Identify the *direct objects* and *indirect objects* in the following sentences.

HELP
Not all sentences in Part A have indirect objects.

1. James Baldwin wrote stories, novels, and essays.
2. Vita made her mother a scarf for her birthday.
3. He handed Amy and me an ad for the concert.
4. A park ranger told Mike the story of Forest Park.
5. Tropical forests give us many helpful plants.
6. Did she tell you about the bear?
7. The senator read the crowd a rousing speech.
8. The tourist gave the pigeons in Trafalgar Square some of his sandwich.
9. On the ferry to Ireland, Mr. McCourt told us the history of Dublin.
10. Bring me the wrench from the workbench, please.

B. Identifying Subject Complements

Identify the subject complements in the following sentences, and label each a *predicate nominative* or a *predicate adjective*.

11. Tuesday is the last day for soccer tryouts.
12. These peaches taste sweet and juicy.
13. Two common desert creatures are the lizard and the snake.
14. My cousin Tena has become an excellent weaver of Navajo blankets.
15. The soil in that pot feels dry to me.
16. The hero of the movie was a songwriter and a singer.
17. Why is Bill Gates so famous and so successful?
18. The three Brontë sisters were Charlotte, Emily, and Anne.
19. *The Adventures of Huckleberry Finn* is probably Mark Twain's best-known book.
20. The movie is shallow, silly, and boring.

Using the Chapter Review

To assess student progress, you may want to compare the types of items missed on the **Diagnostic Preview** with those missed on the **Chapter Review.** You may want to work on specific goals with individual students who are still having difficulty mastering essential information.

C. Identifying Complements

Identify the complements in the following sentences, and label each a *direct object*, an *indirect object*, a *predicate nominative*, or a *predicate adjective*.

21. Madrid is the capital of Spain. **21.** p.n.
22. Did you give me your new address? **22.** i.o./d.o.
23. These sketches of yours are wonderful! **23.** p.a.
24. Dr. Jonas Salk developed a vaccine to prevent polio. **24.** d.o.
25. Pam Adams is my best friend. **25.** p.n.
26. My father sent his mother and father two tickets to Mexico. **26.** i.o./i.o./d.o.
27. Your handwriting is neat and readable. **27.** p.a./p.a.
28. The longest play by Shakespeare is *Hamlet*. **28.** p.n.
29. Hugo handed his teacher the papers. **29.** i.o./d.o.
30. My father tossed the dog an old bone. **30.** i.o./d.o.
31. Whitney Houston is my favorite singer. **31.** p.n.
32. Thunder sometimes gives me a headache. **32.** i.o./d.o.
33. Are these toys safe for children? **33.** p.a.
34. My dad is buying my mother a bicycle. **34.** i.o./d.o.
35. Light reflectors for a bike are a good idea. **35.** p.n.
36. The wizard granted them three wishes. **36.** i.o./d.o.
37. Our trip to Villahermosa was short but exciting. **37.** p.a./p.a.
38. Angelo painted a beautiful picture of his mother. **38.** d.o.
39. Have you eaten lunch yet? **39.** d.o.
40. Miki is one of the best spellers in the class. **40.** p.n.

Writing Application
Using Complements in a Paragraph

Direct Objects and Indirect Objects For National Hobby Month, students in your class are making posters about their hobbies. Each poster will include drawings or pictures and a written description of the hobby. Write a paragraph about your hobby to go on your poster. Use at least three direct objects and two indirect objects in your paragraph.

RESOURCES

Complements

Review
- *Grammar, Usage, and Mechanics,* pp. 104, 105, 106

Assessment
- *Assessment Package*
  —*Chapter Tests,* Ch. 14
  —*Chapter Tests in Standardized Test Formats,* Ch. 14
- *Test Generator (One-Stop Planner CD-ROM)*

Prewriting Choose a topic for your poster project. You could write about any collection, sport, craft, or activity that you enjoy in your free time. You could also write about a hobby that you are interested in starting. Freewrite about the hobby. Be sure to tell why you enjoy it or why you think you would enjoy it. If the hobby is new to you, find out more about it from another hobbyist or from the library.

Writing Begin your paragraph with a main-idea sentence that clearly identifies the hobby or special interest. Check your prewriting notes often to find details you can use in describing the hobby.

Revising Read your paragraph aloud. Does it give enough information about your hobby? Would someone unfamiliar with the hobby find it interesting? Add, cut, or rearrange details to make your paragraph easier to understand. Identify the transitive verbs in your paragraph. Have you used at least three direct objects and two indirect objects? You may need to revise some sentences.

Publishing Read over your paragraph for spelling, grammar, and punctuation errors, and correct any you find. You and your classmates may want to make posters using your paragraphs and some pictures. Cut pictures out of magazines and brochures, or draw your own. Then, attach your writing and art to pieces of poster board and display the posters in the classroom.

Reference Note
For information about **main idea sentences,** see page 279.

GRAMMAR

Writing Application
(pp. 418–19)

OBJECTIVE

- To write a paragraph using three direct objects and two indirect objects

Writing Application

Tip. The assignment requires that students write paragraphs about their hobbies. Students may need further elaboration on what constitutes a hobby. You can tell them that a hobby is anything someone does on a regular basis for enjoyment.

Scoring Rubric. While you will want to pay particular attention to students' use of complements, you will also want to evaluate overall writing performance. You may want to give a split score to indicate development and clarity of the composition as well as grammar skills.

Critical Thinking

Analysis. For students to write paragraphs about their hobbies, they will need to analyze the processes they go through when practicing their hobbies. For example, if they collect things, they will need to discuss where or how the things are obtained and how the collections are kept or displayed.

Writing Application
Extension
- *Grammar, Usage, and Mechanics,* p. 109
- *Language Workshop CD-ROM,* Lessons 26–28

CHAPTER

15 Agreement
Subject and Verb, Pronoun and Antecedent

Diagnostic Preview

A. Choosing Verbs That Agree in Number with Their Subjects

Find the subject of each of the following sentences. Then, choose the form of the verb in parentheses that agrees with the subject.

EXAMPLE 1. Janelle and Brad (*are, is*) in the drama club.
 1. *Janelle, Brad—are*

1. Neither the passengers nor the pilot (*was, were*) injured.
2. There (*are, is*) two exciting new rides at the amusement park.
3. That book of Spanish folk tales (*is, are*) selling out.
4. (*Here are, Here's*) some books about Hawaii.
5. Shel Silverstein and Ogden Nash (*appeal, appeals*) to both children and grown-ups.
6. Velma and her little sister (*was, were*) reading a story by Gyo Fujikawa.
7. (*Was, Were*) your parents happy with the results?
8. Why (*doesn't, don't*) she and Megan bring the lemonade with them to the picnic?
9. The dishes on that shelf (*look, looks*) clean.

420 Chapter 15 Agreement

CHAPTER RESOURCES

Planning
- One-Stop Planner CD-ROM

Practice and Extension
- *Grammar, Usage, and Mechanics*, p. 110
- *Language Workshop CD-ROM*

Internet
- go.hrw.com (keyword: EOLang)

Evaluation and Assessment
- *Assessment Package*
  —Chapter Tests, Ch. 15
  —Chapter Tests in Standardized Test Formats, Ch. 15
- *Test Generator (One-Stop Planner CD-ROM)*

10. Either the cats or the dog (*has, have*) upset the plants.
11. There (*go, goes*) two more deer!
12. I (*am, is*) crocheting an afghan.
13. Why (*wasn't, weren't*) you at the scout meeting yesterday?
14. Several paintings by that artist (*are, is*) now on exhibit at the mall.
15. They (*doesn't, don't*) know how to find their way to the family reunion.

B. Choosing Pronouns That Agree with Their Antecedents

For each of the following sentences, identify the pronoun that agrees with its antecedent.

EXAMPLES
1. Either Eileen or Barbara will bring (*her, their*) notes.
1. her

2. When Dennis and Aaron were younger, (*he, they*) rode the same bus to school.
2. they

16. A student should proofread (*his or her, their*) work carefully before turning in the final copy.
17. Carlos and Andrew finally watched the videos (*he, they*) had borrowed.
18. Everyone on the girls' volleyball team has picked up (*her, their*) equipment.
19. The cat had batted its toy under the sofa and couldn't reach (*it, them*).
20. Jennifer or Sharon will leave early so that (*she, they*) can prepare the display.
21. Most of the trees in the park had lost (*its, their*) leaves.
22. If you aren't going to finish those crossword puzzles, may I do (*it, them*)?
23. Each of the drawings was hung on the wall in (*its, their*) frame.
24. When Martin and Stephanie were not rehearsing onstage, (*he or she, they*) studied their lines in the hall.
25. Did one of the chickens lose (*its, their*) feathers?

USAGE

Number and Agreement of Subject and Verb

Rules 15a, b (pp. 422–425)

OBJECTIVES

- To identify words as singular or plural
- To identify subjects and verbs as singular or plural
- To change the number of subjects and verbs
- To choose verbs that agree in number with their subjects

TEACHING TIP

Motivation. Draw stick figures on the chalkboard in three groups: one single figure, one pair, and one group of three. Tell students the figures are students, and ask volunteers to say how many students are in each group. Then, ask "Would you say 'three student' or 'three students'?" Lead the class to see that nouns are either singular (one item) or plural (more than one item).

Meeting INDIVIDUAL NEEDS

ENGLISH-LANGUAGE LEARNERS

Spanish. In Spanish, *la gente* (people) is a singular noun, so Spanish-speaking students might use sentences such as "The people is going to the game." Provide some practice in subject-verb agreement using *people* as the subject.

---

15 a, b

HELP

Most nouns that end in *–s* are plural (*igloos, sisters*). Most verbs that end in *–s* are singular (*sings, tries*).

EXAMPLES
My **sisters sing**.
My **sister sings**.

However, verbs used with the singular pronouns *I* and *you* do not end in *–s*.

EXAMPLES
I sing.
You sing.

Reference Note

The plurals of some nouns do not end in *–s* (*mice, Chinese, aircraft*). For more about **spelling the plural forms of nouns**, see page 621.

Number

Number is the form a word takes to show whether the word is singular or plural.

15a. Words that refer to one person, place, thing, or idea are generally *singular* in number. Words that refer to more than one person, place, thing, or idea are generally *plural* in number.

Singular	tepee	I	baby	mouse
Plural	tepees	we	babies	mice

Exercise 1   Identifying Singular and Plural Words

Identify each of the following words as *singular* or *plural*.

EXAMPLE 1. activities
          1. *plural*

1. peach   **1.** s
2. libraries **2.** p
3. highway   **3.** s
4. knife   **4.** s
5. shelves   **5.** p
6. children   **6.** p
7. they   **7.** p
8. enchiladas **8.** p
9. women   **9.** p
10. America   **10.** s
11. dirt   **11.** s
12. dress   **12.** s
13. someone   **13.** s
14. feet   **14.** p
15. fantasy   **15.** s
16. society   **16.** s
17. potatoes **17.** p
18. people   **18.** p
19. several   **19.** p
20. fathers-in-law **20.** p

Agreement of Subject and Verb

15b. A verb should agree in number with its subject.

A subject and verb *agree* when they have the same number.

(1) Singular subjects take singular verbs.

EXAMPLES The **ocean roars** in the distance. [The singular verb *roars* agrees with the singular subject *ocean*.]

She plays the violin well. [The singular verb *plays* agrees with the singular subject *She*.]

422   Chapter 15   Agreement

RESOURCES

Number and Agreement of Subject and Verb
Practice
- *Grammar, Usage, and Mechanics*, pp. 111, 112–113
- *Language Workshop CD-ROM*, Lessons 10, 11

(2) Plural subjects take plural verbs.

EXAMPLES **Squirrels eat** the seeds from the bird feeder. [The plural verb *eat* agrees with the plural subject *Squirrels*.]

They practice after school. [The plural verb *practice* agrees with the plural subject *They*.]

When a sentence contains a verb phrase, the first helping verb in the phrase agrees with the subject.

EXAMPLES **Latrice has** been studying Arabic.
They have been studying Arabic.

Reference Note
For information on **verb phrases,** see page 348.

Exercise 2 Identifying the Number of Subjects and Verbs

Identify each of the following subjects and verbs as either *singular* or *plural*.

EXAMPLE 1. flag waves
1. singular

HELP
All verbs in Exercise 2 agree with their subjects.

1. socks match **1. p**
2. lightning crackles **2. s**
3. leaves rustle **3. p**
4. mosquitoes buzz **4. p**
5. Lyle baby-sits **5. s**
6. bands march **6. p**
7. Richelle knits **7. s**
8. they listen **8. p**
9. singer practices **9. s**
10. horses whinny **10. p**
11. crows fly **11. p**
12. Shannon chooses **12. s**
13. boat floats **13. s**
14. we learn **14. p**
15. leg aches **15. s**
16. Roger guesses **16. s**
17. poets write **17. p**
18. cells divide **18. p**
19. he knows **19. s**
20. ice cube melts **20. s**

Exercise 3 Changing the Number of Subjects and Verbs

All of the subjects and verbs in the following sentences agree in number. Rewrite each sentence, changing the subject and verb from singular to plural or from plural to singular.

EXAMPLE 1. Lions roar on the plains of Kenya.
1. *A lion roars on the plains of Kenya.*

1. Maps show the shape of a country.

Agreement of Subject and Verb **423**

MINI-LESSON

Continued on p. 424

Finding the Subject. To determine correct agreement of the subject and verb, students must be able to locate the subject of a sentence. Write the following sentences on the chalkboard, and have volunteers find the subjects by asking *Who?* or *What?* before the verbs.

1. The tired <u>campers</u> built a campfire.
2. <u>Leonie</u> enjoyed her hike through the canyon.

TEACHING TIP

Activity. To introduce subject-verb agreement to students, write these two nonsense sentences on the chalkboard:

1. The ama (*plin, plins*) the corb. [*plins*]

2. The amas (*plin, plins*) the corb. [*plin*]

Ask students to select the correct "verb" and to explain how they were able to make the correct choices. [*Some students will probably say that they chose what "sounded" right.*]

Ask volunteers to replace the nonsense words in each sentence with real words. Tell students to notice how the –s endings in sentence 1 are different from those in sentence 2.

1. The <u>horse jumps</u> the fence.

2. The <u>horses jump</u> the fence.

Meeting INDIVIDUAL NEEDS

LEARNERS HAVING DIFFICULTY
To provide students with practice in subject-verb agreement, have them develop subject-verb pairs like those in **Exercise 2.** You can pair students and have one student in each pair suggest subjects and the other suggest verbs that agree with those subjects. For added practice, have students create complete sentences from their subject-verb pairs as well as from the word pairs in **Exercise 2.**

Exercise 3 Changing the Number of Subjects and Verbs

ANSWERS

1. The (*or* A) map shows the shape of a country.
2. What country is highlighted on the map on the right?
3. Do oceans form Kenya's eastern border?
4. A (*or* The) visitor enjoys Kenya's beautiful scenery.
5. Mount Kenya's peak is covered with snow.
6. A wildlife park has been created in Kenya.
7. In the picture below, a (*or* the) ranger patrols a park to protect the animals.
8. He certainly has unusual transportation.
9. An industry is located in Kenya's capital, Nairobi.
10. A (*or* The) Kenyan farmer grows such crops as wheat, corn, and rice.

TEACHING TIP

Extension. To emphasize map-reading skills, you may want to use the exercise below as an oral activity or write the questions on the board and have students answer in writing.

1. What is the capital of Rwanda? [*Kigali*]
2. Name two countries that border Lake Victoria. [*Kenya, Uganda, Tanzania*]
3. Burundi is directly south of what country? [*Rwanda*]

2. What countries are highlighted on the map below?
3. Does an ocean form Kenya's eastern border?
4. Visitors enjoy Kenya's beautiful scenery.
5. Mount Kenya's peaks are covered with snow.
6. Wildlife parks have been created in Kenya.
7. In the picture below, rangers patrol a park to protect the animals.
8. They certainly have unusual transportation.
9. Many industries are located in Kenya's capital, Nairobi.
10. Kenyan farmers grow such crops as wheat, corn, and rice.

424   Chapter 15   Agreement

MINI-LESSON

3. On the calm waters, the <u>boat</u> rocked gently.
4. My <u>tent</u> offered shelter from the rain.

For additional information and practice, refer students to **Chapter 10: The Sentence,** p. 300.

Exercise 4 Choosing Verbs That Agree in Number with Their Subjects

For each of the following sentences, choose the form of the verb in parentheses that agrees with the subject.

EXAMPLE 1. The kitten (*pounces, pounce*) on the ball.
1. *pounces*

1. Firefighters (*risks, risk*) their lives to save others.
2. The snowplow (*clears, clear*) the road quickly.
3. Some dancers (*like, likes*) reggae music best.
4. St. Augustine, Florida, (*has, have*) many old buildings.
5. Some students (*chooses, choose*) to play volleyball.
6. At the science fair, the winner always (*receives, receive*) a savings bond.
7. Strong winds (*whistles, whistle*) through the old house.
8. Each Saturday, club members (*picks, pick*) up the litter in the park.
9. The principal (*makes, make*) announcements over the loudspeaker each day.
10. Doctors (*says, say*) that listening to loud music can harm people's hearing.

Problems in Agreement
Phrases Between Subject and Verb

15c. The number of a subject is not changed by a phrase following the subject.

EXAMPLES These **shades** of blue **are** my favorite colors.

The **ballerina** with long black braids **has** been my sister's ballet teacher for two years.

However, if the subject is the indefinite pronoun *all, any, more, most, none,* or *some,* its number may be determined by the object of a prepositional phrase that follows it.

EXAMPLES **Some** of the oranges **are** gone. [*Some* refers to the plural noun *oranges.*]

Some of the fruit **is** gone. [*Some* refers to the singular noun *fruit.*]

Reference Note
For information on **phrases,** see Chapter 13.

—HELP—
The subject of a sentence is never in a prepositional phrase.
EXAMPLE
The **apples** in the refrigerator are not cold yet. [*Apples* is the subject. *Refrigerator* cannot be the subject because it is part of the prepositional phrase *in the refrigerator.*]

RESOURCES

Problems in Agreement
Practice
- *Grammar, Usage, and Mechanics,*
  pp. 114, 115–116, 117, 118, 119
- *Language Workshop CD-ROM,* Lesson 12

Problems in Agreement
Rules 15c–m *(pp. 425–435)*

OBJECTIVES

- To choose verbs that agree in number with their subjects when an intervening phrase separates the subject and verb
- To choose verbs that agree in number with indefinite pronouns used as subjects
- To choose verbs that agree with compound subjects
- To read aloud sentences with compound subjects joined by *or* or *nor*
- To choose verbs that agree with subjects that come after the verb
- To read aloud sentences containing *don't* and *doesn't*
- To write *don't* and *doesn't* to agree with subjects in sentences

Meeting INDIVIDUAL NEEDS

INCLUSION
Learning-disabled students often have difficulty focusing their attention. To help them understand agreement rules, create exercises in which students match subjects and predicates to form complete sentences. You may also want to have students skip the chapter's more difficult content.

To provide additional practice, write verbs on flashcards and have the students create sentences by adding subjects that agree with the verbs.

> **NOTE** *As well as, along with, together with,* and *in addition to* are compound prepositions. Phrases beginning with compound prepositions do not affect the number of a subject or verb.
>
> **EXAMPLE** **Myra,** along with her brothers, **helps** with household chores each evening. [The prepositional phrase *along with her brothers* does not affect the number of the subject *Myra*. *Myra* is singular and takes a singular verb, *helps.*]

Exercise 5 Choosing Verbs That Agree in Number with Their Subjects

In each of the following sentences, choose the form of the verb in parentheses that agrees with the subject.

EXAMPLE 1. Islands off the coast (*has, have*) a life of their own.
1. have

1. The second-largest island of the United States (*is, are*) located in the Gulf of Alaska.
2. The thirteen thousand people on Kodiak Island (*is, are*) mostly of Scandinavian, Russian, or Native Arctic descent.
3. The citizens of Kodiak (*calls, call*) Alaska the mainland.
4. Sacks of mail (*is, are*) flown there from the mainland.
5. Industries in the community, originally known as Kikhtak, (*includes, include*) farming, fishing, and mining.
6. One cannery on the island (*cans, can*) salmon eggs, or roe.
7. Many residents on the mainland (*considers, consider*) roe a delicacy.
8. Bears like this one (*catch, catches*) fresh salmon.
9. However, their search for leftovers often (*create, creates*) problems for Kodiak.
10. The officials of one town (*has, have*) had to put a special bear-proof fence around the garbage dump.

Indefinite Pronouns

Personal pronouns refer to specific people, places, things, or ideas. A pronoun that does not refer to a definite person, place, thing, or idea is called an *indefinite pronoun*.

Personal Pronouns	she	you	we	them
Indefinite Pronouns	each	many	anyone	all

15d. The following indefinite pronouns are singular: *anybody, anyone, anything, each, either, everybody, everyone, everything, neither, nobody, no one, nothing, one, somebody, someone,* and *something*.

EXAMPLES **One** of the stars **is** Gloria Estefan.

Each of the tourists **was** given a souvenir.

Does everybody in the restaurant like pita bread?

TIPS & TRICKS

The words *one*, *thing*, and *body* are singular. The indefinite pronouns that contain these words are singular, too.

EXAMPLES
Was every**one** there?

Some**body has** answered.

No**thing works** better.

HELP

Remember that the subject is never part of a prepositional phrase.

Exercise 6 Choosing Verbs That Agree in Number with Their Subjects

In the following sentences, choose the form of the verb in parentheses that agrees with the subject.

EXAMPLE 1. Neither of the teams (*is, are*) on the field.
1. is

1. Nearly everybody in Ruby Lee's family (*enjoy, enjoys*) tomato soup.
2. Neither of them (*was, were*) wearing a helmet.
3. Somebody in the class (*speaks, speak*) French.
4. Nobody in the first two rows (*want, wants*) to volunteer to be the magician's assistant.
5. Each of these songs (*is, are*) by Natalie Imbruglia.
6. Someone in the crowd (*is, are*) waving a pennant, but I can't tell whether it's Nick.
7. Everyone in those exercise classes (*has, have*) lost weight.
8. One of the band members (*play, plays*) lead guitar and sings backup vocals.
9. No one (*was, were*) listening to the speaker.
10. (*Do, Does*) either of them know how?

Meeting INDIVIDUAL NEEDS

ENGLISH-LANGUAGE LEARNERS
General Strategies. The rules in the section on indefinite pronouns might overwhelm English-language learners. To lessen this anxiety, you might pair English-language learners with one or more students who can serve as peer tutors.

MULTIPLE INTELLIGENCES
Linguistic Intelligence. Students can practice making verbs agree with indefinite pronouns by writing their own fairy tales or other stories. Have students discuss possible characters and situations for a fairy tale, such as a youngest child meeting a challenge. Ask students to list indefinite pronouns they might use and to explain how pronouns like *someone*, *anybody*, *nothing*, and *any* would fit into their tales. Have students write their fairy tales or stories and underline the pronouns (and the verbs that agree with them) in their tales.

Cooperative Learning
Arrange students in groups of four. Have three of the group members each select one of the groups of indefinite pronouns listed in **Rules 15d–f**. The fourth group member will be the group illustrator. Each group will decide on a topic on which to write a brief story. Then, each of the three writers in a group will write four sentences for the story. The sentences should contain underlined examples of the writer's pronouns. Group members should divide the story parts among themselves (beginning, middle, end) and write the parts in order. The illustrator can then draw one picture for each part of the story. Have each group post its finished story on a class bulletin board.

COMPUTER TIP

Using indefinite pronouns correctly can be tricky. To help yourself, you may want to create an indefinite pronoun guide. First, summarize the information in Rules 15d–15f. Then, choose several example sentences to illustrate the rules.

If you use a computer, you can create a help file with these rules and examples. Call up your help file whenever you have trouble with indefinite pronouns in your writing. If you don't use a computer, you can keep your guide in a writing notebook.

HELP

The pronouns listed in Rule 15f aren't always followed by prepositional phrases.

EXAMPLES
  All are here.
  Some has spilled.

In such cases you should look at the **context**—the sentences before and after the pronoun—to see if the pronoun refers to a singular or a plural word.

15e. The following indefinite pronouns are plural: *both, few, many, several.*

EXAMPLES **Both overflow** occasionally.

Few of the guests **are** wearing formal clothes.

Many of the newer houses **have** built-in smoke detectors.

Several in the group **say** yes.

15f. The indefinite pronouns *all, any, more, most, none,* and *some* may be singular or plural, depending on their meaning in a sentence.

Often, the object of a preposition that follows the pronoun indicates whether the pronoun is singular or plural. If the object of the preposition is singular, the pronoun usually is singular. If the object is plural, the pronoun usually is plural.

EXAMPLES **All** of the snow **has** melted. [*All* is singular because *snow* is singular. The helping verb *has* is singular to agree with *All*.]

All of the snowflakes **have** melted. [*All* is plural because *snowflakes* is plural. The helping verb *have* is plural to agree with *All*.]

Some of the birdseed **is** left in the feeder. [*Some* is singular because *birdseed* is singular. The helping verb *is* is singular to agree with *Some*.]

Some of the sunflower seeds **are** left in the feeder. [*Some* is plural because *seeds* is plural. The helping verb *are* is plural to agree with *Some*.]

Exercise 7   Choosing Verbs That Agree in Number with Their Subjects

Choose the <u>correct form of the verb</u> in parentheses in each of the following sentences.

EXAMPLE   1. Many of these puppies (*needs, need*) a good home.
          1. need

1. Most of the balloons (*has*, <u>*have*</u>) long strings.
2. All of the girls wearing purple uniforms (*plays*, <u>*play*</u>) on the softball team.

USAGE

LEARNERS HAVING DIFFICULTY

You may want to let students work on **Exercise 7** in small groups. Group members can record their answers on a sheet of paper that all members sign. Then, provide a group grade for the work.

3. Both of the sneakers (*gives*, *give*) me blisters.
4. Most of these recipes (*requires*, *require*) ricotta cheese.
5. Some of the artists (*paint*, *paints*) landscapes.
6. Few of those songs (*was*, *were*) composed by Duke Ellington.
7. None of the apartments (*has*, *have*) been painted.
8. All of the jewels (*is*, *are*) in the safe.
9. Many in the crowd (*waves*, *wave*) signs.
10. All of the writing (*is*, *are*) upside down.

Compound Subjects

A compound subject is made up of two or more subjects that are connected by the conjunction *and*, *or*, or *nor*. These connected subjects share the same verb.

15g. Subjects joined by *and* generally take a plural verb.

EXAMPLES **Red** and **blue are** the school's colors.

New **uniforms** and **instruments were ordered** for the marching band.

Mr. Lewis, Mrs. Kirk, and **Ms. Jefferson have applied** for new jobs.

Exercise 8 Choosing Verbs That Agree in Number with Their Subjects

Identify the compound subject in each of the following sentences. Then, choose the form of the verb in parentheses that agrees with the compound subject.

EXAMPLE 1. Volcanoes and earthquakes (*is*, *are*) common in that area.
1. Volcanoes, earthquakes—are

1. The blanket and the robe (*has*, *have*) Navajo designs.
2. Wind, hail, and freezing rain (*is*, *are*) predicted for Thursday.
3. A desk and a bookcase (*were*, *was*) moved into Ella's room.
4. Savannas and velds (*is*, *are*) two kinds of grasslands found in Africa.

HELP

Some indefinite pronouns, such as *both*, *each*, and *some*, can also be used as adjectives. When an indefinite adjective comes before the subject of a sentence, the verb agrees with the subject as it normally would.

EXAMPLES
Children love playing in the park.

Both children love playing in the park.

The **child loves** playing in the park.

Each child loves playing in the park.

Reference Note

For information on **conjunctions,** see page 364.

Critical Thinking

Metacognition. Have students analyze their results from **Exercise 7**. Students should take note of each sentence they missed or had difficulty with and write an example sentence of their own for each problematic indefinite pronoun. Then, have students answer the following questions:

- What about agreement of subjects and verbs in **Exercise 7** causes you trouble?
- Why do you have difficulty in this area?
- How can you improve your understanding in this area?

TEACHING TIP

Exercise 8 Remind students that compound subjects can be made up of more than two elements. A series of three or more elements can make up a compound subject. No matter how many subjects there are, though, a coordinating conjunction will generally be used before the last item in a series.

Looking at Language

Dialects. Explain that some dialects of American English frequently omit the –s ending from verbs. [*He work hard. She like mysteries.*] Suggest that students take turns reading aloud the following subjects and verbs to hear examples of standard English. You may want to have students work together to expand the list and then read aloud their subjects and verbs.

1. horse jumps
2. girls leave
3. apple tastes
4. Marie talks
5. telephone rings
6. soldier waits
7. sisters want
8. teacher gives
9. car stops
10. Bill works

---

5. A delivery truck and a car with a trailer (*were*, *was*) stalled on the highway.
6. A raccoon and a possum (*raid*, *raids*) our vegetable garden every night.
7. Mandy and her aunt (*goes*, *go*) to the Chinese market every Saturday.
8. Eric and Jarvis (*were*, *was*) asked to introduce the speaker.
9. Mosquitoes and earwigs (*has*, *have*) invaded our backyard.
10. Ketchup, onions, and mustard (*goes*, *go*) well on many sandwiches.

15h. Singular subjects that are joined by *or* or *nor* take a singular verb.

EXAMPLES   A new marble **statue** or a **fountain has been planned** for the park.

On Mondays, either **Manuel** or **Stephie baby-sits** the children.

15i. Plural subjects joined by *or* or *nor* take a plural verb.

EXAMPLES   Either **potatoes** or **beans are served** with the baked chicken.

Tulips or **pansies make** a lovely border for a sidewalk.

15j. When a singular subject and a plural subject are joined by *or* or *nor*, the verb agrees with the subject nearer the verb.

EXAMPLES   Either the **engineers** or their **boss has made** this mistake. [The singular helping verb *has* agrees with the nearer subject, *boss*.]

Either the **boss** or the **engineers have made** this mistake. [The plural helping verb *have* agrees with the nearer subject, *engineers*.]

A soft **blanket** or some warm **booties make** a baby comfortable. [The plural helping verb *make* agrees with the nearer subject, *booties*.]

Some warm **booties** or a soft **blanket makes** a baby comfortable. [The singular verb *makes* agrees with the nearer subject, *blanket*.]

Oral Practice 1 **Using Correct Verbs with Compound Subjects Joined by *Or* or *Nor***

Read each of the following sentences aloud, stressing the words in italics.

1. A *desert* or a *jungle is* the setting for the play.
2. The *table* or the *bookshelves need* dusting first.
3. Neither the *bus* nor the *train stops* in our town.
4. Neither *jokes* nor funny *stories make* Gordon laugh.
5. *Flowers* or a colorful *picture makes* a room brighter and more cheerful.
6. Either the *story* or the *poems are* by Langston Hughes.
7. At this restaurant, *rice* or *potatoes come* with the tandoori chicken dinner.
8. Neither the *Carolinas* nor *Illinois borders* Texas.

Review A **Choosing Verbs That Agree in Number with Their Subjects**

For each of the following sentences, choose the form of the verb in parentheses that agrees with the subject.

EXAMPLE   1. Tara and Chen (*are, is*) reading the same book.
          1. are

1. Many vegetables (*grow, grows*) quite large during Alaska's long summer days.
2. His mother (*teach, teaches*) math.
3. All of the boats in the harbor (*belong, belongs*) to the village.
4. You and your cousins (*are, is*) invited to the party.
5. Either the wall clock or our wristwatches (*tell, tells*) the correct time.
6. The new magazines on the kitchen table (*are, is*) for the hospital waiting room.
7. My list of favorite singers (*include, includes*) Shania Twain and Brandy.
8. Both my big brother and my sister (*deliver, delivers*) the morning newspaper.
9. Neither pencils nor an eraser (*are, is*) permitted.
10. The clowns and jugglers (*has, have*) always been my favorite circus performers.

STYLE TIP

Compound subjects that have both singular and plural parts can sound awkward even though they are correct. Try to avoid such constructions by revising the sentence.

AWKWARD
  Jewelry or flowers make a nice Mother's Day gift.
REVISED
  Jewelry makes a nice Mother's Day gift, and **flowers do,** too.

USAGE

Meeting INDIVIDUAL NEEDS

MODALITIES
Visual Learners. To help visual learners improve their understanding of subject-verb agreement, have each student write nine sentences, varying the sentences to include three sentences with the subject following the verb, three sentences with the subject followed by a prepositional phrase, and three sentences with indefinite pronouns as subjects. Students can exchange sentences with partners. Partners can circle each subject and draw an arrow from it to the verb with which it agrees. Students can then review their marked sentences.

1. celebrate
2. knows
3. C
4. enjoy
5. dresses
6. C
7. have
8. is
9. wears
10. C

TIPS & TRICKS

When the subject of a sentence comes after the verb, the word order is said to be *inverted*. To find the subject of a sentence with inverted order, restate the sentence in normal subject-verb word order.

INVERTED
How much time **has he spent** at the lake?

NORMAL
He has spent how much time at the lake?

INVERTED
Here **are** the **toys**.

NORMAL
The **toys are** here.

Review B Proofreading a Paragraph for Errors in Subject-Verb Agreement

Most sentences in the following paragraph contain a verb that does not agree in number with its subject. If a sentence is incorrect, give the correct verb form. If a sentence is already correct, write *C*.

EXAMPLE   [1] Holiday customs throughout the world is fun to study.

1. are

[1] In Sweden, adults and children celebrates St. Lucia's Day. [2] Everyone there know St. Lucia as the Queen of Light. [3] Many people eagerly look forward to the December 13 holiday. [4] Girls especially enjoys the day. [5] By tradition, the oldest girl in the family dress as St. Lucia. [6] The girl in the picture above is ready to play her part. [7] You surely has noticed the girl's headdress. [8] A crown of lighted candles are hard to miss! [9] Each of the young Lucias also wear a white robe. [10] Early in the morning, the costumed girls bring breakfast to the adults of the household.

Subject After the Verb

15k. When the subject follows the verb, find the subject and make sure that the verb agrees with it.

The subject usually follows the verb in questions and in sentences that begin with *there* and *here*.

EXAMPLES   **Are** the **birds** in the nest?
Is the **nest** on a high branch?

There **go** the **dragons**.
There **goes** the **dragon**.

NOTE   The contractions *there's* and *here's* contain the verb *is*. These contractions are singular and should be used only with singular subjects.

EXAMPLES   There**'s Uncle Max.**
Here**'s** your **allowance.**

Exercise 9 Choosing Verbs That Agree in Number with Their Subjects

Identify the subject of each sentence. Then, choose the form of the verb in parentheses that agrees with the subject.

EXAMPLE 1. There (*was, were*) a baby rabbit hiding in the grass.
1. rabbit—was

1. There (*are, is*) a new foreign-exchange student at my brother's high school.
2. (*Was, Were*) the fans cheering for the other team?
3. (*Has, Have*) the Washingtons moved into their new home?
4. Here (*stand, stands*) one brave, young woman and her only son, Dale.
5. (*Has, Have*) the bees left the hive?
6. (*There's, There are*) several correct answers to that tough question.
7. How long (*has, have*) the Huang family owned this tai chi studio?
8. (*Here are, Here's*) the shells that we collected from Driftwood Beach.
9. (*There's, There are*) a pint of fresh strawberries on the kitchen table.
10. There (*were, was*) Amy and Wanda in the doorway.

The Contractions *Don't* and *Doesn't*

15l. The word *don't* is the contraction of *do not.* Use *don't* with all plural subjects and with the pronouns *I* and *you.*

EXAMPLES **I don't** have my keys.   **Dogs don't** meow.

You don't care.   **Don't they** know?

We don't agree.   The **boots don't** fit.

15m. The word *doesn't* is the contraction of *does not.* Use *doesn't* with all singular subjects except the pronouns *I* and *you.*

EXAMPLES **He doesn't** know you.   **Don doesn't** like thunder.

She doesn't see it.   **Doesn't** the **car** run?

It doesn't work.   A **penguin doesn't** fly.

Reference Note

For more information on **contractions,** see page 602.

TECHNOLOGY TIP

If you have access to tape recorders, you may wish to have students tape each other reading **Oral Practice 2**. Students could then listen to the tapes of themselves to reinforce standard usage of *don't* and *doesn't*.

TEACHING TIP

Activity. To give students extra practice with subject-verb agreement, write a list of subjects and a list of verbs on the chalkboard. Ask students to use the list to compose sentences with compound subjects, sentences with phrases between the subjects and verbs, and sentences with the subjects following the verbs.

Cooperative Learning

Pair students, and have each pair construct flashcards with which to review the rules covered so far in the chapter. Each flashcard should have an incomplete rule on one side and the word missing from the rule on the other. For example, the front of the flashcard for **Rule 15b** could read *A verb should agree in _____ with its subject.* The back should supply the missing word, *number.* Each pair should have a full set of matching cards to which they can add **Rules 15c–m** individually. Before students take the **Chapter Review,** allow partners to meet again to quiz each other with their flashcards. You may want to grade partners together on the **Chapter Review,** adding their scores and dividing by two.

Oral Practice 2 — Using *Don't* and *Doesn't* Correctly

Read each of the following sentences aloud, stressing the words in italics.

1. *He doesn't* want us to give him a party.
2. *Margo* and *Jim don't* have any money left.
3. *Lynna doesn't* remember the punchline.
4. The *bus doesn't* stop here.
5. *They don't* believe that old story.
6. *It doesn't* snow here in October.
7. *You don't* sing the blues anymore.
8. That Zuni *vase doesn't* look very old.

Exercise 10 — Writing *Don't* and *Doesn't* with Subjects

Identify the subject in each of the following sentences. Then, choose the contraction, either *don't* or *doesn't,* that agrees with the subject.

EXAMPLE 1. Our cats _____ like catnip.
 1. cats—*don't*

1. don't — 1. My parents _____ listen to rap music.
2. don't — 2. I _____ have much homework tonight.
3. doesn't — 3. Jerome _____ play the guitar as well as Angela does.
4. doesn't — 4. The pizza _____ have enough onions, mushrooms, green peppers, or cheese.
5. don't — 5. They _____ permit diving into the pool.
6. doesn't — 6. This bedroom _____ look very neat.
7. don't — 7. My ski boots _____ fit me this year.
8. doesn't — 8. Matthew enjoys playing lacrosse, but he _____ like to play soccer.
9. don't — 9. You _____ live on this street anymore.
10. doesn't — 10. It _____ seem possible that Leon grew an inch in one month.

Review C — Proofreading for Errors in Subject-Verb Agreement

Most of the following sentences contain a verb that does not agree in number with its subject. Correct each incorrect verb. If a sentence is already correct, write *C.*

434 Chapter 15 Agreement

EXAMPLE 1. Is the people in the picture worried?
1. Are

1. There is sharks swimming all around them. **1. are**
2. However, the people doesn't seem to care. **2. don't**
3. Has they lost their senses? **3. Have**
4. No, there aren't anything for them to worry about in this shark exhibit. **4. isn't**
5. There's a transparent tunnel right through the shark pool. **5. C**
6. Everyone who visits the exhibit ride a moving walkway through the tunnel. **6. rides**
7. The sharks don't seem to mind the people. **7. C**
8. Actually, sharks in the wild doesn't attack people very often. **8. don't**
9. Of course, sharks does eat almost anything. **9. do**
10. Caution and respect, therefore, is necessary in shark-inhabited waters. **10. are**

Agreement of Pronoun and Antecedent

A pronoun usually refers to a noun or another pronoun called its *antecedent.* When you use a pronoun, make sure that it agrees with its antecedent.

Reference Note
For more information on **antecedents**, see page 328.

15n. A pronoun should agree in gender with its antecedent.

Some singular personal pronouns have forms that indicate gender. Feminine pronouns refer to females. Masculine pronouns refer to males. Neuter pronouns refer to things (neither male nor female) and sometimes to animals.

Feminine	she	her	hers
Masculine	he	him	his
Neuter	it	it	its

RESOURCES

Agreement of Pronoun and Antecedent
Practice
- *Grammar, Usage, and Mechanics,* pp. 120–121, 122, 123

Agreement of Pronoun and Antecedent
Rules 15n, o *(pp. 435–440)*

OBJECTIVE
- To proofread for pronoun-antecedent agreement

TEACHING TIP

Activity. Have students practice using pronouns that agree in gender with their antecedents by asking volunteers to create sentences about people or objects in the classroom. For example:

This *chalkboard* looks clean because I washed *it* yesterday.

Miguel passed the test because *he* studied hard.

You might want to list on the chalkboard the people or objects you want students to refer to in creating their sentences. After each student recites a sentence, ask the rest of the class to identify the pronoun, its antecedent, and its gender.

Meeting INDIVIDUAL NEEDS

ENGLISH-LANGUAGE LEARNERS
Asian Languages. Students whose native languages use pronouns differently from the way English uses them may have difficulty with pronoun-antecedent agreement in English. In Korean, for example, pronouns do not refer to gender. Japanese has no number agreement, and the languages of Vietnam and Laos have no neuter pronouns. To prevent confusion, you can explain which personal pronouns refer to which sorts of antecedents, with special emphasis on the use of *he, she,* and *it.*

STYLE TIP

To avoid the awkward use of *his or her,* try to rephrase the sentence.

AWKWARD
Each of the actors had memorized **his or her** lines.

REVISED
All of the actors had memorized **their** lines.

Reference Note
For more information about **indefinite pronouns,** see page 332.

EXAMPLES Rosa said **she** lost **her** glasses.

Hank took **his** journal to the beach with **him.**

Manny chose that **bike** because of **its** color and styling.

The antecedent of a personal pronoun can be another kind of pronoun. In such cases, you can often look in a phrase that follows the antecedent to tell which personal pronoun to use.

EXAMPLE **One** of those **ladies** left **her** scarf in the car.

Each of the **boys** brought **his** own softball mitt.

Some singular antecedents may be either masculine or feminine. In such cases, use both the masculine and feminine forms of the pronoun.

EXAMPLE **Nobody** in the class finished **his or her** paper early.

NOTE In informal speech and writing, people often use a plural pronoun to refer to a singular antecedent that may be either feminine or masculine.

INFORMAL Every actor in the play had already memorized their lines.

Such usage is grammatically incorrect and should be avoided, especially in formal situations.

15o. A pronoun should agree with its antecedent in number.

A pronoun that refers to a singular antecedent is singular in number. A pronoun that refers to a plural antecedent is plural in number.

EXAMPLES Please put the lawn **mower** away after you have finished using **it.**

These **tools** will last longer if you take good care of **them.**

(1) Use a singular pronoun to refer to the indefinite pronouns *anybody, anyone, anything, each, either, everybody, everyone, everything, neither, nobody, no one, nothing, one, somebody, someone,* **and** *something.*

436 Chapter 15 Agreement

Learning for Life

Informal vs. Formal Language. Explain to students that in casual conversation, many people may use informal or even nonstandard English. However, in formal situations, standard English—including correct agreement—is required.

Tell students that they will be writing letters to obtain information about a summer camp, hobby class, or club. Each student should explain what he or she wants to know about the camp, class, or club, and why. For example, an athlete might want

EXAMPLES Has **one** of the hamsters hurt **its** leg?

Someone left **his or her** jacket on the bus.

Everyone on the girls' team has **her** own locker.

(2) Use a plural pronoun to refer to the indefinite pronouns *both, few, many,* **and** *several.*

EXAMPLES **Both** of the birds had hidden **their** nests well.

Several of the spiders continue to live under that log; it is where **they** hatched.

On a night like this, **few** of the travelers will reach **their** destinations on schedule.

(3) The indefinite pronouns *all, any, more, most, none,* **and** *some* **may be singular or plural, depending on their meaning in a sentence.**

EXAMPLES **None** of the cereal has lost **its** crunch. [*None* is singular because it refers to the singular noun *cereal*.]

None of the cereal flakes have lost **their** crunch. [*None* is plural because it refers to the plural noun *flakes*.]

(4) Use a singular pronoun to refer to two or more singular antecedents joined by *or* **or** *nor.*

EXAMPLES Either **Miguel or Randall** has **his** paintings on display.

Neither **Karli nor Marta** will lend you **her** book.

Using a pronoun to refer to antecedents of different numbers may create an unclear or awkward sentence.

UNCLEAR Neither the kittens nor their mother liked her new food. [*Her* agrees with the nearest antecedent, *mother.* However, it is unclear if the kittens disliked their own new food or if they disliked their mother's new food.]

UNCLEAR Neither the kittens' mother nor the kittens liked their new food. [*Their* agrees with the nearest antecedent, *kittens.* However, it is unclear if the mother disliked her own new food or if she disliked her kittens' new food.]

AWKWARD Neither the kittens nor their mother liked their or her new food.

STYLE TIP

Sentences with singular antecedents joined by *or* can sound awkward if the antecedents are of different genders. If a sentence sounds awkward, revise it to avoid the problem.

AWKWARD
Mark or Sherrie will bring his or her flashlight.

REVISED
Either **Mark** will bring **his** flashlight, or **Sherrie** will bring **hers.**

Agreement of Pronoun and Antecedent 437

It is best to revise sentences to avoid unclear and awkward constructions like the ones on the previous page.

REVISED Neither the kittens nor their mother liked **the** new food.

None of the cats liked **their** new food.

(5) Use a plural pronoun to refer to two or more antecedents joined by *and*.

EXAMPLES When **Tyrell and Davis** get home, **they** will be surprised.

Have **Chelsea and Susan** tried on **their** new outfits?

Exercise 11 Proofreading for Pronoun-Antecedent Agreement

Most of the following sentences contain errors in pronoun-antecedent agreement. Identify the ~~incorrect pronoun~~, and write the correct pronoun. If a sentence is already correct, write *C*.

EXAMPLE 1. Colby and everybody else brought his or her calculators.
1. his or her—their

1. Neither Chile nor Argentina has given ~~their~~ consent to the project. **1.** its
2. These knives are sharp; be careful with ~~it~~! **2.** them
3. Of course, Mrs. Chin and her daughters will give us ~~her~~ assistance. **3.** their
4. Everyone needs to take ~~their~~ project home by Friday. **4.** his or her
5. Many of the houses were decorated with ribbons on ~~its~~ doors for the holidays. **5.** their
6. Neither Frank nor Paul has had ~~their~~ hair cut recently. **6.** his
7. Every one of the dogs is required to have a numbered tag attached to ~~their~~ collar. **7.** its
8. That song on the radio sounds familiar, but I can't remember its title. **8.** C
9. Roseanne and Kimberly, I believe, recently lost ~~her~~ glasses. **9.** their
10. Have any of the horses escaped ~~its~~ corral? **10.** their

TEACHING TIP

Exercises You may wish to use **Exercise 11** as guided practice and have students complete **Exercise 12** as independent practice.

Exercise 12 — Proofreading for Pronoun-Antecedent Agreement

Most of the following sentences contain pronouns that do not agree with their antecedents. Identify each ~~incorrect pronoun~~, and write the correct pronoun. If a sentence is already correct, write *C*.

EXAMPLE 1. On the first day, no one knew their partner.
　　　　　1. *their—his or her*

1. Somebody in the back row left ~~their~~ umbrella behind.
2. At last, all of the kittens were having their nap.
3. Several of the students had large scholarships given to ~~him or her~~ by local businesses.
4. Anybody in the sixth grade should know ~~their~~ mother's maiden name.
5. Neither of the antique cars had ~~their~~ original paint job.
6. Did many of the apprentices later change ~~his or her~~ trade?
7. Yes, anyone can enter ~~their~~ pet in the contest.
8. Few of the boys know the procedure, but ~~he~~ will learn it quickly.
9. None of the girls brought their books.
10. Both of the packages had been opened, and ~~it~~ sat forgotten on the floor.

1. his or her
2. C
3. them
4. his or her
5. its
6. their
7. his or her
8. they
9. C
10. they

Exercise 13 — Proofreading for Pronoun-Antecedent Agreement

Most of the following sentences contain a pronoun that does not agree in number or gender with its antecedent or antecedents. Identify each ~~incorrect pronoun~~, and write the correct pronoun. If a sentence is already correct, write *C*.

EXAMPLE 1. Either Abe or Brian will give their speech first.
　　　　　1. *their—his*

1. Gold and silver gain worth from ~~its~~ rarity.
2. Ask Mr. Reed or Mr. Steinhauer if ~~they~~ will lend you a pen or a pencil.
3. The house at the corner and the house next door have flowers growing in front of ~~it~~.

1. their
2. he
3. them

Crossing the Curriculum

Social Studies. Work with the social studies teacher to develop a list of topics students might use to write a five-sentence paragraph in which they emphasize pronoun-antecedent agreement. Geographical topics would give students practice using *it*; biographical topics would emphasize other third-person singular or plural pronouns.

4. C
5. her
6. itself
7. C
8. its
9. C
10. them

4. The birds and the butterflies have flown south to their winter homes.
5. Can even a princess or a queen have their every wish?
6. Pepper tastes good in a recipe, but not all by themselves.
7. A single red rose or a lily does not cost much, and it will look nice on the table.
8. Each of the grocery stores advertises their sales in the Sunday paper.
9. Neither Dan nor Bob likes onions on his sandwich.
10. More of the oranges have stickers on it than I thought.

Exercise 14 Proofreading for Pronoun-Antecedent Agreement

Most of the following sentences contain a pronoun that does not agree in number or gender with its antecedent or antecedents. Correct each incorrect pronoun. If a sentence is already correct, write *C*.

EXAMPLE 1. Delia and Dawn told me about her idea for a neighborhood show.
  1. their

1. Both of my parents gave us his or her permission, so we used my front yard.   1. their
2. The name of our play, which was actually a rock opera, was *Strange Night,* and I wrote it.   2. C
3. Two trees lent us its trunks for a stage.   3. their
4. Somebody bought popcorn with their allowance and sold it to the audience.   4. his or her
5. Everyone in the neighborhood brought his or her own chair to the show.   5. C
6. Either Matt or Freddy practiced his dance routine.   6. C
7. Lisa and Tanya play guitar, so we asked her to be in our band.   7. them
8. Joan wore a costume with pink flowers and bluebirds on it.   8. C
9. Of course, a few dogs and one unhappy cat made its entrance at an improper moment.   9. their
10. Tickets were only fifty cents, and we sold all of it before the show began.   10. them

440   Chapter 15   Agreement

CHAPTER 15

Chapter Review

A. Choosing Verbs That Agree in Number with Their Subjects

For each of the following sentences, identify the subject. Then, choose the form of the verb in parentheses that agrees with the subject.

1. The flowers in that garden (*need, needs*) water.
2. She and her cousin (*play, plays*) tennis every weekend except in the winter.
3. Either Paulette or Lily (*attend, attends*) all the local performances of the Alvin Ailey dancers.
4. There (*was, were*) several teachers at the game.
5. All of the corn (*has, have*) dried up.
6. (*Was, Were*) Liang and his sister born in Taiwan?
7. None of the trucks (*has, have*) arrived yet.
8. My best friend at school (*doesn't, don't*) live in our neighborhood.
9. (*Was, Were*) you heating some bean and cheese burritos in the microwave?
10. Here (*come, comes*) Elena and James.
11. Only one of my three dogs, my beagle Neptune, really (*enjoy, enjoys*) the beach.
12. Either the students or their teacher (*has, have*) decided on the color of the new bulletin board.
13. (*Doesn't, Don't*) that sweater belong to Ralph?
14. Neither the clerk nor the shoppers (*was, were*) aware of the fire down the street.
15. Where (*was, were*) you last night around supper time?
16. Several houses in our neighborhood (*is, are*) for sale.
17. My brother and I often (*play, plays*) checkers together.
18. Either he or she (*is, are*) next in line.
19. Marilu (*don't, doesn't*) know the name of the author.
20. There (*was, were*) no other people there besides us.

Using the Chapter Review

To assess student progress, you may want to compare the types of items missed on the **Diagnostic Preview** to those missed on the **Chapter Review**. If students have not made significant progress, you could refer them to **Chapter 24: Correcting Common Errors, Exercises 6–9,** for additional practice.

Chapter Review

B. Changing the Number of Subjects and Verbs

ANSWERS

21. A dog barks in the middle of the night.
22. Birds sing in the distance.
23. A book has fallen off the shelf.
24. Camels pass.
25. A car moves down the highway.
26. Does an elephant eat grass?
27. The men have eaten lunch.
28. A person is at the river today.
29. They have an unusual hobby.
30. A police officer protects the people.

B. Changing the Number of Subjects and Verbs

All the subjects and verbs in the following sentences agree in number. Rewrite each sentence, changing the subject and verb from singular to plural or from plural to singular. You may have to add or delete *a*, *an*, or *the*.

21. Dogs bark in the middle of the night.
22. A bird sings in the distance.
23. Books have fallen off the shelf.
24. A camel passes.
25. Cars move down the highway.
26. Do elephants eat grass?
27. The man has eaten lunch.
28. Many people are at the river today.
29. She has an unusual hobby.
30. Police officers protect the people.

C. Proofreading for Errors in Pronoun-Antecedent Agreement

Most of the following sentences contain a pronoun that does not agree in number or gender with its antecedent or antecedents. Write each ~~incorrect pronoun~~. Then, write the ∧pronoun that agrees with the antecedent. If a sentence is already correct, write *C*.

31. their
32. its
33. they
34. C
35. his
36. their

31. We had to call the parking lot attendant because two cars and one truck had ∧its lights on.
32. Each of the ducks was tagged with an electronic device around ∧their left leg.
33. Tim and Donny promised ∧he would bring some snacks to the party.
34. Frances or Donna will sing her favorite number.
35. I can't remember which one of my grandfathers spent ∧their eighteenth and nineteenth years fighting in World War II.
36. Both my brother and my sister might lend me ∧~~his or her~~ favorite videos.

RESOURCES

Agreement

Review
- *Grammar, Usage, and Mechanics*, pp. 124, 125, 126, 127, 128

Assessment
- Assessment Package
  —Chapter Tests, Ch. 15
  —Chapter Tests in Standardized Test Formats, Ch. 15
- Test Generator (One-Stop Planner CD-ROM)

37. Somebody left the engine running in ~~their~~ car. ^his or her^
38. Did one of the applicants forget to sign his or her forms?
39. Most of the customers complained that ~~his or her~~ food was cold. ^their^
40. Neither of the robins had ~~their~~ winter plumage. ^its^

Writing Application
Using Agreement in Instructions

Subject-Verb Agreement   Your family is going on a weekend trip. A neighbor has agreed to look after your pets. Write a note giving your neighbor complete instructions for tending the animals. To avoid confusing your reader, make sure the subjects and verbs in your sentences agree.

Prewriting   Think about pets that you have had or that someone you know has had. If you have never cared for a pet, talk to someone who has. Take notes on caring for each pet.

Writing   Write a draft of your note. Explain the daily care of the pets step by step. The more specific your instructions are, the better. With your teacher's permission, you may use informal, standard English if you are writing to someone you know well.

Revising   Read your note aloud. Can you follow each step of the instructions? Are all the steps in order? Have you included all the necessary information? If not, revise your note to make it clear and complete.

Publishing   After you have revised your note, check each sentence for subject-verb and pronoun-antecedent agreement. Take special care with any verb that is part of a contraction. Check your note for any other errors in grammar, punctuation, and spelling. Find or make pictures that illustrate each of your steps. With your teacher's permission, mount the pictures on a storyboard and display the storyboard in your classroom.

37. his or her
38. C
39. their

40. its

Reference Note
For more about **informal English,** see page 519.

Chapter Review   **443**

RESOURCES
Writing Application
Extension
- *Grammar, Usage, and Mechanics,* p. 131
- *Language Workshop CD-ROM,* Lessons 10, 11, 12

CHAPTER 16

Using Verbs Correctly
Principal Parts, Regular and Irregular Verbs, Tense

PREVIEWING THE CHAPTER

- The first part of the chapter explains the difference between regular and irregular verbs and shows how to form the principal parts of regular verbs. Examples of the present participle, past, and past participle forms of irregular verbs are given. This chapter also discusses verb tenses, including tenses of six verbs that often give students problems.

- The chapter closes with a **Chapter Review** for checking students' mastery of correct verb forms and tenses. Also, a **Writing Application** feature asks students to use correct verb forms in writing a paragraph.

- For help in integrating this chapter with composition chapters, use the **Teaching Strands** chart on pp. T297A–T297B.

USING THE DIAGNOSTIC PREVIEW

- You could use the **Diagnostic Preview** to determine students' understanding of correct verb forms. The parts of the test that students have trouble with should indicate the areas in which students need help and the sections of the chapter on which they should concentrate.

Diagnostic Preview

Revising Incorrect Verb Forms in Sentences

Most of the following sentences contain an ~~error in the use of verbs~~. If a verb form is incorrect, write the correct form. If the sentence is already correct, write *C*.

EXAMPLE 1. The last movie I seen was terrible.
           1. *saw*

1. sat — 1. My friends and I recently have ~~set~~ through several bad movies.
2. written — 2. Has anyone ever ~~wrote~~ a letter to complain about how many bad movies there are?
3. ran — 3. Last Saturday our local theater ~~run~~ two bad movies!
4. gone — 4. My friends J. D. and Carolyn had ~~went~~ with me to the movie theater.
5. C — 5. We had hoped that we would enjoy *Out of the Swamp*.
6. rose — 6. In the beginning of the movie, a huge swamp creature ~~raised~~ out of the muddy water.
7. began — 7. It ~~begun~~ to crawl slowly toward a cow in a field.
8. lying — 8. The cow had been ~~laying~~ under a tree.

CHAPTER RESOURCES

Planning
- One-Stop Planner CD-ROM

Practice and Extension
- *Grammar, Usage, and Mechanics*, p. 132
- Language Workshop CD-ROM

Internet
- go.hrw.com (keyword: EOLang)

Evaluation and Assessment
- Assessment Package
  —Chapter Tests, Ch. 16
  —Chapter Tests in Standardized Test Formats, Ch. 16
- Test Generator (One-Stop Planner CD-ROM)

9. She never even ~~seen~~ the swamp monster.   9. saw
10. I had ~~sank~~ back in my seat, expecting the monster to pounce.   10. sunk
11. Then the lights ~~come~~ back on.   11. came
12. What a disappointment—the film had ~~broke~~!   12. broken
13. It ~~taked~~ a long time before the machine came back on.   13. took
14. Some little children ~~throwed~~ popcorn up in the air.   14. threw
15. Others ~~drunk~~ noisily through their straws.   15. drank
16. I had ~~sat~~ my popcorn on the floor by my seat, and someone kicked it over.   16. set
17. Finally, the theater manager ~~choosed~~ another movie to show us, but it was only a silly cartoon about a penguin and a polar bear.   17. chose
18. The penguin wore a fur coat it had ~~stole~~ from a sleeping polar bear.   18. stolen
19. The bear awoke, ~~become~~ angry, and chased the penguin all over the place.   19. became
20. Finally, the penguin gave back the coat and ~~swum~~ to Miami Beach to get warm.   20. swam

Principal Parts of Verbs

The four basic forms of a verb are called the *principal parts* of the verb.

16a. The four principal parts of a verb are the *base form,* the *present participle,* the *past,* and the *past participle.*

Base Form	Present Participle	Past	Past Participle
start	[is] starting	started	[have] started
wear	[is] wearing	wore	[have] worn

NOTE The words *is* and *have* are included in this chart because present participle and past participle verb forms require helping verbs (forms of *be* and *have*) to form tenses.

HELP
Some people refer to the base form as the *infinitive.* Follow your teacher's directions when labeling this form.

Reference Note
For more information about **helping verbs,** see page 347.

RESOURCES
Principal Parts of Verbs
Practice
- *Grammar, Usage, and Mechanics,* p. 133
- *Language Workshop CD-ROM,* Lesson 13

USAGE

Regular and Irregular Verbs

Rules 16b, c (pp. 446–457)

OBJECTIVES

- To read sentences aloud stressing regular verbs
- To form the principal parts of regular verbs
- To use the principal parts of regular verbs in sentences
- To read sentences aloud stressing irregular verbs
- To identify the correct forms of irregular verbs

TEACHING TIP

Activity. Draw the following chart on the chalkboard, write in the base form, and have students complete the chart without looking in their books.

BASE FORM	PRESENT PARTICIPLE	PAST	PAST PARTICIPLE
walk	(is) [walking]	[walked]	(have) [walked]

Ask students to identify what is different about each verb form. Then, ask them to formulate rules for finding the forms of the verb *walk*. [Add *–ing* to form the present participle; add *–ed* to form the past and past participle.]

As you can see from their names, the principal parts of a verb are used to express time.

PRESENT TIME   She **wears** a blue uniform.

Ray **has been wearing** his baseball cap.

PAST TIME   Yesterday, we **wore** sweaters.

I **had worn** braces for three months.

FUTURE TIME   Jessica **will wear** her new dress at the party.

By next spring, Joey **will have worn** holes in those shoes.

A verb that forms its past and past participle by adding *–d* or *–ed* is called a ***regular verb.*** A verb that forms its past and past participle differently is called an ***irregular verb.***

Regular Verbs

16b. A ***regular verb*** forms its past and past participle by adding *–d* or *–ed* to the base form.

Base Form	Present Participle	Past	Past Participle
wash	[is] washing	washed	[have] washed
hop	[is] hopping	hopped	[have] hopped
use	[is] using	used	[have] used

Reference Note
For more about **spelling rules,** see Chapter 23.

NOTE Most regular verbs that end in *–e* drop the *–e* before adding *–ing.* Some regular verbs double the final consonant before adding *–ing* or *–ed.*

EXAMPLES   cause   **caus**ing   **caus**ed
drop   **dropp**ing   **dropp**ed

Reference Note
For more about **standard** and **nonstandard English,** see page 519.

One common error in forming the past or past participle of a regular verb is to leave off the *–d* or *–ed* ending.

NONSTANDARD   Josh was suppose to meet us here.
STANDARD   Josh was **supposed** to meet us here.

RESOURCES

Regular and Irregular Verbs
Practice
- *Grammar, Usage, and Mechanics,* pp. 134, 135–139
- Language Workshop CD-ROM, Lessons 13, 14

Oral Practice 1 Using Regular Verbs

Read the following sentences aloud, stressing each italicized verb.

1. We *are supposed* to practice sit-ups this morning.
2. With the help of his guide dog, the man *crossed* the street.
3. Carlos and Rita *have ordered* soup and salad.
4. Her family *had moved* from Trinidad to Brooklyn.
5. Some American Indians *used* to use shells for money.
6. Many *called* shell money "wampum."
7. Larry *has saved* most of his allowance for the past two months.
8. My grandmother *worked* at the computer store.

Exercise 1 Forming the Principal Parts of Regular Verbs

Write the four principal parts for each of the following verbs.

EXAMPLE 1. hope
1. hope; [is] hoping; hoped; [have] hoped

1. skate
2. pick
3. live
4. move
5. talk
6. stun
7. enjoy
8. rob
9. laugh
10. love
11. hop
12. snow
13. cook
14. examine
15. imagine
16. question
17. ask
18. worry
19. turn
20. experiment

HELP—
Remember that the spelling of some verbs changes when –*ing* or –*ed* is added.

Exercise 2 Using the Principal Parts of Regular Verbs

Complete each of the following sentences with the correct form of the given italicized verb.

EXAMPLE 1. *paint*   Henry Ossawa Tanner ____ many kinds of subjects.
1. painted

1. *create*   Tanner ____ images showing people, nature, history, and religion.
1. created

Exercise 1 Forming the Principal Parts of Regular Verbs

ANSWERS

1. skate; (is) skating; skated; (have) skated
2. pick; (is) picking; picked; (have) picked
3. live; (is) living; lived; (have) lived
4. move; (is) moving; moved; (have) moved
5. talk; (is) talking; talked; (have) talked
6. stun; (is) stunning; stunned; (have) stunned
7. enjoy; (is) enjoying; enjoyed; (have) enjoyed
8. rob; (is) robbing; robbed; (have) robbed
9. laugh; (is) laughing; laughed; (have) laughed
10. love; (is) loving; loved; (have) loved
11. hop; (is) hopping; hopped; (have) hopped
12. snow; (is) snowing; snowed; (have) snowed
13. cook; (is) cooking; cooked; (have) cooked
14. examine; (is) examining; examined; (have) examined
15. imagine; (is) imagining; imagined; (have) imagined
16. question; (is) questioning; questioned; (have) questioned
17. ask; (is) asking; asked; (have) asked
18. worry; (is) worrying; worried; (have) worried
19. turn; (is) turning; turned; (have) turned
20. experiment; (is) experimenting; experimented; (have) experimented

Viewing the Art

The Banjo Lesson

About the Artist. Henry Ossawa Tanner (1859–1937) was born in Pittsburgh, Pennsylvania. He studied at the Pennsylvania Academy and later moved to Paris, France, where he became famous for his symbolist renderings of Biblical scenes. In 1923, Tanner was elected a Knight of the Legion of Honor. He is a major American artist whose work exhibits a blend of conservatism and innovation. *The Banjo Lesson,* one of Tanner's best works, is an oil on canvas painted in 1893.

Crossing the Curriculum

Social Studies. Point out to students that history is the study of the past, so historical writing uses past and past participle forms of verbs. Ask students to identify the past and past participle forms of verbs in a piece of writing in their history textbooks. Discuss with students how the writing might be confusing or misleading if written with the base and present participle forms.

The Banjo Lesson by Henry Ossawa Tanner, 1893. Oil on canvas. Hampton University Museum, Hampton, Virginia.

2. *learn*	2. learning	What is the boy in this painting ____ to do?
3. *title*	3. titled	Not surprisingly, Tanner ____ this painting *The Banjo Lesson.*
4. *live*	4. lived	The artist, a native of Pittsburgh, ____ from 1859 to 1937.
5. *move*	5. moved	At the age of thirty-two, Tanner ____ to Paris to study and work.
6. *visit*	6. visited	Other African American artists ____ Tanner in France.
7. *admire*	7. admired	For years, people have ____ Tanner's paintings.
8. *plan*	8. planning	Our teacher is ____ to show us more of Tanner's work.
9. *want*	9. wanted	I have ____ to see Tanner's famous portrait of Booker T. Washington.
10. *praise*	10. praised	In his book *Up from Slavery,* Washington ____ Tanner's talent.

Irregular Verbs

16c. An *irregular verb* forms its past and past participle in some other way than by adding *–d* or *–ed* to the base form.

An irregular verb forms its past and past participle in one of the following ways:

- changing vowels

Base Form	Past	Past Participle
win	won	[have] won
sing	sang	[have] sung
hold	held	[have] held

- changing consonants

Base Form	Past	Past Participle
make	made	[have] made
lend	lent	[have] lent
hear	heard	[have] heard

- changing vowels *and* consonants

Base Form	Past	Past Participle
catch	caught	[have] caught
draw	drew	[have] drawn
tear	tore	[have] torn

- making no change

Base Form	Past	Past Participle
burst	burst	[have] burst
cut	cut	[have] cut
hurt	hurt	[have] hurt

NOTE If you are not sure about the principal parts of a verb, look up the verb in a current dictionary. Entries for irregular verbs list the principal parts of the verb.

Reference Note
For more about **using a dictionary,** see "The Dictionary" in the Quick Reference Handbook.

Common Irregular Verbs

Base Form	Present Participle	Past	Past Participle
become	[is] becoming	became	[have] become
begin	[is] beginning	began	[have] begun
blow	[is] blowing	blew	[have] blown
break	[is] breaking	broke	[have] broken

(continued)

Meeting INDIVIDUAL NEEDS

ENGLISH-LANGUAGE LEARNERS
General Strategies. Emphasize that the past and past participle forms of regular verbs are always the same. Once students have learned the past form, they need only add *have* or *has* to use the past participle.

The lists of common irregular verbs here and on the following pages may seem overwhelming to some students. To help students with irregular verbs, have them use the verbs in a personal context. Require students to master only small increments of the material at a time.

LEARNERS HAVING DIFFICULTY
Remind students that to form the past and past participle forms of most regular verbs, they add –*ed* or –*d* to the base forms. Write the following verbs on the chalkboard, and have students volunteer the past and past participle form for each.

1. look [*looked*], (have) [*looked*]
2. taste [*tasted*], (have) [*tasted*]
3. touch [*touched*], (have) [*touched*]

Relating to Literature

If the short story "Stray" by Cynthia Rylant is available in students' literature books, have students list the base forms of five verbs that the writer uses in the selection. Then, ask students to indicate whether the verbs are regular or irregular and have them write the past and past participle forms of each one.

Meeting INDIVIDUAL NEEDS

MODALITIES

Auditory Learners. It may be easier for some students to learn the correct form of an irregular verb by listening to principal parts of the verb being read aloud in sentences. You may wish to read the **Common Irregular Verbs** list aloud and ask for volunteers to use the verbs in sentences. To hold students' attention, suggest sentences that relate to a theme of interest to them.

Critical Thinking

Application. Challenge students to name irregular verbs that are not listed in the charts in this section. Students can organize their irregular verbs in a chart such as the **Common Irregular Verbs** chart.

(continued)

Common Irregular Verbs			
Base Form	Present Participle	Past	Past Participle
bring	[is] bringing	brought	[have] brought
buy	[is] buying	bought	[have] bought
choose	[is] choosing	chose	[have] chosen
come	[is] coming	came	[have] come
do	[is] doing	did	[have] done
drink	[is] drinking	drank	[have] drunk
drive	[is] driving	drove	[have] driven
eat	[is] eating	ate	[have] eaten
fall	[is] falling	fell	[have] fallen
feel	[is] feeling	felt	[have] felt
find	[is] finding	found	[have] found
freeze	[is] freezing	froze	[have] frozen
get	[is] getting	got	[have] gotten *or* got
give	[is] giving	gave	[have] given
go	[is] going	went	[have] gone
grow	[is] growing	grew	[have] grown
have	[is] having	had	[have] had
hear	[is] hearing	heard	[have] heard
hit	[is] hitting	hit	[have] hit
hold	[is] holding	held	[have] held
keep	[is] keeping	kept	[have] kept
know	[is] knowing	knew	[have] known

Oral Practice 2 Using Irregular Verbs

Read the following sentences aloud, stressing each italicized verb.

1. I *have begun* to learn karate.
2. We *chose* to stay indoors.
3. Earline never *had drunk* buttermilk before.
4. We *did* our homework after dinner.
5. Anna and Dee *have* almost *broken* the school record for the fifty-yard dash.

6. The wind *has blown* fiercely for three days.
7. Last Saturday, Isaac *brought* me a tape of reggae music.
8. The water pipes in the laundry room *have frozen* again.

Exercise 3   Identifying the Correct Forms of Irregular Verbs

Choose the correct verb form in parentheses in each of the following sentences.

EXAMPLE 1. The children have finally (*broke, broken*) the piñata.
1. broken

1. We had just (*began, begun*) our project when I got sick.
2. The Ruiz family (*drove, driven*) across the country.
3. Has anyone (*brung, brought*) extra batteries for the radio?
4. I have finally (*chose, chosen*) a book to borrow.
5. Last week the lake (*froze, frozen*) hard enough for skating.
6. My brother and I have (*gave, given*) away all our comic books to the children's hospital.
7. It is amazing that no one has ever (*fell, fallen*) off that old ladder.
8. Everyone (*went, gone*) back to the classroom to watch the videotape of the spelling bee.
9. David's aunt (*came, come*) here to attend his bar mitzvah.
10. Have you (*ate, eaten*) at the new Philippine restaurant?
11. They should not have (*drank, drunk*) so much ice water after playing tennis.
12. After our guests had (*ate, eaten*), we all toured the city.
13. We have (*came, come*) to expect great things from you.
14. By the time Jason arrived, Gina had already (*went, gone*).
15. When they left, Uncle Enrique (*gave, given*) them some Cuban bread.
16. Their team (*chose, chosen*) another topic for the debate.
17. Oh, yes, Chris and I have (*knew, known*) each other since kindergarten.
18. He (*did, done*) the experiment that very afternoon.
19. Lenny had never (*drove, driven*) a tractor before that day.
20. We must have (*blew, blown*) up a hundred balloons for my little brother's birthday party.

ENGLISH-LANGUAGE LEARNERS
General Strategies. As is true in many languages, the verbs that are irregular in English are among the most common. It is especially important, therefore, that your English-language learners learn these verbs well. You may want to pair these students with others who are proficient in English, first for help defining unknown words and learning correct pronunciations (especially of the past and past participle forms, whose pronunciations are often quite different from those of the base forms), and again later for informal quizzing and reteaching of the definitions and pronunciations.

Exercise 4 Identifying the Correct Forms of Irregular Verbs

Choose the correct verb form in parentheses in each of the following sentences.

EXAMPLE 1. Jameel has already (*drank*, *drunk*) a large glass of orange juice, but he is still thirsty.
    1. drunk

1. The wool sweater (*felt*, *feeled*) scratchy, so I did not buy it.
2. Ramón (*got*, *gotten*) a part in the school play.
3. The new houseplant has already (*grew*, *grown*) several inches since we bought it.
4. Leslie (*become*, *became*) my best friend back in first grade.
5. I (*holded*, *held*) on to the dog's leash tightly.
6. Our neighbors have (*buyed*, *bought*) a new doghouse for their German shepherd.
7. Kani has (*kept*, *keeped*) a log of his study time.
8. Yesterday we finally (*finded*, *found*) a copy of Pat Mora's latest book.
9. In last night's ballgame, Heather (*hit*, *hitted*) another home run.
10. Have you ever (*hear*, *heard*) traditional Japanese music?

More Common Irregular Verbs			
Base Form	Present Participle	Past	Past Participle
lead	[is] leading	led	[have] led
leave	[is] leaving	left	[have] left
lose	[is] losing	lost	[have] lost
pay	[is] paying	paid	[have] paid
put	[is] putting	put	[have] put
read	[is] reading	read	[have] read
ride	[is] riding	rode	[have] ridden
ring	[is] ringing	rang	[have] rung
run	[is] running	ran	[have] run
say	[is] saying	said	[have] said

More Common Irregular Verbs			
Base Form	Present Participle	Past	Past Participle
see	[is] seeing	saw	[have] seen
send	[is] sending	sent	[have] sent
shrink	[is] shrinking	shrank *or* shrunk	[have] shrunk
sing	[is] singing	sang	[have] sung
sink	[is] sinking	sank *or* sunk	[have] sunk
speak	[is] speaking	spoke	[have] spoken
stand	[is] standing	stood	[have] stood
steal	[is] stealing	stole	[have] stolen
swim	[is] swimming	swam	[have] swum
take	[is] taking	took	[have] taken
teach	[is] teaching	taught	[have] taught
tell	[is] telling	told	[have] told
throw	[is] throwing	threw	[have] thrown
wear	[is] wearing	wore	[have] worn
write	[is] writing	wrote	[have] written

Oral Practice 3 Using Irregular Verbs

Read the following sentences aloud, stressing the italicized verbs.

1. Despite the blinding snowstorm, the Saint Bernard *had led* the rescue party to the stranded hikers.
2. The school bell *rang* five minutes late every afternoon this week.
3. When she visited New York City, Julia *saw* the Ellis Island Immigration Museum.
4. How many sixth-graders would you guess *have ridden* on this school bus?
5. What is the longest distance you *have swum*?
6. George *ran* to the corner to see the antique fire engine.
7. Gloria Estefan *sang* on the awards show.
8. *Have* you ever *written* haiku?

"You don't say 'He taked my chair'...it's 'My chair was tooken'."

FAMILY CIRCUS reprinted with special permission of King Features Syndicate, Inc.

Meeting INDIVIDUAL NEEDS

MULTIPLE INTELLIGENCES

Intrapersonal Intelligence. Ask students to think about important moments in their lives. Have any of them won prizes, visited interesting places, or switched schools? Have each student write a descriptive paragraph about such a moment. As students write, tell them to pay close attention to the verbs they use. When students have finished, have them circle and identify in their paragraphs the main verbs whose forms match one of the principal parts.

Bodily-Kinesthetic Intelligence. Have students work with a partner to make a list of the base forms of irregular verbs in the **Common Irregular Verbs** chart. Then, have the partners take turns acting out each of the verbs. The other student guesses the verb and writes the verb's present participle, past, and past participle forms next to the verb. This pattern should continue until the completed list shows the four forms of each of the verbs.

Exercise 5

ALTERNATIVE LESSON

To review the parts of speech, have students find the following items in the designated sentences from Exercise 5.

2. adjectives [*cute, little*]
3. adverbs [*never, more, beautifully*]
8. nouns [*rabbit, door, Alice, size*]
16. prepositions [*to, about*]

Relating to Speaking

Divide the class into small groups, and ask each student to name two verbs. Then, have the group members use each verb in a separate sentence. Group members should compose and read aloud their sentences in turns. Tell students that their sentences can be serious or silly, as long as the verb tenses are used correctly.

Exercise 5 Identifying the Correct Forms of Irregular Verbs

Choose the correct verb form in parentheses in each of the following sentences.

EXAMPLE 1. Ms. Toyama (*took, taken*) her new kitten to the veterinarian.
   1. took

1. Who (*ran, run*) faster, Jesse or Cindy?
2. That cute little puppy has (*stole, stolen*) a biscuit.
3. The Boys Choir of Harlem has never (*sang, sung*) more beautifully.
4. Jimmy's toy sailboat had (*sank, sunk*) to the bottom of the lake.
5. Have you (*thrown, throwed*) yesterday's paper into the recycling bin?
6. Maria had (*wore, worn*) her new spring outfit to the party.
7. Until yesterday, no one had ever (*swam, swum*) across Crystal Lake.
8. Before she followed the white rabbit through the tiny door, Alice had (*shrank, shrunk*) to a very small size!
9. The students have (*written, wrote*) a letter to the mayor.
10. I have never (*spoke, spoken*) to a large audience before.
11. An open convertible (*lead, led*) the ticker tape parade.
12. Vulcan's hammer (*rang, rung*) as he worked metal for the Roman gods.
13. Why had the dog (*took, taken*) the portable phone outside?
14. We (*saw, seen*) a whole stack of petri dishes in the back of the lab closet.
15. Not only have I never (*rode, ridden*) a roller coaster, but I probably never will.
16. Have you (*spoke, spoken*) to your parents about taking those tuba lessons?
17. The children simply (*sang, sung*) "The Bear Went over the Mountain" until the baby sitter read them another story.
18. Why have all those people (*swam, swum*) across the English Channel?
19. The detective always (*wore, worn*) a porkpie hat.
20. The clever fox (*threw, throw*) the dog off the trail.

Exercise 6 Identifying the Correct Forms of Irregular Verbs

Choose the correct verb form in parentheses in each of the following sentences.

EXAMPLE 1. Uncle Alberto (*leaded*, *led*) the parade.
 1. led

1. Justin (*putted*, *put*) the soy sauce on the table.
2. Have Grandma and Grandpa (*left*, *leaved*) already?
3. The family (*said*, *sayed*) grace and then ate dinner.
4. The senator (*stood*, *standed*) up and waved to the crowd.
5. Has Leta (*readed*, *read*) the story "Miss Awful" yet?
6. After school Angela (*taught*, *teached*) me the new dance.
7. Each Christmas, Aunt Arlene has (*sended*, *sent*) me a classic children's book.
8. Mom (*paid*, *payed*) for the groceries, and we went home.
9. Ms. Cata (*telled*, *told*) the children a Hopi myth.
10. Lucas has (*losed*, *lost*) his Mariah Carey CD.

Review A Proofreading for Errors in Irregular Verbs

Most of the following sentences contain an incorrect verb form. Identify each error, and write the correct form of the verb. If a sentence is already correct, write *C*.

EXAMPLE 1. Many stories have been wrote about the American athlete Jesse Owens.
 1. wrote—written

1. Owens breaked several sports records during his career.   1. broke
2. At the Olympic games of 1936, he winned four gold medals.   2. won
3. A photographer took this picture of one of Owens's victories.   3. C
4. Owens's career begun in an unusual way.   4. began
5. As a little boy, Owens had been very sick, and later he run to strengthen his lungs.   5. ran
6. In high school, the other boys on the track team done their practicing after school, but Owens had to work.   6. did

Viewing the Illustration

Exploring the Subject. Born in Oakville, Alabama, on September 12, 1913, Jesse Owens grew up to become one of the United States' greatest track and field athletes. When he was a member of the Ohio State University track team, he tied the world record in one event and broke world records in three others in one day. At the 1936 Olympics in Berlin, Germany, Owens set new world records in three events and a new Olympic record in a fourth.

7. Owens's coach encouraged him to practice an hour before school and ~~brung~~ him breakfast every morning. **7. brought**
8. The coach ~~knowed~~ Owens's parents couldn't afford to send their son to college. **8. knew**
9. The coach ~~seen~~ that something had to be done, and he helped Owens's father find a job. **9. saw**
10. Later, Owens went to Ohio State University, where he became a track star. **10. C**

Review B — Writing the Past and Past Participle Forms of Irregular Verbs

For each of the following sentences, write the correct past or past participle form of the italicized verb.

EXAMPLE   1. *take*   Gloria has ____ the last envelope.
　　　　　1. taken

Answer	Verb	Sentence
1. read	1. *read*	Has everyone ____ the assignment for today?
2. burst	2. *burst*	Suddenly, the door ____ open.
3. driven	3. *drive*	We have ____ on Oklahoma's Indian Nation Turnpike.
4. found	4. *find*	Have you ____ your socks yet?
5. spoke	5. *speak*	Who ____ at this year's Hispanic Heritage awards ceremony?
6. grown	6. *grow*	Patricia has ____ two inches in one year.
7. heard	7. *hear*	One of the hikers had ____ the distant growl of a bear.
8. gave	8. *give*	Mrs. Matsuo ____ me a copy of the book *Origami: Japanese Paper-Folding*.
9. frozen	9. *freeze*	The water in the birdbath has ____ again.
10. chosen	10. *choose*	Which play have they ____ to perform?
11. worn	11. *wear*	The Highland School Band has always ____ Scottish kilts.
12. knew	12. *know*	Noriko ____ the way to Lynn's house.
13. taught	13. *teach*	Ms. Brook has ____ all of us how to work together.
14. sent	14. *send*	My sweater was too small, so I ____ it to my cousin.
15. rang	15. *ring*	Who ____ the doorbell a moment ago?
16. held	16. *hold*	The puppy ____ up its injured paw.

Timesaver

To save time grading **Review B** exercises, have students exchange papers. Then, read the sentences aloud with the correct answers and have students circle any verbs that are used incorrectly.

17. *hit*	David ____ a ball past third base in the ninth inning.	17. hit
18. *leave*	Have you ____ your towel at the pool?	18. left
19. *see*	We had never ____ a koala before.	19. seen
20. *buy*	Jerome ____ the decorations for the party.	20. bought

Review C Proofreading for Incorrect Verb Forms

Read each of the following sentences. If the form of a verb is wrong, write the correct past or past participle form. If the sentence is already correct, write *C*.

EXAMPLE 1. Dr. Seuss knowed how to please readers of all ages.
 1. knew

1. Have you ever saw the wacky characters shown here?   1. seen
2. The imagination of Dr. Seuss brought both of them to life.   2. C
3. You may have bursted out laughing at the Cat in the Hat, Horton the elephant, or the Grinch.   3. burst
4. In one story, the mean Grinch stoled Christmas.   4. stole
5. In another, a bird gived Horton an egg to hatch.   5. gave
6. The Lorax spoke out in support of the trees and the environment.   6. C
7. The Cat in the Hat has always wore his striped hat.   7. worn
8. During his lifetime, Dr. Seuss must have wrote about fifty books with unusual characters.   8. written
9. Many children have began reading with his books.   9. begun
10. Dr. Seuss choosed *The Lorax* as his own favorite book.   10. chose

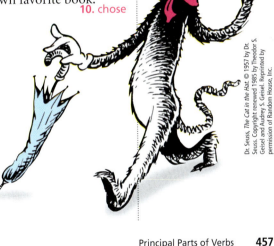

MULTIPLE INTELLIGENCES
Musical Intelligence. Have students practice using the different verb forms by writing a poem or song. Each poem or song should include at least five irregular verbs. You may want to bring to class a book by Dr. Seuss for students to use as a model or inspiration for their own rhymes. Invite volunteers to perform their poems or songs for the class.

Viewing the Art
About the Artist. Dr. Seuss is the pen name of Theodor Seuss Geisel (1904–1991), an American writer and illustrator of many popular and humorous children's books.

Principal Parts of Verbs

Tense

Rules 16d, e (pp. 458–462)

OBJECTIVES

- To identify verb tenses in sentences
- To revise a paragraph for consistency of verb tense

Tense

16d. The *tense* of a verb indicates the time of the action or the state of being that is expressed by the verb.

The six tenses are *present, past, future, present perfect, past perfect,* and *future perfect.* These tenses are formed from the principal parts of verbs. Each of these six tenses has its own uses. The following time line shows the relationships between tenses.

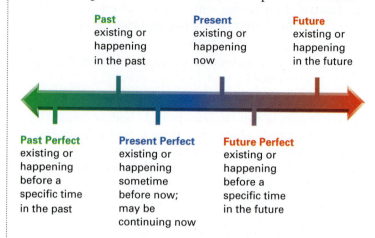

Listing all the forms of a verb is called **conjugating** the verb.

Conjugation of the Verb *Wear*	
Present Tense	
Singular	Plural
I wear	we wear
you wear	you wear
he, she, *or* it wears	they wear
Past Tense	
Singular	Plural
I wore	we wore
you wore	you wore
he, she, *or* it wore	they wore

RESOURCES

Tense

Practice
- *Grammar, Usage, and Mechanics,* pp. 140, 141
- *Language Workshop CD-ROM,* Lesson 15

Conjugation of the Verb *Wear*

Future Tense

Singular	Plural
I will (shall) wear	we will (shall) wear
you will (shall) wear	you will (shall) wear
he, she, *or* it will (shall) wear	they will (shall) wear

Present Perfect Tense

Singular	Plural
I have worn	we have worn
you have worn	you have worn
he, she, *or* it has worn	they have worn

Past Perfect Tense

Singular	Plural
I had worn	we had worn
you had worn	you had worn
he, she, *or* it had worn	they had worn

Future Perfect Tense

Singular	Plural
I will (shall) have worn	we will (shall) have worn
you will (shall) have worn	you will (shall) have worn
he, she, *or* it will (shall) have worn	they will (shall) have worn

STYLE TIP

Traditionally, the helping verb *shall* was used only in certain situations. Now, however, *shall* can be used almost any time that you would use *will*.

Progressive Forms

Each of the six tenses also has a form called the ***progressive form.*** The progressive form expresses continuing action or state of being. It is made up of the appropriate tense of the verb *be* plus the present participle of a verb. The progressive is not a separate tense. It is just a different form that each tense can take.

TEACHING TIP

Activity. Write the following incomplete sentences on the chalkboard. Ask students to fill in the blanks with the tense forms of the verb *eat*.

Before breakfast this morning, I _____ _____ only one bagel in my life. [*had eaten*]

This morning, however, I _____ two. [*ate*]

I _____ _____ many different foods over the years. [*have eaten*]

Usually I _____ different things throughout the day. [*eat*]

Before the day is over, however, I _____ _____ _____ three bagels! [*will have eaten*]

Later tonight I _____ _____ something completely different. [*will eat*]

Point out to students that the verb forms all refer to different times. Tell students that verbs refer to different times by taking different tenses. Label the tenses in order on the chalkboard: *past perfect, past, present perfect, present, future perfect,* and *future.* Ask students to identify the tenses they used in the activity.

Present Progressive	am, are, is wearing
Past Progressive	was, were wearing
Future Progressive	will (shall) be wearing
Present Perfect Progressive	has, have been wearing
Past Perfect Progressive	had been wearing
Future Perfect Progressive	will (shall) have been wearing

The Verb *Be*

The verb *be* is the most irregular of all the irregular verbs in English. Note the many different forms of *be* in the following conjugation.

Conjugation of the Verb *Be*	
Present Tense	
Singular	**Plural**
I am	we are
you are	you are
he, she, *or* it is	they are
Present Progressive: am, are, is being	
Past Tense	
Singular	**Plural**
I was	we were
you were	you were
he, she, *or* it was	they were
Past Progressive: was, were being	
Future Tense	
Singular	**Plural**
I will (shall) be	we will (shall) be
you will (shall) be	you will (shall) be
he, she, *or* it will (shall) be	they will (shall) be

HELP

The present and past progressive forms of *be* are the most common. The other progressive forms of *be* are hardly ever used.

EXAMPLES
will (shall) be being [*future progressive*]

has, have been being [*present perfect progressive*]

Chapter 16 Using Verbs Correctly

MINI-LESSON

Tense. Students may use the past, present, and future tenses easily but may be confused by the perfect tenses. Write the following sentences on the chalkboard:

I had started camp. [*past perfect*]

I have started camp. [*present perfect*]

I will have started camp. [*future perfect*]

Ask students what each sentence has in common besides the subject *I* and the

Using Verbs Correctly

Conjugation of the Verb *Be*

Present Perfect Tense

Singular	Plural
I have been	we have been
you have been	you have been
he, she, *or* it has been	they have been

Past Perfect Tense

Singular	Plural
I had been	we had been
you had been	you had been
he, she, *or* it had been	they had been

Future Perfect Tense

Singular	Plural
I will (shall) have been	we will (shall) have been
you will (shall) have been	you will (shall) have been
he, she, *or* it will (shall) have been	they will (shall) have been

Exercise 7 — Identifying Tenses

Identify the verb's tense in each of the following sentences.

EXAMPLE 1. A trolley noisily rolled down the track.
   1. *past*

1. Oh, no! Who fed this to the paper shredder?
2. Yes, Mom actually drinks that green stuff from the juicer.
3. Benjamin has left Des Moines.
4. Had you heard Andrés Segovia's music before then?
5. A mosaic of colorful tiles will decorate the entryway.
6. By my twenty-first birthday, I will have qualified for my pilot's license.
7. The committee will notify you of its decision.
8. Will you have saved enough money by then?
9. Evidently, I had thought of every possibility but one.
10. They are using the new modem now.

1. past
2. present
3. pres. perfect
4. past perfect
5. future
6. future perfect
7. future
8. future perfect
9. past perfect
10. pres. progressive

ENGLISH-LANGUAGE LEARNERS
General Strategies. Some students may not write or pronounce the endings for present-tense, third-person singular verbs, as in the sentence "She miss the bus almost every day." Similarly, they may have a tendency to omit the *–d* or *–ed* ending for past-tense verbs, as in "She miss the bus yesterday." To give students practice with such endings, create sentences containing present-tense, third-person singular, and past-tense forms. Ask students to underline all of the present-tense endings for third-person verbs. Then, tell students to circle the past-tense endings and to read the sentences aloud. Listen carefully, and model standard pronunciation when necessary.

---

object *camp*. Lead students to see that each perfect form contains the past participle *started* and the past, present, or future form of the verb *have*. Whether the perfect is past, present, or future depends on the tense of the *have* form. Ask students to label the tense in each example sentence; encourage them to look for a past participle and a form of the verb *have* to identify the perfect tenses.

Exercise 8 Revising a Paragraph for Consistency of Tense

ANSWERS

Answers will depend on whether students choose to rewrite in the present tense or in the past tense. Corrected verbs are indicated in italics.

Present Tense

1. We trade essays with other English classes.
2. They read and *comment* on our essays, and we read and comment on theirs.
3. We also share reports with other classes in the school.
4. In Spanish I, we are writing letters to students in Argentina.
5. We *practice* our Spanish.
6. They *write* back to us in English.
7. The computer classes *send* a newsletter to all the other classes every week.
8. Every student has e-mail.
9. Students send messages to each other and to teachers.
10. E-mail *makes* it easy to ask questions about assignments.

Past Tense

1. We *traded* essays with other English classes.
2. They read and commented on our essays, and we read and *commented* on theirs.
3. We also *shared* reports with other classes in the school.
4. In Spanish I, we *were* writing letters to students in Argentina.
5. We practiced our Spanish.
6. They wrote back to us in English.
7. The computer classes sent a newsletter to all the other classes every week.
8. Every student *had* e-mail.
9. Students *sent* messages to each other and to teachers.
10. E-mail made it easy to ask questions about assignments.

COMPUTER TIP

Most word processors can help you check your writing to be sure that you have used verbs correctly. For example, a spell-checker will highlight misspelled verb forms such as *telled* and *growed*. Some style-checking software can point out inconsistent verb tense.

Remember, though, that the computer is just a tool to help you improve your writing. As a writer, you must make all the style and content choices that affect your writing.

HELP

Although the example in Exercise 8 gives two possible revisions, you need to give only one for each sentence.

Consistency of Tense

16e. Do not change needlessly from one tense to another.

To write about events that take place at about the same time, use verbs in the same tense. To write about events that occur at different times, use verbs in different tenses.

INCONSISTENT	The cat jumped onto the counter and steals the sandwich. [The events happen at about the same time, but *jumped* is in the past tense, and *steals* is in the present tense.]
CONSISTENT	The cat **jumped** onto the counter and **stole** the sandwich. [Both verbs are in the past tense.]
CONSISTENT	The cat **jumps** onto the counter and **steals** the sandwich. [Both verbs are in the present tense.]

Exercise 8 Revising a Paragraph for Consistency of Tense

Read the following paragraph, and decide whether to rewrite it in the present or the past tense. Then, rewrite all of the sentences, changing the verb forms to correct any needless shifts in tense.

EXAMPLE [1] Since our school has a computer network, we "chatted" with students from other schools.

1. Since our school has a computer network, we "chat" with students from other schools.

or

Since our school had a computer network, we "chatted" with students from other schools.

[1] We trade essays with other English classes. [2] They read and commented on our essays, and we read and comment on theirs. [3] We also share reports with other classes in the school. [4] In Spanish I, we are writing letters to students in Argentina. [5] We practiced our Spanish. [6] They wrote back to us in English. [7] The computer classes sent a newsletter to all the other classes every week. [8] Every student has e-mail. [9] Students send messages to each other and to teachers. [10] E-mail made it easy to ask questions about assignments.

Six Confusing Verbs

Sit and Set

The verb *sit* means "to be seated" or "to rest." *Sit* seldom takes a direct object. The verb *set* means "to put (something) in a place." *Set* usually takes a direct object. Notice that *set* has the same form for the base form, past, and past participle.

Base Form	Present Participle	Past	Past Participle
sit	[is] sitting	sat	[have] sat
set	[is] setting	set	[have] set

EXAMPLES I **will sit** in the easy chair. [no direct object]
I **will set** the cushion in the easy chair. [I will set what? *Cushion* is the direct object.]

The worker **has sat** there. [no direct object]
The workers **have set** their equipment there. [The workers have set what? *Equipment* is the direct object.]

Oral Practice 4 Using the Forms of *Sit* and *Set* Correctly

Read the following sentences aloud, stressing each italicized verb.

1. Before she left, Josie *had set* two loaves of French bread on the table.
2. The clown *sat* on the broken chair.
3. They *are sitting* down to rest awhile.
4. *Has* she *set* her bracelet on the night stand?
5. The Clarks' car *has sat* in the driveway for a week.
6. My little brother *sits* still for only a few seconds at a time.
7. The teacher *is setting* the best projects in the display case in the hall.
8. The librarian *set* the book about Michael Jordan on the large table.

Reference Note
For more about **direct objects,** see page 405.

If you do not know whether to use *sit* or *set* in a sentence, try substituting *put.* If the sentence makes sense with *put,* use *set.* If not, use *sit.*

EXAMPLE
Jill (*set, sat*) the CDs on the shelf.

TEST
Jill put the CDs on the shelf. [The sentence makes sense with *put.*]

ANSWER
Jill **set** the CDs on the shelf.

Six Confusing Verbs **463**

Six Confusing Verbs
Practice
- *Grammar, Usage, and Mechanics,* pp. 142, 143, 144, 145
- *Language Workshop CD-ROM,* Lesson 15

Meeting INDIVIDUAL NEEDS

ENGLISH-LANGUAGE LEARNERS
General Strategies. You may need to remind some students that there are two strategies for deciding which of these confusing verbs to use. The first strategy, as stated in the textbook, is to look for an object that receives the action of the verb. If there is an object, then *lay, set,* or *raise* is most likely the appropriate verb. Students can also look for a preposition or an adverb immediately following the verb. The presence of either generally indicates that there is no object and thus *lie, sit,* or *rise* is probably correct. However, point out that there are exceptions, such as "Please *set up* the card table," "What questions did you *raise* at the meeting?" and "*Lay down* your pencils!" Take this opportunity to remind students of the importance of using the textbook and other reference sources to double-check their work.

MODALITIES
Visual Learners. Consider demonstrating the definitions of the six confusing verbs. To begin, you could stand up and then sit down on a chair. As you sit down, you might say "I sit on the chair." After sitting, you could lift a book and set it on a desk, saying aloud, "I set the book on the desk."

To demonstrate the verbs *rise* and *raise,* you could sit down for a few moments and stand up while saying, "I rise." Then, pick up a pencil and say, "I raise the pencil."

To demonstrate the verbs *lie* and *lay,* you could pick up a notebook and place it on a desk while saying, "I lay the notebook on the desk." Then, point to the notebook and say, "The notebook lies on the desk."

HELP
You may know that the word *set* has meanings that are not given on page 463. Check in a dictionary to see if the meaning you intend requires a direct object.

EXAMPLE
The sun **sets** in the west.
[Here, *sets* does not take a direct object.]

HELP
The verb *raise* has definitions other than the ones given here. Another common definition is "to grow" or "to bring to maturity."

EXAMPLES
They **raise** wheat.
She **raises** sheep.

Notice that both of these uses also take a direct object.

Exercise 9 Writing the Forms of *Sit* and *Set*

Write the correct form of *sit* or *set* to complete each of the following sentences.

EXAMPLE   1. The girls ____ on the porch swing yesterday.
1. sat

1. At the party yesterday, we ____ the birthday presents on the coffee table. **1. set**
2. Then we ____ on the floor to play a game. **2. sat**
3. Alana had been ____ next to Rosa. **3. sitting**
4. The Jiménez twins never ____ together, even though it was their birthday. **4. sat**
5. Mrs. Jiménez ____ a large cake on the table. **5. set**
6. Mr. Jiménez had already ____ party hats and favors around the table. **6. set**
7. He also ____ out the plates. **7. set**
8. One of the twins ____ on a hat by mistake. **8. sat**
9. At every party we always ____ quietly while the birthday person makes a wish. **9. sit**
10. Yesterday, we ____ still twice as long for the Jiménez twins! **10. sat**

Rise and Raise

The verb *rise* means "to go up" or "to get up." *Rise* does not take a direct object. The verb *raise* means "to lift (something) up" or "to cause (something) to rise." *Raise* usually takes a direct object.

Base Form	Present Participle	Past	Past Participle
rise	[is] rising	rose	[have] risen
raise	[is] raising	raised	[have] raised

EXAMPLES   The winner **is rising** to receive his medal. [no direct object]

The winner **is raising** her arms in triumph. [The winner is raising what? *Arms* is the direct object.]

Taxes **rose** quickly. [no direct object]

Congress **raised** taxes. [Congress raised what? *Taxes* is the direct object.]

464   Chapter 16   Using Verbs Correctly

Learning for Life

Setting Goals for the Future. Discuss with students what they know about contracts. You can bring to class examples of contracts, such as lease agreements or club memberships. Have students take note of the formal language and the use of verb tenses in the contracts. You may want to have students label examples of various tenses in the contracts.

Tell students that they will write a personal contract, entering into an agreement with themselves. The contract should list

Continued on pp. 465–466

Oral Practice 5 **Using the Forms of *Rise* and *Raise* Correctly**

Read the following sentences aloud, stressing each italicized verb.

1. The audience *had risen* from their seats to applaud Bonnie Raitt.
2. They *raised* the curtains for the play to start.
3. Dark smoke *rose* from the fire.
4. They always *rise* early on Saturday mornings.
5. The wind *had raised* the Chinese dragon kite high above the trees.
6. They *are raising* the banners.
7. The huge crane *can raise* the steel beams off the ground.
8. The temperature *was rising* quickly.

Exercise 10 **Writing the Forms of *Rise* and *Raise***

To complete each of the following sentences, supply the correct form of *rise* or *raise*.

EXAMPLE 1. We will ____ a banner.
          1. raise

1. Before the game the color guards ____ the flag. **1. raised**
2. The fans were ____ for the national anthem. **2. rising**
3. The pitcher ____ his arm to throw the ball. **3. raised**
4. The baseball seemed to ____ above the batter's head. **4. rise**
5. Someone in front of me was ____ a sign that blocked my view. **5. raising**
6. I have ____ my voice to cheer a hundred times during one game. **6. raised**
7. When the sun had ____ too high, the players couldn't see the high fly balls. **7. risen**
8. Whenever someone hits a home run, the fans ____ their mitts to catch the baseball. **8. raise**
9. Yesterday, everyone ____ when Marcus Jackson hit a home run. **9. rose**
10. As soon as the ninth inning was over, we ____ to leave. **10. rose**

Cooperative Learning

Divide the class into groups of three. Have each group member study a different pair of the six confusing verbs in the lesson and present an explanation of the differences between the two verbs to the group. Students' explanations should include strategies for using the verbs correctly and example sentences. Group members should then work together to write a paragraph in which all six of the verbs are used correctly. Invite a group spokesperson to read his or her group's paragraph to the class.

Critical Thinking

Synthesis. Have students expand the charts for each of the verb pairs by writing the six tenses of each verb. Students can then write six sentences for each verb, using each of the tense forms of the verb once.

Meeting INDIVIDUAL NEEDS

MULTIPLE INTELLIGENCES
Spatial Intelligence. Ask students to draw comic strips in which they show the differences between *rise* and *raise*. Have them use the verbs *rise* and *raise* in captions to explain the events taking place. This activity can also be done with the other pairs of confusing verbs.

---

personal goals and resolutions to which each student would like to commit. Have students use a pie chart such as the following to brainstorm for goals and resolutions for each area of their lives.

Lie and Lay

The verb *lie* generally means "to recline," "to be in a place," or "to remain lying down." *Lie* does not take a direct object. The verb *lay* generally means "to put (something) down" or "to place (something)." *Lay* usually takes a direct object.

Base Form	Present Participle	Past	Past Participle
lie	[is] lying	lay	[have] lain
lay	[is] laying	laid	[have] laid

EXAMPLES The beam **is lying** near the edge. [no direct object]
The workers **are laying** the beams near the edge. [The workers are laying what? *Beams* is the direct object.]

The newspaper **lay** on the kitchen table. [no direct object]
Sara **laid** the newspaper on the kitchen table. [Sara laid what? *Newspaper* is the direct object.]

The beach blanket **has lain** under the umbrella. [no direct object]
They **have laid** the beach blanket under the umbrella. [They have laid what? *Blanket* is the direct object.]

HELP

The verb *lie* has definitions other than the ones given here. Another common definition is "to tell an untruth."

EXAMPLE
  Little Terry did not **lie** about spilling the milk.

When used this way, *lie* usually does not take a direct object. Its past and past participle forms are *lied* and [have] *lied*.

COMPUTER TIP

If you have trouble using *sit, set, rise, raise, lie,* and *lay* correctly, a computer may be helpful. Use the search function to find and highlight all the uses of these confusing verbs in your writing. Then, look at each case carefully to determine whether you have used the correct form, and revise if necessary.

Oral Practice 6 Using the Forms of *Lie* and *Lay* Correctly

Read the following sentences aloud, stressing each italicized verb.

1. The corrected test paper *lay* on the desk.
2. My teddy bear *lies* on my bed all day.
3. Before the sale, the clerk *laid* samples on the counter.
4. Have those toys *lain* outside too long?
5. The Inuit hunter *was laying* his harpoon on the ice.
6. Last night, I *was lying* on the sofa reading a book when the phone rang.
7. I think the hero *has laid* a trap for the villain.
8. *Lay* the baby gently in the crib.

466 Chapter 16 Using Verbs Correctly

Learning for Life

Have students write their contracts, listing at least five goals and resolutions. Have proofreaders pay special attention to the verb tenses they have used. Point out to students that their goals and resolutions should be written in the future tense.

Tell students they do not have to share their contracts, but they should sign and date them and keep them in a safe place. Encourage students to check their contracts periodically to see how well they are pursuing their goals.

Exercise 11 Writing the Forms of *Lie* and *Lay*

To complete each of the following sentences, write the correct form of *lie* or *lay*.

EXAMPLE   1. Children often ____ toys in the wrong places.
             1. *lay*

1. The remote control for the television is ____ under the rocking chair.   1. *lying*
2. How long has it ____ there?   2. *lain*
3. My brother Ramón probably ____ it there last night.   3. *laid*
4. He was ____ on the floor, watching television.   4. *lying*
5. Julia, my younger sister, is always ____ her toys in front of the television set.   5. *laying*
6. She has ____ little parts from her board games all over the house.   6. *laid*
7. Whenever Mom and Dad find one of these parts, they usually ____ it on the bookcase.   7. *lay*
8. Yesterday, Dad ____ down on some hard plastic pieces on the sofa.   8. *lay*
9. Now those broken bits of plastic ____ at the bottom of the wastebasket.   9. *lie*
10. Today, Julia has ____ every single toy safely in the toy chest in her room.   10. *laid*

Review D Identifying the Correct Forms of *Sit* and *Set*, *Rise* and *Raise*, and *Lie* and *Lay*

Choose the correct verb from the pair in parentheses in each of the following sentences.

EXAMPLE   1. Dad (*sat, set*) the scrapbook from our visit to the Hopi reservation on the table and opened it to the picture shown on the next page.
             1. *set*

1. One of the first people we saw was a young Hopi mother with a small baby (*lying, laying*) in her arms.
2. Around lunchtime, I was glad I had not (*lain, laid*) aside my hat, because the sun was very hot.
3. A Hopi artist (*sat, set*) quietly in the shade, painting a beautiful design on a pot.

TECHNOLOGY TIP

Activity. If students are using word-processing programs, tell them to check their word processor's dictionary, if available, if they have questions about when to use these six confusing verbs. Along with giving the correct definition of each verb, the dictionary will probably provide students with sample sentences they can compare with their own to see if they are using the verbs correctly.

Relating to Literature

After students have read and discussed a poem such as Gary Soto's "Ode to Mi Gato," ask them to list the verbs used in the poem and to identify each verb's tense. Ask students how changing the tense of the verbs would alter the meaning of the poem.

Cooperative Learning

For added review, divide the class into groups of three. Have a member of each group write a paragraph in the present tense. Then, have the other group members rewrite the paragraph in the past and future tenses. Group members should underline each of their verbs and compare the different tenses.

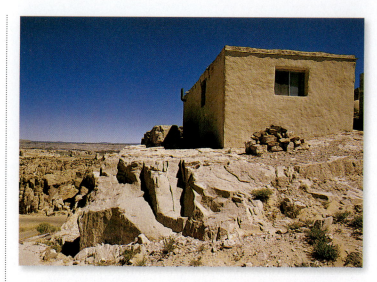

4. At the reservation, everyone (*sat, set*) quietly during the Hopi Snake Dance.
5. One dancer had (*risen, raised*) a snake above his head for the crowd to see.
6. The growing corn (*rises, raises*) high in the Hopi country of Arizona.
7. Hot and very tired, I (*lay, laid*) on a bench at the Hopi trading post.
8. In a moment, Dad had (*rose, raised*) his hat to shade my face from the sun.
9. When we entered the pueblo, a Hopi woman (*rose, raised*) from her chair to greet us.
10. Smiling, the woman (*sat, set*) a beautiful coiled basket on the counter.

Review E Proofreading for Correct Verb Forms

Identify the ~~incorrect verb form~~ in each of the following sentences. Then, write the ∧ correct form.

EXAMPLE 1. Lately, everyone in our neighborhood has did more to keep physically fit.

1. did—done

1. No one is ~~setting~~ down anymore—except on stationary bicycles.   **1. sitting**
2. My mom has ~~rode~~ 150 miles so far.   **2. ridden**
3. In addition, I have never ~~knew~~ so many aerobic dancers.   **3. known**
4. Yesterday afternoon, I ~~swum~~ twelve laps in the pool.   **4. swam**
5. Last month, a famous exercise instructor ~~choosed~~ our neighborhood for her new fitness center.   **5. chose**
6. Many people ~~seen~~ her interviews on local talk shows.   **6. saw**
7. All of a sudden, adults and children have ~~began~~ going to the center.   **7. begun**
8. Each person is ~~suppose~~ to use different kinds of equipment.   **8. supposed**
9. Last night, I ~~rose~~ a fifty-pound weight.   **9. raised**
10. So far, no one has ~~broke~~ a leg on the cross-country ski machine.   **10. broken**
11. Mom had ~~went~~ to several gyms over the years.   **11. gone**
12. After my workout, I just ~~laid~~ on the floor, out of breath.   **12. lay**
13. She and I have ~~took~~ several classes at that gym.   **13. taken**
14. I must have ~~ran~~ a thousand miles on that treadmill.   **14. run**
15. We never ~~worn~~ fancy outfits, only sweat pants and T-shirts.   **15. wore**
16. I had ~~chose~~ an hour soaking in the whirlpool as my first exercise plan.   **16. chosen**
17. However, I ~~seen~~ the dancers and heard the music.   **17. saw**
18. Now I have ~~knowed~~ many of the dancers for a long time.   **18. known**
19. My energy level has ~~raised~~, and I'm happier.   **19. risen**
20. Don't ~~sit~~ those free weights down; keep at it!   **20. set**

Review F Using the Correct Forms of Verbs

Write the correct past or past participle form of the verb in parentheses in each of the following sentences.

EXAMPLE   1. I have (*grow*) tired of this TV program.
          1. grown

1. Grant (*feel*) proud and happy after winning the chess tournament.   **1. felt**
2. Over the years, I have (*keep*) all the postcards from my grandparents.   **2. kept**
3. Mother has (*lose*) the sash for her kimono.   **3. lost**

Six Confusing Verbs   **469**

4. became	4. The room quickly (*become*) crowded with curious fans.
5. told	5. Mr. Shaw (*tell*) us to read about the life of Harriet Jacobs.
6. made	6. Have you (*make*) the hat for your costume yet?
7. stood	7. All night the faithful Irish setter (*stand*) watch over the homestead.
8. ridden	8. Has Yoshi ever (*ride*) a horse before?
9. heard	9. Have you ever (*hear*) the story of Pocahontas?
10. said	10. Juanita (*say*) the biscuits would be ready soon.
11. began	11. As the sun set, the temperature (*begin*) to drop.
12. eaten	12. A squirrel had (*eat*) all the seed we put out for the birds.
13. run	13. Has Darius (*run*) ten laps yet?
14. wore	14. All the band members (*wear*) the same color socks on Friday.
15. led	15. At halftime, our team (*lead*) by two goals.
16. broken	16. The secret agent had easily (*break*) the code and deciphered the message.
17. sang	17. A whippoorwill (*sing*), crickets chirped, and a breeze rustled the leaves.
18. took	18. While I washed the dishes, Diane (*take*) the trash out.
19. fallen	19. A baby raccoon had (*fall*) from the tree into the soft pile of pine needles.
20. given	20. Have you (*give*) Dad his Father's Day present?

FRANK & ERNEST reprinted by permission of Newspaper Enterprise Association, Inc.

Chapter Review

A. Using Correct Forms of Irregular Verbs

For each of the following sentences, write the correct past or past participle form of the verb in parentheses.

1. ridden
2. fallen
3. knew
4. blown
5. went
6. brought
7. lay
8. broken
9. wore
10. froze
11. shrunk
12. sang
13. ate
14. rose
15. drank
16. ran
17. began
18. sat
19. sank
20. come

1. We had (*ride*) in the car for several hours.
2. Six inches of snow had (*fall*) the night before.
3. I never (*know*) snow was so beautiful.
4. The wind had (*blow*) some of it into high drifts.
5. As we (*go*) past them, they looked like white hills.
6. My brother Ernest had (*bring*) some comics to read.
7. I (*lie*) back and looked at the scenery.
8. Unfortunately, the car heater had (*break*).
9. We all (*wear*) our heavy coats and mittens.
10. However, my ears almost (*freeze*).
11. My favorite wool cap had (*shrink*) to a tiny size in the dryer.
12. During the long ride home, we (*sing*) some songs.
13. At noon, we (*eat*) lunch at a roadside cafeteria.
14. The clerk (*rise*) and asked if we would like some hot chocolate.
15. I (*drink*) two cups of hot cocoa.
16. Mom and I (*run*) around the parking lot to wake up.
17. After lunch, Ernie (*begin*) to feel sleepy.
18. I had never (*sit*) so long in a car before.
19. All warmed up, Ernie (*sink*) into a deep sleep.
20. We had (*come*) a long way.

B. Writing the Past and Past Participle Forms of Irregular Verbs

For each of the following sentences, write the correct past or past participle form of the verb in parentheses.

21. heard
22. broke

21. Have you (*hear*) the good news about Barbara?
22. The lower branches of the tree (*break*) in the storm.

Using the Chapter Review

To assess student progress, you may want to compare the types of items missed on the **Diagnostic Preview** to those missed on the **Chapter Review**. If students have not made significant progress, you may want to refer them to **Chapter 24: Correcting Common Errors, Exercises 10–13** for additional practice.

Chapter Review **471**

23. led	23. Our current mayor has (*lead*) three successful administrations.
24. held	24. The train was crowded, so we stood in the aisle and (*hold*) on to the luggage rack.
25. lay	25. The tired dog (*lie*) down as soon as it arrived home.
26. seen	26. As far as I know, they haven't (*see*) that movie.
27. set	27. She has always (*set*) the table herself, but tonight she has no time.
28. flown	28. "So far, children," said Ms. Espinosa, "that robin has (*fly*) all the way from Minnesota on its way to the Gulf Coast for the winter."
29. wore	29. She (*wear*) her blue parka to the parade.
30. risen	30. "Time to get up, everyone!" said Mom from the base of the stairs. "The sun has already (*rise*)."

C. Proofreading for Correct Verb Forms

For each of the following sentences, identify the ~~incorrect verb form~~. Then, write the correct form.

31. kept	31. When Dad was a boy in Iowa, he ~~keeped~~ bees.
32. lay	32. Before I ~~laid~~ down to sleep, I had packed everything I would need for today's trip.
33. set	33. Has Everett ~~sit~~ out the food for the picnic?
34. gone	34. Nobody in our family had ever ~~went~~ to college before Mom did.
35. ridden	35. I have never ~~rode~~ on a camel, but I'd like to someday.
36. began	36. Yesterday's class ~~begun~~ with a speed drill.
37. hit	37. She felt triumphant because she had never ~~hitted~~ a fly ball before.
38. raised	38. The unit stood at attention as Corporal Martinez ~~rose~~ the flag.
39. laid	39. The builder ~~lay~~ the plans on the table.
40. brought	40. Both Leyla and Hussain ~~brung~~ some delicious falafel to the anniversary party.

RESOURCES

Using Verbs Correctly

Review
- *Grammar, Usage, and Mechanics,* pp. 146, 147, 148, 149, 150

Assessment
- Assessment Package
  —Chapter Tests, Ch. 16
  —Chapter Tests in Standardized Test Formats, Ch. 16
- Test Generator (One-Stop Planner CD-ROM)

Writing Application
Using Verbs in a Description

Forms and Tenses of Verbs Many scientists and writers make predictions about the future. They base their predictions on past and present trends. Write a paragraph or two describing how one everyday item such as a car, a house, a home appliance, or a school might be different one hundred years from now. In your description, be sure to use the correct forms and tenses of verbs.

Prewriting Choose a topic that interests you, such as video games or skyscrapers. Based on what you already know about the topic, make some predictions about the future. Write down as many details as you can.

Writing Begin your draft by telling what time period your predictions concern. Then, use your notes to write a clear, vivid description of something in that future time.

Revising Have a classmate read your composition. How does it sound? Do your predictions sound possible? Add, cut, or revise details to make your description clear and believable.

Publishing Read your paragraph carefully to check for errors in grammar, spelling, and punctuation. Take special care with the forms of verbs. Use a dictionary to check the forms of any irregular verbs you are not sure about. You may want to present your final draft to the class as a multimedia computer presentation, an illustrated bulletin board, or a three-dimensional mobile.

Writing Application
(p. 473)

OBJECTIVE
- To use correct verb forms in writing a paragraph about how an everyday item today might be different one hundred years from now

Writing Application
Tip. Before students begin the writing activity, remind them that they are each to write about only one item.

Scoring Rubric. While you will want to pay particular attention to students' use of verb forms and tenses, you will also want to evaluate overall writing performance. You may want to give a split score to indicate development and clarity of the composition as well as usage skills.

Crossing the Curriculum
Science. Students may want to combine their predictions with research on a specific area of scientific development, such as robotics or genetic engineering. Students can conduct their research in the school library and provide copies of their sources along with their descriptions. Discuss students' findings with the class.

RESOURCES
Writing Application
Extension
- *Grammar, Usage, and Mechanics,* p. 153
- *Language Workshop CD-ROM,* Lessons 13–15

CHAPTER 17

Using Pronouns Correctly
Subject and Object Forms

Diagnostic Preview

Revising Incorrect Pronoun Forms in Sentences

Most of the following sentences contain an incorrect pronoun form. If a pronoun is used incorrectly, write the incorrect form of the pronoun and give the correct form. If a sentence is already correct, write *C*.

EXAMPLE 1. The police officer complimented us and they on knowing the rules of bicycle safety.
1. they—them

1. I
2. We
3. us
4. Who
5. me
6. us
7. C
8. they
9. C

1. The members of our bicycle club are Everett, Coral, Jackie, and me.
2. Us four call our club the Ramblers, named after a bicycle that was popular in the early 1900s.
3. Mrs. Wheeler gave an old three-speed bike to we four.
4. Whom explained the special bicycle safety course?
5. Our cousins gave Coral and I their old ten-speed bikes.
6. Each of we Ramblers rides after school.
7. Sometimes we ride with the members of the Derailers, a racing club.
8. On Saturday mornings, we and them meet at the school.
9. Who told us about the bike trail along the river?

PREVIEWING THE CHAPTER

- This chapter first explains the forms of personal pronouns (subject and object). Then, subject forms and object forms are discussed at length in their own sections. Finally, the chapter addresses special problems with the pronouns *who* and *whom* and pronouns used with appositives. All the information, reinforced by multiple exercises and activities, challenges students to use pronouns correctly in their speech and writing.

- The chapter closes with a **Chapter Review** for checking students' mastery of pronoun usage. As part of the Chapter Review, the **Writing Application** feature asks students to use correct pronoun forms in writing a paragraph that describes a proposed skit.

- For help in integrating this chapter with composition chapters, use the **Teaching Strands** chart on pp. T297A–T297B.

USING THE DIAGNOSTIC PREVIEW

- The **Diagnostic Preview** can help you determine areas in which additional instruction may be beneficial. Going over the answers orally may serve as a helpful review for some students, particularly auditory learners.

CHAPTER RESOURCES

Planning
- One-Stop Planner CD-ROM

Practice and Extension
- *Grammar, Usage, and Mechanics*, p. 154
- Language Workshop CD-ROM

Internet
- go.hrw.com (keyword: EOLang)

Evaluation and Assessment
- *Assessment Package*
  —Chapter Tests, Ch. 17
  —Chapter Tests in Standardized Test Formats, Ch. 17
- Test Generator (One-Stop Planner CD-ROM)

10. Everett warned we three about being careful because sometimes the Derailers are reckless. — **10.** us
11. He saw other riders and they at an intersection. — **11.** them
12. A car almost ran over two of them! — **12.** C
13. When the Ramblers ride with the Derailers, it is us who obey all the safety rules. — **13.** we
14. Everett, Coral, Jackie, and I entered a safety contest. — **14.** C
15. Other clubs and us competed for a tandem bike. — **15.** we
16. Everett and her taught Jackie how to ride it and shift gears. — **16.** she
17. One by one, us contestants went through the course. — **17.** we
18. Of all of we riders, the most careless were the Derailers. — **18.** us
19. Jackie and me were nervous as the judges were deciding. — **19.** I
20. Finally, the judges announced that the winners of the contest were us Ramblers. — **20.** we

The Forms of Personal Pronouns

The form of a personal pronoun shows how it can be used in a sentence. Pronouns used as subjects and predicate nominatives are in the ***subject form.***

EXAMPLES **He** and **I** went to the post office. [subject]

The winner of the marathon is **she**. [predicate nominative]

Pronouns used as direct objects and indirect objects of verbs and as objects of prepositions are in the ***object form.***

EXAMPLES Mr. García helped **him** and **me** with yesterday's homework. [direct objects]

The clerk gave **us** the package. [indirect object]

When is Theo going to give the flowers to **her**? [object of a preposition]

Possessive forms (*my, mine, your, yours, his, her, hers, its, their, theirs, our, ours*) are used to show ownership or possession.

EXAMPLES **My** sister had to turn the box on **its** end to get it through the door.

A mother bear is very protective of **her** cubs.

HELP
The subject form of pronouns is also sometimes known as the ***nominative case.*** The object form of pronouns is sometimes known as the ***objective case.***

The Forms of Personal Pronouns **475**

RESOURCES

The Forms of Personal Pronouns
Practice
- *Grammar, Usage, and Mechanics,* p. 155
- *Language Workshop CD-ROM,* Lessons 17, 18

Reference Note

For more information about **possessive pronouns**, see page 601.

Personal Pronouns		
	Singular	Plural
Subject Form	I you he, she, it	we you they
Object Form	me you him, her, it	us you them
Possessive Form	my, mine your, yours his, her, hers, its	our, ours your, yours their, theirs

Notice that the pronouns *you* and *it* are the same in the subject form and object form.

NOTE Some authorities prefer to call possessive forms such as *our*, *your*, and *their* possessive adjectives. Follow your teacher's instructions regarding possessive forms.

Exercise 1 Identifying Pronouns

Identify each of the following pronouns as a *subject form*, an *object form*, or a *possessive form*. If the pronoun can be used as either the subject form or the object form, write *subject or object*.

EXAMPLE   1. they
               1. subject form

1. him   **1. o.**   3. it   **3. s.o.**   5. our   **5. p.**   7. you   **7. s.o.**   9. he   **9. s.**
2. me   **2. o.**   4. we   **4. s.**   6. them   **6. o.**   8. their   **8. p.**   10. your   **10. p.**

Exercise 2 Identifying Pronouns in Sentences

For each of the following sentences, identify the pronoun in italics as a *subject form*, an *object form*, or a *possessive form*.

EXAMPLE   1. Ever since *he* could remember, Edward Bannister had wanted to be an artist.
               1. subject form

Exercise 2

ALTERNATIVE LESSON
To review the parts of a sentence, have students identify the complete subjects, complete predicates, direct objects, and objects of prepositions in the designated sentences from **Exercise 2**. [Complete subjects are shown in bold, complete predicates are shown in italics, direct objects are underlined once, and objects of prepositions are underlined twice.]

5. **The young Bannister** *couldn't afford* paper, *so* **he** *drew on barn* doors *and* fences.

6. *Later,* **Bannister** *met* Christiana Carteaux *and married* her.

9. **Bannister** *treasured his* prize *and regarded* it *as a great* honor.

10. *What do* **you** *think of the* painting?

1. He had to work hard to reach *his* goal. **1. p.**
2. Although Bannister was born in Canada, many consider *him* an American artist. **2. o.**
3. Bannister's parents died when *he* was young. **3. s.**
4. The little money they had was left to *their* son. **4. p.**
5. The young Bannister couldn't afford paper, so *he* drew on barn doors and fences. **5. s.**
6. Later, Bannister met Christiana Carteaux and married *her*. **6. o.**
7. She was from Rhode Island, where *her* people, the Narragansett, lived. **7. p.**
8. In 1876, a Philadelphia artistic society recognized Bannister by awarding *him* a gold medal for the painting shown here. **8. o.**
9. Bannister treasured his prize and regarded *it* as a great honor. **9. o.**
10. What do *you* think of the painting? **10. s.**

Edward Bannister, *Under the Oaks* (1876). Oil on canvas. National Museum of American Art, Washington DC/Art Resource, New York.

The Subject Form

Pronoun as Subject

The *subject* tells whom or what the sentence is about.

17a. Use the subject form for a pronoun that is the subject of a verb.

TEACHING TIP

Activity. Write on the board the following sentence:

Juan and _____ will be outside the auditorium.

Ask students how many different pronouns can fit in the blank. Have them work in pairs to list the pronouns and arrive at a number. [*There are seven pronouns that will fit: I, you, he, she, it, we, they.*] Then, ask what these pronouns have in common. [*They can all be used as subjects.*]

Critical Thinking

Metacognition. Ask students how they figured out which pronouns would work in the sentence above. Ask them whether it is easier for them to rely on position in the sentence or sound. If it is easier for them to use sound, ask students how they can best "hear" the correct form in this sentence. [*It is easier to hear the correct form if the first subject is omitted.*]

Meeting INDIVIDUAL NEEDS

ENGLISH-LANGUAGE LEARNERS

Spanish. Because Spanish verbs have endings that indicate the person and number of the subject, pronouns often are omitted in Spanish. For example, in the sentence *Yo hablo español* (I speak Spanish), the Spanish speaker typically omits *Yo* (I): *Hablo español.* Remind Spanish-speaking students that they should include the subject pronoun in their sentences in English even if to their ears it may sound redundant at first.

TIPS & TRICKS

To test whether a pronoun is used correctly in a compound subject, try each form of the pronoun separately.

EXAMPLE
(*She, Her*) and (*I, me*) practiced hard. [*She practiced* or *Her practiced*? *I practiced* or *me practiced*?]

ANSWER
She and **I** practiced hard.

EXAMPLES I walked to school. [*I* is the subject of the verb *walked.*]

Did **they** get to the theater on time? [*They* is the subject of the verb *Did get.*]

Dan said that **he** and **she** live on the Tigua reservation near El Paso, Texas. [*He* and *she* are the compound subject of the verb *live.*]

Oral Practice 1   Using Pronouns as Subjects

Read the following sentences aloud, stressing the italicized pronouns.

1. *She* and Ahmed solve crossword puzzles.
2. Are *they* very hard puzzles to solve?
3. Dad and *I* finished putting together a jigsaw puzzle last night.
4. *We* worked for three hours!
5. Finally, *you* and *he* found the missing pieces.
6. *He* and *I* liked the completed picture of flamenco dancers.
7. *They* are from Spain.
8. *We* agreed that *we* would like to see them dance.

Exercise 3   Identifying Correct Pronoun Forms

Choose the correct form of the pronoun in parentheses in each of the following sentences.

EXAMPLE 1. Brad and (*me, I*) wrote a skit based on the myth about Pygmalion.

1. *I*

1. (*Him, He*) and I thought the myth was funny.
2. (*We, Us*) asked Angela to play a part in the skit.
3. Neither (*she, her*) nor Doreen wanted to play a statue that came to life.
4. Finally Brad and (*me, I*) convinced Doreen that it would be a funny version of the myth.
5. (*Him, He*) and I flipped a coin to see who would play the part of Pygmalion.
6. The next day (*we, us*) were ready to perform.
7. Doreen and (*me, I*) began giggling when Brad pretended to be the beautiful statue.

8. In the skit, when Pygmalion returned from the festival of Venus, (*him, he*) and the statue were supposed to hug.
9. Instead of hugging, (*they, them*) laughed too hard to say the lines correctly.
10. Doreen, Brad, and (*I, me*) finally took a bow, and the class applauded.

Pronoun as Predicate Nominative

A *predicate nominative* completes the meaning of a linking verb and identifies or refers to the subject of the sentence.

17b. Use the subject form for a pronoun that is a predicate nominative.

A pronoun used as a predicate nominative usually follows a form of the verb *be* (such as *am, are, is, was, were, be, been,* or *being*).

EXAMPLES The next singer is **she**. [*She* completes the meaning of the linking verb *is* and identifies the subject *singer*.]

The first two speakers might be **he** and **I**. [*He* and *I* complete the meaning of the linking verb *might be* and identify the subject *speakers*.]

Was the winner really **she**? [*She* completes the meaning of the linking verb *Was* and identifies the subject *winner*.]

Reference Note
For more information on **predicate nominatives**, see page 410.

TIPS & TRICKS

To help you identify the predicate nominative in a question, try rearranging the words to make a statement.

QUESTION
Was the winner really she?

STATEMENT
The winner was really she.

As you can see in the statement form, the subject is *winner*, the verb is *was*, and the predicate nominative is *she*.

Oral Practice 2 Using Pronouns as Predicate Nominatives

Read the following sentences aloud, stressing the italicized pronouns.

1. The stars of that movie were *he* and *she*.
2. The actors from Australia must be *they*.
3. Of course, the mountain man is *he*.
4. Was the actress really *she*, Jeremy?
5. The director could have been *he*.
6. The villains are *he* and *they*.
7. The movie's biggest fans may be *you* and *I*.
8. The next ones to rent the film will be *we*, I think.

INCLUSION

Some students may have poor decoding skills and may read a different word in place of the one written. The words they insert may be similar in one or more ways to the ones presented: configuration, sound, definition, and linguistic function. Such substitution may or may not affect students' comprehension, but you should monitor them closely when they are doing the **Oral Practice** exercises.

The Forms of Personal Pronouns 479

Relating to Writing

To give students more practice using pronouns correctly as predicate nominatives, have them revise sentences from something they have written and included in their portfolio. Have students rewrite sentences in which pronouns have been used as subjects, making the pronouns predicate nominatives instead.

STYLE TIP

Expressions such as *It's me* and *That's him* are common in everyday speech. However, these expressions contain the object forms *me* and *him* used incorrectly as predicate nominatives.

Such expressions should be avoided in formal writing and speaking. If the subject form of the pronoun sounds awkward as the predicate nominative, revise the sentence.

AWKWARD
The next speakers will be **he** and **I**.

REVISED
He and **I** will be the next speakers.

HELP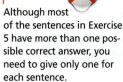

Although most of the sentences in Exercise 5 have more than one possible correct answer, you need to give only one for each sentence.

Answers will vary. Here are some possibilities.
1. he, she
2. he, she
3. they, we
4. she, he
5. I, he, she
6. I, he, she
7. he, she
8. they, we
9. he, she
10. he, she

Exercise 4 Identifying Pronouns Used as Predicate Nominatives

Choose the correct form of the pronoun in parentheses in each of the following sentences.

EXAMPLE 1. The man behind the curtain is (*him, he*).
1. he

1. The winners are you and (*me, I*).
2. It might have been (*he, him*).
3. The cooks for the traditional Vietnamese meal were (*them, they*).
4. Could it have been (*we, us*)?
5. Every year the speaker has been (*her, she*).
6. That was Carl and (*they, them*) in the swimming pool.
7. The volleyball fans in our family are Dad and (*she, her*).
8. First on the Black History Month program will be (*us, we*).
9. Was that (*he, him*) at the door?
10. Last year, the class treasurer was (*he, him*).

Exercise 5 Writing Sentences with Pronouns Used as Predicate Nominatives

Supply pronouns to complete the following sentences correctly. Use a variety of pronouns, but do not use *you* or *it*.

EXAMPLE 1. The man in the silliest costume was ____.
1. he

1. The person in the gorilla suit must be ____.
2. The next contestants will be ____ and ____.
3. The winners should have been ____.
4. Can that singer be ____, Samuel?
5. The one sitting in the back row was ____.
6. The first ones in line were my friends and ____.
7. "Excellent interpreters of Shakespeare's characters were ____ and ____," said Mr. Simmons.
8. Are the next entrants on stage ____?
9. The leader of that dragon team is probably ____.
10. Finalists in the contest will be Ted, Lisa, or ____.

Review A **Identifying Correct Pronoun Forms**

Choose the correct form of the pronoun in parentheses in each of the following sentences.

EXAMPLE 1. Last summer Carl, Felicia, and (*us, we*) went to San Antonio, Texas.

1. we

1. Carl and (*she, her*) took these photographs.
2. Early one morning (*him, he*) and (*she, her*) visited the Alamo.
3. That could be (*him, he*) in the crowd outside the Alamo.
4. Felicia and (*I, me*) listened to a mariachi band on the Riverwalk.
5. Of course, the musicians in the picture at right are (*they, them*).
6. Don't (*they, them*) look as though they're having a good time?
7. Carl and (*I, me*) enjoyed visiting the Spanish Governor's Palace in the afternoon.
8. Felicia, Carl, and (*us, we*) particularly liked the palace.
9. In fact, the first guests there that morning were (*us, we*).
10. Maybe you and (*they, them*) will get a chance to visit San Antonio someday.

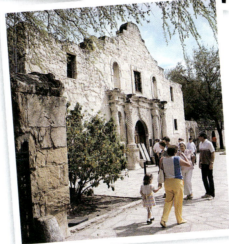

The Object Form

Pronoun as Direct Object

A ***direct object*** completes the meaning of an action verb and tells *who* or *what* receives the action of the verb.

Reference Note
For more about **direct objects**, see page 405.

Viewing the Illustrations

Exploring the Subject. The Alamo was the site of a major battle between defenders and an attacking Mexican army in 1836 during the Texas Revolution. Today the Alamo, Riverwalk, and Spanish Governor's Palace are popular tourist attractions in San Antonio, Texas.

The Object Form

Rules 17c–e *(pp. 481–486)*

OBJECTIVES

- To read sentences aloud and to stress the pronouns used in the objective case
- To identify pronouns used as direct objects, indirect objects, and objects of prepositions

---

RESOURCES

The Object Form

Practice

- *Grammar, Usage, and Mechanics,* pp. 158–159, 160–161
- *Language Workshop CD-ROM,* Lesson 18

Meeting INDIVIDUAL NEEDS

ENGLISH-LANGUAGE LEARNERS

Spanish. Some students may have difficulty positioning direct and indirect object pronouns within sentences. For example, "Lalo gave it to me" can be expressed in Spanish as *Lalo me lo dio*. Object pronouns can come before verbs in several languages.

Relating to Literature

To illustrate the value of object pronouns in literature, have your students read "All Summer in a Day" by Ray Bradbury. Then, have them identify as many object pronouns as possible on the first page. You may want to read those paragraphs aloud and replace the object pronouns with their antecedents to demonstrate how different the language would sound without object pronouns. Ask volunteers to express the grammatical value of object pronouns in literature. [*Without object pronouns, the names of the objects would have to be repeated over and over. This repetition would lead to awkward, tedious sentences.*]

STYLE TIP

Just as there are good manners in behavior, there are also good manners in language. In English, it is polite to put first-person pronouns (*I, me, mine, we, us, ours*) last in compound constructions.

EXAMPLES
Veronica showed **Roberto and me** how to use the software program.

She and I arrived early for softball practice.

TIPS & TRICKS

To help you choose the correct pronoun in a compound object, try each pronoun separately in the sentence.

EXAMPLE
Ms. Stone praised Alonzo and (*we, us*). [*Ms. Stone praised we* or *Ms. Stone praised us*?]

ANSWER
Ms. Stone praised Alonzo and **us**.

17c. Use the object form for a pronoun that is the direct object of a verb.

EXAMPLES The teacher thanked **me** for cleaning the chalkboard. [*Teacher* is the subject of the verb *thanked*. The teacher thanked whom? The direct object is *me*.]

The answer surprised **us**. [*Answer* is the subject of the verb *surprised*. The answer surprised whom? The direct object is *us*.]

Have you told **him** about the change in plans? [*You* is the subject of the verb *Have told*. You have told whom? The direct object is *him*.]

Fred saw **them** and **me** last night. [*Fred* is the subject of the verb *saw*. Fred saw whom? The compound direct object is *them* and *me*.]

Oral Practice 3 Using Pronouns as Direct Objects

Read the following sentences aloud, stressing the italicized pronouns.

1. Kathy found *them* and *me* by the fountain.
2. Mr. Winters took *us* to the rodeo.
3. Did you see *her* and *him* at the Cajun restaurant?
4. Tyrone frightened *us* with his rubber spider.
5. Ellis invited Luis, Jared, and *me* to his party.
6. The mayor met *them* at Howard University.
7. Uncle Ken thanked *her* for the gift.
8. The fans cheered Anthony and *her*.

Exercise 6 Identifying Pronouns Used as Direct Objects

Choose the correct form of the pronoun in parentheses in each of the following sentences.

EXAMPLE 1. Marcus met Howard and (*I, me*) at the game.
1. me

1. Mrs. Freeman invited Leroy and (*I, me*) to a Kwanzaa party.
2. The spectators watched (*we, us*) and (*they, them*).
3. The shoes don't fit (*her, she*) or (*I, me*).

MINI-LESSON

Number of Personal Pronouns. You might want to review with students the singular and plural forms of personal pronouns. Have students alter the sentences in **Oral Practice 3**, changing the singular pronouns to plural and the plural pronouns to singular. Tell them not to change the person of the pronouns.

1. him *or* her, us
2. me
3. them

4. Sean called Marco and (*he*, *him*) on the telephone.
5. Our new neighbors asked (*we*, *us*) for directions to the synagogue.
6. They hired Tía and (*us*, *we*) to rake their yard.
7. The puppy followed Louis and (*he*, *him*) all the way home.
8. Last week, friends from Panama visited (*us*, *we*).
9. Odessa thanked (*her*, *she*) and (*me*, *I*) for helping.
10. The usher showed Greg and (*them*, *they*) to their seats.

Pronoun as Indirect Object

An **indirect object** may come between an action verb and a direct object. An indirect object tells *to whom* or *to what* or *for whom* or *for what* something is done.

Reference Note
For more about **indirect objects,** see page 407.

17d. Use the object form for a pronoun that is the indirect object of a verb.

EXAMPLES   Scott handed **me** a note. [Scott handed what? *Note* is the direct object. To whom did he hand a note? The indirect object is *me*.]

Coretta baked **them** some muffins. [Coretta baked what? *Muffins* is the direct object. For whom did Coretta bake muffins? The indirect object is *them*.]

Elizabeth sent **him** and **me** some oranges from Florida. [Elizabeth sent what? *Oranges* is the direct object. To whom did Elizabeth send oranges? The compound indirect object is *him* and *me*.]

— HELP —

Indirect objects do not follow prepositions. If *to* or *for* precedes a pronoun, the pronoun is the object of a preposition, not an indirect object.

Reference Note
For more information about **prepositions and their objects,** see page 361.

Oral Practice 4 Using Pronouns as Indirect Objects

Read the following sentences aloud, stressing the italicized pronouns.

1. Mr. Krebs showed Bill and *them* the rock collection.
2. Paco told *me* the answer to the riddle.
3. Mr. Thibaut gives *us* lacrosse lessons.
4. We bought *her* and *him* a present.
5. The artists drew *us* and *them* some pictures.
6. The server brought *me* a bagel with cream cheese.
7. A pen pal in Hawaii sent *her* some shells.
8. My uncle Shannon told *us* a funny story about leprechauns.

4. me
5. us
6. him *or* her
7. them
8. them

Meeting INDIVIDUAL NEEDS

MODALITIES
Visual Learners. You may want to write the sentences from **Oral Practice 4** on the chalkboard. After the class reads each sentence, use an eraser, book, or other object to cover the pronouns used as indirect objects. Then, have students read the sentences without the covered indirect objects. Help them see that the direct objects are receiving the action of the verb in each sentence. For example: Mr. Krebs showed the rock collection. Mr. Krebs showed what? [*the rock collection*]

Then, uncover the indirect object and ask to whom or to what the action has been done. For example: Mr. Krebs showed the rock collection to whom? [*Bill and them*]

Meeting INDIVIDUAL NEEDS

LEARNERS HAVING DIFFICULTY
You might want to have students work in pairs to complete **Review B**. Have partners alternate writing sentences. As they write each sentence, the partners should work together to identify and circle the subject and object forms of personal pronouns in the sentences, determine the function of each pronoun (subject, predicate nominative, direct object, or indirect object), and identify the relevant rule from the chapter. The partners should note the rule in the margin of their paper and write the correct pronoun form for any incorrect sentences.

Relating to Writing
As an alternative to **Review B**, ask each of your students to write a brief descriptive paragraph about a pet or favorite animal. Students should include object pronouns in each sentence. When they finish their first drafts, tell them to exchange papers with partners, who will check the correctness of the object pronouns.

Review B Revising Incorrect Pronoun Forms in Paragraphs

ANSWERS
1. me—I
2. she—her; I—me
3. C
4. C

Exercise 7 Identifying Pronouns Used as Indirect Objects

Choose the correct form of the pronoun in parentheses in each of the following sentences.

EXAMPLE   1. At the start of class, Mr. Chou assigned (*we, us*) new seats.
   1. us

1. The store clerk gave (*they, them*) a discount.
2. For lunch, Anthony fixed (*he, him*) and (*she, her*) bean burritos with salsa.
3. Would you please show (*her, she*) and (*me, I*) that Navajo dream catcher?
4. Those green apples gave both Christopher and (*he, him*) stomachaches.
5. The waiter brought (*us, we*) some ice water.
6. Why don't you sing (*she, her*) a lullaby?
7. Have they made (*we, us*) the costumes for the play?
8. An usher handed (*me, I*) a program of the recital.
9. The Red Cross volunteers showed (*we, us*) and (*they, them*) a movie about first aid.
10. Please send (*me, I*) your new address.

Review B Revising Incorrect Pronoun Forms in Paragraphs

In most of the sentences in the following paragraphs, at least one pronoun has been used incorrectly. Identify each incorrect pronoun, and give the correct form. If all of the pronouns in a sentence are already correct, write *C*.

EXAMPLE   [1] Ms. Fisher took several of my friends and I to the museum.
   1. I—me

[1] At the Museum of Natural History, Luisa and me wanted to see the American Indian exhibit. [2] The museum guide showed she and I the displays of Hopi pottery and baskets. [3] Both she and I were especially interested in the kachina dolls. [4] After half an hour, Ms. Fisher found us.

[5] Then Luisa, her, and I joined the rest of the group. [6] Another guide had been giving Ms. Fisher and they information about the Masai people in Africa. [7] Them and us decided to see the exhibit about ancient Egypt next.

[8] A group of little children passed Ms. Fisher and we on the stairway as we were going to the exhibit. [9] The ones who reached the exhibit first were them. [10] Jeff, the jokester, said that they wanted to find their "mummies." [11] Ms. Fisher and us laughed at the terrible pun. [12] She gave him a pat on the back. [13] We asked her not to encourage him. [14] The museum guide led the children and we to the back of the room. [15] There, he showed us and they a model of a pyramid. [16] Then Ms. Fisher and him explained how the Egyptians prepared mummies. [17] Was it her who asked about King Tutankhamen? [18] Of course, Luisa and me recognized this golden mask right away. [19] As we were leaving, the guide gave the children and we some booklets about King Tut and other famous ancient Egyptians. [20] He handed Luisa and I booklets about the builders of the pyramids.

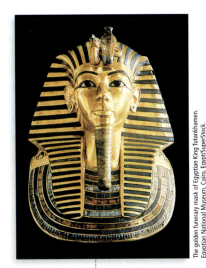

The golden funerary mask of Egyptian King Tutankhamen. Egyptian National Museum, Cairo, Egypt/SuperStock.

Pronoun as Object of a Preposition

The *object of a preposition* is a noun or a pronoun that follows a preposition. Together, the preposition, its object, and any modifiers of that object make a *prepositional phrase*.

Reference Note

For more information about **prepositions**, see page 360.

17e. Use the object form for a pronoun that is the object of a preposition.

EXAMPLES   above **me**   beside **us**   with **them**

                for **him**   toward **you**   next to **her**

Oral Practice 5 Using Pronouns as Objects of Prepositions

Read the sentences on the following page aloud, stressing the italicized pronouns.

The Forms of Personal Pronouns   **485**

Review B Revising Incorrect Pronoun Forms in Paragraphs

ANSWERS CONTINUED

5. her—she
6. they—them
7. Them—They; us—we
8. we—us
9. them—they
10. C
11. us—we
12. C
13. C
14. we—us
15. they—them
16. him—he
17. her—she
18. me—I
19. we—us
20. I—me

Viewing the Illustration

Exploring the Subject. The funeral mask of Tutankhamen is made of solid gold with lapis lazuli eyelids, quartz and obsidian eyes, and blue glass stripes in the headdress. The fact that Tutankhamen was king of both upper and lower Egypt is symbolized by the vulture and cobra on the forehead.

Crossing the Curriculum

Social Studies. Locate a copy of "The New Colossus," a poem by Emma Lazarus that was inscribed on a tablet in the pedestal of the Statue of Liberty in 1903. Tell your students that the Statue of Liberty greeted many of the immigrants who sailed to the United States. Then, write all or some of the poem—particularly the last two sentences—on the chalkboard, and have students identify subject and object pronouns used by the poet.

Exercise 8

ALTERNATIVE LESSON
Before students work on **Exercise 8**, you might want to have them identify the prepositions in the designated sentences.

1. In, against
2. with, at
3. to
4. around

Special Pronoun Problems
(pp. 486–490)

OBJECTIVES

- To read sentences aloud and to stress the pronouns *who* and *whom*
- To identify the correct forms of *who* and *whom* and pronouns with appositives

TIPS & TRICKS

When a preposition is followed by two or more pronouns, try each pronoun alone to be sure that you have used the correct forms.

EXAMPLE
Carrie divided the chores between (*they, them*) and (*we, us*). [Carrie divided the chores between they or Carrie divided the chores between them? Carrie divided the chores between we or Carrie divided the chores between us?]

ANSWER
Carrie divided the chores between **them** and **us**.

1. The lemonade stand was built by Chuck and *me*.
2. The younger children rode in front of *us*.
3. Just between *you* and *me*, that game wasn't much fun.
4. Everyone has gone except the Taylors and *them*.
5. Give the message to *him* or *her*.
6. Why don't you sit here beside *me*, Ben?
7. Were those pictures of Amish families taken by *him*?
8. Donna went to the Cinco de Mayo parade with *them*.

Exercise 8 Identifying Pronouns Used as Objects of Prepositions

Choose the correct form of the pronoun in parentheses in each of the following sentences.

EXAMPLE   1. Someone else should have sent an invitation to (*they, them*).
　　　　　　1. them

1. In the first round, Michael Chang played against (*he, him*).
2. Did you sit with Martha or (*her, she*) at the game?
3. Peggy sent homemade birthday cards to Josh, you, and (*them, they*).
4. There is a bee flying around (*he, him*) and you.
5. If you have a complaint, tell it to Mr. Ramis or (*she, her*).
6. Ms. Young divided the projects among (*us, we*).
7. This secret is strictly between you and (*me, I*).
8. Can you believe the weather balloon dropped right in front of (*we, us*)?
9. Please don't ride the Alaskan ferry without Jim and (*me, I*).
10. One of the clowns threw confetti at us and (*they, them*).

Special Pronoun Problems
Who and *Whom*

The pronoun *who* has two different forms. *Who* is the subject form. *Whom* is the object form.

When you are choosing between *who* and *whom* in a question, follow these steps:

486   Chapter 17   Using Pronouns Correctly

RESOURCES
Special Pronoun Problems
Practice
- *Grammar, Usage, and Mechanics,* pp. 162, 163
- Language Workshop CD-ROM, Lesson 19

STEP 1	Rephrase the question as a statement.
STEP 2	Identify how the pronoun is used in the statement—as a subject, a predicate nominative, a direct object, an indirect object, or an object of a preposition.
STEP 3	Determine whether the subject form or the object form is correct according to the rules of standard English.
STEP 4	Select the correct form—*who* or *whom*.

EXAMPLE (*Who, Whom*) rang the bell?
- STEP 1 The statement is (*Who, Whom*) *rang the bell*.
- STEP 2 The pronoun is the subject of the verb *rang*.
- STEP 3 As the subject, the pronoun should be in the subject form.
- STEP 4 The subject form is *who*.
- ANSWER **Who** rang the bell?

EXAMPLE (*Who, Whom*) does Lindsay see?
- STEP 1 The statement is *Lindsay does see (who, whom)*.
- STEP 2 The pronoun is the direct object of the verb *does see*.
- STEP 3 A direct object should be in the object form.
- STEP 4 The object form is *whom*.
- ANSWER **Whom** does Lindsay see?

EXAMPLE To (*who, whom*) did Jo give the gift?
- STEP 1 The statement is *Jo did give the gift to (who, whom)*.
- STEP 2 The pronoun is the object of the preposition *to*.
- STEP 3 The object of a preposition should be in the object form.
- STEP 4 The object form is *whom*.
- ANSWER To **whom** did Jo give the gift?

STYLE TIP

The use of *whom* is becoming less common in informal English. Informally, you may begin any question with *who*. In formal written and spoken English, however, you should distinguish between *who* and *whom*. *Who* is used as a subject or a predicate nominative, and *whom* is used as an object.

Oral Practice 6 — Using Pronouns Correctly in Sentences

Read the following sentences aloud, stressing the italicized pronouns.

1. *Who* owns the sailboat over there?
2. To *whom* did you throw the ball?
3. *Whom* did Miguel marry?

Special Pronoun Problems **487**

Meeting INDIVIDUAL NEEDS

MULTIPLE INTELLIGENCES

Logical-Mathematical Intelligence. Have students create their own flowcharts showing the process for choosing between *who* and *whom* in a question, using the list of steps on this page as a model. Have students develop their own example sentences to use within the flowchart.

ENGLISH-LANGUAGE LEARNERS

General Strategies. When you are guiding English-language learners, it is important to look for simpler ways of expressing rules and to avoid linguistic labeling whenever possible.

Differentiating the use of *who* and *whom* is sometimes tricky, even for a proficient English speaker. Students need information to be given to them clearly and directly.

To help students learn to use *who* and *whom* properly, tell them these simple rules:

1. *Whom* is used after a preposition.
2. With any form of the verb *be* when *be* is the main verb, always use *who*, not *whom*.

USAGE

Learning for Life

Continued on pp. 488–489

A Letter to the Editor. Explain to students that many people write letters to the editors of newspapers and magazines. The letters typically express an opinion about a newsworthy topic. To make sure the message is clear for readers, the letter writer must take care to use formal, standard English—including the correct use of pronouns.

Have students choose a historical event that they think was important. Students should then imagine that they are writing

Special Pronoun Problems **487**

4. *Who* was the stranger with the ten-gallon hat?
5. For *whom* did you knit that sweater?
6. *Who* is the author of that book about Jackie Robinson?
7. *Whom* did Josh choose as his subject?
8. By *whom* was this work painted?

Pronouns with Appositives

Sometimes a pronoun is followed directly by a noun that identifies the pronoun. Such a noun is called an **appositive.** To help you choose which pronoun to use before an appositive, omit the appositive and try each form of the pronoun separately.

Reference Note
For more information about **appositives,** see page 570.

EXAMPLE (*We, Us*) Girl Scouts swam laps. [*Girl Scouts* is the appositive identifying the pronoun. *We swam laps* or *Us swam laps*?]

ANSWER **We** Girl Scouts swam laps.

EXAMPLE The director gave an award to (*we, us*) actors. [*Actors* is the appositive identifying the pronoun. *The director gave an award to we* or *The director gave an award to us*?]

ANSWER The director gave an award to **us** actors.

Exercise 9 Identifying the Correct Forms of Pronouns in Sentences

Choose the correct form of the pronoun in parentheses in each of the following sentences.

EXAMPLE 1. (*Who, Whom*) can do the most jumping jacks?
1. Who

1. (*We, Us*) baseball players always warm up before practice.
2. (*Who, Whom*) knows how to stretch properly?
3. Coach Anderson has special exercises for (*we, us*) pitchers.
4. To (*who, whom*) did the coach assign thirty sit-ups?
5. (*Who, Whom*) do you favor for tomorrow's game?
6. Would you teach (*we, us*) girls that new batting stance?
7. Please take (*we, us*) fans with you to the next game.

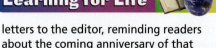

letters to the editor, reminding readers about the coming anniversary of that event. Because space in a newspaper is limited, each letter should be no longer than about 250 words.

The letter should identify the event, the anniversary date, and important individuals involved in the event. For example, one student might choose to write about the anniversary of the 1963 March on Washington, an important civil rights event at which Dr. Martin Luther King, Jr., and

Cooperative Learning
You may want to have students work in pairs for **Exercise 9.** Make one partner responsible for choosing the pronoun and the other for identifying the way the pronoun is used in the sentence. Students should correct any answers that do not follow rules for correct pronoun usage.

8. The ones with the new gloves and jerseys should have been (*we, us*) fielders.
9. (*Who, Whom*) should start the lineup?
10. With (*who, whom*) do you practice after school?

Review C — Revising Incorrect Pronoun Forms in Sentences

Identify each incorrect pronoun in the following sentences. Then, write the correct pronoun. If a sentence is already correct, write *C*.

EXAMPLE 1. At first Karen and me thought that Lucy was imagining things.
   1. me—I

1. Lucy told Karen and I that creatures from outer space had just landed. **1.** me
2. She was certain it was them at the park. **2.** they
3. Whom would believe such a ridiculous story? **3.** Who
4. Us girls laughed and laughed. **4.** We
5. Lucy looked at we two with tears in her eyes. **5.** us
6. Karen and I agreed to go to the park to look around. **6.** C
7. Lucy walked between Karen and me, showing the way. **7.** C
8. In the park she and us hid behind some tall bushes. **8.** we
9. Suddenly a strong wind almost blew we three down. **9.** us
10. A green light shone on Karen and I, and a red one shone on Lucy. **10.** me
11. Whom could it be? **11.** Who
12. One of the creatures spoke to us girls. **12.** C
13. Very slowly, Karen, Lucy, and me stepped out from behind the bushes. **13.** I
14. "You almost scared they and me silly!" shouted a creature, pointing at the others. **14.** them
15. Neither Karen nor her could speak, and I could make only a squeaking noise. **15.** she
16. Then the man inside the costume explained to we three girls that a movie company was filming in the park. **16.** us
17. They and we could have been in an accident. **17.** C
18. The fireworks hidden in the bushes might have hurt one of we girls. **18.** us

Special Pronoun Problems **489**

MODALITIES

Visual Learners. To make students aware of the various uses of pronouns, suggest that students use colored pencils to rewrite the sentences in **Review C,** using one color for writing correct personal pronouns used as subjects and three different colors for writing correct personal pronouns used as direct objects, indirect objects, and objects of prepositions.

others spoke. Each letter should include examples of pronouns used as subjects, predicate nominatives, direct objects, indirect objects, objects of prepositions, and appositives.

After students have finished their letters, invite volunteers to read their work to the class. Have students keep their letters in their portfolios for future reference.

19. him   **19.** Lucy told the director and he about being afraid of the space creatures in the park.

20. we   **20.** If you see the movie, the short purple creatures under the spaceship are us three girls.

Review D — Replacing Nouns with Pronouns

Revise each of the following sentences, substituting pronouns for the words in italics.

EXAMPLE   1. The bird hopped lightly into the *bird's* nest.
                   1. The bird hopped lightly into its nest.

1. you   **1.** David, I have already asked *David* several times to clean your room.

2. it   **2.** The raccoon reached into the water, caught a fish, and ate *the fish*.

3. They   **3.** *Anne and Paula* should be here in a few minutes.

4. She   **4.** *Sandra* will be reading my report to the class tomorrow.

5. him   **5.** Don't forget to return Reginald's book to *Reginald*.

6. he   **6.** As soon as Willis finishes dinner, *Willis* must leave for play practice.

7. your   **7.** Diane, did you turn in *Diane's* permission slip yet?

8. our   **8.** Mario and I have decided to do *Mario's and my* project as a musical skit.

9. him   **9.** In his locker, Felipe has a photograph of WNBA star Sheryl Swoopes with *Felipe*.

10. their   **10.** The dogs came running in as soon as they knew *the dogs'* food dish was filled.

CHAPTER 17 Chapter Review

A. Identifying Correct Pronoun Forms

For each of the following sentences, write the correct form of the pronoun in parentheses.

1. Could that be (*she, her*) at the bus stop?
2. The guest speakers were Dr. Lucia Sanchez and (*he, him*).
3. Are you and (*they, them*) going to the basketball game?
4. You and (*I, me*) have been friends for a long time.
5. Sometimes, even our parents cannot tell (*we, us*) apart.
6. (*We, Us*) players surprised the coach with a victory party.
7. (*Who, Whom*) is bringing the holiday turkey?
8. Laura lent my sister and (*I, me*) a new CD.
9. Mr. Lee will divide the money between you and (*I, me*).
10. To (*who, whom*) is the envelope addressed?
11. Please keep this information between you and (*she, her*).
12. Did Maria or (*she, her*) call Grandmother Lopez?
13. Mom and (*they, them*) have gone shopping.
14. Can you show Charlie and (*she, her*) how to fish?
15. Danny and (*I, me*) are practicing woodcraft for camp.
16. Why didn't you tell me about (*he, him*)?
17. Eldon and (*we, us*) were tired of playing checkers.
18. Mom and Dad promised Keith and (*they, them*) a puppy.
19. Was (*he, him*) the only one in the theater?
20. Would you lend your notes to (*we, us*)?

B. Identifying Pronouns Used as Predicate Nominatives

For each of the following sentences, write the correct form of the pronoun in parentheses.

21. The bus driver was (*he, him*).
22. That was Mr. San Miguel and (*they, them*) at the stadium last night.

Using the Chapter Review

To assess student progress, you may want to compare the types of items missed on the **Diagnostic Preview** to those missed on the **Chapter Review.** If students have not made significant progress, you may want to refer them to **Chapter 24: Correcting Common Errors, Exercises 14–15** for additional practice.

23. The most devoted animal-lovers I know are Melanie and (*her*, *she*).
24. The junior racquetball champion last year was (*her*, *she*).
25. Once or twice a month the lifeguard at the local pool is (*he*, *him*).
26. Was that (*they*, *them*) in the parking lot?
27. Second on the program at the concert was (*he*, *him*).
28. It could have been (*her*, *she*), but I doubt it.
29. The devoted Rangers fans in our class are Gregorio and (*he*, *him*).
30. The visitors from Taiwan must be (*they*, *them*).

C. Identifying the Correct Forms of Pronouns Used as Subjects, Direct Objects, Indirect Objects, and Objects of Prepositions

For each of the following sentences, choose the correct form of the pronoun in parentheses and tell whether it is used as a subject, a direct object, an indirect object, or an object of a preposition.

31. o.p.	31. The one who cheered loudest was the girl behind (*I*, *me*).
32. o.p.	32. Did Isabel travel to Santa Fe with John and (*her*, *she*)?
33. s.	33. (*We*, *Us*) baseball fans welcomed the decision not to move the team.
34. d.o./d.o.	34. Peter called (*her*, *she*) and (*I*, *me*) last night.
35. s.	35. (*We*, *Us*) cousins had a yard sale.
36. i.o.	36. Tomas and José gave (*we*, *us*) their addresses in Mexico.
37. i.o.	37. Her grandmother in Oregon sent (*her*, *she*) some apples.
38. o.p.	38. On the hike, Christie and Maggie walked ahead of (*I*, *me*).
39. d.o.	39. The teacher scolded us and (*he*, *him*) for being late.
40. i.o.	40. I bought (*they*, *them*) an anniversary present.

RESOURCES

Using Pronouns Correctly
Review
- *Grammar, Usage, and Mechanics,* pp. 164, 165, 166, 167

Assessment
- *Assessment Package*
  —Chapter Tests, Ch. 17
  —Chapter Tests in Standardized Test Formats, Ch. 17
- *Test Generator (One-Stop Planner CD-ROM)*

Writing Application
Using Correct Pronoun Forms in Writing

Using Pronouns Health Awareness Week is coming up soon. Your class has been chosen to perform a skit on a health-related topic for the rest of the school. Your teacher has asked each class member to write down an idea for an entertaining, informative skit. Write a paragraph or two describing a skit that your class could perform. Be sure to use correct pronoun forms in your description.

Prewriting First, you will need to decide on a topic for the skit. Think about the health concerns of people your age. For example, you might plan a skit about the dangers of smoking or the importance of regular dental check-ups. After you choose a topic, brainstorm some ideas for a simple, entertaining skit. Be sure to list any props or costumes your class will need.

Writing Use your notes to help you write your draft. First, tell what the skit is about and why it is appropriate for Health Awareness Week. Then, explain what happens in the skit from beginning to end. Be sure to tell in a general way what each character does and says. Describe the props and costumes that your class can make or bring from home.

Revising Ask a classmate to read your paragraph. Is the information given in the skit correct? Does the skit sound entertaining? Is it clear which character does and says what? If not, revise your paragraph. Add details that will make the skit more fun and interesting.

Publishing Check your sentences to be sure you have used pronouns correctly and clearly. Read through your description carefully to check for errors in grammar, spelling, and punctuation. Use this chapter to help you check for errors in pronoun forms.

Your class may want to hold a contest for the best skit idea. Using the best idea, work together to develop the skit in more detail. Then, with your teacher's permission, give a performance of the skit for other classes.

Chapter Review **493**

Writing Application
(p. 493)

OBJECTIVE
- To use correct pronoun forms in writing a paragraph that describes a proposed skit

Writing Application
Tip. This writing assignment provides students with an opportunity to develop descriptive paragraphs in which they will use correct pronoun forms.

Scoring Rubric. While you will want to pay particular attention to students' use of pronouns, you will also want to evaluate overall writing performance. You may want to give a split score to indicate development and clarity of the composition as well as usage skills.

Critical Thinking
Evaluation. Encourage students to be objective about each sentence in their paragraphs. Tell them to examine each sentence separately and to use the following criteria.

1. Does the sentence have a subject and verb and express a complete thought?
2. Does the sentence say exactly what you want it to say?
3. Does it support the topic sentence?
4. Does it contain a subject pronoun or an object pronoun?

RESOURCES
Writing Application
Extension
- *Grammar, Usage, and Mechanics,* p. 170
- *Language Workshop CD-ROM,* Lessons 17–19

CHAPTER 18

Using Modifiers Correctly
Comparison and Placement

Diagnostic Preview

Correcting Errors in the Form, Use, and Placement of Modifiers

Most of the following sentences contain an error in the use of modifiers or negative words. If a sentence has an error, rewrite the sentence correctly. If a sentence is already correct, write *C*.

EXAMPLE 1. The weather looks more worse today.
  1. *The weather looks worse today.*

1. Of the students in class, Odelle writes ~~better~~.
2. Can you type ~~fastest~~ on a computer or on a typewriter?
3. Juan seemed very happy that we had visited him.
4. No one knew ~~nothing~~ about the tornado.
5. The vegetables were eaten by rabbits ~~that we had planted~~.
6. Throughout history, many people have written ~~regular~~ in their diaries.
7. The people who moved in next door are the ~~most~~ friendliest neighbors who have ever lived there.
8. The bread smelled ~~wonderfully~~.
9. Did that armadillo make it across the road ~~with a limp~~?

PREVIEWING THE CHAPTER

- The chapter begins with a discussion of different kinds of modifiers and teaches the degrees of comparison of adjectives and adverbs, both regular and irregular. This section is followed by lessons on the use of *well* and *good*, on the use of adjectives after linking verbs, on avoiding double comparisons and double negatives, and on the correct placement of modifiers.

- The chapter closes with a **Chapter Review** to help you check students' mastery of the use and placement of modifiers and the correct use of negative words. Also, a **Writing Application** feature asks students to use negative words correctly in writing a letter to a friend.

- For help in integrating this chapter with composition chapters, use the **Teaching Strands** chart on pp. T297A–T297B.

USING THE DIAGNOSTIC PREVIEW

- You can use the **Diagnostic Preview** to assess your students' skills in recognizing and correcting errors in the form, use, and placement of modifiers. The **Diagnostic Preview** also checks students' skills in recognizing sentences with double negatives. If your students show a particular weakness in one of these areas, you can skip to the relevant part of the chapter.

Revisions of double negatives may vary.
1. best
2. faster
3. C
4. anything
5. that we had planted
6. regularly

8. wonderful
9. with a limp

CHAPTER RESOURCES

Planning
- *One-Stop Planner CD-ROM*

Practice and Extension
- *Grammar, Usage, and Mechanics,* p. 171
- *Language Workshop CD-ROM*

Internet
- go.hrw.com (keyword: EOLang)

Evaluation and Assessment
- *Assessment Package*
  —*Chapter Tests,* Ch. 18
  —*Chapter Tests in Standardized Test Formats,* Ch. 18
- *Test Generator (One-Stop Planner CD-ROM)*

10. Wynton Marsalis plays the trumpet good.
11. If you don't feel well today, you shouldn't go out.
12. We read a story written by Mark Twain yesterday.
13. Mai is one of the most persistent people I know.
14. I felt sadly at the end of *Old Yeller*.
15. The boy ordered a sandwich that was hungry.
16. The team usually wins the game that has the better defense.
17. Tanya is the youngest of my brothers and sisters.
18. It doesn't make no difference to Brian.
19. I'm not sure which I like best, CDs or tapes.
20. Arthurine's piano playing sounds very nicely to me.
21. The storm came up so sudden that it surprised us.
22. The house looks differently to me.
23. Lena and Ivan are twins, and Lena is the oldest one.
24. We couldn't hardly believe the news!
25. Miyoko looks well in her new school uniform.

10. well
11. C
12. Yesterday
13. C
14. sad
15. that was hungry
16. that has the better defense
17. C
18. makes
19. better
20. nice
21. suddenly
22. different
23. older
24. could
25. good

What Is a Modifier?

A **modifier** is a word, a phrase, or a clause that makes the meaning of a word or word group more specific. The two kinds of modifiers are *adjectives* and *adverbs*.

One-Word Modifiers

Adjectives

18a. *Adjectives* make the meanings of nouns and pronouns more specific.

EXAMPLES   **That** one is my favorite. [The adjective *That* tells which one.]

Does Stephen know the **secret** combination? [The adjective *secret* tells what kind of combination.]

Estéban has saved **more** money than I have. [The adjective *more* tells how much money.]

Four horses grazed peacefully at the foot of the hill. [The adjective *Four* tells how many horses.]

Reference Note
For more about **adjectives**, see page 336. For more about **adverbs**, see page 357.

One-Word Modifiers
Rules 18a, b *(pp. 495–497)*

OBJECTIVE

- To identify modifiers as adjectives or adverbs and to tell what word is modified

RESOURCES

One-Word Modifiers
Practice
- *Grammar, Usage, and Mechanics,*  pp. 172, 173, 174, 175

USAGE

TEACHING TIP

Activity. To help students understand how adjectives and adverbs modify words, consider using the following demonstration. First, identify for the class what you are wearing, using only nouns such as "shirt, pants, shoes." Then, ask students to modify those nouns by using descriptive words called adjectives: "*white* shirt, *blue* pants, *dress* shoes." Invite volunteers to repeat this exercise by describing your classroom, a desk, or another object. Lead students to understand that they are using adjectives to make the meanings of the nouns more specific.

Then, walk quickly to the back of the room and then slowly back to the front of the room. Tell students that you *walked* to the back and then *walked* back to the front. Ask what you did differently each time. [*You walked* quickly *the first time and* slowly *the second time.*] Explain that *walk* is a verb and that *quickly* and *slowly* are adverbs describing how you walked.

TIPS & TRICKS

Many adverbs end in *–ly,* but others do not. Also, not all words with the *–ly* ending are adverbs. Some adjectives end in *–ly.*

ADVERBS
calmly   not
quickly soon

ADJECTIVES
curly   holy
elderly silly

To decide whether a word is an adjective or an adverb, look at how the word is used in the sentence.

Reference Note
For more about **phrases,** see page 374.

Reference Note
For more about **clauses,** see page 387.

Adverbs

18b. Adverbs make the meanings of verbs, adjectives, and other adverbs more specific.

EXAMPLES   The car backfired **loudly.** [The adverb *loudly* makes the meaning of the verb *backfired* more specific.]

The painting is **quite** old. [The adverb *quite* makes the meaning of the adjective *old* more specific.]

The bear traveled **surprisingly** quickly. [The adverb *surprisingly* makes the meaning of the adverb *quickly* more specific.]

Phrases Used as Modifiers

Like one-word modifiers, phrases can also be used as adjectives and adverbs.

EXAMPLES   The cat **with the short tail** is my favorite. [The prepositional phrase *with the short tail* acts as an adjective that modifies the noun *cat.*]

Mr. Rodriguez planted the new bushes **along the fence.** [The prepositional phrase *along the fence* acts as an adverb that modifies the verb *planted.*]

Clauses Used as Modifiers

Like words and phrases, clauses can also be used as modifiers.

EXAMPLES   Spaghetti is the food **that I like best.** [The adjective clause *that I like best* modifies the noun *food.*]

Before Mario went downstairs, he washed his face and hands. [The adverb clause *Before Mario went downstairs* modifies the verb *washed.*]

Exercise 1   Identifying Modifiers as Adjectives or Adverbs

Tell whether the italicized word or word group in each of the following sentences is used as an *adjective* or an *adverb*. Then, identify the word that it modifies.

EXAMPLE   1. Ms. Olivarez is the woman *on the left.*
           1. adjective—*woman*

MINI-LESSON

Using Commas Correctly. Tell students to use commas to set off nonessential clauses, but not essential ones.

My oldest brother, **who is in college,** is studying chemistry. [*nonessential clause*]

The car **that Mom bought** is in excellent condition. [*essential clause*]

For more information on punctuating nonessential elements, see **Chapter 21.**

Using Modifiers Correctly

1. The squirrel <u>darted</u> *quickly* up the tree trunk and hid among the leaves.   1. adv.
2. Wang Wei was a talented <u>painter</u> *of landscapes*.   2. adj.
3. Gabriela can ski <u>faster</u> *than I can*.   3. adv.
4. Is *this* <u>poem</u> the one that you wrote?   4. adj.
5. The <u>man</u> *who has curly hair* is my Uncle Thaddeus.   5. adj.
6. *Soon* you <u>will need</u> to put the bread in the oven.   6. adv.
7. *Before the performance* the actors <u>practiced</u> their lines and gestures.   7. adv.
8. Mountain biking is the <u>sport</u> *that I enjoy most*.   8. adj.
9. Tasmania is an <u>island</u> *off the coast of Australia*.   9. adj.
10. *Because the weather was hot*, we <u>sat</u> with our feet in the stream.   10. adv.

Comparison of Adjectives and Adverbs

When adjectives and adverbs are used in comparisons, they take different forms. The specific form they take depends upon how many things are being compared. The different forms of comparison are called **degrees of comparison.**

18c. The three degrees of comparison of modifiers are the *positive*, the *comparative*, and the *superlative*.

(1) The *positive degree* is used when only one thing is being modified and no comparison is being made.

EXAMPLES   *Felita* is a **good** book.

Shawn runs **quickly.**

The horse jumped **gracefully.**

(2) The *comparative degree* is used when two things are being compared.

EXAMPLES   In my opinion, *Nilda* is a **better** book than *Felita*.

Juanita runs **more quickly** than Shawn.

Which of the two horses jumped **more gracefully**?

TIPS & TRICKS

Here is a way to remember which form of a modifier to use. When comparing two things, use *–er* (the two-letter ending). When comparing three or more things, use *–est* (the three-letter ending).

Comparison of Adjectives and Adverbs   **497**

Comparison of Adjectives and Adverbs

Rule 18c *(pp. 497–502)*

OBJECTIVES

- To write the comparative and superlative forms of modifiers
- To use regular and irregular comparative and superlative forms of modifiers correctly in sentences

TEACHING TIP

Activity. Have students practice the use of the positive, comparative, and superlative forms of modifiers by having them describe a character from a popular television program. Then, have students suggest five adjectives that apply to the character. Finally, ask volunteers to write sentences that use each adjective in its comparative and superlative forms by comparing the character to other characters on the program. [*Sample answers:* taller than Bob, more talkative than Julie, prettiest of all]

RESOURCES

Comparison of Adjectives and Adverbs
Practice

- *Grammar, Usage, and Mechanics,* pp. 176, 177, 178–179, 180–181
- *Language Workshop CD-ROM,* Lesson 20

TEACHING TIP

Mnemonic. Suggest a mnemonic device for the comparative and superlative degrees. Point out that the comparative degree is often formed by adding two letters (*–er*) to a word and is used when two objects are compared. The superlative degree adds three letters (*–est*) and is used when three or more objects are compared.

Meeting INDIVIDUAL NEEDS

MODALITIES
Visual Learners. You can help students understand the difference between the comparative and superlative degrees by letting them make comparisons using tangible objects. Bring to class a grape, a lemon, and a large orange. Working with students in a small group, ask them to tell which is the biggest [*orange*]. Take away the orange and then ask which is bigger [*lemon*]. Explain that *biggest* is used when there are three or more objects and that *bigger* is used when there are only two.

 STYLE TIP

In conversation you may hear such expressions as *Put your best foot forward.* Such uses of the superlative (to compare only two things) are acceptable in informal English. In formal speaking and writing, however, you should follow the rules in this chapter.

 STYLE TIP

Many two-syllable modifiers can form their comparative and their superlative forms either way. If adding *–er* or *–est* makes a word sound awkward, use *more* or *most* instead.

AWKWARD carefuller
  BETTER **more** careful
AWKWARD commonest
  BETTER **most common**

---

(3) The *superlative degree* is used when three or more things are being compared.

EXAMPLES *Nilda* is one of the **best** books I've read.

Which member of the team runs **most quickly**?

Regular Comparison

Most one-syllable modifiers form the comparative degree by adding *–er* and the superlative degree by adding *–est*.

Positive	Comparative	Superlative
near	near**er**	near**est**
sad	sadd**er**	sadd**est**
cute	cut**er**	cut**est**
bright	bright**er**	bright**est**

Two-syllable modifiers can form the comparative degree by adding *–er* or by using *more*. They can form the superlative degree by adding *–est* or by using *most*.

Positive	Comparative	Superlative
fancy	fanci**er**	fanci**est**
lonely	loneli**er**	loneli**est**
cheerful	**more** cheerful	**most** cheerful
quickly	**more** quickly	**most** quickly

 NOTE When you add *–er* or *–est* to some modifiers, you may also need to change the spelling of the base word.

EXAMPLES sad   **sadd**er   **sadd**est
[The final *d* is doubled.]

cute   **cut**er   **cut**est
[The final *e* is dropped.]

fancy   **fanci**er   **fanci**est
[The final *y* is changed to *i*.]

Modifiers that have three or more syllables form the comparative degree by using *more* and the superlative degree by using *most*.

Positive	Comparative	Superlative
difficult	**more** difficult	**most** difficult
interesting	**more** interesting	**most** interesting
skillfully	**more** skillfully	**most** skillfully

Decreasing Comparison

To show a decrease in the qualities they express, modifiers form the comparative degree by using *less* and the superlative degree by using *least*.

Positive	Comparative	Superlative
clean	**less** clean	**least** clean
humorous	**less** humorous	**least** humorous
carefully	**less** carefully	**least** carefully

Exercise 2 Writing Comparative and Superlative Forms

Give the comparative forms and the superlative forms for each of the following modifiers.

EXAMPLES
1. calm
1. calmer, calmest; less calm, least calm

2. happy
2. happier, happiest; less happy, least happy

1. nervous
2. great
3. hot
4. funny
5. noisy
6. easily
7. poor
8. young
9. swiftly
10. intelligent
11. politely
12. efficient
13. old
14. thoughtfully
15. sweet
16. angrily
17. ancient
18. neatly
19. lovely
20. long

—HELP—

A dictionary will tell you when a word forms its comparative or superlative form in some way other than just by adding *–er* or *–est* or *more* or *most*.

Be sure to look in a dictionary if you are not sure whether a word has irregular comparative or superlative forms.

A dictionary will also tell you if you need to double a final consonant (or otherwise change the spelling of a word) before adding *–er* or *–est*.

Reference Note
For more about **how to spell words when adding –er or –est,** see page 619.

—HELP—

Some words in Exercise 2 may have more than one acceptable comparative and superlative form. You need to give only one comparative and one superlative form for each item.

Comparison of Adjectives and Adverbs **499**

TEACHING TIP

Activity. When adjectives end in *e* (as in the **Exercise 3** example), tell students to drop the *e* before adding the comparative or superlative ending. You can help your students arrive at this rule inductively by asking them to write the comparative and superlative forms for the following words on the chalkboard.

1. large [*larger, largest*]
2. close [*closer, closest*]
3. rare [*rarer, rarest*]
4. wide [*wider, widest*]

USAGE

HELP

In Exercise 3, do not use decreasing comparisons.

1. nearest
2. closest
3. brighter
4. smaller
5. more difficult
6. more common
7. more frequently
8. bigger
9. more quickly
10. more slowly

Exercise 3 Using Comparative and Superlative Forms Correctly in Sentences

Give the correct form of the italicized modifier for each blank in the following sentences.

EXAMPLE   1. *large*   As the illustration below shows, the moon appears ____ during the full-moon phase.

   1. largest   Answers may vary slightly.

1. *near*   The moon is the earth's ____ neighbor in space.
2. *close*   At its ____ point to the earth, the moon is 221,456 miles away.
3. *bright*   Seen from the earth, the full moon is ____ than the new moon.
4. *small*   The moon appears ____ during the crescent phase than at other times.
5. *difficult*   It is ____ to see the new moon than the crescent moon.
6. *common*   The word *crescent* is ____ than the word *gibbous*, which means "partly rounded."
7. *frequently* We notice the moon ____ when it is full than when it is new.
8. *big*   Do you know why the moon appears ____ on some nights than on others?
9. *quickly*   The changes in the moon's appearance take place because the moon travels ____ around the earth than the earth travels around the sun.
10. *slowly*   The moons of some other planets move ____ than our moon.

500   Chapter 18   Using Modifiers Correctly

Irregular Comparison

Some modifiers do not form their comparative and superlative degrees by using the regular methods.

Positive	Comparative	Superlative
good	better	best
well	better	best
bad	worse	worst
many	more	most
much	more	most

NOTE You do not need to add *–er/–est, more/most,* or *less/least* to an irregular comparison. For example, *worse,* all by itself, is the comparative form of *bad. Worser* and *more worse* are nonstandard forms.

Exercise 4 Using Irregular Comparative and Superlative Forms

Give the correct form of the italicized modifier for each blank in the following sentences.

EXAMPLE 1. *many* Let's see which of the two teams can wash ____ cars.

1. more

1. *bad* This is the ____ cold I have ever had.
2. *much* We have ____ homework now than we had last year.
3. *well* Derrick feels ____ today than he did last night.
4. *good* This peach has a ____ flavor than that one.
5. *well* Of all the instruments he can play, Shen Li plays the banjo ____.
6. *much* Catherine ate ____ enchilada casserole on Monday than she had eaten on Sunday.
7. *many* Of all the volunteers, Doreen has collected the ____ donations for the animal shelter.
8. *bad* Our team played the ____ game in history.
9. *good* The judges will now award the prize for the ____ essay.

1. worst
2. more
3. better
4. better
5. best
6. more
7. most
8. worst
9. best

COMPUTER TIP

A computer can help you find and correct problems with modifiers. A spell-checker will highlight nonstandard forms such as *worser, bestest,* and *gracefuller.*

However, the computer cannot tell you that you have used the superlative form where you should have used the comparative. You will have to look carefully for such errors when you proofread your writing.

Comparison of Adjectives and Adverbs 501

10. more	10. many	I have ___ baseball cards than John does.
11. best	11. good	Who is the ___ Japanese chef in town?
12. most	12. much	Of all the ranchers, she knows the ___ about lambs and sheep.
13. worst	13. bad	Wow! That was the ___ storm I have ever seen.
14. better	14. well	I think that another variety of blackberry might grow ___ than these do.
15. most	15. many	Who got the ___ signatures for the petition?
16. best	16. well	In my opinion, out of all the artists in the world, these Chinese masters paint landscapes ___.
17. worse	17. bad	Traffic is always ___ at this time of day than at any other time.
18. more	18. many	This year, ___ people attended the ceremony at the reservation than last year.
19. best	19. good	Of the book, the movie, and the play, which was ___?
20. more	20. much	Of these two containers, which holds ___ juice?

Special Problems in Using Modifiers

18d. The modifiers *good* and *well* have different uses.

(1) Use *good* to modify a noun or a pronoun.

EXAMPLES   The farmers had a **good** crop this year. [The adjective *good* modifies the noun *crop*.]

The book was **better** than the movie. [The adjective *better* modifies the noun *book*.]

Of all the players, she is the **best** one. [The adjective *best* modifies the pronoun *one*.]

Reference Note
For more about **standard usage**, see page 519.

Good should not be used to modify a verb.

NONSTANDARD   N. Scott Momaday writes good.
STANDARD   N. Scott Momaday writes **well**.

(2) Use *well* to modify a verb.

EXAMPLES   The day started **well**. [The adverb *well* modifies the verb *started*.]

502   Chapter 18   Using Modifiers Correctly

The team played **better** in the second half. [The adverb *better* modifies the verb *played*.]

Tina Thompson played **best** in the final game. [The adverb *best* modifies the verb *played*.]

Well can also mean "in good health." When *well* has this meaning, it acts as an adjective.

EXAMPLE   Does Sherry feel **well** today? [The adjective *well* modifies the noun *Sherry*.]

18e. Use adjectives, not adverbs, after linking verbs.

Linking verbs, such as *look, feel, seem,* and *become,* are often followed by predicate adjectives. These adjectives describe, or modify, the subject.

EXAMPLES   Mayor Rodríguez should feel **confident** [not *confidently*] about this election. [The predicate adjective *confident* modifies the subject *Mayor Rodríguez*.]

Did Chris seem **sad** [not *sadly*] to you? [The predicate adjective *sad* modifies the subject *Chris*.]

Exercise 5 Choosing Correct Modifiers After Linking Verbs and Action Verbs

Choose the correct modifier of the two in parentheses in each of the following sentences.

EXAMPLE   1. Ellen said that Murray's matzo ball soup tasted (*delicious, deliciously*).
           1. delicious

1. The band became (*nervous, nervously*) before the show.
2. You may get a higher score if you remain (*calm, calmly*) while taking the test.
3. We (*eager, eagerly*) tasted the potato pancakes.
4. Cheryl sews (*good, well*), so she made all the puppets for the show.
5. The mariachi band appeared (*sudden, suddenly*) at our table.
6. Ooh, these wild strawberries taste (*good, well*).
7. The plums tasted (*sour, sourly*).
8. Mr. Duncan was looking (*close, closely*) at my essay.

HELP
Some linking verbs can also be used as action verbs. As action verbs, they may be modified by adverbs.

LINKING VERB
Jeanette looked **alert** [not *alertly*] during the game. [*Alert* modifies the subject *Jeanette*.]

ACTION VERB
Jeanette looked **alertly** around the gym. [*Alertly* modifies the verb *looked*.]

Reference Note
For more about **linking verbs,** see page 351.

TEACHING TIP

Exercise 5   You may wish to use the first five items in **Exercise 5** as guided practice and have students complete the exercise as independent practice.

Timesaver

If you have students complete **Exercise 5** orally, you can add variety by asking the student who answers the first item to call on someone for the second item, that person to call on someone else for the third, and so on.

Exercise 5

ALTERNATIVE LESSON
To review verbs, you might want students to identify linking and action verbs in the designated sentences.

5. appeared—action verb

7. tasted—linking verb

If some students are having problems, you might want the class to review the sections on action and linking verbs on pp. 350–353 in **Chapter 12**.

TEACHING TIP

Activity. Linking verbs that are forms of the verb *be* are relatively easy to identify, but some others may not be. You can point out to your students that a verb is a linking verb if the word *seem* can be substituted for it without significantly changing the meaning of the sentence. For example, one could change *This milk tastes sour* to *This milk seems sour*. *Tastes* is therefore a linking verb.

9. Those trophies certainly look (*good, well*) up there, Piper.
10. The bicyclist looked (*cautious, cautiously*) both ways before crossing the street.
11. Adobe, dried mud brick, stands up (*good, well*) under the hot Southwestern sun.
12. Peg looked at her broken skate (*anxious, anxiously*).
13. Don't you think vanilla smells as (*good, well*) as or better than those expensive perfumes?
14. Akira Kurosawa was (*good, well*) at making Shakespeare's plays into movies.
15. Sylvia certainly looked (*pretty, prettily*) in her new outfit.
16. Even for beginners, green beans grow (*good, well*), and quickly, too.
17. We didn't know that you could vault so (*good, well*).
18. Erica was (*happy, happily*) to help us.
19. Oh, you are too (*good, well*) at chess for me.
20. Some tropical fish don't get along very (*good, well*) with each other.

18f. Avoid using double comparisons.

A **double comparison** is the use of both *–er* and *more* (or *less*) or both *–est* and *most* (or *least*) to form a single comparison. When you make a comparison, use only one of these forms, not both.

NONSTANDARD	That was Salma Hayek's most scariest role.
STANDARD	That was Salma Hayek's **scariest** role.
NONSTANDARD	The kitten is less livelier than the puppy.
STANDARD	The kitten is **less lively** than the puppy.

NOTE Remember that irregular comparisons do not use *–er/–est*, *more/most* or *less/least*. Adding these to an irregular modifier is a double comparison.

NONSTANDARD	more better
STANDARD	**better**
NONSTANDARD	worstest
STANDARD	**worst**

Exercise 6 Revising Double Comparisons

Each of the following sentences contains a double comparison. Identify the ~~double comparison~~, and then write the correct form of each comparison.

EXAMPLE 1. Are you feeling more better now?
            1. more better—better

1. That must be the ~~bestest~~ song you've written yet!
2. Hit the ball ~~less harder~~ next time.
3. Dates are one of the ~~most popularest~~ foods in Africa and Asia.
4. Nicki, this was the ~~most liveliest~~ party ever.
5. The ancient Chinese made paper ~~more earlier~~ than any other people.
6. Yikes, this computer game is the ~~most hardest~~ one I've played.
7. The ~~least jolliest~~ of the characters was Jo.
8. Sure, I think Spanish is ~~more easier~~ to learn than English.
9. Please do visit us ~~more oftener~~.
10. Maybe Friday will arrive ~~more sooner~~ this week.

1. best
2. less hard
3. most popular
4. liveliest
5. earlier
6. hardest
7. least jolly
8. easier
9. more often
10. sooner

Review A Writing Comparative and Superlative Forms in Sentences

For each blank in the following sentences, give the correct form of comparison of the italicized word.

EXAMPLE 1. *noisy*   This is the ____ class in school.
            1. noisiest

1. *bad* Yesterday was the ____ day of my entire life.
2. *good* Tomorrow should be ____ than today was.
3. *old* The ____ American Indian tepee in the world can be seen at the Smithsonian Institution.
4. *soon* Your party ended ____ than I had hoped.
5. *funny* That is the ____ joke I've ever heard.
6. *rapidly* Which can run ____, the cheetah or the lion?
7. *beautifully* This piñata is ____ decorated than the other one.
8. *well* I did well on the first half of the test, but I did ____ on the second half.

1. worst
2. better
3. oldest
4. sooner
5. funniest
6. more rapidly
7. more beautifully
8. better

Meeting INDIVIDUAL NEEDS

LEARNERS HAVING DIFFICULTY
Some students might resist using standard forms in spoken language because of peer pressure. Point out to these students that casual speech among peers and formal English are different forms of communication. Students can express themselves one way with friends and a different way in class.

MULTIPLE INTELLIGENCES
Intrapersonal Intelligence. Have each student write a paragraph describing significant events or important people in their lives. (Tell students they need not write anything they do not want to share with you.) As students write, tell them to pay close attention to comparative forms. When students are finished, have them circle and identify all the comparisons in their paragraphs. Score each correct comparison 1 point; for each use of a double comparison, score 0.

USAGE

9. *joyfully* Of all the songbirds in our yard, the mockingbirds sing ____.

10. *strange* This is the ____ book I have ever read!

9. most joyfully
10. strangest

Review B Proofreading a Paragraph for Correct Forms of Modifiers

Most of the sentences in the following paragraph have errors in English usage. If a sentence contains an error, identify the error and then write the correct usage. If a sentence is already correct, write *C*.

EXAMPLE [1] You may not recognize the man in the picture on the left, but you probably know his more famous characters.

1. more famous—most famous

[1] This man, Alexandre Dumas, wrote two of the most popularest books in history—*The Three Musketeers* and *The Count of Monte Cristo*. [2] Born in France, Dumas was poor but had a good education. [3] As a young playwright, he rose quick to fame. [4] In person, Dumas always seemed cheerfully. [5] Like their author, his historical novels are colorful and full of adventure. [6] Their fame grew rapid, and the public demanded more of them. [7] In response to this demand, Dumas hired many assistants, who probably wrote most of his

Link to Literature

1. popular
2. C
3. quickly
4. cheerful
5. C
6. rapidly
7. more

506 Chapter 18 Using Modifiers Correctly

later books than he did. [8] Dumas's son, who was also named Alexandre, was a writer, too, and he became ~~famously~~ with the publication of *Camille*. [9] At that time, the younger Dumas was often thought of as a ~~more~~ better writer than his father. [10] Today, however, the friendship of the three musketeers remains ~~aliver~~ than ever in film, print, and even comic books.

8. famous

10. more alive

Double Negatives

Negative words are a common part of everyday speaking and writing. These words include the modifiers *no*, *not*, *never*, and *hardly*. Notice how negative words change the meaning of the following sentences.

POSITIVE   We can count in Spanish.
NEGATIVE   We can**not** count in Spanish.

POSITIVE   They ride their bikes on the highway.
NEGATIVE   They **never** ride their bikes on the highway.

Common Negative Words			
barely	never	none	nothing
hardly	no	no one	nowhere
neither	nobody	not (–n't)	scarcely

18g. Avoid using double negatives.

A ***double negative*** is the use of two or more negative words to express one negative idea.

NONSTANDARD   Sheila did not tell no one her idea. [The negative words are *not* and *no one*.]
STANDARD   Sheila did **not** tell anyone her idea.
STANDARD   Sheila told **no one** her idea.

NONSTANDARD   Rodney hardly said nothing. [The negative words are *hardly* and *nothing*.]
STANDARD   Rodney **hardly** said anything.
STANDARD   Rodney said almost **nothing**.

STYLE TIP

Some fiction writers use double negatives in dialogue. This technique can help make certain characters sound more realistic. However, in your formal speaking and writing, you should avoid using double negatives.

Double Negatives
Rule 18g *(pp. 507–509)*

OBJECTIVE

■ To revise sentences by eliminating double negatives

Meeting INDIVIDUAL NEEDS

ENGLISH-LANGUAGE LEARNERS
General Strategies. Some students who use double negatives in speech may be curious about why they should avoid them. You can point out that double negatives may be encountered in informal, everyday speech, but that they're incorrect in formal speech and writing because if read literally, they express the opposite meaning from the meaning intended [*I don't know nothing* means "I know something."] Also, double negatives can sometimes be confusing to careful readers.

RESOURCES

Double Negatives
Practice
■ *Grammar, Usage, and Mechanics*, p. 185
■ *Language Workshop CD-ROM*, Lesson 21

USAGE

Relating to Literature

Sometimes authors of stories use double negatives on purpose to give a special flavor to their writing. Ask your students to read the Uncle Remus tale "He Lion, Bruh Bear, and Bruh Rabbit," as retold by Virginia Hamilton (or any of the other Uncle Remus tales of Joel Chandler Harris). As the students read, ask them to make note of the double negatives the narrator and the characters use. What effects do the double negatives have? [*They make the story seem more like a tale that a person is telling orally, and they reflect the speech of the characters in the story.*]

HELP
Some double negatives in Exercise 7 may be corrected in more than one way. You need to give just one revision for each sentence.

Exercise 7 Revising Sentences to Correct Double Negatives

Revise each of the following sentences to eliminate the double negative. *Revisions may vary.*

EXAMPLE 1. Those books don't have no pictures.
   1. *Those books don't have any pictures.*
      or
      Those books have no pictures.

1. The Plains Indians did not waste ~~no~~ part of a bear, deer, or buffalo.   1. any
2. Ms. Wooster never tries ~~nothing~~ new to eat.   2. anything
3. Movie and TV stars from Hollywood never visit ~~nowhere~~ near our town.   3. anywhere
4. Until last summer, I didn't know ~~nothing~~ about Braille music notation.   4. anything
5. By Thanksgiving, the store didn't have ~~none~~ of the silver jewelry left.   5. any
6. I'm so excited that I ~~can't~~ hardly sit still.   6. can
7. No one brought ~~nothing~~ to eat on the hike.   7. anything
8. Strangely enough, Frieda hasn't ~~never~~ tasted our delicious Cuban bread.   8. ever
9. There isn't ~~no~~ more pudding in the bowl.   9. any
10. Our dog never fights with ~~neither~~ one of our cats.   10. either

HELP
Some double negatives in Review C may be corrected in more than one way. You need to give just one revision for each sentence.

Review C Proofreading Sentences for Correct Use of Modifiers

Most of the following sentences contain errors in the use of modifiers. If a sentence is incorrect, write it correctly. If a sentence is already correct, write *C*.

EXAMPLE 1. Haven't you never made a paper airplane or a paper hat?
   1. *Haven't you ever made a paper airplane or a paper hat?*
      or
      Have you never made a paper airplane or a paper hat?

Chapter 18 Using Modifiers Correctly

1. Making Japanese origami figures is much ~~more~~ easier than I thought it would be.   Answers may vary.
2. Origami, the ancient Japanese art of paper folding, ~~wasn't hardly known~~ in the United States before the 1960s.   2. was hardly known
3. Now, many people know how to fold the ~~most~~ cleverest traditional origami animals.
4. In true origami, artists ~~do not never~~ cut or paste the paper.   4. do not ever
5. A beginner doesn't need ~~nothing~~ but a sheet of paper to create an origami figure.   5. anything
6. With a bit of patience, anyone can make a folded-paper figure rather ~~quick~~.   6. quickly
7. Even kindergartners can do a good job making the simple sailboat shown in the diagram.   7. C
8. Other origami figures require ~~more~~ greater time and patience than this sailboat.
9. Today, there probably ~~isn't no one~~ better at origami than Akira Yoshizawa.   9. isn't anyone
10. Even the most difficult figure is not too hard for him, and he has invented many beautiful new figures.   10. C

Placement of Modifiers

18h. Place modifying words, phrases, and clauses as close as possible to the words they modify.

Notice how the meaning of the following sentences changes when the position of the phrase *from Brazil* changes.

> The singer **from Brazil** gave a radio interview for her fans. [The phrase modifies *singer*.]
>
> The singer gave a radio interview for her fans **from Brazil**. [The phrase modifies *fans*.]
>
> **From Brazil,** the singer gave a radio interview for her fans. [The phrase modifies *gave*.]

A modifier that seems to modify the wrong word in a sentence is called a *misplaced modifier*.

Placement of Modifiers   **509**

Placement of Modifiers

Rule 18h *(pp. 509–514)*

OBJECTIVES

- To correct misplaced prepositional phrases
- To correct misplaced adjective clauses

RESOURCES
Placement of Modifiers
Practice
- *Grammar, Usage, and Mechanics,* pp. 186, 187, 188, 189–190

Adjectives and Adverbs

The placement of an adjective or adverb may affect the meaning of a sentence. Avoid placing an adjective or adverb so that it appears to modify a word that you didn't mean it to modify.

EXAMPLES Jackie borrowed some camping equipment **only** for the weekend. [She borrowed the equipment for the weekend, not for any other time.]

Only Jackie borrowed some camping equipment for the weekend. [Jackie—and no one else—borrowed some equipment.]

Jackie borrowed **only** some camping equipment for the weekend. [She borrowed some camping equipment but nothing else.]

Nearly all of the skaters fell. [Most of the skaters fell.]

All of the skaters **nearly** fell. [All of the skaters came close to falling but did not fall.]

Today Randall said he would help me build a birdhouse. [Randall made the statement today.]

Randall said he would help me build a birdhouse **today**. [Randall will help with the birdhouse today.]

Prepositional Phrases

Reference Note
For more information about **prepositions** and **prepositional phrases,** see pages 360 and 361.

A *prepositional phrase* includes a preposition, the object of the preposition, and any modifiers of that object.

A prepositional phrase used as an adjective generally should be placed directly after the word it modifies.

MISPLACED Ms. Ruiz got a sweater for her dog with a snowflake pattern.

CLEAR Ms. Ruiz got a sweater **with a snowflake pattern** for her dog.

MISPLACED This book describes Nat Turner's struggle for freedom by Judith Berry Griffin.

CLEAR This book **by Judith Berry Griffin** describes Nat Turner's struggle for freedom.

A prepositional phrase used as an adverb should be placed near the word it modifies.

MISPLACED   Roberto read that some turtles can swim quite fast in a magazine.
CLEAR   Roberto read **in a magazine** that some turtles can swim quite fast.

MISPLACED   I watched a movie that George Lucas produced on Friday.
CLEAR   **On Friday,** I watched a movie that George Lucas produced.

Avoid placing a prepositional phrase where it can modify either of two words. Place the phrase so that it clearly modifies the word you intend it to modify.

MISPLACED   Cynthia Ann said after her ballet class she would take out the trash. [Does the phrase *after her ballet class* modify *said* or *would take*?]
CLEAR   Cynthia Ann said she would take out the trash **after her ballet class.** [The phrase modifies *would take*.]
CLEAR   **After her ballet class** Cynthia Ann said she would take out the trash. [The phrase modifies *said*.]

Exercise 8 Correcting Misplaced Prepositional Phrases

Find any misplaced prepositional phrases in each of the following sentences. Then, revise the sentence, placing the phrase near the word it modifies. If a sentence is already correct, write *C*. Answers may vary.

EXAMPLE   1. I read about the car thieves who were caught in this morning's paper.

1. I read in this morning's paper about the car thieves who were caught.

or

In this morning's paper, I read about the car thieves who were caught.

1. Michael went outside ˄ to trim the hedges ~~with Bruce~~.
2. ˄ I saw the ants marching ~~through my magnifying glass~~.

HELP

Some sentences in Exercise 8 may be corrected in more than one way. You need to give just one revision for each.

1. with Bruce
2. Through my magnifying glass,

Placement of Modifiers   **511**

Meeting INDIVIDUAL NEEDS

MODALITIES

Visual Learners. To help students see how the placement of modifiers can change the meaning of a sentence, you might want to have students from your class volunteer to sketch humorous scenes suggested by the example sentences that include misplaced prepositional phrases on this page. For example, a student artist might sketch a dog whose fur has snowflake patterns or turtles trying to swim in a magazine. You might want your students to sketch other scenes suggested by misplaced prepositional phrases in Exercise 8. Later, you might have them illustrate sentences with misplaced adjective clauses.

USAGE

 Learning for Life

Continued on pp. 512–513

Writing a Letter of Appreciation. Tell students that sometimes people like to write to businesses or organizations to thank or praise them for carrying a particular product or providing a valuable service. The recipients use those letters to help them determine how well they are doing their jobs. Have each student write a letter of appreciation to a local business or organization that has provided an important product or service or made a welcome change that the student likes. For example,

Placement of Modifiers   **511**

3. From Kim,
4. with the cellular telephone
5. C
6. in the pond
7. From our back windows
8. In class today
9. in Fred's living room
10. In the attic

3. Angelo borrowed a radio ~~from Kim~~ with a weather band.
4. That man bought the rare photograph of Geronimo ~~with the cellular telephone~~.
5. The robin sat carefully on the eggs in its nest.
6. The frog seemed to be staring at the moon ~~in the pond~~.
7. We could see the wheat growing ~~from our back windows~~.
8. The sound designer told us about recording a herd of gnus ~~in class today~~.
9. Many people watched the televised ballgame ~~in Fred's living room~~.
10. I found the collection of records your father bought ~~in the attic~~.

Adjective Clauses

An **adjective clause** modifies a noun or a pronoun. Most adjective clauses begin with a relative pronoun—*that, which, who, whom,* or *whose.*

Like adjective phrases, adjective clauses should generally be placed directly after the words they modify.

MISPLACED   Mrs. Chu gives the sculptures to her friends that she carves. [Does Mrs. Chu carve her friends?]

CLEAR   Mrs. Chu gives the sculptures **that she carves** to her friends.

MISPLACED   The students met with a tutor who needed help in math. [Did the tutor need help in math?]

CLEAR   The students **who needed help in math** met with a tutor.

Exercise 9 Correcting Misplaced Adjective Clauses

Find any misplaced adjective clauses in each of the following sentences. Then, revise the sentence, placing the clause near the word it modifies. If a sentence is already correct, write *C.*

EXAMPLE   1. The students wanted to work on a project at the school that they had designed themselves.

1. The students at the school wanted to work on a project that they had designed themselves.

Reference Note
For more about **adjective clauses,** see page 389.

COMPUTER TIP
A word-processing program can help you correct misplaced modifiers. First, examine all the modifying words, phrases, and clauses in your writing to make sure they are placed correctly. If you find a misplaced modifier, you can use the cut-and-paste function to place the modifier closer to the word it modifies.

HELP
Some sentences in Exercise 9 may be revised in more than one way. You need to give just one revision for each.

Learning for Life

one writer might want to thank a business for carrying a particular item of sports equipment or a musical instrument that would be otherwise hard to find. Another writer might want to praise a church or youth organization for organizing a field trip or hosting a party. If a student cannot think of a topic for a letter of appreciation, have him or her write a letter asking a business or organization to carry a particular product or provide a special service.

The letters should include reasons why a

1. The girl₍is from my class that won the spelling bee.
2. The blue jay moved carefully₍through the snow with small hops, which had begun to melt.
3. ₍I hardly recognized my uncle Ken when he came for a visit, whose beard had turned white.
4. Kwanzaa, which was first celebrated in 1966, is an African American holiday developed by Maulana Karenga.
5. The expression "that's the ticket," which means "that's the correct thing," comes from a mispronunciation of the French word *etiquette*.
6. My oldest brother₍just graduated from college, who lives in Rhode Island.
7. Jason's favorite shirt₍already has another stain on it, which was just washed.
8. That team₍played in front of a sellout crowd, which was having its best season ever.
9. "The Rum Tum Tugger,"₍is a poem about a cat, which we studied in class.
10. ₍We like to watch the many butterflies in the fields on the weekends, that are behind our house.

Answers may vary.
1. that won the spelling bee
2. with small hops
3. When he came for a visit,
4. C
5. C
6. , who lives in Rhode Island,
7. , which was just washed,
8. , which was having its best season ever,
9. which we studied in class,
10. On the weekends,

Review D — Proofreading a Paragraph for Correct Placement of Modifiers

Most of the following sentences have misplaced modifying words, phrases, or clauses. If the sentence contains an error, revise the sentence by placing the modifier in the correct place. If the sentence is already correct, write *C*.

EXAMPLE [1] Sometimes the person can be a hero who seems least likely.

1. *Sometimes the person who seems least likely can be a hero.*

[1] J.R.R. Tolkien's *The Hobbit* is a wonderful story that has a very complicated adventure about a simple person. [2] Hobbits are very small, quiet people, and most of the world had never heard of them until a few of them began to have adventures. [3] The hero of the story, Bilbo Baggins, is not a typical hero, who likes nothing more than chatting with his neighbors, sleeping, and eating. [4] Bilbo's quiet life is

HELP
Some sentences in Review D may be correctly revised in more than one way. You need to give just one revision for each.

Link to Literature

Review D — Proofreading a Paragraph for Correct Placement of Modifiers

ANSWERS
Revisions may vary.

1. J.R.R. Tolkien's *The Hobbit* is a wonderful story about a simple person who has a very complicated adventure.
2. C
3. The hero of the story, Bilbo Baggins, who likes nothing more than chatting with his neighbors, sleeping, and eating, is not a typical hero.

Review D Proofreading a Paragraph for Correct Placement of Modifiers

ANSWERS continued
Revisions may vary.

4. Bilbo's quiet life is interrupted when the wizard Gandalf chooses him to help a band of dwarves recover their treasure from a dragon.
5. Despite being small and shy, Bilbo saves the dwarves several times on their way to their old home under the Lonely Mountain.
6. Along the way, Bilbo also finds a magical ring that can make him invisible.
7. With the ring and the wizard Gandalf, Bilbo gets the dwarves out of trouble.
8. When they finally reach the mountain, Bilbo tricks the dragon Smaug into revealing a weak spot in his armor.
9. The dragon is very angry and attacks a nearby town, but an archer who has been told about the weak spot kills Smaug.
10. In *The Lord of the Rings,* Bilbo goes back to his quiet life, but his nephew Frodo inherits the ring and saves the world.

---

interrupted when the wizard Gandalf chooses him to help a band of dwarves from a dragon recover their treasure. [5] Bilbo saves the dwarves several times on their way to their old home under the Lonely Mountain, despite being small and shy. [6] Bilbo also finds a magical ring along the way that can make him invisible. [7] Bilbo gets the dwarves out of trouble with the ring and the wizard Gandalf. [8] When they finally reach the mountain, Bilbo tricks the dragon Smaug into revealing a spot in his armor that is weak. [9] The dragon is very angry and attacks a nearby town, but an archer kills Smaug, who has been told about the weak spot. [10] Bilbo goes back to his quiet life, but in *The Lord of the Rings* his nephew Frodo inherits the ring and saves the world.

CHAPTER 18

Chapter Review

A. Identifying the Correct Forms of Modifiers

Choose the correct form of the modifier in parentheses in each of the following sentences.

1. Cool water tastes (*good*, *well*) on a hot day.
2. The wind howled (*fierce*, *fiercely*) last night.
3. Which twin is (*taller*, *tallest*), Marcus or Jim?
4. *Forever Friends* is the (*best*, *bestest*) book I've read this year.
5. Sergio has always played (*good*, *well*) during an important match.
6. The roses in the vase smelled (*sweet*, *sweetly*).
7. They could view the eclipse (*more clear*, *more clearly*) than we could.
8. Which of these two winter coats is the (*best*, *better*) value?
9. Of all the days in the week, Friday goes by (*more*, *most*) slowly for me.
10. Ernesto felt (*good*, *well*) about volunteering to help collect money for the homeless.
11. Is this the (*darkest*, *darker*) copy of the three?
12. The (*faster*, *fastest*) runner is the captain of the track team.
13. Mr. Chen told them to be (*better*, *more better*) prepared tomorrow.
14. Joni's way of solving the math puzzle was much (*more easier*, *easier*) than Ken's.
15. We felt (*sleepy*, *sleepily*) after lunch.

B. Correcting Double Negatives

Most of the following sentences contain errors in the use of negative words. If the sentence is incorrect, write it correctly. If the sentence is already correct, write *C*.   Answers may vary.

16. None of us knows ~~nothing~~ about astronomy.   **16.** anything
17. Wendell can hardly wait to see Serge Laîné in concert.   **17.** C
18. Kathy ~~hasn't never~~ heard of the Romanovs.   **18.** has never

---

HELP

In some cases, a double negative can be corrected in more than one way. However, you need to give only one revision for each sentence in Part B.

Using the Chapter Review

To assess student progress, you may want to compare the types of items missed on the **Diagnostic Preview** to those missed on the **Chapter Review**. If students have not made significant progress, you may want to refer them to **Chapter 24: Correcting Common Errors, Exercises 16–18** for additional practice.

19. could
20. any

19. Last night we ~~couldn't~~ see no stars through the telescope. [could]
20. Whenever I want fresh strawberries, there are never ~~none~~ in the house. [any]

C. Writing Comparative and Superlative Forms

Write the comparative and superlative forms for each of the following modifiers.

21. difficult   26. good
22. new   27. light
23. quickly   28. short
24. cold   29. clearly
25. fantastic   30. noisy

HELP — Remember to include forms showing decreasing comparison in your answers to Part C.

Chapter Review

C. Writing Comparative and Superlative Forms

ANSWERS

21. more difficult, most difficult; less difficult, least difficult
22. newer, newest; less new, least new
23. more quickly, most quickly; less quickly, least quickly
24. colder, coldest; less cold, least cold
25. more fantastic, most fantastic; less fantastic; least fantastic
26. better, best; less good, least good
27. lighter, lightest; less light, least light
28. shorter, shortest; less short, least short
29. more clearly, most clearly; less clearly, least clearly
30. noisier, noisiest *or* more noisy, most noisy; less noisy, least noisy

D. Correcting Misplaced Phrases and Clauses

Find any misplaced phrases and clauses in each of the following sentences. Then, revise each incorrect sentence, placing the phrase or clause near the word it modifies. **Answers may vary.**

31. On the radio
32. with the beard
33. From his friend,
34. In the backyard,
35. From our car
36. that was made of silver
37. On Tuesday
38. In the newspaper
39. At her press conference,
40. who had on the red hat

31. I heard about the bad weather ~~on the radio~~.
32. The man drove the sports car ~~with the beard~~.
33. Arthur borrowed a mountain bike ~~from his friend~~ with eighteen speeds.
34. Uncle Mark and Aunt Jennifer were watching the meteor shower ~~in the backyard~~.
35. We saw the fog rising ~~from our car~~.
36. I gave a bracelet to my friend ~~that was made of silver~~.
37. Mom saw a museum exhibit of ancient pottery made in the American Southwest ~~on Tuesday~~.
38. Una read about the latest political developments ~~in the newspaper~~.
39. The mayor said she would lead the St. Patrick's Day parade ~~at her press conference~~.
40. The woman won the CD player ~~who had on the red hat~~.

RESOURCES

Using Modifiers Correctly

Review
- *Grammar, Usage, and Mechanics,* pp. 191, 192, 193, 194, 195

Assessment
- Assessment Package
  —Chapter Tests, Ch. 18
  —Chapter Tests in Standardized Test Formats, Ch. 18
- Test Generator (One-Stop Planner CD-ROM)

Writing Application
Using Negative Words in Description

Negative Words Everyone has a bad day now and then. Yesterday, it was your turn. You were late for school because your alarm clock did not go off. From then on, things just got worse. Write a letter to a friend giving a funny description of your unlucky day. Make sure that you use negative words correctly.

Prewriting Write down some notes about a real or imaginary bad day in your life. List at least five things that went wrong during the day. The events can be big or small. Tell how you felt when one thing after another went wrong.

Writing In your letter, explain the events of your day in the order they happened. Describe each event in detail. Also describe your reactions to the events. You may want to exaggerate some details for a humorous effect.

Revising Ask a friend to read your letter. Have you described the events clearly? Do your descriptions give a vivid, humorous picture of your day? If not, add or revise details.

Publishing Be sure that your letter follows the correct form for a personal letter. Proofread your letter carefully for errors in grammar, spelling and punctuation. Read through each sentence one more time to check that negative words are used correctly. With your teacher's permission, you and your classmates may wish to present your descriptions in class and vote on who survived the worst day.

Reference Note
For information on **writing a personal letter,** see "Writing" in the Quick Reference Handbook.

Chapter Review **517**

RESOURCES
Writing Application
Extension
- *Grammar, Usage, and Mechanics,* p. 198
- *Language Workshop CD-ROM,* Lessons 20, 21

CHAPTER 19

A Glossary of Usage
Common Usage Problems

Diagnostic Preview

Correcting Errors in Usage

Each of the following sentences contains an ~~error in the use of formal, standard English~~. Rewrite each sentence correctly.

EXAMPLE 1. I knew all the answers accept the last one.
          1. *I knew all the answers except the last one.*

Answers may vary.
1. take
2. rather
3. already
4. well
5. have
6. an
7. to
8. bad
9. can't [*or* can hardly]
10. than
11.
12. their

1. If you're going to the library, would you please ~~bring~~ these books there for me?
2. The water tasted ~~kind of~~ salty.
3. Has Jamila finished the assignment ~~all ready~~?
4. Leon went to the doctor because he didn't feel ~~good~~.
5. They should ~~of~~ asked for directions.
6. We found nothing but a old shoe.
7. Bao will try ~~and~~ fix her bike today.
8. The tuna looked all right but smelled ~~badly~~.
9. Albert ~~can't hardly~~ wait to read that biography of the Olympic star Jesse Owens.
10. Why is this mitt more expensive ~~then~~ that one?
11. He knocked a bowl of plantains off ~~of~~ the table.
12. In rural Vietnam, children often take care of ~~there~~ family's water buffalo.

CHAPTER RESOURCES

Planning
- One-Stop Planner CD-ROM

Practice and Extension
- *Grammar, Usage, and Mechanics*, p. 199
- Language Workshop CD-ROM

Internet
- go.hrw.com (keyword: EOLang)

Evaluation and Assessment
- *Assessment Package*
  —*Chapter Tests*, Ch. 19
  —*Chapter Tests in Standardized Test Formats*, Ch. 19
- Test Generator (One-Stop Planner CD-ROM)

PREVIEWING THE CHAPTER

- This chapter covers usage problems, including those involving adjective and adverb selection, pronoun use, word choice, and verb selection. The chapter is arranged in a glossary format and includes several exercises for students to practice what they have learned.

- The chapter closes with a **Chapter Review** for checking students' mastery of various usage problems. A **Writing Application** feature asks students to use rules they have learned in this chapter to write an informative letter.

- For help in integrating this chapter with composition chapters, use the **Teaching Strands** chart on pp. T297A–T297B.

USING THE DIAGNOSTIC PREVIEW

- The results of the **Diagnostic Preview** will tell you which students are able to recognize and correct nonstandard usage. Some students might have trouble applying the rules from the chapter to their writing. You may want to give each student a checklist of his or her problem areas to refer to when proofreading writing assignments.

13. After school we ~~use~~ to have band practice.
14. Tanya made ~~less~~ mistakes after she had started practicing.
15. Do you know ~~who's~~ pencil this is?
16. Mr. Abeyto assigned me to this ~~here~~ seat.
17. A glitch is ~~when~~ a mistake ~~is~~ made by a computer.
18. Did Ann say ~~how come~~ she won't attend the meeting?
19. The food was shared ~~between~~ the families of the village.
20. At one time, Bessie Coleman was the only black woman pilot ~~anywheres~~ in the world.

13. used
14. fewer
15. whose

18. why
19. among
20. anywhere

About the Glossary

This chapter contains an alphabetical list, or **glossary**, of common problems in English usage. You will notice that some examples in this glossary are labeled *nonstandard, standard, formal,* or *informal.*

The label **nonstandard** identifies usage that is acceptable only in the most casual speaking situations and in writing that attempts to re-create casual speech. **Standard** English is language that is grammatically correct and appropriate in formal and informal situations. **Formal** identifies standard usage that is appropriate in serious speaking and writing situations (such as in speeches and in writing for school). The label **informal** indicates standard usage common in conversation and in everyday writing such as personal letters. When doing the exercises in this chapter, be sure to use only standard English.

The following are examples of formal and informal English.

Reference Note
For a list of **words often confused,** see page 625. Use the **index** at the back of the book to find discussions of other usage problems.

Formal	Informal
angry	steamed
unpleasant	yucky
agreeable	cool
very impressive	totally awesome
accelerate	step on it

A Glossary of Usage

A, An—How Come
(pp. 520–526)

OBJECTIVE
- To identify and correct common errors in usage

Meeting INDIVIDUAL NEEDS

ENGLISH-LANGUAGE LEARNERS

General Strategies. In presenting *a* and *an*, avoid using the terms *vowel* and *consonant*. Instead, emphasize the initial sound of the words that *a* and *an* precede so that students understand more clearly which article is appropriate. You might want to have students hold up objects and identify them by saying, "It's a/an . . . ," or you can hold up pictures from a magazine and ask students to identify the objects shown, using *a* or *an* as appropriate.

TEACHING TIP

Mnemonic. Tell students that one way to remember the difference between *accept* and *except* is by thinking of the *x* in *except* as an X-ing out, or canceling, of something. You might want to use the following example: *All of the dogs accept/except hers will eat now.* Ask students which word is appropriate. [*except*]

Mnemonic. You might want to point out that written as one word, *allright* is *all wrong*.

---

a, an Use *a* before words beginning with a consonant sound; use *an* before words beginning with a vowel sound. Keep in mind that the sound, not the actual letter, that a word begins with tells you whether *a* or *an* should be used.

EXAMPLES The airplane was parked in **a** hangar.

She lives on **a** one-way street. [*A* is used because *one* begins with a consonant sound.]

My father works in **an** office.

They arrived **an** hour early. [*An* is used because *hour* begins with a vowel sound.]

accept, except *Accept* is a verb; it means "to receive." *Except* may be used as either a verb or a preposition. When it is used as a verb, *except* means "to leave out." As a preposition, *except* means "excluding" or "but."

EXAMPLES The winners of the spelling bee proudly **accepted** their awards. [verb]

Because Josh had a sprained ankle, he was **excepted** from gym class. [verb]

All the food **except** the won-ton soup was ready. [preposition]

ain't Avoid using this word in speaking and writing; it is nonstandard English.

all right *All right* can be used as an adjective that means "satisfactory" or "unhurt." As an adverb, *all right* means "well enough." *All right* should be written as two words.

EXAMPLES This tie looks **all right** with that blue shirt. [adjective]

The baby squirrel had fallen out of its nest, but it was **all right.** [adjective]

Lorenzo and I did **all right** on the pop quiz. [adverb]

"Beats me why I ain't gettin' no better marks in English."

520 Chapter 19 A Glossary of Usage

RESOURCES

A, An–How Come

Practice
- *Grammar, Usage, and Mechanics,* pp. 200, 201
- *Language Workshop CD-ROM,* Lesson 52, 53

a lot   *A lot* should be written as two words.

EXAMPLE   I can make **a lot** of my mom's recipes.

already, all ready   *Already* means "previously." *All ready* means "completely prepared" or "in readiness."

EXAMPLES   We looked for Jay, but he had **already** left.

I had studied for two hours on Sunday night and was **all ready** for the test on Monday.

among   See **between, among.**

anyways, anywheres, everywheres, nowheres, somewheres   These words should have no final *s*.

EXAMPLE   They looked **everywhere** [not *everywheres*] for the missing puzzle piece.

at   Do not use *at* after *where*.

NONSTANDARD   Where is the Chinese kite exhibit at?

STANDARD   Where is the Chinese kite exhibit?

bad, badly   *Bad* is an adjective. It modifies nouns and pronouns. *Badly* is an adverb. It modifies verbs, adjectives, and adverbs.

EXAMPLES   The milk smelled **bad.** [The predicate adjective *bad* modifies *milk*.]

Before I took lessons, I played the piano **badly.** [The adverb *badly* modifies the verb *played*.]

between, among   Use *between* when you are referring to two things at a time even when they are part of a group consisting of more than two.

EXAMPLES   Kim got in line **between** Lee and Rene.

Be sure to weed **between** all ten rows of carrots. [Although there are ten rows of carrots, the weeding is done *between* any two of them.]

Use *among* when you are referring to a group rather than to separate individuals.

EXAMPLE   The four winners divided the prize **among** themselves.

STYLE TIP

A lot sounds vague and boring when it is used too often. When you revise your own writing, try to replace *a lot* with a more exact word or phrase whenever possible.

ORIGINAL   Ernie drinks a lot of water every day.

REVISED   Ernie drinks **at least six large glasses** of water every day.

STYLE TIP

The expression *feel badly* is common in informal English. However, in formal English you should use *feel bad*.

INFORMAL   Beth felt badly about hurting José's feelings.

FORMAL   Beth felt **bad** about hurting José's feelings.

TEACHING TIP

Activity. To inspire students to use alternatives for the overused *a lot*, bring in a copy of *An Exaltation of Larks* by James Lipton. This illustrated book lists traditional names for groups of animals, such as a "pride of lions." Lipton then coins a series of modern group names such as a "slouch of models" or a "wince of dentists." Have students work in small groups to come up with collective terms for groupings of numerous items in their world: books, teachers, homework, music videos, and so on.

Meeting INDIVIDUAL NEEDS

ENGLISH-LANGUAGE LEARNERS

General Strategies. When discussing the usage of the adjective *bad* and the adverb *badly,* you may want to list some of the verbs they frequently follow, such as *sound, feel, taste, smell,* and *look.* Write a list of such verbs on the chalkboard, emphasizing that when used to show how something is perceived, these verbs are always followed by the adjective *bad,* not the adverb *badly.* Give students extra practice by asking them to complete the following sentences with a sensory verb and adjective(s):

1. Ice-cold watermelon . . .

2. The thorn on a rosebush . . .

3. Before a thunderstorm, the sky . . .

4. The inside of a garbage dumpster usually . . .

5. During Marie's first piano lesson, her music . . .

Exercise 1
ALTERNATIVE LESSON
Before students attempt to identify the correct words or word groups in **Exercise 1,** ask them to identify the verbs in sentences 6 and 10 as linking or action verbs.
[6. *linking.* 10. *linking*]

Viewing the Art
After Supper, West Chester
About the Artist. Horace Pippin (1888–1946) loved to draw when he was young but worked at various jobs to earn his living. While serving in the infantry during World War I, he suffered a wound that caused paralysis of his right arm. Because he had very limited use of the arm, he returned to his old love, art. He would burn a design into a board with a poker that had been heated in a fire. Then, he would fill in the design with paint.

Exercise 1 Identifying Correct Usage
For each of the following sentences, choose the word or word group in parentheses that is correct according to the rules of formal, standard usage.

EXAMPLE 1. The picture on this page is titled *After Supper, West Chester,* but the scene could be almost (*anywhere, anywheres*).
   1. anywhere

1. This colorful work was painted by (*a, an*) artist named Horace Pippin, who lived from 1888 to 1946.
2. By the time Pippin was in elementary school, he was (*already, all ready*) a talented artist.
3. In fact, he had won a drawing contest and had eagerly (*accepted, excepted*) the prize, a box of crayons and a set of watercolor paints.
4. In World War I, Pippin was once caught (*among, between*) U.S. troops and the enemy.
5. During this battle (*somewheres, somewhere*) in France, Pippin's right arm—the arm he used when painting—was seriously wounded.
6. For a long time, Pippin felt quite (*bad, badly*) about his disability, but he was determined to paint again.
7. After Pippin recovered, he tried (*alot, a lot*) of new ways to paint; the most successful was to hold up his right hand with his left arm.
8. It (*ain't, is not*) surprising that one of his first paintings after the war portrayed a battle scene.
9. When Pippin painted *After Supper, West Chester,* in 1935, he was remembering the small town in Pennsylvania (*where he was born, where he was born at*).
10. I think that the painter of this peaceful scene must have felt (*all right, alright*) about his work and about himself.

Horace Pippin, *After Supper, West Chester* (1935). Collection Leon Hecht and Robert Pincus-Witten, New York. © 1991 Gridley/Graves.

bring, take   *Bring* means "to come carrying something." *Take* means "to go carrying something." Think of *bring* as related to *come* (*to*) and *take* as related to *go* (*from*).

EXAMPLES   Make sure that you **bring** your book when you come to my house.

Always remember to **take** your coat when you go outside during the winter.

could of   Do not write *of* with the helping verb *could*. Write *could have*. Also avoid *ought to of, should of, would of, might of,* and *must of.*

EXAMPLES   Yvetta wished she **could have** [not *could of*] gone to the movie Saturday night.

We **should have** [not *should of*] asked your mom for permission to go to the park.

don't, doesn't   See page 433.

everywheres   See **anyways,** etc.

except, accept   See **accept, except.**

fewer, less   *Fewer* is used with plural words. *Less* is used with singular words. *Fewer* tells "how many"; *less* tells "how much."

EXAMPLES   This road has **fewer** stoplights than any of the other roads in the county.

This road has **less** traffic than any of the other roads in the county.

good, well   *Good* is an adjective. Do not use *good* to modify a verb; use *well*, which can be used as an adverb.

NONSTANDARD   Heather sings good.

STANDARD   Heather sings **well**.

Although it is usually an adverb, *well* is also used as an adjective to mean "healthy."

EXAMPLE   Keiko went home from school today because she didn't feel **well**.

TIPS & TRICKS

Could of, should of, etc., are common errors because they are mistaken for the contractions of *could have, should have*, etc. When spoken, *could've* sounds like *could of*. The difference is hardly noticeable in speech, but it is very noticeable in writing.

TIPS & TRICKS

Use *fewer* with things that can be counted. Use *less* with things that cannot be counted.

EXAMPLE
Yolanda has (*fewer, less*) pets than Kristi does.

ASK
Can you count pets? [yes]

ANSWER
Yolanda has **fewer** pets than Kristi does.

Meeting INDIVIDUAL NEEDS

MODALITIES

Auditory Learners. You might want to have students read aloud the example sentences under *could of*. Make sure that they clearly enunciate the word *have* and that they avoid using the contractions *could've* and *should've*. Tell students that if they emphasize the word *have* when proofreading aloud, they will be less tempted to substitute *of* for *have* in their writing.

Looking at Language

Dialect. Most of the nonstandard usage studied in this chapter appears in various regional dialects. These nonstandard forms are used in such spoken sentences as "Have a apple," "She don't like spinach," and "You did good." Tell your students that standard English is the language of business, government, schools, and colleges. To succeed in any of these settings, it is essential to be fluent in standard English.

Relating to Literature

Show students that although standard English is the form used in formal writing, nonstandard English is often used to establish character in writing dialogue in works of fiction. Some selections from Mark Twain's work (such as parts of *Huckleberry Finn* or *Tom Sawyer*) can be used as examples of such writing. Read aloud some of the dialogue from the selections, and discuss with your students why Twain sometimes uses nonstandard English.

**MULTIPLE INTELLIGENCES
Musical Intelligence.** Challenge musical learners to set any of the rules on this page or any page in the chapter to music. Students may want to create rhyming couplets, use alliteration, or employ other poetic techniques. They may add examples to the rules. The only restriction is that the musical piece must teach a concept in the chapter. If there are enough students interested in this approach, suggest that they work together to create a song of several verses. You may want to record the song or songs for use in other classes.

NOTE *Feel good* and *feel well* mean different things. *Feel good* means "to feel happy or pleased." *Feel well* means "to feel healthy."

EXAMPLES I feel **good** when I'm with my friends.

Rashid had a cold, and he still doesn't feel **well**.

had of   See **of**.

had ought, hadn't ought   The verb *ought* should not be used with *had*.

NONSTANDARD   They had ought to be more careful.
STANDARD   They **ought** to be more careful.

NONSTANDARD   You hadn't ought to have said that.
STANDARD   You **oughtn't** to have said that.
or
You **shouldn't** have said that.

hardly, scarcely   *Hardly* and *scarcely* are negative words. They should not be used with other negative words to express a single negative idea.

EXAMPLES   Pedro **can** [not *can't*] **hardly** wait for the fiesta.

The sun **has** [not *hasn't*] **scarcely** shone today.

hisself, theirself, theirselves   These words are nonstandard English. Use *himself* and *themselves*.

EXAMPLES   Mr. Ogata said he would do the work **himself** [not *hisself*], I believe.

They congratulated **themselves** [not *theirselves*] on their victory.

how come   In informal English, *how come* is often used instead of *why*. In formal English, *why* is preferred.

INFORMAL   How come she can leave early?
FORMAL   **Why** can she leave early?

Exercise 2 **Identifying Correct Usage**

For each of the following sentences, choose the word or word group in parentheses that is correct according to the rules of formal, standard usage.

EXAMPLE 1. There might be (*fewer, less*) accidents if people were more alert around small children.
 1. fewer

1. Everyone knows that children are not always as careful as they (*ought, had ought*) to be.
2. However, young children (*can hardly, can't hardly*) be blamed for being curious and adventurous.
3. Just a few days ago, I was involved in a scary situation that (*could of, could have*) led to a serious accident.
4. After I (*brought, took*) my little brother Gerald home from a walk, I called my friend Susan.
5. Gerald quickly wandered off by (*hisself, himself*).
6. I don't know (*how come, why*) he always disappears when I'm on the phone.
7. I found Gerald climbing onto the stove, and in (*fewer, less*) than a second, I lifted him down.
8. I told him that he (*could have, could of*) been burned.
9. He said he would be (*good, well*) from then on.
10. Although the experience was frightening, it turned out (*good, well*).

Review A **Proofreading a Paragraph for Correct Usage**

Each of the sentences in the following paragraph has at least one error in the use of standard, formal English. Identify each error. Then, write the correct usage.

EXAMPLE [1] The game of soccer has proved to be more popular than the king of England hisself.
 1. hisself—himself

[1] Derby, England, may have been the town where soccer was first played at. [2] Sometime around the third century A.D., an early version of the game was played among two towns.

Review A — Proofreading a Paragraph for Correct Usage

ANSWERS continued

3. Anywhere
4. fewer; well
5. already
6. ought; themselves
7. all right; an
8. didn't obey *or* hardly obeyed
9. bad
10. accept

Its, It's—Them
(*pp. 526–529*)

OBJECTIVE

- To identify and correct common errors in usage

[3] ~~Anywheres~~ from fifty to several hundred people played in a match. [4] Back then, soccer had ~~less~~ rules than it does today and the participants probably didn't behave very ~~good~~. [5] By the fifteenth century, the government had ~~all ready~~ outlawed the sport. [6] The king said that young people ~~had ought~~ to be training ~~theirselves~~ in archery instead of playing soccer. [7] According to the king, archery practice was ~~alright~~ because bows and arrows could be used against ~~a~~ enemy. [8] However, many people ~~didn't hardly obey~~ the king's rule, and soccer continued to grow in popularity. [9] Perhaps later kings felt ~~badly~~ about outlawing soccer. [10] Eventually the government had to ~~except~~ that soccer had become the most popular sport in England.

its, it's   *Its* is the possessive form of the personal pronoun *it*. *Its* is used to show ownership. *It's* is a contraction of *it is* or *it has*.

EXAMPLES   The raccoon washed **its** face in the shallows of the stream. [possessive pronoun]

My grandparents have a dog; **it's** a collie. [contraction of *it is*]

It's been sunny and warm all day. [contraction of *It has*]

kind of, sort of   In informal English, *kind of* and *sort of* are often used to mean "somewhat" or "rather." In formal English, however, it is better to use *somewhat* or *rather*.

INFORMAL   That story is kind of funny.
  FORMAL   That story is **rather** funny.

learn, teach   *Learn* means "to gain knowledge." *Teach* means "to instruct" or "to show how."

EXAMPLES   The students from Vietnam are **learning** English.

Ms. Sanita is **teaching** them.

less   See **fewer, less**.

lie, lay   See page 466.

might of, must of   See **could of**.

RESOURCES

Its, It's–Them
Practice
- *Grammar, Usage, and Mechanics*, p. 202
- *Language Workshop CD-ROM*, Lesson 54

nowheres See **anyways,** etc.

of Do not use *of* with prepositions such as *inside, off,* and *outside*.

EXAMPLES Mrs. Cardona stood **outside** [not *outside of*] the office.

The child stepped **off** [not *off of*] the porch.

We heard a noise **inside** [not *inside of*] the engine.

Of is also unnecessary with *had*.

EXAMPLE If we **had** [not *had of*] known you were hungry, we would have brought some food.

Reference Note
For information on **using** *of* **with helping verbs,** see **could of,** page 523.

ought to of See **could of.**

rise, raise See page 464.

should of See **could of.**

sit, set See page 463.

somewheres See **anyways,** etc.

sort of See **kind of, sort of.**

suppose to, supposed to Do not leave the *d* off *supposed* when you write *supposed to*.

EXAMPLE They were **supposed to** [not *suppose to*] join us at the gate.

take, bring See **bring, take.**

than, then *Than* is a conjunction used in making comparisons. *Then* is an adverb meaning "next" or "after that."

EXAMPLES This cheese is tastier **than** that one.

First the phone rang, and **then** someone knocked on the door.

that there See **this here, that there.**

their, there, they're *Their* is the possessive form of *they*. It is used to show ownership. *There* is used to mean "at that place" or to begin a sentence. *They're* is a contraction of *they are*.

TIPS & TRICKS

Than helps show a contrast between two things. *Then* tells something about time. If you have trouble choosing between *than* and *then*, ask yourself whether you want to (1) show a contrast or (2) specify a time.

EXAMPLE
I think this book is more difficult (*than, then*) the other one.

CONTRAST OR TIME?
contrast [Use *than*.]

ANSWER
I think this book is more difficult **than** the other one.

A Glossary of Usage **527**

MINI-LESSON **Continued on p. 528**

Contractions. Some students might have particular difficulty in distinguishing between possessive pronouns and some contractions. You might want to refer students to the discussion of contractions in **Chapter 22: Punctuation.** Explain that a contraction is a shortened form of a word, number, or group of words. An apostrophe shows where the letters, numerals, or words have been left out. Then, have students identify the full forms of the following contractions:

Meeting INDIVIDUAL NEEDS

ENGLISH-LANGUAGE LEARNERS
General Strategies. To help students differentiate more clearly between *than* and *then*, point out that *than* always involves a comparison, for example, "Lisa is taller than Alberto." On the other hand, *then* specifies a point in time, for example, "She ate breakfast, and then she went to school."

TEACHING TIP

Mnemonic. Point out to students that they can remember that *then* is an adverb by thinking of the phrase *then is when*. This phrase can usually be used (though awkwardly) in a sentence that requires *then,* for example, "First the phone rang, and then (is when) someone knocked at the door." *Then* is an adverb; it answers the question . . . *when?*

A Glossary of Usage **527**

Meeting INDIVIDUAL NEEDS

LEARNERS HAVING DIFFICULTY
Have pairs of students create two sets of flashcards. In one set of flashcards, words and groups of words from this section should be used correctly in sentences. The backs of these cards should be labeled *Standard English*. In the second set of cards, the words, groups of words, and nonstandard constructions (such as *theirselves*) should be used in sentences that do not conform to standard English. The backs of these cards should be labeled *Nonstandard English* and, below the label, should have corrected versions of the nonstandard sentences. Have students shuffle the flashcards and then take turns quizzing each other with the cards, alternating roles after each card. Students should tell whether each sentence uses standard English and correct any sentence written in nonstandard English.

Viewing the Art

Exploring the Subject. The ancient Mayan people were experts in mathematics and developed the most advanced system of record keeping in the world at the time. They also invented and used a calendar that some experts say was very accurate. Ask students to imagine trying to write an assignment in tiny pictures.

EXAMPLES The children played happily with **their** toys. [*Their* tells whose toys.]

We are going over **there** very soon. [*There* tells where we are going.]

There are twelve members in our club. [*There* begins the sentence but does not add to the sentence's meaning.]

They're going to have a Juneteenth picnic. [*They're* is a contraction of *They are*.]

theirself, theirselves   See **hisself**, etc.

them   *Them* should not be used as an adjective. Use *the*, *these*, or *those*.

EXAMPLE   How much are **those** [not *them*] baseball cards?

Exercise 3   Identifying Correct Usage

For each of the following sentences, choose the word or word group in parentheses that is correct according to the rules of formal, standard English.

EXAMPLE   1. For years, scientists have studied Mayan writing on temples and (*inside of, inside*) caves.
1. inside

1. Some scientists are (*learning, teaching*) themselves how to understand this writing.
2. The Ancient Mayas didn't use an alphabet to write (*there, their, they're*) language.
3. Instead, they drew symbols like (*them, these*) small pictures shown at left.
4. As you can see, the sign for jaguar looked (*somewhat, sort of*) like a jaguar.
5. At times, it could be difficult to tell what a picture was (*suppose, supposed*) to represent.
6. (*Its, It's*) meaning was made clear by the use of another small symbol.
7. (*There, Their, They're*) is an example of this technique in the illustration in the middle.

Jaguar

Scarf

Lord

Man

MINI-LESSON

1. it's [*it is* or *it has*]
2. there's [*there is* or *there has*]
3. they're [*they are*]
4. who's [*who is* or *who has*]
5. you're [*you are*]

8. When a scarf symbol was added to the symbol for man, (*then, than*) the picture meant "lord."
9. Mayan writing contained other symbols that stood for syllables rather (*then, than*) entire words.
10. (*Its, It's*) clear we still have a great deal to learn about this beautiful, ancient language.

Review B **Identifying Correct Usage**

Choose the correct word or words in parentheses in each of the following sentences.

EXAMPLE 1. Our club will (*accept, except*) anyone interested in computers.
1. accept

1. Well, I (*should of, should have*) seen that coming.
2. Few chiefs were more powerful (*than, then*) Sitting Bull.
3. Maybe this dog can't find (*its, it's*) way home.
4. You didn't do too (*bad, badly*) in that last race.
5. David sings pretty (*good, well*), doesn't he?
6. Thanks, you've been (*a lot, alot*) of help!
7. We (*had ought, ought*) to plant our garden next week.
8. That book has (*all ready, already*) been checked out.
9. The lenses were dirty, but (*their, there, they're*) clean now.
10. Would you (*learn, teach*) us how to use those castanets?

this here, that there   Do not use *here* and *there* after *this* and *that*.

EXAMPLE   Do you want **this** [not *this here*] book or **that** [not *that there*] one?

try and   In informal English, *try and* is often used for *try to*. In formal English, the correct form is *try to*.

INFORMAL   Pat will try and explain the problem.
  FORMAL   Pat will **try to** explain the problem.

use to, used to   Do not leave the *d* off *used* when you write *used to*.

EXAMPLE   Dr. Chang **used to** [not *use to*] live next door to us.

RESOURCES

This Here, That There–Your, You're
Practice
- *Grammar, Usage, and Mechanics,* pp. 203, 204
- *Language Workshop CD-ROM,* Lesson 54

Relating to Writing

You might want to have students review pieces of writing from their portfolios, identifying and correcting any of the common errors in usage listed in this chapter.

Timesaver

To save time as you write the answers to **Exercise 4** on the chalkboard, you could have students exchange papers and check each other's answers.

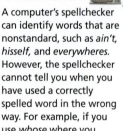

COMPUTER TIP

A computer's spellchecker can identify words that are nonstandard, such as *ain't, hisself,* and *everywheres.* However, the spellchecker cannot tell you when you have used a correctly spelled word in the wrong way. For example, if you use *whose* where you should use *who's,* the computer probably will not find the error. Always proofread your writing carefully to correct such errors in usage.

way, ways   Use *way,* not *ways,* when referring to a distance.

EXAMPLE   We traveled a long **way** [not *ways*] today.

well   See **good, well.**

when, where   Do not use *when* or *where* incorrectly to begin a definition.

NONSTANDARD   A phrase is when a group of words is used as a part of speech.

STANDARD   A phrase is a group of words that is used as a part of speech.

Do not use *where* for *that.*

EXAMPLE   I read **that** [not *where*] the concert has been canceled.

whose, who's   *Whose* is the possessive form of *who.* It shows ownership. *Who's* is a contraction of *who is* or *who has.*

EXAMPLES   **Whose** dog is that? [possessive pronoun]

Who's [*Who is*] the bravest person you know?

He's the only one **who's** [*who has*] turned in a report.

would of   See **could of.**

your, you're   *Your* is the possessive form of *you. You're* is the contraction of *you are.*

EXAMPLES   Do you have **your** watch with you? [possessive pronoun]

You're late today. [contraction of *you are*]

Exercise 4   **Identifying Correct Usage**

For each of the following sentences, choose the <u>word or word group in parentheses that is correct</u> according to the rules of formal, standard English.

EXAMPLE   1. Take a map on (*your, you're*) next camping trip.
1. *your*

1. A trail map is (*when a map shows,* <u>*a map that shows*</u>) trails, campsites, and geographical features for a given area.

530   Chapter 19   A Glossary of Usage

Learning for Life   **Continued on pp. 531–532**

Giving Directions. Tell students they will be writing directions that tell a friend how to get from school to a chosen place. To make sure their directions are clear and specific, have students model their directions on the following sentence: "When you get to the corner, a blue house will be on your right." In addition, the directions should answer the following kinds of questions:

- Are there key landmarks along the way, such as big trees or buildings? What

2. For a safe camping trip, a map like (*this here, this*) one can be very important.
3. Hikers who are not (*used to, use to*) an area often easily lose their way.
4. Every year, rangers report (*where, that*) some campers were lost for a day or more.
5. If you don't want to get lost, (*try and, try to*) get a good trail map.
6. In fact, every hiker in your group (*who's, whose*) able to read a map should have one.
7. With the map, you can choose a (*good, well*) location for your campsite.

should the visitor do at each landmark?
- How will the visitor know whether he or she is following the directions correctly or has made a wrong turn?
- What does the destination look like? Does it lie between two other structures?
- Are there other routes the visitor could take to reach the destination?

Meeting INDIVIDUAL NEEDS

INCLUSION
Learning-disabled students who have visual-processing deficits tend to become overwhelmed when faced with a page of text to read and correct. Enlisting a helper to read the text to the student will draw upon that student's auditory strengths. Have the students answer orally, and then have them write their responses on paper.

USAGE

8. When you begin your hike, mark where (*your*, *you're*) campsite is on the map.
9. If you go quite a (*way*, *ways*) from your campsite, note your path on the map, too.
10. As (*your*, *you're*) walking, your trail map can help you figure out exactly where you are.

Review C Proofreading a Paragraph for Correct Usage

Most of the sentences in the following paragraph contain ~~errors in the use of formal, standard English~~. If a sentence is incorrect, rewrite it correctly. If a sentence is already correct, write *C*.

EXAMPLES [1] Do you know someone who can learn you how to dance the Texas Two-Step?
1. Do you know someone who can teach you how to dance the Texas Two-Step?

[2] Well, your in for a real treat!
2. Well, you're in for a real treat!

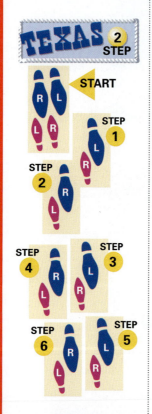

[1] Country music lovers enjoy the two-step because ̭its fun to dance. [2] If you don't know anyone who can teach you the two-step, you can use this ~~here~~ diagram to learn the basic steps. [3] Grab ~~you're~~ ̭partner and get ready. [4] First, listen closely to ~~them~~ ̭musicians. [5] Try ~~and~~ ̭catch the rhythm of the music with a small double shuffle step. [6] Remember, men, ~~your~~ ̭always starting with the left foot; women, you do just the opposite. [7] The man steps to the left, touches his left shoe with his right one, and then steps to the right and does the same thing. [8] Then, he takes two ~~kind of~~ ̭quick steps forward followed by two slow shuffle steps. [9] Some dancers add variety to ~~there~~ ̭steps by doing a sidestep or a turn. [10] Now you've come a long ~~ways~~ ̭toward learning the Texas Two-Step!

1. it's   5. to   8. rather
3. your   6. you're   9. their
4. the   7. C   10. way

532 Chapter 19 A Glossary of Usage

Learning for Life

Tell students to use as many of the words from the **Glossary of Usage** as possible in writing their directions. When students are finished, have them exchange directions with a partner. Partners should circle examples of the correct usage of words discussed in the glossary. They also should mark any sentences that include nonstandard English. Students should then correct their own directions and save them in their portfolios.

CHAPTER 19

Chapter Review

A. Revising Sentences by Correcting Errors in Usage

In each of the following sets of sentences, choose the letter of the sentence that contains an error. Then, write the sentence correctly, using formal, standard English.

1. a. Everyone was at the meeting except Diego.
   b. Does you're dog bite?   **1.** your
   c. Andy waited outside the dentist's office.

2. **a.** The landfill smelled badly.   **2.** bad
   b. No one knew whose knapsack that was.
   c. We could hardly wait for the rain to stop.

3. **a.** Mr. Catalano says that spiders ain't insects.   **3.** aren't
   b. I feel rather tired today.
   c. Do you accept personal checks?

4. a. Nina can run faster than he can.
   b. Anna would have finished, but she was interrupted.
   c. Be sure to bring a extra pencil with you.   **4.** an

5. a. The cow and its calf stood in the meadow.
   b. Less students signed up for tutoring this month.   **5.** Fewer
   c. What is the difference between these brands of basketball shoes?

6. a. We did as we were told.
   b. Everyone was already to go.   **6.** all ready
   c. I used to enjoy playing tennis.

7. **a.** Penny, bring this book when you go home.   **7.** take
   b. Ms. Michaelson told us that our plan was all right.
   c. Julie said that it's already time to go.

8. a. The team had fewer fouls in the last game.
   b. They looked everywhere for him.
   c. Do you know where he is at?

9. a. Water-skiing is more fun than I thought.
   b. We hiked a long way before we pitched camp.
   c. Try ~~and~~ get to the meeting on time, please. **9.** to
10. a. Their team has never beaten your team.
    b. A pop fly is ~~when~~ a ball ~~is~~ batted high into the infield.
    c. I finished my homework; then I called Duane.

B. Revising Sentences by Correcting Errors in Usage

Each of the following sentences contains an ~~error in the use of formal, standard English.~~ Rewrite each sentence correctly.

11. They could have come if the plane had ~~of~~ been on time.
12. That ~~ain't~~ an expensive hotel. **12.** isn't
13. We talked quietly ~~between~~ the three of us. **13.** among
14. That parade was the noisiest I've ever heard ~~anywheres~~. **14.** anywhere
15. This ~~here~~ beach is beautiful!
16. When the semi-trailer drove past the house, the picture fell off ~~of~~ Aunt Edna's wall.
17. I should ~~of~~ taken my camera inside the cave. **17.** have
18. ~~Its~~ one of the nicest beaches near Port Aransas. **18.** It's
19. I wasn't ~~hardly~~ scared on the cable car. **19.** *or* was hardly
20. You ~~hadn't~~ ought to miss the national park. **20.** not
21. After spending most of the weekend in the library, I was ~~already~~ for the exam. **21.** all ready
22. Earlier in the race, I could ~~of~~ caught up with her. **22.** have
23. "I'm doing ~~good~~. How are you doing?" **23.** well
24. Every major country in Western Europe ~~accept~~ Switzerland and Norway belongs to the European Union. **24.** except
25. Mom and Dad treated ~~theirselves~~ to dinner at a fine restaurant on their anniversary. **25.** themselves
26. It ~~hasn't~~ hardly rained all month in west Texas. **26.** has
27. The birds flew toward ~~there~~ nests. **27.** their
28. Boston is a long ~~ways~~ from San Francisco. **28.** way
29. When I was a baby, I ~~use~~ to eat dog biscuits. **29.** used
30. "~~Your~~ late today," said Ms. Jimenez. "Next time, remember to set your watch." **30.** You're

534 Chapter 19   A Glossary of Usage

RESOURCES

A Glossary of Usage

Review
- *Grammar, Usage, and Mechanics,* pp. 205, 206, 207, 208

Assessment
- Assessment Package
  —Chapter Tests, Ch. 19
  —Chapter Tests in Standardized Test Formats, Ch. 19
- Test Generator (One-Stop Planner CD-ROM)

Writing Application
Using Formal English in a Letter

Formal, Standard Usage You are an after-school helper at a day-care center. The teachers at the center plan to take the children on a field trip. One of the teachers has asked you to write a letter to send to the children's parents. The letter should tell where the children will visit and describe some of the things they will do there. The letter should also list any special items the children need to take with them.

Prewriting First, decide where the children will go on their field trip. They might go to a library, a park, a museum, or a fire station. Then, list the kinds of activities in which the children might participate. Note how the children will travel—for example, by bus or car. Also, note any special clothing or other things they might need for the field trip. List all the details you can imagine.

Writing Begin your draft with a polite greeting to the parents. Then, clearly explain why the children are going on the field trip. Invite the parents to call the day-care center with any questions they might have. In your letter, avoid using any informal or non-standard expressions.

Revising Read over your work carefully, and then ask a friend to read your letter. Does your reader understand the information in the letter? Does the letter follow the guidelines for a proper business letter? Revise any information that is unclear.

Publishing Check your letter for correct spelling, punctuation, and grammar. With your teacher's permission, you may want to discuss the planned field trip with the rest of the class. Post your letter on a class bulletin board or Web page.

HELP Use the Glossary of Usage to help you write the letter in formal, standard English.

Reference Note For more about **writing business letters,** see "Writing" in the Quick Reference Handbook.

Writing Application
(p. 535)

OBJECTIVE
- To write a letter using formal, standard English

Writing Application
Tip. The writing assignment gives students an opportunity to use the rules they have learned in this chapter. The rules are numerous, so you might wish to review those that cover errors common to your class.

Scoring Rubric. While you will want to pay particular attention to students' usage, you will also want to evaluate overall writing performance. You may want to give a split score to indicate development and clarity of the composition as well as usage skills.

Critical Thinking
Analysis. To help students think critically and to help them generate writing ideas, ask them to work together to prepare a questionnaire that focuses on where young children might want to go on a field trip. After students have composed the questionnaire, distribute copies and ask students to fill them out. Read the results to the class, and allow students to use in their letters any of the ideas that they like.

Chapter Review **535**

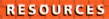 

Writing Application
Extension
- *Grammar, Usage, and Mechanics,* p. 211
- *Language Workshop CD-ROM,* Lessons 52–54

CHAPTER 20

Capital Letters
Rules for Capitalization

Diagnostic Preview

Correcting Sentences by Capitalizing Words

For each of the following sentences, correctly write each word that should be capitalized but is not. If a sentence is already correct, write *C*.

EXAMPLE 1. our guest speaker will be mayor Masella.
         1. Our, Mayor

1. Today i learned the song "simple gifts" from my friend.
2. "Hansel and Gretel" is a well-known fairy tale.   2. C
3. The kane county fall carnival will be held on saturday, october 19.
4. I believe that the recent trip to japan was organized by dr. alexander.
5. Let's ask the club treasurer, ms. lee.
6. Have you met professor martínez, rondelle?
7. Luis valdez filmed *the shepherd's tale*, a traditional mexican play, for tv.   7. TV
8. The greek god of war was ares.
9. My mother wrote to senator smith about the base closing.
10. members of congress often debate issues.
11. The letter began, "dear Ms. Joy."

PREVIEWING THE CHAPTER

- This chapter provides rules for the correct use of capitalization. It includes rules for the capitalization of first words in sentences, the pronoun *I*, and proper nouns and adjectives—including geographical names and names of nationalities, races, and peoples. The chapter also discusses the rules for capitalizing names of school subjects, abbreviations, and titles. Because the chapter emphasizes the importance of capitalization in writing, it can be useful with any writing assignment.

- The chapter closes with a **Chapter Review** including a **Writing Application** feature that asks students to use proper nouns in writing an essay about a proposed visit to a historical place.

- For help in integrating this chapter with composition chapters, use the **Teaching Strands** chart on pp. T297A–T297B.

USING THE DIAGNOSTIC PREVIEW

- You may want to use the **Diagnostic Preview** to identify areas in which students need instruction and practice in capitalization. You may wish to take the diagnosis one step further by evaluating actual writing samples to identify specific areas of confusion.

CHAPTER RESOURCES

Planning
- One-Stop Planner CD-ROM

Practice and Extension
- *Grammar, Usage, and Mechanics*, p. 212
- *Language Workshop CD-ROM*

Internet
- go.hrw.com (keyword: EOLang)

Evaluation and Assessment
- Assessment Package
  —Chapter Tests, Ch. 20
  —Chapter Tests in Standardized Test Formats, Ch. 20
- Test Generator (One-Stop Planner CD-ROM)

12. Have you seen any of Mary cassatt's paintings?
13. I didn't know that there are mummies in the american museum of natural history.
14. A venezuelan exchange student will be living with our family for eight months.
15. The graduation ceremony was held at Newberry college.
16. When is the jewish holiday yom kippur this year?
17. Grandma asked me what i want for my birthday.
18. Monique said, "that movie is about World war II."
19. Next spring uncle William is going to take me on a hiking trip to mount Elbert.
20. Darnell took a rafting trip on the Colorado river.

Using Capital Letters

20a. Capitalize the first word in every sentence.

EXAMPLE   **M**y sister has soccer practice after school. **T**hen she has to do her homework.

The first word of a directly quoted sentence should begin with a capital letter, whether or not the quotation comes at the beginning of your sentence.

EXAMPLE   Reiko asked, "**H**ave you finished your report?"

Traditionally, the first word of every line of poetry begins with a capital letter.

EXAMPLE
Let the rain kiss you.
Let the rain beat upon your head with silver liquid drops.
Let the rain sing you a lullaby.
The rain makes still pools on the sidewalk.
The rain makes running pools in the gutter.
The rain plays a little sleep-song on our roof at night—
And I love the rain.

Langston Hughes, "April Rain Song"

NOTE   Some poets do not follow this style. When you quote from a poem, use capital letters exactly as the poet uses them.

HELP
Capitalize the first word of a sentence fragment used in dialogue.

EXAMPLE
    Helena asked, "Have you read Terry Brooks' new novel?"
    Jenny answered, "**N**o, not yet."

Reference Note
For more about **direct quotations,** see page 590.

Relating to Literature

To support the textbook statement (on the previous page) that the first word of a line of poetry usually begins with a capital letter, have students study poems in their literature textbooks. For example, Gwendolyn Brooks in "Cynthia in the Snow" and Langston Hughes in "Poem" begin all lines with capitals. You may want to challenge students to find poems that are exceptions to the statement and that have lines whose first words do *not* begin with capitals.

Reference Note

For information about **writing letters,** see "Writing" in the Quick Reference Handbook. For information on using **colons in letters,** see page 579. For information on using **commas in letters,** see page 574.

20b. Capitalize the first word in both the salutation and the closing of a letter.

SALUTATIONS	**D**ear Service Manager:
	Dear Adam,
	My dear Brenda,
CLOSINGS	**S**incerely,
	Yours truly,
	Very truly yours,

20c. Capitalize the pronoun *I*.

EXAMPLE   When **I** returned home, **I** walked the dog.

Exercise 1 Proofreading Sentences for Correct Capitalization

If a sentence has one or more errors in capitalization, correctly write each word that should be capitalized. If a sentence is already correct, write *C*.

EXAMPLE   1. What time should i call?
           1. I

1. my library report on Edwin Arlington Robinson is due at the end of next month.
2. My sister memorized the limerick that begins, "a tutor who tooted a flute."
3. Aren't you glad that tomorrow is a holiday?   3. C
4. Elizabeth said, "we need to buy some more shampoo."
5. My grandparents let me watch television only after i have finished all my chores.
6. I used "yours truly" to close my letter.
7. How many yen did you spend during your vacation in Japan, Alexander?   7. C
8. "Everything i need to make the spaghetti sauce is right here," Nanna said.
9. two groups that i like will perform in concert next month in the park.
10. Greg said, "tomorrow is a holiday, so there will be no mail delivery."

20d. Capitalize proper nouns.

A *proper noun* names a particular person, place, thing, or idea. Proper nouns are capitalized. A *common noun* names a kind or type of person, place, thing, or idea. A common noun generally is not capitalized unless it begins a sentence or is part of a title.

Proper Nouns	Common Nouns
Fairview **S**chool	middle school
November	month
Toni **M**orrison	writer
Red **S**ox	team
Kenya	country
Queen **E**lizabeth	queen
Motorola	company

Reference Note
For more about **proper nouns** and **common nouns,** see page 324.

NOTE As you may already have noticed, some proper nouns consist of more than one word. In these names, short words such as prepositions (those of fewer than five letters) and articles (*a, an,* and *the*) are not capitalized.

EXAMPLES   **I**sle **o**f **W**ight   **A**ttila **t**he **H**un

(1) Capitalize the names of persons and animals.

Persons	
Kazue **S**awai	**H**arriet **T**ubman
Golda **M**eir	**E**ric the **R**ed
Heitor **V**illa-**L**obos	**W. C. H**andy

Animals	
Lassie	**R**over
Shamu	**S**ocks

STYLE TIP
Some names consist of more than one part. The different parts may begin with capital letters only or with a combination of capital and lowercase letters. If you are not sure about the spelling of a name, ask the person with that name, or check a reference source.
EXAMPLES
du **M**aurier, **D**u**P**ont, **v**an **G**ogh, **V**an **B**uren, **L**a **V**erne, **d**e **l**a **T**our

Meeting INDIVIDUAL NEEDS

MODALITIES

Kinesthetic Learners. Challenge students to construct a mobile that contains cards with sentences demonstrating each of the subrules of **Rule 20d**. On poster board or construction paper, each student (or small group of students) should write one long sentence for each subrule. Then, they should label the capitalized words; for example, they would write *team* over the capitalized name of a team. They should then cut the board or paper into sentence strips and use the strips to create a mobile. Students could add artwork to the mobiles and hang them from the ceiling.

Cooperative Learning

Organize the class into groups of six. Have the students from each group divide the twelve subrules of **Rule 20d** so that each student is responsible for two subrules. Then, have students regroup so that all of the students having the same two subrules are working together. These groups should study their subrules and then generate three example sentences containing capitalization errors. After they have finished, have the original groups reassemble. Each student should explain his or her two subrules and then have others in the group tell what should be capitalized in the three example sentences.

Meeting INDIVIDUAL NEEDS

ENGLISH-LANGUAGE LEARNERS
General Strategies. In some languages, such as Serbo-Croatian and Vietnamese, it is customary to capitalize only the first word of a geographical name that contains two or more words, while in English we capitalize all the words in the name. For example, *Thai binh duong* means "Pacific Ocean" in Vietnamese. Also, the name of a person's nationality is not capitalized in Spanish, Portuguese, Romanian, or Russian; thus, *a Russian* is *un ruso* in Spanish and *ruskii* in Russian. You may wish to emphasize these two points and give students examples to reinforce these differences between English and their native languages.

Crossing the Curriculum

Social Studies. Tell students that the Corn Belt is a region of the Midwestern United States where farms produce an abundance of corn as well as other crops. Geographers and others sometimes use names such as this to identify important economic or physical features of a region: the Mountain States, the Wheat Belt, the Sun Belt. You might wish to have students suggest descriptive names for their state or community. Remind students that such names are considered proper nouns and should be capitalized.

MECHANICS

---

(2) Capitalize geographical names.

Type of Name	Examples	
Continents	Asia Australia	North America Europe
Countries	Denmark Burkina Faso	Thailand Costa Rica
Cities, Towns	Minneapolis Havana	New Delhi San Diego
States	Maryland West Virginia	Mississippi Oregon
Islands	Hawaiian Islands Leyte	Isle of Wight Key West
Bodies of Water	Yangtze River Hudson Bay	Lake Okeechobee Caribbean Sea
Streets, Highways	Front Street Fifth Avenue	Sunset Boulevard Interstate 55

COMPUTER TIP
You may be able to use your spellchecker to help you correctly capitalize people's names, geographical names, and other proper nouns. Each time you use a proper noun in your writing, make sure you have spelled and capitalized it correctly. Then, add the name to your computer's dictionary or spellchecker.

NOTE In a hyphenated street number, the second part of the number is not capitalized.

EXAMPLE Forty-ninth Street

Type of Name	Examples	
Parks	San Antonio Missions	Yellowstone National Park
Mountains	Adirondacks Pine Mountain	Mount Kilimanjaro Andes
Forests	Sherwood Forest Black Forest	Sierra National Forest
Sections of the Country	the South Corn Belt	the Northwest New England

540 Chapter 20   Capital Letters

Capital Letters

NOTE Words such as *east, west, northeast,* or *southwest* are not capitalized when the words indicate a direction.

EXAMPLES Turn **e**ast when you reach the river. [direction]

Mae goes to college in the **E**ast. [section of the country]

Exercise 2 Writing Proper Nouns

For each common noun given below, write two proper nouns that name the same kind of person or thing. Be sure to use capital letters correctly.

EXAMPLE 1. lake
1. Lake Louise, Lake Ontario

1. river
2. street
3. actor
4. park
5. friend
6. singer
7. island
8. state
9. country
10. ocean
11. dog
12. politician
13. city
14. pet
15. painter
16. explorer
17. mountain
18. lake
19. continent
20. athlete

HELP
A dictionary and an atlas can help you correctly complete Exercise 2.

Exercise 3 Proofreading for the Correct Use of Capital Letters

If a sentence has an error in capitalization, correctly write the word that should be capitalized. If the sentence is already correct, write *C*.

EXAMPLE 1. Huge rigs pump oil from beneath the North sea.
1. Sea

1. María Ayala and eileen Barnes are going to Chicago.
2. Our neighbor Ken Oshige recently moved to canada.
3. Midway island is in the Pacific Ocean.
4. We could see mount Hood from the airplane window.
5. After you turn off the highway, head north for three miles.
6. During the sixteenth century, explorers from Spain brought horses to the west.
7. Several of us went camping near the guadalupe River.
8. My closest friend just moved to Ohio with shadow, her cat.
9. Hawaii Volcanoes National park is in Hawaii.
10. The bookstore is located on Maple street in New Orleans.

(3) Capitalize the names of organizations, teams, institutions, and government bodies.

Type of Name	Examples	
Organizations	Math Club	
	Oakdale Chamber of Commerce	
	Boy Scouts	
Teams	New York Mets	
	Los Angeles Lakers	
	Riverside Raiders	
Institutions	University of Oklahoma	
	Kennedy Middle School	
	Mount Sinai Hospital	
Government Bodies	League of Arab States	
	Department of Education	
	Federal Bureau of Investigation	

STYLE TIP

The names of government bodies are generally abbreviated.

EXAMPLES
FBI   IRS

Reference Note

For more information on **abbreviations,** see pages 548 and 563.

NOTE Do not capitalize words such as *hotel, theater,* and *high school* unless they are part of a proper name.

EXAMPLES	Fremont Hotel	the hotel
	Apollo Theater	a theater
	Ames High School	that high school

(4) Capitalize the names of special events, holidays, and calendar items.

Type of Name	Examples	
Special Events	World Series	Parade of Roses
	New York Marathon	Tulip Festival
Holidays	Thanksgiving	Martin Luther
	Labor Day	King, Jr., Day
Calendar Items	Sunday	December
	Father's Day	April Fools' Day

MECHANICS

ENGLISH-LANGUAGE LEARNERS
General Strategies. In English, the names of days of the week and months of the year are capitalized. In some languages, such as Czech, French, Polish, Portuguese, Romanian, Russian, Spanish, and Vietnamese, those names are written with small letters. For example, *Saturday* is *samedi* in French, *simbata* in Romanian, *sabado* in Spanish, *subbota* in Russian, and *thu bay* in Vietnamese. You may need to remind some students to capitalize these words in English.

NOTE Do not capitalize the name of a season unless it is part of a proper name.

EXAMPLES   a **w**inter storm   the **W**inter **F**estival

(5) Capitalize the names of historical events and periods.

Type of Name	Examples	
Historical Events	**B**oston **T**ea **P**arty **B**attle of **H**astings **W**ar of 1812	**N**ew **D**eal **M**arch on **W**ashington
Historical Periods	**B**ronze **A**ge **R**eformation	**G**reat **D**epression **R**enaissance

Exercise 4 **Correcting Errors in the Use of Capital Letters**

For the following sentences, identify each word that should be capitalized but is not. Then, write the word or words correctly.

EXAMPLE   1. Hart middle school is having a book fair.
            1. Middle School

1. Would you like to go to the movies this friday?
2. I think that the special Olympics will be held in our town this year.
3. What plans have you made for easter?
4. My sister and I were born at memorial Hospital.
5. The Rotary club donated equipment for our school's gym.
6. Did dinosaurs live during the stone Age?
7. My favorite baseball team is the Atlanta braves.
8. I always look forward to the first day of springfest.
9. The united states Congress is made up of the senate and the house of representatives.
10. Did you see any fireworks on the fourth of July?
11. Donna's youngest sister is going to join the girl scouts next Wednesday.
12. Our family has a wonderful time at the Alaska renaissance festival each year.

Meeting INDIVIDUAL NEEDS

ADVANCED LEARNERS
Students who have a firm grasp of **Rules 20a–d** may want to examine some works by writers who use capitalization in creative or unusual ways. As they progress through these rules, students should collect examples of creative capitalization, analyze its effects, and discuss their findings with the class. Students should be prepared to give their opinions about why the authors chose to break or bend the rules. Possible writers to study include Rudyard Kipling and E. E. Cummings. Remind students that creative capitalization is acceptable only in fiction or poetry.

ENGLISH-LANGUAGE LEARNERS
Spanish. Point out to Spanish-speaking students that while adjectives derived from geography, such as those relating to languages, races, peoples, and nationalities, are not capitalized in Spanish, they are capitalized in English. You may wish to ask students about capitalization rules in their native languages and let students discuss how these rules differ from English ones.

MECHANICS

---

13. The Grand hotel used to have Roman and Egyptian statues in its lobby.
14. Dave teaches at either the university of Florida or the university of Miami.
15. Why would you like to have lived during the middle ages?
16. If you like baseball games, you will enjoy watching the Texas rangers play.
17. Mrs. Nelson's class prepared the library display about civil rights day.
18. For fifteen years, spring carnival has been our school's main fund-raiser.
19. During the French revolution, people demanded their freedom and rights.
20. We'll be visiting my cousin's high school in may.

STYLE TIP

The words *black* and *white* may or may not be capitalized when they refer to people. Either way is correct.

EXAMPLE
During the Civil War, many **B**lack [or **b**lack] people joined the Union forces.

(6) Capitalize the names of nationalities, races, and peoples.

Type of Name	Examples	
Nationalities, Races, and Peoples	**M**exican **M**icronesian **C**herokee	**S**wiss **C**aucasian **B**antu

(7) Capitalize the names of businesses and the brand names of business products.

Type of Name	Examples
Businesses	**J.** and **J. C**onstruction, **I**nc. **U**ptown **S**hoe **S**tore **G**rommet **M**anufacturing **C**ompany
Business Products	**G**oodyear **A**quatred **N**ikon **P**ronea **F**ord **R**anger

NOTE Names of types of products are not capitalized.
EXAMPLES Goodyear **t**ires, Nikon **c**amera, Ford **t**ruck

544   Chapter 20   Capital Letters

(8) Capitalize the names of ships, trains, aircraft, and spacecraft.

Type of Name	Examples	
Ships	Santa Maria	Monitor
Trains	Coast Starlight	City of Miami
Aircraft	Air Force One	Spirit of St. Louis
Spacecraft	Columbia	Lunar Prospector

Reference Note
For information on using **italics (underlining) for the names of vehicles,** see page 589.

(9) Capitalize the names of buildings and other structures.

Type of Name	Examples	
Buildings	Flatiron Building Gallier Hall	World Trade Center
Other Structures	Hoover Dam Astrodome	Golden Gate Bridge

(10) Capitalize the names of monuments, memorials, and awards.

Statue of Liberty	Lincoln Memorial	Pulitzer Prize

(11) Capitalize the names of religions and their followers, holy days and celebrations, sacred writings, and specific deities.

Type of Name	Examples	
Religions and Followers	Buddhism Taoism	Christian Jew
Holy Days and Celebrations	Purim Christmas	Ramadan Ash Wednesday
Sacred Writings	Dead Sea Scrolls Bible	Koran Talmud
Specific Deities	Allah God	Vishnu Jehovah

COMPUTER TIP
A computer's spellchecker or style checker might spot some capitalization errors for you.

However, you cannot rely on these programs to find all your mistakes. Since many words are capitalized in some situations but not in others, the computer cannot find every error. Also, the computer might mistakenly highlight a word that is already correct.

Always proofread your writing carefully to make sure you have used capital letters correctly.

Using Capital Letters **545**

Meeting INDIVIDUAL NEEDS

MULTIPLE INTELLIGENCES
Intrapersonal Intelligence. Many young students like to create names for things. Read aloud to students the sentences below. Then, ask students to copy the sentences on a sheet of paper and to fill in the blanks.

1. If I discovered a new continent, I would name it _____.
2. If I could rename my school, I would call it _____.
3. If I raised a racehorse, I would name it _____.
4. If I built a sailboat, I would name it _____.
5. If I could rename a favorite holiday, I would call it _____.
6. If I founded my own country, I would name it _____.
7. If I could rename my (town, city, community), I would call it _____.
8. If I could rename the month when I was born, I would call it _____.

Have students write sentences explaining why they have chosen those names. Then, have them check that all of the proper nouns in their sentences are capitalized, circling the proper nouns and noting to the side the relevant capitalization rule and subrule for each one.

MECHANICS

NOTE The words *god* and *goddess* are not capitalized when they refer to deities of ancient mythology. However, the names of specific mythological gods and goddesses are capitalized.

EXAMPLE   The Roman **g**od of the sea was **N**eptune.

(12) Capitalize the names of planets, stars, constellations, and other heavenly bodies.

Mars	**P**luto	**N**orth **S**tar	**B**etelgeuse
Milky **W**ay	**B**ig **D**ipper	**U**rsa **M**inor	**S**irius

NOTE The word *earth* is not capitalized unless it is used along with the names of other heavenly bodies that are capitalized. The words *sun* and *moon* generally are not capitalized.

EXAMPLES   China is home to one fourth of the people on **e**arth.

How far is Saturn from **E**arth?

The **s**un rose at 7:09 this morning.

Exercise 5 Correcting Sentences by Using Capital Letters Correctly

For each of the following sentences, correctly write the word or words that should be capitalized.

EXAMPLE   1. We went to the leesburg library to learn more about african american history.
    1. Leesburg Library, African American

1. The methodist quoted a verse from the bible.
2. Bob has a chevrolet truck.
3. On a clear night you can see venus from earth.
4. My teacher took a cruise on the *song of Norway*.
5. Meet me in front of the Woolworth building.
6. Pilar received the Junior Achievement award.
7. Otis made a detailed scale model of the spacecraft *nozomi*.
8. Elena wrote a poem about the Greek god zeus.
9. Some navajo make beautiful silver jewelry.
10. Who were the first europeans to settle in Mexico?

Review A **Correcting Sentences by Capitalizing Proper Nouns**

For each of the following sentences, correctly write the word or words that should be capitalized.

EXAMPLE
1. In the late nineteenth century, henry morton stanley explored an area of africa occupied by ancestors of the bambuti.
   1. Henry Morton Stanley, Africa, Bambuti

1. The bambuti people live in the ituri forest, which is located in the northeast area of the Democratic republic of the congo.
2. This forest is located almost exactly in the middle of the continent of africa.
3. It lies north of mungbere, as shown in the boxed area on the map to the right.
4. The bambuti people, also known as twides, aka, or efe, have lived there for many thousands of years.
5. The earliest record of people like the Bambuti is found in the notes of explorers from egypt about 2500 B.C.
6. Other early reports of these people are found on colorful tiles in italy and in the records of explorers from portugal.

TEACHING TIP

Extension. To emphasize map-reading skills, you may want to use the extension of **Review A** below as an oral activity or write the questions on the chalkboard for students to answer in writing.

1. Which city is on the Aruwimi River? [*Avakubi*]
2. What is the capital of the Democratic Republic of the Congo? [*Kinshasa*]
3. What three rivers run through the Ituri Forest? [*Uele, Aruwimi, and Lindi*]
4. What two countries border the Democratic Republic of the Congo to the south? [*Angola, Zambia*]
5. What city is southeast of Mambasa? [*Irumu*]

Using Capital Letters

Rules 20e–h (pp. 548–556)

OBJECTIVES

- To correct errors in sentences in the capitalization of school subjects, proper adjectives, abbreviations, and titles
- To write titles for imaginary works and to capitalize them correctly

TEACHING TIP

Activity. Have your students name all of the school subjects they are taking during the current school year. Using only lowercase letters, list those subjects on the chalkboard. Then, invite volunteers to come to the chalkboard one at a time and to write a sentence about a subject in the list. The sentences can be descriptive or can explain why a subject is fun, easy, or difficult. When each volunteer has finished writing a sentence, have the rest of the class check the sentence to see if **Rule 20e** was correctly followed.

Meeting INDIVIDUAL NEEDS

ADVANCED LEARNERS

Have students work in small groups to analyze the types of changes made in the spellings of proper nouns converted to proper adjectives. Students could develop categories and give examples of the various types of changes. [*Examples may include adding* –n: *Cuban, American; adding* –ese: *Vietnamese, Japanese; and adding* –ian: *Egyptian, Arabian.*]

After students have completed the activity, have them share their findings with the rest of the class.

---

7. Stanley met some of the bambuti people, but he didn't write much about them.
8. In the 1920s, paul schebesta went to africa to learn more about the Bambuti people.
9. He learned that the bambuti are very different from the bantu and from other neighbors.
10. In fact, the bambuti were probably the first people in the rain forest that stretches across central africa from the atlantic ocean on the western coast to the eastern grasslands.

20e. **Do not capitalize the names of school subjects, except course names followed by a numeral and the names of language classes.**

EXAMPLES   **s**ocial **s**tudies, **s**cience, **h**ealth, **a**rt, **W**oodworking II, **C**onsumer **E**ducation I, **S**panish, **E**nglish

20f. **Capitalize proper adjectives.**

A *proper adjective* is formed from a proper noun. Proper adjectives are usually capitalized.

Proper Noun	Proper Adjective
Mexico	**M**exican carvings
King **A**rthur	**A**rthurian legend
Judaism	**J**udaic laws
Mars	**M**artian landscape

Reference Note
For more information on **proper adjectives,** see page 338.

20g. **Most abbreviations are capitalized.**

Capitalize abbreviations that come before and after personal names.

EXAMPLES   **M**r., **M**s., **M**rs., **D**r., **G**en., **M.D.**, **RN**, **J**r., **S**r.

Capitalize abbreviations of the names of organizations, businesses, and government bodies.

EXAMPLES   **I**nc., **C**o., **C**orp., **FBI, UN, NAACP, FDA**

In addresses, capitalize abbreviations such as those for roads, rooms, and post office boxes.

EXAMPLES   **A**ve., **D**r., **R**d., **S**t., **A**pt., **R**m., **P.O. B**ox

Reference Note
For information on using **abbreviations,** see page 563.

RESOURCES

Using Capital Letters
Practice

- *Grammar, Usage, and Mechanics,* pp. 221, 222–223, 224, 225, 226, 227–228
- *Language Workshop CD-ROM,* Lessons 46, 47

Abbreviations of geographical names are capitalized.

EXAMPLES **N.Y.C.**   **S**t. Louis   **N.** America   **O**kla.

NOTE A two-letter state abbreviation without periods is used when the abbreviation is followed by a ZIP Code. Each letter of the abbreviation is capitalized.

EXAMPLES Austin, **TX** 78704-6364

New Orleans, **LA** 70131-5140

Some abbreviations, especially those for measurements, are not capitalized.

EXAMPLES **e**tc., **e.g.**, **v**ol., **c**hap., **i**n., **y**d, **l**b, **c**c, **m**l, **m**m

Exercise 6 Correcting Errors in Capitalization

For each of the following sentences, correctly write each word or abbreviation that should be capitalized.

EXAMPLE 1. I went with mrs. McCain to visit mr. Brennan in the retirement home.
1. Mrs., Mr.

1. The address was p.o. box 32, Green Bay, Wi 54305.   **1. WI**
2. The new student had just moved to our town from st. Petersburg, Florida.
3. Will gen. Scott Quinn be speaking tonight?
4. Mr. Lloyd Mitchell, jr., has been appointed president of Sprockets and Widgets, inc.
5. The next speaker for Career Day will be Chet Patterson, rn, who works at the local hospital.   **5. RN**
6. Blair O'Brien, cpa, has a top-floor office in the Hanley corp. building.   **6. CPA**
7. The Fbi, the Fda, and the Un have decided to cooperate on the investigation.   **7. FBI/FDA/UN**
8. Are you taking art II or spanish?
9. Many scottish people have celtic, scandinavian, and irish ancestors.
10. The Chisholm Trail, which stretched over one thousand miles from San Antonio, tex., to Abilene, kans., was used by cowboys to drive cattle north.

Meeting Individual Needs

MULTIPLE INTELLIGENCES
Logical-Mathematical Intelligence. You might want to have students create a step-by-step process to determine whether a particular abbreviation should be capitalized, as required by **Rule 20g**. (Students may use their processes to complete **Review B**.) Have students write the following five-question process on a sheet of paper:

1. Does the abbreviation come either before or after a personal name?
2. Does the abbreviation stand for the name of an organization, business, or governmental body?
3. Does the abbreviation stand for a geographical name?
4. Is the abbreviation part of an address?
5. Does the abbreviation stand for a measurement?

Point out that if the answer to any of questions 1–4 is *yes*, then the abbreviation should be capitalized. However, if the answer to question 5 is *yes*, then the abbreviation probably should not be capitalized.

Students might want to create a diagram that shows each step (question) in the process and an example for each step. Some students might want to create similar step-by-step processes for other capitalization rules.

MECHANICS

Review B — Proofreading a Letter for Correct Capitalization

Read the following letter. For each numbered word group, identify any words or abbreviations that are not capitalized correctly. Rewrite the words or abbreviations with correct capitalization. If a sentence is already correct, write *C*.

EXAMPLE [1] 1066 south Norman st.
1. South, St.

1. PA

6. C

March 14, 2001

Mr. Leonard Thornton
1234 Windswept Dr.
[1] Lancaster, Pa 17601

[2] dear Mr. Thornton:

   [3] I think that the easiest thing you could do to help make lancaster better is to make it safer to ride bicycles here. [4] My friend James almost got hit by a car on his way to Memorial middle school. [5] As a member of our city's Transportation advisory Board, you can do a lot to encourage cyclists to wear helmets.
   [6] Also, in Earth Science I class, we have learned that if more people used bicycles instead of cars, the air would be cleaner. [7] One company that I know of, Universal Solutions, inc., rewards people who ride bicycles to work. [8] Many cities, such as Boulder, colorado, are building bicycle lanes. [9] maybe you could help with programs like these. Thank you for your attention to this matter.

   [10] yours truly,

   Tate Washington

   Tate Washington

20h. Capitalize titles.

(1) Capitalize a person's title when the title comes before the person's name.

EXAMPLES   **J**udge O'Connor   **P**rincipal Walsh

Mrs. Santos   **D**octor Ellis

Senator Topping   **P**resident Truman

(2) Titles used alone or following a person's name generally are not capitalized.

EXAMPLES   Judy Klein, our club **p**resident, led the meeting.

The **s**ecretary gave a speech to Congress.

However, a title used alone in direct address usually is capitalized.

EXAMPLES   Can the cast come off today, **D**octor?

Good morning, **M**a'am [or **m**a'am].

(3) Capitalize a word showing a family relationship when the word is used before or in place of a person's name.

EXAMPLES   Are **U**ncle Carlos and **A**unt Rosa here yet?

Either **M**om or **D**ad will drive us to the show.

Do not capitalize a word showing a family relationship when the word follows a possessive noun or pronoun.

EXAMPLE   My **c**ousin Dena and her **n**iece Leotie made stew.

HELP

You may capitalize a title used alone or following a person's name if you want to emphasize the person's high office.

EXAMPLE
Please come and meet Texas' native daughter and our country's **S**ecretary of **S**tate.

Exercise 7   Correcting Sentences by Capitalizing Words

For each of the following sentences, correctly write the word or words that should be capitalized. If a sentence is already correct, write *C*.

EXAMPLE   1. Thank you, aunt Shirley, for the pretty sweater.
           1. *Aunt*

1. He says that judge Johnson is very strict.
2. Reuben's mother, mrs. Santos, owns the new restaurant.

TEACHING TIP

Activity. Assign two capitalization rules to each student. Then, ask students to find examples of each use of the rule in newspapers or magazines. Have the students cut out the examples and use them to assemble a bulletin board display of capitalization rules and examples.

While searching for their examples, students might find examples that contradict the capitalization rules they have learned. Explain that newspapers and magazines often use their own styles, which may differ from standard rules.

TECHNOLOGY TIP

If your students use spellchecking, style-checking, or grammar-checking computer software to find grammatical errors, remind them that these programs, although useful, do make mistakes and may incorrectly question the correct use of capital letters in the middle of a sentence.

3. Will your uncle be at the party? 3. C
4. Well, doctor Sakamoto, do I need braces?
5. Did the secretary of state attend the meeting?
6. Is cousin Josie going to Israel? 5. C [or Secretary of State]
7. Please accept my apologies, senator.
8. On Saturday, aunt Latisha will arrive from Savannah.
9. Does professor Jones teach American history?
10. I learned to swim at grandpa Brown's cottage on the lake last summer.

Review C Using Capital Letters Correctly in Sentences

For each of the following sentences, correctly write the word or words that should be capitalized.

EXAMPLE 1. The Civil war is sometimes called the war between the states.
1. War, War Between the States

1. There is a fountain in the middle of lake Eola.
2. dr. jones teaches at York high school.
3. Some of these folk songs are mexican.
4. the atlantic borders the states from maine to florida.
5. Someday i would like to bicycle through europe.
6. all of my friends came to the party.
7. Have you visited the Washington monument?
8. Our history class wrote letters to the secretary-general of the united nations. 8. [or Secretary-General]
9. There's a long detour on highway 50 just east of brooksville, dad.
10. Our first fall camping trip will be in october.

(4) Capitalize the first and last words and all important words in titles and subtitles.

Unimportant words in a title include:

- articles (*a, an, the*)
- coordinating conjunctions (*and, but, for, nor, or, so, yet*)
- prepositions of fewer than five letters (such as *by, for, into, on, with*)

Reference Note

For a list of **prepositions**, see page 361.

552 Chapter 20 Capital Letters

MINI-LESSON

Punctuating Titles. Students might ask why some titles are in italics while others are enclosed in quotation marks. Explain that titles of books, plays, periodicals, films, television programs, works of art, long musical works, ships, aircraft, and spacecraft are italicized in print or on a computer or underlined when handwritten or typed. Titles of short works, such as poems or short stories, are enclosed in quotation marks. Then, ask students whether the titles of the following works should be italicized or

Type of Name	Examples	
Books	The Horse and His Boy	Dust Tracks on a Road
Magazines	Sports Illustrated for Kids	Essence Reader's Digest
Newspapers	Detroit Free Press The Fresno Bee	Tulsa Tribune The Denver Post
Poems	"The City Is So Big" "The Sneetches"	"For a Poet" "Steam Shovel"
Short Stories	"The Day the Sun Came Out"	"The Six Rows of Pompons"
Plays	Once on This Island	A Chorus Line
Comic Strips	Peanuts	Rose Is Rose
Movies	Babe: Pig in the City	A Bug's Life The King and I
Television Programs	Touched by an Angel Sister, Sister	Star Trek: Deep Space Nine
Videos	The Lion King II: Simba's Pride	Basic Sign Language
Video Games	Mario Kart 64	Escape Velocity
Compact Discs	Bringing Down the Horse	Mi Tierra Ray of Light
Audiotapes	Tiger Woods: The Makings of a Champion	My Family Tree: A Recorded History
Works of Art	Delfina and Dimas	Forever Free
Musical Works	"Oh, What a Beautiful Morning"	Peter and the Wolf "Angel of Mine"

Reference Note

For guidelines on using **italics (underlining)** and **quotation marks with titles,** see pages 588 and 595.

TEACHING TIP

Activity. Have students write sentences about titles with which they are familiar. They should each write one sentence about each of the following topics.

1. a favorite television show
2. a favorite book
3. a favorite movie
4. a movie I don't like
5. a song I like
6. a newspaper
7. a short story I've read

Instruct students to write complete sentences and to capitalize titles correctly. Have students exchange papers with partners, and have partners check the work, referring to **Rule 20h(4)**. Allow time for partners to discuss discrepancies in capitalization.

Using Capital Letters 553

---

enclosed in quotation marks.
- this textbook [*italics/underlining*]
- a popular movie [*italics/underlining*]
- a story from the front page of the newspaper [*enclosed in quotation marks*]

For more information on punctuating titles, refer students to **Chapter 22: Punctuation.**

HELP

The official title of a book is found on the title page. The official title of a newspaper or periodical is found on the masthead, which usually appears on the editorial page or the table of contents.

NOTE An article (*a*, *an*, or *the*) before a title is not capitalized unless it is the first word of the official title.

EXAMPLES Do you read **t**he *Sacramento Bee*?

Grandmother showed Nehal and me an article in ***T****he Workbasket.*

My mother reads ***T****he Wall Street Journal.*

Coordinating conjunctions and prepositions that begin a title or subtitle are capitalized.

EXAMPLES I have read ***T****hrough the Looking Glass* three times.

Marcia said that ***B****ut I'll Be Back Again* was very interesting.

Exercise 8 Writing Titles for Imaginary Works

Create a title for each item described below. Be sure each title is capitalized correctly.

EXAMPLE 1. a video about training pet birds
   1. *How to Be Your Bird's Best Friend*

1. a movie about an American Indian detective who solves a murder mystery
2. a magazine for people interested in video games about fly-fishing in Montana
3. a book about choosing the best breed of dog as a pet for your family
4. a song about saving the rain forests
5. a painting about life in a modern suburb somewhere in the United States
6. a poem about a new baby brother or sister coming home for the first time
7. a play about a student's first day at a new school in a South American country
8. a television show about the humorous people who visit the local library
9. a short story about students who go on a field trip to an animal park and get stuck there overnight
10. a newspaper published by the athletics department

554 Chapter 20 Capital Letters

MECHANICS

Exercise 8 Writing Titles for Imaginary Works

ANSWERS

Answers will vary. Titles should be capitalized correctly. Here are some possibilities:

1. *Detective Echohawk*
2. *Video Cast*
3. *How to Choose Your Dog*
4. "Save the Trees"
5. *Suburban Gothic*
6. "Baby, Please Come Home"
7. *Amigo in Argentina*
8. *Literary Giggles*
9. "Lost and Found"
10. *Battling Bobcat News*

Learning for Life

Writing to a Pen Pal. Tell students that many people enjoy writing to pen pals from other parts of the United States or from places around the world. While these pen pals might never meet each other, the correspondence can be a fun way to learn about people and ways of life in other places. Ask your students to each write a letter to a pen pal elsewhere in the United States or in another country. Students can find pen pals by searching appropriate Internet sites or by checking youth-oriented

Continued on pp. 555–556

554 Capital Letters

Exercise 9 Correctly Capitalizing Titles

Correct any incorrect capital or lowercase letters in titles in the following sentences. If a sentence is already correct, write C.

EXAMPLE 1. Mom gave me an article called "the importance Of fitness."
1. "The Importance of Fitness"

1. "Heart And Soul" is the only piano duet we can play.
2. Do you read *National geographic World*?
3. My little sister loves *the Cat in the Hat*.
4. I saw *Around the World in Eighty Days* on television.   4. C
5. We enjoy watching reruns of *The Cosby show*.
6. My mother likes to work the crossword puzzle in *the New York times*.
7. The children look forward to receiving their copies of *Ranger rick* each month.
8. Tony's short story "a few words about Aunt Frederica's dog Smitty and all his friends" certainly has the longest title of any story written by a member of the class.
9. "A Poem About A Poem" is the title of Mary Elizabeth's funny poem.
10. Whitney Houston's music is a special feature of the movie *the preacher's wife*.

Review D Proofreading a Paragraph to Correct Errors in Capitalization

Proofread the following paragraph, correcting any errors in the use of capital and lowercase letters.

EXAMPLE [1] what a huge Ship the *titanic* was!
1. What, ship, Titanic

[1] This magnificent ocean liner sank on april 15, 1912. [2] For more than seventy years, the *Titanic* lay untouched in the icy waters of the atlantic ocean. [3] Then, on September 1, 1985, Dr. Robert Ballard of the woods hole oceanographic institution and his crew found the ship. [4] To view the Ocean floor, the scientists used the remote-controlled vehicle *Argo*, shown on the next page. [5] once they discovered the ship, they attached a special underwater sled to *Argo*. [6] The sled,

with its lights and camera, provided dr. Ballard with more than twenty thousand photographs of the *Titanic*. [7] In 1986, Dr. Ballard and his Team returned to explore the wreck of the british ocean liner once more. [8] using a minisubmarine, the team was able to explore the sunken ship. [9] after years of wondering about the *Titanic*, underwater explorers finally found the Wreck and uncovered the truth about its fate. [10] In his book *The discovery of the Titanic*, Dr. Ballard tells about his underwater adventures.

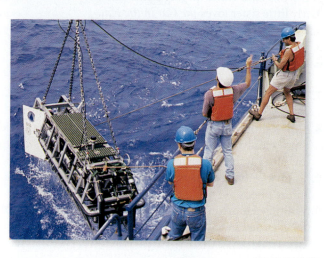

Learning for Life

to include information about his or her birthday, favorite books, movies, foods, and other things. When students have finished, have them check their letter for correct capitalization. Afterward, ask students to mail their letters and to save copies in their portfolios.

CHAPTER 20

Chapter Review

A. Proofreading Sentences for Correct Capitalization

Words that should be capitalized or lowercased are underscored.

For each of the following sentences, correctly write the word or words that contain an error in capitalization.

1. Sean's dog, Ransom, is a <u>german</u> shepherd.
2. Our <u>Spring</u> vacation begins on <u>march</u> 26.
3. Write to me at 439 Walnut <u>street</u>.
4. Mira asked, "<u>do</u> you know why the *Titanic* sank?"
5. In 1998, David Trimble and John Hume of Northern Ireland jointly won the Nobel <u>peace prize</u>.
6. As soon as <u>i</u> finish my English homework, <u>i</u>'ll call you.
7. She would like to go to <u>College</u> someday.
8. We watched a scene from *Romeo <u>And</u> Juliet*.
9. Eric's orthodontist is <u>dr.</u> McCambridge.
10. On Saturday my aunt is taking us to <u>jones beach</u>.
11. Dad used the <u>general</u> Electric waffle iron to make breakfast.
12. <u>have</u> you seen my copy of *<u>newsweek</u>*?
13. The Peace <u>corps</u> volunteers helped build a bridge.
14. The capital of Peru is <u>lima</u>.
15. The French <u>revolution</u> changed <u>european</u> society.
16. The spacecraft *sputnik 2* carried a dog named Laika.
17. Tom's brother is a <u>roman</u> <u>catholic</u> priest.
18. Although I live in Biloxi now, I'm from the <u>north</u>.
19. I answered, "<u>the</u> <u>gulf</u> of Mexico, I think."
20. Are you taking <u>spanish</u> or art this year?

B. Correcting Sentences by Using Capital Letters Correctly

For the following sentences, correctly write each <u>word that contains an incorrect capital or lowercase letter</u>.

21. Malaysia is in the <u>Southeastern</u> part of Asia.

Chapter Review   557

22. Its largest ethnic groups are malay, chinese, and indian.
23. The capital and largest city is kuala lumpur.
24. Much of the world's Rubber comes from Malaysia.
25. Other Major products are Tin and Palm Oil.
26. Most inhabitants of malaysia are muslims.
27. Malaysia is a constitutional monarchy headed by a King.
28. The Prime Minister is the Leader of the Government.
29. Many Malays wear the Sarong, a kind of skirt.
30. The Encyclopedia called *World book* can give you more information about Malaysia.

C. Correcting Errors in Capitalization

For the following sentences and word groups, correctly write each word and each abbreviation that should be capitalized.

31. Todd's new address is 1240 mud road, Setauket, Ny 11733-2851.   **31.** NY
32. The exchange student is from San remo, Italy.
33. My parents' favorite television movie is *Lonesome dove*.
34. We went with mrs. Rigatti to see the floats in the San gennaro Festival.
35. It was a surprise to learn that uncle Elwood had been in the Cia all those years.   **35.** CIA
36. isn't your aunt Etta here?
37. Mont blanc, the highest peak in the alps, was first climbed in 1786.
38. We sent a petition to mayor Moore.
39. Millie enjoyed reading *Anne of Green gables* so much that she rented the movie.
40. yours sincerely, Beth Tewes

RESOURCES

Capital Letters
Review
- *Grammar, Usage, and Mechanics,* pp. 229, 230, 231, 232

Assessment
- *Assessment Package*
  —*Chapter Tests,* Ch. 20
  —*Chapter Tests in Standardized Test Formats,* Ch. 20
- *Test Generator (One-Stop Planner CD-ROM)*

Writing Application
Using Capital Letters in an Essay

Proper Nouns Your social studies teacher has asked you to write about a vacation you would like to take to a historical place. Write an essay telling where you would like to go and why you would like to go there. In your essay, use at least five proper nouns.

Prewriting First, brainstorm a list of historical places that interest you. Which of these places would you most like to visit? Write down notes about what you would do during your visit.

Writing Begin your rough draft by stating where you would like to go and why. Explain what historical event or events happened at that place. Then, tell what particular areas or landmarks you would visit. Be sure to use at least five proper nouns naming places, events, and people.

Revising Ask a friend to read your draft and tell you if any parts seem unclear or uninteresting. Then, revise anything that is confusing or boring.

Publishing Use an encyclopedia or other reference source to check the spelling of any proper nouns you have included. Proofread your essay carefully for any other errors in grammar, spelling, capitalization, and punctuation. Put your essay on poster board, along with pictures or drawings of the place you wrote about in your essay. With your teacher's permission, display your poster in the classroom.

—HELP—
An encyclopedia can help you learn more about historical places.

Writing Application
(p. 559)

OBJECTIVE
- To write an essay about a historical place, using five proper nouns

Writing Application
Tip. The writing assignment gives students practice in using capital letters correctly in an essay. Since students will be writing to explain where they would like to go and why, you may wish to review **Chapter 1: Sharing Our Stories.**

Scoring Rubric. While you will want to pay particular attention to students' use of capital letters, you will also want to evaluate overall writing performance. You may want to give a split score to indicate development and clarity of the composition as well as mechanics skills.

Critical Thinking
Analysis. To ensure effective essays, students should analyze their travel interests. Their reasons for choosing their destinations will serve as topics for their writing and will determine the details included.

Chapter Review 559

RESOURCES
Writing Application
Extension
- *Grammar, Usage, and Mechanics,* p. 235
- *Language Workshop CD-ROM,* Lessons 46, 47

CHAPTER 21

PREVIEWING THE CHAPTER

- The first part of this chapter discusses end marks and abbreviations. Then, comma rules are presented, followed by rules for the use of semicolons and colons.

- The **Chapter Review** offers students the opportunity to test their mastery of punctuation marks. Finally, the **Writing Application** asks students to write a scene for a television show script, using a variety of end marks.

- For help in integrating this chapter with writing chapters, use the **Teaching Strands** chart on pp. T297A–T297B.

USING THE DIAGNOSTIC PREVIEW

- Keep in mind that students who can punctuate the sentences in the **Diagnostic Preview** may not transfer this knowledge to their writing. Therefore, it may be necessary to examine students' writing to determine which punctuation rules students need to practice.

- You could use the results of the test to decide which lessons to teach to the entire class and which ones to assign to cooperative-learning groups.

CHAPTER 21 Punctuation
End Marks, Commas, Semicolons, Colons

Diagnostic Preview

Using Periods, Question Marks, Exclamation Points, Commas, Semicolons, and Colons Correctly

The following sentences lack necessary periods, question marks, exclamation points, commas, semicolons, and colons. Write the letter, word, or words that should be followed by a punctuation mark. Then, add the correct punctuation mark after each word. For numerals, write the entire numeral and insert the correct punctuation mark.

Commas that may be considered optional are underscored.

EXAMPLE   1. Mr. Cotton my next-door neighbor asked me to pick up his mail while he is away

   1. Cotton, neighbor, away.

1. The mangos and papayas and avocados will make a good fruit salad.
2. Before the slide presentation began Ms Jee gave a short, clear history of Korea.
3. Ray Charles a popular singer and musician became blind at the age of seven.
4. I've taken classes in photography, ceramics, and weaving.
5. When will dinner be ready?
6. Here comes a tornado!
7. Cheryl will take gymnastics Eddie will take piano lessons.

560   Chapter 21   Punctuation

CHAPTER RESOURCES

Planning
- One-Stop Planner CD-ROM

Practice and Extension
- Grammar, Usage, and Mechanics, p. 236
- Language Workshop CD-ROM

Internet
- go.hrw.com (keyword: EOLang)

Evaluation and Assessment
- Assessment Package
  —Chapter Tests, Ch. 21
  —Chapter Tests in Standardized Test Formats, Ch. 21
- Test Generator (One-Stop Planner CD-ROM)

8. Ted mowed the lawn, cleaned the garage, and painted the shed.
9. Would 6:30 P.M. be too early?
10. This Zuni ring was made in Santa Fe, N. Mex.
11. I finished the letter, but I haven't proofread it yet.
12. Dear Senator Hutchison:
13. We will learn about the federal court system; then we will visit the county courthouse.
14. Sara, Eric, and Manuel can speak both Spanish and English.
15. Hurry, get me some ice!
16. Yes, I did clean my room.
17. When you go cross-country skiing, bring the following items: skis, boots, poles, and ski wax.
18. Shall we leave at 9:00 A.M.?
19. Mr. Pak, when is the Chinese New Year?
20. The Scouts' annual dinner will be held February 19, 2001.

End Marks

An **end mark** is a punctuation mark placed at the end of a sentence. *Periods*, *question marks*, and *exclamation points* are end marks. Periods are also used after some abbreviations.

21a. Use a period at the end of a statement (a declarative sentence).

EXAMPLES French is the official language of Haiti, but many people there speak Haitian Creole.

I will write to you soon.

21b. Use a question mark at the end of a question (an interrogative sentence).

EXAMPLES Have you heard Gloria Estefan's new song?

Where should I meet you?

21c. Use an exclamation point at the end of an exclamation (an exclamatory sentence).

EXAMPLES What a cute puppy that is!

This egg drop soup is delicious!

Reference Note

For more information about **classifying sentences by purpose**, see page 316.

HELP

Periods (decimal points) are also used to separate dollars from cents and whole numbers from fractions.

EXAMPLES

$6.57 [six dollars and fifty-seven cents]

2.7 [two and seven tenths]

In some countries a comma is used instead of a period in such cases.

End Marks
Rules 21a–e (pp. 561–565)

OBJECTIVES

- To correct sentences by adding appropriate punctuation
- To correct paragraphs by adding the proper end marks and capital letters to sentences

Meeting INDIVIDUAL NEEDS

ENGLISH-LANGUAGE LEARNERS
General Strategies. In some languages, punctuation is the same as in English; however, certain languages do punctuate sentences differently. A period is a vertical line in Hindi, a circle in Japanese, and four dots in Aramaic. In languages such as Greek, Korean, Persian, and Arabic, the period is slightly raised. The Greek question mark looks like an English semicolon, and Spanish question marks and exclamation points are placed both before and after a question or exclamation, with the first punctuation mark inverted.

RESOURCES

End Marks
Practice
- *Grammar, Usage, and Mechanics,* pp. 237, 238, 239
- *Language Workshop CD-ROM,* Lesson 39

Meeting INDIVIDUAL NEEDS

MULTIPLE INTELLIGENCES

Linguistic Intelligence. An exclamation point indicates emotion, but it does not indicate a specific emotion. The emotion that is being expressed is usually indicated by the words in the sentence. Have students compose five exclamatory sentences, each expressing a different emotion such as anger, joy, surprise, disbelief, or love. Ask volunteers to write sentences on the chalkboard. Have other students guess which emotion is being expressed in each sentence.

Critical Thinking

Metacognition. Ask students how they know which emotion is being expressed in the sentences written by students in the activity above. [*the content of the sentence; the emphasis on certain words when the sentences are read aloud*] Point out to students that using more than one exclamation point at the end of a sentence is unnecessary and inappropriate.

Relating to Writing

Students might discover that exclamation points rarely appear in articles published in news periodicals. In fact, many journalists avoid the use of exclamation points in news articles because they may make such articles appear excessively dramatic or even biased.

STYLE TIP

In your own writing, make sure to use exclamation points only when you want to emphasize a strong feeling. Do not overuse exclamation points, or they will lose their effectiveness.

ORIGINAL
The little gray cat looked up at Judy! With one look, Judy knew this was the kitty for her! How lucky that she had visited the animal shelter today!

REVISED
The little gray cat looked up at Judy. With one look, Judy knew this was the kitty for her. How lucky that she had visited the animal shelter today!

HELP—
When you finish Exercise 2, you should have ten complete sentences.

21d. Use either a period or an exclamation point at the end of a request or a command (an imperative sentence).

Use a period after an imperative sentence that makes a request or a mild command. Use an exclamation point after a strong command.

EXAMPLES Please sit down. [a request]

Sit down. [a mild command]

Sit down right now! [a strong command]

Exercise 1 Correcting Sentences by Adding End Marks

Write the last word of each sentence, and add a period, a question mark, or an exclamation point.

EXAMPLE 1. What time is it
1. it?

1. When does the bus come?
2. What a great game that was!
3. Did you bring your lunch today?
4. Hyo was born in Korea.
5. I don't understand the assignment.
6. Who can identify the subject of this sentence?
7. Pardon me, sir.
8. Imagine me at the White House! 8. [*or* House.]
9. Get the iguana back into your room right now! 9. [*or* now.]
10. The legend for this map is in the lower right-hand corner.

Exercise 2 Correcting a Paragraph by Adding Capital Letters and End Marks

Decide where the sentences in the following paragraph begin and end. Rewrite each sentence, providing the needed capital letters and end marks.

EXAMPLE what an ancient art weaving is
What an ancient art weaving is!

have you ever been to Hawaii? the first Europeans who landed there found chiefs dressed in beautiful feather cloaks.

feathers for cloaks like the one shown here came from thousands of birds. different-colored feathers were arranged in royal designs. the feathers were then attached to a base of woven fibers. cloaks were worn in battle and for ceremonies. most of the islanders did not wear such fine garments. colorful prints are worn by all kinds of people on the islands. every Friday is Aloha Friday. on that day many people wear Hawaiian prints and live flowers.

Robert Dampier, *Kamehameha III* (1825). Oil on canvas (24 3/8" × 20 1/16"). Honolulu Academy of Arts, gift of Mrs. C. Montague Cooke, Jr., Charles M. Cooke III, and Mrs. Heston Wren, in memory of Dr. C. Montague Cooke, Jr., 1951.

21e. Many abbreviations are followed by periods.

Types of Abbreviations	Examples			
Personal Names	I. M. Pei	J. C. Watts		
	Vicki L. Ruíz	M.F.K. Fisher		
Titles Used with Names	Mr.	Mrs.	Ms.	Jr.
	Dr.	Sr.	Ph.D.	D.D.S.
Organizations	Assn.	Co.	Corp.	Inc.

NOTE Abbreviations for government agencies and some widely used abbreviations are written without periods. Each letter of such abbreviations (which are called **acronyms**) is capitalized.

EXAMPLES CIA (**C**entral **I**ntelligence **A**gency)

NOS (**N**ational **O**cean **S**ervice)

PC (**p**ersonal **c**omputer)

RFD (**R**ural **F**ree **D**elivery)

TV (**t**ele**v**ision)

STYLE TIP

When writing the initials of someone's name, place a space between two initials (as in *I. M. Pei*). Do not place a space between three initials (as in *M.F.K. Fisher*).

Reference Note

For more on **using capital letters for abbreviations,** see page 548.

End Marks 563

TEACHING TIP

Activity. To give students practice in using end marks and abbreviations, ask volunteers to go to the chalkboard to write specific types of sentences containing specific types of abbreviations.

Cooperative Learning

Pair students and tell them to make flashcards for the abbreviations in the charts and **Notes** on pp. 563–564, using one side of each card for the abbreviation without periods and the other side for the correctly punctuated abbreviation. Have partners shuffle the cards and then use them to drill each other on the correct punctuation of abbreviations.

STYLE TIP

The abbreviations *A.D.* and *B.C.* need special attention. Place *A.D.* before the year and *B.C.* after the year.

EXAMPLES
231 **B.C.**

A.D. 590

There is one exception to this rule. For centuries expressed in words, place both *A.D.* and *B.C.* after the century.

EXAMPLES
fifth century **B.C.**

second century **A.D.**

HELP

If you are not sure whether to use periods with an abbreviation, look up the abbreviation in a dictionary, an encyclopedia, or another reliable reference source.

HELP

Some sentences in Review A need more than one punctuation mark.

Types of Abbreviations	Examples		
Times	A.M.	B.C.	Aug.
	P.M.	A.D.	Sat.
Addresses	Ave.	Blvd.	Ct.
	P.O. Box	Rd.	St.
Geographical Names	Ark.	Colo.	D.C.
	St. Paul	P.R.	U.S.

NOTE A two-letter state abbreviation without periods is used only when it is followed by a ZIP Code. Both letters of the abbreviation are capitalized. No mark of punctuation is used between the abbreviation and the ZIP Code.

EXAMPLES   Washington, **DC** 20013

San Juan, **PR** 00904

Abbreviations for units of measure are usually written without periods and are not capitalized.

EXAMPLES   cc, kg, ml, m, ft, lb, qt

However, you should use a period with the abbreviation *in.* (for *inch*) to prevent confusing it with the word *in*.

When an abbreviation that has a period ends a sentence, another period is not needed. However, a question mark or an exclamation point is used in such situations if it is needed.

EXAMPLES   The game lasted until 8:30 P.M.

Did it start at 5:00 P.M.?

Review A **Correcting Sentences by Adding Punctuation**

Write the following sentences, adding periods, question marks, and exclamation points where they are needed.

EXAMPLE   1. Some caterpillars become butterflies
   1. *Some caterpillars become butterflies.*

1. Will Mr. Highwater be teaching the science course?

2. Just after 3:00 P.M., the sun came out.
3. The letter from Ms. E. J. Hunter was dated Fri., Nov. 12.
4. How heavy the traffic was on First Avenue!
5. Do your measuring cups say *ml* or *oz*?
6. Address comments to 7890 E. Kyle Dr., Oswego, New York.
7. By 300 B.C., Chinese cooks already had a philosophy of five tastes.
8. The city of St. Petersburg is situated on a peninsula.
9. Apply at the loading dock at H. J. Movers, Inc.
10. On TV tonight, Dr. Melba West will explain nutrition.

Review B Using Punctuation Correctly

For each of the following sentences, write the word or words that should be followed by a period, question mark, or exclamation point. Add the proper punctuation after each word.

EXAMPLE   1. My neighbor Mr Nhuong showed me this picture of people celebrating the Vietnamese holiday Tet

1. *Mr., Tet.*

1. Unlike New Year's Day, which is always on Jan. 1, Tet can fall on any day in late January or early February.
2. Moreover, Tet isn't just one single day; the celebration lasts a whole week.
3. Wouldn't you like a week-long holiday?
4. Even here at 8420 Beaconcrest Ave, the Nhuong family still enjoy their traditions.
5. According to Mr. Nhuong, the name of the first person to visit a house can bring good or bad luck to the family.
6. Since my nickname is Lucky, the Nhuongs asked me to be their first visitor and to arrive by 7:00 A.M.
7. I tried hard not to be late.
8. One of the Nhuongs' relatives flew in from Santa Barbara, Calif, later that morning.
9. Mrs. Nhuong prepared a huge breakfast, and we all sat down to enjoy it.
10. What a great meal that was!

MODALITIES

Auditory Learners. Ask students to read aloud sentences 1, 2, 3, 6, 7, 8, 9, and 10 in **Review A,** spelling out the abbreviations as they are written and using a click of the tongue or a snap of fingers to indicate the periods in each.

Commas

Rules 21f–l *(pp. 566–576)*

OBJECTIVES

- To proofread sentences for correct use of commas
- To correct compound sentences by adding commas
- To correct errors in the punctuation of sentences with appositives and appositive phrases
- To add commas to sentences with words used in direct address
- To add commas to sentences with introductory elements
- To use commas correctly in conventional situations

Meeting INDIVIDUAL NEEDS

ENGLISH-LANGUAGE LEARNERS
General Strategies. In some languages, such as Japanese, Persian, and Arabic, the comma is raised above the line of writing and inverted or reversed. You may find that some of your English-language learners will write the comma in that way when they write in English. Remind them that they should place the comma level with the bottom of the letters, with the tail pointing down and curving left.

STYLE TIP

Some writers do not use a comma before the conjunction *and, or,* or *nor* when it joins the last two items in a series. However, sometimes such a comma is needed to make the meaning clear. Notice how using a comma before *and* changes the meaning in these examples.

EXAMPLES
Grandma, Mom, and Dad came to the game. [Three people were at the game.]

Grandma, Mom and Dad came to the game. [Grandma is being told who came to the game.]

Including the comma before the conjunction in such a series is not incorrect, so it is best always to use this comma.

Commas

End marks are used to separate complete thoughts. ***Commas,*** however, are generally used to separate words or groups of words within a complete thought. If you fail to use necessary commas, you may confuse your reader.

CONFUSING — The members of the team are Jo Ann Jerry Lee Darrin Marcia and Jeanne. [How many members?]

CLEAR — The members of the team are Jo Ann, Jerry Lee, Darrin, Marcia, and Jeanne. [five members]

Items in a Series

21f. **Use commas to separate items in a series.**

A ***series*** is three or more items written one after the other. The items may be single words or word groups.

Words in a Series
Sugar cane, bananas, and citrus fruits are grown in Jamaica. [nouns]
Yesterday I dusted, vacuumed, and mopped. [verbs]
The day was wet, cold, and windy. [adjectives]

Word Groups in a Series
At the beach we swam, built sand castles, and played volleyball. [predicates]
I searched for the lost contact lens in the sink, on the counter, and on the floor. [prepositional phrases]
Please punch the time card when you arrive, when you take lunch, and when you leave. [clauses]

When all the items in a series are joined by *and, or,* or *nor,* do not use commas to separate them.

EXAMPLES — I've seen snakes **and** lizards **and** toads in our yard.

Shall we go bowling **or** rent a movie **or** listen to CDs?

566 Chapter 21 Punctuation

RESOURCES

Commas

Practice
- *Grammar, Usage, and Mechanics,* pp. 240, 241, 242, 243, 244–245, 246, 247–248
- *Language Workshop CD-ROM,* Lessons 36–38

Punctuation

Exercise 3 **Proofreading Sentences for the Correct Use of Commas**

Most of the following sentences need commas. If a sentence needs commas, write the word before each missing comma; then, add the comma. If a sentence is already correct, write C. Commas that may be considered optional are underscored.

EXAMPLE 1. Beverley DeGale Claire Jackson and Iman won Candace Awards in 1997.
  1. DeGale, Jackson,

1. I finished my dinner, brushed my teeth, combed my hair, and ran out the door.
2. The nurse checked the patient's pulse, took his temperature, and gave him a glass of water.
3. For lunch we had milk, tuna sandwiches, and pears.
4. Cora, Jack, and Tomás all entered the contest.
5. Marcus plays golf and football and volleyball.   5. C
6. The U.S. Marine Corps is prepared for battle on land, on the sea, and in the air.
7. For her birthday on September 27, my sister wants a dog and a cat and a hamster and a bird.   7. C
8. Jan told Raul where she had been, where she was, and where she was going.   8. C
9. This project is fun, easy, fast, and inexpensive.
10. Balloons were floating in the living room, the kitchen, the bedrooms, and the dining room.

21g. Use commas to separate two or more adjectives that come before a noun.

EXAMPLES Pita is a round, flat bread of the Middle East.

James Earl Jones certainly has a deep, strong, commanding voice.

Do not place a comma between an adjective and the noun immediately following it.

INCORRECT Alexandra and I found an old, rusty, bicycle in the vacant lot down the street.

CORRECT Alexandra and I found an old, rusty bicycle in the vacant lot down the street.

HELP

Use a semicolon rather than a comma between phrases in a series when the phrases contain commas.

EXAMPLE
The three sections of this project will be due on Tuesday, March 3; on Thursday, March 19; and on Friday, April 3.

Reference Note

For more information about **semicolons**, see page 577.

Exercise 3

ALTERNATIVE LESSON
Before students attempt to proofread for errors in **Exercise 3**, ask them to identify the subjects in the example sentence and the verbs in sentence 1. [*Beverley DeGale, Claire Jackson, Iman*; 1: *finished, brushed, combed, ran*]

Remind students that the nouns or pronouns of a compound subject or the verbs of a compound verb can be listed in a series separated by commas.

Meeting INDIVIDUAL NEEDS

INCLUSION
Some students have difficulty taking in many new concepts at one time. The numerous rules of comma usage presented in this chapter might be frustrating if presented simultaneously. Be prepared to spend ample time on each rule before proceeding to the next.

MULTIPLE INTELLIGENCES
Spatial Intelligence. Show students that a series of items can be visualized as the branching of three or more limbs of a "sentence tree." You might want to use the following sentence: The colors of our flag are red, white, and blue.

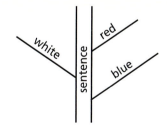

Point out that the commas separate the limbs. You might want to have students adapt the tree diagram for a series of four or more items.

TEACHING TIP

Activity. Have each of your students write three or four descriptive sentences about his or her favorite animal. Emphasize the use of vivid, colorful adjectives. Remind students to use commas correctly when separating adjectives in their sentences. Have the students proofread each other's papers for vivid adjectives and the proper use of commas.

Meeting INDIVIDUAL NEEDS

MULTIPLE INTELLIGENCES
Bodily-Kinesthetic Intelligence. Have students divide a piece of paper into six slips by folding and tearing. Tell them to write an adjective on each slip of paper. Collect the slips, shuffle them, and redistribute them. Each student will receive six slips of paper. Tell students to create two sentences using three adjectives from the slips for each sentence. Have several volunteers write their sentences on the chalkboard, and have the other students check the punctuation.

Timesaver

When students do the exercises in this chapter, you could have them write the words in one color of ink and then use a different color for punctuation, or you could have them alternate pencil and ink in the same manner. This process will make the punctuation visually striking and easier to check.

TIPS & TRICKS

To see whether a comma is needed between two adjectives, insert *and* between the adjectives (*tall and pine*, for example). If *and* sounds awkward there, do not use a comma.

Another test you can use is to switch the order of the adjectives. If the sentence still makes sense when you switch them, use a comma.

STYLE TIP

In your reading, you may see very short compound sentences that do not use commas.

EXAMPLE
I'm tired and I'm hungry.

However, a comma before a conjunction in a compound sentence is always correct.

Sometimes the last adjective in a series is thought of as part of the noun. In that case, do not use a comma before the last adjective.

EXAMPLES The tall pine tree [not *tall, pine tree*] swayed.

Kimchi is a spicy Korean dish [not *spicy, Korean dish*] made with pickled cabbage.

Exercise 4 Proofreading Sentences for the Correct Use of Commas

For each of the following sentences, write the word that should be followed by a comma; then, add the comma. If a sentence is already correct, write *C*.

EXAMPLE 1. Mrs. Hirata taught us several beautiful old Japanese folk songs.

1. beautiful,

1. His calm wrinkled face told a story.
2. François Toussaint L'Ouverture was a brilliant patriotic Haitian leader.
3. The huge lively wriggling kingfish dropped from the hook.
4. There's a sleek shiny bicycle in the store window.
5. The sound of the soft steady rain put me to sleep.
6. We read Chief Black Hawk's moving farewell speech.   6. C
7. I washed my hands in the cold clear spring water.
8. May I please have some of that spicy delicious soup?
9. The old diary had ragged yellowed pages.
10. The crowded dining room is filled with people celebrating my parents' anniversary.   10. C

Compound Sentences

21h. Use a comma before *and, but, for, nor, or, so,* or *yet* when it joins independent clauses in a compound sentence.

EXAMPLES Theo will bring the potato salad, and Sarah will bring the apple juice.

Congress passed the bill, but I believe the president vetoed it.

I went to bed early, for I had a big day ahead of me.

NOTE Do not confuse a compound sentence with a simple sentence containing a compound verb. No comma is needed between the parts of a compound verb.

COMPOUND SENTENCE   We ran relay races first, and then we ate lunch.

SIMPLE SENTENCE   We ran the relay races first and then ate lunch. [The sentence contains a compound verb.]

However, a compound verb made up of three or more verbs generally does require commas.

EXAMPLE   We **ran** the relay races, **ate** lunch, and then **prepared** for the individual races.

Reference Note
For more information on **compound sentences,** see pages 274 and 395. For more information on **compound verbs,** see page 312.

Exercise 5 Correcting Compound Sentences by Adding Commas

Some of the following sentences are compound and need to have commas added. If a sentence needs a comma, write the word or numeral before the missing comma; then, add the comma. If a sentence is already correct, write *C*.

EXAMPLE   1. The storm brought heavy rain but a tornado did the most damage.
          1. rain,

1. At the Native American Heritage Festival, Mary Johns wove baskets from sweet grass, and Alice Billie made rings from beads.
2. The sailboat was almost hidden by the fog, yet we could see part of the mast.
3. German Silva of Mexico was the fastest male runner in the 1994 and 1995 New York City Marathons, and Tegla Loroupe of Kenya was the female winner in both races.
4. Would you like to play checkers, or shall we go to the lake instead?
5. I called my friends and told them the news.   5. C
6. Jim practiced the piano piece all month, for he wanted to do well at the recital.

Meeting INDIVIDUAL NEEDS

MODALITIES

Visual Learners. To help students distinguish a compound sentence from a simple sentence with a compound verb, write the following sentence pairs on the chalkboard:

1. **Fred** *loves* to eat yet *hates* meat.
   Fred *loves* to eat, yet **he** *hates* meat.

2. **Pam** *swims* often and *jogs* daily.
   Pam *swims* often, and **she** *jogs* daily.

3. **Maria** *reads* books but *sees* no movies.
   Maria *reads* books, but **she** *sees* no movies.

Underline the subjects (shown above in bold) in one color and underline the verbs (shown above in italics) in another color. Circle the comma in each compound sentence, and emphasize that compound sentences have two independent clauses, each of which has a subject and a verb. Therefore, the clauses are separated by a comma and a coordinating conjunction.

MECHANICS

Commas   **569**

7. Many people are used to celebrating New Year's Day on January 1,but the Chinese New Year begins between January 21 and February 19.
8. The lake contains fish and is home to several alligators.
9. The old oak tree shaded the house,but the shade kept the grass from growing.
10. I wanted to buy a camera,so I mowed yards in the neighborhood to earn extra money.

8. C

Interrupters

21i. Use commas to set off an expression that interrupts a sentence.

Two commas are used to set off an interrupting expression—one before and one after the expression.

EXAMPLES   My favorite gospel singers, BeBe and CeCe Winans, were on TV last night.

As you leave, Jesse, please close the door quietly.

Sometimes an "interrupter" comes at the beginning or the end of the sentence. In such cases, only one comma is needed.

EXAMPLES   Yes, I'll call back later.

How did you do in karate class today, Kami?

(1) Use commas to set off appositives and appositive phrases that are not necessary to the meaning of a sentence.

An *appositive* is a noun or a pronoun that identifies or describes another noun or pronoun beside it. An *appositive phrase* is an appositive with its modifiers.

EXAMPLES   A gymnast, **Mrs. Shaw,** will coach us. [The appositive *Mrs. Shaw* identifies the gymnast.]

This book is about geology, **the science of the earth and its rocks.** [*The science of the earth and its rocks* is an appositive phrase that identifies *geology*.]

Do not use commas when an appositive is necessary to the meaning of a sentence.

570   Chapter 21   Punctuation

TEACHING TIP

Motivation. To show students that some phrases are nonessential, write on a large strip of paper a sentence containing an unnecessary appositive phrase. You might want to use one of the examples on this page or p. 571. Fold the strip to hide the appositive phrase to show students that the sentence makes sense without the phrase. Emphasize that when the phrase is reinserted, it must be set off from the sentence by commas.

EXAMPLES My cousin Roberto lives in Puerto Rico. [I have more than one cousin and am using his name to identify which cousin I mean.]

The character Alice is based on Alice Liddell. [Alice is one of several characters; the appositive tells which character is meant.]

Exercise 6 Punctuating Appositives

Most of the following sentences contain at least one error in the punctuation of appositives and appositive phrases. Write each word that should be followed by a comma, and add the comma. If a sentence is already correct, write *C*.

EXAMPLE 1. Two cold drinks lemonade and punch were available to the guests.
  1. *Two cold drinks, lemonade and punch, were available to the guests.*

1. The park a beautiful place for a party was lit by streetlights and had a bandstand.
2. Our hosts Mr. and Mrs. Worthington greeted us at the entrance.
3. Some of the men were wearing boaters straw hats popular at the time.
4. My friend Eliza Wolcott sat in the shade at our table. **4. C**
5. Do you see an empty table a quiet place for conversation?
6. Somehow a puppy the pet of one of the guests got onto the dance floor.
7. Edward Finch, the best dancer has his choice of partners.
8. Music mostly waltzes filled the air.
9. A young woman in a striped dress a new bride, is remembering her wedding.
10. Listen to laughter and lively conversation, the sounds of happy people. **10. C**

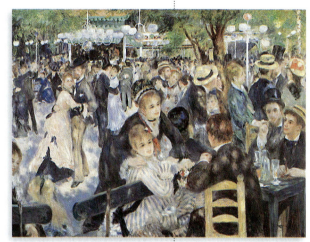

Pierre Auguste Renoir, *Ball at the Moulin de la Galette* (1876). Paris, Musée d'Orsay, Paris, Giraudon/Art Resource, New York.

TEACHING TIP

Exercise 6 You may wish to use the first two or three items in **Exercise 6** as guided practice. Then, have students complete the exercise as independent practice.

Viewing the Art

***Ball at the Moulin de la Galette*
About the Artist.** Pierre Auguste Renoir (1841–1919) was one of the innovators of French Impressionism. Among his innovations was the use of pure, unmixed colors—an integral element of Impressionist technique.

Crossing the Curriculum

History. Have students think of their favorite historical figure. Tell them to write a sentence about this person's life addressed to the person.

Example: Abe Lincoln, I wish you hadn't gone to see that play.

Students may be able to think up serious or humorous sentences. Students could write their sentences under a drawing of that person. Remind them to use commas to set off nouns of direct address. (If the noun of direct address is at the beginning or end of the sentence, only one comma is needed.)

Relating to Literature

To reinforce comma usage, you may want to have students read a short story such as "President Cleveland, Where Are You?" by Robert Cormier. Have students find examples of compound sentences, introductory expressions, nonessential phrases, and so forth in the story. Then, have students copy in their writer's logs the sentences they find, paying careful attention to correct comma placement. You may want to pair students for this activity and to limit the type of comma usage each pair is searching for. When students have found examples, have students copy their examples onto poster board for a classroom poster. Allow students to write sentences in different colors, but have all students use the same color for commas.

---

(2) Use commas to set off words used in direct address.

EXAMPLES   Ms. Jacobs, please explain the assignment.

Do you know who Santa Anna was, Beth?

You're right, Inés, to say he was a Mexican general.

In the sentences above, the words *Ms. Jacobs, Beth,* and *Inés* are **nouns of direct address.** They identify the person or persons spoken to or addressed.

HELP — Some sentences in Exercise 7 need more than one comma.

Exercise 7   Correcting Sentences by Adding Commas

For each of the following sentences, write each word that should be followed by a comma; then, add the comma.

EXAMPLE   1. Are you sure you left your book in the room James?
1. room,

1. Michi will you read the haiku you wrote?
2. Carla please bring me the newspaper when you finish with it.
3. Did you bring the tickets Jorge?
4. After all the work we've done Ann it would be a shame to turn it in late.
5. If you mow the lawn Kelly I'll rake the clippings.
6. Please Mom can you drive me to rehearsal?
7. Mr. Ferguson you have a telephone call.
8. You are dismissed class.
9. How long have you worked here David?
10. The problem my friends is simply lack of effort.

Introductory Words, Phrases, and Clauses

21j. Use a comma after certain introductory elements.

(1) Use a comma after *yes, no,* or any mild exclamation such as *well* or *why* at the beginning of a sentence.

EXAMPLES   **Yes,** you may use my pencil.

Why, it's Arthur!

Well, I think you should apologize.

MINI-LESSON

Interjections. Tell students that an interjection is one kind of introductory word. Students will find a list on p. 366 in **Chapter 12: Parts of Speech Overview.** Explain that an interjection is a word used to express an emotion and has no grammatical relationship to the rest of the sentence.

Often, an interjection is followed by an exclamation point: "Oops! I don't want to make that mistake again." Sometimes an

(2) Use a comma after two or more introductory prepositional phrases.

EXAMPLE **In the valley at the base of the hill,** a herd of buffalo grazes.

Also, use a comma after a single long introductory prepositional phrase.

EXAMPLE **On the winter morning when Kenan discovered the strange visitor,** the rosebush burst into bloom.

Use a comma after a single short introductory prepositional phrase when the comma is necessary to make the sentence clear.

CONFUSING In the evening sunlight faded in the western sky.

CLEAR **In the evening,** sunlight faded in the western sky. [The comma is needed so that the reader does not read "evening sunlight."]

(3) Use a comma after an introductory adverb clause.

EXAMPLE **After the show is over,** we will go out to eat.

NOTE An adverb clause that comes at the end of a sentence usually is not preceded by a comma.

EXAMPLE We will go out to eat **after the show is over.**

Reference Note
For more about **prepositional phrases,** see page 361. For more about **adverb clauses,** see page 391.

Exercise 8 Using Commas with Introductory Elements

If a comma is needed in a sentence, write the word before the missing comma and add the comma. If a sentence is already punctuated correctly, write *C*.

EXAMPLE 1. After he left we noticed that his hat was on the table.
  1. left,

1. Before eating the birds were singing noisily.
2. On the table in the kitchen dinner was getting cold.
3. Although he trained hard for a month, Juan could not break his own record.   3. C
4. Yes that is a cardinal.
5. On her way to school in the morning Roseanne was thinking about her project.

Commas   573

Meeting INDIVIDUAL NEEDS

ADVANCED LEARNERS
Divide the class into groups, and have each group use a television and a VCR or a radio and a tape recorder to tape several small portions of dialogue from a show. Have the students write out the dialogue, punctuating it correctly. To shorten this assignment, you could also specify that each group concentrate on only one portion of dialogue. Groups can then present their tapes and punctuated transcripts to the class.

---

interjection is set off by a comma: "Oh, we don't have time to see both movies anyway."

Ask students when they think an interjection should be followed by an exclamation point rather than a comma. Lead them to see that writers use an exclamation point after an interjection to emphasize a particular emotion the speaker is experiencing, such as surprise or joy.

Relating to Writing

Have each student check that he or she has correctly used commas in an essay or other writing assignment completed for a social studies class. Students should pay particular attention to sentences that include references to dates and places.

6. When I have time on the weekends, I like to hook rugs.
7. Well, you had better make up your mind soon.
8. With the decorations in the living room in place, Julie was ready for her mother's birthday party.
9. In the corner of the room, a night light showed the way to the door.
10. Because the snow cover was so thin, the deer had no trouble finding food.

Conventional Uses

21k. Use commas in certain conventional situations.

(1) Use commas to separate items in dates and addresses.

EXAMPLES Bill Cosby was born on July 12, 1937, in Philadelphia, Pennsylvania.

Saturday, May 10, will be the day of the soccer playoff.

My aunt has lived at 41 Jefferson Street, Northfield, Minnesota, since 1998.

Notice that a comma separates the last item in a date or in an address from the words that follow it. However, a comma does not separate a month from a day (*July 12*) or a house number from a street name (*41 Jefferson Street*).

NOTE No punctuation is used between the state abbreviation and the ZIP Code.

EXAMPLE Cerritos, **CA 90701**

STYLE TIP

Business letters use a colon, not a comma, after the salutation.

EXAMPLE
Dear Ms. Hinojosa:

Reference Note

For more about **writing letters**, see "Writing" in the Quick Reference Handbook.

(2) Use a comma after the salutation of a personal letter and after the closing of any letter.

EXAMPLES Dear Grandma and Grandpa,   Love,

Dear Tyrone,   Sincerely,

Exercise 9 Using Commas Correctly in Conventional Situations

Write the following items and sentences, inserting or deleting commas as needed.

EXAMPLE　1. Friday February 11 is the first day of the fair.
　　　　　1. *Friday, February 11, is the first day of the fair.*

1. Yours truly,
2. Shirley Chisholm was born on November 30, 1924, in New York City.
3. The first female principal chief of the Cherokee Nation is Wilma Mankiller, who was born near Rocky Mountain, Oklahoma.
4. Write to me at 327 Adams Way, Darrouzett, TX 79024.
5. The Harvest Carnival is on Friday, October 29, 2001.
6. Dear Uncle Sig,
7. Address orders to Pretty Good Camping Supplies, P.O. Box 528, Southborough, MA 01772.
8. He made his stage debut on May 25, 1928, in London, England.
9. Friday, July 5, 2002, will be my grandparents' golden wedding anniversary.
10. The main office in Santa Barbara, California, has a new fax number.

―HELP―

Commas are also used in numbers greater than and including one thousand. Use a comma before every third digit to the left of the decimal point.

EXAMPLE
7,386,149.00 [seven million three hundred eighty-six thousand one hundred forty-nine]

Unnecessary Commas

21l. Do not use unnecessary commas.

Too much punctuation can be just as confusing as not enough punctuation, especially where the use of commas is concerned.

CONFUSING　My friend, Jessica, said she would feed my cat and my dog while I'm away, but now, she tells me, she will be too busy.

CLEAR　My friend Jessica said she would feed my cat and my dog while I'm away, but now she tells me she will be too busy.

　Have a reason for every comma or other mark of punctuation that you use. When there is no rule requiring punctuation and when the meaning of the sentence is clear without one, do not insert any punctuation mark.

TEACHING TIP

Activity. Refer students to the example sentence under **Rule 21l**. Ask students to explain why *Jessica* should not be enclosed in commas and why a comma should be placed between *away* and *but*. [*Jessica* is an appositive that identifies the noun *friend*, but unless Jessica is the speaker's only friend, the name is necessary to indicate which friend will be taking care of the animals. *But* is preceded by a comma because it joins two independent clauses in a compound sentence.]

Review C **Proofreading a Letter for the Correct Use of Commas**

The sentences in the following letter each contain an error in the use of commas. Rewrite the letter, adding or deleting commas as needed.

EXAMPLES [1] July, 6, 2001
1. July 6, 2001

[2] Dear Tom
2. Dear Tom,

Dear Tom,

  [1] Well, on July 4, 2001, Aunt Lil kept her promise and took me up in her airplane. [2] Wow! What a view of the canyons, valleys, and plateaus we had! [3] We flew over a hill, and saw a small herd of mustangs. [4] Aunt Lil circled above the horses, and the plane's shadow frightened the stallion. [5] The whole herd stampeded with tails, and manes and hooves flying in a storm of dust all the way down into the valley. [6] One black colt trailed behind, but his mother quickly nudged him onward. [7] In a moment the swift, sturdy mustangs, descendants of the fiery steeds of the Spanish conquistadors, were galloping into the woods. [8] I wish you could have seen them, Tom! [9] At least I remembered my camera, so here is a picture of those beautiful horses.

  [10] Yours truly,

  Sal

576 Chapter 21 Punctuation

Semicolons

A semicolon is part period and part comma. Like a period, it can separate complete thoughts. Like a comma, it can separate items within a sentence.

21m. **Use a semicolon between parts of a compound sentence if they are not joined by *and*, *but*, *for*, *nor*, *or*, *so*, or *yet*.**

EXAMPLES Todd's report is about Arizona; mine is about Utah.

The rain clouds are moving in quickly; let's head home.

NOTE Use a semicolon to join independent clauses only if the ideas in the independent clauses are closely related. Otherwise, use a period to make two separate sentences.

EXAMPLES Do not touch that tree frog; it may be poisonous.
[The two ideas are closely related.]

Do not touch that tree frog. Everyone stay together.
[The two ideas are not closely related.]

HELP
Use a semicolon rather than a comma between phrases in a series when the phrases contain commas.

EXAMPLE
The acrobats are traveling from Albuquerque, New Mexico; through Phoenix, Arizona; and finally to San Diego, California.

Exercise 10 Proofreading Sentences for the Correct Use of Semicolons

Most of the following sentences have commas where there should be semicolons. If a sentence needs a semicolon, write the words before and after the missing semicolon; then, insert the semicolon. If a sentence is already correct, write *C*.

EXAMPLE 1. Mary Vaux Walcott treasured her box of watercolor paints, she took it with her everywhere she went.

1. paints; she

Carets indicate placement of semicolons.

1. As a young girl, she visited the Canadian Rockies each year, there she began to paint wildflowers.
2. She loved mountain climbing, she often crossed rugged areas to find new wildflowers.
3. She painted her flowers from life, for she did not like to rely on pencil sketches.   3. C
4. You can see five of her paintings on the next page, aren't they beautiful?

Semicolons 577

RESOURCES
Semicolons
Practice
- *Grammar, Usage, and Mechanics,* p. 249
- *Language Workshop CD-ROM,* Lesson 38

ALTERNATIVE LESSON
Before students correct semicolon errors in **Exercise 10,** ask them to identify the subjects and verbs in the sentences designated below.

  6. Painting B, is; it, grows
  7. American wisteria, is; you, can see
  10. Mary Vaux Walcott, is known; she, painted

Remind students that a semicolon is used between two independent clauses, each of which has a subject and a verb.

5. Painting A shows a western red lily, such lilies wither quickly when picked.
6. Painting B is of a bottle gentian, a fall flower, it grows in bogs and swamps.   6. [*or* flower; it]
7. American wisteria is a climbing plant, and you can see in Painting C that it has many showy flowers.   7. C
8. Painting D shows blossoms of the American waterlily opening in early morning, their aroma draws insects.
9. Painting E is of Carolina jessamine, it spreads its fragrant flowers through treetops.
10. Mary Vaux Walcott is known as "the Audubon of North American wildflowers," for she painted more than seven hundred species.   10. C

A   B   C

D   E

Mary Vaux Walcott, *Bottle Gentian.* Watercolor. National Museum of American Art

578   Chapter 21   Punctuation

Colons

A colon usually signals that more information follows.

21n. Use a colon before a list of items, especially after expressions such as *the following* and *as follows*.

EXAMPLES   These are the winners of the poetry contest: Carmen Santiago, Justin Douglass, and Steven Yellowfeather.

Pack the following items for your overnight trip: a toothbrush, toothpaste, and your hairbrush.

The order of the colors seen through a prism is as follows: red, orange, yellow, green, blue, indigo, and violet.

NOTE Do not use a colon between a preposition and its object or between a verb and its object. Either omit the colon or reword the sentence.

INCORRECT   My report includes: a table of contents, three chapters, illustrations, and a list of sources.

CORRECT   My report includes a table of contents, three chapters, illustrations, and a list of sources.

CORRECT   My report includes **the following parts:** a table of contents, three chapters, illustrations, and a list of sources.

Colons may also be used to introduce long, formal statements and quotations.

EXAMPLE   Mark Twain had a very definite opinion on happiness: "The best way to cheer yourself is to try to cheer somebody else up."

21o. Use a colon between the hour and the minute when you write the time.

EXAMPLES   8:55 A.M.   9:15 P.M.   6:22 this morning

21p. Use a colon after the salutation of a business letter.

EXAMPLES   Dear Sir or Madam: Dear Mrs. Jordan:

Dear Sales Manager: To Whom It May Concern:

STYLE TIP

Personal letters use a comma, not a colon, after the salutation.

EXAMPLE
Dear John,

Colons   579

RESOURCES
Colons
Practice
- *Grammar, Usage, and Mechanics,* p. 250
- *Language Workshop CD-ROM,* Lessons 37, 45

Meeting INDIVIDUAL NEEDS

MULTIPLE INTELLIGENCES

Musical Intelligence. It might be helpful for some students to think of sentences being similar to a musical composition, with words functioning as musical notes. Commas, semicolons, and colons would then be like the musical notations, rests: quarter rests, half rests, and whole rests. Symbols for rests indicate the duration of a silence or pause in a musical composition. Have a student who knows musical notation draw these rests on the chalkboard. (They have been reproduced below.) Explain to students that while musical rests indicate the length of a pause, the punctuation marks in sentences indicate the structure of sentences as well as subtle pauses.

quarter rest   half rest   whole rest

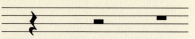

ENGLISH-LANGUAGE LEARNERS

General Strategies. Some students might confuse the colon and the semicolon or think that they are interchangeable. Tell your students that a colon usually indicates the part of the sentence the writer wants to emphasize, whereas a semicolon helps the reader avoid confusion. You may want to have students make and display a poster illustrating the uses of the colon and the semicolon. Students can refer to the poster throughout the year.

MECHANICS

Exercise 11 Using Colons Correctly

Most of the following items contain an error in the use of colons. Rewrite each incorrect sentence to correct the error. If a sentence is already correct, write *C*.

EXAMPLE   1. Bring the following items to class your notebook, a pencil, and your textbook.

1. *Bring the following items to class: your notebook, a pencil, and your textbook.*

1. We visited the following cities:Bayamón, Ponce, and San Juan.
2. A good baby sitter should have the following qualities: promptness, reliability, an interest in children, and common sense.
3. To stay healthy, you should not smoke or chew tobacco. 3. C
4. Add these items to your shopping list:tissues, toothpaste, and shampoo.
5. A good friend should be: loving, loyal, and honest.
6. The first bell rings at 8:10 A.M., and the second bell rings twenty minutes later.
7. Your homework includes: your spelling worksheet, one chapter of reading, and a rough draft of your English composition for Monday.
8. The recipe for Brunswick stew called for these ingredients: lamb, carrots, potatoes, and onions.
9. Every time we see her, Grandmother likes to remind us of her favorite Ben Franklin saying: "Whatever is begun in anger ends in shame."
10. Dear Sir or Madam:

HELP—
Some of the sentences in Review D contain more than one punctuation error.

Review D Proofreading a Letter for the Correct Use of Punctuation

Proofread the following letter for errors in punctuation. Then, rewrite the letter, adding the necessary periods, question marks, commas, semicolons, and colons.

EXAMPLE   [1] 1200 E Halifax Avenue

1. *1200 E. Halifax Avenue*

Commas that may be considered optional are underscored.

580   Chapter 21   Punctuation

Learning for Life

A Short Speech. Tell students that as they get older, there may be various occasions when they will be asked to speak to groups of people. A person may be asked to say a few words about a guest of honor at a birthday party, about the bride and groom at a wedding, or about people at some other celebration.

Have each student write a short speech (no more than one or two minutes) about a friend or family member who is celebrating an important event. The speech should

Continued on pp. 581–582

[1] January 11, 2001

Superintendent of Schools
Baltimore City Board of Education
200 E. North Avenue
Baltimore, MD 21202

[2] Dear Superintendent:

[3] Would your students be interested in visiting an African American wax museum? [4] The only one of its kind is right here in Baltimore. [5] The Great Blacks in Wax Museum features life-size wax models of famous African Americans. [6] These wax images include leaders in education, civil rights, and science. [7] The museum displays statues of the following people: Rosa Parks, Phillis Wheatley, Crispus Attucks, Carter G. Woodson, Dred Scott, Harriet Tubman, Booker T. Washington, Frederick Douglass, and many others.

[8] Our company offers students and teachers discount tours of the museum during Black History Month; discount tours of other historic attractions are also available then. [9] For more information, please call me between 8:30 A.M. and 5:30 P.M.

[10] Yours truly,

Jane Lee Harper

Jane Lee Harper
President
Uhuru Guided Tours

Colons   581

Relating to Writing

To reinforce the use of colons in sentences introducing quotations and to give students practice in speaking before a group, have them select quotations that they like. If they need help, refer them to *Bartlett's Familiar Quotations* or *Poor Richard's Almanac*. Then, have them write sentences containing the quotations (for example, *"I'll never forget Patrick Henry's stirring words: 'Give me liberty, or give me death.'"*).

Have students write their sentences on the chalkboard. Then, ask students to read the quotations and to tell why they chose them. Check sentences for correct colon usage.

MECHANICS

---

recognize the person by name, congratulate him or her on the occasion, and include comments about the person's special qualities. In addition, at least five of the sentences in the speech should include the following punctuation marks and sentence structures:

- an exclamation point
- a series of adjectives
- an appositive
- a colon preceding a list
- a semicolon

Colons   581

HELP
Some of the sentences in Review E contain more than one punctuation error.

Review E: Using End Marks, Commas, Semicolons, and Colons Correctly

Each of the following items contains at least one error in the use of end marks, commas, semicolons, or colons. Rewrite the items, adding or changing punctuation to correct each error.

EXAMPLE 1. Mrs. Hunter how long will the leaves remain that color.

1. Mrs. Hunter, how long will the leaves remain that color?

Commas that may be considered optional are underscored.

1. Liechtenstein, a country not quite as large as Washington, D.C., is one of the smallest countries in Europe.
2. The students gathered signatures on a petition, and a spokesperson presented their argument for better sidewalks.
3. That must be the biggest fish in the whole lake? . 3. [or lake!]
4. Did you find out which president created the Peace Corps in 1961.?
5. Dear Sir:
6. No, I haven't seen that new movie, but I've heard it's absolutely terrific.
7. Fort Sumter, the site of the first shots fired in the Civil War, is located in Charleston, South Carolina.
8. After the sparrows finished in the birdbath, they flew up to the feeder.
9. A long, white, shiny limousine pulled into the parking lot; after that came a bus and a police officer on a motorcycle.
10. Before you may read your mystery novel, you must finish your homework, clean your room, and walk the dog.

Learning for Life

Tell students that these punctuation marks and sentence structures do not have to be used in the order shown and can be used more than once. However, each punctuation mark and sentence structure should be circled and identified in the margin of the speech. Students should save their speeches in their writing portfolios.

CHAPTER 21

Chapter Review

A. Using Punctuation Correctly

Periods, question marks, exclamation points, commas, semicolons, and colons are missing in the following items. Write the word or numeral before each missing punctuation mark, and add the correct mark.
Commas that may be considered optional are underscored.

1. Flora, please pass the pepper.
2. Did Fred once work for Interactive Corp.?
3. We are learning about meteorology, the study of weather.
4. The shirts come in the following four colors: blue, green, brown, and red.
5. Yasunari Kawabata won the 1968 Nobel Prize in literature; he was the first Japanese writer to win the prize.
6. Watch out! 6. [or out.]
7. I wish I could go to camp this summer, but I have to stay home because I caught chickenpox.
8. Dear Mom and Dad,
9. I taught Zachary how to swim.
10. While Dr. Sanchez is on jury duty, Dr. Kelley is seeing his patients.
11. My youngest sister was born on April 12, 1997.
12. She is a bright, lively child.
13. His address is 2330 River Rd., Sterling, VA 22170-2322.
14. The Mandan and Hidatsa peoples in North Dakota harvested wild rice, and they traded it for buffalo hides and dried meat.
15. Have you ever been to Austin, Texas?
16. Well, Eric, my favorite actor is Denzel Washington.
17. Tom Brokaw, a national newscaster, was born in South Dakota.
18. I get up at 6:00 A.M. on school days.
19. Yes, a taco is a fried, filled tortilla.
20. The meeting will be held Sunday, February 23, at 2:00 P.M.

Chapter Review **583**

B. Using Punctuation Correctly

Periods, question marks, exclamation points, commas, semicolons, and colons are missing in the following items. Write the word or numeral before each missing punctuation mark, and add the correct mark.
Commas that may be considered optional are underscored.

21. Wow! Thanks for the new bike, Grandpa.
22. What a friendly, obedient dog you have!
23. Dawn finished her report, read the paper, cooked dinner, and set the table.
24. Can you tell me his address, or should I ask someone else?
25. Write to 637 West Elk Ave., Washington, DC 20015-2602.
26. Our mechanic could not find anything wrong with the water pump; the problem must be somewhere else.
27. Answer the following questions:
    (1) Was Lincoln a successful leader?
    (2) Could the Civil War have ended sooner?
    (3) How important was the naval blockade?
28. One of our troop leaders, Ms. Wells, is teaching us photography.
29. We'll need some minnows; worms aren't good bait in salt water.
30. Ned, the oldest in my family, has many responsibilities.
31. Aren't you going to Glasgow, Scotland, this summer?
32. She hid the lantern, the keys, two maps, and the gold.
33. Before June 1, 1998, I had never heard of Christine; then she was on the front page of every paper.
34. Get those filthy, muddy cowboy boots of yours out of this house now!
35. Chiles rellenos are very spicy; you'll like them.
36. Go to the cave, build a fire, and wait for Sabrina.
37. No, Teresa, there was no TV in those days.
38. Color this one yellow; Mr. Papastratos won't mind.
39. Let's finish this; we'll see about starting something new tomorrow.
40. Dear Mr. President:

Writing Application
Using End Marks in a Screenplay

Kinds of Sentences You are a scriptwriter for a popular TV show. You are writing a scene in which one of the characters wins one million dollars in a sweepstakes. Write down the character's response to the good news. Use a variety of end marks to help express the character's feelings.

Prewriting First, you will need to make up a character or use one from a TV show you have seen. How would that person feel if he or she won a million dollars? Write down some notes on how you think your character would react.

Writing Using your prewriting notes, write a draft of what your character will say. Make your draft at least one paragraph long. Use end punctuation to help express the character's emotions.

Revising Read your character's response aloud. Does it sound realistic? Check to make sure you have used a variety of end marks to express your character's feelings.

Publishing Check your writing for any errors in grammar, spelling, and punctuation. In small groups, exchange papers with another student. Take turns reading the papers to the group as if you each were one of the characters. Use the punctuation as a guide to what the character is feeling and to how you should read the response.

Chapter Review **585**

Writing Application
(p. 585)

OBJECTIVE
- To write a scene for a script using a variety of end marks

Writing Application

Tip. This activity calls for a script; however, because the script is to include only what one person will say, it does not need to be written in dialogue form. A single paragraph will do.

Scoring Rubric. While you will want to pay particular attention to students' use of end marks, commas, semicolons, and colons, you will also want to evaluate overall writing performance. You may want to give a split score to indicate development and clarity of the composition as well as punctuation skills.

Critical Thinking

Application. The exclamation point is the punctuation mark most associated with expressing feeling, but other punctuation marks can express feeling as well. If students overuse the exclamation point, the feeling expressed will seem contrived and the punctuation will be ineffective. Remind students that the assignment calls for a variety of end marks. Challenge them to convey feeling with what is said as well as with punctuation.

MECHANICS

RESOURCES
Writing Application
Extension
- *Grammar, Usage, and Mechanics,* p. 258
- *Language Workshop CD-ROM,* Lessons 36–39, 45

Chapter Review **585**

CHAPTER 22

PREVIEWING THE CHAPTER

- This chapter provides students with practice in using several marks of punctuation. The first section explains the use of underlining (italics) for titles. The next section helps students to distinguish between indirect and direct quotations, to punctuate and capitalize direct quotations, and to use quotation marks with titles of short works. The following section explains the use of apostrophes in possessives, in contractions, and in the plural forms of letters, numerals, symbols, and words used as words. The final section focuses on the use of hyphens.

- The chapter concludes with the **Chapter Review,** including a **Writing Application** that asks students to use apostrophes correctly in writing a personal letter.

- For help in integrating this chapter with composition chapters, use the **Teaching Strands** chart on pp. T297A–T297B.

USING THE DIAGNOSTIC PREVIEW

- To avoid unnecessary reteaching, you may want to analyze students' responses to the **Diagnostic Preview** and assign specific sections to individuals or groups. For students who do exceptionally well on the **Diagnostic Preview,** you may want to assign only **Reviews A, B,** and **C** within the chapter, the **Chapter Review,** and the **Writing Application.**

CHAPTER 22 Punctuation
Underlining (Italics), Quotation Marks, Apostrophes, Hyphens

Diagnostic Preview

A. Proofreading Sentences for the Correct Use of Underlining (Italics) and Quotation Marks

Each of the following sentences contains at least one error in the use of underlining (italics) or quotation marks. Rewrite each sentence correctly.

EXAMPLE 1. The recent movie of Shakespeare's "Hamlet" is true to the original play.
    1. The recent movie of Shakespeare's <u>Hamlet</u> is true to the original play.

1. 'All Summer in a Day,'   1. "The next short story we will be reading is called <s>All Summer in a Day</s>," Mr. Willis told us.
2. My younger brother learned how to play the song "Yesterday" on the piano.
3. Isn't your favorite poem "The Unicorn"?
4. "Wasn't that a song?" asked Carrie.
5. "I think a folk singer wrote it," answered Tony.

586   Chapter 22   Punctuation

CHAPTER RESOURCES

Planning
- One-Stop Planner CD-ROM

Practice and Extension
- Grammar, Usage, and Mechanics, p. 259
- Language Workshop CD-ROM

Internet
- go.hrw.com (keyword: EOLang)

Evaluation and Assessment
- Assessment Package
  —Chapter Tests, Ch. 22
  —Chapter Tests in Standardized Test Formats, Ch. 22
- Test Generator (One-Stop Planner CD-ROM)

6. Juanita said that "she would hum a bit of it."
7. Brad commented, "I think my parents have a copy of it."
8. "Can you bring it to class?" Elena asked.
9. "Who said, 'Time is money'?" Gerald asked.
10. "Benjamin Franklin wrote it," answered Karen, "in a book called Advice to a Young Tradesman."
11. "I think," said Theo, "that you're right."
12. "Into the Woods" is a musical comedy in which characters from several different fairy tales meet in the same forest.
13. Kelly's favorite episode of *Star Trek: Voyager* is titled "Message in a Bottle."
14. Sean often wonders what makes van Gogh's painting "Twelve Sunflowers in a Vase" so interesting.
15. Melba built a model of the Merrimack for extra credit in social studies.

B. Proofreading Sentences for the Correct Use of Apostrophes and Hyphens

Each of the following sentences contains at least one error in the use of apostrophes or hyphens. Rewrite each sentence correctly.

EXAMPLE   1. We havent finished dinner yet.
          1. We haven't finished dinner yet.

The ‸ symbol indicates a hyphen.

16. My teacher's house is being painted.
17. Each classroom has thirty-four desks.
18. This recipe I'm trying calls for fresh greens, potatoes, car-rots, and onions.
19. The assembly then featured a speech by the new president-elect of the student council.
20. Who's going to sample this dish?
21. Don't forget the soy sauce.
22. The three chefs' recipes were prepared by the chefs themselves on television.
23. Jiro's last name has two *l*'s.
24. Have you tried those new fat-free potato chips?
25. In the quiet early evening, we could hear the flapping of the geese's wings.

Diagnostic Preview   587

Underlining (Italics)

Rules 22a, b (pp. 588–590)

OBJECTIVE

- To use underlining (italics) correctly in sentences

Meeting INDIVIDUAL NEEDS

MULTIPLE INTELLIGENCES

Interpersonal Intelligence. Write on the chalkboard the following list of categories:

book
play
newspaper/magazine
movie
television series
painting
long musical work

Have each student write his or her favorite specific title for each category. Tell students to underline all titles. Remind students that names of ships, aircraft, trains, and spacecraft also are underlined. Then, have each student use his or her favorite title for each category in a sentence. Ask volunteers to write some of their sentences on the chalkboard, and have the rest of the class check to make sure the title has been underlined.

MECHANICS

---

22 a, b

COMPUTER TIP
If you use a computer, you may be able to set words in italics yourself. Most fonts can be set in italic type.

TIPS & TRICKS
Generally, use italics for titles of works that stand alone, such as books, CDs, and television series. Use quotation marks for titles of works that are usually part of a larger work, such as short stories, songs, and episodes of a television series.

Reference Note
For examples of **titles that require quotation marks** instead of italics, see page 595.

Underlining (Italics)

Italics are printed letters that lean to the right—*like this*. When you handwrite or type, you show that a word should be italicized by underlining it. If your writing were printed, the typesetter would set the underlined words in italics. For example, if you wrote

Zora Neale Hurston wrote Mules and Men.

the sentence would be printed like this:

Zora Neale Hurston wrote *Mules and Men*.

22a. Use underlining (italics) for titles and subtitles of books, plays, periodicals, films, television series, works of art, and long musical works.

Type of Name	Examples
Books	*Number the Stars* *To Kill a Mockingbird* *Tibet: Through the Red Box*
Plays	*Song of Sheba* *Romeo and Juliet* *Life with Father*
Periodicals	*Sioux City Journal* *The Dallas Morning News* *Highlights for Children*
Films	*Babe: Pig in the City* *The Wizard of Oz* *Oliver & Company*
Television Series	*Under the Umbrella Tree* *Fun with Watercolors* *Reading Rainbow*

588 Chapter 22 Punctuation

 **RESOURCES**

Underlining (Italics)
Practice
- *Grammar, Usage, and Mechanics,* pp. 260, 261
- *Language Workshop CD-ROM,* Lesson 42

Type of Name	Examples
Works of Art	The Old Guitarist Mona Lisa Confucius and Disciples
Long Musical Works	The Pirates of Penzance The Nutcracker Suite A Little Night Music

NOTE An article (*a, an,* or *the*) before the title of a magazine or a newspaper is not italicized or capitalized when it is part of a sentence rather than part of the title.

EXAMPLES I deliver **the** *Evening Independent.* [*The* is part of the sentence, not part of the title.]

Is that the latest issue of ***The*** *New Yorker*? [*The* is part of the magazine's title.]

HELP
If you are not sure whether an article is part of a title, check the periodical's masthead (the section that lists the publisher, owners, editors, etc.) or the table of contents to find out the official title.

22b. Use underlining (italics) for names of trains, ships, aircraft, and spacecraft.

Type of Name	Examples
Trains	Stourbridge Lion Best Friend of Charleston The City of New Orleans
Ships	Lusitania Flying Cloud USS Lexington
Aircraft	Solar Challenger Hindenburg Spirit of St. Louis
Spacecraft	Landsat-7 Discovery Enterprise

Relating to Literature

Have students write a one-page review of a book such as *Woodsong, Harriet Tubman: Conductor on the Underground Railroad,* or *The Secret Garden.* In writing their reviews, students should answer the following questions.

1. What is the theme of the book?

2. How is the theme developed through plot, character, setting, or mood? (Have students choose one or two of these elements.)

3. Did you enjoy the book? Why or why not? Would you recommend it to a friend?

MECHANICS

Exercise 1

ALTERNATIVE LESSON
Point out to students that the titles in sentences 1 and 4 in **Exercise 1** are appositives. Ask why the title in sentence 1 is not set off by commas, while the title in sentence 4 is. [In sentence 1, the title is necessary to the meaning of the sentence. There are many magazines, and the title *Popular Science* tells which one. The title in sentence 4 is not necessary to the meaning of the sentence. The Wright brothers had only one first airplane, the *Flyer*.]

Quotation Marks

Rules 22c–l *(pp. 590–597)*

OBJECTIVES

- To use punctuation and capitalization correctly in quotations
- To recognize indirect quotations and to rewrite them as direct quotations
- To use single and double quotation marks correctly in sentences

Meeting INDIVIDUAL NEEDS

MODALITIES

Visual Learners. Distribute to each student a short newspaper or magazine article that uses direct and indirect quotations. Then, have each student circle direct quotations and underline indirect quotations in his or her article. Afterward, have students trade articles with partners and check each other's work.

---

22 c–l

STYLE TIP

Now and then, writers will use italics (underlining) for emphasis, especially in written dialogue. Read the following sentences aloud. Notice that by italicizing different words, the writer can change the meaning of the sentence.

EXAMPLES
"Are you going to wear the *red* shoes?" asked Ellen. [Will you wear the red shoes, not the blue ones?]

"Are *you* going to wear the red shoes?" asked Ellen. [Will you, not your sister, wear them?]

"Are you going to *wear* the red shoes?" asked Ellen. [Will you wear them, or are you just trying them on?]

Italicizing (underlining) words for emphasis is a handy technique that should not be overused. It can quickly lose its impact.

Exercise 1 Using Underlining (Italics) Correctly

For each of the following sentences, write each word or item that should be printed in italics and underline it.

EXAMPLE 1. We saw Rodin's famous statue The Thinker.
1. *The Thinker*

1. The magazine Popular Science reports news about science.
2. Have you ever seen the movie The Shaggy Dog?
3. My favorite painting is Morning of Red Bird by Romare Bearden.
4. The Wright brothers built their first airplane, the Flyer, in 1903.
5. We read the play You're a Good Man, Charlie Brown.
6. On his famous voyage in 1492, Christopher Columbus acted as captain of the ship named the Santa Maria.
7. Which newspaper do you read, the Chicago Sun-Times or the Chicago Tribune?
8. My sister watches Sesame Street every day.
9. Aboard Vostok 1, Yuri A. Gagarin orbited Earth.
10. The book Stuart Little is by E. B. White.

Quotation Marks

22c. Use quotation marks to enclose a **direct quotation**—a person's exact words.

Be sure to place quotation marks both before and after a person's exact words.

EXAMPLES Our team leader says, "I try to practice every day."

"Let's go home," Jeanne suggested.

Do not use quotation marks for an **indirect quotation**—a rewording of a direct quotation.

DIRECT QUOTATION	Juan said, "The bus is late." [Juan's exact words]
INDIRECT QUOTATION	Juan said that the bus was late. [not Juan's exact words]

590 Chapter 22 Punctuation

RESOURCES

Quotation Marks
Practice

- *Grammar, Usage, and Mechanics,* pp. 262, 263, 264, 265, 266–267
- *Language Workshop CD-ROM,* Lessons 43-44

| DIRECT QUOTATION | Juan asked, "Is the bus late?" [Juan's exact words] |
| INDIRECT QUOTATION | Juan asked whether the bus was late. [not Juan's exact words] |

22d. A directly quoted sentence begins with a capital letter.

EXAMPLES Mrs. Talbott said, "**P**lease get a pencil."

Kristina asked, "**I**s it my turn?"

22e. When an expression identifying the speaker interrupts a quoted sentence, the second part of the quotation begins with a lowercase letter.

EXAMPLE "Will you take care of my lawn and my pets," asked Mr. Franklin, "**w**hile I'm on vacation next month?"

When the second part of a divided quotation is a new sentence, it begins with a capital letter.

EXAMPLE "Yes, we will," I said. "**W**e can use the extra money."

22f. A direct quotation can be set off from the rest of the sentence by a comma, a question mark, or an exclamation point, but not by a period.

(1) If a quotation comes at the beginning of a sentence, a comma, question mark, or exclamation point usually follows it.

EXAMPLES "Dogs make better pets than cats do**,**" said Frank.

"Have you ever had a cat**?**" Donna asked.

"No, and I never will**!**" he replied.

(2) If a quotation comes at the end of a sentence, a comma usually comes before it.

EXAMPLE Maria asked**,** "What makes you say that?"

(3) If a quoted sentence is divided, a comma usually follows the first part and comes before the second part.

EXAMPLE "Oh**,**" Donna commented**,** "he's probably just saying that because he's never had a cat."

HELP

To set off means "to separate."

Meeting INDIVIDUAL NEEDS

ENGLISH-LANGUAGE LEARNERS
Spanish. Although quotation marks are not unheard of in Spanish, it is far more common to use dashes to set off quotations. For example:

—No—he said—I don't believe you.

—¿Why not?—she asked.

When quotation marks are used, they look like this: « ».

INCLUSION
Some students may have difficulty identifying an unpunctuated direct quotation, especially if it is interrupted by explanatory or declarative text. Have students who have difficulty copy an exercise sentence that contains a direct quotation. Next, pair each student having difficulty with a partner who can read the sentence aloud, emphasizing the quoted words. Tell the student having difficulty to repeat only the quoted words.

LEARNERS HAVING DIFFICULTY
Some students may be able to create dialogue but may not know how to punctuate it. You might have students work in pairs, pairing each student having difficulty with a student who has a good grasp of punctuation. Have the student having difficulty dictate some dialogue to the other student. Then, have the other student punctuate the dialogue and discuss the punctuation with the student having difficulty. Finally, you may wish to have students switch roles so that the student having difficulty can practice punctuating quotations offered by his or her partner.

22g. A period or a comma should be placed inside the closing quotation marks.

EXAMPLE "I can't wait to see Shirley Caesar's new video," James said. "It's supposed to come out next week."

22h. A question mark or an exclamation point should be placed inside closing quotation marks when the quotation itself is a question or an exclamation. Otherwise, it should be placed outside.

EXAMPLES "What time will you be home from work, Mom?" asked Michael. [The quotation is a question.]

Who said, "All the world's a stage"? [The sentence, not the quotation, is a question.]

"Stop!" yelled the crossing guard. [The quotation is an exclamation.]

What a surprise to hear Susana say, "We're moving back to Puerto Rico in June"! [The sentence, not the quotation, is an exclamation.]

Exercise 2 Punctuating and Capitalizing Quotations

Rewrite the following sentences, using commas, end marks, quotation marks, and capital letters where they are needed. If a sentence is already correct, write *C*.

EXAMPLE 1. We're going tubing next Saturday said Carlos.
1. "We're going tubing next Saturday," said Carlos.

1. May I go with you I asked.
2. We'd like to go, too added Barbara and Tranh.
3. Barbara asked who will bring tubes for everyone?
4. Jim said I'll bring them.
5. I offered to bring sandwiches and lemonade.   **5. C**
6. My dad will drive said Carlos he has a van.
7. Tranh told us that the river is fed by a glacier.   **7. C**
8. That means said Barbara that the water will be cold.
9. It should feel good I pointed out if Saturday is as hot as today is.
10. Carlos told all of us to meet him at his house at 8:30 A.M.   **10. C**

MODALITIES

Kinesthetic Learners. Some students will learn punctuation rules more easily if sentences are broken into parts. For this activity, you may want to use sentences 1, 2, 4, 8, and 9 from **Exercise 2,** which require only punctuation and not additional capitalization. Have a volunteer write parts of each sentence on pieces of stiff cardboard; one or two pieces will contain the quotation itself (depending on whether or not the quoted sentence is divided), and the other piece will contain the text identifying the speaker(s). For example, for sentence 8 the words *That means* should be written on one card, the words *said Barbara* on another, and the words *that the water will be cold* on the last card. Then, the volunteer should create a set of eight punctuation marks: two large opening quotation marks, two large closing quotation marks, two large commas, one large question mark, and one large period. Finally, select students to come to the front of the class and arrange the cards correctly for each sentence. (The one set of cards of punctuation marks will be reused for each sentence.)

Exercise 3 **Punctuating and Capitalizing Quotations**

Rewrite each of the following sentences correctly, using punctuation and capitalization as needed.

EXAMPLE 1. Clementine Hunter was born in 1887 said María and she died in 1988.

1. "Clementine Hunter was born in 1887," said María, "and she died in 1988."

1. Staci said here is a photograph of this self-taught American artist.
2. Clementine Hunter was born in Natchitoches, Louisiana Staci remarked.
3. She started working on a plantation when she was only fourteen María added.
4. When she was fifty-three years old said Staci Hunter decided to do what she loved most—paint.
5. Staci continued she began painting on almost any surface that would hold the paint!
6. Her early pieces were painted on brown paper bags and cardboard boxes María remarked and then on canvas, wood, and paper.
7. Hunter used bright colors Mike explained to paint everyday scenes like this one, called *Wash Day*.
8. It may surprise you to learn added Mike that her paintings sold for as little as twenty-five cents fifty years ago!
9. María asked Mike didn't you say that her paintings are now worth thousands of dollars?
10. Moreover Staci concluded Clementine Hunter's paintings have been exhibited throughout the United States.

9. [*or* María asked Mike, "Didn't you . . ."

Clementine Hunter (c.1945). Photo from the Mildred Bailey Collection, Natchitoches, Louisiana.

Clementine Hunter, *Wash Day*. The collection of Thomas N. Whitehead, courtesy of the Association for the Preservation of Historical Natchitoches, Louisiana, Melrose Plantation.

Quotation Marks **593**

Meeting INDIVIDUAL NEEDS

LEARNERS HAVING DIFFICULTY
To increase students' self-esteem, choose one or two students to be your helpers or graders for selected exercises in the chapter. Pass around the responsibilities so that each student feels needed and important. It will save you grading time, and it will also make students feel more responsible, and checking other students' work will reinforce their understanding.

Viewing the Art

About the Artist. Born in the 1880s to former slaves, Clementine Hunter, creator of *Wash Day*, dropped out of school after three years to work in the cotton fields of Melrose Plantation near Natchitoches, Louisiana. In her late 50s, Hunter became a house servant.

The Melrose mistress, an amateur painter, often entertained artists. One evening Hunter found some discarded tubes of paint and created her first painting on an old window shade.

Hunter went on to paint thousands of canvases—colorful representations of African American life on a Southern plantation. Her paintings celebrate life and depict only her happy memories. Internationally renowned in her lifetime, Hunter lived to be 101 years old.

Exercise 4 Revising Indirect Quotations to Create Direct Quotations

ANSWERS
Revisions may vary.
1. The cashier replied, "I'm not allowed to make change unless a purchase is made."
2. "I need a new pen," I said.
3. "It costs seventy-nine cents," the cashier told me.
4. I said, "I will give you $1.79."
5. "I can give you change for a dollar," she told me.
6. "How do you want the change?" the cashier asked.
7. I said, "Three quarters, two dimes, and a nickel would be good."
8. "I do not have any more dimes in my cash register," she replied.
9. "Then," I said, "I will gladly take four quarters."
10. "That's okay, but why do you want change?" she said.

Relating to Literature

Some excellent dialogue for discussion can be found in the "Riddles in the Dark" chapter of J.R.R. Tolkien's *The Hobbit*. To illustrate how Tolkien uses dialogue for characterization, read aloud several examples and ask your students to identify the speaker as Bilbo or Gollum. Ask students to identify places where Tolkien's use of punctuation contributes to meaning.

—HELP—
You will need to change some pronouns and verb forms in Exercise 4.

Exercise 4 Revising Indirect Quotations to Create Direct Quotations

Revise each of the following sentences to change the indirect quotation to a direct quotation. Be sure to use capital letters and punctuation marks where they are needed.

EXAMPLE 1. I asked the cashier for change for a dollar.
1. "May I please have change for a dollar?" I asked the cashier.

1. The cashier replied that she was not allowed to make change unless a purchase was made.
2. I said that I needed a new pen.
3. The cashier told me that it cost seventy-nine cents.
4. I said that I would give her $1.79.
5. She told me she could give me change for a dollar.
6. The cashier asked how I wanted the change.
7. I said that three quarters, two dimes, and a nickel would be good.
8. She replied that she did not have any more dimes in her cash register.
9. Then I said that I would gladly take four quarters.
10. She said that was okay but asked why I wanted change.

22i. When you write dialogue (conversation), begin a new paragraph every time the speaker changes.

EXAMPLE   In Khanabad, Mulla Nasrudin was sitting in a tea house when a stranger walked in and sat down beside him.
   The newcomer said:
   "Why is that man over there sobbing his heart out?"
   "Because I have just arrived from his hometown and told him that all his winter camel fodder was lost in a fire."
   "It is terrible to be a bearer of such tidings," said the stranger.
   "It is also interesting to be the man who will shortly tell him the good news," said Nasrudin. "You see, his camels have died of a plague, so he will not need the fodder after all."

Idries Shah, "Camel Fodder"

22j. When a quotation consists of several sentences, put quotation marks only at the beginning and the end of the whole quotation.

EXAMPLE "Will Bao help with the play? Zachary has offered to make costumes," Aaron said.

22k. Use single quotation marks to enclose a quotation within a quotation.

EXAMPLE "Mrs. Engle distinctly said, 'Your book reports are due Thursday,'" Krista told me.

22l. Use quotation marks to enclose the titles of short works such as short stories, poems, newspaper or magazine articles, songs, episodes of television series, and chapters and other parts of books.

Type Of Name	Examples
Short Stories	"The Stone" "All Summer in a Day"
Poems	"Jetliner" "Song of the Sky Loom"
Articles	"Celebrating Our Heritage" "The Giants of Easter Island"
Songs	"Georgia on My Mind" "America the Beautiful"
Episodes of Television Series	"Kali the Lion" "The Trouble with Tribbles"
Chapters and Other Parts of Books	"Energy from the Stars" "I Go to Sea"

NOTE Titles that appear in quotation marks are set in single quotation marks when they appear within a quotation.

EXAMPLE Kris said, "Our class learned 'America the Beautiful' today."

TIPS & TRICKS

In general, the title of a work that can stand alone (for instance, a novel, a TV series, a collection of poems) is in italics. The title of a work that is usually part of a collection or series (for instance, a chapter of a book, an episode of a television series, a poem) is in quotation marks.

Reference Note

For examples of **titles that require italics** instead of quotation marks, see page 588.

Cooperative Learning

Divide the class into groups of five, and give each group a list of books, plays, stories, articles, and poems taken from the table of contents of a literature textbook. Have each group member take responsibility for one of the five types of works. Each member should decide for each title in his or her category whether it should be underlined or placed in quotation marks. Then the five members should correctly write their titles on poster board, noting to the side of each title the relevant rule from this section (**Rules 22a–l**). Ask a volunteer from each group to present the group's poster to the rest of the class.

Timesaver

Prepare on an overhead transparency an answer key to **Exercise 5**. After they complete the exercise, have students check their own work while you circulate through the room to answer questions and to make sure students understand the items they have missed. You can use this technique with many of the exercises in this chapter.

Exercise 5 Punctuating Quotations and Titles

Rewrite the following sentences, adding single and double quotation marks where they are needed.

EXAMPLE 1. I just finished the chapter The Circulatory System in our health book, Dell told me.

1. "I just finished the chapter 'The Circulatory System' in our health book," Dell told me.

1. Diane is learning the song "This Little Rose" for her recital.
2. "Angelo, can we meet after school tomorrow? We need to practice our presentation," Sam said.
3. "I'm sure I heard the announcer say, 'Schools are closed because of the storm,'" I said.   3. storm,'"
4. "I can pronounce all the words in Lewis Carroll's poem 'Jabberwocky,'" Nina told Lou.   4. 'Jabberwocky,'"
5. Ted said, "My dad will pick us up on Saturday at 7:30 A.M. After the race, he is taking us to Lucy Chang's for lunch. Do you like Chinese food?"
6. "The weather should be nice tomorrow. Let's plan on hiking in the woods," Eric said.
7. Mrs. Banister said, "'The Fun They Had' is a good short story, don't you think?"
8. "Have you read 'The Toaster?'" Sue May asked. "It's the funniest poem I know."
9. One article in the newspaper this morning is titled "Black Scientists Make History."
10. "Strong's new song is 'Be True, Not Blue,' and it's great!" Marcie said.

Review A Punctuating Paragraphs in a Dialogue

Rewrite the following paragraphs, using capital letters as well as quotation marks and other marks of punctuation where they are needed.

HELP
All of the punctuation marks already in Review A are correct.

EXAMPLE [1] What are you writing my grandfather asked.

1. "What are you writing?" my grandfather asked.

[1] "Grandpa, I said, "I'm writing a report about your hero, Octaviano Larrazolo. Can you tell me how he helped Mexican Americans?"

596 Chapter 22 Punctuation

Learning for Life

Keeping a Journal. Personal journals give writers a window into their pasts. A writer can look back on journal entries to recall important events or favorite artistic works or moments. Have students compose journal entries about their favorite books, magazines, music, movies, television programs or series, short stories, and poems. Explain that in a few years they will be able to read about some of the things that were important to them in the sixth grade.

In writing these journal entries, students

[2] Grandpa got out his scrapbook. "Octaviano did many things for our people," he began. "In 1912, New Mexico became a state. Octaviano and other Hispanic leaders wanted to be sure that Mexican Americans could hold political office. They wanted to make certain that they would always be allowed to vote. When New Mexico's new constitution was written, Octaviano and the other leaders fought for these rights."

[3] "How did Mr. Larrazolo know how to protect the rights of people?" I said.

[4] Grandpa replied, "he had studied law. His knowledge of the law helped him understand the constitution. It also helped him later when he became interested in politics."

[5] "When did Mr. Larrazolo become involved in politics?" I asked.

[6] "In 1916, he campaigned for Ezequiel Cabeza de Baca for governor," said Grandpa. "De Baca was elected, but he died a month later. Another election was held, and Larrazolo became New Mexico's governor."

[7] I asked, "what are some things that Mr. Larrazolo felt strongly about?"

[8] He answered, "Octaviano believed that public schools should teach children about Mexican American culture. He also was in favor of both English and Spanish being spoken in schools. Here is a picture of him with his daughters."

[9] "What else should I know about Octaviano Larrazolo," I asked Grandpa.

[10] "Octaviano was elected to the United States Senate in 1928," Grandpa said. "He continued to work hard for the rights of Hispanic Americans until he died. If you want to read more about him, I have a copy of an article, Octaviano Larrazolo: New Mexico's Greatest Governor, here in my scrapbook."

Photo: Wesley Bradfield. Courtesy Museum of New Mexico, #47660.

Relating to Writing

Octaviano Larrazolo (in **Review A**) is obviously a hero to Grandpa. Ask students to write brief essays about their own heroes. Students can write about someone they know or about a historic person. Tell students to answer the following questions in their essays:

1. Who is your hero?
2. What heroic actions has this person performed?
3. What heroic qualities does this person have?
4. Will others consider this person a hero? Why or why not?

should correctly underline (or italicize if they complete this assignment using a computer) or place in quotation marks titles of their favorite works. When they are finished, students should place their journal entries in their personal portfolios.

Apostrophes and Hyphens

Rules 22m–w *(pp. 598–608)*

OBJECTIVES

- To use apostrophes to write the singular and plural possessives of nouns
- To use apostrophes to write the possessive forms of indefinite pronouns
- To use apostrophes correctly in contractions
- To form correctly the plurals of numbers, letters, words used as words, and symbols using apostrophes
- To use hyphens correctly

Meeting INDIVIDUAL NEEDS

LEARNERS HAVING DIFFICULTY
Select or borrow several specific, recognizable objects from members of the class. For example, you might choose a backpack, a jacket, and so forth. Be sure that students will recognize who owns each object. Then, hold the objects up in front of the students and have them write down the name of each object and its owner. Have students use the possessive form of the name with the item, for example, *Roberto's backpack*.

Apostrophes

Possessive Case

The *possessive case* of a noun or a pronoun shows ownership or possession.

EXAMPLES
Heidi's comb	no **one's** fault
his jacket	**two weeks'** vacation
our dog	**my** stepbrother

22m. To form the possessive case of a singular noun, add an apostrophe and an *s*.

EXAMPLES
| a student's grant | Tanaka's store |
| the child's toy | Tess's painting |

NOTE A proper noun ending in *–s* may take only an apostrophe to form the possessive case if adding *–'s* would make the name awkward to say.

EXAMPLES the Netherlands' climate

Ms. Andrews' class

Exercise 6 Using Apostrophes for Singular Possessives

For each of the following sentences, identify the word that needs an apostrophe. Then, correctly write the word.

EXAMPLE 1. Kenyans celebrate 1963 as the year of their countrys independence.

1. country's

1. Soon that young nations athletes were setting records in international sports.
2. Leading Kenyas world-class distance runners was Kipchoge Keino, shown on the next page.
3. Keino increased his endurance by running many miles in his homelands mountains.
4. In 1965, he burst into his sports top ranks by setting world records for both the 3,000-meter and the 5,000-meter races.

598 Chapter 22 Punctuation

RESOURCES

Apostrophes and Hyphens
Practice
- *Grammar, Usage, and Mechanics,* pp. 268, 269, 270, 271, 272, 273, 274
- *Language Workshop CD-ROM,* Lessons 40–41, 45

5. Training in the mountains helped Keino win a gold medal at Mexico City's 1968 Olympics.
6. His record in that year's 1,500-meter race stood until 1984.
7. In fact, the Kenyan team's runners took home a total of eight medals in 1968.
8. In the 1972 Olympics, Keino's performance won him a second gold medal, this time for the 3,000-meter steeplechase.
9. A silver medal in the 1,500-meter race marked his career's remarkable completion.
10. His victories won Keino the world's praise and set new standards for all runners.

22n. To form the possessive case of a plural noun that does not end in *s*, add an apostrophe and an *s*.

EXAMPLES   geese's feathers   men's clothing
           children's books   feet's bones

22o. To form the possessive case of a plural noun ending in *s*, add only the apostrophe.

EXAMPLES   boxes' lids   ten minutes' time
           beetles' shells the Ozawas' address

> **NOTE** In general, you should not use an apostrophe to form the plural of a noun.
> INCORRECT   Two boy's left their books here.
> CORRECT   Two **boys** left their books here.

Reference Note
For information about **using apostrophes to form the plurals of letters, numerals, symbols, and words used as words,** see page 605.

Exercise 7 Writing Plural Possessives

For each of the following sentences, identify the word that needs an apostrophe. Then, correctly write the word.

EXAMPLE 1. Wild creatures survival depends on their ability to adapt.
         1. creatures'

1. Animals ways of dealing with cold are fascinating.

Viewing the Illustration
Exploring the Subject. The modern Olympic games are based on the ancient Olympic games, whose winners were first recorded in 776 B.C. The ancient games were held at the stadium at Olympia, which lies at the foot of Mount Olympus, reputed home of the Greek gods and goddesses. The pure amateur spirit of the ancient games was lost in modern times as rules were relaxed and professional athletes were allowed to compete. The ancient games officially ended in A.D. 393.

Meeting INDIVIDUAL NEEDS

ENGLISH-LANGUAGE LEARNERS
Romance Languages. Some students who speak Spanish or French may have difficulty using possessive nouns in English because their native languages do not have a possessive ending that resembles –'s. The most common way of expressing possession in those languages is with the preposition *de*, which means "of." Students may, therefore, generate phrases such as *the book of Lisa*, or they may use correct English word order but simply omit the possessive suffix, resulting in *Lisa book*. You may want to create an exercise such as the following one.

1. That pen belongs to Felipe. [*That is Felipe's pen.*]
2. This suitcase belongs to Martha. [*This is Martha's suitcase.*]

Exercise 7

ALTERNATIVE LESSON
Before students work on **Exercise 7**, ask them to identify the objects being possessed in the designated sentences.

[1. *ways*, 2. *feathers*, 4. *coats*, 5. *underwear*]

2. At night, chickadees' feathers are fluffed over the soft down next to their skin.
3. In addition, the birds' breathing rates and heartbeats slow, and their body temperatures fall, saving energy.
4. Deer's winter coats, made of hollow hairs filled with air, keep body heat from escaping. 4. [or Deers']
5. Soft undercoats of fine hair are many animals' thermal underwear.
6. In the picture on the left, you can see how squirrels' tails, flattened against their backs and necks, keep them warm when they leave their nests.

7. The picture on the right shows how red foxes' tails are used as muffs curled around their heads while they sleep.
8. On grouses' toes are comblike structures that make walking in snow easier.
9. In cold weather, fur grows on the bottom of snowshoe hares' feet for protection.
10. Some wild creatures' survival during freezing temperatures and snow depends on traits like these.

Review B Writing Possessives

Rewrite each of the following expressions by using the possessive case. Be sure to add apostrophes where they are needed.

EXAMPLE   1. the speeches of the politicians
          1. *the politicians' speeches*

1. the books of the children   **1. the children's books**

2. the prize of the winner **2. the winner's prize**
3. the bed of the kittens **3. the kittens' bed**
4. the home of my friend **4. my friend's home**
5. the streets of the city **5. the city's streets**
6. the fish of the teacher **6. the teacher's fish**
7. the cars of the women **7. the women's cars**
8. the dens of the foxes **8. the foxes' dens**
9. the fables of Aesop **9. Aesop's fables**
10. the medal of Rowan **10. Rowan's medal**
11. the hiding place of the mice **11. the mice's hiding place**
12. the idea of the boss **12. the boss's idea**
13. the plans of the builders **13. the builders' plan**
14. the diet of moose **14. the moose's diet**
15. the climate of the Cook Islands **15. the Cook Islands' climate**
16. the lawnmower of the Barkers **16. the Barkers' lawnmower**
17. the shoes of the girls **17. the girls' shoes**
18. the elephants of the zoo **18. the zoo's elephants**
19. the roads of the cities **19. the cities' roads**
20. the computer of the company **20. the company's computer**
21. the desks of the students **21. the students' desks**
22. the driveway of the neighbor **22. the neighbor's driveway**
23. the tail of the dog **23. the dog's tail**
24. the stories of Mark Twain **24. Mark Twain's stories**
25. the history of Texas **25. Texas's history [*or* Texas' history]**

22p. Do not use an apostrophe with possessive personal pronouns.

EXAMPLES   Is this pencil **yours** or **mine**?

Our apartment is smaller than **theirs**.

Her enchiladas are spicier than **his**.

22q. To form the possessive case of many indefinite pronouns, add an apostrophe and an *s*.

EXAMPLES   either**'s** topic

everyone**'s** favorite

somebody**'s** notebook

Reference Note

For more information about **possessive personal pronouns,** see page 475. For more information about **indefinite pronouns,** see page 332.

Relating to Writing

Rules 22p and **22q** explain the use of apostrophes with possessive pronouns. To help students distinguish between the punctuation of possessive personal pronouns and that of possessive indefinite pronouns, give them the practice exercise below and ask them to insert apostrophes where needed. Remind students that possessive personal pronouns do not require apostrophes, whereas many possessive indefinite pronouns do.

theirs	anybodys ['s]
everyones ['s]	ours
his	everybodys ['s]
yours	eithers ['s]
someones ['s]	hers
nobodys ['s]	anothers ['s]

MINI-LESSON   Continued on p. 602

Personal Pronouns. You might want to review briefly common usage problems involving possessive pronouns. Some usage problems are discussed in **Chapter 19: A Glossary of Usage,** p. 518. Ask students to choose the correct word to complete each of the following sentences.

1. Rafael and Lisha forgot to bring (*they're, their*) project to class this morning. [*their*]

Relating to Literature

Select an example of literary dialogue from your textbook or from a story such as Gary Soto's "La Bamba" or Isaac Asimov's "The Fun They Had." Be sure that the passage contains several contractions. Read the passage aloud as it is written. Then, read it aloud again, reading the contractions as separate, complete words. For example, say *are not* for *aren't*. Ask students which version they like and why. Discuss with students the importance of representing oral language realistically in dialogue.

Exercise 8 Writing the Possessive Case of Personal Pronouns and Indefinite Pronouns

Rewrite each of the following expressions by using the possessive case. Be sure to add apostrophes where they are needed.

EXAMPLE   1. the speeches of everybody
          1. everybody's speeches

1. the wishes of everyone **1. everyone's wishes**
2. the fault of him **2. his fault**
3. the answer of no one **3. no one's answer**
4. the album of someone **4. someone's album**
5. the guess of me **5. my guess**
6. the job of neither **6. neither's job**
7. the color of something **7. something's color**
8. the deal of anyone **8. anyone's deal**
9. the sweaters of them **9. their sweaters**
10. the notebook of you **10. your notebook**

STYLE TIP
Some people consider contractions informal. Therefore, it is generally best not to use them in formal writing and speech.

Contractions

22r. Use an apostrophe to show where letters, numerals, or words have been left out in a contraction.

A *contraction* is a shortened form of a word, a numeral, or a group of words. The apostrophe in a contraction shows where letters, numerals, or words have been left out.

Common Contractions			
I am	I'm	they have	they've
1999	'99	here is	here's
let us	let's	you are	you're
of the clock	o'clock	she is	she's
movie is	movie's	Bill has	Bill's
he would	he'd	you will	you'll

The word *not* can be shortened to *n't* and added to a verb. The spelling of the verb usually does not change.

602 Chapter 22 Punctuation

MINI-LESSON

2. May Donna borrow (*your, you're*) pencil? [*your*]
3. The cat licked (*its, it's*) paws. [*its*]
4. (*Whose, Who's*) book is this? [*Whose*]

EXAMPLES	is not . . . . isn't	has not . . . . hasn't
	are not . . . . aren't	have not . . . . haven't
	does not. . . . . doesn't	had not. . . . . hadn't
	do not . . . . don't	should not. . . . shouldn't
	was not . . . . . . wasn't	would not . . . . wouldn't
	were not . . . . weren't	could not . . . . . . couldn't
EXCEPTIONS	will not . . . . . . won't	cannot. . . . . can't

Do not confuse contractions with possessive pronouns.

Contractions	Possessive Pronouns
It's [*It is*] raining. **It's** [*It has*] been a long day.	**Its** tires are flat.
Who's [*Who is*] your coach? **Who's** [*Who has*] been in my room?	**Whose** watch is this?
You're [*You are*] welcome.	**Your** sister won.
They're [*They are*] late.	**Their** house is next door.
There's [*There is*] the bell.	That car is **theirs**.

Exercise 9 Using Apostrophes in Contractions

For the following sentences, write the word or numeral that requires an apostrophe and insert the apostrophe. If a sentence is already correct, write *C*.

EXAMPLE   1. Well be leaving soon.
    1. We'll

1. Youve been a big help.
2. Youd better hurry up.
3. Whose umbrella is this?   3. C
4. Were having a fund-raiser for the homeless.
5. I cant find my skateboard.
6. He promised hed wear his seat belt.
7. Lets get tickets to see the concert.

Apostrophes   **603**

8. It's time to leave for the party.
9. Its wings are painted blue. 9. C
10. I'll wash the car tomorrow morning.
11. Daniel asked the decoration committee who's going to be in charge.
12. Isn't this the book we need?
13. Remember to give your dog fresh water. 13. C
14. Stephanie said she'll bring a cardboard box from home.
15. This is a picture of my parents in '99, the year before my half-brother was born.
16. If that hummingbird returns to the feeder, I'm going to take a picture.
17. Theirs will be the last band to perform. 17. C
18. The cold weather doesn't bother Jeremy much.
19. We should be back to school by three o'clock.
20. Have you found out yet if you're on the team?

Exercise 10 Writing Contractions

For each of the following sentences, write the contraction of the *italicized* word or words.

EXAMPLE   1. *We will* see a performance of the puppet theater when we visit the Japan America Theatre in Los Angeles.
   1. We'll

1. *Have not* you always wondered what goes on backstage at a puppet show? 1. Haven't

604 Chapter 22 Punctuation

2. *Here is* an illustration that takes you behind the scenes at a seventeenth-century puppet theater in Japan. **2.** Here's
3. The audience *cannot* see all the backstage action because of the curtain. **3.** can't
4. The men *who are* handling the puppets in the picture are very highly trained. **4.** who're
5. They *do not* speak the characters' lines, though. **5.** don't
6. *It is* the man sitting on the right on the platform who narrates the play. **6.** It's
7. As you can see, *he is* accompanied by a musician. **7.** he's
8. On the right are more puppets; *they have* been hung there for future use. **8.** they've
9. In the box at the top, *that is* the Japanese word that means "puppet." **9.** that's
10. As *you will* notice, the Japanese system of writing is very different from ours. **10.** you'll

Plurals

22s. Use an apostrophe and an *s* to form the plurals of letters, numerals, and symbols, and of words referred to as words.

EXAMPLES   I think the word *Mississippi* has four *i*'s, four *s*'s, and two *p*'s.

Your *1*'s and *7*'s look alike.

You wrote +'s instead of *x*'s in these math problems.

Try not to use so many *you know*'s when you talk.

Exercise 11 Forming Plurals by Using Apostrophes

Correctly form the plural of each of the following items.

EXAMPLE   **1.** 9
   1. 9's

1. *I*'s
2. *t*'s
3. @'s
4. *it*'s
5. *6*'s
6. #'s
7. *A*'s
8. .com's
9. *too*'s
10. *thou*'s
11. *14*'s
12. %'s
13. *at*'s
14. ?'s
15. *and*'s
16. *B*'s
17. *3*'s
18. +'s
19. !'s
20. *of*'s
21. $'s
22. *'s
23. *uh oh*'s
24. ='s
25. /'s

TEACHING TIP

Activity. Place students in small groups. Give each group a list of ten words. Have the groups determine which words can be divided and then divide them correctly with hyphens. Possible words are *carpet, kitchen, basketball, desk, tortilla, poster, sweater, friend,* and *football.* Include one or two one-syllable words, which cannot be divided, on each list. Provide a dictionary for each group of students.

Relating to Literature

In his poetry, E. E. Cummings often uses hyphens and compound words to contribute to his meaning. For example, in "hist whist" he makes up the compound *ghostthings* and uses hyphens in the words *tip-toe, twinkle-toe,* and *hob-a-nob.* If this poem is available in your library, read it aloud to your students, carefully quickening your speed when you get to these words to indicate the poet's intention to emphasize the poem's rhythm. Then, ask students what effect the poet achieves by using these hyphenated words.

HELP

You may need to look up words in a dictionary to be sure of how to divide them into syllables.

STYLE TIP

Hyphens are often used in compound names. In such cases, the hyphen is thought of as part of the spelling of the name.

EXAMPLES
　Margaret Bourke-White
　Kung-sun Lung
　Terry-Jo
　Edward Levy-Lawson

If you are not sure whether a compound name is hyphenated, ask the person with that name, or look up the name in a reference source.

Hyphens

22t. Use a hyphen to divide a word at the end of a line.

When you divide a word at the end of a line, remember the following rules:

(1) Divide a word only between syllables.

INCORRECT　Uncle Payat, Aunt Nina, and Ayita will jou-
　　　　　　rney eighty miles to join us.

CORRECT　　Uncle Payat, Aunt Nina, and Ayita will jour-
　　　　　　ney eighty miles to join us.

(2) Do not divide a one-syllable word.

INCORRECT　They are bringing a salad, ham, and rye bre-
　　　　　　ad.

CORRECT　　They are bringing a salad, ham, and rye
　　　　　　bread.

(3) Do not divide a word so that one letter stands alone.

INCORRECT　Is that your family's brand-new car parked a-
　　　　　　cross the street?

CORRECT　　Is that your family's brand-new car parked
　　　　　　across the street?

22u. Use a hyphen with compound numbers from *twenty-one* to *ninety-nine*.

EXAMPLE　　Until 1959, the United States had only forty-eight stars in its flag.

22v. Hyphenate a compound adjective when it comes before the noun it modifies.

EXAMPLES　an activity that is well planned
　　　　　　a **well-planned** activity

　　　　　　a flavor that is long lasting
　　　　　　a **long-lasting** flavor

Some compound adjectives are always hyphenated, whether they come before or after the nouns they modify.

EXAMPLES   a **brand-new** bicycle
a bicycle that is **brand-new**

an **up-to-date** encyclopedia
an encyclopedia that is **up-to-date**

22w. Use a hyphen with the prefixes *all–, ex–, great–, self–,* **and with the suffixes** *–elect* **and** *–free.*

EXAMPLES   all-purpose   self-confidence

ex-students   governor-elect

great-grandfather   sugar-free

HELP
If you are not sure whether a compound adjective is always hyphenated, look up the word in a dictionary.

Exercise 12 Using Hyphens Correctly

Write each of the following words. Add hyphens to show where the word may be divided at the end of a line or where they are needed in a compound number or word. If a word should not be hyphenated, write *do not hyphenate*.

EXAMPLES
1. tomorrow
1. *to-mor-row*

The ‸ symbol indicates a hyphen.

2. thirty nine
2. *thirty-nine*

3. theme
3. *do not hyphenate*

1. loose   1. d.n.h.
2. twenty‸nine
3. temp‸o‸rary
4. self‸esteem
5. chil‸dren
6. elect   6. d.n.h.
7. prin‸ci‸pal
8. dec‸o‸rate
9. president‸elect
10. through   10. d.n.h.
11. im‸me‸di‸ate‸ly
12. eighty‸three
13. seize   13. d.n.h.
14. broom‸stick
15. great‸aunt
16. pi‸ano
17. pre‸ferred
18. gram‸mar
19. lint‸free
20. among   20. d.n.h.

HELP
The prefix *half–* often requires a hyphen, as in *half-life, half-moon,* and *half-truth.* However, sometimes *half* is used without a hyphen, either as a part of a single word (*halftone, halfway, halfback*) or as a separate word (*half shell, half pint, half note*). If you are not sure how to spell a word containing *half,* look up the word in a current dictionary.

Word breaks are based on *Webster's New World College Dictionary, Third Edition.*

TEACHING TIP

Exercise 12 You might want to use the first ten items of **Exercise 12** as guided practice. Then, have students complete the exercise as independent practice. You might want to provide a dictionary so that each student can check that he or she has hyphenated the words correctly.

COMPUTER TIP

Some word-processing programs will automatically divide a word at the end of a line and insert a hyphen. Sometimes the program will divide a word at the wrong place. Always check a printout of your writing to see how the computer has hyphenated words at the ends of lines. If a hyphen is used incorrectly, move the word to the next line or divide the word yourself by correctly inserting a "hard" hyphen (one that the computer will not move).

Review C Using Apostrophes and Hyphens Correctly

Correctly write the word or letter that needs an apostrophe or a hyphen in each of the following sentences.

EXAMPLE
1. Wheres my history book?
1. Where's

The ‸ symbol indicates a hyphen.

1. Do you know where the atlases and the two diction‸aries are?
2. There are two i's in *tomorrow*.
3. The last speaker was the ex‸president of the Town Council.
4. The tiger cubs aren't on view yet.
5. Is that one of Bessie Smith's songs?
6. Someone's gold bracelet is on the counter in the bath‸room.
7. Forty‸nine students signed the get-well card.
8. Is that salad dressing fat‸free?
9. Who's going to the fair this weekend?
10. It's almost time to leave.

CHAPTER 22

Chapter Review

A. Using Underlining (Italics), Quotation Marks, Apostrophes, and Hyphens

Each of the following sentences contains at least one error in the use of underlining (italics), quotation marks, apostrophes, or hyphens. Write each sentence correctly.

1. While taking a bath, I like to sing "This Land Is Your Land."
2. Washington's largest city is named for Chief Seattle.
3. Chapter two is called "The Siamese Cat."
4. I read Robert Louis Stevenson's novel *Treasure Island*.
5. "I remember making a barometer in the fourth grade. "I had to start over twice before it would work," I said.
6. "Deva, will you please show me how to make a weather vane?" asked Todd.
7. "It took me only forty-five minutes to make a sundial," Carlos remarked.
8. We built a model airplane, but it crashed on its test flight.
9. All students' projects are due next Friday.
10. Raymond read a fascinating article called "The Standing Stones of Wales and Brittany."
11. When in Corpus Christi, try to visit the USS "Lexington."
12. Which newspaper do you prefer, *The New York Times* or *Newsday*?
13. "Next time, please be prompt, Joe," said Ms. Lomazzi as I walked through the door ten minutes late.
14. The children's bikes were in the driveway.
15. "Everyone's project must be in on time," Mrs. Tolliver said.
16. "Bill's exact words," said Sean, "were 'I'll be back at noon.'"
17. In his English class, my brother Julio is reading the Dylan Thomas poem "Fern Hill."
18. Do you know the magazine "Highlights for Children"?
19. Please don't use so many *like*s when you speak.
20. Isn't twenty questions the average length for an exercise of this kind?

Using the Chapter Review

To assess student progress, you may want to compare the types of items missed on the **Diagnostic Preview** to those missed on the **Chapter Review**. If students have not made significant progress, you may want to refer them to **Chapter 24: Correcting Common Errors, Exercises 27–29,** for additional practice.

Chapter Review **609**

Chapter Review

B. Revising Indirect Quotations to Create Direct Quotations

POSSIBLE ANSWERS

21. "You cannot take any breaks during the exam," the teacher warned us.
22. "I will call you at eight o'clock," Lisa said.
23. "Don't be late," Mom told us.
24. "Will you wait behind the fence?" the police officer asked us.
25. "Where is the *Mona Lisa*?" I asked the museum guard.
26. "Two hours should be long enough," Taylor said.
27. "I will be in the city for five days," Stephanie replied.
28. Dr. Grizzard reminded us, "Take your vitamins every day."
29. Wendy asked her father, "Will you drive me to the library?"
30. "I have never been so surprised in my life!" Giulio exclaimed happily.

C. Punctuating a Dialogue

[31]¶"Oh, Travis," said Lucy, "when are you leaving?" [32]¶"I told you, Lucy," replied Travis. "I'm planning to leave soon. At around ten o'clock." [33]¶"Oh," said Lucy, "Listen, Trav, I'm afraid I won't be able to come with you after all. Something has come up." [34]¶"Well, Grandma will certainly be disappointed," remarked Travis. "She's been looking forward to seeing her two grandkids on her birthday." [35]¶"Yes, but that's just it," said Lucy. "I haven't bought anything for her birthday yet. I just haven't had the time." [36]¶"Well, guess what, Sis. I took care of that yesterday." Travis went over to the desk and took something out of the drawer. [37]"Your present to Grandma is this framed photograph of me." [38]¶"You're kidding," said Lucy. [39]¶"And," continued Travis, "my present to her is this framed photograph of you. What do you think?" [40]¶"I think you're crazy, but we can discuss that on the way there. Let's go!"

HELP
You will need to change some pronouns and verb forms in Part B.

B. Revising Indirect Quotations to Create Direct Quotations

Revise each of the following sentences by changing the indirect quotation to a direct quotation. Be sure to use capital letters and punctuation marks where they are needed.

21. Our teacher warned us that we could not take any breaks during the exam.
22. Lisa said that she would call me at eight o'clock.
23. Mom told us not to be late.
24. The police officer asked us to wait behind the fence.
25. I asked the museum guard where the *Mona Lisa* was.
26. Taylor said that two hours should be long enough.
27. Stephanie replied that she would be in the city for five days.
28. Dr. Grizzard reminded us to take our vitamins every day.
29. Wendy asked her father if he would drive her to the library.
30. Giulio exclaimed happily that he had never been so surprised in his life.

C. Punctuating a Dialogue

Rewrite the following dialogue, using quotation marks and other marks of punctuation where they are needed. Remember to begin a new paragraph every time the speaker changes.

[31] Oh, Travis, said Lucy, when are you leaving? [32] I told you, Lucy, replied Travis. I'm planning to leave soon. At around ten o'clock. [33] Oh, said Lucy. Listen, Trav, I'm afraid I won't be able to come with you after all. Something has come up. [34] Well, Grandma will certainly be disappointed, remarked Travis. She's been looking forward to seeing her two grandkids on her birthday. [35] Yes, but that's just it, said Lucy. I haven't bought anything for her birthday yet. I just haven't had the time. [36] Well, guess what, Sis. I took care of that yesterday. Travis went over to the desk and took something out of the drawer. [37] Your present to Grandma is this framed photograph of me. [38] You're kidding, said Lucy. [39] And continued Travis, my present to her is this framed photograph of you. What do you think? [40] I think you're crazy, but we can discuss that on the way there. Let's go!

RESOURCES

Punctuation
Review
- Grammar, Usage, and Mechanics, pp. 275, 276, 277, 278, 279

Assessment
- Assessment Package
  —Chapter Tests, Ch. 22
  —Chapter Tests in Standardized Test Formats, Ch. 22
- Test Generator (One-Stop Planner CD-ROM)

Writing Application
Using Apostrophes in a Letter

Contractions and Possessives You have been so busy at summer camp that you have not had time to write to your best friend. Write your friend a letter telling about your first week at camp. Be sure to use apostrophes correctly to make your meaning clear.

Prewriting If you have never been to a summer camp, ask a friend or relative who has been to one to tell you about it. Write down some notes on your activities at summer camp. Use your experience or your imagination to describe activities such as sports, crafts, and hiking trips. Also, make some notes about the camp itself.

Writing Include specific details about the natural setting and special or daily activities at the camp. Tell your friend what you have enjoyed most. Try to give your friend a clear, vivid picture of your first week.

Revising Ask a friend or a family member to read your letter. Can he or she imagine the activities you have described? If not, revise your letter to make it clearer and more descriptive.

Publishing Be sure you have used the correct form for personal letters. As you proofread your letter, take extra care with apostrophes. Check your use of contractions and pronouns like *its, it's, your, you're, their,* and *they're*. Also, look for any other errors in grammar, spelling, and punctuation. Exchange letters with a classmate, and see how your camp experiences, real or imagined, are similar and how they are different.

Reference Note
For information about **writing a personal letter,** see "Writing" in the Quick Reference Handbook.

Chapter Review **611**

RESOURCES
Writing Application
Extension
- *Grammar, Usage, and Mechanics,* p. 282
- *Language Workshop CD-ROM,* Lessons 40–43, 45

CHAPTER 23 Spelling
Improving Your Spelling

PREVIEWING THE CHAPTER

- The chapter begins with a discussion of the methods students can use to improve their spelling and presents a series of basic spelling rules, including rules for adding prefixes and suffixes and for forming the plurals of nouns. Exercises are provided to reinforce the understanding of the spelling rules. The chapter also contains lists of homonyms and other words that are often confused and concludes with a list of spelling words.

- A **Chapter Review** on pp. 637–639 includes a **Writing Application** asking students to use correct spelling in a personal letter.

- For help in integrating this chapter with composition chapters, use the **Teaching Strands** chart on pp. T297A–T297B.

USING THE DIAGNOSTIC PREVIEW

- You may wish to use the **Diagnostic Preview** to determine what kinds of spelling problems your students have. Keep in mind that students may have a variety of such problems. You could use the results of the test to decide which lessons to teach to the entire class and which lessons to assign to cooperative-learning groups.

Diagnostic Preview

A. Proofreading Sentences for Correct Spelling

Correctly write the word that is misspelled in each of the following sentences.

EXAMPLE 1. The dog is diging in the flower garden again.
  1. *digging*

1. The children are ~~happyest~~ when swimming in the pool on a hot afternoon.   **1.** happiest
2. The porch ~~chaires~~ look newer than the tables.   **2.** chairs
3. Our ~~nieghbor~~ was born in Texas, I believe.   **3.** neighbor
4. The Tolbys bought ~~blueberrys~~ for the party.   **4.** blueberries
5. Uncle Steven is ~~driveing~~ through seven foreign countries on his trip.   **5.** driving
6. Is the weather in Arizona ever ~~changable~~?   **6.** changeable
7. Five ~~womans~~ auditioned for the leading role in the Broadway production.   **7.** women
8. Have you heard the ~~tunful~~ Peter, Paul, and Mary songs of the sixties?   **8.** tuneful
9. Matthew and Kim ~~bravly~~ rescued the baby raccoon from the muddy ditch.   **9.** bravely
10. Would you kindly dig up the ~~potatos~~ and let them dry in the cellar?   **10.** potatoes

CHAPTER RESOURCES

Planning
- *One-Stop Planner CD-ROM*

Practice and Extension
- *Grammar, Usage, and Mechanics*, p. 283
- *Language Workshop CD-ROM*

Reinforcement
- *Spelling*

Evaluation and Assessment
- *Assessment Package*
  —Chapter Tests, Ch. 23
  —Chapter Tests in Standardized Test Formats, Ch. 23
- *Test Generator (One-Stop Planner CD-ROM)*

B. Proofreading Sentences to Correct Spelling Errors

Choose the correct word or words from the choices in parentheses in each of the following sentences.

EXAMPLE 1. Please give (*you're, your*) book orders to me today.
1. your

11. Angela is taking five (*courses, coarses*) this semester.
12. Nora said she was (*already, all ready*) for the banquet.
13. "Please pass me a (*peace, piece*) of bread," Gary said.
14. The (*altar, alter*) at the Spanish mission is marble.
15. The (*plain, plane*) to Ontario is ahead of schedule.
16. People often (*loose, lose*) pennies in stores and on streets.
17. We saw the (*principal, principle*) pass by twice.
18. Whose (*stationery, stationary*) has initials at the top?
19. (*There, Their*) shop sells shirts, dresses, and scarves.
20. "You'd better get these (*breaks, brakes*) fixed right away," the mechanic said.

Good Spelling Habits

The following techniques can help you spell words correctly.

1. **To learn the spelling of a word, pronounce it, study it, and write it.** Pronounce words carefully. Mistakes in speaking can cause mistakes in spelling. For instance, if you say ad•je•tive instead of ad•jec•tive, you will be more likely to spell the word incorrectly.
   - First, make sure that you know how to pronounce the word correctly, and then practice saying it.
   - Second, study the word. Notice any parts that might be hard to remember.
   - Third, write the word from memory. Check your spelling.
   - If you misspelled the word, repeat the three steps of this process until you can spell the word correctly.
2. **Use a dictionary.** If you are not absolutely sure about the spelling of a word, look it up in a dictionary. Do not guess about the correct spelling.

HELP

If you are not sure how to pronounce a word, look it up in a dictionary. In a dictionary, you will usually find the pronunciation given in parentheses after the word. The information in parentheses will show you the sounds used, the syllable breaks, and any accented syllables. A guide to the pronunciation symbols is usually found at the front of a dictionary.

23 a–g

Good Spelling Habits and Spelling Rules

Rules 23a–g (pp. 613–620)

OBJECTIVES

- To spell correctly words that contain the letters *ie* or *ei*
- To add prefixes and suffixes to words

Meeting INDIVIDUAL NEEDS

MODALITIES

Auditory Learners. Choose one of the words from the spelling word list at the end of the chapter, and pronounce the word carefully for the class. For example, you might want to use *varied, political, constitution,* or *reconstruction*. Ask a volunteer first to repeat the pronunciation carefully and then to write the word on the chalkboard, making sure to spell the word as it sounds. If a volunteer misspells the word, ask him or her to divide the word into syllables. Then, pronounce the word again slowly and ask the volunteer to match sounds in the pronunciation to each syllable of the word. Lead the class to see that pronouncing a word correctly may help in spelling it correctly.

Internet
- go.hrw.com (keyword: EOLang)

RESOURCES

Good Spelling Habits and Spelling Rules

Practice
- *Grammar, Usage, and Mechanics,* pp. 284, 285, 286, 287, 288, 289, 290, 291
- *Language Workshop CD-ROM,* Lesson 48

Meeting INDIVIDUAL NEEDS

MULTIPLE INTELLIGENCES

Logical-Mathematical Intelligence. Some students might find a flowchart useful for remembering techniques for spelling words correctly. Have students use the good spelling habits listed in this section to develop a process for spelling an unfamiliar word. For example:

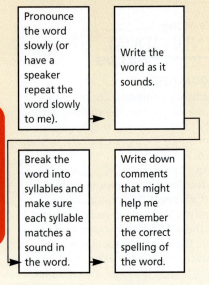

Students might want to number and illustrate steps along the flowchart.

TEACHING TIP

To help students syllabicate words for their spelling notebooks, explain that words can be divided after a vowel if the vowel is long (an **open syllable**) and after a consonant if the vowel is short (a **closed syllable**). Students might use the following list of words as examples: be-come, co-bra, de-tail (open) beck-on, cop-per, det-o-nate (closed).

MECHANICS

STYLE TIP

In some names, marks that show how to pronounce a word are considered part of the spelling.

PEOPLE
Muñoz   Søren   Fauré

PLACES
Neuchâtel   Košice
Cap-Haïtien

If you are not sure about the spelling of a name, ask the person with that name or look it up in a dictionary or other reference source.

---

3. **Spell by syllables.** A *syllable* is a word part that can be pronounced as one uninterrupted sound.

EXAMPLES   ear•ly [two syllables]

av•er•age [three syllables]

Instead of trying to learn how to pronounce and spell a whole word, break it into its syllables whenever possible. It is easier to learn a few letters at a time than to learn all of them at once.

4. **Keep a spelling notebook.** Divide each page into four columns:

COLUMN 1   Correctly spell any word you have misspelled. (Never enter a misspelled word.)

COLUMN 2   Write the word again, dividing it into syllables and indicating which syllables are accented or stressed. (You will probably need to use a dictionary.)

COLUMN 3   Write the word once more, circling the spot that gives you trouble.

COLUMN 4   Write down any comments that might help you remember the correct spelling.

Here is an example of how you might make entries for two words that are often misspelled.

5. **Proofread for careless spelling errors.** Re-read your writing carefully, and correct any mistakes and unclear letters. For example, make sure that your *i*'s are dotted, your *t*'s are crossed, and your *g*'s do not look like *q*'s.

614   Chapter 23   Spelling

Spelling Rules

ie and *ei*

23a. Write *ie* when the sound is long *e*, except after *c*.

EXAMPLES   ch**ie**f, bel**ie**ve, br**ie**f, rec**ei**ve, c**ei**ling

EXCEPTIONS   **ei**ther, n**ei**ther, prot**ei**n, s**ei**ze

Write *ei* when the sound is not long *e*, especially when the sound is long *a*.

EXAMPLES   n**ei**ghbor, w**ei**gh, r**ei**ndeer, h**ei**ght, for**ei**gn

EXCEPTIONS   fr**ie**nd, f**ie**rce, anc**ie**nt, misch**ie**f

Exercise 1 Writing Words with *ie* and *ei*

Complete the following letter by adding *ie* or *ei* to each numbered word.

EXAMPLE   I wrote Aunt Hannah a **[1]** br____f thank-you note.
1. brief

December 12, 2001

Dear Aunt Hannah,

   Thank you very much for the **[1]** sl_ei_gh you recently sent me. I **[2]** rec_ei_ved it on the **[3]** _ei_ghth of this month, just in time for our first big snowstorm. My new **[4]** fr_ie_nds and I have great fun pulling each other across the **[5]** f_ie_lds in it. The **[6]** n_ei_ghbor's dog races alongside us, barking **[7]** f_ie_rcely all the way.

   So far, I like living here in Vermont, but I can't quite **[8]** bel_ie_ve how different everything is from life in California. Thank you again for your gift.

            Your loving **[9]** n_ie_ce,

            Mai

P.S. If only we had some **[10]** r_ei_ndeer to pull us!

TIPS & TRICKS

This verse may help you remember the *ie* rule:
   I before *e*
   Except after *c*,
   Or when sounded like *a*,
   As in *neighbor* and *weigh*.
If you use this rhyme, remember that "*i* before *e*" refers only to words in which these two letters are in the same syllable and stand for the sound of long *e*, as in the examples under Rule 23a.

Meeting INDIVIDUAL NEEDS

INCLUSION

Learning-disabled students typically have difficulty learning to spell contractions and words that are not spelled as they sound. For most students, repeated exposure through reading enhances spelling ability. To improve students' spelling abilities, copy misspelled words taken from their writing assignments. Ask students to write each word correctly at least three times and to use the words in sentences. Constant repetition in writing, as well as increased exposure to silent reading, can enhance spelling ability.

TEACHING TIP

Looking at Language. To help students with the syllabication of two-syllable words, point out that syllables have boundary patterns. Common patterns include vowel-consonant-consonant-vowel (VCCV), for example p*il-l*ow or v*el-v*et, and vowel-consonant-vowel (VCV), for example b*a-s*is or l*o-c*al. Explain that in a VCCV pattern the first syllable usually has a short vowel sound. In two-syllable words with the VCV pattern, the first syllable usually has a long vowel sound.

Prefixes and Suffixes

Prefixes

A ***prefix*** is a letter or a group of letters added to the beginning of a word to create a new word that has a different meaning.

23b. When adding a prefix to a word, do not change the spelling of the word itself.

EXAMPLES   dis + satisfy = dis**satisfy**

mis + lead = mis**lead**

un + done = un**done**

pre + view = pre**view**

a + typical = a**typical**

Exercise 2   Spelling Words with Prefixes

Combine each of the following prefixes and words to create a new word.

EXAMPLE   1. mis + place

1. misplace

1. fore + word **1. foreword**
2. un + natural **2. unnatural**
3. in + dependent **3. independent**
4. mis + use **4. misuse**
5. un + common **5. uncommon**
6. im + patient **6. impatient**
7. pre + historic **7. prehistoric**
8. mis + spell **8. misspell**
9. dis + satisfied **9. dissatisfied**
10. re + assert **10. reassert**

Exercise 3   Spelling Words with Prefixes

Create ten different words by combining the prefixes given below with the words listed beside them. (You may use a prefix or word more than once.) Check each of your new words in a dictionary. Then, use each word in a sentence.

Prefixes			Words			
un–	mis–	dis–	able	do	judge	place
pre–	over–	re–	cover	trust	pay	informed

EXAMPLE   1. repay—I'll repay you when I get my allowance.

616   Chapter 23 Spelling

Exercise 3   Spelling Words with Prefixes

ANSWERS

Words and sentences will vary. Here are some possibilities:

1. unable—The cat was unable to catch the mouse.
2. misplace—My parents always misplace their keys.
3. overdo—Some athletes overdo their workouts.
4. discover—I wonder what secrets the scientist will discover.
5. replace—Please replace the air filter when it gets clogged.
6. disable—My sister is careful to disable the lawn mower before storing it.
7. undo—It is difficult to undo the damage a lie does.
8. prejudge—Be careful not to prejudge a situation before you know all the facts.
9. overpay—Sir, did you overpay the utility bill for which you got a refund?
10. misinformed—We were misinformed about the time for the picnic.

Exercise 3

ALTERNATIVE LESSON

Ask students to circle and identify the part of speech of each word they create from the chart and use in a sentence. In the example sentence, the word *repay* is a verb.

Suffixes

A *suffix* is a letter or a group of letters added at the end of a word to create a new word that has a different meaning.

23c. When adding the suffix *–ness* or *–ly* to a word, do not change the spelling of the word itself.

EXAMPLES   kind + ness = **kind**ness

tough + ness = **tough**ness

sincere + ly = **sincere**ly

slow + ly = **slow**ly

EXCEPTIONS   For most words that end in *y*, change the *y* to *i* before adding *–ly* or *–ness*.

happy + ly = happ**ily**

friendly + ness = friendl**iness**

23d. Drop the final silent *e* before adding a suffix that begins with a vowel.

Vowels are the letters *a, e, i, o, u,* and sometimes *y*. All other letters of the alphabet are *consonants.*

EXAMPLES   cause + ing = **caus**ing

reverse + ible = **revers**ible

strange + er = **strang**er

adore + able = **ador**able

Spelling Rules

TEACHING TIP

Activity. Word games can help students learn to spell. Write a long word on the chalkboard, and have students make as many other words of four or more letters as they can by using letters from the word. Allow them to use dictionaries. For example, the word *dictionary* could be used to produce words such as *yard*, *icon*, and *radio*.

Exercise 4 — Spelling Words with Suffixes

ANSWERS
1. activity
2. surely
3. statement
4. location
5. courageous
6. silliness
7. suspenseful
8. littlest
9. decorated
10. traceable

Meeting INDIVIDUAL NEEDS

MULTIPLE INTELLIGENCES

Musical Intelligence. Have students work in pairs to create short songs about the rules in this section. Students might want to begin their songs with the rhyme "*i* before *e* except after *c*" and then create other rhymes or lyrics for other rules in the section. They might spell words within the lyrics as examples of each rule. Invite volunteers to perform their songs for the class.

MECHANICS

HELP

Some words that end with a silent *e* can either keep the *e* or drop it when a suffix is added.

EXAMPLES
judge + ment = judg**ment** *or* judg**ement**

acknowledge + ment = acknowledg**ment** *or* acknowledg**ement**

love + able = lov**able** *or* lov**eable**

TIPS & TRICKS

When you proofread your own writing, you will find more spelling errors by looking at each word separately. To focus on each word, try using a piece of paper to hide some of the nearby words or lines. You can even cut a slit in a sheet of paper and move it over your writing to show just a few words at a time.

EXCEPTIONS	Keep the silent *e* in words ending in *ce* and *ge* before adding a suffix beginning with *a* or *o*.
	manage + able = manag**eable**
	courage + ous = courag**eous**
	notice + able = notic**eable**

23e. Keep the final silent *e* before adding a suffix that begins with a consonant.

EXAMPLES	hope + less = hop**eless**
	place + ment = plac**ement**
EXCEPTIONS	argue + ment = argu**ment**
	true + ly = tru**ly**

Exercise 4 — Spelling Words with Suffixes

Combine each of the following words and suffixes to create a new word.

EXAMPLE 1. sudden + ness
1. sudden**ness**

1. active + ity
2. sure + ly
3. state + ment
4. locate + ion
5. courage + ous
6. silly + ness
7. suspense + ful
8. little + est
9. decorate + ed
10. trace + able

23f. For words that end in a consonant plus *y*, change the *y* to *i* before adding a suffix.

EXAMPLES	cry + ed = cr**ied**	lonely + est = lonel**iest**
	pretty + er = prett**ier**	lazy + ness = laz**iness**
EXCEPTION	Keep the *y* if the suffix begins with an *i*.	
	carry + ing = carr**ying**	

NOTE Keep the *y* if the word ends in a vowel plus *y*.

EXAMPLES	stay + ed = sta**yed**	key + ed = ke**yed**
EXCEPTIONS	day + **ly** = daily	pay + **ed** = paid

23g. Double the final consonant before adding *–ing*, *–ed*, *–er*, or *–est* to a one-syllable word that ends in a single vowel followed by a single consonant.

EXAMPLES beg + ing = be**gging**   sad + er = sa**dder**

chat + ed = cha**tted**   big + est = bi**ggest**

When a one-syllable word ends in two vowels followed by a single consonant, do not double the consonant before adding *–ing*, *–ed*, *–er*, or *–est*.

EXAMPLES sleep + ing = slee**ping**   cool + er = coo**ler**

treat + ed = trea**ted**   fair + est = fai**rest**

Exercise 5 Spelling Words with Suffixes

Combine each of the following words and suffixes to create a new word.

EXAMPLE 1. creep + er
1. creeper

1. say + ing   **1. saying**
2. slim + er   **2. slimmer**
3. squeak + ing **3. squeaking**
4. rainy + est **4. rainiest**
5. steady + ness **5. steadiness**
6. beat + ing   **6. beating**
7. rely + ing   **7. relying**
8. easy + ly   **8. easily**
9. chop + ed   **9. chopped**
10. play + ed   **10. played**

Review A Proofreading Sentences for Correct Spelling

Most of the following sentences contain a misspelled word. Write each misspelled word correctly. If a sentence is already correct, write *C*.

EXAMPLE 1. My grandma often says, "Let sleepping dogs lie."
1. sleeping

1. It's unnusual weather for this time of year. **1. unusual**
2. In 1991, Lithuania regained its independence from the Soviet Union. **2. C**
3. With Sacagawea's help, the explorers Lewis and Clark maped out the Northwest. **3. mapped**
4. Now that Bao Duc is on the team, our hiting has improved. **4. hitting**

HELP
In Review A, none of the proper nouns are misspelled.

5. Serita and I can easyly make enough rice for the class. **5.** easily
6. We visited my grandmother in the Dominican Republic during the rainyest month of the year. **6.** rainiest
7. Please resstate the question. **7.** restate
8. My sister has the loveliest voice I've ever heard. **8.** C
9. Former astronaut Sally Ride earned recognition for her courage and steadyness. **9.** steadiness
10. The temperature has droped at least ten degrees. **10.** dropped

Review B — Proofreading a Paragraph for Correct Spelling

ANSWERS
1. truly
2. neighbors
3. getting; dissatisfied
4. Fortunately
5. C
6. loving; receive
7. closing; putting
8. happily
9. retrieves; dropped
10. joking; writing

HELP
Some sentences in Review B contain more than one misspelled word.

Review B Proofreading a Paragraph for Correct Spelling

For each sentence in the following paragraph, correctly write the word or words that are misspelled. If a sentence is already correct, write *C*.

EXAMPLE [1] My cousin Chris was very couragous after she was baddly hurt in a car accident.

1. courageous; badly

[1] After the accident, Chris found that she truely needed other people. [2] Her friends, family, and nieghbors gladly helped her. [3] However, Chris liked the idea of geting along on her own as much as she could, so she was disatisfied. [4] Fortunatly, she was able to join an exciting program called Helping Hands. [5] This program provides monkeys like this one as friends and helpers for people with disabilities. [6] Chris said that the baby monkeys are raised in loving foster homes for four years and then they go to Boston to recieve special training. [7] There, they learn how to do tasks on command, such as opening and closeing doors, turning lights on and off, and puting tapes into a VCR or tape player. [8] Chris has been happyly working with her own monkey, Aldo, for six months now. [9] Aldo retreives anything that Chris has droped, works the TV remote control, and even scratches Chris's back when it itches! [10] Chris is always jokeing, "Pretty soon Aldo will be writting my book reports for me!"

Forming the Plurals of Nouns

23h. Follow these rules for spelling the plurals of nouns:

(1) To form the plurals of most nouns, add s.

SINGULAR	snack	oven	Juliet	breeze	umbrella
PLURAL	snack**s**	oven**s**	Juliet**s**	breeze**s**	umbrella**s**

NOTE Make sure that you do not confuse the plural form of a noun with its possessive form. In general, you should not use an apostrophe to form the plural of a word.

INCORRECT The boy's stayed after school for choir practice.
CORRECT The **boys** stayed after school for choir practice. [plural]
CORRECT The **boys' choir** has practice today. [possessive]

Reference Note
For a discussion of **possessive forms of nouns**, see page 598. For information on using an apostrophe and an *s* to form **plurals of letters, numerals, symbols, and words used as words**, see page 605.

(2) Form the plurals of nouns ending in *s, x, z, ch,* or *sh* by adding *es*.

SINGULAR	glass	fox	buzz	itch	bush	Jones
PLURAL	glass**es**	fox**es**	buzz**es**	itch**es**	bush**es**	Jones**es**

HELP
Some one-syllable words ending in *z* double the final consonant when forming plurals.

EXAMPLES
quiz   fez
qui**zz**es   fe**zz**es

Exercise 6 Spelling the Plurals of Nouns

Spell the plural form of each of the following nouns.

EXAMPLES 1. scratch
          1. *scratches*

          2. ax
          2. *axes*

1. night 1. *nights*
2. dish 2. *dishes*
3. address 3. *addresses*
4. lens 4. *lenses*
5. box 5. *boxes*
6. branch 6. *branches*
7. loss 7. *losses*
8. peach 8. *peaches*
9. waltz 9. *waltzes*
10. Smith 10. *Smiths*
11. complex 11. *complexes*
12. faucet 12. *faucets*
13. cobra 13. *cobras*
14. doctor 14. *doctors*
15. ditch 15. *ditches*
16. Sanchez 16. *Sanchezes*
17. tax 17. *taxes*
18. glue 18. *glues*
19. occurrence 19. *occurrences*
20. radish 20. *radishes*

Spelling Rules **621**

Forming the Plurals of Nouns
Rule 23h (pp. 621–625)

OBJECTIVE
- To spell the plural and singular forms of nouns

TEACHING TIP

Exercise 6 You might wish to use the first ten items in **Exercise 6** as guided practice. Then, have students complete the exercise as independent practice.

MECHANICS

RESOURCES
Forming the Plurals of Nouns
Practice
- *Grammar, Usage, and Mechanics,* pp. 292, 293, 294, 295
- *Language Workshop CD-ROM,* Lesson 49

TEACHING TIP

Activity. Have students work in small groups to generate lists of the plurals of the last names of students in the class. They may need to refer to the rules in this lesson to complete the activity. After each group has a complete list, go over it to make certain each name is correct.

As an alternative to this activity, provide phone books or other directories and have groups list twenty-five names and their plurals.

Meeting INDIVIDUAL NEEDS

ENGLISH-LANGUAGE LEARNERS
General Strategies. Some of your English-language learners might speak languages such as Chinese or Vietnamese, which have no plural forms. Others might speak languages such as Portuguese, Spanish, or Turkish, which have plurals formed according to rules that seldom vary. These students might find English irregularities (such as *wife—wives*) and seemingly arcane rules (such as changing a final *y* to *i* between a consonant and a suffix beginning with a vowel) difficult to master. Remind the students a few times on different days of the importance of the English-language rules.

MECHANICS

---

(3) Form the plurals of nouns that end in a consonant plus *y* by changing the *y* to *i* and adding *es.*

| SINGULAR | country | mummy | berry |
| PLURAL | countr**ies** | mumm**ies** | berr**ies** |

EXCEPTION   With proper nouns, just add *s.*

the Shelby**s**   the Mabry**s**   the O'Grady**s**

(4) Form the plurals of nouns that end in a vowel plus *y* by adding *s.*

| SINGULAR | boy | turkey | holiday | Riley |
| PLURAL | boy**s** | turkey**s** | holiday**s** | Riley**s** |

(5) Form the plurals of nouns that end in a vowel plus *o* by adding *s.*

| SINGULAR | rodeo | patio | kangaroo | Romeo |
| PLURAL | rodeo**s** | patio**s** | kangaroo**s** | Romeo**s** |

HELP
Form the plurals of most musical terms ending in *o* by adding *s.*

SINGULAR
piano   trio
soprano cello

PLURAL
pianos trios
sopranos cellos

(6) Form the plurals of nouns that end in a consonant plus *o* by adding *es.*

| SINGULAR | tomato | echo | veto | torpedo |
| PLURAL | tomato**es** | echo**es** | veto**es** | torpedo**es** |

EXCEPTIONS   auto—auto**s**   Latino—Latino**s**   Soto—Soto**s**

Exercise 7   Spelling the Plurals of Nouns

Spell the plural form of each of the following nouns.

EXAMPLE   1. story
1. *stories*

1. toy **1. toys**
2. apology **2. apologies**
3. valley **3. valleys**
4. try **4. tries**
5. piano **5. pianos**
6. potato **6. potatoes**
7. emergency **7. emergencies**
8. chimney **8. chimneys**
9. radio **9. radios**
10. video **10. videos**
11. journey **11. journeys**
12. stereo **12. stereos**
13. county **13. counties**
14. hero **14. heroes**
15. delay **15. delays**
16. scenario **16. scenarios**
17. agony **17. agonies**
18. solo **18. solos**
19. O'Malley **19. O'Malleys**
20. zoo **20. zoos**

Chapter 23   Spelling

Spelling

(7) The plurals of a few nouns are formed in irregular ways.

SINGULAR	woman	mouse	foot	man	child
PLURAL	wom**en**	m**ic**e	f**ee**t	m**en**	child**ren**

(8) Some nouns are the same in the singular and the plural.

SINGULAR AND PLURAL   fowl   sheep   spacecraft   Sioux

(9) Form the plurals of numerals, letters, symbols, and words referred to as words by adding an apostrophe and s.

SINGULAR	1990	A	+	and
PLURAL	1990**'s**	A**'s**	+**'s**	and**'s**

Exercise 8   Spelling the Singular and Plural Forms of Nouns

Spell the singular form and the plural form of each italicized word in the following sentences.

EXAMPLES
1. We use strong line to fish for *salmon*.
   1. salmon—singular; salmon—plural

2. Field *mice* invaded the food supplies in the tent.
   2. mouse—singular; mice—plural

1. Our guide, Robert Tallchief, a *Sioux*, knows all about the animals called llamas.
2. Robert and his father use llamas like the ones shown below to carry equipment people need for hiking and for catching *fish*.
3. The trips are very popular with both men and *women*.

STYLE TIP

When it refers to the computer device, the word *mouse* can form a plural in two ways: *mouses* or *mice*. Someday one form may be the preferred style. For now, either is correct.

STYLE TIP

In your reading, you may notice that some writers do not use apostrophes to form the plurals of numerals, letters, symbols, and words referred to as words.

EXAMPLE
Her great-grandparents moved here from Italy sometime in the **1940s**.

However, using an apostrophe in such cases is not wrong and is sometimes necessary for clarity. Therefore, it is usually best to use the apostrophe.

HELP

If you do not know the plural form of a word, look up the word in a dictionary.

Spelling Rules   623

> **Exercise 8** Spelling the Singular and Plural Forms of Nouns
>
> **ANSWERS continued**
>
> 4. child—singular; children—plural
> 5. tooth—singular; teeth—plural
> 6. Japanese—singular; Japanese—plural
> 7. moose—singular; moose—plural
> 8. deer—singular; deer *or* deers—plural
> 9. sheep—singular; sheep—plural
> 10. goose—singular; geese—plural

4. *Children* especially are fascinated and amused by the sure-footed llamas.
5. However, the llama has one very disagreeable habit—if upset, it bares its *teeth* and spits.
6. The Tallchiefs' llama trips have attracted tourists from all over the world, including many *Japanese*.
7. One highlight of these trips is viewing *moose* in their natural habitat.
8. *Deer* thrive in this area of the Northwest.
9. In addition, families of mountain *sheep* clamber up the steep cliffs.
10. Most people who go on the llama trips take many pictures of the wild *geese*.

Review C Proofreading Sentences for Correct Spelling

For each of the following sentences, correctly write the word or words that are misspelled. If a sentence is already correct, write C.

EXAMPLE 1. Aunt Dorothy's old-time sayings are echos of her childhood.
   1. echoes

>
> **HELP**
> Some sentences in Review C have more than one misspelled word.
>
> 1. earlier
> 2. mischief/monkeys
> 3. brothers
> 4. C
> 5. taxes
> 6. Wishes/dishes
> 7. Joneses
> 8. Kellys

1. Aunt Dorothy Kelly talks mostly in expressions from the 1930's and ~~earlyer~~.
2. If we get into ~~mischeif~~, she exclaims, "You little ~~monkies~~!"
3. When my ~~brother's~~ run through the house, she shakes her head and mutters, "Boys will be boys."
4. Every time she can't find her eyeglasses, Aunt Dorothy says, "I've beaten the bushes, looking for them."
5. Aunt Dorothy believes that there are only two things in life that are certain: death and ~~taxs~~.
6. We've heard her say "There's no use crying over spilled milk" and "~~Wishs~~ won't wash ~~dishs~~" about a thousand times apiece.
7. When we want something because our friends have it, Aunt Dorothy says we're trying to keep up with the ~~Jones'~~.
8. Sometimes we get tired of hearing these little bits of folk wisdom, especially when Aunt Dorothy and all the little ~~Kellies~~ come over to visit for the holidays.

9. However, Aunt Dorothy is so sweet that we just smile and listen to her proverbs and ~~storys~~. **9.** stories
10. Sometimes she says something really worthwhile, like "There are only two things that money can't buy—true love and home-grown ~~tomatos~~." **10.** tomatoes

Words Often Confused

People often confuse the words in each of the following groups. Some of these words are **homonyms.** They are pronounced the same, but they have different meanings and spellings. Other words in this section have the same or similar spellings, but have different meanings.

already	[adverb] *at an earlier time* The show has *already* begun.
all ready	[adjective] *all prepared; completely prepared* The floats are *all ready* for the fiesta.
altar	[noun] *a table or stand used for religious ceremonies* My uncle Chee wove the cloth for the *altar*.
alter	[verb] *to change* A flood can *alter* a riverbed.
altogether	[adverb] *entirely* I'm *altogether* lost.
all together	[adjective] *in the same place;* [adverb] *at the same time or place* Is everyone *all together*? Let's sit *all together* at the movie.
brake	[noun] *a device to stop a machine* The front *brake* on my bike squeaks.
break	[verb] *to fracture; to shatter;* [noun] *a fracture; an interruption; a rest* Try not to *break* your promises. Let's take a five-minute *break*.

Reference Note

In the Glossary of Usage in Chapter 19, you can find many other words that are often confused or misused. You can also look them up in a dictionary.

Meeting INDIVIDUAL NEEDS

ENGLISH-LANGUAGE LEARNERS
General Strategies. Homonyms might seem strange to many English-language learners whose native languages have few or none of such pairs of confusing words. Ask the students to find in their native languages the equivalent words of the English homonyms that give them trouble. The corresponding words in their native languages may serve as mnemonics to help them remember which homonym to use.

LEARNERS HAVING DIFFICULTY
Some students might need extra help to master homonyms. Write the following pairs of words on the chalkboard, and ask volunteers to circle the letters that differentiate each pair. Ask other volunteers to look up the words in dictionaries and to report on the different definitions.

1. compliment, complement [*i, e*]
2. stationary, stationery [*a, e*]
3. their, there [*ir, re*]
4. threw, through [*ew, ough*]
5. weak, week [*a, e*]
6. capital, capitol [*a, o*]

MECHANICS

Exercise 9 Choosing Between Words Often Confused

For each of the following sentences, choose the correct word or words from the pair in parentheses.

EXAMPLE 1. Can the artist (*altar, alter*) the design?
1. alter

1. Did you help (*brake, break*) the piñata, Felipe?
2. Who arranged the flowers on the (*altar, alter*)?
3. I've (*all ready, already*) seen that movie.
4. My mom was (*all together, altogether*) pleased with my report card.
5. Don't forget to set the emergency (*brake, break*) when you park on a hill.
6. Our family will be (*all together, altogether*) at Thanksgiving this year.
7. "Will you (*altar, alter*) this sundress for me, Mom?" Angie asked.
8. You were (*all together, altogether*) right about the show times for the movie.
9. The Great Circus Parade is (*already, all ready*) to begin.
10. Unfortunately, handblown glass figurines (*break, brake*) very easily.

TIPS & TRICKS
Here's a way to remember the difference between *capital* and *capitol*. There's a d**o**me on the capit**o**l.

capital	[noun] *a city; the location of a government* Havana is the *capital* of Cuba.
capitol	[noun] *a building; statehouse* Our state *capitol* is made of granite.
choose	[verb, rhymes with *shoes*] *to select* Did you *choose* the movie for today?
chose	[verb, past tense of *choose*, rhymes with *shows*] Who *chose* the movie yesterday?
cloths	[noun] *pieces of cloth* My aunt brought these kente *cloths* home from Ghana.
clothes	[noun] *wearing apparel* Bob irons his own *clothes*.

Chapter 23 Spelling

coarse	[adjective] rough; crude; not fine
	Some cities still use *coarse* salt to melt snow on streets and roads.
course	[noun] a path of action; a series of studies; [also used in the expression *of course*]
	What *course* should we follow to accomplish our goal?
	The counselor suggested several *courses* for us to take.
	I can't, *of course*, tell you what to do.
desert	[noun, pronounced des'•ert] a dry, sandy region; a wilderness
	Plants and animals of the *desert* can survive on little water.
desert	[verb, pronounced de•sert'] to abandon; to leave
	Don't *desert* your friends when they need you.
dessert	[noun, pronounced des•sert'] the final, sweet course of a meal
	What's for *dessert* tonight?

Exercise 10 Choosing Between Words Often Confused

For each of the following sentences, choose the correct word from the pair of words in parentheses.

EXAMPLE   1. The sand on the beach is (*coarse, course*).
         1. coarse

1. The Mojave (*Desert, Dessert*) is located in California.
2. Juan packed lightweight (*clothes, cloths*) to wear on his trip.
3. The sailor set a (*coarse, course*) for the port of Pago Pago.
4. When was the (*capital, capitol*) built, and how long has the state legislature been meeting there?
5. For (*desert, dessert*) we had pears and cheese.
6. Each team must (*choose, chose*) a captain.
7. The polishing (*cloths, clothes*) are by the wax on the shelf.
8. "Of (*coarse, course*) you may go!" Mr. Vance said.
9. The (*capital, capitol*) is the second-largest city in the state.
10. The cooking (*coarse, course*) lasted six weeks last summer.

TEACHING TIP

Mnemonics. The following memory tricks can help some students with confusing words.

1. dessert—When *dessert* is served, we often want two (two *s*'s).
2. hear—We *hear* with our *ears*.
3. piece—A *pie* contains a *piece*.
4. stationery—You might write a lett*e*r on station*e*ry.
5. Tell students to remember the round *o* in *capitol* by thinking of the rotunda, a large round room that lies under a domed roof in many capitol buildings.

Cooperative Learning

Divide the class into small groups of three or four students. Have each group compose a short poem, a series of cartoons, or song or rap lyrics that use three or four sets of confusing words from the charts in this section. Each group's project can be serious or funny, but students must correctly use or illustrate each word in their sets of words. The group should first decide on the theme or topic for their project. Then, each student in the group should be responsible for writing lines or creating illustrations for one set of words. One student should be responsible for arranging the group's work onto a piece of poster board or large sheet of paper. Invite groups to share their completed projects with the rest of the class.

Review D   Proofreading Sentences for Words Often Confused

ANSWERS

1. desert
2. all ready
3. all together
4. course
5. break
6. clothes
7. altars
8. alter
9. capital
10. dessert

Crossing the Curriculum

Geography. Challenge pairs of students to use as many words from this section as they can in descriptive sentences about various parts of the world. Students should circle each word that they use from this chapter and note in the margin the word with which it is often confused, for example, *The Spree River flows* through *Berlin, the* capital *of Germany. The* course *of the Spree River takes it across the North German* Plain. (*threw, capitol, coarse, plane*). Students may need to use encyclopedias and other classroom and library resources.

TECHNOLOGY TIP

You might want to discuss the use of spellchecking features for students who use word processors. Explain that the computer will search for words not in its dictionary, highlight the words, and suggest alternative spellings. Remind students that they cannot depend entirely on computers for spelling. Most spellchecking programs will not recognize the misuse of a homonym. Tell students that they must carefully proofread in addition to using spellchecking features.

Review D   Proofreading Sentences for Words Often Confused

For each of the following sentences, correctly write the word that is misused.

EXAMPLE   1. The students are already for the Fall Festival.
   1. *all ready*

1. Throughout history, most societies and cultures, from the hot dessert regions to the cold northern regions, have celebrated the harvest.
2. The Jewish celebration of Sukkot marks the time when the harvest was gathered and the people were already for winter.
3. The most important tradition of Sukkot called for the family to live altogether in a temporary shelter called a sukkah.
4. Today, of coarse, many Jews still celebrate Sukkot but simply eat a meal outdoors under a shelter like the one pictured below.
5. Native Americans believed that without the help of the gods, there would be a brake in their good fortune.
6. During their planting ceremonies, most Native Americans, like the ones at left, dressed in special cloths.
7. To thank their harvest gods, the Chinese and Japanese placed wheat on alters.
8. Today, the Japanese do not altar this tradition much.
9. In most Japanese cities, including the capitol, the people hold parades to thank the ocean for the food it provides.
10. Many families in the United States celebrate Thanksgiving by sharing a meal, often with pumpkin pie for desert.

hear	[verb] *to receive sounds through the ears* When did you *hear* the news?
here	[adverb] *in this place* The mail is *here*.
its	[possessive form of *it*] *belonging to it* You should not judge a book by *its* cover.
it's	[contraction of *it is* or *it has*] *It's* your turn, Theresa. *It's* been a long day.
lead	[verb, rhymes with *need*] *to go first; to be a leader* Will you *lead* the singing, Rachel?
led	[verb, past tense of *lead*, rhymes with *red*] *went first; guided* The dog *led* its master to safety.
lead	[noun, rhymes with *red*] *a heavy metal; graphite used in pencils* *Lead* is no longer used in household paints. Use a pencil with a softer *lead* if you want to draw dark, heavy lines.
loose	[adjective, rhymes with *goose*] *not tight* A *loose* wheel on a bike is dangerous.
lose	[verb, rhymes with *shoes*] *to suffer loss* That sudden, loud noise made me *lose* my place.

Exercise 11 Choosing Between Words Often Confused

For each of the following sentences, choose the correct word from the pair of words in parentheses.

EXAMPLE 1. Rabbi Epstein (*lead, led*) our group during our tour of Israel.

1. led

1. We could (*hear, here*) the patter of the rain on the (*lead, led*) roof from a block away.
2. A kimono is a (*loose, lose*) Japanese garment with short, wide sleeves and a sash.
3. Mom said that (*its, it's*) your turn to wash the dishes.

Words Often Confused **629**

Cooperative Learning

For a class project, have students compile a thesaurus from some of the words often confused listed in this chapter and any other words students may discover on their own. Divide the class into teams of two or three, and assign each team words often confused from this chapter.

Give each team a stack of index cards. Instruct the teams to write one word on each card, followed by synonyms found in a dictionary, a usage book, or a thesaurus.

Once the cards have been completed, proofread, and corrected, ask for volunteers to alphabetize the cards. Enter the words on a word processor, and print a copy of the finished thesaurus for each member of the class.

Timesaver

Any of the exercises in this lesson can be graded quickly by having the students exchange papers and mark corrections as you write the answers on the chalkboard.

Looking at Language

British English. Tell students that some English words have two spellings, depending on whether the word is written in British English or American English. For example, *labor* is spelled *labour* in British English. Ask students if they know other words that are spelled differently by U.S. and British writers. [*color, colour; curb, kerb; jail, gaol*]

4. (*Hear, Here*) is a good article about Black History Month.
5. I hope the team doesn't (*loose, lose*) its opening game.
6. Who will (*lead, led*) the team to victory tomorrow?
7. "Wait (*hear, here*) while I open the door," Peter ordered.
8. The weights were as heavy as (*led, lead*).
9. (*Its, It's*) taken too long to respond to your letter.
10. The (*lead, led*) in this mechanical pencil is almost gone.

passed	[verb, past tense of *pass*] went by We *passed* you on the way to school.
past	[noun] time that has gone by; [preposition] beyond; [adjective] ended You can learn much from the *past*. The band marched *past* the school. The *past* week was a busy one.
peace	[noun] quiet, order, and security People all over the world long for *peace*.
piece	[noun] a part of something I had a delicious *piece* of spinach pie at the Greek festival.
plain	[adjective] simple; common; [noun] a flat area of land Raul's directions were *plain* and clear. The coastal *plain* was flat and barren.
plane	[noun] a flat surface; a tool; an airplane A rectangle is a four-sided *plane* with four right angles. Wood shavings curled from the *plane* to the workshop floor. The *plane* flew nonstop to Atlanta.
principal	[noun] the head of a school; [adjective] chief, main The vice *principal* is at the high school. The committee's *principal* task is preserving the park.
principle	[noun] a rule of conduct; a basic truth Freedom of speech is one of the *principles* of democracy.

TIPS & TRICKS

Here's a way to remember the difference between *peace* and *piece*. You eat a pi**e**ce of **pie**.

TIPS & TRICKS

To remember the spelling of *principal*, use this sentence: The princi**pal** is your **pal**.

Exercise 12 **Choosing Between Words Often Confused**

For each of the following sentences, choose the correct word from the pair of words in parentheses.

EXAMPLE
1. The (*passed, past*) president served two terms, not three.
   1. past

1. The Old Order Amish wear (*plain, plane*) clothes.
2. Many Americans believe that the golden rule is a good (*principal, principle*) by which to live.
3. Mark likes the (*piece, peace*) and quiet of the country.
4. One (*piece, peace*) of the puzzle was missing.
5. Komako used a (*plain, plane*) to smooth the rough edge of the door.
6. We flew in an enormous Singapore Airlines (*plain, plane*) to Frankfurt, Germany.
7. By studying the (*passed, past*), we understand the present.
8. She was (*principal, principle*) of the school for years.
9. Gail Devers quickly (*passed, past*) the other runners.
10. The trees are just (*passed, past*) their lovely fall colors.

Review E **Proofreading a Paragraph to Correct Errors in Words Often Confused**

For the sentences in the following paragraph, correctly write each incorrect word.

EXAMPLE
[1] Often, people don't know how precious something is until they loose it.
1. lose

[1] Several months ago, my aunt had what we all thought was a plane old cold. [2] In the passed, her doctor had told her there was no cure for a cold, so my aunt didn't even seek treatment. [3] No one knew that she had an ear infection that would led to a hearing loss in one ear. [4] Very soon, my aunt realized that she was hearing only peaces of conversations and could no longer hear out of her left ear. [5] When she went to the doctor, he explained that an infection had caused her to loose hearing in that ear. [6] The doctor gave her a chart showing the principle types of hearing aids. [7] He suggested

1. plain
2. past
3. lead
4. pieces
5. lose
6. principal

Words Often Confused 631

7. it's
8. Its
9. course
10. hear

the in-the-canal hearing aid because ~~its~~ barely noticeable when in place. **[8]** ~~It's~~ small size really surprised me. **[9]** The doctor told my aunt that, of ~~coarse~~, new advances in hearing technology are being made every day now. **[10]** Some people who could not ~~here~~ at all before can now be helped.

TIPS & TRICKS

Here is an easy way to remember the difference between *stationary* and *stationery*. You write a lett**er** on station**er**y.

stationary	[adjective] *in a fixed position* The desks are *stationary,* but the chairs can be moved.
stationery	[noun] *writing paper* Sarah designs her own *stationery*.
their	[possessive form of *they*] *belonging to them* *Their* pitcher struck out six players.
there	[adverb] *at or to that place;* [also used to begin a sentence] I'll see you *there.* *There* are more than two million books in the Harold Washington Library in Chicago.
they're	[contraction of *they are*] *They're* right behind you.
threw	[verb, past tense of *throw*] *tossed* Zack *threw* the ball to me.
through	[preposition] *in one side and out the other* Let's walk *through* the park.

Exercise 13 Choosing Between Words Often Confused

For each of the following sentences, choose the correct word from the choices in parentheses.

EXAMPLE 1. (*Their, They're, There*) goes the space shuttle!
1. There

1. The 100-yard dash will begin over (*their, there, they're*) by the fence.
2. In a flash, the girls (*threw, through*) everything into (*their, there, they're*) lockers and ran onto the field.
3. The planet earth was once thought to be (*stationary, stationery*) in space.
4. (*Threw, Through*) the door bounded a large dog.
5. Are you sure (*their, there, they're*) not coming?
6. "Who (*through, threw*) the pass that led to the touchdown?" Jill asked.
7. I think that the red envelopes do not go with the pink (*stationery, stationary*) at all.
8. (*They're, Their*) planning to see a Will Smith movie sometime this weekend.
9. We drove (*threw, through*) Kansas and Oklahoma on the way to Texas.
10. (*Their, There*) is a Cajun band playing in the park this afternoon until 4:00.

to	[preposition] *in the direction of; toward* We drove *to* Carson City.
too	[adverb] *also; more than enough* Am I invited, *too*? Your poem has *too* many syllables to be a haiku.
two	[adjective or noun] *one plus one* Ms. Red Cloud's last name is *two* separate words. *Two* of the pandas woke up then.
weak	[adjective] *feeble; not strong* People with *weak* ankles have difficulty ice-skating.
week	[noun] *seven days* The club meets once a *week*.

(continued)

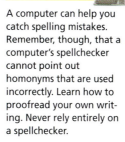

COMPUTER TIP

A computer can help you catch spelling mistakes. Remember, though, that a computer's spellchecker cannot point out homonyms that are used incorrectly. Learn how to proofread your own writing. Never rely entirely on a spellchecker.

Relating to Writing

If students are having problems finding misspelled words as they proofread, suggest that they go over their work starting at the end of a sentence and working backward in order to look at words out of context. Tell them to pay attention to each word and to circle any word about which they are uncertain. After they have gone over their papers, they should check each circled word in a dictionary.

Learning for Life

Continued on pp. 634–636

Writing a Yearbook Article. Tell students that one of the most treasured mementos of some students is the school yearbook. Students who serve on a yearbook staff gather photographs and write articles about events that occurred during a particular school year. High schools and universities produce most yearbooks, but some elementary and middle schools also publish annuals.

Have each student imagine that he or she is writing an article for a class yearbook for

(continued)

who's	[contraction of *who is* or *who has*] *Who's* wearing a watch? *Who's* seen Frida Kahlo's paintings?
whose	[possessive form of *who*] belonging to whom I wonder *whose* backpack this is.
your	[possessive form of *you*] belonging to you Rest *your* eyes now and then when you read.
you're	[contraction of *you are*] *You're* next in line.

Exercise 14 Choosing Between Words Often Confused

For each of the following sentences, choose the correct word from the choices in parentheses.

EXAMPLE 1. I wonder (*who's, whose*) won the election.
  1. who's

1. (*Who's, Whose*) story did you like best?
2. Walking (*to, too*) the grocery store, he began to feel (*weak, week*).
3. Does (*your, you're*) dad work for the newspaper, (*to, too, two*)?
4. It took me a (*weak, week*) to complete my project for history class.
5. If (*your, you're*) not making that noise, (*who's, whose*) making it?
6. "Is there (*too, two*) much flour in the tortilla dough?" Alinda asked.
7. Always fasten (*you're, your*) seat belt when (*you're, your*) riding in a vehicle.
8. They asked (*who's, whose*) painting was chosen (*to, too*) be entered in the contest.
9. (*Too, Two*) of the foreign exchange students are from southern India.
10. "See you next (*weak, week*)!" the ballet teacher said to the students cheerfully.

634 Chapter 23 Spelling

Learning for Life

the current academic year at your school. Each student should write a short article about a particular event in which his or her class has been involved. Students might write about a class play, a special program, a field trip, a band or choir concert, or another interesting event. Students should keep in mind that their articles will serve collectively as a record of events that occurred during the school year. You might want to assign certain events to students and gather articles from existing school

Review F — Choosing Between Words Often Confused

For each of the following sentences, choose the correct word or words from the choices in parentheses.

EXAMPLE   1. Don't (*loose, lose*) your house key.
           1. lose

1. Oh, Rebecca, which of these (*to, too, two*) boxes of (*stationary, stationery*) do you like better?
2. The Israelis and the Palestinians met in Madrid, the (*capital, capitol*) of Spain, for the (*peace, piece*) talks.
3. (*Principal, Principle*) Wong raised his hand for silence, and the students waited to (*hear, here*) what he would say.
4. These curtains will likely be hard to (*altar, alter*) because the fabric is so (*coarse, course*).
5. (*Its, It's*) (*all together, altogether*) too easy to confuse similar words.
6. Ruth vowed to (*lead, led*) the life of an exile rather than to (*desert, dessert*) Naomi.
7. Can that (*plain, plane*) (*brake, break*) the sound barrier?
8. We're (*all ready, already*) for the big game against our rivals this (*weak, week*).
9. (*Your, You're*) next chore is to dust; the dust (*clothes, cloths*) are on the counter.
10. The two friends (*passed, past*) the time pleasantly reading (*there, their, they're*) books.

Review G — Proofreading a Paragraph to Correct Spelling Errors and Errors in Words Often Confused

For each sentence in the following paragraph, correctly write each misspelled or misused word. If a sentence is already correct, write *C*.

EXAMPLE   [1] Its time to test you're knowledge of South American history.
           1. It's; your

[1] Starting about A.D. 1200, people known as the Incas began too take over the western portion of South America. [2] Look at the map on the next page, and you'll see that thier

1. to

2. their/deserts
3. capital
4. their
5. developed

6. principal

7. C
8. living

9. 1500's [or 1500s]
10. break

territory included mountains, seacoasts, river valleys, and deserts. [3] The capitol of the Incan empire was Cuzco. [4] The Incas created an impressive road system that connected Cuzco with the rest of there empire. [5] These hard-working people also built storehouses and developped large irrigation projects. [6] To help them manage their huge empire, they used a device called a quipu as their principle method of keeping records. [7] The quipu (shown below) is a series of knotted, colored cords. [8] With it, the Incas recorded such information as the number of people liveing in an area, the movements of the planets, and the amount of goods in storage. [9] The Incan civilization lasted until the Spanish arrived in the mid-1500s'. [10] In only a short time, Spanish conquistadors were able to defeat the Incas and brake up their empire.

636   Chapter 23   Spelling

the homonym for each word in the margin.
   You might want to make copies of the articles so students can collect them in special folders or notebooks to serve as their class yearbooks.

636   Spelling

CHAPTER 23

Chapter Review

A. Proofreading Sentences for Correct Spelling

For each of the following sentences, correctly write the word that is misspelled.

> **HELP**
> No proper nouns in the Chapter Review are misspelled.

1. The company's cheif accountant wrote the schedule. **1.** chief
2. Mr. Santander gave a breif speech before the ceremony. **2.** brief
3. Breatheing hard, we finally reached the summit. **3.** Breathing
4. Chickens and gooses are common fowl. **4.** geese
5. We changed the subject to avoid having an arguement. **5.** argument
6. How many Is did you use in your letter to Irene? **6.** I's
7. Mom and Dad have no tolerance for lazyness. **7.** laziness
8. Spain and Portugal are two countrys I have always wanted to visit. **8.** countries
9. The new store on the corner will sell computer disks, computers, and stereoes. **9.** stereos
10. My grandmother's recipe calls for half a clove of garlic and two garden tomatos. **10.** tomatoes
11. Three small active childs came running out of the house. **11.** children
12. We cut several large branchs off the pine tree. **12.** branches
13. After she ran through the patch of stinging nettles, Alice had itchs up and down her legs. **13.** itches
14. We were surprised to see two pianoes on the stage instead of only one. **14.** pianos
15. I am very interested in the history of anceint Egypt. **15.** ancient
16. "The last thing we want," said the new sales manager, "is a disatisfied customer." **16.** dissatisfied
17. The first thing you notice in San Miguel is the friendlyness of the people. **17.** friendliness
18. That dinosaur skeleton must have been the bigest thing in the whole museum. **18.** biggest
19. Aunt Rina has lost weight; she looks much slimer than she has in a long time. **19.** slimmer
20. Strawberrys are my favorite fruit. **20.** Strawberries

Using the Chapter Review

To assess student progress, you may want to compare the types of items missed on the **Diagnostic Preview** to those missed on the **Chapter Review.** If students have not made significant progress, you may want to refer them to **Chapter 24: Correcting Common Errors, Exercises 30–32,** for additional practice.

B. Choosing Between Words Often Confused

For each of the following sentences, choose from each pair in parentheses the word that will make the sentence correct.

21. Nothing would persuade him to (*altar*, *alter*) his plans.
22. Berlin is the (*capitol*, *capital*) of Germany.
23. Sometimes the wisest (*course*, *coarse*) of action is to do nothing.
24. Samantha tried on the new (*cloths*, *clothes*) she received on her birthday.
25. For (*desert*, *dessert*) we had red grapes, strawberries, frozen yogurt, and melon.
26. The vast (*planes*, *plains*) of Patagonia stretch from the mountains to the ocean.
27. "Your cousins are over (*their*, *there*)," said Mr. Octavius. "I think this is (*there*, *their*) luggage."
28. In all the confusion, it was difficult to tell (*whose*, *who's*) things belonged to whom.
29. We were somewhat surprised when an overloaded pickup truck (*past*, *passed*) us going uphill.
30. On their way (*too*, *to*) the train station, they were held up in the (*stationary*, *stationery*) traffic.

C. Proofreading a Paragraph to Correct Spelling Errors

For each sentence in the following paragraph, correctly write the word or words that are misspelled. If a sentence is already correct, write *C*.

31. capital/location
32. past
33. Vikings
34. there
35. C
36. peace
37. C
38. Its

[31] Dublin, the capitol of Ireland, has a beautiful locateion between the sea and the mountains. [32] The city has a rich and interesting passed. [33] The Viking's established Dublin in the mid-800's, though a small settlement had existed previously on the site. [34] Norman soldiers from England captured Dublin in 1170 and built St. Patrick's Cathedral and Dublin Castle their. [35] The castle remained the center of British rule in Ireland throughout the next 700 years. [36] War and piece came and went. [37] By the 1700's, Dublin was growing fast. [38] It's cultural life flourished, and manufacturing and trade increased.

Chapter 23 Spelling

RESOURCES

Spelling
Review
- *Grammar, Usage, and Mechanics*, pp. 300, 301, 302, 303, 304

Assessment
- Assessment Package
  —Chapter Tests, Ch. 23
  —Chapter Tests in Standardized Test Formats, Ch. 23
- Test Generator (One-Stop Planner CD-ROM)

Spelling

[39] ~~Unfortunatly~~, between 1916 and 1922, much property was destroyed during the war of independence and a civil war.
[40] Today, Dublin is growing and prosperous and is ~~faceing~~ the challenges common to most modern big ~~citys~~.

39. Unfortunately

40. facing/cities

Writing Application
Using Correct Spelling in a Personal Letter

Following Spelling Rules You are writing a letter to congratulate your cousin Mary, who has been awarded first prize in a spelling bee. Write a paragraph expressing your congratulations and saying how important you think it is to use correct spelling. In your paragraph, use at least five words often confused.

Prewriting Jot down a list of reasons correct spelling is important. You might mention making a good impression and making communication easier. Also, compose sentences about how difficult it must be to remember correct spelling in front of an audience and how impressed you are that Mary managed to do so.

Writing Begin your rough draft by stating how hard it is to spell correctly in English and how important it is to continue developing that skill. Then, congratulate Mary on her award and say that her success will inspire you to continue working hard at learning correct spelling.

Revising Have a friend or classmate read your draft. Have you clearly stated the importance of correct spelling? Is your pleasure at your cousin's success clearly described?

Publishing Make sure you have not used any homonyms incorrectly. Then, proofread your letter for any errors in grammar, punctuation, and spelling. You and your classmates may wish to post your letters on a class bulletin board or Web page.

Reference Note
For more about **writing a personal letter,** see "Writing" in the Quick Reference Handbook.

Chapter Review   639

RESOURCES

Writing Application
Extension
- *Grammar, Usage, and Mechanics,* p. 307
- *Language Workshop CD-ROM,* Lessons 48–51

TEACHING TIP

In the **Spelling Words** list, the numbers of the word groups correspond to lessons in the *Spelling* workbook.

Lesson 1: OBJECTIVE
- To spell words that demonstrate these sound-letter relationships: /a/*a*; /e/*e*; /i/*i*; /o/*o*; /u/*u*

Lesson 2: OBJECTIVE
- To spell words that have a long vowel sound

Lesson 3: OBJECTIVE
- To spell words that demonstrate these sound-letter relationships: /ou/*ou*; *ô*/*o, a, au, aw*; /ōō/*ou, oo, u*

Lesson 4: OBJECTIVE
- To spell words that demonstrate these sound-letter relationships: /är/*ar*; /âr/*ar, are*; /ôr/*oar, ar, our*; /ûr/*ur, or, er*

Lesson 6: OBJECTIVE
- To spell words that include unusual spellings of the short *i*, short *u*, long *a*, and long *o* vowel sounds

Lesson 7: OBJECTIVE
- To spell words that include the vowel combination *ei* or *ie*

Lesson 8: OBJECTIVE
- To spell open, closed, and hyphenated compound words

Lesson 9: OBJECTIVE
- To spell homophones

Lesson 10: OBJECTIVE
- To spell words that sound similar and have spellings that are somewhat alike

Lesson 12: OBJECTIVE
- To spell words ending with consonant *y* in which *y* changes to *i* before *es* or *ed* is added

Lesson 13: OBJECTIVE
- To spell words that demonstrate these sound-letter relationships: /ər/*er*; /əl/*al*; /ən/*en, an*

MECHANICS

Spelling Words

1. - contact
   - contract
   - advance
   - depth
   - comment
   - summit
   - sketch
   - nonsense
   - splendid
   - ethnic
   - liquid
   - impulse

2. - globe
   - grove
   - slope
   - slice
   - roast
   - spike
   - choke
   - praise
   - squeeze
   - breathe
   - gross
   - thigh

3. - shout
   - youth
   - amount
   - pounds
   - mountain
   - thousands
   - proof
   - crawled
   - account
   - launched
   - rumors
   - saucer

4. - turtle
   - nightmare
   - burnt
   - curb
   - purse
   - declare

   scarce
   inserts
   sparkling
   source
   nervous
   warrant

6. - enough
   - though
   - straight
   - rough
   - courage
   - eighth
   - system
   - although
   - sleigh
   - boulder
   - biscuit
   - dough

7. - freight
   - foreign
   - receive
   - receiver
   - belief
   - relief
   - weighed
   - reins
   - fierce
   - heights
   - thieves
   - achieve

8. - grandfather
   - fairy tales
   - bedtime
   - cupboard
   - upright
   - teenager
   - thunderstorm
   - barefoot
   - middle-class
   - middle-aged
   - bodyguard
   - so-called

9. - grown
   - groan
   - guest
   - guessed
   - creek
   - creak
   - weather
   - whether
   - sore
   - soar
   - stake
   - steak

10. - angle
    - angel
    - costume
    - custom
    - affect
    - effect
    - adopt
    - adapt
    - device
    - devise
    - decent
    - descent

12. - varied
    - centuries
    - colonies
    - applies
    - occupied
    - identified
    - enemies
    - activities
    - denied
    - allied
    - industries
    - qualified

13. - beaten
    - musical
    - rotten
    - German
    - Indian
    - Roman

    explorer
    stretcher
    critical
    criminal
    political
    original

14. - escape
    - gotten
    - velvet
    - engine
    - insist
    - admire
    - index
    - intense
    - further
    - frantic
    - convince
    - instinct

15. - agent
    - evil
    - local
    - eager
    - famous
    - fiber
    - razor
    - vital
    - rival
    - basis
    - cheetah
    - scenic

16. - speaking
    - spelling
    - wondered
    - bragged
    - healed
    - scrubbed
    - answered
    - threatened
    - admitted
    - committed
    - referring
    - preferred

640 Chapter 23 Spelling

Lesson 14: OBJECTIVE
- To spell two-syllable words that contain a vowel-consonant-consonant-vowel pattern (VCCV)

Lesson 15: OBJECTIVE
- To spell two-syllable words that contain a vowel-consonant-vowel pattern (V/CV)

18.
- insurance
- conference
- ambulance
- absence
- instance
- audience
- allowance
- intelligence
- assurance
- appearance
- obedience
- presence

19.
- activity
- ability
- argument
- personality
- electricity
- championship
- community
- majority
- responsibility
- curiosity
- necessity
- authority

20.
- approach
- accuse
- applause
- affection
- accompany
- assign
- appreciate
- accurate
- association
- apparent
- accustomed
- assistance

21.
- continued
- commander
- commit
- constitution
- confusing
- commence
- commotion
- commercial
- communicate
- communities
- communication
- committee

22.
- elephant
- confident
- instant
- element
- servant
- excellent
- opponent
- permanent
- assistant
- innocent
- significant
- sufficient

24.
- talent
- novel
- treason
- comic
- profit
- token
- weapon
- gopher
- pleasant
- siren
- frigid
- spiral

25.
- habit
- display
- clever
- gather
- empty
- chaos
- suspense
- Saturn
- oval
- orphan
- fatal
- crystal

26.
- media
- fungi
- bacteria
- stimulus
- stimuli
- larvae
- radius
- nucleus
- nuclei
- species
- salmon
- hippopotamus

27.
- curious
- tremendous
- enormous
- obvious
- delicious
- mysterious
- executive
- creative
- fabulous
- legislative
- negative
- sensitive

28.
- unpredictable
- disagreement
- renewal
- unemployment
- unexpectedly
- unfortunately
- unusually
- reproduction
- reconstruction
- disagreeable
- unsuccessful
- uncomfortable

30.
- wonderfully
- thoughtfully
- relationship
- respectively
- naturally
- nervously
- gracefully
- actively
- joyfully
- beautifully
- successfully
- accidentally

31.
- illegal
- impolite
- impossible
- invisible
- irregular
- inexpensive
- impure
- inability
- impatient
- indigestion
- indefinite
- incredible

32.
- descriptive
- description
- prescribed
- inspector
- spectacle
- spectacular
- scribbled
- inscription
- subscription
- spectrum
- spectators
- transcripts

33.
- erupt
- abrupt
- bankrupt
- inject
- disrupting
- disruption
- eject
- reject
- rejected
- rupture
- corrupt
- interrupt

Lesson 19: OBJECTIVE
- To spell words with the suffixes –ship, –ment, or –ity

Lesson 20: OBJECTIVE
- To spell words with the prefix ad– (ac–, af–, ap–, as–)

Lesson 21: OBJECTIVE
- To spell words that begin with the prefix com– (con–)

Lesson 22: OBJECTIVE
- To spell words that end in –ant or –ent

Lesson 24: OBJECTIVE
- To spell two-syllable words that contain a V/CV or a VC/V pattern in the middle

Lesson 25: OBJECTIVE
- To spell two-syllable words having mixed spelling patterns

Lesson 26: OBJECTIVE
- To spell words whose plural form has an unusual spelling

Lesson 27: OBJECTIVE
- To spell adjectives having an –ive or –ous suffix

Lesson 28: OBJECTIVE
- To spell words with both a prefix and a suffix

Lesson 30: OBJECTIVE
- To spell words that have two suffixes

Lesson 31: OBJECTIVE
- To spell words that include one of these variations of the prefix in–: im–, il–, ir–

Lesson 32: OBJECTIVE
- To spell words with the Latin root –scrib–/–script– or –spect–

Lesson 33: OBJECTIVE
- To spell words with Latin roots –rupt– and –ject–

MECHANICS

Lesson 16: OBJECTIVE
- To spell words ending with –ed or –ing

Lesson 18: OBJECTIVE
- To spell words with the suffix –ance or –ence

CHAPTER 24 Correcting Common Errors

PREVIEWING THE CHAPTER

- This chapter provides application and review of some aspects of grammar, usage, and mechanics that cause students particular difficulty. You may find this chapter useful in a variety of ways. You could use the exercises and tests in this chapter as diagnostic tests, judging by student scores which areas need most attention; as a resource for reteaching and remediation, providing extra practice for concepts you feel need added emphasis; as a review of key concepts, helping to prepare students for standardized tests of language skills mastery; or in any combination of these ways.

HELP
The exercises in Chapter 24 test your knowledge of the rules of **standard, formal English.** These are the rules you should follow in your schoolwork.

Reference Note
For more information about **standard** and **nonstandard English** and **formal** and **informal English,** see page 519.

Key Language Skills Review

This chapter reviews key skills and concepts that pose special problems for writers.

- Sentence Fragments and Run-on Sentences
- Subject-Verb Agreement
- Pronoun-Antecedent Agreement
- Verb Forms
- Pronoun Forms
- Comparison and Placement of Modifiers
- Double Negatives
- Standard Usage
- Capitalization
- Punctuation—Commas, End Marks, Semicolons, Colons, Quotation Marks, and Apostrophes
- Spelling

Most of the exercises in this chapter follow the same format as the exercises found throughout the grammar, usage, and mechanics sections of this book. You will notice,

642 **Chapter 24** Correcting Common Errors

CHAPTER RESOURCES

Planning
- One-Stop Planner CD-ROM

Practice and Extension
- *Grammar, Usage, and Mechanics,* pp. 308–338

Internet
- go.hrw.com (keyword: EOLang)

Evaluation and Assessment
- *Assessment Package*
  —Chapter Tests, Ch. 24
  —Chapter Tests in Standardized Test Formats, Ch. 24
- *Test Generator (One-Stop Planner CD-ROM)*

however, that two sets of review exercises are presented in standardized test formats. These exercises are designed to provide you with practice not only in solving usage and mechanics problems but also in dealing with these kinds of problems on standardized tests.

Exercise 1 Identifying Sentences and Sentence Fragments

Identify each of the following word groups as a *sentence* or a *sentence fragment*. If a word group is a sentence, rewrite it correctly, using a capital letter at the beginning and adding an end mark.

Reference Note
For information on **sentences** and **sentence fragments**, see page 302.

EXAMPLES
1. the squirrel hopped across the branch
   1. sentence—The squirrel hopped across the branch.

   2. Jeremy's collection of comic books
   2. sentence fragment

1. near the door of the classroom   1. frag.
2. all members of the safety patrol   2. frag.
3. sumo wrestling is popular in Japan.   3. sent.
4. please pass me the fruit salad.   4. sent.
5. will become a member of Junior Achievement   5. frag.
6. after school Sonya repaired her backpack.   6. sent.
7. what an active puppy that is!   7. sent.
8. lived in British Columbia for many years   8. frag.
9. do you like the sound of ocean waves?   9. sent.
10. on the top shelf of the refrigerator   10. frag.
11. ate goat cheese every day in Norway   11. frag.
12. that's a fantastic idea! [or .]   12. sent.
13. because rap music is still popular   13. frag.
14. not everyone wants to play the game.   14. sent.
15. a tree was placed on top of the completed building.   15. sent.
16. when the armadillos enter another state   16. frag.
17. stopped traffic for half an hour   17. frag.
18. John the plumber around noon   18. frag.
19. please return the books by tomorrow afternoon.   19. sent.
20. plugged in the computer and nothing happened   20. frag.

Exercise 1

OBJECTIVE

- To distinguish complete sentences from sentence fragments and to punctuate complete sentences correctly

COMMON ERRORS

Grammar and Usage

Exercise 2

OBJECTIVE

- To identify and correct sentence fragments

Exercise 2 Revising Sentence Fragments

ANSWERS

Answers may vary. Sample responses are given.

1. The book is titled *The Case of the Missing Cutthroats.*
2. It is a book for young detectives who love nature.
3. S
4. S
5. Most people thought cutthroat trout had died out where she was fishing in the Snake River.
6. S
7. They are puzzled by the presence of a cutthroat trout.
8. S
9. Spinner and her cousin Al go on an adventure.
10. They hope to find clues that will help them solve the mystery.

Cooperative Learning

If students need more practice revising sentence fragments, bring in some classified ads that contain fragments. Have students work in groups of two or three to revise the ads to create complete sentences.

Exercise 3

OBJECTIVE

- To revise run-on sentences by making two sentences or adding a comma and a coordinating conjunction

COMMON ERRORS

Reference Note

For information on **sentence fragments**, see page 302.

Link to Literature

HELP

Most of the sentences in Exercise 3 can be correctly revised in more than one way. You need to give only one revision for each sentence.

Reference Note

For information on **run-on sentences**, see page 265.

Exercise 2 Revising Sentence Fragments

Some of the following word groups are sentence fragments. First, identify the fragments. Then, make each fragment a complete sentence by adding (1) a subject, (2) a verb, or (3) both. You may need to change the punctuation and capitalization, too. If the word group is already a complete sentence, write *S*.

EXAMPLE   1. Finished reading an exciting book by Jean Craighead George.
   1. I finished reading an exciting book by Jean Craighead George.

1. Titled *The Case of the Missing Cutthroats.*
2. A book for young detectives who love nature.
3. In the book, a girl named Spinner goes fishing.
4. During the trip, she catches a giant cutthroat trout.
5. Thought cutthroat trout had died out where she was fishing in the Snake River.
6. Both she and her family are surprised by her catch.
7. Puzzled by the presence of a cutthroat trout.
8. What has happened to the cutthroat trout?
9. Spinner and her cousin Al on an adventure.
10. Hope to find clues that will help them solve the mystery.

Exercise 3 Identifying and Revising Run-on Sentences

Decide which of the following word groups are run-on sentences. Then, revise each run-on sentence by (1) making two separate sentences or (2) using a comma and a coordinating conjunction. You may have to change the punctuation and capitalization, too. If the word group is already a complete sentence, write *S*. Revisions will vary. Sample responses are given.

EXAMPLE   1. Both girls enjoy playing soccer one is usually the goalie.
   1. Both girls enjoy playing soccer, and one is usually the goalie.
   or
   Both girls enjoy playing soccer. One is usually the goalie.

644   Chapter 24   Correcting Common Errors

1. Puffins are shorebirds, they have brightly colored beaks and ducklike bodies.
2. Cement is a fine powder. it is mixed with sand, water, and small rocks to make concrete.
3. Alicia collects birth dates, she has recorded the birthdays of all her friends and of her favorite movie stars.
4. We may go to the Zuni arts and crafts fair on Saturday, we may wait until next weekend.   **4. or**
5. The band placed first in regional competitions, it did not win at the state contests.   **5. but**
6. I plan to go to the Florida Keys someday, I want to skin-dive for seashells.   **6. for**
7. Kerry is having a party tomorrow night, we are planning to go.   **7. and**
8. The school board could vote to remodel the old cafeteria, or they may decide to build a new one.   **8. S**
9. My brother would like to live on a space station someday, I would, too.   **9. and**
10. These rocks are too heavy for me to lift, I asked Christy to help me move them.   **10. so**

Exercise 4 Identifying and Revising Run-on Sentences

Identify which of the following word groups are run-on sentences. Then, revise each run-on sentence by (1) making two separate sentences or (2) using a comma and a coordinating conjunction. You may have to change the punctuation and capitalization, too. If the word group is already a complete sentence, write S. **Revisions will vary. Sample responses are given.**

EXAMPLE
1. The Navajo woman allowed the children to try on jewelry, it was made out of silver and beautiful turquoise.

1. *The Navajo woman allowed the children to try on jewelry. It was made out of silver and beautiful turquoise.*

1. Sheila liked a ring with one stone in the middle, it didn't fit her fingers.   **1. but**
2. She found another ring with three small stones, it was a perfect fit for her.   **2. and**

HELP

Most of the sentences in Exercise 4 can be correctly revised in more than one way. You need to give only one revision for each sentence.

Reference Note

For information on **run-on sentences,** see page 265.

TEACHING TIP

To help students eliminate run-on sentences, have them try the following suggestions:

1. Read sentences aloud. If you hesitate at certain places, you may need to make two separate sentences or use a comma and a conjunction.
2. Watch for changes in ideas.
3. Check for especially long sentences.

Exercise 4

OBJECTIVE

- To revise run-on sentences by separating them into two sentences or by adding a comma and a coordinating conjunction

Cooperative Learning

To give students additional practice in checking for sentence fragments and run-on sentences, take a passage from your students' literature textbook or from a magazine or newspaper article. Revise the passage so that it contains no end marks and sentences begin with lowercase letters. Organize students into small groups, and give each group a copy of the revised passage.

Ask each group to add punctuation to the passage and to capitalize letters at the beginning of sentences. Groups should not change the wording of the passage, but they should use correct punctuation to avoid run-ons and fragments. Students can check their results against the original text.

Exercise 5

OBJECTIVE

- To correct run-on sentences and sentence fragments

COMMON ERRORS

HELP

Most of the sentences in Exercise 5 can be correctly revised in more than one way. You need to give only one revision for each sentence.

Reference Note

For information on **sentence fragments,** see page 302. For information on **run-on sentences,** see page 265.

3. Aaron picked out a turquoise watchband, and he also found a ring with blue stones and fire agates.   **3. S**
4. The watchband had little pieces of turquoise in the shape of a star he really wanted to buy it.
5. Both Maria and Francine spied a necklace a rough chunk of turquoise was hung from a silver chain.
6. Thad may spend his allowance on a turquoise ring he may save up his money for a watchband.   **6. or**
7. Several children had never seen turquoise before they wanted to know if the stones were real.   **7. and**
8. The saleswoman's arms were covered with bracelets everyone noticed her.   **8. so**
9. Ruben put six bracelets on his arms, and then he couldn't get all of them off.   **9. S**
10. The group wanted to see more turquoise jewelry the woman had sold many pieces earlier in the day.   **10. but**

Exercise 5 Correcting Run-on Sentences and Sentence Fragments

Decide which of the following word groups are run-on sentences and which are sentence fragments. Then, revise each word group to make one or more complete sentences. Remember to use correct capitalization and punctuation. If a word group is already a complete sentence, write *S*.

EXAMPLES
1. Do you like brightly colored art you should see Faith Ringgold's paintings.
   1. *Do you like brightly colored art? You should see Faith Ringgold's paintings.*

   2. Uses color boldly and imaginatively.
   2. *Ringgold uses color boldly and imaginatively.*

Revisions may vary. Sample responses are given.
1. Ringgold was born in Harlem in 1930 at a young age, she knew she wanted to be an artist.
2. Today her artwork in museums around the world.   **2. is**
3. Paints on fabric and sometimes uses fabric to frame her paintings.   **3. She**
4. Her creativity led her to invent a whole new art form she decided to call it the "story quilt."
5. Story quilts blend storytelling with painting.   **5. S**

646   Chapter 24   Correcting Common Errors

6. One of Ringgold's series of story quilts about an African American woman in Paris.   **6.** is
7. Much of her work represents her African American roots.   **7.** S
8. Ringgold's painting *Tar Beach* is based on her childhood experiences she completed the work in 1988.   **9.** *Tar Beach*
9. Shows a playground on the roof of an apartment building.
10. Behind the rooftop lies the George Washington Bridge, a bridge whose string of lights reminded Ringgold of a diamond necklace.   **10.** S

Exercise 6 Choosing Verbs That Agree in Number with Their Subjects

For each of the following sentences, choose the form of the verb in parentheses that agrees with the subject.

EXAMPLE   1. Everyone except my twin sisters (*want, wants*) to go to the powwow.
   1. wants

1. Here (*come, comes*) the marching bands in the parade!
2. Several of my friends (*has, have*) trail bikes.
3. I (*don't, doesn't*) like to swim when the water is cold.
4. Neither the guinea pigs nor the hamster (*is, are*) awake yet.
5. (*Has, Have*) Mr. Baldwin and Sherry been talking long?
6. One of the scientists (*was, were*) Isaac Newton.
7. Thunderstorms usually (*don't, doesn't*) bother me.
8. (*Is, Are*) the Chinese cookbooks still on sale?
9. All of the movie (*was, were*) filmed in Vietnam.
10. The boy in the red shoes (*run, runs*) fast.

Exercise 7 Proofreading Sentences for Correct Subject-Verb Agreement

Most of the following sentences contain a verb that does not agree in number with its subject. If a verb form is incorrect, write the correct form. If a sentence is already correct, write *C*.

EXAMPLE   1. A carved slice of potato make a good stamp.
   1. makes

1. Images from this type of stamp are called potato prints.   **1.** C

Reference Note

For information on **verb forms,** see page 445. For information on **subject-verb agreement,** see page 422.

Exercise 6

OBJECTIVE

- To choose verbs that agree in number with their subjects

Reference Note

For information on **subject-verb agreement,** see page 422.

Exercise 7

OBJECTIVE

- To write correct verb forms

Grammar and Usage

2. Both my cousins and my younger brother Michael ~~creates~~ potato prints. **2.** create
3. It ~~don't~~ cost much to make these prints. **3.** doesn't
4. A firm potato, a knife, paint, a paintbrush, and paper ~~is~~ the necessary supplies. **4.** are
5. My friend James ~~find~~ unique shapes and patterns in his mother's old magazines. **5.** finds
6. He then carves these designs on the flat surfaces of cut potatoes. **6.** C
7. Next, each carved design on the potato slices ~~are~~ coated with paint. **7.** is
8. Pieces of fabric or a sheet of paper ~~offer~~ a good surface for stamping. **8.** offers
9. Each of my cousins ~~like~~ to make greeting cards with stamped designs. **9.** likes
10. Other uses for a potato stamp ~~includes~~ making writing paper and wrapping paper. **10.** include

Exercise 8

OBJECTIVE

- To choose pronouns that agree with their antecedents

Reference Note

For information on **pronoun-antecedent agreement,** see page 435.

Exercise 8 **Choosing Pronouns That Agree with Their Antecedents**

For each of the following sentences, choose the pronoun in parentheses that agrees with its antecedent.

EXAMPLE 1. The engineers showed (*his, their*) plans for the new bridge.
 1. their

1. J. W. and I hope to have (*our, their*) skits ready in time for the talent show.
2. Two boys and one girl have received honors, and all of (*her, their*) parents are very proud.
3. During the last serve, with the crowd watching, Danny's tennis racket flew out of (*his, our*) hand.
4. We treated (*ourselves, themselves*) to Chinese noodles and stir-fried vegetables for supper.
5. The table is made of oak and is quite solid, but one of (*his, its*) legs is broken.
6. The members of the Asian Students Club asked to have (*its, their*) picture taken with the school mascot.

7. Neither Jack nor Charles wants to have (*his*, *their*) hair cut by Lisa.
8. Arlene asked Samuel to go on the picnic, but (*he*, *she*) hasn't given an answer yet.
9. The squirrels and the rabbits play in the yard; (*they*, *it*) seem to have a lot of fun.
10. Each of the girls will receive (*their*, *her*) own directions.

Exercise 9 Proofreading for Pronoun-Antecedent Agreement

Most of the following sentences contain a pronoun that does not agree with its antecedent. If a sentence is incorrect, write the correct pronoun. If a sentence is already correct, write *C*.

EXAMPLES
1. The asteroids will not hit Earth, but it will come close.
1. they

2. Each of the boys thought that their independent project was the best one.
2. his

1. Dad wrote out the check to the painters although he had not finished the painting job for him.   1. they
2. Tom Sawyer tricked his friends into doing his work, but they enjoyed it.   2. C
3. Jesse Owens, Willie Mays, and Joe Louis were sports stars in their day, and many people still remember him.   3. them
4. Have you ever noticed how the bears at the zoo really enjoy sunning itself?   4. themselves
5. Several of the men in our town plan to donate his time to Habitat for Humanity.   5. their
6. Each of the girls wanted to read their report first.   6. her
7. Did Randy or Tomás finish cleaning their desk first?   7. his
8. Our grandparents gave us a surprise party when we came home from camp.   8. C
9. Either José or Andrew will arrive early so that they can help us finish the posters.   9. he
10. Each of the cats was chasing their toys.   10. its

Reference Note
For information on **pronoun-antecedent agreement**, see page 435.

Exercise 9

OBJECTIVE

- To proofread for pronoun-antecedent agreement

Exercise 10

OBJECTIVE

- To use the principal parts of regular verbs

Meeting INDIVIDUAL NEEDS

ENGLISH-LANGUAGE LEARNERS
General Strategies. Students acquiring English may not realize that a past or past participle verb form that they hear every day is spelled with a –d or an –ed ending. This confusion arises because native English-speakers often barely pronounce the d sound or pronounce it with a t sound. In addition, native English-speakers often "drop" or "swallow" the n sound on the ends of some irregular past participle forms, so that this sound cannot be heard. Point out these discrepancies between pronunciation and spelling, and have students pay particular attention to these forms as they complete **Exercise 10**.

HELP

Some sentences in Exercise 10 may have more than one correct answer. You need to give only one answer for each sentence.

Reference Note

For information on **regular verb forms,** see page 446.

1. climbed
2. joking
3. shopped
4. filled
5. entering
6. watching
7. called
8. measured
9. loaded [or load]
10. jumped
11. laughed [or laugh]
12. fixing
13. washed
14. played
15. walked
16. talking
17. hammered [or hammers]
18. observing
19. helped
20. dressing [or dressed]

Exercise 10 Using the Principal Parts of Regular Verbs

Give the form of the italicized verb that will correctly complete each of the following sentences.

EXAMPLE 1. roll   The dog ___ on its back for us to pet it.
1. rolled
or
rolls

1. climb — Yesterday the cat ___ the tree.
2. joke — I can never tell when Bob is ___.
3. shop — My friend and I once ___ all day at a mall in Bloomington, Minnesota.
4. fill — Have the fans ___ the auditorium yet?
5. enter — Too many cars are ___ the parking lot.
6. watch — The class is ___ a film about the ancient Incan culture in Peru.
7. call — Who ___ my name a few seconds ago?
8. measure — My mother has ___ the space for the new bookcase.
9. load — Two men ___ our furniture into the truck.
10. jump — A deer has ___ over the fence.
11. laugh — We ___ for a long time over Ira's joke.
12. fix — Steven is ___ the computer.
13. wash — Cora's brother has ___ his new car at least a dozen times.
14. play — Have you ___ the soundtrack from that movie for Isaac yet?
15. walk — Mother and I ___ three miles on the county road yesterday morning.
16. talk — The young boys are ___ about starting their own soccer team.
17. hammer — The carpenter ___ the nails into the crossbeam in almost no time at all.
18. observe — Benjamin's family is ___ Yom Kippur in the traditional way.
19. help — Regular exercise has ___ many people to stay physically fit.
20. dress — Are you ___ up for the banquet tonight?

Exercise 11 Using Irregular Verbs

For each italicized verb, give the past or the past participle form that will correctly complete the sentence.

EXAMPLE 1. *drink* The guests ____ all of the raspberry tea.
   1. drank

1. *blow* The wind has ____ the kite out of the tree!
2. *shrink* The boy in the movie had ____ to the size of a squirrel.
3. *steal* "I've never ____ anything in my life," Abe declared in his defense.
4. *drive* Pat and Justin ____ go-carts at the park.
5. *freeze* The water in the birdbath has ____.
6. *sink* The toy boat has ____ in the sudsy bath water.
7. *throw* Each athlete has ____ the javelin twice.
8. *sing* The choir ____ at the celebration last night.
9. *swim* Have you ever ____ in warm mineral water?
10. *burst* The balloon ____ when the cat clawed it.
11. *teach* Mrs. Randall has ____ at Rosenwald Middle School for years.
12. *give* Last year I ____ part of my allowance to the United Way.
13. *run* Our car is old and unattractive, but it has ____ well for many years.
14. *eat* Sharon baked two small potatoes and ____ both of them.
15. *fly* "That hawk has ____ over the yard twice," Justin said.
16. *write* Many people have ____ about the Mexican myth of Quetzalcoatl.
17. *begin* It has ____ to snow, but the flakes are very small and dry.
18. *come* "Who ____ to Dad's surprise birthday party?" Miriam asked.
19. *speak* Lin and Jeff have ____ about their tickets to everyone in class.
20. *do* It's a good feeling to know that you have ____ your best.

Reference Note
For information on **irregular verb forms**, see page 448.

1. blown
2. shrunk [*or* shrunken]
3. stolen
4. drove
5. frozen
6. sunk
7. thrown
8. sang
9. swum
10. burst
11. taught
12. gave
13. run
14. ate
15. flown
16. written
17. begun
18. came
19. spoken
20. done

Exercise 11

OBJECTIVE

- To complete sentences by supplying the past or past participle form of given irregular verbs

Meeting INDIVIDUAL NEEDS

ENGLISH-LANGUAGE LEARNERS
General Strategies. Point out to students that when they have questions about the principal parts of irregular verbs, they can often find the answers in a dictionary. Tell them that the base forms of verbs are listed as entry words and that the past, past participle, and present participle forms of irregular verbs are given in the entries. For example, if students look up *sink*, they will find *sank*, *sunk*, and *sinking*. As practice, have each student look up three irregular verbs and find the verbs' principal parts in the dictionary entry.

INCLUSION
Students with learning disabilities may have limited vocabularies or experience difficulties with abstract concepts such as irregular verbs.

For each student, make a chart with four columns. Label the first column "Base Form," the second "Present Participle," the third "Past," and the fourth "Past Participle." In the first column, list ten irregular verbs. Next, using the charts in **Chapter 16**, fill in two of the three remaining columns with the correct present participle, past, or past participle forms of the irregular verbs. Then, have students fill in whichever columns are blank with the appropriate verb forms. Students can then return to the charts in **Chapter 16** to check their answers. Students can keep their corrected charts in their notebooks as a reference and can repeat this practice whenever they need review of specific irregular verb forms.

COMMON ERRORS

Exercise 12

OBJECTIVE

- To proofread sentences for errors in irregular verbs

Reference Note
For information on **irregular verb forms,** see page 448.

Exercise 12 Proofreading for Errors in Irregular Verbs

Most of the following sentences contain incorrect verb forms. Identify each error, and write the correct form of the verb. If the sentence is already correct, write *C*.

EXAMPLE 1. We have went to the African art exhibit two weekends in a row.
1. went—gone

1. Sarah ~~done~~ well at yesterday's track meet.
2. My stepfather ~~brung~~ me a stuffed animal when I was in the hospital.
3. Nickelodeon movie theaters ~~begun~~ to be quite popular in the United States around 1905.
4. Manuel's grandfather ~~come~~ to the United States forty years ago.
5. We ~~seen~~ the Rio Grande when we drove through the state of New Mexico.
6. Chris knew that a basement was a good place to take shelter during a tornado.
7. Judy ~~taked~~ a few minutes to decide what to say.
8. Maria's team ~~choosed~~ the oak tree in her front yard as home base.
9. The poison ivy in the woods ~~gived~~ me a rash.
10. Dr. Seuss wrote the poem "The Sneetches."
11. The blue pitcher that my godparents ~~buyed~~ for me in Denmark is on the table in the living room.
12. Do you remember what running records Carl Lewis ~~breaked~~?
13. The girls on the front porch have ~~drank~~ their lemonade too quickly.
14. My shirt and pants tore on the barbed wire as I climbed through the fence.
15. Jina's mother and stepfather have ~~went~~ to the same church for thirty-five years.
16. A raccoon ~~felled~~ from the roof of our house, but it was not injured.
17. In a very generous mood, Marsha ~~lended~~ her favorite scarf to Natalie.

Answers:
1. did
2. brought
3. began
4. came
5. saw
6. C
7. took
8. chose
9. gave
10. C
11. bought
12. broke
13. drunk
14. C
15. gone
16. fell
17. lent

18. The family made the giant scarecrow to scare away the grackles from their backyard garden.
19. The young artist ⟨drawed⟩ a lovely picture of the waves and rocks on the Oregon coast.
20. Gwen ⟨catched⟩ the ball even though Craig threw it fast and high.

18. C
19. drew
20. caught

Exercise 13 Using the Past and Past Participle Forms of Verbs

For the italicized verb in each of the following sentences, give the past or past participle form that will correctly complete the sentence.

EXAMPLE 1. *establish* Robert D. Ballard, a marine geologist, _____ the JASON Foundation for Education.

1. established

1. *create* — JASON, an underwater robot, was _____ for scientific research.
   1. created
2. *build* — JASON was _____ to dive much deeper than humans can dive.
   2. built
3. *sink* — More than 1,600 years ago, the Roman ship *Isis* _____ in the Mediterranean Sea.
   3. sank 3. [or sunk]
4. *know* — Ballard _____ that students would want to share in the exploration of the wrecked ship.
   4. knew
5. *make* — A network of satellites _____ it possible for many students to see JASON explore the wreck.
   5. made
6. *see* — Some 250,000 schoolchildren _____ JASON on giant video screens.
   6. saw
7. *ask* — While JASON searched the ship, students _____ questions of Ballard and his team.
   7. asked
8. *take* — Ballard has _____ students on some amazing electronic field trips by televising himself working with JASON.
   8. taken
9. *give* — He has _____ much of his time and energy to involving students in scientific discoveries.
   9. given
10. *write* — Ballard has _____ about finding the *Isis* and about the 1985 discovery of the *Titanic*, which sank in 1912.
    10. written

Reference Note
For information on **verb forms**, see page 445.

Exercise 13

OBJECTIVE

- To use the correct past and past participle forms of verbs

COMMON ERRORS

Grammar and Usage 653

Exercise 14

OBJECTIVE

- To choose correct pronoun forms

Reference Note

For information on **pronoun forms,** see page 475.

Exercise 14 Choosing Correct Pronoun Forms

Choose the correct form of the pronoun in parentheses in each of the following sentences.

EXAMPLE   1. The catcher gave (*she, her*) the signal.
            1. *her*

1. The winners may be you and (*her, she*).
2. Gregory asked (*her, she*) to the dance.
3. The ending of the movie really amazed Andrew and (*us, we*)!
4. Should Emily and (*they, them*) make the spaghetti?
5. The bus driver gave (*he, him*) a warning.
6. The competition is really between Mario and (*I, me*).
7. Who bought (*her, she*) that opal necklace?
8. The best player on our team is (*him, he*).
9. The next step for Michael and (*them, they*) is to check with the principal.
10. My cousin and (*me, I*) are learning to do origami in our class at the community center.
11. You and (*I, me*) can work together on a report about American Indians of the Southwest.
12. The physical education teacher designed a special exercise program for (*her, she*).
13. The ones who asked to see our pictures from the Miami zoo are (*they, them*).
14. (*Us, We*) always enjoy the plays at the children's theater, especially when they are performed outdoors.
15. (*He, Him*) plays the guitar quite well and has performed in a band.
16. Ms. Ruel asked Kei and (*I, me*) to recite the French nursery rhyme.
17. "I'd like to go to the movies with (*they, them*)," Thi said after meeting Carmela and Tony.
18. Aunt Edna is buying new backpacks for Carl and (*I, me*).
19. Last week (*them, they*) began taking tennis lessons after school.
20. Will you or (*I, me*) be the first one with the correct answer?

Exercise 15 Proofreading for Correct Pronoun Forms

Most of the following sentences contain a pronoun that has been used incorrectly. Identify each incorrect pronoun. Then, write the correct form. If a sentence is already correct, write *C*.

EXAMPLE   1. Cassie sat between Melissa and I at the concert.
                1. I—me

1. Who did you meet at the skating rink last night?
2. You and them are the only ones who are going on the hike.
3. My pen pal in Vietnam will soon receive another letter from me.
4. Just between you and I, the other book was much easier to understand.
5. One of the actors in that play was her.
6. The pencils, paints, and colored paper belong to Kimiko and he.
7. Matthew has invited you and I to his party next weekend.
8. Either her or I will make a poster for Black History Month.
9. Who is the fastest runner on the baseball team?
10. They and us went swimming in Lake Travis.

Reference Note
For information on **pronoun forms,** see page 475.

1. Whom
2. they
3. C
4. me
5. she
6. him
7. me
8. she
9. C
10. we

Exercise 16 Choosing Correct Regular and Irregular Modifiers

Choose the correct form of the adjective or adverb in parentheses in each of the following sentences.

EXAMPLE   1. The stars tonight look (*more bright, brighter*) than usual.
                1. brighter

1. This puzzle book is (*difficulter, more difficult*) than the other one.
2. Kevin is the (*taller, tallest*) of the four Sutherland brothers.
3. The (*most exciting, excitingest*) day of our trip to Indonesia was still to come.
4. I like drawing, but I like painting (*best, better*).
5. If you blend strawberries, bananas, and yogurt really (*good, well*), you'll have a great drink.
6. Felicia had the (*worst, worse*) case of chickenpox of anyone in the sixth grade.

Reference Note
For information on **using modifiers correctly,** see Chapter 18.

Grammar and Usage   655

Exercise 15

OBJECTIVE

- To proofread for correct pronoun forms

Exercise 16

OBJECTIVE

- To choose the correct forms of adjectives or adverbs to fit sentences

TECHNOLOGY TIP

Some word-processing programs include a dictionary that students might use to check regular and irregular modifiers. For example, if students are not sure whether *gracefuller* or *more graceful* is the correct form of the modifier, they might see whether *gracefuller* is listed in their spellchecking programs. If not, *more graceful* is correct.

COMMON ERRORS

Exercise 17

OBJECTIVE

- To correct errors in the use of modifiers

Exercise 17 Correcting Errors in the Use of Modifiers

POSSIBLE ANSWERS

1. Ernest runs very well, but William can run even better.
2. Katherine is the most curious of the four Matsuo children.
3. Which flavor of frozen yogurt do you think would be worse, cheddar or carrot?
4. Tell me, did you do better on this week's spelling test than on last week's?
5. Annie brings to her friends homegrown tomatoes that she picks from her garden.
6. The astronaut who had commanded a mission aboard the space shuttle met with children.
7. Gloria became more worried as the storm grew worse.
8. Of the Amazon, Nile, and Mississippi rivers, the Nile is the longest.
9. At the video store we rented that scary movie from which the filmmakers spun off a television series.
10. Have you ever read *Fahrenheit 451*, the novel by Ray Bradbury about book burning?

COMMON ERRORS

---

7. My brothers and I were taught how to wash, iron, and mend clothes, and we are (*gladder, glad*) that we were.
8. Rachel can't decide which of the two wallpaper patterns would look (*prettier, prettiest*) in her room.
9. Our schoolyard has been (*cleanest, cleaner*) since the Ecology Club asked people not to litter.
10. I am going to practice American Sign Language until I sign (*good, well*) enough to communicate easily.

Reference Note
For information on **using modifiers correctly**, see Chapter 18.

Exercise 17 Correcting Errors in the Use of Modifiers

Rewrite each of the following sentences, correcting any errors in the use or placement of modifiers.

EXAMPLE 1. Do you like Western boots or hiking boots most?
        1. most—more

1. Ernest runs very good, but William can run even better.
2. Katherine is the more curious of the four Matsuo children.
3. Which flavor of frozen yogurt do you think would be worser, cheddar or carrot?
4. Tell me, did you do gooder on this week's spelling test than on last week's?
5. Annie brings homegrown tomatoes to her friends that she picks from her garden.
6. The astronaut met with children who had commanded a mission aboard the space shuttle.
7. Gloria became more worriedly as the storm grew worse.
8. Of the Amazon, Nile, and Mississippi rivers, the Nile is the longer.
9. We rented that scary movie at the video store from which the filmmakers spun off a television series.
10. Have you ever read *Fahrenheit 451*, the novel about book burning by Ray Bradbury?
11. After carefully rehearsing several times, Toni felt confidently about giving her speech.
12. Vincente made a cover for his textbook with his initials on it.
13. Janelle found a recipe for broiling catfish in a cookbook.

Chapter 24 Correcting Common Errors

14. If you look close at the painting, you can see how tiny the brush strokes are.
15. We looked through the old photo album in the kitchen that we had just found in the attic.
16. It was a large crop, and it grew good, too.
17. Icarus foolish flew nearer to the sun than he should have.
18. In different parts of the world, we have read about unusual customs.
19. Aunt Dee and Uncle Mike enjoyed the CD of the symphony in their living room.
20. We found the sheet music for songs your mother used to sing in the piano bench.

Exercise 18 Correcting Double Comparisons and Double Negatives

Revise each of the following sentences to correct the double comparison or double negative.   *Answers may vary.*

EXAMPLE   1. Grandma thought learning to swim would be more harder than it was.
   1. Grandma thought learning to swim would be harder than it was.

1. My sister gave me her soccer ball because she never plays soccer ~~no more~~.
2. You can get a ~~more~~ clearer idea of what the trail is like by looking at this map.
3. We ~~couldn't~~ hardly believe our eyes when we saw what was under the rock!
4. You shouldn't stand ~~nowhere~~ around a tall tree during a thunderstorm.
5. Keisha's uncle Anthony just adopted the ~~most~~ strangest pet I've ever seen.
6. My little sister ~~can't~~ scarcely reach the doorknob without standing on tiptoe.
7. I'm not going to put off practicing my bongo drums ~~no more~~.
8. That was the ~~most~~ worst movie we've ever seen.

Reference Note
For information on **double comparisons** and **double negatives**, see pages 504 and 507.

1. anymore

3. could

4. anywhere

6. can

7. anymore

Exercise 17 Correcting Errors in the Use of Modifiers

POSSIBLE ANSWERS continued

11. After carefully rehearsing several times, Toni felt confident about giving her speech.
12. Vincente made a cover with his initials on it for his textbook.
13. In a cookbook, Janelle found a recipe for broiling catfish.
14. If you look closely at the painting, you can see how tiny the brush strokes are.
15. In the kitchen we looked through the old photo album that we had just found in the attic.
16. It was a large crop, and it grew well, too.
17. Icarus foolishly flew nearer to the sun than he should have.
18. We read about unusual customs in different parts of the world.
19. In their living room, Aunt Dee and Uncle Mike enjoyed the CD of the symphony.
20. In the piano bench we found the sheet music for songs your mother used to sing.

Exercise 18

OBJECTIVE

- To correct double comparisons and double negatives

Exercise 19

OBJECTIVE

- To identify correct usage

INCLUSION
You may want to suggest that students with learning disabilities try using strategies that involve more than one of the senses when they attempt to identify errors in **Exercise 19** and **Exercise 20**. Suggest to students that they use rulers or pieces of paper to cover all sentences on the page except the one on which they are working. This strategy involves using the sense of touch to help students focus on the task at hand without letting their eyes wander or be distracted by other text on the page. Another strategy is to have students point to words as they proofread. This tactile technique can help them focus and isolate words that do not sound or look correct.

Exercise 20

OBJECTIVE

- To correct errors in usage

Reference Note
For information on **common usage errors,** see Chapter 19.

9. either

Reference Note
For information on **common usage errors,** see Chapter 19.

9. Didn't ~~neither~~ of the books have the information you needed?
10. I've read that potbellied pigs learn ~~more~~ faster than dogs do.

Exercise 19 Identifying Correct Usage

For each of the following sentences, choose the word or word group in parentheses that is correct according to the rules of formal, standard English.

EXAMPLE 1. My aunt Claire was working in Athens, Greece, (*then, than*).
  1. then

1. Everyone from the volleyball team is here (*accept, except*) Roseanne.
2. Steve said he thought the new batting lineup looked (*alright, all right*).
3. The two friends felt (*bad, badly*) after arguing.
4. The children helped (*theirselves, themselves*) to the curry.
5. Do you know (*whose, who's*) sunglasses these are?
6. The boys will (*try to, try and*) finish painting today.
7. Be sure to (*bring, take*) your lunch when you go to the park.
8. The ten students in the art class divided all of the construction paper and markers (*between, among*) themselves.
9. (*Who's, Whose*) going to show them how to dance?
10. Heat lightning occurs too far from people for them to hear (*its, it's*) accompanying thunder.

Exercise 20 Correcting Errors in Usage

Each of the following sentences contains an error in the use of formal, standard English. Identify each error, and then write the correct usage.

EXAMPLE 1. Them fish are called sea horses.
  1. Them—Those

1. Where are sea horses found ~~at~~?
2. Sea horses are found in tropical and temperate waters—not ~~anywheres~~ that is very cold. 2. anywhere

3. Baby sea horses often use ~~they're~~ curved tails to hold on to each other. **3.** their
4. That ~~there~~ sea horse used its tail to grasp some seaweed.
5. Don't you think that ~~it's~~ head looks amazingly like a tiny horse's head? **5.** its
6. The little fin on a sea horse's back moves so fast that you ~~can't~~ hardly see it. **6.** can
7. Several students asked the teacher ~~how come~~ the eyes of a sea horse work independently of each other. **7.** why
8. My stepsisters and I ~~use~~ to look for sea horses when we lived near the coast in California. **8.** used **9.** take
9. The teacher reminded us to ~~bring~~ home a parental approval form for the field trip to the city aquarium.
10. When ~~your~~ at the aquarium, remember to stop by the sea horse exhibit. **10.** you're

Exercise 21 Proofreading Sentences for Correct Usage

Each of the following sentences contains an error in English usage. Identify each error. Then, write the correct usage.

EXAMPLE 1. Do you all ready know about the Pantanal?
1. all ready—already

1. The Pantanal is the largest wetland ~~anywheres~~ on earth.
2. To get an idea of ~~it's~~ size, imagine an area about the size of Arkansas.
3. Most of the Pantanal is located ~~inside of~~ Brazil.
4. The area contains ~~a~~ enormous wealth of wildlife.
5. Our science teacher is ~~learning~~ us about the jaguar, the giant anteater, and other animals that live there.
6. The Pantanal may be more important for wading birds such as storks ~~then~~ any other place in South America.
7. In addition, ~~alot~~ of other birds, such as toucans and macaws, live there.
8. The Pantanal has swamps that sometimes have absorbed heavy rains that otherwise might ~~of~~ flooded nearby areas.
9. However, the Pantanal ~~ain't~~ all swamps; it also contains forests.
10. Although the Pantanal is a long ~~ways~~ from where I live, I hope to have a chance to explore it someday.

Reference Note
For information on **common usage errors,** see Chapter 19.

1. anywhere
2. its
3. inside
4. an
5. teaching
6. than
7. a lot
8. have
9. isn't
10. way

Exercise 21

OBJECTIVE

- To proofread sentences for correct usage

COMMON ERRORS

Grammar and Usage Test: Section 1

DIRECTIONS In each of the following sentences, a word group is underlined. Using the rules of formal, standard English, choose the answer that most clearly expresses the meaning of the sentence. If there is no error, choose A. Indicate your response by shading in the appropriate oval on your answer sheet.

EXAMPLE 1. The fish smelled badly, so we didn't buy any.
  (A) smelled badly
  (B) smells badly
  (C) smelled bad
  (D) smelling bad

ANSWER 1.

1. Roz and I catched fireflies in a jar.
   (A) I catched
   (B) me catched
   (C) I caught
   (D) me caught

2. Fun hiking in the wilderness preserve.
   (A) Fun hiking in the wilderness preserve.
   (B) While having fun hiking in the wilderness preserve.
   (C) Hiking in the wilderness preserve was fun.
   (D) Have had fun hiking in the wilderness preserve.

3. The election resulted in a runoff between he and I.
   (A) he and I
   (B) him and me
   (C) him and I
   (D) he and me

4. In bowling, a strike is when a bowler knocks down all ten pins on the first throw in a frame.
   (A) is when
   (B) occurs when
   (C) is where
   (D) is because

5. Have you heard of Lawrence and Lorne <u>Blair, two brothers who traveled in Indonesia for ten years?</u>
   - (A) Blair, two brothers who traveled in Indonesia for ten years?
   - (B) Blair? Two brothers who traveled in Indonesia for ten years.
   - (C) Blair, two brothers whom traveled in Indonesia for ten years?
   - (D) Blair and two brothers who traveled in Indonesia for ten years?

6. <u>Is this here</u> drill bit the right size?
   - (A) Is this here
   - (B) Is that there
   - (C) Is this here kind of
   - (D) Is this

7. <u>Here your car keys.</u>
   - (A) Here your car keys.
   - (B) Here are your car keys.
   - (C) Here's you're car keys.
   - (D) Here is your car keys.

8. <u>The dog barked the baby awoke.</u>
   - (A) The dog barked the baby awoke.
   - (B) The dog barked, the baby awoke.
   - (C) The dog barked, and the baby awoke.
   - (D) The dog barking and the baby awoke.

9. I <u>shouldn't of</u> waited to start my essay.
   - (A) shouldn't of
   - (B) shouldn't have
   - (C) ought not to of
   - (D) oughtn't not to have

10. Mrs. Levine asked <u>how come Darnell and he aren't</u> ready to leave yet.
    - (A) how come Darnell and he aren't
    - (B) how come Darnell and him aren't
    - (C) why Darnell and he isn't
    - (D) why Darnell and he aren't

Grammar and Usage 661

Grammar and Usage Test: Section 2

DIRECTIONS Read the paragraph below. For each of the numbered blanks, select the word or word group that best completes the sentence. Indicate your response by shading in the appropriate oval on your answer sheet.

EXAMPLE Two species of elephant __(1)__ today: the African elephant and the Asian elephant.

1. (A) does exist
   (B) exists
   (C) have been existing
   (D) exist

ANSWER 1. (A) (B) (C) ●D

Each of these species has __(1)__ own unique features; for example, the African elephant has __(2)__ ears and tusks than the Asian elephant does. Although different in some ways, both species of elephant __(3)__ strong, intelligent, and social. Both have poor sight and are colorblind but can smell and hear quite __(4)__. Elephants can detect the scent of __(5)__ human who is over a mile away. __(6)__ hearing is so good that they can communicate over distances of more than two miles, using sounds __(7)__ any that humans can hear. Unfortunately, human population growth, farming, industry, and illegal hunting __(8)__ a decline in the elephant population. For instance, poachers have killed thousands of African elephants for their ivory tusks; in fact, from 1979 to the early 1990s, the number of elephants in Africa __(9)__ from 1,300,000 to fewer than 600,000. __(10)__ protect elephants, the trade of ivory was outlawed worldwide in 1989.

---

1. (A) it
   (B) its'
   (C) it's
   (D) its ✓

2. (A) larger ✓
   (B) more larger
   (C) the more larger
   (D) the most largest

3. (A) they are
   (B) are ✓
   (C) are being
   (D) is

4. (A) well ✓
   (B) good
   (C) better
   (D) best

662 Chapter 24 Correcting Common Errors

5. (A) a
   (B) an
   (C) the
   (D) this

6. (A) They're
   (B) There
   (C) Their
   (D) They

7. (A) more lower than
   (B) lower than
   (C) more low then
   (D) lower then

8. (A) will have caused
   (B) causes
   (C) are causing
   (D) is cause

9. (A) shrinks
   (B) shrank
   (C) shrinked
   (D) is shrinking

10. (A) 2
    (B) Too
    (C) Two
    (D) To

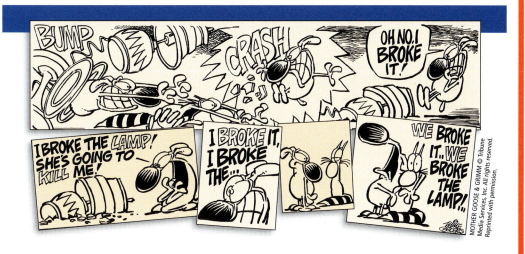

Exercise 22

OBJECTIVE
- To correct errors in capitalization

Reference Note
For information on **capitalization rules**, see Chapter 20.

Exercise 22 Correcting Errors in Capitalization

Each of the following word groups contains at least one error in capitalization. Correct the errors either by changing capital letters to lowercase letters or by changing lowercase letters to capital letters.

EXAMPLE
1. abilene, texas
1. *Abilene, Texas*

1. the smoky mountains
2. rutherford B. hayes
3. *Alice In Wonderland*
4. university of kansas
5. labor day
6. near lake Placid
7. it's already tuesday!
8. english or Art II
9. washington monument
10. marta Hinojosa, m.d.
11. neptune and other planets
12. second day of hanukkah
13. my Uncle Jack
14. an airplane called *spirit of st. louis*
15. a river running South
16. Bryce canyon national park
17. 912 valentine st.
18. president Cleveland
19. "i'm home!"
20. newbery medal

Exercise 23

OBJECTIVE
- To correct sentences with errors in capitalization

Reference Note
For information on **capitalization rules**, see Chapter 20.

Exercise 23 Correcting Errors in Capitalization

Correct the capitalization errors in the following sentences either by changing capital letters to lowercase letters or by changing lowercase letters to capital letters.

EXAMPLE
1. i went to see a play last saturday.
1. *I went to see a play last Saturday.*

1. Our drama teacher, ms. soto, took us to see it.
2. the new play was first performed by the south Texas performance company.

3. this theater group's founder and director is the translator, playwright, and theater scholar joe rosenberg.
4. He has established an exchange program for theater students from the united states, mexico, and south america.
5. In addition, mr. rosenberg has written a full-length play titled *saturday stranger,* which was published in germany.
6. Mr. Rosenberg has also edited a Book called ¡aplauso! hispanic Children's theater.
7. the book includes plays by héctor santiago, roy conboy, and lisa loomer, among others.
8. the plays are printed in both english and spanish.
9. these plays draw on hispanic literary traditions native to such places as mexico, puerto rico, and cuba.
10. Next month the southwest middle school drama club plans to perform one of the plays from this book.

Exercise 24 Using Periods, Question Marks, and Exclamation Points Correctly

For each of the following sentences, write each letter or word that should be followed by a period, question mark, or exclamation point, and add the proper punctuation.

EXAMPLE 1. Senator Jackson, can you meet with our class at 8:15 A M

1. A.M.?

1. Please follow me.
2. Will you please help me carry my books?
3. Where in the downtown library is the new display of Peruvian pottery?
4. Watch out for that car! 4. [*or* car.]
5. Dr. Williamson taught me to fly a model helicopter.
6. Anthony asked Rose whether her favorite cartoonist is Charles M. Schulz.
7. One fossil recently discovered in these mountains dates back to 3 million B.C.
8. What a surprise that was!
9. Have you ever brought your skateboard to school?
10. The letter addressed to 4613 Sleepy Hollow Blvd, Kingston, NY 12401, must be for Mrs. C. R. Smith.

Reference Note
For information on **using end marks,** see page 561.

HELP
Some sentences in Exercise 24 need more than one punctuation mark.

Exercise 24

OBJECTIVE

- To use periods, question marks, and exclamation points correctly

COMMON ERRORS

Exercise 25

OBJECTIVE

- To proofread sentences for correct use of commas

Timesaver

Ask students to write the sentences for **Exercise 25** and **Exercise 26** in one color (such as blue) and then use a different color (such as red) for punctuation marks so that these marks stand out. Students could also alternate pencil and ink in the same manner, or if two distinct marking methods are not available, they can write the sentences neatly and then circle the punctuation marks they have added to the sentences. These procedures will make the punctuation more visually striking and easier to grade.

Exercise 26

OBJECTIVE

- To use semicolons and colons correctly

Reference Note
For information on **using commas,** see page 566.

Reference Note
For information on **using colons and semicolons,** see page 577.

Exercise 25 Proofreading Sentences for the Correct Use of Commas

Each of the following sentences is missing at least one comma. Write the word or numeral that should be followed by a comma, and add the comma. Optional commas are underlined.

EXAMPLE 1. Oh I hope we win the track meet when we go to Salina Kansas next week.

1. Oh, Salina, Kansas,

1. Sheila ran laps on Monday, Tuesday, and Wednesday.
2. On February 20, 1999, my family had a reunion in San Juan, Puerto Rico.
3. Yes, that is the dog they adopted from the animal shelter.
4. Because my father is going to teach me to play the guitar soon, he is showing me how to tune one now.
5. No, I have never read *The Hobbit*.
6. Scissors, pins, tacks, and other sharp items should be kept out of the reach of young children.
7. Athena, the Greek goddess of crafts, wisdom, and war, is often shown with an owl on her shoulder.
8. Douglas never leaves shopping carts in parking spaces set aside for people who have disabilities, and neither should anyone else.
9. My aunt and I bought nails, lumber, and paint for the birdhouses we plan to build.
10. Professor Chang, will you explain the differences between these two kinds of cells?

Exercise 26 Using Semicolons and Colons Correctly

The following sentences lack necessary colons and semicolons. Write the words or numerals that come before and after the needed punctuation, and insert the proper punctuation.

EXAMPLE 1. My grandmother is coming to visit we will meet her at the airport.

1. visit; we

1. We picked subjects for our reports: I chose sea turtles.
2. Our school day used to start at 8:15; now it starts at 8:00.

666 Chapter 24 Correcting Common Errors

COMMON ERRORS

3. The following items will be needed for the new playground: swings, slides, and picnic tables.
4. The rain just ended; maybe we will get a chance to see a double rainbow.
5. We can save water in these ways: turning off the faucet while brushing our teeth, pouring only as much as we plan to drink, and taking showers instead of baths.
6. At the farmers' market, shoppers were discussing the recent election; they were discussing the weather, too.
7. "Dear Sir or Madam:" is one proper way to begin a business letter, but not the only way.
8. Plains Indians include the following peoples: Comanche, Osage, Pawnee, Crow, and Blackfeet.
9. At 6:30 A.M. my alarm went off; I couldn't believe it was time to get up.
10. My wish list is as follows: a mountain bike, good grades, and a happy home.

Exercise 27 Punctuating and Capitalizing Quotations

Revise the following numbered items, using quotation marks, other marks of punctuation, and capital letters where needed. If a sentence is already correct, write *C*.

EXAMPLE 1. I admire Marian Wright Edelman said Paul she has worked hard for children's rights.

1. "I admire Marian Wright Edelman," said Paul. "She has worked hard for children's rights."

1. "In 1973, Edelman founded the Children's Defense Fund, a nonprofit organization that has helped many people," said Mr. Knepp.
2. Paul commented that just the other day he had read an article titled "Edelman: The Children's Defender."
3. Justin said, "I'd like to work to protect children's rights, too, one day."
4. "Edelman was born in 1939," Paul told us. "She grew up in Bennettsville, South Carolina."
5. Mr. Knepp said that Marian Wright Edelman is one of our country's greatest civic leaders.   5. C

HELP

Some sentences in Exercise 27 may be correctly revised in more than one way. You only need to give one revision for each sentence.

Reference Note

For information on **using quotation marks,** see page 590. For information on **using capital letters,** see Chapter 20.

Exercise 27

OBJECTIVE

- To punctuate and capitalize quotations correctly

Exercise 28

OBJECTIVE

- To punctuate dialogue correctly

Exercise 28 Punctuating Dialogue

ANSWERS

1. "Bobby was a special dog," Jennifer said, "and extremely loyal to his master."
2. ¶Tony asked, "Can you believe that Bobby actually lived by his master's grave for fourteen years?"
3. ¶Jennifer said, "My cousin went to Edinburgh, Scotland, and saw Bobby's grave. **4.** It is in Greyfriars churchyard, near his master's grave."
5. ¶"When did Bobby die?" Tony asked.
6. ¶"He died in 1872," Jennifer replied. **7.** "The people in the town fed Bobby and cared for him until his death."
8. ¶"Bobby slept during the day," Tony recalled, "because, before his master died, they had worked together at night."
9. ¶Jennifer said, "Yes, his master, old Jock, guarded cattle that were sold at the market."
10. ¶Tony said, "In Edinburgh there is a statue of Greyfriars Bobby on top of a drinking fountain for dogs."

Reference Note

For information on **punctuating dialogue,** see page 594.

6. "Please tell me more about Edelman's career as a lawyer," Ashley said.
7. "She graduated from Yale Law School in 1963," he said. "And soon became the first African American woman licensed to practice law in Mississippi."
8. Mr. Knepp added, "Edelman has handled many civil rights cases and has always made community service a priority."
9. "did Edelman say that she had been taught as a child to make service a central part of her life?" Justin asked.
10. "Yes," Ashley answered. "I remember reading that in her autobiography, *The Measure of Our Success: A Letter to My Children and Yours.*" **10.** [*or* "Yes," Ashley answered. " I. . .]

Exercise 28 Punctuating Dialogue

Revise the following dialogue, adding quotation marks and other marks of punctuation and replacing lowercase letters with capital letters where necessary. Remember to begin a new paragraph each time the speaker changes.

EXAMPLE [1] The legend of Greyfriars Bobby is so moving, Jennifer exclaimed, that I'll never forget it.

1. "The legend of Greyfriars Bobby is so moving," Jennifer exclaimed, "that I'll never forget it."

[1] Bobby was a special dog, Jennifer said, and extremely loyal to his master. [2] Tony asked, "can you believe that Bobby actually lived by his master's grave for fourteen years?" [3] Jennifer said, My cousin went to Edinburgh, Scotland, and saw Bobby's grave. [4] It is in Greyfriars churchyard, near his master's grave. [5] When did Bobby die? Tony asked. [6] He died in 1872, Jennifer replied. [7] "the people in the town fed Bobby and cared for him until his death."

[8] "Bobby slept during the day, Tony recalled because, before his master died, they had worked together at night."

[9] Jennifer said, "yes, his master, old Jock, guarded cattle that were sold at the market." [10] Tony said, In Edinburgh there is a statue of Greyfriars Bobby on top of a drinking fountain for dogs.

Exercise 29 Using Apostrophes Correctly

Rewrite the following word groups, inserting an apostrophe wherever one is needed.

EXAMPLE 1. the womens class
1. the women's class

1. if theyve gone
2. no ones fault
3. that statues condition
4. so lets try
5. since youre going home
6. that giants castle
7. theirs werent faded
8. the Rockies highest peak
9. when there isnt time
10. these books authors
11. Arkansas governor
12. if everybodys there
13. made all As in school
14. one pueblos history
15. the five camels saddles
16. born in 84
17. and theres the dog
18. the sheeps wool
19. when youll find out
20. two os in the word *igloo*
21. arent able to
22. the one whos late
23. when Im tired
24. around 10 oclock
25. those two books pages

Reference Note
For information on **using apostrophes,** see page 598.

Exercise 30 Correcting Spelling Errors

Most of the following words are misspelled. If a word is not spelled correctly, write the correct spelling. If a word is already spelled correctly, write *C*.

EXAMPLE 1. mispeak
1. *misspeak*

1. percieve
2. disolve
3. gladest
4. charging
5. comedies
6. sillyness
7. taxs
8. tryed
9. potatos
10. traceing
11. classes
12. sleigh
13. matchs
14. videoes
15. funnyer
16. toyes
17. schoolling
18. wieght
19. loosness
20. Gomezs
21. managable
22. unatural
23. ladys
24. runing
25. finaly

Reference Note
For information on **spelling rules,** see page 615.

Exercise 29

OBJECTIVE

- To use apostrophes correctly

Exercise 30

OBJECTIVE

- To correct errors in spelling

Exercise 30 Correcting Spelling Errors

ANSWERS

1. perceive
2. dissolve
3. gladdest
4. C
5. C
6. silliness
7. taxes
8. tried
9. potatoes
10. tracing
11. C
12. C
13. matches
14. videos
15. funnier
16. toys
17. schooling
18. weight
19. looseness
20. Gomezes
21. manageable
22. unnatural
23. ladies
24. running
25. finally

Mechanics 669

Exercise 31

OBJECTIVE

- To choose correctly between words often confused

Cooperative Learning

If students need further review of words often confused, divide the class into teams of students and assign each team such words from **Exercise 31** or from those covered in **Chapter 23.**

Give each team a stack of index cards. Instruct teams to write one word on each card, followed by as many synonyms as they can come up with on their own. Then, have students augment their lists of synonyms by consulting dictionaries, usage books, and thesauruses.

Once the cards have been completed, proofread, and corrected, the words can be entered on a computer word-processing program. Each member of the class could then be given a copy of the compiled list. Suggest that students keep the lists in their notebooks for future reference.

COMMON ERRORS

Reference Note
For information on **words often confused,** see page 625.

Exercise 31 Choosing Between Words Often Confused

For each of the following sentences, choose the word or word group in parentheses that will make the sentence correct.

EXAMPLE
1. Matthew suggested that I (*altar, alter*) the first paragraph of my story.
1. alter

1. Have you (*all ready, already*) finished your latest painting?
2. (*Your, You're*) pets need good food, clean water, warm shelter, and loving attention.
3. Be careful not to (*lose, loose*) any of those puzzle pieces, or we'll have to buy a new puzzle.
4. Chuckwallas are harmless lizards that may grow to be two feet long and live in rocky (*desserts, deserts*) in the United States and Mexico.
5. Manuel dreamed of finding a sunken ship and (*it's, its*) treasure chest.
6. The school (*threw, through*) away tons of paper and cardboard before the recycling program was started.
7. (*Whose, Who's*) planning to bring food and drinks to the fiesta tomorrow?
8. We drove (*passed, past*) the park, across the bridge, and around the lake to the dock.
9. Marcie's enthusiasm for playing in the marching band was (*plain, plane*) to see.
10. The guide (*lead, led*) the scouts through the museum.
11. Former President Jimmy Carter has been greatly involved in efforts to bring (*piece, peace*) to various countries all over the world.
12. In less than one (*weak, week*), Sandra's mother will begin her new job as editor-in-chief of the newspaper's new Washington bureau.
13. (*There, Their*) are many kinds of trees in our neighborhood, and they provide plenty of shade.
14. The gravel in the driveway is (*coarse, course*), but it still feels good on my bare feet.
15. The flagpole itself was (*stationary, stationery*), but the flag flapped in the breeze.

Chapter 24 Correcting Common Errors

16. "The lamp may (*brake*, *break*) if you try to carry it on its side and with one hand," Dad cautioned.
17. What is the (*capital*, *capitol*) of Puerto Rico?
18. Mr. Edgars is a good man whose (*principles*, *principals*) include honesty and fairness.
19. When we sit outside on the porch, we can't (*hear*, *here*) the phone ring.
20. We read (*threw*, *through*) Gary Soto's book of poetry and picked out some poems to memorize.

Exercise 32 Proofreading Sentences for Errors in Spelling and Words Often Confused

For each of the following sentences, identify and correct any error in spelling or usage.

EXAMPLE 1. The Iroquois people's name for themselfs means "we longhouse builders."
         1. themselfs—themselves

1. In our American history coarse, we learned that the Iroquois constructed large dwellings called longhouses.
2. Years ago, nearly all Iroquois lived in forests and built they're longhouses out of logs and strips of bark.
3. Several individual familys lived in each of these longhouses.
4. When a couple marryed, the husband would move into the longhouse of his wife's extended family, called a clan.
5. Each family had it's own separate area with a sleeping platform that was raised about a foot above the ground.
6. They kept the longhouse neat by storing many of their belongings on shelfs above their sleeping platforms.
7. Fires were made in hearths in a central corridor, and smoke rose threw holes cut in the longhouse roof.
8. When it rained or snowed, slideing panels were used to close the holes.
9. The bigest longhouses measured more than two hundred feet in length.
10. Such large longhouses could shelter 10 or more individual families at a time.

Reference Note
For information on **spelling rules,** see page 615. For information on **words often confused,** see page 625.

1. course
2. their
3. families
4. married
5. its
6. shelves
7. through
8. sliding
9. biggest
10. ten

Exercise 32
OBJECTIVE
- To revise sentences for errors in spelling and in words often confused

Exercise 33

OBJECTIVE

- To proofread a paragraph for errors in mechanics

HELP— Many of the sentences in Exercise 33 contain more than one error.

7. C

9. lining

Exercise 34

OBJECTIVE

- To proofread a business letter for correct grammar, usage, and mechanics

HELP— Most items in Exercise 34 contain more than one error.

Exercise 33 Proofreading a Paragraph for Errors in Mechanics

For the sentences in the following paragraph, correct each error in mechanics. If a sentence is already correct, write *C*.

Optional commas are underlined.

EXAMPLES
1. Have you ever seen the movie *the Wizard of Oz*?
1. *The Wizard of Oz*

2. You may not know that its based on a book.
2. it's

[1] The book was written by l. frank Baum. [2] He was born on May 15, 1856, in the state of New York. [3] When he was a teenager, he was interested in the theater; and his father, a wealthy oilman, gave him several theaters to manage. [4] In 1881, he wrote *The maid of Arran*, a successful play. [5] For many years, he worked at several jobs, including storekeeper, newspaper reporter, and traveling salesman. [6] In 1900, he published a childrens book called *The Wonderful Wizard of Oz*, which was a bestseller for two years in a row. [7] Baum adapted the book into a successful play, and he even made several silent movies about Oz. [8] Baum died in Hollywood, California, in 1919; and twenty years later, the famous film starring Judy Garland as Dorothy was made in the same city. [9] During the making of the film, the actor who played the wizard discovered that L. Frank Baum's name was sewn into the lineing of the wizard's coat. [10] According to Baum's wife, it really was Baum's old coat; the movie studio's wardrobe department had bought it at a secondhand clothing shop.

Exercise 34 Proofreading a Business Letter for Correct Grammar, Usage, and Mechanics

Correct the errors in grammar, usage, and mechanics in the numbered items in the following letter.

EXAMPLE [1] 254 Thirty second street
1. 254 Thirty-second Street

254 Thirty-second Street
Syracuse, NY 13210
[1] November 5 2001

Ms. Susan Loroupe
[2] *Syracuse daily times*
598 Seventh Avenue
Syracuse, NY 13208

[3] Dear Ms Loroupe

[4] Thank you for taking time during you're busy workday to show the Van Buren Middle School Journalism Club around the Newspaper's offices.

[5] Us club members are glad to have had the chance to see how newspaper articles are wrote and printed. [6] Especially enjoyed seeing the presses—even more then talking with the design artists and editors! [7] We were surprised that the presses were so loud and we were impressed by how quick and efficient everyone worked. [8] Please thank the artists, to, for showing us how they use computer's to arrange the art and photos on the pages.

Sincerely,

Carlos Lopez

Carlos Lopez
[9] journalism club Secretary
[10] Van Buren middle school

Reference Note

For information on **writing business letters,** see "Writing" in the Quick Reference Handbook.

Exercise 34 Proofreading a Business Letter for Correct Grammar, Usage, and Mechanics

ANSWERS
Underscores in text below show corrections.

1. November 5, 2001
2. *Syracuse Daily Times*
3. Dear Ms. Loroupe:
4. Thank you for taking time during your busy workday to show the Van Buren Middle School Journalism Club around the newspaper's offices.
5. We club members are glad to have had the chance to see how newspaper articles are written and printed.
6. The club especially enjoyed seeing the presses—even more than talking with the design artists and editors!
7. We were surprised that the presses were so loud, and we were impressed by how quickly and efficiently everyone worked.
8. Please thank the artists, too, for showing us how they use computers to arrange the art and photos on the pages.
9. Journalism Club Secretary
10. Van Buren Middle School

COMMON ERRORS

Mechanics

TEACHING TIP

Using the Mechanics Tests. A *Correcting Common Errors Standardized Test Answer Sheet* that students may use for this **Mechanics Test** is provided in *Chapter Tests in Standardized Test Formats.*

Mechanics Test: Section 1

DIRECTIONS Each numbered item below contains an underlined word or word group. Choose the answer that shows the correct capitalization, punctuation, and spelling of the underlined part. If there is no error, choose answer D (Correct as is). Indicate your response by shading in the appropriate oval on your answer sheet.

EXAMPLE   [1] <u>Quincy, MA 02158</u>

(A) Quincy, Mass. 02158
(B) Quincy MA, 02158
(C) Quincy, M.A. 02158
(D) Correct as is

ANSWER   1.

```
    147 Hickory Lane
    Quincy, MA 02158
[1] May 11 2001

    The Hobby Shop
[2] 2013 forty-First Street
    Los Angeles, CA 90924

[3] Dear Mr. Shaw

    While I was visiting [4] my aunt Laura, who's
    house is near your store, she bought a model
    airplane from you. [5] Two of my freinds have
    [6] already tryed to help me get the plane to
    fly, but we haven't been able to. [7] Putting
    the plane together was not difficult; the
    problem is that the engine will not start.
    Also, I found no stickers in the box when I
    opened [8] it and the box says that there
    should be stickers for the plane's wings. I
    have enclosed the engine and my [9] aunt's
    reciept. I hope that [10] youre able to send
    me stickers and a new engine soon.

    Sincerely,
    Timothy Martin
    Timothy Martin
```

674   Chapter 24   Correcting Common Errors

1. (A) May, 11 2001
   (B) May 11, 2001
   (C) May, 11, 2001
   (D) Correct as is

2. (A) 2013 Forty First Street
   (B) 2013 Forty-first street
   (C) 2013 Forty-first Street
   (D) Correct as is

3. (A) Dear Mr. Shaw,
   (B) Dear Mr. Shaw:
   (C) Dear mr. shaw:
   (D) Correct as is

4. (A) my aunt Laura, whose
   (B) my Aunt Laura, whose
   (C) my Aunt Laura, who's
   (D) Correct as is

5. (A) Two of my friends
   (B) To of my freinds
   (C) Too of my friends
   (D) Correct as is

6. (A) all ready tryed
   (B) already tried
   (C) all ready tried
   (D) Correct as is

7. (A) Puting the plane
   (B) Puting the plain
   (C) Putting the plain
   (D) Correct as is

8. (A) it and the box says that their
   (B) it, and the box says that their
   (C) it, and the box says that there
   (D) Correct as is

9. (A) aunt's receipt
   (B) Aunt's receipt
   (C) aunts' reciept
   (D) Correct as is

10. (A) your
    (B) you're
    (C) your'
    (D) Correct as is

Mechanics Test: Section 2

DIRECTIONS Each of the following sentences contains an underlined word or word group. Choose the answer that shows the correct capitalization, punctuation, and spelling of the underlined part. If there is no error, choose answer D (Correct as is). Indicate your response by shading in the appropriate oval on your answer sheet.

EXAMPLE   1. Today the school <u>librarian Mr. Woods</u> will show us a film.

   (A) librarian, Mr. Woods
   (B) librarian, Mr. Woods,
   (C) librarian Mr. Woods,
   (D) Correct as is

ANSWER   1.

Mechanics **675**

1. I wonder what the capital of Spain is?
   (A) capital of Spain is.
   (B) capitol of Spain is.
   (C) capitol of Spain is?
   (D) Correct as is

2. The mouses' nest may be in the garage.
   (A) mouses
   (B) mices
   (C) mice's
   (D) Correct as is

3. "What did you see at the park?" asked my grandfather.
   (A) see at the park"? asked my grandfather.
   (B) see at the park," asked my grandfather?
   (C) see at the park? asked my grandfather."
   (D) Correct as is

4. Felix, you've been a naughty kitten this passed week!
   (A) passed weak
   (B) past weak
   (C) past week
   (D) Correct as is

5. Aisha exclaimed, "see how much these crystals have grown!"
   (A) exclaimed, "See
   (B) exclaimed! "See
   (C) exclaimed "see
   (D) Correct as is

6. The Olympic team waved at the crowd, the audience cheered.
   (A) crowd; the audeince
   (B) crowd: the audience
   (C) crowd, and the audience
   (D) Correct as is

7. The Kalahari Desert is in southern Africa.
   - (A) Kalahari Dessert
   - (B) kalahari desert
   - (C) Kalahari desert
   - (D) Correct as is ✓

8. "Its snowing," observed Mrs. Daniels.
   - (A) "It's snowwing,"
   - (B) "It's snowing," ✓
   - (C) Its snowing,
   - (D) Correct as is

9. The Red Cross is asking for: blankets, sheets, and pillows.
   - (A) for; blankets,
   - (B) for, blankets,
   - (C) for blankets, ✓
   - (D) Correct as is

10. Robert Frost's poem The Road Not Taken is famous.
    - (A) poem *The Road Not Taken*
    - (B) poem "The Road Not Taken" ✓
    - (C) poem "the Road not Taken"
    - (D) Correct as is

RESOURCES

Correcting Common Errors

Review
- *Grammar, Usage, and Mechanics,* pp. 339, 340, 341, 342

Assessment
- *Assessment Package*
  —*Chapter Tests,* Ch. 24
  —*Chapter Tests in Standardized Test Formats,* Ch. 24
- *Test Generator (One-Stop Planner CD-ROM)*

COMMON ERRORS

PART 4
Quick Reference Handbook

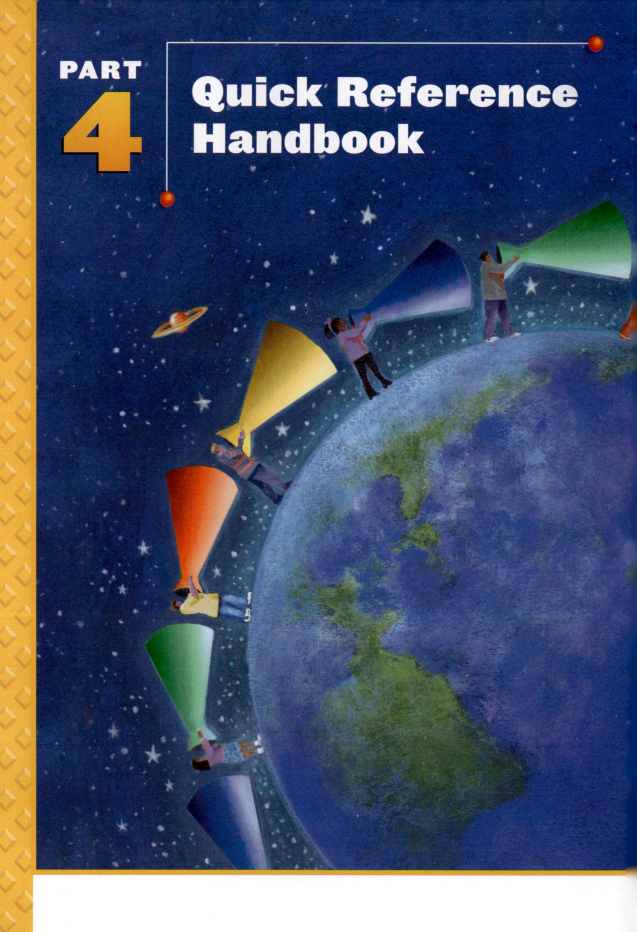

- The Dictionary
- Document Design
- The History of English
- The Library/Media Center
- Reading and Vocabulary
- Speaking and Listening
- Studying and Test Taking
- Viewing and Representing
- Writing
- Grammar at a Glance

Quick Reference Handbook

The Dictionary

TEACHING TIP

Dictionary Entry
Encourage students to use a dictionary as a tool for improving spelling, not just for checking it. For example, students often have difficulty spelling final stable syllables such as *–le, –tion,* and *–age.* When students confirm the spelling of a word containing a final stable syllable, have them pause to compare the syllable breaks shown in the entry word and those in the phonetic spelling that follows. By comparing the syllable breaks, they may begin to see spelling patterns among syllables with the same pronunciation. For example, the sound "ell"—as an unaccented final syllable that follows a consonant (as in *babble*)—is almost always spelled *–le.*

Types and Contents

Types of Dictionaries   Different types of dictionaries provide different kinds of information. You should choose a dictionary that will have the kind of information you need. The following chart shows the types of dictionaries.

Types of Dictionaries

An **abridged** dictionary is the most common type of dictionary. The word *abridged* means shortened or condensed, so an abridged dictionary contains most of the words you are likely to use or encounter in your writing or reading.

Example
Merriam-Webster's Collegiate Dictionary, Tenth Edition

A **specialized** dictionary defines words or terms that are used in a particular profession, field, or area of interest.

Example
Stedman's Medical Dictionary

An **unabridged** dictionary contains nearly all the words in use in a language.

Example
Webster's Third International Unabridged Dictionary

Dictionary Entry

When you look up a word in the dictionary, the entry gives the word and other information about it. Look at the dictionary entry on the next page. The following explanations of the parts of the entry will help you get the most out of your dictionary.

1. **Entry word**   The entry word is printed in boldface (thick) letters. It shows the way the word should be spelled and how to divide the word into syllables. It may also show whether a word should be capitalized or if the word can be spelled in other ways.

2. **Pronunciation**   The pronunciation of a word is shown with symbols. These

cloud (kloud) **n.** ⟦ME *cloude, clude,* orig., mass of rock, hence, mass of cloud < OE *clud,* mass of rock: for IE base see CLIMB⟧ **1** a visible mass of tiny, condensed water droplets or ice crystals suspended in the atmosphere: clouds are commonly classified in four groups: *A* (high clouds above 6,096 m or 20,000 ft.) CIRRUS, CIRROSTRATUS, CIRROCUMULUS; *B* (intermediate clouds 1,981 m to 6,096 m or 6,500 ft. to 20,000 ft.) ALTOSTRATUS, ALTOCUMULUS; *C* (low clouds, below 1,981 m or 6,500 ft.) STRATUS, STRATOCUMULUS, NIMBOSTRATUS; *D* (clouds of great vertical continuity) CUMULUS, CUMULONIMBUS **2** a mass of smoke, dust, steam, etc. **3** a great number of things close together and in motion [a *cloud* of locusts] **4** an appearance of murkiness or dimness, as in a liquid **5** a dark marking, as in marble **6** anything that darkens, obscures, threatens, or makes gloomy —**vt. 1** to cover or make dark as with clouds **2** to make muddy or foggy **3** to darken; obscure; threaten **4** to make gloomy or troubled **5** to cast slurs on; sully (a reputation, etc.) —**vi. 1** to become cloudy **2** to become gloomy or troubled —**in the clouds 1** high up in the sky **2** fanciful; impractical **3** in a reverie or daydream —**under a cloud 1** under suspicion of wrongdoing **2** in a depressed or troubled state of mind

symbols help you pronounce the word correctly. In the sample entry, look at the *k* symbol. It shows you that the *c* in *cloud* sounds like the *c* in *can*, not like the *c* in *ice*. Special letters or markings that are used with letters to show a certain sound are called **phonetic symbols**. **Accent marks** show which syllables of the word are said more forcefully. Look in the front of a dictionary for an explanation of the symbols and marks it uses.

3. **Part-of-speech labels**   These labels are abbreviated and show how you may use the word in a sentence. Some words may be used as more than one part of speech. For each meaning of a word, the dictionary shows the part of speech. In the sample entry, *cloud* can be used as a noun or as a verb, depending on the meaning.

4. **Etymology**   The *etymology* tells how a word entered the English language. The etymology also shows how the word has changed over time. In the sample entry, the abbreviations *ME* and *OE* trace the history of the word *cloud* from Middle English back to Old English. The final abbreviation *IE* tells the word's parent language, which is Indo-European. (See also **History of English** on page 690.)

5. **Definitions**   If the word has more than one meaning, the different definitions are numbered. To help you understand the different meanings, dictionaries often include a sample phrase or sentence after a numbered definition. (See also **Examples** below.)

6. **Examples**   A dictionary may show how the entry word is used. The examples are often in the form of phrases or sentences using the word in context.

7. **Idioms**   A dictionary entry may sometimes give examples and definitions of *idioms* that include the word. An *idiom* is a phrase that means something different from the literal meanings of the words. Dictionaries provide definitions because you cannot always define idioms using the usual meanings of the words.

Document Design

Manuscript Style

Whether you write your paper by hand or use a word-processing program, you should always submit a paper that is neat and easy to read. The guidelines in the chart below can help. You should also ask your teacher for help. He or she may have additional guidelines for you to follow.

Guidelines for Manuscript Style

1. Use only one side of each sheet of paper.

2. Type your paper using a word processor, or write it neatly in blue or black ink.

3. For handwritten papers, ask your teacher if you should skip lines. For typed papers, many teachers prefer that you double-space your assignment.

4. Leave one-inch margins at the top, bottom, and sides of your paper.

5. The first line of every paragraph should be indented five spaces (letter lengths), or half an inch. You can set a **tab** on a word processor to indent five spaces automatically.

6. Number all pages in the top right-hand corner. Do not number the first page.

7. Make sure your pages look neat and clean. For handwritten papers, use correction fluid to correct your mistakes. However, if you have several mistakes on one page, write out the page again. For papers typed on a computer, you can make corrections and print out a clean copy.

8. Use the heading your teacher prefers for your name, your class, the date, and the title of your paper.

9. Include graphics if they will make your ideas clearer to the reader. (See also **Graphics** on page 687.)

Desktop Publishing

To produce professional-looking reports, newsletters, and other documents, writers use *desktop publishing*. **Desktop publishing** describes all of the techniques involved in using a computer to make attractive documents. A computer's desktop publishing program contains many features. These features help a writer create eye-catching documents that contain text (words) and graphics (images and pictures). You can also apply many of the following desktop publishing techniques to handwritten papers.

The following section explains how you can effectively arrange, or lay out, the text of your document. For information about how graphics can make your ideas clearer to readers, see page 687.

Page Layout

Page layout refers to the design, or appearance, of each page in a document. As you plan the design of your page, consider each of the following elements.

Alignment The word *alignment* refers to how lines of text are arranged on the page. Aligning your text the right way can give your page a neat, attractive look.

- **Center-aligned** Text that is *center-aligned* is centered on an imaginary line that runs down the middle of the page or column. You may have used center-alignment for titles of papers or reports. You might also find centered text on posters, advertisements, and invitations.

   EXAMPLE
   >These lines are center-aligned.
   >The text is centered on
   >an imaginary line that runs down
   >the middle of this column.

- **Left-aligned** When text is *left-aligned,* each line begins on the left margin of the page or column. Because English is read from left to right, most blocks of text are left-aligned.

   EXAMPLE
   These lines of text are left-aligned.
   Each line in this column starts at
   the same place on the left margin.

- **Right-aligned** Text that is *right-aligned* is lined up on the right side of the page or column. Right alignment makes short, important bits of information stand out. For instance, when you write reports, you may right-align your name, the date, and the page numbers so that the teacher can find them.

   EXAMPLE
   >These lines are right-aligned.
   >Each line in this column
   >ends at the same place
   >on the right margin.

- **Justified** Text that is *justified* forms a straight edge along the right and the left margins. Spaces may be added to the lines so that the lines are the same length. (The last line in justified text may be shorter than the other lines if it contains only a few words.) You often see justified text in books, newspapers, and magazines.

> **EXAMPLE**
> This text is justified. The text forms a straight edge along the right and left margins of this column.

- **Ragged** Text that is *ragged* lines up along only one margin. Use ragged text for your reports.

> **EXAMPLE**
> This text is ragged. The text lines up along the left margin but not along the right.

Bullet A *bullet* (•) is a large dot or other symbol used to separate items in a list. Bullets attract the reader's eyes and make information easier to read and remember. Consider these guidelines when using bullets.

- A bulleted list should contain at least two items.
- Each item in your list should begin with the same type of wording. For example, each item in this bulleted list begins with a declarative sentence, or a sentence that makes a statement.

Contrast The balance of light and dark areas on a page is called *contrast*. Light areas have very little text and few, if any, pictures or graphics. Dark areas contain lots of text and perhaps pictures or graphics. Pages of high contrast—or a good mix of both light and dark areas—are easier to read than pages with low contrast.

Emphasis *Emphasis* is a way of showing readers the most important information on a page. In a newspaper, a headline in large and heavy type can create emphasis. Color, graphics, and boxes around the text can also create emphasis.

> **EXAMPLE**
> **Sunken Treasure Discovered**
> SUNNY SEA—Diving students made an amazing discovery Saturday one mile off the Texas coast. . . .

Gutter A *gutter* is the inner margin of space from the printed area of a page to the binding.

Headers and Footers A writer uses *headers* and *footers* to provide information about the document. Headers are lines of information that appear at the top of each page in a document. *Footers* are lines of information that appear at the bottom of each page in a document. Headers and footers frequently contain the following information.

- author's name
- name of magazine, newspaper, or document
- publication date
- chapter or section title
- page numbers

Headings and Subheadings Titles within a document are called *headings* and *subheadings* (also called *heads* and *subheads*). Headings and subheadings show readers how information in a document is organized.

- *Headings* tell readers the title or topic of a major section of text. A heading appears at the beginning of a section of text and is usually in bold or capital letters. (See also **Type** on this page.)

- *Subheadings* are more descriptive headings within a major section. Subheadings break a section into smaller sections. Subheadings help readers find the information they need. To separate the subhead from the main text, subheadings may be in a different size or style of type than that of the main text.

EXAMPLE

Keeping Our Parks ——— (heading)
Clean

Weekend Cleanups Give ——— (subheading)
Parks a Whole New Look

The biggest commitment Girl ——— (text)
Scout Troop #912 is making
to the city this year is a program
called Weekend Cleanups. Every
Saturday, five girls from the troop
pick an area park and clean up
trash that people have left behind.

Indentation When you *indent* a line, you move the first word a few spaces to the right of the left margin. Always indent five spaces or half an inch at the beginning of a new paragraph.

Margins The *margin* on a page is the blank space that surrounds the text on the sides, top, and bottom. Some word-processing programs automatically set margins at 1.25 inches for the sides and 1 inch for the top and bottom. You can change the margins, however, to be larger or smaller. Changing the margins will allow you to fit more or less text on a page. Check with your teacher before changing your margins on an assignment.

Rules *Rules* are vertical or horizontal lines in a document. Rules can be used to separate columns of text or to set off text from other elements, such as headlines or graphics.

Title and Subtitle The *title* of a document is its name. A *subtitle* is a secondary, more descriptive title. Subtitles are sometimes joined to titles with a colon. However, if the subtitle is on its own line, no colon is needed. A title and subtitle appear on a separate page at the beginning of a book.

EXAMPLE

The 5 in 10 Pasta and
Noodle Cookbook (title)
5 Ingredients in 10 Minutes or Less (subtitle)

Type

Type refers to the characters (letters and other symbols) in a printed text. Thanks to computer programs, a writer can experiment with the size and design of type in a document until the right look is achieved. When you create a document, there are many different aspects of type that you should consider.

Fonts A *font* is a set of characters (such as numbers, letters, and punctuation marks) of a certain size and design. For example, 12-point Courier is a font. The font size is 12 points (see below); the font design is called Courier. A computer program will let you use many different fonts. A font design is also called a *typeface*.

Font Size The size of type in a document is called the *font size* or *point size*. The size of type is measured in points, which are $\frac{1}{72}$ of an inch. School assignments are usually printed in 10- or 12-point type. Captions for pictures are usually printed in smaller point sizes than the main text is. Titles may be printed in larger point sizes.

EXAMPLE

Title ———— 24 point
Text text text text ———— 12 point
Caption caption caption ———— 9 point

Font Style The *font style* of type refers to the way the type is printed. You may use a font style, such as italic, to show that you are typing a book title. You may also use a different font style, such as boldface, to call attention to important words in your writing. Look at the examples of font styles below and in the next column.

- **Boldface** A *boldface* word is written in thick, heavy type. You can use boldface to show important information.

    EXAMPLE
    This entire sentence is written in boldface type.

- **Capital letters** A *capital* (or *uppercase*) *letter* usually signals a proper name, the beginning of a sentence, or a title. You can put titles and headings in all capital letters. To make an idea stand out, you can put a word or a sentence in text in all capital letters. However, if you put too many words in all capital letters, the idea may not stand out as much.

- **Condensed** When type is *condensed*, the letters in a word will have less space between them. A writer uses condensed type to save space.

    EXAMPLE
    This sentence is written in condensed type.

- **Expanded** When type is *expanded*, the letters in a word will have more space between them. Writers use expanded type to fill up space.

    EXAMPLE
    This sentence is written in expanded type.

- **Italics** Type that is *italic* has a slanted style. Like boldface, italic type can be used to call attention to information. Italic type is also used in text to signal titles. (See also page 588.)

    EXAMPLE
    This sentence is written in italic type.

- **Lowercase letters** A *lowercase letter* is not a capital or a small capital. (See **Small capitals** below.) Lowercase letters are the letters we use most often.

- **Shadow**   A word written in *shadow* style appears to cast shadows. Shadow style may be used for titles and headings.

  EXAMPLE
  This sentence is written in shadow style.

- **Small capitals**   Use *small capitals* when writing abbreviations referring to time. For example, when typing the time 5:45 P.M. and the year A.D. 1812, you should use small capitals.

Leading   Another word for *line spacing* is *leading* (rhymes with *wedding*). **Leading** is the distance between each pair of lines of text. When a text is single-spaced, there is no extra space between lines. Books, magazines, and newspapers are usually single-spaced. Assignments for your teacher are usually double-spaced. Double-spacing your papers makes it easier for your teacher to read your assignment and make corrections or comments on the page.

Legibility   A document is *legible* when its text and graphics are clearly readable. A document with high legibility uses a simple, easy-to-read font size and design for the main text. Well-designed graphics are another key to legibility.

Typeface   See **Font** on page 685.

Graphics

Graphics can often communicate information more quickly and effectively than words. Graphics you can use in your document include *charts, graphs, tables, diagrams,* and *illustrations.* They can

- show information
- explain how to do something
- show how something looks, works, or is organized
- show what happens over a period of time

The main purpose of a graphic is to support or explain the text of your document. Whether you create graphics by hand or by computer, make sure that they are informative and easy to read.

Arrangement and Design

Use the following ideas to create informative and effective graphics.

Accuracy   Make sure all of your graphics contain **accurate** information. In other words, the information in your graphics should be true and from reliable sources.

Color   Readers are attracted to colorful graphics, especially when colorful graphics appear on a page of black-and-white text. You can use *color* to do the following:

- get a reader's attention
- call attention to certain information
- group items on a page
- help organize a page or even an entire document

Keep these tips in mind when you choose colors for your graphics.

- **Use warm colors sparingly.** Red, orange, yellow, and other warm tones seem to jump off the page. Overusing warm tones will decrease their dramatic effect.
- **Use cool colors to create a calming effect.** Cool colors, such as blue and green, make readers feel calmer. Use them as background colors.

Labels, Captions, and Titles You can explain your graphics by adding *labels* and *captions*. **Labels** appear within the graphic or are connected to specific areas of the graphic by thin lines called *rules*. Labels identify different parts of graphics, charts, tables, and diagrams. **Captions** are phrases or sentences that describe a graphic. Many photographs and illustrations have captions. Captions appear directly beside, above, or under the graphic. If your graphic has no labels or captions, give it a descriptive *title*.

Types of Graphics

Use the definitions and examples below to help you decide which graphics to use in your document.

Chart A *chart* helps show how pieces of information relate to each other. Two of the most common types of charts are flowcharts and pie charts.

- **Flowcharts** show an order of events. The boxes in a flowchart contain text, and appear in order from left to right or from top to bottom. Flowcharts usually contain arrows to direct readers from one box to the next.

EXAMPLE

How to Start a Flower Garden

- **Pie charts** show percentages, or how parts of a whole relate to each other. (See also **Charts** on page 711.)

Diagram A *diagram* uses symbols, such as arrows, to show how to do something or how something works. As with the other graphics in this section, diagrams can be drawn by hand or by using a computer program.

EXAMPLE

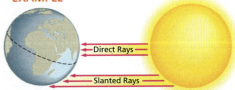

Graph   A *graph* can show changes over time in a way that allows readers to understand the changes at a glance. The horizontal axis (the line that runs across the page) of a line or bar graph usually shows periods or points in time. The vertical axis (the line that runs up and down) shows quantities. (See also **Line graphs** and **Bar graphs** on page 712.)

Illustration   An *illustration* is a drawing or photograph that can show readers items or events that are unfamiliar, new, or hard to describe. It can also show how something works, how to do something, or what someone or something looks like. (See also **Diagrams** on page 712 and **Illustration** on page 748.)

Storyboard   *Storyboards* illustrate the different moments, or scenes, of an event or story. Storyboards are frequently used to map out a story or to plan a video segment. Storyboards contain boxes that each represent one scene in the sequence. The boxes contain drawings and text to be spoken by a narrator or actors within the scene. Example storyboards appear below.

Table   A *table* contains information such as numbers and statistics, but it does not show trends the way a graph does. While a reader of a graph can immediately see an increase or decrease, readers of tables must look at all of the information and draw their own conclusions. For example, after studying the following table, a reader could conclude that membership in the Park Hills Computer Club rose for three years in a row.

EXAMPLE

Number of Middle School Students in the Park Hills Computer Club	
Year	Number of Members
1999	10
2000	19
2001	21

Time Line   A *time line* shows events that happen over a period of time. The points along a time line show years or groups of years. The events that happen during a given year or period of years are described above, below, or to the side of the time line. (See also **Time Lines** on page 713.)

EXAMPLE

Clarissa finds a nest of baby sea turtles on the beach. They head toward the ocean.

One of the turtles cannot walk to the ocean with its brothers and sisters. It struggles on its back.

Clarissa turns the baby sea turtle over so it can walk toward the ocean.

The History of English

Origins and Uses

A Changing Language

No one knows exactly when or how English got started. We do know that English and many other modern-day languages come from an early language that was spoken thousands of years ago. The related languages still resemble that parent language, just as you resemble your parents. For example, notice how similar the words for *mother* are in the following modern-day languages.

ENGLISH mother   FRENCH mère
SPANISH madre   ITALIAN madre
SWEDISH moder

Over 1,500 years ago, a few small tribes of people invaded the island that is now Britain. These tribes, called the Angles and Saxons, spoke the earliest known form of English, called **Old English.** Old English was very different from ours.

English continued to evolve through a form known as **Middle English.** While our language has always changed and grown, some of our most basic words have been around since the very beginning.

EARLY WORD
hand   dohtor   andswaru   hleapan

PRESENT-DAY WORD
hand   daughter   answer   leap

Changes in Meaning It may be hard to believe that the word *bead* once meant "prayer." Many English words have changed meaning over time. Some of these changes have been slight. Others have been more obvious. Below are a few examples of words that have changed their meanings.

naughty—In the 1300s, *naughty* meant "poor or needy." In the 1600s, the meaning changed to "poorly behaved."

lunch—In the 1500s, a *lunch* was a large chunk of something, such as bread or meat.

caboose—*Caboose* entered the English language in the 1700s when it meant "the kitchen of a ship."

Even today the meanings of words may vary depending on where they are used. For example, in America a *boot* is a type of shoe, but in Great Britain, a *boot* may refer to the trunk of a car.

Changes in Pronunciation and Spelling
If you traveled back in time a few hundred years, you would probably have a hard time understanding spoken and written English.

- **Changes in pronunciation** English words used to be pronounced differently from the way they are pronounced today. For example, in the 1200s, people pronounced *bite* like *beet* and *feet* like *fate*. They also pronounced the vowel sound in the word *load* like our word *awe*.

You may have wondered why English words are not always spelled as they sound. Changes in pronunciation help account for many strange spellings in English. For example, the *w* that starts the word *write* was not always silent. Even after the *w* sound that started the word *write* was dropped, the spelling stayed the same. The *g* in *gnat* and the *k* in *knee* were once part of the pronunciations of the words, too.

- **Changes in spelling** The spellings of many words have changed over time. Some changes in spelling have been accidental. For example, *apron* used to be spelled *napron*. People mistakenly attached the *n* to the article *a*, and *a napron* became *an apron*. Here are some more examples of present-day English words and their early spellings.

EARLY SPELLING

| jaile | locian | slæp | tima |

PRESENT-DAY SPELLING

| jail | look | sleep | time |

- **British vs. American spelling and pronunciation** Pronunciations and spellings still vary today. For instance, the English used in Great Britain differs from the English used in the United States. In Great Britain, people pronounce *bath* with the vowel sound of *father* instead of the vowel sound of *cat*. The British also tend to drop the *r* sound at the end of words like *copper*. In addition, the British spell some words differently from the way people in the United States do.

AMERICAN

| theater | pajamas | labor |

BRITISH

| theatre | pyjamas | labour |

Word Origins English grows and changes along with the people who use it. New words must be created for new inventions, places, or ideas. Sometimes, people borrow words from other languages to create a new English word. Other times, people use the names of people or places as new words.

- **Borrowed words** As English-speaking people came into contact with people from other cultures and lands, they began to borrow words. English has borrowed hundreds of thousands of words from French, Hindi, Spanish, African languages, and many other

TEACHING TIP

Word Origins
Show students that the source language of a word can determine its spelling. First, have students brainstorm words that are not pronounced as they would expect based on the word's spelling. For example, the spelling *ou* is usually pronounced *ow*, but several words from French contain this spelling pronounced *oo*, including *souvenir* and *mousse*. Then, divide the class evenly into four groups and assign each group to research one of the following spelling patterns: *j* pronounced *h* (Spanish) [jalapeño, junta], silent *h* (French) [honor, hour], *ae* (Latin) [aerial, aerobic], and *sch* pronounced *sk* (Greek) [schedule, scheme]. Each group member should use a dictionary to search for two words from the source language that contain the spelling pattern. Then, group members should compile a list of all of the words found and create a poster that lists the words with the spelling pattern in a different color. At the top of the poster, have students identify the spelling pattern and the source language. Each group should present its poster to the rest of the class and explain how the spelling pattern is pronounced in words from the source language.

languages spoken around the world. In many cases, the borrowed words have taken new forms.

FRENCH ange
ENGLISH angel

HINDI champo
ENGLISH shampoo

AFRICAN banjo
ENGLISH banjo

SPANISH patata
ENGLISH potato

- **Words from names** Many things get their names from the names of people or places. For example, in the 1920s, someone in Bridgeport, Connecticut, discovered a new use for the pie plates from the Frisbie Bakery. He turned one upside down and sent it floating through the air. The new game sparked the idea for the flying plastic disk of today.

Dialects of American English

You probably know some people who speak English differently than you do. Different groups of people use different varieties of English. The kind of English we speak sounds most normal to us even though it may sound unusual to someone else. The form of English a particular group of people speaks is called a *dialect*. Everyone uses a dialect, and no dialect is better or worse than another.

Ethnic Dialects Your cultural background can make a difference in the way you speak. A dialect shared by people from the same cultural group is called an *ethnic dialect*. Because Americans come from many cultures, American English includes many ethnic dialects. One of the largest ethnic dialects is the Black English spoken by many African Americans. Another is the Hispanic English of many people whose families come from places such as Mexico, Central America, or Cuba.

Regional Dialects Do you *make* the bed or *make up* the bed? Would you order a *sub* with the *woiks* or a *hero* with the *werks*? In the evening, do you eat *supper* or *dinner*? How you answer these questions is probably influenced by where you live. A dialect shared by people from the same area is called a *regional dialect*. Your regional dialect helps determine what words you use, how you pronounce words, and how you put words together.

Not everyone from a particular group speaks that group's dialect. Also, an ethnic or regional dialect may vary depending on the speaker's individual background and place of origin.

Standard American English

Every dialect is useful and helps keep the English language colorful and interesting. However, sometimes it is confusing to try to communicate using two different dialects. Therefore, it is important to be familiar with **standard American English**. Standard English is the most commonly understood variety of English. You can find some of the rules for using standard English in the **Grammar, Usage, and Mechanics** section of this textbook beginning on page 298. Language that does not follow these rules and guidelines is called **nonstandard English**. Nonstandard English is inappropriate in situations where standard English is expected.

NONSTANDARD I don't want *no* more spinach.

STANDARD I don't want *any* more spinach.

NONSTANDARD Jimmy was *fixing* to go hiking with us.

STANDARD Jimmy was *about* to go hiking with us.

Formal and Informal
Read the following sentences.

> Many of my friends are excited about the game.
>
> A bunch of my friends are psyched about the game.

Both sentences mean the same thing, but they have different effects. The first sentence is an example of **formal English,** and the second sentence is an example of **informal English.**

Formal and informal English are each appropriate for different situations. For instance, you would probably use the formal example if you were talking to a teacher about the game. If you were talking to a friend, however, the second sentence would sound natural. Formal English is frequently used in news reports and in schools and businesses.

- **Colloquialisms** Informal English includes many words and expressions that are not appropriate in more formal situations. The most widely used informal expressions are *colloquialisms*. **Colloquialisms** are colorful words and phrases of everyday conversation. Many colloquialisms have meanings that are different from the basic meanings of words.

EXAMPLES
I wish Gerald would *get off my case*.
Don't get *all bent out of shape* about it.
We were about to *bust* with laughter.

- **Slang** *Slang* words are made-up words or old words used in new ways. Slang is highly informal language. It is usually created by a particular group of people, such as students or people who hold a particular job, like computer technicians or artists. Often, slang is familiar only to the groups that invent it.

  Sometimes slang words become a lasting part of the English language. Usually, though, slang falls out of style quickly. The slang words in the sentences below will probably seem out of date to you.

  That was a really *far-out flick*.
  Those are some *groovy duds* you're wearing.
  I don't have enough *dough* to buy a movie ticket.

The Library/Media Center

Using Print and Electronic Sources

Libraries contain huge amounts of information. In a library you can read about your favorite celebrities in the latest magazine, research breeds of dogs to choose a family pet, or find tips to help you in a sport. Whatever information you are looking for, your library has the tools to help you find it. Knowing how to use the library can bring you hours of enjoyment.

The information in a library takes many forms. The resource you use depends on the type of information you need. The following chart shows ways that information is classified.

Print Sources	
Fiction	Stories (novels, short stories, and plays)
Nonfiction	Factual information about real people, events, and things; includes biographies and "how-to" books
Reference books	General information about many subjects
Magazines and newspapers	Current events, commentaries, and important discoveries
Maps, globes, atlases, and almanacs	Geographic information, facts, dates, and statistics
Pamphlets	Brief summaries of facts about specific subjects
Nonprint Sources	
Audiotapes, records, films, filmstrips, slides, videotapes, CD-ROMs	Stories (narrated, illustrated, or acted out), music, instructions and educational material, facts and information about many specific subjects
Computers	Information stored electronically, allowing for easy access and frequent updates

Books Many books that you can use as sources are packed full of information. The specific information that you might need can sometimes be hard to find. You will find information more easily if you know how to use every part of a book. The following chart shows the types of information you will find in a book.

Information Found in Parts of a Book
The **title page** gives the full title, the name of the author (or authors), the publisher, and the place of publication.
The **copyright page** gives the date of the first publication of the book and the date of any revisions.
The **table of contents** lists titles of chapters or sections of the book and their starting page numbers.
The **appendix** provides additional information about subjects found in the book; it sometimes contains tables, maps, and charts.
The **glossary** defines, in alphabetical order, various difficult terms or important technical words used frequently in the book.
The **bibliography** lists sources used to write the book and provides names of books about related topics.
The **index** lists topics mentioned in the book, along with the page or pages on which they can be found; it sometimes lists the page where a certain illustration may be found.

Call Number When you need to find a book in the library, first find its *call number.* A call number is a code using letters and numbers that is assigned to a source in a library. Call numbers indicate the category a book is in and where it is located. Books in school and community libraries use the *Dewey Decimal Classification system.* (See also **Card Catalog** below.)

The *Dewey Decimal Classification system* assigns a number to each nonfiction book. These numbers are assigned according to the book's subject. Using this system of arrangement, books that contain factual information about similar subjects are placed near each other on the library shelves. **Biographies** are arranged differently from other nonfiction books. Most libraries arrange biographies alphabetically by the name of the subject in a separate section. **Fiction** books are arranged alphabetically by author in their own section of the library.

Card Catalog The easiest way to locate a book in the library is to look up the call number in the library's card catalog. There are two kinds of card catalogs: the traditional card catalog and the online catalog.

The traditional *card catalog* is a cabinet of small drawers. Each drawer holds many small file cards. There are cards in this file for every book in the library. The cards are arranged in alphabetical order by title, author, or subject. Each fiction book has a *title card* and an *author card.* A nonfiction book will also have a *subject card.* The graphic on the next page shows the information contained in the card catalog.

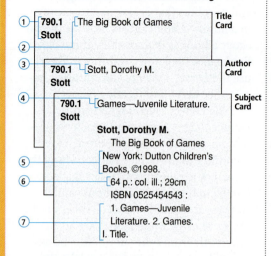

Information in the Card Catalog

1. The **call number** assigned to a book by the Library of Congress or the Dewey Decimal Classification system
2. The full **title** of a book
3. The **author's full name,** last name first
4. The general **subject** of a book; a subject card may show specific headings
5. The place and date of **publication**
6. A **description** of the book, such as its size and number of pages, and whether it is illustrated
7. **Cross-references** to other headings or related topics under which you can find additional books

Many libraries now use electronic or online card catalogs instead of traditional card catalogs. (See also **Online Catalog** on page 698.)

CD-ROMs *CD-ROM* stands for **C**ompact **D**isc-**R**ead **O**nly **M**emory. A CD-ROM is a computer disc that holds visual and audio information. "Read Only" tells you that you can get information from the disc, but you cannot make changes to the disc. In order to use a CD-ROM, you must have a computer with a CD-ROM disc drive. CD-ROMs are popular because they can hold as much as 100,000 pages of information per disc. CD-ROMs can also perform searches, provide interactive graphics, and supply sound. You might use an encyclopedia, dictionary, or other programs on CD-ROM.

Indexes When researching a topic, you might start by consulting an *index,* which lists topics, sources, or authors. The *Readers' Guide to Periodical Literature,* for example, helps readers find articles, poems, and stories from more than two hundred magazines and journals. The guide lists articles alphabetically both by author and by subject. Each entry has a heading printed in boldface capital letters. In the front of the *Readers' Guide* is a guide to abbreviations that appear in the entries. Below is an example of an online *Readers' Guide* entry. The next page shows an example from the printed version.

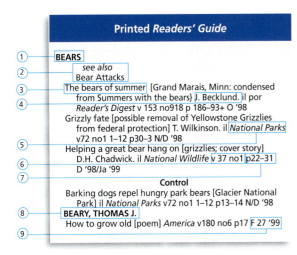

Internet The *Internet* does not exist in one place. Instead, it is a network, or web of connections, among computers all over the world. While the Internet was originally created to share science information, it has expanded today to include sites on virtually any topic. Many libraries have computers that you can use to connect to the Internet. The most popular way to view information on the Internet is through a World Wide Web browser. (See also **World Wide Web** on page 699.)

Microforms *Microforms* are photographs of articles from newspapers and magazines that have been reduced to take up less space. Two types of microforms are *microfilm,* a continuous roll of film, and *microfiche,* small cards of film. To use microforms, you must also use machines that magnify the information and project it onto a screen for you to read.

Newspapers Newspapers include different types of reading materials that are often contained in several separate sections. As a reader, you probably read the various parts of a newspaper for different reasons.

If you are reading to learn about differing viewpoints or opinions on an issue, read the editorial section. The editorial section is also a good place to get ideas for persuasive papers. As you read an editorial, identify points with which you agree or disagree. Also, try to identify the reasons and evidence the writer uses.

If you want to find information or gain knowledge, try reading the city, state, or national news sections. For each news story you read, ask yourself the *5W–How?* questions (see page 60). If you use the news story as a source for one of your papers, be sure to put the information into your own words.

If you want to be entertained, you might want to read the comics or the entertainment section.

Online Catalog
The *online catalog* is stored on a computer. To find the call number for a book, type in the title, the author, or the subject of the book. The computer will show the results of your search. The results are a little different in each library, but the search results that follow are typical.

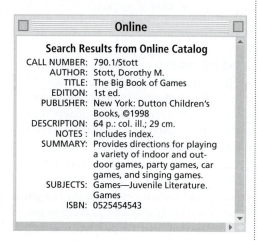

Online Databases
Online databases are collections of information stored on a computer. You can use online databases to search for information. They are usually created for specific groups or organizations. Many databases require users to pay a fee, but other databases are free. You can use the World Wide Web to access some databases.

Once you have accessed a database, search for specific topics by typing in a *keyword* or key phrase. You can print out the information you find. The results of the search for articles about bears in the *Online Readers' Guide* on page 696 is an example of an online database.

Online Sources
An *online source* is a source of information that can be accessed only by computer. You can find and access online information through computer networks. A network is a group of computers connected by telephone lines, by fiber-optic cables, or via satellite. Computer networks make the Internet and the World Wide Web possible.

Radio, Television, Film, and Video
Some of the most common sources of information today are *radio* and *television.* You can find news broadcasts, newsmagazines, and documentaries on radio and television stations every day. Additional educational programs are available on *film* or *video.* To find shows that might have information you need, consult magazines or newspaper listings that contain descriptions of radio and television programs. If you want to rent or borrow a video, check out books that have descriptions of educational videos. You might find several books of video listings at your local library. Before using a film or video as a source of information, check the ratings to make sure it is appropriate. (See also **Critical Viewing** on page 746 and **Media Messages** on page 732.)

Reference Sources

Type	Description	Examples
Encyclopedias	• many volumes • articles arranged alphabetically by subject • good source for general information	*Collier's Encyclopedia* *Compton's Encyclopedia* *The World Book Multimedia Encyclopedia™*
General Biographical References	• information about birth, nationality, and major accomplishments of outstanding people	*Current Biography* *Dictionary of American Biography* *The International Who's Who* *World Biographical Index on CD-ROM*
Atlases	• maps and geographical information	*Atlas of World Cultures* *National Geographic Atlas of the World*
Almanacs	• up-to-date information about current events, facts, statistics, and dates	*The Information Please Almanac, Atlas and Yearbook* *The World Almanac and Book of Facts*
Books of Synonyms	• lists of more interesting or more exact words to express ideas	*Roget's International Thesaurus* *Webster's New Dictionary of Synonyms*

Reference Sources There are many different kinds of reference sources, print and nonprint, that you can use to find specific kinds of information. Most libraries devote an entire section to reference works. The chart above lists some of the reference sources you might use.

Vertical File Many libraries have a **vertical file,** a filing cabinet containing up-to-date materials such as newspaper clippings, booklets, and pamphlets.

World Wide Web (*WWW* or the *Web*) The *World Wide Web* is part of the Internet. It is a system of connected documents, called **Web pages** or **Web sites.** These pages or sites contain text, graphics, and multimedia presentations such as video and audio. The documents on the Web are connected by *hyperlinks.* By clicking on a **hyperlink** you can navigate from one Web site to another. To use the World Wide Web, you must use a computer that has Internet software installed. The following terms will help you.

TEACHING TIP

World Wide Web
If students search the World Wide Web for information about their research projects, remind them that Internet resources are sometimes public forums and their content can be unpredictable.

- **Browser**   A *browser* is software that allows you to find and view Web pages. A browser also allows you to download, or get and save, software or files. Using a browser to read your way around the Web is called *browsing*. (See also **Web site** on this page.)

- **Hyperlink**   A *hyperlink* is a connection from one place on the Web to another. Hyperlinks, also known as *links*, might appear as words or icons. By clicking on them, you can move to another place on the same Web page or to a different Web page or site. Hyperlinks are usually a different color from the other text and underlined.

- **Search engine**   A search engine is a program used for searching for information on the World Wide Web. (See also **World Wide Web, Searching** on page 701.)

- **URL**   (*U*niform *R*esource *L*ocator) A *URL* is the specific address of a Web page. URLs may include words, abbreviations, numbers, and punctuation. Below is a URL with its parts labeled.

  ```
        1              2              3
  http://www.go.hrw.com/programs/science
  ```

  1. The language used by the Internet service
  2. The *hostname.* The hostname is made up of a series of domains. Reading from right to left, each domain gives your computer more and more specific information when you send it out to look for a Web site. In the example above, *com* tells your computer that the Web site you want is a part of a commercial network. In the same example, *hrw* is the name of the company whose computer contains the Web site, and *go* is the specific machine within *hrw* that contains the Web site.

  Here are the abbreviations of the most common networks.

Common Networks on the World Wide Web	
com	commercial or individual
edu	educational
gov	governmental
org	usually nonprofit organization

  3. The specific address of the page requested. Not all URLs contain this last part.

- **Web site** (or **Web page**) A Web site or Web page is a location on the World Wide Web. The **home page** is the first page on a Web site. A typical home page gives you an overview of the Web site's contents. It also contains hyperlinks to pages within the Web site and sometimes hyperlinks to other Web sites. (See also **Hyperlink** on this page.) Other information on a home page includes information about the site's author or sponsor as well as the date the site was last updated. On the next page is an example of a Web page viewed with a browser program.

1. **Toolbar** The buttons on the toolbar let you move back to previous pages, move forward, print a page, search for information, or see or hide images.
2. **Location indicator** This box shows you the address (URL) of the site you are currently viewing.
3. **Content area** The area of the screen where the Web page appears.
4. **Hyperlink** Click on these buttons to find information and other Web sites available through the browser.
5. **Scroll bar** Clicking along the horizontal or vertical scroll bar (or on the arrows at either end) allows you to move left to right or up and down in the image area.

World Wide Web, Searching The World Wide Web is full of information, but you must find it before you can use it. Luckily, there are tools to help you find what you need. You can search the Internet by using a *search engine* or a *directory*.

- **Search engines** When you use a search engine, you look for Web sites by doing a *keyword search*. A **keyword search** lets you look for Web sites that contain specific words or phrases. Type important words about your topic in the space provided on the search engine screen. Then press the Return key or click on the Search or Find button. The search engine will provide a list of sites that fit your search. Sites that contain all of your keywords will be at the top of the list.

Sometimes your keyword search will list too many Web sites to look at, or sometimes it may not find any sites at all. When this happens, you need to narrow your keyword search. Try the following strategies to narrow your searches, or consult the Help section of your search engine for other ideas.

Refining a Key Word Search	
Tip	**How It Works**
Use specific terms.	Words have many different, and sometimes unexpected, meanings. Using more specific words can help you get just the right results. EXAMPLE To find information on making videos, enter *video production* instead of *movies*.
Put words that go together as a phrase into quotation marks.	If you are searching for a phrase, type it in quotation marks. The search engine will find sites that use the words exactly as they are typed. EXAMPLE Type in "computer games" to find information on the latest gaming software instead of information on types of computers or board games.
Use *AND* and *NOT*.	You can narrow your search by using the words *AND* and *NOT*. Placing *AND* between two words will narrow your results to pages that contain both words. Putting *NOT* between two words will help exclude sites with information you do not want. EXAMPLE Type in "Brooklyn Bridge" AND "Golden Gate Bridge" to find sites on both the Brooklyn and Golden Gate bridges. To find sites about the human heart, but not romance, enter "heart NOT love."
Use *OR*.	Using *OR* can make your search broader. The results list will include sites that contain any of your important words. EXAMPLE Type in "Brooklyn Bridge" OR "Golden Gate Bridge" to find sites that discuss either the Brooklyn Bridge or Golden Gate Bridge.

■ **Directories**   A directory is an organized list of Web sites. Directories organize sites into categories, such as *sports*. Each category is broken down into smaller and smaller categories, helping you narrow your search. Most search engine sites include directories.

World Wide Web, Web Site Evaluation   The World Wide Web is full of information because anyone can post sites there. Since no one supervises the Web, you are much more likely to find false information there than you are in a newspaper or book. Follow the tips on the next page to **evaluate** Web sites you use.

Evaluating Web Sites

Questions to Ask	Why You Should Ask
Who created the Web site? Who is the Web site's sponsor?	The creator or sponsor of a Web site chooses its content. Look on the site's home page to find the author or sponsor. Make sure you use only Web sites that are sponsored by trustworthy organizations, such as government agencies, universities, and museums. To help identify these sites, look for URLs containing *edu, gov,* or *org*. National news organizations are also good sources of information.
When was the page first posted? Has it been updated?	Look for this information at the end of the home page. It sometimes includes the copyright notice, date last updated, and a link to the creator's e-mail. Make sure you use only up-to-date information.
What links to other Web pages does the site include?	The most trustworthy Web sites will usually provide links to other trusted sites. Look at the links provided to get hints about the quality of this site.
Is the Web site objective?	Objective sites present ideas from both sides and focus on facts rather than opinions.
Is the Web site well designed?	Look for easy-to-read type, clear graphics, and working links. Well-designed and well-maintained Web sites are easy to read and navigate. Sites should also have correct spelling, punctuation, and grammar.

TEACHING TIP

Evaluating Web Sites
Inform students that the World Wide Web is a good resource for information about writing. As students write, revise, and edit their next writing project, you may want to have them visit and use some of the writing-related hyperlinks on *Elements of Language's* Web site, whose address is given on p. 642.

Quick Reference Handbook

Reading and Vocabulary

Reading

Skills and Strategies

You can become a better reader by using the following skills and strategies.

Author's Point of View, Determining
The opinion or attitude an author expresses is called *point of view*, or *bias*. Figuring out the author's point of view can help you evaluate what you are reading. (See also page 157.)

EXAMPLE Philately (fə•lat′′l•ē), or the study of postage stamps, is an interesting way to learn about the world. When you examine stamps from around the world, you learn about history, different cultures, and art all at the same time.

Author's point of view: Collecting stamps is interesting and educational.

Author's Purpose, Determining
An author has a reason, or *purpose*, for writing. An author may write to inform, to persuade, to express feelings, or to entertain. Determining an author's purpose will help you decide if his or her conclusions are fair.

EXAMPLE Skateboarding is an exciting and athletic sport. It combines speed with control and is safe as long as it is done in a properly designed park with safety pads and helmets. If you want a fun way to stay fit, pick up your skateboard!

Author's purpose: To persuade people that skateboarding is a good form of exercise.

Cause-and-Effect Relationships, Analyzing
A *cause* makes something happen, and an *effect* is what happens as a result of that cause. Ask "Why?" and "What are the effects?" as you read to examine causes and effects. (See also page 65.)

EXAMPLE Many traditional medicines of Asia use the bones and body parts of tigers. Local people can make a large amount of money by poaching, or illegally hunting, and selling parts of tigers. Because their parts are so valuable, tigers are close to extinction.

Analysis: The *cause* is killing tigers to sell their parts for medicines. The *effect* is that tigers are threatened with extinction.

Clue Words, Using Writers often use certain *clue words* to connect their ideas. The type of clue words a writer uses can help readers understand what type of organization the author is using. (See also **Text Structures** on page 709.)

Clue Words	
Cause-Effect Pattern	
as a result	since
because	so that
if . . . then	therefore
nevertheless	this led to
Chronological Order	
after	first, second
as	now
before	then
finally	when
Comparison-Contrast Pattern	
although	however
as well as	on the other hand
but	unless
either . . . or	yet
Listing Pattern	
also	most important
for example	to begin with
in fact	
Problem-Solution Pattern	
as a result	this led to
nevertheless	thus
therefore	

Conclusions, Drawing You draw *conclusions* about a text by combining information that you read with information you already know. (See also page 192.)

EXAMPLE   The ancient Egyptian process of mummification was expensive and time-consuming. The entire process took seventy days and involved various ceremonies. Tombs where the mummies were laid to rest were sometimes crowded with furniture and models of other everyday items.

Conclusion: Most ancient Egyptians who were mummified were wealthy people in life.

Fact and Opinion, Distinguishing
A *fact* is a statement you can prove with an outside source. An *opinion* gives a personal belief or attitude, so it cannot be proved true or false. Writers often support their opinions with facts. Distinguishing facts from opinions can help you be a better reader. (See also page 231.)

EXAMPLE

Fact: The earliest armor of European knights of the Middle Ages was a short leather or cloth tunic known as a *hauberk*. [You could look this up in an encyclopedia or dictionary and find that it is true.]

Opinion: Knights of the Middle Ages were kindhearted soldiers. [This is what one writer thinks or believes. The statement cannot be proved true in every case.]

Generalizations, Forming
Generalizations are formed by gathering information as you read and connecting it to your own experiences to make a

judgment or statement about the world in general. (See also page 21.)

EXAMPLE Students at Jordan Middle School are now eating healthier meals at lunch. Inspired by student requests, cafeteria workers have stopped cooking fried, greasy foods and have created new recipes using fresh fruits and vegetables. While some school officials worried that students would not like the new menu, cafeteria sales have actually gone up. It seems that healthy food is the newest trend at Jordan Middle School.

Generalization: Many young people prefer healthy choices for lunch to fatty, fried foods.

Implied Main Idea, Identifying

Sometimes the main idea of a piece of writing is not directly stated but only suggested or *implied.* To identify an implied main idea, read the text and think about the details in it. Then, create a statement that expresses the text's overall meaning. (See also page 53 and **Stated Main Idea** on page 709.)

EXAMPLE Many students sleep less than seven hours a night. In a school survey, sixty percent of the students complained of being tired during the school day. Fifteen percent of the students admitted that they had fallen asleep during class. This sleepiness makes it difficult to pay attention and learn at school.

Implied main idea: Students should get more than seven hours of sleep.

Inferences, Making

Making an *inference* is making a guess based on what you read and what you already know about the topic. *Conclusions, generalizations,* and *predictions* are types of inferences. Making inferences helps you to understand ideas about the situation in the text even though the author does not directly state them. (See also **Conclusions** and **Generalizations** on page 705 and **Predicting** on page 707.)

EXAMPLE Aruna sprang out of bed and quickly put on her soccer uniform, making sure she had her lucky socks. She ate a nutritious breakfast and tried not to be worried. As her dad drove her to the field she rehearsed the plays in her mind. When she met her team, each girl had an air of nervous determination about her.

Inference: Aruna is about to play in an important soccer game.

Paraphrasing

To *paraphrase* is to express an author's ideas in your own words. Paraphrasing helps you understand complicated readings. *Plagiarism* is copying someone else's words and ideas and claiming that they are your own. Since a paraphrase is a rewording of another piece of writing, a paraphrased passage is usually around the same length as the original. A brief rewording that explains the key ideas of the original passage is called a *summary.* (See the chart on page 735 for **Paraphrasing Guidelines**.)

EXAMPLE A well-known French marine scientist and filmmaker, Jacques Cousteau spent much of his life exploring underwater. He contributed to the invention of the Aqua-Lung™, a breathing apparatus that allowed divers to stay underwater longer. Cousteau made films about his ocean explorations and won Academy Awards for *The Silent World* in 1956 and *World Without Sun* in 1966.

Paraphrase: Jacques Cousteau was a French filmmaker who explored the ocean as a diver and marine scientist. He contributed to the creation of the Aqua-Lung™, a breathing device for divers. Two of Cousteau's films about the ocean, *The Silent World* and *World Without Sun,* won Academy Awards.

Persuasive Techniques, Analyzing

When writers want to convince readers to think or act in a certain way, they may use *persuasive techniques.* Some persuasive techniques include using facts, reasons, and evidence. Other persuasive techniques use words and ideas that create an emotional reaction. Watch out for persuasive arguments that use only *emotional appeals.* (See also page 257.)

EXAMPLE   Homelessness is a problem that will not be solved until more people get involved in the solution. Many programs exist to help homeless citizens, including programs that build houses, distribute food, and give temporary shelter. The government recognized the importance of caring for the homeless with the passage of the McKinney Homeless Assistance Act in 1987. If you want to make a difference, you should get involved with solving the problem of homelessness. After all, not everyone is fortunate enough to have a place to call home.

Analysis: The second and third sentences use facts to support the opinion in the first sentence. The last sentence is an emotional appeal aimed at readers' sympathy. It may not be persuasive because it assumes that the readers probably have homes.

Predicting

Predicting is deciding what will happen next. To make predictions, read the passage and use your past experiences to help you guess what will happen next. The point of predicting is to get involved with what you are reading, not to be correct every time. Therefore, it is all right to make a wrong guess. (See also page 86.)

EXAMPLE   Jackie Joyner-Kersee approached the starting line at the 1992 Olympics in Barcelona. She had won track competitions since she was fourteen years old. At the 1984 Olympics, Joyner-Kersee won a silver medal in the heptathlon. She won two gold medals in the 1988 Olympics in Seoul, Korea. As Joyner-Kersee took her stance for this latest race, she was once again ready to run for gold.

Prediction: Jackie Joyner-Kersee is about to win another Olympic gold medal.

Problem-Solution Relationships, Analyzing

A *problem* is an unanswered question, while a **solution** is a suggested answer. Authors who write about problems often also write about one or two solutions and try to explain what effects the solutions will have. When you read, ask "What is the problem?" and "Who has the problem?" Then, identify the solutions that the writer suggests.

EXAMPLE   A vacant lot in the west side neighborhood of Journeyville had become a dumping area filled with trash. Tired of this eyesore, several neighbors approached the city council about creating a community center building. While the council was in favor of the proposal, they did not have the budget to build the center. Another group of neighbors got together on weekends and began to move the trash. As the land was cleared, they built swing sets and even started a community garden. Now the lot is a bustling center of the community.

Analysis: The problem was that the west Journeyville neighborhood had a vacant lot with too much trash in it. This problem disturbed the neighbors. One possible solution was to have the city create a community center there. Another solution was to create a community park and garden.

Reading Log, Using a When you write informally about what you read, you are keeping a *reading log.* In a reading log, you can write down questions, write about personal connections you make with the reading, or make note of important sections. In addition to writing down your thoughts during reading, you can use your reading log to write down ideas you have before reading (prereading), or after reading (postreading).

Reading Rate, Adjusting *Reading rate* is the speed at which you read something. Readers adjust their reading rates based on their purpose for reading, the difficulty of the reading material, and their knowledge about the subject. The chart at the bottom of this page shows how you can adjust your reading rate for different purposes.

SQ3R *SQ3R* is a study strategy that you can use when you read. SQ3R is an abbreviation of the five steps in this process:

S *Survey* the passage. Look over the headings, titles, illustrations, charts, and any words in boldface or italics.

Q *Question* yourself about the passage. Make headings, subtitles, and boldface words into questions that you can answer after you read.

R *Read* the entire passage. Answer your questions as you read.

R *Recite,* or say out loud, the answers to your questions.

R *Review,* or look back over, the passage. Read it again quickly and quiz yourself with the questions.

Reading Rates According to Purpose		
Reading Rate	**Purpose**	**Example**
Scanning	Quickly reading for specific details	Finding the last name of a character in a novel
Skimming	Quickly reading for main points	Previewing a chapter from your science textbook by reading the headings before you read the text
Reading for mastery (reading to learn)	Reading to understand and remember	Reading and taking notes from a book for a research report
Reading at a comfortable speed	Reading for enjoyment	Reading a novel by your favorite writer

Stated Main Idea and Supporting Details, Identifying The *main idea* of any piece of writing is its most important idea. Sometimes main ideas are found at the beginning of a paragraph in a topic sentence. Other times, the main idea may be found at the end of the passage, as a conclusion. Main ideas are backed up by *supporting details* that explain and give more information about the main idea. When a main idea is directly stated, it is called an *explicit main idea*. (See also page 53 and **Implied Main Idea** on page 706.)

EXAMPLE Even though they are known as disease-causing organisms, today viruses are being used to fight illnesses. Scientists are using the organisms to produce proteins for research and industry. Also, since viruses carry genetic information, they are being used to carry correct genetic information to defective cells.

Stated main idea: Viruses are being used to combat illnesses.

Supporting details: Viruses are used to produce proteins for research and industry, and they carry correct genetic information to defective cells.

Summarizing A *summary* is a brief restatement of the main points expressed in a piece of writing. Summarizing can help you understand a difficult reading passage. Summaries are similar to paraphrases since summaries restate someone else's ideas in your own words. Summaries, however, are usually much shorter than the original passage because they do not include every detail. (See also **Paraphrasing** on page 706. See the chart on page 736 for **Summarizing Guidelines**.)

EXAMPLE Virtual reality lets even the most couch-bound television watcher feel like he or she is skiing in the Swiss Alps. Virtual reality combines computer-created worlds with a headset that enables a person to see images in three dimensions. By using data gloves that transmit hand motions, a person can seem to be inside the computer environment.

Summary: Virtual reality is a system combining computers, headsets, and data gloves to make a person feel that he or she is within a different setting.

Text Structures, Analyzing *Text structures* are patterns of organization that a writer uses. There are five common patterns: *cause-effect, chronological order, comparison-contrast, listing,* and *problem-solution*. Sometimes a writer may use one pattern, and other times a writer may combine two or more patterns. By understanding the way a piece of writing is organized, you can better understand the information you are reading. These guidelines can help you analyze a text structure:

1. Look for clue words that might hint at a specific pattern of organization. (See also **Clue Words** on page 705.)
2. Look for important ideas and connections between those ideas. Is there an obvious pattern?
3. Draw a graphic organizer to help you understand the text structure. Your graphic organizer may look like one of the five common text structures illustrated on the next two pages.

- *Cause-effect pattern* focuses on the relationship between causes and their effects or results. (See also page 65.) The following chain shows how nutritional education can lead to health and energy.

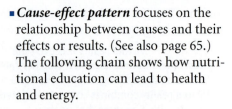

- *Chronological order* shows events or ideas in the order in which they happen. (See also page 23.) The sequence chain in the next column lists the steps for blowing up a balloon.

- *Comparison-contrast pattern* focuses on how two or three ideas or events are alike or different. (See also page 124.) The Venn diagram at the bottom of the page compares a human brain and a computer.

- *Listing pattern* organizes information in a list form using classifications such

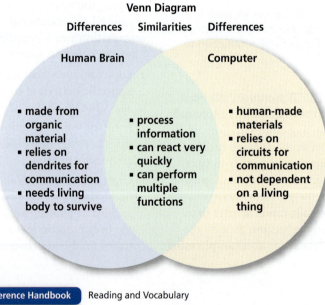

as importance, size, location, or other important criteria. The list below organizes dogs by size.

List
Dogs of Different Sizes
1. Chihuahua (small)
2. cocker spaniel (medium)
3. Saint Bernard (large)

- *Problem-solution pattern* focuses on one or more problems and solutions to the problem. The pattern also explains the outcomes of each solution and the final results of the problem and solution. (See also page 74.) The following example shows a problem and some possible solutions.

Cluster

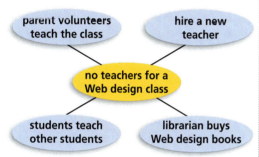

Transitional Words and Phrases, Identifying
Transitions are words and phrases writers use to connect ideas and to make writing read more smoothly. By identifying transitions, you can understand how the ideas in a piece of writing fit together. (See page 287 for a chart of **Transitional Words and Phrases.**)

Visuals and Graphics, Interpreting
Visuals and *graphics* communicate information with pictures or symbols. Visuals and graphics can communicate very complex information in a simple way. When you read writing that contains visuals or graphics, examine the information and draw your own conclusions.

- **Elements** Effective visuals and graphics contain the following elements. (See also page 687.)
    1. A *title* identifies the subject or main idea of the graphic.
    2. The *body* of the visual gives information in the form of a graph, chart, time line, diagram, or table.
    3. *Labels* identify and explain the information shown in the visual or graphic.
    4. A box called a *legend* may be included to identify symbols, colors, or scales to help the reader interpret the graphic.
    5. The *source* tells where the information in the graphic was found; knowing the source helps readers evaluate the accuracy of the graphic.

- **Types** Several common types of visuals are *charts, diagrams, graphs, tables,* and *time lines*.
    1. **Charts** show how the parts of something relate to the whole thing. In the *pie chart* on the next page, notice how all of the segments contribute to the whole picture. Pie charts often do not show specific numbers but focus on percentages instead.

Reading 711

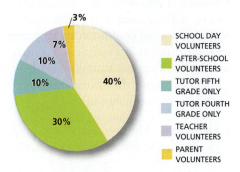

Types of Volunteers

- 40% SCHOOL DAY VOLUNTEERS
- 30% AFTER-SCHOOL VOLUNTEERS
- 10% TUTOR FIFTH GRADE ONLY
- 10% TUTOR FOURTH GRADE ONLY
- 7% TEACHER VOLUNTEERS
- 3% PARENT VOLUNTEERS

2. **Diagrams** use symbols (such as circles or arrows) or pictures to compare ideas, show a process, or show how an object is built. The following diagram shows how to make a "valley fold," a typical starting step in the Japanese art of origami.

3. **Graphs,** including bar graphs and line graphs, show changes or trends over time. In a graph, the horizontal line, called an axis, represents points in time such as hours, days, or years. The vertical axis shows quantities or amounts. When you read graphs, check to see that the amounts on the axes are clearly marked. Also, look at the starting points of both axes to help you read the graph correctly. Notice that the same information is presented in the following bar graph and line graph.

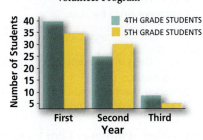

Number of Students Tutored Through Volunteer Program

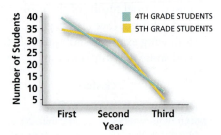

Number of Students Tutored Through Volunteer Program

4. **Tables** give information in a simple way. Tables do not include symbols or graphics that show patterns in the information. Instead, readers must think carefully about the information found in a table and draw their own conclusions. For example, a reader might conclude based on the following table that the number of volunteer tutors increases every year.

Number of Volunteers in the Peer Tutoring Program	
First year	8
Second year	10
Third year	15

5. **Time lines** place events in order as they take place over a period of time. In the example below, the events are identified below the time line, while segments of time are shown above it.

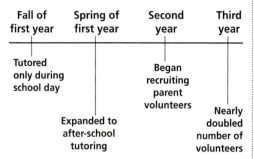

Development of the Tutoring Program

- **Viewing tips** When you come across graphics or visuals, stop and examine the information. Use the tips below to help you understand graphics.
  1. Read the title, labels, and legend of a graphic before you try to analyze the information.
  2. Draw your own conclusions from the graphic and compare them to the writer's conclusions.
  3. Ask yourself if the graphic might be leaving out information. Sometimes, an author leaves out information that does not agree with his or her conclusions.

Vocabulary

Skills and Strategies

You can use the following skills and strategies to become a more effective reader.

Context Clues One way to figure out the meaning of an unfamiliar word is by finding clues in its *context,* the words and sentences surrounding it. This chart shows some of the most common types of context clues. (See also page 25.)

How to Use Context Clues

Type of Clue

Definitions and Restatements: Look for the meaning of the unfamiliar word restated in other words somewhere in the sentence.

*Dionne's little brother continued to **aggravate** her, doing all the things that bother her.* [*Aggravate* must mean "bother."]

Examples: Look for an example that gives you clues to the meaning of the unfamiliar word.

*Malik had many **aspirations,** such as his dream of being a doctor.* [*Aspirations* must be "dreams."]

Synonyms: Look for a word that has a similar meaning used in the context.

*The **faculty** of our school is well-educated. Most of the teachers have advanced degrees.* [*Faculty* must mean "teachers."]

(continued)

(continued)

How to Use Context Clues
Type of Clue
Antonyms or Contrasts: Look for words that have an opposite meaning of the unfamiliar word. *My favorite aunt is **eccentric**. Her attitudes are anything but typical.* [*Eccentric* must mean "not typical."]
Cause and Effect: Look for clues that an unfamiliar word is related to the cause or is the result of a cause. *When Jaime **ridiculed** my hat, I felt embarrassed and took it off.* [*Ridicule* must mean "make fun of."]

Word Bank You can create a *word bank* by making a list of unfamiliar words you encounter. Creating your own word bank can help you improve your vocabulary. When you add a word to your bank, look up its definition in the dictionary. You might keep your word bank in a notebook or in a computer file.

Word Meanings The meanings of words change over time or in the situations in which they are used. You always want your words to say exactly what you mean. The following definitions and examples can help.

- **Clichés and tired words** A *cliché* is an overused expression. These expressions were once fresh and expressive, but their overuse has made them seem dull and tired. Clichés weaken your writing.

  EXAMPLES *fresh as a daisy, easy as pie, so hungry I could eat a horse*

A *tired word* has been used so often and so carelessly that it has become worn out and almost meaningless.

EXAMPLES *nice, fine, pretty, terrific*

- **Denotation and connotation** A word's direct, "dictionary" definition is called its **denotation.** Words also have a **connotation,** the emotional meanings a word suggests. Connotations can have powerful effects on readers and listeners.

  EXAMPLES The words *firm* and *strict* have very similar denotations. However, *firm* has the positive connotation of being stable. *Strict* has more a negative connotation of being harsh and severe.

- **Figurative language** *Figurative language* is the imaginative use of words and phrases to describe one thing by comparing it to something else. Figurative language requires the reader to look beyond the literal, or usual, meaning of the words.

Type of Figurative Language	Example
A **metaphor** directly compares one thing to another.	*Daisies are little suns shining in a field.*
Personification uses human characteristics to describe non-human things.	*The plants stretched their arms toward the sun.*
A **simile** compares two different things using the words *like* or *as*.	*The dancers floated across the floor like leaves blowing in the wind.*

Reading and Vocabulary

- **Idioms** *Idioms* are phrases with a different meaning than each word's literal, or usual, meaning. Idioms are frequently common to a particular region, culture, or time period. They cannot be explained grammatically or translated word-for-word.

    EXAMPLES

    She was *sitting on pins and needles* as she waited.
    Jim went *out on a limb* and asked another question.
    Last night Sarah and Javier went out and *cut a rug*.

- **Loaded words** *Loaded words* are terms that are used to have a strong positive or negative impact on the reader or listener. Loaded words can be very persuasive since they appeal to the reader's or listener's emotions.

    EXAMPLES

    Leah *frowned* at her dog's *misbehavior*.
    Leah *scowled* at her dog's *disobedience*.

- **Multiple meanings** Many words have several different meanings. To determine which meaning is being used, look at the word's context. If you still have difficulty figuring out the meaning, look up the word in the dictionary and read each meaning. Then, try each meaning in the sentence to pick the correct one. (See also page 56.)

    EXAMPLE As we sailed out on the choppy waves of the lake, my brother looked *green*.
    green (grēn) *adj.* **1.** relating to the color found in grass and plants; **2.** naive and inexperienced; **3.** sickly and nauseated [The third definition best fits the context.]

Word Origins See **The History of English** on page 690.

Word Parts Many words in English are made up of smaller **word parts.** These word parts are known as *roots, prefixes,* and *suffixes*. Knowing the meanings of word parts can help you understand the meanings of unfamiliar words.

- **Roots** The *root* is the foundation on which a word is built. The root contains the word's basic meaning. Prefixes and suffixes are added to the root. (See also page 196.)

Commonly Used Roots		
Root	Meaning	Example
–audio–	hearing, sound	audience
–bibli–, –biblio–	book	bibliography
–log(ue)–, –logy–	study, word	geology
–magni–	large	magnificent
–micro–	small	microscope
–ped–	foot	pedestrian
–phon–	sound	telephone

- **Prefixes** A *prefix* is a word part that is added before a root. When a prefix is added to a root, the word it forms is a combination of the prefix and the root meaning. (See also page 126.)

QUICK REFERENCE HANDBOOK

TEACHING TIP

Words to Learn
For more help with vocabulary instruction, see the *Vocabulary Workshop* program. *Vocabulary Workshop* includes vocabulary instruction and practice with the three hundred words that make up the Words to Learn list.

Commonly Used Prefixes

Prefix	Meaning	Example
anti–	against, opposing	antiwar
bi–	two	bicycle
dis–	away, opposing	disagree
mis–	wrong	mistake
non–	not	nonfat
over–	above, too much	overdone
pre–	before	preread
re–	again	replace
semi–	half	semicircle
sub–	under	submarine
un–	not	unhappy

■ **Suffixes** A *suffix* is a word part that is added after a root. Adding a suffix may change both a word's meaning and its part of speech, as in *joy/joyful*. (See also page 126.)

Commonly Used Suffixes

Suffix	Meaning	Example
–able	can, will	respectable
–dom	state, condition	kingdom
–en	make	weaken
–ful	full of	stressful
–hood	state, condition	neighborhood
–ish	suggesting, like	feverish
–less	without	penniless
–ly	characteristic of	quickly
–ment	result, act of	commitment
–ness	quality, state	goodness, sadness
–ous	characterized by	luxurious

Words to Learn You can study the 300 words below to improve your vocabulary this year. Try to learn as many unfamiliar words from this list as you can.

abdomen
absorb
abundant
acquire
adjust
amateur
ambitious
analyze
anthem
apologize
applaud
application
appreciate
appropriate
architect
arid
associate
assume
astonish
aviation

ballot
barrier
benefit
betray
biography
boast

bombard
Braille
bureau

campaign
candidate
captivity
career
caution
ceremony
characteristic
collapse
collide
commotion
competition
complaint
complex
compliment
conceal
conduct
conference
congratulate
conscience
consent
contrast
contribute
conviction

716 Quick Reference Handbook Reading and Vocabulary

cooperate
corporation
counterfeit
courteous
cultivate

dainty
debate
debt
decrease
definite
demonstration
deny
departure
descendant
descriptive
desirable
desperate
destination
detect
determination
disadvantage
disastrous
discomfort
discourage
disguise
disgust
dissolve
district
disturb
document
doubtful
doubtless
dramatic
dread
duplicate

earnest
eavesdrop
eliminate
employer
engage
entertain
envy

error
escort
essential
establish
eternal
exception
exclaim
exert
export
extraordinary

fatal
feat
flammable
flexible
flourish
foe
foul
foundation
fragrant
frantic
furious

gasp
generation
generous
genuine
glimpse
gorgeous
gossip
gratitude
guidance

hazard
hearty
heir
heroic
hesitate
hibernate
hoist
honorable

identical
ignite
imitate

impatience
import
impostor
inaccurate
incident
inexpensive
inform
inhale
innumerable
inspiration
instinct
interrupt
interview
intrusion
investment
inviting
involve
irregular
issue

jeopardy
journalism
justify
juvenile

keen
knapsack

legend
leisure
license
linger
locally
lunar
luscious
luxurious

majority
mammoth
management
marvel
maximum
merchandise
migrate
miraculous

mobile
mourning

navigator
nominate
notion
nuisance
numerous

oath
obvious
occasion
offense
offspring
omit
ordinary
ornamental

paralysis
particle
persuade
pharmacy
pierce
plead
plot
pollute
portion
possess
precipitation
predict
prehistoric
previous
prey
privacy
profession
prohibit
promotion
protest
portrait
provoke
pry
publicity

qualify
quantity

Vocabulary 717

QUICK REFERENCE HANDBOOK

quarantine
quote

ransom
rash
reaction
realm
rebel
receipt
reckless
reduction
reference
regret
regulate
rehearsal
reign
relate
reliable
remedy
request
requirement
resemble

reservoir
resident
resign
respectable
responsibility
revolution
routine

sacrifice
satisfy
scheme
scholar
security
self-confidence
self-respect
separation
session
severe
simplify
solitary
specify
static

stray
suburbs
summarize
superior
surgery
survey
survival
suspicion
symbol
sympathy

temporary
tension
terminal
terrain
text
theme
thorough
threat
toll
toxic
tradition

tragedy
transparent
twilight

unexpectedly
unfavorable
unfortunate
unite
urge

vacuum
vault
vicinity
victim
victorious
villain
visual
vivid
vocal

wardrobe
widespread

yacht

Speaking and Listening

Speaking

You probably enjoy having conversations with your friends. You can build on the skills you use in conversations to develop new speaking skills for different situations. Use the strategies in this section to become a more effective speaker.

Formal Speaking

In formal speaking, a specific time and place are set aside for someone to give a presentation to a group. The purpose of this presentation may be to inform, to persuade, to discuss problems and solutions, or to entertain.

Content and Organization of a Presentation
The following steps can help you create an effective presentation.

1. **Choose a topic.** Sometimes, your topic will be assigned. However, when you are free to choose your own topic, try one or more of these ideas.
   - Consider turning a piece you have written into a presentation.
   - Brainstorm a list of topics.
   - Re-read your journal to find ideas.
   - Ask friends, family members and teachers for ideas.
   - Look through magazines and newspapers.
2. **Identify the purpose and occasion of your presentation.** Your *purpose* is why you are speaking—what you want your presentation to accomplish. The purpose of your presentation will help you determine your word choice and usage (formal or informal). Here are some common purposes for presentations.

Purposes for Presentations	
Purpose	**Examples of Presentation Titles**
To inform give facts, explain how to do something, or present a problem and propose a solution	• Life Aboard a Covered Wagon • How to Choose a Bike Helmet • How We Can Protect Coral Reefs

(continued)

(continued)

Purposes for Presentations	
Purpose	**Examples of Presentation Titles**
To persuade attempt to change opinions or get listeners to take action	• Where's Our School Spirit? • Hidden Dangers on the Playground
To entertain share a funny or interesting story or event	• A Birthday to Remember • My First Home Run

The *occasion* is the event or situation that prompts you to speak. Often, the occasion may be a class assignment. At other times it may be a meeting of a club you belong to or an awards ceremony. Reviewing what you know about the occasion will help you prepare a presentation. For example, think about the date, the time of day, the place, and how much time you will have.

3. **Think about your audience.** Knowing the occasion will give you a general idea of who your audience will be. Consider your listeners' needs and interests and use words they will understand. The questions in the following chart can help you. Your answers may also help you decide on your *point of view,* or the way you will approach your topic.

Analyzing Your Audience		
Question	**If your answer is . . .**	**Your presentation should . . .**
How much does the audience already know about the topic?	not much	provide background information about the topic
	some	connect information the audience may not know to what they already know
	a lot	share new and interesting information
How interested in the topic do you think the audience will be?	very interested	keep the audience interested by spacing out surprising ideas or information
	a little interested	get the audience more interested by beginning with a question or a surprising fact
	not interested	show the audience how the topic affects them personally

Speaking and Listening

4. **Gather information.** For some topics, you can draw information from your own experience or papers you have already written. For others, you may need to do research. You can read newspapers and magazines, check the Internet, or talk to people who know the topic well. (See also **Library/Media Center** on page 694.)

5. **Organize your information.** Organizing your ideas for a presentation is like arranging information for a written paper. You will include an introduction that states your main idea, support your main idea with evidence, examples, and elaboration, and summarize your main points in a conclusion. Below is an example of a plan for a specific kind of presentation, one that explores a problem and a possible solution.
   - Define the problem.
   - Support your definition with evidence (reasons, facts, and the opinions of experts).
   - Present your ideas about the problem's causes (*Why is this happening?*) and effects (*What are the results?*).
   - Suggest a solution, and show how it is connected to the problem.
   - Present evidence showing why your solution is a good one.

   See the Writing Workshops in this book for ways to arrange information for other purposes.

6. **Make note cards.** Each note card for your speech should have notes on only one major point and include supporting details that elaborate on that point. Make a special note on the card to remind you when to show or refer to a visual in your speech. Number your note cards to help you keep them in order.

7. **Use media.** Consider including media such as visuals or sounds in your speech if they will make your ideas clearer or help listeners remember an important point. Media should be easy for you to use and easy for your audience to see, hear, and understand. Otherwise, you may lose your train of thought or confuse your listeners. Here are forms of media you might consider using.
   - electronic media, including Web pages
   - audio recordings such as CDs or cassettes
   - audiovisual recordings, including videotapes, videodiscs, and short films
   - slides or filmstrips
   - traditional visuals such as charts, graphs, illustrations, and diagrams

   (See also **Creating Visuals to Share Information** on pages 220–221.)

Delivery of a Presentation These steps will help you give your presentation.

1. **Practice.** Practice your presentation until you are sure you know it well. Ask friends or family members to listen to your speech and suggest ways to make it better. If you plan to use visuals or other media, be sure to include them in your practice.

TEACHING TIP

Deliver Your Presentation
Remind students that they may need to adjust verbal elements for the speech to fit the audience or setting. Make the concept vivid by having students imagine these audiences and settings: a large group of elementary school students in a cafeteria early in the morning and a small group of parents in a corner of the library after school. Have students act out the following line, in the role of someone speaking to each group:

"I'd like to explain our new tutoring program to you."

How would the rate, volume, pitch, and tone vary for each of these audiences? How would the location affect these verbal elements? What adjustments might need to be made when speaking to a group early in the morning (to capture their interest) or after a full day of work or school (to avoid annoying them)? Why? Have students explain their interpretations of the line.

---

2. **Deliver your presentation.** Use these tips to help you deliver your presentation effectively.

- *Stay calm and confident.* Before you begin speaking, take a deep breath. Stand up straight, look alert, and pay attention to what you are saying.
- *Use body language.* The chart below lists nonverbal signals, or body language, that will add to your message.

Nonverbal Signals
Eye contact
Look into the eyes of your audience members
Purposes
▪ Shows that you are honest or sincere
▪ Keeps audience's attention
Facial expression
Smile, frown, raise an eyebrow
Purposes
▪ Shows your feelings
▪ Emphasizes parts of your message
Gestures
Give thumbs up, shrug, nod, or shake your head
Purposes
▪ Emphasizes your point
▪ Adds meaning to the speech
Posture
Stand tall and straight
Purpose
▪ Shows that you are sure of yourself

- *Use your voice effectively.* Here are verbal elements to consider as you practice and deliver your speech. You may adjust these elements depending on your **audience** and the **setting**. For example, you might use a soothing tone with children. If you are giving a morning talk, you might vary your pitch to capture your audience's attention.

Verbal Element	Definition
Diction	Pronounce words clearly, or *enunciate*. Speak carefully so that your listeners can understand you.
Mood (or tone)	Your speech or oral interpretation may make your listeners feel a certain emotion. Making listeners feel happy, angry, or sad about what you are saying can help them remember your points better.
Pitch	Your voice rises and falls naturally when you speak. If you are nervous, your voice may get higher. To control your pitch, take deep breaths and stay calm as you give your speech.
Rate (or tempo)	In conversations you may speak at a fast rate, or speed. When you make a speech, you should talk more slowly to help listeners understand you.
Volume	Even if you normally speak quietly, you will need to speak loudly in a formal speech. Listeners at the back of the room should be able to hear you clearly.

- *Use standard English.* Pronounce words correctly, and use correct grammar. You should avoid using slang or jargon. If you use any technical terms in your speech, define them for your listeners.

Other Formal Speaking Situations

Here are two other types of formal speeches and strategies you might use to give each type of speech.

- **Making an announcement** An *announcement* is a short speech that provides information to a group of listeners. Often, it includes instructions about a current situation or an upcoming event. Write out your message ahead of time, and use the following tips.

How to Make an Announcement

1. Include all the important facts. Most announcements provide the following information:
   - the kind of event or situation
   - who is involved in the event or situation
   - the time and location of the event or situation
   - why the event is important
   - any special information, such as the cost of admission
2. Add interesting details that will catch your listeners' attention.
3. Announce your message slowly, clearly, and briefly.
4. If necessary, repeat the most important facts.

- **Introducing a speaker** To introduce a speaker to an audience, identify the speaker and tell listeners a little about his or her background. Your introduction should also prepare the audience to hear what the speaker has to say. Make the speaker feel welcome, but keep your comments brief.

Informal Speaking

When you speak informally, you do not plan in advance what you will say. The guidelines that follow will help you to speak more effectively in discussions and in social situations.

Group Discussion Group discussions are an important part of many clubs and classes. To get the most from such discussions, follow these tips.

1. **Set a purpose.** Setting a purpose will help your group identify what you need to accomplish in the time you have. This purpose may be
   - to connect ideas, insights, and experiences with others
   - to cooperate in gaining information
   - to solve a problem
   - to reach a decision or recommend a course of action
2. **Assign roles.** Each person in the group has a role to play. For example, your group may choose a chairperson, whose role is to keep the discussion moving smoothly. Another person may be named the recorder. This person's role is to take notes of what is said during

Cooperative Learning

Group Discussion. Have students practice listening and speaking in groups on the topic of culture. Ask each student to identify a culture to which he or she belongs. (This response could be as broad as "American" or as specific as "skateboarders.") Then, have students give at least one example of an experience he or she has had as a member of that culture. Finally, ask students to share insights about what "culture" means, based on their experiences as members of particular groups. (One definition is "the customary beliefs and social practices of religious or social groups.")

Prior to the discussion, provide instruction about the process of collaboratively composing, organizing, and revising a record of group discussion. Different members of the group should take responsibility for different stages of development. For example, the student designated as the recorder will take notes during the discussion. After the discussion, another group member may organize the notes in logical order (for example, by grouping similar ideas about culture together), and a third can revise them, incorporating suggestions from the group and then sharing the notes with the class.

the discussion. No matter what your role in the group is, use the guidelines in the following chart to contribute effectively to the discussion.

> **Guidelines for Group Discussions**
>
> **1. Prepare for the discussion.** If you know what topic your group will discuss, find out some information about the topic ahead of time.
>
> **2. Listen to what others say.** Be willing to learn from the other members of your group. Do not interrupt when someone is speaking. Instead, listen and wait until it is your turn to speak.
>
> **3. Do your part.** Contribute to the discussion by sharing your ideas and knowledge. Encourage other members of the group to do the same.
>
> **4. Stay on the discussion topic.** Although the discussion may give you other, related ideas, keep your group's purpose in mind. You can make a note for yourself about an idea, but only discuss ideas that fit your group's topic and purpose.
>
> **5. Ask questions.** If you are not sure you understand the point a member of your group is making, ask him or her to explain it more clearly. Others in the group may also be confused.

Speaking Socially

In any social situation, remember to speak politely and clearly. The following strategies will help.

- **Giving directions or instructions** When you need to give directions or explain how to do something, make sure your directions or instructions are clear and complete. Here are some pointers.

> **How to Give Directions or Instructions**
>
> **1.** Before you give information, plan what you want to say. Think of the information as a series of steps.
>
> **2.** Explain the steps in order. Be sure you have not skipped any steps or left out important details.
>
> **3.** If necessary, repeat all of the steps to be sure your listener understands them.

- **Making introductions** Use these tips to introduce people who do not know each other or to introduce yourself to someone new.

> **How to Make Introductions**
>
> **1.** You can use first names if you are introducing people your own age. ("Mirha, this is Josh.")
>
> **2.** Speak first to the older person of the people you are introducing. ("Dad, this is my friend Keisha.")
>
> **3.** Introduce yourself to others if no one introduces you first. Start a conversation by asking a question.
>
> **4.** When you need to introduce someone to a large group of people, introduce him or her to just a few people at a time. ("Class, this is Gordon Delgado. Gordon, meet Letrice, Michael, and Bao.")
>
> **5.** If someone you are meeting offers to shake your hand, do so. You may offer to shake hands with someone your own age.
>
> **6.** Mention something the two people you are introducing to each other have in common. ("Trey, meet my cousin Li. Li runs as much as you do.")

- **Speaking on the telephone** It is important to use the telephone courteously. Here are some suggestions.

Guidelines for Telephoning

1. Call at a time that is convenient for the person you are calling.

2. Be sure to dial the correct number. If you reach a wrong number, apologize for the error.

3. Speak clearly. Say who you are when the phone is answered. If the person you are calling is not there, you may want to leave your name, phone number, and a short message.

4. Do not stay on the telephone too long.

Oral Interpretation

An *oral interpretation* is a dramatic reading of a written piece. The purpose of the reading is to entertain.

1. Choose a selection. Poems, short stories, and plays can provide you with good material for an oral interpretation.

Type of Literature	Characteristics of a Good Selection
Poem	- tells a story (an epic or a narrative poem) - has a speaker (uses the word *I*) or has dialogue (a conversation between characters) - expresses a particular emotion
Short story	- has a beginning, middle, and end - has characters whose words you can act out (a narrator who tells the story or characters who talk to one another)
Play	- has a beginning, middle, and end - has one or more characters with dialogue

When you choose a selection, think about the occasion. Should you be serious, or can you have some fun? How much time will you have? Also, consider your audience. Will your listeners find the selection interesting? Will they understand its meaning?

2. Adapt the material. Sometimes, you may need to shorten a story, poem, or play to make it work as an oral interpretation. To make a shortened version, or ***cutting,*** follow these suggestions.

How to Make a Cutting

1. Decide where the part of the selection you want to use should begin and end. Follow that part of the story in time order.

2. Cut dialogue tags, such as *she said*.

3. Cut out parts that do not have anything to do with the part of the story you are telling.

3. **Present your interpretation.** Once you have chosen a selection, you can use the following guidelines to help you present it.
   - *Prepare a reading script.* A *reading script* is a neatly typed or handwritten copy of the selection marked to show exactly how you will present it.

How to Mark a Reading Script
1. Underline words or phrases you plan to stress.
2. Use a slash (/) to show each pause.
3. Make notes in the margin about when you will raise or lower your voice, use gestures, or create a particular mood.

   - *Write an introduction.* You may need to introduce your interpretation to your audience. In your introduction, you can tell what happened before your scene in the story, describe the characters involved, or tell listeners from whose point of view the story is being told (one of the characters, for example).
   - *Practice.* Rehearse your selection carefully. Practice reading the material aloud, using voice tone, movements, and emphasis, or stress. Think about how you can make the meaning and mood of the selection clear to your audience. Practice in front of a friend or family member or in front of a mirror until you feel confident about your presentation.

Self-Evaluation

Evaluating means judging. Evaluating your formal speaking is a good way to improve your speaking skills. When you can judge what went well and what did not, you can focus on the areas that need work. After you give a speech or present an oral interpretation, take some time to review your performance. Coming up with a set of *evaluation criteria,* or standards, will help you cover all the bases. In general, evaluation criteria for speaking should look at

- content (what you say—"Did I state a main idea and support it with evidence? Were the media I used easy to see, hear, and understand? Did I handle them well?")
- organization (how you group and order your ideas—"Did I explain my ideas in a clear and logical way?")
- delivery (how you use language and present your ideas)

To come up with specific criteria for delivery, look at the charts on page 722. Ask a question about each of the important ideas covered. For the term *rate,* for example, you might ask "Did I speak at a steady rate?"

You can use these criteria during practice sessions as well as after you speak. They will help you to measure your progress during the year and judge for yourself just how far you have come as a speaker. (See also the **Points to Evaluate** chart on page 731.)

Listening

Active listening means making sense of the information you hear. Becoming an active listener will help you understand and evaluate a speaker's ideas.

Basics of the Listening Process

Like reading, listening is a process. Here are strategies you can use before, during, and after listening to get the most from a spoken message.

Before Listening Take these steps before you begin to listen.

1. **Know why you are listening.** You will be a more effective listener if you remember your purpose for listening. The amount of attention you give to a speaker depends on your purpose for listening. For example, you would probably pay closer attention to your teacher giving directions than to friends discussing a topic that does not interest you. Some common purposes for listening are
   - for enjoyment, entertainment, or appreciation
   - for information or explanation
   - for forming opinions or evaluating ideas

2. **Limit distractions.** Listening is not always easy. The room you are in may be too hot or too cold or too stuffy. You may have other things on your mind. These guidelines will help you make the best of the situation.

Eliminating Barriers to Effective Listening

Stay positive, and focus on the speaker. As you sit down, clear your mind to help you concentrate on what the speaker will say.

Adjust to your surroundings. Be sure to sit where you can see and hear the speaker well.

Prepare to think about the message. Focus on what the speaker is saying, not on how he or she looks, talks, stands, or moves.

Listening to a Speaker Follow these guidelines to be a courteous and effective listener.

- Look at the speaker, and pay attention.
- Do not interrupt the speaker. Do not whisper, fidget, or make distracting noises or movements.
- Respect the speaker's race, accent, clothing, customs, and religion.
- Try to understand the speaker's point of view. Remember that your own point of view or attitude toward the topic affects your judgment.
- Listen to the entire message before you form an opinion about it.
- Take notes. Do not try to write down every word. Instead, focus on the speaker's most important details. (See also **Notes** on page 734.)

TEACHING TIP

Before Listening
Students may have trouble determining their purposes for listening. Tell students that their purpose will often be influenced by to whom or what they are listening. For example, if students are listening to a teacher, they will probably be listening for information; if they are attending a poetry reading, they will probably be listening for appreciation.

To help students determine the purposes for listening, provide examples of a variety of listening situations. Then, have students figure out which purpose suits which of the following situations.

- a teacher is about to give instructions on how to convert a decimal into a fraction
- a political candidate is about to give a speech on why you should vote for her
- a librarian is about to read a story to young children
- a friend is about to describe his new pet

To give students practice listening for a number of purposes, arrange students in groups of four or five and have each group member read a short piece of writing of his or her choice. After each reading, group members should discuss their purposes for listening to the piece. Encourage students to provide reasons for their choices.

Responding to a Speaker Your role as a listener does not end when a presentation is over. Here are some ways to respond to the speaker and add to your understanding of the topic.

- Ask questions. If you did not understand something the speaker said, ask about it. The speaker's response to your question can clear up any confusion, which can help you and others.
- Give positive feedback. Point out one or two things the speaker did well. If you disagree with the speaker's message, find something else to praise, such as the use of media.
- Give constructive criticism. Politely point out something the speaker could do even better the next time.
- Use body language to give positive feedback. Listen to the questions and answers that follow the presentation. Stay seated until the speaker turns to leave.
- Compare your response to the presentation with the responses of others. You may gain a new insight or help someone else gain one.

Listening with a Purpose

Different strategies can help you achieve different purposes for listening. The strategies that follow will help you listen more effectively to appreciate (or be entertained), to comprehend (or understand), and to evaluate a speech.

Listening to Appreciate When you listen to appreciate, you are listening to enjoy what you hear. Usually, you listen to literature or oral tradition for appreciation.

- **Listening to literature** In a way, listening to literature is like reading it yourself. In both situations, you carry out a process, or series of steps.

Listening to Literature

Before you listen

- Preview the work by asking questions. What kind of literature is it—a story, a poem, a play? What is the title? Who wrote it? What is it about?
- Make **predictions** about what you will hear. (A prediction is a guess based on what you already know.) Do not worry about whether your predictions are correct. Making them is a way of sharpening your focus, not a test you must pass.

As you listen

- Picture the characters, actions, and scenes the writer describes.
- Identify the **tone** (the writer's attitude toward the topic) and the **mood** (the emotions, or feelings, the work creates in the listener).
- Connect the work with your own life. Which experiences or feelings seem similar to ones you have had?
- Jot down questions or comments the work brings to mind. Are there any parts you do not understand? What would you like to ask the writer?

Listening to Literature

After you listen

- Respond personally to the work. What did you like or dislike about it? How did it make you feel? What did you learn from it?
- Summarize the selection. What happened in the selection? What did you learn about life from listening to this work?
- Confirm or adjust your predictions. Which ones were right on target? Which ones did you need to change and in what ways?
- Identify how the writer uses elements of literature, such as rhyme, suspense, and imagery. How did these elements help shape the work?

■ **Listening to oral tradition** *Oral traditions* are messages that are passed down from older people to younger people through the spoken word. These messages often take the form of folk tales and songs that use stories to teach a moral—a lesson for living—or to pass down history or culture. The following tips will help you be an active listener when you have the chance to hear such stories.

Strategies for Listening to Oral Tradition

1. **Compare the elements of literature in different stories.** Many folk tales and folk songs have similar characters, settings, plots, and themes. As you listen, recall stories you know that have similar elements. How are the stories alike, and how are they different?

2. **Compare how storytellers use language.** A storyteller sometimes uses labels (names for objects or ideas) or sayings that reflect his or her culture or region. For example, depending on a storyteller's region, he or she might use the label *stoop* or *porch* to mean a covered entrance to a house. As you listen to a speaker from a different region or culture, compare his or her sayings and labels with your own.

3. **Compare the way the story is told in different regions.** Among Native Americans, for example, trickster tales appear widely. Depending on the region, though, the main character—the trickster—could be a raven, a coyote, a mink, a blue jay, a rabbit, a spider, or a human. Often, the geography, wildlife, or weather patterns mentioned are clues to where the story (or the storyteller) is originally from.

Listening to Comprehend Use the steps in the chart below and the strategies on the next page to help you get information from a message you hear.

How to Listen for Information

Find the major ideas.

Identify the most important points the speaker makes. Listen for clue words, such as *major* or *most important*.

Identify supporting evidence.

How does the speaker support the main idea? What details does the speaker emphasize with gestures, visuals, or verbal cues, like "for example"?

(continued)

Meeting INDIVIDUAL NEEDS

MULTIPLE INTELLIGENCES
Linguistic Intelligence. Inform students that the language a person uses when telling a story may depend on the speaker's region of origin. He or she might say "hoagie" rather than "submarine sandwich," for example.

List the following items on the chalkboard: *cornbread, faucet, tennis shoes, bucket,* and *sack.* Then, have students copy the list and ask people from other regions what they call each item. If students find someone who calls the item something different, they should write the new word and the person's place of origin next to the original word on the list. Have students share their findings with the class.

TEACHING TIP

Strategies for Listening to Oral Tradition
Find two oral traditions from different regions that each have an animal "trickster" as a main character, such as an African American tale involving Brer Rabbit and an African tale about Ananse, the Spider. Read the stories aloud. Then, ask questions about the similarities found in the two stories.

1. Why do you think the African American story used a rabbit and the African story used a spider? [Possible answer: Rabbits are common animals in the South; spiders are common in Africa.]
2. What do the trickster animals in each story have in common? [Possible answer: They both use the power of intelligence to trick a more powerful foe.]
3. Why do you think stories like these were so popular with Africans and African Americans? [Possible answer: They could identify with the plight of the less powerful, yet intelligent, character.]

Meeting INDIVIDUAL NEEDS

LEARNERS HAVING DIFFICULTY
Have students practice listening to learn by reading aloud from a selection and having them take notes on it. To prepare students to take notes, suggest that they use either an outline or a conceptual map to organize the ideas in the selection. Then, have students write down their purpose for listening.

Review the strategies listed in the chart titled "How to Listen for Information." Emphasize the instructions for identifying the major ideas and supporting evidence and for distinguishing fact from opinion. Tell students to listen for words that signal an opinion, such as *should, ought, best, worst, I think,* and *I feel;* to note opinions; and to mark them with an *O.*

Informative texts from which you might read include the Writer's Models on pp. 67 and 211, the Reading Selections on pp. 121 or 229, or another text containing information you would like your class to learn. Read aloud the selection a few paragraphs at a time, and ask students to summarize orally the major ideas. Finally, allow students to use their notes during a quiz on the material in the selection.

MULTIPLE INTELLIGENCES
Interpersonal Intelligence. Give students a chance to practice their listening skills by reading aloud a set of directions for them to follow. Choose a landmark that requires only five or six steps to reach from your school. Read the directions to the class, and encourage students to use the LQ2R method to jot down the directions as they hear them. You may want to draw a map on the chalkboard after students have taken their notes so that they can check the accuracy of their directions. Then, have students meet in small groups to compare their notes and add or correct information.

(continued)

How to Listen for Information

Distinguish between facts and opinions.
A fact is a statement that can be proved to be true. An opinion is a belief or judgment about something. It cannot be proved to be true.

Listen for comparisons and contrasts.
The speaker may emphasize a point or explain an idea by comparing or contrasting it to something familiar to you.

Pay attention to causes and effects.
Does the speaker say or hint that some events cause others to happen? Does the speaker suggest that some events are the results of other events?

Predict outcomes and draw conclusions.
Connect the speaker's words and ideas to your own experiences. What conclusions can you draw about the topic? What might happen as a result of events the speaker discusses?

■ **LQ2R** The LQ2R study method is especially helpful when you are listening to a speaker who is giving information.

L *Listen* carefully to information as it is presented.

Q *Question* yourself as you listen. Make a list of your questions as you think of them.

R *Recite* to yourself, in your own words, the answers to your questions as the speaker presents them. Summarize the information in your mind, or jot down notes as you listen.

R *Relisten* as the speaker concludes the presentation. The speaker may repeat the major points of the speech.

■ *5W-How?* **questions** When you are listening for details, try to sort out information that answers the basic *5W-How?* questions: *Who? What? When? Where? Why?* and *How?* For example, when you are introduced to someone new, you may want to listen for the person's name (*Who?*) and their hometown (*Where?*).

■ **Listening to instructions and directions** Instructions and directions are usually made up of a series of steps. To understand the steps, follow these guidelines.

How to Listen to Instructions

1. Listen to each step. Listen for words that tell you when each step ends and the next one begins—for example, *first, second, next, then,* and *last.*

2. Listen for the number of steps required and the order you should follow. Take notes if necessary.

3. In your mind, make an outline of the steps you should follow. Then, picture yourself completing each step in order.

4. Make sure you have all the information you need and understand the instructions. Ask questions if you are not sure about a particular step.

5. If the situation allows, repeat the instructions back to the speaker. Listen to any further corrections or comments the speaker makes.

Listening to Interpret and Evaluate
Evaluating a presentation involves judging its content, organization, delivery, and believability. The questions in the chart on the next page will help you.

Points to Interpret and Evaluate

Content and Organization

Interpret the speaker's message and purpose
- Can you sum up the main idea?
- Why is the speaker giving the presentation?

Evaluate how clearly the content was organized
- Does the speaker explain ideas in a clear and logical order?
- Can you list each of the main points?

Delivery

Evaluate the speaker's use of verbal and visual elements
- Did the speaker speak loudly and clearly?
- Did the speaker use visuals? If so, did the speaker handle them well? Were the visuals clear and easy to understand?

Evaluate the use of nonverbal elements
- Did the speaker use body language—posture, gestures, facial expressions?
- Did the nonverbal elements match the speaker's words? For example, did the speaker use hand gestures or a raised voice when making an important point?

Believability (Content + Delivery = Believability)

Interpret the speaker's perspective or point of view
- What is the speaker's attitude toward the topic?

Analyze the speaker's techniques
- Did the speaker try to *convince* by using reasons and evidence or *sell* his or her point by appealing to listeners' emotions? Did the speaker use propaganda? (See page 751.)

Special Listening Situations

Group Discussion See page 723.

Interviews An *interview* is a good way to gather firsthand information for a project or a report. The suggestions that follow can help when you interview.

How to Conduct an Interview

Before the interview
- Make an appointment with the person you would like to interview. Make sure you arrive on time.
- Decide what you want to know.
- Make a list of questions. Avoid questions that require only yes or no answers.

During the interview
- Listen carefully. Be respectful, even if you disagree with the person.
- Take notes. If you do not understand something, ask questions about it.
- Thank the person before you leave.

After the interview
- Make sure your notes are clear.
- Write a summary as soon as you can.

TEACHING TIP

Points to Interpret and Evaluate
Provide students with a persuasive audio message to evaluate, such as a radio ad or an editorial. Review the persuasive techniques on p. 257. As students listen, have them answer the questions in the chart on p. 731, using the following pointers:

- **content and organization**—To interpret the speaker's message, students should first understand that the speaker's purpose is to persuade them to do or believe something. Have students identify the speaker's perspective on the topic by listening for opinion clue words such as *should, ought to,* and *I think*. Students should also consider whether the speaker is trying to convince listeners to share his or her opinion or to sell a product. What propaganda or persuasive techniques are used in the message? To evaluate the speaker's support for his or her opinion, students should consider whether the speaker uses facts that can be proved or only more opinions. Only an expert opinion is strong enough to serve as evidence.

- **delivery**—Have students consider what the delivery adds to the message. Does it make ideas clearer? Students should monitor their understanding of the message to decide whether the speaker's delivery makes the message easier to understand or more confusing.

- **believability**—Students should understand that the believability, or credibility, of a speaker depends on both content and delivery, but is based on an overall impression rather than several specific points. Have students discuss the speaker's believability, comparing their ideas and perceptions and giving reasons for them.

COOPERATIVE LEARNING

Discussion. Have students help each other analyze how listening experiences vary depending on the listener's preferences and purpose. Divide the class into four groups to discuss listening to narrative, dramatic/poetic, persuasive, or informative selections. To prepare for the discussion, have students complete these two steps.

1. Have students choose and tape-record themselves reading aloud a short narrative, persuasive, dramatic/poetic, or informative selection (for example, a published piece or a speech written for school). Students should label tapes with the title, author, or subject of the selection. Alternatively, choose pre-recorded selections from each of these categories.

2. Students should then choose to listen to a selection. From the tapes at the listening station, students may choose a specific reading based on its title, author, or subject. Before they listen, remind them to consider their purpose for listening. Have them refer to the guidelines beginning on p. 728 depending on their purpose.

Finally, students should discuss their listening experiences with other students who listened to the same type of selection. Have them discuss these questions.

- Describe the selection to which you listened. Was it similar to the one you read aloud? If so, how?
- Did the selection fulfill your purpose for listening? Explain.

Media Messages The *media* are communication forms that you read and hear. Media include newspapers, magazines, radio, television, and the Internet. They are sometimes called the *mass media* because they reach masses, or large numbers, of people. Much of the information we receive comes to us by listening to the media. For that reason, it is important to be a critical listener.

■ **Analyzing media messages** *Analyzing* means identifying the parts of something and understanding how those parts work together. To analyze a media message, use the following questions.

Analyzing Media Messages

What is the purpose of the message? Many media messages have more than one purpose. For example, most news programs give information. To make money, though, a program will sell time to advertisers, who pay according to how many viewers will see their ads. Therefore, the program will also try to entertain so it can attract more viewers.

Is the information correct and up-to-date? What is the source of the information? If no sources are given, you have no way of knowing whether the information can be trusted.

How does the message use language? Does it include persuasive words, such as *you should*? Does it use persuasive techniques (see page 707)? Are you being given straight information, or are you being sold a product, service, or idea?

What ideas does the message take for granted? What is left out is as important as what is included. For example, a program on teens that tells only about the problems they cause presents a one-sided message.

What is your opinion of the message? Based on your answers to the questions in this chart, form your own opinion about the message. If you think the message may not be accurate, you may want to find more information on your own.

■ **Identifying lack of objectivity in the media** The following chart lists some signs to watch for in media messages. Seeing any of these signs in a message is a clue that the message may be unfair or unbalanced.

Evaluating Media Messages

Bias—leaning toward one side of an issue. A biased speaker may not give opposing views equal time or may not mention them at all.

Misleading Information—bending facts or statistics to support an idea. A speaker may bend facts to move an audience to take action or to win over an undecided audience.

Prejudice—judging people or situations, most often in a negative way, before the facts are known. Prejudiced speakers may ignore facts that do not agree with their views.

Studying and Test Taking

Studying

Skills and Strategies

One purpose of studying is to learn information a little bit at a time so you can do well on tests and earn good grades. However, studying also helps you remember important information you may need later in life. (See also **Test Taking** on page 737.)

Making a Study Plan Set up a study schedule that will help you succeed. Follow the suggestions below to make effective use of your study time.
1. **Know your assignments.** Write down your assignments for each class and the date when each one is due. Make sure you understand the instructions for each assignment.
2. **Plan to finish your work on time.** Break larger assignments into smaller steps. Use a calendar to set deadlines and keep track of when you should be finished with each step.
3. **Study.** Set aside a time and a place where you can work on your assignments without becoming distracted.

Organizing and Remembering Information There are many different ways you can study because there are many different ways to handle information. The strategies listed on the following pages can help you organize and remember information as you study.

- **Classifying** When you *classify* items, you sort them into groups, or categories, with other items that are related to them. The name of the category describes the relationship between the items in the group. If you break your notes into categories, you will have an easier time learning the information.
  EXAMPLE In what category do the following things fit?
  dolphin, shark, whale, octopus
  Answer: ocean animals

■ **Graphic organizers** New information is sometimes easier to understand if you organize it visually. The process of classifying and organizing information in a *graphic organizer* will help you learn the information. Studying information in a *graphic organizer,* such as a map, chart, or diagram, is often more effective than studying the same information in a paragraph. (See also **Text Structures** on page 709).

■ **Memorization** Sometimes you need to *memorize* information. To develop memorization skills, follow the tips below. Information is easier to memorize if you practice in frequent, short, focused sessions. You may also find that working with another person who can quiz you helps you commit information to memory.

> **How to Memorize**
>
> **Memorize only the most important information.** Whenever possible, shorten the material you need to remember.
>
> **Practice the material in different ways.** For example, write the material by hand onto a sheet of paper. Read the paper aloud. Put it away. Then, write out the material again from memory.
>
> **Invent memory games.** Find words that have the same first letters as the important terms and string them together into a sentence, or make up poems or songs that help you remember facts and details.

■ **Notes on reading or lectures** Taking accurate *notes* is worth the extra effort. As you read at home or listen in class, you should record detailed information in your notebook. Then, you will be ready to study for even the most challenging tests.

> **How to Take Study Notes**
>
> **1.** Identify and write down the main ideas presented in class or your reading. These main ideas should be headings in your notes. In class, listen for key words and phrases, such as *first, most important,* or *therefore.* These words often introduce main ideas and tell you how ideas are related. In a textbook, look for chapter headings and subheadings. They usually contain key ideas.
>
> **2.** Keep your notes brief. Use abbreviations, and sum up source material in your own words.
>
> **3.** Include brief examples or details from the source material. Important examples or details can help you recall the key ideas more easily.
>
> **4.** Look over your notes as soon as you write them. Be sure you have included the most important information.

At the top of the next page is an example of careful study notes one student wrote after reading a passage about the Cherokee Nation. The notes show the main ideas as headings. Underneath each main heading, you will find a group of important details that relate to that heading. Notice that the notes are brief.

Background information
- Cherokee leaders wanted to modernize
- 1827—formed a legislature, wrote a constitution, started a judicial system
- built a capital—New Echota in Georgia

Causes for removal
- New settlers of European descent did not want to share land in the Southeast with Indians
- 1828—gold discovered on edge of Cherokee territory and Andrew Jackson was elected president. Jackson believed Indians should not have nations within the U.S.

Effects
- 1830—Indian Removal Act passed
- Jackson gives the Five Civilized Tribes (Cherokee, Chickasaw, Choctaw, Creek, Seminole) land in Indian Territory (Oklahoma)
- Cherokees must leave their lands in Georgia and Tennessee

How to Paraphrase

1. Read the selection carefully before you begin.

2. Be sure you understand the main idea of the selection. Look up any unfamiliar words in a dictionary.

3. Determine the tone of the selection. (What is the attitude of the writer toward the subject of the selection?)

4. Identify the speaker in fictional material. (Is the poet or author speaking, or is a character speaking?)

5. Write your paraphrase in your own words. Shorten long sentences or stanzas. Use your own, familiar vocabulary, and keep the ideas in the same order as they are in the selection.

6. Be sure that the ideas in your paraphrase match the ideas expressed in the original text.

- **Outlines** An *outline* can help you organize ideas. When you write an outline, you group ideas in a pattern that shows their relationship to one another. (See also **Prewriting Techniques** on page 761.)

- **Paraphrasing** When you *paraphrase,* you explain someone else's idea in your own words. When you put an idea in your own words, you will understand it better and remember it longer. (See also **Paraphrasing** on page 706.)

- **SQ3R** *SQ3R* stands for *Survey, Question, Read, Recite,* and *Review.* It is a reading strategy that helps you learn information from a book. (See also **SQ3R** on page 708.)

- **Summarizing** A *summary* is a brief restatement of the main ideas expressed in a piece of writing. A summary is similar to a paraphrase because you express another person's ideas in your own words. However, a summary is usually shorter than a paraphrase because you only note the most important points. (See also **Summarizing** on page 709.)

How to Summarize

1. Skim the selection you wish to summarize.
2. Read the passage again closely. Look for main ideas and supporting details.
3. Write your summary in your own words. Include only the main ideas and the most important supporting points.
4. Evaluate and revise your summary. Check that you have covered the most important points. Make sure that the information is clearly expressed and that the reader can follow your ideas.

■ **Writing to learn** *Writing* is a valuable study tool. Writing helps you organize your thoughts, solve problems, make plans, and get your mind ready to learn. The chart below contains some kinds of writing that can help you learn about yourself and your world.

Types of *Writing to Learn*

Freewriting helps you focus your thoughts.
Example writing for five minutes to brainstorm everything you know about a subject you are studying

Autobiographies help you examine the meaning of important events in your life.
Example writing about a personal event that showed you the importance of learning

Diaries help you recall thoughts, express feelings, and clear your mind.
Example expressing the feelings you have about a subject about which you are learning

Journals help you record observations and descriptions or explore answers to questions.
Example recording questions that you develop about a topic, and exploring possible answers to them

Learning logs help you define or analyze information or propose a solution.
Example listing and defining words you learned in Spanish class

---

Meeting INDIVIDUAL NEEDS

ADVANCED LEARNERS

You might want to suggest to students that they use a journal to discover or learn about how the world around them works. Suggest that they do the following:

1. Carry a journal every day.
2. Jot down observations about how something works, how something came into being, or why something is the way it is.
3. Seek answers, explanations, or opinions from people or other sources throughout the day.
4. Set aside ten or fifteen minutes daily to read over the observations made or questions generated. Record any answers or insights gathered during the day.

Test Taking

Studying for Tests

There are two common tests you are likely to take in school: essay tests and objective tests. The information in this section will help you prepare for both kinds of tests.

Essay Tests   An *essay test* measures your understanding of the material you have learned in class by asking you to explain your answers. Essay answers are usually a paragraph or more in length.

> **How to Study for Essay Tests**
>
> **1.** Read the assigned material carefully.
>
> **2.** Make an outline of the main points and important details.
>
> **3.** Invent your own essay questions, and practice writing out the answers.
>
> **4.** Evaluate and revise your practice answers by checking your work against your notes and textbook. You can also use the **Writing Workshops** in this book to help you write an essay answer.

Objective Tests   *Objective tests* measure your ability to remember specific information, such as names, terms, dates, or definitions. Most objective test questions have only one correct answer.

> **How to Study for Objective Tests**
>
> **1.** Identify important terms or facts in your textbook and class notes.
>
> **2.** Review the information in more than one way. For example, for a science test, you may need to learn the definitions for scientific terms. Make flashcards. Practice identifying the definition from the term, then the term from the definition.
>
> **3.** Practice and repeat information to remember it. Go over difficult information more than once.
>
> **4.** If possible, briefly review all the information shortly before the actual test.

Types of Test Questions

The following section describes the different types of questions you may find on tests you take in school. Read about these questions to find tips and strategies for answering them.

- **Essay questions**   To answer an *essay question,* you usually write a paragraph or several paragraphs. Your essay should have a topic sentence, supporting details, and a conclusion. The following steps can help you answer essay questions. (See also the **Key Verbs That Appear in Essay Questions** chart on page 738.)

1. Scan the directions on the test. How many questions are you required to answer? Select the ones you think you can answer best. Plan how much time you can afford to spend on each answer. Then, stick with your plan.

2. **Read each question carefully.** Be sure you understand exactly what the question is asking before you plan your response. If a question contains several parts, your answer should contain several parts as well.

3. **Pay attention to important terms in the question.** Identify the task that the essay question asks you to complete. You can tell what the task is by looking at the key verb that appears in the essay question. Refer to the chart below.

\multicolumn{3}{c}{Key Verbs That Appear in Essay Questions}		
Key Verb	**Task**	**Sample Question**
analyze	Take something apart to see how each part works.	Analyze the effects that a balanced diet has on a growing body.
compare	Point out ways that things are alike.	Compare cross-country skiing to water skiing.
contrast	Point out ways that things are different.	Contrast the schools in Japan and the United States.
define	Give specific details that make something unique.	Define the term *personification*.
demonstrate	Give examples to support a point.	Demonstrate how the Internet helps people communicate.
describe	Give a picture in words.	Describe the appearance of a test tube of water after another substance is added.
explain	Give reasons.	Explain why the moon looks different at various times each month.
identify	Point out specific characteristics.	Identify the types of figurative language.
list	Give all steps in order or all details about a subject.	List the countries that make up the United Kingdom.
persuade	Give your opinion on an issue and provide reasons to support it.	Persuade your science teacher that your science class should or should not start a vegetable garden.
summarize	Give a brief overview of the main points.	Summarize the story told in "Raymond's Run."

4. **Use prewriting strategies.** After you identify the key verbs in the question, make notes and an outline to help you decide what you want to say. Write your notes or a rough outline on a piece of scratch paper.

5. **Evaluate and revise as you write.** You may not have time to write your whole essay over, but you can edit your essay to strengthen it. Correct any spelling, punctuation, or grammatical errors, and make sure you have answered every part of the question.

Qualities of a Good Essay Answer
The essay is well organized.
The main ideas and supporting points are clearly presented.
The sentences are complete and well written.
There are no distracting errors in spelling, punctuation, or grammar.

■ **Matching questions** *Matching questions* ask you to match the items in one list to items in another list.

EXAMPLE

Directions: Match the animals in the left-hand column to the correct kind of animal in the right-hand column.

_B_ 1. Greyhound A. Amphibian
_D_ 2. Sparrow B. Mammal
_A_ 3. Bullfrog C. Reptile
_C_ 4. Crocodile D. Bird
_E_ 5. Sea Bass E. Fish

How to Answer Matching Questions

1. **Read the directions carefully.** Some items may be used more than once. Others might not be used at all.

2. **Scan the columns.** Match the items you know first. That way you can spend more time thinking about more difficult items you are less sure about.

3. **Complete the rest of the matching.** Make your best guess on the remaining items.

■ **Multiple-choice questions** A *multiple-choice question* provides a number of possible answers and asks you to select the one that is correct.

EXAMPLE

1. Which of the following items is *not* a characteristic of poison ivy?
   A. Its oil causes people to itch.
   B. Each leaf has three leaflets.
   C. It produces white berries.
   (D.) It grows into a tall tree.

How to Answer Multiple-Choice Questions

1. **Read the question or statement carefully.** Before you look at answer choices, make sure you understand the question or statement. Watch for words such as *not* and *only.* These words limit your choice of possible answers.

2. **Read all the choices before answering.** If you know an answer choice is incorrect, rule it out. Think carefully about the remaining choices, and select the one that makes the most sense.

On-demand reading questions

On-demand questions are ones you cannot study in advance. *On-demand reading questions* ask you about a reading passage. In some cases, you will find answers to the questions in the passage. Other times, you may need to draw from your own experiences or understanding of the passage.

EXAMPLE

Directions: Read the passage below, and answer the question that follows.

   Julia threw her roller skates down on the sofa. She plopped down next to them and pouted. Didn't anyone remember that it was her birthday? No one in her family had said "Happy birthday" to her before she went skating this morning. She walked into the kitchen to get lunch, and her face brightened. Her family was there and so were all her friends! On the table, there was a cake with twelve candles. It was surrounded by presents.

1. Why does Julia pout?
   - **(A.)** She thinks her family has forgotten that it is her birthday.
   - B. She fell while roller-skating.
   - C. Her friends did not come to her birthday party.
   - D. Her family forgot her presents.

> **How to Answer On-Demand Reading Questions**
>
> **1. Read the passage carefully.** Make sure you know the main idea and important details.
>
> **2. Read the questions that follow the reading passage.** Usually the questions are multiple-choice. (See also **Multiple-Choice Questions** on page 739.) Sometimes you will be asked to write short, precise answers to questions. (See also **Short-Answer Questions** on page 742.)
>
> **3. Notice which words from the passage are repeated in the questions.** In the example above, the question includes the word *pout*, which is part of the word *pouted* from the second sentence of the reading passage. That clue tells you that the answer is in the second sentence of the reading passage or somewhere near it.
>
> **4. If the language of the passage does not appear in the question, you must draw your own conclusions.** Your conclusion may be based on your own experiences and knowledge.

On-demand writing questions

On-demand writing questions are the core of many state writing tests. They are essay questions that ask you to write a persuasive, informative, narrative, or descriptive essay. Since these questions are broad and related to your experience, you cannot study for the content of an on-demand writing question. However, you can prepare by writing a practice essay and asking for feedback from your teacher or classmates.

EXAMPLE

   Your principal is thinking about requiring all students to take a class about career selection. Persuade your principal that such a class is or is not a good idea.

How to Answer On-Demand Writing Questions

1. Read the question and decide what it is asking. Look for the key verbs in the question. These verbs will tell you whether your answer should be persuasive, informative, narrative, or descriptive. (See also the **Key Verbs That Appear in Essay Questions** chart on page 738.)

2. Plan your answer. Use prewriting strategies to help you plan before you begin writing. (See also **Prewriting Techniques** on page 761.)

3. Evaluate and revise your answer as you write. Make sure your answer has a clear topic sentence, supporting details, transitions between ideas, and a conclusion.

How to Answer Reasoning or Logic Questions

1. Make sure you understand the instructions. Reasoning or logic questions are often multiple-choice. On some tests, however, you may need to write a word or phrase, complete a number sequence, or draw a picture for your answer.

2. Analyze the relationship implied in the question. Look carefully at the question to gather information about the relationship of the items.

3. Draw reasonable conclusions. Evaluate the relationship of the items to decide your answer.

■ Reasoning or logic questions

Reasoning or *logic questions* test your reasoning skills rather than your knowledge of a specific subject. Reasoning or logic questions may ask you to identify the relationship among several items, to identify a pattern in a sequence of numbers, or to predict the next item in a sequence.

EXAMPLE

What comes next?

1   2   3   4

In this sequence of drawings, the hour hand on the clock starts at noon and moves three hours forward in each picture. In the fourth position, the hour hand will have reached the nine o'clock position.

■ Sentence-completion questions

Sentence-completion questions test your knowledge of vocabulary words. These types of questions ask you to choose an answer that correctly completes the meaning of a sentence.

EXAMPLE

1. On stage the two performers seemed like good friends. In reality, however, the two were _____ who were always competing for the same roles.

   A. cousins
   B. pals
   C. rivals
   D. equals

How to Answer Sentence-Completion Questions

1. Read the sentence carefully. Make sure you understand the words in the sentence. Some sentences may contain

(continued)

Test Taking

(continued)

> **How to Answer Sentence-Completion Questions**
>
> clues to the meaning of the word or words that go in the blanks. In the example on the previous page, *however* is a clue that the two performers were not friends offstage. Therefore, the correct answer is *rivals*.
>
> **2. Rule out incorrect answer choices.** If you can immediately rule out an answer choice, mark through it.
>
> **3. Fill in the blank with the remaining choices, and choose the best answer.** If you are not sure which choice is correct, use each one in the blank of the sentence and choose the answer that makes the most sense.

- **Short-answer questions** *Short-answer questions* ask you to write brief, precise responses. Short-answer questions vary in length. You may be asked to fill in a blank, label a map, or write one or two sentences.

EXAMPLE Why do whales frequently rise to the surface of the sea?

Answer: Whales cannot breathe underwater. They come up to the surface to get air through their blowholes.

> **How to Answer Short-Answer Questions**
>
> **1. Read the question carefully.** Some questions have more than one part. Be sure to answer the entire question.
>
> **2. Plan your answer.** Briefly decide what ideas and details you need to include in the answer.
>
> **3. Be as specific as possible.** Write a full, exact answer.
>
> **4. Budget your time.** Answer the questions you know first. Save time for more difficult questions.

- **True-false questions** *True-false questions* ask you to determine whether the statement you are given is a true statement or a false statement.

EXAMPLE
1. T (F) Cockroaches never fly.

> **How to Answer True-False Questions**
>
> **1. Read the statement carefully.** If any part of the statement is false, then the whole statement is false. A statement is true only if it is entirely and always true.
>
> **2. Look for word clues.** Words such as *always* or *never* limit a statement's meaning.

Viewing and Representing

Understanding Media Terms

People who work in and write about the media often use special terms. Learning some of those terms will help you evaluate or judge the media messages you see and hear. It will also help you create your own media messages.

The terms in this section are divided into three lists: **Electronic Media Terms, General Media Terms,** and **Print Media Terms.** If a term is used in both print media and electronic media, it is defined under **Print Media Terms** only. For information on the Internet and the World Wide Web, see the **Library/Media Center** section beginning on page 694. For more on using type and graphics, see **Document Design** beginning on page 682.

Electronic Media Terms

Advertising   See **Advertising** on page 751.

Animation   *Animation* is a way of making photographs of drawings appear to move. Each drawing in an animated film is only slightly different from the ones before and after it. When the photographs of these drawings are projected very quickly (at 24 images per second), the figures in them seem to move.

Broadcasting   *Broadcasting* is sending television or radio signals through the airwaves over a wide area. *Commercial broadcasting* is sending these signals to make money. Commercial broadcasters are paid by advertisers to air commercials along with the broadcasters' programs. *Public broadcasting* refers to nonprofit radio and television. The Public Broadcasting Service (PBS) in the United States has more than three hundred member TV stations. Companies, viewers, and listeners pay most of the cost of public broadcasting. Some money comes from the federal government.

Cable Television *Cable television* uses powerful antennas to pick up television signals and then delivers the signals to homes and businesses through cables. Some cable companies only provide the signals to viewers. Others create original programs as well. (See also **Broadcasting** on page 743.)

Camera Angle The *camera angle* is the angle at which a camera points toward a subject. Placing the camera at a high angle above the subject makes the subject look small. Placing the camera at a low angle makes the subject look tall and powerful. Tilting the camera makes the subject seem off-balance.

Camera Shot A *camera shot* is the way an image in a film or video is presented to viewers. The following are the three most common shots used in film production.

- **Close-up shot** a shot made from very close to the subject, for example, a shot of a person's eyes
- **Medium shot** a shot made from a midrange distance, for example, a shot of a person from the waist up
- **Long shot** a shot made from far away, for example, a shot of a football field from a blimp

Commercial Broadcasting See **Broadcasting** on page 743.

Copy See **Copy** on page 751.

Credits *Credits* list the people who worked on a presentation. Credits are usually listed at the end of a television program, film, or video.

Documentary A *documentary* is a film or television program that explores the meaning of an actual event. Most documentaries include a combination of interviews and footage of actual events. Some documentaries include reenactments of events by actors and an offscreen narrator. A documentary's main purpose may be to inform, to persuade, or to entertain. In addition, some documentaries are intended to make money for their producers. A documentary may have more than one purpose. For example, a filmmaker might create a documentary that both informs viewers about the problem of pet overpopulation and tries to persuade them to take actions to help solve that problem.

Editor See **Editor** on page 751.

Feature News See **Feature News** on page 752.

Film *Film* is a medium for recording sounds and images. Message makers who need sounds and images to be crisp and clear, to last a long time, or to be presented on a large screen will film their messages. Filmed images can appear more sophisticated than images recorded on videotape, but film is more expensive to buy and develop than videotape is. (See also **Videotape** on page 746.)

Hard News   See **Hard News** on page 752.

Internet   The *Internet* is a network of computers that lets computer users communicate with each other. Using the Internet requires a computer with a modem and Internet software. The modem links the computer with a telephone or cable line. For a monthly fee, Internet service providers (ISPs) provide access to the Internet. (See also **World Wide Web** on page 699.)

Lead   See **Lead** on page 752.

Medium   See **Medium** on page 752.

Message   See **Message** on page 750.

News   See **News** on page 753.

Newsmagazine   See **Newsmagazine** on page 753.

Photography   See **Photography** on page 753.

Producer   A *producer* is the person who oversees the production of a movie or a radio or TV program. He or she decides what overall message to present. The producer also gathers a crew or staff, raises and manages the money needed to create the film or program, and keeps the production on schedule. (See also **Production** on page 753.)

Public Broadcasting   See **Broadcasting** on page 743.

Reporter   See **Reporter** on page 754.

Script   A *script* is the words to be spoken during a play, a film, or a TV or radio program. TV, film, and play scripts also include notes about the images to be shown and the movements or emotions that actors will perform. The script for a news broadcast is called *copy*. (See also **Copy** on page 751.)

Soft News   See **Soft News** on page 754.

Sound   In film and video, sound is all of the recorded material that you hear, including dialogue, music, sound effects, and so on. In addition to getting the spoken words across to viewers, producers and filmmakers use sound to achieve the following goals.

- **Create an illusion**   You might see two actors in a film rushing to get farm animals into a barn. Sound effects, such as wind noise and thunder, can signal to you as a viewer that these characters want to protect their livestock from an approaching storm. It is unlikely that the scene was shot on a stormy day, though.

- **Create a mood**   The music that a producer chooses to play while certain images are on screen can guide the audience to feel a certain way about those images. For example, music with a strong rhythm played during a chase scene can make viewers feel tense, as if they are moving quickly, too.

Understanding Media Terms   **745**

TEACHING TIP

Sound. Have students also consider the effects of silence in a movie, television show, or documentary. First, have them brainstorm about times when there are pauses or silent periods in a program. In what situations is there silence? Why might a director include silent periods or pauses in a program? Emphasize that no sound or silence is in the scene by chance; everything is a result of choices the director has made.

Then, show a scene from a program that includes a silent period, or have students watch a program at home. Students should make notes on the following questions:

- What is the situation when the pause or silent period occurs? Who are the people involved?

- Why is this silent period included? What point might the director be making?

- How are people's thoughts or emotions communicated when no words or sounds are used? How is this method of communicating ideas more or less effective than using sound would be?

Source   See **Source** on page 754.

Storyboard   A *storyboard* is a set of drawings that show the order of shots and scenes in a script. A storyboard may also include dialogue, narration, and audio and visual cues. For an example of a storyboard, see page 689.

Target Audience   See **Target Audience** on page 754.

Text   See **Text** on page 754. (See also **Script** on page 745.)

Videotape   *Videotape* is a medium used to record sounds and images. Message makers may use videotape because the medium and equipment needed are relatively inexpensive when compared with film. Videotape equipment may also be more accessible and easier to use than film equipment. When using videotape, message makers must consider that images and sounds recorded on videotape tend to have less *resolution*, or clarity, than filmed images. They must also keep in mind that videotape does not last as long as film. (See also **Film** on page 744.)

General Media Terms

Audience   An *audience* is a group of people who see or hear a media message. Advertisers aim their messages at the audiences they think will buy their products or services. (See also **Advertising** on page 751 and **Target Audience** on page 754.)

Authority   The term *authority* means how well the source of a message seems to know the subject. If a message appears to come from an expert source, you will think it has authority.

Bias   A *bias* is a slanted point of view, either in favor of an issue or against it. A biased message maker may not even mention information that supports views other than his or her own. (See also **Point of View** on page 751.)

Context   *Context* is the material that surrounds a media message. For example, the context of an ad on a children's TV program is the other ads on the program and the program itself. Context may affect the way people respond to a message.

Credibility   *Credibility* means being believable. Whether or not a speaker or writer seems believable is up to the audience to decide. (See also **Message** on page 750.)

Critical Viewing   *Critical viewing* means analyzing visual messages to understand them and evaluate or judge them. Visual messages include photographs, editorial cartoons, films, and television programs, to name just a few.

Keeping the five key ideas on the next page in mind as you view messages will help you become a more critical viewer.

Key Ideas for Critical Viewing

Key Idea 1: All messages are put together by people.

People who create visual messages must make many choices. They must decide which elements (words, images, sounds) to include and how to arrange them. One of the most important decisions the creator of a visual message makes is what to leave out. When you understand that visual messages are constructed, you can analyze how the elements work together. You can also recognize the skill that went into creating the message.

Key Idea 2: Messages are one person's version of reality.

When you see something in a visual message, remember that the reality may be quite different. For a TV ad for a theme park, for example, everything from the actors to the camera angles to the background music is carefully chosen and arranged to make the park seem even more fun than it is. When you understand that a visual message is a version of reality, you can evaluate how authentic (true-to-life) the message seems.

Key Idea 3: People make their own meanings from messages.

The meaning you draw from a visual message depends on your prior knowledge (what you already know) and on your experience. Everyone's prior knowledge and experience are different, so different viewers may draw different meanings from the same message. When you connect the message to your own knowledge and experience, you can form your own ideas about what the message means.

Key Idea 4: Messages have a wide range of purposes.

Every message has a purpose. Usually, that purpose is to inform, to persuade, to entertain, or to express thoughts and feelings. Most mass-media messages also have another purpose: to make money for the message makers and for the people who own and run the media. Knowing that a visual message might be presented to make money can help you decide for yourself whether you will let it influence you.

Key Idea 5: The medium shapes the message.

Different visual media have different strengths and weaknesses. For example, a still photograph shows just one moment in time, but it can be studied over and over. Film has movement and sound, but the images flash by quickly. The people who create visual messages must choose the medium that will best help them achieve their purpose. Understanding how the medium shapes the message can help you see why a message affects you in a certain way.

Evaluating Media Messages

The following questions will help you analyze and evaluate media messages.

- Who created the message?
- What elements (words, images, or sounds) does the message include?
- How are the elements arranged?

TEACHING TIP

Key Ideas for Critical Viewing

To practice critical viewing, divide the class into three or four groups. Assign each group a different media form to analyze and evaluate (such as print ad, TV ad, radio ad, or billboard). If possible, all media forms should discuss a similar idea or advertise a similar product.

In their groups, students should answer the eleven questions beginning on p. 747. (The first three questions are analysis questions; the fourth through seventh questions are evaluation questions; the eighth and ninth questions discuss purposes and effects.) As a class, discuss the last two questions and arrive at an evaluation of each media form.

- How well are the elements used?
- What may have been left out of the message?
- How is this version of reality similar to and different from what I know from my own experience or from other sources?
- How authentic (true-to-life) does the message seem? Why?
- Of what does the message make me think? How does it make me feel about the world? about myself? about other people?
- What seems to be the main purpose of the message? Is there also another purpose? If so, what is it?
- What medium carries the message?
- How do the characteristics of the medium (image, sound, motion) shape the message?

Formula A *formula* is a set way of doing something. In television and film, it refers to a common way of presenting material or combining characters. For example, situation comedies often use this formula: A character gets into an uncomfortable situation, which is usually caused by a misunderstanding or by one of the character's own faults. The situation gets sillier and sillier until finally, someone or something comes along and solves the character's problem. By the end of the show, the character is out of trouble and everything is back to normal.

Genre A *genre* is a category of art forms or media products that share certain common ways of doing things. Genres found on television include

- children's programming
- documentary
- drama
- game show
- infomercial
- music video
- news broadcast
- sitcom (situation comedy)
- soap opera
- talk show

Illustration An *illustration* is a picture created as a decoration or to explain something. Drawings, paintings, photographs, and computer-generated artwork can all be illustrations. The following are some elements of illustration.

- **Color** Color creates a certain mood or draws attention to a certain part of an illustration.
- **Form** Form refers to the three-dimensional look of an illustration. Depth and weight make an illustration more effective. Illustrators can create shadows and bright spots to make an illustration look three-dimensional.
- **Line** Everything you see around you has some sort of line. Some lines are obvious, like the vertical line made by walls meeting in a corner. However, you might not notice other lines, for example, the lines made by the fur of a cat. Illustrators use line to show depth in

a drawing and to show viewers where the horizon in a drawing is.

- **Shape** Shape is the two-dimensional outline of something. Lines come together to make a shape, and all of the shapes in an illustration are connected.

Images An *image* is a visual representation of something. It may be a painting, a photograph, a sculpture, or a moving picture, among other things. An image may be *still* or *moving*.

- A *still image,* such as a photograph, allows viewers to notice detail and spend time considering the meaning of the image. Still images may also be easier than moving images for message makers to manipulate through cropping or using computer programs.

- A *moving image* is a series of still images projected quickly onto a television or film screen. A moving image may show an actual event (called *documentary footage*), or it may show an event arranged by the message maker (a *dramatization*). Documentary footage includes scenes shown on the evening news; dramatizations include fictional movies. Both kinds of moving images are the message maker's version of an event and may be incomplete or altered in some way.

To analyze how message makers create certain effects using images, consider the points in the chart below.

Creating Effects with Images

Technique	Definition/Effects
Color	Color can emphasize certain parts of an image or guide viewers to feel a certain way about an image. When a spot of color suddenly appears in a black-and-white movie, the director wants viewers to pay special attention to that part of the image. Photographing an image through a yellow filter can create a happy mood in the image.
Juxtaposition	This technique involves putting two or more images next to each other to create meaning. For example, a comedy show that cuts between images of a person happily walking down a city street and a piano dangling from an apartment window tells its viewers that the person's walk will be rudely interrupted by the piano. Editing moving images together or placing still images side by side can sometimes communicate more meaning than an individual image.
Slow or Fast Motion	A message maker may speed up or slow down a moving image to create a certain effect. Making an image move faster than normal can create a comic effect, while slowing an image down can create a tense, dramatic effect.

TEACHING TIP

Media Law
Have groups of three students each work collaboratively to write a letter inviting an editor, a producer, or a reporter from a local TV station or newspaper to speak to the class about media law. Students can follow the format for a formal request letter on p. 760. Encourage students to include specific requests for information from the speaker. Students can ask questions such as the following examples:

- How does the First Amendment affect your daily work?
- How do you make sure you do not violate any copyright laws?
- Have you ever been censored? Do you ever censor your own work?

One group member can draft the letter while a second revises it for content and organization. The third can make sure it is error-free and that it follows the guidelines.

Media Law The First Amendment of the U.S. Constitution states that Congress shall pass no law that limits the freedom of the press. One effect of this amendment is that, except during wartime, the United States government seldom uses *censorship*. *Censorship* is any attempt by a government or other group to limit the amount or type of information people receive. However, there are laws that regulate, or control, the media. The Federal Communications Commission (FCC) enforces U.S. laws dealing with electronic media, including radio, television, and the Internet. A person whose reputation has been hurt by lies that were printed or broadcast about him or her may sue the people responsible for the false statements. The creator of a media message may *copyright* that message to stop anyone from *plagiarizing*, or stealing his or her work.

Media Literacy *Media literacy* is the ability to find, analyze, evaluate, and communicate messages in many different forms. (See also **Critical Viewing** on page 746.)

Message A *message* is an idea communicated using symbols (things that stand for ideas). Symbols may be language, gestures, images, or sounds. The *content* of a message is the information it presents. (See also **Credibility** on page 746, **Realism** on page 751, and **Source** on page 754.)

Multimedia Presentation A *multimedia presentation* is any presentation that uses two or more forms of media. For example, when you give an oral presentation including visuals (such as slides, transparencies, or posters), you are giving a multimedia presentation. One medium is your voice, and the other is the visuals you use to support your presentation. A multimedia presentation that involves the use of presentation software or Web sites is sometimes called a *technology presentation.*

Newsworthiness *Newsworthiness* is the quality that makes a news event seem worth reporting. An event may be considered newsworthy if it meets any of the following criteria, or standards.

Criteria	Definitions
Timeliness	events or issues that are happening now or that people are interested in right now
Impact	events or issues that have a direct effect on people's lives
Human Interest	stories about people's basic needs or stories that affect the audience's emotions
Celebrity Angle	stories about famous people

Persuasion See **Propaganda** on page 751.

750 Quick Reference Handbook Viewing and Representing

Point of View A message maker's *point of view* is the way he or she approaches a topic. The message maker's background and beliefs often affect his or her point of view. For example, in a newspaper story about a local zoo, one reporter might focus on how the zookeepers are helping save endangered species. Another reporter with different experiences might focus on what the animals are missing by not being in the wild. (See also **Bias** on page 746 and **Propaganda** below.)

In photography, point of view refers to the photographer's approach to his or her subject. Choices that affect the photographer's point of view include selecting the subject and the camera angle. (See also **Photography** on page 753.)

Propaganda *Propaganda* is the use of certain techniques to make a message as persuasive as possible. The word *propaganda* has a negative connotation as it originally referred to messages that lied or distorted the truth in order to influence public opinion. However, the practice of using some propaganda techniques—such as the celebrity testimonial—is widely accepted in the field of advertising. Many of these techniques work by leading you to make a generalization about the ad. Suppose, for example, a company uses a basketball star to advertise its shoes. The company wants you to generalize that anyone who wears those shoes will play as well as the basketball star does. (See also **Advertising** on this page, **Bias** on page 746, and **Point of View** above.)

Realism *Realism* means showing people and events just the way they appear, without making them seem better or worse in any way.

Stereotypes *Stereotypes* are beliefs (usually negative ones) about a whole group of people. For example, some adults do not trust teenagers even though relatively few teenagers ever cause problems. Such beliefs are usually based on too little evidence or on false or misleading information.

Visual Literacy *Visual literacy* is the ability to understand how the visual media communicate meaning. (See also **Critical Viewing** on page 746.)

Print Media Terms

Advertising *Advertising* is using images or words to persuade an audience to buy, use, or accept a product, service, or idea. Advertisers pay the media for time or space in which to run their ads.

Byline A *byline* lists the name of the reporter or writer of a print article or a broadcast presentation.

Copy *Copy* is the text in a media message. (See also **Script** on page 745.)

Editor An *editor* oversees the work of reporters. Editors decide what news stories will appear, check facts, and correct mistakes.

TEACHING TIP

Stereotypes. To help students consider stereotypes in media messages, have them complete the following activity. You may wish to provide advertisements with clear stereotypes for in-class analysis.

Have students watch several advertisements that are shown during a television program for teens or children and look for stereotypes in the ads. For example, are teenage girls shown as being concerned only with clothes and makeup? When students find an ad with obvious stereotypes, they should make a note of what the stereotype is and answer these questions about the ad.

- What is the main concept or overall message of the ad? What information, sounds, or images in the ad support this message?

- What do the stereotype and the message tell you about the producer's bias? In other words, why do you think the producer of the ad chose to use this stereotype? How does the producer seem to feel about the product advertised? What does the producer seem to think about the potential customers for the product?

Then, students should write a paragraph analyzing the ad's stereotypes based on their answers. If possible, have students show the ads in class and explain their answers.

Editorial Cartoon An *editorial cartoon* is a cartoon, usually found in the editorial section of a newspaper, that shows the cartoonist's opinion about a current event or issue. An editorial cartoonist may make his or her point in the following ways.

- exaggerating the impact of an event or issue
- drawing people involved in the event as *caricatures,* or giving them exaggerated features that make it obvious to readers who is being represented
- connecting the event to another event or story with which readers will be more familiar

Feature News The primary purpose of *feature news* (or soft news) is to entertain. These stories may or may not be timely. They may be about ordinary people or celebrities or about animals, events, places, or products. A profile of a neighborhood volunteer who brings food to homeless people is an example of a feature-news story. (See also **Hard News** below and **Soft News** on page 754.)

Font A *font* is a style of lettering used for printing. (See also **Font** on page 685.)

Hard News *Hard news* is reporting based on facts. It covers important current events and issues such as politics. Usually, it answers the basic *5W-How?* questions. A hard-news story might provide information about a flood that occurred today or about the problem of overcrowded classrooms in local schools. (See also **Feature News** on this page and **Soft News** on page 754.)

Headline A *headline* is the title of a newspaper article. Headlines are usually set in large, bold type. They have two purposes: to hook the reader's attention and to tell the reader the topic of the article.

EXAMPLE: Fido Fetches Family from Flames

Lead A *lead* is the first few words or the first paragraph of a news story. It answers some or all of the *5W-How?* questions and tries to hook the audience's attention with a surprising fact or idea.

EXAMPLE: (HOBBS, NM) A family pet proved himself a hero early yesterday when he alerted the sleeping occupants of a burning home here. Even though he could have easily escaped through his doggie door, Fido the terrier chose to stay and bark until the Yellowbird family had all woken up and fled the house.

Medium The *medium* of a message is the means by which it is sent. (*Medium* is the singular form of *media.*) **Print media** include newspapers and magazines. **Electronic media** include radio and television, audio and video recordings, film, and the Internet. The **mass media** are the media that reach a very large audience.

Message See **Message** on page 750.

News *News* is the presentation of current information. The people who own and run *media outlets,* such as newspapers or television stations, decide which stories to cover. They try to choose stories that will interest or affect their audience. Local news outlets present stories about their region of the country. National news outlets cover national and world issues and events.

Newsmagazine A *newsmagazine* is a publication that discusses recent events and issues. Most print newsmagazines appear once a week. In television the term refers to a news program that airs one or more times a week. Such programs usually analyze and explore the meanings of events.

Photography *Photography* is the process of recording a still image on film with a camera. Like any other visual message, a photograph records only the parts of an image that the message maker chooses to include. The choices a photographer can make about an image include the following.

- **Camera angle** By placing the camera at different angles relative to the subject, a photographer can guide viewers to feel a certain way about the subject. (See also **Camera Angle** on page 744.)
- **Film type** A photographer may choose color or black-and-white film depending on what he or she wants viewers to get from the image. Black-and-white film can emphasize shapes or create a dramatic effect, while color images appear more realistic.
- **Lighting** A photographer may have control over the light available when the photo is taken. If so, he or she can use just a few lights set at dramatic angles for effect, or use full light for a more natural-looking image.
- **Subject** When taking a photo of a scene, a photographer may position the camera to get only the most important part of the scene or to eliminate images that take away from his or her message. Even after the photo has been taken, *cropping* can be used to cut out an unwanted part of the scene. Message makers can also add *captions* that guide viewers to draw a conclusion about the photo. (See also **Message** on page 750.)

Political Cartoon See **Editorial Cartoon** on page 752.

Production *Production* is the process of creating a publication, a film, a video, or a radio or television program. Production takes place in three stages.

- **Preproduction** Copy or scripts are gathered and fine-tuned. Money is raised, and plans are made for how it will be spent. Staff and crew are hired, and schedules are planned.
- **Production** The work is filmed, recorded, or printed.
- **Postproduction** Finishing touches are added. Books and newspapers are bound or gathered. Films and tapes

are edited, soundtracks are recorded, and sound and special effects are added.

Reporter   A *reporter* is a journalist who gathers information. Reporters work with editors to create print or electronic reports.

Soft News   *Soft news* is general-interest material, such as information on fashion trends, presented in a news format. The purpose of soft news is to entertain. For example, a soft-news story might explain how the special effects for a new science fiction movie were created. (See also **Feature News** and **Hard News** on page 752.)

Source   A *source* is a person or publication that gives a journalist information or ideas. Journalists try to use sources that have authority and seem credible. (See also **Authority** and **Credibility** on page 746, and **Message** on page 750.)

Target Audience   A *target audience* is a group of people for whom a message or product is designed. For example, the target audience of advertisements for acne medications is teenagers.

Text   The term *text* refers to the words, printed or spoken, that are used to create a message. (See also **Message** on page 750.)

Writing

Skills, Structures, and Techniques

Good writing does not just happen. A writer must work at his or her writing. You can use the following ideas and information to become a more effective writer.

Applications See **Forms** on page 757.

Composition A *composition* is a piece of writing that has several paragraphs. Compositions have three main parts: *introduction*, *body*, and *conclusion*. All three parts work together to communicate the author's main idea or point.

- **Introduction** The *introduction* is the first paragraph of your composition. An introduction should do two things: Get your readers' attention and tell them the main idea of the composition.
  1. **Grab the readers' attention.** Your introduction should make your readers want to read more. The chart in the next column gives some strategies for drawing in your reader.

How to Catch Your Readers' Attention

Begin by asking a question.
Do you wonder what to do with all of your free time after school and on the weekends?

Begin with an anecdote or a funny story.
House painting has always been something I do well, so when I showed up at the volunteer building site, I was ready to paint. Little did I know that my friend Joaquin was ready to paint me.

Begin with a startling fact.
You may not think that you can help to build a house, but with the teamwork of young people and adults, a house can be quickly built, painted, landscaped, and prepared for a family to move in.

2. Present the main idea statement, or thesis. The *main idea statement*, or *thesis*, is a sentence or two that tells your topic and your main idea about it. Use your main idea as a guide as you plan, write, and revise your paper. Here are some strategies for writing a main idea statement.

> **How to Write a Main Idea Statement**
>
> **1. Ask yourself, "What is my topic?"**
> *volunteering*
>
> **2. Review your prewriting notes.** Think about how the facts and details fit together. Identify the idea that connects the details to one another.
> *Volunteering is good, hard work.*
>
> **3. Use specific details to make the main idea clear.** Zooming in on specific details will make the main idea more focused.
> *Volunteering to build homes taught me to respect all kinds of people, to work hard, and to challenge myself.*

■ **Body** The main idea is supported and developed in the *body* of the composition. The body usually contains several paragraphs with supporting statements, facts, and details. Each paragraph has its own main idea, called a *topic sentence,* and all of the topic sentences support the main idea statement. As you write the body of a composition, keep the following tips in mind.

1. Make sure that you arrange the information in your composition in a way that will make sense to your reader. (See also page 283.)
2. Do not include details that distract from your main idea.
3. Show how your ideas are connected by using *transitional words and phrases*. (See also page 287.)

■ **Conclusion** The *conclusion* of your paper sums up your information and makes your final points. Your conclusion should do the following things.

1. **Give the readers a sense of completion.** Good conclusions leave the readers feeling satisfied, not as if they have been left hanging.
2. **Restate the main idea.** The conclusion is your last chance to make your point. In addition to summing up your main points, restate your main idea in different words.

> **How to Write a Conclusion**
>
> **Refer to your introduction.**
> *When I thought that I was in for an easy day of fun and painting, I was only partly right. I had fun with my friends. We even had a paint fight. However, I also learned how to work with others to help others.*
>
> **Restate your main idea.**
> *I now know that by giving up a Saturday, I did not miss out on fun. I had a great time and felt that my day was spent in an important way.*

Close with a final idea or example.

I enjoyed my Saturday of painting so much that I have decided to spend one day each month volunteering in some way.

E-mail Electronic mail, or *e-mail,* is a way of sending messages over the Internet rather than through the post office. E-mail is used for both personal and business correspondence. Since e-mail messages are instant, people sometimes write casually. Casual messages are fine for informal e-mail with friends. When e-mailing teachers or businesses, however, you should follow the guidelines below.

E-Mail Guidelines

- Keep your message short, since reading through long e-mails can be difficult and confusing.

- When you have several questions or points, use a bulleted list or indentations to make your e-mail easier to read.

- Use correct spelling, grammar, punctuation, and standard English.

- Include salutations (or greetings) and closings, especially if you are writing to someone for the first time.

- Do not send angry or rude messages. E-mail is easily forwarded. Therefore, someone other than the person you originally wrote to may end up receiving your message.

- Avoid using all capital letters in your messages. Writing in capitals in e-mail is similar to shouting. If you need to emphasize a word or phrase, place an asterisk (*) before and after it.

- Double-check the address in the address line of your message to make sure you are sending your message to the right person.

- Fill in the subject line in your message. Giving your readers an idea of the topic of your message allows them to read the most important messages first.

- Do not forward e-mails to others unless you have the original author's permission.

Forms You will be called upon to fill out forms many times throughout your life. You fill out forms or applications for library cards, savings accounts, even school club memberships. Below is an example of a simple information form.

Information Form

Date 7/26/01

Name Bliss Winston

Address 705 E. Oak St.

City Oakland   State CA   ZIP 90821

Home Phone 555-0141

Date of Birth 12/21/90

Parent or Guardian Joseph Winston

The following tips will help you fill out forms correctly.
1. Read all instructions before you begin. Look for special instructions to see whether you should use a pen or pencil.
2. Read each item carefully.
3. Print neatly all the information that is requested.
4. Proofread the form to make sure you did not leave anything blank. Also, check for errors and correct them neatly.
5. Mail the form to the correct address or give it to the correct person.

Letters   Most people like to receive mail. To get letters, though, you need to write letters. That is why it is important to develop good writing skills for social and business letters. There are several different kinds of letters. All of them have a purpose and an audience. The chart at the bottom of this page lists some common types, purposes, and audiences for letters.

Letters, Business   *Business letters* have specific purposes. People write business letters to apply for a job or communicate about a business. Make sure your business letters look professional. Type or use your best handwriting, and use standard, formal English.

- **Envelopes**   To make sure that your letter goes where you want it to go, address the envelope neatly and correctly. Follow these tips.
  1. Place your return address in the top left-hand corner of the envelope.
  2. Write the name and address of the person to whom the letter is being sent in the center of the envelope.
  3. Use the standard two-letter postal abbreviation for the state name, followed by the ZIP Code.

Return address

```
Sudi Foster
63 Washington Ave.
Salem, OR 97305


        Aola Washington
        2119 Brushcreek Ave. #302
        Independence, MO 64055
```

Mailing address

Letters		
Type of Letter	**Purpose for Writing**	**Probable Audience**
Business	to inform a business about a service you need or how a service was performed	a business or organization
Informal or Personal	to tell about your ideas or feelings, to be polite, to thank someone, or to tell someone about a planned event	close friends, relatives, or social acquaintances

- **Forms for business letters** The six parts of a business letter are usually arranged in one of the two following styles.
  1. **Block form** In the block form, every part of the letter begins at the left margin of the page. A blank line is left between paragraphs, which are not indented.
  2. **Modified block form** In the modified block form, the heading, the closing, and your signature are placed to the right of an imaginary line down the center of the page. The middle parts of the letter begin at the left margin. Paragraphs are indented.

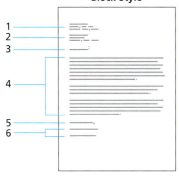

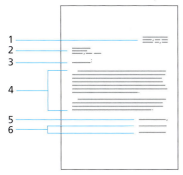

- **Parts of a business letter** There are six parts to a business letter.
  1. The **heading** of a business letter has three lines: your street address; your city, state, and ZIP Code; and the date you are writing the letter.
  2. The **inside address** gives the name and address of the person to whom you are writing. If you are directing your letter to someone by name, use a courtesy title (such as *Mr., Ms., Mrs.,* or *Miss*) or a professional title (such as *Dr.* or *Professor*) in front of the person's name. After the person's name, include the person's business title (such as *Principal* or *Business Manager*). If you do not have a person's name, use a business title or position title (such as *Refunds Department* or *Editor in Chief*).
  3. Your **salutation** is your greeting to the person to whom you are writing. In a business letter, the salutation usually ends with a colon (such as in *Dear Professor García:*).
     If you are writing to a specific person, you can use the person's name (such as *Dear Ms. Lyon*). If you do not have a specific name, use a general greeting (such as *Dear Sir or Madam:* or *Ladies and Gentlemen:*). You can also use a business or position title instead (*Dear Committee Leader:*).
  4. The **body** contains the message of your letter. Leave a blank line between paragraphs in the body of the letter.
  5. Conclude your letter politely. The **closing** of a business letter often uses one of several common phrases (such as *Sincerely, Yours truly,* or *Respectfully*

TEACHING TIP

■ **Types of Business Letters**
Have students compose letters of request to local authors, asking about the challenges the writers face and the writing strategies they use. You can help students identify local authors by contacting a local writer's guild, newspaper, or magazine. Students can ask for specific information in their letters and invite the authors to speak to the class. After writing, students can exchange letters with partners for peer evaluation. After revising, students can exchange letters with new partners to check for errors and to make sure the letters follow the correct format.

---

yours). Capitalize only the first word. End the closing with a comma.

6. Your *signature* should be written in ink directly below the closing. Your name should be typed or printed neatly just below your signature.

■ **Types of business letters** Types of business letters include the following.

1. **Adjustment or complaint letters** When you write an *adjustment* or *complaint letter,* you state a problem and explain how you think it should be solved. For example, if you are unhappy with a product you bought, you might write a letter like the one below.

```
5208 Range Drive
St. Louis, MO 63117
June 15, 2001

Gadgets Mail Order
1992 Highland Road
Albany, NY 12212

Dear Sir or Madam:

I am returning science kit #609
that was delivered yesterday. It
arrived with a broken microscope.

Please replace the kit or refund
my purchase price of $69.95 plus
$4.30 that I paid for postage
and handling.

Sincerely,
Ramiro Sanchez
Ramiro Sanchez
```

2. **Appreciation letters** When you write an *appreciation letter,* you tell people in a business or organization that they did a good job. Give details about what they did that you liked. For example, perhaps you want to tell the manager of a restaurant that you appreciate the good service you received there.

3. **Request or order letters** In a *request letter,* you ask for specific information about a product service. An *order letter* tells a business about a product or service you want such as a free brochure (an excerpt is shown below). Be sure to include all important information, such as the item number, size, color, brand name, and price.

```
I would like to order three back
issues of Zip! magazine. Please
send the issues from March,
April, and May 2001. In the mag-
azine, you state that back
issues are $3 each, including
postage. I have enclosed a money
order for $9. Thank you for
sending the issues as soon as
possible.
```

Letters, Informal or Personal An *informal* or *personal letter* is a good way to communicate with a friend or relative. A personal letter is like a conversation, only much better. Conversations may be interrupted or forgotten, but a letter is often treasured and read many times.

A personal letter is a token of friendship. It usually contains a personal message from you, the sender, to the person you are writing to, the receiver. For example, you might write a friend to congratulate him or her for receiving a school award. You might write to tell a friend about the new school you attend.

When you are sending a personal letter, remember to write about a subject that interests you and the person you are writing.

■ Types of informal or personal letters

There are three common types of informal or personal letters. Each of these types is meant for a particular purpose.

1. **Invitations** You write an invitation to ask someone to an event. Include specific information about the occasion, such as the type of event, time, and place, and any other information your guests might need to know (such as how to dress and what to bring, if anything).

2. **Letters of regret** You will need to write a letter of regret when you receive an invitation to an event that you will not be able to attend. You should always respond in writing to invitations that include the letters *RSVP*. (These letters are an abbreviation for the French words that mean "please reply.")

3. **Thank-you letters** When you receive a gift or a favor, you should write a thank-you letter. The purpose of a thank-you letter is to express your appreciation when someone has spent time, trouble, or money to do something for your benefit. In addition to thanking the person, you might include a paragraph or so of personal news or friendly, chatty information. Try to think of something about the person's effort or gift that made it special to you. In the following example, the writer explains why she enjoys a gift from her grandfather.

> 9300 Leon St.
> Burlington, VT 05401
> October 6, 2001
>
> Dear Grandpa,
>   Thank you so much for the wonderful beagle puppy you brought down from the farm. She must have been the smartest one in the litter. She already knows her name after only two days. We named her Waggles because her tail wags all the time. She's the greatest gift. Thanks!
>
>   Love,
>   Rita

Prewriting Techniques One of the hardest parts of writing is getting started. The following prewriting techniques can help you find topics for writing. They can also help you gather information and ideas about a topic. As you try the different techniques, you may find some are more helpful to you than others. You might even use more than one technique when writing a composition.

Prewriting techniques often include the use of a *graphic organizer*. A **graphic organizer** is a visual way of representing thoughts or ideas. Graphic organizers can help you "see" what you are thinking. You can use graphic organizers to find a subject to write about, to gather information, and to organize your information.

1. **Finding ideas** Use the following techniques to find ideas for writing.

   - **Asking *5W-How?* questions** To gather information, news reporters often ask the *5W-How? questions: Who? What? Where? When? Why?* and *How?* You can do the same for any topic. Some questions may not apply to your topic. For other topics, there may be many answers to one question. Here are some *5W-How?* questions about Native American cliff dwellings.

WHO?	*Who* lived in cliff dwellings?
WHAT?	*What* was their daily life like?
WHERE?	*Where* are cliff dwellings found?
WHEN?	*When* did people live in cliff dwellings? *When* did they leave them?
WHY?	*Why* did they build their villages on or into cliffs? *Why* did they leave their villages?
HOW?	*How* did they get food and water?

   - **Asking "What if?" questions**
   "What if?" questions can help you think creatively. Let your imagination wander to find as many answers as you can.

   What if I could change one thing in my life? (What if I could make myself invisible? What if I had a car and a driver's license?)

   What if some everyday thing did not exist? (What if the earth had no moon? What if radios had not been invented?)

   What if I could change one thing about the world? (What if everyone in the world had enough food and a home? What if animals could talk with people?)

   - **Brainstorming** When you *brainstorm,* your thoughts fly in all directions. Start with a broad subject, then quickly list everything you can think of about the subject. You can brainstorm alone or with a group.

Guidelines for Brainstorming
Write any subject at the top of a piece of paper or on a chalkboard.
Write down every idea that occurs to you. If you are brainstorming in a group, one person should record all the ideas.
Do not stop to judge what is listed.
Do not stop until you run out of ideas.

   Here are some brainstorming notes on the subject *astronauts.* When you are brainstorming, it is fine to list unusual ideas. Unusual ideas may lead to the perfect topic.

   <u>Astronauts</u>

Sally Ride	space explorers
Neil Armstrong walking on the moon	floating without gravity
space shuttle	cramped space, food in tubes
spacesuits	man in the moon
diving suits	woman in the moon
lunar rover	Astrodome

- **Clustering** *Clustering* is sometimes called *mapping* or *webbing*. It is a visual kind of brainstorming.

Guidelines for Clustering
Write your subject in the center of your paper and then circle it.
Around the subject, write related ideas that come to you. Circle these, and draw lines to connect them with the subject or with other ideas.
Keep going. Write new ideas, circle them, and draw lines to show connections.

The following is a cluster diagram on the topic of Hispanic grocery stores, or *bodegas*.

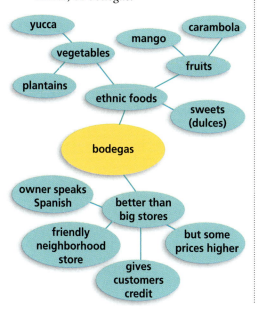

- **Freewriting** *Freewriting* means just that—writing freely. Begin with a word or phrase, and then write whatever comes to mind.

Guidelines for Freewriting
Time yourself for three to five minutes, and keep writing until the time is up.
Write your topic first. Then, write down the ideas your topic gives you.
Do not stop or pause. If you can't think of anything to write, keep writing the same word or phrase until something else pops into your head.
Do not worry about spelling, punctuation, or complete sentences.

EXAMPLE

Bicycling. I like pedaling pedaling pedaling. Aching muscles, biking in the rain. Ride everywhere—school, soccer, down to lake. Never without my helmet, remember Travis's accident. Dangerous at night—reflectors, headlight, reflective tape on jacket. Safety, safety rules—driver's license for bike riders?

In *focused freewriting* (or *looping*), you begin with a word or phrase from freewriting you have already done. You might choose "biking in the rain" and do three minutes of freewriting on this limited topic.

Skills, Structures, and Techniques

- **Writer's notebook or journal**
Fill your *writer's journal* with experiences, feelings, and thoughts. You can put in cartoons, quotations, song lyrics, and poems that have special meaning for you. When you need a writing topic, look through your journal to find an idea you want to expand. You can also have a section called a *learning log,* where you write about things you learn. Keep your journal in a notebook, file folder, or computer file.

Writer's Notebook Guidelines
Write every day, and date your entries.
Write as much or as little as you want. Do not worry about spelling, punctuation, or grammar.
Give your imagination some space. Write about dreams, daydreams, and far-out fantasies.

EXAMPLE

July 12, 2001. Saw people doing strange exercise in the park Sat. morning. They moved SO slowly like in a dream. A slow-motion dance. Seven people following movements of an old Chinese woman, few old, mostly young, all moving together. We watched a long time. They call it tai chi—it made me feel good.

2. **Gathering information** When you run out of ideas from your imagination or you need facts, you can turn to other sources. Use the following strategies to find more information on a topic.

- **Listening with a focus** You can find information by listening to radio and TV programs and tapes or by interviewing someone who knows something about your topic. Before you listen, write out some questions about your topic. Then, listen for answers and take notes. (See also **Listening** on page 727.)

- **Reading with a focus** When you look for information in print, follow the guidelines in the chart below.

Reading Guidelines
Find your topic in a book's table of contents or index. Turn to the pages listed.
Do not read every word. Skim pages quickly, looking for your topic.
When you find information on your topic, slow down and read carefully.
Note main ideas and key details.

3. **Arranging ideas** The following strategies will help you to organize and summarize your ideas. These strategies can be especially helpful for organizing ideas from a number of different sources.

- **Charts** A *chart* is a way of classifying information. Charts help you begin to gather and organize your facts and details before you write. One type of chart is a table like the one below made by a student who is researching types of armor worn by knights in the Middle Ages.

Armor in the Middle Ages	
Type of Armor	Description
hauberk	a tunic made from chain mail with a hood
surcoat	a coat worn over the chain mail suits to protect them from the sun; the coats are decorated with identifying emblems
plate armor	plates of solid metal designed to deflect arrows

- **Conceptual mapping** *Mapping,* or *conceptual mapping,* is similar to clustering. The difference is that it is used to organize information that you have gathered rather than to find ideas. You can use conceptual mapping to group your main ideas and supporting details before you write your paragraphs. An example of a conceptual map is shown at the bottom of the page.

- **Outlines** An *outline* is another way to organize important information. When you make an outline, you arrange the ideas to show the main ideas and the supporting details. You can use the outline as a guide to writing.

  You may need to use different types of outlines. For a report, your teacher might require you to write a *formal outline,* like the one at the top of the next page, with Roman numerals for headings and capital letters for subheadings.

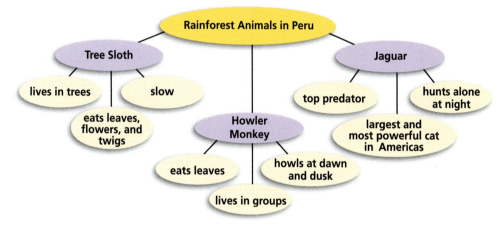

Conceptual Map

TEACHING TIP

- **Time Line**
Point out to students that time lines are not only a good way to organize information, but also a way to organize a narrative or instructions during the prewriting stage. If students choose to organize a paper using a time line, they should make sure the body paragraphs each treat a single event and are presented in clear chronological order. For information on how to organize steps for a "how-to" paper on a time line, have students refer to **Chapter 3**, p. 96.

```
                Formal Outline
Title: Kids About Town
Main Idea: After-school activi-
ties are good, but you should
limit how many you do.
I. Benefits
   A. Group Activities (soccer
      team)
      1. learn teamwork
      2. make friends
      3. physical fitness
   B. Individual Activities
      (violin lessons)
      1. develop self-discipline
      2. learn a skill
II. Drawbacks
   A. Less Study Time
   B. Stress
```

To organize your writing quickly, you can use an *informal outline* like the one below.

Informal Outline	
Topic: After-School Activities	
Benefits	**Drawbacks**
group activities (soccer): learn teamwork make friends physical fitness	sometimes too busy to study
	stress caused by worrying about my grades and when I will have time for everything
individual activities (violin lessons): develop self-discipline learn a skill	

- **Sequence chain**   See **Text Structures, Analyzing** on page 709.

- **Time line**   A *time line* organizes information by the date it happened. The time line below shows one student's progress in learning to use a personal computer.

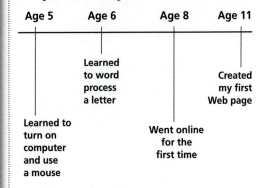

- **Venn diagram**   A *Venn diagram* uses circles to show how two subjects are alike and different. Each subject has its own circle, but the circles overlap. In the overlapping part, you write details that are the same for both subjects. In the parts that do not overlap, you write details that make these subjects different. (See also page 132.)

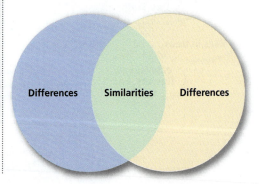

Symbols for Revising and Proofreading

Symbol	Example	Meaning of Symbol
≡	I will see you on saturday morning.	Capitalize a lowercase letter.
/	My Dog's name is Spot.	Lowercase a capital letter.
∧	Do not walk away from me.	Insert a missing word, letter, or punctuation mark.
⌒	After you go go home, give me a call.	Leave out a word, letter, or punctuation mark.
∽	peice	Change the order of letters.
¶	¶ After you finish the first steps, continue on to the next.	Begin a new paragraph.
⊙	Dr. Chavez	Add a period.
∧	Yes, I like strawberry smoothies.	Add a comma.

Revising and Proofreading Symbols When you are revising and proofreading, indicate any changes by using the symbols in the chart above.

Style When you act a certain way or dress a certain way, you are creating your personal style. When you write, you decide what words you are going to use and how you are going to arrange those words in sentences. The choices you make create your *style* of writing. Your writing style is personal because you are the one who created it.

Transitions *Transitions,* or *transitional expressions,* are words and phrases that show the connections between ideas in a piece of writing. Transitions make your writing *coherent,* or smooth and easy to read. (See page 287 for a chart of **Transitional Words and Phrases.**)

Voice The way a piece of writing "sounds" is its *voice.* As you write, try to express your ideas clearly and naturally. Although some writing requires a formal voice because of its audience and purpose, the writing should still sound like you. Your writing voice also reveals your attitude about your topic and your audience. Treat both with respect by choosing your words carefully.

Grammar at a Glance

HELP

Grammar at a Glance is an alphabetical list of special terms and expressions with examples and references to further information. When you encounter a grammar or usage problem in the revising or proofreading stage of your writing, look for help in this section first. You may find all you need to know right here. If you need more information, **Grammar at a Glance** will show you where in the book to turn for a more complete explanation. If you do not find what you are looking for in **Grammar at a Glance**, turn to the index.

abbreviation An abbreviation is a shortened form of a word or a phrase.

- **capitalization of** (See page 548.)

TITLES USED WITH NAMES	**M**r.	**D**r.	**J**r.	**Ph.D.**
KINDS OF ORGANIZATIONS	**C**o.	**I**nc.	**D**ept.	**C**orp.
PARTS OF ADDRESSES	**B**lvd.	**A**ve.	**S**t.	**P.O. B**ox
NAMES OF STATES	[without ZIP Codes]		**K**y.	**W**yo.
			Wis.	**N.J.**
	[with ZIP Codes]		KY	WY
			WI	NJ
TIMES	A.M.	P.M.	B.C.	A.D.

- **punctuation of** (See page 563.)

WITH PERIODS	(See preceding examples.)			
WITHOUT PERIODS	VCR	UN	PBS	NASA
	DC (D.C. without ZIP Code)			
	kg	ft	lb	yd	cm

[Exception: in.]

action verb An action verb expresses physical or mental activity. (See page 350.)

EXAMPLES   Stefan **rode** the bike over the bridge.

Teresa **trimmed** the hedge and **raked** the leaves.

I **thought** about the problem.

adjective An adjective modifies a noun or a pronoun. (See page 336.)

EXAMPLE **The** Nobles live in **a beautiful, old** house.

adjective clause An adjective clause is a subordinate clause that modifies a noun or a pronoun. (See page 389.)

EXAMPLE The woman **who directs the City Ballet** is from Romania.

adjective phrase A prepositional phrase that modifies a noun or a pronoun is called an adjective phrase. (See page 377.)

EXAMPLE Fruit **from Mr. Park's market** always seem fresher than the produce **in the grocery store.**

adverb An adverb modifies a verb, an adjective, or another adverb. (See page 357.)

EXAMPLE **Occasionally,** when he's feeling **especially** energetic, Dino goes ice-skating.

adverb clause An adverb clause is a subordinate clause that modifies a verb, an adjective, or an adverb. (See page 391.)

EXAMPLE **Before I watch TV,** I have to do my homework.

adverb phrase A prepositional phrase that modifies a verb, an adjective, or an adverb is called an adverb phrase. (See page 381.)

EXAMPLE **At the shore,** Trish and Sandy played volleyball.

agreement Agreement is the correspondence, or match, between grammatical forms. Grammatical forms agree when they have the same number and gender.

- **of pronouns and antecedents** (See page 435.)

  SINGULAR **Marcie** could not check out the book because **she** did not have **her** library card with **her.**

PLURAL **Readers** who do not have **their** library cards with **them** cannot check out books.

SINGULAR Every afternoon, **each** of the students is given time to write in **his or her** journal.
PLURAL Every afternoon, **all** of the students are given time to write in **their** journals.

- **of subjects and verbs** (See page 422.)

SINGULAR That **box** of blankets **is** for the homeless shelter.
PLURAL The **blankets** in that box **are** for the homeless shelter.

SINGULAR **Mixed vegetables, roasted potatoes, or rice pilaf comes** with any seafood entree.
PLURAL **Rice pilaf, mixed vegetables, or roasted potatoes come** with any seafood entree.

SINGULAR **Each** of these books **was written** by Amy Tan.
PLURAL **All** of these books **were written** by Amy Tan.

SINGULAR **Neither Eli nor Leo wants** to go skateboarding.
PLURAL **Both Eli and Leo want** to go skateboarding.

SINGULAR Here **is** my **collection** of baseball cards.
PLURAL Here **are** the most valuable baseball **cards** in my collection.

SINGULAR Where **is** my **wallet**?
PLURAL Where **are** the **tickets**?

SINGULAR **He doesn't** know how to play jai alai.
PLURAL **They don't** know how to play jai alai.

antecedent An antecedent is the word or word group that a pronoun stands for. (See page 328.)

EXAMPLE **Patricia** told **Aunt Sally** and **Uncle Ted** that **she** was thinking of **them**. [*Patricia* is the antecedent of *she*. *Aunt Sally* and *Uncle Ted* are the antecedents of *them*.]

apostrophe

- **to form contractions** (See page 602. See also **contractions**.)

  EXAMPLES   hasn't   you'll   let's   o'clock   '01

- **to form plurals of letters, numerals, symbols, and words used as words** (See page 605.)

  EXAMPLES   *a*'s, *e*'s, *i*'s, *o*'s, and *u*'s

  A's, *I*'s, and *U*'s

  v's and *w*'s

  1900's

  UFO's

  +'s and –'s

  using *and*'s instead of *&*'s

- **to show possession** (See page 598.)

  EXAMPLES   the astronaut's spacesuit

  the astronauts' spacesuits

  someone's book bag

  Kim's and Mariah's math projects

  Kim and Mariah's math project

appositive
An appositive is a noun or a pronoun placed beside another noun or pronoun to identify or describe it. (See page 570.)

EXAMPLE   The manager, **Max,** always brought his lunch to work.

appositive phrase
An appositive phrase consists of an appositive and its modifiers. (See page 570.)

EXAMPLE   Claude Baker, **the manager of our local branch,** has been in banking for ten years.

article
The articles, *a*, *an*, and *the*, are the most frequently used adjectives. (See page 520.)

EXAMPLE   **The** jetliner, **a** new model, had **an** eventful voyage.

Grammar at a Glance   **771**

bad, badly (See page 521.)

NONSTANDARD   This tuna salad smells badly.
STANDARD   This tuna salad smells **bad**.

base form The base form, or infinitive, is one of the four principal parts of a verb. (See page 445.)

EXAMPLE   Lee helped me **lift** the heavy box.

capitalization

- **of abbreviations** (See page 548. See also **abbreviation**.)
- **of first words** (See page 537.)

EXAMPLES   **I**n Norse mythology, Thor is the god of thunder.

His sister asked him, "**H**ave you already fed our goldfish today?"

Dear Mrs. Yellowfeather:

Yours truly,

- **of proper nouns and proper adjectives** (See pages 539 and 548.)

Proper Noun	Common Noun
Col. **C**urtis **L. B**rown, **J**r.	astronaut
Charles the **W**ise	leader
North **A**merica	continent
Argentina	country
Elk **P**oint, **S**outh **D**akota	city and state
Kodiak **I**sland	island
Yukon **R**iver	body of water
Guadalupe **P**eak	mountain
Cheyenne **M**ountain **Z**oological **P**ark	park
Siuslaw **N**ational **F**orest	forest
Luray **C**averns	caves
the **S**outhwest	region
Twenty-**f**ourth **S**treet	street

Proper Noun	Common Noun
World **H**ealth **O**rganization (**WHO**)	organization
Federal **A**viation **A**dministration (**FAA**)	government body
North **C**arolina **S**tate **U**niversity (**NCSU**)	institution
Klondike **G**old **R**ush	historical event
Ice **A**ge	historical period
Little **L**eague **W**orld **S**eries	special event
Hana **M**atsuri, or **F**lower **F**estival	holiday
February, **M**ay, **A**ugust, **N**ovember	calendar items
winter, spring, summer, fall (autumn)	seasons
Nez **P**erce	people
Islam	religion
Protestant	religious follower
God (*but* the Greek **g**od **A**pollo)	deity
Rosh **H**ashanah	holy days
Koran	sacred writing
Joshua **T**ree **N**ational **M**onument	monument
Metropolitan **M**useum of **A**rt	building
Caldecott **M**edal	award
Uranus	planet
Canopus	star
Delphinus, or **D**olphin	constellation
HMS *L*eopard	ship
Lunar Prospector	spacecraft
Physical **S**cience **I** (*but* **p**hysical **s**cience)	school subject
Cherokee	people or language

- **of titles** (See page 552.)

  EXAMPLES   **M**ayor Maria Sanchez [preceding a name]

  Maria Sanchez, the city's **m**ayor [following a name]

  Welcome, **M**ayor. [direct address]

  Uncle Darnell [*but* our **u**ncle Darnell]

  The **C**all of the **W**ild [book]

Grammar at a Glance

Saved by the **B**ell [television series]

Amahl and the **N**ight **V**isitors [musical composition]

"**O**ver the **R**ainbow" [song]

"**T**he **S**mallest **D**ragonboy" [short story]

"**I A**m of the **E**arth" [poem]

Reader's **D**igest [magazine]

The **W**ashington **P**ost [newspaper]

Rose **Is R**ose [comic strip]

case of pronouns Case is the form a pronoun takes to show how it is used in a sentence. (See page 475.)

NOMINATIVE   Louis and **she** were the finalists in the spelling bee. [part of the compound subject of the verb *were*]

The only sixth-graders in the contest were Felicia and **he.** [part of the compound predicate nominative referring to the subject *sixth-graders*]

We volunteers spent Saturday afternoon making piñatas for the fiesta. [subject followed by the noun appositive *volunteers*]

Who painted *Cow's Skull: Red, White and Blue*? [subject of the verb *painted*]

Who is the author of *Yolanda's Genius*? [predicate nominative referring to the subject *author*]

OBJECTIVE   On Friday, Ms. Yabuuchi took **them** on a field trip to the planetarium. [direct object of the verb *took*]

Gwen sent **me** an invitation to her family's Kwanzaa party. [indirect object of the verb *sent*]

I went with Carla and **her** to a Japanese tea ceremony. [part of the compound object of the preposition *with*]

The judge awarded each of **us** contestants a certificate of achievement. [object of the preposition *of*, followed by the noun appositive *contestants*]

Whom did the coach select as the captain of the team? [direct object of the verb *did select*]

In the last line of the poem, to **whom** is the speaker referring? [object of the preposition *to*]

POSSESSIVE **Your** birthday is the same day as **mine** is. [*Your* is used as an adjective before the subject *birthday*; *mine* is used as the subject of the verb *is*.]

clause A clause is a group of words that contains a subject and a verb and that is used as part of a sentence. (See page 387. See also **independent clause** and **subordinate clause**.)

INDEPENDENT CLAUSE   she stripped the walls of the living room
SUBORDINATE CLAUSE   before I painted them

colon (See page 579.)

- **before lists**

EXAMPLES   Amber's favorite fables by Aesop are as follows: "Belling the Cat," "The Fox and the Grapes," and "The Frogs Who Wished for a King."

I need to get a few items at the pet shop: a bag of colored gravel for the aquarium, a small mirror for the birdcage, and a new collar for my pet Chihuahua.

- **in conventional situations**

EXAMPLES   9:15 A.M.

Genesis 4:1–16

State Names, Seals, Flags and Symbols: A Historical Guide

Dear Dr. Kawabata:

comma (See page 566.)

- **in a series**

EXAMPLES   Dad made chicken quesadillas and topped them with a relish of diced tomatoes, onions, and chilies.

The book is a collection of stories that tell about the daring exploits of Heracles, King Arthur, Gilgamesh, and fourteen other heroes of ancient times.

- **in compound sentences**

    EXAMPLES   My neighbor Mr. Kim owns a hardware store, and occasionally he hires me to restock the shelves.

    We should leave now, or we may not get home before curfew.

- **with introductory elements**

    EXAMPLES   Well, were you able to get Sammy Sosa's autograph after the ballgame?

    Yes, here's the baseball that he autographed!

- **with interrupters**

    EXAMPLES   The Jaw-Dropper, the world's tallest and fastest roller coaster, is at the amusement park near my house.

    On Saturday afternoon, Tyrone, let's play miniature golf after we finish our chores.

- **in conventional situations**

    EXAMPLES   San Antonio, Texas, is the home of the Alamo.

    I was born on July 17, 1988, in Des Moines, Iowa.

    Is 483 Cottonwood Way, Columbia, SC 29250-3840, your current address?

comparison of modifiers (See page 497.)

- **comparison of adjectives and adverbs**

Positive	Comparative	Superlative
sharp	sharp**er**	sharp**est**
friendly	friendl**ier**	friendl**iest**
loyal	**more** loyal	**most** loyal
cheerfully	**less** cheerfully	**least** cheerfully
good/well	**better**	**best**

- **comparing two**

    EXAMPLES   These red grapes are **sweeter** than those.

    Jiro speaks the language **more fluently** than Anzu does.

- **comparing more than two**

    EXAMPLES Of the nine planets, Mercury is **nearest** the sun.

    Of a gazelle, a cheetah, and an ostrich, which animal can run **most swiftly**?

    Alaska is the **largest** of all the U.S. states.

complement A complement is a word or word group that completes the meaning of a verb. (See page 403. See also **direct object, indirect object, predicate nominative** and **predicate adjective.**)

EXAMPLES Ed gave **Martha** a **nod**.

Rei is the **leader** because he is so **organized**.

complex sentence A complex sentence has one independent clause and at least one subordinate clause. (See page 397.)

EXAMPLES Two of my favorite writers are Katherine Paterson, who wrote *Bridge to Terabithia,* and Beverly Cleary, who wrote *Dear Mr. Henshaw.* [one independent clause and two subordinate clauses]

When Jason and I were stargazing last night, we clearly saw the planets Venus, Mars, Jupiter, and Saturn. [one subordinate clause and one independent clause]

compound-complex sentence A compound-complex sentence has two or more independent clauses and at least one subordinate clause. (See page 398.)

EXAMPLES Most people think of dolphins as gentle, playful creatures, but as the documentary film shows, they can become fiercely aggressive predators in the wild. [one subordinate clause between two independent clauses]

When we were in Boston last summer, we visited The Computer Museum; we were especially impressed by the exhibit called The Giant Walk-Through Computer. [one subordinate clause followed by two independent clauses]

compound sentence A compound sentence has two or more independent clauses and no subordinate clauses. (See page 395.)

EXAMPLE This Saturday, the Library Club at our school will hold a book fair; the price of each hardcover book will be one dollar, and the price of each paperback will be fifty cents. [three independent clauses]

conjunction A conjunction joins words or groups of words. (See page 364.)

EXAMPLE **Both** Sy **and** Ben went to the Chinese restaurant, **but** they had to wait before being served, **for** the power was out.

contraction A contraction is a shortened form of a word, a numeral, or a group of words. Apostrophes in contractions indicate where letters or numerals have been omitted. (See page 602. See also **apostrophe**.)

EXAMPLES we'd [we had *or* we would]   it's [it is *or* it has]
who's [who is *or* who has]   won't [will not]
'98 [a year ending in *98*]   o'clock [of the clock]

declarative sentence A declarative sentence makes a statement and is followed by a period. (See page 316.)

EXAMPLE Birmingham is the second-largest city in the United Kingdom**.**

direct object A direct object is a word or word group that receives the action of the verb or shows the result of the action. A direct object answers the question *Whom?* or *What?* after a transitive verb. (See page 405.)

EXAMPLE Ms. Echavarría saw **John** and **Peter**.

double comparison A double comparison is the nonstandard use of two comparative forms (usually *more* and *–er*) or two superlative forms (usually *most* and *–est*) to express comparison. In standard usage, the single comparative form is correct. (See page 504.)

NONSTANDARD	King's Holly, a shrub growing in Tasmania, is considered the world's most oldest living plant.
STANDARD	King's Holly, a shrub growing in Tasmania, is considered the world's **oldest** living plant.

double negative A double negative is the nonstandard use of two or more negative words to express a single negative idea. (See page 507.)

NONSTANDARD	Without her eyeglasses, Ally couldn't hardly read the letters in the bottom line of the eye chart.
STANDARD	Without her eyeglasses, Ally **could hardly** read the letters in the bottom line of the eye chart.

end marks (See page 561.)

- **with sentences**

EXAMPLES At the state fair, we rode in a hot-air balloon. [declarative sentence]

Have you ever ridden in a hot-air balloon? [interrogative sentence]

Wow! [interjection] What a thrilling adventure that was! [exclamatory sentence]

Don't be afraid to look down. [imperative sentence]

- **with abbreviations** (See **abbreviation**.)

EXAMPLES Your tae kwon do class begins at 7:00 P.M.

Doesn't your tae kwon do class begin at 7:00 P.M.?

exclamation point (See **end marks**.)

exclamatory sentence An exclamatory sentence expresses strong feeling and is followed by an exclamation point. (See page 317.)

EXAMPLE How kind you are!

fragment (See **sentence fragment**.)

G

good, well (See page 502.)

EXAMPLES Doreen is a **good** saxophone player.
Doreen plays the saxophone **well** [not *good*].

H

hyphen (See page 606.)
- to divide words

EXAMPLE The bright star Sirius is part of the constellation Canis Major.

- in compound numbers

EXAMPLE In a leap year, February has twenty-nine days.

I

imperative sentence An imperative sentence gives a command or makes a request and is followed by either a period or an exclamation point. (See page 316.)

EXAMPLES Please close the window**.** [request]
Close the window**!** [command]

independent clause An independent clause (also called a *main clause*) expresses a complete thought and can stand by itself as a sentence. (See page 387.)

EXAMPLE After you get home, **don't forget to water the plants.**

indirect object An indirect object is a word or word group that often comes between a transitive verb and its direct object and that tells to whom or to what or for whom or for what the action of the verb is done. (See page 407.)

EXAMPLE Give the **dog** a bath.

interjection An interjection expresses emotion and has no grammatical relation to the rest of the sentence. (See page 366.)

EXAMPLE **Wow,** look at that sunset!

interrogative sentence An interrogative sentence asks a question and is followed by a question mark. (See page 316.)

EXAMPLE Is Clay Regazzoni still racing**?**

intransitive verb An intransitive verb is a verb that does not take an object. (See page 353.)

EXAMPLE   The crowd **laughed,** but Bob only **smiled.**

irregular verb An irregular verb is a verb that forms its past and past participle in some way other than by adding –d or –ed to the base form. (See page 448. See also **regular verb.**)

Base Form	Present Participle	Past	Past Participle
be	[is] being	was, were	[have] been
begin	[is] beginning	began	[have] begun
bring	[is] bringing	brought	[have] brought
burst	[is] bursting	burst	[have] burst
fall	[is] falling	fell	[have] fallen
go	[is] going	went	[have] gone
make	[is] making	made	[have] made

italics (See **underlining.**)

its, it's (See page 526.)

EXAMPLES   **Its** [the snow leopard's] scientific name is *Panthera uncia.*

It's [It is] considered an endangered species.

It's [It has] been overhunted for **its** fur.

lie, lay (See page 466.)

EXAMPLES   Anxious about his first day at a new school, Harry **lay** awake most of the night. [past tense of *lie*]

Aunt Una **laid** the map on the table and showed us the route we would travel. [past tense of *lay*]

linking verb A linking verb connects the subject with a word that identifies or describes the subject. (See page 351.)

EXAMPLE   Cousin Marty **became** a clarinetist.

M

misplaced modifier A misplaced modifier is a word, phrase, or clause that seems to modify the wrong word or words. (See page 509.)

MISPLACED Ms. Osaka said on Friday the sixth-grade students would elect class officers. [Does the phrase *on Friday* modify the verb *said* or the verb phrase *would elect*?]

REVISED **On Friday,** Ms. Osaka said the sixth-grade students would elect class officers. [The phrase *On Friday* clearly modifies the verb *said*.]

REVISED Ms. Osaka said the sixth-grade students would elect class officers **on Friday.** [The phrase *on Friday* clearly modifies the verb phrase *would elect*.]

modifier A modifier is a word or word group that makes the meaning of another word or word group more specific. (See page 495.)

EXAMPLE **The loud** chirping **of sparrows** filled **the** air.

N

noun A noun names a person, place, thing, or idea. (See page 323.)

EXAMPLE During the **drive, Ms. Washington** asked **Tommy** and **Sarah** to sing their **version** of the **song.**

number Number is the form a word takes to indicate whether the word is singular or plural. (See page 422.)

EXAMPLES The **dove** dipped **its head** as **it** drank.
The **doves** dipped **their heads** as **they** drank.

O

object of a preposition An object of a preposition is the noun or pronoun that ends a prepositional phrase. (See page 361.)

EXAMPLE Do you have any books about **elephants**? [*About elephants* is a prepositional phrase.]

P

period (See **end marks.**)

phrase A phrase is a group of related words that does not contain both a verb and its subject and that is used as a single part of speech. (See page 374.)

EXAMPLE   Marcia **is designing** a dress **for her cousin Francine's wedding.** [*Is designing* is a verb phrase. *For her cousin Francine's wedding* is a prepositional phrase.]

predicate The predicate is the part of a sentence that says something about the subject. (See page 307.)

EXAMPLES   She **is waiting for the bus.**

Does Walter **know Rebecca?**

predicate adjective A predicate adjective is an adjective that completes the meaning of a linking verb and that modifies the subject of the verb. (See page 412.)

EXAMPLE   At the farm, the cows looked **sleek** and **healthy.**

predicate nominative A predicate nominative is a noun or pronoun that completes the meaning of a linking verb and identifies or refers to the subject of the verb. (See page 410.)

EXAMPLE   The first passengers to exit were **Ron** and **Dee.**

prefix A prefix is a word part that is added before a base word or root. (See page 616.)

EXAMPLES   un + solved = **un**solved

im + mature = **im**mature

dis + satisfied = **dis**satisfied

preposition A preposition shows the relationship of a noun or a pronoun to some other word in a sentence. (See page 360.)

EXAMPLE   **At** the market, Tancredo bought green peppers, cheese, and tomatoes **for** the meal he was planning.

prepositional phrase A prepositional phrase is a group of words that includes a preposition, an object of the preposition, and any modifiers of that object. (See page 361.)

EXAMPLE   A book **of swashbuckling adventure** is *Treasure Island*, **by Robert Louis Stevenson**.

pronoun A pronoun is used in place of one or more nouns or pronouns. (See page 328.)

EXAMPLE   Julie told Mom and Dad **she** would be happy to drive **them** to the airport.

question mark (See **end marks**.)

quotation marks (See page 590.)

- **for direct quotations**
    EXAMPLE   "On our vacation in Mexico," said Mrs. Tamayo, "we visited Chichén Itzá, where we saw the ruins of pyramids and temples that the Maya had built."

- **with other marks of punctuation** (See also preceding example.)
    EXAMPLES   "In what year was the first Earth Day celebration held?" asked Megan.

    Who is the main character in Gary Soto's story "The No-Guitar Blues"?

    The teacher asked, "What do you think Benjamin Franklin meant when he wrote the proverb 'Hunger is the best pickle'?"

- **for titles**
    EXAMPLES   "Amigo Brothers" [short story]

    "Madam and the Rent Man" [short poem]

    "Under the Sea" [song]

regular verb A regular verb is a verb that forms its past and past participle by adding *–d* or *–ed* to the base form. (See page 446. See also **irregular verb**.)

Base Form	Present Participle	Past	Past Participle
ask	[is] asking	asked	[have] asked
drown	[is] drowning	drowned	[have] drowned
move	[is] moving	moved	[have] moved
risk	[is] risking	risked	[have] risked
suppose	[is] supposing	supposed	[have] supposed
use	[is] using	used	[have] used

rise, raise (See page 464.)

EXAMPLES When the sun **rose,** the restless scouts were still awake. [past tense of *rise*]

The orchestra conductor **raised** the baton to begin the concert. [past tense of *raise*]

run-on sentence A run-on sentence is two or more complete sentences run together as one. (See page 265.)

RUN-ON Nishi and I have been computer pen pals for two years she lives in Tokyo, Japan I live in Omaha, Nebraska.

REVISED NishI and I have been computer pen pals for two years**;** she lives in Tokyo, Japan**, and** I live in Omaha, Nebraska.

REVISED Nishi and I have been computer pen pals for two years**.** **S**he lives in Tokyo, Japan**, and** I live in Omaha, Nebraska.

semicolon (See page 577.)

EXAMPLE In 1993, Ramon Blanco from Spain became the oldest person to scale Mount Everest**;** he was sixty years old at the time.

sentence A sentence is a group of words that contains a subject and a verb and that expresses a complete thought. (See page 302.)

                 S   V
EXAMPLE The fish swam lazily in the clear water.

sentence fragment A sentence fragment is a group of words that is punctuated as if it were a complete sentence but that does not contain both a subject and a verb or that does not express a complete thought. (See pages 262 and 302.)

FRAGMENTS	Hera, the queen of the Greek gods, casting a spell on Hercules. Because she was jealous of him.
SENTENCE	Hera, the queen of the Greek gods, cast a spell on Hercules because she was jealous of him.

simple sentence A simple sentence has one independent clause and no subordinate clauses. (See page 394.)

EXAMPLE	On the Internet, Milo and I accessed a search page and searched for information about King Tutankhamen. [one independent clause with a compound subject and a compound verb]

sit, set (See page 463.)

EXAMPLES	Carmen **sat** on the bench, anxiously waiting for Coach Engle to send her back into the game. [past tense of *sit*]
	Anthony **set** the box of dominoes on the table, hoping that someone in his family would play the game with him. [past tense of *set*]

stringy sentence A stringy sentence is a sentence that has too many independent clauses. Usually, the clauses are strung together with coordinating conjunctions like *and* or *but*. (See page 266.)

STRINGY	One day, the gods Jupiter and Mercury decided to come down to the earth to test the people of Phrygia for their hospitality, so the gods disguised themselves as peasants who were in desperate need of food and shelter, and they stopped at hundreds of houses, and at each one the "peasants" were turned away, but finally, they came to the very small house of a poor, elderly couple named Baucis and Philemon.
REVISED	One day, the gods Jupiter and Mercury decided to come down to the earth to test the people of Phrygia for their

hospitality. The gods disguised themselves as peasants who were in desperate need of food and shelter. They stopped at hundreds of houses, and at each one the "peasants" were turned away. Finally, they came to the very small house of a poor, elderly couple named Baucis and Philemon.

subject The subject tells whom or what a sentence is about. (See page 305.)

EXAMPLE   The **geraniums** bloomed early this year.

subject complement A subject complement is a word or word group that completes the meaning of a linking verb and identifies or describes the subject. (See page 410. See also **predicate adjective** and **predicate nominative**.)

EXAMPLES   My cousin Brian is a **software technician.**

   The art room was **messy.**

subordinate clause A subordinate clause (also called a *dependent clause*) does not express a complete thought and cannot stand alone as a sentence. (See page 388. See also **adjective clause** and **adverb clause**.)

EXAMPLE   **After I read that article,** I changed my opinion.

suffix A suffix is a word part that is added after a base word or root. (See page 617.)

EXAMPLES   steady + ly = steadi**ly**
    forgive + ness = forgive**ness**
    obey + ing = obey**ing**
    adore + able = ador**able**
    shop + ing = shop**ping**

tense of verbs The tense of verbs indicates the time of the action or of the state of being that is expressed by the verb. (See page 458.)

Present Tense

I do	we do
you do	you do
he, she, it does	they do

Past Tense

I did	we did
you did	you did
he, she, it did	they did

Future Tense

I will (shall) do	we will (shall) do
you will (shall) do	you will (shall) do
he, she, it will (shall) do	they will (shall) do

Present Perfect Tense

I have done	we have done
you have done	you have done
he, she, it has done	they have done

Past Perfect Tense

I had done	we had done
you had done	you had done
he, she, it had done	they had done

Future Perfect Tense

I will (shall) have done	we will (shall) have done
you will (shall) have done	you will (shall) have done
he, she, it will (shall) have done	they will (shall) have done

transitive verb A transitive verb is an action verb that takes an object. (See page 353.)

EXAMPLE   Their dog **chased** our cat.

underlining (italics) (See page 588.)

- **for titles**

  EXAMPLES *The Way to Rainy Mountain* [book]

  National Geographic World [magazine]

  Sleeping Gypsy [work of art]

  Duke Bluebeard's Castle [long musical composition]

- **for names of vehicles**

  EXAMPLES *Orient Express* [train]

  Air Force One [aircraft]

verb A verb expresses an action or a state of being. (See page 347.)

EXAMPLE Evelyn **wore** a blue blazer.

Is the desert nearby?

verb phrase A verb phrase consists of a main verb and at least one helping verb. (See page 348.)

EXAMPLES The helicopter **should have been** here by now.

I **have** never **heard** Michael Bolton sing.

well (See *good, well*.)

who, whom (See page 486.)

EXAMPLES **Who** was the first astronaut to walk in space? [nominative form used as the predicate nominative referring to the subject *astronaut*]

Whom have you invited to your bat mitzvah party? [objective form used as the direct object of the verb phrase *have invited*]

Grammar at a Glance   789

Diagramming Appendix

Diagramming Sentences

A *sentence diagram* is a picture of how the parts of a sentence fit together. It shows how the words in the sentence are related.

Subjects and Verbs

Reference Note
For more about **subjects** and **verbs,** see page 305.

To diagram a sentence, first find the simple subject and the simple predicate, or verb, and write them on a horizontal line. Then, separate the subject and verb with a vertical line. Keep any capital letters, but leave out sentence punctuation.

EXAMPLES Dogs bark.

| Dogs | bark |

Children were singing.

| Children | were singing |

The preceding examples are easy because each sentence contains only a simple subject and a verb. Now, look at a longer sentence.

EXAMPLE   My older brother is studying Arabic in school.

To diagram the simple subject and the verb of this sentence, follow these three steps:

Step 1:   Separate the complete subject from the complete predicate.

complete subject	complete predicate
My older brother	is studying Arabic in school.

Step 2:   Find the simple subject and the verb.

simple subject	verb
brother	is studying

Step 3:   Draw the diagram.

brother	is studying

Exercise 1   Diagramming Simple Subjects and Verbs

Diagram the simple subject and verb in each of the following sentences.

EXAMPLES   1. Aunt Carmen is teaching me to cook.

1. | Aunt Carmen | is teaching |
   |---|---|

2. The dog sleeps in the garage.

2. | dog | sleeps |
   |---|---|

1. My family goes to the store together every Saturday.
2. We shop at the grocery store at the corner of our street.
3. I select the red beans, rice, meat, and cheese.
4. Grandma López must have written the shopping list.
5. Rosita is buying the chile peppers and cilantro.

HELP

Remember that simple subjects and verbs may consist of more than one word.

Exercise 1   Diagramming Simple Subjects and Verbs

ANSWERS

1. | family | goes |
   |---|---|

2. | We | shop |
   |---|---|

3. | I | select |
   |---|---|

4. | Grandma López | must have written |
   |---|---|

5. | Rosita | is buying |
   |---|---|

Compound Subjects

To diagram a compound subject, put the subjects on parallel lines. Then, put the connecting word (the conjunction, such as *and*, *but*, or *or*) on a dotted line between the subject lines.

EXAMPLE   **Koalas** and **kangaroos** are found in Australia.

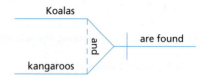

Reference Note
For more about **compound subjects**, see page 311.

Compound Verbs

To diagram a compound verb, put the two verbs on parallel lines. Then, put the conjunction on a dotted line between the verbs.

EXAMPLE   Callie **washes** and **dries** the dishes after dinner.

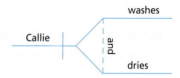

Reference Note
For more about **compound verbs**, see page 312.

Compound Subjects and Compound Verbs

A sentence with both a compound subject and a compound verb combines the two patterns you just learned.

EXAMPLE   The **cat** and her **kittens ate** and then **slept**.

HELP
Sentences in Exercise 2 may contain compound subjects, compound verbs, or both.

Exercise 2   Diagramming Compound Subjects and Compound Verbs

Diagram the simple subjects and verbs in the following sentences.

EXAMPLE 1. Spike Lee and Robert Townsend made and released movies recently.

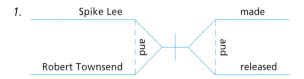

1. Ursula LeGuin and Nicholasa Mohr are my favorite authors.
2. Ms. Sanchez and Mr. Charles teach Spanish.
3. Bill Russell first played and later coached in the NBA.
4. My friends and I hurried home and told our parents the good news.
5. The students and the teacher visited the museum but did not have time for a complete tour.

Questions

To diagram a question, first make the question into a statement without changing or dropping any words. Then, diagram the sentence.

EXAMPLE Can all insects fly? [question]
All insects can fly. [statement]

Notice that the diagram uses the capitalization of the original sentence.

Understood Subjects

In an imperative sentence (a request or command) the subject is always understood to be *you*. Place the understood subject *you* in parentheses on the horizontal line.

EXAMPLE Look over there.

(you) | Look

Reference Note
For more information about **questions,** see page 316.

HELP
Remember that in a diagram, the subject always comes first, even if it does not come first in the sentence.

Reference Note
For information about **imperative sentences** and **understood subjects,** see page 316.

Exercise 2 Diagramming Compound Subjects and Compound Verbs

ANSWERS

1.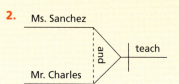

2. Ms. Sanchez / and / Mr. Charles — teach

3.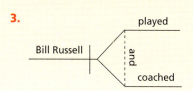

4.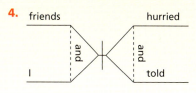

5.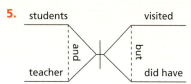

Diagramming Sentences 793

Exercise 3 — Diagramming Questions and Commands

ANSWERS

1. (you) | Eat
2. you | Do know
3. driver | is going
4. (you) | help
5. they | are standing

Exercise 3 Diagramming Questions and Commands

Diagram the simple subjects and verbs in the following sentences.

EXAMPLE 1. Please wash the dishes.

1. (you) | wash

1. Eat the rest of your jambalaya.
2. Do you know much about the Jewish holidays?
3. Where is the driver going?
4. Please help me with these cartons.
5. Why are they standing in line?

Adjectives and Adverbs

Adjectives and adverbs are written on slanted lines connected to the words they modify. Notice that possessive pronouns are diagrammed in the same way adjectives are. Also notice that the articles *a*, *an*, and *the* are included as adjectives.

Reference Note
For more information about **adjectives**, see page 336.

Adjectives

EXAMPLES **yellow** bird   **her best** blouse   **a playful** puppy

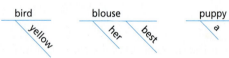

Exercise 4 Diagramming Sentences with Adjectives

Diagram the subjects, verbs, and adjectives in the following sentences.

EXAMPLE 1. A strong, cold wind blew all night.

794 Diagramming Appendix

1. My favorite singer is coming to town.
2. The long, grueling hike tired us.
3. Red, ripe tomatoes grow there.
4. The two brave astronauts stepped into space.
5. Is a funny movie playing downtown?

Adverbs

When an adverb modifies a verb, the adverb is placed on a slanted line below the verb.

EXAMPLES   wrote **quickly**   walked **there slowly**

Reference Note
For more about **adverbs**, see page 357.

When an adverb modifies an adjective or another adverb, it is placed on a slanted line connected to the word it modifies.

EXAMPLES   **incredibly** large poster   runs **very** fast

Exercise 5 Diagramming Sentences with Adverbs

Diagram the subjects, verbs, adjectives, and adverbs in the following sentences.

EXAMPLE   1. We almost always recycle newspapers.

1. Gloria Estefan recently recorded that song.
2. That new band plays very loudly.

Exercise 4 Diagramming Sentences with Adjectives

ANSWERS

1.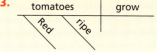

2.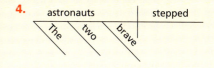

3.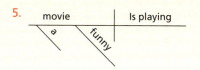

4.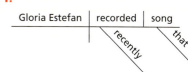

5.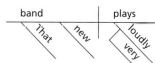

Exercise 5 Diagramming Sentences with Adverbs

ANSWERS

1.
Gloria Estefan	recorded	song
	recently	that

2.
band	plays
That new	loudly / very

> **Exercise 5** Diagramming Sentences with Adverbs
>
> ANSWERS continued
>
> 3.
>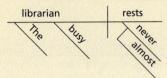
>
> 4.
>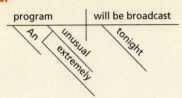
>
> 5.

3. Her two brothers visited Chinatown yesterday.
4. The busy librarian almost never rests.
5. An extremely unusual program will be broadcast tonight.

Prepositional Phrases

Prepositional phrases are diagrammed below the words they modify. Write the preposition on a slanting line. Then, write the object of the preposition on a horizontal line connected to the slanting line. Notice that the slanting line extends a little beyond the horizontal line.

> **Reference Note**
> For more information about **prepositional phrases**, see page 361.

Adjective Phrases

EXAMPLES time **of day**   several **in a row**

> **Reference Note**
> For more about **adjective phrases**, see page 377.

Adverb Phrases

EXAMPLES walked **on the moon**   are ready **for the test**

> **Reference Note**
> For more about **adverb phrases**, see page 381.

moves quickly **for an old dog**

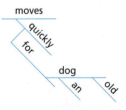

Exercise 6 — Diagramming Sentences with Prepositional Phrases

Diagram the following sentences.

EXAMPLE   1. The freighter slowed for the first lock.

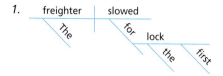

1. Tamales are wrapped in corn husks.
2. The soccer team from Brazil ran onto the field.
3. My friend from India skis very well.
4. The students in his class went to the library.
5. Catherine Zeta-Jones and Will Smith may star in that new movie.

Direct and Indirect Objects

Direct Objects

A direct object is diagrammed on the horizontal line with the subject and verb. A short vertical line separates the direct object from the verb.

EXAMPLE   We have been playing **tapes**.

Compound Direct Objects

EXAMPLE   Rachel enjoys **soccer** and **basketball**.

Reference Note
For more about **direct objects,** see page 405.

Reference Note
For more information about **compound direct objects,** see page 405.

Exercise 6 Diagramming Sentences with Prepositional Phrases

ANSWERS

1.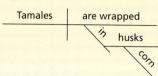

2.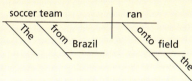

3.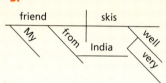

4.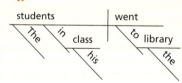

5.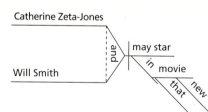

Reference Note
For more about **indirect objects,** see page 407.

Indirect Objects
The indirect object is diagrammed on a horizontal line beneath the verb. The verb and the indirect object are joined by a slanting line.

EXAMPLE   Dad fixed **us** some spaghetti.

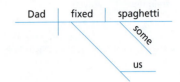

Compound Indirect Objects
EXAMPLE   Marisa gave her **brother** and **me** some grapes.

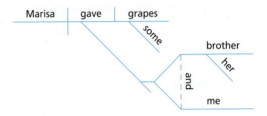

Reference Note
For more information about **compound indirect objects,** see page 408.

HELP
Not every sentence in Exercise 7 contains an indirect object.

Exercise 7 Diagramming Direct Objects and Indirect Objects

Diagram the following sentences.

EXAMPLE   1. He handed her the report.

1. Amy Tan wrote that book.
2. Marcus made a touchdown.

Exercise 7 Diagramming Direct Objects and Indirect Objects

ANSWERS

1.
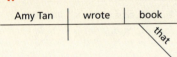

2.
Marcus | made | touchdown
                         \a

3. My grandmother knitted me a sweater.
4. Marilyn won a bronze medal in the Special Olympics.
5. I bought Jolene and her sister a present.

Subject Complements

A subject complement is diagrammed on the horizontal line with the subject and the verb. The complement comes after the verb. A line slanting toward the subject separates the subject complement from the verb.

Predicate Nominatives

EXAMPLE   Mickey Leland was a famous **congressman** from Texas.

Compound Predicate Nominatives

EXAMPLE   Aaliyah is a **singer** and a **dancer**.

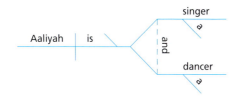

Predicate Adjectives

EXAMPLE   The guitarist was very **skillful**.

Reference Note
For more information about **predicate nominatives,** see page 410.

Reference Note
For more information on **compound predicate nominatives,** see page 411.

Reference Note
For more information on **predicate adjectives,** see page 412.

Exercise 7 Diagramming Direct Objects and Indirect Objects

ANSWERS continued

3.
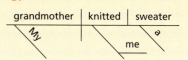

4.
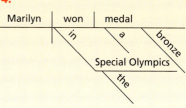

5.
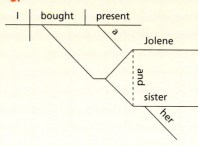

Exercise 8 Diagramming Sentences with Subject Complements

ANSWERS

1.
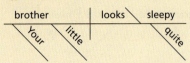

2.
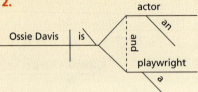

3.
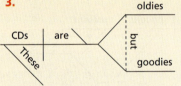

4.
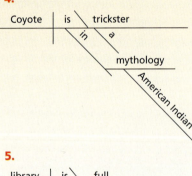

5.
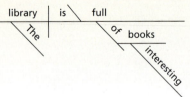

Reference Note
For more about **compound predicate adjectives**, see page 413.

Compound Predicate Adjectives

EXAMPLE   They were **weary** but **patient**.

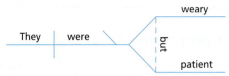

Exercise 8 Diagramming Sentences with Subject Complements

Diagram the following sentences.

EXAMPLE   1. Ms. Chang is an excellent teacher and a fine lawyer.

1.
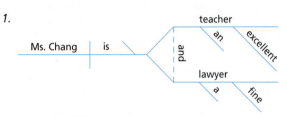

1. Your little brother looks quite sleepy.
2. Ossie Davis is an actor and a playwright.
3. These CDs are oldies but goodies.
4. Coyote is a trickster in American Indian mythology.
5. The library is full of interesting books.

Subordinate Clauses

Adjective Clauses

Diagram an adjective clause by connecting it with a broken line to the word it modifies. Draw the broken line between the relative pronoun and the word to which it relates. The adjective clause is diagrammed below the independent clause.

Reference Note
For more information about **independent clauses,** see page 387. For more about **adjective clauses** and **relative pronouns,** see page 389.

EXAMPLE   Certain land crabs **that are found in Cuba** can run fast.

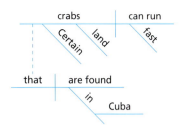

Adverb Clauses

Diagram an adverb clause by using a broken line to connect the adverb clause to the word it modifies. Place the subordinating conjunction that introduces the adverb clause on the broken line. The adverb clause is diagrammed below the independent clause.

EXAMPLE   **When Halley's Comet returns,** I will be a very old man.

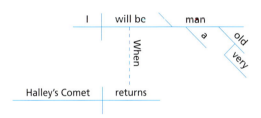

Reference Note

For more information about **adverb clauses,** see page 391. For a list of **subordinating conjunctions,** see page 388.

HELP

The words *after, because, if, since, unless, when,* and *while* are often used as subordinating conjunctions.

HELP

The words *who, whom, whose, which,* and *that* are often used as relative pronouns.

Diagramming Sentences   **801**

Exercise 9 — Diagramming Sentences with Adjective Clauses and Adverb Clauses

ANSWERS

1.
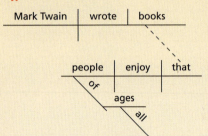

2.
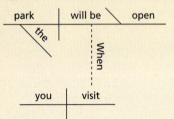

3.
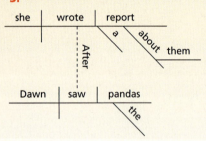

4.
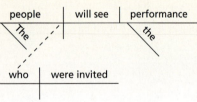

5.
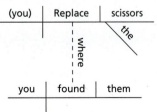

Exercise 9 — Diagramming Sentences with Adjective Clauses and Adverb Clauses

Diagram the following sentences.

EXAMPLE 1. If you go to the library, will you return this book for me?

1.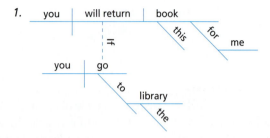

1. Mark Twain wrote books that people of all ages enjoy.
2. When you visit, the park will be open.
3. After Dawn saw the pandas, she wrote a report about them.
4. The people who were invited will see the performance.
5. Replace the scissors where you found them.

The Kinds of Sentence Structure

Simple Sentences

A simple sentence contains one independent clause.

EXAMPLE The coach gave Alfonso a pat on the back. [one independent clause]

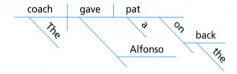

Compound Sentences

A compound sentence contains at least two independent clauses. The second independent clause in a compound sentence is diagrammed below the first and is joined to it by a coordinating conjunction.

Reference Note
For more about **simple sentences,** see page 394.

EXAMPLE   Ostriches walk in a funny way, but they can run fast.
[two independent clauses]

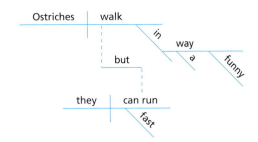

Reference Note
For more information about **compound sentences,** see page 395. For more about **coordinating conjunctions,** see page 364.

NOTE   The coordinating conjunctions are *and, but, for, nor, or, so,* and *yet.*

Exercise 10 Diagramming Compound Sentences

Diagram the following compound sentences.

EXAMPLE   1. Genna went to the mall, but I stayed home.

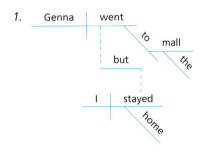

1. Lisa likes soccer, but I prefer basketball.
2. Gabriela Mistral is a poet, but she has also written essays.
3. Cactuses are desert plants, yet they can grow in milder climates.
4. I can give Jewel the news tonight, or you can call her now.
5. Chinese immigrants worked on the railroad in the West, but Irish immigrants built the railroad in the East.

Exercise 10 Diagramming Compound Sentences

ANSWERS

1.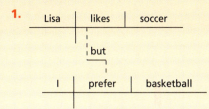

2.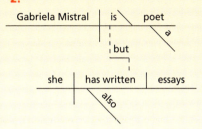

3.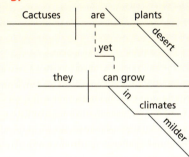

4.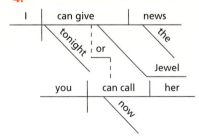

5.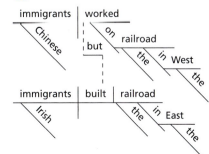

Complex Sentences

A complex sentence contains one independent clause and at least one subordinate clause.

EXAMPLE Leon received a letter that was mailed from Germany. [one independent clause and one subordinate clause]

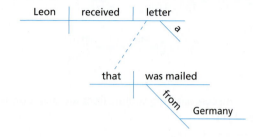

Reference Note
For more about **complex sentences,** see page 397.

Compound-Complex Sentences

A compound-complex sentence contains two or more independent clauses and at least one subordinate clause.

EXAMPLE After we rehearse this scene, we will move to another room, and the stage crew will work on the set. [two independent clauses and one subordinate clause]

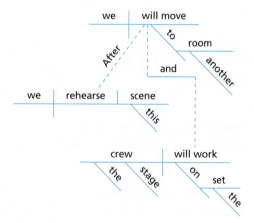

Reference Note
For more about **compound-complex sentences,** see page 398.

Exercise 11 **Diagramming Complex and Compound-Complex Sentences**

Diagram the following complex and compound-complex sentences.

EXAMPLE
1. If the Bulldogs win their last two games, they will finish in first place.

1. Hector walked to school because his bicycle had a flat tire.
2. Rosa was the contestant who knew the correct answer.
3. Unless the rain stops soon, the umpire will cancel the game.
4. As the lights dimmed, the audience grew quiet.
5. The student that designs the best cover receives a free yearbook, so many students will be entering designs.

Exercise 11 **Diagramming Complex and Compound-Complex Sentences**

ANSWERS

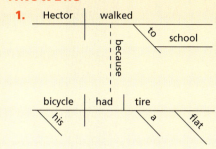

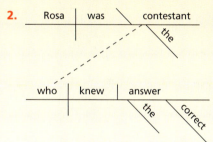

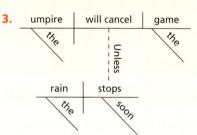

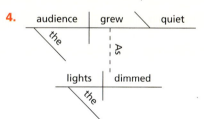

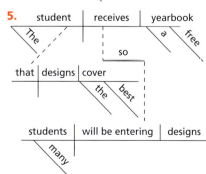

INDEX

A, an, 520
***A, an, the,* as articles,** 336
    capitalization of, 554
    italicizing in title, 589
Abbreviations
    for addresses, 564
    capitalization of, 548–49
    for geographical names, 564
    of names of government bodies, 542
    punctuation of, 563–64
    for time, 564
    for units of measure, 564
Abridged dictionary, 680
Accent marks, in dictionary entry, 681
Accept, except, 520
Accurate information, in graphics, 687
Acronyms, 563
Action details, 30
Action verbs, 350, 768
    in headline, 73
    and linking verbs, 352, 410
Actors, feelings expressed by, 183
A.D., 564
Adding (as revision technique) 12, 36, 69, 103, 104, 139, 171, 214, 248
Addresses
    abbreviations in, 564
    commas in, 574
Adjective(s)
    commas with, 567–68
    comparative form of, 142
    comparison with adverbs, 497–501
    compound, 606–607
    definition of, 336
    demonstrative adjectives, 339
    diagram of, 794
    after linking verbs, 503
    as modifiers, 495
    placement in sentences, 510
    possessive pronouns as, 330
    proper adjectives, 338, 548
    word endings for, 270
Adjective clauses, 389–90, 769
    definition of, 512
    diagram of, 800–801
Adjective phrases, 377–78, 379, 769
    diagram of, 796
Adjustment letter, 760
Adverb(s)
    comparative form of, 142
    comparison with adjectives, 497–502
    definition of, 357
    diagram of, 795
    after linking verbs, 503
    as modifiers, 495, 496
    placement in sentences, 358, 510
    prepositions distinguished from, 363–64
    word endings for, 270
Adverb clauses, 391, 769
    diagram of, 801
    placement in sentences, 392
    punctuation of introductory, 573
Adverb phrases, 381–83, 769
    diagram of, 796
Advertising
    humorous, 254–55
    in media, 751
    in print, 255
    on radio, 255
    relationship, documentary filmmakers and advertisers, 146
    on television, 255
Advice column, 74
Affixes. *See* Prefixes; Suffixes.
Agreement (pronoun-antecedent), 435–38, 769–70
    antecedent gender, 435–36
    antecedents joined by *and,* 438
    antecedents joined by *or* or *nor,* 437
    indefinite pronouns as antecedents, 436–37
    his or her construction, 436
    in number, 436
Agreement (subject-verb), 422–23, 770
    compound subjects, 429–30
    of *don't/doesn't* and subject, 433
    indefinite pronouns and, 427–28
    in number, 422
    and phrases between subject and verb, 425–26
    subject following verb, 432
Ain't, 520
Aircraft
    capitalizing names of, 545
    italicizing names of, 589
Alignment, of page, 683–84
Alliteration, 42
All right, 520
Almanacs, 699
A lot, 521
Alphabetization, of source list, 205
Already, all ready, 521, 625
Altar, alter, 625
Altogether, all together, 625
American English. *See also* Standard English.
    dialects of, 692
    spelling and pronunciations, 691
Among, between, 521
Analyzing
    of cause and effect, 65

media messages, 732
sound effects in poetry, 179
Anchor, for television news segment, 79, 80, 82
And. See also Conjunctions.
    subjects joined by, 429
Anecdotes, 755
Animation, in electronic media, 743
Announcements, 723
Antecedents
    definition of, 328–29
    pronoun agreement with, 435–38
Anyways, 521
Anywheres, 521
Apostrophes, 598–605, 771
    with contractions, 602–603
    with personal pronouns, 601
    with plurals, 605, 623
    with possessives, 598–601
    and possessive personal pronouns, 251
Appendix, in a book, 695
Appositive(s), 174, 488, 570–71, 771
Appositive phrases, 570–71, 771
Appreciation letter, 760
"April Rain Song" (Hughes), 537
Arguments. *See also* Facts; Opinions; Persuasion; Persuasive essay (reading); Persuasive essay (writing).
    counterarguments and, 233
Arranging ideas, 31
Art and artwork. *See also* Graphic(s); Illustrations; Visuals.
    designing a newspaper, 77
    details in illustrations, 151
    editorial cartoons, 76, 83, 259
    underlining (italicizing) names of, 589
Articles
    capitalizing in titles, 217, 554
    italicizing in titles, 589
At, 521
Atlases, 699
Audience, media and, 746
Audience (speaking)
    adapting word choice for, 45
    analyzing for presentation, 720
    and verbal elements of speech, 722
Audience (writing). *See also* Advertising; Target audience.
    for autobiographical incident, 29
    for book review, 163–64
    for business letters, 758
    for comparison-contrast essay, 130–31
    for "how-to" paper, 95
    identifying, 10
    for informal or personal letters, 758
    for news article, 60
    for persuasive letter, 239, 240, 241–42
    for research report, 200

Audio. *See* Television.
Author(s)
    bias of, 704
    of book, 168
    point of view, 704
    purpose of, 188, 194–95, 704
Authoritative sources, 202
Authority, in media, 746
Autobiographical incident (reading)
    chronological order, 18, 23–24
    making inferences (forming generalizations), 18, 21–22
    reading selection, 19–20
Autobiographical incident (writing)
    prewriting, 27–31
    proofreading/publishing, 39–40
    revising, 36–38
    Student's Model, 35
    Writer's Model, 33–34
    writing, 32
Autobiographies, writing to learn and, 736
Auxiliary verbs. *See* Helping verbs.
Awards, capitalization of, 545

B

Babbitt, Natalie, 169
Background information for telling a story, 11, 29, 45
Background knowledge. *See* Prior knowledge.
Bad, badly, 521, 772
Bandwagon technique, 257
Banta, Natalie, 68
Bar graphs, 143, 712
Barriers to effective listening, eliminating, 727. *See also* Listening.
Base forms of verbs, 445, 772
Basic situation, 165
B.C., 564
Be. See also Helping verbs; Irregular verbs.
    conjugation of, 460–61
    as linking verb, 351, 412
Become, **principal parts of,** 449
Begin, **principal parts of,** 449
Believability
    evaluation and, 731
    of persuasive speaker, 256
Beowulf, 690
Between, among, 521
Bias. *See also* Point of view.
    of author, 704
    media and, 746
Bibliographic references, 210
    in a book, 695
Biography. *See also* Autobiographical incident; Autobiographies.

in the library, 695
Block style (of business letter), 759
Block style (of comparison-contrast essay), 124
Blow, **principal parts of,** 449
Body
 of book review, 168
 of business letter, 759
 of comparison-contrast essay, 136
 of composition, 756
 of "how-to" paper, 98
 of news article, 66
 of persuasive letter, 244
 of research report, 210
 of visual and graphic, 711
Body language
 movement and feelings, 183
 as positive feedback, 728
 in presentation, 722
Boldface fonts, 5, 686
Book(s)
 call number of, 695, 696
 comparing with film and television, 181–84
 information in card catalog, 695–96
 underlining (italicizing) titles of, 588
 information found in parts of, 695
 as sources, 132, 202, 203
Book jacket, 162
Book review (reading)
 elements of a novel, 154, 156
 point of view, 154, 157
 reading selection, 155
Book review (writing)
 gathering and organizing details, 164–66
 identifying plot elements, 165
 preparing your evaluation, 167
 prewriting, 161–67
 proofreading and publishing, 174–75
 purpose and audience for, 163–64
 revising, 171–73
 Student's Model, 170
 Writer's Model, 169
 writing, 168–70
Borrowed words, 691–92
Brainstorming, 10. *See also* Prewriting.
 for clarification essays, 219
 for comparison-contrast essay, 129
 for "how-to" paper, 94
 for humorous advertisement, 255
 for presentation topic, 719
 prewriting and, 762
 for research report, 199
 for short story, 176
Brake, break, 625
Brand names, capitalization of, 544
Break, **principal parts of,** 449
Bring, **principal parts of,** 450
Bring, take, 523

British English, spelling and pronunciations, 691
Broadcasting, 743
Brochures, 225
Browser, World Wide Web, 697, 700
Buffalo Book, The (Dary), 280
Buildings and other structures, capitalization of, 545
Bullet, in page layout, 684
Bulletin board display, 259
Businesses, capitalization of, 544
Business letters. *See also* Letters (correspondence).
 envelopes for, 758
 format of, 246
 forms of, 759
 parts of, 759–60
 punctuation in, 574, 579
 purposes for, 758
 types of, 760
Buy, **principal parts of,** 450
Byline, 751

C

Cable television, 744
Calendar items, capitalization of, 542
Call number, 695, 696. *See also* Card catalog.
Call to action, in persuasive letter, 242–43
"**Camel Fodder**" (Shah), 594
Camera person, for television news segment, 79, 82
Cameras, 753
 camera angle, 148, 744
Camera shot, 744
Capital, capitol, 626
Capitalization, 537–56, 772–74
 of abbreviations, 548–49
 of aircraft, 545
 of animal names, 539
 of awards, 545
 of brand names, 544
 of buildings and other structures, 545
 of businesses, 544
 of calendar items, 542
 of constellations, 546
 of deities, 545
 of directions, 541
 of directly quoted sentence, 591
 of first word in sentence, 537
 of geographical names, 540–41
 of government bodies, 542
 of heavenly bodies, 546
 of historical events and periods, 543
 of holidays, 542
 of holy days and celebrations, 545
 of institutions, 542
 in letter salutation and closing, 538
 of memorials, 545

of monuments, 545
of names, 539
of nationalities, 544
of organizations, 542
of peoples, 544
of personal names, 539
of planets, 546
of pronoun *I*, 538
of proper adjectives, 338, 548
of proper nouns, 39, 324, 539
of races, 544
of religions and followers, 545
of sacred writings, 545
of school subjects, 548
of ships, 545
of spacecraft, 545
of special events, 542
of stars, 546
of teams, 542
of titles and subtitles of works, 217, 552–54
of titles of persons, 551
of trains, 545

Capital letters, 559, 686

Captions
in graphics, 688
in photography, 149–50, 753

Card catalog, 162, 695–96. *See also* Online catalog.

Career development activities
comparing and contrasting by journalists, 151
expert guidance, 225
film or book review, 185
in journalism, 83
letter writing, 117
persuasion and, 259
reading and writing used in careers, 15
writing journal entry about person who interests you, 47

Career guide, 225

Carroll, Lewis, 178

Cartoons. *See* Editorial cartoons.

Case. *See* Personal pronouns, forms of.

Categories, for ideas in research, 207. *See also* Organizing ideas.

Catherine, Called Birdy (Cushman), 155

Cause, definition of, 704

Cause-and-effect order, 6

Cause-and-effect pattern, 293, 705, 710
in expository paragraphs, 293

Cause-and-effect relationships
analysis of, 65, 704
as context clues, 713

CD-ROM, as source, 202, 696

Censorship, 750

Center-aligned text, 683

Characterization, 182–83

Characters
main character, 162, 163
in novel, 156
in short story, 176–77
in *Tuck Everlasting*, 164

Charts, 197, 221, 711–13, 764–65. *See also* Diagrams; Graphic(s).
answering questions about, 197
flowcharts, 112–13, 688
learning "how-to" from graphics and, 112–13
pie chart, 688, 712
T-chart, 145

Choose, chose, 626

Choose, **principal parts of,** 450

Choppy sentences, combining, 141

Chronological order, 166
analysis of text pattern of, 710
for autobiographical incident, 31
chart of, 24
clue words, 705
definition of, 283
to develop paragraphs, 285–86
for explaining a process, 286
in "how-to" paper, 96, 98
plot summary in, 168
for story, 45
for telling a story, 285

Clarification, of speech, 224, 258

Clarification essay, 219

Classification
of information as study skill, 733
of sentences by purpose, 316–17

Classification essay, 145

Clauses
adjective clauses, 389–90, 512
adverb clauses, 391
definition of, 387
independent clauses, 303, 387, 397, 577
as modifiers, 496
subordinate clauses, 303, 388, 397

Cleary, Beverly, 285

Clichés, 172, 173, 714. *See also* Tired words.

Clincher sentences, 279, 282, 283

Closing, of business letter, 759

Cloths, clothes, 626

Clue words, 705. *See also* Context clues; Text structures.

Clustering, 10
prewriting and, 763

Coarse, course, 627

Coherence. *See also* Organizing ideas; Rearranging (as revision technique); Specifical language; Transitional words and phrases.
in book review, 168
in "how-to" paper, 98
in paragraphs, 283–88

Cohesive. *See* Unity.

Collaborative writing
database records, 185
forms, 185, 259

short story, 185
skit, 15
Collection of written works. *See* Portfolio building.
"Collection Question, A" (Hester), 138
Colloquialisms, 693
Colons, 579, 775
    in business letter salutation, 579
    with list of items, 579
    used in writing expressions of time, 579
Colors
    cool colors, 688
    creating effects with images, 749
    in graphics, 687–88
    illustrations and, 748
    in visuals, 221
    warm colors, 688
Columns, in newspaper article, 73
Combining (as revision technique), 12, 70, 140
Combining sentences, 71, 141
    and complex sentences, 275
    and compound sentences, 274
    and compound subjects, 273
    and compound verbs, 273
    with connecting words, 273–75
    with groups of words, 271–72
    by inserting words, 269–70
    simple sentences, 395
    to smooth writing style, 314
Comic book form, 192, 194
***Come,* principal parts of,** 450
Commas
    and appositive phrases, 570–71
    and appositives, 174, 570–71
    in compound sentences, 568–69
    with conjunctions connecting sentences, 71
    conventional uses of, 574
    definition of, 566
    with interjections, 366
    with interrupters, 570–71
    after introductory elements, 572–73
    for items in a series, 106, 566
    with quotations, 591–92
    and run-on sentences, 265
    to separate two or more adjectives coming before a noun, 567–68
    to set off word group, 271–72
    to set off words in direct address, 572
    in stringy sentences, 267
    unnecessary, 575
Commercial broadcasting, 743
Common nouns, 39
    definition of, 324, 539
Community, sharing information with, 240
Comparative degree, 497–98, 499
Comparative form
    of adjectives, 142
    of adverbs, 142

Comparing and contrasting
    adjectives and adverbs used in, 497–501
    of film and book in same genre, 183–84
    comparative adjectives and adverbs, 142
    decreasing comparison, 499
    double comparison, 504
    of film, TV, and literature, 181–84
    of ideas in photography, 147–50
    irregular comparison, 501
    oral traditions, 47, 729
    perception of spoken message with others, 258, 728
Comparison-contrast essay (reading)
    comparison-contrast structure, 120, 124–25
    points of comparison, 120, 123–24
    reading selection, 121–22
Comparison-contrast essay (writing), 128–45
    choose and narrow two subjects, 128–30
    main idea statement for, 133
    organizing information for, 132–33
    prewriting, 128–35
    proofreading and publishing, 142–44
    purpose and audience for, 130–31
    revising, 139–41
    Student's Model, 138
    support for, 132–33
    Writer's Model, 137
    writing, 136–38
Comparison-contrast pattern, 705, 710
Comparison-contrast structure, 120, 124–25
Complaint letter, 760
Complements. *See also* Direct objects; Indirect objects; Predicate adjectives; Predicate nominatives.
    definition of, 403
    diagrams of, 797–800
    finding in sentences, 404
    subject complements, 410–13
Complete predicate, compared with simple predicate, 309
Complete sentences, 262–63
Complete subject, 306
Complex sentences, 397, 777
    combining sentences and, 275
    diagram of, 804
Complications, in plot, 165
Composition
    body of, 756
    conclusion of, 756–57
    introduction of, 755–56
Compound adjectives, 606–607
Compound-complex sentences, 398, 777
    diagram of, 804
Compound nouns, definition of, 323
Compound numbers, hyphenating, 606
Compound prepositions, 361
Compound sentences, 395, 778
    combining sentences and, 274
    commas in, 568–69

diagram of, 802–803
run-on sentence changed to, 72
semicolons used to separate parts, 577
Compound subjects, 311, 429–30
combining sentences with, 273
diagram of, 792
using correct pronouns in, 478
Compound verbs, 312
combining sentences with, 273
diagram of, 792
Compound words, 92
Comprehension, listening and, 729–30
Computers. *See also* Internet; World Wide Web.
cut and paste commands for sentence fragments, 264
desktop publishing, 683–87
editing with, 38, 107, 264
evaluating writing, 248
headings, 209
networking for collaborative writing, 287
networks, 698
online card catalog, 698
online databases, 698
online sources, 698
revising with, 141, 171
spellchecker on, 107, 530
thesaurus for replacing dull verbs, 38
Computer software
learning "how-to" from, 112, 114–15
presentation software, 224
Conceptual maps, 208, 765
Concluding paragraphs, 294
Conclusion of written work
book review, 168
comparison-contrast essay, 136
composition, 756–57
"how-to" paper, 98
persuasive letter, 244
research report, 210
Conclusions. *See* Drawing conclusions.
Condensed type, 686
Confirming your understanding, 4
Conflict, in short story, 176–77
Conjugating verbs, 458–61
Conjunctions, 272–73, 364–65, 778
combining sentences, 71, 72
commas used with, 566
coordinating conjunctions, 364–65
correlative conjunctions, 365
definition of, 364
stringy sentences and, 250
Connecting cultures, 46
ethnic dialect, 692
comparing folk tales, 47
Connecting ideas. *See also* Transitional words and phrases.
in paragraphs, 287–88

Connecting words
in compound subjects, 311
in compound verbs, 312
conjunctions as, 273
for creating complex sentences, 275
Connections to life, 74–75, 146, 220–21, 254–55
Connections to literature. *See* Literature connections.
Connecting with others through speaking and listening, 17, 85, 119, 187, 723–24. *See also* Making connections.
Connotation, definition of, 714
Consonants, 617
suffixes with, 618–19
Constellations, capitalization of, 546
Constructive criticism, 728
Content and Organization Guidelines for Self-Evaluation and Peer Evaluation
autobiographical incident, 36
book review, 171
comparison-contrast essay, 139
"how-to" paper, 103
news article, 69
persuasive letter, 248
research report, 214
Content (speaking), evaluating, 256
Context, 25, 159, 160
of media message, 746
Context clues, 25, 160, 194, 195
identifying meanings of words with, 713–14
Contractions
agreement with *don't* and *doesn't,* 433
apostrophes with, 602–603
definition of, 602
Here's, there's, 432
in informal English, 602
possessive pronouns compared with, 603
Contrasting. *See* Comparing and contrasting.
Conversation. *See also* Dialogue; Speaking.
using correct end punctuation in writing of, 318
Convincing, in persuasive speech, 256, 258, 731
Coordinating conjunctions, 364–65
definition of, 364
run-on sentences and, 265
Copy. *See also* Script.
media, 751
Copyright page, of a book, 695
Correlative conjunctions, 365
Corresponding with others. *See* E-mail; Letters (correspondence).
Could of, 523
Counterargument, 233
Cover of novel, 162
Creative writing
as author's purpose, 194
humorous poem, 151
about research topic, 225

story writing with group of classmates, 185
writing about reading process, 15
Credibility. *See also* Believability.
media definition of, 746
Credits, in electronic media, 744
Criteria (speaking)
developing, to evaluate persuasive speech, 257–58
developing, to evaluate self, 726
Criteria (writing). *See* Content and Organization Guidelines for Self-Evaluation and Peer Evaluation; Style Guidelines.
Critical thinking. *See* Mini-lesson (critical thinking).
Critical viewing, of visual messages, 746–48
Critics, careers as, 185
Cropping, of photographs, 149, 753
Cross-curricular activities (art)
details in illustrations, 151
editorial cartoons, 83
Cross-curricular activities (music), multimedia presentation, 151
Cross-curricular activities (physical education), trading cards, 225
Cross-curricular activities (science)
articles about, 83
flowchart or graphic for process in, 117
Cross-curricular activities (social studies), letters and forms for field trips, 259
Cross-curricular activities (speech), class "how-to" demonstration, 117
Cross-references, in card catalog, 696
CSSD (context, structure, sound, dictionary), 159
Culture. *See* Connecting cultures.
Cursive writing, 41
Cushman, Karen, 155
Cutting, 725

Dary, David A., 280
Database
online, 698
of reports on educational computer games (creating), 185
Dates, commas in, 574
Decimal points, 561
Declarative sentences, 316, 778
punctuation of, 561
Definitions
as context clues, 713
in dictionary entry, 681
Degrees of comparison, 497–502
Deities, capitalization of, 545
Deleting (as revision technique), 12, 139, 171
Delivery, of presentation, 223, 224, 256, 721–22
Demonstrative adjectives, 332, 339

Demonstrative pronouns, 332, 339
Denotation, definition of, 714
Dependent clauses. *See* Subordinate clauses.
Description
definition of, 291–92
details in, 30
explanation of, 292
as literary technique, 177, 182
in short story, 177
writing, 41, 109–11
Desert, dessert, 627
Designing your writing
bar graph, 143
business letter format, 246
headings, 209
illustrating steps in a process, 101
for newspaper production, 77
quotations in book reviews, 166
Desktop publishing
definition of, 683
page layout, 683–85
type, 685–87
Details. *See also* Evidence.
action details, 30
arranging and organizing, 63–64, 134, 164–66
elaboration and, 289–90
evaluation of, 63–64, 135
gathering, 60–63, 164, 166
in illustrations, 151
in news article, 66
organizing in spatial order, 110
relevant, 135
sensory details, 10, 30, 46, 109, 281
supporting details, 6, 127
Dewey Decimal classification system, 695, 696
Diagrams, 113, 688, 712
sentence diagrams, 790–804
Venn diagram, 132, 766
Dialects, of American English, 692
Dialogue, 4, 182
informal English for, 45
quotation marks in, 594
in short story, 177
Diaries, studying and, 736
Diction, 722
Dictionary, 159, 235
comparative and superlative forms in, 499
parts of entry, 680–81
pronunciation in, 613
types of, 680
Differences, 129, 131, 145. *See also* Comparing and contrasting.
Direct address, punctuation of, 572
Directions (geographical), capitalization of, 541
Directions (instructions). *See also* Instructions.
for demonstration to class, 117

guidelines for giving, 724
listening to, 730
Direct objects, 405–406, 481, 482, 778
compared with predicate nominatives, 411
definition of, 481
diagram of, 797
Directory, for Internet search, 204, 701, 702
Direct quotations, 66, 590–91
setting off with punctuation, 591
Discover, writing to. *See* Writing to discover.
Distractions, listening and, 727
Do, **principal parts of,** 450
Documentaries, 744. *See also* Producer.
comparing documentaries, 146
definition of, 146
footage, 749
as research source, 202
Document design
desktop publishing and, 683–86
graphics in, 687–89
manuscript style, 682
page layout, 683–85
type, 685–87
Documenting sources, 202–203, 210
Don't, doesn't
agreement with subject, 433
Double comparisons, 504, 778
Double negatives, 507, 779
Double-spaced text, 687
Drafting. *See* Writing (first draft).
Dramatic interpretation. *See also* Oral interpretation.
of experience (telling a story), 45–46
of poem, 44
of play, 47
of story, 177
Drawing conclusions, 4, 8, 188, 192–93, 705
Drink, **principal parts of,** 450
Drive, **principal parts of,** 450
Dudley, William, 229–30

E

Earth, **capitalization of,** 546
Eat, **principal parts of,** 450
–ed **(word ending), adding to verb,** 446
Editing, 13, 251. *See also* Grammar Links; Revising (writing); Proofreading.
for appropriate word choice, 38, 173, 216
of book review, 171
of news article, 55, 69
of persuasive essay, 253
for sentence variety, 71, 141
Editor, in media, 751
Editorial cartoons, 76, 83, 259, 752
Editorials (writing), 15, 76

Effect, definition of, 704
Effects, of media messages, 182, 224, 747–48
***ei, ie,* spelling rule for,** 615
Elaboration
of description, 110
explanation of, 289–90
in persuasive letter, 244
with specific language, 97
as revision technique, 36, 69, 103, 139, 171, 214, 248
to support spoken ideas, 222, 721
supporting evidence and, 242
in writing, 9, 11
Electronic mail. *See* E-mail.
Electronic media terms, 743–46
Elements
of novels, 154, 156
of plot, 165
Eliminating barriers to effective listening. *See* Barriers to effective listening, eliminating.
E-mail, 47
guidelines for, 757
persuasive letter and, 252
response to novel in, 185
Emotional appeals, 233
as persuasive technique in speech, 257
Emotions. *See* Feelings.
Emphasis, in page layout, 684
Encyclopedias, 202, 699
End marks (sentence punctuation), 318, 779
definition of, 561
exclamation points, 561, 562
periods, 561, 562
question marks, 561
English language
American English dialects, 692
changes in, 690–91
colloquialisms in, 693
formal, 45, 519, 535, 693
history of, 690–93
informal, 45, 519, 693
Middle English, 690
nonstandard, 519, 692–93
Old English, 690
slang in, 693
standard English, 519, 535, 692–93
word origins, 691–92
Entertaining
as author's purpose, 194
documentary for, 146
Entry word, in dictionary entry, 680
Envelopes, addressing, 758
Essay
capitalization in, 559
proofreading of, 39
publishing, 40
reflecting on, 40

Essay tests
  evaluating and revising, 739
  key verbs in, 738
  prewriting, 739
  qualities of good answer, 739
  questions, 737–39
  studying for, 737
Ethical appeals, 233
Ethnic dialect, 692
Etymology, in dictionary entry, 681
Evaluation. *See also* Content and Organization Guidelines for Self-Evaluation and Peer Evaluation; Peer review; Revising (writing); Style Guidelines.
  of book, 167
  of details in a news article, 63–64
  of event in a news story, 58–59
  of oral presentation, 729
  of persuasive speech, 256–58
  of research presentation, 223–24
  of self, in formal speaking, 726
  of Web sites, 702–703
  of writing, 12, 248
  of written draft, 12
Evaluation criteria, 726
Events, newsworthy, 58–59
Everywheres, 521
Evidence, 228, 232–34
  to clarify and support spoken ideas, 222, 721
  elaboration and, 242
  in persuasive essay, 253
  for persuasive letter, 241, 242
Exact verbs, 37, 38
Exaggeration, in humorous advertisement, 255
Examples
  definition of, 281
  in dictionary entry, 681
  for persuasive letter, 241
  to support spoken ideas, 222
Except, accept, 520
Exclamation points, 561
  with interjection, 366
  with quotations, 591, 592
  uses of, 317
Exclamatory sentences, 317, 780
Expanded type, 686
Experience, personal. *See* Life experience.
Experts, career guidance from, 225
Explanations
  in comparison-contrast essay, 136
  in "how-to" paper, 98
Exploring your reading, 4, 8
Expository paragraphs
  cause-and-effect pattern in, 293
  definition of, 291
  discussion of, 293
Expository writing, 58
  book review, 161–75

  comparison-contrast essay, 128–44
  "how-to" paper, 94–107
  informative essay, 219
  newspaper article, 58–73
  research report, 198–218
Expressing, as author's purpose, 194
Expressive writing, 15, 17, 27–40. *See also* Autobiographical incident.
Extending ideas, 4, 8
Extending your reading, 8
Eye contact, 722

Facial expressions, 183, 722
  of Cinderella, 184
Facts, 228, 231–32, 233. *See also* Opinions.
  definition of, 281
  distinguishing from opinions, 705
  in news article, 60–61
  in persuasive letter, 241
  test on, 236
Fall, principal parts of, 450
Faulty generalizations, 22
Feature news, 752. *See also* Soft news.
Feedback, 728
Feelings, expressed by actors, 183
Feel, principal parts of, 450
Feminine pronouns, 435–36
Fewer, less, 523
Fiction books, 695
Figurative language, 42, 43, 109, 714
  metaphor, 109
  simile, 109
Films. *See also* Documentaries; Videos and videotapes.
  comparing with TV and literature, 181–84
  definition of, 744
  documentary, 146
  as information source, 698
  underlining (italicizing) titles of, 588
Find, principal parts of, 450
First impressions, of poems, 179
First-person pronouns
  in compound constructions, 482
  intensive pronouns, 330
  personal pronouns, 329, 330
  reflexive pronouns, 330
5W-How? questions, 697
  listening to comprehend and, 730
  news article and, 50, 54–55, 60–62, 63, 66
  prewriting and, 762
Fix-it strategies, 4, 6
Flowcharts, 23–24, 31, 112–13, 688
  diagrams and, 113
Focused topic, 199

Focused writing, 763
Fonts (typefaces), 248, 685–87, 686. *See also* Underlining (italics).
    boldface, 5, 686
    in print media, 752
    size of, 686
    style of, 686–87
Footers, 684
Formal English, 45, 519, 693
Formal outlines, 765–66
Formal speaking, 719–23
    announcements, 723
    introductions to presentations, 723
    presentations, 719–23
Format, of business letter, 246
Forming generalizations. *See* Generalizations.
Form of writing, choosing, 9, 10, 15
Forms
    for evaluating, 185
    for field trips, 259
    filling out, 757–58
Formula, in media, 748
Foul Shot (Hoey), 43
Four *W*'s (What? When? Who? Where?), 29
Fragments. *See* Sentence fragments.
Freewriting, 10
    focused, 763
    guidelines for, 763
    studying and, 736
Freeze, **principal parts of,** 450
Future perfect progressive tense, 460
Future perfect tense, 458, 459, 461
Future progressive tense, 460
Future tense, 458, 459

G

Games, writing instructions for, 117
Gender, pronoun-antecedent agreement in, 435–36
Generalizations, 4, 8, 18, 21–22, 184, 705–706
Genres in media, 748
Genres of literature, 181
Geographical names
    capitalization of, 540
    abbreviation of, 564
Gersh, Harry, 288
Get, **principal parts of,** 450
Give, **principal parts of,** 450
Glossary
    in a book, 695
    definition of, 519
    of usage, 519–30
Go, **principal parts of,** 450
Goals, for writing improvement, 107
God, goddess, **capitalization of,** 546

"**Gold Rush**" (Wilmore), 189–91
Good, well, 502–503, 523, 780
Government bodies
    acronyms for names of, 563
    capitalization of names of, 542
Grammar Links
    capitalizing and punctuating titles, 217
    capitalizing proper nouns, 39
    correcting run-on sentences, 72
    punctuating possessives correctly, 251
    using commas in a series, 106
    using comparatives correctly, 142
    using appositives, 174
Graphic(s), 682. *See also* Illustrations.
    arrangement and design of, 687–88
    charts, 112–13, 197
    cool colors in, 688
    creating, 221
    diagrams, 113
    elements of effective graphics, 711
    functions of, 687
    interpreting, 711–13
    for science process, 117
    for television advertisements, 255
    types of, 688–89, 711–13
    warm colors in, 688
Graphic organizers, 8, 10
    for comparison-contrast essay, 130
    for conceptual maps and time lines, 208
    flowcharts, 23–24, 31
    prewriting and, 761
    of reasons and evidence, 234
    studying and, 734
    time line, 31, 208, 211
Graphs, 221, 712
    bar graph, 143
    using in documents, 688–89
Group activities, story writing as, 185
Group discussion
    guidelines for, 724
    purpose of, 723
    role assignment in, 723–24
Grow, **principal parts of,** 450
Gutter, 684

H

Had of. See Of.
Had ought, hadn't ought, 524
Half-, **hyphens with,** 607
Handwriting, 41
Handwritten papers, 682
Hardly, scarcely, 524
Hard news, 752
Have, **principal parts of,** 450

Headers, 684
Headings, 209, 684–85
    of business letter, 759
    of document, 682
    in outline, 207
    in outlining research report, 207
Headline, of news article, 73, 752
Hear, here, 629
Hear, **principal parts of,** 450
Heavenly bodies, capitalization of names of, 546
Helping verbs, 347–48, 371, 445
Hisself, 524
Historical events and periods, capitalization of, 543
Hit, **principal parts of,** 450
Hoey, Edwin A., 43
Hold, **principal parts of,** 450
Holy days, capitalization of names of, 545
Home page, 700
Homonyms (words often confused), 625–34
Hop, **principal parts of,** 446
How come, 524
"How Doth the Little Crocodile" (Carroll), 178
"How-to" article (reading)
    forming mental images and, 86, 91
    making predictions and, 86, 87–88
    reading selection, 89–90
"How-to" instructions (viewing)
    in charts and graphics, 112–13
    in computer software, 114–15
    in TV and video programs, 115–16
"How-to" paper (writing)
    audience for, 95–96
    elaborating, 97
    illustrating steps in a process, 101
    planning of, 96
    prewriting, 94–96
    proofreading and publishing, 106–107
    purpose of, 95
    revising, 103–105
    Student's Model, 102
    for test, 108
    transitional words and phrases in, 104, 105
    Writer's Model, 99–100
    writing of, 98–102
"How-to" videos, 112, 115–16
Hughes, Langston, 537
Humor
    poem, 151
    writing humorous advertisement, 254–55
Hyperlinks, 699, 700
Hyphens
    compound adjectives with, 606–607
    in compound names, 606
    compound numbers with, 606
    prefixes with, 607
    suffixes with, 607
    word division and, 606

I (pronoun), capitalization of, 538
Ideas, prewriting and organizing, 764–66
Idioms
    definition of, 715
    in dictionary entry, 681
    ie, ei, spelling rule for, 615
Illustrations. *See also* Diagrams; Graphic(s); Photographs and photography.
    of autobiographical incident, 34
    details in, 151
    elements of, 748–49
    media choice in, 150
    photographs, 147–50
    of steps in a process, 101
    style of, 150
    using in documents, 689
Images
    moving, 749
    still, 749
Imperative sentences, 316, 780
    punctuation of, 562
Implied main idea, 50, 279. *See also* Main idea.
    identifying, 706
Indefinite pronouns, 427–28
    number of subject and, 425
    plural, 428
    plural pronouns with, 437
    possessive case of, 601
    singular, 427, 428
Indentation
    in page layout, 685
    for paragraphs, 682
Independent clauses, 303, 387, 780
    semicolons used in, 577
Indexes
    in a book, 695
    as information sources, 696–97
Indirect objects, 407–408, 483, 780
    compared with object of preposition, 408
    diagram of, 798
    finding in sentences, 407
Indirect quotation, 590–91
Inferences, 26, 706
    forming generalizations and, 18, 21–22
Infinitive. *See* base form.
Influencing, as author's purpose, 194
Informal English, 45, 519, 693
    contractions in, 602
Informal or personal letters. *See* Personal letters.
Informal outlines, 10, 207–208, 766
    subtopics in, 207, 210
Informal speaking, 723–25

Information. *See also* Sources.
    in card catalog, 696
    gathering, 9, 10
    in graphics, 687
    listening for, 729–30
    organizing for presentation, 721
    in photographs, 148–50
    for presentation, 721
    prewriting and gathering, 764
    print and electronic sources, 694–703
    on World Wide Web, 204
Informative article (reading)
    author's purpose, 188, 194–95
    drawing conclusions, 188, 192–93
    making inferences, 188, 192–93
    reading selection, 189–91
Informative essay, 219
Informative writing. *See* Expository writing.
Informing
    as author's purpose, 194
    documentary for, 146
–ing, **adding to verb,** 446
Inside address, of business letter, 759
Institutions, capitalization of names of, 542
Instructions. *See also* Directions (instructions); "How-to" paper.
    in charts, 112–13
    in chronological order, 96
    for computer software, 114–15
    demonstrations to class, 117
    for games, 117
    guidelines for giving, 724
    for "how-to" paper, 95
    listening to, 730
    writing, 108
Intensive pronouns, 330, 331
Interesting beginning, of persuasive letter, 244
Interjections, definition of, 366
Internet, 132. *See also* World Wide Web.
    definition of, 745
    as information source, 697
    online catalog, 162
    as source, 202
Interpreting, 6
Interrogative pronouns, 334
Interrogative sentences, 316, 780
    diagram of, 793
    punctuation of, 561
Interrupters, commas used with, 570–71
Interviews
    conducting, 225, 731
    for news article, 61
    as sources, 202
Intransitive verbs, 353–54, 781
Introduction
    to book review, 168
    of comparison-contrast essay, 136
    of composition, 755–56
    drafting of, 11
    to "how-to" paper, 98
    to persuasive letter, 244
    to presentations, 723
    to research report, 210
Introductory paragraphs, 294
Inverted pyramid structure, 50, 54–55, 63, 66
Inverted word order, 432
Invitations, 761
Irony, in humorous advertisement, 255
Irregular comparison, 501
Irregular plurals, 623
Irregular verbs, 446, 448–50, 781
    list of common irregular verbs, 449–50, 452–53
Italics, 686. *See also* Underlining (italics).
Its, it's, 330, 526, 629, 781

Journal
    career interests, 47
    entry-writing activities, 15, 47
    studying and, 736
    writer's, 764
Journalism, careers in, 83
Judgment words, 231
Justified text, 683–84
Juxtaposition, creating effects with images, 749

Keep, **principal parts of,** 450
Key words
    in skimming, 207
    in Web search, 204, 698, 701, 702
Kind of, sort of, 526
Know, **principal parts of,** 450
K-W-L chart for researching, 201, 205

Labels (for graphics)
    on diagrams, 113
    on flowcharts, 112–13
    for graphics and visuals, 688, 711
Labels (regional or cultural), 692, 729
Langewiesche, Wolfgang, 284
Language. *See also* English language.
    figurative, 714

"Last Night I Dreamed of Chickens" (Prelutsky), 178
Lay, lie, 466, 782
Lead, in news story, 63, 66, 752
Leading, 687
Lead, led, 629
Lead, **principal parts of,** 452
Learn, teach, 526
Learning log, 3, 6, 764
    comparison-contrast essay and, 144
    news article and, 73
    studying and, 736
Leave, **principal parts of,** 452
Left-aligned text, 683
Legend, for visuals and graphics, 143, 711
Legible handwriting, 41
Less, fewer, 523
Letters (alphabet), plurals of, 605, 623
Letters (correspondence). *See also* Personal letters.
    adjustment or complaint letter, 760
    appreciation letter, 760
    book review in, 185
    business, 246, 758–60
    for career development, 117
    for class field trip, 259
    envelopes for, 758
    informal or personal, 758, 760–61
    invitation, 761
    persuasive letter, 237–53
    of regret, 761
    request or order letter, 760
    about research topic, 225
    salutations and closings of, 538, 574
    thank-you letter, 761
Library/Media center, print and electronic sources of, 694–703
Lie, lay, 466, 782
Life experience, writing about. *See* Autobiographical incident (writing).
Lights! Camera! Scream! (Mooser), 286
Line graphs, 712
Line spacing. *See* Leading.
Linking verbs, 351, 371, 781
    and action verbs, 352, 410
    adjectives and, 503
Listening
    analyzing persuasive techniques, 257
    to appreciate, 728–29
    asking questions (for clarification), 223, 258, 728
    comparing perceptions, 116, 258, 728
    to comprehend, 729–30
    connecting with others through, 17, 85, 119, 187, 723–24
    distinguishing between fact and opinion, 256, 257, 730
    distractions in, 727
    eliminating barriers to, 224, 727
    to evaluate, 730–31
    evaluating a persuasive speech, 256–58
    evaluating a research presentation, 223–24
    5W-How? questions and, 730
    with a focus, 764
    guidelines for, 727
    to "how-to" TV programs and videos, 115–16
    for information, 729–30
    to instructions and directions, 730
    interpreting speaker's message, 223–24, 257, 258, 731
    interpreting speaker's purpose and perspective, 256, 258, 731
    interviews and, 731
    to literature, 728–29
    LQ2R study method and, 730
    for major ideas and supporting evidence, 223, 257, 729
    to media messages, 732
    monitoring understanding, 223, 258
    for nonverbal-message elements, 224, 257, 731
    to oral tradition, 729
    organizing spoken ideas, 116
    preparing to listen, 727
    purpose for, 256, 727, 728–31
    researching music and, 225
    and responding to speaker, 728
    summarizing spoken ideas, 116
    taking notes and, 116, 224, 727
Listing pattern, 705, 710–11
List of sources, of research report, 202–203, 210
Lists
    bulleted, 684
    of sources, 202–203, 205
Literature connections. *See also* Genres of literature.
    comparing with film and television, 181–84
    listening to, 728–29
    narrative poem, 42–44
    poetry, 178–80
    short story, 176–77
    writing a descriptive paragraph, 109–11
Loaded words, 715
Location words, 109
Log. *See* Learning log.
Logical order, 134
    in paragraph organization, 286
Logical support, 135, 139, 241. *See also* Support.
Logic questions, 741
Looping. *See* Freewriting.
Loose, lose, 629
Lose, **principal parts of,** 452
Lowercase letters, 686
LQ2R study method, and listening for information, 730
–ly, –ness, 617

Magazines, 202
    as sources, 132
Mail. *See also* E-mail.
    persuasive letter and, 252
Main character, 162, 163
Main clauses. *See* Independent clauses.
Main idea, 6, 10
    answering questions about, 57
    in composition, 756
    elaboration and, 289–90
    implied main idea, 50, 53, 279, 706
    of paragraph, 279
    stated main idea, 50, 53–54, 709
Main idea statement, 133, 136, 210
    for research report, 209
Main verbs, 347
"Make It Grow" (Thompson), 102
Making connections, 4
    in storytelling, 46
Making inferences, drawing conclusions and, 188, 192–93
Making predictions. *See* Predicting.
Manuscript style, guidelines for, 682
Maps. *See* Clustering; Conceptual maps.
Margins, 682. *See also* Alignment.
    page layout and, 685
Masculine pronouns, 435–36
Mass media, 732. *See also* Media; Media messages.
Matching questions, 739
Meaning(s)
    changes in English and, 691
    multiple, 715
    word, 714–15
Media. *See also* Films; Internet; Multimedia presentations; Videos and videotapes.
    comparing film, TV, and literature, 181–84
    definition of, 732
    producing a television news segment, 79–82
    using in presentation, 721
Media center. *See* Library/Media center.
Media law, 750
Media literacy, 750. *See also* Critical viewing.
Media messages, 732
    analyzing, 732
    evaluating, 747–48
    objectivity in, 732
Media terms
    electronic media terms, 743–46
    general media terms, 746–51
    print media terms, 751–54
Medium
    definition, 752
    of message, 752

Memorials, capitalization of names of, 545
Memorization, as study skill, 734
Mental images, forming, 86, 91, 111
Messages, 750. *See also* Media messages.
    critical viewing of visual messages, 746–48
Metaphors, 42, 109, 714
Microfiche, 697
Microfilm, 697
Microforms, 697
Middle English, 690
Might of, must of. See Could of.
Mini-lesson (critical thinking)
    arranging ideas, 31
    cause and effect, 65
    elements of a plot, 165
    evaluating details, 135
    searching World Wide Web, 204
    understanding your audience, 240
Mini-lesson (test taking), 26, 41, 57
    answering main idea questions, 57
    answering questions about charts, 197
    clarification essay, 219
    classification essay, 145
    fact and opinion, 236
    informative essay, 219
    making inferences, 26
    making predictions, 93
    persuasive essay, 253
    supporting details, 127
    unfamiliar vocabulary and, 160
    writing description for tests, 41
    writing instructions, 108
Mini-lesson (vocabulary). *See also* Vocabulary.
    compound words, 92
    context clues, 25
    dictionary and thesaurus, 235
    multiple-meaning words, 56
    prefixes and suffixes, 126
    wordbusting strategy (CSSD), 159
    word roots, 196
Mini-lesson (writing)
    elaboration with specific language, 97
    paraphrasing, 206
Misplaced modifiers, 509, 782
    correction of, 512
Modified block style (of business letters), 759
Modified block style (of comparison-contrast essay), 134
Modifiers. *See also* Adjective(s); Adverb(s); Comparative form.
    clauses used as, 496
    comparison of, 497–501
    definition of, 336, 495, 782
    double comparisons, 504
    double negatives, 507
    good, well, 502–503
    irregular comparison, 501
    misplaced, 509

one-word modifiers, 495–96
phrases used as, 496
placement in sentences, 509–12
regular comparison, 498–99
Money making, documentary for, 146
Monitor, for oral research presentation, 224
Monitoring understanding, 223, 258. *See also* Listening.
Monuments, capitalization of names of, 545
Mood, 722, 728
creating with sound, 745
Moon, **capitalization of word,** 546
Mooser, Stephen, 286
More, most, 498–99, 501
Movies. *See* Films.
Moving image, 749
"**Mr. Sagers Moves to Cyprus High**" (Banta and Tidwell), 68
Multimedia presentations, 750. *See also* Media.
music activity and, 151
visuals in, 220–21
Multiple-choice questions, 739
Multiple-meaning words, 56
Musical terms, plural formation of, 622
Musical works
underlining (italicizing) names of, 589
multimedia presentation and, 151
researching, 225

N

Names. *See* Capitalization; Personal names; Titles (works).
Narration, in film and literature, 182
Narrative paragraphs
definition of, 291
discussion of, 292
Narrative (writing)
autobiographical incident, 27–40
narrative poem, 42–44
short story, 176–77
Nationalities, capitalization of names of, 544
Negatives
double negatives, 507
negative words, 157–58
-ness, -ly, 617
Networks, computer, 698
Neuter pronouns, 435–36
News, 753
feature news, 752
hard news, 752
producing a TV news segment, 79–82
reporting, 49
soft news, 754
Newsmagazine, 753
Newspaper

production of, 76–78
school newspaper, 59
as source, 202, 697
Newspaper article (reading)
inverted pyramid structure for, 50, 54–55, 63, 66
main idea, 50, 53–54
reading selection, 51–52
Newspaper article (writing), 58–73
advice column, 74–75
audience, 60
columns in, 73
prewriting, 58–64
proofreading and publishing, 72–73
revising, 69–71
Student's Model, 68
varying sentences, 71
Writer's Model, 67
writing, 66–68
Newsworthiness, criteria for, 750
"**Nixon-Kennedy Presidential Debates, The**" (Wakin), 121–22
Nominative case, 475
Nonstandard English, 519, 692–93
Nonverbal signals, 722
Not **and contraction** *n't,* 602
as adverbs, 358
Notebook, writer's, 764
Note cards, for presentation, 721
Note taking. *See* Taking notes.
Noun(s), 323–24, 782
as appositives, 488
common nouns, 39, 324, 539
compound noun, 323
definition of, 323
of direct address, 572
plurals, 599, 621–23
possessive case of, 598–601
precise nouns, 215, 216
proper nouns, 39, 324, 539, 598
spelling plurals of, 621–23
Novels
elements of, 154, 156
previewing, 162
writing a review of, 161–75
Nowheres, 521
Number (grammar)
agreement in, 422
pronoun-antecedent agreement in, 436–38
Numbers (numerals)
hyphenation of, 606
plurals of, 605, 623
punctuation of, 561

Object form of personal pronouns, 475, 476, 481–85
Objections
    addressing, 240–42
    to arguments, 233
    by audience, 240
Objective case, 475
Objective tests, 737, 739–42
Objective voice, 61
Objectivity, in media messages, 732
Objects of prepositions
    compared with indirect objects, 407, 408
    definition of, 361, 375, 782
    placement in sentences, 362
    pronouns as, 485
    using correct pronoun forms for, 487
Objects of verbs, 353, 354
    definition of, 353
    diagrams of, 797–98
    direct objects, 405–406
    indirect objects, 407–408
Occasion, of presentation, 223, 720
Of, 527
Offerman, Genna, 213
Old English, 690
On-demand reading questions, 740
On-demand writing questions, 740–41. *See also* Multiple-choice questions; Short-answer questions.
Online catalog, 162, 695, 698
Online databases, 698
Online Readers' Guide, 698
Online sources, 698
Opinions, 163, 228, 231–32. *See also* Persuasive essay (reading); Persuasive letter (writing).
    distinguishing from facts, 236, 705
    persuasion and, 237
    in persuasive essay, 253
    sharing of, 15
Opinion statement, 234
    in persuasive letter, 238, 244
Or, nor, **joining singular and plural subjects with,** 430
Oral interpretation. *See also* Dramatic interpretation.
    choosing selection for, 725
    cutting for, 725
    definition of, 725
    presenting, 726
Oral response, book review as, 175
Oral traditions, 45. *See also* Storytelling.
    comparing folk tales in different cultures, 47
    listening to, 729
Order letter, 760
Order of ideas. *See also* Chronological order; Logical order; Organization.
    cause-and-effect order, 6
    logical order, 134
    spatial order, 110
    in writing, 11, 283–86
Order of importance, in paragraph organization, 286
Organizing ideas, 10. *See also* Arranging ideas; Content and Organization Guidelines for Self-Evaluation and Peer Evaluation; Plan (writing).
    for book review, 164, 166
    for comparison-contrast essay, 132–33
    during listening, 116
    of news article, 63–64
    within paragraphs, 283–86
    for presentation, 721
    for research report, 207
Organization, patterns of, 4, 6. *See also* Text structures.
Organizations (groups)
    capitalization of names of, 542
    abbreviation of names of, 563
Ought to of. *See* Could of.
Outlining
    formal, 765–66
    informal, 10, 207–208, 210, 766
    prewriting and, 765–66
    of research report, 207
    studying and, 735
Out of the Storm (Willis), 170
Overhead projector, for oral research presentation, 224

Page alignment, 683–84
Page layout, 683–85
Paper(s). *See* Document design.
Paragraphs
    clincher sentences in, 282
    coherence in, 283–88
    concluding paragraphs, 294
    connecting ideas in, 287–88
    definition of, 278
    descriptive, 109–11, 291, 292
    elaboration in, 289–90
    expository, 291, 293
    indentation of, 682
    introductory, 294
    in long pieces of writing, 32, 98, 136, 210, 244, 294–95
    main idea of, 279
    narrative, 291, 292
    order of ideas in, 283–86
    parts of a paragraph, 279–82
    persuasive, 291, 293–94
    in persuasive letter, 244
    reasons for using paragraphs, 278
    supporting sentences in, 281

topic sentences in, 279
transitions within, 287–88
types of, 291–94
unity in, 288
Paraphrasing, 206, 706–707
studying and, 735
Parks, Rosa, 19–20
Parts of speech
adjectives, 336–39
adverbs, 357–58
conjunctions, 364–65
determining parts of speech, 368
interjections, 366
nouns, 323–24
prepositions, 360–64
pronouns, 328–35
verbs, 347–54
Passed, past, 630
Past participle, 445, 446, 448–50
Past perfect progressive tense, 460
Past perfect tense, 458, 459, 461
Past progressive tense, 460
Past tense, 445, 458, 460
Pay, **principal parts of,** 452
Peace, piece, 630
Peer evaluation, 12. *See also* Content and Organization Guidelines for Self-Evaluation and Peer Evaluation; Peer review.
Peer review, 37, 70, 104, 140, 172, 215, 249
Peoples, capitalization of names of, 544
Periodicals, italicizing titles of, 588
Periods, 561
with abbreviations, 563–64
with quotations, 591, 592
Perrault, Charles, 183
Person (pronouns)
first person, 329–30
second person, 329–30
third person, 329–30
Personal letters
commas used in salutation of, 574
purpose for, 758, 760–61
types of, 761
Personal names
capitalization of, 539
hyphens in, 606
punctuating abbreviations of, 563
Personal pronouns, 329–30
antecedent of, 436
forms of, 475–85
object form, 475, 476, 481–85
possessive form, 475–76, 601
as predicate nominative, 479
subject form, 475, 476, 477–79
Personification, 42, 714
Persons
capitalization of names of, 539

capitalization of titles of, 551
Perspective (of a speaker). *See* Bias; Point of view.
Persuasion. *See also* Advertising; Persuasive essay (reading); Persuasive letter (writing); Propaganda.
analyzing techniques of, 707
as author's purpose, 194
and careers, 259
documentary for, 146
Persuasive essay (reading)
preparing to read, 228
reading selection, 229–30
Persuasive essay (writing), 253
Persuasive letter (writing), 237–53
audience and purpose for, 239
call to action in, 242–43
choosing an issue, 237–38
opinion statement for, 238
prewriting, 237–43
proofreading and publishing, 251–52
reasons and evidence for, 241–42
revising, 248–49
Student's Model, 247
Writer's Model, 245–46
writing, 244–47
Persuasive letter, call to action in, 242–43
Persuasive paragraphs
definition of, 291
discussion of, 293–94
Persuasive speech, 259
evaluating, 256–58
Persuasive techniques, in speech, 257
convincing, 256, 257, 258
propaganda, 257, 732
selling, 257, 258
Persuasive writing, 15
Phonetic symbols, in dictionary entry, 681
Photographs and photography
comparing ideas in photographs, 147–50
information in, 148–50
media and, 753
vs. reality, 147
Phrases
adjective phrases, 377–78, 379
adverb phrases, 381–82, 383
definition of, 374, 783
diagrams of, 796
as modifiers, 496
moving to beginning of sentence, 271
prepositional phrases, 375
punctuating series of, 567
between subject and verb, 425–26
transitional, 287–88, 711
verb phrases, 348
Pie chart, 221, 688, 711–12
Pitch, as verbal element
speaking in a different voice, in storytelling, 46
in speech presentation, 722

Plagiarism, 206, 706
Plain, plane, 630
Plan (study plan), 733
Plan (writing). *See also* Order of ideas; Organizing ideas.
    of "how-to" paper, 96
    writing essay about poem, 179
    in writing process, 11
Planets, capitalization of names of, 546
Plays, underlining (italicizing) of names of, 588
Plot, 156, 162, 163
    elements of, 165
Plot line, 165
Plurals
    adding –*s* to nouns, 621–23
    formation of, 605, 623
    indefinite pronouns, 428
    irregular formation of, 623
    of letters, numerals, and symbols, 605, 623
    nouns ending in *o,* 622
    nouns ending in *s, x, z, ch, sh,* 621
    nouns ending in *y,* 622
    pronouns, 437
    words referred to as words, 605, 623
Plural subjects, 430
Plural words, 422
Poem
    humorous (writing), 151
    narrative (writing), 42–44
    about research topic (writing), 225
    writing essay on sound effects, 178–80
Point-by-point style, 124, 125
Point of view. *See also* Bias; Propaganda.
    in book review writing, 167
    determining author's point of view, 154, 157–58, 704
    media and, 751
    in presentation, 720
    voice and, 167
Points of comparison, 120, 123–24, 136
    choosing, 131–32
Political cartoons. *See* Editorial cartoons.
Portfolio building, 13. *See also* Writing portfolio.
    autobiographical incident and, 40
    book review and, 175
    comparison-contrast essay and, 144
    "how-to" paper and, 107
    to identify strengths and weaknesses, 13–14, 252
    news article and, 73
    persuasive letter and, 252
    research report and, 218
    to set goals, 14, 107, 252
Positive degree of comparison, 497, 498, 499
Positive feedback, 728
Positive words, 157–58
Possessive adjectives. *See* Possessive pronouns.
Possessive case
    of indefinite pronouns, 601
    of nouns or pronouns, 598
    of personal pronouns, 601
    of plural nouns, 599
    of singular nouns, 598
Possessive pronouns
    contractions compared with, 603
    definition of, 330
    personal pronouns, 251, 475–76, 601
Possessives
    plural nouns compared with, 621
    punctuation of, 251
Precise nouns, 215, 216
Predicate(s)
    complete compared with simple, 309
    definition of, 307, 783
    position of, 307
    simple predicate, 309
Predicate adjectives, 412–13, 783
    diagram of, 799–800
Predicate nominatives, 410–11, 783
    finding in questions, 479
    diagram of, 799
Predicting, 4, 5, 86, 93
    as reading skill, 707
Prefixes, 126, 196, 783
    definition of, 126, 616, 715–16
    hyphens with, 607
    list of, 716
    spelling of words with, 616
Prelutsky, Jack, 178
Preposition(s). *See also* Objects of prepositions.
    adverbs distinguished from, 363–64
    capitalization in titles, 217
    commonly used prepositions, 361
    compound prepositions, 361
    definition of, 360, 783
Prepositional phrases, 361–62, 375, 485, 784
    adjective phrases, 377–78, 379
    adverb phrases, 381–82, 383
    definition of, 361, 375, 510
    diagrams of, 796
    placement in sentences, 510–11
    punctuation of introductory, 572–73
Prereading, 4, 5, 708
Presentation. *See also* Technology presentation.
    content and organization of, 719–21
    delivery of, 721–22
    multimedia, 151, 220–21, 750
    purposes for, 719–20
    research, 222–24
Presentation software, for oral research presentation, 224
Present participles, 445
Present perfect progressive tense, 460
Present perfect tense, 458, 459, 461
Present progressive tense, 460
Present tense, 458

Previewing, 4, 162
Prewriting, 9. See also Text structures; Writing applications.
    arranging ideas, 764–66
    audience and, 10
    autobiographical incident, 27–31
    book review, 161–67
    brainstorming, 762
    charts and, 764–65
    clustering, 763
    comparison-contrast essay, 128–35
    conceptual mapping and, 765
    essay tests and, 739
    5W-How? questions and, 762
    freewriting and, 763
    graphic organizer and, 761
    "how-to" paper, 94–97
    listening and, 764
    news article, 58–65
    on-demand writing questions and, 740–41
    outlining and, 765–66
    persuasive letter, 237–43
    purpose of writing and, 10
    reading and, 764
    research report, 198–209
    time line and, 766
    Venn diagram and, 766
    "What if?" questions and, 762
    writer's notebook or journal, 764
Pride of Puerto Rico (Walker), 280
Principal, principle, 630
Print, advertisements in, 255
Print media terms, 751–54
Printed handwriting (manuscript), 4
Prior knowledge, 4, 5
    drawing conclusions and, 193
Problem solution
    in advice column, 74–75
    analyzing relationships, 707–708
    pattern, 705, 711
Process. See also "How-to" article (reading); "How-to" instructions; "How-to" paper (writing).
    flowchart or graphic for, in science, 117
Producer, 745
    of TV news segment, 79, 81
Product(s), humorous advertisement for, 254–55
Production, stages of media, 753–54
Progression (order of details) 63–64, 96, 164–66. See also Arranging ideas; Organizing ideas; Rearranging (as revision technique).
Progressive verb forms, 459–61
Pronoun(s). See also Personal pronouns.
    antecedents and, 328–29, 435–38
    appositives and, 488
    choosing in compound object, 482
    definition of, 328, 784
    demonstrative pronouns, 332, 339
    as direct objects, 481, 482
    indefinite, 332–33, 427–28
    as indirect objects, 483
    intensive pronouns, 330, 331
    interrogative pronouns, 334
    as object of preposition, 485
    personal pronouns, 329–30, 475–85
    placement of first-person pronouns in compound constructions, 482
    possessive case of, 598, 601
    as predicate nominative, 479
    reflexive pronouns, 330
    relative pronouns, 335, 512
    usage of, 475–88
    who, whom, 486–87
Pronoun-antecedent agreement. See Agreement (pronoun-antecedent).
Pronunciation
    British *vs.* American, 691
    changes in English and, 691
    in dictionary, 613, 680–81
    spelling and, 613
Proofreading. See also Publishing (writing); Revising (writing).
    autobiographical incident, 39
    book review, 174
    compare-contrast essay, 142
    guidelines for, 13
    "how-to" paper, 106
    news article, 72
    by a peer, 13, 39, 72, 106, 142, 174
    persuasive letter, 251
    research report, 217
    for spelling errors, 614
    symbols for, 767
    techniques for, 618
Propaganda, 257, 751
Proper adjectives, 338
    capitalization of, 548
Proper nouns
    capitalization of, 39, 539–41
    definition of, 324, 539
    possessive case and, 598
Public broadcasting, 743
Publishing for various audiences. See also Writing applications.
    of book review, 174–75
    of comparison-contrast essay, 142–44
    of "how-to" paper, 106–108
    news article, 72–73
    of persuasive letter, 251–52
    of research report, 217–18
Punctuation
    of abbreviations, 563–64
    apostrophes, 598–603
    of appositives, 174
    colons, 579

commas, 566–75
end marks, 318, 561–64, 585
exclamation points, 317, 561
hyphens, 606–607
of interjections, 366
of numerals, 561
periods, 561
of possessives, 251
question marks, 561
quotation marks, 590–92
semicolons, 577
of sentences, 302
to set off direct quotations, 591
of titles of works, 217
underlining (italics), 588–89
"Puppy Love or Hamster Heaven," 137
Purpose (of media messages)
of informative video, 116, 146, 224, 747–48
Purpose (reading) 4, 5
author's purpose, identifying, 188, 194–95
Purpose (speaking and listening)
adapting word choice in speech to, 719
interpreting speaker's purpose, 256, 731
listening with a, 256, 727, 728–31
for formal speaking, 719–20
Purpose (writing)
of autobiographical incident, 29
of book review, 163–64
of comparison-contrast essay, 130–31
evaluating achievement of, 107, 218
of "how-to" paper, 95
in writing process, 10
of persuasive letter, 239
of research report, 200
Put, **principal parts of,** 452

Questioning
in interviews, 61
K-W-L method of, 201
about text, 4
Question mark, 561
with quotation marks, 591, 592
Questions
for analyzing media messages, 732
finding predicate nominatives in, 479
diagram of, 793
as response to speaker, 728
Quotations
in book reviews, 166
direct, 66, 590–91
indirect, 590–91
punctuation of, 590–92
within quotations, 595

Quotation marks, 590–92, 784
in dialogue, 594
in long quotations, 595
single quotation marks, 595
with titles of short works, 217, 595

Races, capitalization of names of, 544
Radio
advertisements on, 255
as information source, 698
Ragged text, 684
Raise, rise, 464
Ramona Forever (Cleary), 285
Rate (or tempo)
talking slowly, for audience, 46, 223
as verbal element in speech presentation, 722
Read, **principal parts of,** 452
Readers' Guide to Periodical Literature, 696
Reading for enjoyment, 708
Reading with a focus, 764
Reading log, 708
Reading for mastery (reading to learn), 708
Reading process, 4
after reading, 8
prereading, 5
while reading, 6–7
Reading rate, adjusting, 708
Reading script, marking, 726
Reading skills and focuses
adjusting reading rate, 708
analyzing text structures, 709–11
author's point of view, 704
author's purpose, 188, 194–95, 704
cause-and-effect relationships, 704
chronological order, 18, 23–24
clue words, 705
comparison-contrast structure, 120, 124–25
drawing conclusions, 188, 192–93, 705
fact and opinion, 228, 231–32, 705
forming generalizations, 18, 21–22, 705–706
forming mental images, 86, 91
implied main idea, 706
inverted pyramid structure, 50, 54–55
main idea, 50, 53–54
making inferences, 18, 21–22, 188, 192–93, 706
making predictions, 86, 87–88
paraphrasing, 706–707
persuasive techniques, analyzing, 707
points of comparison, 120, 123–24
predicting, 707
problem-solution relationships, 707–708
reading log, 708
reasons and evidence, 228, 232–34

SQ3R, 708
    stated main idea and supporting details, 709
    summarizing, 709
    using transitional words and phrases, 711
    visuals and graphics interpretation, 711–13
Reading-writing connection, 14
Realism, 751
Real life, photographs compared to, 147
Rearranging (as revision technique), 12, 36, 69, 103, 214
Reason(s)
    for buying product, 254
    in persuasive essay, 228, 232–34, 253
    in persuasive letter, 241–42, 244
Reasonable request, 243
Reasoning or logic questions, 741
Record, writing to. See Writing to record.
Reference materials and resources for writing. See also Sources.
    bibliographies as, 695
    dictionary, 40, 69
    to edit and revise, 69
    reference sources chart, 699
    sources for research, 202–204
    using library as resource in prewriting, 162
    to verify facts in prewriting, 132
    word-processors thesaurus, 38
Reflecting on writing. See Writing to reflect.
Reflexive pronouns, 331
    definition of, 330
Regional dialect, 692
Regular comparison, 498–99
Regular plurals, 621–22
Regular verbs, 446, 784–85
Rehearsing, for oral interpretation, 726
Relative pronouns, 335, 512
Relevant details, 135
Religions, capitalization of names of, 545
Repetition, in poetry, 178
Report(s). See also Research report (writing).
    comparison-contrast in, 151
    database of, 185
    on journalism careers, 83
Reporters, 754. See also Newspaper article (writing).
    for television news segment, 80
Request letter, 760
Research presentation, giving and evaluating, 222–24
Research report (writing). See also Informative article (reading).
    asking questions, 201
    categorizing ideas, 207
    documenting sources, 202–203, 210
    K-W-L chart (to organize prior knowledge), 201
    making a source list, 202–203, 210
    main idea statement, 209
    oral presentation of, 222–24
    organizing information for, 207
    outlining, 207–208
    paraphrasing, 206
    prewriting, 198–209
    proofreading and publishing of, 217–18
    purpose and audience for, 200
    reviewing outline and revisiting research, 208
    revising, 214–16
    sources for, 202–203
    Student's Model, 213
    summarizing information for, 205
    taking notes, 205
    Writer's Model, 211–12
    writing, 210–13
Resolution, of plot, 165
Resources for writing. See Reference materials and resources for writing.
Responding to others' writing. See Content and Organization Guidelines for Self-Evaluation and Peer Evaluation; Peer evaluation; Peer review.
Restatements, as context clues, 713
Review. See also Book review (reading); Book review (writing).
    of music recording (writing), 225
Revising (writing), 6, 9, 12. See also Content and Organization Guidelines for Self-Evaluation and Peer Evaluation; Style Guidelines; Writing applications.
    autobiographical incident, 36–38
    of book review, 171–73
    of comparison-contrast essay, 139–41
    of "how-to" paper, 103–105
    of news article, 69–71
    of persuasive letter, 248–50
    and proofreading symbols, 767
    research report, 214–16
    and writing process, 12
Rhyme, 178
Rhythm, 178
Ride, **principal parts of,** 452
Richardson, Lisa, 51–52
Right-aligned text, 683
Ring, **principal parts of,** 452
Rise, raise, 464, 785
Road map, as graphic organizer, 28
Roots, 196
    definition of, 126, 715
    list of, 715
Rosa Parks: My Story (Parks), 19–20
Rules (lines), 685
Run, **principal parts of,** 452
Run-on sentences, 72, 265, 785

Sacred writings, capitalization of titles of, 545

Salutation
    of business letter, 759
    punctuation of, 574, 579
Say, **principal parts of,** 452
Sayings, 46, 729
Scanning of text, 708
Scarcely, hardly, 524
School subjects, capitalization of names of, 548
Science, articles about, 83
Script
    for electronic media, 745
    for TV news segment, 80–81
Search, computer
    on Internet, 701–702
    in online card catalog, 698
    on World Wide Web, 204
Search engine, 204, 700, 701
Second person
    of personal pronouns, 329, 330
    of reflexive and intensive pronouns, 330
See, **principal parts of,** 453
Self-expression, documentary for, 146
Selling, in persuasive speech, 256–58, 731
Semicolons, 577, 786
    between parts of a compound sentence, 577
Send, **principal parts of,** 453
Sensory details, 10, 30, 109
    definition of, 281
    in short story, 177
    in storytelling, 46
Sentence(s). *See also* Sentence fragments.
    adjective placement in, 510
    adverb placement in, 510
    capitalization of direct quotations, 591
    classified by purpose, 316–17
    classified by structure, 394–98
    clincher sentences, 279, 282
    combining sentences, 141, 269–75
    complete sentences, 262–63
    compound-complex sentences, 398
    compound sentences, 274–75, 395, 568–69, 577
    declarative sentences, 316, 561
    definition of, 302, 785
    diagrams of, 802–804
    exclamatory sentences, 317, 561
    fragments, 262–63
    imperative sentences, 316, 562
    interrogative sentences, 316, 561
    joining two related sentences, 274–75
    prepositional phrase placement in, 510–11
    revision of, 12
    run-on sentences, 72, 265
    simple sentences, 394–95, 569
    stringy sentences, 250, 266–67
    supporting sentences, 279, 281
    topic sentences, 279
    transitional words in, 104, 105
    varying for interest, 71, 321
Sentence-completion questions, 741–42
Sentence fragments, 262–63
    definition of, 302, 786
    identification of, 302
    in speech, 303
    subordinate clause as, 388
    use by professional writers, 303
Sentence parts
    predicate, 307–10
    subject, 305–306
Sentence punctuation. *See* End marks.
Sentence structure
    complex sentences, 397
    compound-complex sentences, 398
    compound sentences, 395
    simple sentences, 394–95
    stringy sentences, 266–67
Sequence chain. *See* Text structures.
Sequential order. *See* Chronological order; Organization.
Series
    commas with, 106, 566
    semicolons with, 567, 577
Set, sit, 463–64, 786
Setting, 162, 163
    for novel, 156
    for short story, 176
    and verbal elements of speech, 722
Shadow style, 687
Shah, Idries, 594
Ships
    capitalization of names of, 545
    underlining (italicizing) names of, 589
Short-answer questions, 742
Short stories, 83, 176–77
    about research topic, 225
Should of. See Could of.
Show and tell, in storytelling, 46
Shrink, **principal parts of,** 453
Signature, of business letter, 760
Silent *e*, suffixes with, 617–18
Silliness, in humorous advertisement, 255
Similarities, 129, 131, 145. *See also* Comparing and contrasting.
Simile, 42, 109, 151, 714
Simple predicate, 309
    compared with complete predicate, 309
Simple sentences, 394–95
    with compound verb, 569
    diagram of, 802
Simple subjects, 306
Sing, **principal parts of,** 453
Single-spaced text, 687
Singular nouns, possessive case of, 598
Singular pronouns
    indefinite pronouns, 427, 428

pronoun-antecedent agreement and, 436
Singular subjects, 422, 430
Singular words, 422
Sink, **principal parts of,** 453
Sit, set, 463, 464, 786
Skimming, 5, 162, 708
    key words in, 207
Slang, 45, 693
Slow motion, creating effects with images, 749
Small capitals, 687
Social situations, speaking in, 724–25
Social studies, letters and forms for field trips, 259
Soft news, 754. *See also* Feature news.
Software. *See* Computer software.
Somewheres, 521
Sort of, kind of, 526
Sound
    in film and video, 745–46
    in humorous advertisement, 254
Sound effects, in poems, 178, 180
Sources, reference, 699. *See also* Authority; Credibility; Dictionary; Information; Messages; Reference materials and resources for writing; Thesaurus.
    books, 695
    card catalog, 162
    electronic, 694, 696–703
    interviews, 61
    lists of, 203, 210
    media, 754
    online catalog, 162
    print and electronic, 694–703
    reference sources, 69
    for research reports, 202–203
    visual and graphic, 711
    on World Wide Web, 204
"South American Guanaco, The," 211–12
Spacecraft
    capitalization of names of, 545
    underlining (italicizing) names of, 589
Spacing, line. *See* Leading.
Spatial order, 110, 284
Speak, **principal parts of,** 453
Speakers
    listening to, 727
    responding to, 728
    as sources, 202
Speaking. *See also* Listening; Speech.
    connecting with others through, 17, 85, 119, 187, 723–24
    formal, 719–23
    giving a research presentation, 222–24
    informal, 723–25
    oral interpretation, 725–26
    persuasive speech, 259
    self-evaluation, 726
    supporting ideas in, 222, 721
    television advertisements and, 255

    in television news segment, 80, 81–82
Special events, capitalization of, 542
Specialized dictionary, 680
Specific language
    elaboration with, 97, 98
    forming mental images and, 86, 91
Specific request, 243
"Spectacle of Niagara, The" (Langewiesche), 284
Speech. *See also* Parts of speech; Presentation; Speaking.
    evaluating persuasive speech, 256–58
Spellchecker, on computer, 107, 530
Spelling
    British *vs.* American, 691
    changes in English and, 691
    correcting, in final drafts, 40, 73, 107, 175, 218, 252
    good habits for, 613–14
    ie, ei, 615
    list of spelling words, 640–41
    plurals of nouns, 621–23
    prefixes and, 616
    rules for, 615–23
    suffixes and, 617–19
    by syllables, 614
    using resources to correct, 40, 107
SQ3R (Survey, Question, Read, Recite, Review) strategy, 708
    studying and, 735
Stand, **principal parts of,** 453
Standard English, 519, 692–93
    using in presentation, 723
Stars, capitalization of, names of, 546
Start, **principal parts of,** 445
Stated main idea. *See* Main idea.
Statement. *See* Declarative sentences.
States
    abbreviation of names of, 549
    capitalization of names of, 540
Stationary, stationery, 632
Steal, **principal parts of,** 453
Stereotype, 751
Stevenson, Robert Louis, 179, 180
Still image, 749
Stories. *See also* Short stories.
    elements of, 156
Storyboards, 689
    for script, 746
Storytelling, 45–46
    chronological order for, 285
Street numbers, capitalization of, 540
Stringy sentences, 250, 266–67, 786
Structure
    comparison-contrast structure of essay, 120, 124–25, 134
    inverted pyramid, in a news article, 50, 54–55, 63
    of texts, 709–11
Student's Model
    autobiographical incident, 35

book review, 170
comparison-contrast essay, 138
"how-to" paper, 102
news article, 68
persuasive letter, 247
research report, 213
Study skills, 733–36. *See also* Reading skills and focuses; Tests.
Style. *See also* Style Guidelines; Style (sentence style); Style (word choice).
adapting to audience, 29, 141
adapting to purpose, 29, 250
definition of, 767
revising to improve, 12
Style guidelines
clichés, 172
combining sentences, 140
exact verbs, 37
precise nouns, 215
stringy sentences, 249
transitional words, 104
varying sentences, 70
Style (sentence style)
combining sentences, 141
stringy sentences, 250
transitional words, 105
varying sentences, 71
Style (word choice)
exact verbs, 38
clichés, 173
precise nouns, 216
Style-checking computer programs, 304
Subheadings, 684–85
Subject(s)
agreement with verb, 422–23, 432
complete subject, 306
compound subjects, 273, 311, 429–30
definition of, 305
diagrams of, 790–92
finding of, 310
plural, 430
position of, 305
simple subject, 306
singular, 430
Subject complements
definition of, 410
diagrams of, 799–800
finding in sentences, 410
predicate adjectives, 412–13
predicate nominatives, 410–11
Subject form of personal pronouns, 475, 477–79
Subject-verb agreement. *See* Agreement (subject-verb).
Subordinate clauses, 303, 787
adjective clause, 389–90
adverb clause, 391
definition of, 388
diagrams of, 804

placement in sentences, 397
Subtitle, 685
capitalization of, 552–54
Subtopics
in informal outline, 210
in outline, 207
Suffixes, 126, 196
definition of, 126, 617, 716
final consonants and, 618–19
final *e*, 617–18
hyphens with, 607
list of, 716
-ness, -ly, 617
Summarizing. *See also* Paraphrasing.
in book review, 164
in captions, 150
in chronological order, 168
definition of, summary, 706, 709, 735
information gathered in research, 205
in interviews, 61
as note-taking strategy, 116
in persuasive letter, 244
as reading strategy, 709
as study skill, 735–36
Sun, **capitalization of word,** 546
Superlative degree of comparison, 498, 499
Support
for comparison-contrast essay, 132
details, 6, 127
evidence as, 242
logical support, 135, 241
revising to add 69, 139, 248
stated main idea and supporting details, 709
supporting sentences, 279, 281
Suppose to, supposed to, 527
Suspense, 45
in short story, 177
Swim, **principal parts of,** 453
Syllable, 614
Symbols
on diagrams, 113
plurals of, 605, 623
Synonyms, 235
books of, 699
as context clues, 713
finding in computer thesaurus, 337
Syntax. *See* Sentence structure.

T

Tab, setting, 682
Table of contents, **of a book,** 695
Tables, 197, 712
using in documents, 689
Take, bring, 523

Take, **principal parts of,** 453
Taking notes, 205, 207
    from authoritative sources, 202
    guidelines for, 116
    informal outline and, 207–208
    about persuasive speech, 258
    from relevant sources, 202
    for studying, 734–35
    about television programs, 15
Tall tale, writing a, 47
"Ta-Na-E-Ka," 176
Target audience. *See also* Audience.
    for media, 754
T-chart, 145
Teach, **principal parts of,** 453
Teams, capitalization of names of, 542
Technology. *See also* Computers; Computer software; Presentation; Television; Videos and videotapes; Web sites.
    collaboration in database of reports, 185
    e-mail messages, 47
    for oral research presentation, 224
    technology presentation, 750
Telephones, guidelines for speaking on, 725
Television
    advertisements on, 255
    comparing with film and literature, 181–84
    learning "how-to" from TV and videos 112, 115–16,
    producing a news segment, 79–82
    as source, 202, 698
    taking notes about television programs, 15
    video and, 115–16
Television series, underlining (italicizing names of), 588
Tell, **principal parts of,** 453
Tenses. *See also* Verb(s).
    consistency of, 462
    definition of, 458
Testimonial, as persuasive technique, in speech, 257
Tests, 737–42. *See also* Study skills.
Test taking. *See* Mini-lesson (test taking).
Text
    arranging in document, 683–85
    in media message, 754
Text structures, 709–11. *See also* Clue words.
Than, then, 527
Thank-you letter, 761
That there, this here, 529
The, a, an
    as articles, 336
    capitalization of in titles, 554
    underlining (italicizing) in titles, 589
Their, there, they're, 527, 632
Theirself, theirselves, 524
Them, 528
Thesaurus, 235
    on computer, 38
    precise nouns and, 216
Thesis and thesis statement, 10, 133, 209. *See also* Main idea; Main idea statement.
    for composition, 756
    opinion statement as, 238
Third person
    of personal pronouns, 329, 330
    of reflexive and intensive pronouns, 330
This here, that there, 529
This, that, these, those
    as demonstrative adjectives, 339
    as demonstrative pronouns, 332
Thompson, Stephanie, 102
Threw, through, 632
Throw, **principal parts of,** 453
Tidwell, Amy, 68
Time
    abbreviations used for, 564
    colons used between hour and minute, 579
Time lines, 31, 96, 208, 221, 689, 713. *See also* Road map.
    prewriting and, 766
Tired words, 714
Title page, 695
Titles (personal)
    capitalization of, 39, 551
    punctuating abbreviations of, 563
Titles (works), 685
    of books, 168
    of books in card catalog, 696
    capitalization of, 217, 552–54
    punctuation of, 217
    quotation marks and, 217, 595
    underlining (italicizing) of, 217, 588–89
    for visual and graphic, 711
Tone (mood) in speaking
    changing, in storytelling, 46
    identifying, in oral interpretations, 728
    as verbal element, 722
Topics. *See also* Subtopics.
    in book review, 168
    choosing, in writing process, 10
    of "how-to" paper, 94–95
    of persuasive letter, 238
    for presentation, 719
    of research report, 198–99
Topic sentences
    in composition, 756
    in paragraph, 279
To, too, two, 633
Trading card, for athlete, 225
Trains
    capitalization of names of, 545
    underlining (italicizing) names of, 589
Transitional words and phrases (transitions), 136, 287–88, 767

in book review, 166, 168
composition and, 756
revising, in "how-to" paper, 104, 105
identifying, 711
Transitive verbs, 353, 354, 790
True-false questions, 742
Try and, 529
Tuck Everlasting (Babbitt), 169
Typed papers, 682
Typefaces. *See* Fonts (typefaces).

Unabridged dictionary, 680
Underlining (italics), 588–89, 590, 686
with titles of works, 217, 588–89, 595
for names of trains, ships, aircraft, spacecraft, 589
Understanding
confirming, 4, 8
monitoring, 224, 258
"U.S. Has a Garbage Crisis, The" (Dudley), 229–30
Units of measure, abbreviations for, 564
Unity, in paragraphs, 288
Uppercase letters. *See* Capital letters.
URL, 700
Usage. *See also* English language; Modifiers; Pronoun(s); Verb(s).
common problems in, 519–30
double negatives, 507
formal English, 519, 535
informal English, 519, 602
Use, **principal parts of,** 446
Use to, used to, 529

VCR, for oral research presentation, 224
Venn diagram, 132
prewriting and, 766
tools for writers, TV producers, and filmmakers, 183
Verb(s)
action verbs, 350
agreement with subjects, 422–23, 432
compound verbs, 273, 312
definition of, 347
diagrams of, 790–92
in essay questions, 738
exact, 37, 38
helping verbs, 347–48
intransitive verbs, 353–54
irregular verbs, 446, 448–50
lie, lay, 466
linking verbs, 351–52
main verbs, 347–48
objects of verbs, 405–406, 407–408
principal parts of, 445–53
progressive forms of, 459–61
regular verbs, 446
rise, raise, 464
sit, set, 463, 464
tenses of, 458–62
transitive verbs, 353–54
Verbal elements, in speech delivery, 722
Verb phrases, 348
definition of, 309
Vertical file, 699
Videos and videotapes. *See also* Documentaries; Films.
in electronic media, 746
"how-to" videos, 112
producing a television news segment, 79–82
as sources, 202–203, 698
for television advertisements, 255
television and, 115–16
Viewing and listening to learn, about charts and graphics, 112–16
Viewing and representing, 743–54
analyzing an editorial cartoon, 259
analyzing visual media, 112–16, 146, 148, 149–50, 183–84
assessing language, medium, and presentation of TV news segment, 82
comparing documentaries, 146
comparing film, TV, and literature, 181–84
comparing ideas in photographs, 147–50
creating a graphic showing a process, 117
creating a humorous advertisement, 254–55
creating an editorial cartoon, 83
creating charts comparing folk tales, 185
creating illustrations, 34, 151
evaluating how various media influence or inform, 150, 747–48
giving a multimedia presentation, 151, 225
interpreting and evaluating visual media, 116, 146, 147, 150, 181–84, 224
interpreting visuals and graphics, 711–13
key ideas for critical viewing, 747
making a trading card, 225
newspaper production, 76–78
producing a TV news segment, 79–82
producing visual media, 34, 76–78, 79–82, 101, 220
sharing information through visuals, 220–21
taking notes about television programs, 15
using visuals to complement meaning, 34, 101, 220
viewing to learn, 112–16
Visualizing, 91
Visual literacy, 751
Visuals, 221. *See also* Graphic(s); Illustrations; Photographs and photography.
creating, 220–21

elements of effective visuals, 711
in humorous advertisement, 254
interpreting, 711–13
types of, 711–13
using visuals to complement meaning, 34, 101, 220

Vocabulary. *See also* English language; Mini-lesson (vocabulary); Word(s).
skills and strategies, 713–18
unfamiliar vocabulary, 160
word meanings, 714–16
word origins, 691–92
word parts, 715–16
words to learn list, 716–18

Voice (writing)
adapting to audience, 29, 239
adapting to purpose, 29, 95, 131, 200
defined, 767
for news article, 61
revealing writer's point of view, 167

Volume
speaking loudly, for audience, 46, 223
as verbal element in special presentations, 722

Wakin, Edward, 121–22
Walker, Paul Robert, 280
Warm colors, in graphics, 688
Wash, **principal parts of,** 446
Way, ways, 530
Weak, week, 633
Wear, **conjugation of verb,** 458–59
principal parts of, 453
Webbing. *See* Clustering.
Web pages, 699, 700, 701
Web search, 204
Web sites, 699, 700
evaluation of, 702–703
presentation and, 750
Well, good, 523
"Whale Watch: Kids Use Internet to Track Progress of Newly Freed J. J." (Richardson), 51–52
"What if?" questions, prewriting and, 762
When, where, 530
Who, whom, 486–87, 789
Whose, who's, 530, 634
Willis, Patricia, 170
Wilmore, Kathy, 189–91
"Windy Nights" (Stevenson), 179, 180
Women Who Made America Great (Gersh), 288
Word(s). *See also* Compound words; Vocabulary.
borrowed, 691–92
changing forms of, 270
clichés, 172–73
commonly confused (homonyms), 625–34

loaded, 715
location words, 109
from names, 692
plurals of words referred to as words, 605, 623
positive and negative words, 157–58
punctuation of introductory, 572
tired, 714
transitional, 287–88, 711
Word bank, 714
Wordbusting strategy (CSSD), 159
Word choice, revising for, 12. *See also* Style (word choice).
Word division. *See* Hyphens.
Word endings, changing forms of key words, 270
Word groups, for combining sentences, 271–72
Word meanings, 714–15
Word order, inverted, 432
Word origins, 692
Word parts
prefixes, 715–16
roots, 715
suffixes, 716
Word pictures, 210
Word processing. *See* Computers.
Word roots. *See* Roots.
Works Cited list, 210. *See also* Sources.
World Wide Web. *See also* Internet; Web pages; Web sites.
browser and, 700
databases, 698
evaluating Web sites on, 702–703
hyperlink and, 700
as information source, 699–701
searching, 204, 701–702
URL of, 700
Would of. See Could of.
Writer's journal or notebook, 764
Writer's Model
autobiographical incident, 33–34
book review, 169
comparison-contrast essay, 137
"how-to" paper, 99–100
news article, 67
persuasive letter, 245–46
research report, 211–12
Writing (first draft). *See also* Description; Narrative writing; Persuasive writing; Writing applications; Writing to learn.
autobiographical incident, 32–35
of book review, 168–70
comparison-contrast essay, 136–38
"how-to" paper, 98–102
news article, 66–68
persuasive letter, 244–47
research report, 210–13
starting to write, 11
Writing applications
agreement in instructions, 443

apostrophes in a letter, 611
capital letters in an essay, 559
complements in a paragraph, 418–19
correct pronoun forms in writing, 493
correct spelling in a personal letter, 639
end marks in a screenplay, 585
formal English in a letter, 535
negative words in description, 517
prepositional phrases in a story, 401
pronouns in a plot summary, 345
sentence variety in a comic strip, 321
using verbs in a description, 473
using verbs in a list, 371

Writing portfolio, tall tales, 47

Writing process, 9–14. *See also* Writing to learn.
prewriting, 10
publishing, 13–14
reading-writing connection, 14
revising, 12
writing stage of, 11

Writing to develop ideas, 285–86. *See also* Chronological order; Prewriting.

Writing to discover, 736. *See* Expressive writing; Journal; Prewriting.

Writing to express, 17
documentary for self-expression, 146

Writing to learn
autobiographies, 736
diaries, 736
freewriting, 736
journals, 736
learning logs, 736
studying and, 736

Writing to persuade. *See* Persuasion; *headings beginning with* Persuasive.

Writing to problem solve, 74–75
in advice column, 74–75

analyzing problem-solution relationships, 707–708

Writing to record, 107, 116, 175, 218, 252
details in autobiographical incident, 30
news article, 73
note-taking guidelines, 116

Writing to reflect, 9
on autobiographical incident, 40
on book review, 175
comparison-contrast essay, 144
on "how-to" paper, 107
on news article, 73
persuasive letter and, 252
on research report, 218

Writing Workshop
autobiographical incident (life experience), 27–41
book review, 161–75
comparison-contrast essay, 128–45
"how-to" paper, 94–108
newspaper article, 58–73
persuasive letter, 237–53
research report, 198–219

Written works. *See also* Quotation marks.
correct end punctuation in written conversations, 318
underlining (italicizing) titles of, 588–89

Your, you're, 530, 634

ZIP Codes, commas used in punctuation of, 574

ACKNOWLEDGMENTS

For permission to reprint copyrighted material, grateful acknowledgment is made to the following sources:

Neil Armstrong: Quote by Neil Armstrong from Apollo 11 on January 23, 1969.

Ballantine Books, a division of Random House, Inc.: From review of *Catherine, Called Birdy* by Karen Cushman from *Great Books for Girls: More Than 600 Books to Inspire Today's Girls and Tomorrow's Women* by Kathleen Odean. Copyright © 1997 by Kathleen Odean.

Cobblestone Publishing Company, 30 Grove Street, Suite C, Peterborough, NH 03458: From "Making a Flying Fish" by Paula Morrow from *Faces: Happy Holidays,* vol. 7, no. 4, December 1990. Copyright © 1990 by Cobblestone Publishing, Company.

Dial Books for Young Readers, a division of Penguin Putnam Inc.: From "You're Under Arrest" from *Rosa Parks: My Story* by Rosa Parks with Jim Haskins. Copyright © 1992 by Rosa Parks.

Tyler Duckworth: From "Let's Clean Up the Planet for Future Generations" by Tyler Duckworth from *Time for Kids Archive,* February 1, 1997. Copyright © 1997 by Tyler Duckworth.

Farrar, Straus and Giroux, LLC.: From *Tuck Everlasting* by Natalie Babbitt. Copyright © 1975 by Natalie Babbitt.

Friends of Volunteers, Inc.: From "Side View of Complex" from *Friends of Volunteers,* Online, March 8, 1999. Copyright © 1999 by Friends of Volunteers, Inc. Available at http://fov.org/side.html.

Girl Zone: From "Volunteering—It's So Easy, a Kid Can Do It" by Liv Learner from *Girl Zone,* Online. Copyright © 1998 by Girl Zone. Available at http://www.girlzone.com/html/care_project.html.

Greenhaven Press, Inc.: From "The U.S. has a garbage crisis" from *The Environment: Distinguishing Between Fact and Opinion* by William Dudley. Copyright © 1990 by Greenhaven Press, Inc.

Greenwillow Books, a division of HarperCollins Publishers, Inc.: From "Last Night I Dreamed of Chickens" from *Something Big Has Been Here* by Jack Prelutsky. Copyright © 1990 by Jack Prelutsky.

Alfred A. Knopf, Inc.: "April Rain Song" from *Collected Poems* by Langston Hughes. Copyright © 1994 by the Estate of Langston Hughes.

Los Angeles Times Syndicate: From "Whale Watch; Kids Use Internet to Track Progress of Newly Freed J. J." by Lisa Richardson from *Los Angeles Times: Orange County Edition,* April 3, 1998, Metro, p. 1. Copyright © 1998 by Los Angeles Times.

Lothrop, Lee & Shepard Books, a division of HarperCollins Publishers, Inc.: From *How TV Changed America's Mind* by Edward Wakin. Copyright © 1996 by Edward Wakin.

Macmillan General Reference, a division of IDG Consumer Reference, part of IDG Books Worldwide, Inc.: Dictionary entry for "Cloud" from *Webster's New World College Dictionary,* Third Edition, Editor in Chief: Victoria Neufeldt, and Editor in Chief Emeritus: David B. Guralnik. Copyright © 1988, 1991, 1994, 1996, 1997 by Simon & Schuster, Inc.

Morrow Junior Books, a division of HarperCollins Publishers, Inc.: From "Picky-picky" from *Ramona Forever* by Beverly Cleary. Copyright © 1988 by Beverly Cleary.

The Octagon Press, Ltd., London: "Camel fodder" from *The Subtleties of the Inimitable Mulla Nasrudin* by Idries Shah. Copyright © 1983 by The Octagon Press, Ltd.

Ohio University Press/Swallow Press, Athens, Ohio: From "The Wild Plains Buffalo" from *The Buffalo Book* by David A. Dary. Copyright © 1974 by David A. Dary.

Mary Roach: From "Meteorite Hunters" by Mary Roach from *Muse,* vol. 3, no. 6, July/August 1999. Copyright © 1999 by Mary Roach.

Scholastic Inc.: From "Ta-Na-E-Ka" by Mary Whitebird from *Scholastic Voice,* December 13, 1973. Copyright © 1973 by Scholastic Inc. From "The California Gold Rush" by Kathy Wilmore from *Junior Scholastic* magazine, December 1, 1997, vol. 100, no. 8. Copyright © 1997 by Scholastic Inc.

Weekly Reader Corporation: "Foul Shot" by Edwin A. Hoey from *Read* ®. Copyright © 1962 and renewed © 1989 by Weekly Reader Corporation. All rights reserved.

The H. W. Wilson Company: Entry for "Bears" from *Reader's Guide to Periodical Literature.* Copyright © 1999 by The H. W. Wilson Company

SOURCES CITED:

From *Women Who Made America Great* by Harry Gersh. Published by HarperCollins Publishers, New York, 1962.

From *The Pride of Puerto Rico: The Life of Roberto Clemente* by Paul Robert Walker. Published by Harcourt Inc., Orlando, 1988.

Screen shot for "Grizzly fate" from *FirstSearch* database. FirstSearch and WorldCat are registered trademarks of OCLC Online Computer Library Center, Incorporated. *OCLC Online Computer Library Center, Inc.* Available online at http://firstsearch.oclc.org/:next=NEXTCMD%...recs=1:/fsrec9.tx1%22%3Asessionid=658964.

PHOTO CREDITS

Abbreviations used: (tl)top left, (tc)top center, (tr)top right, (l)left, (lc)left center, (c)center, (rc)right center, (r)right, (bl)bottom left, (bc)bottom center, (br)bottom right.

COVER: Comstock.

TABLE OF CONTENTS: Page xv, Image Copyright ©2001 PhotoDisc, Inc.; xvi, M.K. Denny/Photo Edit; xvii, SuperStock; xviii, Rod Planck/Photo Researchers, Inc.; xix, Image Copyright ©2001 PhotoDisc, Inc.; xx, H. Knaus/SuperStock; xxii, Mike Okoniewski /The Image Works; xxiii, Fred Bavendam/Peter Arnold, Inc.; xxiv, Egyptian National Museum, Cairo, Egypt/SuperStock; xxv, Carl Purcell/Photo Researchers, Inc.

INTRODUCTION: Page 7, Richard Elliott/Tony Stone Images.

PART OPENERS: Page xxii, 1, 260, 261, 298, 299, 678, 679, Kazu Nitta/The Stock Illustration Source, Inc.

CHAPTER 1: Page 34, Randal Alhadeff/HRW Photo.

CHAPTER 3: Page 89, SuperStock.

CHAPTER 4: Page 148 (bl) (br), Peter Van Steen/HRW Photo; 149 (tl) (tr), Peter Van Steen/HRW Photo; 149 (bl), CORBIS/Kennan Ward; 150 (tr), CORBIS/Kennan Ward 150 (bl) (br) Peter Van Steen/HRW Photo.

CHAPTER 5: Page 158, From *Catherine, Called Birdy* by Karen Cushman/ copyright © 1994 by Karen Cushman. Jacket Illustration copyright © 1994 by Trina Schart Hyman. Jacket calligraphy by Iskra. Reprinted by permission of Clarion Books/Houghton Mifflin Co.

CHAPTER 6: Page; 220, F. Gohier/Photo Researchers, Inc.

CHAPTER 7: Page 230, Tim Davis/Photo Researchers, Inc.; 254, Photos by John Langford/HRW Photo and Sam Dudgeon/HRW Photo (bottle).

CHAPTER 8: Page 262, Jim Corwin/Stock Boston; 267, Image Copyright ©2001 PhotoDisc, Inc.; 268 (bl), Patti Murray/Animals Animals/Earth Scenes; 268 (bc), SuperStock; 268 (br), Toni Angermayer/Photo Researchers, Inc.; 270, Huntington Library/SuperStock; 271, CORBIS; 274, Zigmund Leszczynski/Animals Animals/Earth Scenes.

CHAPTER 9: Page 280 Sports Illustrated; 282, Digital Stock Corp.; 284 Hubertus Kanus/Photo Researchers, Inc.; 288 ALLSPORT USA/IOC, 290, E.R. Degginger/Earth Scenes; 293 (tr), Image Copyright ©2001 PhotoDisc, Inc.; 293 (br), M.K. Denny/Photo Edit; 295, Robert & Linda Mitchell.

CHAPTER 10: Page 303, SuperStock; 307, Russell Dian/HRW Photo; 308, Comstock; 313, CORBIS/ David Allen; 318, Spencer Swager/Tom Stack & Associates.

CHAPTER 11: Page 325, Orion Press, Japan; 327, Image Copyright ©2001 PhotoDisc, Inc.; 328, Bob Daugharty, AP/Wide World Photos; 337, HRW Photo Research Library; 340, Image Copyright ©2001 PhotoDisc, Inc.; 341, SuperStock.

CHAPTER 12: 350, Jerry Jacka Photography/Courtesy: The Heard Museum, Phoenix, Arizona; 353, Johnson Publishing Company, Inc.; 355, Image Copyright ©2001 PhotoDisc, Inc.; 356 (l), Image Copyright ©2001 PhotoDisc, Inc. (bc), Dr. Ronald H. Cohn/ The Gorilla Foundation/Koko.org; 359, Lionel Delvigne/Stock Boston.

CHAPTER 13: Page 383, Michael Newman/Photo Edit; 385 (c), Lowell Georgia/Photo Researchers, Inc.; 385 (br), Katherine Feng/Viesti Collection; 396, Tom Stack & Associates; 397, Michele Burgess/Stock Boston.

CHAPTER 14: Page 415, H. Knaus/SuperStock.

CHAPTER 15: Page 424 (bc), Bruce Davidson/Animals Animals/ Earth Scenes; 426, CORBIS/© Kennan Ward; 432, Joe Viesti/Viesti Collection; 435, Bob Couey/Seaworld Inc. © 1998. All rights reserved. Reproduced by permission.; 440, Image Copyright ©2001 PhotoDisc, Inc.

CHAPTER 16: Page 455, Corbis/Bettmann-UPI; 469, ©1997 Radlund & Associates for Artville.

CHAPTER 17: Page 481 (cr), Joe Jaworski/HRW Photo; 481 (br) Mike Okoniewski /The Image Works; 488, Image Copyright ©2001 PhotoDisc, Inc.

CHAPTER 18: Page 506 (bc) Giraudon/Art Resource, NY.; 506 (br), Corbis-Bettmann.

CHAPTER 19: Page 526, Image Copyright ©2001 PhotoDisc, Inc.; 532 (br), Photo Image Technologies.

CHAPTER 20: Page 547 (bc), SuperStock; 556, Margaret Sulanowska/Woods Hole Oceanographic Institution.

CHAPTER 21: Page 563 (tr), Carl Purcell/Photo Researchers, Inc.; 565, Michael Newman/Photo Edit; 571, Giraudon/Art Resource, New York; 576, Eastcott/Momatiuk/ Animals Animals/Earth Scenes.

CHAPTER 22: Page 599, Keystone/Sygma; 600 (cl), Rod Planck/Photo Researchers, Inc.; 600 (cr), Gordon and Cathy Illg/Animals Animals/Earth Scenes.

CHAPTER 23: Page 615, CORBIS/Aaron Horowitz; 620, Chris Brown/SIPA Press; 623, A. Ramey/Photo Edit; 628, T. Harmon Parkhurst/Courtesy Museum of New Mexico; 628 (bc) Photo Edit; 632 (tl), Aaron Haupt/Photo Researchers, Inc.; 632 (tr), Aaron Haupt/Photo Researchers, Inc.; 636 (bc), Werner Forman Archive/Museum fur Volkerkunde, Berlin/Art Resource, NY.

CHAPTER 24: Page 646, Richard Weiss/HRW Photo; 653, News Office, Woods Hole Oceanographic Institution; 659, Fred Bavendam/Peter Arnold, Inc.; 665, Courtesy of Joe Rosenberg; 668, Robert Trippett/SIPA Press.

ILLUSTRATION CREDITS

TABLE OF CONTENTS: Page viii (tl), Melinda Levine; (bl), Tom Voss/Vicki Prentice Associates Inc. NYC; ix (cl), Christin Ranger; x (cl), Susan Sanford; xi (cl), Susan Tolonen/Wilson-Zumbo; xii (tl), Tim Spransy/Wilson-Zumbo; xiii (cl), Fred Lynch; xiv (tl), John Ceballos/Carol Guenzi Agents.

INTRODUCTION: Page 2 (all), Melinda Levine.

CHAPTER 1: Page 16 (all), Tom Voss/Vicki Prentice Associates Inc. NYC.

CHAPTER 2: Page 48 (all), Christin Ranger.

CHAPTER 3: Page 84 (all), Susan Sanford; 90 (b), Leslie Kell; 91 (bl), 101 (cl), HRW; 113 (cl), Leslie Kell.

CHAPTER 4: Page 118 (all), Susan Tolonen/Wilson-Zumbo.

CHAPTER 5: Page 152 (all), Tim Spransy/Wilson-Zumbo.

CHAPTER 6: Page 186 (all), Fred Lynch; 189 (cl), Ortelius Design; 199 (bl), Leslie Kell; 221 (tr), HRW; (br), Ortelius Design.

CHAPTER 7: Page 226 (all), John Ceballos/Carol Guenzi Agents; 254 (c), HRW.

CHAPTER 12: Page 363 (c), HRW; 367 (b), Linda Kelen.

CHAPTER 13: Page 376 (c), Rich Lo; 380 (c), Rondi Collette.

CHAPTER 15: Page 424 (c), Ortelius Design.

CHAPTER 16: Page 468 (tc), Chris Ellison.

CHAPTER 18: Page 500 (br), 509 (tr), Rondi Collette.

CHAPTER 19: Page 528 (bl), Tom Gianni; 531 (c), Ortelius Design; 532 (bl), Leslie Kell.

CHAPTER 20: Page 547 (cr), Ortelius Design.

CHAPTER 22: Page 604 (bc), Rondi Collette.

CHAPTER 23: Page 636 (br), Ortelius Design.

QRH: Page 688 (br), Precision Graphics; 689 (b), HRW; 701 (tl), Leslie Kell.

Grade 6 ATE, Acknowledgments

For permission to reprint copyrighted material, grateful acknowledgment is made to the following sources:

E. L. Doctorow: Quote by E. L. Doctorow. Copyright © 1993 by E. L. Doctorow.

Greenhaven Press, Inc.: From "The U.S. has a garbage crisis" from *The Environment: Distinguishing Between Fact and Opinion* by William Dudley. Copyright © 1990 by Greenhaven Press, Inc.

Scholastic Inc.: From "The California Gold Rush" by Kathy Wilmore from *Junior Scholastic* magazine, December 1, 1997, vol. 100, no. 8. Copyright © 1997 by Scholastic Inc.

Simon & Schuster Division Books for Young Readers, an imprint of Simon & Schuster Children's Publishing Division: From *Volcano* by Patricia Lauber. Copyright © 1986 by Patricia Lauber.

SOURCES CITED:
Quote by Gore Vidal from *The New York Times*, February 24, 1976. Published by The New York Times, New York, 1976.

Grade 6 Reading Selection Amendments

CHAPTER 1, PAGES 19–20
Excerpted as an example of an autobiographical incident
CHAPTER 2, PAGES 51–52
Excerpted, with some word and mechanics changes and internal deletions, as an example of a newspaper article
CHAPTER 3, PAGES 89–90
Excerpted, with some mechanics changes and internal deletions, as an example of a how-to article
CHAPTER 4, PAGES 121–122
Excerpted as an example of a comparison-contrast essay
CHAPTER 5, PAGE 155:
Used as an example of a book review, with some word changes and internal deletions
CHAPTER 6, PAGES 189–191
Used as an example of an informative article, with some mechanics changes and internal deletions
CHAPTER 7, PAGES 229–230
Used an example of a persuasive essay, with some internal deletions
CHAPTER 9, PAGE 280
Excerpted as a practice assignment for students to identify the main idea
CHAPTER 9, PAGE 280
Excerpted as a practice assignment for students to identify the main idea
CHAPTER 9, PAGE 280
Excerpted as a practice assignment for students to identify the main idea
CHAPTER 9, PAGE 282
Excerpted, with some mechanics changes, to focus on the concept of clincher sentences presented in this chapter
CHAPTER 9, PAGE 284
Excerpted, with some internal deletions, to focus on concept of spatial order presented in this chapter
CHAPTER 9, PAGE 285
Excerpted to focus on concept of chronological order to tell a story presented in this chapter
CHAPTER 9, PAGE 286
Excerpted to focus on concept of chronological order to explain a process presented in this chapter
CHAPTER 9, PAGE 288
Excerpted, with some mechanics changes, to focus on concept of transitional words and phrases presented in this chapter
CHAPTER 9, PAGE 292
Excerpted, with some mechanics changes and internal deletions, to focus on concept of narrative writing presented in this chapter
CHAPTER 9, PAGE 292
Excerpted, with some mechanics changes and internal deletions, to focus on concept of descriptive writing presented in this chapter
CHAPTER 9, PAGES 293–294
Excerpted, with some mechanics changes and internal deletions, to focus on concept of persuasive writing presented in this chapter
CHAPTER 20, PAGE 537
Excerpted to focus on concept of capitalization presented in this chapter
CHAPTER 22, PAGE 594
Excerpted to focus on concept of quotation marks presented in this chapter